THE NOVEL IN
THE ANCIENT WORLD

THE NOVEL IN THE ANCIENT WORLD

Revised Edition

EDITED BY

GARETH SCHMELING

Brill Academic Publishers, Inc.
Boston • Leiden
2003

Library of Congress Cataloging-in-Publication Data

The novel in the ancient world / edited by Gareth Schmeling.—Rev. ed.
   p. cm.
Includes bibliographical references and index.
  ISBN 0-391-04134-7
  1. Classical fiction—History and criticism. 2. Civilization, Ancient, in literature. I. Schmeling, Gareth L.

PA3040.N68 2003
880.09—dc21

2002067251

ISBN: 0-391-04134-7

© Copyright 1996 by E.J. Brill, Leiden, The Netherlands
Revised Edition © Copyright 2003 by Koninklijke Brill NV, Leiden, The Netherlands

All rights reserved. No part of this publication may be reproduced, translated stored in a retrieval system, or transmitted in any form or by any means, electronic, mechanical, photocopying, recording or otherwise, without prior written permission from the publisher.

Authorization to photocopy items for internal or personal use is granted by Brill provided that the appropriate fees are paid directly to the Copyright Clearance Center, 222 Rosewood Drive, Suite 910 Danvers, MA 01923, USA. Fees are subject to change.

PRINTED IN THE UNITED STATES OF AMERICA

IN MEMORIAM

J.P. SULLIVAN
(1930–1993)

ille sapit quisquis, Postume, vixit heri
Martial 5.58.8

(obituary in *PSN* 27 (1993) 14)

CONTENTS

Introduction xi

1. *Preface* 1
   Gareth Schmeling, Professor of Classics
   University of Florida

2. *The Genre: Novels Proper and the Fringe* 11
   Niklas Holzberg, Professor of Classics
   Universität München

3. *The Rise of the Greek Novel* 29
   Consuelo Ruiz-Montero, Professor of Classics
   Universidad de Murcia

4. *The Ancient Readers of the Greek Novels* 87
   Ewen Bowie, Fellow and Tutor in Classics
   Corpus Christi College, Oxford, and University
   Lecturer in Classical Languages and Literature

5. *Popular and Sophisticated in the Ancient Novel* 107
   Graham Anderson
   University of Kent at Canterbury

6. *Characterization in the Ancient Novel* 115
   Alain Billault, Professor
   Université Jean Moulin, Lyon

7. *Mystery Religions, Aretalogy and the Ancient Novel* 131
   Roger Beck, Professor of Classics
   University of Toronto

8. *Women in the Ancient Novel* 151
   Renate Johne, Fellow of the Research Group of
   the Berlin-Brandenburg Academy of Sciences, Berlin

9. *A Study on the Margin of the Ancient Novel:*
   "Barbarians" and Others 209
   Heinrich Kuch, Berlin

10. *The Social and Economic Structures of the Ancient Novels* 221
    Antonio M. Scarcella, Professor of Classics
    Università degli Studi di Perugia

11. *Modern Critical Theories and the Ancient Novel* 277
   Massimo Fusillo, Professor of Classics
   Università degli Studi di Messina

12. *Major Authors: Greek and Roman* 307

Greek

   A. *Chariton* 309
      B.P. Reardon, Professor Emeritus of Classics
      University of California-Irvine

   B. *Xenophon of Ephesus* 336
      Bernhard Kytzler, Professor of Classics
      University of Natal, Durban

   C. *Longus*, Daphnis and Chloe 361
      Richard Hunter, University Lecturer in Classics and
      Fellow of Pembroke College, Cambridge

   D. *Achilles Tatius* 387
      Karl Plepelits, Graz

   E. *Heliodoros* 417
      J.R. Morgan, Lecturer in Classics
      University of Wales, Swansea

Roman

   F. *The* Satyrica *of Petronius* 457
      Gareth Schmeling, Professor of Classics
      University of Florida

   G. *Apuleius'* Metamorphoses 491
      S.J. Harrison, Fellow and Tutor in Classics
      Corpus Christi College, Oxford, and University
      Lecturer in Classical Languages and Literature

   H. Historia Apollonii Regis Tyri 517
      Gareth Schmeling, Professor of Classics
      University of Florida

13. *Novel-like Works of Extended Prose Fiction I*

   A. *Lucian's* Verae Historiae 555
      Graham Anderson
      University of Kent at Canterbury

B. *The Truth and Nothing but the Truth: Dictys and Dares* 563
Stefan Merkle
Ludwig Maximillians Universität, München

C. *Xenophon of Athens: the* Cyropaedia 581
Bodil Due, Fellow of the Danish Academy in Rome

D. *The Metamorphoses of the* Alexander Romance 601
Richard Stoneman
Institute of Classical Studies, London

E. *Philostratus on Apollonius of Tyana: the Unpredictable on the Unfathomable* 613
Graham Anderson
University of Kent at Canterbury

14. *Novel-like Works of Extended Prose Fiction II* 619
Niklas Holzberg, Professor of Classics
Universität München
   A. *Utopias and Fantastic Travel: Euhemerus, Iambulus* 621
   B. *History: Ctesias* 629
   C. *Fable: Aesop. Life of Aesop* 633
   D. *Rhetoric: Dio Chrysostom* 640
   E. *Letters: Chion* 645

15. *Fragments of Lost Novels* 655
Susan Stephens, Professor of Classics
Stanford University

16. *The Ancient Novel Becomes Christian* 685
Richard Pervo, Professor of New Testament
and Patristics, Seabury-Western Theological Seminary,
Evanston

17. *The Byzantine Revival of the Ancient Novel* 713
Roderick Beaton, Professor of Modern Greek and
Byzantine History, Language and Literature,
King's College, London

18. *The Heritage of the Ancient Greek Novel in France and Britain* 735
Gerald Sandy, Professor of Classics
University of British Columbia

19. *The Nachleben of the Ancient Novel in Iberian Literature in the Sixteenth Century* 775
   M. Futre Pinheiro, Professor of Classics
   University of Lisbon

20. *Maps* 801
   Jean Alvares, Assistant Professor of Classics
   Franklin and Marshall College, Lancaster
   A. *The World of the Ancient Novels*
   B. *Chariton—Chaireas and Callirhoe*
   C. *Xenophon of Ephesus—An Ephesian Tale*
   D. *Achilles Tatius—Leucippe and Clitophon*
   E. *Heliodorus—An Ethiopian Tale*
   F. *Petronius—The Satyricon*
   G. *Apollonius King of Tyre*
   H. *Homer—The Odyssey*
   I. *Apollonius of Rhodes—Voyage of the Argo*
   J. *Virgil—The Aeneid*
   K. *Paul's Journey to Rome*
   L. *Travelers to the Holy Land*

Bibliography 815

Index 865

INTRODUCTION TO THE REVISED EDITION

Analytic and Thematic Bibliographies of The Ancient Novel
and Notes on Ways Teachers and Students of Classics,
Early Christian/Jewish/Byzantine Literature,
Modern Languages Might Use This Book
to Explore The Ancient Novel

Gareth Schmeling

Though this is a large book, it can be approached easily in smallish pieces. The Table of Contents to this book sets out its design (references in bold type indicate pages in this book; references to authors with dates in parentheses can be found in the bibliography at the end of this book or in the supplemental listing at the end of the Introduction): the opening pages, **11–305**, contain 10 essays on the most discussed aspects of the ancient novel (e.g., origins, readership, gender, theory); **309–456** discuss each of the 5 Greek authors, his novel, plot summary and special problems like dating, sources, and intent; **457–551** present similar types of discussions of the three Roman novels; **555–683** contain 7 studies of complete works and numerous fragments in Greek and Latin which are novel-like (fringe novels), which probably should be classified as novels but which also fall into various sub-genres of the novel, works which might be seen as imitating the novel, developing toward the novel or running parallel to it; **685–799** interpret the reception of the ancient novel in early Christian and Jewish narratives, the Byzantine novels, and in modern literature; **803–814** lay out in a series of 12 maps the journeys of characters in the ancient novels, epics, early Christian writings (St. Paul) and by juxtapositioning them invite the reader to compare journeys; **815–865** contain a comprehensive bibliography arranged by author; **865–876** are an index of names, themes and crucial points.

This book is a good place to begin a study of the ancient novel, to examine essential matters, to review the novels themselves, and to become acquainted with a wide range of issues and problems concerning the ancient novel and its relevance to the ancient world and to modern literature. For the ancient novel surely spills over into the narratives of early Christian and Jewish narratives and has meaning for the study and history of the modern novel: the novel is an enduring and surprisingly resilient genre from which countless sub-genres (e.g. science fiction) have arisen and which continues today as the most popular form of literature. In this book the ancient works of extended narrative prose fiction are referred to as novels. This designation [**2–3, 11–28**; Tatum (1994) 1–7] is not without detractors among classicists [Selden (1994); Ademietz (1995)] and scholars of modern languages [Watt (1957); Hunter (1990)], but the classification is defended by scholars of English literature like Heiserman (1977).

Analytic Bibliography

Comprehensive Works on All Greek and Roman Novels

In addition to sections on the ancient novel in histories of Greek and Latin literature and in encyclopedias we have several excellent one-volume studies which cover most facets of the ancient novel. The grandfather of scholars writing on the ancient novel is surely Rohde (1914 [1876]) whose towering intellect could not in all instances overcome his low regard for the subject. Because the novel papyri, which help to date the novels, had not yet been uncovered, Rohde dated the novels many centuries too late, but had made a significant beginnning; Swain (1999) 12–20 sets Rohde's work in its cultural context. Perry (1967) can rightly be viewed as the father of scholarship on the ancient novel; the start of great interest in the ancient novel can be said to date to him. In what is unfashionable today Perry credits the first novel to an author who decided to write a novel "on a Tuesday afternoon in July" for an audience very much like the audience of the modern novel, living in an open and cosmopolitan society; Swain (1999) 24–25. In this family of novel scholars Reardon (1971) (1989) (1991) holds the position of son and rightful heir of Perry. It was Reardon who in 1976 to mark the 100th anniversary of Rohde's *Der griechische Roman* sponsored the first International Conference on the Ancient Novel (ICAN). To date there have been three such conferences whose proceedings and published papers are required reading; Reardon (1977); Tatum (1990) (1994); Zimmerman/ Panayotakis/Keulen (2003).

A comfortable way for readers to approach the ancient novel might be in fact through the grandchildren of Rohde: Schmeling, editor of this volume; Hägg (1983) who deals lavishly and learnedly with the novel—better on the Greek than the Roman novel; Holzberg (1986) (1995) (2001a) who by regularly refining his book offers a current assessment of work on the ancient novel. He dissects each of the Greek and Roman novels, the fringe novels, papyrus fragments, early Christian narratives, and adds a superb bibliography. There is also profit in Heiserman (1977), Anderson (1982) (1984) and Wolff (1997). Books on the Greek novel by Fusillo (1989) and Billault (1991a) and on the Roman novel by Sullivan (1968), Walsh (1970), and Conte (1996) should also be included here because, while they emphasize either Greek or Roman novels, they address many issues in both.

Closely related to such studies of the wider corpus of the ancient novels are collections of commissioned essays which address the major and fringe novels and their reception in the modern world: Tatum (1994) and Zimmerman (2003) represent selections of papers of two international conferences; Kuch (1989a) speaks to issues and characteristics shared by novels rather than examining the novels individually; Baslez (1992) and Pouderon (2001) analyze just the Greek novel but do so in depth; Pecere/Stramaglia (1996) focus on the novel as popular literature. The most comprehensive work in this format, and thus the most useful for the reader is the matched set of books by Morgan/ Stoneman (1994) [Greek novel] and Hofmann (1999) [Roman novel] which comment on core novels, fringe novels, the novels and historiography, and the novel in the religious turmoil of the first/ second centuries A.D. Special notice should be given to the nine volumes (1988–1998) of the *Groningen Colloquia on the Novel (GCN)* edited by Hofmann and then by Hofmann and Zimmerman. They contain a wealth of information about the ancient novels. The role and function of *GCN* have been assumed by an electronic journal which can be accessed at http://www.ancientnarrative.com. This new journal *Ancient Narrative (AN)* also publishes an annual hardcover journal and special issues.

The most important research done on the ancient novel has occurred in the last 100 years or so (preparation of critical editions, discovery of papyri containing novel fragments, work on translations of quality, research across academic disciplines to set the novel into its historical and cultural framework), and summaries/outlines of this work are discussed in many places, but I shall list just four: Bowie/ Harrison (1993); Swain (1999) 1–35; Harrison (1999) xi–xxxix; *Petronian*

Society Newsletter (*PSN*), published since 1970, now subsumed under *Ancient Narrative*, and available (including all back issues) at http://www.ancientnarrative.com, where each year's work on the ancient novel is available, as well as information about new books, conferences, and the *piccolo mondo antico*.

A. Greek Authors and Novels

(those consulting the bibliography listed chronologically under each author/novel/subject will find a well balanced approach to the subject; references in bold type indicate pages in this book)

1. Chariton, *Callirhoe*. Greek texts: Blake (1938); Molinié/Billault (1989); Goold (1995); Reardon (2003, Teubner). Commentary: Plepelits (1976). English translations: Blake (1939); Reardon in Reardon (1989) 17–124; Goold (1995). Critical studies: **Reardon 309–335**; Hägg (1971a) (1987a); Schmeling (1974); C.W. Müller (1976); Plepelits (1976); Reardon (1982); Elsom (1992); Hunter (1994); Hernandez Lara (1994); Egger (1994a); Ruiz-Montero (1994a); Edwards (1996); Hock (1996).
2. Xenophon of Ephesus, *Ephesiaca*. Greek texts: Dalmeyda (1926); Papanikolaou (1973a). English translations: Hadas (1953); Anderson in Reardon (1989) 125–169. Critical studies: **Kytzler 336–360**; Zimmermann (1949–50); Hägg (1966) (1971a) (1971b); Schmeling (1980); Konstan (1994c); Ruiz-Montero (1994b); O'Sullivan (1995); Chew (1998).
3. Longus, *Daphnis and Chloe*. Greek texts: Thornley/Edmonds (1916); Dalmeyda (1934); Reeve (1986^2, 1994^3). Bibliography: Morgan (1997). English translations: Thornley/Edmonds (1916); Hadas (1953); Turner (1968c); Gill in Reardon (1989) 284–348. Critical studies: **Hunter 361–386**; Chalk (1960); Mittelstadt (1966) (1967); McColloh (1970); Effe (1982); Hunter (1983); Pandiri (1985); Merkelbach (1988); Wouters (1989–90) (1994); MacQueen (1990); Winkler (1990b); Zeitlin (1990); Teske (1991); Morgan (1994b); B. Zimmermann (1994).
4. Achilles Tatius, *Leucippe and Clitophon*. Greek texts: Gaselee (1917); Vilborg (1955). Commentary: Vilborg (1962); Plepelits (1980). English translations: Gaselee (1917); Winkler in Reardon (1989) 170–284. Critical studies: **Plepelits 387–416**; Durham (1938); Sedelmeier (1959); Bartsch (1989); Reardon (1994); Nimis (1998); B. Zimmermann (1999).

5. Heliodorus, *Ethiopica*. Greek texts: Colonna (1938); Rattenbury (1960). English translations: Hadas (1957); Lamb (1961; 1997); Morgan in Reardon (1989) 349–588. Critical studies: **Morgan 417–456**; Hefti (1950); Szepessy (1957) (1976); Mazal (1958); Morgan (1982) (1989b) (1989c) (1991) (1994a); Sandy (1982a) (1982b); Winkler (1982); Bartsch (1989); Bowie (1995); Dowden (1996); Futre Pinheiro (1998); Hunter (1998).

B. Roman Authors and Novels

1. Petronius, *Satyrica*. Latin texts: Bücheler (1862); K. Müller (1961¹) (1983³) (1995⁴). *Cena Trimalchionis*, text and commentary: Friedländer (1906²); Maiuri (1945); M.S. Smith (1975). Bibliographies: Gaselee (1910); Schmeling (1977); M.S. Smith (1985); *Petronian Society Newsletter* (1970–). English translations: Arrowsmith (1959); Sullivan (1986); Branham (1996); Walsh (1996). Critical studies: **Schmeling 457–490**; Heinze (1899); Raith (1963); Arrowsmith (1966); Sullivan (1968); Stöcker (1969); Walsh (1970); K. Rose (1971); Zeitlin (1971); Schmeling (1971b) (1991) (1994b) (1994c) (1999a); Beck (1973) (1975) (1982a); Astbury (1977); Petersmann (1977); C.W. Müller (1980); Bodel (1984) (1994) (1999); Barchiesi (1984) (1996); Horsfall (1989); Slater (1990); Boyce (1991); Elsner (1993); Richardson (1993); Panayotakis (1995); Conte (1996); Connors (1998); Courtney (2001).
2. Apuleius, *Metamorphoses (The Golden Ass)*. Latin texts: Helm (1931³); Robertson (1940–45); Hanson (1989). Bibliography: Schlam (1971); Schlam/Finkelpearl (2001). Commentaries: Scobie (1975); Mal-Maeder (2001); Paardt (1971); Hijmans (1977) (1981) (1985) (1995); Kenney (1990a); Zimmerman (2000); Griffiths (1975). English translations: Lindsay (1962); Hanson (1989); Walsh (1994). Critical studies: **Harrison 491–516**; Bernhard (1927); Callebat (1968); Walsh (1970); Smith (1972); Penwill (1975); Hijmans (1978a); Tatum (1969) (1979); Millar (1981); Paardt (1981); Dowden (1982) (1994); Scobie (1983); Winkler (1985); James (1987); Krabbe (1989); Schlam (1992); Hofmann (1993); Shumate (1996); Sandy (1997); Mal-Maeder (1997); Finkelpearl (1998); Zimmerman (1998); Harrison (2000); Kahane/Laird (2001).
2a. Pseudo-Lucian, *Lucius or the Ass*. Greek text: Macleod (1967). English translations: Macleod (1967); Sullivan in Reardon (1989) 589–618. Critical studies: **Harrison 500–502**; Anderson (1976b); Effe (1976); Mason (1978) (1994) (1999); Holzberg (1984); Kussl (1990).

3. Unknown author, *History of Apollonius King of Tyre*. Latin texts: Kortekaas (1984); Konstan (1985); Schmeling (1988), plus Hunt (1994). English translations: Sandy in Reardon (1989) 736–772; Archibald (1991). Critical studies: **Schmeling 517–551**; Klebs (1899); Lana (1975); Ziegler (1977) (1984); Chiarini (1983); Mazza (1985); Schmeling (1989) (1998) (1999b); Holzberg (1990); Archibald (1991); Kortekaas (1991) (1998); C.W. Müller (1991); Konstan (1994b); Robins (1995) (1996) (2000); Wolff (1998) (2001); Botermann (1999).

C. Novel-Like Works: The Fringe Novels

1. Lucian, *True History*. Greek texts: Macleod (1972); Harmon (1913). English translations: Harmon (1913); Reardon in Reardon (1989) 619–649. Critical studies: **Anderson 555–561**; Bompaire (1958); Anderson (1976a) (1976b); Fredericks (1976); Fauth (1979); Swanson (1979); Morgan (1985); C.P. Jones (1986); Fusillo (1988a); Billault (1994); Swain (1994); Larmour (1997); Rütten (1997).
2. Dares Phrygius, *Acta Diurna Belli Troiani*, and Dictys Cretensis, *Ephemeris Belli Troiani*. Latin texts: Meister (1873); Eisenhut (1973²). English translation: Frazer (1966). Critical studies: **Merkle 563–580**; Schetter (1987) (1988); Merkle (1989) (1990) (1994a) (1999); Beschorner (1992a).
3. Xenophon of Athens, *Cyropaedia*. Greek texts: Marchant (1910); W. Miller (1914). English translation: W. Miller (1914). Critical studies: **Due 581–599**, (1989a) (1989b); Tatum (1989) (1994); B. Zimmermann (1989); Stadter (1991); Gera (1993); Reichel (1995).
4. Pseudo-Callisthenes (Greek), Julius Valerius (Latin), *The Romance of Alexander* and historiography. Greek texts: Kroll (1926); van Thiel (1983). Latin text: Rosellini (1993). English translations: Dowden in Reardon (1989) 650–735; Stoneman (1991). Critical studies: **Stoneman 601–612**; Merkelbach (1977²); Konstan (1998); Stoneman (1991) (1994b) (1994c) (1995) (1999).
5. Philostratus, *Life of Apollonius, Heroikos*. Greek texts: Kayser (1870); Conybeare (1912); de Lannoy (1977). English translations: Conybeare (1912); Maclean (2001). Critical studies: **Anderson 613–618**; Dzielska (1986); Billault (1991b) (1993) (2000); Bowie (1994a); Francis (1998); Maclean (2001).
6. Utopias and Fantastic Travel: Euhemerus, *Sacred Scripture* and Iambulus, *Blessed Isle*. Greek texts and English translation: found

most conveniently in Diodorus Siculus, *Bibliotheca Historica* 5.41–46, 6.1 (Euhemerus) and 2.55–60 (Iambulus), in Oldfather (1939) and (1935). Critical studies: **Holzberg 621–628**; Brown (1955); Ferguson (1975); Kytzler (1988); Ehlers (1985); Holzberg (1993c); R.J. Müller (1993). [Antonius Diogenes, *Marvels Beyond Thule* and Lucian, *True History* share some aspects with the subject above.]

7. History and the Novel: Ctesias, *Persica* (and *Indica*). Greek texts: summary in Photius, *Bibliotheca* 72; *P. Oxy.* 2330, Lobel (1954). English translation: Wilson (1994). Critical studies: **Holzberg 629–632**, also on the *Ninus Romance*; Jacoby (1922); Bigwood (1965) (1980) (1986); Brown (1978); Kussl (1991).

8. Fables, Aesop, *Life of Aesop*, and the Novel. Greek text of *Life of Aesop*: Perry (1952). English translation: Daly (1961); Wills (1997). Bibliography: Beschorner/Holzberg (1992b). Critical studies: **Holzberg 633–639**; Adrados (1979); Winkler (1985) 276–291; Holzberg (1992a) (1992c) (1993a) (1993b) (2001²); Hopkins (1993); Merkle (1996); Hägg (1997); Pervo (1998); Shiner (1998); Dillery (1999).

9. Rhetoric and the Novel, Dio Chrysostom, *The Hunters of Euboea* (*Oration 7, Euboicus*). Greek text: Cohoon/Crosby (1932–51). English translations: Cohoon/Crosby (1932–51); Hadas (1953). Commentary: Russell (1992). Critical studies: **Holzberg 640–644**; Reuter (1932); Anderson (1976b); Jouan (1977); C.P. Jones (1978); Swain (1994).

10. Chion of Heraclea, *Letters*, and other collections of letters which make up novels. Greek text with English translation and commentary of Chion: Düring (1951); Greek texts and translations of other collections are listed in Holzberg (2001a) 147–148. Critical studies: **Holzberg 645–653**; Penwill (1978); Doenges (1981); Konstan (1990); Brodersen (1994); Holzberg (1994a) (1994b); Rosenmeyer (1994) (2001).

D. Fragments of Lost Novels. For convenience all fragments are grouped here; most fragments, however, have resemblances and similarities to previously listed novels. The Greek texts are available in Kussl (1991) and Stephens/Winkler (1995). Commentaries and bibliography: Kussl (1991); Stephens/Winkler (1995); Morgan (1998). English translations: in Reardon (1989) 775–827; Stephens/Winkler (1995).

Idealistic—Romantic Novels

1. *Parthenope and Metiochus*. Critical studies: **Stephens 657–660**; Maehler (1976); Dihle (1978); Utas (1984–86); Hägg (1984) (1985) (1986) (1987a) (1989).
2. *Chione*. Critical studies: **Stephens 660–661**; Wilcken (1901); Gronewald (1979b); Marini (1993).
3. *Apollonius*. Critical studies: **Stephens 661–662**; Kussl (1991) 143–159.

Nationalistic Novels

1. Iamblichus, *Babyloniaca*. Critical studies: **Stephens 662, 667–669**; Schneider-Menzel (1948); Beck (1982b); Danek (2000).
2. *Calligone*. Critical studies: **Stephens 662, 666–667**; Körte (1927).
3. *Ninus*. Critical studies: **Stephens 663–665**; Wilcken (1893); Gronewald (1993).
4. *Sesonchosis*. Critical studies: **Stephens 665–666**; Ruiz-Montero (1989a).

Comic-Satiric Novels

1. Lollianus, *Phoenicica*. Critical studies: **Stephens 669–672**; Henrichs (1972); Szepessy (1978); Sandy (1979a); C.P. Jones (1980); Winkler (1980a); Stramaglia (1992) (1998).
2. *Iolaus*. Critical studies: **Stephens 673–674**; Parsons (1971); Merkelbach (1973); Astbury (1977).
3. *Tinouphis*. Critical studies: **Stephens 673–674**.
4. *Daulis*. Critical studies: **Stephens 674**.

Attempt to Diversify from the Idealistic Novel [Holzberg (1995) 57–60]

1. Antonius Diogenes, *Unbelievable Things Beyond Thule*. Critical studies: **Stephens 674–680**; Di Gregorio (1968); Reyhl (1969); Fauth (1978); Morgan (1985); Romm (1992) (1994); Swain (1992).

E. The Ancient Novel Becomes Christian

1. Jewish Fiction: *Esther, Daniel, Ruth, Judith, Tobit, Barlaam and Ioasaph, Joseph and Aseneth*. For Hebrew and Greek texts and English translations see **Pervo 710–711**. Critical studies: **Pervo 687–689**; Braun (1938); Pervo (1975); Wills (1994) (1995).
2. Early Christian Narrative and Ancient Fiction. For Greek texts

and English translations see **Pervo 710–711**. Bibliographies: see reports by R. Hock in the *Petronian Society Newsletter* (this is on-line including all back issues at: http://www.ancientnarrative.com). See, for example, C. Hedrick, "Ancient Fiction and Early Christian and Jewish Narrative Working Group," *PSN* 24 (1994) 6–7.

   a. Gospels, Luke-Acts, Apocryphal Acts: Andrew, John, Paul (includes Acts of Thecla), Peter, Thomas; Wills (1997); Ramelli (2001).
   b. Pseudo-Clement, *Homilies, Recognitions*
   c. *Xanthippe and Polyxena*

For critical studies on No. 2 above with some references also to No. 1 above, see: **Pervo 685–711**; Söder (1932); Plümacher (1978) (1988); Pervo (1987) (1994); Hock (1988) (1998a); M. Edwards (1992); Perkins (1994a) (1994b) (1995) (2001); Szepessy (1995); Cooper (1996); D. Edwards (1996); Hansen (1997); Bremmer (1998); Hock/Chance/Perkins (1998)—15 essays interpreting the intersection of the ancient novel and early Christian narrative; Lalleman (1998); Huber-Rebenich (1999); Vielberg (2000); Thomas (2003); Reiser (1984).

F. Byzantine and Late Greek Reception of the Ancient Novel

For Greek texts and translations into modern languages, see **Beaton 713–733**; MacAlister (1994a) (1994b). For bibliographies see C. Jouanno's reports in the *Petronian Society Newsletter* available (with all back issues) under the *Ancient Narrative* web site: http://www.ancientnarrative.com. Critical studies: **Beaton 713–733**; Gigante (1960); Mazal (1967); Cupane (1974); Alexiou (1976) (1977) (1986); H.G. Beck (1984); Kazhdan (1984); Dyck (1986); Beaton (1987) (1988) (1989a, new edition 1996) (1993) (1994); Jouanno (1989) (1992) (1998); Ricks (1990); Agapitos (1991); Holton (1991a) (1991b); MacAlister (1991) (1994a) (1994b) (1996); Magdalino (1992) (1993); Wilson (1992).

G. Reception-Heritage-Influence-Nachleben of the Ancient Novel

1. Greek Novel in France and England

The most convenient place to start an investigation into the reception of the Greek novel in France is **Sandy 735–764**, and in England it is **Sandy 764–773**. Hägg (1983) 192–227 offers a short but illuminating review of the influence of the Greek novel across France, England, Spain, and Germany. Soon after the first translations of the Greek novel into French and English [Wolff (1912) 8–10 provides a chart] modern writers began to make use of the plots, descriptions, characterizations, and erotic interests.

For the reception in France beginning with the 16th century. Critical studies: Huet (1670); Daele (1946); Weinreich (1950); Sandy (1979) (1982a) (1982c) (1984–85) (1992); Molinié (1978) (1982) (1992); Barber (1989); Romm (1994); Plazenet (1997) (2002).

For the reception in England beginning with Elizabethan fiction and Shakespeare. Critical studies: Reeve (1785); Wolff (1912); Gesner (1970); Hägg (1987a); Doody (1994); Plazenet (1997).

Another way to appreciate the influence of the ancient Greek novel in modern literature is to study it not by place but by chronology. Such a method has been adopted by Doody (1996) who proceeds by "ages" or centuries. First she deals with survival of the ancient novel in the Middle Ages (175–212), its growing security in the age of printing and the Renaissance (213–250), novels in the 17th century (251–273), 18th century (274–300), and then a study of the modern era (303–485), which she calls "Tropes of the Novel," and in which she shows how contemporary writers use themes/motifs/tropes in ways similar to the ancient novelists. A major motif which runs through Doody's book is that the ancient novel (by birth, development, maturity) is tied (closely or not) to various aspects of ancient religion: as ancient religion is ever more dominated by female deities, so the ancient novel is a story of women becoming heroines, becoming goddesses. And this motif continues into the modern novel. On the contemporary novel, see Turner (1968b) and Montague (1994).

2. Greek Novel in Spanish and Portuguese Literature

The most convenient place to begin is with the essay by **Futre-Pinheiro 775–799**, who concentrates her study on the earliest influences beginning in the 16th century; Billault (1992); Romm (1994); Doody (1996) *passim*.

3. Greek Novel in Italy

Work on the influence of the ancient Greek novel in Italy has been slight: Wilson (1992); Sandy (1992); W. Stephens (1994).

4. Greek Novel in Greece and Byzantium

The influence of the ancient novel in the Byzantine world is set out in F above: **Beaton 713–733**, (1988) (1989a, reedited 1996); Bien (1994) on 19th and 20th century Greece.

5. Roman Novel in the Modern World: Petronius

Of all the ancient novelists and novels, Greek and Latin, Petronius and his *Satyrica* are surely the best known in the contemporary world. Petronius, the *arbiter elegantiae* under the notorious emperor Nero, has become a character in his own right, detached at times from the author of the *Satyrica*, and the listed author of such scandalous works as the *Memoirs of the Present Countess of Derby* (London 1797); *New York Unexpurgated: an Amoral Guide for the Jaded* ... (New York 1966); Eurydice, *Satyricon USA: a Journey Across the New Sexual Frontier* (New York 1999); and such mundane works as *Thorne's Complete Contract Bridge* (London 1939), said to be "revised and partly rewritten by Petronius."

For general works on the reception of Petronius and his *Satyrica*, see **Schmeling 487–490**, (1975) (1977) nos. 2045–2074; Smith (1985) 1665; Walsh (1970) 224–243 (more sympathetic to Apuleius).

Reception in France: Collignon (1893) (1905); Gagliardi (1993); Martin (1999) 91–130.

Reception in Italy: Rini (1937); Gagliardi (1993).

Reception in Spain: Walker (1971); Gagliardi (1993); Martin (1999) 91–130.

Reception in England: Stuckey (1966) notes that 17th century England is influenced by St. Evremond and the Restoration of Charles II (1660) who aid the study of Petronius; Kelly (1970) on Rochester, Dryden, Swift, Addison, Steele, Pope, Fielding, Smollett, Johnson, Goldsmith, Walpole, Reynolds; Schmeling (1975) with notes on Peacock, Stevenson, Wilde, Joyce [see also Killeen (1957)], D.H. Lawrence, the Bloomsbury Group, Huxley, Durrell, Sienkiewicz (*Quo Vadis*), Huysman, Synge, Christopher Fry, F. Scott Fitzgerald [see also MacKendrick (1950)], Ezra Pound, Henry Miller, T.S. Eliot.

Menippean Satire in the *Satyrica* and later: Dronke (1994); de Smet (1996).

The Influence of the Widow of Ephesus: Grisebach (1889); Carleton (1988); Boldrini (1989); Huber (1990).

Forgeries in the *Satyrica* by Nodot and Marchena: Stolz (1987); Laes (1998).

The movie *Fellini Satyricon* (1969) [so-called because Polidoro produced his *Satyricon* in Italy just before Fellini did]. Fellini (1970); Highet (1970); Grossvogel (1971); Segal (1971); Bondanella (1992).

The *Satyrica* on stage and in music: *Satyricon*, an opera by Bruno Maderna, premier 16 March 1973, see Fusillo (1997a); *The Satyricon*, a musical with book and lyrics by T. Hendry and music by S. Silverman, 1969 Stratford, Ontario Festival; *Overture Satyricon* by John Ireland, recorded by Sir Adrian Boult and the London Philharmonic; *Scena* (1983) by Geert van Keulen was recorded in Amsterdam, chapters 33 and 36 of the *Satyrica* sung in Latin; the *Süddeutsche Zeitung* of 20 January 1996 notes that on 19 January a stage performance of the *Cena Trimalchionis* was given in a fringe theater (Fest-Spiel-Haus) in Munich, and the audience was treated not only to the sights on stage but to the food and wine of Trimalchio.

6. Roman Novel in the Modern World: Apuleius

Haight (1927) wrote a general book (now out of date) on the influence of Apuleius, but we can supplement this with Walsh (1970) 224–243 and Doody (1996) 216–226, *passim*.

Reception in France: Rollo (1994).
Reception in Italy: Scobie (1978); Mass (1989); Moreschini (1994).
Reception in Spain: Walker (1971); Scobie (1978); Wilson (1994).
Reception in the Netherlands: Paardt (1989).
Reception in England: Tobin (1984); Carver (1991).
Apuleius and the Movies: Elsom (1989).
Apuleius and the Opera: *The Golden Ass*, an opera by R. Peters with libretto by R. Davies, performed by the Canadian Opera Company, Toronto, April 1999.

7. The Roman Novel in the Modern World: *Apollonius of Tyre*

The reception of this work is limited to the Middle Ages and Renaissance. See **Schmeling 550–551**; Singer (1895); Klebs (1899); Archibald (1988) (1991).

INTRODUCTION   xxiii

Thematic Bibliography

(references in bold type indicate pages in this book)

Bakhtin, M. *on* Menippean Satire, structure, time, *see* **Fusillo 277ff.**; Bakhtin (1974) (1975) (1993); Branham (2002) (2002a) (he is editing a book on Bakhtin, Russian Formalists, and the ancient novels)

Canon of literature *see* F.R. Leavis, *Revaluation* (Harmondsworth 1978 [1936]) who lists the works which he believes belong to the canon of English literature. For Old and New Testament scholars (and believers) the canon (i.e., books accepted by one group but not by another) is a contentious issue (apocryphal books): D. Russell, *Between the Testaments* (Philadelphia 1960) 58–91. Bowie/Harrison (1993) note that the ancient novel has moved to the fringe of the Classics' canon. The Oxbridge reading list for the tripos has traditionally established the Classics' canon.

characterization *see* **Billault 115–129**

Christian narrative (including the *Apocrypha*) and its relationship to the ancient novel *see* **Pervo 685–711**; Söder (1932); Pervo (1987) (1994); Hock (1988) (1998a); Perkins (1994a) (1994b) (1995) (2001); Cooper (1996); Shumate (1996 on conversion); Wills (1997); Bremmer (1998); Hock/Chance/Perkins (1998); Huber-Rebenich (1999); W. Smith (2001); Ramelli (2001)

cinema *see* **Schmeling 489**; Fellini (1970); Elsom (1989); Bondanella (1992)

codes, decoding *see* Merkelbach (1962) (1994); Bartsch (1989); Swain (1996) (1999:28)

conversions, confessions *see* Shumate (1996) on Apuleius and St. Augustine; Schmeling (1994b)

country life (*locus amoenus*) vs. city life *see* e.g. Chariton 2.3 who describes a peaceful country (*locus amoenus*); Horace *Serm.* 2.6 (country mouse); Juvenal 3 (Courtney); Dio Chrysostom *Oration 7* (*Euboicus*); Saïd (1987); Winkler (1980); MacMullen (1967); Shaw (1984)

cultural (social settings) influences *see* **Scarcella 221–276**; Reardon (1971); Bowersock (1994); Swain (1996) 101–131; Goldhill (2001) (2001a)

economics *see* **Scarcella 221–276**; D'Arms (1981); Bodel (1984)

dreams *see* **Index 868**; Stark (1989) 141–144; MacAlister (1996)

ecphrasis *see* Hägg (1983) 46–49, passim; Bartsch (1989); Shea (1998)

English novel, rise of, and ancient novel *see* Doody (1996) and such novelists as Richardson, Fielding, Smollett; Scholes (1966)

epistolary novels *see* Düring (1951); Penwill (1978); Konstan (1990); Holzberg (1994a); Rosenmeyer (1994) (2001)

erotics *see* **Fusillo 300–305**; Foucault (1984a) (1984b); Fusillo (1989) 179–234; Winkler (1990a) (1990b); Zeitlin (1990) (1994); Montague (1992) (1994); Richlin (1992) (1992a); Konstan (1994a); Goldhill (1995); Doody (1996) *see* her Index under *sex*; Larmour (1998)

eye-witness (autopsy) *see* **Merkle 563–580**; Fusillo (1988a)

fable *see* **Holzberg 633–639**; Holzberg (2001[2])

family novel *see* Szeppessy (1985–88)

fantastic travel, utopias *see* **Holzberg 621–628; Ruiz-Montero 38–42**; Ferguson (1975); Kuch (1989c) 52–62

feminist reading *see* **Fusillo 304–305; Johne 151–207**; Egger (1988); Liviabella Furiani (1989a); Wiersma (1990); Elsom (1992); Montague (1992); Richlin (1992) (1992a)

fiction, lies, make-believe *see* Winkler (1982); Gill (1993); Holzberg (1995a); Konstan (1998a)

first-person narrative *see* **Index 869**: Veyne (1964); Paardt (1981); Hägg (1983) 42–44, 55, 74–75, 79, 110, 118; Reardon (1994); Holzberg (1995) 20–21, 68, 72, 77, 88, 90; Kahane (2001)

Foucault, M. *see* also erotics; **Fusillo 303–305**; Goldhill (1995); Larmour (1998); Balot (1998)
gaze *see* Egger (1994a) 36–38; Goldhill (1995) 70–72, 76, 143; Slater (1998); Goldhill (2001a)
gender *see* Lefkowitz (1981) (1986); Egger (1988) (1990); Winkler (1990b); Zeitlin (1990); Elsom (1992); Montague (1992); Richlin (1992) (1992a); Konstan (1994a); Goldhill (1995)
genre *see* **Holzberg 11–28; Ruiz-Montero 29–85**; Kuch (1985) (1989b) (1992); Selden (1994)
happy ending *see* Perkins (1995) 15–40 ["Death as a Happy Ending"]; 41–76 ["Marriages as Happy Endings"]
historical novel *see* Hägg (1987a)
history and the novel *see* **Ruiz-Montero 42–48**; Hägg (1984) (1985) (1987a); Tatum (1989); Alvares (1993); Bowersock (1994); Hunter (1994); Edwards (1996)
humor, laughter *see* Stöcker (1969); Rütten (1997); Plaza (2000)
imperialist, colonial, postcolonial *see* also *travel*; F. Azim, *The Colonial Rise of the Novel* (London 1993) and J. Newman, *The Ballistic Bard: Postcolonial Fictions* (London 1995) note that geographical mobility encourages the importance of the novel; Swain (1996); Goldhill (2001); Schmeling (2003)
interpolated tales *see* Sandy (1970); Shumate (1999)
intertextuality *see* Kristeva (1970) 139–146; Barchiesi (1986); Fusillo (1988a) (1990c); Harrison (1986b); Bremmer (1998); Finkelpearl (2001); Gibson (2001); Gowers (2001); W. Smith (2001)
Isis and the ancient novel *see* Merkelbach (1962) (1994) (1995); Witt (1971); Griffiths (1975) (1978a) (1978b); Shumate (1996)
Jewish narratives/novels *see* **Pervo 687–689**; Wills (1994) (1995)
labyrinth, losing one's way *see* Doody (1996); Bodel (1999); protagonists of novels seem at times to wander around the ancient world, as if they were in a maze; *see travel*
Liebespaar *see* **Index 871**
love-at-first-sight *see* **Index 871**; Rohde (1914) 159; Hägg (1983) 6, 24, 36, 51, 56, 68, 123; Maehler (1990); as a Hellenistic motif *see* R. Heinze, *Virgils epische Technik* (Leipzig 1928³) 122; Apollonius Rhodius 3.275ff.; Terence *Phor.* 111; Catullus 64.86; Virgil *Ec.* 8.41; *see* Thompson (1966) N202.1; N711.4; T15
on the margins, slaves, barbarians, others *see* **Kuch 209–220**; Kuch (1989d)
marriage *see* Egger (1994); Perkins (1995) 15ff., 41ff.; Alexander (1998)
Milesian Tales *see* Trenkner (1958) 174ff.; Perry (1967) 92–95; Mason (1978); Lefèvre (1997); Harrison (1998a)
mystery religions, aretalogy *see* **Beck 131–150**
narratology *see* **Fusillo 280–288**; Hägg (1971a); Winkler (1985)
open form of novel *see* **Fusillo 277–280**
physicians, medicine *see* McLeod (1969); Amundsen (1974); Nutton (1985); *see* Scheintod
popular literature *see* **Anderson 107–113**; Hägg (1983) 125ff.; Fusillo (1994) (1996a); Pecere/Stramaglia (1996); Hansen (1998) xi–xxix, plus introductions to each section; R. Peacock, *Criticism and Personal Taste* (Oxford 1972) 17–18
poststructuralism *see* **Fusillo 300–305**
power and religion *see* Edwards (1996)
psychoanalysis, approach of *see* **Fusillo 293–300**; Sullivan (1968) 232–253
readers/audience *see* **Bowie 87–106**; Perry (1967) *passim*; Levin (1977); Hägg (1983) 90–101, (1994); Wesseling (1988); Stephens (1994); Bowie (1994b); Dowden (1994)
readers, women *see* Egger (1988) (1994a) (1994b); Wiersma (1990)
reader-response *see* **Fusillo 288–293**
recognition scenes, anagnorisis *see* **Index 874; Pervo 706–707**

religion, ancient *see* **Beck 131–150**; Kerényi (1927); Chalk (1960); Merkelbach (1962) (1988) (1994) (1995); Bowersock (1994); Shumate (1996); Edwards (1996); Maclean (2001)
resurrection (opposite to or resulting from Scheintod) *see* Cabaniss (1970); Bowersock (1994); Ramelli (2001); Maclean (2001)
riddles *see* Kortekaas (1984) (1998); Schmeling (1988) (1998); C.W. Müller (1991)
sacrifice, human *see* Cueva (2001)
Scheintod a common motif in the ancient novel, e.g.: Chariton 1.5–6; Xenophon of Ephesus 3.6–7; Achilles Tatius 3.15 among several; Apuleius *Metamorphoses* 4.33. This motif is listed by Aarne (1964) as Type 990 and is employed for the apparent deaths of young women on (soon after, soon before) their wedding day. This motif develops from or into the real death of a youthful bride: Sophocles, *Antigone*; *AP* 7.182–188, 711–712; Seneca *Cont.* 6.6; Silius Italicus *Punica* 13.547–548; Heliodorus 2.29, 10.16; Lattimore (1942) 192–194; Szepessy (1972); Knoles (1981); Seaford (1987); Rehm (1999). And this real death of a youthful bride is one of the categories of the motif of the young girl who dies too young even to have had a chance to marry: Pliny *Ep.* 5.16; *CIL* 6.16630–32 (6.16631 = *ILS* 1030); Vrugt-Lentz (1960); Griessmair (1966); Bodel (1995). A variant shows the suicide of a young woman (about to become the bride of a man whom she does not love) prevented by a kindly physician (another motif), who turns suicide into Scheintod (Xenophon of Ephesus 3.6–7); Amundsen (1974). Another variant of the motif of the death of the young is found in the story of Protesilaus and Laodamia, in which the youthful husband is killed, but the laments of his wife cause the gods to allow him to return from the dead (motif of resurrection). It seems that heroes like Protesilaus return from the dead [or from journeys, Campbell (1949)] to aid mortals, Bowersock (1994), and become part of written fiction as in Philostratus' *Heroicus*; Bowie (1994a); Maclean (2001). In the "death" and "resurrection" of the Widow of Ephesus in Petronius 111–112, Cabaniss (1970) sees a parody of examples of resurrection motifs (resurrection of Christ).
science fiction, fantastic travel *see* **Anderson 555–561**; Fredericks (1976); Swanson (1979); Larmour (1997)
sexuality *see* erotics
shipwrecks *see* **Index 875**; Hägg (1983) 17, 21, 102–103, 148, 160, 163, 174, 203; Alexander (1995a) (1995b) (1998)
social history *see* **Scarcella 221–276**; D'Arms (1981); Millar (1981); Bodel (1984); Saïd (1987); Hopkins (1993); Bowersock (1994); Swain (1996); Goldhill (2001)
suicides *see* Hooff (1990); MacAlister (1996)
theater and the novel *see* **Ruiz-Montero 48–52**; Panayotakis (1995)
theorizing the ancient novel *see* **Fusillo 277–305**, (1986) (1988a) (1988b) (1989); Frye (1976); Winkler (1994); Selden (1994); Morgan (1996); Branham (2002a)
travel, journeys *see* **Holzberg 621–628; Alvares 801–814 (Maps)**; Rohde (1914); Nethercut (1969); Hägg (1983) 89, 118, *passim;* Reardon (1991) 15–45, 97–126; Stoneman (1991) (1994b) (1994c); Alexander (1995a) (1995b); J. Hawthorne, *Studying the Novel* (London 1997³) 38–39: "From its first appearance in the world the novel is associated with movement and travel—and, in a more general sense, with mobility. In the passage I quote above from *Moll Flanders* we are reminded how important being able to move from place to place was for Moll, but we should remember, too, that for her *geographical* movement was closely linked to her desire for *social* movement or advance." Such movement is possible only in imperialist or colonial periods; *see* imperialist, colonial
virginity, chastity, enkrateia *see* **Fusillo 301–302** (on Foucault); **Pervo 699–702** (on Paul and Thecla); **Johne 151–207**; Fehrle (1910); Goldhill (1995); Cooper (1996); Alexander (1998); Aubin (1998)

virginity ordeals/tests *see* Rattenbury (1926)
women and the ancient novel *see* **Johne 151–207**; Lefkowitz (1981) (1986); Egger (1988) (1990) (1994) (1994a); Liviabella Furiani (1989a); Wiersma (1990); Perkins (1995)
women writers *see* **Johne 156–164**; Lefkowitz (1991)

INTRODUCTION   xxvii

*Notes on Ways Teachers and Students of Classics, Early Christian/
Jewish/Byzantine Literature, Modern Languages Might Use This Book
to Explore The Ancient Novel*

1. Classics courses in which the Greek and Latin novels are read in the original languages:

   A. Greek novels. There are good and available texts for Chariton, Achilles Tatius, and Longus; for Xenophon of Ephesus and Heliodorus texts might be a problem, but with good preparation these can be secured. Texts of Lucian, Xenophon of Athens, Philostratus, Pseudo-Callisthenes, and novel fragments are easily found. Information about texts is found in this book listed under the individual authors, which also introduces each author and offers a literary history of the ancient novel. While whole courses are, of course, devoted to the text of each author, or the pairings of authors for likenesses/differences/developments, novels are often read in conjunction with (when appropriate) works of New Comedy, epic (Homer, Apollonius of Rhodes), Euripides' *Helen* (e.g.), historians, Theocritus, epistolary fictions, texts dealing with erotics or religion. The reason for the popularity of Greek novel courses is the creativity of faculty in finding a place in the curriculum for this late-appearing genre. The novel rounds out the offerings in Greek prose with a genre which is the predominant form of literature in the modern world.

   B. Latin novel. Texts of all Latin novels are readily available. Because of its colorful manuscript tradition and resulting textual criticism, valuable insights into everyday life and language of slaves, the *Cena Trimalchionis* is popular as a separable piece of literature, and because of the author's connection to the notorious Nero, the *Satyrica* of Petronius has for some years been a popular part of the Classics canon. Its popularity/notoriety among modern writers keeps the title a living icon among modern literate students. Part of the fun in reading the *Satyrica* is the students' search for Petronian borrowings from earlier writers and comparisons of the Latin dialogues of freedmen in the *Cena* with inscriptions from Pompeii. The *Metamorphoses* or *Golden Ass* of Apuleius is also regularly read and enjoyed because of its baroque and musical Latin and for the sheer fun of its narrative. The inserted tale of

Cupid and Psyche almost makes a novel within a novel, and it is often read separately from the whole. The *Metamorphoses* is often read together with texts relating to the cult of Isis. The anonymous *Historia Apollonii Regis Tyri* lies somewhere between the Greek novels to which it is related and the Latin "family novel" of which it is the only extant example. It is often read with Late Latin texts.

2. Classics courses in which the Greek and Latin novels are read in translation. This is perhaps the most popular format today for presenting the ancient novel. Almost all of the Greek and Latin novels can be made available to students in just three books: 1) Reardon (1989); 2) Sullivan (1986) or Branham (1996) or Walsh (1996); 3) Lindsay (1962) or Walsh (1994). Translations of the "fringe-novels," which are discussed at **555–653**, or fragments at **655–683**, are available in a variety of formats. The high quality of the translations makes these courses in the ancient novel very appealing.

#1. "Novels Ancient and Modern." For this course the ancient novels could be divided into four non-exclusive groups: 1) Ideal. Chariton (historical), Achilles Tatius (comedy-parody), Longus (pastoral), Heliodorus (serious/religious), *Apollonius of Tyre* (family). Modern novels read for comparison might be Mitchell, *Gone with the Wind*, Prevost, *Manon Lescault*, Flaubert, *Madam Bovary*, Brontë, *Jane Eyre*, or almost any of the novels on the library shelves listed under "modern romance." Discussions: a) similarities and differences in characters; b) are plots well developed or unimportant? c) are ancient or modern characters more plausible? General comparisons of ancient and modern love stores. 2) Picaresque. Apuleius' *Metamorphoses, Lucius or the Ass, Lazarillo de Tormes*. 3) Menippean. Petronius' *Satyrica, Iolaus*, the Alice books. 4) Utopian Fiction. Lucian's *True Story*, Antonius Diogenes' *Wonders Beyond Thule*, Swift's *Gulliver's Travels*, the Alice books. Questions for the class to discuss and to write about: a) consider the narrators, Lucius in the *Metamorphoses*, Encolpius in the *Satyrica*, and Lazarillo; do genre differences arise from differences in the narrator? Achilles Tatius' novel might also be considered here. b) under Menippean satire Frye (1957) 308ff. would add Thomas Love Peacock, Swift, Huxley and the Alice books; does this make sense? c) attack or defend the statement that Carroll's *Through the Looking Glass* is utopian fiction. d) read the first quarter of Defoe's *Robinson Crusoe* and describe the differences with all ancient novels read.

#2. "Novel and History." **Ruiz-Montero 42–48, Holzberg 629– 632**. The ancient novel is read as a social history and an alternative to political history. Students will have to acquire some knowledge of ancient literary and social history. What do ancient novels tell us about the Graeco-Roman world and its literature, if anything? about the same amount as the modern reader obtains from a "romance novel" he acquired in a supermarket? If the ancient novel is proto-feminist literature and women buy most of the "romance novels" in supermarkets, can we draw any conclusions? Or are the ancient novels really imitations of early genres of literature (epic, drama, comedy), and the reader is expected to see the imitations of Homer, Thucydides, and Euripides? Do we learn anything about social realities in the novel (**Scarcella 221–276**)? about religious beliefs and practices (**Beck 131–150**)? Are the ancient novels best studied as literature, novels of separation-search-recognition, crime novels, science fiction, novels of travel in which, if there were no mobility, there would be no novel? Ancient novels might speak to certain social realities: use of torture, treatment of slaves, marriage customs, sexual attitudes, attitudes towards barbarians, labor, wealth. Ancient texts: Xenophon's *Cyropaedia; Alexander Romance*; Chariton's *Callirhoe* and the historical novel, Hägg (1987a); *Parthenope* as history, Hägg (1984) (1985).

#3. "Novels, Utopias, Fantasy and Science Fiction." Travel is an important element in almost every novel: mobility marks the novels' protagonists and the important people in the social structure. Utopian fiction like other types of novels utilizes travel and like several other types adds a strong element of fantasy. On utopias and travels of fantasy which include Euhemerus and Iambulus, see **Ruiz-Montero 38–42** and **Holzberg 621–628**. For a parody of this see Lucian's *True Story*, **Anderson 555– 561**, and Antonius Diogenes' *Wonders Beyond Thule*, **Stephens 674–680**, who seems to parody fantastic travel but intends to entertain rather than amaze; Ferguson (1975). In its nature as a development from epic where characters roam the Mediterranean world, the novel imitates the *Odyssey* and Apollonius' *Voyage of the Argo*. Fantastic travel is a major element of the *Alexander Romance* (**Stoneman 601–612**) and reminds the reader of the ability of ancient gods to move through space. A strong travel element, though not fantastic, appears also in novels like the Clementine *Recognitions* (**Pervo 706–707**) where travel is a journey in search of identity, knowledge, adventure, loved ones. The role played by travel in the novel can be seen from the maps prepared by **Alvares 801–814**. If the reader concentrates on the fantasy (playing down the utopia) and the travel, some of the ancient novels might be read as science fiction; Fredericks (1976); Swanson (1979); Larmour (1997).

#4. A course in "The Novel and Mythology." The novel can be seen as a record or a retelling of stories which over time (out of which the Classical world runs) would become myths. Alexander the Great dead in 323 BC enjoyed a marvelous afterlife in the *Alexander Romance*, first in Greek and then in Latin, and in geography all the way to India. The great/holy man does not really die and leave the scene but is transformed into a kind of hero who appears, participates in fantastic adventures, and benefits many of the people around him. Just so Protesilaus is thought to be alive and like Alexander becomes the subject of novel-like myths in Philostratus' *Heroicus* [Maclean (2001)]. Later on in the eastern part of the Roman Empire Nero was believed to have survived assassination attempts and to be alive as late as the reign of Trajan (Dio Chrysostom *Oration* 21.9–10), and for Christians (the best of mythographers) Nero is written into apocalyptic literature as the sign of the Antichrist at the end of the world. Could the similarities in Greek novel plots arise from the fact that the novels are variations of a single myth or a series of related myths? Can we say that some Greeks perhaps rethought their own history in terms of myth by reading or hearing such novels as the *Alexander Romance*, and that the *Heroicus* and stories like the myths of Nero represent some of the ways in which people continued to rethink (re-imagine) their own history?

#5. "The Novel as Epic for Everyman." Many scholars of the ancient novel see in Homer's *Odyssey* the beginnings of the prose novel, the mother of all novels; Sullivan (1968) 92ff.; Hägg (1983) 110: "The *Odyssey* is the prototype of the Greek novel, and as such is simply the first novel of love, travel, and adventure in Greek." This course would begin with the students reading the *Odyssey* and perhaps some of the *Voyage of the Argo* for narrative style, manipulation of the plot, episodes/motifs/themes. After Petronius'

Satyrica and Heliodorus have been read, the students are asked to discuss what Petronius borrows, how he uses it. For Heliodorus the students are led to discover that the *Odyssey* is an intertext. Myths of the journey of discovery and maturation [Campbell (1949)] like those of Telemachus and Perseus can be used to show that the novel is a latter day "epic for Everyman."

#6. A course in the "Ancient Novel, Magic, and Ancient Religion." **Beck 131–150; Pervo 685–711**. The class reads Apuleius' *Metamorphoses* (**Harrison 491–516**) with special emphasis on Book 11 [Griffiths (1975)]. There are, however, many other passages in the *Metamorphoses* describing in detail scenes about witches and religious charlatans [the mendicant priests of the Syrian goddess; Winkler (1985)] which are illuminating and can be compared with other such episodes in other novelists. Achilles Tatius (magic to cure bee-stings) and Heliodorus (raising the dead) provide vivid examples of ancient magic; fragmentary novels, such as *Iolaus*, Iamblichus' *Babyloniaca* and Lollianus' *Phoenicica* (**Stephens 655–683**) have episodes of the occult; Petronius has stories about werewolves and witches, and Philostratus' *Life of Apollonius* provides tales of ghosts, spirits, and vampire-like creatures. Apuleius' *Metamorphoses* is perhaps the best place to start discussions about mystery religions, but there are many images from mystery religions in most of the novels and echoes of Orphism in Longus. Heliodorus and Philostratus' *Life of Apollonius* paint a picture of the ancient holy-man/miracle worker which can be used in a course about New Testament society. The Apocryphal Acts of the Apostles, particularly the *Acts of Andrew and Matthias in the City of the Cannibals,* demonstrate how the novels are used by early Christians, particularly those with wild imaginations and those prone to repeat miracle reports.

#7. A course entitled "The Ancient Novel as Escape Literature: the Fantastic and Miraculous." This course is related to the preceding one. Rather than seeing literature as traditional material, the class learns to recognize, then to isolate, the fantastic in often-told tales: Homer's *Odyssey*, Apollonius' *Voyage of the Argo*, Heliodorus [e.g., both of Charicleia's parents are black, but she is born white; Reeve (1989)], Lucian's *True Story*, the *Alexander Romance*, Antonius Diogenes' *Wonders Beyond Thule*, Euripides' *Alcestis*, Plato's "Atlantis Myth," Phlegon of Tralles, *Book of Marvels*, selections from the New Testament and Apocrypha.

#8. "The Ancient Novel as Post-Colonial Literature." In the last few years there has occurred a heightened interest in what many call post-colonial literature, which explores the writings, lives, and mentalities of formerly colonialized people (some are still colonialized): how do the colonizers and the colonized view each other, inscribe themselves on each others' culture, view the past as if it were the present? For example, what would this mean for Apuleius? He was born in Madauros in North Africa, probably with strong connections to the local Punic language and culture (in *Apology* 24 he refers to himself as *seminumidam et semigaetulum*), to a father who attained the highest office in a *colonia*, who received an excellent Roman education and spoke Greek and Latin well (he studied in Rome and Athens), who became a "Latin Sophist" and developed a great interest in Middle-Platonic philosophy; Harrison (2000) 2: "It is important for a true appreciation of Apuleius to realize that he belongs not to an African sub-culture but to the mainstream of Latin culture and literature . . ." This Apuleius writes a novel about a man named Lucius who has an important Greek lineage, a Roman career and traditional Greek religion, but who abandons everything to become a follower of the exotic Egyptian goddess Isis. While the travels of Philostratus' Apollonius of Tyana reinforce the opinion about the superiority of Greek wisdom, the Phoenician Heliodorus from the Syrian city of Emesa makes Ethiopia, not Greece, the source of true enlightenment; Whitmarsh (1999). Chariton of Aphrodisias in Asia Minor wrote a novel about Callirhoe of Syracuse and placed it in the late 5th century BC. An important character in Chariton is Dionysius of the Greek city of Miletus, first in *paideia* in Ionia, but his home is luxurious enough to receive the Persian king, and he is so acclimated to the political/cultural realities that he performs the patriotic act of *proskynesis* to the king. Dionysius' *paideia* and status in the Persian Empire reflect the prestige sought by many Greeks from their colleagues and from their Roman overlords. Chariton neatly dissects the conflicted attitudes of the Greek elite under Rome; Swain (1996).

#9. "Ancient Novel as Popular Literature." In the Introduction to his edited volume, *Anthology of Ancient Greek Popular Literature* (Bloomington 1998) xvii, W. Hansen defines popular literature: "The popular aesthetic, as expressed in literature, manifests itself typically as writing that is easy to read, quickly and continually engaging, and replete with action and sensation. Its opposite is literature that is aesthetically or intellectually demanding, inviting the reader to savor its texture or ponder its implications." Hansen has in fact prepared a course text with a valuable introduction at the beginning of the volume and at the beginning of each section, and assembled a collection of readings which would make a most interesting semester course. To the novels by Xenophon of Ephesus, he has added *The Acts of Paul and Thecla, Secundus the Silent Philosopher, Lucius or the Ass, The Aesop Romance, The Alexander Romance*, Phlegon of Tralles' *Book of Marvels*, and various other items of popular literature. Hansen's arrangement of materials provides a most useful approach to the ancient novel, which deemphasizes the literary quality of the works in favor of their immediate entertainment value.

#10. "Biography Becomes Novel." As factual history becomes "dramatic history," so reliable biographies become fictitious and novel-like. The strength in the plots of Xenophon's *Cyropaedia*, *The Alexander Romance*, Philostratus' *Life of Apollonius of Tyana*, and the works of Dictys and Dares about the fall of Troy, is its connection or relationship to biography. A way to approach the ancient novel and to try to understand better extended narrative prose fiction might be to do so through the form of biography; Holzberg (1995) 14–19; Hägg (1983) 115–117.

3. Course in an English Department about the Ancient Novel for Surveys of Western Literature

#1. "Modern Literature and its Recognition of the Ancient Novel." For background resources see **Sandy 735–773; Futre Pinheiro 775–799**; Hägg (1983) 192–227; Gagliardi (1993); Doody (1996). In such a course it has proved successful in the past to have students begin by reading a selection of ancient novels and comparing them with early English novelists like Swift, *Gulliver's Travels*, Defoe, *Robinson Crusoe* and *Moll Flanders*, Richardson, *Pamela*, Fielding, *Joseph Andrews* and *Tom Jones*, Smollett, *Roderick Random*. The earliest of the English novels often display narrative strategies and experimentations with the form which seem similar to those in the ancient novels. Boccaccio, *Decameron*, Chaucer, *Canterbury Tales*, *Lazarillo de*

Tormes, and Cervantes, *Don Quixote,* might be read with Petronius, Apuleius, and Heliodorus. Sir Philip Sidney, *Arcadia,* shows influences of Achilles Tatius, Longus, and Heliodorus; Jean Racine seems to have been acquainted with Heliodorus, and Goethe with Longus. Doody (1996) is the only scholar who has in a systematic and comprehensive way followed and uncovered the tracks of the ancient novel from the classical world to the contemporary. For the first half of her book Doody adopts an historical approach, tracing the novel in chronological steps. But when she gets to the late 19th century, she argues that the forms, ideas, motifs, "stuff" of the earlier novels are by then so pervasive that she must find a new approach to deal with the subject in a meaningful way, an approach which could demonstrate that the "stuff" of the ancient novel is spread everywhere in contemporary fiction. Doody (1996) 304: "From now on, the discussion will concentrate not on history but on what I prefer to think of as the 'deep rhetoric' of the Novel rather than its 'form.' I concentrate on what I call 'Tropes of Fiction' in the Novel—as Tropes of the Novel itself. These tropes, I maintain, rather than anything describable in terms of spatial shape, characterize and thus define the Novel (insofar as it may be definable). These tropes are figures not of phrasing but of narrative. They are not techniques (like manipulating point of view). Nor are they modes of narrative (such as epistolary narration). The 'Tropes of Fiction' are to be understood as something more like narrative symbols that move us through a novel's story." Instead of showing connections between the ancient novel and the contemporary, Doody chooses a series of tropes and then shows how novels from the ancient to the modern employ the same tropes in the same way. One example, Chapter 18, "Breaking and Entering," the trope is named "The Cut, The Break" (pp. 309–313): Heliodorus, de Scudéry, *Artamène,* Doyle, *A Study in Scarlet,* Carroll, *Through the Looking Glass,* Joyce, *Finnegans Wake,* Richardson, *Pamela.*

4. Course for a Religion Department about the Ancient Novel and the New Testament

#1. "The World of the New Testament." In addition to reading the ancient novels and comparing them with works in the New

Testament and other early Christian texts, the students use novels as sources for reconstructing the social and intellectual world of the early Church and the early Roman Empire. Though the novels show an overriding interest in the theme of love, they also offer the reader a "detailed, comprehensive, and coherent account of the social, economic, and religious institutions of the people and regions that witnessed the spread of Christianity into the Greek East of the early Roman Empire" [Hock (1998a) 123]. For example, Chariton is seen to comment on aspects of social history: on friendship, *peristasis* catalogues, empty tomb stories, letter conventions, role of household managers, strategies used by slaves to mitigate punishment, courtroom speeches. Longus on social history: practice of exposure, rhythm of work in the *chora*, social hierarchy in the chora, danger of brigands, slave role of the *syntrophos*, aristocratic household, visit of householder to his estate. Hock (1998a) sets out a detailed rationale and methodology for making the ancient novel an integral part of courses on the early Church and early New Testament writings; in fact, he provides a virtual course outline. Of all New Testament scholars Hock probably makes the greatest use of the ancient novels in course work in Religion. Hock can be reached at hock@usc.edu. A short bibliography on the ancient novel and early Christian church and its narratives would include: **Pervo 685–711**, (1987); Hedrich (1994); Alexander (1995a) (1995b) (1998); Perkins (1995); Cooper (1996); Edwards (1996); Hock/Chance/Perkins (1998); Hock (1998a); Huber-Rebenich (1999).

(In preparing these suggestions on ways teachers might use the ancient novels in various courses, I have benefited much from the help and guidance of Professer J. Alvares, Montclair State University, Professor Ronald Hock, University of Southern California, and Professor Joel Relihan, Wheaton College. Jean Alvares is a former student of mine, now friend and colleague; Ron Hock has done much to close the gap between the disciplines of Religion and Classics.)

Bibliography

[Supplemental entries to the Bibliography found at the end of this book.]

Adamietz, J. (1995) "Circe in den *Satyrica* Petrons und das Wesen dieses Werkes," *Hermes* 123: 320–334.
Alvares, J. (1993) *The Journey of Observation in Chariton's Chaereas and Callirhoe*. Diss. Austin.
Alexander, L. (1995a) "'In Journeyings Often:' Voyaging in the Acts of the Apostles and in Greek Romance," in *Luke's Literary Achievement: Collected Essays*, ed. C. Tuckett (1995) 17–39. Sheffield.
Alexander, L. (1995b) "Narrative Maps: Reflections on the Toponymy of Acts," in *The Bible in Human Society: Essays in Honor of John Rogerson*, ed. M. Carroll (1995) 17–57. Sheffield.
Alexander, L. (1998) "'Better to Marry than to Burn:' St. Paul and the Greek Novel," in Hock (1998) 235–256.
Amundsen, D. (1974) "Romanticizing the Ancient Medical Profession: the Characterization of the Physician in the Graeco-Roman Novel," *Bulletin of the History of Medicine* 48: 320–337.
Arrowsmith, W., trans. (1959) *The Satyricon of Petronius*. Ann Arbor.
Aubin, M. (1998) "Reversing Romance? The *Acts of Thecla* and the Ancient Novel," in Hock (1998) 257–272.
Balot, R. (1998) "Foucault, Chariton, and the Masculine Self," *Helios* 25: 139–162.
Barber, G. (1989) *Daphnis and Chloe: the Markets and Metamorphoses of an Unknown Bestseller*. London.
Barchiesi, A. (1996) "*Extra legem:* consumo di letteratura in Petronio," in Pecere (1996) 191–208.
Bien, P. (1994) "The Reemergence of Greek Prose Fiction in the Nineteenth and Twentieth Centuries," in Tatum (1994) 370–390.
Billault, A. (1992) "Cervantès et Héliodore," in Baslez (1992) 307–314.
Billault, A., ed. (1994) *Lucien de Samosate*. Lyon.
Billault, A. (2000) *La littérature grecque*. Paris.
Billault, A. (2000) *L'Univers de Philostrate*. Brussels.
Bodel, J. (1995) "Minicia Marcella: Taken Before her Time," *American Journal of Philology* 116: 453–460.
Bodel, J. (1999) "The *Cena Trimalchionis*," in Hofmann (1999) 38–51.
Boldrini, S. (1989) "Il pasto della vedova: cibo, vino, sesso, da Petronio a J. Amado," *Groningen Colloquia on the Novel* 2: 121–131.
Bondanella, P. (1992) *The Cinema of Federico Fellini*. Princeton.
Botermann, H. (1999) "König Apollonius von Tyrus und seine Vorbilder," *Geschichte in Wissenschaft und Unterricht* 50: 678–688.
Bowie, E.L. (1995) "Names and a Gem: Aspects of Allusion in Heliodorus' *Aethiopica*," in *Ethics and Rhetoric*, ed. D. Innes (1995) 269–280. Oxford.
Boyce, B. (1991) *The Language of Freedmen in Petronius' Cena Trimalchionis*. Leiden.
Branham, R., Kinney, D., trans. (1996) *Petronius: Satyrica*. London.
Branham, R., ed. (2002) *Bakhtin and the Classics*. Evanston.
Branham, R., (2002a) "A Truer Story of the Novel," in Branham (2002) 161–186.
Bremmer, J. (1998) "The Novel and the Apocryphal Acts: Place, Time and Readership," *Groningen Colloquia on the Novel* 9: 157–180.
Callebat, L. (1998) *Langages du roman latin*. Hildesheim.
Carleton, S. (1988) "The Widow of Ephesus in Renaissance England," *Classical and Modern Literature* 9: 51–63.
Carver, R. (1991) *The Protean Ass: the Metamorphoses of Apuleius from Antiquity to the English Renaissance*. Diss. Oxford.

Chew, K. (1998) "Inconsistency and Creativity in Xenophon's *Ephesiaca,*" *Classical World* 91: 203–213.
Cohoon, J., Crosby, H. (1932–51) Dio Chrysostom, *Orations*, 5 vols. Cambridge, MA.
Collignon, A. (1893) *Pétrone au moyen âge*. Paris.
Connors, C. (1998) *Petronius the Poet: Verse and Literary Tradition in the Satyricon*. Cambridge.
Conybeare, F. (1912) *Life of Apollonius of Tyana*, 2 vols. Cambridge, MA.
Coon, L. (1997) *Sacred Fictions: Holy Women and Hagiography in Late Antiquity*. Philadelphia.
Cooper, K. (1996) *The Virgin and the Bride. Idealized Womanhood in Late Antiquity*. Cambridge, MA.
Courtney, E. (2001) *A Companion to Petronius*. Oxford.
Cabaniss, A. (1970) *Liturgy and Literature*. University, AL.
Cueva, E. (2001) "Euripides, Human Sacrifice, Cannibalism, Humor and the Ancient Greek Novel," *Classical Bulletin* 77: 103–114.
Daly, L., trans. (1961) *Aesop Without Morals*. New York.
Danek, G. (2000) Iamblichs *Babyloniaka* und Heliodor bei Photios. Referattechnik und Handlungsstruktur," *Wiener Studien* 113: 113–134.
Dillery, J. (1999) "Aesop, Isis, and the Heliconian Muses," *Classical Philology* 94: 268–280.
Doody, M. (1994) "Heliodorus Rewritten: Samuel Richardson's *Clarissa* and Frances Burney's *Wanderer,*" in Tatum (1994) 117–131.
Doody, M. (1996) *The True Story of the Novel*. New Brunswick, NJ.
Dowden, K. (1982) "Apuleius and the Art of Narration," *Classical Quarterly* 32: 419–435.
Dowden, K. (1994) "The Roman Audience of the *Golden Ass,*" in Tatum (1994) 419–434.
Dowden, K. (1996) "Heliodoros: Serious Intentions?," *Classical Quarterly* 46: 267–285.
Dronke, P. (1994) *Verse with Prose: From Petronius to Dante*. Cambridge, MA.
Dzielska, M. (1986) *Apollonius of Tyana in Legend and History*. Rome.
Edwards, D. (1996) *Religion and Power: Pagans, Jews, and Christians in the Greek East*. New York.
Edwards, M. (1992) "The *Clementina:* a Christian Response to the Pagan Novel," *Classical Quarterly* 42: 459–474.
Elsner, J. (1993) "Seduction of Art: Encolpius in a Neronian Picture Gallery," *Proceedings of the Cambridge Philological Society,*" 39: 310–347.
Elsom, H. (1989) "Apuleius and the Movies," *Groningen Colloquia on the Novel* 2: 141–150.
Fehrle, E. (1910) *Die kultische Keuschheit im Altertum*. Giessen.
Fellini, F. (1970) *Fellini's Satyricon*, ed. D. Zanelli. New York.
Finkelpearl, E. (1998) *Metamorphoses of Language in Apuleius: a Study of Allusion in the Novel*. Ann Arbor.
Finkelpearl, E. (2001) "Pagan Traditions of Intertextuality in the Roman World," in *Mimesis and Intertextuality in Antiquity and Christianity*, ed. D. MacDonald (2001) 78–90. Harrisburg.
Francis, J. (1998) "Truthful Fiction: New Questions to Old Answers on Philostratus' *Life of Apollonius,*" *American Journal of Philology* 119: 419–441.
Frangoulidis, S. (2001) *Roles and Performances in Apuleius' Metamorphoses*. Stuttgart.
Fusillo, M. (1996b) "Il romanzo antico come paraletteratura? Il *topos* del racconto di ricapitolazione," in Pecere (1996) 47–67.
Fusillo, M. (1997) "How Novels End: Some Patterns of Closure in Ancient Narrative," in *Classical Closure: Reading the End in Greek and Latin Literature*, ed. D. Roberts (1997) 209–227. Princeton.
Fusillo, M. (1997a) "Il *Satyricon* di Bruno Maderna: un'opera poliglotta," *Kleos* 2: 231–234.

Futre Pinheiro, M. (1998) "Time and Narrative Technique in Heliodorus' *Aethiopica*," *Aufstieg und Niedergang der römischen Welt* II 34.4: 3148–3173. Berlin.
Gagliardo, D. (1993) *Petronio e il romanzo moderno*. Florence.
Gaselee, S. (1910) "The Bibliography of Petronius," *Transactions of the Bibliographical Society* 10: 141–233.
Gera, D. (1993) *Xenophon's Cyropaedia: Style, Genre, and Literary Technique*. Oxford.
Gibson, B. (2001) "*Argutia nilotici calami*: a Theocritean Reed?," in Kahane (2001) 67–76.
Goldhill, S., ed. (2001) *Being Greek under Rome. Cultural Identity, the Second Sophistic and the Development of Empire*. Cambridge.
Goldhill, S. (2001a) "The Erotic Eye: Visual Stimulation and Cultural Conflict," in Goldhill (2001) 154–194.
Gowers, E. (2001) "Apuleius and Persius," in Kahane (2001) 77–87.
Griessmair, E. (1966) *Das Motiv der Mors Immatura in griechischen metrischen Grabinschriften*. Innsbruck.
Grisebach, E. (1889) *Die Wanderung der Novelle von der treulosen Wittwe durch die Weltliteratur*. Berlin.
Grossvogel, D. (1971) "Fellini's *Satyricon*," *Diacritics* 1: 51–54.
Hadas, M., trans. (1953) *Three Greek Romances*. Indianapolis.
Hadas, M. trans. (1957) *Heliodorus: an Ethiopian Romance*. Ann Arbor [Philadelphia 1999].
Hägg, T. (1997) "A Professor and his Slave: Conventions and Values in the *Life of Aesop*," in *Conventional Values of the Hellenistic Greeks*, ed. P. Bilde (1997) 177–203. Aarhus.
Haight, E. (1927) *Apuleius and his Influence*. New York.
Hansen, D. (1997) "Die Metamorphose des Heiligen. Clemens und die *Clementina*," *Groningen Colloquia on the Novel* 8: 119–129.
Hansen, W., ed. (1998) *Anthology of Ancient Greek Popular Literature*. Bloomington.
Hanson, J.A., trans. (1989) *Apuleius: Metamorphoses*, 2 vols. Cambridge, MA.
Harmon, A., trans. (1913) *Lucian*, vol. 1. Cambridge, MA.
Harrison, S.J. (1998a) "The Milesian Tales and the Roman Novel," *Groningen Colloquia on the Novel* 9: 61–73.
Harrison, S.J. (1998b) "From Epic to Novel: Apuleius as Reader of Vergil," *Materiali e discussioni* 39: 53–73.
Harrison, S.J., ed. (1999) *Oxford Readings in the Roman Novel*. Oxford.
Harrison, S.J. (2000) *Apuleius: A Latin Sophist*. Oxford.
Hedrick, C. (1994) "Ancient Fiction and Early Christian and Jewish Narrative Working Group," *Petronian Society Newsletter* 24: 6–7.
Hedrick, C. (1998) "Conceiving the Narrative: Colors in Achilles Tatius and the Gospels of Mark," in Hock (1998) 177–197.
Hijmans, B., et al. (1995) *Apuleius Madaurensis Metamorphoses Book IX*. Groningen.
Hock, R. (1988) "The Greek Novel," in *Greco-Roman Literature and the New Testament*, ed. D. Aune (1988) 127–146. Atlanta.
Hock, R. (1996) "An Extraordinary Friend in Chariton's *Callirhoe*: the Importance of Friendship in the Greek Romances," in *Greco-Roman Perspectives on Friendship*, ed. J. Fitzgerald (1996) 145–162. Atlanta.
Hock, R., Chance, J., Perkins, J., eds. (1998) *Ancient Fiction and Early Christian Narrative*. Atlanta.
Hock, R. (1998a) "Why New Testament Scholars Should Read Ancient Novels," in Hock (1998) 121–138.
Hofmann, H., ed. (1999) *Latin Fiction: the Latin Novel in Context*. London.
Holzberg, N. (2001^2) *Die antike Fabel: eine Einführung*. Darmstadt.
Holzberg, N. (1993c) "Zweivorläufer des utopischen Romans: die Inselbeschreibungen des Euhemeros und Iambulos," *Anregung* 39: 244–250.

Holzberg, N. (2001a) *Der antike Roman: ein Einführung*. Düsseldorf.
Huber-Rebenich, G. (1999) "Hagiographic Fiction as Entertainment," in Hofmann (1999) 187–212.
Hunter, J. Paul (1990) *Before Novels: the Cultural Contexts of Eighteenth-Century English Fiction*. New York.
Hunter, R., ed. (1998) *Studies in Heliodorus*. Cambridge.
James, P. (1987) *Unity in Diversity: a Study of Apuleius' Metamorphoses*. Hildesheim.
Jouanno, C. (1998) *Digénis Akritas, le héros des frontières. Une épopée byzantine*. Turnhout.
Kahane, A., Laird, A., eds. (2001) *A Companion to the Prologue of Apuleius' Metamorphoses*. Oxford.
Kayser, K., ed. (1870) *Flavii Philostrati Opera*. Leipzig.
Kelly, E. (1970) *Petronius Arbiter and Neoclassical English Literature*. Diss. Rochester.
Killeen, J. (1957) "James Joyce's Roman Prototype," *Comparative Literature* 9: 193–203.
Knoles, T. (1981) "'The Spurned Doxy' and the Dead Bride: Some Ramifications for Ancient *Topoi*," *Classical World* 74: 223–225.
Konstan, D. (1994c) "Xenophon of Ephesus: Eros and Narrative in the Novel," in Morgan (1994) 49–63.
Konstan, D. (1998) "The *Alexander Romance*: the Cunning of the Open Text," *Lexis* 16: 123–138.
Konstan, D. (1998a) "The Invention of Fiction," in Hock (1998) 3–17.
Kortekaas, G., ed. (1984) *Historia Apollonii Regis Tyri*. Groningen.
Kortekaas, G. (1991) "The *Historia Apollonii Regis Tyri* and Ancient Astrology," *Zeitschrift für Papyrologie und Epigraphik* 85: 71–85.
Kortekaas, G. (1998) "Enigmas in and around the *Historia Apollonii Regis Tyri*," *Mnemosyne* 51: 176–191.
Krabbe, J. (1989) *The Metamorphoses of Apuleius*. New York.
Laes, C. (1998) "Forging Petronius: François Nodot and Fake Petronian Fragments," *Humanistica Lovaniensia* 47: 358–402.
Lalleman, P. (1998) "The Canonical and the Apocryphal Acts of the Apostles," *Groningen Colloquia on the Novel* 9: 181–192.
Lamb, W., trans. (1961 [1997]) *Ethiopian Story*. London.
Lannoy, L. de, ed. (1977) *Flavii Philostrati Heroicus*. Leipzig.
Larmour, D. (1997) "Sex with Moonmen and Winewomen: the Reader as Explorer in Lucian's *Vera Historia*," *Intext* 1: 131–146.
Larmour, D., Miller, P., Platter, C., eds. (1998) *Rethinking Sexuality: Foucault and Classical Antiquity*. Princeton.
Lattimore, R. (1942) *Themes in Greek and Latin Epitaphs*. Urbana.
Lefèvre, E. (1997) *Studien zur Struktur der Milesischen Novelle bei Petron und Apuleius*. Stuttgart.
Lefkowitz, M. (1991) "Did Ancient Women Write Novels?," *Women Like This: New Perspectives on Jewish Women in the Greco-Roman World*, ed. A. Levin (1991) 199–219. Atlanta.
Levin, D. (1977) "To Whom Did the Ancient Novelists Address Themselves?," *Rivista di Studi Classici* 25: 18–29.
Lindsay, J., trans. (1962) *Apuleius: the Golden Ass*. New York.
MacAlister, S. (1994a) "Byzantine Developments," in Morgan (1994) 275–287.
MacAlister, S. (1994b) "Ancient and Contemporary in Byzantine Novels," in Tatum (1994) 308–322.
MacAlister, S. (1996) *Dreams and Suicides: the Greek Novel from Antiquity to the Byzantine Empire*. London.
MacKendrick, P. (1950) "The Great Gatsby and Trimalchio," *Classical Journal* 45: 307–314.
Maclean, J., Aitken, E., trans., comm. (2001) *Flavius Philostratus: Heroikos*. Atlanta.
Macleod, M., ed. (1972) *Luciani Opera*, vol. 1. Oxford.

MacMullen, R. (1967) *Enemies of the Roman Order: Treason, Unrest and Alienation in the Empire.* Cambridge, MA.
Maehler, H. (1990) "Symtome der Liebe im Roman und in der griechischen Anthologie," *Groningen Colloquia on the Novel* 3: 1–12.
Mal-Maeder, D. van (1997) "The Enigma of the Last Book of Apuleius' *Metamorphoses*," *Groningen Colloquia on the Novel* 8: 87–118.
Mal-Maeder, D. van (2001) *Apuleius Madaurensis Metamorphoses. Livre II. Texte, Introduction et Commentaire.* Groningen.
Marini, N. (1993) "Osservazioni sul *Romanzo di Chione*," *Athenaeum* 80: 587–600.
Martin, R. (1999) *Pétrone, le Satyricon.* Paris.
Mason, H.J. (1994) "Greek and Latin Versions of the Ass-Story," *Aufstieg und Niedergang der römischen Welt* II 34.2, 1665–1707. Berlin.
Mason, H.J. (1999) "The *Metamorphoses* of Apuleius and its Greek Sources," in Hofmann (1999) 103–112.
Mass, E. (1989) "Tradition und Innovation im Romanschaffen Boccaccios," *Groningen Colloquia on the Novel* 2: 87–107.
McLeod, A. (1969) "Physiology and Medicine in a Greek Novel: Achilles Tatius' *Leucippe and Clitophon*," *Journal of Hellenic Studies* 89: 97–105.
McMahon, J. (1998) *Paralysin Cave: Impotence, Perception, and Text in the Satyrica of Petronius.* Leiden.
Merkelbach, R. (1995) *Isis regina—Zeus Serapis.* Stuttgart.
Merkle, S. (1996) "'Anecdote' and 'Novella' in the *Vita Aesopi*: the Ingredients of a 'Popular Novel'," in Pecere (1996) 209–234.
Merkle, S. (1999) "News from the Past: Dictys and Dares on the Trojan War," in Hofmann (1999) 155–166.
Montague, H. (1994) "From *Interlude in Anarchy* to *Daphnis and Chloe*: Two Thousand Years of Erotic Fantasy," in Tatum (1994) 391–401.
Moreschini, C. (1994) *Il mito di Amore e Psiche in Apuleio.* Naples.
Morgan, J.R. (1994b) "*Daphnis and Chloe*: Love's Own Sweet Story," in Morgan (1994) 64–79.
Morgan, J.R. (1996) "The Ancient Novel at the End of the Century," *Classical Philology* 91: 63–73.
Morgan, J.R. (1997) "Longus, *Daphnis and Chloe*: a Bibliographical Survey, 1950–1995," *Aufstieg und Niedergang der römischen Welt* II 34.3, 2208–2276. Berlin.
Morgan, J.R. (1998) "On the Fringe of the Canon: Work on the Fragments of Ancient Greek Fiction," *Aufstieg und Niedergang der römischen Welt* II 34.4, 3293–3390. Berlin.
Müller, K., ed. (1995[4]) *Petronius. Satyricon Reliquiae.* Leipzig.
Nethercut, W. (1969) "Apuleius' *Metamorphoses*: the Journey," *Agon* 3: 97–134.
Nimis, S. (1998) "Memory and Description in the Ancient Novel," *Arethusa* 31: 99–122.
Nutton, V. (1985) "Murders and Miracles: Lay Attitudes towards Medicine in Classical Antiquity," in *Patients and Practitioners: Lay Perspectives of Medicine in Pre-Industrial Society*, ed. R. Porter (1985) 23–53. Cambridge.
Oldfather, C., trans. (1935) *Diodorus Siculus*, vol. 2. Cambridge, MA.
Oldfather, C., trans. (1939) *Diodorus Siculus*, vol. 3. Cambridge, MA.
Paardt, R. van der (1989) "Three Dutch Asses," *Groningen Colloquia on the Novel* 2: 133–144.
Pecere, O., Stramaglia, A., eds. (1996) *La letteratura di consumo nel mondo greco-latino.* Cassino.
Penwill, J. (1975) "Slavish Pleasures and Profitless Curiosity: Fall and Redemption in Apuleius' *Metamorphoses*," *Ramus* 4: 49–82.
Perkins, J. (1994a) "Representation in Greek Saints' Lives," in Morgan (1994) 255–271.

Perkins, J. (1994b) "The Social Work of the *Acts of Peter*," in Tatum (1994) 296-307.
Perkins, J. (1995) *The Suffering Self: Pain and Narrative Representations in the Early Christian Era*. London.
Perkins, J. (2001) "Space, Place, Voice in the *Acts* of the Martyrs and the Greek Romance," in *Mimesis and Intertextuality in Antiquity and Christianity*, ed. D. MacDonald (2001) 117-137. Harrisburg, PA.
Pervo, R. (1994) "Early Christian Fiction," in Morgan (1994) 239-254.
Pervo, R. (1998) "A Nihilist Fabula: Introducing the *Life of Aesop*," in Hock (1998) 77-120.
Plaza, M. (2000) *Laughter and Derision in Petronius' Satyrica: a Literary Study*. Stockholm.
Plazenet, L. (1997) *L'Ébahissement et la délectation. Réception comparée et poétiques du roman grec en France et en Angleterre aux XVIe et XVIIe siècles*. Paris.
Plazenet, L. (2002) "Jacques Amyot and the Greek Novel: the Invention of the French Novel," in *The Classical Heritage in France*, ed. G. Sandy (2002) 237-280. Leiden.
Pouderon, B., ed. (2001) *Les personnages du roman grec*. Lyon.
Ramelli, I. (2001) *I romanzi antichi e il Cristianesimo: contesti e contatti*. Madrid.
Reardon, B.P. (1994) "Achilles Tatius and Ego-Narrative," in Morgan (1994) 80-96.
Rehm, R. (1999) *Marriage to Death: the Conflation of Weddings and Funeral Rituals in Greek Tragedy*. Princeton.
Reichel, M. (1995) "Xenophon's *Cyropaedia* and the Hellenistic Novel," *Groningen Colloquia on the Novel* 6: 1-20.
Reiser, M. (1984) "Der Alexanderroman und das Markusevangelium," in *Markus-Philologie. Historische, literargeschichtliche und stilistische Untersuchungen zum zweiten Evangelium*, ed., H. Cancik (1984) 131-161. Tübingen.
Richlin, A. (1992a) *Garden of Priapus. Sexuality and Aggression in Roman Humor*. New York.
Robins, W. (1995) *Ancient Romance and Medieval Literary Genres: Apollonius of Tyre*. Diss., Princeton.
Robins, W. (1996) "Latin Literature's Greek Romance," *Materiali e discussioni* 35: 207-215.
Robins, W. (2000) "Romance and Renunciation at the Turn of the Fifth Century," *Journal of Early Christian Studies* 8: 531-557.
Rollo, D. (1994) "From Apuleius's Psyche to Chrétien's Erec and Enide," in Tatum (1994) 347-369.
Romm, J. (1994) "Novels beyond Thule: Antonius Diogenes, Rabelais, Cervantes," in Tatum (1994) 101-116.
Rosenmeyer, P. (2001) *Ancient Epistolary Fiction: the Letter in Greek Literature*. Cambridge.
Ruden, S., trans. (2000) *Petronius. Satyricon*. Indianapolis.
Rütten, U. (1997) *Phantasie und Lachkultur. Lukians Wahre Geschichten*. Tübingen.
Sandy, G. (1979) "Notes on Lollianus' *Phoenicica*," *American Journal of Philology* 100: 367-376.
Sandy, G. (1997) *The Greek World of Apuleius: Apuleius and the Second Sophistic*. Leiden.
Schlam, C. (1971) "The Scholarship on Apuleius Since 1938," *Classical World* 64: 285-309.
Schlam, C., Finkelpearl, E. (2001) *A Review of Scholarship on Apuleius' Metamorphoses 1970-1998. Lustrum* 42. Göttingen.
Schmeling, G. (1998) "Apollonius of Tyre: Last of the Troublesome Latin Novels," *Aufstieg und Niedergang der römischen Welt* II 34.4, 3270-3291. Berlin.
Schmeling, G. (1999a) "Petronius and the *Satyrica*," in Hofmann (1999) 23-37.
Schmeling, G. (1999b) "*The History of Apollonius King of Tyre*," in Hofmann (1999) 141-152.
Schmeling, G. (2003) "Myths of Person and Place: the Search for a Model for the Ancient Greek Novel," in Zimmerman (2003, forthcoming).

Scholes, R., Kellogg, R. (1966) *Nature of Narrative*. New York.
Seaford, R. (1987) "The Tragic Wedding," *Journal of Hellenic Studies* 107: 106–130.
Segal, E. (1971) "Arbitrary *Satyricon:* Petronius and Fellini," *Diacritics* 1: 54–57.
Shea, C. (1998) "Setting the Stage for Romances: Xenophon of Ephesus and the Ecphrasis," in Hock (1998) 61–71.
Shiner, W. (1998) "Creating Plot in Episodic Narrative: the *Life of Aesop* and the Gospel of Mark," in Hock (1998) 155–176.
Shumate, N. (1996) *Crisis and Conversion in Apuleius' Metamorphoses*. Ann Arbor.
Shumate, N. (1999) "Apuleius' *Metamorphoses*: the Inserted Tales," in Hofmann (1999) 113–125.
Singer, S. (1895) *Apollonius von Tyrus: Untersuchungen über das Fortleben des aniken Romans in spätern Zeiten*. Halle.
Slater, N. (1990) *Reading Petronius*. Baltimore.
Slater, N. (1998) "Passion and Petrification: the Gaze in Apuleius," *Classical Philology* 93: 18–48.
Smet, I. de (1996) *Menippian Satire and the Republic of Letters 1581–1655*. Geneva.
Smith, M.S. (1985) "Petronius: a Bibliography 1945–82," in *Aufstieg und Niedergang der römischen Welt* II 32.3, 1628–1665. Berlin.
Smith, W. (2001) "Apuleius and Luke: Prologue and Epilogue in Conversion Texts," in Kahane (2001) 88–98.
Stephens, W. (1994) "Tasso's Heliodorus and the World of Romance," in Tatum (1994) 67–87.
Stoneman, R. (1999) "The Latin Alexander," in Hofmann (1999) 167–186.
Stramaglia, A. (1998) "Il soprannaturale nella narrativa greco-latina: testimonianze papirologiche," *Groningen Colloquia on the Novel* 9: 29–60.
Swain, S. (1994) "Dio and Lucian," in Morgan (1994) 166–180.
Swain, S. (1996) "The Greek Novel and Greek Identity," in *Hellenism and Empire: Language, Classicism and Power in the Greek World AD 50–250*, 101–131. Oxford.
Swain, S., ed. (1999) *Oxford Readings in the Greek Novel*. Oxford.
Szepessy, T. (1972) "The Story of the Girl Who Died on the Day of her Wedding," *Acta Antiqua Academiae Scientiarum Hungaricae* 20: 341–357.
Szepessy, T. (1995) "Les Actes d'apôtres apocryphes et la roman antique," *Acta Antiqua Academiae Scientiarum Hungaricae* 36: 133–161.
Tatum, J. (1994) "The Education of Cyrus," in Morgan (1994) 15–28.
Thiel, H. van (1983) *Leben und Taten Alexanders von Makedonien nach der Handschrift L*. Darmstadt.
Thomas, C. (2003) *The Acts of Peter, Gospel Literature, and the Ancient Novel: Rewriting the Past*. New York.
Thornley, G., Edmonds, J., eds. (1916) *Longus. Daphnis and Chloe*. Cambridge, MA.
Tobin, J. (1984) *Shakespeare's Favorite Novel: a Study of the Golden Asse as Prime Source*. Lanham, IL.
Turner, P., trans. (1968c) *Longus. Daphnis and Chloe*. Harmondsworth.
Vielberg, M. (2000) *Klemens in den pseudoklementinischen Rekognitionen. Studien zur literarischen Form des spätantiken Romans*. Berlin.
Vrugt-Lentz, J. ter (1960) *Mors Immatura*. Groningen.
Walker, J. (1971) *The Satyricon, the Golden Ass, and the Spanish Golden Age Picaresque Novel*. Diss., Provo.
Walsh, P.G., trans. (1994) *Apuleius: the Golden Ass*. Oxford.
Walsh, P.G., trans. (1996) *Petronius: the Satyricon*. Oxford.
Watt, I. (1957) *The Rise of the Novel*. Berkeley.
Whitmarsh, T. (1999) "The Writes of Passage: Cultural Imitation in Heliodorus' *Aethiopica*," in *Constructing Identities in Late Antiquity*, ed., R. Miles (1999) 16–40. London.

Wills, L. (1997) *The Quest of the Historical Gospel: Mark, John and Origins of the Gospel Genre*. London.
Wilson, D. de Armas (1994) "Homage to Apuleius: Cervantes' Avenging Psyche," in Tatum (1994) 88–100.
Wilson, N., trans. (1994) *Photius. The Bibliotheca*. London.
Wolff, E. (1997) *Le roman grec et latin: thèmes et études*. Paris.
Wolff, E. (1998) "Réflexions sur *l'Historia Apollonii Regis Tyri*," *Recherches et Travaux* 54: 181–188.
Wolff, E. (2001) "Les personnages du roman grec et *l'Historia Apollonii Regis Tyri*," in Pouderon (2001) 233–240.
Zimmerman, M., ed. (1998) *Aspects of Apuleius' Golden Ass* II. Groningen.
Zimmerman, M. (2000) *Groningen Commentaries on Apuleius. Apuleius Madaurensis Metamorphoses Book X*. Text, Introduction and Commentary. Groningen.
Zimmerman, M., Panayotakis, S., Keulen, W., eds. (2003) *The Ancient Novel and Beyond*. Leiden.
Zimmermann, B. (1999) "Poetische Bilder. Zur Funktion der Bilderbeschreibung im griechischen Roman," *Poetica* 31: 61–79.

1. PREFACE

Gareth Schmeling

I

The present volume attempts to take a comprehensive look at the ancient classical Greek and Roman novel.[1] Here the reader will find discussions on the major issues of concern to those working on the ancient novel, essays on the eight canonical novels and novelists as well as on those novel-like narratives often included with the ancient novels, papers on fragments of novels and the life of the ancient novel among the Christians and Byzantines, and on the novel's rediscovery in the late Renaissance. We hope to provide here in a single work more information and in-depth studies than are currently available in introductions, handbooks, histories, and other studies on the ancient novel, and in general works on classical literature.

The ancient novel is the subject of this volume. By ancient we mean the later classical periods in Greece and Rome, and by novel we mean that group of works of extended prose narrative fiction which bears many similarities to our modern novel. Frye[2] calls these ancient works romances, Heiserman[3] refers to the ancient corpus as proto-novels before the real novels, and in *The Rise of the Novel* (London 1957) Ian Watt defines the novel so narrowly so as to exclude any fiction before Richardson and Defoe—in fact, his definition now excludes some contemporary novels.[4] We will do little in the pages which follow to settle this dispute. In fact, we will in all likelihood

---

[1] Fictional narratives from Egypt which might have some influence on our classical novels are not extensively considered here, nor are the Jewish novels, which Wills (1995) discusses.
[2] Fry (1976).
[3] Heiserman (1977).
[4] M. Doody, a scholar of English literature, contends that Watt and others in the English academic profession are mistaken in their belief that the novel is "the defining achievement of the English middle class". The idea that the novel was created by the English is one of the "profession's 'most successful literary lies'". In *The True Story of the Novel* (Rutgers University Press 1996) Doody argues that the novel is in fact a product of the Graeco-Roman mind; cf. *Lingua Franca* (July–August 1995) 22–23.

make it worse, since this volume is inclusive rather than exclusive in dealing with works of ancient prose fiction. Thus the model for this volume is German scholarship, not British. The reader will probably be more familiar with the *Satyrica, Metamorphoses,* and *Daphnis and Chloe* than with some of the other works, to which we may seem to give unwarranted and generous attention.

In addition to Watt, scholars of English literature like J. Paul Hunter have vigorously attacked all who attempt "to broaden or diffuse the definition of the novel—to include a variety of... classical prose of several kinds—[because they] muddle the cultural and formal issues in similar ways, however useful they are in extending knowledge of narrative generally".[5] To these English scholars the subject of our volume is not the novel but something like a loose collection of longish bits of prose. In an interesting and well reasoned argument Tatum[6] explains how Hunter and some of his colleagues, who have isolated themselves within one national literature, protect their turf by keeping others away from it and protect their power by controlling (in this instance) the name of a genre.

According to the *Oxford English Dictionary* a novel is a "fictitious prose narrative or tale of considerable length in which characters and actions representative of the real life of past or present times are portrayed in a plot of more or less complexity". If the name Oxford still possesses its magical powers, the genre argument is soon settled. If we must resort to an even higher authority, let us recall the judgment of a novelist, E.M. Forster: "Perhaps we ought to define what a novel is before starting... It is... 'a fiction in prose of a certain extent'... and if this seems to you unphilosophic will you think of an alternative definition, which will include *The Pilgrim's Progress, Marius the Epicurean, The Adventures of a Younger Son, The Magic Flute, A Journal of the Plague Year, Zuleika Dobson, Rasselas, Ulysses* and *Green Mansions,* or else will give reasons for their exclusion?"[7] If the name of a novelist does not persuade the jury, we must resort to the highest authority in the land, an academic critic, former president of the Modern Language Association (MLA), Wayne Booth: "The novel began we are told, with Cervantes, with Defoe, with Fielding, with Richardson,

---

[5] J. Paul Hunter as quoted by Tatum (1994) 4. Selden (1994), the classicist, cautions against using the term novel.
[6] Tatum (1994) 4.
[7] E.M. Forster, *Aspects of the Novel* (London 1974 [1927]) 3.

with Jane Austen—or was it with Homer? It was killed by Joyce, by Proust, by the rise of symbolism, by loss of respect for—or was it the excessive absorption with?—hard facts. No, no, it still lives, but only in the works of..."[8] Retrospectively we apply the term novel to the works of extended imaginative prose fiction presented in this volume. Tatum[9] mischievously observes that ancient novel is an oxymoron.

Respect for and interest in the ancient novel had grown only grudgingly until about twenty-five years ago. At the 1971 annual meeting of the American Philological Association in Cincinnati, the newly formed Petronian Society held an especially well attended session for reading papers. The reaction to this new society and to the content of its session was not universally positive. Agnes Kirsopp Lake Michels, then president of the APA and speaking for some in that organization, proposed that the Petronian Society be prohibited from participating in future APA meetings because it was a "splinter" group, because it was not subject to the quality control of the APA, and because its interests were on the fringe of classical studies. Henry Rowell objected to the motion and argued that, if there were something valuable in splinter groups, they would survive and benefit the larger group. Academic forces especially should have appreciated how difficult it is to kill (a) fiction. The Petronian Society and its *Newsletter* went on to embrace not only Nero's *arbiter elegantiae* but also the whole genre of the ancient novel. The *Newsletter* has just celebrated its 25th anniversary.

Bowie and Harrison provide a most comprehensive look at the current status of studies in the ancient novel and reasons for its popularity, and we quote a small portion of their observations:[10]

> Students of the ancient world are falling for the ancient Greek and Latin novels in increasing numbers, a state of affairs of which there were few intimations a generation ago. To be sure, the *Satyrica* of Petronius and the *Metamorphoses* of Apuleius were given standing-room on the edge of the classical canon... The Greek novels were still wallflowers... Now the ancient novel has become one of the hottest properties in town... Some factors that have made the novel so alluring can readily be suggested. As the "central" texts of the classical period have become progressively over-grazed scholars have looked to new

---

[8] W. Booth, *The Rhetoric of Fiction* (Chicago 1983) 36.
[9] Tatum (1994) 2.
[10] Bowie (1993) 159.

pastures. The rediscovery of the Greek novel is part of the rediscovery of imperial Greek literature as a whole. But within that literature the Greek novels, like Petronius and Apuleius in Latin literature, stand outside canonical genres, and such forbidden fruit is especially enticing to a generation that esteems the non-canonical and potentially subversive.

Those working on the ancient novel traditionally date the origin of its modern scholarship to 1876 and the publication of Erwin Rohde's magisterial *Der griechische Roman*[11]—some also with a nod to Pierre Daniel Huet's *Traité de l'Origine des Romans* of 1670.[12] Rohde's work, which is still in print, caused only a small stir and no large following. Almost a century later in 1967, however, the appearance of Perry's *The Ancient Romances*[13] stirred a great deal of interest and reflected a growing awareness of the importance of the ancient novel. This new enthusiasm was celebrated in 1976—to mark the centenary of the publication of Rohde's great book—when B.P. Reardon hosted the first International Conference on the Ancient Novel (ICAN-I) in Bangor, Wales.[14] Many of those working on the ancient novel met for the first time a large number of other like-minded individuals. The origins of the "novel mafia" can be traced to that chilly July conference on Conwy Bay. Thirteen years later in the hills of New England an even larger group of scholars met for ICAN-II at Dartmouth College, hosted by James Tatum.[15] Scholars focusing their efforts on the ancient novel could no longer be referred to as a splinter group.

The ancient novel has become popular not only among students of literature but also among historians, some of whom employ the ancient novels as if they were "alternative histories": Chariton provides, as it were, in his novel a "popular" view of several aspects of history of fifth-fourth century Magna Graecia, Greece and Asia Minor. Duncan-Jones[16] uses various prices and costs cited in the Roman novels as a control group for prices established by other means; Millar[17] employs Apuleius' novel to construct a picture of the social history

---

[11] Rohde (1914). Though originally published in 1876, scholars generally cite the 1914 edition.
[12] Huet (1670).
[13] Perry (1967).
[14] For the conference proceedings cf. Reardon (1977).
[15] For conference proceedings cf. Tatum (1990).
[16] Duncan-Jones (1982).
[17] Millar (1981).

of part of the eastern Roman Empire; D'Arms[18] reconstructs a first century A.D. successful businessman from Petronius' description of Trimalchio in the *Satyrica*; Hopkins[19] manipulates a slave's biography, the novel-like *Life of Aesop*, to enrich our meager knowledge of what people in the ancient world thought about their own society; and Bowersock[20] treats ideas and motifs from the ancient novel, which recur also in historical records, as information to enhance our appreciation of the history of culture or social history of the classical world.

Scholars of religion have also found a rich treasure in the ancient novel. The Society of Biblical Literature, an American association with connections to the American Academy of Religion, has established an organization which calls itself the "Ancient Fiction and Early Christian and Jewish Narrative Working Group" which meets regularly "to bring into focus the early Greek and Roman novels as the narrative matrix in which early Christian/Jewish narrative is most at home."

There exist excellent introductions to the study of the ancient novel, some of which are collections of essays [Tatum (1994), Morgan (1994), Baslez (1992), Kuch (1989)], and others monographs [Holzberg (1995), Konstan (1994), Reardon (1991), Billault (1991), Fusillo (1989), Hägg (1983), Perry (1967)]. For many of the ancient novels and novel-like pieces of fiction there are useful texts, commentaries, translations, and bibliographies. Each year the *Petronian Society Newsletter* (*PSN*) chronicles the previous year's work on the ancient novel; each year the Rijksuniversiteit Groningen hosts a small conference on the ancient novel; and each year H. Hofmann edits a collection of papers for the *Groningen Colloquia on the Novel* (*GCN*).

II

The first eleven sections of our volume offer essays dealing with a selection of some of the most important issues for our understanding and appreciation of the ancient novel and represent topics of concern and interest to those studying these novels. The basis for these essays ranges from the empirical to the theoretical, from traditional

---

[18] D'Arms (1981).
[19] Hopkins (1993).
[20] Bowersock (1994).

deutsche philologische Wissenschaft to modern approaches. But this volume necessarily reflects also the make-up of the discipline. Statements and strategies in one essay might be contradicted in another; no attempt is made to seek a compromise and smooth out these differences. Depending on the nature of the subject or the methodology employed, some essays are descriptive, some summary statements, some discursive, some directed at the whole field of the ancient novel, some more restrictive. The nature of the topic often dictates the style of the essay. Through it all, however, a serious attempt is made to discuss those questions most often raised about the ancient novel.

The essays in section twelve are divided into Greek and Roman and within each division arranged chronologically. Though some arrangement had to be devised for this large section of eight novels, the division does not imply setting Greek novels against Roman or earlier works against later. These works and their authors are called major because they constitute the canon of the ancient novel. The essayists follow no uniform approach. What makes Apuleius' *Metamorphoses* interesting and significant differs from that of Longus' *Daphnis and Chloe*. Because we have historical information about Petronius and Apuleius and none for Xenophon of Ephesus, Longus, or the author of the *Historia Apollonii*, emphases in essays about their works will vary. For many years there has been a debate about whether or not Xenophon's *Ephesiaca* and the *Historia Apollonii* are epitomes, while a discussion of *Daphnis and Chloe* must take into account its relationship with pastoral poetry and Theocritus. Chariton's imitation of Greek historiography requires treatment different from that for Achilles Tatius' sense of playfulness and parody. Heliodorus' gamesmanship, manipulation of structure, unreliable narrators, powerful heroine, and sheer size all demand a different strategy from that for the straightforward narrative of Xenophon. Several of the essays on individual authors contain detailed discussions of manuscripts because so much of the scholarly research on these authors involves the manuscript tradition and textual problems. Just a few of these essays (e.g., Plepelits') have brief, specialized bibliographies as appendices to their essays, which pertain only to their essays and are included for the convenience of the reader.

Following the section on the canonical texts, we discuss in section thirteen works which are novel-like, that is works of extended narrative prose fiction which in many respects can be termed novels. They do not fit exactly into any genre classification but fit best into the novel category, and are included in this volume because they represent works closely associated historically and literarily with the canonical novel texts. The works discussed in section thirteen could all be termed something like historical novels, fictional histories, histories as fiction. The last three essays in this section deal with biography (a form of history), as it develops from the subject-as-model to the subject-as-holy man.

Section fourteen is a unified collection of essays on novel-like works, which are similar to those in the preceding section but are not necessarily novels based on historiographical models. These works are often referred to as fringe novels.

Because so many fragmentary works recently discovered have been identified as novels, the essay on novel fragments tells a most exciting story. Papyrus fragments are also important because they help to date the canonical novels and because they give witness to their popularity.

The first four centuries of the modern era mark out not only the temporal span of the ancient novel but also the origin, rise and assumption of power of the Christian church. The novelists and Christian writers work in the same milieu, the same hot-house of change and local experimentation. Narrative is no longer inspired by the Muses; edification of the faithful and glorification of their God have removed entertainment as the primary intention of the novels. Byzantine writers, recognizing their rich Greek heritage in the ancient novels, creatively re-form the pagan narratives. And then after a prolonged sojourn in the lightless ages, the ancient novels attract the attention of creative artists and thinkers in France, Britain, Spain and Portugal. Sections seventeen-nineteen report on the *Nachleben* of the novel and mark the end of our story.[21]

We include a list of maps as a kind of appendix. The first seven maps are pictorial representations of the travels of heroes and heroines of the novels. Travel is such a delineating and integral strategy of the ancient novels (except for Longus and Apuleius) that we felt obliged to highlight them. These maps will, we hope, also aid the reader in identifying those cities, islands, routes or areas which ancient writers considered fascinating, exotic, enchanting or mysterious enough to warrant visits by their heroes and heroines. The similarities

---

[21] The want of essays on the *Nachleben* of the ancient novel in Germany, Italy, The Netherlands is owing to the inability of the editor to secure them.

and differences in routes and places used by the various novelists are instructive. The novelists write fiction, and our illustrations of those fictions by the use of maps do not indicate any attempt to render them more realistic. The remaining five maps represent the most famous journeys in the ancient world, and we believe it worthwhile to compare these with the travels of heroes and heroines in the novels. Whether the travels were real, imaginary or only wished for, they clearly engaged the imagination of both writer and reader.

Certain editorial attempts at uniformity in this volume have been made, but not so rigidly so as to repress or restrict national conventions or characteristics: uniformity is imposed only at those places where readers could be confused. The reader is invited to look past variations in spelling among contributors (*Satyrica, Satyricon, Satiricon* are the same work by Petronius; *Aithiopica* and the *Ethiopian Story* are the same; Calasiris = Kalasiris); capital letters in titles and the use of double-single quotation marks reflect the American background of the editor; in footnotes citations of multiple-authored works are listed by first author only. Styles of essays necessarily differ even for the eight major Greek and Roman novels (Section 12): problems with the texts of some novels are at times of major concern; our knowledge of individual novelists varies from nothing (Xenophon of Ephesus) to a great deal (Apuleius); interests of contributors vary—just as do their egos. Serious scholarship based on acknowledged fiction presents an interesting paradox: we are asking readers to take seriously critical studies of something that never happened; maps of real places are provided at the end of this volume to demonstrate imaginary journeys of fictional characters and beg to be compared with journeys of Odysseus, Jason, Aeneas, and Christian saints.

The twenty-five contributors to this volume reflect the international pedigree of scholarship on the ancient novel: one scholar each from Austria, Denmark, France, Portugal, Republic of South Africa, Spain; two from Canada and Italy; four from Germany and the U.S.A.; seven from the U.K.

The volume which follows is a natural reaction and response to the growing interest in the study of the ancient novel and is directed at the serious students of Classics, i.e. graduate students and faculty; at those in modern languages interested in the complete history of the novel; at those fascinated by the survival of classical literature into the postmodern age of advertizing; and at cultural historians familiar with Greece and Rome. It is hoped that this present volume covers many of the important issues dealing with the novels, novelists, novel-like works of fiction, and the literary/historical/philological/theoretical/religious matters of concern to the scholars in the field. If the reader wants more than he can find here, we hope that we have at least whetted his appetite, pointed him in one or more profitable directions, and provided him with a bibliography and a starting place for future study.

2. THE GENRE: NOVELS PROPER AND THE FRINGE

Niklas Holzberg

If the terms "romance" and "novel" are applied in discussions of Greek and Latin prose fiction to any of the texts in hand, this is only done so in full awareness of the fact that these generic labels were coined for medieval and modern narrative prose, but not for that of antiquity. We know of no ancient *termini* even remotely similar in meaning to "romance" or "novel". In those days it was clearly not even considered at all necessary to find any kind of generic heading under which to place the very texts which, today, are immediately associated with medieval and modern romances and novels.[1] Some scholars consequently still refuse now to talk of the prose narratives of antiquity as "romances" or "novels".[2] A certain degree of scepticism as to the proper use of the terms may actually be justifiable, in so far as there has been much rash drawing of parallels between the ancient and modern texts in question. However, genre studies on medieval and modern narrative prose are by no means entirely agreed that the labels "romance" and "novel" are always quite applicable,[3] so that, in classifications of ancient narrative prose, it seems unnecessary to avoid using terms which signify something that is at least similar to the type of text under consideration.

The real problem that presents itself in any attempt to evolve a theory on the generic nature of ancient narrative prose is not one of terminology—there simply are no ancient names and we must be allowed the anachronism of working with modern ones. What is genuinely troublesome is the decision as to which ancient texts can be labelled "novel"—this being, incidentally, the nomenclature I intend to use here—and thus classed as belonging to one and the same "genre". And the very concept of a genre will only be legitimate in

---

[1] Reardon (1991) 77ff. considers what a theory of the genre could have looked like. On the various isolated references to Greek and Latin novels made by ancient and Byzantine authors see esp. Müller (1976) 115–8; Kuch (1985) 8–12; (1989b) 13–4; Morgan (1993) 175–93.
[2] See esp. Schmidt (1989), Vessey (1991–93) and Selden (1994).
[3] Kuch (1985) 3. More recent literature on the theory of the novel is listed by Schmidt (1989) 21–3.

this context, if fixed criteria can be found which permit us to assign a selection of ancient prose narratives to one homogeneous group. These criteria, moreover, must not only conform with modern dictates, but also, and most especially, with ancient literary standards.

A first look at the works customarily included in discussions of the ancient novel[4] reveals a picture that is anything but homogeneous. The texts are many and various, the spectrum is utterly confusing. And most of the attempts made so far to order this chaos are just as confusing. These began in 1948 with Rudolf Helm's *Der antike Roman*. The author states briefly at the outset that "ancient novels" come "in all shapes", and then proceeds to list the various types; they all, for Helm, clearly belong to the same genre, simply because they all "sprang forth from the same root". He distinguishes between "historical novels, mythological novels, travel novels and utopias, erotic novels, Christian novels, biographies, parodies on the novel, comic-satirical novels".[5] In order to justify his amassing of heterogeneous texts under one and the same heading, then, Helm puts himself in line with Rohde (1876), using the observations made by this scholar and his successors on the origins of ancient fiction. Tomas Hägg, who deals with a very similar assortment of texts in his *The Novel in Antiquity* (1983), dispenses, by contrast, with a discussion of his conception of the genre. For readers, Hägg assumes, the genre's "main characteristics will emerge, in due course, through comparison with related literature, and are also mirrored in the *Nachleben*".[6] There is reasonable doubt that ancient critics would have been able to follow Helm's classification of texts as the one, vast genre "ancient novel", his arguments being based on the "*Vorleben*" of Greek and Latin prose fiction. And doubt seems even more permissible in Hägg's case—a definition on the basis of the *Nachleben* would, of course, have been impossible.

A different approach is taken by Heinrich Kuch, whose thoughts on the genre appear in the 1989 collection of essays *Der antike Roman* and elsewhere.[7] He quite rightly stresses that a major role is played in the genesis of a genre by the political and social circumstances under which the texts in question were written. Unfortunately, not

---

[4] For surveys of generic studies to date see Kuch (1985) 3–8; (1989b) 18–9; Merkle (1989) 295–7; Selden (1994) 43ff.
[5] Helm (1956) 6.
[6] Hägg (1983) vii.
[7] Kuch (1989b); see also Kuch (1985) (1992).

very much is made of this observation. Kuch merely concludes that the changes in the conditions which, over the centuries, determined the production of novels, explain the disparity between the various texts, e.g. the "contrariety" (*Gegensätze*) between Euhemerus' "utopian novel" and the "Troy novel" of Dares.[8] Does Kuch mean that the texts may differ from one another in terms of their phenotype—one describes an exotic island, the other a war—but that in terms of their genotype, of their social breeding grounds then, they are at least comparable? Even if this were the case—and we shall in fact see below that Kuch's theory does offer some scope for development when the intended effect of the respective works is taken into account—we can, nevertheless, scarcely assume that ancient readers would appreciate this basis for comparison.

Sounder than the above-mentioned attempts to typologize ancient narrative prose is the approach first taken by Wehrli and Perry. Scholars following this line base their examination of the genre on a comparison of the texts, focusing on the authors' treatment of the subject-matter, on their use of motifs, and on narrative structure. There are two methods by which this can be executed. Either the definition sought is restricted *ab initio* to that of the "Greek novel", in which case the conclusion reached is that only the following texts can be considered as belonging to the genre: the fully extant love-and-adventure tales of Chariton, Xenophon of Ephesus, Achilles Tatius, Longus and Heliodorus, together with those partially or completely lost works which surviving fragments or summaries show to have been very similar to the other five.[9] Or this "canon" of Greek love-and-adventure stories is extended to include two Latin narratives, these being Petronius' *Satyrica* and Apuleius' *Metamorphoses*, further Pseudo-Lucian's *The Ass* (an epitome of the now lost Greek text used by Apuleius) and the fragment of a narrative known as *Iolaus*; these are then divided into the two sub-categories "idealistic novel" and "comic-realistic novel".[10] One conclusion commonly reached, whichever of the two methods is applied, is that all other narrative prose texts of antiquity must be banished to the "fringe" of the genre.

This line of reasoning certainly has one argument in its favour: the remarkable homogeneity between the eight fully extant (or epito-

---

[8] Kuch (1985) 16; (1989b) 25–6.
[9] Müller (1981) 387–92; Reardon (1991) 3–7; Morgan (1994) 1.
[10] Wehrli (1965); Perry (1967); Holzberg (1995).

mized) prose narratives as regards contents and form. Particularly striking is the similarity of the narrative motifs they each use to depict the protagonists' erotic experiences and the adventures they meet with on their journeys. The plots of the five "idealistic novels" even follow the same stereotype pattern. A handsome young man falls in love with a beautiful young girl, the two pledge that they will be eternally faithful; very early in the story their happiness begins to seem blighted, when, for example, they are torn asunder; after a series of adventures the couple are eventually reunited, thenceforth to spend a married life blessed by Fortuna. The adventures, undergone during travels across the entire eastern Mediterranean, consist mostly of separation and between times brief reunions, enslavement and threats to their lives, be it from robbers, a storm, shipwreck or from rivals. There is nothing in the narratives of Petronius, Pseudo-Lucian and Apuleius that corresponds directly to this pattern of action, but the said texts do contain variants of all the above-mentioned adventures. Here the idealizing presentation of events that characterizes the narratives of Chariton, Xenophon, Achilles Tatius, Longus and Heliodorus is supplanted by satirical caricature or gross realism. Whether the allusions in the three "comic-realistic novels" to the five "idealistic novels" are interpreted as harmless play on motifs or as the vehicle for a profound intellectual statement, they certainly provide one convincing argument for grouping together the eight narratives—and those fragments or only indirectly known texts that are closely related to them in content and motifs—and labelling them "the ancient novels".

Or perhaps, for the moment, we should say "the ancient novels proper". Very few scholars who look upon the eight texts named above, or only the five Greek ones, as a homogeneous group are absolutely rigorous in their differentiation between these and the "fringe". The vast majority is not opposed to styling the one or the other of those "peripheral" texts as "novel" too, or as "romance" or, at least, something very similar.[11] However, opinions vary widely as to which "fringe" text is still or nearly still a "novel" and which can no longer be regarded as such. The main reason for this is probably that the "fringe" texts have so far not been subjected to such thor-

---

[11] On the grounds for such differentiation see Perry (1967) 70–1; 84–7; Reardon (1969) 303 (= 230) n. 32; Müller (1981) 379, 392; Anderson (1982) 59–62; Kytzler (1983) 7–8; Bowie (1985a) 687; Holzberg (1995) 11–26; Reardon (1989) 3–4; (1991) 5.

ough scrutiny as have the "novels proper". Judgements on the "novel-ness" of ancient prose narratives consequently tend to be overly subjective. Only one scholar, Bernhard Kytzler, actually rests his case for the extension of the list of eight "canonical" novels and their fragmentary congeners on the evidence of an ancient reference to Greek and Latin prose fiction.[12] The passage cited is found in Macrobius' commentary on Cicero's *Somnium Scipionis* (1.2.7–8). It reads:

> *Fabulae, quarum nomen indicat falsi professionem, aut tantum conciliandae auribus voluptatis, aut adhortationis quoque in bonam frugem gratia repertae sunt. auditum mulcent vel comoediae, quales Menander eiusve imitatores agendas dederunt, vel argumenta fictis casibus amatorum referta, quibus vel multum se Arbiter exercuit vel Apuleium non numquam lusisse miramur. hoc totum fabularum genus, quod solas aurium delicias profitetur, e sacrario suo in nutricum cunas sapientiae tractatus eliminat.*

> The stories of which the very title points to an account of fictional events were made up either purely to entertain their audiences or also for the purpose of giving practical advice. The ear is pleased by comedies such as those staged by Menander and his imitators, or by narratives full of the fictional adventures of lovers, a theme which Petronius frequently tried his hand at and which even Apuleius, as we note with amazement, played with on occasion. This whole class of stories, the sole aim of which is to entertain the audience, a philosophical treatise banishes from its sanctuary to nannies' cradles.

The term used here by Macrobius for "narratives" is *argumenta*. This shows him to be familiar with the ancient literary theory whereby narrative texts are classified according to the truth of their contents.[13] Three types of narrative are distinguished: 1. those which deviate from the truth (Gr. *muthos, muthikon*, Lat. *fabula*) or which are entirely untrue (*pseudos*); 2. those which are consistent with the truth (*alethes, historia, historikon*); 3. those which are made up, but still seem very realistic (Gr. *hos alethes, plasmatikon, peplasmenon, dramatikon*;[14] Lat. *argumentum*). Macrobius assigns the works of Petronius and Apuleius to the third category, plausibly fictional narratives, and this provides confirmation to those scholars who look upon the two Latin authors, together with their Greek "relations", Chariton, Xenophon, Achilles Tatius, Longus, Heliodorus and Pseudo-Lucian, as the "novelists proper".

---

[12] Kytzler (1983) 5–8.
[13] Müller (1976) 115–8; Morgan (1993) 189–90; Fuchs (1993) 217–8.
[14] On Byzantine use of the term *dramatikon* for "novel" see Müller (1976) 116; Kuch (1985) 11–2; (1989b) 16–7.

And since the *Historia Apollonii regis Tyri*, the descriptions of exotic islands summarized by Diodorus Siculus, and Lucian's *True History* can also be regarded as fiction of the third category,[15] Kytzler quite legitimately interprets Macrobius' remarks as justification for including these texts together with the "idealistic" and "comic-realistic" novels on the list of "ancient novels".

But does this list really cover all the ancient prose narratives that fall under the category *diegema plasmatikon*? Where, for example, do the fictional eye-witness accounts of the Trojan War by "Dares" and "Dictys" stand? On the face of it these would naturally seem to belong to the first of the three categories, because their subject-matter is taken from mythology. However, "Dares" and "Dictys" have in fact both stripped this particular myth of all the very things which, for ancient theorists, would have made it appear to diverge from reality: they omit all miraculous events and the entire cast of gods. Both authors claim to be describing what "really" happened in the famous war between the Greeks and Trojans. They have thus turned a *diegema muthikon* into a *diegema plasmatikon* where, as Cicero put it (*De inv.*1.27), a *ficta res, quae tamen fieri potuit* forms the subject-matter.

It would seem, then, that ancient authors did not always distinguish clearly between the theorists' narrative categories, or at least that they occasionally enjoyed a game of mixing the three. A literary *lusus* of this kind is certainly being played in one of the few examples of a *diegema plasmatikon* where the author actually uses a specific *terminus* to describe his work—in the prologue to *Daphnis and Chloe*. Longus promises his readers here a *historia erotos*. If we apply the theorists' division of *diegemata* into three types, this can only mean "a true, erotic story". In his prologue and in a remark which he makes at the end of the tale, clearly referring back to the prologue, Longus does indeed allow the impression to arise that he has simply put the protagonists' autobiography, which previously existed only in the form of a painting, into words.[16] A play on truth and fiction, then, and at the same time a connecting link between the author of an ancient

---

[15] On the question of genre regarding the *Historia* see Müller (1991) and Konstan (1994b), regarding the island accounts Holzberg, below p. 621ff. The *True History* does not offer much in the way of *ficta res, quae tamen fieri potuit*, but there is a reason for this: here a satirist is taking fictional narrative to absurd extremes. This text is thus comparable to the *Ass Romance*, where the motif "transformation into an ass" serves the same purpose: satirical variation on a *diegema plasmatikon*.

[16] Wouters (1989–90).

text generally held to be a "novel", and "Dares" and "Dictys", authors whose narratives are usually allocated to the "fringe". We must therefore ask whether it is perhaps ultimately wiser not to differentiate all too strictly here. One key to the answer is found in a letter written by Emperor Julian in the year 363 A.D. Discussing the kind of reading he considers most suitable for his priests, Julian notes (89, 301B):

> ὅσα δέ ἐστιν ἐν ἱστορίας εἴδει παρὰ τοῖς ἔμπροσθεν ἀπηγγελμένα πλάσματα παραιτητέον, ἐρωτικὰς ὑποθέσεις καὶ πάντα ἁπλῶς τὰ τοιαῦτα.
>
> All made-up stories of the type published by writers of earlier ages in the shape of historical accounts—love stories and all that kind of narrative—are to be rejected.

When the emperor singles out one kind of *plasmata* in historical guise, the *erotikai hupotheseis*, there can be no doubt that he is referring to narratives like that of Longus.[17] In addition to *Daphnis and Chloe*, there are amongst the fully and partially extant "idealistic" novels several in which the author poses as a historian. In what is probably the oldest "novel", *Ninus*, and in *Sesonchosis*, which perhaps too represents an early stage in the history of the genre, the protagonist is a genuinely historical figure. Minor roles are played by famous characters from Greece's glorious past in Chariton's *Callirhoe*, in the *Parthenope Romance* and in Antonius Diogenes' *The Wonders Beyond Thule*. While Achilles Tatius merely "authenticates" the events he relates by maintaining that the protagonist himself told him the whole story, Antonius Diogenes, Xenophon, Iamblichus (*Babyloniaca*) and the author of version RB of the *Historia Apollonii regis Tyri* all explicitly cite "real" spoken or written sources for their accounts.[18] Heliodorus' *Aethiopica*, finally, reads at times like a *historia*. The narrator writes of various events that he "believes" or that it "appears" to him that they "perhaps" took place as he describes them, or he considers it possible that things were in fact entirely different.[19] The very title "Aethiopica" is reminiscent of the names given to historical works, and we have a number of "novels" with this type of title: *Ephesiaca, Babyloniaca, Phoenicica* and—Petronius' play on tradition—*Satyrica*.[20]

---

[17] See Morgan (1993) 178 n. 6.
[18] These and other such authentication devices are listed in Wouters (1989–90) 474–6 and Fuchs (1993) 209–12; see also Maeder (1991) 23–32.
[19] More on this in Morgan (1982).
[20] On the fiction of historicity in the "idealistic novels" see esp. Perry (1967).

For Julian, the category "pseudo-history" includes, however, not only *erotikai hupotheseis*, but also *panta haplos ta toiauta*. What could he mean here? One clue to the answer can be found in the proem to Lucian's *True History*. There is one passage here which, in its wording, is very reminiscent of Julian's above-quoted remarks. Lucian says that he has presented in his work "a colourful selection of lies with a convincing ring of truth" (*pseusmata poikila pithanos te kai alethos*), alluding therein to "certain poets, historians and philosophers of old", who had written "many wondrous and fantastic things". Two such writers, at least, are specifically named by Lucian in the sentence following: Ctesias of Cnidus and Iambulus. Both are prose authors and are quite certainly not classed by Lucian as philosophers, but as historians (*sungrapheis*). Their respective accounts of far-off lands rank for Lucian as fiction; in connection with Iambulus he uses the verb *plattesthai*. Here, therefore, we have two examples of the *plasmata* which were "published by writers of earlier ages in the shape of historical accounts", but which could not be defined as *erotikai hupotheseis*. And perhaps this is the kind of "pseudo-history" referred to by Julian with the words *kai panta haplos ta toiauta*.

For Lucian, at any rate, the category "pseudo-history", which formed the target of his *True History*, most probably denoted those works which tell of historical events in an account that is itself "untruthful", i.e. pseudo-historical. Whether or not the writings of Ctesias and Iambulus did actually belong to this category, is not a question that we need discuss here.[21] The texts themselves no longer survive, and a genre study ought reasonably to confine itself to the extant texts. Our next step must therefore be to draw up a list of the ancient prose narratives which present historical events in pseudo-historical form and which are also generally classed as "fringe novels".

Fictional Biography

Xenophon of Athens, *The Education of Cyrus*
Pseudo-Callisthenes, *Life and Deeds of Alexander of Macedon*
Life of Aesop

78–9; Müller (1976) 123–6; Müller (1981) 378–9; Morgan (1982); Treu (1984); Hägg (1987a); Maeder (1991); Fuchs (1993) 213–6; Morgan (1993) 187, 197–215; Hunter (1994).

[21] See below p. 621ff. and p. 629ff.

Philostratus, *Life of Apollonius of Tyana*
Apocryphal Acts of the Apostles: *Andrew*
                                             John
                                             Paul
                                             Peter
                                             Thomas

Fictional Autobiography

Pseudo-Clementines

Pseudepigraphic Letters Reflecting in their Sequence the Development of a Particular Story

Letters of Aeschines
       Chion
       Euripides
       Hippocrates
       Plato
       Socrates and the Socratics
       Themistocles

This list must also include two texts which present, in pseudo-historical form, events which are neither historical nor entirely made-up, but are taken from mythology: the fictional eye-witness accounts of the Trojan War written by "Dares" and "Dictys".

We do not know whether for Julian not only the "idealistic novels", but also these texts listed here—if indeed he knew them at all—were *plasmata*, "published by writers of earlier ages in the shape of historical accounts". Many such works were probably taken at face value and regarded by Julian and their other ancient readers as genuine biographies, letters or eye-witness accounts. But the authors themselves, at least, knew quite well that their writings were as fictional as the "idealistic novels" of those authors who chose to wear the mask of a historian. And all these pseudo-historians and authors of pseudepigrapha must have known that educated readers with a knowledge of history and literature would see through the fiction. This audience would realize that, when "Dictys" poses as historian, he is playing the same literary game as Longus with his historian's pose.

In this respect, then, we may regard the "novels proper" and the "fringe novels" as akin, and we should ask of each individual text the same questions. What were the authors' underlying intentions in their respective games of make-believe historicity? Are there any common denominators in this area which would allow us to attempt a more exact definition of the genre?

We shall start by considering Xenophon's *Education of Cyrus*, the oldest of the "fringe" texts. Written about 360 B.C., this fictional biography paints the portrait of an ideal ruler. Taking a free and easy approach to the historical facts, and adding to these others that he has quite simply made up, Xenophon presents the life of the Persian king in such a way that Cyrus must appear to readers in every respect as a model of excellence. Here, then, pseudo-historical narrative serves as a vehicle for political and moral instruction. The text is addressed not so much to readers who find themselves in a position comparable to that of Cyrus—Xenophon could hardly expect to attract a large audience of that kind, not in his own time at any rate. The *Education of Cyrus* is aimed instead at members of the Athenian nobility, who, for the aristocratically-minded author, were most suited as occupants of the leading political positions in the city-state.[22] They were supposed to follow in particular the example of Cyrus the politician, reading with the eyes of *polis* citizens rather than of private individuals. After all, the man they were meant to emulate does actually refuse even to take one look at the female prisoner Panthea, although he has been told of her great beauty: he feels that he might be tempted to take a second look and thus allow his affection to wander from affairs of state (5.1.4–8).

A good 300 years later, when Chariton wrote his *Callirhoe*, likewise pretending to record historical events, the *polis* as autonomous state no longer existed. Chariton's readers are, accordingly, private individuals with their own private concerns. They still perhaps dream about the glory that was Greece, and so Chariton chooses as the setting for *Callirhoe* the age in which Xenophon of Athens lived; the motifs he uses and his narrative technique are a deliberate allusion to the historian's works.[23] However, when Chariton too writes about an *anabasis*, it is here no more a political and military operation, but instead an expedition of a more delicate nature: its end is a court-

---

[22] See Stadter (1991) 468–9.
[23] See esp. Plepelits (1976) 12, and, more recently, Hunter (1994) 1058–9.

room hearing to decide who shall be the lawful husband of the story's beautiful female protagonist (4.6.8ff.). The theme "love", which in the *Education of Cyrus* had been relegated to the periphery, has been made the focal point here. And this corresponds exactly to the changed interests of readers, for whom life now centres round the family and private sphere. An aristocratic audience that could put the knowledge gained from political instruction into practice, no longer existed.

Xenophon's Cyrus had gone off to war to take possession of other countries, whereas Chaereas, the male protagonist in *Callirhoe*, goes to war to regain possession of the wife that had been taken away from him. This "hero" is no model politician, he is simply a faithful husband. In this respect his behaviour is, however, exemplary and is rewarded with a happy ending. If Xenophon wrote a utopia for statesmen, then this is an escapist dream for private persons. It tells them that life without responsibility for the *polis* can still be meaningful: all problems can be solved if only personal virtue, e.g. in the form of conjugal fidelity, is upheld.[24] On the other hand, *Callirhoe* does have one thing in common with the *Education of Cyrus*: as in all pseudo-historical "idealistic novels", here too the fiction that this is an account of events which took place long ago, gives added weight to the message. The deeds of men from former ages generally tend to be taken as shining examples, and the more romanticized the better.

In the *Alexander Romance* it is again the prospect of conquering other countries that induces the protagonist to go to war. However, this particular king entirely lacks all the virtues which had made Xenophon's Cyrus an ideal ruler. In the 3rd century A.D., when the fictional biography was probably written, an Alexander endowed by Pseudo-Callisthenes with such merits would in any case scarcely have been very suitable as a proposed role model for the Roman emperor's Greek-speaking subjects—these potential readers were still given no opportunities to prove their worth as statesmen anyway. But even readers without any political voice would find this Alexander facing situations which they could easily picture for themselves: they would

---

[24] Perry (1967) and Reardon (1969) developed the theory that the early "idealistic novels" are essentially escapist literature, written as a reaction to the changed political and social situation of the individual citizen in the age of the *Diadochi*. This has very recently been questioned in studies by Bowie (1994b) and Stephens (1994) on ancient readership. See, however, the latest arguments brought forward by Hägg (1994); these are also based on readership considerations and confirm nicely the ideas of Perry and Reardon.

see him mastering some difficulties in the manner of a picaresque hero. There is, for example, the episode in which Alexander fights a duel with King Porus of India. His opponent is considerably taller, but can nevertheless be overcome, because a sudden noise distracts him for a brief second, and Alexander turns this swiftly to his own advantage, dealing the crucial blow with his sword (3.4). Here, long before Chaplin's time, it is clearly the daydreams of the "little fellow" that are to be indulged. These will have been fired by Alexander's letter to Aristotle describing the *mirabilia* of India (3.17)—a world of adventure as an alternative to the humdrum of everyday life. The picture is, however, marred somewhat by the great king's untimely death. He has the whole world at his feet, is looked upon as a god (two things he has in common with the Roman Caesars!), and yet he must die so young and so wretchedly. But this may have been in some sense a comfort for the little fellow: the escapist dreams inspired by the *Alexander Romance* could never become reality for him, but at least he would be spared an end such as that.[25]

An element of ambivalence which seemingly renders the proffered role model less attractive is also found in the figure of Aesop as it is presented in a fictional biography dating from the 2nd/3rd century A.D. Like Pseudo-Callisthenes' Alexander, the slave Aesop is characterized as something of a *pícaro*. He manages to rise from his lowly social position to become adviser to kings. He owes his initial success to a gift bestowed upon him by the Muses in reward for a pious deed: in every situation, however hopeless it may seem, he is always able to find the right words and thus solve all problems. But even such wisdom has its limits, as the reader sees at the end of the tale. This becomes manifest when the man made so wise begins to put on airs and rate himself higher than a deity. With an act of hubris, Aesop incurs the wrath of Apollo and, like Alexander, ends as a victim of murder. Just as all the king's horses and all his men cannot protect him, all Aesop's wisdom and all the eloquence he summons up cannot stop his enemies from throwing him off a cliff.[26] In both fictional biographies, then, two goods that are generally considered extremely desirable—power and wisdom—are made to appear relative, but this in a way that would appeal strongly to many readers in the Greek-speaking world. The exemplary character is, here too,

---

[25] Stoneman (1994b) 125–7.
[26] Holzberg (1993b) 10–1.

heightened by the fact that, in both biographies, the events treated take place in an age which for readers belongs to the distant past. And the two men whose lives are described were both particularly well-known figures in Imperial times.

For Greeks forced to live under Roman rule, the most important thing that they had been able to preserve from the more glorious past was their culture, which had reached full bloom during the Classical period of Greek history. Philosophy formed the heart of this heritage and as such was cultivated with particular care all over the Greek-speaking world. Amongst the numerous schools which had come into existence in the meantime, the ones founded in Hellenistic times were all agreed as to what the basis for a philosophical approach to life must be for subjects of an arbitrary monarch: to be free of any desire for things that are in any case not within the control of individuals, above all, then, to renounce all striving for power and riches. This did not prevent the occasional clash between philosophers and the authorities. Nero and Domitian, for example, both had philosophers who taught in Rome arrested and banished at various times. This confrontation between Greek intellect and Roman supremacy was frequently taken up in literature. In order not to aggravate the situation, it was usually represented not as a clash between contemporary forces, but as one which had taken place in the past. Some such literary airings took the form of fictional letters of famous philosophers and rhetors from the 5th and 4th centuries B.C. The letters were published anonymously as collections, and these appeared for the most part in late Hellenistic and Imperial times.[27]

A number of these "letter-books" are of particular significance for our generic discussion of ancient narrative prose, because their contents, like the letters in modern epistolary novels, are ordered in such a way as to reflect a specific course of events. In all there are seven collections which may be counted as narrative prose texts. The letter-writers in these either describe the happenings referred to in detail—letter no. 10 of Aeschines even relates an erotic episode—or they reflect on them, as we find the protagonists of narrative texts doing in their monologues. In six of the seven "epistolary novels"[28]

---

[27] For the editions of "letter-books" of famous Greeks and for further literature see Beschorner (1994).

[28] The exception: the *Letters of Hippocrates*, where the theme relationship letter-writer/ruler is merely hinted at in letters 5 and 6.

the dominant theme running through the accounts and reflections is the relationship between the letter-writer and a ruler, with whom he is in some way personally involved.[29] We can differentiate between two basic situations. Either the letter-writer finds himself faced with a tyrant: Euripides, Socrates and Plato must ask themselves whether they can reasonably accept an invitation to attend the court of such a ruler, while Chion knows, as a student of Plato's philosophy, that he must assassinate the despot who governs his home, Heraclea. Or the writer has been banished from his home and his letters represent his reaction to this: Themistocles and Aeschines describe how they reach their place of exile, and try at the same time to come to terms with their new form of existence. The opportunities created for readers somehow to identify with the "narrative I" in each of these "letter-books" are in many ways similar to those afforded in other Hellenistic and Imperial texts we have considered here. Again the problems addressed are not unlike those faced by private citizens in the aftermath of Alexander's death, with all the political and social upheavals that ensued for the Greek states. And again it is well-known figures from Greece's glorious past that are called upon to give readers the benefit of their experience.

One of the Greek sages who came into conflict with the authorities lives on not only in pseudepigraphic letters, but also in a fictional biography: Apollonius of Tyana, a Pythagorean from the 1st century A.D. His *vita* was written down at the beginning of the 3rd century by Philostratus and contains more of its author's fantasy than of actual fact. Great pains are taken at the outset to make this pseudo-biography appear authentic. Philostratus refers, amongst other things, to the notes of a certain Damis, who had allegedly accompanied Apollonius on his travels as teacher and miracle-worker across the Mediterranean world, India, Egypt and Ethiopia. This time the fiction that the narrative is true history serves as mainstay for the edifying intentions behind the work. If readers are to be persuaded to accept the doctrines propagated by Apollonius, then they must first be utterly convinced that he really was able to prove the reliability of his teachings by backing them up with prophecies, instant healing and, on one occasion, the resuscitation of a corpse.[30]

This also applies *mutatis mutandis* to the fictional biographies of the

---

[29] See below p. 650.
[30] On the *Vita Apollonii* and its "novel" connections see esp. Bowie (1994a).

apostles Andrew, John, Paul, Peter and Thomas, and to the fictional autobiography of Clement, the first successor to St. Peter as bishop of Rome. The sudden deaths and miraculous returns to life in some episodes of the various 2nd- and 3rd century *Acts of the Apostles* do seem to come in series, and at times the holy men take to converting animals, even bugs (*Acts of John* 60f.). Nevertheless, these narratives too are deliberately made to appear historical in order that their contents be given credence.[31] It is at least thinkable that the above-quoted *panta haplos ta toiauta* in Emperor Julian's letter actually refers to the apocryphal *Acts*. The various stories about the adventures which befall an unswervingly faithful disciple of Christ and the apostle's own equally devout followers bear, of all the extant "fringe" texts, the closest resemblance to *erotikai hupotheseis* of the kind represented by Chariton's *Callirhoe*. And as an apostate, Julian will have been anxious to prevent his priests from being shaken in their pagan faith by the *eidos historias* of these *Acts*.

The portrayal of the apostles in the fictional *vitae* is such that even the very ordinary and average amongst ancient readers likely to have read this kind of texts would be able to identify with the heroes.[32] This applies similarly to the last texts on our "fringe" list, the fictional eye-witness accounts of "Dares" and "Dictys". In these "authentic" versions of the Trojan War, both of which are based on now lost Greek originals dating probably from the 2nd/3rd century A.D.,[33] the heroes do not appear as the kind of hero familiar from Homer, but instead as fighting men whose military feats are anything but heroic. The Achilles of the *Ephemeris*, for example, does not kill Hector in open combat, but in an ambush (3.15). A recent study has shown that the modifications to the myth and the characterization of the figures involved both contribute towards a negative image of soldiery and war in the work of "Dictys".[34] If this really was intended by the unknown author of the *Ephemeris*—"Dares" offers nothing comparable—then, here too, pseudo-historical narrative will have served as a vehicle for a specific message.

---

[31] Plümacher (1978) 62–3.
[32] In the apocryphal *Acts of the Apostles*, too, we find "the whole apparatus of repetitive material", which Hägg (1994) quite rightly interprets as evidence that narrative prose texts were read aloud to an illiterate audience.
[33] Merkle (1989) 243–6; Beschorner (1992a) 250–4.
[34] Merkle (1989) 240–2; (1994a) 191.

Having ended our survey of the fictional narratives in pseudo-historical guise that survive from antiquity, we can return immediately to the first question posed above before our consideration of the texts—what was in each case the intention underlying the literary game of make-believe historicity? In answer to this we can now say that, in the same measure as "idealistic novels" like Chariton's *Callirhoe*, the fictional biographies, the "letter-books" and the fictional eye-witness reports of the Trojan War from late Hellenistic and Imperial times are all designed to meet quite specific consumer needs. The works are written for Greek readers whom the course of history following Alexander's death has rendered politically impotent. They offer their audience the chance to re-orient themselves in their dreams and moral standards by looking back at the exemplary behaviour of men of old. And, from the targeted readers' point of view, the most attractive form of "packaging" for these days of yore is the one used in the texts just considered above: the author of prose fiction wears the mask of a historian. The said texts were not all written in the same age, but over a period of almost 500 years, and the political and social conditions under which their respective readers lived were, of course, subject to constant change. Nevertheless, the thematic resemblances between some works are striking, however far apart they may have been written; *Callirhoe* and the *Acts of Paul* are but one good example of this. We must therefore assume that there existed a certain continuity in the escapist dreams and moral sentiments of the individual, an unvarying factor and one even common to Christian and pagans alike.

Turning now to the second question posed above, we must consider whether the observations we have made allow us to attempt a more exact definition of the genre, excluding from it or adding to it any of the works discussed here. A recapitulation may be helpful at this point.

It was stipulated at the outset that the term "novel" should only be used here for a group of ancient prose narratives which both by modern and by ancient standards can be considered homogeneous. One such group was found to exist, comprising the so-called "idealistic" and "comic-realistic" novels. We then looked at a passage from Macrobius, where he refers to the type of fictional narrative represented by Petronius' *Satyrica* and Apuleius' *Metamorphoses*. This showed us that, in antiquity, prose narratives with a plot which was entirely fictitious, but which consisted of events that could feasibly have taken place in the way described, were classified as one of the three possible categories of narrative: in Greek as *diegema plasmatikon* (or similar), in Latin as *argumentum*. We established that not only the "idealistic" and "comic-realistic" novels, but also the *Historia Apollonii regis Tyri*, the narratives describing exotic islands (extant in the form of Diodorus' summaries), and Lucian's *True History* all conform to what an ancient reader would expect of a *diegema plasmatikon* or an *argumentum*. It therefore seemed reasonable to follow Kytzler and class these texts too for present purposes as "novels".

The reference made by Julian to a particular type of *plasmata* seemed, as we then saw, to suggest that the Emperor and other ancient readers of narrative prose made no clear distinction between, on the one side, fiction in pseudo-historical guise, for example Chariton's *Callirhoe* and similar "idealistic" novels, and on the other texts which gave an account of genuinely historical events, but in the form of pseudo-history. And since our survey of the texts has now shown us that both types of pseudo-historical writing are comparable in their intended effect, we have no reason not to attach the label "novel" to the fictional biographies, "letter-books" and fictional eye-witness reports from Troy as well, rather than confining them to the "fringe".

However, one consideration ought not to be overlooked here. As mentioned briefly above, only the ancient reader with a very thorough knowledge of history and literature, in other words only a very small number of readers in antiquity will have realized and appreciated that the make and ideological message of works like Chariton's *Callirhoe* and the "fringe" texts are tailored to meet roughly the same kind of consumer needs. Only this minority amongst ancient readers of narrative prose would have seen the "idealistic" novels and the "fringe" works as one generic group. And yet, paradoxical as it may seem, these erudite few—amongst them the literary theorists themselves—, these readers who alone could have made the connection, did not even deem it necessary to give the genre a name.

The far greater part of antiquity's audience for prose fiction—readers all over the Greek world who found food for their dreams in exciting accounts of what seemed to be historical events[35]—quite

---

[35] No analogous assumptions can be made about the ancient Roman readers of fictional prose, because the only Latin texts we have from early Imperial times are Petronius' *Satyrica* and Apuleius' *Metamorphoses*. Readers of these works are more likely to have come from educated background. Nevertheless, it is scarcely possible to decide now whether or not they would have appreciated fully the literary character

certainly remained unaware of the literary ties between *Callirhoe*, the *Life of Aesop* and the *Letters of Chion*. And indeed there was no real need for them to recognize such kinship. Whether Chion's letters were read as an epistolary novel or as a posthumous edition of genuine letters written by the historical Chion, the unknown epistolographer's message would come across either way. In fact, the role model offered here to contemporary readers will even have been more readily accepted, if the text was taken to be an authentic document and not a "novel". It is these readers, the ones who were taken in by the *eidos historias* of the fictional biographies, "letter-books" and fictional eye-witness reports from Troy known to us, who must provide the yardstick for our decision as to which texts can be included in the genre "ancient novel". In the final count, then, the only texts that we can properly class as novels are those which the majority of ancient readers will have understood as fiction in the sense of the theoretical definition *diegema plasmatikon* or *argumentum*. Thus the term can only be applied to the group of narratives which, on the basis of Macrobius' remarks, can be considered homogeneous. The other texts must remain "fringe novels", even if the boundaries between these and the "novels proper" cannot be as clearly marked as some scholars demand.

---

of any fictional biographies or "letter-books" they may have happened to read. The 3rd–6th century Latin versions of the *Alexander Romance*, of the fictional eye-witness accounts from Troy, and of the *Historia Apollonii* were very probably consumed, even before the Middle Ages, by readers who did not differentiate between pseudo-history and the real McCoy.

3. THE RISE OF THE GREEK NOVEL

Consuelo Ruiz-Montero

I. *Introduction*

The study of the formation and origins of the Greek novel must begin with an attempt to define the genre, which in turn implies an acceptance that that category exists. (The two questions are not, as we shall see, unrelated.) At the same time we need to determine whether the Greek novel comprises a single type or a number of different subtypes and, in the latter case, to specify which subtype is to be the object of study. Fragments of Greek novels that have come to light in recent years make it impossible to accept the traditional split between "serious or ideal romance" (e.g., *Callirhoe* by Chariton of Aphrodisias, *Ephesiaca* by Xenophon of Ephesus, the *Pastoral Tales* of Longus, the *Babyloniaca* of Iamblicus, *Leucippe and Cleitophon* by Achilles Tatius) and "comic, or unideal romance" (e.g., the *Satyricon* by Petronius, the *Metamorphoses* by Apuleius and the *Ass* attributed to Lucian).[1] That comic or parodic novels also existed in Greek is confirmed by the fragments of *Iolaus* and Lollianus's *Phoenicica*, while the remaining fragments might also include novels that are similar to the ones just mentioned or even different from the forms known today.[2] Nor should we forget the layers of parody in the novel by Achilles Tatius or, as we shall see below, the fact that some authors have doubted the seriousness of the *Wonders beyond Thule* by Antonius Diogenes. And if we accept as novels mixed texts like the *Life of Alexander*, *Chion of Heraclea* or the apocryphal *Acts of Paul and Thekla*, the genre would have to be widened considerably.[3]

---

* This paper has been possible thanks to a grant from the Alexander von Humbolt Foundation at the University of Munich.

I should like to express my gratitude to Prof. E. Vogt, to whom I respectfully and affectionately dedicate this paper.

[1] Perry (1967) 87–88.

[2] *Suda* mentions a *Rhodiaca* by Philippus of Anphypolis, a highly bawdy work, and describes its author as a *historikos*, attributing to him also a *Coaca*, *Thasiaca* and other works. In this respect Hägg (1994) 53 is right when he states: "our gravest mistake would be to construct a building using only the few scattered remains—and believe the result to be historically true".

[3] Pervo (1987) 114 cites more than fifty Graeco-Roman titles and authors.

The mosaic-like variety of these works of prose fiction has brought thematic classifications such as *Reiseromane, utopische Romane, Liebesromane, Christliche Romane, Biographien, Romanparodie, komisch-satirische Romane*, to confine ourselves to the terms used by Helm.[4] The group studied here is what, traditionally, has been termed "novels of love and adventure", including the "idealist" works cited above. Though there are differences among them, these novels share a unity of structure, that is, the same structural model. The group, which could be said to comprise fragments such as *Ninus, Metiochus and Parthenope* and possibly *Sesonchosis*, is not a homogeneous group, and a traditional distinction between "pre-" or "non-sophistic" and "sophistic" novels has also been made.[5] The first group would include the fragments cited above, Chariton and Xenophon. But we need first to define the term "sophistic", to decide whether it applies to the atmosphere or spirit of the work, its narrative technique, its rhetorical expression or its chronology. As far as the latter is concerned, the Second Sophistic begins in the second half of the first century A.D.; and so only *Ninus* could with any certainty be said to predate it,[6] since Chariton may well have written under the reign of Trajan and Hadrian, with Xenophon emerging slightly later.[7] As examples of rhetorical works (more rhetorical than Xenophon's) we have *Ninus* and *Callirhoe*, as we shall see below.[8] The narrative technique is far more sophisticated in novels after Chariton and, as far as "spirit"

---

[4] Helm (1956²) for this and other classifications see Kuch (1985) 3ff.

[5] For example Perry (1967) 108 and Reardon (1971) 339n. for the "pre-sophistic" novels; Hägg (1983) 34 for the "non-sophistic" ones. In his 1994 study Hägg continues to use the term "non-sophistic" though, despite his awareness of the problems presented by novels such as the *Ephesiaca*, which belong to the first group by spirit and to the second by chronology, he retains the distinction.

[6] This is the oldest work of its kind: it probably dates back to the 1st century B.C.—maybe earlier, according to Wilcken (1893)—or to the beginning of the Empire. For a commentary of the fragments see Kussl (1991) 15ff.; Dostálová (1991) 30–35. The papyri of *Metiochus and Parthenope* belong to the 2nd century A.D. and those of *Sesonchosis* to the 3rd century A.D., though the fact that they deal with historical or legendary characters suggests they might belong to the origins of the genre: see the commentaries by Maehler (1976), Dostálová (1991) 35–41, O'Sullivan (1986). I have not been able to consult the book by Stephens, S., Winkler, J. *Ancient Greek Novels. The Fragments* (Princeton 1995).

[7] The chronology for Chariton is taken from a study of the language and social context of the work: see Ruiz-Montero (1989) (1991) (1994a) for a summary of opinions. Later studies place the work in the period of Hadrian: Baslez (1992a), or in the first half of the 2nd century A.D.: C.P. Jones (1992a). For Xenophon see Ruiz-Montero (1994b).

[8] Cf. n. 77.

goes, the naive and romantic idealism of *Ninus*, Chariton and Xenophon differs from that of later writers.

The chronology of *Wonders beyond Thule* is uncertain, but it belongs probably to the 2nd century A.D., for its narrative technique is quite subtle, a fact which casts doubt on its pertinence to the early stages of the genre. Besides, the idealist, sentimental, more rough-and-ready nature of the novels of Chariton and Xenophon is incompatible with this later novel.[9]

One other key element allows us to separate the novels into two groups, namely: their structure. Indeed the underlying structure of the early novels is based on the lover's search for the beloved after the enforced separation of the main couple, who have overcome an initial obstacle to get married. In the meantime both undergo their own adventures until the final encounter and the return to their native land. In my structural analysis of Greek novels I tried to show how their narrative morphology is comparable to that found by Propp in his study of character functions in the Russian folktale.[10] Propp distinguished a *hero-searcher* and a *hero-victim*, who are not usually found together in the tales but who do coexist in the earliest Greek novels, those of Chariton and Xenophon. The common structural element in the genre is neither love nor the adventures along the way but the *search* itself, which is particularly marked in the early novels, a fact of some relevance to our purposes. The semantics of love in that search are a specific feature of the Greek novel. In Longus there is no journey as such: both of the young lovers seek to satisfy their sexual desires, and the work culminates in marriage, as in Achilles and Heliodorus. Achilles omits the search, while Heliodorus merges it with the return to the native land.[11]

As the earliest works, then, the fragments cited above and the novel by Chariton are the texts on which this study of the origins and formation of the Greek novel as a genre will be based.

---

[9] See *infra*, p. 40.

[10] See Ruiz-Montero (1988) and Propp (1928). The central motif for the search is to be found in the *quest for the vanished wife* in folklore: see Thompson (1966) H 1385.3; Aarne-Thompson (1964) 400–425; types 705–712: *the banished wife or maiden*.

[11] The same structure appears in tales such as Apuleius's tale of Amor and Psyche, *Met.* IV 27ff., and a modified version (an allomorph) in the *History of Apollonius, King of Tyre*, where the erotic element is secondary and the hero is presented as a *searcher* at the start, albeit in a debilitated form. The likely Greek original of the novel could belong to the early stage of the genre: see Ruiz-Montero (1983) for a study of its structure. The *Recognitions* by Ps. Clement would belong to the same group: cf. *infra*, (note 89).

B. *The Genre in Antiquity*

Ancient treatises on rhetoric carry no specific reference to the genre. Barwick correctly noted that the *narratio in personis posita* in *ad Herennium* I 8,12–13 and Cicero's *De inv.*I 19,27 bear no relation to the novel, though they do have some relevance to the genre.[12] The ultimate source for these texts is Plato's celebrated *Republic* 392d–394c, where the διήγησις of poetry is divided into the imitative (tragedy and comedy), the enunciative (dithyramb) and the mixed (epic). Obviously the novel has no place in this division, which was held for a considerable length of time,[13] and this is one of the reasons later rhetoric does not mention it as a genre. On the other hand, of the three genres into which the *narratio a causa civili remota* is divided—*fabula*, *historia* and *argumentum*—one of them had surely to provide the basis for the novel: in this case the third genre (in Greek, πλάσμα), whose example was comedy, later termed διήγημα δραματικόν.[14] Following the Platonic division, the novel would be a mixed genre, like the epic, since the author's speech mingles with that of the characters. Hence, to the dramatic model we should add the narrative genre *par excéllence*: the epic. To be sure, when the novel emerges at the close of the Hellenistic period the mixture of genres and literary forms, ποικιλία is a fact, and, as the presence of the novel itself reveals, the phenomenon persists through the imperial age.

Scholars have stressed that in Greece poetry was traditionally reserved for the "fictional" genres and prose for the true ones;[15] nevertheless, both tragedy and comedy were written in verse and were not regarded by Greeks as being equally fictional: only comedy constituted "pure fiction".[16] At the same time, as historiography, philosophical utopias and rhetorical declamation reveal, there was no hard

---

[12] Barwick (1928). Compare the cited text of Cicero ("pleasure, the fruit of a variety of situations, of different states of mind, severity, sweetness, hope, fear, suspicion, desire, dissembling, error, compassion, changes of fortune, an unexpected setback, a sudden joy, a happy unwinding of the situations") with that of Chariton V 8,2 ("It was as if one were at a theatre filled with a thousand feelings, all of them felt at once: tears, joy, admiration, compassion, incredulity, supplications"). See n. 69.

[13] We still find it in Nicolaus (5th century A.D.): cf. Rohde (1914) 375ff.

[14] Besides Barwick (1928), see Kerényi (1927) 2–4; Gutu (1972).

[15] Perry (1967) 66ff.; Fusillo (1990b) 35–6.

[16] Hesiod, *Theog.*27–8 had already called for a poetry which would communicate the truth, thus acknowledging the fact that there was a poetry that did not. That poetic form is not a hindrance to scientific treatises was also noted by Aristotle, *Po.*1447e.

and fast separation between the real and the marvellous in prose either. Hence, not all poetry was fictional and not all prose was true.[17]

Traditional rhetoric was in any case more concerned with the formation of the orator, so that literature which had no practical function, literature for its own sake, hardly came up for discussion. Such literature belonged to the so-called "epideictic" or "panegyric" genre. This explains why, in the 2nd century A.D., an important critic like Hermogenes (in his work *On Types of Style* 404–407) could cite as the prime exponent of the genre Xenophon of Athens (with examples from the *Cyropaedia*), the Socratic Aeschines—the author of myths and fables—and Nicostratus, an author who "has invented lots of myths, some like those of Aesop, but also some that are in one way or another even dramatic" (p. 407), "dramatic" here being used to refer to certain kinds of intrigue, a form perhaps closer to the theatre than to the novel.

Elsewhere Hermogenes calls non-oratorical prose "logography" (pp. 389; 404; 1–11; 19–20), with Plato as the stylistic model, though there is no reference to the contemporary novel. This is hardly surprising given that the only contemporary authors cited are Aristides and Nicostratus. Following the trend of the Second Sophistic Hermogenes cites only classical authors and genres.

Interestingly enough, on page 405 he describes the story of Abradates and Pantheia in the *Cyropaedia* IV–VII as πάθος, at the same time as the mythical basis of the work is said to make the style pleasurable (p. 306).[18] On page 333 he also describes as sweet all thoughts that have to do with being in love.

I am not sure whether Philostratus (*Letters* 66) has our Chariton in mind,[19] but if he does, it would indicate his scorn for the genre—as well as the popularity of Chariton. The same scorn is said to exist in the *Lives of the Sophists* I 524, where there is a mention of "Araspes, the lover of Pantheia" which cannot, because of its rhythm, other

---

[17] That the distinction between fictional discourse and real discourse is typical not just of Plato but of Greek culture in general has been noted by Gill (1993a). Gill's article, as well as the others included in the book edited by Gill and Wiseman (1993), are highly relevant to the subject of "fiction" in antiquity: see also Reardon (1991) 46ff.

[18] The same term is used to describe the story of Tigranes and Armenia in *Cyropaedia* III 1,36.

[19] "To Chariton. You think the Greeks will remember your work when you die. What importance can those who are nothing in life possibly have when they are no longer alive?"

stylistic features and enthymemes, be by the sophist Dionysius of Miletus, but is rather the fruit of the work (φρόντισμα) of Celer, the rhetorician, a good imperial secretary, but not a good declaimer. Yet, from the context, it is clear that Philostratus is referring to a work of declamation, not to a novel.

In the second half of the 4th century A.D. the emperor Julian, in a well-known text, recommends that the priests of Asia Minor read true stories, not fictions (πλάσματα) in story form (ἐν ἱστορίας εἴδει), love intrigues (ἐρωτικὰς ὑποθέσεις) and similar works, recounted by the ancients.[20] Here he seems to be referring to the novels. Julian presents them as ancient works, though it is hard to know whether ἱστορία is to be understood as a "work pertaining to the genre of historiography" or as a "tale", as used in the proem by Longus and (possibly) in *Suda*, where three "Xenophons" and Philippus of Anphipolis are referred to as ἱστορικοί.[21]

The works of Petronius and Apuleius are mentioned by the Neoplatonist Macrobius (ca. 400 A.D.) in his commentary of Cicero's *Somnium Scipionis* I 2,7ff.: like the works of Menander, their sole function is to delight, and they are comparable to the *nutricum cunae*.[22] Though Macrobius does not cite the Greek novels, they might well belong to those *argumenta fictis casibus amatorum referta* (I 2,8), that is, "intrigues full of fictional stories of lovers", where *casibus amatorum* recalls the πάθος of Hermogenes, as we shall also see in Parthenius and Chariton.[23]

Finally in various passages of the *Library* by Photius (9th century), the term δραματικόν is used to define the novels of Antonius Diogenes, Iamblichus, Achilles and Heliodorus,[24] and δράματος πρόσωπα to de-

---

[20] *Letters* 300c–301d. Shortly before he had banned the reading of Aristophanes: these works were considered pernicious, inducing base desires. It is worth recalling that Theodorus Priscianus, a 5th century physician, recommended reading Iamblichus and similar authors as a cure for impotence: see Wesseling (1988) 68. Photius, cod. 87, regarded the novel by Achilles Tatius as highly immoral and Iamblichus's as slightly less so, though more so than the novel by Heliodorus (cod. 94).

[21] This was the opinion of Rohde (1914) 376, n. 1. For the first sense see C.W. Müller (1976).

[22] They are distinguished from the *narratio fabulosa* of poetry and philosophy, and from the *fabulae* of Aesop.

[23] This interpretation of the term is not certain in X.E.III 9,4, or in Luc., *De salt*.54 (referring to Polycrates). Kerényi (1927) 19, gives the same sense to the term ἄκουσμα in X.E.I 1,4.

[24] Cod. 166; 94; 87; 73. The term is not used to describe the *Metamorphoses* of Lucius of Patrae (cod. 129), whose tales are characterised by their fantasy (τὴν ἐν τοῖς διηγήμασι τερατείαν), as well as the fact that they are full of fantastic fictions (πλασμάτων μυθικῶν).

scribe the protagonists of the *Babyloniaca*. In cod. 94 Photius also states that Iamblichus, Achilles and Heliodorus "composed intrigues on amorous subjects" (ἐρωτικῶν δραμάτων ὑποθέσεις ὑπεκρίθησαν).[25] His opinion is clear when he argues that the style of Iamblichus merits more serious attention than these *divertimenti* and fictions (παιγνίοις καὶ πλάσμασιν). The definitions δραματικόν/δρᾶμα /ὑπόθεσις, which are theatrical in origin, could be interpreted as "intrigues" in the narrative sense; this at least would seem to be the meaning of δρᾶμα in Achilles Tatius.[26] What is not clear is how we should interpret Antonius Diogenes's description of his work as κωμῳδία παλαιά in Phot. cod. 166: either as Aristophanic comedy or comedy developed at an earlier stage.[27]

The authors' own definitions of the genre are equally varied. Chariton opens his novel with the expression πάθος ἐρωτικὸν διηγήσομαι, (I 1,1), which evokes the ἐρωτικὰ παθήματα of Parthenius, a collection of love stories that provides the model for later works like the *Love Narrations* (ἐρωτικαὶ διηγήσεις) attributed to Plutarch, and the *Metamorphoses* of Antoninus Liberalis, and which comprises a kind of *novelle*, discussed in part VI of this study. Chariton's πάθος ἐρωτικόν would refer to the ἱστορία ἔρωτος of Longus's proem, where the amorous intrigue is also defined as τύχην ἐρωτικήν, εἰκόνα γραπτήν, and also γραφή, that is, as the rhetorical description of a painting, an ἔκφρασις, a genre very much in vogue in the imperial period.

Meanwhile, the verb διηγέομαι and the noun διήγημα, frequent in the novel, are typical of contemporary rhetoric, though the verb had already been used by Xenophon of Athens.[28]

The act of counterfeiting a story (πλάσασθαί τι διήγημα) also appears in Chariton I 10,6. Another of the terms Chariton uses to refer to his work is σύγγραμμα or the verb συγγράφω (VIII 1,5; 8,16), a word used previously by Thucydides (I 1, 1), to characterise writing in prose.

Chariton himself defines his novel in terms borrowed from the theatre[29] and refers to it as a θέατρον with emotions included,[30] or compares himself to a dramatic poet.[31] These concepts appear in other

---

[25] Photius's terminology may be based on words used by the novelists themselves.
[26] Cf. *infra*, n. 29.
[27] C.W. Müller (1976) accepts the second sense: cf. *infra*, p. 40.
[28] Cf. n. 77. See also *infra*, n. 156.
[29] Cf. IV,3,11; 4,2; V 8,2; VI 3,6; 8,1. The myths of Andromeda (III 7,9) and Philomela (V 3,4), as well as the very plot of the novel (VIII 15,4) are defined by Achilles Tatius as δρᾶμα. The same name is given to the myths by Luc., *De salt.*54.
[30] I 9,3; II 4,4; III 7,6; V 8,2; VIII 5,8.
[31] III 8,6; IV 7,6.

novelists.[32] In II 27,2 Longus classes his novel as a μῦθος, that is, as a myth in the traditional sense.[33] Achilles gives the same name to certain episodes in his novel in VIII 4,12; 15,4.

Πάθος, διήγημα, ὑπόθεσις, δρᾶμα, ἱστορία, μῦθος, τύχη are, then, the terms used by novelists to refer to their intrigue. There is also a divergence when it comes to giving the works titles: while Chariton chooses *Callirhoe*, others link their novels to local historiography, with names such as *Ephesiaca, Babyloniaca,* or *Aethiopica.*[34]

These facts help to explain the lack of references to the genre amongst contemporaries. At the same time, the genre's formal variety, its ποικιλία, explains the wide range of definitions, as well as revealing rhetoric's own equivocations on the matter. In the last part of this study we shall consider how "humble" the origins of the genre really were.

Let us state finally that we are aware of the excesses of the "genetic" approach to the novel; bent as they were on discovering a direct line of filiation between the novel and some earlier genre, scholars have used concepts such as "development" and "evolution" which are no longer in common currency. But in the affairs of man there is no such thing as creation *ex nihilo*, and the Greek literary tradition is no exception. The fact that there is no single definition for the genre precludes the possibility of a mythical inventor with a clear idea of what he was doing; even if such an inventor existed, the gulf between intentions and actual achievement would have been as vast as the gulf between the continent Columbus discovered and the continent he thought he had discovered. We are also aware of the risk of talking about the birth not of the genre, but of one particular novel—a birth that may have been different in the case of another novel—, or of giving a version of the start of the genre that is actually more relevant to the situation in the 2nd century A.D., the period we

---

[32] Xenophon and Longus use none of them. For Achilles and Heliodorus see Conca (1989) s.v. δρᾶμα, and O'Sullivan (1980): "tale of action, action in narration or in painting" for the same term.

[33] The term seems to bear the same meaning in A.T. I 2,2. In the Italian lexicon cited above μῦθος has the sense of "story" in novelists, never of "theatrical intrigue". The same goes for μυθολόγημα in Longus and μυθολογία in Longus and Achilles as synonyms for the former. λόγος also appears in Chariton, Achilles and Heliodorus with the sense of "racconto, storia, narrazione". But for O'Sullivan (1980) s.v. μῦθος, the sense of "theatrical works" is retained in I 8,4, where the noun appears in the plural.

[34] Heliodorus sets this title by the names of his protagonists at the end of his novel.

have most information about. We hope, therefore, to avoid the wrath of the gods by presenting and analysing the material as impartially and rigorously as possible. With this aim in mind, we shall focus on an aspect of the novel that has often been neglected, but that strikes us as crucial when it comes to making comparisons with other genres: the structure.[35] We intend to complement our comments on the structure of the novel with Segre's distinction between the four levels of analysis, namely: (in order of increasing abstraction) discourse, intrigue, *fabula* and narrative model.[36]

Also worth bearing in mind are the findings of comparative literature, though scholars of historical poetics have, sadly, devoted little attention to the study of ancient texts.[37]

In the pages that follow we shall revisit the different factors that, in some way or another, have contributed to the formation and emergence of the genre, starting with the literary tradition. We shall underline the importance of that tradition, and the endless dialogue between innovation and imitation, in the construction of the novel. We shall point to similarities and differences between the novel and other genres. Still within the Greek tradition, we shall go on to look at the rhetorical context, as well as to consider the scope of possible influences from the East. Our final comments will be on the social context surrounding the genre.[38]

---

[35] Hölscher (1988) 226 gives it equal importance, and adds that no scholar of the novel has thought of the folk tale as an antecedent. But cf. *supra*, n. 10.

[36] Segre (1974) 14ff.: *discorso, intreccio, "fabula", modello narrativo*. Discourse refers to the surface appearance of the text, that is, as it is perceived by the reader. Plot is the events narrated in the order they are presented in the text. These two levels are the object of study in literature, whereas the following two are more the concern of ethnography and folklore. Indeed, the *fabula* and narrative model are theoretical constructs: *fabula* is used to describe the plot in its logical, causal-temporal order, which cannot coincide with the order of the text. Finally, *narrative model* helps us to give a uniform description of texts of different natures and historical periods, i.e., to abstract their invariable elements. We should avoid the confusion between "narrative model", understood in this semiological sense, and "literary model", as used in the habitual way in philology. Fusillo (1989) is also aware of Segre's distinction, and this strikes me as useful when it comes to drawing comparisons between genres.

[37] An example is Genette (1986) 155, who asserts that autobiography is only possible in the modern age.

[38] For general treatments of the subject, see Giangrande (1962); Reardon (1971) 309–39; Ruiz-Montero (1981); Pervo (1987) 86–114; Fusillo (1989) 24ff.; Dubielzig (1991); Grimal (1992).

II. *The Utopian Tradition*

According to Frye, there are two social concepts that can only be expressed in terms of myth—the social contract and utopia. The latter generally takes the form of a journey through space or time, a journey narrated in the first person by a traveller who relates what he sees.[39] This literary form serves as the vehicle for a set of ideas, be it the proposal of some ideal society, an ideal education or both. Satire and pastoral literature are the genres in which these ideas can be expressed.

In Greece utopian features have already been noted in Homer's presentation in the *Odyssey* of the Phaeacians, a race whose king is a paragon of virtue and a friend of the gods, and whose ships steer themselves.[40] Utopian concerns figure also in the comedy of Aristophanes when he suggests that a city be governed by women, or founded by birds, as it is in the ideal political constructs of Socrates and his disciples, Plato, Antisthenes and the Cynic Diogenes of Sinope. The tradition persists in the works of the Stoics. Plato establishes links with the utopian tradition in *Timaeus* and *Critias*, works that, like the *Odyssey*, present a fantastic and distant land. A blend of pedagogical utopia and novelistic biography, Xenophon's *Cyropaedia* is set in an idealised Persia, ruled over by an idealised monarch. We shall return to this work, whose importance for the development of Greek literature was immense. For the moment, suffice it to say that if Plato sought a philosopher as king, Xenophon seeks a soldier, who is well-educated and polite. With the conquests of Alexander, the horizons of utopia begin to expand and the genre is consolidated. Cynicism helped in this respect, as an increasingly travel-oriented and novelistic utopia begins to emerge.

The first utopia is said to have been Euhemerus's *Sacred Inscription*, written after the author's embassy to Cassander, an enlightened and philanthropically-minded monarch, in Arabia Felix of around 300 B.C. The information comes from Diodorus of Sicily V 41–46, whose tale has a philosophical and religious content and is set within a real political context. Ferguson called it a "philosophical novel".[41] Following

---

[39] Frye (1973).
[40] For an extended treatment of the subject see Ferguson (1975) 246ff. Homer also idealises Ethiopians, Egyptians and Indians.
[41] Ferguson (1975) 108. For differences from Antisthenes and Plato see p. 104.

the utopian tradition, whose roots are in folklore, the novel includes a number of famous personages.

Amongst other authors of utopias the most relevant for the novel is Iambulus. Diodorus II 55–60 provides an extensive report of his work when he deals with the wonders of Arabia. Iambulus was extremely interested in education, but on the death of his father, a merchant, he too became a merchant and, in this capacity, undertook a journey to Arabia. He was captured by pirates and later by the Ethiopians, who took him to Ethiopia as a sacrificial victim. In accordance with an oracle, he and a companion were thrown into a boat until, with storms raging all around them, they reached an island of happy and kindly inhabitants. Diodorus describes the latters' physical features, their interest in education, especially astronomy, as well as their customs and other peculiarities. Iambulus and his companion remain on the island for seven years, but are exiled as a result of their misdemeanours. On leaving, they are shipwrecked off the coast of India, where the companion is drowned and Iambulus reaches a city whose king is both educated and an admirer of the Greeks. The king helps Iambulus on his way to Persia and he eventually reaches Greece. Here he writes his work, a chronicle (ἀναγραφή), as well as many other stories about India.

Iambulus almost certainly existed and would have written between 250 and 225 B.C. His ideas on education and the natural life are apparently based on Stoic principles.[42] Motifs such as the journey of the hero with one or more companions, the capture by pirates, storms and shipwrecks are typical of the genre of the novel as a whole. Oracles and purifying rituals are found in Xenophon and Heliodorus, where Ethiopia is the sought-for land. Iambulus, however, adds certain ideals of conduct, the praise of education and an admiration for the traditional Greeks of literature, themes which will extend to the Second Sophistic and can be found in Chariton.

Utopias such as Iambulus's reveal a connection with paradoxography, though this work confines itself to description, not to the proposal of a new and ideal community. The account of the wonders is presented in the first person, which lends a certain credibility to the incredible things described by the author.[43] The device once more recalls Ulysses at the court of the Phaeacians. This seems to be

---

[42] See Ferguson (1975) 126–9.
[43] See Scobie (1969) 42–3.

the case in Iambulus, though the qualifying term παράδοξον applies not only to the description of portentous creatures in Achilles and Heliodorus, but to the power of Eros. Chariton uses it frequently in this sense, so much so in fact that he himself seems to regard his novel as a παράδοξόν τι.[44]

But it is in the *Wonders beyond Thule* by Antonius Diogenes that the paradoxographical tradition reaches its highpoint.[45] Here is a first-person narration in which the journey "in search of knowledge" (κατὰ τὴν ζήτησιν τῆς ἱστορίας) by Dynias and his son is the framework both for a love story and for the story of the wicked magician Paapis's persecution of a brother and sister. The work includes fantastic tales and elements of Pythagorean astronomy.[46] Photius's summary provides one clear impression of the plot, namely: that it is a complex one.[47] The context of the story is historical: Alexander's soldiers discover tablets relating events in the 5th century B.C. (a device Cervantes would later employ in *Don Quixote*).[48] As we noted above, Photius described the work as an "ancient comedy", and Morgan has suggested that it may even have been a comic parody, whose obscene and fantastic-parodic elements were censored by the patriarch.[49]

The search for the wife, typical of the love novels, is not present here. Instead, we find only one erotic episode and a quest for knowledge or information, a journey inspired perhaps by a kind of "curiosity" or a desire to "see the sights", as in *Ephesiaca* I 10,3. In *Ninus* there may have been a prior journey or military campaign that served as a frame for Ninus's later journey in search of his wife. But the compositional structure and the tone of Antonius Diogenes's work seem different from those of Chariton and other love novels. Meanwhile, the journey to see more of the world is already made by Solon in Herodotus I 29–30, who travels to Egypt and Sardes.

---

[44] See Kerényi (1927) 9–12.
[45] See the introduction to Fusillo (1990b).
[46] See Fauth (1978), who finds traces of "philosophischer Aretalogie" in this novel. The text was used by Porphyrius (3rd century A.D.) for his *Life of Pythagoras*: cf. C.W. Müller (1981) 394.
[47] Fusillo (1990b) speaks of the "passion of narrating". According to Photius, Diogenes cited the sources of his tales at the start of each book.
[48] Morgan (1985) 426 notes that Balagrus and Phile are historical personages too. Photius gave such credit to the fiction that he believed the work to be close chronologically to Alexander.
[49] Whether the *True Tales* of Lucian imitate the work or not is secondary, but, as Morgan himself points out, writing a parody of another parody would be meaningless.

Rohde believed the travel stories could have influenced the origins of the new genre. The genre would have developed out of the fusion of two elements: a "material" element (the travel stories or *Reisefabulistik*) and an erotic element appended to the former and with its source in Hellenistic poetry. Rohde assumes the fusion took place in the last centuries before Christ and posits the existence of an inventor (*Erfinder*) for the first novel, with later novels (except that of Longus) being variations on the first.[50] The fusion would have already been effected in the extant novels, but it is in the work of Antonius Diogenes that the first stages of the process begin. For Rohde the novel would have been written during the reign of Alexander, and would provide the model for later works. It would, in other words, have been pre-sophistic. According to Rohde, the genre would have been formed some time between Diogenes and Iamblicus—i.e., the 3rd century B.C. and the 2nd century A.D.—when the erotic element is strengthened under the Second Sophistic. We shall return to this point, though, as already stated, we now know that Diogenes was not the first novelist. To place the intrigue in the classical period is a typical gesture of the Second Sophistic, and this is what happens in Chariton, though the characters are now fictional, however historical the framework might be.

According to Ferguson, utopian literature ends with Iambulus, the sole exception being the *True Tales* by Lucian, who expressly cites Iambulus and Ctesias. Only political utopia would survive in the doctrine of the Stoics and Roman political theory. Nevertheless, escapism persists in the tradition of the bucolic. An example is the *Euboic* by Dio of Prusa, a first-person narration containing a eulogy of the good life, set on an island visited much earlier by the author.

Yet to what extent are Greek novels not simply fantastic constructs of an ideal society, an *Erotopolis* founded on a single emotion, love, before which all men are rendered equal? A world in which love is the overlord and the best subject is the best lover? A world in which to woo the beloved is to be "the same as the gods", ἰσόθεος, to quote Chariton VII 5,15. Though the plots of these novels develop in a particular place and time, they are to this extent members of the utopian tradition. The most utopian of novels, that is, the novel least fixed to a time and space, is that of Longus, an encomium of

---

[50] Rohde (1914) 262–64; 296.

Love and Nature.[51] Heliodorus also describes an idealised Ethiopia owing to its king and its great wealth. Utopia is a genre with a message, but the Greek novel might also contain one: Chariton stresses the importance of φιλανθρωπία and Greek παιδεία, and a religious interpretation is feasible in almost all of the novels, a subject we shall return to below.

As we have seen, besides paradoxography, the travel story tradition intersects with other narrative genres, such as historiography, the epic and the folktale. It is time now to consider the historiographical tradition.

III. *The Historiographical Tradition*

It is a fact that the first known novel, *Ninus*, presents characters from history or legend. The heroine, whose name does not appear in the fragments, may have been the Assyrian queen Semiramis.[52] Ninus seems to have been a legendary, rather than a historical, king, though Semiramis was certainly famous for her deeds.[53] Both figure in the Greek historiographical tradition: both Ctesias and Diodorus mention them.[54] The latter presents Ninus as the great Assyrian conqueror, the founder of the first world empire, while Semiramis is described as the fairest, cruellest, mightiest and most sensual of the eastern queens. The conquests of Ninus are cited in the fragments, though the presentation of both characters as love heroes clashes with what we actually know about them, especially where Semiramis is concerned: here she is presented as a shy young girl who blushingly confesses to her aunt her love for her cousin Ninus. History has been tampered with, the characters transfigured and transformed

---

[51] The action takes place in Mytilene, "almost an island" within another island, Lesbos. The novel's innocent and optimistic heroes, their primitivism, their vegetarianism, their insistence on love and sexual longing, are all features to be found in one type of utopia described by Frye (1973). The novel also includes real-life characters such as Xenophon of Ephesus included, an element that comes from folklore: see Ruiz-Montero (1988) 212ff. Despite this, Longus is, as Hunter (1983) demonstrates, a cultivated and sophisticated novelist.

[52] See *supra*, n. 6. For the "Forschunggeschichte", see Kussl (1991) 68–83. He opts for AB, the order favoured by the first editor, Wilcken; Dostálová (1991) prefers the order BA.

[53] See Pettinato (1985).

[54] For Ctesias, see Auberger (1991); D.S. II 1–20, who highlights the παράδοξον nature of his account. Herodotus hardly cites them.

into the protagonists of a romantic tale. Strikingly, there is no precedent for the novel in either written or oral sources.

As in Chariton's novel, the heroes wed after an initial impediment—a law. After the wedding the wife accompanies Ninus on a military operation, as in *Cyropaedia* IV 3,1–2 and *Callirhoe* VI 9,6–7; it is here, possibly after a defeat, that she is taken prisoner. He searches for her and, whether after a battle (in alliance with the enemies of his aggressor as in Chariton VII 1,10ff.; see VII 6) or by pure chance, eventually finds her, as in the *History of Apollonius*. Meanwhile, she has possibly been the object of her conqueror's amorous advances, remaining in his custody (as in *Callirhoe* under Dionysius and Artaxerxes) or, as in the *History of Apollonius*, with no particular role in the intrigue.[55]

Much the same romantic features are to be found in the *Sesonchosis* novel.[56] The hero represents the great Egyptian conqueror, the perfect pharaoh, whom popular tradition has linked to several different kings.[57] According to Herodotus and Diodorus, Sesonchosis is another founder of a huge empire.[58] It is not hard to see how the Macedonian conqueror becomes the model for other conquerors from the peoples he has subdued: legends existed in the oral tradition that evince a desire for national self-assertion, the championing of traditions and local kings who have stood up to the conquerors, and any of these novels in turn may have been the basis for an *Assyriaca* or *Babyloniaca*, and an *Aegyptiaca*.[59]

Certain facts related by Diodorus, such as the education of Sesonchosis with other youths of his age and the conquest of Arabia, are corroborated in the fragments; what is less clear is whether the treason of the brother of Sesonchosis while the latter is abroad is present or not in Greek historiography, though fragment C does report that

---

[55] Dostálová (1991) 34, relates the mosaic in Antioch, in which Ninus is seen contemplating the picture of a woman, to Chariton I 14 and II 11,1, in which Callirhoe contemplates a picture of Chaereas in her ring.

[56] Cf. *supra*, n. 6.

[57] See Lloyd (1982); Gaggero (1989).

[58] Hdt.II 102–11; D.S.I 53–58. The name can also appear in Greek as Sesostris or Sesoosis.

[59] *Suda* is known to have mentioned a certain Xenophon of Antiochia as the author of a *Babyloniaca*, together with Xenophon of Ephesus and Xenophon of Cyprus, the author of a *Cypriaca*. The three are termed ἱστορικοί (*supra*, n. 2 and 21, and below, n. 237). Bowie (1994b) 451 believes it is unnecessary to talk of nationalism, and adds that the reliefs of Ninus and Semiramis found could serve to place the birth of the genre in Aphrodisias.

Sesonchosis has foregone his lofty status. This fact is to be viewed as another instance of shifting Fortune, and is already borne out in fragment C of *Ninus* and is a typical feature of Chariton's *Callirhoe*.[60] Herodotus tells us that, thanks to the astuteness of Sesonchosis's wife, both he and his family were saved, though the possible love story presented in fragment C is unique to the novel. Diodorus calls him εὐεργέτης, his subjects εὖνοι and describes his treatment of the vanquished as ἐπιείκεια. These are qualities that belong to the biographical tradition and are comparable to those found in Chariton.[61]

The emergence of these novels would seem to be influenced by a process of folklore which, true to the model of a romantic oral legend, affects both characters, dates and other details. On the subject of Sesonchosis Diodorus mentions Egyptian priestly and poetic traditions, as well as Greek prose ones. Dostálová adds that, from the 6th dynasty, gravestone inscriptions adopt a narrative character and even include letters from the pharaohs.[62] We do not know how far the novel predates the papyri preserved from the 3rd century A.D., though the legendary nature of the hero suggests it may belong to the early phase. Gaggero believes that the period from Augustus to the end of the 2nd century A.D. is "conclusivo" for the Sesonchosis legend.

The historical context is highlighted in the fragments of *Metiochus and Parthenope*, which features the Phrygian Metiochus and the daughter of Polycrates of Samos, who goes from East to West in search of her husband.[63] The symposium scene, with the debate on the nature of Eros, is typically sophistic. A symposium can also be found in *Callirhoe* IV 5,7, a novel probably quite close, chronologically, to *Metiochus and Parthenope*. The central motif of the search is also present here, as in Chariton and Xenophon. We also find the same contamination of dates and characters as in *Callirhoe*. Chariton introduces Hermocrates of Syracuse, the Persian king Artaxerxes and his wife Statira, and

---

[60] Hdt.II 102–11 states, moreover, that Sesostris reached the banks of the Phasis, in Colchis, a fact that, if the conjecture is correct, coincides with *Ninus* C 13.

[61] See Ruiz-Montero (1989) 134 ss.

[62] Dostálová (1991) 80–1; D.S.II 17–8 includes a letter from the king of India to Semiramis, which recalls the letter in the *Life of Alexander*.

[63] Hdt.VI 39–41: Luc., *De salt*.54 relates Parthenope's pilgrimage to the Persians, a possible reference to the novel. In 2 he presents Parthenope together with Phaedra and Rhodope as highly erotic and lascivious women, an image which bears no resemblance to the feminine ideal in the Greek novels. They are subjects for dance, as the stories of Ninus, Metiochus and Achilles in *Pseud*.25 are for popular theatre (*infra*, n. 174). See Dostálová (1991); Hägg (1984) (1985) for their reconstructions from Persian imitations.

the world of Persian satraps and eunuchs.[64] The heroine is the daughter of Hermocrates, though the author's aim is not history, but a love story whose setting is Syracuse. This would also seem to be the case for *Ninus, Metiochus and Parthenope* and *Sesonchosis*.

It is hardly surprising that the novel was viewed as a derivation from historiography. If Schwartz noted the possibility of a disintegration (*Zersetzung*), Ludvíkovský would devote an entire study to the matter.[65] Ludvíkovský regarded *Ninus* as a link between the two genres: historiography would undergo several developments before becoming the product of Asia Minor rhetoric, which is the novel. The presence of rhetoric in the novel would be explained from its connection with Hellenistic historiography, though the roots of the novel were not to be found in the schools of rhetoric but, on the contrary, as a response to the official literature of the "intelligentsia". It would be a popular genre written for the masses, and this is why it is sentimental and its earliest authors remain anonymous.

Following Brunetière's theory that one genre grows from the dismantling of another, Ludvíkovský believes that both the historical novel (*Life of Alexander*) and the erotic novel derive from the novel of "adventure", constituting two phases of internal development within the genre. The *Cyropaedia* would play a decisive part in the process, the order being: *Cyropaedia – Alexander – Ninus – Callirhoe*. *Ninus* would mark the transition between the two types. Finally, the erotic element would stem from the idealist *novella*, such as that of Pantheia. For Dostálová also Greek historiography, with its eastern legends, would eventually lead to the novel.[66]

Clearly the biographical tradition, represented by works such as *Cyropaedia, Anabasis* or the Hellenistic version of the present *Life of Alexander*, is an important link in the development of Greek prose fiction. It should be stressed that, from its appearance in the 4th century B.C., biography figures as an encomium of the hero,[67] that is, as an object of rhetorical analysis, a status which grows and is strengthened in the Hellenistic period. It is in this way that the hero

---

[64] For the historical context of Chariton see now Baslez (1992a) and C.P. Jones (1992a) (1992b).
[65] Schwartz (1943) 142ff.; Ludvíkovský (1925).
[66] Dostálová (1991) 84.
[67] For his moral virtues see *supra*, n. 61. Useful here are the studies by Fraustadt (1909) and Dihle (1987); Momigliano (1971) 43–64 already noted the influence of rhetoric on 4th century B.C. biography.

can assume epic proportions, as the case of Alexander, transformed into another Achilles and another Ulysses, demonstrates.[68] Epic permeates biography as drama did in its turn. The result is a hybrid form, a typical instance of Hellenistic ποικιλία which has also been found in Cicero's *Letter to Lucceius*.[69]

Certainly, the μεταβολή in fragment C of *Ninus* is a typical example of so-called Hellenistic "tragic history" represented by authors like Duris and Philarchus, features of which are, as Walbank has indicated,[70] already discernible in the classical period in authors like Herodotus and Ctesias. Walbank also notes the connection between history and tragedy as genres, in so far as they avail themselves of the same material and purpose.[71] Pédech has recently found in Theopompus the "tragic history" model, and in his characters the actors of a drama whose aim is to move the audience.[72] I am not concerned here with the problem of this type of historiography, though I believe Walbank is right. Nevertheless, if, as Pédech asserts, the influence of Duris and Phylarchus on Plutarch is clear (and we have good examples in *Agis* and *Cleomenes*), the atmosphere and details of the episodes narrated by these authors strike us as perfectly compatible with others that appear in Chariton. The techniques of dramatisation and suspense, the psychological interest in the characters, the importance of women and the tragic conception of the facts we find in Phylarchus are equally evident in Chariton, whose novel reveals other features attributed by Bartsch and Zegers to "tragic history".[73]

---

[68] See Centanni (1988) XXVI–XXVIII; Stoneman (1994b).

[69] *Ad fam.*V 12. Zegers (1959) discerns a tragic model in the text, while stating that Reitzenstein and Ullmann can only think of it in terms of a historical monograph. In his letter Cicero asks the historian Lucceius to write of his political achievements in a fashion more ornate than truthful (*rogo ut et ornes vehementius etiam quam fortasse sentis et in eo leges historiae neglegas gratiamque illam... eam ne aspernare amorique nostro plusculum etiam quam concedat veritas, largiare*). He should center on *quasi fabula rerum eventorumque nostrorum; habet enim varios actus multasque actiones et consiliorum et temporum,* in order to be celebrated like Alexander and Agesilaus. See also *Brutus* 11; *De orat.*II 36; *De inv.*I 27; *Part.Or.*31–2; 72–3. These *temporum varietates fortunaeque vicissitudines* will give pleasure to the reader. See in this regard n. 12.

[70] Walbank (1955) (1960). See also Sacks (1981).

[71] Cf. *infra*, p. 49.

[72] Pédech (1989).

[73] See Pédech (1989) 356ff.; 449–66. It is hard to see how original Duris and Phylarchus really were when our only source is Plutarch, though I still think Pédech overstates their veracity when they describe certain details unknown in other sources, as well as understating the importance of rhetoric. We would have also to discover if other *Lives* of Plutarch follow similar descriptive lines to the ones found in *Demetrius, Agis* and *Cleomenes*.

Phylarchus might be the source for the Chilonides episode in *Agis* 17–18,3, with the appearance of the devoted wife who follows her husband into exile. Episodes such as the discussion with a friend on the possibility of suicide (*Cleomenes* 31), the journey to Egypt, where he receives all manner of honours (*ibid.*, 32), the friendly treatment via a confidant by the new Egyptian king and Cleomenes's subsequent valour, recall similar episodes in Chariton VII.[74] The biography also includes some lines from the *Iliad*, a comparison with Achilles (Chapter 34) and a secret letter leading to imprisonment (chap. 35, 6). Of still more interest is the episode (chap. 22, 4) in which Cleomenes does not dare to speak before his mother, who suspects the truth, laughs and asks him some questions, an episode that finds an echo in *Ninus* I 5,6ff.[75] Other similarities between Plutarch and Chariton might be adduced.[76] The presence of Xenophon and Hellenistic historiography have also been detected in *Ninus*, whose heavily rhetorical nature needs stressing.[77]

We share Hägg's opinion that the oldest Greek novels can be regarded as "historical novels", that they are linked to the biographical tradition and that history seems to precede and explain the novel.[78] Of relevance here is the fact that works of chivalry are presented in the form of historical chronicles, imitating the style of the historians.[79] It is no coincidence that, as Müller has rightly observed, the word "history" figures in titles of novels right up to the 19th century.[80]

The influence of the historiographical and biographical traditions,

---

[74] I am happy to find that Professor Jones also notes Hellenistic historiographical sources in Chariton, developed and adapted to the new contexts, in his highly interesting (1992b) article.

[75] See Flacelière (1976). If this is the case, we have yet another fact to help us reconstruct these lines. Gronewald (1993) confirms Zimmermann's supposition that in line 14 a question is to be placed. The French editors cited assume that the source for Plutarch was Phylarchus. Could this have been the model for Chariton? The discussion scene might ultimately date back to the *Odyssey* VI 66–7.

[76] See Ruiz-Montero (1992). Papanikolaou (1973) 16–22 supplies a list of texts by this novelist which he compares to others of the historiographical tradition.

[77] See *infra*, n. 173. Episodes showing the training of the young hero appear in *Ages*.I 25; *Cyr*.I 18–19; being sent off on an expedition by his father in *An*.I 9,7; *Cyr*.I 18; the expedition against Babylonia in *An*.I 7,11; *Cyr*.V 2,28; rivalry between Egyptians and Persians in *Ages*.II 28; *An*.II 2,13, etc. The verb διηγέομαι is used frequently in the *Cyropaedia*.

[78] Hägg (1987a). The appearance of non-historical kings and princes as characters in the later novels is an archaism, which is highly accentuated in the case of Heliodorus.

[79] Bobes (1993) 66.

[80] C.W. Müller (1976).

closely linked in Greece, plays a crucial part in the formation of the novels; it is discerned in both narrative techniques and *topoi* and particular episodes that the author copies or adapts to the new contexts. That is to say, the traditions provide the literary flesh for the new genre (as is the case in other literary genres), though as literary models they strike me as superficial and with no impact on the underlying structure of the plot: Egypt, Persia, Assyria, their kings and deeds are well-known from Herodotus and Ctesias, but the story of two lovers who are married and then separated against their will, etc., as described above, is not a part of that tradition. For this reason, neither the rationale for their structure nor what we might describe as their purpose—a pedagogical and moralistic one—provides the basis for a possible *Ninopaedia*.

IV. The Dramatic Tradition

We have seen above that some of the novelists compare their texts to dramatic works, using terms like δρᾶμα, μῦθος, σκήνη, θέατρον. The tragedy of Euripides and the New Comedy no doubt had a special influence as models. Let us begin with tragedy.

A. *Tragedy*

Monologues in which the heroine, above all, laments for her fate are very frequent in Chariton and Xenophon.[81] The first lines of fragment C of *Ninus* would also seem to contain a complaint on the part of the hero.

Aristotle had already noted the pleasure (ἡδονή) to be drawn from tears and lamentations, as well as from adventures (περιπέτεια) and from being saved at the last moment from dangers, all of which provoked the spectator's admiration (θαυμαστά).[82] In the *Poetics* he also notes the importance of the element of surprise in tragedy, and even more so in the epic, as a way of heightening our admiration; he even accepts the impossible (τὰ ἀδύνατα) if it achieves a greater impact (ἔκπληξις).[83] Of the three tragedians Euripides displays these

---

[81] See Ruiz-Montero (1988) 82; 152.
[82] *Rh*.1370b 25; 1371b 10.12, respectively.
[83] *Po*.1460b.

qualities most clearly, and the importance of the unexpected is expressly mentioned as a facet of the final lines of five of his tragedies: *Alcestis, Medea, Andromache, Helen* and *Bacchae*.[84] The happy end, usually associated in Euripides with the *deus ex machina* device, provides a link with the novels and comedies of Menander. The influence of the tragic model, however, extends even further, operating at the level of composition.

In strict accordance with the theoretical principles of the *Poetics*, we could say that tragedy and the novel differ in terms of imitation: the medium (the novel imitates by means of prose) and the manner of representation (narration is in the third person and adopts the mixed form of the epic). As to the object, i.e., the characters, the novel presents them as average, though a hero like Chaereas continues to display certain virtues:[85] in any case, the error of judgement (ἁμαρτία) is present in I 4,7–5,1, where, trusting in false accusations, Chaereas kicks his wife and thus encourages the expulsion of the heroine and the subsequent search for her.

In extent the novel seems closer to the epic. Novel and tragedy share certain elements: recognition, *peripéteia* and *metabolē*,[86] while the adventures following the heroes' separation (in tragedy, excluded from the μῦθος) remain unique to the novel. In this the novel's proximity to the epic is clear. We have already pointed to the importance of *metabolē*, in *Ninus* C 41ff., a device common to both Chariton and Hellenistic historiography.[87] If in tragedy the *metabolē* may take the form of a shift from happiness to disaster or vice versa, in the novel there is an initial change from happiness to disaster, but then another change back to happiness. It is also clear that verisimilitude (εἰκός) dominates the plot of *Callirhoe*. In this case the duration of the complication (δέσις) would be shorter than its denouement (λύσις): the development of the λύσις is the novel's specific feature, with recognition being the end-point of that development.

Recognition is one of the cornerstones of both tragedy and the novel, as it was previously in the *Odyssey*. It is a key component of Euripides's theatre (e.g., *Orestes*, or other works described as "tragicomedies",

---

[84] Traditionally, doubt has been cast on the authenticity of these lines (except in the case of *Alcestis*), but see the recent arguments of Roberts (1987), who adduces information from 3rd century B.C. papyri.
[85] See Ruiz-Montero (1989).
[86] These would be the only coincidences, as far as "intrigue" is concerned.
[87] See allusions to the shifts of Fortune in *Ion* 1512–14; *IT* 722.

"romantic pieces" or "intrigues" like *Ion, Iphigenia in Tauris* and *Helen*).[88] The novel presents two kinds of recognition after the splitting up of a family, be it by the husband and wife or by the parents: *Ninus, Metiochus and Parthenope, Callirhoe, Ephesiaca* belong to the first group, the *Pastoral Tales* and the *Aethiopica* to the second.[89] Tragedy gives us examples of recognition between spouses (*Helen*), and between parents and offspring and even sister and brother (*Ion* and *Iphigenia in Tauris*), the latter a particularly common motif in the New Comedy. The novel, then, has a complex plot (πεπληγμένη πρᾶξις), like certain tragedies, and, together with that plot, shares a beginning, middle and end, as well as a different fate for the good characters and for the bad.

The element of πάθος is also present in the novel. Indeed, if tragedy involves destructive and painful action, such as deaths on stage, grief, wounds and similar events (*Po.*1452b), the novel has its supposed deaths (a commonplace from *Callirhoe* I 5,1)—some of them quite brutal (e.g., *Phoenicica* B I, *Leucippe and Cleitophon* III 15)—, attempted rapes of the heroine (*Ephesiaca* III 11,4; IV 5,4–5) or woeful scenes, referred to at the start of this chapter.

The use of language is an important point of contrast between the genres: in the novel the style is uniform throughout, though there is also the use of an ornate, i.e., rhetorical, language already patent in *Ninus* and *Callirhoe*.[90]

As for the effect and aim of the novel, they could be said to have been above all to entertain and please the public, while not excluding the communication of some message or ideals, or the use of ἔλεος and φόβος to shock the audience (particularly evident in the *Ephesiaca*).[91] Nevertheless, the effect of catharsis also seems to have been acknowledged by Chariton when he states (VIII 1,4) that the book is to be a καθάρσιον of the sadness of the previous ones. In this, Chariton

---

[88] See Kitto (1939); Conacher (1967).

[89] The *History of Apollonius* involves both kinds, with the reencounter between both husband and wife and parents and daughter. Its relation to the theatre of Euripides has been noted for years, though while Trenkner (1958) 40–44 looks elsewhere for the origin of the novel, Szepessy (1985–88) finds it in this work. My own feeling is that the origin for the *History* is in folklore and is not necessarily dependent on Euripides. The motif is as old as the *Odyssey*, for Telemachus had already gone in search of his father.

[90] Cf. pp. 42–3.

[91] The confrontation between Hymen and Death is to be found in previous texts like *IT* 362–68.

could be said to reinterpret or trivialise Aristotle,[92] since according to the Stagyrite, the effect would not be produced by this book, but by the suffering described in the earlier ones.[93]

To the qualitative elements Aristotle adds certain quantitative ones, namely: prologue, episode, exodus and chorus. From Reitzenstein on a five-act division of *Callirhoe* has been proposed, the basis being purely one of content, a criterion I find both subjective and neglectful of the work's compositional structure.[94]

Another characteristic of tragedy, irony, is also present in the novel, which nonetheless never attains the tragic depth of Sophocles's *Oedipus Rex*. But the play between appearance and reality, fundamental in (say) the *Ion*, can be found in Chariton: Callirhoe believes Chaereas to be dead and vice versa (I 5,1; III 10,3). At the same time, in Euripides's tragedy Xuthus is led to believe that Ion is his son, just as Dionysius is convinced that the son of Chaereas is his own.[95]

Euripides anticipates not just certain intrigues, but also certain subjects involving love: *Helen*, described by Kitto as "high comedy", presents us with a heroine who is both chaste and faithful (rejecting a marriage to King Proteus), and clear-minded and intelligent, like the future heroines of the novel. Like Callirhoe later, she despises her own beauty (27; 236–37; 305). The tragedy also involves the separation and reencounter of the spouses, who are prepared to die for their love (834–42). The vow of fidelity on v. 835 also featured in *Medea* 492–95 between Jason and Medea, anticipates the εὐορκήσας in *Ninus* A 2,1.

For many critics the modern novel is characterised by a journey into the soul, a journey which is not to be found in the ancient novel. Nevertheless, that inner journey and the desire to penetrate the psychology of the characters had already existed in tragedy; and though Chaereas may not be a stable character, endowed with

---

[92] This fact is also noted by C.W. Müller (1976): see Ruiz-Montero (1994a). Some comparisons between Chariton and the *Poetics* are recorded in Cicu (1982).

[93] In *Ion* 1605 Athena announces a happy destiny (*potmon*) as a relief from fatigue, comparable to the final words on the heroes in the oracle of Apollo in *Ephesiaca* I 6,2.

[94] Reitzenstein (1906). Amongst followers of the division, we could mention Perry, Schmeling, Plepelits and Molinié: see Ruiz-Montero (1994a) 1021, where I also cite scholars who reject the division.

[95] In *IT* 1487–88 Athena beseeches the winds to lead Orestes to Athens, an event comparable to Char.III 5,9, where Chaereas implores the sea, though the scene is reminiscent of the epic.

psychological depth, Chariton reveals himself to be a master of the inner portrait in his presentation of Dionysius, a character who is particularly well developed. Indeed the work's denouement—after believing himself to be the most fortunate of mortals through the love of Callirhoe, whom he adores, he is left without the woman he believed to be his wife—transforms Dionysius into a tragic hero.[96]

Tragedy persists, then, in the Greek and Roman epochs, if not as a genre in itself, then in its invasion and conquest of other genres such as historiography, the epic, rhetorical declamation and the novel.

B. *New Comedy*

That major formal features of New Comedy had already appeared in the tragedy of Euripides has already been noted by us and by other critics.[97] Scenes of recognition, capture, slaves and pirates provide the usual links. The love theme itself is of great importance within the genre, since it is here that we find the young couple who fall in love at first sight, express their feelings and even try to take their own lives.[98] Chariton also offers episodes of this type: capture at the hands of pirates (I 9,7) or episodes such as the heroine's pregnancy, resolved thanks to the serving-maid Plangon (II 10 ss.), recall comic models. And indeed, traces of Menander have been found here;[99] names such as Chaereas, Plangon or Theron are derived from him. The comic influence persists and is even intensified in successive novels, where the princely personages of the early novels are replaced increasingly with characters from everyday life (the phenomenon is similar to that found in epistolography). The genre becomes more and more bourgeois. The question is to see what role comedy had in the formation of the genre.

An allusion to subjects appropriate to the genre appears in *Ninus* A 41–45, where the hero talks of the night, drunkenness, a servant and a nurse as accomplices of his passion.[100] Bourgeois comedy is also evoked in the scene where both mothers meet to arrange their

---

[96] Molinié (1989) 34 also makes this point. The description of the soul in love has, as Cataudella (1927) wisely observed, a celebrated predecessor in Dido in the *Aeneid* IV.
[97] See Webster (1974) 175; 184, and the recent Vogt-Spira (1992) 5.
[98] See Trenkner (1958) 110–11.
[99] See Borgogno (1971).
[100] Noted already by Calderini (1913).

children's wedding. (The scene from *Ninus* B I might also be seen in the same light.) The influence of the genre is also evident in Hellenistic poetry. The rationale for these scenes is what we might describe as the Greeks' taste for scenes from family life; and indeed, it is the private lives that interest the early novelists, military campaigns (still present in the last two books of *Callirhoe*) playing second fiddle.

The similarities between comedy and the novel have been noted for some time now: Menander has even been regarded as the originator of the novel, which would thus have emerged in the 1st century A.D.[101] It should nonetheless be stated that the formal parallels discerned, as in the case of Euripides, pertain to the level of *narrative model*,[102] that is, to the material from folklore, not to the *intrigue* or to the "*fabula*", comedy also featuring as a literary model for the genre. That is to say, there is no more reason for deriving the novel from comedy than there is for deriving it from the type of Euripidean tragedy discussed above. Obviously, the introduction of a prologue explaining the sources of the plot (sources which nonetheless remain outside it) is an important compositional element that links the dramatic μῦθος to the last narrative model, the *folktale* (or *novella*, according to Trenkner), a popular narrative genre practised right up to the appearance of the novel.[103] It is from this genre that the astute and audacious heroine finally emerges. The title Chariton chooses for his work, *Callirhoe*, may be dramatic in origin, though the name also appears in elegy and local legends.[104]

We have seen that for ancient rhetoric comedy and the novel are instances of πλάσμα ("fiction"), which, as Aristotle noted, is not entirely alien to tragedy,[105] and provides the bond between the two genres. But rather than simply conflate them, we should recall a possible definition of comedy by Theophrastus: "a change or inversion of private themes or matters stripped of all danger";[106] in this case, we

---

[101] See especially Corbato (1968). Corbato does not regard *Ninus*, *Chion* or *Sesonchosis* as novels.

[102] Fusillo (1989) also makes this point.

[103] See n. 155. For themes of recognition, fidelity and chastity, female astuteness, adultery, capture, etc., see also Trenkner. It should be recalled that Ion is disposed to look for his mother in *Ion* 1356.

[104] See Roscher (1890-94) s.v., and Plut. *Love Narrations* IV.

[105] *Po*.1451b, in his comments on Agathon, who invented the plot and names of the characters. Aristotle only demands that the facts have verisimilitude (εἰκός).

[106] ἰδιωτικῶν πραγμάτων ἀκίνδυνος περιοχή as quoted by Diomedes: see Webster (1974) 179. The basis for his interpretation of περιοχή is a gloss by Photius: περιπέτεια. See also Blanchard (1983) 56, n. 107.

would have an obvious point of contrast between each genre, for if anything characterises the novel it is the dangers faced by the heroes, and, consequently, there would (initially at least) seem to be no basis by which Greek criticism could assimilate it to comedy.

In a recent study Vogt-Spira stresses the importance of Tyche in the conception of the intrigue in Menander's comedy, Menander being viewed as the chief source for the study of this notion.[107] Comedy would center on the κακὴ τύχη, which would eventually become ἀγαθή in the novel.[108] The concept of *Tyche* is typical of Hellenism, though its most ancient and important origin is Euripides. We have already noted its presence in *Ninus*. Chariton uses it as a device to develop the plot.[109] The notion is thus common to several genres.

V. *The Epic Tradition*

It is a proven fact that Chariton cites some thirty hexameters of Homer, used either to compare the heroine with goddesses or to relate scenes of the novel to those of Homer, while imbuing them with new meaning.[110] The author himself states at the start of Book VIII that Chaereas wandered from East to West as a consequence of the wrath of Aphrodite, who finally took pity on him and granted him a happy end. Particular scenes such as the prayer to the sea and Poseidon in III 5,9,[111] or techniques such as the use of repetitions (formulae, recapitulations) are epic in origin. Basic structural elements such as the separation of husband and wife, the journey of adventures or the final reencounter after a series of recognition scenes

---

[107] Vogt-Spira (1992) 10–18, who cites the four types of τύχη studied in Ar. *Physics* II 4–6.

[108] *Ibid.*, 43, and n. 56: cf. in this respect *supra*, p. 44. Vogt-Spira also notes the importance of *tyche* in Euripides (19, n. 2; 51–59).

[109] Ruiz-Montero (1988) 85.

[110] See Papanikolaou (1973) 14–16; Müller (1976) stresses the functional nature of these hexameters, no mere ornament, which install Homer as an authority for the narration. Some authors have found here a connection between Chariton and the Menippean, after the fashion of Petronius's *Satyricon*. My own view is that these poetic citations are rhetorical in origin: see Ruiz-Montero (1994a) 1023, n. 29 and 67. To the works cited there we could add Barchiesi (1986) (1988), who finds the quotations in Chariton different from those of Petronius, who distinguishes his work from the genre of the novel precisely through the ironic use of *Verseinlagen*. D.S.II 56–7 also cites hexameters from the *Odyssey* concerning Iambulus.

[111] See also the scenes quoted by Müller (1976); Laplace (1980); Hölscher (1988) 222ff.; Fusillo (1989) 29–32.

link even the novel's *"fabula"* to the Odyssey. Heliodorus constructs his novel around a conscious imitation of the *Odyssey*, basing it on the hero's return to his homeland and beginning *in medias res*, something that does not occur in the first novels. The further appearance of these elements in the dramatic tradition has already been noted, and it is worth recalling that Aristotle (*Po.*1449a) found the roots of tragedy in the *Iliad* and the *Odyssey*.

Müller saw in Chariton a "Homernachfolger", a "Homeride der Prosa"; the novel was thus an epic in prose, with the common purpose of pleasing, a fact that distinguishes it from historiography which, nevertheless, already employs epic techniques.[112] And Hölscher is right to regard Ulysses as a narrator (*Urheber*) who invents a fantastic tale, and thus lifelike fiction, when he tells the whole truth to Alcinous.[113] However, even if we accept the *Odyssey* as a literary model, we should remember that there was another epic, a Hellenistic epic, closer both chronologically and aesthetically to the novel, namely: Apollonius's *Argonautica*, a work which was more successful in antiquity than certain modern critics are prepared to admit.[114]

As epic genre, the *Argonautica* is based also on a folk model, the sending of the hero, Jason, to fulfil a difficult task, his encounter with helpers and attackers and, once the task has been completed, his return to the point of departure. The poem is endowed with a beginning, middle and end, as we noted with regard to tragedy. The hero's chief helper, Medea, retains the traditional features of the wise but terrifying sorceress, who is more active than the hero himself. But, as the literary epic it also is, the work employs a narrative technique which is far more advanced than in the archaic epic: this reaches its climax in Book III, where the dramatic technique is particularly intense. Five different acts have been discerned, in which psychological scenes alternate with "epic" ones, as well as four simultaneous and independent pieces of action in 439–64, with a complexity which is rarely found in the epic or novel, the genre which it prefigures.[115] Apollonius makes quite remarkable use of the technique of anticipation by means of prophecies, dreams or authorial

---

[112] C.W. Müller (1981). But see Barchiesi (1986).
[113] Hölscher (1988) 234.
[114] The point is made by Hunter (1993).
[115] Vian-Delage (1980) II,5; Beye (1982) 124. The episodic structure of Books I, II and IV will appear in Xenophon and Achilles. The sudden ending to the novel of the latter also recalls Apollonius's poem.

comments,[116] scenes of contrast,[117] intrigue and suspense,[118] as well as πάθος.[119] Many scholars have viewed particular scenes of the *Argonautica* as providing the model for scenes in the novel: Brioso, for instance, notes that Chariton's description of the heroes' departure in III 5 bears a strong resemblance to the *Argonautica* I 238ff.[120] However, a detailed comparison between both genres is still needed.[121]

If the sea voyage lends itself to episodes of danger and subsequent salvation, as well as paradoxographical descriptions, another key element in common with the novel is the presence of the erotic. Medea, indeed, inherits from folklore the function of the sorceress and, from tragedy, her dramatic character, evident both in the battle of her emotions and in her capacity to express them, yet she also reveals a new quality: that of the young bourgeois woman in love, whose vacillations are masterfully described by Apollonius in III 681ff. Like the female protagonist of *Ninus* I A 4,35–9 and 5,28–30, Medea blushes and is tongue-tied before her sister, and feels the same confusion when faced with the beauty of Jason,[122] who asks her what the object of her fear is, as—and his self-defence recalls the reaction of Ninus in fr. B 1,13 in the novel of that name—his intentions are honourable. As in *P.Mich. inv.n.* 5 Medea is the sorceress who has a cure for everything except love (IV 65), and at the same time the young woman who flees her father's punishment.

Jason, the modern, civilised and pacific hero, who persuades with his "honeyed words", who is in frequent ἀμηχανίη compared to the active nature of Medea, has more in common with the heroes of the novel than with those of Homer.[123] He has been described as a "love hero", though this is only true to the extent that women fall in love

---

[116] See III 627–31; 837; 940–43; 961–1133; 1026–62; IV 1166–67; 1380–92; 1313–29; 1216.

[117] I 449ff.; III 1163–72.

[118] See the novelistic intrigue of IV 1140.

[119] IV 1232ff., where Medea and the Argonauts are trapped in an area from which there is no escape; the pilot declares that navigation is impossible (cf. *Ninus* III C 9), and the characters prepare themselves for death. The serving-maids, huddling around Medea, spend the night wailing (cf. *Callirhoe* VII 6,5). Fortunately three goddesses appear to Jason (cf. *Longus* II 23) and salvation is made possible.

[120] Brioso (1989).

[121] Heisermann (1977) 11–29 has devoted most attention to the subject. See also Beye (1982).

[122] In Chariton II 5,4 the roles are inverted: it is Dionysius who falls in love with, and is struck dumb by, the heroine when they meet.

[123] See the comparison between Aeetes and Jason in III 171–5; 484–8; 491ff.; 566–71: the Greek notion of *paideia* is set against eastern despotism and cruelty, in

with him as a result of his beauty; he is not, in other words, the enamoured hero who does everything to win his beloved that we find in the novel—the tradition of the character still weighs heavily here. Circumstances force Jason to promise wedlock to Medea, and they even swear an oath to do so, as in *Ninus*.[124] The power of Eros is such for Apollonius that the poem's central motif, the search for the fleece, takes a secondary role to Medea: when the Colchians reach the city of Alcinous, they do not demand the stolen fleece, but rather the sorceress herself, whose main preoccupation from now on is to justify her crazy love-provoked conduct to Aeetes and (here she appears to be a worthy predecessor of the chaste heroines of the novel) to assure him her maidenhead is still intact.[125] The fleece plays second fiddle, and book IV centers on the adventures of a pair of lovers who flee, manage to get married and undergo a series of dangers at sea, dangers which Ninus also appears to have undergone after his separation from his wife in frg. C, where, by all accounts, he also reaches Colchis. The separation of the lovers does not, however, take place in Apollonius.

As a narrative genre, the novel resembles the epic, whose length it shares and, as we saw in the last chapter, the mixed nature of its manner of representation; from the epic it inherits the function of entertaining, prompting its description as "latter-day epic".[126] From Hegel on, the novel is frequently described as the "epopee of decadence", a notion which is inherited by Lukács.[127] Bakhtin saw the classical novel as closer to the epic and the folktale than to the modern novel: the former was an "embryo" only of bivocal and bilingual prose, while the latter, as a piece of polyphonic discourse, is characterised by its plurilinguism, or dialogism.[128] That no such straightforward opposition can be set up has been shown in modern studies of the Greek novel, such as Fusillo's.[129]

---

similar fashion to the comparison between the Greek and the barbarous in Chariton: see *supra*, n. 61.

[124] ὅρκιος ἔστω IV 95; see also 194–5; 388: cf. *supra*, p. 51.

[125] IV 1014ff.: ἄχραντος καὶ ἀκήρατος are the terms she uses, the first of which appears in X.E.II 9,4; 13,8; IV 3,3.

[126] Perry (1967) 46, who deals only with the Homeric epic, not the *Argonautica*.

[127] García Gual (1972); Bobes (1993) 63–4.

[128] Bobes (1993) 79. For the rest, I agree with Barchiesi (1986) 232, n. 27, in that Bakhtin's comparison of the novel with the Menippean has brought more confusion than anything else.

[129] Fusillo (1989), whose title is already programmatic. From a different view-

Bakhtin's definition of the novel as a genre that represents "the vicissitudes of a private man, alone in a hostile world" would apply to the Greek novel also, which is not without its analysis of the inner life, though, if we set it against the five categories which, for Bobes, characterise the modern novel in relation to the epic, Chariton's novel clearly possesses epic features:

1. Theme restricted to a world viewed in a partial, individualised form.
2. Choice of themes from ordinary life.
3. Time period set in the present and with a contemporary feel.
4. Characters lacking in greatness, subject to tests which reveal their value or values.
5. Lack of any religious transcendence.

As far as points 2 and 3 are concerned, Chariton and his predecessors remain within the framework of the epic (Xenophon's case is already different), and, in accordance with point 5, the genre still clearly contains a religious message. In this respect the *Argonautica* is closer to the modern novel, with points 1 and 4 also highlighting the proximity. This kind of comparison is useful in that, firstly, it brings out the tonal differences between the *Odyssey*—a tone which already differs from that of the *Iliad*—and the *Argonautica* and, secondly, it shows the dangers of generalisations and simplifications when it comes to distinguishing between genres.

As a mimetic narrative fiction based on a folk structure, the *Argonautica* is, then, a worthy predecessor of the genre; certain structural parallels can also be observed between this epic and the first novels at the levels of *"fabula"* and *intrigue*, though there are major semantic differences as far as the object to be sought is concerned. The simultaneity of the heroes only exists here when the Argonauts return with Medea after winning the fleece, though it is not a case here of one searching for the other, but of the couple's adventures during the journey, a fact which has no parallel in the structure of the older novels. In the *Odyssey* the prevailing scheme is the journey of adventures, and there is no development of the adventure cycle of the heroine (*hero-victim* in Propp's terminology), which is simultaneous to that of the hero and a characteristic structural component of the

---

point, recent studies by Elsom and Montague include aesthetic judgements which compare the novels of Chariton and Longus to the modern novel: see Richlin (1992).

novel. Nevertheless, not only does the epic provide a literary model for the novel, but both genres feed off the same *narrative model*, together with the tragedy of Euripides and the comedy of Menander.

It is almost a universal of historical poetics that the epic as genre precedes the novel.[130] In the study of medieval literature the passage of the *chanson de geste* to the *roman courtois* (12th century), and from the latter to the French prose novel (13th century), has already been noted.[131] Even if we accept the existence of such a transition in French literature, its equivalent in Greek literature has yet to be proven; at most, we should talk of a substitution, not a derivation, of genres.[132]

VI. *The Alexandrian Elegy. Local Legends*

The love theme is known to be one of the favourite themes of Hellenistic poetry, and so the novel can be said to have its roots in Hellenistic literature. The chief thematic novelty of the first novels is the centrality given to the vicissitudes of the pair of lovers who marry at the start of the work and are separated against their will. Nevertheless, an obstacle prior to the wedding, an obstacle quickly overcome, seems an essential part of the genre and is what distinguishes it from the New Comedy.[133] In particular, there are clear similarities between the initial narrative sequence leading up to the marriage in Chariton and Xenophon and stories such as those of Acontius and Cydippe in Callimachus, or Pyramus and Thisbe in Ovid.[134] In the former we find the novelistic motifs of falling in love at a party, love sickness and the consultation of the oracle, who proposes the heroes' marriage. The obstacle may be a law (*Ninus*), or family opposition

---

[130] Japanese literature provides an exception: cf. Meletinsky (1993) 217–54 (from the Russian original of 1986), an essential text for students of historical poetics.

[131] See Jauss (1986) an article first published in 1970.

[132] In order to explain the origin of the French medieval novel, Meletinsky (1993) adds to the epic genre an element from the local folktale and another from the lyric, elements he discerns in the narrative morphology of the works of Chrétien de Troyes. But he finds no genetic relation between the ancient epic and novel. Perry (1967) 50 denies the existence of such a relation both for the ancient novel and for the medieval and modern ones.

[133] See *Ninus* I A 2,32ff.; Char.I 1,2–3; X.E.I 1,2–5.

[134] Cal. *Aetia* III 65–75, reconstructed from Ov. *Her*.XX–XXI; Ant.Lib.I; Aristaen.I 10; for Pyramus and Thisbe see Ov. *Met*.IV 55–66. In this case Cydippe has sworn an oath to Artemis. Callimachus cites the testimony of the mythographer Xenomedes of Ceos.

(*Callirhoe*), but the type of story is comparable. As for Pyramus and Thisbe, we are faced with family opposition, which will have tragic consequences in the suicide of the two lovers.[135] Bourgeois taste dictates that the ending in the novel be a happy one.

We know of the existence of collections of love stories, used in metamorphic literature, which are Hellenistic in origin and survive right through the imperial epoch.[136] An important collection is that of Parthenius of Nycaea, whose 36 *Love Stories* (ἐρωτικὰ παθήματα) have remained intact.[137] These stories, most of them with tragic endings, provided the material for Latin elegies and the epic,[138] and, like those of the poets cited above, were connected with local legends.

Rohde regarded these elegiac love stories as the first love novels— later to be imitated, even stylistically, by the novelists—, and, as already stated, as the nucleus of the genre.[139] Other authors followed suit, the theory still being held today by Giangrande:[140] the novel would emerge from the paraphrase in prose of the Alexandrine elegy, a rhetorical paraphrase evident in papyri from the 1st century B.C. Paraphrase would provide the spark, later to be kindled by σοφισταί. Giangrande also distinguishes thematic motifs common to the novel and to Parthenius's collection.[141]

Clearly, these love stories constitute the literary source of the novel, that is to say, the elegy features amongst its models, and this type of story continues to be written in the Empire, as demonstrated by the five *Love Narrations* (ἐρωτικαὶ διηγήσεις) attributed to Plutarch,[142] and

---

[135] Other instances of love stories with tragic ends are Ov. *Met*.XII 393–428; X 560–707; Paus.VII 19,2; VII 21,1–5; IX 32,2: see Rohde (1914) 132, n. 2. In the novels: X.E.III 2; V 1,4–11. Paus.VIII 10,2 says he writes what he has heard.

[136] See Lafaye (1904) and the introduction by Papathomopoulos (1968) to his edition of Antoninus Liberalis, an important author for the reconstruction of lost poetic precedents. The tradition survives right up to Museus, whose *Hero and Leander* is a Greek-origin epyllion, as Rohde (1914) 142 assumed.

[137] On the title see above p. 35.

[138] That the ἔπος in the proem by Parthenius should be interpreted as a synonym for "epyllion", which used similar techniques to those of the elegy, is, as Giangrande (1984) remarks, highly likely.

[139] Rohde (1914) 154ff.; he also noted the differences in style and tone (149–52).

[140] Giangrande (1962) (1984) (1991).

[141] (1962) 148–9: the motifs are the historical background, oracles, wars, bandits and captures.

[142] Giangrande (1991) defends the authenticity of the work from linguistic details. The stylistic and thematic similarities between these tales and the novels of Chariton and Xenophon are obvious, especially in the case of the latter: see Ruiz-Montero (1982a), an article where I deduce that Xenophon consciously imitates the oral style to suit the material.

the work of authors such as Athenaeus and Pausanias.[143] Lavagnini established that these local legends based on an erotic theme and theoretically linked to some god, cult or custom, were the source of the elegy and the novel.[144] At the outset they would be narrations less "pretenziose" than the learned ones, formally suited to the needs of the people and influenced by local historiography. They would, in other words, be the object of a twofold development: local historiography and Hellenistic poetry. The titles of the novels would recall that historiography.[145]

We have already noted the local character of the legends on which the first novels are based, their national self-assertiveness in the face of a centralised administration, first Greek and then Roman in the 2nd century A.D., a "romantic" period in which local folklore and the Hellenistic "antiquarian" spirit once more come to the fore. Hence there are two pathways by which the local legends reached the novel: the written or literary (Parthenius, the elegy) and direct oral folklore. Elegiac material of the "Acontius and Cydippe" kind gives rise to a series of brief, partial and introductory intrigues within the structure of the novel itself. In the earliest of these the initial marriage is, as we have said already, indispensable.[146]

For the expression of amorous feelings the novel finds a suitable model in the elegiac: already in *Ninus* A 2,19; 25–6; B 1,28 the power of Aphrodite and Eros is well-known. The narrative nature of the Greek elegy is well-known, though a nuclear structure that is comparable *in all respects* to the genre of the novel is yet to appear, so that it is impossible to say that *Ninus* is a development of Hellenistic elegy.

It would seem more relevant to seek the sources of the novel in the oral legends. The latter form short self-enclosed stories, comparable to the type of narration known as the *novella*. The genre finds precedents in Homer, and is particularly common in Herodotus, which

---

[143] See Lavagnini (1950, original of 1921), 31, n. 3 and 4; 33, n. 5; Cataudella (1957) 79.
[144] *Ibid.*, 1–105.
[145] The criticism that the development from local historiography was a gratuitous one was answered by Lavagnini (1985), who defines the concept more clearly, likening it to Ionian periegesis, as found in Pausanias, with whose titles it coincides.
[146] The closest example we can find is Parthenius VIII: a married couple is separated after the wife is seized by a Gallic chief; this prompts the search by the husband who, on finding her, discovers that she has deceived him and allows her to die at the hands of the Gaul. There is no trace here, however, of the pair of young lovers, and neither the tone nor the denouement is comparable to that of the Greek novels.

is why it is traditionally linked to Ionia, though Trenkner also adduced ample evidence of an Attic *novella*.[147]

We should turn now to the relation of the first novels with the so-called *fabula Milesia*, on the one hand, and of the *novella* with the novel, on the other. Indeed, there are no remnants of the *Milesiaca*, a collection of *novelle* attributed to Aristides of Miletus, who may have lived in the second half of the 2nd century B.C., as the *novelle* were translated into Latin by Cornelius Sisenna in the times of Sulla. Citations in several ancient texts suggest the *fabulae Milesiae* enjoyed enormous popularity amongst their readers.[148] We know that they delighted both officers in Crassus's army and even the emperor Clodius Albinus himself, that they were preferred to the texts of Plato, and that the *turba cirratorum* repeated them by heart at school.

Nor is there really anything left of the Latin version, though the novel of the *Ass* is traditionally linked to the genre from Apuleius's own acknowledgement at the start of his *Metamorphoses: at ego tibi sermone isto Milesio varias fabulas conseram.* . . . The *Milesia* question and its tradition are extremely complex and have been much discussed; hence we shall confine ourselves here to those points that relate to the Greek novel, though we shall also have to turn to the Latin novel, especially Apuleius.

A characteristic of the genre is the apparent union of author and protagonist, that is, the first-person narrative in which the author is a guarantor of the story either as an eye-witness of the events or, through the technique of framing, as a facilitator of the narrations of other character-guarantors. We have seen already that the technique is typical of paradoxography, and we find it both in Hellenistic utopias and in the fantastic stories told by Ulysses to the Phaeacians.[149] A series of *novelle* surrounding the protagonist is to be found in the cycle of adventures around Anthia in *Ephesiaca*.[150] The technique is a biographical one, appearing both in the *Life of Aesop* and in the sacred

---

[147] Trenkner (1958); Cataudella (1957).

[148] See Pepe (1972) 402ff. for a detailed study of the topic. The *fabulae* are cited by Plutarch, Arrian, *Amores*, Harpocration, Tertullian, Martianus Capella, Hieronimus and Sidonius Apollinaris.

[149] The "autopsia" of Ionian ἱστορίη or the journey that frames Plato's *Phaedrus* are of the same order. Lucian adopts the technique in the *Lover of Lies*, where the framing device is a philosophers' reunion at the house of a sick friend.

[150] See the structural analysis of the novel in Ruiz-Montero (1988) 97–167; (1994b) 1096ff. The novel includes two autobiographies inserted at the start of books III and V respectively.

legends, and extending as far as the picaresque. If the *Ephesiaca* does not adopt the autobiographical form, Achilles Tatius, who is here much closer to Petronius and Apuleius, does. If the first-person narrative were an obligatory technique in the *Milesia* we would have a major technical difference between this work and the first Greek novels.

As far as content is concerned, the *fabulae* seem to have contained local stories, though not necessarily referring to Miletus, if we are to judge by the tale of the "Widow of Ephesus" in *Sat*.111–12 or by the tales of the Greek *Ass* and Apuleius's *Metamorphoses*.[151] Ovid and Plutarch record the licentious nature of the tales,[152] though the *Milesiae* would also include stories of a sentimental or idealist kind.[153] The most celebrated instance is the story of "Love and Psyche" in Apul. *Met*.IV 27ff., whose origins are, as the phraseology and very structure suggest, most probably Greek:[154] in *Metiochus and Parthenope* the search is also carried out by the wife herself.

If this story is to be viewed as *Milesia*, and if we bear in mind that the teller is an old woman, it is possible to establish a further link between the *anilis fabula* and the *Milesia*. In X.E.III 9,8 there is a similar tale told by an old woman and described by the author as a διήγημα; the tale is set in Tarsus and is none other than the story of Anthia, i.e. an episode from the same novel. We can thus conclude that assimilations are possible between the *Milesia*, Xenophon's novel and the *anilis fabula* or γραώδης μῦθος of Greek tradition.[155] We also

---

[151] We know of the existence of other short works whose names derived from their place of origin: Sybaritic, Lybian, etc. legends (cf. Theon, *Progymn*.73). Schissel (1913a) 94–105, in his reconstruction of Aristides's work, assumed the existence of a "rahmengessprāch, nicht rahmenerzählung", an erotic dialogue held in Miletus during a lascivious night-time celebration. The stories would be erotic in theme and with a happy end, would take place in Miletus or Ionia and would be presented as ἀληθεῖς ἱστορίαι. The first suppositions of Schissel are extremely hypothetical.

[152] Ov. *Tristia* II 413; 443ff.: *historiae turpes inseruisse iocos*. Plut. *Crass*.32,4: ἀκόλαστα βιβλία/διηγήματα. See also Ps.Luc. *Am*.I 1.

[153] Pepe (1972) 405–6 cites here the evidence of Hieronimus and S. Apollinaris VII 2, who in his letter to the bishop of Marseille uses the term *fabula Milesia* to refer to the (non-licentious) story of an adventurer. Along the same lines see Moreschini (1990) 124–5.

[154] See Rohde (1914) 371. That the model was, in any case, the Greek novels is obvious. Eros and Psyche already appear in Hellenistic art: see Pollitt (1989) 212. For the structure see Mantero (1973) and Ruffinato (1981), both based on Proppian methodological principles: cp. Ruiz-Montero (1988). The folk structure is here endowed with symbolic value, and is thus converted into a myth. See also the works cited by Bowie (1993).

[155] It already appears in Plato, *Lys*.205c–d; *Hp.Ma*.286a; *R*.I 350e. To give this

see that the material of Xenophon and Apuleius has certain parallels, and that μῦθος and διήγημα are assimilated here also.[156]

Meanwhile, Xenophon presents his novel as a local history of Ephesus, city of the famous "matron" of Petronius. And indeed, a great deal of the action of *Callirhoe* takes place in Miletus, so that the story of Callirhoe and Dionysius of Miletus may well constitute a *fabula Milesia*.[157] Asia Minor is the geographical frame for *Ninus* and *Metiochus and Parthenope* also.

So it is that the folk material and its local character become points of contact between the *Milesia*, the stories compiled by Parthenius and writers like him,[158] and the Greek novels of the early phase. To what extent Aristides's work affected the birth of a novel like *Ninus* is unclear: they may have constituted parallel literary formations, just as their subsequent development was also a parallel development, though, in any case, Aristides's work stood as an important literary precedent of prose fiction whose purpose was entertainment. We might also add that the facts show that Rohde's old assumption that the *novelle* could never lead to the *Roman* is false: the *Roman* might also be considered as a collection of *novelle* or (depending on the term we choose) fairy tales.

The coexistence of folk material and literary sources is a phenomenon that can be observed in the birth of the novel in other countries (e.g., the French *roman courtois* or the Spanish *Lazarillo de Tormes*),[159] and is a fact that needs further highlighting in Greek.

---

anilis fabula the name of "fairy tale" or *novella* is debatable: see Ruiz-Montero (1981) 291–2.

[156] Διήγημα is the term preferred by Chariton to convey the concept of "tale, story", to the extent that he is the novelist who most uses it, followed by Heliodorus (14 times) and Xenophon, where its usage is frequent given the shortness of the novel (9 times). Neither Chariton nor Xenophon employs διήγησις, which is used by Achilles and Heliodorus as a synonym of the former. Μῦθος, which does not feature in Xenophon, does in the rest, with the sense of "story, tale" or "mythical tale, myth": cf. Conca (1989), Beta (1993) s.v. διήγημα and μῦθος are used interchangeably in Chariton (cf. IV 2,13; VI 3,6). Kerényi (1927) 19, notes the equivalence between διήγημα and Latin *historia* in Apul. *Met*.II 12: *historiam magnam et incredundam fabulam*. . . . If this is so, this is a further instance of the union of the same two Greek terms translated into Latin.

[157] This does not mean that Chariton's knowledge of Miletus was purely literary, as seems to be the case with Xenophon: see Ruiz-Montero (1989) (1994a); Jones (1992b). Chariton links his story initially to Syracuse, though, as with Ephesus in Xenophon, the city is soon of secondary importance: Ruiz-Montero (1994a) 1015–16.

[158] The stories of Herippe (Parthenius VIII) and Antheus (XIV) also take place in Miletus.

[159] Bobes (1993) 72; Meletinsky (1993) 217ff.

Let us turn now to the consideration of how a short story is put together: this is the function of rhetoric.

VII. *The Rhetorical Context*

Theon establishes six basic elements for narration or the tale: character, fact, place, time, mode and cause. Each is subject to variations and expansions. He also discusses the appropriate style and procedures such as exposition, declination, linking, abbreviation and expansion and the inverting of disposition, the latter exemplified by the *Odyssey*, Thucydides and Herodotus. Exposition also is comprised of certain modes (enunciation, interrogation, investigation, doubt, order, supplication, oath, appellation, supposition, conversation). Tales can also be refuted or confirmed, a category that includes not just historical tales but the mythical tales of poets and historians.[160]

There are other rhetorical devices for the literary transformation of a thematic motif, scene or episode taken from a particular literary source. We have already mentioned paraphrase. Ethopoeia and prosopopoeia contributed to characterisation, to finding the appropriate nuance or the words that best suited each occasion.[161]

The romantic triangle in *Callirhoe* V 8,4–6 is a fine example of rhetorical *controversia*, with its respective speeches.[162] In sum, feigning situations and creating atmospheres is a hallmark of rhetoric, and in this respect we should underscore the importance of declamation or μελέτη as a fictional exercise.

Prose fiction dates back to the birth of rhetoric in the 5th century B.C., the period of Antiphon's *Tetralogies*, the first totally fictitious speeches in Greek literature. Equally important for the development of rhetorical fiction are the *Encomium of Helen* and the *Defence of Palamedes*

---

[160] Theon, *Progym.*78ff. Many of these devices are common to the fable (μῦθος). διήγημα and διήγησις are treated as equivalents: it is a case of "a composition that reveals facts that have taken place or are acknowledged to have taken place". The fable is "a false composition that stands for the truth". For a comparison between these preparatory exercises and Chariton, see Ruiz-Montero (1994a) 1042–43.

[161] Bartsch (1934) noted this in Chariton. A related concept is that of τὸ πρέπον, Latin *decorum*. Bartsch also highlighted the ἐνάργεια and πάθος, that is, the capacity to visualise the events narrated and to provoke emotions in the reader. He also cites examples of encomium and exhortative discourse.

[162] See Ruiz-Montero (1994a) 1041. Besides letters and speeches Chariton has a predilection for introducing tales: see Ruiz-Montero (1988) 81–2.

by Gorgias. These works show how, from its very beginnings, rhetoric makes use of myth as a point of reference, a device which would prove a typical feature in its later development. Plato condemned the lack of truthfulness in rhetoric,[163] though he himself should figure as one of the sources of prose fiction, not just in his use of myth but by the very nature of his dialogues.[164] The importance of Xenophon's *Cyropaedia* as fiction has already been stated.

With the use of declamation, fully constituted in the Hellenistic period,[165] the role of fiction is increased: declamation is a practical exercise in a legal context, but its status as imaginative literature grows steadily.[166] The importance of narrative fiction is shown above all in κατάστασις or the narration of facts. Controversy and declamation take their references from both myth and true history, and so the action may involve anyone from Orestes or Ajax to Demosthenes or Alexander.[167] The generalisation of historical facts consisted in the omission of names.[168] The context was usually the historical past, particularly the glorious epoch of Athens, though the exercise involved an appreciable lack of historical accuracy. The use of ethopoeia and the dramatic are equally striking tendencies of declamation. Amongst its main literary sources are oratory and comedy, though for some time now the *novella*, including folk material, tales and legends, has also been seen to have had an influence.[169] It is unclear whether this origin includes, or rather the novel itself has had an influence on, an example given by Choricius (6th century A.D.) of a young hero who returns victorious from the war and seeks

---

[163] Bornecque (1967, original of 1902) 86–7 and Schamberger (1917) 11ff. note that Cicero and Seneca, however, accepted rhetorical convention.

[164] Aristotle regarded them as both dramatic and narrative literature. Reardon (1991) 62–70 also notes the importance of Plato: see also Gill (1993a) and Morgan (1993) 182ff.

[165] There are papyri from the 3rd century B.C. See Russell (1983) 4, who notes that the real beginnings occur with the introduction of fixed themes, which would seem to date back to 4th century Athens, rather than to 5th century Ionia.

[166] Russell *ibid*.

[167] Suet. *de rhet*.I states that these themes come *aut ex historiis aut ex veritate ac re*, taking as *historiae* "traditional tales": cf. Schamberger (1917) 7; Bonner (1969) 18–9; Trenkner (1958) 184. The same phenomenon is seen in Parthenius, whose characters include Cyrus (XXII) and Periander of Corinth (XVII) together with Io (I), Ulyssees (II; III), Daphne (XV) and Achilles (XXI; XXVI).

[168] Cf. Schamberger (1917) 22; Russell (1983) 120–22.

[169] Cataudella (1957). Aly (1936) noted that the *novella* had already slipped into the work of Lysias and Xenophon, and Manganaro (1958) noted the same for Aristotle and his school.

as a recompense from his father a girl with whom he has fallen in love at a party. The paternal opposition, the young man's words on the respect he feels towards her, on his lack of violence, on the fact she is his first love, as well as the allusions to her beauty and chastity, are highly familiar and remind us particularly of *Ninus* and its young ἀριστεύς. At the same time, the example is proof of a nexus between novel and declamation, a nexus that has not escaped the attention of scholars of declamation from Bornecque on.[170] Indeed, its themes include capture, pirates, falling in love, adultery, poisoning or chaste young ladies in brothels. Another favourite rhetorical theme is the Athenian expedition to Sicily, used by Chariton, together with the verb μελετάω in V 5,6, in which Chaereas prepares for the future trial.[171] This is not unexpected in the case of the secretary of a rhetor, namely: Athenagoras.[172]

As a series of fictional exercises, then, rhetoric enhances the power of that fiction in permeating the different literary genres of the Hellenistic and Roman periods; they thus collaborate in the construction of the fictional genre *par excéllence*—the novel. The increasing autonomy of declamation as a parallel literary exercise to the novel throughout the Empire is a conclusion that begins to emerge clearly from Russell's study. That the Greek love novel is born mechanically in the rhetorical laboratory (the Second Sophistic, for Rohde) is an assertion that is unacceptable in its present form and obeys a concept of literature as a purely material, formal product, not as a cultural phenomenon bound up with the context in which it emerges. Rhetoric is another socio-cultural phenomenon—this is particularly evident in the imperial period—and not just a set of exercises and rules. These exercises are instruments at the service of the creativity and talent of each author; they are not a beginning and end in themselves, but rather a *means*.

Novel and rhetoric are inseparable travelling companions, and this

---

[170] Bornecque (1967) 130 saw the origin of the novel in declamation. Pepe (1972) 469 also cites here Thiele, Schmid, Haight and Cataudella, though the latter (1957) posits a reciprocal influence between *novella* and declamation. Russell (1983) 38–9 finds common elements between the novel and declamation, but attributes them to an identical milieu.

[171] The verb also appears in III 2,8 and VII 1,5. In V 11,4 he uses ῥητορεύω; in V 4,11 the expression δικανικῶς λέγω.

[172] Robert noted that his name did not figure amongst the rhetors of Aphrodisias but in Smyrna, a fact that could shed some biographical light on Chariton: see C.P. Jones (1992a).

has been the case from the beginnings of the genre. Fiction exists before the rhetoric of the 5th century B.C., but rhetoric is crucial for fiction's crystallisation as a literary genre. The novel as a genre is born, like the rest of the literature of the age, in a rhetorical-literary context. This is evident not just in the aspects of content discussed above, but in the very expression and style of the text: Jenistová detected metrical clauses, rhetorical figures, Atticistic influences on the use of vocabulary and other rhetorical signals in fragments of *Ninus*, and Hernández-Lara has found the same in *Callirhoe*.[173] These analyses reveal the high level of rhetorical awareness and mastery of both authors, and are proof that the novel is not a marginal development outside the official cultivated literature of the period, but, on the contrary, is a genre that bears its seal.[174] We must, that is, abandon the idea that these texts are simple, unpretentious or unrhetorical works, and above all avoid conflating the term "pre-sophistic" with that of "pre-rhetorical": the novels of Longus, Achilles and Heliodorus are more sophistic in so far as the rhetoric of the period is more sophisticated, more precious than that of the 1st century A.D., as the works of Aelius Aristides, Lucian and the Philostratuses confirm. And obviously we should bear in mind the personal stylistic urges of each author: Xenophon of Ephesus writes in the midst of the Second Sophistic, and Chariton not long before.

Final mention should be made of a genre that epitomises the tight nexus between fiction and rhetoric: the epistolary novel. We know that the collection of letters centering on a historical figure, letters that may be authentic like Plato's,[175] leads on in the Hellenistic period to the collection of feigned letters about famous personages, literary

---

[173] Jenistová (1953); Hernández-Lara (1990); on lexical Atticisms see also the latter's 1994 study: cf. also Ruiz-Montero (1991). Chariton's style strikes me as more ἀφελής than that of *Ninus*. The stylistic simplicity of *Sesonchosis* also reveals a certain care, as I indicated earlier (1989a) 56–7.

[174] This is also apparent in the ideological study of Chariton: cf. Ruiz-Montero (1989). Meanwhile, Ninus and Semiramis are characters who appear in the rhetorical handbooks: the former, if Szepessy (1982–84) is right, amongst the handsome heroes, together with Sesostris; the latter amongst the husband killers (Hyg. *Fab*.CCXLI, together with Clytaemnestra and Deianeira) and the suicides (CCXLIII, together with Ajax, Hecuba, Pyramus and Thisbe). This is not to mention the historiographical sources. If the testimony of Luc. (cf. n. 63) refers to novels, the fact would indicate that the stories of Ninus and of Metiochus and Parthenope are admitted into the mythical-legendary tradition and are well-known by the spectators. Quet (1992) 138ff. adds that the same conclusion may be drawn from the appearance of these characters in mosaics; cf. n. 185.

[175] D.L.III 62 cites letters of Plato's edited by Aristophanes of Byzantium.

celebrities, politicians or philosophers, that may well constitute a unified narrative, that is, a novel.[176] We know also of the existence of a *Briefroman* on Alexander, already formed in the 1st century B.C., while the rest of the texts preserved date from the 1st century A.D. on.[177] The former period includes the best-known epistolary novel, that of Chion of Heraclea, the assassin of Clearchus, a tyrant of Pontus's Heraclea in the mid 4th century B.C.[178] All scholars of the subject accept the rhetorical origin of these epistolary fictions, which proliferated during the Empire.

Epistolography allows us to recognise two facts: first, that epistolary fiction based on historical personages precedes the fiction that places other private persons on stage (e.g., Alciphron, Aelian, Philostratus). Second, the supposedly autobiographical character of the epistolary novel links it to the biographical tradition, a fact which shows that this tradition, in its different forms, precedes the love novel, as well as explaining the appearance of historical characters in the earliest forms of the love genre. This implies the acceptance neither of a genetic relationship nor of a natural evolutionary development: we are merely noting the presence of a narrative precedent that strikes us of the greatest importance.

Everything said so far is perfectly compatible with the development of the Greek literary and ideological traditions. But Sykutris noted that the literary letter had attained great perfection long beforehand in Egypt, where a feigned letter already existed; nor should we forget that at the start of the 2nd century B.C. *Nectanebus* papyrus seems to adopt the form of a letter.[179] As this text is often purported

---

[176] On this subject see Sykutris (1931a); Holzberg (1994b); Rosenmeyer (1994). Holzberg studies seven supposed *Briefromane*, but believes that it is possible to accept the existence of others. Common features of these and the love novel are the framing of the action in the 5th/4th centuries B.C., the use of anachronisms, the importance of ethopoeia, the dramatic tendency and narrative techniques such as retardation. For the rest, these texts are the vehicle for philosophical-political ideology and thus, as we noted in respect of Antonius Diogenes, coincide with the utopian tales.

[177] On Alexander see the recent article by Merkelbach (1989). The epistolary novel on Hippocrates may, according to Holzberg and Rosenmeyer, date from the 1st century B.C.

[178] On this novel see also the introduction by Düring to his 1951 edition (re-edited in 1979).

[179] Cf. the heading of Philippus's letter to the Thessalian *tagoi* (Schw. *Del.*590), where the sender's name appears in the genitive and the receiver's in the accusative preceded by the preposition ποί (*pros*), as in the papyrus in question. Nevertheless, what follows in the papyrus is written in the third person, by way of a chronicle: see Koenen (1985).

to be a precedent of the Greek novel, together with other demotic tales, we shall go on to revise the relations between the love novel and, on the one hand, these Egyptian tales and, on the other, tales from the Orient as a whole.

VIII. *The Eastern Influence*

With *Ninus* and *Sesonchosis* we come to Assyria, Babylonia, Egypt, Arabia and other peoples who reached India. The scene is a Greek one in *Metiochus and Parthenope* and *Callirhoe*, though in the former the heroine does reach the Persians in her search for her husband, and in the latter the Persians appear together with their Egyptian underlings, whose structural role in the plot is crucial.[180] The Babylonian episode in book V is the climax of the intrigue. The confrontation between Asia and Europe goes back to the *Iliad* and Herodotus, but it is after the Medic wars that the Persians become literary characters and the tyranny they represent a stylised *tópos* used in contraposition to the democratic and free spirit of the Greeks. This is one of the key ideas of the Second Sophistic: the superiority of Greek *paideia* to the "barbarians". Chariton conveys it clearly in V 4,10 when he comments on the eunuch Artaxerxes's attempt to coerce Callirhoe: "Indeed he thought the deed simple, as a eunuch, as a slave, as a barbarian. He ignored the nobility of the Greek spirit, and especially of Callirhoe, who was chaste and faithful to her husband." This is not the idealised Persia of the *Cyropaedia*.[181]

Egypt had, from Herodotus, exercised a powerful fascination over the Greeks. As frequent historiographical matter, the novel could be said to fit into the historiographical tradition in its introduction of eastern themes, though with a typically Greek focus. But as Egypt is, in one way or another, a theme and compulsory setting for practically the whole genre,[182] we need to know if the phenomenon is

---

[180] The Egyptian uprising corresponds to 4th century B.C. historical fact: cf. Baslez (1992a) 201.

[181] On Persia in Chariton see Baslez (1992a). The author highlights the influence of Ctesias, as well as the popularity of Rodogune from Aeschines on. For the rest, Auberger (1991) 156, n. 3 notes apropos of Ctesias that the powerful eunuchs he presents—comparable to those of Chariton—did not in fact exist.

[182] Besides Chariton, Xenophon, Achilles, Heliodorus, *Historia Apollonii, Sesoncosis*, Egyptian characters feature in the fragments of *Amenophis, Severis, Tinuphlis*, the epiphany of the god Asclepius: cf. Dostálová (1991) 67ff.

explicable as a literary mimesis within the framework of a tradition, a cultural fashion, or even as a result of Egypt's decisive role in the origins of the genre. This last hypothesis has been offered by scholars from two standpoints: one based on the existence of demotic texts translated into Greek in the Hellenistic and Roman periods, the other founded on religious reasons. Let us start with the demotic texts.

A. *The Egyptian Tales*

It was Barns who in 1956 drew our attention to a papyrus found in 1839, containing a fragment of a possible demotic novel translated into Greek in the 2nd century B.C. and, from its content, generally known as *Nectanebus' Dream*.[183] Nectanebus was the last Egyptian pharaoh, expelled by Artaxerxes III in 343 B.C. Diodorus XVI 51,1 tells how he took refuge in Egypt, taking all the money with him. The rest is legend, reconstructed from the *Life of Alexander* and the *Demotic Chronicle*, a collection of oracles probably written under Ptolemy III Euergetes (246–21 B.C.) and which announces the return of Nectanebus, younger and stronger, to liberate Egypt from the Persians. Ps. Callisthenes tells of his reincarnation as Alexander, his son. As a magician, Nectanebus would have seduced Olympia in the form of Ammon. The Egyptians thus tried to undercut the Greeks' might by relating the foreign king to their traditional dynasty.[184]

The *Nectanebus* papyrus would form the beginning of the supposed novel: within the frame of a letter or report addressed from Petesis to Nectanebus, the story tells how the said king sees in dreams a reunion of the gods presided over by Isis, in which Onuris-Ares complains that Nectanebus has neglected his temple. Nectanebus tries to soften the gods' wrath by hiring the best sculptor to finish the work, for which he offers him a huge sum of money. But the sculptor decides to amuse himself before he starts the job, and by chance he meets a beautiful young woman.... Here the papyrus breaks off, leaving us intrigued, though it is easy to imagine that an erotic episode would ensue whose upshot would be an unfinished temple and, thence,

---

[183] Cf. Koenen (1985); Dostálová (1991) 78–9; Sandy (1994b).

[184] Cf. *supra*, p. 43. Braun (1938) stressed the nationalism of these heroes (Ninus, Alexander, Nectanebus) and concluded that they did not derive from Ctesias, but rather that his works had more in common with books of Eastern folklore, and that the same could be said of Moses and Jesus.

the gods' ire against Nectanebus. This would prompt his disgrace and subsequent flight to Ethiopia and Macedonia.

Barns cites other Egyptian tales from even earlier dates which have obvious folk features and are based on a journey. His theory is that these Egyptian stories, translated into Greek, would serve as a model for Greek novels, which would be born in the literary city of Alexandria. The origin, that is, would not be far away.

As the papyri come from Egypt, Egyptian nationalism is the most likely source, but the phenomenon is not restricted to that country.[185] Fraser and, later, Lloyd[186] have examined the forms of Ptolemaic nationalist propaganda, whose atmosphere of hostility to the invader sweeps through novels such as *Sesostris/Sesonchosis*, legends such as *Nectanebus*, and the oracle of the potter which announces the end of Greek power.[187] It is precisely due to the nationalistic character of these writings that they must coincide with the beginnings of the Ptolemaic era and not with the dates of the texts preserved.[188] Their translation into Greek may have been encouraged by an enhancement of Egyptian influence over Greece from the reign of Ptolemy Philometor. The social context for this literature would have been the middle and lower classes. The *Nectanebus* papyrus in particular would, according to Fraser in an interesting theory, have been copied by a person of limited learning, as the errors of handwriting reveal.

These texts, of which there are even cycles, emerge, according to Fraser, in a priestly ambit, and, he insists, the Greek and the Egyptian are inseparable.[189] More recently, Tait has provided an interesting overview of Egyptian narrative in demotic and in Greek, many of

---

[185] As an example of the phenomenon Quet (1992) interprets the survival of the Ninus and Metiochus mosaics in Antiochia. Morgan (1994) *intrd*.7 shares her opinion; Dostálová (1991) 34 believes that *Ninus* may have been at the service of Seleucid propaganda. Barns also acknowledged, however, other possible Eastern sources for the Greek novel.

[186] Fraser (1972) 674–87; Lloyd (1982), who speaks of the novel of "Sesostris", not of Sesonchosis. Cf. *supra*, n. 58.

[187] The oracle is made up of three fragmentary papyri, a probable 2nd and 3rd century A.D. translation from the demotic.

[188] Nevertheless, as the fragments of Egyptian based novels and the very copy of previous texts on the topic suggest, nationalism and Egyptian themes also stretch right through the 2nd and 3rd centuries A.D.

[189] He cites a 3rd century B.C. Greek ostracon which contains sentences of the Seven Wise Men attributed here to the Egyptian Amenotes. The priestly atmosphere and genuinely Egyptian character of these *Königsnovelle* are also highlighted by Koenen (1985).

these papyri remaining unpublished.[190] Production begins in the second half of the 4th century B.C. or the start of the Ptolemaic period; the extant texts are fragmentary, normally in prose, consisting of shortish, mainly first-person tales (some in letter form), which may be extended through the "story-within-a-story" technique. The characters are usually kings, priests or magicians, the latter occupying practically a genre to themselves.[191] The tales mingle names and historical facts from the different dynasties. No happy end is to be expected, as the tales transmit quite traditional Egyptian ideas. In a few cases (e.g., *Tefnut*)[192] both the demotic and the Greek versions exist, though in others (Tinuphis [2nd century A.D.], Amenophis, Sesonchosis [3rd century A.D.]) only the Greek texts have survived. These texts would seem to have no versions in demotic.

Fraser did not believe Egypt was the birthplace of the Greek novel, either in its embryonic or more advanced forms,[193] but other authors have found in these texts translated from the demotic the model required for the emergence of the Greek novel. Thus Reardon, who likens the phenomenon to that which occurred in the Renaissance:[194] these Egyptian tales would find their way into the Greek tradition via the schools of rhetoric.

The theory is attractive: clearly, Egypt is the homeland of *Nectanebus* and *Alexander*,[195] and possibly a plausible site for *Sesonchosis* and other stories. But the issue begs several questions, as well as needing a few adjustments.

First of all, of all the texts adduced only *Nectanebus* can with any certainty be said to precede *Ninus*. Second, of all the texts adduced only *Sesonchosis* would seem comparable to *Ninus*, though it is not clear whether the erotic component is structural or episodic.[196] If it

---

[190] Tait (1994) 203–22.

[191] There are cycles centered on one or more characters, such as that of Setna (3rd/2nd centuries B.C.), or that of "Inaros (Petubastis)" in the 2nd century, which would seem to refer to a 7th century B.C. king.

[192] The myth of *Tefnut* ("Sun Eye") tells the story of the god's wrath and Thoth's attempts to placate him in long speeches. The demotic text is from the 2nd century, and the Greek translation from the 3rd century A.D.

[193] Fraser (1972) 676; Koenen (1985) is another who does not identify the *Nectanebus* papyrus with the Greek novel.

[194] Reardon (1971) 329ff.

[195] On Alexander see Macuch (1989).

[196] Winkler (1994) 35 finds the "love-in-marriage" model alien to Greek culture, and so suggests it comes from the Near East. Against this opinion see Ruiz-Montero (1989) 132–3.

were structural and the text preceded *Ninus* we could state that in all probability the Greek novel was born in Egypt. But it should be noticed that there are two conditions to be met here, and while that certainty is lacking, we would have to say that the likely source for *Ninus, Metiochus and Parthenope* and *Callirhoe* is Asia Minor.[197] Naturally, these might well be parallel developments also.

Clearly *Nectanebus* is comparable to *Ninus* neither in structure, stylistic and rhetorical level, social context nor, probably, in extension. The Greek *paideia* displayed in form and content by the texts cited above is nowhere to be found in *Nectanebus* or the Setna cycle. On the contrary, the survey presented by Tait gives a clear idea of the markedly Egyptian personality of these demotic-born texts,[198] whose brevity makes their inclusion in the genre we are studying impossible to prove.[199] Their extension would seem to suggest that we are dealing rather with *novelle*, and with strongly drawn characters into the bargain.[200]

Coexisting as the Greeks did with other Eastern cultures, there was a natural transfer of elements from one culture to the other; yet, when it comes to comparing narratives from different cultures, we should not forget that the laws of folklore are also operating, that is, that oral narrative might also have an impact here. This does not mean that a putative Eastern influence on the novel should be excluded; rather, the Greek fantastic tradition is very rich and is in contact with the Orient from the earliest times.[201] What *is* relevant to determining the originality and specificity of the Greek novel is not so much what Eastern elements are found there as what characteristic structural elements of the genre figure in the Orient, and, in

---

[197] The opinion is shared by Hägg (1983) (1994) 70, n. 32; Bowie (1994b), amongst others.

[198] Dostálová (1991) reaches the same conclusions as the ones we are presenting.

[199] Dostálová (1991) considers it improbable for Severis and Tinuphis, whose papyri are from the 2nd century A.D., Tinuphis's in metric prose. The Tefnut papyrus is clearly different to the Greek novels. Stoneman (1994) wrongly asserts this to be the oldest Greek novel: we assume he is referring to *Nectanebus*.

[200] We do not know when priests and magicians make their first appearance in the novel. If the *Ass* were included in Aristides's *Milesiae* the magic would not originate in Egypt. Lloyd (1982) remarks that the magic and astrology in *Nectanebus* are eastern in origin, but are not Egyptian.

[201] Dostálová (1991) argues correctly that if we class the novel as Eastern, then we could class the *Cyropaedia* in the same way. He also makes the point that Barns changed his mind in 1978, accepting the possibility of a mutual influence between the novel and Egypt, though none of the modern scholars seems to have taken him up on this.

this respect, it should be stated that no love stories have so far been discovered in the East that bear any resemblance to *Ninus* or *Callirhoe*. This is not, of course, to forget the rhetorical treatment and ideology, typical of the Greeks.

The search for a remote eastern origin is an old and much criticised project,[202] though recently Anderson has joined the hunt in a study which, in my view, is mistaken in both its methodology and its conclusions.[203] For Anderson, the novel emerges above all in Sumer, in texts of the third millenium, a conclusion based on the comparison of isolated episodes from the different novels with episodes in the Eastern texts, analysed atomistically not structurally, with assimilations that are, in most cases, highly dubious and unconvincing (as when *Callirhoe* is compared to the story of Enlil and Ninlil on the grounds that it contains motifs such as pregnancy or a journey). The eastern texts would form models from which the genre is developed. The medium would be translation, and there would be prior oral versions.

In his stress on the importance of the oral tradition Anderson is, I believe, on the right path: we have seen it at work in the legends of Ninus, Semiramis, Sesonchosis or Alexander himself. In the oral origin of narrative fiction we do indeed find precedents in the Orient (the *Life of Aesop* is a possible example). Though the oldest Greek papyri are from the 2nd/3rd centuries A.D., they refer back to a much older text, since an Aramaean work, the novel of Ahikar (preserved on a 5th century B.C. papyrus) served as its basis.[204] Aesop is the astute hero of folklore, who, like the later picaro, successfully negotiates a series of adventures.[205] Stoneman has found the same qualities in the *Life of Alexander*,[206] though he adds that his death at

---

[202] It was proposed already in 1670 by P.D. Huet in *Traité de l'origine des romans*. In 1911 Lacôte suggested India. The influence of the Greek novel on Arabian narrative is indicated by Barchiesi (1988) 350–51.

[203] Anderson (1984). They are accepted by Grotanelli (1987).

[204] See Holzberg (1993a) 84–93, with a study of the text's structure. Adrados (1979) also studied it, along with the sources, without excluding the possible influence of *Ninus* and the *Life of Alexander*, as well as the Cynics.

[205] Cf. *supra*, p. 62. To the novels of Petronius and Apuleius cited by Holzberg, as predecessors of the picaresque we might also add the Greek *Ass*, as Adrados (1979) points out. The German author finds a likeness in biographies of characters such as Hesiod, the Seven Wise Men, Socrates and Diogenes.

[206] Stoneman (1994b). Kussl (1992) rightly relates the Tinuphis fragment to the Ahikar-Aesop tradition, and cites two demotic papyri on Ahikar from the 1st century A.D. For the rest, several traditions converge in the *Life of Aesop*, which, as Adrados's study shows (1979), makes the text a highly complex one.

the end approximates him to real "Life", not to the picaresque. The *History of Apollonius* gives us another wise hero capable of solving enigmas. All of them are protagonists of popular and well-circulated *Volksbücher*. This kind of story has parallels in the Orient.[207] Knowing the formative stages of the *Life of Aesop* would help us to establish the dates of the episodes in Babylonia and Egypt, under Nectanebus, though the latter may be quite late, possibly influenced by Greek fiction.[208] Babylonia would be a point of union between *Alexander* and *Ninus*, but from a structural point of view, the novelistic biography of Aesop, like that of Alexander, is comparable neither to *Ninus* nor to *Callirhoe*: they simply belong to different folk traditions, to different narrative models.

B. *The Religious Model*

A remote origin is posited mainly in the theory held by Kerényi in 1927,[209] by which the mysteries of death and resurrection of Isis and Osiris would serve as the model for the novel's pair of lovers, whose adventures would echo those of the gods and follow the same order. In his tremendously erudite study Kerényi likened situations in the novels to Christian or Isiac aretalogies. This would explain the lovers' search, their comparison to the gods, or virtues such as σωφροσύνη. Even the erotic element would have religious roots.

Merkelbach took Kerényi's thesis to an extreme in 1962[210] when he argued that the structure of the Greek novel was a reproduction of the mysteries of Isis and Osiris, Mithras or Dionysus, as the case determined. He reaches this conclusion after analysing each novel and comparing each episode with the respective rites. The novels would be aretalogical texts to be explained in public by an aretalogist with a wide repertoire: the powers or *aretai* of a god, mythical stories, *novelle*, tales, Milesian fables, etc. They would be oral tales at first (whence the stereotyped formulae), which eventually became literary

---

[207] For instance that of the prophet Daniel, who travels to the courts of Babylonia, Media and Persia: cf. Wills (1994), who calls it a *novella*. Ahikar was a functionary in the Assyrian court.
[208] Centanni (1988) XXV notes the influence of the love novel in the *Life of Alexander*—not surprising in a version from the 3rd century A.D.
[209] Reprinted in 1973.
[210] In his (less radical) 1994 article (p. 291) he suggests that it comes *not just* from the aretalogies.

ones. The disposition of literary material would, then, be Greek, but the religious content would be Eastern.

Kerényi's correspondences were already strained,[211] but Merkelbach displays a greater imagination and, in asserting that the novels are the prime source of information for the mystery religions, is caught in a vicious circle: the pirates are initiates of Isis who comfort the heroes in their ritual tests (p. 97); the slave Satyrus owes his name to the fact that every satyr is a servant of Dionysus-Osiris (p. 118); the description of animals has a religious significance (p. 138), etc. One of the most serious difficulties Merkelbach has is what to do with Chariton: as he discounts a mystic interpretation here, he places Chariton at the end of the series of novelists (which is impossible chronologically), and concludes that Chariton would have misunderstood the mystic value of the novels and a potential reader found his work irritating (p. 339).

The theory has been frequently attacked and rarely accepted as a global mystic interpretation.[212] But to reject it out of hand is equally extreme.[213] Religious elements are undeniably present in the novel, but the important point is to decide how deep they go, what their structural function is and how all this is incorporated into the early novels.

First of all, as far as the central thesis goes, we have already pointed out that the novel's underlying structure is comparable to the search in the fairy tale. Scholars of folklore have highlighted the structural equivalence between the folktale and the myth that forms its base,[214] but the novelists remain unaware of that myth: the possible symbolic significance of novels such as those by Longus or Apuleius does not stem from the material used, but is rather an element added by the author, who is trying to endow the simple tale of entertainment with a deeper significance. This significance is a function of the exaltation of some godhead, be it the miracle-performing Isis of Xenophon or the Aphrodite of Chariton. The heroes of the *Ephesiaca* consecrate their deeds in writing in the Ephesian temple of Artemis, which

---

[211] See the criticisms in Reardon (1971) 319-20. Nock in his review of *Gnomon* (1928) 485-92 already noted the popular nature of the novels' danger-salvation episodes, as well as the fact that the liturgical cadences which Kerényi finds in Chariton and Achilles are not restricted to religious formulae but appear in other literary forms and are rhetorical in origin.
[212] See the opinions reviewed in Ruiz-Montero (1981) 284, n. 21.
[213] This is what Perry (1967) 336 does: "This is all nonsense".
[214] Besides Propp (1928), see Meletinsky (1974).

establishes a clear link with aretalogy.[215] Chariton uses the epic recourse in VII 1,3 to explain Aphrodite's wrath with Chaereas, and so establishes the link with the Greek literary tradition. But at the same time he underscores the faith in the goddess manifested by Callirhoe. Indeed, the author ends the novel with the latter's prayer to Aphrodite thanking her for her salvation, just as in I 1,7–8 she asks that Chaereas be given to her.[216] Callirhoe herself is even taken for the goddess in III 8,3–5. Chariton is exalting in his novel the goddess of his homeland, Aphrodite, whose cult was of great local importance.[217] We must, then, conclude that aretalogy and the novel can indeed be linked, and that this was a given fact by the 2nd century A.D. That said, aretalogy is not the same thing as mystic ritual and, in the case of Chariton, that ritual does not seem to be operative.

With regard to the issue that concerns us, it has to be acknowledged that the highpoint of the genre in the 2nd century A.D. coincides with that of the mystic religions (apart from coinciding with that of the Second Sophistic), and this is due to the fact that both phenomena fulfil the need for escape from the concerns of everyday life which, as Altheim noted,[218] was a constant of the age. Hence the religious element is a cultural component of the genre, which thus played lip service to the desires of the audience. The audience would appreciate, perhaps even demand, that element. This is a key factor in the study of the genre's social context, a subject we shall return to below. But are we to give the genre a religious interpretation that is ritual in origin, as in tragedy, or would that element have emerged gradually? What happened in the novels which preceded Chariton?

There is no clear evidence of aretalogical exaltation in the fragments which came before him. *Ninus* only speaks of Aphrodite and the Eros of Alexandrian literature, *Metiochus and Parthenope* and *Sesonchosis* do not mention the gods, though Diodorus links the Egyptian pharaoh

---

[215] For Xenophon see Ruiz-Montero (1994b). The same motif appears in the *History of Apollonius* 51; cf. Merkelbach (1994) 285.

[216] For other supplications and epiphanies of the goddess see Ruiz-Montero (1989) 125–6. These phenomena were habitual in the Empire.

[217] The lengthy final recapitulation in the theatre of Syracuse (VII 7) recalls both a dramatic practice and a declamatory and even aretalogical session, typical of the period.

[218] Altheim (1948a) also included in *Literatur und Gesellschaft in ausgehenden Altertum* I, Halle (1948) defends the religious character of the novel.

to Hephaestus.[219] A religious element would seem to figure in the fragment called *Asclepius*. If we turn to the comic or parodic novel, the *Ass* contains no divine exaltation whatever, though *Iolaus* does present a parody of a mysteries scene, which also figures in the *Satyricon*. Moreover, lists of healings attributed to Asclepius were known to exist in Epidaurus as early as the 4th century B.C. Together with aretalogy *sensu stricto*, i.e., religious aretalogy, mention should be made of the ἀρεταλόγοι cited by Philodemus[220] along with μιμογράφοι and other συγγραφεῖς, by which he appears to refer to a professional prose writer, though what that *aretalogus* wrote is unknown.

The religious theory of the novel takes aretalogy in the first sense, though some scholars have made a further distinction between temple-based and profane αρεταλόγοι, the common denominator between them being the use of the same folk material.[221] Precisely through this use of the same oral-based material, Kerényi identifies novelist with *aretalogus*, though he does not explain how one then becomes the other, as clearly the coincidence between priestly class and literate class found in Egypt is not necessarily a feature of Greek culture.

Scobie also brings in a detail from comparative literature when he notes the importance of aretalogy in the hands of Buddhist monks for the birth of the novel in China, something which—and Scobie notes the use of similar narrative techniques in Chariton and Xenophon and in the Chinese novels—may also have taken place in the ancient novel.[222]

Scobie's observations are interesting and show that aretalogy is a universal phenomenon. Lavagnini had already remarked that the local legends may be connected to a divinity, and indeed the story of Acontius and Cidyppe is associated with Artemis.[223] But even assuming

---

[219] D.S. I 53,9; 57,8.

[220] *On poems* IX.

[221] Thus Longo (1969) 33ff. distinguishes between pure aretalogy and *novellistic* aretalogy, and believes that, on losing its religious component, the aretalogical *novella* is transformed into the profane. Longo and Scobie (1969) 24–27 and (1973) 53ff. identify the Roman *fabulator* with the non-religious aretalogist. When Kerényi (1927) 200 called the style of the tale "aretalogical style" he was also identifying aretalogy with the fantastic tale, thus following the tradition of authors such as Reitzenstein (1906), who use the term in a dual sense. We use it here in its genuine religious sense.

[222] Scobie (1979).

[223] Lavagnini (1950). Longo (1969) also cites examples of love stories linked to a divinity: Paus.VII 19,1–4; 21,1–5; VIII 47,6. In VIII 23,2 says that he is relating what he has heard.

the existence of an aretalogist with an erotic repertoire, how does he then become an expert in rhetoric like the author of *Ninus*?[223 bis] Could Philodemus's aretalogist be the link in the chain? Were the first novelists reproducing an aretalogical model, whether taken or not from the Orient? The existing evidence is not conclusive proof, but even if we could accept that model, something else is needed, something that explains the reason for the interest in this type of tale. And so it is we come to the question of the novel's social context.

IX. *The Social Context*

Up to now we have seen how the literary tradition influences the novel, how together with these written sources there are also oral ones, how a "fictionalising" rhetorical process was necessary and to what extent the Orient had an impact: we have, in other words, tried to answer the questions how, when, where and whence the genre was formed, distinguishing between origins that were close and others that were more remote. We need now to answer a question that is equally crucial in explaining the rise of the genre: Why was it born? Why was it not born in the 4th century B.C., if prose fiction had already been invented? What material and spiritual elements converge in the 1st century B.C. which did not exist in previous periods? Or, in parallel terms: what elements exist in the 8th century B.C. to explain the appearance of the *Iliad* and the *Odyssey*? Why does drama emerge in the 5th century B.C.? A tight link is known to exist between literature and the society that produces it and to which it is addressed—like art—, whose demands, needs, dreams and aspirations it somehow reflects.[224] Literature is the vehicle for the ideas belonging to the particular social class which patronises it, or through which the author may even try to influence his audience. The social function of Greek literature in the archaic and classical periods is quite clear. But what is the function of the novel? What kind of ideas does it transmit? To what social class is it addressed?[225]

[223 bis] It has been thought that the intermediaries may have been Cynic-Stoic philosophers, perhaps in the 2nd century B.C.: cf. Merkelbach (1962) 334 and Miralles, in his review of Longo (1969), *BIEH* 5 (1971) 60–61.

[224] Todorov (1988) 38–39: each period has its own system of genres which relates to the dominant ideology. But Wellek-Warren (1953) 156–86 already observed that the relationship between society and art is never a direct one, since in the Middle Ages there are few social transformations and many literary ones.

[225] Köhler (1974) wondered whether the novel of chivalry was a genre of escap-

We have already mentioned certain social factors which enhance the rise of the novel, when referring to phenomena such as nationalism, religion or the social importance of rhetoric. The progression of Greek prose in relation to poetry from the 2nd century B.C. (in art, reflected in the taste for classicism apparent in the sculptures preserved)[226] is a fact that needs stressing. This progression is accompanied by the rise of schools of rhetoric, a rise which is enhanced during the Empire, when rhetoric enjoys extraordinary social prestige.[227] In this respect, the novel aligns itself with biography, epistolography and declamation, though fiction permeates practically all of the literature of the period.[228] Obviously, this love of fiction responds to the public taste. Escapism is a social demand, and the same goes for the love theme, which in its idealistic, passionate, tragic or bourgeois forms, triumphed in the Hellenistic period. If the novels favour an idealised, chaste and conjugal love, this also is a product of the audience's taste: there are naturally examples of the "other" love in the Latin and Greek novels, but it is also revealing how in epitaphs in the Empire the allusions to conjugal love increase, and how from the age of Hadrian a coin is minted with the inscription PUDICITIA.[229] The idealisation of the genre's protagonists responds to something in the age. In this, the ideology of the novel coincides with the dominant, and the same conclusion can be drawn from the exaltation of certain ideals by Chariton.[230] Let us recall finally that both *Ninus* and *Callirhoe* presuppose a cultivated author and readership. To see the novel as a genre born in a way not alien to other forms of literature in the period seems to me a basic criterion in the study of the social (not just literary) context of the genre. The latter seems addressed to a cultivated public seeking prose fiction, with love as the theme and entertainment as the prime objective.

Studies on the origins of the genre prior to Perry's 1967 work had little or nothing to say about the social context. Underlining its

---

ism or combat: on these questions see Ruiz-Montero (1989) 124–5.

[226] See Zanker (1979).

[227] See Bowersock (1969), expanded by Bowie (1982); Reardon (1971); Anderson (1989b).

[228] Reardon (1971) offers a good survey of the 2nd and 3rd centuries A.D.

[229] Ruiz-Montero (1989) 132. Also worth recalling is the exaltation of this type of love in Plutarch and the philosopher Musonius Rufus: cf. *ibid.*, 132–3. This did not prevent the *Milesia* from also enjoying a great deal of success.

[230] The ideals are those of *paideia* and *philanthropia*, ideals of the upper classes, the *pepaideumenoi*. I draw this conclusion from the ideological study of *Callirhoe* based on literary and non-literary evidence: Ruiz-Montero (1989).

importance was one of Perry's insights, together with his opposition to the genetic fixation of scholars insisting that it was a question of a new genre. Perry believed in the conscious purpose of an author, who invented the genre to meet new social demands.[231] Later scholars, starting with Reardon, have signalled the importance of knowing *why* the novel, a genre accurately defined by Reardon as *mythe hellénistique*,[232] was born. This implies the study of the public to whom the genre is addressed, the social class which backs it, its level of education, etc. These questions are vital for our complete understanding of the genre, but also controversial given the lack of information on the degree of literacy of the readers of the Empire's eastern provinces, as well as on their social history. If we could fix the dates in which each novel was written we would gain a greater knowledge of that society;[233] at the same time, in order to establish the degree of realism of the novels we need a more rigorous knowledge of the historical context. In this respect, the collaboration of philologists and historians strikes me as necessary.[234]

In 1930 Perry made some remarks on the public for the first novels—Chariton in particular—which imply their rejection of the genre:[235] his unfortunate view of Chariton as an ignorant writer who wrote for the "poor in spirit", women and the young above all, are well known. The conclusion was a view of the novel as a popular genre, aimed at the masses and ignored by the cultivated official literature. The lack of reference to the genre amongst its contemporaries has led scholars to find here proof of the scorn the genre inspired in the age, or to see it as a marginal literary development. Though we have outlined the reasons that explain (in part) the silence of the

---

[231] Perry (1967) 175. The theory of the inventor is not a new one. Rohde (1914) had already referred to an "Erfinder", meeting the objection of Giangrande (1962) that this was a facile answer to the problem.

[232] Reardon (1971) 332ff. Reardon adds that Perry is also biologistic, since he replaces the concept of the development of genres with that of the development of societies.

[233] An observation shared by Bowie (1993).

[234] The historical orientation inspired the 1987 Paris conference, edited in 1992 by Baslez-Hoffman-Trédé, and whose interest for this discussion (especially the articles by Baslez, Bowie, Jones and Quet) is immense. Social issues are the focus of the book edited by Liviabella (1989). Situating the novels in their literary and social context is the aim of the work edited by Morgan (1994), but its contributors, though worth reading, focus more on the literary than on the social.

[235] Also in his 1967 book (pp. 89–90; 98–99): the novel may have been a low-quality genre but it sold well, was written by people with no literary name but with a smattering of rhetoric, for money and popularity.

genre's contemporaries, a certain amount of contempt on the part of the official sophistic is undeniable,[236] at least at the outset.[237]

In his 1983 book Hägg included a chapter on the social context and the first readers of the novel in which he makes an interesting survey and concludes that "literacy" extended to the non-urban population and to women. Hägg argues that sentimentalism does not imply social class, and suggests that there were scribes and secretaries who helped spread the genre by means of public readings in villages or family settings (whence the frequent repetitions found in Chariton and Xenophon). The public would have been the same as for the mystery religions.

Other commentators have been less optimistic, however, about how "widespread" and especially how "popular" the genre was. Thus Wesseling insists that higher education was for an (above all) male minority, that books were dear and that the oral character is explicable from the folk material, though she does admit the possibility of readings aloud and the oral nature of a society whose functioning we are unaware of.[238] Treu does not exclude the possibility of readings in social circles, and posits a medium-culture public from his study of the material of the papyri; however, from literary citations and mosaics with scenes from novels he posits a high-class public and does not exclude possible summaries—such as Xenophon of Ephesus's—for a lower-ranking audience.[239]

Stephens is more radical: from her study of the material of the papyri she concludes that it is impossible to conceive of any other

---

[236] Cf. *supra*, 32 ff. Gill (1993a) 79–81 believes the novel has been ignored by critics not just because of its "unambitious" nature, but because it could not have been the vehicle for the traditional, ethical or political truths of the community in the way other genres had been, and, finally, because its purely fictional status makes it a hard genre to pigeon-hole. We have already discussed the first and last of these reasons. As for the second one, it is obvious that the novel offers new "truths" to a new society, namely: ideals of human behaviour, religious values, etc.

[237] The lack of a known author may be interpreted in this way, but the use of the pseudonym "Xenophon" in at least three causes tends, rather, to make the fact a phenomenon of rhetorical *mimesis*.

[238] Wesseling (1988), a good overall analysis. Harris notes that "literacy" in the 1st–3rd centuries A.D. was around 15%: cf. Stephens (1994).

[239] Treu (1989), who gives an even more impressive display of his imagination when he states that the rooms decorated with these mosaics would be the place where the novels would be read (p. 196). His remarks on the ostracon containing a fragment of *Metiochus and Parthenope* as proof of a low-class reading public (p. 192) are, nonetheless, interesting. A middle-class audience was suggested by Schmeling (1974) 32–3, who in 1980 opted rather for a sentimental audience.

readers than those similar to the authors of the novels. Like Bowie, she finds the hypothesis of readings by scribes a gratuitous one. The novel would be entertainment for an educated elite, and it makes no sense to talk of a "mass literature" in antiquity: there was no middle class, only a pyramid structure. The papyri were expensive, the level of literacy low. As far as the female readership was concerned, any comparison with the modern novel or (on theory) the possibility of female authors writing under a pseudonym, are rightly rejected by Wesseling, Bowie and Stephens.[240] Certainly, the thought of a genre aimed especially at women because of its eroticism and sentimentalism is hardly credible: the number of educated women was even lower than that of men, even if women did manage to attain higher levels of culture and political power during the Empire.[241] Like Isidora, the sister of Antonius Diogenes, who dedicates his novel to her, that minority may well have been readers of the genre.[242]

The studies of Bowie and Stephens, then, posit a minority and cultivated audience, the same as for the rest of the literature (Plutarch, Lucian or the historians) or for the sophists. The few extant fragments of the novel in comparison to other genres, would also disprove Perry's earlier belief in a widely read genre. These facts match the opinions cited above of the cultivated character of the novel from its inception. And, besides Isidora, we know that novels were also read by Porphyrius, perhaps Philostratus, Julian and the priests of Asia Minor, the physician Theodorus Priscianus and Photius.

Is another less educated public, then, to be excluded? This is the question posed in a recent article by Hägg, who, adopting both extrinsic and intrinsic criteria, answers in the negative.[243] He notes the inadequacy of statistics when it comes to judging the genre's

---

[240] Hägg (1983) 96 reviews the theory, which he does not share. Bowie (1992) (1994b) gives examples of typically male scenes and episodes. The masculine nature of the novels' ideas is noted already by Hägg (1983) 91; Ruiz-Montero (1989) 146.

[241] Treu (1989) 188-9 is of the same opinion. See Nollé (1994) for high-ranking aristocratic women; he believes that the fact does not lead to the conclusion that there was a "female emancipation".

[242] Photius, cod. 166, 111a. For women as readers see the fine analyses of Egger (1987) (1994). Parthenope and Callirhoe show themselves to be quite cultivated, but they obviously belonged to the aristocracy. The women of this social class are the only ones that can identify with the ideal of the cultivated and capable woman of the love novels.

[243] Hägg (1994): Hägg's arguments are as subtle and intelligent as those of Bowie and Stephens. Hägg adds that the number of literary papyri surviving from the 1st centuries B.C. and A.D. is scant, and that Harris's figures only apply to Rome and Italy. In any case, Hägg always has in mind the "upper strata" of society (p. 58),

popularity, and above all stresses the possibility of public, or other kinds of, readings that would have increased, if not the reading, then the listening-public. Hägg's hypothesis is not, in my mind, unreasonable, even though Chariton may talk specifically of readers in VIII 1,4: it seems obvious that there may have been different levels of "reading" or "enjoyment" of the text, some more literary and others more superficial which would not look beyond the external elements of love and adventure.[244] These are the themes of universal literature which obviously do not depend on sex or social status, though perhaps we are taking a modern perspective here. The question for research is how that circulation took place, though the possibility will have to remain open,[245] since we are clearly dealing with a far more orally-oriented society than our own. In the meantime, the evidence from Lucian and the mosaics in Asia Minor implies the transmission and acceptance of novelistic themes, just as the parody of Chariton and Xenophon in the *Ass* implies the popularity, or even the success, of the genre. And the same conclusion may be drawn from the fact that consummate sophists such as Longus, Achilles Tatius and Heliodorus devote themselves to it, that it enters Christian apocryphal literature and that certain novels are translated into Latin.

Let us add finally that it is clear that the novel shares elements from many other genres, but is to be identified with none of them and, in consequence, to be derived from none. Its structure is that of the marvellous tale, a story in which the rational is fused with fantasy and imagination, as in dream, because that is what it expresses: the dreams of society, part of its consciousness, its search for answers and its desire for happiness and transcendence. That is why it continues to intrigue us and why it has become the modern genre *par excéllence*.

---

members of the administration, the professional classes and commerce (p. 57). Thus also Wesseling (1988) 75ff.

[244] I make this point in my 1994a article (p. 1040). The modernity of the themes of sex and violence is, if contemporary cinema is anything to go by, beyond any doubt. Hägg compares Xenophon's technique to series such as "Dallas" and "Dynasty".

[245] Hägg (1994) talks of dual readings for Middle Ages, classical drama or Islandic sagas. I recall how in *Don Quixote* I, chap. 32, the inn-keeper talks of readings aloud of chivalric novels by a mower who knows how to read, with more than thirty people listening, though, obviously, this does not mean the same thing necessarily occurred in the Roman period. Hägg is wrong to state (p. 53) that *Ninus* contained no erudite quotations (*supra*, n. 173). Nor is it clear that the repetitions and anticipations in Chariton are due to its "oral performance", not to its literary origin. Xenophon, in my opinion, addresses a different audience.

4. THE ANCIENT READERS OF THE GREEK NOVELS

Ewen Bowie

I

As Cleitophon begins to fall passionately in love with Leucippe in Achilles Tatius' novel, he hits on a strategem for catching glimpses of her in the part of his parental home that had been set aside for her and her mother when they arrived as refugees from Byzantium (1.6.6 cf. 5.1). He takes a book and perambulates the house in such a way that from time to time, facing the doorway behind which Leucippe is to be found, he can raise his eyes from the book over which he is bent and glimpse his beloved. Achilles does not tell us what sort of a book it was, and we are free to suppose that it might be precisely the sort of book that he has written and that we are reading. The uncertainty left by this brief mention of a (presumably) literary text, the only such mention in our extant corpus of Greek novels whether complete, summarised or fragmentary, is an appropriate metaphor for the obscurity attaching to the readership of these works in the ancient Greek world. The issue has been alive since Rohde, and has been much debated since Perry's Sather lectures were published in 1967, particularly over the last decade.[1] Yet although some more evidence has been gathered and arguments and distinctions have been refined, the subject is still one where the best that can be offered is plausible inference and not proof.

The lack of what can reasonably be termed evidence is at the heart of our problem. Hence it is possible for some scholars to hold that the novel developed in the late Hellenistic period precisely as a literature designed for a new category of reader, men and women who were literate but not intellectual, residents of huge Hellenistic cities whose *déracinement* encouraged them to identify with the often isolated characters in the novels and to find meaning for their own lives in the pattern of their adventures, and for others to hold that the texts were primarily produced for and read by the same social

---

[1] Hägg (1983) and (1994), Wesseling (1988), Treu (1989), Harris (1989), Bowie (1985a) and (1994b), Stephens (1994).

and intellectual élite who read Plutarch and historians or attended philosophy lectures. The following discussion will necessarily traverse ground already much trodden by both these groups (the latter of which has included me) and the most my reader can hope for is map with clearer definition of important features, not one in which The Answer is unambiguously marked.

A definition that must be essayed at the outset is that of the novels themselves. Are we dealing with a single genre, or should the "ideal" romances, in which a pair of heterosexual lovers is central and chastity esteemed, be seen as different from a more lubricious form apparently represented by Lollianus' Φοινικικά and the Iolaus story, and should yet a third type be seen in the 24-book Τὰ ὑπὲρ Θούλην ἄπιστα of Antonius Diogenes, in which the central couple are brother and sister, not lovers, and extensive and fantastic travel is a more important element than love? In the absence of ancient literary theory we are again denied any demonstrable conclusion. But we may argue that both Lollianus and Antonius Diogenes read more effectively if they are taken to involve some parody of the "ideal" romance, and that any propositions about readership should take account both of generic links and of diversity between individual specimens.

A similar question must be addressed concerning the relation between the novels that have been argued to be less ambitious and that in most cases also seem to be earlier (*Ninus, Parthenope and Metiochus*, Chariton's *Chaereas and Callirhoe*, Xenophon's *Anthia and Habrocomes* and arguably the supposed Greek original of *Apollonius king of Tyre*) and those by common consent described as sophistic" (Achilles Tatius' *Leucippe and Cleitophon*, Longus' *Daphnis and Chloe* and Heliodorus' *Charicleia and Theagenes*). Can a conclusion about readership reached for the one group be expected to hold in any degree for the other? Again the sorts of intertextuality with the earlier works that have been detected in the sophistic novels do something to hold the two groups together. At the least the readers of the sophistic novels are, it seems, expected to know what the stereotypical features of the earlier novels were and to admire the adroitness with which the sophistic novelist handles them: such features are the pirates, perhaps even Phoenician pirates, that invade Longus' pastoral Lesbos, or the sort of story implied as gripping by the responses of Cnemon to Calasiris' narrative in Heliodorus.[2]

---

[2] Longus 1.28.1 (Τύριοι V, retained by Vieillefond; Πύρριοι F; Πυρραῖοι Reeve). For Cnemon as a simple-minded audience, Winkler (1982).

A final preliminary: it is clear that an investigation should consistently distinguish between actual and intended readers, and that the sorts of result we might in principle expect in trying to establish these two categories are likely to be different. If we had comprehensive data on *actual* readership in the ancient world (though of course we have almost no data at all) we would be able to draw up an inventory of all individuals who actually read novels and allocate them to different groups by criteria of income, geographical location, and level of education and come up with some hard-and-fast generalisations. But the question of an author's "intended readership" is much more slippery. Some authors of certain sorts of work (intermediate Greek language-teaching manuals; travel-guides to Disneyworld) have a very precise category of reader in mind; authors of other sorts of work (Histories of the Second World War; crime fiction; "soft" pornography) might be thought often to have a much looser conception of their intended readership: at the time they start writing they may envisage four or five possible categories, in the course of composing their work they may admit a further two, and if pressed by an interviewer might concede that certain other categories might also furnish appropriate readers. Finally (of my selective list, though not of course of any possible list) there are some authors who (like musicians and like pictorial or plastic artists) may claim to have no regard to prospective audiences at all, and may explain their creativity in terms of some inner compulsion, or (with less mystification) as adoption of a fashion: *semper ego auditor tantum?*[3]

This last point abuts on an issue that has often been closely bound up with that of readership, viz. the reasons for the development of this post-classical genre. Perry saw its genesis as a response to the reading needs of late Hellenistic man, and Tomas Hägg has recently suggested that such positions as my own which do not connect readership with the emergence of the genre are for that reason flawed.[4] I am not embarrassed that my view of a predominantly intellectual readership takes us back "to square one" on the question of origins. The hard question we have to ask is this: did the writers of either the first novels (of which we are statistically unlikely to have any examples in our selective remains) or of their immediate successors (by which I mean *Ninus, Parthenope and Metiochus, Chaereas and Callirhoe* and *Anthia and Habrocomes*) have any idea, whether inchoate or clear,

---

[3] Juvenal *Sat.*1.1.
[4] Hägg (1994) 52–3.

of the sort of reader for whom they were writing, and did the *way* that they wrote take account systematically of that envisaged readership? Like so many of the fundamental questions in this enquiry, it is probably unanswerable. But we can exclude, at the one end of the spectrum, extensive consumer-research resulting in the designer-novel; and we might equally wish to exclude an extreme form of the *semper ego auditor tantum*? approach. We should be ready to admit familiarity with the sorts of literature that have proved to go down well in the (necessarily) limited environment of the writer, but we might also be wise to admit an impulse to try out a new formula in an age when all the established genres were already overcrowded with past masters and contemporary aspirants. A scribbler in a city of Egypt, Syria or Asia Minor might thereby hit on a recipe that was to catch the attention of certain sorts of reader all over the Eastern Mediterranean (just as a Jewish mystic from Nazareth hit on a winning religious formula) but we may doubt that he could have had good reason to believe that this was what he was doing. And unless we endorse some relatively strong form of the "designer-text" hypothesis, we should beware of claiming too close a link between the reasons for which the first novels were written and their intended readership.

If we are to insist that some link must be supposed between the reasons for writing novels and their earliest readers, another *caveat* should perhaps be entered at this point. Like Hägg, I have seen hints in the earliest extant novels that suggest that not only *Callirhoe* (which explicitly purports to be by a man from Aphrodisias) but also *Ninus* and perhaps *Parthenope* were composed or intended for a readership in Western Asia Minor.[5] Recently Bowersock has also claimed Antonius Diogenes, persuasively if unprovably, for Chariton's city Aphrodisias.[6] These novels' presumptive predecessors may of course have been written elsewhere, but in an era when most works must have had a geographically restricted circulation it is at least *more likely* that such predecessors should also be associated with Western Asia Minor. Now whether or not the picture of Hellenistic man as suffering a sense of loss and isolation as a result of the breakdown of the society and shared values of the classical *polis* is a correct diagnosis of inhabitants of huge cities like Antioch and Alexandria,[7] it is hardly

---

[5] Hägg (1994) 70 n. 32; Bowie (1994b) 450–2.
[6] Bowersock (1994) 38–41.
[7] Scepticism concerning the applicability of this *mentalité* to Hellenistic Athens has already been voiced by Gruen (1993). Note Gruen's conclusion (drawn admittedly

applicable even to the biggest cities of Western Asia Minor. Although this too is treacherous ground, the citizen population of Pergamum in the high Roman empire is put by Galen at 40,000, with guesses that this implies a total population of between 160,000 and 200,000, and that the Hellenistic city was substantially smaller.[8] Ephesus and Smyrna may well have been of the same order. We are not here in a different world from that of fifth-century Athens or Syracuse, the former with at least 20,000 citizens in the first three Solonian classes in 432/1 B.C. and arguably a total male citizen population over 30,000.[9] Of the remainder of the reputedly 500 cities of *provincia Asia* very few can have been as large as classical Athens, and the vast majority were on the same small scale as the classical *polis*. A recent estimate allows few cities more than 25,000 inhabitants and puts the majority in the range between 5,000 and 15,000.[10] All these cities about which we know anything, large and small, seem to have been highly conscious of their identities in the Hellenistic and Roman period, to have elaborated traditions which authorised that identity, and sometimes to have enjoyed benefactions whose founders were in varying degrees careful to use their benefaction to create a structure in which all but the lowest echelons of the citizen body were given a place.[11] Things were no doubt different in Antioch-on-the-Orontes and Alexandria, both cities created *de novo* and from very heterogeneous

---

from evidence that is chiefly for the third century B.C.): "Civic spirit had not evaporated in the Hellenistic age. The polis held its place as a centre of allegiance and a source of pride. Hellenistic individuals were not all driven to seek inner solace or to reach out longingly to the cosmos. They could still find support in the familiar institutions of the polis" (354). Note too the arguments (not all cogent) of Martin (1994) 117, that "neither the Hellenistic idea nor ideal can be held to value in any way an individualistic view of the self." (I am grateful to Mark Golden for drawing my attention to these discussions).

[8] Magie (1950) 585 and n. 50 on 1446. Galen *de cogn. curand. animi morbis* 9 (= 5.49 Kuhn) attests 40,000 citizens for Pergamum, totalling 120,000 with wives and slaves: from this a total population of between 180,000 and 200,000 is estimated by Mitchell (1993) vol. 1, 244, while Radt (1988) 175 estimated 160,000 for the later second century A.D. and only ca. 25,000 to 40,000 for the Attalid period. It was thought by Magie (and others have followed him) that the inscription published in *Jahreheft des Österreichischen Archäologischen Instituts* 26 (1930) Beiblatt 57ff. attested the same number of citizens as entertained by Aur. Varenus at Ephesus late in the second century A.D.: but cf. Warden and Bagnall (1988).

[9] For interpretations of the key passage, Thucydides 2.13.6, see Gomme (1927), (1956) 33–9 and (1959); A. Jones (1957) 161–80, Hansen (1981).

[10] Mitchell (1993) vol. 1, 244.

[11] The closest and most illuminating study of such a benefaction is of that of C. Vibius Salutaris at Ephesus in A.D. 104 by Rogers (1991). For discussion of interest in local foundation legends cf. Strubbe (1984–6).

populations: the latter's free residents in the middle of the first century B.C. are numbered at 300,000 by Diodorus Siculus, from which a population of ca. 500,000 has been inferred.[12] Scholars who ascribe isolation and *déracinement* to Hellenistic man are doubtless influenced by our image of these two huge cities, but any who hold that the novel may have been first written in Western Asia Minor must reckon with a different sort of environment. Indeed the enthusiasm for true or forged traditions and for local history that characterises these cities might more appropriately be associated with precisely that orientation in *Parthenope* and *Callirhoe*.

After these preliminaries I return to the main theme of this chapter, and attempt to outline the state of the question (as I see it) under six heads.

II

1a *The "Sophistic" Novels: Intended Readership*

This seems now to be a relatively uncontested aspect of the problem. Tomas Hägg is happy to allow that Achilles Tatius, Longus and Heliodorus were themselves highly educated and envisaged similarly educated readers as the primary readership of their works. The argument is based on the frequency and subtlety of intertextuality with earlier literature, some of it more recondite than the stuff of basic secondary educational curricula.[13] At the same time it may be reasonable to insist (as Hägg does for Chariton)[14] that in the "sophistic" novels too "narrative suspense, emotional impact, the escapist function were there for all," and that their writers *may* have envisaged a few less highly educated readers who would turn to them for these and would not find the more complicated narrative structure of Heliodorus or the Atticizing Greek of all three an obstacle to understanding. We must remember, however, that quite a high level of education must be assumed in a prospective reader of Atticising Greek—an education acquired by studying classical texts in one's youth and reinforced by encounters with these texts or with their imperial written or spoken imitators in adult life.

---

[12] Diodorus Sic. 17.52; Bowman (1986) 208.
[13] Bowie (1994b) 438, 451–3.
[14] Hägg (1994) 54.

1b *The "Sophistic" Novels: Actual Readership*

Paradoxically, we are little better off for evidence of actual readers of the big three than of other species of the genre. True, we have six papyri of Achilles Tatius, two of the second century and four of the third.[15] But we have only one of Heliodorus, and that as late as the sixth century,[16] and none of Longus. We know, then, that some Greek speakers in Oxyrhynchus and in other parts of Egypt read or thought they might like to read Achilles Tatius in the later second and in the third centuries. The format of the book and the type of writing do not mark off these papyri from those of high literary texts,[17] the numbers of novel papyri remain much smaller than those of the most-read of such high literary texts, and it remains tempting to infer that their readers are indeed the same as the readers of these texts. It is also tempting to ascribe the greater popularity of Achilles Tatius (if a mere six papyri can attest "popularity" of any sort) to the Alexandrian origin claimed for him by the Suda and the prominence of Egypt in his narrative. But then Heliodorus also sets the largest single section of his narrative in Egypt, and so far has no known readers in Egypt before the sixth century.

He does, however, have a possible reader in the emperor Julian. Julian's account of the siege of Nisibis in A.D. 350, to be found in his orations 1 and 3 of A.D. 357, is either influenced by Heliodorus' narrative of the siege of Syene or influences it.[18] Proof of a later fourth-century date for Heliodorus would compel the latter conclusion, but so far this has not been forthcoming, and I still regard the issue as open, with a greater readiness to believe that Julian read Heliodorus than *vice versa*. If so, our first known reader of Heliodorus is indeed highly educated, even if he is one who in a letter of A.D. 363 to the *archiereus* of Asia proscribed the reading of erotic fiction.[19]

---

[15] Listed by Garnaud (1991) xxiii–xxv; three from Oxyrhynchus, one from Hermoupolis and the others of unknown provenance.

[16] Gronewald (1979a) 19–21.

[17] See Stephens (1994) 412–14, though note the slightly different emphasis of Treu (1989) 190f., who allocates the novel papyri to the middle and bottom part of a scale running from luxurious to simple. What is important, however, is that the novel papyri "in the aggregate look different both from the early New Testament material and from unskilled productions": Stephens (1994) 413.

[18] For the evidence and arguments see Bowie (1994b) 446 with n. 54, to which should now be added Chuvin (1991) 321–5 and Bowersock (1994) 149–60.

[19] Letter 89, p. 169 in the Budé edition of Bidez, cf. Bowie (1994b) 446. The case for use of Julian by Heliodorus and against a third-century date has been

A further fourth-century reader for Heliodorus has been enticingly proposed by Bowersock.[20] In the Augustan History's life of Aurelian his successor-to-be Tacitus, praising his achievements, lists the Seres among the peoples he conquered alongside the Blemmyes and the people of Aksum (*Exomitae*, 41.10). Bowersock has suggested that the idea of associating the Seres with these African peoples came to the historian from reading Heliodorus' account of envoys sent to Hydaspes by his allies (10.25-7), and notes that an earlier list of Aurelian's conquests, in the description of his triumph (*Aurelian* 33.4) mentions Blemmyes, the people of Aksum and a giraffe offered by the latter (but no Seres): a giraffe also figures in Hydaspes' triumphal parade at Meroe. The suggestion is attractive but its foundations precarious. Giraffes could be found in other Latin texts by the writer of the Augustan History,[21] and the bizarre location of the Seres, as Bowersock himself notes, was already offered by Lucan (*Pharsalia* 10.292-3). Their conjunction in the Augustan History, written in the last two decades of the fourth century, *may* arise from its author's familiarity with Heliodorus' work (presumably the Greek text: we have no hint that there was ever a Latin translation) but need not.

The first man, therefore, to show certain knowledge of Heliodorus is Socrates Scholasticus whose history of the church, written in Constantinople and stopping at A.D. 439, alleges that he became bishop of Trikka in Thessaly.[22] Although eschewing Atticism himself, Socrates undoubtedly belongs to the highly educated élite, and defended Christians' reading of pagan literature. That he actually read Heliodorus, we have no proof. There is even less support for his reading rather earlier in the fifth century by the doctor Theodorus Priscianus, who prescribed the reading of erotic novels as a cure for impotence. He names Iamblichus and Herodian: in the absence of a known novelist Herodian it might be that the name is a corruption

---

reaffirmed by Bowersock (1994) 149-160. Much turns on whether the description of the siege works at Nisibis by the Syriac term *talâla* (plural of *tall*) assimilates them to or differentiates them from the *chomata* of Heliodorus 9.3. I am not competent to pronounce. But even if the terms describe the same phenomenon, that simply removes an argument for seeing Julian as dependent on Heliodorus and does not constitute an argument for the reverse relation. Heliodorus' interest in cataphracts (157-60) does indeed match their fourth-century prominence, but the armed cavalryman goes back at least as far as Crassus' debacle at Carrhae in 53 B.C. (as of course Bowersock concedes).

[20] Bowersock (1994) 150-60.
[21] E.g. Varro *de Lingua Latina* 5.100, Pliny, *Hist.Nat.*8.69.
[22] *Hist.Eccl.*5.22.

of Heliodorus, with whom Iamblichus and Achilles Tatius are grouped by Photius.[23]

Between its second-century composition and this mention by Photius in the latter half of the ninth century influence of Achilles Tatius' *Leucippe and Cleitophon* has been detected only in one text, Musaeus' *Hero and Leander* (?ca. 470). Musaeus is a learned poet, well deserving the epithet γραμματικός given him by his manuscripts.[24] The second- and third-century owners of papyri of Achilles Tatius may indeed not have been so learned, but given the similarity of their books to those of high literature, we have no warrant for supposing that they were from a significantly less-educated stratum.

2a The "Early" Novels: Intended Readership

Of all the issues discussed in this chapter this is perhaps the one most fought over and least susceptible of a confident answer. The early novels' sentimentality and preference for simpler forms of narrative have led scholars to suppose they were aimed at some class other than the readers of high literary texts—whether women, children, or simple a lower social and cultural level of reader (the alleged silence concerning novels in higher literary genres has reinforced this position, but of course it bears not on intended but actual readers, and is discussed below under **2b**). In an earlier discussion I have drawn attention to the limited number of women likely to have been educated to a level at which they could both read literary texts with ease and appreciate allusions in them to earlier literature, and have stressed that the importance of such allusions in Chariton (and their presence in *Metiochus and Parthenope*) points rather to the same sort of reader who read classical texts and contemporary writers such as Plutarch.[25]

Tomas Hägg (1994) has recently advanced important criticisms of these arguments and restated the case for a wider audience—not simply, that is, a wider readership, but aural access to novels by

---

[23] Theodorus Priscianus, *Euporista* 2.11.34 (133 Rose) (a Latin translation by Theodorus of his own Greek text), Photius *Bibliotheca Codex* 94, 73b: cf. Bowie (1994b) 457 n. 55.

[24] 1.4 is the chief model for expressions in lines 58, 92, 96, cf. Orsini (1968) vi–xvii; Kost (1971) 29ff.

[25] For further discussion of literary influences on and allusions in Chariton see the excellent article of Hunter (1994), and for citation in the novelists in general Fusillo (1990c).

audiences who either lacked literacy or found it tedious to activate, and who listened while another read aloud.

Many of Hägg's points have considerable force. It is fair, for example, to insist that the survival of positive evidence for certain sorts of readers cannot establish the non-existence of other sorts of reader for whom our surviving witnesses would be unlikely to offer testimony. It is also fair to insist that a work may be intended to entertain on several levels, or may actually do so, and that "the narrative suspense, the emotional impact, the escapist function were there for all, the rhetorical and classicizing embellishment for some"[26] and so that Chariton may have had several different audiences in mind.

Some other points made by Hägg strike me as less convincing. In support of a female readership he lays stress on "the early novels' preoccupation with women—particularly evident in *Callirhoe* and *Parthenope*—and with psychology, sentiments and private life." The problem remains that a considerable interest in all these subjects can well be supposed of a male readership, and certainly the classical Greek male poet who has often seemed to critics ancient and modern to have shown especial interest in women's psychology, Euripides, composed and produced his plays for audiences that were predominantly or—in my view—wholly male. It is one thing to demonstrate, as Hägg rightly judges that Brigitte Egger (1988) has, that novel heroines are described in a way that would make them suitable objects of identification for women in the Roman empire, relatively more emancipated than those of classical Greece, and another to show that a novelist had such women in mind as a significant element in his readership.

Another point seen by Hägg to support a "partly, some would say predominantly, female audience" is the phenomenon that the early novels' heroines are "sympathetically drawn and altogether more alive than their pale husbands and lovers."[27] It is perhaps dangerous to claim this for the shadowy Parthenope (and on present evidence the claim could not be extended to Semiramis) though it is certainly true of Callirhoe and Anthia: but it is also, unfortunately, true of Charicleia in Heliodorus' *Aethiopica*, a work that Hägg agrees to envisage a predominantly male readership. An explanation for the relative weakness of the hero and strength of the heroine in terms of the novels'

---

[26] Hägg (1994) 54.
[27] Hägg (1994) at n. 43.

internal dynamics that applies to the genre as a whole has recently been offered by David Konstan and if accepted would make an explanation in terms of prospective readers redundant.[28]

Hägg's main arguments, however, are drawn from the style and form of the early novels, on the basis of which he had already in 1971 formulated his hypothesis that the early novels were intended for "oral" delivery.[29] The four key features are these:

(a) stereotyped linking phrases between episodes which summarise preceding action in a clause with the particle μέν and begin the new action with a δέ clause. As examples Hägg notes Chariton 4.2.1 and Xenophon 2.14.1.

As Hägg points out, however, these devices are found throughout Greek narrative prose, and their presence in such texts as that of Thucydides makes it hard to associate their use with intended oral performance, even if they may originally have been welcomed into Greek narrative at a time when that was oral (our earliest instances are of course in Homer).

(b) Recapitulations of earlier events, in Xenophon mostly in indirect speech (Hägg notes 3.3.1), in Chariton either in a character's words or reflections (e.g. 2.5.10, 8.7.8) or in his own authorial voice—above all 5.1.1–2, but also more briefly, and combined with foreshadowing, at 8.1.1).

(c) Foreshadowing (of which 8.1.1 is but one example).

Hägg concludes that "This whole apparatus of repetitive material must have some kind of functional explanation" and he finds this explanation in the hypothesis that the novels were intended for "people who had not yet moved definitely from orality to literacy, i.e. to inexperienced readers, or to listeners."[30] Of course it may be wrong to suppose that all these features—and others that Hägg goes on to consider, (c) and (d) below—are correctly to be subjected to the same explanation. The μέν ... δέ transitions, for example, might, as I suggest above, be there for a different reason. As to Chariton's recapitulations at the beginnings of books, Hägg himself notes the relevance

---

[28] Konstan (1994a) esp. 3–59. Konstan himself suggests (78) that the presence of implied male and female audiences within the novel may be Chariton's way of suggesting a complex readership for his work.
[29] Hägg (1971a) ch. 7, and the oral hypothesis at 332.
[30] Hägg (1994) at n. 50.

of the appearance of such recapitulations in our manuscripts of Xenophon's *Anabasis* (at the beginnings of books 2, 3, 4, 5 and 7), recapitulations which Chariton and his readers probably had in their texts. At least part of their function, then, may be to corroborate Chariton's historiographic pose; another is to reinforce the sense of closure with which Chariton clearly seeks to mark the ends of his books.[31]

I would suggest too that the most striking example of recapitulation, that which occupies 17 lines in the Budé text at 5.1.1, may serve the same function as was presumably served by the interpolated summaries in Xenophon, i.e. to offer orientation to readers who had access only to the roll or rolls which began with that book-opening and not to earlier rolls. Chariton may have felt a particular need to place such a full recapitulation at the beginning of book five. In literary terms, it is the mid-point of the work. From a codicological point of view (if this technical term can be transferred to a discussion of *volumina*) the chances that book five would begin on a new roll must be high. On the one hand our extant and attested novels (Xenophon and Longus excepted) are too long to fit on one roll (not surprisingly the beginning of our Oxyrhyncus papyrus roll of Antonius Diogenes was also the beginning of a book, probably book four).[32] On the other hand more than one book *could* be accommodated on a roll, as the fragments of Lollianus, spanning three books, show. Chariton's 150 Budé pages would certainly exceed one roll, but could be comfortably divided between two. A weaker form of this argument could be offered in terms of where a reader who had access to a complete set of rolls of Chariton's novel might most likely pause. The format of division into books encourages such pauses to be at the end of books, so that a reader resuming the reading of the work after a pause (of minutes? hours? days?) might welcome reminder of the story-so-far at the beginning of a book.

The stronger version of this explanation cannot be offered for 8.1 (unless we were to suppose that Chariton envisaged each book occupying a separate roll, which I would not). Here, however, the function must be taken alongside that of the foreshadowing which immediately follows (8.1.2–5). Now it must be agreed that if Chariton did

---

[31] On the historiogaphical frame see esp. Hunter (1994) 1056–64, and on closure at book-ends 1064 with n. 43.
[32] *P.Oxy.*42.3012, ed. P.J. Parsons.

envisage "inexperienced" readers, or listeners who lacked the opportunity to remind themselves of how the story had developed, both the recapitulation and the foreshadowing could have a specific function in relation to them. However it is also clear that the way in which such foreshadowing raises the dramatic temperature can be as rewarding for experienced as for "inexperienced" readers. It is not only "inexperienced" readers whom suspense and increased expectations encourage to continue reading. Moreover the terminology of this case of foreshadowing, with its apparent allusion to the *catharsis* theory of Aristotle's *Poetics*,[33] seems to be aimed to some extent at a well-educated reader.

These recapitulations and foreshadowings may, then, be an indication that Chariton envisaged "inexperienced" readers, but it is not an unambiguous indication. It might also be observed that if Hägg's model of an individual reading aloud to a group is adopted, we lose one constraint which may have generated recapitulations in genuinely oral performances, i.e. the lack of opportunity (in theory always open to a solo reader) to go back to check what has happened in earlier parts of the text: an individual reading aloud to others can always be asked to go back and check (as many parents must know!). Moreover we should remember that such checking is much harder for users of rolls than for users of codices: thus even for a solo reader, of whatever level of experience, recapitulations have a useful function.

(d) Hägg also adduces in favour of an "inexperienced" readership the stereotypical phraseology that is especially noticeable in Xenophon and the stereotypical scenes, motifs and plots that characterise the whole genre. That the latter mark even the "sophistic" novels naturally weakens their force as indicators of inexperienced readers, and since many "high" genres of ancient Greek literature also have stereotypical scenes and motifs I doubt if they can be given much weight. The stereotypical phraseology of Xenophon is another matter: perhaps Hägg's explanation should be considered seriously, but it must compete with the more common view that such phraseology is part of a broader limitation in Xenophon's literary skills.[34] Even if the explanation is to be linked to features of "oral" narrative, it remains possible that these are present either because the early novels are

---

[33] καθάρσιον γάρ ἐστι, 8.1.4, cf. Hunter (1994) 1070.
[34] See also Zanetto (1990).

successors of oral narratives or that they are consciously evoking them.[35]

2b The "Early" Novels: Actual Readership

In the Greek world the papyri are again our first witnesses. Our earliest Greek evidence for the "ideal" romance remains the *Ninus* fragments, written on a papyrus whose verso bears accounts of A.D. 101, while the hand of the novel text itself seems to belong between 50 B.C. and A.D. 50. Our four papyri of Chariton stretch unevenly from the mid-second century (P. Michaelides 1, P. Fayum 1) through the third (*P.Oxy.*1019 + 2948) to Wilcken's codex of ca. 600. The *Chione* story that was also on that ill-fated codex also looks like an "early" novel. The other work in this group, *Parthenope and Metiochus*, is represented by two papyrus rolls, both late second century, and by an ostracon (*Bodl.* 2175). Once again it is worth stressing that the books here represented are similar to the texts of classical authors. It has been claimed that the ostracon is different: Kurt Treu, whose scholarly integrity was never compromised by his DDR environment in Berlin, took the ostracon as one of the few pieces of evidence for the impact of the novel on classes lower than the educated élite.[36] Perhaps he was right, but ostraca were used for a wide range of purposes, high and low, and the appearance of a literary text on an ostracon does not establish that its owner was of a lower social class. That is certainly unlikely to have been true of the owner of the ostracon which preserved Sappho fr. 2, who must have had a taste and a capacity to read difficult Lesbian poetry. The person who copied (or had copied) part of *Parthenope* onto an ostracon need have belonged to a social group no different from that to which those who owned papyrus rolls belonged.

There may also, however, be evidence that the early novels were known in the Latin world, evidence that may antedate the *Ninus* fragments. Niklas Holzberg has argued that Ovid's version of the Pyramus and Thisbe story in *Metamorphoses* (4.55–166) parodies the literary conventions both of New Comedy and of the "ideal" novel: the setting in adjacent houses and love between members of the families

---

[35] For oral features in Xenophon and Chariton see Scobie (1983) 32–5.
[36] Treu (1989) 192. Treu's terms are "Kreisen eines mittleren Bildungshöhe" and "auf soziale Unterschichten."

that occupy them are to be recognised as taking off New Comedy, while the flight from city to country and the decision to commit suicide on misleading evidence of a partner's death hints at the novel, with its exploitation of *Scheintod*, its impulsive and easily overwrought hero and heroine, and their commitment to a love unto death. The idea is an attractive one, but suicide-decisions on mistaken grounds are also found in earlier mythology, and although the fact that Ovid's couple dies can be seen as an unexpected reversal of the novel's convention whereby they improbably survive all manner of perils, it can also be argued to give so different a flavour to the story that any allusion to novels becomes difficult to pick up. I regard the case as not proven. But if Holzberg is right, then we have not just our earliest hard *terminus ante quem* for the composition of novels (the first years of our era) but evidence that its readers in the Latin West included both Ovid and (on Ovid's calculation) those people whom he expected to entertain with his *Metamorphoses*—the one a poet as *doctus* as any and the others people of substance and culture.

Again, if Holzberg is right, then the case is strengthened for seeing Persius' half-line *post prandia Callirhoen do* (1.134) as alluding to recitation from a novel, our *Chaereas and Callirhoe*. It need hardly be said that both the audience of a recitation such as the *eques Romanus* Persius imagines and the readership he is likely to have conceived for his rebarbative satires (composed in the years immediately preceding his death in A.D. 62) belong well up the economic and cultural scale.

If doubts remain about Ovid and Persius, it is harder to maintain them for Petronius. Although Petronius parodies the *Odyssey* and, from time to time, other established genres, his *Satyrica* arguably (if again unprovably) also either parodies the ideal romance, with the pair Encolpius and Giton a deformation of that genre's hero and heroine, or draws on a Greek comic version of the genre (like the *Iolaus*) that does. In either case a Roman of the writing classes in the reign of Nero emerges as a fancier of one or other sort of Greek novel, and as a writer who expects *his* readers to appreciate the parody.

Our next candidates for witnesses to knowledge of the early novels are from the Severan period. Two mosaics from a substantial house in Antioch's hill-suburb, Daphne, depict Metiochus and Parthenope, clearly identified by name; a third depicts Ninus looking at a portrait, identifiable by its similarity to a mosaic portrait from nearby Alexandria ad Issum labelled "Ninus". However since Lucian links

Ninus and Metiochus as (it seems) characters in some form of theatrical performance, and since one of the two mosaics of Metiochus and Parthenope depicts them standing on a level surface most plausibly interpreted as a stage, it is perhaps more likely that the owner of the house knew the three characters from theatrical performances, presumably mimes, than from reading novels.[37] If, however, the novels played a part in his interest, we have here a man from the propertied classes who could, like Petronius' Trimalchio, be deficient in education, but is more likely to belong to the well-educated.

It is one of this man's best-educated contemporaries, Philostratus, who affords us what is probably our first glimpse of Chariton outside Egypt. In *Letter* 66 he attacks a Chariton whose claim to distinction in λόγοι makes him hard to dissociate from the novelist:

> Χαρίτωνι
> Μεμνήσεσθαι τῶν σῶν λόγων οἴει τοὺς Ἕλληνας ἐπειδὰν τελευτήσῃς. οἱ δὲ μηδὲν ὄντες, ὁπότε εἰσιν, τίνες ἂν εἶεν ὁπότε οὐκ εἰσίν;

> To Chariton
> You think that the Greeks will remember your words when you are dead; but those who are nobodies when they are alive, what will they be when they are dead?

As in his critical reference to Plutarch in *Letter* 73, Philostratus treats as if alive a writer who is long dead. As he must see, his claim that Chariton will not be remembered is falsified both by his very mention of him and by his assumption that his readers will know who this is. We may infer that Philostratus expected these readers to share a low literary evaluation of Chariton—though even that inference may be questioned—but we must also conclude that they were expected to know enough about Chariton to understand why it was witty to write in these terms about him.

---

[37] For a fuller discussion Bowie (1994b) 448–9. The Daphne mosaics are published by Levi (1947) vol. 1, 117–9, vol. 2 pll. xx, cviif.; cf. Levi (1944) 420–8; that from Alexandria ad Issum is discussed on p. 118. See further Maehler (1976) 1–20; Quet (1992) 125–60. The Lucian text is *Pseudologistes* 25. That plots or characters might appear both in the mime and the novel may contribute to the linking of Antonius Diogenes and the mime composer Philistion by Epiphanius *Adv.haer.*1.33.8 = *Patrologia Graeca* 41.568, cf. below **3b**.

3a Other Novels: Intended Readership

Antonius Diogenes is said by Photius to have written a preface in which he dedicated his 24-book Τὰ ὑπὲρ Θούλην ἄπιστα to his sister Isidora. This is perhaps the only ancient evidence that supports the hypothesis of a female readership, envisaged or actual, for a Greek novel, and it should at least be admitted as evidence that Antonius and his readers might imagine an educated woman (she is described as φιλομαθῶς ἔχουσα) as a reader of τὰ ἄπιστα. But this dedication was stated in a letter not to Isidora herself but to one Faustinus (perhaps her husband, so Antonius' brother-in-law) and at least one of her functions may be to stand for the avid but gullible reader who will take Antonius' elaborated authenticated and encyclopaedic information at face value, contrary to his indication to Faustinus that he is a fabricator of the fantastic in the tradition of Old Comedy.[38] The more plausible target remains the male reader to whom the term Old Comedy was meaningful and who was familiar enough with encyclopaedic writers given to citing their sources (in the manner of the Elder Pliny) to appreciate literary humour at their expense.

The *Metamorphoses* which Photius took to be by Lucius of Patrae, and which (with some other scholars) I think likely to be the work of Lucian, had a lower moral tone than either Antonius Diogenes or the apparently typical "ideal" novels and, as far as can be told from Photius' epitome, showed no sign of these works' recurrent urge to purvey recondite knowledge. We might, therefore, more readily suppose that its author envisaged a rather lower level of readership, and certainly less elevated than we know it actually got (below **3b**). The similarity of some of its narrative to Milesian tales (signalled by Apuleius in the prologue of his Latin adaptation) may entitle us to recall Plutarch's story of the copy of Aristides' *Milesian Tales*, allegedly found in a Roman's kit after the battle of Carrhae,[39] and the fact that Aristides' work was translated into Latin by Sisenna, probably the historian who was *praetor* in 78 B.C.[40] Reading of *Milesian Tales* might be lambasted as immoral (as it is by Epictetus[41] as well as by Plutarch) but both Plutarch and Arrian expect their readers to know the work, and its Latin translator was of praetorian rank. Lucian

---

[38] See Photius *Bibliotheca, Codex* 166, 111a30, and more fully Bowie (1994b) 437–8.
[39] Plutarch, *Crassus* 32.4–6.
[40] Ovid, *Tristia* 2.443–4 cf. 413–4.
[41] Arrian, *Diss.Epicteti* 4.9.6.

may have expected some less well-educated readers, but he is unlikely to have excluded πεπαιδευμένοι.

It may be right to group Lollianus' *Phoenikika* and the prosimetric Iolaus with the *Metamorphoses*. Sensationalism and a coarser treatment of sex certainly separates them from the "ideal" novels, and Lollianus' failure to avoid hiatus may corroborate a tentative inference that here we come nearer than elsewhere to a work written for readers who, though literate, were not from the well-educated élite.[42]

3b Other Novels: Actual Readership

For two, rather different novels in this broad category we have some indication of actual readership. For Egypt two papyri, one of the second or third century, the other no earlier than A.D. 200, attest readers (or would-be-readers) of Antonius Diogenes.[43] Rather earlier it may be that Lucian read Antonius Diogenes and exploited some of his ideas in his *True Histories*. So Photius thought (*Bibliotheca, Codex* 166), but the relationship has been forcefully challenged by Morgan (1985), and at the least the absence of Antonius Diogenes' name from Lucian's text might be taken to indicate that he could not rely on his readers to recognise that author or his work.

By the middle of the third century, however, Antonius Diogenes is being used by Porphyrius of Tyre in his *Life of Pythagoras*.[44] In the second half of the fourth century Epiphanius brackets him with the writer of mimes, Philistion, as a byword for incredible invention.[45] Soon after Servius refers to him when commenting on the reference to Thule by Vergil at *Georgics* 1.30;[46] and about the same time Synesius of Cyrene refers to Thule as a place about which untestable fictions

---

[42] For the sensationalism cf. Winkler (1980a); for the relation to Apuleius, C.P. Jones (1980). For hiatus see Reeve (1971b).

[43] *PSI* 1177 (no earlier than A.D. 200), *P.Oxy*.3012: this latter from a very handsomely set out book roll (Stephens) and assigned to second/third century by its first editor (Parsons). *P.Mich.* inv. 5 (a magician's speech) has also been claimed for Antonius Diogenes by Reyhl (1969) 14–20 but is not accepted by Fusillo (1990b) or by Stephens and Winkler (1995).

[44] Porphyrius, *Opuscula selecta*, ed. A. Nauck (Leipzig 1886), *Vita Pythagorae* sections 10–17, 32–47, 54–5, cf. Reyhl (1969).

[45] *Adv.haer*.1.33.8 = *Patrologia Graeca* 41.568.

[46] Stephens and Winkler (1995) *ad loc*. suggest that Servius' ascription of wonders concerning Thule to Sammonicus may indicate that Servius' knowledge of Antonius came to him *via* Sammonicus. If so Serenus Sammonicus (murdered A.D. 212) rather than Servius becomes his earliest Latin reader.

circulate, a reference easiest understood if he expects his readers to recognise a particular work (and has knowledge of it himself). The final testimony before Photius is that of John the Lydian in his work *On Months*.[47]

Although of course (as always) this documentation of readers (only one of them dismissive) drawn from the educated classes cannot show that other and less well educated people did not read Antonius Diogenes, it at least demonstrates that he *was* known among these classes. It is unfortunate that the papyri of the *Iolaus* narrative and of Lollianus cannot establish to what class their readers belonged.

For the *Metamorphoses* of Lucius we can be certain only of two readers before Photius: the compiler of the epitome that has been transmitted in the works of Lucian, and the Platonist philosopher who was the nearest thing in Latin culture to a Greek sophist, Apuleius of Madaurus. Of course they cannot be seen as typical readers, since each had a special purpose, to create a new literary work on the basis of the *Metamorphoses*. But it is of some relevance to the question of whether the novels were known or "recognised" in elevated literary circles that Apuleius should have encountered the *Metamorphoses* at all; and it might be argued that the perception of the compiler of the epitome, entitled Λούκιος ἢ Ὄνος, that there were certain readers for whom the full-length *Metamorphoses* was too long or complicated, offers some support to the view that the *Metamorphoses* was being tackled by readers with greater pretensions as well as to the view that there were other potential readers lower down the cultural scale for whom it was too challenging.

III

What conclusions can be drawn from the evidence and arguments set out above?

As to the "sophistic" novels, I would conclude that they were principally intended for and chiefly read by well educated readers. Less educated readers may in fact have attempted them, and some may have persevered, though their level of appreciation of the texts must have been different from that of the former group.

---

[47] Johannes Lydus, *De mensibus*, ed. R. Wünsch (Leipzig 1898) 3.5, 4.42 (with specific ref. to Bk. 13).

Of our surviving "early" novels that of Chariton comes closest to the "sophistic" novel in its exploitation of allusion to classical texts (*Metiochus and Parthenope* may not have been far behind) and I would not doubt that Chariton aimed at and reached well-educated readers. It is also possible that he both expected and got less educated readers, but the nature of our evidence is such that we cannot expect these readers to be documented even in the haphazardly selective way that our more elevated readers are documented, and the argument must depend on indications within Chariton's text, indications that are susceptible of different explanations.

The different character of Xenophon's work—the fact that it is not similarly dependent on allusion to classical literature, its stereotyped phrases and its unsophisticated and sometimes clumsy use of stereotyped motifs—may point to a rather lower level of reader: but not, I suspect, dramatically lower, and any scholar who holds that we have only an epitome of a longer original may postulate that that original was better fashioned and aimed at a more exacting class of reader than the supposed epitome. I remain sceptical about the hypothesis that novels might have been read aloud to illiterates or "inexperienced" readers, but if any of our extant complete texts was intended or exploited for this purpose Xenophon's work is a better candidate than Chariton's.

Of other novels Antonius Diogenes' 24 books seem intended rather for the light relief of the πεπαιδευμένοι than for the bafflement of simpler readers, and there is adequate evidence that he was indeed read by the πεπαιδευμένοι. I suspect—but we are back with guesswork—that Lucian destined his *Metamorphoses* for the same class of reader as his other works, but that the epitome Λούκιος ἢ Ὄνος may be going for a slightly different market, one for which Lollianus and the author of the *Iolaus* were also catering. I would be reluctant, however, to come far down the economic scale, or to shift the likely target group from adult male either to female or to juvenile readers. Of the diverse novels considered one might well expect an example of any category to have been in Cleitophon's hands in that early scene in Achilles Tatius: but, had the reader been Leucippe and not Cleitophon, I would be as surprised to learn that it was from the last and most lubricious class as that it was one of the more learned and allusive texts that Achilles himself writes. More likely, if Leucippe had been presented reading a novel at all, that of Xenophon, or, if Leucippe were as educated as Parthenope or Charicleia (which Achilles does not tell us that she is!) that of Chariton.

5. POPULAR AND SOPHISTICATED IN THE ANCIENT NOVEL

Graham Anderson

The ancient novel has a strong claim to be regarded as part of the history of popular storytelling, however the latter might itself be defined. The genre has a humble place in any hierarchy of genres, if indeed it should be felt to have a place at all; and the three sophisticated products of extended romantic storytelling in prose are all from the Roman Imperial period.[1] But beyond that point we can expect less unanimity from scholars on the character of popular narrative itself, or on the ways we can attempt to relate it to the novels we have: does popular narrative consist in theme and outlook as well as style of narration? Is it possible to construct any scale from popular to sophisticated among the extant materials? Is the former to be equated with "folktale", taking on the methods of what has long been established as an autonomous discipline? And what if anything is its contribution to the perennial question of "origins" of the novel?

I. *Cultural Horizons*

We may find that a negative approach is useful in the first instance; it may be easier to say what popular narrative is not, or what it might be relied upon to avoid. The first characteristic to my mind might be "unawareness of education or high culture", and of the self-consciousness which that awareness confers on the narrator. A popular narrator will deal with basic experiences of a very simple civilisation. A writer might think of calls of nature rather than theatres or schools: in Greek terms, the thought-world of Hesiod at most. One does not expect that Aesopic fables will mention schoolmasters or scribes.

Moreover popular subject-matter might be associated with some

---

[1] Relevant discussions embrace a large cross-section of the recent novel bibliography as a whole, but are not always focussed directly on these terms, e.g. Perry (1967) 98–101; Hägg (1983); Anderson (1984) 136–151 (juxtaposing Longus and Xenophon as "sublime" and "subliterary"; Holzberg (1986); Kuch (1989a).

elementary notion of a repertoire: the kind of things "people" think about, talk about, or do—or might be thought to like to. Such a repertoire would embrace what in a modern society might be the subject of television soaps, pulp novels, or tabloid newspapers: love, marriage, adultery, melodramatic disasters, and the like.[2]

At the same time one looks for limitations in the storyteller's means of execution. One expects a certain clumsiness, particularly in matters of organisation: a popular narrator will tend on the whole simply to add episodes in a linear way, without a great deal of concern for the overall shape of his narrative. He may have difficulty in matters of language and style, or stylistic consistency and congruity. Lastly, one looks also for a certain naivety of outlook, tending to indulge in simple direct emotions such as pathos or anger, with a strong sense of polarisation between good and bad, or right and wrong.

Nor dare we say that "sophisticated" is easy to define either, though we shall always tend to assume that we know what we mean by it. Again this is largely connected with notions of education and high culture, including differentiation of highly literary language. One of the most obvious traits of the three "sophistic" novels is their sophistication:[3] while schools as such do not figure prominently in the actual subject-matter, the notion that the *Liebespaar* have the best possible education certainly does, and there will be at least secondary characters, if not the hero himself, to maintain digressions or other show-pieces to establish the whole business of connoisseurship.[4] In this respect the author of *Daphnis and Chloe* has a special problem, insofar as the exposure of infants and upbringing among peasants compromises their educational prospects; but as usual in Longus the author is able to find an elegant way of side-stepping the problem: the couple are given a proper education (i.e. at least they are taught to read and write)[5] because of auspicious dreams for their future. The summit of sophistication will often be seen in an author's ability to smile at the most sophisticated educational pretentions: Achilles is perhaps

---

[2] Useful orientation from a cultural perspective e.g. in Reardon (1974) 23–29, who notes the popularity of sophistic literature itself, and the relative respectability and stylistic pretention even at the lower end of the sophistic romances (27f.).

[3] That of Achilles, Longus, and Heliodorus is well underlined in a trio of monographs from the turn of the last decade: Fusillo (1989); Billault (1991a); and Reardon (1991).

[4] Anderson (1984) 43–61.

[5] Longus 1.8.1.

not wholly supportive of the pretentions of Clitophon's wooing of Leucippe with highly recondite mating habits of poisonous snakes, nor Petronius of Encolpius' melodramatic and overeducated soliloquies.

The other criteria applied to popular narrative can of course be reversed in turn: subtlety rather than directness of outlook, with skilful use of irony or humour;[6] complex, convoluted and competently managed narrative with ambitious structural features; and the absence of naive emotional preoccupations, at least on the part of the author.

A further criterion of sophistication is the ability to present "the popular" from the outside, by showing detached amusement at those perceived to be culturally inferior. Writers require considerable sophistication before they can set out to present the horizons of the uneducated: the very structure of the plot in *Daphnis and Chloe* calls for a certain detachment on the part of the writer from the life of the peasants among whom his *Liebespaar* have found themselves. The *locus classicus* of sophisticated narrative in this sense is the freedmen's conversations in Petronius, not least in its perception of the subliminal popular hostility to the pretentions of the educated when exacerbated by a generation gap, as in Hermeros' criticism of Giton.

II. *The Popular in Practice*

We can go through a cross-section of fictional narratives noting what seem to be obvious "popular" characteristics in each case. The two romantic novels closest to the "popular" world are unquestionably Xenophon of Ephesus' *Anthia and Habrocomes*[7] and the anonymous Latin *Apollonius of Tyre*.[8] In the case of Xenophon we might wish to draw some distinction between "popular" subject-matter and simple inferior workmanship.[9] There is, for example, an attempt at anticipatory ecphrasis, a technique which sophisticated novelists are able to operate with distinction. But in particular the unresourceful use of language, the taste for melodrama, and the rather indifferent grind

---

[6] Apart from Anderson (1982), see now G. Bretzigheimer (1988) 515–555.
[7] Cf. Dalmeyda (1926) xxvii ("physionomie de conte populaire").
[8] For characterization see now E. Archibald (1991) (on education, learning and riddles, 22–26). Kortekaas (1984) 4, approves Enk's characterization of the work as a fairy-tale. But where are the fairies, or their equivalent?
[9] Cf. Anderson (1984) 144–148.

of inconsequential adventures tend to betray a popular taste as well. The case is perhaps more clear-cut in the case of *Apollonius of Tyre*. Here there is actually a teacher-pupil relationship, a feature which on our initial criterion should mark out a sophisticated novel; but the fact that the princess is merely at school level rather than studying declamation or philosophy confirms the crudity of the storyteller's conception.[10] Again an actual literary inset, such as an ambitious paraphrase of Virgil, confirms the crudity of the operation still further by its sheer clumsiness and its isolation in such a text.[11] So, more markedly, does the inclusion of a set of riddles almost in defiance of the logic of the plot.

But the horizons of what can be seen as "popular" extend well beyond the relatively stereotyped formulae of the sentimental romantic love-and-travel plot. It is only when we come to the so-called *Aesop-romance* that we come face to face with unsophistication in its most direct and undiluted form.[12] Here at last is a *Volksbuch* whose written form does virtually nothing to disguise its oral character: this is often little more than an assembly of "did-you-hear-the-one-about?" stories, which appear to have agglutinated round a central core rather than to have been shaped into a story with any sense of form. And we have the language to match: a vulgar Greek with no pretence of aspiration to any standard of literary ambition. Here, too, we have a story shaped round a sympathetic character of obstinately lower-class origins, who is elevated to the level of a counsellor of the Samians or even of an adviser at Royal Courts, but not by any New Comic recognition machinery.

Here the image of the droll, disadvantaged underdog might be seen as a theme with guaranteed popular appeal: in the broadest sense such a figure embodies a paradigm of life with which any audience can identify. In the case of the *Alexander Romance*,[13] however, we can recognise a subject who is no less charismatic and for just the opposite reason. Alexander's attainment was unique enough for his achievements to be felt to reach the borderline between history and myth. And the reshaping of history attracts to itself a whole apparatus of characteristically popular materials: prophecies, proverbial

---

[10] *Historia Apollonii* 18–22, with the remarks of Archibald (1991) 22f.
[11] *Historia Apollonii* 11.
[12] One is especially grateful for Holzberg's variorum (1992a). For the social-historical implications for slavery itself, K. Hopkins (1993) 3–27.
[13] On its popularity, e.g. Hägg (1983) 125–153.

elements, wonder-narrative, trivial anecdotage; all these are juxtaposed in a relatively unassimilated form, as well as being invested with a crudely nationalistic pro-Egyptian angle.

III. *Some Shifting Borderlines?*

A number of the most central items serve to remind us that the contrast of popular and sophisticated is not always so straightforward. Even in the cases of Xenophon and *Apollonius of Tyre* we have a certain contrast between the natural level of the storyteller's competence and his literary ambition. One text however remains deservedly fascinating for its refusal to fall exclusively into the category of either popular or sophisticated, while still maintaining the impression of competence and consistency. Chariton's *Chaereas and Callirhoe* might well be seen as marking the very middle of the middle-brow: on the one hand the author can be seen as smiling at the mannerisms of social underlings, but maintaining a naive outlook in relation to the behaviour of a Persian King as if he were a character in New Comedy; and there is room for variety of interpretation as to the degree to naivety to be attached to the author himself.

On the other hand it should be stressed how often in our limited sample the most sophisticated authors fall back on quite clearly popular material. One need look no further than the ass-romance, where two essential components, *Cupid and Psyche* and the framing ass-romance itself, have all the appearances of popular tales. The accumulation of supernatural tales in the first three books of Apuleius' *Metamorphoses* alone is testimony to the very different ambience from the world of the ideal romances where magic is kept on the fringe. The one-time existence of two Greek versions of the frame-tale, the extant *Onos* and the lost *Metamorphoses*, reflect the vitality of a tale to be told in at times only slightly different versions.

Yet Apuleius' handling of his complex string of tales is no less artistic and sophisticated on that account, even if there is a certain carelessness about the overall organisation. And in the case of Petronius we can look at for example the tale of Niceros or the "Widow of Ephesus"; or in that of Achilles at his treatment of Conops and the exchange of fables. One has the impression that inset tales in particular are perhaps closer to the roots of popular narrative than the sometimes grandiose ensembles of which they are now a part.

There is a special point to noting Hägg's[14] argument vis-à-vis the *Parthenope Romance*, which he sees as transformed into a medieval vernacular *Romance of Bartanuba*. The extant portions of the former belong to a relatively sophisticated world: a philosopher present at a banquet, and conceptions of love that include scientific theory as opposed to the poetic notion of a winged Eros. The *Romance of Bartanuba* appears to be a Christian martyr-story based on such material. If this link is accepted we have a popular recycling of sophisticated material, though arguably in this case for a very specific and narrow purpose. But we also have a corresponding adaptation to a rather different cultural milieu.[15] Here we should suggest however that the transition from sophisticated to popular is not necessarily straightforward, for in a sense we have an instance of one popular motif supplanting another: with the disappearance of Metiochus from the Christian version we have the loss of the *Liebespaar* and a more aggressive reassertion of chastity than is already implied in the name Parthenope itself.

IV. *Future Prospects*

It should be plain enough that the traditionally clear-cut distinctions between sophisticated and popular overlap considerably, and while they remain obvious enough at either end of the spectrum, there is considerable room for typically inept experiment in the middle: *Apollonius of Tyre* and *Anthia and Habrocomes* in particular have authors less resourceful than their narrative ambitions require. And in the case of the sophisticated Latin comic novels we have bold experimentors who will allow sophisticated narrators to interact amusingly and incongruously with low life. It is worthwhile at this point to challenge the viewpoint of B.E. Perry on the general theory of

---

[14] Hägg (1984) 61–92.
[15] I have not attempted a systematic survey of where each single novel or fragment might be situated: *Joseph and Aseneth* is once again to be assigned within the ranks of the popular, as confirmed by the story's particularly fruitful transmission: see now Burchard (1986) 543–667. It should also be seen in the context of the burgeoning popularity in the Near East of erotic stories about Joseph and Potiphar's wife, culminating in *Yusuf and Zuleikha*. Philostratus' work on Apollonius is discussed elsewhere in this volume: for its relation to this theme, pp. 614ff. The *Phoenikika* might well be seen to belong in this respect not too far distant from Xenophon of Ephesus on the one hand, for ghoulishness and general lack of taste, and to represent like *Iolaus* a distinctly "lower" version of picaresque narrative than Petronius.

romantic narrative: he allowed the crude polarisation into naive ideal romance and sophisticated comic narrative, with a correspondingly implied distinction in readership. Fiction need be no more like that than life itself.

A further challenge for the future is to relate the materials of the available fictional works to the staggering amount of data available in modern folktale. I shall argue elsewhere that some of the best-known fiction in antiquity can be related to often quite familiar folktales already known in antiquity. In particular it can be argued that the novels of Xenophon of Ephesus and Achilles Tatius, and the Tarsia-romance that forms the latter half of *Apollonius of Tyre*, embody or incorporate substantial parts of the story of Snowwhite (Aarne-Thompson Type 709). Examination of modern versions of the latter does not take long to show that robbers rather than seven dwarfs are just as characteristic companions of the heroine, and that the Grimm Brothers' version is very far from definitive of the type as a whole. Xenophon's heroine Anthia has companions Leucon (White) and Rhode (Rose); her envious rival is not a mirror-gazer as such, but is noneless named Manto ("prophetess"). And there were "snowwhites" in antiquity, although folklorists have not quite caught up with them: apart from several sketchy mythical versions with Artemis as the villain, there was one novel whose title is known, that of Chione, which embodies the name "Snowey" or the like in the title itself. It can also be argued that *Joseph and Aseneth*, *Daphnis and Chloe*, and Heliodorus' *Aethiopica* use plots related to ancient (and already widely divergent) versions of the Cinderella story represented in Aarne-Thompson Types 510/11 (of which Perrault's version is again far from typical): in all three cases versions of the story incorporate the critical recognition test of a maltreated heroine, as well as a number of unusual secondary features characteristic of the modern popular Cinderella complex as a whole. These identifications are complementary to my arguments that *Daphnis and Chloe* draws on the traditions of the Dumuzi myths,[16] since these can also be shown to embody a substantial stock of materials related to both tales. The aversion of recent decades of scholarship to "origins" need not stand in the way of showing that some stories are resilient enough to appear in the form of myth, folktale or novel indifferently, a matter not without consequence for the early history and nature of all three forms of narrative.

---

[16] Anderson (1984) 5–14 *passim*; and now (1993) 65–79.

6. CHARACTERIZATION IN THE ANCIENT NOVEL

Alain Billault

If the point of writing a novel is to communicate with the reader, then reference has to be made somehow in the story to the real world where he lives. Characterization provides a good example of this rule of the game. Characters do not exist in the real world, but they bear a relation to it. They represent real persons along lines that are specific to fiction.[1] Those lines belong to the core of the novelist's craft. In the ancient novel they are many and diverse. Greek novels represent the bigger part of the extant texts and therefore they will constitute the main basis of this study; but of course Latin novels will not be ignored. Greek and Latin novelists picture a crowd which they endow with specific attributes. To portray their characters as individuals, they grant them a social position, some personal features, and also compare them with prominent figures in literature, mythology and religion. As for the heroes, their individuality gradually emerges as the result of the adventures through which they are going before the eyes of the gods.

The Specific Attributes of the Whole Crowd of Characters

A girl and a boy who belong to good families and are wonderfully good-looking meet and fall madly in love. To the risk of their chastity and life, they endure many adversities. They are often forced to lead separate lives, but in the end they will be happy together ever after: this may be a correct abstract of the plot of the ancient novels, but it does not offer an accurate view of their world. As a matter of fact, these novels are crowded with characters[2] and the heroes are by no means all alone. They are often surrounded by many people who play major roles in their story and their characterization. Some of them are protagonists, others are extras.

---

[1] Ducrot and Todorov (1972). Jouve (1992), 9–11.
[2] Billault (1991), 121ff.

1) *Protagonists and Extras*

The protagonists stand in the foreground for a long time, and their role in the plot is prominent. To this kind, for instance, belong Dionysius, Mithridates and the king of Persia in Chariton's novel, Kalasiris, Thyamis, Knemon and Arsake in the *Aithiopika*, Philetas in *Daphnis and Chloe*, Hippothous in the *Ephesiaka* and Melite in Achilles Tatius. Others, such as the tyrant of Acragas who tricks Chaereas into believing that Callirhoe is unfaithful to him, Demainete, the adulterous and criminal woman who accuses Knemon of trying to murder his father, or Lampis who kidnaps Chloe for a short time, are just passing through the story. Each one of them has an important share in the development of the story, and the extras supply the décor.

Some of them appear as individuals, others only in groups. The heroes often rise from among a crowd of people who enhance their flashing presence. Chaereas and Callirhoe meet and fall in love at first sight, while the whole people of Syracuse are worshiping Aphrodite (1.1). In the *Ephesiaka* (1.2-3) Anthia and Habrocomes have the same experiences during the festival of Artemis that all the assembled Ephesians encounter. In the *Aithiopika* (2.34-3.6) the sacred embassy of the Ainianes in Delphi affords Charikleia and Theagenes an opportunity to meet in the temple of Apollo where the Delphians have gathered. The ensuing scene of love at first sight is very important in the novelistic tradition,[3] but we may also cite this moment as a model instance of the way in which the presentation of heroes is magnified. This is a recurrent feature of the novelists' narrative technique. In Chariton's novel Chaereas and Callirhoe undergo many adventures before the eyes of the crowd in Syracuse (1.1; 1.5.3ff.; 3.3.2ff.; 3.4.5; 8.6.2ff.), in Miletus (3.2.14ff.; 4.1.7ff.), in Persia (5.1.8) and in Babylon (5.3.6ff.; 5.5.8ff.; 6.1.1ff.; 6.2.1ff.). In the *Aithiopika* the unravelling of the plot takes place in the presence of the people of Meroe; in the *Ephesiaka* the Rhodians escort the heroes (1.12, 1-3; 5.13); in Achilles Tatius' novel (8.3-14) the Ephesians crowd together to attend the trial of Leukippe and Kleitophon. Even in Longus' pastoral novel where the characters are less numerous, rustic men and women admiringly surround Daphnis and Chloe as they gather the grapes (2.2.1-2). These crowds serve as a background against which the characters are made to stand out, and at various moments in their story virtues

---

[3] Rousset (1981).

of their nature are highlighted in those scenes. This is the main function of the extras, and the novelists often resort to it. But the distinction between protagonists and extras is not the only one we should make, if we want to be better acquainted with the crowd of characters. According to the part they are playing, some characters belong to types that preexisted the novel or were invented by the novelists.

2) *Types from the stage*

When the novel arose, the audience, thanks to Greek New Comedy and Latin Comedy, had become familiar with certain types of characters. Though some of the figures appearing in the ancient novel are derived from the tradition of the stage, the novelists do not limit themselves to mere borrowing.

In the ancient novel, for example, we do not find the typical youngster of New Comedy who is casual and careless and whose faults are redeemed by his pleasant nature. Neither the passionate lovers in the Greek novels nor the wandering profligates in the *Satiricon* resemble him; Lucius, the sharp and imaginative hero of the *Golden Ass*, does not fit the description. Other protagonists, such as Astylus, the landlord's son in *Daphnis and Chloe*, who visits the countryside to enjoy pleasures he cannot find in the city and behaves kindly to everyone (4.10ff.), come close to it. He reminds the reader of Sostratos in Menander's *Dyskolos*, Kleinias and Menelaos in Achilles Tatius' novel, and Knemon in the *Aithiopika*, all of whom come close to the type, but are still different from it: Kleinias and Menelaos are homosexual, and Knemon's adventures are too tragic to make one think of comedy.

Comedians often portray faithful slaves, such as Leucon and Rhode in the *Ephesiaka* and other servants who are loyal to their master and can cleverly and zealously help his love-affairs. Kleitophon's manservant Satyros and Dionysius' devoted maid Plangon belong to this type of the *servus callidus*. Thanks to Plangon's clever schemes, Dionysius succeeds in marrying Callirhoe. Other servants, however, are quite different: in the *Aithiopika* Thisbe and Kybele are skillful at achieving criminal goals and die violent deaths. They have nothing to do with comedy. On the other hand, the parasite is a well-known comic character.

Gnathon in *Daphnis and Chloe* typifies the parasite. He likes boys as well as food, but such is not the case with parasites on the stage. Gnathon has their gift of constant ostentation and is as eloquent and kind as they are. In Chariton's novel another parasite who bears no name is close to the tyrant of Acragas and helps him to lure Chaereas into a trap baited by jealousy (1.4). Thus Chariton and Longus borrow characters from the New Comedy, as does Achilles Tatius: Melite, the alleged widow who marries Kleitophon, is as eager, determined and smart as the heroines of any comedy. Lycaenion who initiates Daphnis into the mysteries of love also resembles them. We may also mention Araxus, the veteran soldier in the *Ephesiaka*, Arsinoe, the courtesan in the *Aithiopika*, and Callirhoe's wet nurse, all of whom may remind the reader of the actors on the comic stage. Thus we see that the novelists at times take their inspiration from the New Comedy without resorting to unadorned plagiarism. Some characters in novels are drawn close to comic types but do not duplicate them. Lastly, we should note that some types from comedy are seldom seen in the novels, but that all types of characters go into making up the crowds in the novels. Then too, the novelists delineate new types of characters.

3) *New types*

Contrary to the pitiful and cynical protagonists of the *Satiricon* and to Lucius, the witty adventurer of the *Golden Ass*, who are peculiar and unclassable characters, the heroes of the Greek novels belong to a type of their own. They are radiant with youth, and their exceptional beauty arouses admiration and desire within many men and women. They are well-bred and gifted and thus their misfortunes all the more stand out against their privileges. Adversity makes them complain and cry. Though superior to ordinary people, they turn out to be as vulnerable. Boys actually seem to be hurt more easily than girls. Chaereas is always on the brink of suicide, Daphnis and Kleitophon frequently shed tears, and Theagenes tends to despair. On the other hand, Callirhoe haughtily faces misfortune. After she has been sold to Dionysius, she does not allow him to suspect her real past (2.5.8). When the eunuch of the king of Persia utters some threats in order to compel her to bestow her favours upon his master, she does not waiver (6.7.8). Charikleia too can brave danger: she defies Arsake (8.8.5ff.) and, when she is back in Ethiopia and understands that she is in peril of being sacrificed, she resolutely carries out her plan to be recognized as the king's daughter and does not give in to panic. Love, however, is something else and becomes the most terrible ordeal for the heroes.

When they fall in love, the heroes feel vanquished. After he has seen Callirhoe, Chaereas is "like a hero mortally wounded in battle".[4] "You have won, Eros... You have set up a great trophy over the self-possessed Habrocomes,"[5] shouts the hero of the *Ephesiaka* after he has met Anthia. Passion strikes them down. Callirhoe, Anthia, Habrocomes and Charikleia lie in bed, wasting away. They are not aware anymore of who they are. When Chloe watches Daphnis bathing, she is upset, a feeling which will last until the end of the story (1.13-14). She kisses Daphnis who looks at her as if it were the first time. From this moment onwards, he will have no peace (1.17-18). Thus for the heroes passion equals suffering. Since all the subsequent misfortunes put obstacles in the way of their love, they are all the more cruel to them. They are tossed on the waves of adversity and carried away from their dear ones, first of all from their parents.

Mothers and fathers of heroes compose a new type of character in ancient novels. They are not all of the same rank: Charikleia is the daughter of the king of Ethiopia, Callirhoe's father is Hermocrates, the famous strategus of Syracuse. In Achilles Tatius' novel and in the *Ephesiaka* the heroes' parents are well-to-do people, just like Chloe's father in the *Pastorals*, and Daphnis' father is a landlord. But they all behave in exactly the same way towards their children. They do not oppose their children's love affairs. Hermocrates allows his daughter to marry his political enemy's son, when the people of Syracuse ask him to do so. The parents of Habrocomes and Anthia watch them waste away but quickly decide to arrange their marriage. The adoptive and the real parents of *Daphnis and Chloe* turn out to be equally caring. In the *Aithiopika* Kalasiris, whom we may consider the third adoptive father of Charikleia, helps her to flee with Theagenes, whom she will marry later with her real parents' consent. Leukippe and Kleitophon alone have trouble with their families, but theirs is a particular case: at the beginning of the story Kleitophon falls in love with Leukippe, who does not reciprocate, and therefore he is forced to seduce her. However, when his father encourages him to marry

---

[4] 1.1.7. Translation by B.P. Reardon, see Reardon (1989).
[5] 1.4.4. Translation by G. Anderson, see Reardon (1989).

his half-sister, the lovely Kalligone, he does not rebel against him nor does he disclose his true feelings. He just waits for the help of fate. As for Leukippe, her mother suspects her of sexual misbehaviour. But as soon as the youngsters get away, their parents consent to the marriage. While generations do not fight with each other in Greek novels, and parents do not oppose their children's feelings, but assume a noble attitude, the chief of the bandits usually does not cooperate.

The bandit is another type of character designed by the ancient novelists, and he is present in every Greek novel with the exception of *Daphnis and Chloe*. The outlines of his temper are easy to describe: he is prone to use violence, he falls passionately in love, and he has a tremendous ability to cope with new situations and frequently one cannot predict how he will behave. He rushes into the story to capture the heroes, holds them prisoners, and sometimes molests them: in the *Ephesiaka* (2.13.5), Anthia has a narrow escape from being sacrificed by Hippothous and his band. In Achilles Tatius' novel (3.15ff.), Leukippe experiences the same trial after she has fallen into the hands of the Boukoloi of the Nile. Later on in Xenophon of Ephesus' novel (4.6), Hippothous throws Anthia to wild dogs, but she contrives to tame them. In the end he takes care of her and falls in love with her, but respects her and returns her to Habrocomes. Other chiefs of bandits do not exercise such self-restraint: in the *Aithiopika* (1.30.4ff.), Thyamis despairs of his future and kills a girl he mistakes for Charikleia. He is in love with the latter and does not want her to live without him. Later on he will protect her and Theagenes as well who had previously been his prisoner. Eventually he turns out to be as honest a fellow as Hippothous. The reason why they behave so is that they both have become outlaws from respectable motives. Thyamis was unjustly deprived of a priesthood he was to inherit and therefore decided to revolt against society. Hippothous devoted himself to banditism after he had killed a man who was trying to attract his beloved boyfriend who later was drowned at sea. His life is in total disarray: his band is destroyed several times, but he resolutely gathers a new one and displays an ability to overcome failures and to adapt himself to the most diverse circumstances. In Chariton's novel Theron, the chief of the pirates who rescue and at the same time capture Callirhoe in her tomb, has the same adaptability, but he is a genuine criminal and never behaves honestly. On the other hand, the enforcer of the law may drift into evil.

This new character, a kind of ancient policeman, often happens to have two faces. First, he saves the heroes, then he threatens them. In the *Ephesiaka* (2.13.3ff.), Perilaus sets Anthia free and falls in love with her and at his urgent request, she promises to marry him. Though she decides to commit suicide on the day of the wedding, she will survive. Later on (5.4.4ff.) we see that Polyidus has less respect for her and wants to force her to sleep with him, but she wards off the danger by invoking the protection of Isis. In Achilles Tatius' novel, Charmides dies just in time not to become a menace to Leukippe, with whom he has become infatuated after he has saved her. Thus the enforcer of the law often assumes swiftly varying attitudes and may change the process of the story. He may also be unreliable when he uses his power: in the *Ephesiaka* (4.2.4ff.), Kyno denounces Habrocomes and the prefect of Egypt orders him to be executed. The gods save him and later on the prefect acknowledges that he is innocent, protects him, and orders Kyno to be executed. Chaereas goes through the same vicissitudes (4.2.5ff.): Mithridates, the Persian satrap, orders him to be crucified and later on becomes his friend. In both cases, the heroes at first are victims of the arbitrariness of power and then benefit by it. They save their life because they have the opportunity to speak to the men who had condemned them to death without even meeting them. But this picture must be tinged with brighter colours. The enforcer of the law also has good qualities. He is an honest man and an eloquent speaker and fears the gods: when Anthia invokes Isis, Polyidus stops threatening her, and the prefect of Egypt agrees to listen to Habrocomes because of the miracles that the Sun and the Nile have worked to save him. When Pan orders him to release Chloe, Bryaxis, the strategus of Methymnus, immediately obeys him (2.28.1). The most prominent enforcer of the law is Hermocrates in Chariton's novel. Shortcomings are not found in his nature, and he transcends the outlines of the type we are describing. Crowned with the glory of his victory over the Athenians, he appears to be the protector of his city, and his name is often invoked and symbolizes perfection itself.[6] The prefect of Egypt bears no name, but his title similarly signifies his power[7] and refers to the social system. The novelists also draw a picture of that system when they portray their characters.

---

[6] Billault (1989).
[7] Hägg (1971b) 31.

Character—Portraying in the Ancient Novel

To portray their characters as individuals, the novelists provide them with a social position and some personal features, and also compare them with gods and heroes and lead them to become identified with their adventures.

1) *Social position*

Many characters are defined by their social position. They are a part of a social system which appears not to be unlike the social reality of the Roman Empire. Many of them are wealthy and powerful. Some are rich landlords such as Dionysius in Chariton's novel, Dionysophanes in *Daphnis and Chloe* and Melite, Kleitophon's second wife. Others, such as the king of Persia in Chariton's novel or the king of Ethiopia in the *Aithiopika*, are reigning over oriental countries. There are also high-ranking Persian dignitaries, such as Mithridates in Chariton's novel and Oroondates in the *Aithiopika*, Greek and barbarian priests and Greek citizens in charge. To that list we must add many subordinate officials. The novelists sometimes differentiate between wealth and power and emphasize the former or the latter, but both are linked to one another. For instance, Dionysius is a rich man who faithfully serves the king of Persia, and who actually reminds the reader of the Greek elite of Ionia who support Roman rule in Asia Minor.[8] Thanks to those powerful characters, the novels bear a seal of aristocratic distinction. They dominate over a hierarchical world.

Aristocrats are surrounded by a large household where various grades can be distinguished. Administrators, such as Sosthenes in Melite's house and Phocas who runs Dionysius' estates are above the anonymous mass of servants in rank. Though other servants exercise no authority, the master trusts them: in Chariton's novel, Dionysius relies on Plangon. The places where the servants live are also hierarchical. In *Daphnis and Chloe* (4.19.1-2), Dionysophanes wants Daphnis to serve his son Astylus in town and means it as a promotion. There is also a hierarchy in the world of the bandits who seem to be living in a kind of counter-society which Xenophon of Ephesus, Achilles Tatius and Heliodorus strikingly describe.[9] Thus only a few

---

[8] Bowersock (1965), 86-8, 140-9.
[9] Billault (1991), 136ff.

characters live on their own. Among the humble we may mention Tyrrhenus and Aegialeus, the fishermen in the *Aithiopika* and the *Ephesiaka*. The learned professions scarcely figure in the plot of the novels: there are a few physicians in Achilles Tatius, Xenophon of Ephesus and Heliodorus, a philosopher in Chariton, some Egyptian scholars and a craftsman in the *Aithiopika*, a group of traders in the *Ephesiaka*. Several barristers and an actor appear in Achilles Tatius, a rhetor and a poet in Petronius. Between the wealthy and the humble, there is a wide gap. Freedmen hold noticeable places in the *Satiricon*. Their class played an important part in the Roman Empire but is practically ignored by the Greek novelists who seem to draw a somewhat faithful picture of the society of their time without providing its complete reproduction. Character-portrayal plays a part in creating this picture and also involves some personal features.

2) *Personal features*

The name comes first. The number of characters who bear a name is not the same in every novel. The ratio is 75% in the *Ephesiaka*, less than 50% in the *Satiricon*, about 33% in Chariton and Achilles Tatius, a little less in Apuleius and 25% in the *Aithiopika*. In *Daphnis and Chloe*, almost everyone bears a name. From those figures we must not draw hasty conclusions about the care the novelists use when throwing their characters into relief. It would be wrong to assume that the characters who bear no name are always poorly delineated whereas those who bear a name are always well drawn. Name, however, is essential for character-portraying most of the time. Chariton, for instance, discloses it before any other information.[10] Is the name in harmony or in contrast with the part the characters are playing? In the *Ephesiaka*, Habrocomes narrowly escapes death after he has been denounced as a murderer by a woman who has unsuccessfully tried to sleep with him. Her name is Kyno, which means "the whore" (3.12.3ff.). On the other hand, one of the pirates who takes the heroes prisoner is called Euxinus, that is to say "the hospitable" (1.15.3ff.). Thus Xenophon of Ephesus sometimes gives ironical names to his characters. It is a kind of game which belongs to the literary tradition of significant names that goes back to Homer. The other novelists play this game too. They sometimes define a character by

---

[10] Hägg (1972).

his name: in the *Aithiopika* Kalasiris bears the name of a long linen gown worn by initiates into mystery religions of the East. Therefore, he is first of all a priest, even if he has a personal and often surprising way of understanding his functions.[11] Petronius mocks significant names when he calls (36) Carver a servant who carves slices of meat. In the *Golden Ass*, the relation of the names of some characters to their parts in the plot is often complicated.[12] The hero's name, Lucius, presumably is connotative of light, but he will see the real light only at the end of the story (11.3ff.). Then he will escape darkness into which he had been thrust by the black magic of Photis, a servant whose name also symbolizes light, but a light of error and roaming.[13] However, the name of a character sometimes refers not to the part he is playing, but to the whole world of the story.

In *Daphnis and Chloe* the hero's adoptive mother is named Nape, that is to say "the girl from the small valley"; Nape's husband is Dryas, "the man of oak", and Chloe means "the growing green girl". Such a concentration of rustic names points to the pastoral world where the story takes place. The name of Daphnis is the novel's main symbol. Daphnis was a legendary shepherd whose name figures for the first time in a poem by Stesichorus,[14] and often appears in Theocritus' *Idylls* and in Vergil's *Eclogues*.[15] Thus, the name of the hero sets the story within the sphere of the pastoral tradition. Similarly Philetas, the old man who tells the heroes that Eros is taking care of them (2.3ff.), is the archetype of the shepherd as described by the poets. Moreover, he bears the name of a pastoral poet of the 3rd century B.C., and Theocritus admired him and may well have been inspired by him.[16] Philetas, the shepherd of myth, fell in love when he was young with Amaryllis who is a young girl we are told about in Theocritus' *Idylls* and in Vergil's *Eclogues*.[17] In those poems, there appears another shepherd named Tityrus,[18] and in Longus' novel Philetas' son is called Tityrus. This network of names points to the close connection between the story and the pastoral tradition. Thus

---

[11] Sandy (1982a), 65ff.
[12] Hijmans Jr., see Hijmans Jr. and van der Paardt (1978), 107–122.
[13] Sandy, see Hijmans Jr. and van der Paardt (1978), 136–7.
[14] Aelianus, *VH* 10.18.
[15] Theocritus 1,19ff.; 5,20,81; 6.7,72ff.; 8.9. *Ep*.2.3.5. Virgil, *Ecl*.2,26; 3,12; 5 *passim* 7,1,7; 8 *passim* 9,46,50.
[16] Bowie (1985b).
[17] Theocritus 3.4,38ff. Virgil, *Ecl*.1.2,14,52; 3,81; 8,77–78,101; 9,22.
[18] Theocritus 3,3–4; 7,72. Virgil, *Ecl*.3,20,96; 5,12; 6,4; 8,55; 9,23–24.

the name of a character may refer to something else than his part in the plot, but the characters also have other personal features.

With the exception of the heroes and some protagonists, the physiques of other characters are seldom and briefly described. On the other hand, the novelists often make psychological remarks. Sometimes, a character is defined only as good or bad. For example, Chariton emphasizes right away Theron's dishonesty (1.7.1), and Longus immediately states that Lamon is humane (1.3.1). But the novelists sometimes go deeply into the details of some natures. In Chariton's novel, for example, Dionysius' personality is described first by his administrator (1.11.6) and then by his maids (2.2.1). Chariton himself mentions other features (2.1.5; 2.3.3; 2.4.1 and 4), and then Dionysius draws a fragmentary self-portrait (2.4.4; 2.5.4). These successive remarks uttered by different people as the story develops provide the character with a true psychological existence. As traits are repeated, the image of a noble, virtuous and cultured man gradually emerges in the story. There are, however, shortcomings in Dionysius' character: he is in love with Callirhoe and resorts to lies in order to drive his rival Chaereas to despair (7.1.3–4). Because of this defect in character, his good qualities seem to be less unreal. Charikleia also displays imperfections: *Aithiopika* (6.8.3ff.): when she is alone and attends the unexpected marriage between Nausikleia and Knemon, she feels so miserable that she cannot bear the sight of their happiness. She locks herself in her room and gives way to despair, resentment and envy. We discover that this servant of Artemis, the sublime caring girl who graces the beginning of the story (1.2), the self-assured and resourceful heroine who steadily faces the events of her destiny[19] sometimes yields to mean feelings. Thus she comes close to ordinary people. Chariton and Heliodorus can picture characters whose nature is not a collection of stereotyped and unreal features, but a complex whole of various qualities and contradictions, which seems to be the real thing.[20] Xenophon of Ephesus, on the other hand, appears not to have such talent.[21] But Longus can subtly describe his heroes' psychology: they are sensitive to compliments, prone to jealousy (2.2.1ff.) and quick to joy and grief (1.31.1; 2.21.2–30.1). They triffle with each other's feelings when they swear

---

[19] Sandy (1982a), 61ff.
[20] Schmeling (1974), 156ff.
[21] Schmeling (1980), 86–7, 122–4.

oaths (2.39); the picture of their temper is lightly tinged with humour. In Achilles Tatius' novel, the accent on humour is more pronounced, as Kleitophon relates his misfortunes and is inclined to make fun of himself (2.23.4ff.; 3.17ff.; 5.23.5ff.; 6.3.1; 6.5; 8.1ff.). His style often comes close to Lucius' in the *Golden Ass*, where the latter narrates his eventful roaming in a detached, elegant and funny tone. On the other hand, in the *Satiricon*, the protagonists display a self-depreciating humour. They have a true insight into social comedy but are pitiless when they describe the ludicrous events of their own sexual life. They are obviously dissatisfied with themselves, and Petronius shows genius in achieving his satirical novel through the eyes and the words of disillusioned and pitiful men. In the portrayal of characters, the ancient novelists also resort to comparisons.

3) *Comparisons*

They often compare their characters with deities. Chariton states that Callirhoe is as beautiful as Aphrodite (1.1.2), is often mistaken for her (2.3.6 and 9; 3.2.14 and 17; 3.9.1; 8.6.11) or for Artemis (1.1.16; 4.7.5). In the *Aithiopika* (1.2.6) Charikleia is mistaken for Artemis and Isis, and according to Achilles Tatius (7.15.2) Leukippe is second in beauty only to Artemis. In the *Ephesiaka* (1.2.7) the Ephesians see Anthia and believe she is the goddess, while Daphnis thinks Chloe is as beautiful as a nymph (1.24.2) and is himself compared with Dionysus (2.2.1) and Apollo (4.14.2). This kind of comparison that suggests unimaginable radiance and absolute superiority to ordinary people goes back to Homer and his godlike heroes. The characters in novel are also compared to heroes.

Achilles holds the first place in this type of comparison. According to Chariton Chaereas looks like him (1.1.3) and the friendship he has formed with Polycharmus is compared with Achilles' relationship with Patroclus (1.5.2). In the *Aithiopika* Theagenes is also compared with the hero fighting against the Scamander (4.3.1) and is said to display the same beauty and nobility (4.5.5). In Achilles Tatius' novel (6.1.3) Kleitophon reminds Melite of a portrait of Achilles, Chariton makes reference to works of art when he describes Chaereas "like Achilles and Nireus and Hippolytus and Alcibiades as sculptors and painters portray them".[22] We must notice that this comparison does

---
[22] 1.1.3.

not concern only the world of Homer; tragedy and history are also involved. The Greek novelists have inherited the whole Greek tradition with its poetical and historical myths, and they draw parallels between those myths and their heroes in order to delineate the latter, but also to establish their positions vis-à-vis other actors.[23] Thus that kind of parallel provides an image of the protagonists, but also explains and intensifies the drama. When Heliodorus compares Charikleia with Andromeda (4.8.5), he wants the reader to compare her misfortunes with this mythological figure's hapless destiny. Chariton has the same intention when he mentions Ariadne in order to describe Callirhoe's beauty as she is lying in her coffin (1.6.2) or to allude to the vanishing of her corpse (3.3.5) and to the possibility of Chaereas forgetting her (8.1.2). In the same way Callirhoe wonders whether she will keep the baby she is expecting or kill him and become a new Medea (2.9.3). Other comparisons are made just in passing: in the *Aithiopika* (1.10.2), Demainete falls madly in love with Knemon and calls him a new Hippolytus; Achilles Tatius (2.23.3) compares Kleitophon with Ulysses and the servant who prevents him from entering Leukippe's room with the Cyclops; Kleitophon compares himself with Niobe when he attends the contrived scene of Leukippe's death (3.15.6). He jestingly draws a parallel between themselves as a couple and the pair of Herakles and Omphale (2.6.2). Petronius parodies this rhetorical device when he compares with Ulysses Giton and Encolpius who are in lewd and even obscene positions (97–98; 105). But other comparisons really aim at defining a character: in the *Aithiopika* (2.24.4) Knemon compares Kalasiris with Proteus. This parallel is suitable for this learned, resourceful and elusive priest. By referring to well-known figures and stories of the tradition, the novelists draw more accurately the aesthetic, psychological and dramatic outlines of their characters. The latter seem to drift for a while toward another story where they do not belong, but then the reader can see them better. In the end their identities emerge from their own adventure.

4) *Adventure as a source of the characters' identity*

The heroes change: they are not the same persons in the end as they were in the beginning of the story. The trials they have undergone,

---

[23] Steiner (1969).

the deeds they have done have left their mark on them and shaped their nature. In Chariton's novel (7.2ff.) Chaereas becomes a leader of the uprising of Egypt; in the *Aithiopika* (10.28ff.) Theagenes performs feats of valour before the Ethiopian people. Longus always pays particular attention to the passing of time and turning two young shepherds into a married couple. He underlines every stage of their initiation. In the *Golden Ass* Lucius treads a longer and more uneven path to truth. On the other hand, the extant fragments of the *Satiricon* do not entitle us to perceive any development of the characters' personality. Neither do the heroes of the *Ephesiaka* undergo any change. But in Achilles Tatius' novel (1.2.1ff.), Kleitophon describes himself as a man to whom love did a lasting harm. Character development through suffering actually is a favourite theme.

As the actors go through their adventures, they often pathetically recapitulate them and identify themselves with their misfortunes. In Chariton's novel Callirhoe frequently retraces and laments her fate. Whenever she complains, she sums up her whole destiny as a long string of unfortunate events. Thus she is constructing and claiming an identity that results from her misadventures. Chaereas, the heroes of the *Ephesiaka* and of the *Aithiopika*, and the protagonists of Achilles Tatius' novel do the same as well.[24] Since there are few dramatic events in *Daphnis and Chloe*, Longus does not develop the theme. But that mode of self-portrayal influences the style and the tone of the other Greek novels. Petronius of course makes fun of it when his characters find themselves in ridiculous or base situations and yet pathetically produce monologues (80, 94, 115). His parody points to the importance of that type of character-portrayal. At the end of the story, we recognize that the heroes are those persons who went through a lot of trouble and could still survive. They have been driven along a dangerous path before the eyes of the gods.

5) *The portraying of the gods*

The gods are supposed to direct the course of the events, but they are more often called upon than they appear in person in the story.

---

[24] Callirhoe: 1.11.2ff.; 2.5.10ff.; 3.2.12ff.; 3.7.5ff.; 3.10.4ff.; 5.1.4ff.; 6.6.2ff.; 6.7.8ff.; 7.5.2ff. Chaereas: 3.3.4ff.; 3.6.6ff.; 4.3.10ff.; 5.2.4ff.; 5.10.6ff.; 6.2.8ff. *Ephesiaka*: 1.4 and 9; 2.1.4,8,10 and 11; 3.5.6.8 and 10; 4,2,3,4 and 6; 5.1.5, 7,8 and 10. *Aithiopika*: 1.8.2ff.; 2.1.2ff.; 2.4; 5.2.7ff.; 5.6.2ff.; 7.14.4ff. Achilles Tatius: 3.10; 4.9.4ff.; 5.7.8ff.; 5.11.1ff.; 5.18.2ff.; 7.5.

In the *Golden Ass* (11.5) Isis appears to Lucius, tells him that his trials have come to an end and shows him the light of truth. In *Daphnis and Chloe* (2.4ff.) Eros reveals to Philetas that he is looking after the two young shepherds in the same way he was looking after Philetas and his beloved Amaryllis. Actually Eros never ceases to take care of them with the kindly and vigilant help of the Nymphs and of Pan. In that story he is a gentle and caring god. *Daphnis and Chloe* is an exception among the Greek novels which stand in the mainstream of Greek tradition that pictures him as an all-powerful and fearsome deity. Chariton says (1.1.3) that the story he is telling took place because Eros wanted to arrange an exceptional marriage. Therefore Chaereas and Callirhoe had to suffer. Aphrodite too plays a part in their suffering and this is why Callirhoe often prays to and reproaches her. In the *Ephesiaka* the whole story is built on Eros' desire to take revenge on Habrocomes who arrogantly claimed that he would be able to escape his power (1.1.5ff.). Achilles Tatius often insists upon the god's absolute rule and the resulting torments that men are suffering.[25] In the *Aithiopika* the destiny of the heroes is under the protection of Apollo and Artemis (3.11.5), and therefore everything goes according to the plan the gods have formed to get rid of human sacrifices in Ethiopia (10.39). This plan, however, plays havoc with men and events. Thus in the ancient novels the gods are more often harsh than kindly. Even if the heroes' adventures end happily, they nevertheless contain many misfortunes. Wandering men stand one trial after another before the eyes of the gods until the latter decide to put an end to their suffering: such is the picture of the deities that the ancient novelists draw.

Their novels are densely peopled and include a wide range of characters, some of which are derived from the stage, others are new. The novelists portray them by referring to gods, heroes, myths and by emphasizing the marks which their adventures have left upon them. They also link them to the real world and thus provide a somewhat faithful image of the society at their own time. Novelists can create wonderful stories and develop believable characters as well. To write a history of characters in prose fiction, one would have to begin with the ancient novels.

---

[25] 1.2.1–2; 1.17.1; 2.3.3; 2.4.5; 2.5.2; 4.7.5; 5.25.6.

7. MYSTERY RELIGIONS, ARETALOGY AND THE ANCIENT NOVEL

Roger Beck

Whether there exists some special relationship between ancient narrative fiction on the one side and the mystery religions on the other has long been a standard critical *topos*, at least in the scholarship of the former. A systematic relationship, both causal and formal, was first postulated by K. Kerényi.[1] It was that the ancient novels derive from, and are the "secularized" expressions of, the legends of the mysteries, in particular the core myth of the Isis cult: the story of Isis and Osiris, which in its narrative essence is a story of love, separation, wandering and eventual reunion.[2]

A yet more integral connection between the novels and the mystery cults was propounded by R. Merkelbach.[3] For Merkelbach, the relationship was functional and fully intentional. The novels did not merely develop from the myths of the mysteries; rather they belonged to the mysteries as their sacred texts, composed within and for the cults. Necessarily, as befits texts of the mysteries, they are in code. The details of their narratives intimate the specifics of cult ritual and theology in ways transparent to the initiates but opaque to the profane and casual reader. The critic's task is accordingly one of decipherment, to read the riddles and to lift the veils of the mysteries. For Merkelbach, the paradigmatic text was Apuleius' story of Cupid and Psyche, and the Isis cult the paradigmatic referent. To those mysteries belonged not only the *Metamorphoses* but also the novels of Xenophon and Achilles Tatius. To the cult of Dionysus was assigned the work of Longus, to the cult of the Sun that of Heliodorus, and

---

[1] Kerényi (1927), (1971). See A.D. Nock's review (reprint 1972) of the former; also I. Stark's critique in her admirable survey of religion in the novel: (1989), 145f.

[2] The story is related and interpreted allegorically and with reference to cult and ritual by Plutarch *De Iside et Osiride*: see the edition of Griffiths (1970), especially for the elements of native Egyptian religion.

[3] Merkelbach (1962). The fullest and in many ways the best critique of Merkelbach's theory is still R. Turcan's review (1963). Turcan approaches the theory primarily from the perspective of religion. From the literary perspective, see esp. Reardon (1971), 393–399 (and 318f. on Kerényi). See also Stark (1989), 147–149; Reardon (1976b).

to the cult of Mithras that of Iamblichus.[4] Recently, Merkelbach has restated his case for *Daphnis and Chloe* as a text of the mysteries of Dionysus in a monograph in which a comprehensive treatment of the cult in the Roman imperial age precedes the analysis of the novel.[5]

Merkelbach's theory is the extreme case on the role of religion in the novel. In effect it collapses the latter into the former as a subtype of allegorical religious literature. Predictably, it has proved unpersuasive, especially to literary critics, who have not welcomed so narrow a prescription for the authorial intent and function of works of imaginative fiction. It fits ill with those widely held views, most forcefully enunciated by Perry,[6] that the novels are works of autonomous literary creation and must be treated as such (though of course with all due regard for the social context of their composition, in which religion figured so largely). Moreover, as a generic model for the ancient novel, it has certain weaknesses both as a whole and in its detailed application, and to these we shall in due course turn. Nevertheless, easy though it is to criticize the theory, it would be mistaken to dismiss it altogether, for it raises considerations which are central to the novel. Let us rather reformulate it as a question: what is it about these novels that seems to resonate so deeply with the mystery cults—and vice versa?

Thus reformulated, the question frees us from the constraints of narrow and inappropriate categorization. As long as one is asking about the novels as mystery-texts, one is restricted to the limited canon of the extant and fragmentary ancient novels on the one hand and to the even more limited group of the pagan mysteries to which they may be assigned. But what is actually at issue is both larger and more diffuse: the relationship between the imaginative narrative prose of a particular era and a certain type of religious experience which found expression, typically though not solely, in certain new (or renewed) forms of cult association.

What is common and central to these cults is that they were re-

---

[4] That the *Babyloniaca* is a Mithraic story was again argued by Merkelbach in an appendix to his study of that cult (1984), 252–259, though his emphasis there is more on the derivation of the story from Iranian (Armenian) sources (about which he is probably correct) than on its supposed allusions to Mithraic initiations. For a critique of the latter, see Beck (1982).

[5] Merkelbach (1988). An excellent dossier of iconographic material (fresco, mosaic, sculpture, etc.) rounds out the study. Like Merkelbach's initial work (1962), this study too has been reviewed with great thoroughness by R. Turcan (1989).

[6] Perry (1967).

ligions of individual salvation which claimed to bring their initiates into special relationship with the god or gods on whom their mysteries were focused. This, the reader should be warned, is both an old-fashioned and an unfashionable definition of the mysteries, but it is still sustainable provided that an inclusive construction is placed on that heady term "salvation".[7] The initiates of the Aventine Mithraeum hailed their god with the words "you have saved us... with the blood shed" (*nos servasti... sanguine fuso*),[8] meaning, presumably, a rather different salvation, and certainly a very different mode of salvation, from that accomplished by the Christian saviour. Functionally, however, in the context and economy of both mysteries, the two "salvations" are equivalent.

In any event, the key terms here are not so much "salvation" as "individual" and "initiation". Neither of the latter is particularly controversial; the second, indeed, is virtually tautologous, since etymologically and in practice a "mystery" (μυστήριον, τελετή) *is* an "initiation". Both elements are stressed by W. Burkert in his definition of the mystery cults in his admirable survey of these religions:[9] "Mysteries were initiation rituals of a voluntary, personal, and secret character that aimed at a change of mind through experience of the sacred". The change wrought by initiation is personal, not social, and it changes the initiate in relation to the divine: "From the perspective of the participant, the change of status affects his relation to a god or goddess; the agnostic, in his view from the outside, has to acknowledge not so much a social as a personal change, a new state of mind through experience of the sacred."[10] Initiation itself was not only a highly charged emotional and psychic experience but also an objective event taking place in the actual world—or on the boundaries

---

[7] The trend in current scholarship is to lessen the divide between the mystery religions and the public cults, seeing the concerns of the former as a more personal expression of the traditional concerns of the latter. The "salvation" sought in the mysteries is construed less as a plea for transcendental or posthumous rescue and more as the same old quest for material well-being, health and long life. The mysteries are now seen as very much more tentative in their promotion of bliss for their initiates in the afterlife. Burkert (1987), 12–29, strikes a good balance on these matters (see also MacMullen (1981), 49–57). Burkert's book provides a much-needed and sensible overview of the major mystery cults (Isis, Eleusis, the Great Mother, Dionysus, Mithras). For the sake of economy, it will be used here as the gateway reference to specialized source material on the mysteries.
[8] Burkert (1987), 111f., with n. 148.
[9] *Ibid.*, 11.
[10] *Ibid.*, 8.

of this world and the other. Something was done to, for and by the initiate. As all authorities agreed, what mattered was not so much what was taught but what was performed (τὰ δρώμενα).[11] Appositely, at the close of his study, Burkert quotes Proclus, who, even at that late date, had knowledge of the mysteries from the daughter of the last Hierophant at Eleusis: "They [the mysteries] cause sympathy of the souls with the *dromena* in a way that is unintelligible to us, and divine, so that some of the initiands are stricken with panic, being filled with divine awe; others assimilate themselves to the holy symbols, leave their own identity, become at home with the gods, and experience divine possession."[12]

Arguably, these actions and experiences resonate with imaginative narrative, and especially with the new prose fiction of the Roman imperial age, in a way quite beyond the capacities of the traditional religion of the public cults. The public cults were corporate, not personal, and they were essentially static. They were designed to maintain society in a prosperous and mutually agreeable relationship with the gods. Profound change and individual psychic adventure, the stuff of novels, were not to be looked for there. But it was precisely in the newer religions of initiation that these goods were on offer.[13]

Incomparably the best description of an initiation, both as experience and event, is that of Lucius' in *Metamorphoses* 11 (22–24). Given its provenance, however, it would be illogical to deploy it in order to demonstrate resonances between life and art without being absolutely sure that it has a foot in each camp rather than both feet planted firmly in the latter—a question, unfortunately, which seems destined to remain moot.[14] As second best, let Plutarch's description of the experience serve:

> The soul [at death] suffers an experience similar to those who celebrate great initiations.... Wanderings astray in the beginning, tiresome

---

[11] *Ibid.*, 89–114 (a chapter appositely entitled "The Extraordinary Experience"). From the initiate's standpoint, as Aristotle appreciated (Fr. 15 = Synesius *Dio* 10 p. 48a), the mystery was undergone as an experience (παθεῖν), not learnt as a lesson (μαθεῖν). Even the language of the mysteries intimates that they were grasped not by the mind but directly by the eye as something shown (cf. *hierophant*) and seen (cf. *epopteia*).

[12] Burkert (1987), 114; Proclus *In Remp*.II 108.17–30 Kroll (Burkert's translation).

[13] Appropriately, MacMullen (1981) terms them the "dynamic" cults. His chapter thereon (112–130) contrasts them well with the larger and more static background of imperial-age paganism.

[14] Historians of religion tend to be much more sanguine about the verisimilitude

walkings in circles, some frightening paths in darkness that lead nowhere; then immediately before the end all the terrible things, panic and shivering and sweat, and amazement. And then some wonderful light comes to meet you, pure regions and meadows are there to greet you, with sounds and dances and solemn, sacred words and holy views; and there the initiate, perfect by now, set free and loose from all bondage, walks about, crowned with a wreath, celebrating the festival together with the other sacred and pure people, and he looks down on the uninitiated, unpurified crowd in this world in mud and fog beneath his feet.[15]

The *dromena* themselves will have varied from mystery to mystery, and their specific actions are seldom recoverable, still less their precise meaning and intent or the way in which they replicate sacred myth. Again, a single example must suffice, relevant here for its dense evocation of "story". It is Mesomedes' brief Hymn to Isis, in which the matters "danced through the *anaktora*" are rapidly alluded to:[16]

A single hymn on land
and on seagoing ships
is sung, a single rite
in manifold orgies.
Deep-horned Isis
whether in spring or summer
or in winter drives
new-furnished harnesses.
You the fire of Hades summons
and the Chthonian wedding song,
the labour pangs of plants,
the desires of the Cyprian,
you the birth of the child,
the perfect, unspeakable fire,
the Curetes of Rhea,
the reaping of Kronos,
the cities chariot-travelled:
all these through the *anaktora*
are danced for Isis.

---

of Lucius' initiation and about Apuleius' intent in describing it than literary critics can afford to be. A.D. Nock, for example, although of course aware of the danger, treats the description as substantially factual and thus as a prime instance of the phenomenon of religious "conversion" in antiquity: (1933), 138–155.

[15] Fr. 168 Sandbach = Stobaeus 4.52.49, trans. Burkert (1987), 91f.

[16] *Hymn*.5 Heitsch = Totti (1985) no. 25 (my translation); see Burkert (1987), 94. Although the hymn is addressed to Isis, the specific allusions and the final reference to the "*anaktora*" as the venue suggest rather the Eleusinian mysteries of Demeter and Persephone. The intent, then, is syncretistic. A "generic" mystery here serves our purpose well.

Πάντα δι' ἀνακτόρων/"Ἴσιδι χορεύεται. The *anaktoron* was the heart and focus of the Hall of Initiation (*telesterion*) at Eleusis. Although we should not read Mesomedes' short hymn too literally as the programme notes for initiation, it reminds us sharply of two key facts. First, initiation is drama (as well as simple *dromenon*); it is an imitation of action, not just its narration.[17] Secondly, what it imitates is divine story in relationship to human story. The initiate in some sense treads in the footsteps of the god.

In delimited sacred contexts and in sacred places the initiations of the mysteries gave formal and intense expression to individual experience, both psychic and physical, which the novels expressed as narratives set in the larger arena of "life" and the "world". Those quotation marks must be applied because the life and world of the novels are of course as artificial as the rituals of the mysteries. The difference is that they are artistic, not sacral, constructs. They are built on their authors' imaginative views of human experience and, more importantly, on certain set ways in which the genre came to present the features of life and the world. But unlike the mysteries, which are enacted in their own special dimensions of sacred space and time, the novels pretend at least to be taking place in the actual world and in real time or in some plausible facsimile thereof.

The world of the novels, no less than the world of the mysteries, was a god-ridden world.[18] The stories are those of men and women acted upon by the divine and reacting to it, of men and women who, like initiates, are the particular darlings of providence and the gods, though at times they appear rather the particular objects of

---

[17] The *telesterion* at Eleusis was functionally a theatre for revelation and spectacle ("showing" and "seeing" the mysteries). Initiation as drama is perhaps best captured, despite his hostility and satiric exaggeration, in Lucian's description of the play constructed by the contemporary mystagogue Alexander for the cult of Asclepius-Glycon at Abonuteichos: *Alexander or the False Prophet* 38f. Cult drama was widespread in the imperial age and attracted large audiences; many "mysteries," as MacMullen (1981), 18–24, reminds us, were anything but secret and discriminating in this regard. Among the novelists, Heliodorus, with his persistent dramatic similes, might be said to reflect something of the idea of fate's theatre of initiation (e.g., 7.6.4–5).

[18] R. Lane Fox (1986), 102–261, conveys well the imperial age's sense of the immediacy of the gods' presence. Men and women took it as a matter of fact that the gods appeared and spoke to them, whether directly or through formal intermediaries such as oracles. Literature here reflected at least the expectations of real life, if not its actualities. This fact is as relevant to sceptical as to pious works. Was Priapus "really" hounding the *Satyrica*'s Encolpius? Of course not. But it was "realism" on Petronius' part to contrive a character who might so fantasize.

their wrath. But the novels are not the only narratives of the interplay of men and gods, and it is important to glance now beyond their confines at other forms which tell of this interplay and which present the stories of persons uniquely blessed—or cursed—by the gods. It is only in that larger narrative context that it makes sense to inquire about the novel as in any way a type of religious literature.

The road out from the narrower confines of the novel proper leads in two directions, one to aretalogy, the other to the biography of god-like or holy men (θεῖοι ἄνδρες). The latter comprises works of more or less the same scope and weight as the novels, the former pieces of altogether shorter compass. Let us consider aretalogy first, because it is to this source that those who favour a religious genesis for the novel look, seeing the novel as a type of developed or specialized aretalogy.[19] An aretalogy is an account of wonders wrought by a god. It is a functional thing, an expression of gratitude and awe towards the god by the recipient of the marvel and a proclamation of the god's power in working the marvel. Ideally, it is something posted in the god's temple as an *ex voto*. To view aretalogy as a literary genre is to look at it through an inappropriate and overly powerful lens.[20] Although we hear of *aretalogoi* as professional storytellers, aretalogy itself was quite unknown to antiquity as a literary form and it has left no identifiable corpus.[21] What we have instead are the scattered primary remains, mostly dedications directly from cult contexts (especially of course the healing cults), preserved on stone or papyrus.[22] The cult of Sarapis furnishes some good examples of the stories and their telling: a priest on Delos is subjected to a criminal charge over the construction of his god's temple but acquitted when the god strikes his accusers dumb;[23] the god arranges an

---

[19] See above, nn. 1, 3, 5, on Kerényi and Merkelbach.
[20] The approach taken by the fullest study of the form, Reitzenstein (1906). Of considerable interest is M. Smith (1971), which emphasizes wonder-tales as contributory material to the gospels. Unfortunately, Merkelbach's article on the form (1994) was not available to me at the time of writing, only the abstract and hand-outs of the conference paper on which it is based (Tatum and Vernazza (1990), 108).
[21] The distinction (*aretalogoi*, but no genre of aretalogy) is well drawn by J.J. Winkler (1985), 233–242. *Aretalogoi* operated in secular as well as sacred contexts: Augustus liked them as dinnertime entertainment (Suetonius *Aug.*74). They did not enjoy much of a reputation.
[22] Collected and studied by V. Longo (1969). On the records of healing miracles, see Weinreich (1909).
[23] *IG* XI.4.1299 = Longo no. 63 = Totti (1985), no. 11 (ca. 200 B.C.); Engelmann (1975).

exchange of fates between two invalids, one whose imminent death was preordained, the other in agony but not yet doomed to die;[24] the god furnishes fresh drinking water to a storm-tossed crew;[25] the god orders the introduction of his cult to Opus, and in so doing reconciles two political enemies.[26] The colophon to the third example captures well the essence of the aretalogy as record of the marvellous intervention of a god on behalf of some thus privileged human: Διὸς 'Ηλίου μεγάλου Σαράπιδος ἀρετὴ ἡ περὶ Συρίωνα κυβερνήτην.

Though brief and sometimes rudimentary, the aretalogy is by no means formless. Nor as a narration is it always simple. The Delian Sarapis aretalogy, for example, tells its story twice, once in rather direct prose and a second time in clunking hexameters. Dreams foreshadow actual events, and stories within stories occur, as in an aretalogy of Imuthes-Asclepius in which a scribe recounts his own episodes of sickness and healing as he sets about translating an earlier account of the god's *aretai*.[27] As a record formally dedicated, the aretalogy frequently takes cognizance of the act and context of narration. Both the witnessing of the event related and its memorializing are matters of explicit concern.[28] Hence the marvelling throng on the occasion and the subsequent injunction to those who read or hear of it to praise the god. As the Delos aretalogy rounds off its story, ἅπας δ' ἄρα λαὸς ἐκείνῳ/σὴν ἀρετὴν θάμβησεν ἐν ἤματι,[29] and as Syrion the helmsman concludes his, καὶ καταχωρίζεται ἡ ἀρετὴ ἐν ταῖς Μερκουρίου βιβλιοθήκαις. οἱ παρόντες εἴπατε "Εἷς Ζεὺς Σάραπις.[30]

The aretalogies are stories anchored in the real world. They relate what happened to real individuals of no great prominence—or, rather, the construction that these people chose to put on what happened to them in some special crisis of their lives when for a time, as they imagined, they became the special objects of the gods' attention and the admiration of bystanders. Can one view the novels as in some sense aretalogies writ large, narratives about the gods' more permanent favourites, ideal types rather than actual individuals, moving in a world like but not quite identical with the contemporary? Cer-

---

[24] *P.Berol.*10525 = Longo no. 66 = Totti no. 12 (3rd century A.D.).
[25] *P.Oxy.*11.1382 = Longo no. 64 = Totti no. 13 (2nd century A.D.).
[26] *IG* X.2.1.255 = Totti no. 14 (1st century A.D.).
[27] *P.Oxy.*11.1381 = Longo no. 58 = Totti no. 15 (2nd century A.D.).
[28] Merkelbach (above, n. 20) rightly emphasizes these features of the aretalogy.
[29] (above, n. 23), lines 90f.
[30] (above, n. 25), lines 19–21.

tainly, the novels are replete with episodes which are the stuff of aretalogies: the miraculous salvation of Habrocomes by Helios and the Nile from death on the cross and the pyre;[31] Charicleia's similar rescue from the pyre as the very flames draw back, choosing not to harm her but to frame her in glory;[32] Chloe's rescue from the Methymneans as Pan turns nature topsy-turvy on her behalf.[33] Above all, the two great episodes of the final book of the *Metamorphoses*, the transformation of Lucius back into human form and his initiation into the mysteries of Isis, are redolent of the aretalogy both in their content and in their telling:[34] the miraculous reversal, the peculiar favour of the god, the explication by holy men and divine dream, the admiring multitude,[35] the awe and gratitude of the beneficiary.[36]

In a larger sense, certain at least of the novels might be equated with aretalogies in that they pretend to derive from a dedication to

---

[31] X.Eph.4.2. Note the bystanders' reaction: "to those who witnessed it the event seemed like a miracle" (translation, as elsewhere unless specified, from *Collected Ancient Greek Novels* = Reardon (1989)).

[32] Hld.8.9.11–16. Again, note the emphasis on popular reaction and awe; the spectators draw the appropriate conclusion: "... whereupon, as with one voice, the city exclaimed in joyful awe and invoked the gods' majesty."

[33] Longus 2.25–29. Again: "everyone was gripped by amazement and shouted out in praise of Pan." Note too the god's dream appearance, typical in an aretalogy, to explicate the underlying realities to the Methymnian general—and to warn of worse should he not release Chloe.

[34] It is mistaken to focus on the rehearsal of Isis' manifestations, names and powers in Lucius' prayer (11.2) or Isis' theophany (11.5) as *the* aretalogies in the *Metamorphoses*. Certainly, they are the passages most closely paralleled by actual sources from the Isis cult which proclaim the god's universal powers and various manifestations (e.g., the Kyme inscription, IG XII Suppl. 14 = Totti 1(A); cf. Walsh (1970), 252f.). But they are not aretalogies in the proper and relevant sense of *stories* of the god's marvels. Only when narrated and duly dedicated to the god, will the prayer of 11.2 and the prediction of 11.5–6 become aretalogies in the strict sense. On the religious specifics of these two passages, see Griffiths' commentary (1975) *ad loc.*

[35] Though the initiation is private, its aftermath (11.24), the display of Lucius in a sort of theophany (*ad instar solis exornato me et in vicem simulacri constituto*) is witnessed by the public; that, indeed, is its purpose: ... *quippe quod tunc temporis videre praesentes plurimi*; ... *in aspectum populus errabat*.

[36] As often, one looks for the antitype in Petronius. One finds it perhaps in Encolpius' recovery from impotence, which he attributes to Mercury: *"dii maiores sunt qui me restituerunt in integrum, Mercurius enim, qui animas ducere et reducere solet, suis beneficiis reddidit mihi, quod manus irata praeciderat...."* Haec locutus sustuli tunicam Eumolpoque me totum approbavi, at ille primo exhorruit, deinde ut plurimum crederet, utraque manu deorum beneficia tractat* (140.12–13). It is all there: the god's favour, the grateful recipient, the token of salvation, the admiring witness. Not that Petronius is deliberately parodying the aretalogy; rather, as so often, his game is to capture and satirize the fantasies and verbal posturings of minds which apprehend their "actual" world through a filter of formal sterotypes and genres.

a god or a record in a temple. The primary purpose of this contrivance is of course to authenticate the story, and a quasi-aretalogy is an obvious device for achieving that purpose when the story is about the god's favourites. Thus, Xenophon's *Ephesiaca* derives from the inscription, "commemorating all their sufferings and all their adventures," which Anthia and Habrocomes dedicate to Artemis in her temple at Ephesus,[37] and Longus' *Pastorals* from a painting in a grove of the Nymphs in Lesbos (praef.). The latter novel is ostensibly an *ekphrasis* of the picture, which the author constructs on the basis both of autopsy and of an explication by a local *exegetes* and which he in turn dedicates to Eros, the Nymphs and Pan. It is tempting, too, to hear the voice of the *exegetes* and confessor in the narrator of the *Metamorphoses* and thus to read the work almost as an extended aretalogy.[38] Lucius (or is it now the "poor man from Madaurus" (11.27)?) relates the marvels of his adventures, his final salvation and his several initiations in the shadow of the cult and temple of Isis and the Egyptian gods in Rome. So heard, it is a credible narrating voice set in a credible narrating context, and it returns a certain unity to the narration, for in the culture to which it belongs the *aretalogos* of marvellous tales, the grateful confessor and the somewhat fussy temple *exegetes* can plausibly be one and the same person.

The aretalogies are not the only narrative records of real humans in their dealings with the gods. Our second analogue to the ancient novel in this regard is the biography of the god-like or holy man (θεῖος ἀνήρ).[39] Like the aretalogy, of which it may well be seen as an amplification, it is set in the actual world of Hellenistic or Graeco-Roman society. Like the novel, it appears to answer a need to hear

---

[37] 5.15.2. The story is thus brought full circle to the cult and temple context in which it had started. The formal conclusion at Ephesus follows the more dramatic thanksgiving to Isis in her temple at Rhodes immediately after the recognition and reunion of the lovers—a sort of instant or mini-aretalogy (5.13.3–4): "The Rhodians cheered and shouted in their excitement, hailing Isis as a great goddess and exclaiming, 'Now once again we see Habrocomes and Anthia, the beautiful pair!' They [H. and A.] recovered, sprang up, and came into the temple of Isis, saying, 'To you, greatest goddess, we owe thanks for our safety; it is you, the goddess we honor most of all, who have restored us.'"

[38] The idea was brilliantly developed by Winkler (1985), 233–242, though as a final portrait of the narrator he found it wanting.

[39] The most exhaustive treatment of this figure is Bieler (1967). On the literature discussed in this paragraph and on its intellectual milieu, the best study is Reardon (1971), esp. 21–26.

about individuals moving in that real world, or in something akin to it,[40] within the compass of a work of some scope. Unlike the novel, its heroes are real people, or people whom we are meant to accept as real, not ideal types.[41] Its leading pagan exemplars are the *Sacred Tales* of Aelius Aristides and Philostratus' *Life of Apollonius of Tyana*: the former the meticulous diary of a hypochondriac sophist in his relation to the healing god Asclepius, a story of dream remedies, cures both marvellous and pedestrian and the inevitable relapses requiring yet further divine attention, insufferably self-indulgent stuff were it not for Aristides' palpable and touching love for his saviour god;[42] the latter the hagiographic account, written a century after his actual life, of a Neopythagorean sage, his wanderings, teachings, miracles and heroization.[43] The antitype, valuable for its negative spin, is Lucian's *Alexander or the False Prophet*, the debunking story of the brilliant entrepreneur of the cult and oracle of Asclepius-Glycon at Abonuteichos.[44] The common theme of these sacred biographies is the insistent claim on special access to the supernatural and on their heroes' right and duty to mediate the fruits of that intercourse back to the world—not to some remote world of myth or long ago but to the teeming actual world of the *oikumene*. In the words of the autobiography of Thessalus the magician, ἔχειν γάρ με ἀνάγκην θεῷ

---

[40] This is not the place to explore the realism or otherwise of the novels' settings. Suffice it to note that the biographies are set in their contemporary Roman imperial world (with forays into the fantastical beyond), while the novels generally archaize (e.g., independent Greek polis society, the Achaemenid empire) but still set themselves within socio-political contexts broadly familiar to contemporaries. The two great Roman novels are of course firmly located in their current contexts.

[41] This is not to assert that the biographies are particularly realistic in their execution or that they were intended to tell us about their subjects "as they really were"—unless by "really" one means *sub specie aeternitatis*. Given their bias to the supernatural, the biographies rapidly part company with the objective realities of their subjects as the distance between a subject's life and the composition of his biography widens. Apollonius of Tyana (see below) is a good case in point. However, the important distinction here is that while there really was an Apollonius there never was a Theagenes or a Chariclea. Philostratus, Heliodorus and their readers, one hazzards the conjecture, appreciated that distinction.

[42] Behr (1968). For further portraits of this figure, see Phillips (1952), Reardon (1973); and for a psychological sketch, Dodds (1965), 39–45.

[43] For the work in its literary context, see Reardon (1971), 265–268.

[44] See above, n. 17. Cf. Lucian's equally hostile and sceptical essay, *On the Death of Peregrinus*, concerning the troubled life and spectacular self-immolation of this wandering holy man. Peregrinus was nicknamed Proteus from the various religious personae he assumed at one time or another in his career (for a tentative psychological profile, see Dodds (1965), 59–63).

ὁμιλῆσαι.[45] "I gotta speak to a god": these are folk who batter on the doors of heaven.

Most biographies of this type are Christian. This is not merely an accident of Christianity's triumph and the consequent privileging of its literature. It stems from the fact that the Christian saviour, so it was claimed, was an historical figure, precisely locatable in the *oikumene* in place and date; also from the fact that the developing cult chose, for whatever reason, to promote and publicize certain of its charismatic leaders.[46] The vehicle for publicity was to hand in the form of prose narrative that manifests itself equally as aretalogy, sacred biography and novel.[47] The Christian exemplars of this form are the subject of separate treatment in this volume,[48] so I note them here only because it is impossible to consider anything to do with "religion" in the novel without taking them into account.[49] In terms of the development of literary form, the most interesting model is that of T. Hägg:[50] a bifurcation of narrative types into popular biography

---

[45] Ed. Friedrich (1968), p. 51.9-10. Thessalus' letter, which serves as an introduction to a work of astrological botany, is a nice proto-typical exemplar of this genre of biography and autobiography. For a spirited explication, see J.Z. Smith (1978); also, Winkler (1985), 258-260. The distinction between biography and autobiography, both here and in the aretalogies, while important narratologically, is functionally insignificant. The autobiographical mode has, of course, its own label: the "confession."

[46] The contrast with the major pagan mystery cults is quite striking. Although the empire's "epigraphic habit" has preserved the names of scores of members and dedicators/patrons, especially in the Mithras cult (see Clauss (1992)), from the cults themselves we do not even learn the names, let alone the deeds, of their movers and shakers. Yet great innovators there must have been, e.g. "the unknown religious genius" (Nilsson's phrase: (1974), 675) who transformed Mithraism from a Persian to a Graeco-Roman religion. Retaining the same example, if Mithraism did in fact have a sacred biography, it would probably have been that of its putative "prophet," Zoroaster (see Porphyry, *De antro nympharum* 6).

[47] Medium affects message: the image of itself that early Christianity presented to the world was in large measure molded by the vehicle to hand. This is essentially M. Smith's point (1971), that the Jesus of the gospels was shaped by the form of aretalogy.

[48] See below, the contribution of R.I. Pervo.

[49] A most salutary development in the criticism of the ancient novel, especially on topics such as this, has been the extension of the field to include Christian and other sacred biography as parts of essentially the same genre of imaginative prose narrative. In addition to Pervo's study in the present volume and his (1987) monograph on the Acts of the Apostles, see D.R. Edwards' survey of research (1987). Especially germane to the present topic are Hägg (1983), 154-165, and Heiserman (1977), 183-219. The Jewish contribution, especially *Joseph and Aseneth* (the most allegorical of all the "novels"?), should not be overlooked: Pervo (1987), 119-121; Heiserman (1977), 184-186.

[50] (1983), 161. Reardon (1971), 303-308, is also valuable on the relation of Christian to pagan literature here.

on the one side, dominated by Christian exemplars such as Acts, *Paul and Thecla*, and the *Pseudo-Clementines*, and on the other side the sophistic novel with its three extant exemplars, the works of Longus, Achilles Tatius and Heliodorus. The more primitive novel (Chariton, Xenophon) peters out as its market is glutted with the marvel-filled biographies of holy men.

These biographies, in their promotion of their subjects, are manifestly religious. Their precise intent—whether they are meant as *kerygma* to win and confirm faith or whether, as R.I. Pervo has persuasively argued for the canonical Acts,[51] they function in a cooler mode as a type of paideia, instructing, edifying and even entertaining the faithful—may be debated, but their status as works from "within the temple" is not really open to doubt. They are thus the proper comparators in assessing the religious dimensions of their narrative cousins the novels, which are less straightforward in this regard. Certainly, the biographies often deploy their matter in much the same way as we have already observed in both the aretalogies and in the novels, that is, in episodes of public encounter: the marvel wrought with the aid of the god, the adversary routed, the wondering throng, the explication of supernatural significance (often by the protagonist in a sermon), the enhancement of the hero's claims and status.[52] It is by these means that we learn what it is to be a saint, whether Christian such as Paul or Neopythagorean such as Apollonius of Tyana.[53]

Against this larger background of narrative from manifestly religious contexts we may now more readily address the question of the religious dimension of the ancient novels. In what sense, collectively or individually, are they religious works? In what sense are any of them works from within particular religions? Finally, to return to our starting point, what is their link with the mysteries?

---

[51] (1987), *passim*.

[52] It is scarcely necessary to cite Christian examples: one may pick them at will virtually anywhere in the gospels or Acts (canonical or apocryphal). On the pagan side, from the *Life of Apollonius* I cite (e.g.) the hero's unmasking of the plague demon at Ephesus (4.10) and the vampire at Corinth (4.25). It is interesting that these public encounters of exorcism and miracle—or the reports of them—were among the principal triggers of mass conversion: MacMullen (1984), 19–29. Whether as events or "events," they were potent occasions in the actual as well as the imaginative world.

[53] Arguably, Philostratus' presentation parallels that of the gospels and Acts so closely because, intentionally or not, he is setting up a philosophical counterpart to the Christian saviour/hero. Certainly, his construction of "Apollonius" was subsequently so used, most notably by the pagan polemicist (and persecutor) Hierocles in a work entitled the *Lover of Truth*.

Over and above a measure of religious content, inevitable in works purportedly set in a "real" world in which religion was paramount and everywhere in evidence,[54] and over and above their god-like and god-favoured heroines and heroes—individuals who, we have seen from aretalogy and sacred biography, are modelled to the religious aspirations of the age—over and above these characteristics, which are common in a greater or lesser degree to all the novels, one may detect in three of them certain qualities which give them a more thoroughgoing religious aspect. The three are the *Aethiopica*, *Daphnis and Chloe*, and the *Metamorphoses*. What makes them seem particularly "religious" is first their architecture and secondly their apparent intent. By "architecture" I mean the broad structure and movement of the novels together with certain explicit pointers thereto. "Intent" is a more subjective and dangerous matter, but I mean it only in the sense that a work may fairly be said to be headed in a particular direction without implying any driving authorial agenda in its back seat. Suggesting a religious architecture and a religious intent does not of course locate the novels within specific religions. To establish that a work is *of* a particular cult is another step involving other criteria.

Burkert, in his monograph on the mystery cults, describes the *Aethiopica* as the novel "that most diligently exploits a religious dimension."[55] Lest we overlook the significance of its author's name, its colophon proclaims him "a Phoenician from the city of Emesa, one of the clan of Descendants of the Sun" (Ἡλίου γένος). Its ending reveals that the destiny of its hero and heroine were to become priest and priestess of the Sun and the Moon, the deities whose servants and types the attuned reader has sensed them to be all along,[56] and who are manifested and worshipped in most authentic form in Ethiopia, blessed Land of the Sun and the goal of recognition and recon-

---

[54] Religious incidents do not of course make the novels religious. Winkler (1980a) was right in asserting that the episode of gruesome initiation now extant from Lollianos *Phoenikika* in no way makes that work a mystery text. It establishes it only as what it appears to be on the surface, sensational popular entertainment. Likewise the *Iolaus*-fragment, although parody may also be at work here: Merkelbach (1973); Reardon (1976b), 90–93.

[55] (1987), 67 (in a paragraph which nonetheless dismisses both it and the other novels as writings of the mysteries).

[56] Most obviously with Charicleia in the opening scene: bandits mistake her for a goddess (Artemis or Isis) or a "priestess possessed" (1.2.6). Actually, they are not mistaken at all, although, unlike the reader, they never discover how near the mark was their awestruck first impression.

ciliation. As the novel wends its complex way through time, place and culture, it unfolds a hierarchy of religious enlightenment from Greek (good) to Egyptian (better) to Ethiopian (best). Mediating and explicating all but the final stages of this theosophical pilgrims' progress is the mystagogic figure of Calasiris, priest of Isis and mentor of the lovers. The *Aethiopica*, then, may fairly be called a religious novel, a product of the solar piety of late antiquity intended to edify within that context. What it is not is a solar mystery text, for the very good reason that there were no solar mysteries, in the sense of an organized cult to which the work might be assigned as *hieros logos*, other than the "Persian" mysteries of Mithras the Unconquered Sun; and no one, to my knowledge, has ever staked a serious Mithraic claim to the *Aethiopica*.[57] Rather than shrinking the novel within the frame of some minor and hypothetical solar cult, it is better to view it as an expanded deployment of the metaphors of the mysteries,[58] in a composition of solar theosophy, on an altogether broader imaginative canvas.

A similar view may be taken of *Daphnis and Chloe*. It is perfectly just to call it a religious novel. It is self-billed "as an offering to Love, the Nymphs, and Pan."[59] Its lovers come to maturity under the protection of those deities, and, as H.H.O. Chalk so elegantly demonstrated,[60] its architecture is that of their progressive revelation, especially of the greatest of the triad, Eros, into whose mysteries— the term is here loosely intended—the lovers are initiated. That indeed is the *telos* of the novel.[61] Perhaps, too, there looms a yet more puissant divinity, Dionysus, intimated in his "manifestation" Dionysophanes, the lord of the estate where all this pastoral activity transpires and the true father of Daphnis the goatherd. Dionysus was the focus of organized mysteries in the technical sense, and it is to those

---

[57] The absence of relevant solar mysteries was pointed out by Turcan (1963), 195–198, and is routinely deployed as the counterargument to Merkelbach's theory (1962), 234f., on the *Aethiopica*.

[58] Notice (e.g.) how in the very last clause of the novel its erotic goal (marriage) is expressed in the language of mystic initiation: τῶν ἐπὶ τῶι γάμῳ μυστικωτέρων κατὰ τὸ ἄστυ φαιδρότερον τελεσθησομένων.

[59] Praef. (see above).

[60] (1960).

[61] As the final sentence reads, Daphnis enacts (ἔδρασε) what his initiatrix Lycaenion had taught (ἐπαίδευσε) him and Chloe learns (ἔμαθεν) "that what had happened in the woods had been mere child's play (παίγνια)" (4.40.3, my trans.). Winkler (1990b) puts a social and rather sinister construction on the lovers' initiation, especially Chloe's: acculturation into the licensed world of male sexual violence.

mysteries that Merkelbach accordingly ascribes the novel.[62] Again, a similar problem obtrudes as with the *Aethiopica*. Dionysus has his mysteries, but the main god of *Daphnis and Chloe*, Eros, does not, at least in the formal sense.[63] Nevertheless, it is fair to say that *Daphnis and Chloe* resonates with the actual mysteries of Dionysus in a way that the *Aethiopica* does not so resonate with any known mysteries of a solar or other cult. The bucolic environment, the seasonal cycle, initiation into sex and marriage, an ethos of sweetness, prettiness, and sensual enjoyment: these are features—and important ones— equally of the novel and of the Dionysiac mysteries of the imperial age. Without needing to concede that *Daphnis and Chloe* is a sacred text of those mysteries, one may well allow that the novel would have been that much more meaningful to an initiate (as it is to the modern reader armed with Merkelbach's elegant and informative dossier on the cult)[64] and that it makes good interpretative sense to construe the novel's implied author/narrator as an initiate too, whether or not the historical Longus was so himself.

With the *Metamorphoses* there is no dissonance between the postulated mysteries and the deity whose presence and providence inform the novel. Both, moreover, are explicit. The novel's climactic episode is the initiation of Lucius, re-transformed by Isis' grace, into the goddess' mysteries; and in theophany, dream, and the explications of her servants—not to mention the pomp of her cult—she is finally and fully manifest, whatever the reader may sense (or perceive in retrospect or re-reading) about her earlier presence as the misapprehended goal of Lucius' quest.[65] These are truisms, challengeable only

---

[62] (1988); see above, n. 5.

[63] The mismatch between the actual gods of the novel and the god of the mysteries is pointed out by Turcan (1989), 176f. It can be bridged to some extent through the equation of Dionysus with the Orphic Eros-Phanes-Protogonos: Merkelbach 130–136, Turcan 176.

[64] Above, n. 5.

[65] Here of course one touches on a central topic of Apuleian criticism, the relation of the "Isis book" to what precedes and the integrity of the novel as a whole. For present purposes, I have adopted a middle-of-the-road position that can accommodate most readings except the extremes that would either (i) subordinate everything to Isiac piety or (ii) read Book 11 as no more than the application of essentially empty epideictic strategies on yet another front. That there is massive and serious foreshadowing, e.g. in the episode of Byrrhaena's warning and the statue of Artemis and Actaeon (2.4–5), seems to me inescapable. Among many reasonable statements of this broadly moderate interpretation, a good recent example is that of E.J. Kenney (1990a), esp. 10f. The intense relevance of the Cupid and Psyche story I touch on below.

when it is claimed, on a pietistic interpretation of the novel, that they are primary, that this and only this is what the novel is "all about." If one allows, as one surely must, that this is *a* legitimate reading of the novel, then one may proceed to a more strictly germane question: does this make the *Metamorphoses* a text of the mysteries of Isis? It was suggested above that the narrator adopts the persona of confessor, temple *exegetes*, and *aretalogos* (the last in the twin functions of story-teller and herald of the god's favours).[66] By adopting this guise, the narrator places himself, and thus his narration *qua* aretalogy, within the temple and within the mysteries. The location is, however, a narrative strategy. It must not be confused with the author's actual stance, still less with the status of his work. Apuleius may or may not have been an initiate of Isis (we may infer at least a sympathetic knowledge of the cult), but the *Metamorphoses* most certainly was not a sacred text of her mysteries. Nothing in the extant written remains of the mystery cults suggests that they possessed *hieroi logoi* remotely resembling the *Metamorphoses*,[67] and only its thoroughgoing allegorization into processes of initiation can force it into that mould.

It is here that we finally confront Merkelbach's hypothesis directly. Space precludes a detailed rebuttal, and in any case that has been done often enough by others.[68] It is a difficult hypothesis to disprove because refutation involves establishing a set of essentially negative facts, that the "apparent deaths" in which the novels abound are *not* initiation experiences, that the pirates and brigands who fill their pages are *not* disguised fellow-initiates putting one to the test, and so on. Demonstrating that such matters are better accounted for as narrative features of an imaginative genre with their origins in literature and life rather than in the halls of initiation can never be final— though it can perhaps be sufficient. Two criteria come to mind. First, if the novels are "really" about initiation into the mysteries, they are a form of allegory. If they are allegories, they will have a certain quality of strangeness and illogicality in detail which indicates that while the narrative appears to be telling a story it is actually signalling something altogether different. This criterion is by no means new. Before constructing an allegory of his own, the philosopher-emperor

---

[66] Note 38.
[67] On the evidence for mystery texts, see Burkert (1987) 66–72.
[68] See above, nn. 3–5.

Julian rightly drew attention to the characteristic "incongruity" (τὸ ἀπεμφαῖνον) in allegorical narrative.[69] Using this benchmark, we may ask if the details of the novels are by and large so extraordinary, such a "paradoxical and prodigious enigma" in Julian's words, as to compel us to reject the superficial narrative and look for a more coherent but hidden system of reference beneath. Oddities of incident are certainly to be encountered here and there in the novels,[70] but the consensus of scholarship since *Roman und Mysterium* has been that in general the narratives are coherent and comprehensible on their own terms *qua* stories. It is not a very exciting conclusion, but the pirates really are pirates. As R. Turcan wisely sensed, Merkelbach's reductionism of detail finally subverts the theory's credibility: "... en voulant tout et trop expliquer, on risque de tout fausser."[71]

The second criterion is more stringent, and if it were to be met it would surely establish the novels as allegories of actual mystery initiations. It is not enough to suggest that various details in the narratives of the novels appear to echo various details in the practice and theory of initiation. What one desiderates is *system*, a demonstration that a sequence of incidents in some way, whether temporal or logi-

---

[69] *Oration 7 (To the Cynic Heracleius)* 217 C, 222 C. Julian maintained that allegories were particularly appropriate to the mysteries, but what he had in mind were allegories about theology, doctrine and, in his own example, the soul's enlightenment, not allegories about initiation processes. Porphyry, drawing on an earlier source, Cronius, had formulated a similar criterion of literal implausibility as the warrant for explicating allegorically Homer's description of the "cave of the nymphs" in *Od.* 13.102–112 (*De antro nympharum* 2, cf. 4). Homer, he argues, would have been unconvincing (ἀπίθανος) if he had tried, by poetic license (κατὰ ποιητικὴν ἐξουσίαν), to get us to imagine a realistic cave on Ithaca with separate entrances for men and for immortals. Therefore, in describing the cave in those terms he must have had another goal—allegory. Porphyry's argument is skilful: the fact that he is wrong reminds us that oddity and obscurity of detail (4: τοιούτων ἀσαφειῶν πλήρους ὄντος τοῦ διηγήματος), although it might be an index of allegory, is not a sufficient condition. On late antique allegory, see Lamberton (1986), 144–161 (esp. n. 1 on Synesius' *Egyptian Tale*, the myth of Osiris told as an allegory of contemporary political events, and pp. 148–157 on "Philip the Philosopher's" allegorizing interpretation of the *Ethiopica*).

[70] Most notably in the details of Psyche's trials and her descent to the underworld in *Met.*6.9–22. Not surprisingly, it is here that Merkelbach is at his most convincing: (1962), 44–46. Oddity of detail also characterizes much of the *Babyloniaca* and the *Ephesiaca*, in both of which it might be mistaken for a sign of allegory (on the former, see Beck (1982), 533; on the latter, Reardon (1976b), 78–82). More probably, the frenetic speed of the narrative and the fact that the *Babyloniaca* survives mostly in Photius' epitome are responsible for the bizarre impressions conveyed by these two novels.

[71] (1963), 176.

MYSTERY RELIGIONS, ARETALOGY AND THE ANCIENT NOVEL 149

cal, actually tracks a sequence of initiation within the postulated mystery. The economies of the novels ought to parallel the economies of the mysteries. Again, one may quote Turcan: "... on ne décèle aucunement dans l'économie du récit la moindre séquence initiatique, la transposition consciente et voulue d'un rituel mystique."[72] The *Babyloniaca* of Iamblichus provides a good test case. Merkelbach claimed the novel for the mysteries of Mithras. Mithraism, as is well known, had a distinctive cursus of seven grades of initiation. However, try as one may, no sign of progression through that cursus is detectable in the plot of the novel.[73]

Nevertheless, as most of Merkelbach's critics have acknowledged, to set the novels alongside the mysteries as mutual comparators is a most fruitful line of criticism. At heart, as we have seen, this is because each in its different way answered to the aspirations of individuals in their encounters with divine providence and human fate. To be less circumlocutory, both were routes for going to meet the gods. "Routes" is an appropriate metaphor to close with. The novels are characteristically stories about travel,[74] and the major exception to this principle, *Daphnis and Chloe*, proves it by substituting for the spatial journey a temporal journey through the cycle of the seasons. Travel is seldom haphazard, though it may at times appear so to those caught up in it; for all its meanderings, it has its proper end. The metaphor of the journey is likewise firmly embedded in the mysteries and in their rituals of initiation, where it is seen as a voyage of the soul to that other and larger world where one can indeed encounter the gods. Typically, the metaphor is that of descent and/or ascent. Its clearest expression is in Mithraism, where, it was said, "they induct the initiate by leading him in a mystery along the downward path of souls and the route back out again."[75] The same sense

---

[72] *Ibid.*, on *Leucippe and Clitophon*.
[73] Beck (1982).
[74] As are the sacred biographies, e.g., Acts and Philostratus' *Life of Apollonius*.
[75] Porphyry *De antro nympharum* 6: . . . τὴν εἰς κάτω κάθοδον τῶν ψυχῶν καὶ πάλιν ἔξοδον μυσταγωγοῦντες τελοῦσι τὸν μύστην. Because Mithraic initiation replicates a journey through the universe, Porphyry explains, it takes place within a real or artificial cave, the cave being "an image of the universe" (εἰκόνα κόσμου). To function as the setting for this cosmic journey, the cave is accordingly equipped with "symbols of the cosmic elements and climes" (σύμβολα . . . τῶν κοσμικῶν στοιχείων καὶ κλιμάτων, *ibid.*). Interestingly, one of those two terms is used in the enigmatic description of Lucius' initiatory journey in *Met.*11.23: . . . *per omnia vectus* elementa *remeavi*. In both instances it probably refers to the planetary spheres as stations in a mimetic celestial voyage: Beck (1988), 78 n. 187 (74 n. 180 for bibliography on the

of journeying, through perils and terrors to a joyous homecoming, speaks through the fragment on initiation from Plutarch with which our brief sketch of the mysteries opened. In the myths of the mysteries, too, journeying is of the essence, for initiates travel in the footsteps of their gods. Isis journeys in search of the scattered limbs of her murdered husband, Demeter journeys in search of her abducted daughter, and Persephone descends to the underworld and back again. So does Psyche in the great and playful myth which the "Platonic philosopher" from Madaurus sets at the centre of his novel.[76] In explicating the story of the journeying Psyche as an allegory of initiation Merkelbach was surely right, but he was right not because its details signify in code the details of an actual initiation, but because it is deeply true of the experience and essence of initiation in general. *Accessi confinium mortis et calcato Proserpinae limine per omnia vectus elementa remeavi, nocte media vidi solem candido coruscantem lumine, deos inferos et deos superos accessi coram et adoravi de proximo*, says Lucius at the climax of the novel. Journeys out and back, descents to suffering and disintegration, ascents to joy and reintegration, these are the stuff of the mysteries and of the novels too.[77]

wider topic of the soul's celestial journey). The *Babyloniaca*'s Rhodanes and Sinonis undergo a sequence of adventures in a cavern (Epit.3f., Frs. 11–17); the episode is accordingly Merkelbach's best candidate for a disguised Mithraic initiation: Beck (1982), 530–533.

[76] On Apuleius in this guise, see Tatum (1979), 105ff.

[77] The polarities of descent/disintegration and ascent/reintegration are explored with profundity and brilliance by Northrop Frye (1976), 97–157. They are key themes of the romance, the tradition which originates with the ancient novel.

8. WOMEN IN THE ANCIENT NOVEL

Renate Johne

1. *Social Background*

"The greatest honour for a woman consists in the fact that neither for better nor for worse she is thought of by men."[1] This sentence put into the mouth of the great statesman of classical time, Pericles, sounds quite strange to modern people, especially to the women. The historian Thukydides records this sentence from a fictitious speech of Pericles for the soldiers who died within the first year of the Greek fratricidal Peloponnesian War. It is true that women—meant are women who were born as free people—especially in the polis of Athens played a secondary role in the 5th century, the epoch of the genius Phidias and the three great dramatists Aischylos, Sophokles and Euripides: they had few rights, were unauthorized to act by themselves, needed legal advisers and were not allowed to hold public positions. Nevertheless it is necessary to avoid generalizations and attempts to impose standards from a prejudiced feminist point of view, because sources for the study of the role of women in the ancient world are rare. Most likely we are able to get a picture of women of the upper and middle classes only. Female self-reflections are very rare, but within a newly conceived social history investigations on women[2] should be changed into a study of the relation between the sexes.[3]

It is remarkable how the literary record of Thukydides agrees with the artistic depictions of that time as far as women of the polis are concerned. Marriage between full members of the society in Athens

---

[1] Thucydides 2.45.
[2] Survey of the development of research excluding antiquity: Bock (1983) 22–60. Referring to antiquity, Schmitt-Pantel (1989) 199–223, Wagner-Hasel (1988a) 11–50.
[3] Within a complete edition of *Women's History* in 5 volumes—G. Duby and M. Perrot as editors—Volume I, *Antike*, edited by P. Schmitt-Pantel; editorial charge for the German edition, B. Wagner-Hasel, Frankfurt/New York, which was published in 1993. The description of women's role, restricted to politics and social history, is not sufficient; a corresponding history of men is necessary before history as a whole could be interpreted.

was mainly an economic union and served for the procreation of legitimate descendants. The sentence often quoted in this concern is meant to emphasize the role of the wife and is derived from the court speech "Against Neaira",[4] dated about 340 B.C.: "The hetaira serves our pleasure; the concubine daily personal hygiene, but the wife bears us legitimate children and is reliable in housekeeping." In this case a former hetaira was accused, who earlier in her life after being set free had lived as a wife of a respected citizen of Athens together with her children for a long time and got her daughter married to a high religious official under false pretenses. A wife should stand out for her sense of decency and dignified tactfulness within the philosophically supported ideology for moderation. A wife is always shown dressed and asexual according to the existing female behavioural role. Obviously the physical component of marriage had been deliberately suppressed within the public consciousness of Athens. This part was covered sufficiently by deeds of the hetaira and paederasty.[5] Also in this way the gods of Mount Olympus— Aphrodite as the symbol of love or Dionysus as the god of ecstasy— were never shown in sexual arousal, because Sophrosyne dominated physical urges.

In connection with the changed conditions in the Hellenic world and later in the Roman Empire the life of women had also changed with the relaxation of the oikos-structure. The public and military commitment of men to the polis does not decide everything any more; in the new states the king or the emperor is the supreme legislator and nearly the only authority. So private life, the private person and everyday life become important. As a result of the increasing retreat towards the private sector, to the house, where the wife has been busy for a long time, the wife's importance comes to the fore. Women and girls are granted more opportunities to broaden their minds; women of the prosperous strata, because of their improved economic and legal situation, gained influence.

Women had gained independence by the right of disposal of their private means, even if it was limited. Financial independence was followed by gains in writing. Gains are seen, for example, in Egypt,[6]

---

[4] Pseudo-Demosthenes 59.118–122, especially 122; inaccurately repeated at Athenaios 13.573b.

[5] Recently added Reinsberg (1993); literary and artificial evidence are also analysed. More one-sided Siemens (1988).

[6] Ziebarth (1914) 39f.; Marrou (1957) 149,212,328,341f., 361f.,401; Pomeroy (1975) 131f.; (1981) 309f.; Specht (1989).

but likely in other Hellenized areas. At school girls learned to read and write—little Heraidous, daughter of the strategist of Apollinopolis, is the most well-known example of that.[7] Furthermore we have hundreds of papyri written by women or addressed to them. Also epigraphic texts[8] and pictures[9] are recorded.

Certain progressive views of some philosophical trends met these new tendencies; above all the Stoa, which proclaimed the "natural" equality of the sexes and even propagated that all people, also slaves, were related to each other. Because of this attitude women were more highly valued. So their feelings, their views and also their desires became important and were expressed in the aesthetic creation of a distinctive personal image of female characters in literature, especially in the ancient novel.

The Stoics were able to refer to older examples with their ideas: Plato had already intended to treat men and women as equals in the upper classes in *The Republic*.[10] This statement, which was intended for Athens, was contradicted by Aristotle. In the following balanced words he describes the necessary community between man and wife as a married couple: "People do not live together only to get children, but also because of things concerning their life. At first work is distributed; it is different for husband and wife: so they help each other and put their own skills and talents to one another's disposal."[11] The Stoics took up the earlier classical ideas and expanded them. The Roman knight C. Musonius Rufus[12] pleaded for the same education for son and daughter, because both sexes had the same mental abilities, the same *logos*, gifts of the gods.

With expanded opportunities in the Hellenistic world and Roman Empire educated women are often mentioned by name. In some cases women from royal families could themselves influence high politics: in Ptolemaic Egypt Arsinoe and Cleopatra, the empress Livia, wife of Augustus, and the Syrian sovereigns from the dynasty of the Severi, Julia Domna, Julia Maesa and Julia Mammaea. All of them had their origin in the ambient Greek culture and participated in

---

[7] First time in detail in Préaux (1929) 772f.; recently Lewis (1983) 62.
[8] Pleket (1969).
[9] Cf. section 2 of this article.
[10] Plato, *Republic* 451D; there should be exceptions only in times of war. Plato's few negative remarks on women are not mentioned here; e.g. *Timaios* 42C and 90E.
[11] Aristotle, *Nicomachean Ethics* 1162a. Similar to 1242a 23ff.: "The human is a being that is made for living within a (lasting) community of his equals."
[12] Musonius (Edition of O. Hense, Freiburg 1905) 8ff., 13ff.

ruling the Roman Empire. In the 3rd century A.D. there was Zenobia,[13] the forceful and artistic princess of Palmyra, a serious opponent of the emperor Aurelianus. From Alexandria there is recorded the name of the mathematician and Neo-Platonist Hypatia, who was murdered by Christian fanatics in 415. Important and very influential women such as Perpetua, Felicitas, Paula, Eustochium and Monnica were known to the early Christian and old church.[14] Also female martyrs and ascetics are well represented.

As we turn to the more private sphere of life in the Hellenistic-Roman world, we see also a change in religiousness and belief. Art is also influenced by the increasing importance of women and their world to which, of course, children belong. So the figure of the once bearded god of love is rejuvenated to a little playful child. Not until Hellenism is this genre intensified in lyric poetry and discovered in art: women with children at play are described, children with animals, the wonderful "foam born" Aphrodite together with old and ugly subjects, as they also exist in real life, plus strange and ludicrous figures and masks. In the classical period unapproachable, godlike male statues generally dominate, e.g., the handsome but severe Apollo from the west gable of the temple of Zeus in Olympia.

Mystery religions with their acting male and female priests have always played a special role in the life of Greek women; religious celebrations were often the only public activity for women[15] also including women who held non-ritual posts. At religious celebrations it seemed to be normal that men and women treated each other informally; this can be assumed as far as the acquaintance of the parents of Alexander the Great at the Samothracian mysteries is concerned.[16] Even clearer, the syncretism of functions of hitherto female gods into one omnipotent goddess takes on a tangible form. The nature of the former Egyptian goddess Isis has been generalized: she is identified with the goddess of love Aphrodite or Venus, with the goddess of heaven Hera or Juno and the goddess of destiny Tyche or Fortuna. This omnipotent goddess is now the One Goddess: "*Una, quae es omnia,*

---

[13] At last, from a deliberately pro-woman point of view: Stoneman (1992c).

[14] Still excellent as a general survey Thraede (1972) 197–269; (1977) 31–182. As bibliographies, *inter alia,* Southwell (1973) 149–159. Against one-sided interpretation see now: Heine (1986) and Küchler (1986). Recently, especially from a more conservative point of view, Krumeich (1993).

[15] Compare Jones (1940); Pleket (1969); van Bremen (1983) 223–241.

[16] Plutarch, *Alexander* 2.2.

dea Isis."[17] This one goddess (or separated goddesses Isis and Aphrodite) plays an essential role as protector of love in the ancient novel, which is a product of the Hellenistic age. By the 2nd and 3rd centuries A.D. at nearly all Graeco-Roman sites there existed richly decorated small shrines of Isis built by rich benefactors. The frescoes in private houses and small temples in Pompeii and Herculaneum give eloquent testimony to the spread of this cult,[18] in which women could function as priests.

Unlike the situation of women in classical Athens, relative self-determination of Roman women is provided with a certain entitlement. This arrangement is certainly due to the social structure and the laws of Rome, whose people were subdivided according to status, the senators and knights with their nearly constant high reputation for centuries—including women, of course. Roman women routinely appeared in public and it was a custom that they went to symposia, theatres or the circus. They were respected as wives. Couples are often represented on memorial sculptures: this rite is of Etruscan origin but was spiritualized by the Romans. With the formation of the Empire the formerly strict patriarchal conditions for matrons and young girls were relaxed, and their legal capacity increased as far as civil law was concerned—inspite of their basic lack of rights in politics. Women by themselves were allowed to lease estates[19] or to obtain divorces. It is interesting that in 2,500 cases of imperial legal advice in the Codex Iustinianus 600 cases are addressed to women.[20] It is also evident that women took part in the local elections of Pompeii, even if participation was limited to election campaigns, as inscriptions tell us.[21] Economic independence of wealthy women is often attested: e.g., Terentia, wife of Cicero, was able to help her husband with money when he was in debt; Eumachia, a woman from Pompeii, donated the meeting house of the tanners' guild from her own means. Besides opinions about virginity in Greece and Rome which we will deal with later, moral concepts, which were often

---

[17] "You one and only who is everything, o Goddess Isis," *CIL* (*Corpus Inscriptionum Latinarum*) 10.3800.
[18] To the spreading and importance of the worship of Isis: Roeder (1916) 2084–2132; Vidman (1970), esp. 48–50 (on female priests); 138 and 159f. (about Fabia Aconia Paulina in the 4th century).
[19] Caesennia in Cicero, *pro Caecina* 6.17. Cp. also Waldstein (1983) 559–571.
[20] Huchthausen (1974) 199–228.
[21] Franklin (1980).

discussed in the Roman Empire, certainly find a place in the novels;[22] for example, the concept of the *univira*, that a wife gets married to one man only, is stressed with special praise on tombstones. An especially good example of a *coniunx carissima*[23] is the following epitaph from Puteoli:

> LOLLIAE•VICTORINAE
> COIVGI•DVLCISSIMAE
> LOLLIANUS•PORRESMUS
> PROCURATOR
> BENE•MERENTI•EMIT
> CVM•QVA•VIXIT•ANNOS XX
> SENE•REPREHENSIONE•VLLA ET•ALTERVTRVM
> HOC•EST•AMASSE.[24]

Beside the commonly praised female virtues such as housekeeping, spinning wool, chasteness, obedience, kindness, obliging nature, religiousness and a restrained outward appearance, for Lollia Victorina "love" is added. And so we are within the subject matter of novels in the Empire of the 1st and 2nd centuries A.D.

2. *Women as Readers—and as Authors?*

Emile Zola tells us about a woman: "She demanded books dealing with affairs, adventures and long journeys".[25] Such desires could already have been decisive for the ancient public which included females, because it seems that already a large part of Hellenistic love poetry was meant for female readers who, for some time, had enjoyed improved opportunities for education. Over a century ago the doyen of ancient novel studies, Erwin Rohde, noted "den überall bemerkbaren moralischen Vorrang der weiblichen Charaktere" as an

---

[22] On the problem see Alföldy (1980).
[23] v. Hesberg-Tonn (1983). In this outstanding paper the way in which the Roman woman "sees herself officially" seems to be a little too much "determined by the rigid ideas of the *mos maiorum*" (*inter alia*, 250).
[24] "The procurator Lollianus Porresmus bought (this plot for a graveyard) for Lollia Victorina his sweetest wife, who deserves it. They lived together for 20 years without accusing each other. That means (really) having loved (= love)."—*CIL* 10.1951.
[25] Quotation from Emile Zola, *The Family Home*, Chapter 11. Original: Pot-Bouille, 11: "Et elle lui demanda des histoires où il y eût beaucoup d'amour, avec des aventures et des voyages dans des pays étrangers."

unconscious admission of the relationship that existed (scil. between the sexes). He notices the better characterization of the main female figures, although he wants to brush them aside as "Typen weiblicher Tugend zu abstrakt" and as a whole only "schablonenmäßige Gestalten der Rhetorenschule".[26] This seems to be symptomatic of the regrettable "Verfallszeit".

What is the fascination of these love novels among—but not only among—women? Why is it run down as "Trivialliteratur",[27] but cannot be hushed up? Are these possibly fairytales for adults, where unfulfilled dreams of ever-lasting love and faithfulness can be dreamed without loosing touch with reality? Are some of these female characters meant to be role models so that female readers willingly elope to a strange world, only to return after a happy ending, fully aware of their own reality which is dreary and dull? Reality and the world of dreams stand in a varied contrast. One cannot deny that the ancient novel has a certain trivial and automated feel. The basic scheme of finding themselves, the separation at the risk to heart and soul, and last (but not least) the (re)unification at the end illustrate this as well as certain other sentimental and macabre motifs. In general, however, ancient novels represent a new genus within Graeco-Roman literature, which nevertheless looks back to ancient traditions and cannot be compared with the "mass literature" of the modern age. As far as style the novel required the involved erudite digressions and the frequent allusions to classical literature, especially Homer; for an audience the novel required a really interested public with an appropriate educational background (which was relatively rare in antiquity). As a late product of literature it was judged to be unclassical by erudite contemporaries as well as by literary sociologists from the 18th century until the middle of our century.[28] Nevertheless the prose of the novels must have been a favourite reading material for a long

---

[26] Rohde (1914 = 1960) 355f. (= 382f.).

[27] It is difficult to find a standard definition for the term "Trivial Literature". It is not reasonable to use it antihistorically, compare Fetzer (1980). The attempt to differentiate between so called higher and lower literature with the concomitant sociological counterpart "elite" and "mass" is problematic and will remain a problem.

[28] See Egger (1988) 35f.; on the philological history of the effects of Greek novels see Egger (1990). I have B. Egger to thank for the valuable hints she gave in stimulating talks. On trivial literature in antiquity and modern age, cf. Kuch (1989a) 23,103,149,196.

period of time.[29] This is all the more remarkable, because the novels were not promoted by schools or references in public literature. For the first time in the private sphere it became possible for women to be readers or audiences: they read themselves or they were read to. With this direct or indirect access to literature they seemed to be reckoned by authors as important recipients with special interests. An often repeated motif in nearly all novels is love-at-first-sight, which falls as a bombshell on the actors and makes a special impression on female emotions. Symptoms of that motif are seen at the first meeting of Charikleia and Theagenes in the novel by Heliodorus:

> When the young people saw each other they loved each other, as if their souls had recognized their relationship when they first met and flew towards each other aware of their destination for one another. At first they were standing still with inner excitement. Hesitating she gave him the torch, hesitating he took it. They looked at each other steadfastly for a long time, as if they had already seen each other, knew each other somehow and tried to remember. They were both smiling but only furtively so that their eyelashes were fluttering brightly for a moment. Then they blushed, as if they were ashamed about this and grew pale again, moved deeply. In a word they expressed a lot with their faces, and the frequent change of colour and expression in their eyes showed their emotion.[30]

This motif of love-at-first-sight is not a new one. Though it had often appeared since Sappho, in the poems of Theokritus and in *Akontios and Kydippe* by Kallimachos, only in the novels has it become a constitutive element.

Another subject seemingly enjoyed by women is the preservation of chastity at any cost, nearly as a religious requirement, until marriage. It was stressed when lovers slept separated,[31] or when a virgin, the heroine Antheia, became the wife of a poor goatherd who let her remain unspoiled because of his sympathy[32]—a motif that Euripides used in his *Electra* for the first time. Certainly opinions about virginity[33] result from an old religious tradition, and are also comprehensible in fairytales like that of the unicorn.

---

[29] Examples in Pack (1965), Montevecchi (1973) 360–394, especially 391.
[30] Heliodorus 3.5 in the translation after H. Gasse. In love-at-first-sight Platonic thought is clearly perceptible.
[31] Heliodorus 5.18.8.
[32] Xenophon of Ephesus 2.9ff.
[33] Fehrle (1910); Rattenbury (1926) 1,59 and 71; Marrou (1953) especially 39–49.

In Rome the Vestal Virgins enjoyed an especially high reputation and certain privileges, but in cases of religious transgressions they were buried alive. Maiden goddesses like Athena and Artemis were always privileged. In the novel the principle of chastity is strictly kept, even aggressively so by the main female figures, and amazingly so by the heroes with two exceptions: in the Melite episode[34] and in the Lykainion scene.[35] In the ancient world the demand for chastity was valid only for women and not typical for men. Perhaps the authors of the novels tried to introduce a reform for men[36] with a certain demand to break through the usual catalogue of motifs or more probably with respect for the female readership. So, of course, private imaginations and secret desires of women played a considerable role as far as the characterization of ideal lovers was concerned. Artistic descriptions of young girls and women with writing utensils, wax-slate and slate-pencil, are found on wall-paintings at Pompeii. Also mosaic floors in residential buildings of rich landowners are a witness to the relatively wide spread interest in the novel: narrative scenes from fragmentary novels still engage the viewers.[37] (Ill. 1) They differ clearly from the scenarios of comedies because of the inscriptions of names of exciting characters.

Direct testimonies concerning readers, especially female readers, are very rare, but are useful for some conclusions. A satirical allusion of Persius to "Kallirhoe" is regarded to be a quite early piece of evidence; the narrative is recommended to men as post-prandial reading.[38]

The Neo-Platonist emperor Julian made no secret of his antipathy to novels. In his 89th letter he referred to the heathen priests in the Greek East and warned against the *erotikai hypotheseis* ("love stories") which were told as true history, although they were *plasmata* ("fictions") only.[39] On the other hand physicians recommended that their male patients read novels as stimulants.[40] The direct effect of a drama

---

[34] Achilleus Tatios 5.27.
[35] Longus 3.18-20.
[36] "Eine spektakuläre Innovation, ein einkalkuliertes Spiel mit den Gattungsschablonen" for Effe (1982) 110, 68, note 10. On this also see Reardon (1969) 23,300.
[37] For the Metiochus-Parthenope novel, Levi (1974), vol. 1, 117ff.; vol. 27 Ill. XX a–c; on attempts to interpret the novel of Ninus, see Müller (1981) 384f., 390.
[38] Persius 1.131: his *mane edictum* (probably meant legal edicts and forum matters), *post prandia Callirhoen do*.
[39] Julian 89. Letter 300C–301D.
[40] Theodorus Priscianus 2.11.34.

1. Metiochus and Parthenope. Floor mosaic at Daphne near Antioch on the Orontes, circa 200. Repro-photograph, M.E. Hamann, Berlin.

and reading material on the physical and psychic disposition has been analysed since Plato. So especially women have been censored strictly from antiquity via Byzantium until the modern age because a demoralizing and unrealistic effect was feared, if they should read novels.

The happy ending of the "chaste love of a married couple" and the "legitimate love" (*erotes dikaioi*) or the "legal marriages" (*nominoi gamoi*) are said to be the aims of the novel for the implicitly addressed reader.[41] This wishful thinking is thought to meet the specific interests of women in antiquity and so female readers are included here and elsewhere. Because of the phenomenon of grammatical classification and subordination of the feminine to the masculine, which is especially picked up as a principal theme in ancient juridical literature,[42] women often are not mentioned *expressis verbis* in written documents but obviously are included. Certainly this is true for Apuleius when he addressed the reader: "*Lector intende: laetaberis.*"[43]

Owing to a fortunate circumstance we get to know the name of one female reader of novels in antiquity, the "story-loving Isidora". Isidora is the sister of the novelist Antonios Diogenes, probably from the first century A.D., who began his novel *About the Miracles Beyond Thule* as a letter to her.[44] Unfortunately there is nothing else recorded about her, but it is important that a female reader with appropriate interests is called by name as addressee.[45]

Perhaps Sallust offers us a glimpse of an emancipated female Roman of that time who was possibly also a female reader of novels: "Fortune had smiled on this lady because of her background and beauty and her husband and children. She was well-versed in Greek and Latin literature and was able to play musical instruments and to dance skilfully, as it was necessary for a respectable woman... She had excellent mental abilities and was able to write verses and to joke and to start conversations, sometimes with restraint or just sentimental or

---

[41] Leukippe's praise of the so-called philosopher Leo, *Anthologia Palatina* 9.203.7f., printed in the Achilleus Tatios edition of Vilborg 163. Directly addressed to the reader in Chariton 8.1.

[42] Compare Servius, *Digest* 32.62: *semper sexus masculinus etiam femininum sexum continet.*

[43] Apuleius 1.1.4.

[44] Antonios Diogenes 5.51, recorded in Photios, *Bibliotheka*, cod.166, pp. 111a–111b.

[45] It is not important for the question of female readers whether the dedication to Isidora is only fictitious, according to Müller (1981) 395. In this connection also the present situation in the research of "book culture" is important; compare, e.g., Kenyon (1951), Havelock (1982), Pöhlmann (1988) 7–20, Knox (1985).

cheeky—briefly, she had a lot of wit and charm."[46] Because there is no further hard evidence for female readership apart from Isidora, it is necessary to look for signals in the text regarding female readers. It is interesting to note that the domestic traditional female sphere plays only a minor role in the ancient novel;[47] it is not yet acceptable in literature. The heroines in the novel and so probably female readers are not yet reading just for fun, but the ability to read and write is always presupposed and practiced. Letters of many different kinds, e.g., love letters, identification and farewell letters are written and read to move the plot forward or to interpret psychological conclusions only:[48] each has a function in the novel.

It is important to note that women of the upper and middle classes assume reading and writing as a matter of course. For the novelists this is a natural observation gathered from a social reality valid for women of the Hellenistic as well as the Roman period. The wife of Apuleius and the Christian martyr Perpetua wrote *manu sua*. It is instructive to observe that in Attic tragedy Phaidra is the only woman[49] able to write, especially when outstanding hetaerae were more likely to be educated.

Education according to the classical term *paideia* is connected with a social self-confidence and meets the ideas of rank of the middle and upper class readers. *Pepaideumenos* or *pepaideumene* is often stressed as a behavior befitting the rank of the Greek heroes in contrast to the barbarians of the Orient.[50] In Longus it is said as a matter of course that the foster parents, who were ordinary shepherds, let both foundlings give lessons, feeling obliged to do this because of the rich gift.[51] It was worthwhile at the end.

One single bookreader in the Greek novels is found in the figure of Kleitophon in Achilleus Tatius. He has just fallen hopelessly in

---

[46] Sallust, *Catilina* 25. Probably Sempronia is meant, daughter of the reform politician C. Gracchus, wife of the former consul D. Junius Brutus and mother of one of the murderers of Caesar.

[47] Achilleus Tatios could be an exception: Books 1 and 2 are about home to a large extend. There is a report about walks in the evening, about the cithara-playing of a young girl, etc.

[48] E.g., Chariton 8.4.5; Xenophon of Ephesus 2.5.1; 2.12.1; Achilleus Tatios 5.18.3; Heliodorus 2.10.1; 9.2.11.

[49] Euripides, *Hippolytos* 856ff.

[50] Especially in Chariton 2.4.1; 6.5.8; 7.5.6; Xenophon of Ephesus 1.1.2; Heliodorus 7.14.2.

[51] Longus 1.8.1; *grámmata epaídeuon*.

love with Leucippe and tries to meet her again "by accident": he is walking to and fro and pretends to be absorbed in a book (*biblion*).[52] Reading is not presented for its own sake but for speeding up the events. Only the heroine of the last love novel in antiquity, Charikleia of Heliodorus, as a beautiful and clever woman[53] is self-confident enough and, so to speak, emancipated enough to maltreat her theological-philosophical interests for her own sake. With her serious ambitions as an "intellectual" she probably did not have the desire to read adventure and romantic novels. Her special position we will deal with later.

In Heliodorus the Athenian Knemon comments that men were "keen on" romances. Just like the "story-loving" Isidora, he is listening raptly to a romantic love story, the drama of Charikleia and Theagenes. He identifies himself as listener = reader of the story of the priest Kalasiris, so to speak the novel in the novel.[54] Knemon is really greedy for stories;[55] his "craze for reading" is almost amusing.[56] Heliodorus describes the ironic picture of the naive and inexhaustible reader[57] to dissociate himself from what is traditionally expected from the genre. On the other hand he offers it in his novel, but with cunning.[58]

We have already seen and will see it again still more clearly that the texts of novels offer many possibilities for the reader to identify with acting females. These females, especially the protagonists, are often characterized as more intelligent, active and on the whole more sympathetic than their male partners. The names of some authors are not very meaningful and in my mind it seems reasonable to assume that some authors are females who used pen-names. If we think of Aristophontes of Athens and Xenophon of Ephesus it is tempting to assume this, but there is no evidence existing, and so it must stay a hypothesis.[59] Pen-names were and are not unusual in the history of

---

[52] Achilleus Tatios 1.6.6. About "book culture"; also compare note 45.
[53] Heliodorus 3.4.1: *kalé kai sophé*.
[54] Heliodorus 3.2.3; 4.3.4; 4.4.2.
[55] Heliodorus 4.4.2f.; 5.13f., and more.
[56] Heliodorus 4.4.3; 5.1.4: *akórestos, seirénion*.
[57] Heliodorus 2.23–5.3.
[58] About the expectations of listeners and readers of Knemon, compare Winkler (1982) 27, 138f.
[59] Very certain, Hägg (1983) 96f. In *Eros und Tyche* (1987b) 122ff., Hägg is even more certain. Met with approval by Holzberg (1986) 42, and Kuch (1989a) 158, but sceptically *ibid.*, 188f.

literature; there were and are many explanations for this precaution. Socio-politically pen-names are reasonable in times of crises and radical changes, e.g., the so called *Epistolae obscurorum virorum* or satirical writings (*Eccius dedolatus*) by renaissance humanists like Willibald Pirckheimer.[60] At the end of the 19th century the widely read writer of adventure stories Karl May used several pen-names without being able to escape from the attacks of his literary opponents. Popular female authors (E. Marlitt) used pen-names to survive in the world of men: Amatine-Aurore-Lucile Dupin became famous as George Sand. Even today female authors of detective stories look for anonymity (Tom Wittgen). There is no reason why this practice should not have existed already in antiquity, when it was much more necessary than later. Women wrote for women about women! Nothing is there against this theory, but it cannot be proven. In this connection a new interpretation of the young charming woman with slate-pencil and wax-slate as "a woman novelist in her hour of inspiration"[61] is worth thinking about. (Ill. 2) Hitherto this Roman wall-painting from Pompeii from the first century B.C. was identified as Sappho. Even that could be a compliment to a great and exceptionally gifted lyricist of antiquity who came into fashion again in the period in question. But why should not a female author of the new genre of novels be portrayed in full self-confidence? So this painting would be a reflexion of an actual female ability to write and read and beyond this of emancipated intellectualism.

3. *Love as a Central Issue*

The subject of love or Eros is as old as literature itself. Already in Homer the famous farewell scene between Hector and Andromache before the last battle expressed the closeness of the couple. Erotic motifs[62] and the depiction of true love existed long before the flowering of the novel, especially in lyric poetry since Sappho, in the elegies, epic poetry as well as in drama, but such an exclusive reference to love only, with subordination of all other things, was for the

---

[60] In addition to that Johne (1992) 48–59.
[61] Hägg (1983) 96.
[62] Lesky (1976) makes a difference between the frivolity of the novella (135–138) and the overaction in the Greek novel (139–145).

2. Young woman with wax tablet and stylus. Wall painting from Pompeii, 1st century B.C. Naples, National Museum. Repro-photograph, M.E. Hamann, Berlin.

first time created by the Greek novel which, so to speak, picked up the problems and yearnings of the "middle-class" couple, i.e., of individuals. The limitation of emotions only to love means, of course, a reduction of the scope for human action.

Sappho calls Eros a "bitter-sweet monster" and so she describes the cosmic elemental power by which each person—man or woman, poor or rich, young or old—could be bewitched without hope of resistence. In the wedding song of Sappho, as it is called, the physical effects of the highest love passion in the melancholy of the farewell hour is expressed:

> He is more than a hero
>
> He is a god in my eyes—
> the man who is allowed
> to sit beside you—he
>
> who listens intimately
> to the sweet murmur of
> your voice, the enticing
>
> laughter that makes my own
> heart beat fast. If I meet
> you suddenly, I can't
>
> speak—my tongue is broken;
> a thin flame runs under
> my skin; seeing nothing,
>
> hearing only my own ears
> drumming, I drip with sweat;
> trembling shakes my body
>
> and I turn paler than
> dry grass. At such times
> death isn't fear from me.[63] (Ill. 3)

The opinion of ennobled nature of Eros is influenced by philosophers like Plato. His mythical story of the spherical man, recited by the ingenious comic poet Aristophanes in the *Symposion*, shows the extreme and endless yearning for the other part of oneself. Full of sinful high spirits the spherical people cause jealousy and anger in the gods and they are separated—the proof is seen at the navel. In

---

[63] Sappho 31 LP (Lobel-Pager 1959) in the translation by Mary Barnard (*Sappho*, Berkeley, 1962). This motive is picked up again later, e.g. by Theokritus.

3. Childlike head of Eros, god of love. Roman marble copy after an original by Lysippos about 340 B.C. Staatliche Museen zu Berlin, Preußischer Kulturbesitz, Antikensammlung. Photograph by Staatliche Museen zu Berlin.

the Platonic dialogue Sokrates interprets the yearning for each other as the striving for a whole, which is to be rendered as the good and at the same time as beauty and perfection. The individual human being is conscious of his imperfection and strives for the corporal and mental union by Eros.[64] It is remarkable that in Athens, where society was dominated by men, a wise woman, the priest Diotima, was able to get to the bottom of the mysteries of the real Eros, when her pupil Sokrates appeared. Eros is a demon, in conflict as a son of Poros (abundance) and Penia (poverty) but nevertheless a mediator between divinity and human nature on the bumpy way to the right thing, the truth and the good. This philosophical sublimation of Eros, which is also latent in the novel, stands in opposition to the modern propagation of the "sexual liberation" without any ethical aim.

In classical tragedy Eros is described as a pining, irrational and corrupting passion. In Deianeira of Sophokles the loving woman is marked. Her youth is fading and she fears that she is losing her beloved husband to a much younger woman. Even more comprehensible are the individual tragedies of the heroines in the female tragedies of Euripides, as they are called. The passionate Medea, the non-Athenian, becomes the murderer of her own children, because her husband, for whom she sacrificed all, plans to leave her. When she talks to herself before the horrible decision, she uncovers the emotional life of a wife: in the yoke women are determined to look at only one soul,[65] which means that they depend completely on the one man to whom they belong. The love-hate relationship of Phaidra leads to the decision to put an end to her life and to the accusation of her stepson as supposed seducer. On the other hand Alkestis with her true love until death seems to be the "ideal of a wife". With her readiness to make sacrifices she shames even the parents of the husband and surpasses by far male figures in her human greatness. Perhaps Euripides wanted to express the discontent with the subordinated social status of women at that time by his characterization of his female actors.[66] In spite of their ability to act, heroines have no ability to effect changes; they are still too much shaped by the general standards system[67] immortalized in depictions of happy couples

---

[64] Plato, *Symposion* 192E: there is a vivid illustration of the "melting together" (*syntékein*).
[65] Euripides, *Medea* 247.
[66] Compare epilogue by Kuch (1976) 237–260, especially 242–248; quotation 260.
[67] Harder (1993) especially 156–158. Similar to Seidensticker (1987) 7–42.

in burial poems and on monuments. The couple's joined hands, the dexiosis, and the looks in their eyes express the intensity of the relationship.[68] *Helena* of the ageing Euripides, this fairytale of female love and truth in an exotic atmosphere of adventures, is rightly seen to be an early stage of the romantic novel. The comedies of Menander provide another source: love and the efforts at the legitimate union of lovers play an important role. In comedy as well as later in the novel problems are caused and solved by accident, but by proving themselves in critical situations actors get their just rewards at the end. Different motifs in the novel are already to be found in the New Comedy, e.g., regret about violent outbursts and wrongful charges. A certain similarity[69] between novels and comedy can be explained by the shift of poetic interest from the civic to the individual sphere. So in Menander there was a change from the political satire of Aristophanes to the "middle-class" comedy with private conflicts and an end in harmony. His dramatic figures are very human,[70] non-heroic, without close ties to the polis and the state cult, but with new traits which had a lasting influence on later literature because of their general humanity. These are completely fictitious characters acting on the stage, similar to the fictitious persons in the Graeco-Roman novels.

When comparing the main female characters in comedy and in the novel,[71] we see that in spite of different *genera* but with nearly the same preconditions the figures in Menander somehow stay pale and passive. In this connection we can cite Pamphile, the young Athenian in *Schiedsgericht*. In other plays the concubine or the young wife often does not even have a name. The sensitive depiction of the hetaira Habrotonon is different. She is characterized by Menander as a "noble hetaira" who can solve all problems because of her quick mental grasp and her clever intriguing: she takes the abandoned child back to the young unlucky mother, Pamphile, calms the husband about supposed unfaithfulness, and achieves her own longed-for freedom.

In the romantic novel the heroine is the young, free citizen of the polis, unlike comedy where often the hetaira, the non-citizen, is the

---

[68] Convincing examples in Diepolder (1931).
[69] See Schmeling (1980) 101–104.
[70] Körte (1937); Treu (1981) 211–214.
[71] Johne (1988) 12–15.

main figure. For this reason there must be no "indiscretion" as far as ideal lovers are concerned. As a reminiscence of tragedy the novel is very demanding of high morals, but unlike comedy it is not possible to bring this very human story to a good end in an amusing fashion. Thus it is not surprising that the heroine in the novel appears as an equal being and fully recognized partner of the man—a phenomenon which was unthinkable in comedy. The private sphere by itself, as in the comedy of Menander, is not a sufficient stage for the novel. The main characters, the couple, are involved in social duties, sometimes even as public authorities of a priesthood. For this reason private happiness has to be brought into line with political and social tasks. The process of maturity and a certain development of the heroine in the novels of the individual authors will be dealt with later.

To my mind there was another genre that played a part in the creation of the novel's heroines: the epos. I offer this as an example to support my theory.

With the figure of Dido, Queen of Carthage and superior partner with the Roman national hero Aeneas, we have an example of a psychologically complex heroine: her counterpart in the novel is Charikleia of Heliodorus. "Love as a destiny" is the title we could give to the Dido-episode of the 4th book in Vergil's *Aeneid*: it plays a pivotal role and is regarded as a highly dramatic story with external and internal completeness. In the focus is a woman deserted by her lover, her struggle for him, her despair, her self-accusation, her madness and eventually her death for love she chose herself. Dido is no goddess or demigoddess but a sorely afflicted person like Aeneas himself. As a woman she tries to perform a man's business in building a new city as a home, but she is defeated by the conflict between her duty and her passionate love. After a short but full love affair which she—and only she!—wants to legitimize in public,[72] *pius Aeneas* leaves her to build his own new Troja in Italy according to the divine will of *fatum*. With the curse of the dying Dido on the man and his descendants enmity between Rome and Carthage has been insured. Only in dying does she recognize the power of destiny and finds her real nature. She dies as a royal woman deserves to. In this epos a happy ending is not possible: there are only a few ex-

---

[72] Vergil, *Aeneid* 4.171f. Dido talks about the *coniugium*. Compare the complications in Johne (1985) 75–82.

amples either in literature or real life which show the possibility of correspondence between private happiness and political and social activities.

When looking at female characters in the different *genera*, it is necessary to stress that only in the novel does love become the central issue. It is, so to speak, "the power of heaven" that is staged in highly pathetic and dramatic moments. A single person is at the mercy of superhuman power, but this condition also elicits superhuman strength. Because of Eros he is able to overcome all threats and temptations. Love is the challenge which gives human life its deepest sense. The individual is brought out of the restrictions on his life in the polis, and the mortal approaches the nature of god.

"Love" especially in the novel is considered to be the totality of physical and psychological affections that direct people and express their comprehensive personal relationship with the other sex. Sexual intercourse alone cannot be love; it is tied to love but, without it, is insignificant. Eros including physical as well as psychological love in the main female character in the novel brings about a long-term relationship that should lead to matrimony and overcome all sufferings and dangers. There is another Eros in Petronius and Apuleius in the Roman satirical novel[73] (which is also seen in the picaresque novel): marital love and truth is made fun of—now and then there can be assumed a pastiche on the romantic novel—, suggestive stories of adultery and other erotic narratives of homosexual and bisexual jealousy are told in a racy way and full of realism. The Enkolpius of Petronius as a "Freibeuter der Liebe",[74] who acts in a way similar to the egocentrical TV-heroes of the present, is a consciously portrayed antihero in comparison with the heroic couple of the Greek romantic novel.

4. *About the Image of the Human Being in the Ancient Novel*

The structures in the romantic novel are relatively inflexible and the catalogue of subjects as a whole is not really variable. These principles are due to the *genus*.

---

[73] The figure of Trimalchio in Petronius and of Lucius in Apuleius; compare Johne (1989a) 172–177.
[74] Quotation of Kytzler (1983), in the introduction to Vol. 1, 10.

On these conditions the figures acting within a certain framework have only a limited possibility of development and autonomy apart from a few exceptions. When shaping their characters, the authors were able to consider their task especially in a framework of variation and nuance. They created a large number and quite varied range of persons differing in sex, geographical origin, social status and age. With this variety they conform to their Hellenistic-Roman surroundings from where they took the ideas for their work. In spite of the similar structure of some couples, especially of the male actors, we can recognize a differentiation; but the genre of novels is open for a certain individualization of its "types",[75] although they are fixed to a large extent without being looked at as mere "puppets".[76] Because this is especially to be seen in the main female figures a more comprehensive description in this chapter seems to be justified.[77] In the following, four groups are especially scrutinized from texts I have stressed:

1. the heroine herself,
2. the female antagonist,
3. the close girl-friend, mostly the servant and
4. the mother.

There is a repeated and prevailing pattern to the beginnings of the Greek romantic novel: a young man and a young girl meet by accident, usually at a public religious celebration. Both are not older than 17 years, sometimes even younger. Often they are caught by "love-at-first-sight", but Leukippe, the main character in Achilleus Tatios, has to be conquered step by step by her male partner. We get to know the heroines as young wives in the novels by Chariton and Iamblichus. The lovers are separated soon after their wedding

---

[75] In the terminology of the science of literature there is no standard use of "Figur", "Gestalt", "Person" and "Typ", but these expressions are used as synonyms; compare *inter alia* Kasper and Wuckel (1982) 108–120. Stimulating for the definition of "Typen" is Milbradt (1974) 1413–1449, especially 1420.

[76] Too simple is the assertion of Anderson (1984) 62–74. He says (62): "The main criticism of the heroes in the novel is that they are puppets." On the other hand he stresses the differentiated expressions of different figures, especially of women, and at the beginning of his book he talks about individuality.

[77] Links arise from the results of the research in Kuch (1989a). Also the world of the opera, e.g., Mozart's *Magic Flute*, deals with the noble heroic couple who are lucky enough to come together again after a long period of tests, in the style of the ancient novel as well as the worship of Isis, even as far as the figure of the heroine is concerned.

and will come together after a time of ordeals and temptations. Before the happy unification or reunification with the wedding or the celebration at the end, there will be sufferings of all kinds like the attempted rape of the bride, dark oracular statements and serious nightmares, escape, storms on the deep sea, shipwrecks, attacks of buchaneers, even captivity and sale into slavery, apparent death, court trials and several intrigues are essential parts of each novel with the catalogue of varying motifs. There is always the happy ending as "reward" of true love and of two people becoming one. In the wedding poem by Simon Dach from the 17th century, which became a German folk song as "Ännchen von Tharau", there is expressed in brief form the contents of a Greek romantic novel as, so to speak, a "timeless" subject.[78]

> 1. Ännchen von Tharau ist's, die mir gefällt.
> Sie ist mein Leben, mein Gut und mein Geld.
> Ännchen von Tharau hat wieder ihr Herz
> auf mich gerichtet in Leib und in Schmerz.
> // Ännchen von Tharau, Mein Reichtum, mein Gut,
> // du meine Seele, mein Fleisch und mein Blut!
>
> 2. Käm alles Wetter gleich auf uns zu schlahn,
> wir sind gesinnt, beieinander zu stahn.
> Krankheit, Verfolgung, Betrübnis und Pein
> soll unsrer Liebe Verknotigung sein.
>
> 3. Recht als ein Palmenbaum über sich steigt,
> hat ihn erst Regen und Sturmwind gebeugt,
> So wird die Lieb in uns mächtig und groß
> nach manchem Leiden und traurigem Los.
>
> 4. Würdest du gleich einmal von mir getrennt,
> lebtest du, wo man die Sonne kaum kennt:
> Ich will dir folgen durch Wälder, durch Meer,
> Eisen und Kerker und feindliches Heer.
> // Ännchen von Tharau, mein Licht, meine Sonn,
> // mein Leben schließt sich um deines herum.

In the novel a special image of the human being is produced: on the one hand there is almost no change between the start and the end

---

[78] The poem "Anke von Tharaw" was written in Samland dialect by Simon Dach (1605–1659) in 1637. He was professor of poetry at Königsberg. It became better known only in the High German version by Johann Gottfried Herder in 1778; it was musically arranged by Fr. Silcher in 1825.

of the action as far as the characters are concerned, the passion at the beginning and wedding at the end of the novel which must have biographical relevance for the heroes—the evil person as well as the buchaneer stay bad, the venal physician stays venal, the respectable widow stays respectable, the true slave stays true and so on; on the other hand the main characters and several others show possibilities of change, e.g., the robber-chief Thyamis in Heliodorus gets into difficulties through no fault of his own. His sins are forgiven as "precious robber" and so he can function again as priest in Memphis. In Longus, e.g., the continuous development "from innocence to experience"[79] of the very young couple is to be viewed outside the physical sphere.[80] In general the lovers are young and beautiful at the beginning, so to speak without age. Also their true feelings for one another stay unchanged—with the temporary exception of Sinonis in Iamblichus. Nevertheless an attempted "psychology" of the heroes is possible. We can observe that there are changes and floods of emotions in the dramatic and rhetorical tradition, detailed monologues and dialogues, comparisons of the heroes with certain gods,[81] and also conspicuous are certain expressions (the frequent "I thought so") and the descriptions of the physical effects (to blush, to turn pale and quite often the fainting fits of women). All this shows a capacity for empathy and so individualization in a certain sense.

The influence of irrational powers starts with the things which happen by accident to each hero of a novel, so that—apart from exceptions—as soon as he takes the initiative something happens to him, so to speak, under duress. Kleitophon in Achilleus Tatios expresses this as follows: "Often the demon foretells people's future while they are sleeping, not because they should protect themselves from the evil, the predicted undoing cannot be made undone—but to bear it more easily when they will be confronted with it."[82]

Already these words make it clear that heroes of novels not only behave passively and lack initiative,[83] they are lively people who

---

[79] So Philippides (1980) 194.
[80] Longus 4.40.3.
[81] Here the concept of *parousia* is expressed as in the religious literature, which means that in a man the *parousia* of a god can be developed and show its power.
[82] Achilleus Tatios 1.3.3.
[83] The "absolutely passive" man in the Greek novel and "total" invariability: like Bakhtin (1974) tries to get us to believe in a connection in the investigation of two pictures of the human being in the ancient novel; it is out of the question (1161–1191; quotation on 1172).

endure, overcome and also influence the game of destiny as "playthings of destiny". They prove themselves in all situations and keep their whole identity, as the eternal "silent sufferer" Odysseus has already shown. The central problem of the novel in antiquity is and will stay the examination of the heroes as far as their steadfastness, their chastity and truthfulness, their courage, strength and fearlessness, humanity and common sense are concerned. Nearly always they pass all examinations and temptations in a brilliant and honourable way. They do not have identity crises like the main figures of the modern middle-class novel.[84] There is no self-estrangement; the ethos of the hero or the heroine translated into action is the basis for the self-assertion of the individual in spite of all attacks of Tyche and the prevailing metaphysical powers. Since the hero and the heroine react essentially on external influences, they are no force to organize history according to the present sense.

An originally aristocratic ideal, the *"kalokagathia"*, is silently taken for granted as far as the main heroes are concerned. In this Greek term aesthetic and ethical advantages, the beautiful (kalon) and the good (agathon), are formed into an integrated whole. The *kalokagathia* means the perfect harmony of the body as well as harmonic mental and moral education. With the end of the classical age the educational and so the individual-ethical aspect came to the fore, which became relevant to the main figures. Also this should be stressed: all experiences and actions of the figures are of a private nature and do not have any socio-political importance. The appearance of the individual and his private sphere in the literature of Hellenism resulted to a large extent from the loss of the participation in public-social life. This tendency met the conditions of reality which caused the desire for compensation in the world of novels.

There is another kind of image of a human being in the Roman-satirical novel, mainly in Petronius and Apuleius but also in a part of the early Christian novel-like biographies.[85] There the close connection of adventures with colourful everyday life is typical. These events with their social background give more maturity to the heroes. A certain caesura in the biography of the hero, which he

---

[84] See *inter alia* Naumann (1978) especially 7f. and 265.
[85] Compare *inter alia* Soeder (1932); Delahaye (1921). Lately several separate studies have been conducted considering the "new hero", which means the apostles, martyrs and saints.

himself often causes, changes all that previously happened—as far as Lucius is concerned it is the transformation, the "metamorphosis". The Psyche-figure in Apuleius we will deal with later in this connection. The scheme presented as stages of development up to purification we can find in early Christian literature: a life full of sins and temptations is followed by crisis and eventually by spiritual reincarnation as a saint.

The utopian novel is an exception. It shows the enormous extension of the world view since the classical time. The idealized state of the Ethiopians in Heliodorus can be understood as political utopia.[86] The imaginations and desires, which emerge at the beginning of the production of novels, are felt to be still relevant at the end of late antiquity. The hero of a utopian novel has a special position. As far as we can see from the fragments, he behaves passively to a large extent. He is brought by chance to an exotic realm with ideally described conditions. He has no part in this and is driven out of this again. We can assume that the author wanted to create an alternative picture and to express veiled social criticism because of discontent with his own time.[87] (Ill. 4)

There is still another aspect to consider as far as the picture of the human being in all novels is concerned: with the new possibilities in the East neither Athens nor Rome are in the focus, which has shifted to the provinces, where most of the novel authors come from. In the male and female Egyptian mummy portraits from the Roman imperial period there is shown a picture of human beings in the provinces in an epoque of relatively high material prosperity which seems to be nearly identical with the readers of the novels. And the papyri of novels and the mummy portraits have their origin in the same area: Egypt.

5. *Female Characters in Selected Novels*

Of course a young man and a young woman belong in each romantic novel. Ideally each partner should contribute according to his ability to a happy end of the relationship. As already mentioned several

---

[86] Szepessy (1981) 203–207.
[87] Compare *inter alia* Kytzler (1973) 45–68; Ferguson (1975); partially overinterpreted by R. Müller (1983); Müller (1987) 10–52.

4. Portrait of Paquius Procules with his wife. Wall painting from Pompeii, 1st century B.C. Naples, National Museum. Repro-photograph, M.E. Hamann, Berlin.

times, women protagonists are amazingly the more active part within the partnership. They are not only more beautiful (this alone would not be extraordinary), they have not only a better social status, more strength of character, intelligence, drive and they are not only better in their practical lifestyle than their lovers, but they enjoy also because of the narrative techniques of the Greek novels moral superiority including faithfulness and steadfastness as central figures. In comparison to the heroines the heroes seem to be weak characters, so to speak "softies", colourless, nearly unimportant and often absolutely well-behaved. They are rarely beset with doubt, they are never on the edge, their behaviour is rarely sensual, and consequently they seem unable to awaken the imagination of their female readers. Powerful and manly behaviour is shown only in sports fights and in war and then only to be able to get a sweetheart for ever at the end. Here I am thinking of Chaireas and of Theagenes. On the other hand heroines play the central role in the true sense of the word. In spite of all conventional restraints they are strong and clever. In situations where men hesitate, they behave self-confidently and make correct decisions—often of necessity but independently. Kallirhoe, e.g., contemplates an abortion but eventually makes a decision in favour of her life and the life of her unborn child. Or Charikleia, who several times pretends that her lover is her brother so that she is not separated from him. Heroines are forced to live surprisingly autonomous existences. They are the more interesting and complex personalities when men appearing like shadows are set beside them.[88]

Using heroines of the following selected novels we will try to show the gradual development of the strong image of the woman. We will also examine the female antagonist, the intimate girl-friend and the mother of the heroine, before we venture to come to a final position.

a. *The Novel of Ninus*

The novel of Ninus, which survives in three fragments A, B, and C, is probably the oldest extant romantic novel[89] and was obviously very popular in imperial times to judge from several surviving mosaics with inscriptions. This novel takes its name from Ninus the legend-

---

[88] Sociological investigations on female roles in films of the Third Reich strangely show a similar tendency; compare Beyer (1991). Of course comparisons of such heterogeneous kinds have to be handled with great care.

[89] Compare Kuch (1989a) 202f.

ary founder of Nineveh. According to the legend this Assyrian king married his cousin Semiramis who later founded Babylon. In the novel both heroes are quite young, the girl is only thirteen years old but already wounded by the arrow of Eros. Since the young prince as head of a big army has to fight the Armenians, he tries to marry Semiramis as soon as possible. The mothers, who are also the aunts of the lovers, are ready to serve as advocates. During his courting speech Ninus' behaviour appears aggressive and imperious because he must act decisively and quickly. He is concerned for the welfare of the state as well as for Semiramis, and the uncertainty and unpredictability of the time make it necessary to hurry. On the other hand the girl can only bashfully make her request: "She asked for some time and cried. She wanted to say something, but, before she could start, she fell silent. Soon she herself expressed the intention to speak, opened her lips and looked as if she wanted to say something, but she didn't say a word at the end. Tears were running down her cheeks and she blushed, ashamed of speaking, but suddenly when she tried again to speak she grew pale with fear. She was between hope and yearning on the one hand and fear and shame on the other hand. Her passionate love encouraged her, but she lacked determination and so she connected violent excitement with serious dejection."[90]

We can assume that the intended marriage took place soon. In fragment B a scene of jealousy ends with the reconciliation before a battle. After the military catastrophy Ninus wanders about (fragment C) the beach of Kolchis in despair and worries about the future of his captured wife.

This early novel already includes many important motifs of the genre: the central part of the lovers, the demand on one another's faithfulness, separation and great misfortune, the magic world of the Orient. The young girl is still described according to the old regime of the role of a woman: shy, blushing with shame and full of tears, subordinated, in the background as it was expected of a woman in the polis and as it is performed in comedy.

b. *Chariton of Aphrodisias*

The heroine Kallirhoe with her almost celestial beauty stands in stark contrast to the heroine of the novel of Ninus—she appears as an

---

[90] Ninos novel, Fragment A 140–159.

incarnation of Aphrodite—and is obviously in the focus of the events. The author from Asia Minor, Chariton, who calls himself a secretary of an orator and lawyer, concludes his novel with the name of the heroine alone (thus emphasizing that he told *her* love-story) because the heroine determines the actions in the novel.

Kallirhoe is purposely included in the opening historical section as the authentic daughter of the commander Hermokrates from Syracuse, who destroyed the Athenian fleet in the Peloponnesian War. The plot of the (arguably) oldest extant novel is said to take place at the time of King of Persia, Artaxerxes II (404 to about 360 B.C.). The love-at-first-sight unites the couple at a festival of Aphrodite. In spite of the rivalry between their fathers they are allowed to marry. But the early days of joy soon end, because Kallirhoe for her erotic aura becomes the desired object of many men. The line of admirers starts with the rejected suitors in Syracuse, later Dionysios, a prince in Miletus and her second husband, then Mithridates and Pharnakes, two Persian satraps, and last but not least the Persian King Artaxerxes himself. So the ranks of the suitors is really arranged as a socially ascending line. But Kallirhoe does not see her beauty as fortunate, because it was disastrous, even dangerous to her life. In a desperate soliloquy she admits to feel "like a household appliance",[91] going from hand to hand, to Greeks, then to "Barbarians" and even to robbers. In monologues her subsequent action is anticipated, especially when she rationally decides not to commit suicide because of the child that she expects and to get married for a second time to Dionysios. In a quite touching dialogue with the still unborn child of Chaireas, who must assume that she is dead, she thinks about an abortion— a unique passage in Greek literature—but finally she makes up her mind to save the child both from death and slavery on the warning of a dream and the wise advice from the older slave Plangon.[92] In the fight for her woman's respect and the child of her true love, her vital energy wins. She marries the overjoyed Dionysios—who has just lost his family.

Kallirhoe the young mother presents problems as a defective human being, when at the end of the novel she leaves her baby behind in Miletus to go back to her native country with her first husband.

---

[91] Chariton 1.14.9: *hos skeúos*.
[92] Chariton 2.8.3; 2.9.1; 2.10.7; 2.11.5. For the whole difficult passage Schmeling (1974) 98f.

In the military battle against the King, Chaireas wins her back and recovers totally from his jealousy and his violent temper, which had almost killed her. Kallirhoe is willing to leave the child with the lonely Dionysios out of gratitude and loyalty: the child's future is safeguarded, but information about legitimate paternity is deliberately withheld. According to the laws of the literary genre her relationship to her lover is stronger than her relationship to the child born abroad, which is to be considered only as an episode. A happy life (further children can be expected because of the ages of the couple) and a common death for the heroes is predicted at the end.

Chariton is able to portray the pure human struggles in his heroine so well that one can say that it is probably the most "psychological" novel of Greek antiquity. In long monologues and descriptions of her thoughts her innermost life is exposed and insights into her emotions and intentions are given. With so-called insight, a term of the modern theory of novels, the sympathy of the readers is gained for a fictitious figure. Private and erotic life influence political and public life—in Syracuse women participate in the assemblies which considers the relationship between Kallirhoe and Chaireas. Comments are made: the chorus of tragedy is virtually replaced by the reactions of the intended readers. An identification of the female reader with the heroine is possible without any sense of guilt. The theme of pursued innocence which has "an informal power"[93] has become very effective in world literature, even if the beautiful and desired woman is acting in a world dominated by men. She has to maintain her position, but she stays more an object than a subject. The dialectics between the restrictions placed on female activities on the one hand and the erotic-emotional strength of the heroine on the other hand are profound and increase the attraction of the Greek novel.

c. *Apuleius*

Extensive works survive from the pen of Lucius(?) Apuleius Madaurensis Platonicus,[94] an outstanding representative of the Second Sophistic. Without any doubt his most important work is the *Metamorphoses*,

---

[93] Expressed correctly by B. Egger in a speech on "Der griechische Roman und der Spielraum der Frauen" at Humboldt University, Berlin, in June, 1990.
[94] He calls himself like that in the *Apologia* 9.10.

the so-called *Golden Ass*, some of which was written from a Greek model about 160.

The adventures and sufferings of a Lucius from Corinth are told as a first-person narrative. His inherent and unreasonable curiosity connected with improprieties and a certain lecherousness ruins him. At the beginning of the story he admits: "I'm not nosy, but I'd like to know all or at least very much."[95]

In Thessaly he is turned into an ass but keeps his human mind and feelings. Apuleius uses as a means of the narrative a voice outside the human being, a means usually associated with satire. The ass is stolen, sold, maltreated and endures adventures and sufferings at the hands of nearly all classes of Romans, all of which offer a satirically distorted genre-picture. The non-heroic moaning of the pack-ass can surely be understood as an allusion to the monologues of complaints in the novel. Only when the "human" in the ass is recognized, when he is presented as a quick-to-learn, weird and wonderful animal who can even be a lover of a distinguished lady can a quite unexpected and surprising end occur. The hero resumes his old form and out of thankfulness he lets himself be initiated into the mysteries of Isis. We seem to have here an interpretation of the history of religion: the confused and, so to speak, brutish man is released and purified only after sufferings and tests.[96] The work of Apuleius is a successful mixture of entertainment with a strong satirical and erotic character rolled into a cycle of novellas. The happy ending is characteristic of the genre of the ancient novel and appears to be automatic. Of course we cannot yet speak of a development of the character in the modern sense of the word, but a "purpose" towards improvement seems clear. This metamorphosis is especially well told in the brilliant inserted tale of the novel, the one and only fairytale of antiquity, that of Cupid and Psyche.[97] (Ill. 5) It has had a lasting influence in art, literature, and musical adaptations.[98]

The connection between Lucius and the figure of Psyche in the fairytale rests on their shared curiosity. She is honoured as Venus on

---

[95] Apuleius 1.2.4.
[96] Research is not in agreement on this: Merkelbach (1962) and Kerényi (1927), (1971) 51–66 with vehement stand for the religious interpretation; Heiserman (1977) wants to regard the whole work as a comedy; Tatum (1979) considers it an integrated whole from the beginning to the end.
[97] Apuleius 4.28–6.24. Weinreich (1923) 89–132.
[98] Blümner (1903) 648–673; Haight (1943); Rüdiger (1963); Scobie (1969), (1973).

5. Cupid and Psyche. Terracotta from Smyrna, Hellenistic period. Staatliche Museen zu Berlin, Preußischer Kulturbesitz, Antikensammlung. Photograph by Staatliche Museen zu Berlin.

earth and cannot find a husband. An oracle of Apollo says that she won't get a mortal to be her husband but a fiend. The husband of Psyche turns out to be no fiend but the god of love, Cupid himself—but he stays invisible, is only present at night and warns her of various evils. "Nosiness and determination of Psyche let her forget her sex" and in the light of a lamp she recognizes Cupid. But a drop of hot oil awakens Cupid, sad and disappointed in Psyche who broke her promise not to identify him. Reconciliation is achieved, and Psyche, the "soul", is connected to Eros, love, as immortal in an everlasting marriage—in the same way that the main characters in the romantic novel are. The child of both is called "Bliss".

In this fairytale women do not show themselves at their best, but Psyche can amend her negative characteristics and as a reward she is raised to a goddess. The couple deserve only the happy ending after they have understood their errant behaviour.[99]

d. *Iamblichus*

The Hellenized Syrian Iamblichus, who probably lived in Armenia under King Soaimos, who was appointed by Rome, wrote a long romantic novel[100] in 35 or 39 books about the destiny of Sinonis and Rhodanes, *The Babyloniaka*, after 165. Only fragments and the summary of Photios survive, which end at the 16th book, but allow a kind of reconstruction.[101]

The married couple is separated because Garmos, a cruel despot, pesters the beautiful Sinonis. The lovers have to suffer much before they are rescued: put in chains, nailed to a cross, abducted, humiliated when they are misidentified, exposed to intrigues by eunuchs, suffer doubts about each other, and are influenced by magic. At the happy ending the legal husband and wife are reunited, and Rhodanes becomes the new King of Babylon.

The Middle Eastern colour of this novel rubs off on the heroine. Her beauty can cast spells, and her passion does not shy from cruelty and jealousy. Her love for Rhodanes doesn't always translate into faithfulness in all situations. Because of her boundless jealousy

---

[99] Because of the suffering a "reformation" has set in; in contrast with this Helm (1956) 75f.
[100] *Dramatikon* after Photios, *Bibliotheka* 94. Still in the Byzantium era the novel must have existed complete.
[101] The fragments are collected: Habrich (1960).

she develops such a hatred towards her lover, who always keeps faith with her, that she marries the young King of Syria. The matter becomes explosive because the young king is an opponent of Garmos, who just got his hands on Rhodanes. In Chariton's novel Kallirhoe is forced to get married for a second time, but here Sinonis acts for very egotistical reasons to hurt Rhodanes.[102] Sinonis doesn't shrink even from murder, and she kills the rich lecher Setapos with a sword when he is drunk and helpless: "She covered the mouth of the dying man with her hand so that no sound of his soul could come out."[103]

After this act of aggressiveness she also wanted to eliminate a pretty farmer's daughter, who had just become a widow. She is jealous of the pretty widow because of a kiss that Rhodanes gave her as a way of saying thank you for her help. She explains her determination with the following words: "The first fight is done. Now let's try the second one, for we have acquired experience just at the right moment!"[104] This girl, who is only called Kore helps the strangers in a selfless and courageous way, but Sinonis is ungrateful and out of her senses: the ordinary woman can be taken as the model for a real heroine.

The aggressiveness of several female actors is stressed by Iamblichus. Sinonis is to be seen as a "barbarian" and so loses her right to idealization. The conventional role of the heroine is turned on its head. Sinonis acts like a man and goes beyond what is permissible for women. Her emotions know few limits and her mistrust of her partner is new to this genre. Nevertheless the happy ending is preserved.[105]

e. *Xenophon of Ephesus*

In the "most conventional" Greek novel[106] that of the unknown Xenophon of Ephesus, both main characters suffer the same and parallel fate, and in fact the plot is marked by parallelism.

---

[102] The fragments 70 and 57 of the Habrich edition show further remarks of her hatred, but one has to be careful in any interpretation. Because of the fragmentary condition of the novel a lot has to be left open. Before the scene where Sinonis is married to the young Syrian, a considerable part of the text is missing.
[103] Fragment 68 Habrich.
[104] Fragment 70 Habrich.
[105] Still stimulating Schneider-Menzel (1948) 48–92. In an interpretation of the history of religion they claim that it is a "Mithras Novel" [Merkelbach (1962) 178–191]; the same (1984) 253–258, more restricted.
[106] We can completely agree with Müller (1981) 399.

The lack of description, the arrangement of unmotivated events and adventures, frequent and almost hectic change of scenes, and references to future events which among other things do not take place, all give some reason to assume an epitome of an original work of 10 books.[107]

In this novel man and woman are dealt with in similar fashion, side by side with the same rights without any special stress on female or male, the handsome but conceited Habrokomes and the young Anthia, a radiant beauty. Also the influence of divine powers is very strong, beginning with the wrath of Eros, who is offended because the young Habrokomes claims that he is more beautiful and more clever than the deity himself. This hubris of course must be punished. The love of the young Ephesians and their dazzling wedding do not change their fate (a happy ending!), as it is predicted in the dark oracle poem of Apollo:

> Why do you long to learn the end of a malady, and its beginning?
> One disease has both in its grasp, and from that the remedy must be accomplished.
> But for them I see terrible sufferings and toils that are endless;
> Both will flee over the sea pursued by madness;
> They will suffer chains at the hands of men who mingle with the waters;
> And a tomb shall be the burial chamber for both, and fire the destroyer;
> And beside the waters of the river Nile, to Holy Isis.
> The savior you will afterwards offer rich gifts;
> But still after their sufferings a better fate is in store.[108]

Before the couple find each other again on Rhodes in the temple of Isis, the tutelary goddess of lovers, they have to overcome shipwreck, a state of apparent death, separation, fear of death, and tortures. Though the heroine was sold to a brothel, she remained faithful, and though she planned suicide, she escaped its worst consequences. Full of tears and tearing her hair she promised in a monologue:

> Oh no, ghost of Habrokomes, my one and only lover, don't be full of sorrow because of me! I will never agree to do you wrong. I'll come to you. Until death I will stay your faithful wife.[109]

---

[107] On the other hand Hägg [(1966) 118–161; the same (1987b) 39f.] sticks to the extant 5 books with reasons which are not quite convincing.

[108] Recommendable German translation by Kytzler (1983) Vol. 1, 106.

[109] German translation by Kytzler (1983) 133f.

Of course the hero stays faithful, "so no other girl seemed to be so beautiful to him and no other woman that he had seen". His meeting with the noble robber Hippothoos, which can be interpreted as "homoerotic relationship",[110] was only an episode and never a threat to his wife. One can almost comment that their life became a fairytale "and they lived happily ever after".[111]

f. *Achilleus Tatius*

In the novel *Leukippe and Kleitophon* the main heroes are cousins, as in the novel of Ninus. Among the many dramatic effects in this novel the use of the Scheintod motif three times for the heroine stands out. Another woman, who is conveniently present, dies as a substitute or the incident is only an apparent death. Still more astonishing in this novel is the explicit erotic component, surpassing even Longus. Neither theoretical nor practical points are handled with restraint. In spite of the original convention of romantic novels, which requires that both partners remain faithful to one another, the hero here lets himself be seduced, using as an excuse the need to rescue or to cure a lovelorn soul. Longus deals with a similar situation, but in a more natural way.

Far more piquant and with distinct love of details Achilles Tatius offers a debate about the advantages or disadvantages of homosexuality in comparison with heterosexual love; Leukippe had earlier withdrawn and only men are present. Though the author wanted to maintain the proprieties in this debate, at other times he discusses the erotic properties of glances, touches, kinds of kisses, affection and suspicion, jealousy and confidence, refusal and devotion.

Near the beginning of the novel when the couple are about to consummate their love, the heroine's mother interrupts them. The mother was dreaming, woke up with a start and suddenly stood in the couple's room. Kleitophon barely escaped and the defiant girl justly affirmed her innocence—which was preserved by a speedy mother. Because of the absence of her husband, the mother adopts excessive parental authority and fans the flames of conflict between

---

[110] See Schmeling (1980) 52; but it is interesting that homosexual friendships between men occur as a central theme in Xenophon of Ephesus and Achilles Tatius. Perhaps this variant is to be understood as broadening of horizons by these novelists.

[111] Quotation from Kirsch (1981) 80. Good observation of the characters also in Garson (1981) 47-55.

generations. In her fury towards her sexually (almost) active daughter she behaves as a representative of patriarchal-restrictive norms and represents the power structures.[112] Obviously she thinks of Leukippe as a rival who attracts the admiration of men. She naturally tries to suppress the arresting sexuality of her daughter as long as possible.

The girl is ashamed, sad and angry after the mother leaves. She considers her situation in a long psychological digression which makes the readers turn all their sympathy to her, while the mother is portrayed negatively. The daughter would like most to defend herself "with the same means", but, of course, she is too weak for that. In a desperate rage and a fit of emotions she had not known previously, she decides to escape with her lover to foreign parts "out of her mother's sight". The desire for erotic self-determination without any parental restriction arises for the first time. As an alternative she could think only of suicide to avenge her humiliation, typical as punishment for the uncomprehending mother from an infantile point of view. At the end of the novel only the reunion with her father is described, who forgives his daughter and sanctions the contact with Kleitophon.[113] A reconciliation between mother and daughter is not mentioned.

Of course the escape over the sea with friends brings difficult situations for the lovers: storms at sea, shipwrecks, and prisons. Leukippe is separated from Kleitophon, kidnapped, and murdered apparently three times. The young man, who must have thought that Leukippe was dead, lets himself be married to a beautiful, rich widow from Ephesus—which event he does nothing to avoid. Of course Leukippe becomes the slave of this Melite, whose husband Thersander, who had been declared dead, reappears. A complicated adultery trial follows, but with the help of Eros, Artemis and Tyche the happy end in marriage for the heroes is achieved after successful tests of truth and chasteness: the hero has only to swear to the truth but not to the "whole" truth, while Melite is able to declare with sophistic reasoning that "when Thersander was absent only mutual talks" took place between her and Kleitophon.[114] So Melite is exonerated and Kleitophon marries his young friend after he recovers her—curiously

---

[112] Especially Achilles Tatius 2.29.5.
[113] Achilles Tatius 7.16f.
[114] At the end of the 5th book in Achilles Tatius.

enough he did not recognize her at Melite's estate when she was a slave, her head shaved, workworn and in unbecoming clothes. The voice of the heart had no effect in this case, since he must have thought her dead—besides he was to be deeply impressed by Melite's erotic charms.

In her innocence and virginity, which she defended vigourously, Leukippe acts according to the convention of the romantic novel, in spite of all the unfavourable vicissitudes of life. On the other hand Kleitophon and his account of his actions seem to be relaxed, lax and weak as far as the unusual moral code is concerned; he is probably representative of his generation and his time. Melite is portrayed with great sympathy and as one of the most pleasant persons in the world of ancient novels.[115] She is recognized as the counterpart of the heroine, as the "other woman", who is allowed to be erotically active, and therefore she is not destined to die. She passes the ordeal, though it was not very difficult, and becomes almost equal to the heroine. She is allowed to radiate human warmth and to be a realistic figure, because she is not subject to unrealistic restrictions. Of course she has special freedoms and privileges as a rich widow, and she knows how to use them. This novel, read as mystery text,[116] sees Melite as a representative of the goddess or as mystagogue in the initiation ritual of the Holy Marriage. The young yet innocent girl faces the mature beautiful woman in a confrontation, which we can also find in Longus, but still more forgiving.

g. *Longus*

The couple in Longus[117] need not go through adventures of travel, because they go on a completely different kind of journey through the exotic land of emotional experience, as two young people who discover physical love step by step.[118] Only on her wedding night does Chloe realize that all previous encounters were only childs' play,

---

[115] See Cresci (1981); Perry (1967) 106; Plepelits (1980) 35f., and Vilborg (1962) 11.

[116] This is also the case for the Lykainion scene in Longus 3.18–20; compare Merkelbach (1962) 144 and 213f.; similar in Chalk (1960) 44.

[117] For Effe (1982) 68: "a spectacular innovation, an intended play with the patterns of the genre". This novel stands out from the ancient examples in connecting a love story and bucolic poetry.

[118] So Holzberg (1986) especially 111, stresses a specific feature of the novel, which he characterizes as a connection between sexual psychology and the bucolic world

mere "pastoral plays". Unconsciously Chloe has had the first emotional feeling of her heart since the moment when she saw Daphnis bathing naked: "She didn't know what happened to her, because she was young and grew up in rural inexperience and even from the others she didn't hear the name of love."[119] In a stylistically polished up masterly performance Longus is able to express the love of Chloe with Daphnis that is growing in spring:

> I'm certainly ill, but I don't know what kind of disease it is; I feel pains,
> but I don't have any wound: I'm sad though no sheep died; I'm burning,
> but I'm sitting in a cooling shadow...
> But the stabbing pain in my chest is aching more than all of that.
> Daphnis is handsome, but also beautiful are the flowers; his syrinx sounds wonderful,
> but so is the voice of the nightingale: nevertheless I don't pay attention.
> For I'd like to be his syrinx to be able to take his breath in!... Oh, nasty water!
> Only to him you gave beauty; but I took a bath for nothing!
> I'll die, my dear nymphs, even you won't be able to rescue the girl...[120]

The eternal love they swear to remain faithful until death unites the couple for ever. It is interesting that Chloe, in spite of her naivety and her girlish behaviour, requires Daphnis to swear an additional oath by his foster-mother, the goat, because Pan is said to be an unfaithful god, who often falls in love.[121] The young couple come closer together, but the kiss and the embrace and lying together without clothes as "the utmost of the ecstasy of passion"[122] do not satisfy them, especially not Daphnis. Even when they tried to imitate the animals they were not successful.

They must obtain external help and this proves again that Longus was a good observer of human nature. Daphnis receives his sex education from a young woman of the neighbourhood, who is married to an elderly farmer. Lykainion has sympathy for the young man and warns him when he wants to hurry to Chloe immediately

---

of salvation. Stanzel (1991) 153–175, almost pleads for a structure of a novel of education, but without dealing with the moral aspect as special subject.

[119] Longus 1.13.
[120] Longus 1.14.
[121] Longus 1.39.
[122] Longus 1.11.

after the "act", of the physical and psychological pain that is connected with a defloration. Daphnis understands this and feels completely responsible for the young girl.[123]

The sophisticated Lykainion is described as a lovable woman. Perhaps she is living with her husband as "Frauchen" (gynaion) only in concubinage.[124] Although she stands in contrast to the heroine, she is not reduced in character—the opposite is the case. Because of her wise advice Chloe keeps her virginity until her marriage and so can have a respectable marriage. Lykainion also takes part in the wedding party as a neighbour,[125] because the novel exudes a tolerant atmosphere as in a fairytale, where the good overcomes the bad at the end. In the interpretation of the history of religion Lykainion emerges as a mystagogue in the ritual of *hieros gamos* at the initiation.[126]

Daphnis suppresses his sexuality until marriage because of love for his bride and this is fortunate, since her father, who is identified again, insists on virginity before the marriage.

We cannot speak of a real "development" of the young heroine in the modern sense, but love as an internal experience is clearly described and is unique in the ancient novel. In the model of erotic development which was created recently by D. Teske,[127] the elements *physis* and *techne* play an important role: *physis* has the function to characterize the sexual awakening as a natural instinct, and *techne* in the form of theoretical and practical instruction by Philetas and Lykainion functions to make people necessarily aware of this instinct.

Already in 1831 Johann Wolfgang von Goethe regarded Daphnis and Chloe as a masterpiece of psychological art of observation and so of world literature:[128] "Es ist darin der hellste Tag... und keine Spur von trüben Tagen, von Nebel, Wolken und Feuchigkeit, sondern immer der blaueste, reinste Himmel, die anmutigste Luft..." During the erotic voyage of discovery "die größten menschlichen Dinge" are brought up, and he recommends reading this novel "alle Jahre einmal".[129]

---

[123] The episode of Lykainion in Longus 3.15–20.
[124] Referred to for the first time by Scarcella (1972a) 65f. The figure of Lykainion also in Levin (1977).
[125] Longus 4.38.1.
[126] E.g., Merkelbach (1962) 144 and 213f.; similar in Chalk (1960) 44.
[127] Teske (1991) especially 114f.
[128] Conversation between Goethe and Eckermann on March 9, 18 and 20, 1831.
[129] Misjudgements pale into insignificance beside comments of Helm (1956) 51, who denounces the supposed "sexual perversity" and "the sensuous lewdness" of the

h. Heliodorus of Emesa

The latest extant Greek novel *The Ethiopian Adventures of Theagenes and Charikleia* was written by Heliodorus.[130]

It is informative that 10 of the 37 people dealt with in detail by Heliodorus are women. These have different geographical origins, social backgrounds and ages. All levels are represented here: from the slave and servant (Kybele, Thisbe) to the hetaira (Arsinoe, Rhodopis), from the middle-class women (Demainete, Isias, Nausiklea) to the queen (Persinna, Arsake) and the priest (Charikleia). So the range (from good to bad) of Greek and "barbarian" female figures is quite comprehensive. In the subplots women, who are to be despised, are in the majority and thus cast Charikleia in the role of the "ideal of a woman".[131] Her chief counterpart is her opponent, the Persian noblewoman Arsake.

The secluded life[132] required of most of the young girls is clearly illustrated by Nausiklea, daughter of the Greek businessman Nausikles at Naukratis. She accepts her father's choice of the Athenian Knemon to be her future husband, because this meets her own secret wishes.[133] Only at her urgent request is she allowed to accompany her more independent friend Charikleia to special events, when she may take part in banquets or welcome guests when her father is absent.[134] To a large degree the picture of this supporting figure in the novel corresponds to the picture of classical and post-classical Athens, which is also reflected in New Comedy.[135]

The female Egyptians seem to be allowed more independent

---

pastoral novel. Of course there is a slight voyeuristic tendency in some episodes, but it does not harm the total work.

[130] Regarding the date 3rd or 4th century, also see Johne (1989) 221–224, especially 222 and literature cited. Convincing reasons for the 3rd century given by Szepessy (1976) 241–276. Also the new *Cambridge History of Classical Literature* of 1985 agrees with him. Heliodorus is the "classic" among the Greek romantic novels [Hägg (1987b) 95].

[131] Quotation in Kowarna (1959). One chapter of her dissertation is entitled "Charikleia—des Dichters Idealbild einer Frau" (233–238; 244–246), but in my opinion the "ideal" is slightly overinterpreted.

[132] In spite of the separation of Greek women from the political-public sphere, we have to be careful of a modernistic and feminist interpretation; also compare Cameron (1989) 6–17, and Wagner-Hasel (1988b) 18–29 and (1993) 535–543. On the "Wissenschaftliche Kontroverse über den sozialen Status der Athenerin", compare Pomeroy (1985) 86–90.

[133] Heliodorus 6.8.
[134] Heliodorus 6.11 and 6.22.
[135] About that see Johne (1988) 12–15.

behaviour. Isias from Chemnis represents a free woman with quite modern attitudes. She no longer adheres to practices of magic, and she often has new ideas to keep her husband on the go, for she is mentally superior to him and this is recognized ironically and humorously.[136] On the other hand in the old Egyptian from Bessa we see a picture of a primitive woman from the lower classes, who knows about the secrets of life and who is also able to call up the dead at full moon,[137] which will be her undoing.

The situation of the female Ethiopians is, according to Heliodorus, similar to that of the Greeks, e.g., women of Meroe are excluded from taking part in the ceremony of the victorious king mainly to avoid desecration of the sacrificial animals.[138] Thus the respected position of the Ethiopian queen Persinna, mother of Charikleia stands out the clearer: as a priest of Selene she is obliged to take part in the ceremony. Of course she is able to read and write[139] and she can even speak Greek. Even when she abandoned her white daughter, she acted wisely and with regard to the future, because she had to protect the child and especially herself from the possible disgrace of an illegitimate birth.[140] She found a way to Charikleia, whom she recognized as her only child, and was able to help her to be legitimized and to save Theagenes from death.

The novelist seems to have chosen powerful and intelligent female rulers from Hellenistic-Roman times as the model of this figure. This is even more evident in the model for Charikleia.

Some female Greeks are mentioned by name. Demainete is described as a middle-class woman from Athens, who as a young girl from a good family married a man, who was much older but respected. Such was common practice. She is quite well-educated[141] but her life is unfulfilled, and her unrequited love for her young stepson Knemon brings disaster. She suffers the fate of Phaedra,[142] but she is not up to the level of her servant Thisbe.

---

[136] Heliodorus 6.3. Isias is possibly a native Greek; see Kowarna (1959) 223.
[137] Heliodorus 6.12 and 14. Of course the priest Kalasiris disapproves of these magic procedures.
[138] Heliodorus 10.4; Queen Persinna is excluded.
[139] Heliodorus 10.8.2; 10.13.
[140] Also she as a queen is threatened with possible punishment for adultery (Hel. 4.8). Really she observed a picture of her white-skinned ancestress Andromeda during sexual intercourse.
[141] Heliodorus 1.9.
[142] Heliodorus 1.10.

As a servant of Demainete, the slave Thisbe got an education similar to that of a hetaira: she is able to write and she is better than a number of hetaerae as singer and player of the cithara, but she enjoys little freedom. As a young slave she always has to serve her mistress or to fear penalty.[143] She shows her superiority to her mistress, who is keen on winning her stepson's love, with very helpful advice. This role is similar to that of the clever slaves of Attic comedy. She always knows a way out for herself, e.g., the revenge on Demainete in a critical situation, her escape out of Athens, or the message to Knemon among the Egyptian pirates.

The atmosphere around a Greek hetaira named Arsinoe is very well described by Heliodorus: she is alone in the world and earns her living at Athens as a flautist and lady of the night. With cleverness, erotic charm and cunning she becomes rich. Later she puts her house at the couples' disposal with whom she is friendly and is able to travel around with her lovers.[144] She does not hesitate to accuse Thisbe who used to be her friend.[145] In the Kalasiris subplot, there is the beautiful and rich hetaira Rhodopis, a native of Thrace, who seems to become a danger even to the priest during her frequent visits to the temple of Isis at Memphis. Her skills in the field of love—one harassed lover talks about "getting caught by a certain device"—were notorious.[146]

Another negative picture of a woman we find is that of another subordinated female character. Although she comes from Lesbos, Kybele, the old Greek wet nurse of the Persian Arsake, lost almost everything that was Greek. She does not educate her son to be a Greek. As a prisoner of war[147] she came to Egypt and was forced to adapt. Dependent on her tyrannical mistress, she uses a lot of coaxing to survive. She uses any flattery, lie and even attempts murder. She is privileged, because she is Arsake's confidante in love affairs, but the poison she makes for the main heroine becomes lethal for her, because the poisoned goblets are mixed up. She dies for her mistress—as a substitute—as Thisbe did.

In contrast to many heroines in ancient novels Charikleia, "the beautiful and clever one",[148] knows exactly from the very beginning

---

[143] Heliodorus 1.16 or 1.11.
[144] Heliodorus 1.15,16,17.
[145] Heliodorus 2.9.
[146] Kalasiris' declaration: Heliodorus 2.25.1.
[147] Heliodorus 7.12.
[148] Heliodorus 3.4.1.

what she wants. Her strong character influences the European novel of the baroque period and also the figure of Leonore in Goethe's *Tasso*.[149] In some respects she is "a self-conscious and emancipated intellectual".[150] Growing up motherless and not in the seclusion of the women's house, she has good common sense and a very good, almost male, education, and at Delphi she associates with educated men. As a priest of Artemis she shows boldness and courage in hunting and archery, and defends her virginity obstinately and aggressively, thus denying her original nature and her female destiny.[151] She drives her foster-father to despair, because he chose her as wife for his nephew. "For the sake of a pure life" she had her own apartment in the temple precinct as a priest, a fact which emphasizes her independence and makes her insistence on her virginity more distinct.[152] According to her predisposition and her education, she despises Eros and Aphrodite as lower passions and intends to stay a virgin all her life.[153] She fights against love-at-first-sight for Theagenes and despises herself for her feelings. During the procession at Delphi in honour of Neoptolemos the couple meets for the first time as she hands over the torch: "When the young people saw each other they loved each other, as if their souls had recognized their relationship when they first met and flew towards each other aware of their destination for one another. At first they were standing still with inner excitement. Hesitating she gave him the torch, hesitating he took it. They looked at each other steadfastly for a long time, as if they had already seen each other, knew each other somehow and tried to remember. They were both smiling but only furtively so that their eyelashes were fluttering brightly for a moment. Then they blushed, as if they were ashamed about this and grew pale again, moved deeply. In a word they expressed a lot with their faces, and the frequent change of colour and expression on their eyes showed their emotion."[154]

After the procession Charikleia loses her balance: struggles among

---

[149] From the copious literature: Oeftering (1901); Prosch (1956); Sandy (1979) 41–55; Berger (1984) 177–189. As far as the influence on art is concerned, Stechow (1953) 144–152.
[150] Expressed by Egger (1988) 43.
[151] Heliodorus 2.33.6. On this subject see Lefkowitz (1981) 41f.
[152] Heliodorus 3.6. We cannot speak of an intentionally curious touch in Heliodorus' topos of chastity, as Anderson (1982) 38, did. We can assume that sexual morals are respectable according to the general concern of the novel.
[153] The whole chapter 33 of the 2nd book is important for this statement.
[154] Heliodorus 3.5.

her emotions seem to become dangerous to her health.[155] Only the knowledgeable Kalasiris, whom she trusts, is able to convince her of the omnipotence of Eros against whom even the gods are powerless. She declares herself for her strong and only love of her life so thoroughly that she leaves her adopted country and her admired fosterfather for ever.[156] If she recognizes something to be correct she will do it even if it is difficult, but she will maintain a certain proud reservedness when she does not feel immediately to be understood.[157] As the main figure in the novel she shows a brave, clever, considered and even adaptable behaviour in each situation. According to Feuillâtre[158] she has "qualities of a boss", because most of the bright ideas, e.g., the disguises as a beggar, are hers. She tries to turn tragic accidents into good things, if possible,[159] but of course she influences the fight and wounds her enemies with a sure shot of her arrow.[160] At the beginning of the novel it is characteristic that she is introduced not only as a beauty of a godlike appearance with long golden hair and shiny eyes, but also full of energy and ready to die, because her life depends on that of the seriously wounded Theagenes. She is prepared to use the sword to save her good name,[161] and her character is delineated by this first speech. She does not present the self-defence of a woman; she is prepared to put such into action only in case of emergency. She also shows her courage when she returns to the battlefield alone at night, something Kalasiris does not dare.[162] When Theagenes intends to give up contrary to his male instincts, she at times offers encouragement.[163]

Her intelligence and presence of mind are shown in several scenes in which she knowingly tries to deceive: "Deception can be a noble thing, if it is useful in what we are striving for."[164] She uses a bit of cunning when it seems to be promising, e.g., several times she declares Theagenes to be her brother,[165] because she does not want to

---

[155] Heliodorus 3.18 and 19; 4.5 and 9.
[156] Heliodorus 4.10, 13 and 17.
[157] Heliodorus 10.18, 29 and 33.
[158] Feuillâtre (1966) 19f.: "les qualités de chef."
[159] Heliodorus 7.21.
[160] Heliodorus 5.32.
[161] Heliodorus 1.1–4.
[162] Heliodorus 5.33.
[163] Heliodorus 5.6.2; 8.11: *thársei*.
[164] Heliodorus 1.26.6.
[165] Heliodorus 1.27 to Thyamis; 7.12 to Kybele and Arsake; 9.25 to Hydaspes.

be separated from him. She also cleverly prepares her parents to recognize her as their daughter, but she has a hard time with her suspicious father: because a large inheritance is at stake she must prove that she is no trickster who somehow learned the marks of identification. She comes through her chastity ordeal in a splendid way, but only the birthmark and her resemblance to Andromeda resolve the problem.

Charikleia cannot understand insufficiencies in other people, because she herself seldom shows any weakness.[166] Only when the situation becomes hopeless does she consider putting an end to her life—when Theagenes is seriously wounded in the palace of the governor of Memphis or at Meroe, when they were to be sacrificed.[167] Her aggressive character, distinctive in emergency, finally can be recognized by these words: "Death can be a sweet thing, if we are lucky enough to see our enemies die before ourselves."[168]

With her strong personality she is also able to get her lover to swear by the gods that she will be his only wife.[169] In the modern age it seems to be unrealistic to insist on virginity in a bride, but in Heliodorus virginity is demanded even of the groom. The highest standard of sexual morality is reached, a requirement that obviously did not meet social reality and middle-class life. But in the Christian novels the subject of virginity and chastity was maintained and even regularized.[170]

Charikleia is respected and appreciated as though a man. As the more active and educated part of the couple she seems to be an example of the Platonic Diotima. In overstressing the ideal of chastity and physical training she is similar to a Valkyrie of the Nordic-Germanic sagas or more likely to an Amazon of Greek saga. When delineating his heroine, Heliodorus seems to use as his model the beautiful Penthesileia, queen of the Amazons, who fought against the Greeks on the side of the Trojans, and was killed by Achilleus in single combat. According to the legend the Greek fell in love with the dying woman, as it can be seen in the "Münchener Schale". In this novel we can define the lovers thus: Charikleia is the spiritual

---

[166] Heliodorus 1.8.3; 5.34.1.
[167] Heliodorus 1.33; 8.7; 10.9.
[168] Heliodorus 8.15.9.
[169] Heliodorus 5.18.
[170] The apocryphal Acts of the Apostles with their speeches of chastity are especially typical, on that see Sœder (1932) 119f.; Sandy (1982a) 95f.

Amazon, and Theagenes, an ancestor of Achilleus, becomes Achilleus and together this latter day mythological pair enjoy a happy ending.

The behaviour of Charikleia is moderate in contrast to her opponent, the "other" woman in the novel. Arsake is the sister of the Persian king and wife of the governor of Egypt, Oroondates. She is very proud of her descent[171] and she combines beauty with intelligence and craving for power. As representative of her husband her authority is far-reaching. She gives audiences requiring *proskynesis*, and is allowed to summon the council of state. Charikleia and Theagenes are at her mercy, because she has her eye on our Greek hero. Arsake exceeds her legal authorization, falls out of favour with her brother, and so decides to put an end to her life.[172]

Heliodorus does not characterize this female from the Middle East as an exclusively negative figure.[173] Her rhetorical skill is stressed, e.g., in her personal accusation of Charikleia,[174] as well as her diplomatic cleverness in debates with her enemies.[175] She even speaks a little Greek.[176] So she is credibly portrayed as a domineering person, as, e.g., Cleopatra or Zenobia, but on the whole she is situated as the background scenery for Charikleia. She is a modern Persian and well educated, but as a barbarian her moods and passions[177] mean more to her than law and order.

Arsake flaunts her emancipation and it destroys her: "Define what is law, decency and benefit, ... (it will not help you) ... Those who have the power do not need it. Their own will determines these words."[178] Heliodorus thus disqualifies her as heroine and defines her as antiheroine and barbarian.[179] Charikleia is recognized in the world

---

[171] Heliodorus 7.2.
[172] Heliodorus 8.15.
[173] In my opinion it is exaggerated to speak of "a real terrifying vision" with a "dissipated sexuality" in the case of Arsake, according to Egger (1988) 54. As far as the difference between the Greek (Charikleia) and the barbarian (Arsake) is concerned, we must also consider that the "good" protagonist is a barbarian by birth as well, but ennobled because of her classical Greek education. It is also inappropriate to declare Arsake to be a "kalte Schönheit", according to Johne (1989a) 171, because this expression is incorrect. Rather we should speak of a beautiful woman, who was able to use her instruments of power with cold calculation in spite of her hot temper.
[174] Heliodorus 7.9.
[175] Heliodorus 7.3f.
[176] Heliodorus 7.19.
[177] Helm (1956) 38 calls her "zuchtlos", "boshaft" and "grausam", and so he downgrades the "Satrapenfrau" with exaggerated moral indignation.
[178] Heliodorus 8.5.
[179] It is interesting to note how the Egyptian archeologist and historian of civili-

of men as an exception, and it is logically consistent that Theagenes gives up his Greek native country forever in order to live and to work with her in a leading position in the land of happiness and justice.[180]

6. *Woman Antagonist—Intimate Girl-friend—Mother*

As the first fictional prose, novels became a great literary genre with a certain large impact that was especially supported by women. This is owing to the fact that novels could be read privately in houses to people who gathered there, in contrast to heroic epic poems with a typical masculine character and to dramas, which generally referred to men in Athens.

In this new genre where the relationship between the sexes played such an important role, the private sphere is not the only subject. Within this myth of the private lives of individuals[181] the heroine is the outstanding figure and not the hero, who is similar to the type of the young man in New Comedy.

Even if the novels should be directed primarily to female readers, it doesn't mean automatically that also the writers were females—though pen-names could lead us to assume that. The picture of a positive woman, who is described as good, beautiful, chaste and faithful, corresponds rather to the typical male ideal. On the other hand

---

zation Auguste Mariette transposed some episodes from the Heliodorus novel for the festive opera *Aida* by Giuseppe Verdi, which was originally planned to be performed on the occasion of the opening of the Suez Canal, but the first performance was given at Cairo on December 24, 1871. It concerns not only the famous triumphal procession after scenes of the 10th book, but especially the confrontation of the two outstanding female characters. In the opera the Ethiopian princess Aida is a beautiful black slave, who is taken captive into Egypt. Like the Egyptian princess Amneris she falls in love with the young, successful commander Radames. The conflict between the love of the main actors and their loyalty to their native country can only be solved romantically, when they die together. The figure of the proud Amneris (Arsake was partially the model for her) shows a clear development of character in the psychological performance of the 19th century. The woman becomes tangible. She is able to bring herself to a human forgiveness after a disappointed love and jealous hatred.

[180] As far as the utopian state of Ethiopia is concerned, see the 10th book of Heliodorus, and compare *inter alia* Lesky (1959) 36–38; Szepessy (1957) 241–259, especially 245–251.

[181] The explanation for the popularity of the Greek novel according to Reardon (1969) 307; (1971) 401.

the novels make nearly the same high moral demands on the hero as they do on the heroine—and this could indicate the interests of women.[182]

Apart from the female protagonists and the few female subcharacters, which we can pass over here, three female groups are singled out in all ancient romantic novels with different significance and regard—the antagonist, the intimate friend, the mother. The person to whom they all relate is the heroine.

The antagonist who is more or less stressed as antiheroine in contrast to the exemplary main figure, plays the most important role. The principal difference between them is the sexual behaviour as well as the standard of education. While the heroine remains chaste and faithful at all costs according to the generic convention until the happy ending (with the understandable exception of Kallirhoe), "the other woman" is allowed to be erotically active. The two sides of the female coin so to speak are presented, "the two sisters of the female archetype, the sensual and the virtuous woman" and "the dual aspects of the archetypal feminine".[183] The distinction between these two types nearly always can be established: Leukippe and Melite in Achilleus Tatius, Chloe and Lykainion in Longus, Charikleia on the one hand and Arsake, Demainete and Rhodopis on the other hand in Heliodorus. In Iamblichus the opposition between Sinonis and the farmer's wife with no name, the Kore, nearly seems to be inverted, but only fragments of this novel have been preserved.

In Chariton's novel, in Ninus and in Apuleius' fairytale of Cupid and Psyche no antagonist can be determined.

Obviously virginity or abstinence is meant to be the positive principle and necessary requirement for the bride. In the course of evolution chastity, however, becomes a problem of historically increasing explosive nature. Kallirhoe's virtue is still subordinated to motherly love,[184] but in the case of Persinna the purity of the daughter has priority.[185] The future father-in-law seeks assurance of virginity from the child of nature Chloe,[186] but most awkward is the position of Leu-

---

[182] Up to now the investigations on the image of women and the role of the sexes in the novel still belong unfortunately to the peripheral tasks of the traditional science of literature.
[183] In Segal (1984) 87 and 91. There is a lack of historical support for this interpretation.
[184] Chariton 2.9.1.
[185] Heliodorus 4.8.
[186] Longus 4.31.3.

kippe towards her father, who cannot believe in her virginity after all her terrible adventures abroad.[187] Nearly carried too far is the constant emphasis on Charikleia's chastity,[188] but she is a priestess and also daughter of a king and therefore this emphasis should appear to be commensurate.

The antagonist, who uses the weapons of a woman in a calculating fashion, is not always caricatured or even defamed, as we see in the case of Lykainion and especially Melite. No Greek novel deals with extramarital affairs of legitimate wives. Kallirhoe, who has to live in bigamy because of her unborn child, is an exception.[189]

The contrasts between the good and the bad women are especially stressed in Xenophon and Heliodorus. Sometimes almost pathological feminine eroticism is demonized in Heliodorus, a phenomenon that was used too much in the history of the genre.[190]

Far less emphasized is the role of girlfriends and intimate friends of the heroines. In all novels the impression is given of a certain isolation of the heroine. Neither at home nor during her odysseys, when she is separated from her lover, does she have an intimate girlfriend. While as a sheltered young girl of the upper class she seldom left her house according to the topos,[191] in foreign parts heroines often prove clever and equal to most troubles. Here we can see social reality under the cover of preserved idyll. Though in the Greek novel there is no special word for "girlfriend" or friendship, there exist several distinctive names for male comrades. Of course the heroes are socially connected through a network built from their education. On their journeys the heroes are in general accompanied by a companion who stands by them come rain or shine, as, e.g., Polycharmos in Chariton or Kleinias in Achilleus Tatius.

Chariton is the one who constructs a deeper relationship between women, e.g., between Kallirhoe and the sympathetic servant Plangon.[192] In most cases the confidantes are slaves and so restricted to

---

[187] Achilleus Tatius 8.7. It is remarkable that the heroine changes her part in the middle of the narration, an intended "curious", parodistic "move of the author"; compare Egger (1988) 52.
[188] Especially Heliodorus 10.8f.
[189] Concerning this compare Egger (1994a) 31–48, (1994) 260–280.
[190] Though I think that the "terrible visions" and "the mortal threatening" of Heliodorus' antiheroines are overinterpreted in view of the whole work [Egger (1988) 54]. In the social utopia of the novel the good must triumph over the bad, just as in fairytales.
[191] E.g., Chariton 1.1.5; Heliodorus 6.11.1.
[192] Chariton 2.8.6f.; 3.10.3; 8.4.5. Help and solidarity is literally dictated in the

the oikos. Though friendship between women is socially debased, the restricted scope is nevertheless varied and also emotionally determined, as foster-mother, wet nurse, matchmaker, girlfriend, companion. Such roles are assumed by Thisbe and Kybele in Heliodorus, Kleio[193] in Achilleus Tatius, and Rhode in Xenophon. Leukippe appears in a special isolation: even at the Egyptian army camp when she is seriously ill, no female attends her.[194] Seldom is there solidarity between women. Melite's woman to woman request for help with her unhappy love affair (when she refers to Leukippe who is her strongest rival) is piquant and sarcastic.[195] In Heliodorus there is little solidarity[196] because Charikleia as an exception is sufficient unto herself.[197] Real possibilities for women to be active in public were restricted[198] and in general these activities concerned the regular service of priestesses at temples. The fact that women are in the focus of the plot and so in the centre of sympathy reflects a discrepancy between reality in novels and in life. Female figures' contact with men is usually restricted to an accompanying lover or husband or the other "bad" men who want to take their virginity. A mere comradely relationship between heroines and other young men is rare: Antheia is safe from the attentions of Hippotheos as the wife of his best friend, Leukippe is outside the circle of Kleitophon's friends, Charikleia and Theagenes have a friend together, Knemon.[199]

Mothers in the novels have a strange position. They appear only for a short time in standard situations like weddings or farewells, and

---

case of foisting a child on someone and procuring; cf. Ahlers (1911) 66f.; Oeri (1948) 53f., 67f.

[193] There is a special explanation as far as the character of Kleio is concerned: because she knows about the aborted love affair of her mistress, she is secretly brought out of the house, placed on a ship, and so forgotten as not useful for the author any longer (Achilleus Tatios 2.27.1). On the other hand the slave Satyros, who knows about it, stays the devoted companion of Kleitophon.

[194] Achilleus Tatios 4.10.

[195] Achilleus Tatios 5.22.

[196] Heliodorus 5.6 and 11.

[197] In contrast to Egger (1988) 50, note 53, I think it is exaggerated to speak of a "part of the misogynistic touch of this novel" in this case. Firstly, this opinion cannot be proved as far as the whole course of the plot is concerned, since even Arsake is not described as completely detestable, and, secondly, it is intended to show Charikleia as the ideal woman who should be considered as normal and as an example.

[198] Cf. Jones (1940) 175. On the whole problem see Pleket (1969) and for the field of medicine van Bremen (1983) 223–241.

[199] Xenophon 5.9; Achilleus Tatios 2.35.1; 4.6f.

relations between heroines and their mothers in almost all preserved literature are strained. They abandon their children because of social difficulties or moral reasons (in Longus and Heliodorus),[200] they leave them (in Chariton) or get them to go away (in Achilleus Tatius). Sometimes a wet nurse takes the place of the mother. At any rate the relationship between mother and child is ambivalent. After a long period of emotional conflicts Chariton's heroine Kallirhoe is married for a second time in order to rescue the unborn child of her first marriage, but then she leaves the child behind without any complaint.[201] The first husband is the lover to whom the heroine is joined together forever. In Longus on the one hand there are complaints about the missing joy of motherhood,[202] but on the other hand it is taken for granted that women sacrifice their newborn children at the request of their husbands without offering any resistence.[203] This fact is proved by the right of the father to decide on the life of his descendants at that time.[204]

Achilleus Tatius describes a perfect mother-daughter conflict, and our sympathies are with the heroine, who is striving for self-determination. In this generation gap the jealous mother represents a negative principle.[205]

Charikleia in Heliodorus appears to have four fathers but her mother is absent. This may explain why this female figure is different.

7. Summary

The last chapter dealt with the most important female figures after the heroines, namely the antagonist, the intimate friend and the mother, and anticipated a part of the summary. Now it is only left to summarize the indicated development of the heroine from the beginning until the end of the genre of Greek novel.

---

[200] In the letter of Persinna to her abandoned daughter (Heliodorus 4.8) the attempt is made to explain logically why she accepts the convention: because it is not possible to explain a white daughter to a black father (2.31.1).

[201] Chariton 8.4.5.

[202] Longus 4.19.4.

[203] Longus 4.21.3; 4.24.1. As far as the psychologizing Euripides is concerned, the painful feelings of the mother Kreusa are reflected in the *Ion*.

[204] Abandoning children and *patria potestas inter alia* Vatin (1970); Krenkel (1971) 443–452; Pomeroy (1983) 207–222; Eyben (1980) 5–81.

[205] Kyno in Xenophon 3.12.3; Demainete in Heliodorus 1.10f.

The social background was very important for the creation and further development of the new literary form of the novel. Since Hellenism and later in the Imperium Romanum the life of women has changed considerably in connection with the easing of the oikos-structure. The polis with its mainly male character is not decisive any longer, but in the large states private life and the individual person himself (or herself) becomes the centre of attention. Religiousness and faith of the Hellenistic-Roman world as well as art are changing. Educational opportunities for women of the upper and middle classes become better in a way that women as readers and even as authors are given true colours.

Of course love becomes the central issue and the exclusive point of reference in the novel. That was not the case in earlier descriptions of erotic motifs. Problems of the "middle-class" couple are shown therefore as problems of individuals. The young free citizen of the polis is the main heroine and no more the mythical figure of the drama or, as it was often the case, the hetaira of the comedy. To a certain degree her part can be compared with that in tragedy, in the epos and especially in New Comedy. Following tragedy, the novel is ambitious also regarding morality but cannot bring what is too human easily to a satisfactory conclusion as in comedy. So the heroine in novel appears as a human equal to, and a completely respected partner of, the man. In the general, the private sphere is not sufficient and the couple is included in the circle of social duties such as the public priesthood. If possible private luck has to correspond to political-social tasks.

The scripts of the novels offer opportunities to identify with the characters, especially with the heroines who are often described as more intelligent, more active and on the whole more sympathetic than their male partners, who are not strong men or eroticised father figures, but as young as the women themselves. The figures in ancient novels do not only live "at the mercy of fate", because as characters they try to come to grips with their lives despite all unfavourable circumstances. Women have to go the long and difficult way of the majority. The story of their efforts at emancipation takes shape and is fascinating.

Within the frame of the rigid structure of the novels the different figures have only restricted opportunities to display autonomy. An unfavourable fate abducts the young man and woman, who had fallen in "love-at-first-sight", from their native country and removes them as far as the magic world of the Orient. They get acquainted with the provinces of the East, where the power of Athens or Rome is not strong. In an epoque of relative financial prosperity the East is the home of the authors, the heroes and heroines, and the readers.

I hope to have shown that in the cases of the heroines in the novels there can be recognized a process of maturity and a certain development. To take stock let us begin with the novel of Ninus, the hitherto oldest romantic novel and preserved only in fragments. The young girl is still delineated according to the old understanding of roles. Semiramis is shy and subordinates herself voluntarily as befits a woman in the polis and in New Comedy. On the other hand Chariton's heroine Kallirhoe is obviously at the centre of attention with her almost celestial beauty. Because of her erotic aura she becomes the desired object of many men who represent different social levels, from the robber to the Persian king. Kallirhoe, however, considers her beauty as an undoing. In monologues of thoughts the plot is anticipated. The touching dialogue with the unborn child of her first husband, whom she must think to be dead, is unique in all of Greek literature. She decides against abortion and so for life and, of course, at the happy ending she finds her Chaireas again. The dialectics between female restriction of action in a world characterized by men on the one hand and the erotic-emotional power of the heroine Kallirhoe on the other hand determines the attraction of the "most psychological" Greek novel.

The only fairytale of antiquity, that about Cupid and Psyche, is the center piece of the *Metamorphoses* or the *Golden Ass* of Apuleius. The beautiful princess Psyche is celebrated as Venus on earth and so arouses the jealousy of the goddess. The invisible god of love marries the female human, who is bothered by an unreasonable curiosity, just as is the main hero in the novel. Punishment is swift, but the heroine is purified and rewarded with immortality, because she recognizes her wrong behaviour and deserves to be happy at the end. In Iamblichus the Middle Eastern atmosphere is transferred to the heroine. As a "barbarian" she possesses a wild passion and does not recoil even from cruelty and blind jealousy. The ordinary role expectation seems to have swung to the other extreme. Sinonis acts like a man and so goes beyond what is decent for a woman. Her mistrust of her partner is an innovation within the genre, but nevertheless the happy ending is predetermined.

In the most conventional novel, that of Xenophon of Ephesus, the parallelism of the two main heroes is maintained in the plot, i.e., their fate is parallel. Perhaps this is due to the epitome. The lovers appear somehow stereotyped as equals side by side without the usual stress on the female part. The novel best representative of the second sophistic, that of Achilleus Tatius, has a pronounced erotic component in theory and practice. The hero for example lets himself be "seduced", but the explanation is reasonable. The heroine Leukippe has to represent the figure of the "persecuted innocent", but the "other" woman, the white widow Melite, is allowed to be the erotically more active antiheroine and becomes sympathetic and human. The generation gap between mother and daughter is also pronounced.

The pastoral novel of Longus is something special. The foundlings *Daphnis and Chloe* grow up as children of nature. They take a journey through the land of emotional experiences reserved for young people who can realize the quality of physical love. Especially in the case of the girl, budding love is described as an experience deep inside. Logically consistent, the naive Daphnis gets "sex education" from a city-dweller who accompanied her husband to the country. Lykainion as a contrast to the heroine is not, however, reduced in character. Because of her wise advice Chloe keeps her virginity and at the happy ending she is able to enjoy a respectable marriage.

In the last preserved romantic novel, which is obviously the best, the heroine Charikleia is most outstanding in comparison to all female figures. Regarding her intellect and education she is superior to her partner and to the other women, although she was born as a "barbarian", she grew up at Delphi. As a strong female character she influenced the European novel of the baroque period as well as Leonore in Goethe's *Tasso*. Motherless and not restricted to the seclusion of the women's house she was educated mentally and physically as if a man. Despite a certain girlish shyness she appears as a self-confident and almost emancipated intellectual, who defends her virginity obstinately and aggressively and even demands unconditional faithfulness and chastity from her bridegroom. But as "prisoners of a pure love" the couple is the personification of an ennobled passion. In a moderate way and in the belief in divine justice in a human world, witnesses for new religious trends in the late empire are discernible in the novel and even more so in Christian writings.

The antiheroine Arsake who is the "other" woman in Heliodorus' novel contrasts sharply with Charikleia. Nevertheless this woman from the Middle East is not a completely negative figure; her passions and her domineering nature overstep the mark of law and order. On the other hand Charikleia is described as an ideal, because she is able to control her emotions.

In the Greek romantic novel which was the first functional prose with a widespread impact, upper and middle-class women could feel writers addressing them. Women found many opportunities for identification, since there could be recognized a certain development from the novel of Ninus to that of Heliodorus. In the nostalgic view of the novelists on classical antiquity unintentional anachronisms from their own age are included. The heroines as fictitious figures have much more freedom than would have been possible in contemporary social reality. In classical Athens women had none at all.

9. A STUDY ON THE MARGIN OF THE ANCIENT NOVEL: "BARBARIANS" AND OTHERS

Heinrich Kuch

Preface

Marginal aspects of literary works tend to be of little relevance to the general effect, and, in principle, this holds true for the ancient novel as well. However, it remains to be seen whether "barbarians" from the Greek point of view, non-Greeks in general[1] and "others" (i.e., strangers, robbers, pirates, and slaves) are entirely without importance in the genre of the ancient novel.

Certainly the focus of the novels' events is on figures who cannot be fit into the categories mentioned above. Main characters are generally Greeks of middle or higher provenance. For example, Euhemerus, the author and the epic character of his utopian adventure novel, enjoyed the friendship of the Macedonian King Kassander (305–298). In Chariton's romance the central characters Callirhoe and Chaereas came from the leading families of Syracuse. But these characters, about whom the action of the novel is centered, are in constant contact with the aforementioned marginal groups. Such contacts are not always harmless meetings; often, they are life-threatening, demanding combat and assertiveness.

The representatives of marginal groups, whether they are "barbarians"[2] or "others", often prove to be serious opponents that the main characters must defeat in order to reach the positive ending of the novel. In ancient literature interactions between main characters and their antipodes form important preconditions for the whole, and only the interplay of the central and peripheral figures can create an ancient novel.

---

[1] Cf. Frisk (1960) 219f. For a discussion of "barbarians", see Jüthner (1923), Jüthner (1950) 1173–6, Christ (1959) 273–288, Bacon (1961), Dörrie (1972) 146–175, Heubner (1985) 91–108, Long (1986), Cunliffe (1988), Kuch (1989d) 80–86, Burkert (1990), Speyer (1992) 813–895, de Romilly (1993) 283–292. Also see notes 2 and 15.

[2] Regarding βάρβαρος and its derivations in novels, consult Conca-De Carli-Zanetto (1983) 136, Papanicolaou (1983) 18, O'Sullivan (1980) 59.

Epic Space

The genre of the ancient novel can be traced to 300 B.C.[3] The conquests of Alexander the Great in the Orient extended the Greek world enormously, and of course anyone who crossed the borders of the Greek realms as Alexander did, inevitably entered the lands of the "barbarians". It was the seductive distance that the ancient novel as a literary genre sought from the very first. The utopian adventure novels created by Hecataeus of Abdera, Euhemerus of Messene, and Iambulus were already taking place in the distant Hyperborean north, as in the case of Hecataeus, or on islands far to the south, as in the case of Euhemerus and Iambulus. In general, the Greek romances, such as those of Chariton or of Xenophon of Ephesus, also move away from familiar regions. Not uncommonly they mention the Orient in their titles.[4] *Phoenicica* is the title Lollianus gave his novel. The same title may have been used by Achilles Tatius.[5] Iamblichus wrote his *Babyloniaca*, while Heliodorus assembled his *Ethiopica*. The Ninus novel, probably written in the second century B.C., deals with the story of the Assyrian King Ninus and the Semiramis (?). The Sesonchosis novel has Egyptian characteristics. We may at least wonder whether these works may also have indicated their non-Greek settings in their titles.[6] In any case, many of the authors seem to have been intent on offering the lure of faraway lands in the titles of their books. Evidently this was an appeal to the public expectation formed by novels that set out for distant horizons.

The promise of these titles was amply repaid by their content. The epic space frequently employed "barbarian" lands.

The characteristic attraction to faraway lands in the Greek novel may be explained in part by the historical foundations of Hellenism. Immense new territories, extending to the borders of India, were opened when Alexander the Great overthrew the Persian Empire. Territorial expansion seems to have been a source of inspiration for authors. The Orient was a favorite setting, even when a novel's title contained no reference to it. In Chariton's *Callirhoe*,[7] the characters travel as far as the Persian royal court at Babylon.

---

[3] On understanding the genre of the ancient novel, cf. Kuch (1992) 223–233, Kuch (1989a).
[4] Cf. Treu (1984) 457f.
[5] Holzberg (1986) 103, Holzberg (1995) 88.
[6] According to Holzberg (1986) 46, the Ninus novel may have been named *Assyriaca*.
[7] Lucke and Schäfer (1985) 181.

Thus a clearly visible trend toward the so-called barbarian lands can be found in the Greek novel. However, contacts with the Near East and with Egypt are not limited to the epic space.

Authors

One must keep in mind that Greek novels were also written by non-Greeks. It is appropriate to begin with the utopian adventure novels. Deserving of mention along with the Greeks Hecataeus of Abdera and Euhemerus of Messene is Iambulus, who at least has a Syrian name. After his adventurous South Sea voyage he returns to Greece (cf. Diodorus 2.60.3). Chariton of Aphrodisias, author of the earliest wholly extant Greek romance, and Xenophon of Ephesus,[8] the novelist who followed in his footsteps, both appear to be Greeks, but they lived in Asia Minor. A special problem is formed by the question of whether Xenophon of Ephesus is a pseudonym in honor of Xenophon of Athens.[9] Longus is probably native to Lesbos, the scene of his work, and he may be one of its Pompeii Longi.[10] It is difficult to decide whether Iamblichus was a native of Babylon or of Syria;[11] in any case, he was very much at home in the Near East. Achilles Tatius may have been of Egyptian origin.[12] At the end of his work, Heliodorus presents himself as a Phoenician from Emesa and thus a Syrian (10.41.4). Lucian, who parodied the Greek novel in his "True Story," was also a Syrian, born in Samosata in the Commagene. And we should not forget that the Roman author Apuleius came from Madaura, in Numidia.

However, it would be off the mark to present the noble author of the *Metamorphoses* as a Romanized "barbarian"; after all, Thomas Mann referred to *The Golden Ass* as a "masterly achievement of world novel-literature" in his essay "The Art of the Novel".[13] Likewise, authors who wrote in Greek but were born in the Near East and in Egypt cannot be called Hellenized "barbarians". As a result of their work, they were doubtless part of a cultural elite that has nothing to do with "barbarians".

---

[8] Papanikolaou (1984) 279–294.
[9] Schmeling (1980) 16.
[10] Schönberger (1989) 9f.
[11] Hägg (1987b) 51.
[12] Hägg (1987b) 51f.
[13] Mann (1965) 459.

The group of authors subsumed in the genre of the ancient novel is as diverse as it is heterogeneous. It is not characterized by strong coherence, but rather by continuous transformation, in a more dynamic evolution of genre. In addition, these authors were open to the world in a way that we would now call "international". The representatives of the genre intellectually transcended their own *poleis*, their own communities, and may therefore be compared with the Sophists of the fifth century B.C. An even more apt comparison might be with the intellectual movement of the later Sophists of the second century A.D.—at a height of the novel's development—who also included representatives from so-called barbarian lands. The differences between the individual novelists are a result not only of the long tradition of the ancient novel (from ca. 300 B.C. to at least ca. 400 A.D.), but also of the individual writing styles so imaginatively developed by the authors, despite the generic conventions. This is especially characteristic of those authors who came from "barbarian" lands. Not only extremely well-versed in the Greek language, these authors also had command of the novel as a genre, so that the Greek tradition easily found continuance. At the same time, they produced an enlivening and loosening of the conventional novelistic scheme. Presumably the non-Greek authors were also working toward a favorable reception of their works in their own countries.

Heroes and Marginal Characters

The choice of main characters for a novel depended on different factors: above all on the author, on his audience, and therefore also on the function of the novel as a counterexample to contemporary conditions. Novelists employed an aesthetic of alternatives to create attractive fictional prospects in contrast with contemporary life. Heroes had to be equal to this task, and also had to be relatively easy for the reader to identify with. Understandably, the profile of the leading roles was also partly determined by the ambience of the intended audience.

For the utopian adventure novels the way was marked. The main character and narrator are the author himself, who claims to have personally visited the wondrous foreign land he describes. But it is the foreign environment, not the author, that is the focus, at least in the presumptive main body dedicated to describing the imagined country. Not so in the case of the romances, the heart of which, so to speak, consists of the fates of the lovers. In consideration of their Greek audiences, Chariton and other classicistically oriented novelists made use of Greek central characters through whom readers could experience the "barbarian" country. On the contrary, in the *Babyloniaca* of Iamblichus we find a heroic couple from Mesopotamia: Sinonis and Rhodanes. They probably offered identification especially for Hellenized Orientals. Heliodorus' *Ethiopica*, set during the Persian rule of Egypt (after 525 B.C.), seem tailored to a Greek and Roman audience as well as to Hellenized inhabitants of the Near East. The central roles in this novel are occupied by the Greek Theagenes, a Thessalian aristocrat whose pedigree extends to the Greek heroic idol Achilles, and Charikleia, a Delphic priestess of Artemis. As it turns out, Charikleia is the daughter of an Ethiopian royal family.

The literary variation to which an ancient novelist resorted again and again to loosen up the traditional form also resulted in a change in the social status of central characters. In Longus' pastoral romance, Daphnis and Chloe are members of free and respectable families, but are abandoned at birth and raised by shepherd slaves. As a result the erstwhile orphans remain slaves until the end of the work. The confusing whims of Tyche can easily lead to other instances of abrupt social decline; Chariton's Callirhoe is sold as a slave in Ionic Asia Minor, and Chaereas also falls into slavery. Both soon regain their freedom, since the Greek novel thrives on the constant changes wrought upon its main characters before the happy ending.

Marginal characters, especially "barbarians," strangers, robbers, pirates, and slaves, are not so lucky in the literature of the novel. These characters fall victim to the dangers that main characters escape, being prominent by their beauty and solid social background. Clitophon watches from a distance as Leucippe is apparently decapitated by pirates (Achilles Tatius 5.7.4f.), but he is in error. The heroine must live on, and the victim is another, an "unlucky woman"—one who, as it is called, sells the joys of Aphrodite for money (8.16.1f.). Likewise, in Heliodorus, the attractive slave girl Thisbe (cf. 1.11.3) falls prey to the murderer's sword (2.5.4; 2.6.2) while Charikleia, who was actually to be murdered and who even appeared to have been murdered (cf. 2.3.3) escapes death as the heroine of the novel. Such victims are not, however, limited to mere individuals. Supporting characters are slaughtered *en masse*. Their lucklessness is accepted as unquestioningly as the constant escapes of the beautiful, privileged heroes.

Robbers and pirates likewise usually come to a bad end, aside from some special exceptions. A coalition of bandits and "barbarians", called βουκόλοι, is formed in Achilles Tatius (3.9.2). These are fearsome and wild black-skinned robbers who speak in a "barbaric" idiom. Nevertheless not all robbers turn out to be as bad as Chariton's Theron. Heliodorus creates his Thyamis as the noble robber type, after Xenophon of Ephesus has also given his robber chieftain Hippothous some admirable traits. The same Xenophon allows the goatherd Lampon, a slave, to show pity and resist the order to kill Anthia. Thus some attempt at differentiation is made, amongst robbers and slaves just as amongst the "barbarians". However, when compared with the "barbarian" component and its importance to the ancient novel, robbers, pirates, and slaves are of less significance, however dangerous they may become.

The category of "strangers" also occurs. In connection with the main character's status—which is subject to rapid changes in the course of his or her adventures—it must be noted that travelers into these distant lands are regarded as strangers. Thus they have few rights, if any, beyond hospitality—and even that is often not extended. In principal, strangers are always susceptible to attacks of all kinds.

Innovations

The novelists of the Near East who wrote in Greek—in any case Iamblichus and Heliodorus—understood how to enrich the traditional structure with new inventions. In the formal realm, Heliodorus achieved the *non plus ultra* of the literature of the ancient novel. He knew how to make engrossing use of the narrative introduction *medias in res*, already employed in the Homeric *Iliad*. His development of the action is so many-layered that the reader has some difficulty finding his way around the artistically arranged narrative labyrinth as its twisted paths offer ever more illusive perspectives. In comparison with such a complicated composition, the real world must have appeared dull and colorless to Heliodorus' readers.

But beyond the structural aspects of his work, Heliodorus sought to excel in content as well. The humane attitude of the work seems, in its glorification of Helius, to be indebted to a religious ethic in which Helius is elevated to the status of Apollo (10.36.3); it peaks in the concluding abolishment of human sacrifice (cf. 10.39.3–40.1). Only this humane act clears the way for the almost ever obligatory happy ending, which in this case occurs through a religious cult—as when Theagenes and Charikleia are able to marry once they have been ordained as priest of Helius and priestess of Selena. Here Heliodorus individually adapted the ancient novel's role of providing a counterexample to contemporary conditions.

The Syrian author's portrayal of his heroine Charikleia,[14] the characteristically Greek princess of Ethiopian ancestry, is a remarkable performance. She displays the initiative of a strong personality, careful yet also heroically fierce in a dangerous situation. Charikleia is undoubtedly an enrichment of the Greek novel as a genre, which contains more than enough emotionally weak and tearful figures.

The inventions of Iamblichus, another man of the East, are no less drastic, and they considerably enhance the dangers that must be overcome by the novel's central characters. Hence the ghost of a ram that appears to threaten the heroine with his love (Epitome of Photius [*Bibliotheca* 94], p. 10, 9 in the Iamblichus edition of E. Habrich; cf. fr. 9f.). In *Babyloniaca* the popular form of the robber becomes a cannibal (*ibid.* p. 18, 8f. Habrich), and there are bees with poisonous honey (*ibid.* p. 14, 6–13 Habrich). Cruel punishments are applied, including the removal of ears and noses (*ibid.* p. 10, 1f. Habrich) and burial alive, in which the wives and children of those convicted must die as well (*ibid.* p. 58, 6–9 Habrich).

These outward horrors are not the only innovations of Iamblichus, who, according to Suda, compiled 39 books (cf. p. 3, 3f. Habrich). The profile of the heroine Sinonis is an impressive accomplishment. In her passion and energy, visible in conjunction with her great jealousy (cf. fr. 70; cf. also p. 8, 4–6 Habrich and fr. 61), she far outpaces the female characters of classicistic novel authors.

There is no doubt that the so-called barbarian novelists were able to create innovations. They skillfully carried on the traditions of the genre, but at the same time they were so inventive as to refresh the form and content of the conventional novel with new elements.

The contributions of nonhellenic novelists to the evolution of the genre cover a broad ground that could only barely be outlined by these examples. For instance, further insights could be gained from the work of Achilles Tatius, who pushed the art of the novel

---

[14] Johne (1987) 30–33.

forward with attempts of psychological analysis and the portrayal of the sensational.

The Hellenes-"Barbarians" Antithesis and Further Innovations

Regardless of all these pioneering innovations, it is impossible to overlook the continued influence of the Hellenes-"barbarians" antithesis[15] of classical and post-classical times in ancient novels. A thorough awareness of this contrast can be taken for granted wherever a non-Greek (to the Greek, a "barbarian") fictional paradise is created— that is, in the utopian adventure novel.

Surprising notions are described, foremost by Euhemerus and Iambulus, who developed models of a more just society to contrast with the Hellenic *status quo*. It is significant that their utopian constructions are located outside Greece, in the "barbarian" realms, but without mention of the term βάρβαρος. Differences that were present in contemporary society are put aside in such places. There is no division of citizens and non-citizens, or of the free and the enslaved there; no one is politically or socially set apart.

Iambulus presented the most determinedly socially critical alternative to the conditions of his own time to be found in any ancient novel. In his imaginary country, the potential "barbarian" realizes a principle of universal equality that is without counterpart in the historical reality of the third century B.C. These ideas surpass even the democratic principles of the Greek *poleis*, which in the fifth century B.C. undertook to include the middle and lower strata of the *demos* in their political life. The domestic peace of the "communities" into which Iambulus divides his fabulous construction (cf. Diodorus 2.57.1) seems to be assured by their social harmony. As a result of the utopia's great distance from the known nations of the earth (cf. Diodorus 2.55.6), external security appears to be guaranteed as well. The novelist's utopia—his constructed counterexample to his own surroundings—was certainly segregated from contemporary civilization—cut off, and practically impossible to reach. His principle of hope, mixed with some paradox (cf. Diodorus 2.55.1; 2.56.6) was situated in the outermost periphery.

---

[15] Regarding the Hellenes-"barbarians" antithesis, cf. Diller (1962) 37–82, Reverdin (1962) 83–120, Laurot (1981) 39–48. Cf. also note 1.

Although this life is referred to as "joyous" (cf. Diodorus 2.55.4), it includes some questionable aspects with a barbaric flavor. Its rigorous social equality also extends to the human constitution (cf. Diodorus 2.56.2). To demonstrate their physical and mental fitness, children must pass a test flight on a large bird; those who fail are expelled (Diodorus 2.58.5). Cripples and the infirm are required by law to part with their lives (Diodorus 2.57.5). Thus the principles of equality are harshly enforced, tainting the idealized non-Greek conditions. In any case, the distant paradisiacal situations of the utopian adventure novel are a marked antithesis to contemporary Greek culture.

Such suggestions were not taken up by the authors of Greek romances. Chariton and Xenophon of Ephesus, attached to the value system of the fifth and fourth centuries B.C., show a considerable prejudice against "barbarians". Nonetheless, Chariton takes pains to differentiate his characters, as do other novelists within the confines of their art. Real "barbarians," as the Greek understood them, are created—albeit not without clichés—in the form of the autocratic, humanly problematic ruler of the Persians, in his faithful and agile eunuch Artaxates, and in the scheming Mithridates, regent of Caria. By way of contrast, the Persian Queen Statira and the wealthy Miletian Dionysius are endowed with considerable individuality and a great deal of noble character—not to overlook the fact that Dionysius, while a Persian subject (6.9.1) and the rival of the hero Chaereas, is a Greek.

When Chariton describes extraordinary martial achievements in the war of the Persians against the rebellious Egyptians, it is characteristic of the author's point of view that these take place under the leadership of a Greek. The Dionysius just mentioned bravely leads the final land battle in favor of the Persian monarch (7.5.12–14), but Chaereas, who has joined the Egyptian side, leads his forces to naval victory over the Persian fleet. This success corresponds to the fifth century B.C. tradition of the Persian wars. With this the novelist connects, *in maiorem gloriam* of his Syracusan hero Chaereas, a further historical tradition: the Athenians, victorious over the Persians, were later defeated by the Syracusans (7.5.8). So one who defeats the Athenians has every hope of also defeating the Persians—a thought which is presented to the audience of the novel by three differently preparatory signals (6.7.10; 7.2.3f.; 7.5.8). And in fact, Chaereas easily wins the naval battle (7.6.1). Thus the absolute superiority of the Greeks over their opponents is manifest in the novel.

Given such preconditions, the Greek couple Chaereas and Callirhoe are also able to secure their personal happiness. The two overcome all the remaining Persian dangers and arrive at their happy ending.

In other romances as well, the Greek main characters (i.e., the lovers) prevail against their "barbarian" antagonists—as described by Xenophon of Ephesus, who also here follows in Chariton's footsteps, and by Achilles Tatius. There is opportunity to observe the Hellenic conception of the "barbarian" as a type. Xenophon of Ephesus, for instance, is able in relatively little space to endow Manto, the daughter of the Phoenician chieftain Apsyrtus, with negative characteristics such as an absence of self-control (2.3.2f.), rage that is described as "barbaric rage" (2.3.5 twice), cruelty (cf. 2.4.4), and vengefulness (2.5.2; 2.5.5 along with other emotions). The "barbaric" is repeatedly emphasized (2.3.5 twice; 2.3.8; 2.4.2; 2.4.5) and is clearly intended to be seen in marked contrast with Hellenic traits.[16]

Even the Syrian novelist Heliodorus is not completely free of the influence of the Hellenes-"barbarians" antithesis. At the end of the *Ethiopica*, his central character, Theagenes, is required to wrestle an Ethiopian athlete whose tremendous strength leaves Theagenes little chance of success (10.31.1–32.2). But because of his Hellenic athletic training (cf. 10.31.5), the hero is able to defeat his massive and stupid opponent. The Greek, familiar with the art of fighting, which is governed by Hermes (cf. 10.31.5: τήν τε ἐναγώνιον Ἑρμοῦ τέχνην ἠκριβωκώς), is able to use his experience to trick raw, untrained power (*ibid.*: ἐμπειρίᾳ δὲ τὴν ἄγροικον ἰσχὺν κατασοφίσασθαι).

The bias expressed here, however, did not prevent Heliodorus from idealizing Ethiopia and expanding it into a humane, friendly utopia in his work.[17] The country is ruled by Hydaspes, a brave, humane, and generous king (9.6.2; 9.21.3; 9.23.5) who follows the advice of wise Gymnosophists (10.2.1). His actions are guided by the φιλάνθρωπον (9.6.2; cf. 9.27.2). As we may conclude from the text, Hydaspes is no τύραννος but rather, a βασιλεὺς ἀληθής (cf. 9.21.3), and the reign of the "Father of the People" (10.17.2: ὁ τοῦ δήμου πατήρ. Cf. also 10.16.8) is accompanied by law and justice (10.3.3; 10.10.3; cf. also 9.27.2; 10.1.1). But anyone in the third or fourth century A.D.—the exact dates for Heliodorus are debatable—who designs a utopian state headed by a monarch is certainly consciously distancing himself from

---

[16] Cf. also Schmeling (1980) 62 and 117.
[17] Szepessy (1981) 203–207, Szepessy (1957) 244–251.

the *Imperium Romanum* of late antiquity. With this critical distance the Phoenician, i.e. Syrian, author has brought out yet another variation in the role of the ancient novel as a contemporary counterexample.

In the *Imperium Romanum*, the Hellenes-"barbarians" antithesis was modified to favor the Romans, who strictly speaking were after all not Greek, but "barbarians". In view of their Hellenization, however, they could approximate Greeks. Thus the classical preconceptions continued to find justification and carried over into Roman thought. In Petronius' *Satyricon* Trimalchio declares that he is native to Asia Minor (75.10; cf. 29.3). His name can be traced to Semitic *malk*, "king".[18] That is, he hails from the Orient and was once a slave. The character of Trimalchio, the affluent and successful freedman who stands out because of his bad taste and lack of culture, is described with condescension by the aristocratic author. If this character treatment is taken in conjunction with the advancement of the wealthy freedmen who were gradually gaining influence in opposition to the aristocracy of the Senate in Nero's time, then we may observe the *elegantiae arbiter* (Tacitus, *Annales* 16.18.2) taking literary revenge upon the foreign parvenus.

A similar attitude is expressed by Apuleius in his *Metamorphoses*. The novel's hero, Lucius, who is driven far and wide after having been transformed into an ass, has the bad luck to fall in with a group of Syrian beggar priests (cf. 8.24–30; 9.4; 9.8–10). He is forced to carry their statue of the *dea Syria* (cf. 8.24.2; 9.10.3), the Syrian goddess, and so becomes witness to their unholy doings, which he describes in repellent detail: orgiastic and amoral practices, betrayals, and finally, the theft of a golden vessel from the shrine of the mother-goddess (9.9.4: *matris deum*). This sacrilege, a *scelus* (cf. 9.9.4)— even a *nefarium scelus* (cf. 9.10.2), a "ruthless, frivolous crime"—is said to have been committed by simulation of "solemn, holy acts" (9.9.4: *simulatione sollemnium*). The criminals are called *impuratissima . . . capita* (9.10.2), that is, "the worst miscreants". With these and other connotations, Apuleius decidedly distances himself from the Syrian group.

The image of the "barbarian" that the Greek novel acquired from the fifth and fourth century B.C. had now found entry and new forms in the Roman novel. However, it should be obvious merely from the illustrious reputation of the novelist from Madaura that here also, one must distinguish between biases.

---

[18] Bauer (1983) 17.

Conclusion

The Greek novel is generally not questioned as a Greek art form. Yet one who considers this literary genre with respect to its "barbarian" components can perceive largely a non-Greek epic space, non-Greek authors, non-Greek heroes, and, it follows naturally, non-Greek audiences. There can be no doubt that the "barbarians" not only preserved the traditions of the ancient novel, but also evolved them further. From Iamblichus to Heliodorus, and even from Iambulus on, this included innovations, new structures, new ideas. That they themselves made use of the classical Hellenes-"barbarians" antithesis should not be overlooked.[19] The Greek novel and, as becomes apparent, also the Roman novel—a wide field of contacts and conflicts between the most varied forces: Hellenes, "barbarians", and "others"— is prolifically molded also by the so-called barbarian elements.

---

[19] Regarding the reception of the ancient novel in the medieval Orient, cf. Hägg (1986) 99–131, Hägg (1989) 36–73.

10. THE SOCIAL AND ECONOMIC STRUCTURES OF THE ANCIENT NOVELS

Antonio M. Scarcella
(translated by Aldo Setaioli)

It is well known that the few chronological and biographical hints we are restricted to concerning the authors of Greek novels as well as the works themselves are totally insufficient to locate them surely and finally in time and geographical area or to assess their social and economic standing. We can doubtfully say that the five novels surviving in their complete form (if we may say this much),—the so called "Big Five"—go back to the imperial period; many other novels, only fragmentarily preserved, and their unnamed and completely unknown authors, probably covered an even greater period of time. Consequently, the conclusion that may be reached by an enquiry on the social and economical conditions reflected in such works cannot possibly be referred to or supported by an actual social and economic background historically testified to by other sources. It is significant, in this connection, that in none of these works any mention is made of the Roman empire, within whose political jurisdiction and cultural and ideological framework these authors and their works must presumably be located.

On the other hand, the form of state, the civil institutions, the war conventions, the law implications, the social structure, the economic background (as well as the religious and ideological attitudes) of such novels are largely to be referred to Greek tradition: or, if related to other countries and peoples, they are made to agree with the general Greek imagination, thus often reflecting manneristic behaviors and ideas. However—and luckily—besides these intended, unequivocal and predictable representations (or in between them), ways and actions sneak in, that are not consistent and appropriate, e.g., democratic elements in monarchical states, individual attitudes of solidarity and generosity in the midst of a legal situation spelling social humiliation and rejection, independent handling of one's affections where habits of submission and surrender to another's will prevail. It is to be surmised that this takes place beyond the authors' awareness and consistency; they thus mix old ideas with new and different experiences. It is precisely in this gap, that the Greek novelists do not try to close, however, that their documentary contribution and value clearly lie. In other words, it is in the breaches, so to speak, of the tale[1] that historical information is hidden, which is all the more precious in as much as it is unconscious and all the more authoritative by being uncalled for. In relation to the reality of the facts, which is set as a model but made into a myth rather than faithfully reproduced, and perhaps adventurously reflected rather than carefully reconstructed, such naive suggestions, disturbing contradictions and quiet inconsistencies, witness an unstable and culturally intricate situation. They are the precarious but precious indication of a change centering on confined and secondary things (down to eating habits, dressing fashions, medical proceedings, means of communication), which, however, eventually affect important affairs (such as the conception and use of power, the political activity of cities or states, the administration of justice, the circulation of consumers' goods and precious metals, minted or otherwise), up to the supporting structures, constituting the most conspicuous and prominent materializations of that society (the relation between the ruling and the ruled, the division of the people into ranks, if we wish to avoid the word "classes", the legal position of free individuals and of slaves, the areas of personal independence either in compliance or in opposition to ethical principles inwardly assimilated, if not actually written).

Of such transformations, which appear as plain and deep to a wide-range examination as they seem flimsy and unconspicuous from a limited point of view, the Greek erotic novels too can be respectable witnesses. Even though their authors may often appear unattentive economists, unheedful historians and incompetent philosophers, the information with which they unwittingly present us constitutes a noteworthy endowment, truly an alluring and durable acquisition.

The societies portrayed by Chariton[2] belong to different states: the democratic *polis* of Syracuse, the monarchical states of Persia and Egypt (the latter at first a province subject to a foreign power, later on an independent state). Unequivocal indications force us to place the story in the fifth century B.C. The tale takes place within the

---

[1] Genette (1972) 75 works out a subtle tripartition of narrative reality. The passage (and the book) are read with profit.
[2] Guiding text: Molinié (1989).

higher social levels, as far as power and prestige are concerned: and the opportunity for a further social climbing is left open (Chaereas). The appearance of democratic attitudes within despotic monarchical structure is surprising. In Syracuse popular masses have some political relevancy; elsewhere they only serve the purpose of decoration. There are lowly and outcast groups: these are the many pirates that wander the sea and replenish the slave market through their robberies and kidnappings. Slaves are everywhere. There appear fortunes and riches, which are boundless in the case of kings (and their associates). The social structure and the economic features of these states, in their main lines, follow a well-known pattern; however, the appreciation of culture as a justification for power is noteworthy.

The young protagonists belong to prominent Syracusan families,[3] though their political (and social) prestige differs. Callirhoe is the daughter of Hermocrates.[4] The girl is full of pride (1.3.6 φρονήματος πλήρης) and boasts of her lineage (2.5.9; 3.1.6; etc.) to the point of being haughty (2.8.1 τὸ μεγαλόφρον) and ironic (6.5.8 κατειρωνεύσατο). Coming from a very prominent family, she has received an excellent education[5] (1.12.9 πεπαίδευται... ἱκανῶς; 6.5.8 πεπαιδευμένη καὶ φρενήρης; 7.6.5; etc.), which combines in her with native qualities (5.6.7 σωφροσύνην... φιλανδρίαν; not to mention further endowments, such as steadfastness and a high level of cynicism). Hermocrates appears to his daughter as an admirable specimen of family virtues (3.8.8: "Grant—I pray you—that my son be more fortunate than his parents, and like his grandfather. May he too sail on a flagship— and when he is in action, may people say 'Hermocrates' grandson is greater than he was!' His grandfather too will be happy to see his

---

[3] Schmeling (1974) 77 doubts the historical pertinence of the information on the two protagonists' lineage, but judges this an irrelevant shortcoming in relation to the narrative ("For Chariton's novel it is most important, however, to provide both heroine and hero with famous and noble, if unhistorical, parents").

[4] Billault (1989) 548: "Il est là comme une autorité dont le seul mot suffit. Ce nom, souvent répété, représente l'aboutissement de la synthèse réussie par Chariton: un personnage construit à partir d'une référence historique unique simplifiée dans sa présentation, riche de mille exploits jamais contés et qui sont comme le piédestal légendaire d'un protagoniste peu actif, presque toujours muet, mais dont la seule présence, parce qu'elle figure une sorte d'idéal de perfection incarné, confère au recit un incontestable cachet de noblesse." But this manipulation, or rather displacement of historical data, is extremely common in Greek novels; if it is not one of their merits, it is, however, their most prominent feature.

[5] Ruiz-Montero (1989) 136ff., on the importance of the παιδεία in Chariton's novel; but her article also offers many useful notes on the different aspects, both realistic and ideological, of the work.

courage inherited; and we shall be happy, his parents, even if we are dead'; also 2.11.2), and of social virtues too (1.11.2). Others agree (4.3.1ff. Polycharmus; 5.8.5 Dionysius; 5.8.8 the Great King), being aware of the reputation or acknowledging the deserts of the distinguished statesman (5.8.7 the counselors of the king of Persia; 7.2.3f. the king of Egypt; 8.8.11 Chaereas, all the more). Blood nobility[6] (which can be recognized at first sight: 1.14.9) supported by culture entitles one to wield power: this is considered transmissible by right of inheritance.

Chaereas' family is also prominent, though less so. His father, Ariston, holds second place in the city, after Hermocrates, his political opponent (1.1.3 τὰ δεύτερα ... μετὰ Ἑρμοκράτην ... τὶς ἦν ἐν αὐτοῖς πολιτικὸς φθόνος). In the novel too his role is limited (1.3.1; 3.5.4f.; 8.6.10). The reasons for this choice are self-evident: Chaereas' personal merits must be exalted, the two main figures in the novel must be balanced. Historical information remains indeterminate. Notwithstanding this fault of lineage, Chaereas attains high reputation among his fellow-citizens (6.7.10 εὐγενής ... πόλεως πρῶτος); actually he gains renown (and wealth) all through Sicily, and this he combines with his natural beauty (4.3.1). Thus, in him natural virtues and acquired qualities merge. Even Callirhoe's suitors are of high lineage (1.1.2 δυνάσται τε καὶ παῖδες τυράννων; 1.1.9 πλουσίους καὶ βασιλεῖς). They gather "from Southern Italy too and farther North." This being so, in Sicily and elsewhere there must be monarchical states or states ruled through a personal regime.

Chaereas' career is extremely brilliant (7.3.10f. he is appointed a general), mainly because of his capabilities as a soldier (8.2.2 στρατηγὸς ἀγαθός); however, he also possesses more refined and human qualities (7.3.11 he cares more for other people's glory than for his own; 8.2.10 his soldiers are συστρατιῶται καὶ φίλοι to him). He is popular with his soldiers (7.3.11 εὔνοιαν ... καὶ πίστιν; 8.2.13) and they trust him; on the other hand he reciprocates their fondness by entrusting them

---

[6] Baslez (1990) 122: "De 'bonne naissance', ce qu'elle signifiait au départ, εὐγένεια devient 'comportement noble'; elle résulte à la fois d'une nature d'élite et d'une éducation soignée." This already profound conception is further developed by other novelists, such as Achilles Tatius and Heliodorus, who acknowledge the existence of noble and highly cultured personalities even outside the Greek world (ibid., 127: "[Ils] prennent davantage en compte l'ouverture de la société impériale aux élites non-grecques, les *Éthiopiques* developpant même une conception proprement orientale à cette date, où la véritable noblesse n'est pas seulement celle du sang mais celle de la caste sacerdotale").

to the king (8.4.3) and presents each one of those that have come back with him with the exorbitant sum of one talent each (8.8.14). From the king of Egypt, though the latter considers and calls him a "kid" (7.2.5), Chaereas obtains not only familiarity (7.2.5 ὁμοτράπεζον ... σύμβουλον; he becomes his table companion and his counselor), but also generous presents (7.5.7 κτῆμα Συρία: Chaereas, however, seems to have no concern for nor recollection of this country with which the king so unrestrainedly presents him). The capability he shows on the battlefield[7] (7.8.7f. εὐγενείᾳ ... καὶ ἀρετῇ διαφέρειν; 8.2.5; 8.2.10; etc.) proves him a strong (7.2.6; 7.3.4f.) and a free man (7.1.1), which is the highest virtue for a Greek. Therefore he can afford to recommend mercy to the king (8.4.3: "more than anyone, a king should show forbearance"; also 7.1.6ff.). Chariton plays down some excesses of Chaereas (1.3.3ff. mad jealousy; 7.2.3; 7.3.4 defection from the king of Persia); he also diminishes Callirhoe's cruelty (6.5.8 she would fain tear out an enemy's eyes). What matters to him is to show that both his protagonists possess (or acquire) qualities that enable them to rise to the peak in their society (and in the novel).

Demetrius, the Egyptian, though a minor character, rises to an important role in the tale. He is appointed an admiral by Chaereas because of his intellectual and moral qualities (8.3.10 φιλόσοφος, βασιλεῖ γνώριμος, ἡλικίᾳ προήκων, παιδείᾳ καὶ ἀρετῇ: "a philosopher who was known to the king of Persia; he was advanced in years and superior to the other Egyptian in culture and character"). He is wealthy, too (8.7.9 πλούτῳ ... γένει ... δόξῃ). The idea of aristocracy is by now less settled: friendship with the powerful, possession of riches and acquired cultural qualities count more than family traditions.

Hermocrates' official position within the Syracusan community is unclear. His definition as μέγας στρατηγός (1.1.11) is abstract, as he is active in the political rather than in the military sphere (3.4.3 he

---

[7] Wars abound in the novels; but their function is mostly (or even solely) related to the narrative. Scarcella (1992) 71: "La fureur collective des peuples ou des foules se mobilise pour bouleverser la douce folie délirante d'un couple d'amoureux, pour l'exaspérer par l'attente et pour l'enrichir par la souffrance. Et alors la guerre voit pâlir, dans le récit romanesque, ses motivations authentiques: elle prend à la tradition historique et littéraire sa physionomie et ses techniques, mais elle accomplit une fonction narratologique, à la fois mineure et sérieuse, qui est celle de l'invention de l'amour." See also Fusillo (1989) 62f.: "esistono ... momenti in cui l'imitazione della matrice storiografica prende un respiro più autonomo: è il topos della guerra ... La guerra è ... un episodio autonomo ed esteso che riscrive nella consueta tonalità 'borghese' la prosa storiografica, ma che resta funzionalizzato al racconto primario."

summons the assembly; 3.4.16f. he influences its judgment, thus bringing about a criminal's execution and he decides the sailing of the state ship; etc.). He is the object of general respect, as is shown by his being escorted by the counselors and the archons (1.1.12); he provokes both admiration and abashment. Near him are the archons, public officials whose functions conform to rule and custom (1.5.2 they choose court members by lot; 1.10.5 they act as judges in conjunction with the people; 3.4.8 they question the defendant; 3.4.12 they summon a witness). Mention is also made of the officials of Athens, who have a reputation for refusing to compromise (1.11.7), as well as of those of Arados (7.6.4 these possess a building specially allotted to their sessions). In spite of the subtleness of the archons' functions, the writer is more interested in remarkable individuals who were able to make it to the top owing to their exceptional endowments.

In Persia[8] the highest authority is reserved for the king by right of inheritance. He is called king of kings (4.6.3. βασιλεῖ βασιλέων) by his subjects, who consider themselves, with no exception, as his servants. Therefore he enjoys a despotic power (6.7.3: "when the king commands, none may argue"). Consequently, everything is easy for the king (6.3.4; 8.4.8 ῥᾴδια ... πάντα βασιλεῖ). Given his institutional and social position (as well as the flattery on the part of his subjects), his figure may be compared with the gods', in as much as he is the offspring of Helios (6.1.10 Ἥλιος προπάτωρ). He is looked at with fear as a god (6.7.12 θεὸν φανερόν). The king avails himself of the help of officials, the satraps: Pharnaces is the satrap of Lydia and Ionia (4.1.7 geographical boundaries are not clear), Mithridates of Caria, being called either σατράπης (4.2.4) or ὕπαρχος (4.1.9; 4.5.7; 4.6.1 Pharnaces), perhaps in relation to some hierarchical scale. Other satraps remain unnamed (5.4.1) as they are irrelevant to the narrative. The king, who bestows political and military authority on them, can freely do as he pleases with whole regions of his state (6.5.7 Miletus, all of Ionia, Sicily and other areas: here, however, a eunuch's derangements are portrayed). Surely the king does not refrain from displaying his anger and his despotism towards his satraps (4.7.1

---

[8] Baslez (1992a) 199 : "utilisant un décor Perse pour la moitié, à peu près, de son roman, Chariton fait preuve de connaissances assez nombreuses, variées et en général exactes, mais l'usage qu'il en fait révèle moins un souci de précision historique qu'un goût du pittoresque;" *ibid.*, 204: "le roman de Chariton tient autant de l'histoire vécue que de l'histoire lue ... Il propose ... une image populaire de l'Orient, qui est donc composite, séléctive et actualisée, bien que son information soit correcte."

Mithridates). He surrounds himself with outward lavishness (6.2.4; 6.4.2); the *proskynēsis* (kowtow) is due him (5.4.8). He unites the functions of head of state, commander of the armed forces, supreme justice in court: such a mixing of powers, with the further ability to consider the whole territory of the state as his own property (6.5.9 τὸν γῆς ἁπάσης κύριον), makes him an autocrat—repulsive to Greek mentality—in accordance with an ossified nationalistic conception. In the actual narrative, however, the king's behavior is marked by democratic feelings, that can only be found historically in the development of Greek civilization. He is the guardian of the law (5.6.4) but may not be the authority that issues it;[9] he presides over the supreme court, but keeps a jury near himself (5.4.8 οἱ συνδικάζοντες), which includes military authorities (5.4.5 ἡγεμόνες ἡγεμόνων), with rather equivocal connections. Decisions are made with the cooperation of the king's friends, who are only perfunctorily alluded to (5.8.6 ἐβουλεύετο μετὰ τῶν φίλων); the verdict, however, is read with all judges present (5.8.8). The sovereign is entitled to grant the request of adjournment made by one of the parties (5.4.13). The procedure seems rather vague, since Chariton is preoccupied with endowing the king's figure with a delicacy of feelings which, though it is intended to appear democratic, is most of all plainly human.

His military abilities are less conspicuous: he calls to arms all able-bodied men (6.9.1) in what appears to be a sort of general mobilization (7.1.1) and personally takes the troops' command and obtains some successes on the field (7.5.12ff.; etc.); on the sea, however, he is defeated by Chaereas (7.6.1ff.; 8.1.1). Anyway, he faces danger in person (6.9.2 δῆλος ἦν πράξων τι γενναῖον) and though his satraps (including Dionysius, 6.9.2) are present, he does not lay on others the burden of the war. In this connection the king once more espouses democratic behavior: he summons the dignitaries (6.8.4 τοὺς ὁμοτίμους) and promptly heeds their advice to leave Babylon (6.9.1). Having learned of his opponent's successes, he sets out against him with the

---

[9] The Great King states that he himself issues the laws (6.3.8: "I am mindful of the laws I myself established and the justice I practice among all men"). But this statement counters the mention of a provision of the oracle at Delphi, which had been quoted by the eunuch Artaxates (6.3.7: "he who hurts shall heal"). Two different conceptions of the source of law appear to clash here (the sovereign, the god); but if the Great King obviously supports the former, his subjects, in the eunuch's person, seem to agree with the second. On the other hand the idea that the king should see with uncompromising scrupulousness to the application of the law, seems to be unchallenged: Scarcella (1990) 251f.

choicest part of the army (7.4.12). The sovereign, who wishes to acquire his people's esteem (6.6.7 εὐδοκιμεῖν), is in fact considered just and good (5.7.1 δίκαιος ... φιλάνθρωπος; 5.9.3 χρηστός; 6.5.10). The Persian king's prerogatives are certainly counterbalanced by human qualities (which foreshadow and justify his falling in love). On the other hand, the figure of the eunuch Artaxates, his extremely powerful (5.2.2 μέγιστος ... δυνατώτατος) and faithful (6.3.1 πιστότατος) prime minister (so to speak), is portrayed in a more manneristic fashion. The king treats him with an almost incredible benevolence (6.4.8): "he put his arm round the eunuch and embraced him. 'I am right to hold you in esteem,' he said. 'You are the most well disposed to me; you protect me well'"). Artaxates' extolment incurs Chariton's disapproval. It is to be submitted that the novelist has created his king of Persia with an eye not just to the suggestions of Greek collective imagination but also to a nobler and purer conception of power—a power which is tempered and enriched by personal qualities. This results in ambiguity and even inconsistency which might stem more from cultural pressure upon the writer,[10] than from a rash manipulation on his part.

Owing to his prominency in the narrative, Dionysius takes up an institutional position that appears to be distinct. His titles to power are wealth, nobility, culture, and reputation (1.12.6 πλούτῳ καὶ γένει καὶ παιδείᾳ; 8.7.9 δόξῃ). No mention is made of his family's importance; on the contrary much stress is laid on the availability of a huge fortune, particularly in real estate (2.3.1 ἐν τοῖς παραθαλασσίοις ... χωρίοις): this is judged extremely opulent (1.13.1 τὸ μέγεθος καὶ τὴν πολυτέλειαν; 1.13.5 πολυτελῶς; 2.3.2 τῇ πολυτελείᾳ τῶν οἰκιῶν) and his fields are so vast that a bailiff and an assistant are needed to run them: their names are Leonas and Phocas (2.1.1). Dionysius' traveling equipment is sumptuous (2.3.3: "the order was passed along the line; coachmen got their coaches ready; grooms prepared their horses, boatmen their boats. Dionysius' friends were invited to join him on the journey, and so were a large number of freedmen"). Unbounded extravagance is displayed in the frequent wedding banquets (3.2.10; 4.5.7). The child to be born, reputedly Dionysius' son, will be extremely rich (2.10.4) and will be part of a family that attained

---

[10] C.P. Jones (1992a) 165: "[Chariton] partage beaucoup des traits de l'époque impériale, et ... comme ses contemporains il voit le monde classique avec les yeux d'un homme cultivé de son temps."

high prestige through the merits of his putative father. Dionysius is a handsome, tall and noble-looking man (2.5.2 φύσει καλός τε καὶ μέγας καὶ μάλιστα πάντων σεμνός) but his first quality is education (2.4.1 πεπαιδευμένος; 3.2.6; 4.7.6). He comes from a cultured city (2.5.11) and his dress conforms to Greek fashion; he is sensible and educated (5.5.1 φρόνιμος... καὶ πεπαιδευμένος), has his own natural modesty (2.10.1 δι' αἰδῶ καὶ σωφροσύνην) and can not join pity and violence (2.6.3). Of course he has male and female slaves at his orders, but forbids them to call him master in front of his bride-to-be (2.4.2), and though lustful, would not stoop to carnal intercourse with female slaves (2.1.5: "Dionysius was glad to learn that the woman was beautiful—he was deeply attached to women—but not glad to learn she was a slave, for he was a true aristocrat, preeminent in rank throughout Ionia and would not contemplate taking a slave as a concubine"). He will not be this woman's κύριος, as the law entitles him to be (2.3.6) and though the woman herself regards him as such (2.9.2), he will not keep her as his παλλακή (2.11.5): he will be a lawful bride's husband and his son will be born according to Greek law (3.2.2). This conception of interpersonal relations is unheard of even in the Greek outlook (at least in the fifth century B.C., when the story supposedly takes place): and Dionysius appears as a strictly Greek figure in Oriental surroundings. The presence of a girl child of tender age (1.12.9), his grieving widowhood (2.1.2), his reluctance to take part in public life (2.1.1), finally the loneliness to which the tale condemns him (8.5.15) makes him the most endearing character in the novel,[11] but also the surest embodiment of a new and exquisite mentality. If power is bestowed upon him through an unprovoked act of the sovereign (5.3.10), he deserves it nevertheless because of his rich humanity. On the contrary his supremacy among all Ionians (4.6.4) appears to count for nothing, since the same is stated about Mithridates too (4.4.3). His native shrewdness calls to mind the statement of the tyrant of Agrigentum (1.2.5: "after all, that is how we become tyrants, by cunning not by force"). In conclusion: power without culture is blameful; if kings become such through natural qualities (2.3.10 φύσει γίνονται βασιλεῖς), if only two beautiful things

---

[11] Molinié (1989) 33: "Dionysos, la splendide conscience du roman, vit donc pathétiquement toute l'ambiguïté des profondeurs inconscientes du sentiment amoureux; il repart, accablé et detruit, à travers l'Asie vers la côte d'Ionie, jouir de ses souvenirs, de ses illusions, sans avoir réussi à fixer le bonheur qui lui échappe sans cesse et en cette aventure, pour la dernière fois: il va vieillir."

exist (love and power: 4.7.2), then whoever wields power cannot be wanting in delicacy and dignity. Dionysius is the embodiment of an ideal prominent man; the needs of the narrative may play a part in his portrayal, but surely a weighty factor lies in the new conception of royalty set out by Chariton for his readers. Dionysius really deserves his king's gratitude (7.5.15; 8.5.12) and the author's admiration.

An element of the Persian court, which appears exotic to the Hellenized reader but is fully representative of Oriental culture, is, of course, the harem. There lives Statira, the king's lawful wife (6.1.12). Other harems house the most prominent Persians' wives (5.3.1 τῶν ἐνδοξοτάτων Περσῶν). As a matter of fact, "it is customary for the king himself and the Persian nobility, when they go off to war, to take along with them their wives, children, gold, silver, clothing, eunuchs, concubines, dogs, dining-room furniture, their costly treasures, and luxuries" (6.9.6). One of these wives is the ravishing Rhodogyne (5.3.4). The capture of the harem (7.6.2; 7.6.5; 8.1.1) triggers the king's anxiety and later his rejoicing, as he recovers his wives safe and sound (8.5.5ff.). These are the features of a fabled Orient; and Chaereas, who captures and then frees the women, is the fervent witness to a by now respectful, if disenchanted, way to understand it.

The representation of Egypt's ruling class is less careful and assured. The country is first ruled by a satrap appointed by the king of Persia; he is killed by the Egyptians during a popular uprising (6.8.2). The reasons for this murder are not explained:[12] one may assume this to be connected with a nationalistic attitude, refusing to endure foreign domination. In the satrap's place a king is elected (6.8.2 κεχειροτονηκέναι). An elected king in fifth century B.C. Egypt is rather startling. In war he acts ably and effectively. He too avails himself of a war council's cooperation (7.3.1). Chaereas, who dubs the Persian the worst of men, calls him a real king (7.3.4 ἀληθῶς βασιλεύς . . . κάκιστος). What we have here, we believe, is the mixing of a likely situation and some highly unlikely elements.

At the opposite end of the social range we find the masses, which

---

[12] This type of indifference is ingrained in all Greek novels. Létoublon (1993) 20: "Certes les romans grecs ne montrent qu'un aspect de la société, familles aisées et parfois aristocratiques. Aucun d'entre eux ne cherche à interesser son public au sort du menu peuple ou d'une famille d'esclaves." On the other hand, it must be recalled that (*ibid.*, 60) "ce n'est nullement de l'espace réel du romancier qu'il est question dans le roman, mais d'une géographie, d'une société et de *realia* médiatisés par la répresentation."

are differently described in accordance with their living either in a democratic or a monarchical society. The people (δῆμος) of Syracuse meet in assembly at first in the theater (1.1.11f.), wherein they ask that the two young people be married; a second assembly (in which, strangely enough, women also take part—certainly a romantic touch) encourages Chaereas (3.4.4); an expedition is also petitioned and two ambassadors appointed to search for Callirhoe (3.4.17); the people (πλῆθος) meet once more of their own accord with the participation of women (8.7.1). They bestow Syracusan citizenship upon 300 foreign soldiers who had come back to the city with Chaereas (8.8.13). The mass of citizens, we gather, is entitled to share in the direction of government. The scope of decisions, however, extends to matters that, though ostensibly private, touch on the whole city's dignity. Their action is therefore largely democratic. At other times we shall have to admit that the Syracusan people have a largely sentimental function, namely to express and broaden the emotions provoked by the tale's vicissitudes. For instance, they become astonished and bow down before Callirhoe (1.1.16 θάμβος), are moved to pity (3.4.10), are bewildered (8.6.8), and applaud (8.6.10). Such city masses are differently assessed. Theron tells his listeners they are "people celebrated for *their* humanity" (3.4.9), whereas Chariton considers the crowds (ὄχλος) naturally curious (8.6.5ff.). Unfortunately Chariton's terminology is regrettably unprecise: he calls the Syracusan people either δῆμος (which should hint at their political function) or πλῆθος (which should refer to numbers), or again ὄχλος (which supposedly marks their rash and emotional nature), or lastly λαός, a poetic and affected word. Different terms are used in relation to the same mass of people: so we have ὄχλος ~ πλῆθος in 8.6.5 ~ 8.6.8; elsewhere (8.7.3 ~ 8.7.5) πλῆθος, λαός ~ δῆμος appear in succession. We might say Chariton is aiming more at dramatic effectiveness than at historical (and terminological) exactitude, and with the appearance of a general "all" (8.6.8; etc.) could perhaps strengthen this impression. Undoubtedly, though, the fact remains as a mark of the writer's limited documentary validity.

Popular masses also appear in Asia Minor, Persia, and Egypt and are generally indicated by the comprehensive term πόλις (3.7.7 Miletus; 4.7.6) or by the name of the city (6.1.2 Babylon is split into two groups of diverging opinion; etc.), or again with a more indefinite "all" (5.3.8; 6.2.5; etc.). Terms like δῆμος (6.2.1) or ἄνθρωποι (5.3.10) are seldom used. Such masses, anyway, are just a decoration of the scene; they do not bring about the occurrences. In oriental society their weight approximates zero; the author records their irrational impulses but does not analyze their rational motives. On the other hand, if no one can oppose the king's will (6.7.3), the masses obviously have no part in decision making.

The way military masses are portrayed is also of interest, all the more so as the story involves numerous military actions. These masses reveal a remarkable independence of judgment (7.3.10f. they choose Chaereas as their commander; 8.2.14 they show a will of their own which it is advisable to learn; 8.4.1 they freely tend to different activities in a colorful glimpse of military daily life: "there were people praying, saying good-bye, rejoicing, grieving, giving each other instructions, writing home"). Among them are mercenaries, who easily refer us to Hellenistic and Roman times; most are free men who fight unrewarded for their own or someone else's country (8.3.12 Cyprians and Phoenicians in Egypt). Discipline is not forced upon them; acts of generosity and dedication are frequent (8.3.11 all would gladly follow Chaereas; etc.). Moreover, even the vanquished Egyptians could behave as loyal and loving soldiers of the Persian king (8.4.3 στρατιώτας ἀγαθοὺς φιλοῦντάς σε). The amount of materials offered by the writer is considerable; what is missing is their interpretation. The picture, so to speak, remains at the sketching stage; the real value of popular will in an unchallenged autocratic regime remains to be appraised.

At the center of the social framework the existence of a middle class must be surmised, but testimonies are indeed as scarce as their occupations and economic worth are vague. The youths at the gymnasium (1.1.10 they are Chaereas' συγγυμνασταί, and their mutual relationship seems to imply homosexual overtones) have probably yet to enter the production process owing to their age or because of their families' wealth. They are the representatives of the *jeunesse dorée* missing nowhere among the upper classes. Others do carry out a working activity: court members fulfil their tasks at the archons' command, and the archons themselves, at Syracuse and at Athens, are only loaned to politics, since it must be assumed they are not professional politicians. Excise men (1.13.4 τελώνας), bankers (2.1.4), notaries (2.1.6) are mentioned; many work as farmers (8.8.14 the soldiers dismissed at Syracuse), including women (2.2.1 αἱ ἄγροικοι γυναῖκες). These are bits and pieces of a world, which appear irrelevant to Chariton's awareness. As it is, the vicissitudes of his novel concern the great of the earth, no matter what their claim to greatness may be.

There is, however, a surely lucrative and therefore widespread activity: piracy. One pirate chief, Theron, is condemned to death by a popular meeting (3.4.15) and executed by crucifixion (3.4.18). His companions are the drunkard (1.7.3) and sacrilegious (1.7.5) Zenophanes of Thurii and Menon of Messene (1.7.2). They cruise with their merchandise, looking for wealthy customers (1.11.5 such are numerous at Athens); later on (1.10.1ff., after a highly unlikely democratic debate) they cast anchor in Ionia (1.11.7), since Miletus is a market for royalty and the wealthy (1.12.1). These people are, in popular opinion (which means in their victims' views), wicked and godless (1.12.3 πονηροτάτους; 3.3.11 ἀνοσίους). Their convenient fictional function and their cumbersome social presence are equally conspicuous.

On the other side of an impassable legal wall in the societies of all the countries involved in the narrative are slaves—of both sexes and with the most diversified duties. About them we read disparaging and contemptuous opinions expressed by characters of the story (Dionysius, 2.1.5: "a person not freeborn cannot be beautiful"), as well as the author's comments in a statement detached from the narration (2.10.7: "she was a young lady of quality and knew nothing of slaves' tricks"). There are wicked slaves (4.5.7 δοῦλοι πονηροί). Slaves are threatened with atrocious tortures (4.2.6; 8.8.2 crucifixion; 3.9.7 scourging and the wheel), which sometimes are actually inflicted upon them (1.5.2; 4.2.1f. Chaereas, slave in Caria, is imprisoned and beaten, 4.2.10; 4.2.12f. Polycharmus is beaten; 4.2.6 a group of 16 workers, locked in a dungeon, attempt to escape but are captured and crucified; 4.5.5; etc.). The bleakness of the slaves' condition is confirmed by the dread expressed by free people of falling into slavery (1.11.3; 1.14.10; 2.8.7; etc., Callirhoe; 8.3.5; etc., queen Statira). In the Greeks' eyes really miserable and despicable characters are the eunuchs, so haughtily present in Oriental societies (6.2.2f.; 6.3.1; 6.4.10; 7.6.3 πάντα τὰ εὐωνότερα σώματα: "They collected the eunuchs and maidservants and all the less valuable personnel into the town square, which offered an extensive area"). On the other hand, the tasks assigned to the slaves are neither burdensome nor humiliating; sometimes they are official duties (3.4.7), more often humble and common household activities, both for men (4.3.7; 4.5.1ff.) and for women (1.1.15; 1.3.4; 1.4.12; 1.12.8; etc.). Nothing in this appears disturbing;

quite the contrary. Masters often acknowledge their slaves' merits
(3.1.8 Πλαγγώνιον φιλοδέσποτον, "my loyal Plangon", or "ma petite
Plangon, si dévouée à ton maître," Molinié); in one case the master
promises to free his female slave and declares his survival depends
on her action (2.8.2). The freeing of slaves is in fact rather frequent
(2.3.3 πλῆθος ἀπελευθέρων; 2.5.1; 5.7.4 τὸ γραμμάτιον τῆς ἀπε-
λευθερώσεως). Chaereas has never hit a slave (1.14.7). Even eunuchs
climb to positions of high responsibility at the Persian court (6.3.1;
6.4.8; 8.5.6ff.; etc.). Extremely delicate and secret assignments are
entrusted to slaves because of the deep confidence placed in them
(4.5.1 Ὑγίνῳ τῷ πιστοτάτῳ: this is Mithridates; Dionysios tells Phocas,
3.9.11: "You are my benefactor, you are my true guardian, the most
faithful partner in my secrets"). The slaves' legal position is certainly
bleak, and Chariton has no reason to emphasize it, as it is a well
established and traditional matter of fact; in the unobtrusive unfolding of the tale, however, they are the object of acts of gratitude and
mercy which mitigate the harshness of their life.

The story of Chariton's novel is all contrived within the highest,
most powerful, and wealthiest social level. All excel, one way or
another, and to many primacy is conceded, because of some special
endowment within their people and country. This prominent position
may stem from lineage (kings may presume to be descended from
Helios), wealth, but also culture; and if beauty, so common among
these characters, is a precious inborn endowment, other qualities may
be acquired. To justify authority and authoritativeness other values
concur and are needed, which are produced, strengthened, or refined
by education. The haughtiness of the strong is instigated by delicacy
of feelings and generosity; at the political level democratic understanding and behavior become more and more widespread (even
within a despotic state and a criminal band). The macho prejudice,
so tiresomely present in Greek conventional ideals, leaves ample space
to women in the field of both initiative and inventiveness[13] (e.g.
Callirhoe's second marriage and the lies therewith connected). Compassion soothes the slaves' condition, which is more miserable in the

---

[13] Liviabella Furiani (1989a) 54: "Calliroe ... è senz' altro una donna nuova, che inaugura subito, dopo il ricongiungimento, un nuovo clima matrimoniale, fatto di autonomia di giudizio e insieme di collaborazione familiare, sebbene alterato da qualche bugia e sotterfugio. Ella, infatti, fornisce avveduti consigli a Cherea, che prontamente li accetta (VIII 2, 4 s.) e lo invita (quasi gli intima) a rimandare al re Statira e Rodogune sottolineando l'inopportunità di tenerle come ancelle (VIII 3, 1 ss.)."

law's provisions than by the will of men. The dutiful and predictable happy ending in no way erases the sufferings and anxieties everywhere endured, but a new and recurring solidarity (towards the miserable, the foreigners, the slaves) amends the harshness of an old and by now void tradition. To all of this Chariton, perhaps unwittingly turns out to be a witness.[14]

The society portrayed by Achilles Tatius[15] is located in the cities of Byzantium, Ephesus, Tyre, and Alexandria; rather than to a state's outlook, what we have here conforms to the features of single cities. The ruling class has obviously "bourgeois" limitations. A royal dynasty is mentioned, but has no role in the story; there is also a generic mention of archons, and they act in capacities unusual in Greek historical reality; στρατηγοί carry out unlikely assignments (they are judges, like the πρυτάνεις). Also surprising is a priest's participation in a forensic debate. A ruling class might be said not to exist. Beyond all legal inconsistencies and contradictions, however, a sense for law clearly appears. Characters often possess wealth and prestige, but none of them rules. Popular masses are allotted a limited space. More active are slaves, whose individuality is acknowledged. Achilles Tatius, through a work of correction and erosion,[16] brings the story

---

[14] It is well known that the placing of Chariton in time is a difficult and controversial problem; no easier task is determining his social standing (though an autobiographical hint of his own, 1.1.1, seems to point to a lowly rank). As for his cultural position the scholars' opinions are helplessly at variance. Permit me to quote some of their conclusions based on his language and style. Zanetto (1990) 237: "Si può parlare... per Caritone, di una dizione alquanto stereotipa, caratterizzata da una costante ricerca del tono medio e preoccupata di uniformarsi a una sorta di linguaggio standard. Il lessico di Caritone accoglie... massicce intrusioni di 'Umgangssprache', ossia di forme che fanno pensare al linguaggio parlato imperiale"; Hernández-Lara (1990) 274: "We can say that Chariton's romance is a clear case of artistic prose. The author is conscious of the rhetorical precepts of the time and uses them. Of course, his style is not so extreme as the one in the so-called sophistic romances, but the presence of rhetoric is unquestionable." Ruiz-Montero (1991) 489: "Chariton uses two linguistic styles: that which corresponds to his time and that which was inherited from literary tradition. It is, then, a mixed language in which various levels of language are combined; yet the *koiné* itself is not homogeneous, as together with vulgarisms it contains technical terms... and other terms belonging to the literary tradition... Whatever the case may be, it is the prose written by literary authors with evident rhetorical concern, who represent the historical period in which we must place Chariton." What we must clearly reckon with, however, is the fact that such mainly aesthetic-oriented appraisals cannot completely dispense with the involvement of personal tastes on the part of the scholars, no matter how careful and subtle.

[15] Guiding text: Garnaud (1991).

[16] Supposedly this is not just a literary intention aiming at changing and perhaps

back into the perspective of common people, at least such as are endowed with ardent and impetuous feelings. And society appears to dissolve into the individuals.

In this society prominent personalities are to be sought for outside the ruling class. The president of the court comes from a royal family[17] (7.12.1: "The president of the judges—he was of the royal house and sat in judgment of cases of murder; according to the law he was advised by elders whom he took as arbiters for each decision"). Besides these forensic functions the novel ascribes no other activity to him. How debased the idea and the very name of king (βασιλεύς) had become is shown, on the other hand, by the very fact that even a bandit chief is called a king (3.9.3; elsewhere the term is metaphorically applied to flowers, animals, etc.: 2.1.2; 2.12.3; 2.15.4; 2.22.1). The existence of this court, however, is fundamental: for this reason further information is given about its president (8.7.6; 8.8.5 τῶν προέδρων καὶ τῶν συμβούλων τὸ δόγμα: "the decree of the presidents and their counselors", with the disturbing mention of several presidents, whereas the president elsewhere is only one: 8.8.7; 8.9.8). The jury is at times called δικαστήριον (2.34.6; 7.7.1; 7.9.1; 7.13.4; 8.8.7;

---

renewing the genre of the novel; it might apply to and unfold in the very contents, the story, of Achilles Tatius' work. This is of course in accordance with the *"roman de formation"* thesis. Laplace (1991) 36: "Chez Achilles Tatius, l'image florale est associée aux figures de la fable dont les personnages de Leucippé et de Clitophon gardent le souvenir, Hélene d'une part, Adonis et Ulysse d'autre part, pour signifier en Leucippé l'épanouissement de le féminité, en Clitophon celui de la virilité et de l'éloquence. De sorte que le récit de leurs aventures amoureuses apparaît comme un roman de formation."

[17] The title and juridical position of this official raise problems: at first sight his presence in a court seems to place the city and institution in which he acts within a monarchical frame—which is historically untenable. To heal this difficulty the following has been said (Gaselee, ed. of Achilles Tatius, London 1969, *ad loc.*): "This, with the mention of the satrap of Egypt in Book III, suggests that the story takes place under the Persian rule. But we had better conclude that Achilles knew that the 'King-archon' at Athens managed murder cases, but misapplies his knowledge". However, the king-archon's functions at Athens were different. He was [Biscardi (1982) 167] "il magistrato competente a istruire le cause di omicidio ... dopo aver fatto la solenne intimazione all' omicida di non frequentare i luoghi sacri e pubblici, teneva tre successive προδικασίαι, vale a dire tre sessioni istruttorie, che dovevano aver luogo ad un mese di distanza l'una dall' altra, e quindi provvedeva ad introdurre (εἰσάγειν) la causa dinanzi al tribunale cui spettava di giudicare." In Achilles Tatius' passage, instead, we do not know if he instituted the proceedings, but he certainly takes part in the debate. It is true, on the other hand, that at Athens the king-archon [Biscardi (1982) 56]: "era a capo dei sacerdoti" and that he "esercitava ... la giurisdizione sacrale." But this is not the case here, either. We must therefore conclude that the writer has carelessly tampered with historical data.

8.9.9, in reference to the court), at other times βουλή (8.7.6; 8.8.6; 8.9.7; etc.). The judge, however, is always δικαστής (1.11.3; 2.34.6; 6.9.2; 7.12.1; etc.). The totality of institutions seems to be summed up in the reproach to Thersandros (8.9.10) for appointing himself δῆμος, βουλή, πρόεδρος, and στρατηγός. Archons take part in judicial proceedings,[18] but the term is generic (at 3.19.1 the archons are the village's chiefs; at 7.1.2 the commander of a prison). The court has judicial police under itself (8.15.1) which includes executioners (7.10.4 τοὺς δημοσίους); witnesses (8.1.1) and lawyers (7.7.1) dutifully appear; the prytanies carry out the function of judges (8.8.6 ὑπό ... τῶν πρυτάνεων κατεγνωσμένους). In spite of this elaborate setup, the trial is only outwardly legal and the verdict only formally just. The jury's appointment as well as the procedure turn out to be incorrect. However, such a heartening statement as "without a judgment passed, no man has more rights than another" (8.9.9), as well as the ample space allotted to the trial, reveal Achilles Tatius' deep sense of law.[19] That the latter turns out to be distorted and manipulated may result from its captious application, which can be historically ascertained. What remains really disturbing is the presence in this court of a priest (at 7.16.2 he stands surety), who delivers a long harangue (8.9.1–8.9.14). He also holds other offices, but we do not know whether public or private (8.3.1 he reproaches Thersandros; 8.7.6 he organizes a θεωρίαν). The statement that he has been elected to his office (8.9.5 τὸν ὑφ' ὑμῶν ἱερωσύνῃ τετιμημένον), from which he might be forced to resign (8.10.6), rules out his belonging to a priestly class with a right to administer justice (even though in cooperation with lay judges). The novel's institutional and juridical frame appears to be inaccurate.

The office of στρατηγός appears in several cities of different countries.[20] In Egypt a στρατηγός rules an island and leads a police

---

[18] In truth [Biscardi (1982) 67]: "ἄρχειν indica la sovranità dello Stato, che si esercita mediante l'attività di tutti i suoi magistrati. Corrisponde indubbiamente al potere esecutivo ed amministrativo della concezione moderna, o, per meglio dire, lo comprende". Therefore the indefiniteness of the term corresponds to the plurality of state officials and their different functions.

[19] Scarcella (1990) 249: "La sollecitudine ad evidenziare le nervature giuridiche dei comportamenti sociali è ... ben forte, in Achille Tazio: e può comprensibilmente culminare nell' esaltazione della sovranità universale e della maestà delle leggi (A.T.8.9.8 ὁ νόμος αὐτόν, ὁ καὶ σοῦ καὶ πάντων κύριος, δησάτω: "che sia la legge, che ha autorità su di te e su tutti, a farlo imprigionare"). Il νόμος πάντων κύριος di Achille Tazio mi sembra un' eco del νόμος πάντων βασιλεύς di Pindaro, con una più muscolosa intenzione legalistica, per il valore pregnante di κύριος."

[20] The στρατηγοί normally held the military command; in classical Athens, since

operation against bandits (5.7.3 the "rangers", βουκόλοι) at the satrap's command (4.11.1). At Byzantium Sostratos and Callisthenes are mentioned as στρατηγοί: the former has political and military capacities, as is shown by his proposal to dispatch an embassy to Tyre (2.14.2); the latter, who is higher in standing because of his Tyrian origin (2.14.6; a generic hint at 8.17.10), confirms this provision. A further στρατηγός has military functions (3.14.1), and a last one, Charmides, στρατηγός of Egypt, in love with Leukippe, turns out to be preoccupied with scientific disquisitions (4.3.2ff., the elephant) and to face amorous disappointments. His office seems to be an easy and useless decoration. A war between the Byzantians and the Thracians is in progress[21] (1.3.6; 2.24.3; 8.18.1), which appears to be waged for long time and with no interruption, contrary to the war customs of the Greeks, who normally carried out military operations only from spring to fall. This war also seems to have a limited influence on the story (1.3.6). The same may be said about Kallisthenes' bravery in battle (8.18.4). The warriors' greatness and determination on the field is replaced by the strangeness of the facts, which are either theatrical (3.15.2 Leukippe's false immolation) or magical (4.15.3f. the potions of Gorgias the Egyptian; 5.22.7 the herbs sought for by Leukippe;

Pericles, they [Biscardi (1982) 57]: "divennero il principale organo esecutivo dello Stato." But in Egypt, by right and practice, military power is exercised by the satrap through the στρατηγοί placed under him. We get the impression that in Achilles Tatius' novel a merging of different legal structures takes place, perhaps to enhance the narrative's likelihood or effectiveness. It must be added that the same office appears elsewhere: determining its legal consistency seems to be a hopeless task.

[21] The reference to this war has been used to try to determine the work's and the author's chronology [Manni (1991) 472]: "in Achille Tazio troviamo indicata la guerra dei Bizantini come Θρακικὸς πόλεμος (I 3) e la prima domanda che ci dobbiamo porre riguarda il nome stesso della guerra, tanto più che anche in III 24 si parla di un Θρᾷξ, che farebbe pensare al popolo di quel nome. Che si trattasse di Traci ribelli è però praticamente impossibile pensare; ma la Tracia stessa è stata spesso invasa da orde barbariche e da esse attraversata. L'indicazione va dunque presumibilmente presa in senso geografico, non in senso etnico. Ciò premesso, si può pensare alla sola invasione dalla quale i Bizantini dovettero difendersi senza il concorso di un comandante romano, quella del 267, ricordata dalla *Vita Gallieni* 13,6, per la quale Gallieno affidò il compito di difendere Bisanzio ed altre città ai duci bizantini Cleodamo ed Ateneo." As for the pseudo-scientific disquisitions of the στρατηγός Charmides, they are prompted not so much by scientific interest as by a sentimental urge of the character [Bartsch (1989) 155]: "Charmides" lengthy digression on the habits of the hippopotamus and the Indian elephant (4.3.2–5.3) had the purpose of keeping Leucippe by him as long as possible", ἵν' ἔχῃ τοῖς ὀφθαλμοῖς αὐτοῦ χαρίζεσθαι (4.3.2: "so that he could gratify his eyes"). From the reader's point of view we might say that such digressions were inserted in the narrative (*ibid.*) "perhaps simply because their readers found them interesting and of genuine educational worth."

8.6.12f. Pan's pipes; 8.12.9 the spring called Styx; etc.).

Though they do not wield power, the novel's main characters show some kind of social and economical preeminence. The unnamed mother of Sostratos, Kleitophon's uncle, owns a considerable fortune at Byzantium (1.3.1); the girl who is offered in marriage to Kleinias is wealthy (1.7.4f.), and so is the Byzantian Kallisthenes (2.13.1); Menelaos has sizable possessions at his disposal (3.19.1); Melite of Ephesus is very rich (5.11.5 πλοῦτος πολύς; 8.10.7): in her city she owns a grand palace with elegant furnishing and numerous servants (5.17.1) and can offer luxurious banquets (5.13.3 πολυτελές; 5.14.3). She owns property that she manages personally (5.17.10 διοικήσασα δέ τινα τῶν κατὰ τοὺς ἀγρούς, with an independence of decision exceptional for a woman; also 5.14.2); she has a bailiff under her, whom she can at will remove from his appointment (5.17.10). The property is four stades away from the city (6.4.4), is fruitful and thick with trees (5.17.3); Melite goes there in a carriage (5.17.2) which is the vehicle she and people normally use for travel overland (2.31.4; 5.23.2; etc.). She also is in possession of much gold, in minted form (6.1.4 one hundred gold pieces; 6.2.5 ten gold pieces; 4.15.5 four gold pieces), as is the case with other characters (3.2.9; 4.16.1; 5.18.5 Leukippe is bought for 2000 drachmas; etc.). Money is used to give a contribution to one's city (8.17.10) and also for an attempt at bribery (8.10.6). So the novel's main characters live in ease and are able to employ considerable amounts of money in totally frivolous affairs; but their estates have nothing extravagant (or romantic) about them: the property may afford just a humble little house (6.4.2; 6.6.1 δωμάτιον; 6.15.4); city houses, where some of the story's scenes are set, show strictly "bourgeois" interiors.

Nevertheless we hear time and again that the main persons in the work are also the most prominent in their cities. Kleitophon, a Phoenician,[22] comes from no obscure city: Tyre (1.3.1), and is second to no Tyrian (6.9.2); Thersandros is first among all Ionians, owns riches even greater than his nobility, and his goodness is even greater than his riches (6.12.2). Kallisthenes is a nobleman, second to no one in Byzantium (8.17.3 δεύτερος οὐδενός). As for Menelaos, finally, "a fine young man he was, and deserved every blessing from heaven"

---

[22] Esogamy is one of the constituent elements of Hellenistic culture [Baslez (1984) 72 and *passim*]; in this novel both sentimental liaisons and marriage are esogamous.

(5.15.1). None of these people, however, sways or leads his city's fates, nor are known beyond his city. None of them can really be counted among the great of the earth. Achilles Tatius' society, in short, has been scaled down to middle class level: we do not catch it at extraordinary conjunctures, as it is described, so to speak, at the everyday level. Nor does any woman in the novel occupy an important position from the point of view of law, politics or administration. Not Leukippe, though she is the daughter of the στρατηγός of Byzantium (7.12.3); nor Melite, though she is considered the most prominent woman among the Ephesians (5.19.4 πρώτην Ἐφεσίων; 7.3.6 τῶν ἐνταῦθα πρώτη γυναικῶν; 8.10.7 the family and the estate). Rather, we are tempted to say, these women's primacy might lie in the strength of their character (6.22.4 Leukippe's memorable words).[23]

Masses of free people appear in several cities: at Byzantium they support the sending of a θυσία to Tyre (2.15.1); at Ephesos the crowd (ὄχλος) in the temple censure Thersandros (8.3.1); the people witness the trial of a girl's virginity (8.6.12; 8.13.1 ὁ δῆμος ... ἄπας) and a bride's chastity (8.14.3). In short, they do effectively share in some events, including crucial ones (8.14.2), but at most they resort to violence (8.14.4): to Achilles Tatius the presence of these masses is an option he can dispense with.

Information about the middle class is hardly more detailed. In spite of the existence of land property, no farmers are mentioned (1.17.4 and 2.2.3 do not relate to the narrative). Several other activities are present, however: soothsayers and interpreters (2.12.2), sailors (2.32.1; 3.3.1; etc.), fishermen (pirates can also be recruited from among the latter: 2.17.3), physicians (4.10.2; 4.10.3; 4.10.5), merchants (5.10.1; 5.17.9; 8.16.7; etc.), a man attached to the temple (though this might be a slave: 7.15.1), workers of undefined description (6.4.1 ἐργατῶν), perhaps an hotel manager (7.3.2). We cannot be sure about the legal status of the brothel manager (8.8.3) and the girls who work there. No doubt can be entertained about the existence of such places (8.8.11 οἴκημα; 8.8.11 οἰκία μοιχῶν ... πόρνης θάλαμος; 8.8.12 ἐν χαμαιτυπείῳ). The presence of women there is of course equally undoubtable: πόρναι are often mentioned (8.11.2; 8.16.1), though they can hardly be free women. That prostitution could be practised by free people,[24] though

---

[23] This nineteen-year old girl's personality is so strong that we are justified in calling her a "feminist" [Liviabella Furiani (1989a) 64ff.].

[24] By Attic law it was possible to bring an action against anyone who had pros-

this entailed disgrace, however, is proved by the insult against Kleitophon (8.10.9) and Thersandros (8.9.1). Middle class has no weight in Achilles Tatius and in some ways seems to have no dignity either (a striking baseness marks the debate in court). The polarization of society, as described by the writer, shoves intermediate groups aside.

At the other end of the social and economical range, in a totally different legal situation, we find slaves. Male and female slaves are everywhere: a crowd of them escorts the two women in their moving from Byzantium to Tyre (1.4.1 πλῆθος οἰκετῶν καὶ θεραπαινίδων); chamber maids wait on Leukippe (2.4.2; 2.8.1; 6.10.1; 7.9.12; etc.); Kleio, one of Leukippe's maid servants, is threatened with torture by Pantheia (2.28.1) and must flee (2.26.3); a young man servant plays the lyre and sings in Hippias' house (1.5.4); another servant, devoted to Kallisthenes, is charged with hiring some bandits (2.16.2) and carrying out a kidnapping with their assistance (2.18.1ff.); there is an uncompromising entrance guardian in Kleinias' house (2.26.1), who must be put to sleep by means of a drugged potion (2.31.2); and two servants escort Kleinias on his trip to Sidon (2.31.5). Numerous personnel are to be found at Melite's house (5.17.1): a slave is ordered to have intercourse with Leukippe (5.17.4); two others stand guard at Kleitophon's prison (5.25.1); still another of Melite's slaves stands guard too (6.2.2). Melite has Melantho, a trustworthy maid servant, by her (6.8.1); a young boy directs Kleitophon in his escape (6.1.2), while another one is sent to the fields to look for Leukippe (6.1.2 νεανίσκος). At Thersandros' house there are perhaps even more servants (5.23.3; 5.23.4; etc.). Kallisthenes avails himself of the slave

---

tituted herself/himself (γραφὴ ἑταιρήσεως); but the accusation was considered to be slander if conviction did not follow (this entailed ἀτιμία); Biscardi (1982) 137f.: "poiché... non risulta in alcun modo che la legge sanzionasse espressamente la nullità degli atti contrari al buon costume, bisognerà rifarsi, caso per caso, alla moralità corrente della società ateniese. Facciamo al riguardo, e come paradigma, l'ipotesi della prostituzione maschile, ovverosia del contratto di prostituzione fra il pederasta e il suo 'partner': se è vero che l'atimia totale colpiva coloro che si prostituivano, che un' azione penale pubblica... poteva essere intentata contro chi, essendosi prostituito, avesse esercitato i diritti politici del cittadino, e che i corruttori degli adolescenti potevano essere perseguiti con un' altra azione criminale (γραφὴ ὕβρεως)..., nessuno potrà stupirsi, considerata la vivissima riprovazione sociale del fenomeno, che il contratto di pederastia (seppure abbastanza frequente in età classica) fosse, proprio per la turpitudine della causa, un contratto invalido". The portrayal of the position of Tatius' characters, in relation to the trial and the procedure, is ossified, to say the least. Therefore, the writer's attitude is either disappointing or uncaring. But, predictably enough, he behaves as the writer he is.

Zenon, a strong man with a pirate's disposition (2.17.3 the statement about his natural inclination is marked by an unveiled fierceness). In short, slaves are in every house and receive even important and delicate assignments: and rightly so, as there are trustworthy ones, such as Sosthenes at Thersandros' (5.17.5; 6.4.1; 6.7.8; 6.9.7; 6.17.1; etc.) or Kleio by Leukippe (1.16.1; 2.7.1; 2.10.1; 2.19.2; 2.23.3; etc.). These servants, who may show even inventiveness and courage (8.15.1ff. Sosthenes is imprisoned, and the tale leaves him there; 2.28.1 Kleio runs the risk of being tortured), are always at the mercy of their masters: they may be freed (6.2.2); but they may also be severely judged. The slave (οἰκέτης) Konops is "a busybody, a gossip, a Nosy Parker and every name you can think of" (2.20.1). The breed of slaves is cowardly by nature (7.10.5). Sosthenes himself is considered a scoundrel by Melite (5.17.8 κακὴ κεφαλή). Torture is a recurrent threat and sometimes a reality (6.21.1 βασάνους... τροχόν... μάστιγας... πῦρ... σίδηρον; 7.9.4; 8.15.11; etc.). Cruelty, so widespread in Achilles Tatius' society (8.16.6ff. Chaereas is beheaded and thrown into the sea; 8.16.1f. a prostitute is also beheaded), does not certainly spare slaves (who, on their part, show adaptability at the same time as submissiveness, fear, and cowardice, no different in this from the more important characters of the novel); on the other hand, it was customary to conduct the court questioning of slaves under torture (8.8.12). In this novel, however, slaves often have a name, a sign of their being endowed with a personality of their own. In other words, slaves emerge from anonymity and indistinction: in a world scaled down to "bourgeois" level, in which social and spiritual standards have become lower, they acquire a greater relevance exactly because they take an active and conscious part in their masters' adventures. If these are often to be blamed, their caring and obedient servants have no fault. The acquisition of the conscience of their rights and strength by the enslaved masses is absolutely incompatible with the novelist's society and the first centuries of the imperial age.

There appear also groups of outcasts, such as pirates at sea[25] and

---

[25] Sea voyages and pirates are among the most widely spread τόποι (and the most fatal misfortunes) in love novels. Létoublon (1993) 175f.: "Les autres (i.e. with the exception of Longus) ont tous compliqué l'intrigue romanesque—jusqu'à l'excès, lassant pour le lecteur moderne—en suscitant divers obstacles à l'amour. Les plus extérieurs et les plus constamment répétés sont des conséquences directes du voyage auquel, sauf Longus, tous les romanciers grecs ont cru nécessaire d'astrendre le couple d'amoureux, qui parcourent ainsi inlassablement la Méditerranée et ses rivages à la recherche l'un de l'autre, quittant un endroit précisément au moment où l'autre y

bandits (the βουκόλοι)²⁶ on land. Especially in Egypt society is forced to organize police operations on the scale of an actual war (3.13.1ff. fifty hoplites with ποδήρεις shields or peltasts against even greater numbers of bandits; two thousand more hoplites are added against ten thousand bandits). These βουκόλοι, so relevant in the Greek novels, occupy all the coast of Egypt (3.5.5); they are tall, dark-skinned, terrible and wild (3.9.2); they are bareback riders (3.12.1), have shaven heads (3.9.2) or long and flowing hair (3.12.1), practice cannibalism²⁷ (3.15.4ff.), and—most ignominious—do not speak Greek (3.10.2). They are not really poor, if their elders can plausibly offer the enormous sum of one hundred silver talents (4.13.4). They are depicted as poor and primitive because they are separated from society, living on an island (4.12.1ff.) in makeshift huts. These robbers (3.5.5 λησταί), however, have a state organization, a chief (3.9.3 βασιλεύς), who is the strongest man among them, and priests (3.15.3; 3.15.7 ἱερεύς); they are also bravely determined to defend themselves (3.13.1). They are detestable and detested just because they are "different".

The other group of outcasts is the pirates, ever-present on the Mediterranean. They have an imposing height (5.7.1f.) and are armed with daggers (2.18.3) and swords (5.7.2 μαχαίρᾳ). They are easily recruited and come from the lowest underproletariat (5.7.6 the murex fishermen). They are despised, and it is a grievous insult when someone is dubbed more merciless than pirates (6.22.1). They are sexually wanton (6.21.3). They are active in the slave trade and kidnap guiltless citizens on commission (2.18.2 there are eighteen of them: ten on a boat and eight in ambush on land). Their chief Chaereas' bloody death is a witness to the revulsion they provoke.

Achilles Tatius' societies are more hellenized than linked to the Orient. The characters belong to preeminent families of their several cities, but their prestige is totally private and confined to their single communities. Public life is contracted, as it were: though a war between

---

parvient le plus souvent... Le voyage par mer est plein de périls, essentiellement les pirates et les tempêtes, souvent conjugués, les unes sauvant parfois les héros du péril des autres."

[26] Scarcella (1981) 90ff.

[27] On bloody sacrifices and particularly on cannibalism, Liviabella Furiani (1991). 530ff.: "Il romanzo di Achille Tazio evidenzia del sangue entrambi gli aspetti, quello energetico e quello distruttivo, con l'accentuazione della forte carica di ambiguità al rosso umore propria. Perfino la pratica del sacrificio umano, che avrebbe dovuto enfatizzarne l'orrore e dilatarne la negatività, si risolve in un *coup de théâtre* che ne svilisce la potenzialità distruttiva." See also Liviabella Furiani (1985b) 26ff.

Byzantium and the Thracians is in progress and police operations against criminals are organized, nobody in any circumstance seeks (or attains) glory (the word δόξα appears in a completely different meaning: 1.10.6; 3.15.6; 7.13.1). This is a reality made baser[28] by coarse elements (menstruation 4.7.6ff.; beatings 8.1.3f.; physiological needs 5.7.1), in which, however, music is known and practiced[29] (2.1.1; 2.2.1; 2.7.1; etc.). Political offices are conferred with procedures and functions that are anything but clear; people, however, seem to have a vigilant sense of the law[30] (though this is actually only formally applied); religiousness does not progress beyond external behavior (8.2.2f.). The fondness for theatricality, in a society that has an experience of theater, substitutes for life's own theatricality (3.15.5 the sword used in a make-believe beheading is a theatrical instrument; the final court trial has a pronounced theatrical coloring; the night judge mentioned in passing, 8.9.11 ὁ νυκτερινὸς δικαστής,[31] is evocative and mysterious at the same time, and more fit for the stage than the court room). Popular masses are devoid of any relevance, given the story's totally individual and private perspective; on the contrary, considerable importance is attached to slaves, who at times seem to acquire a personality of their own and a new genuineness. Still, spite, not just confidence, is heaped upon them. On the other hand, bandits and pirates provoke only revulsion and terror; nevertheless, even they are physically imposing and not devoid of reason. Only some particulars of their behavior make an understanding impossible.

In Xenophon Ephesius' novel[32] any structure of the societies there depicted has all but disappeared. Some historically traceable magistracies are mentioned: so Egypt's ἄρχων, established by Augustus, and Cilicia's εἰρηνάρχης, appointed by Trajan. The distinction between Italy and Sicily—which was abolished by Diocletian—is important. There is no portrayal of politics and administration, though single elements thereof are sketchily mentioned. The involvement of people who are foreigners in relation to the novel's main couple is a most creative invention along with the recording of personal and cultural

---

[28] Fusillo (1990a) 207: "Chez Achille Tatius... les figures narratives et les figures thématiques fournissent... par rapport aux autres romanciers, une vision de l'héros moins glorifiée et moins cristallisée, plus proche du quotidien de la comédie."
[29] On music in Greek love romances, Liviabella Furiani (1984).
[30] All the sentimental vicissitudes leading up to the conclusive trial are involved with the law; Liviabella Furiani (1989a).
[31] Liviabella Furiani (1985a).
[32] Guiding text: Papanikolaou (1978).

exchanges. The middle class, in their diversified but humble activities, are allotted no great space. Slaves are not numerous, and they have rarer occasions to make themselves conspicuous, owing to the mistreatment and spite of which they are the object. Pirates and bandits are sundered from society, but in one case (Hippothous) we witness the social and economical downfall and resurrection of a man who, in spite of his criminal activity, succeeds in becoming a positive figure.

High-ranking personalities meet the heroine, Anthia (and fall in love with her). Besides passion, which is irrelevant here, they all share the fact of being foreign to the girl's country. Perilaus is εἰρηνάρχης of Cilicia (2.13.3 ὁ τῆς εἰρήνς τῆς ἐν Κιλικίᾳ προεστώς); the officer arrives with huge police forces (2.13.4). Psammis, an Indian maharajah staying at Alexandria for unlikely touristic and organizational reasons (3.11.2), falls in love with the girl (3.11.4). On the way back home, with a train of camels, donkeys, and pack horses loaded with gold, silver, and precious materials, however, he is attacked, robbed and killed by bandits (4.3.1ff.). The governor of Egypt (3.12.6; 4.2.1 ἄρχοντα) wields power over the country entrusted to him (4.4.1; 4.4.2), but he remains unnamed, perhaps to retain the highest possible indetermination. In the case of Perilaus the reader learns that he comes from a distinguished family (3.9.5 ἀνὴρ τῶν τὰ πρῶτα δυναμένων) and holds an elective office (3.9.5 ἐχειροτονήθη); but about the governor of Egypt we do not even know whether he is Roman or Egyptian; anyway, he is a foreigner in relation to Habrocomes, a Milesian who meets him by chance: and the young man, after being sentenced first to be crucified (4.2.1) and then to be burned at the stake (4.2.8), ends up being protected by him (4.4.2), whereas Kyno, the woman who accused him, is punished by crucifixion (4.4.2). The governor's powers seem unlimited: he has both civil (3.12.6 the rash accusation of murder) and military (5.3.1) authority. He is also entitled to hire an assistant (5.3.1 Polydus, a relative of his, shows a touch of nepotism). In any case all these figures are foreigners in relation to the protagonists.

The male party of the young couple, Habrocomes, belongs to a distinguished family of Ephesus, and his father is one of the most prominent citizens (1.1.1 τῶν τὰ πρῶτα ἐκεῖ δυναμένων).[33] The nobility of his lineage has provided him with wealth and culture (1.1.2: music, hunting, horseback riding, military training, mentioned in this order).

---

[33] For recourse to stereotyped expressions, Zanetto (1990) 233f.

On her part Anthia is only beautiful, though the most beautiful of the city's women[34] (1.2.5). Both take part in civil and religious public ceremonies (1.2.2; 1.5.1), but of course only Habrocomes can hope to become a preeminent citizen (women are constitutionally excluded from city government). But he is still extremely young (only sixteen: 1.2.2) and has therefore no part in the community's political life. Hippothous, so important for the two young people's fate, is also a foreigner: he comes from Perinthus, in Thrace, and is a member of one of that city's most prominent families (3.2.1 τῶν τὰ πρῶτα ἐκεῖ δυναμένων, a stereotypical expression). He becomes a murderer for love (3.2.10: he kills his rival Aristomachus, a Byzantian nobleman) and a bandit by chance (3.2.14). His first ἐρώμενος, Hyperanthes, is the son of a greedy and despicable man (3.2.7): the intention is perhaps to associate a young man of the lowest social extraction with a still blamable man. Cleisthenes, his next ἐρώμενος, has a different social position: he belongs to a respectable Sicilian family (5.9.3); but by now Hippothous is a reformed bandit (5.2.2ff.): he can adopt the boy, who belongs to the same class as he, and is able to live according to his social rank again, with Anthia and Habrocomes (5.15.4). The author wanted all the girl's suitors to be foreigners in relation to Ephesus, her city; Anthia herself is aware of this: "No one persuaded me to go astray: not Moeris in Syria, Perilaus in Cilicia, Psammis or Polyidos in Egypt, not Anchialus in Ethiopia, not my master in Tarentum" (5.14.2). But Hippothous too is a foreigner, though he seeks her for sex (5.9.11f.) or solidarity (5.9.15), not for love. The two situations are remarkable and original: her suitors are all foreign, she is Ephesian and married to a fellow citizen, whose parents are also Ephesian. Hippothous is a noteworthy figure, whose originality resides in a quasi-pathological social and economical instability (from nobility to abjection, then again from an outcast's condition to

---

[34] Del Corno (1989) 84: "Certo, la protagonista del romanzo greco è una figura ideale, per non dire irreale: come già la stessa eccezionalità dei suoi connotati fisici e anagrafici esplicitamente ammette. Ma essa è il prodotto di una letteratura che, pure nelle sue tenui ambizioni di intrattenimento, recepisce certe tendenze di fondo del suo tempo, e le esprime secondo la logica di una stilizzazione che non trascende dalla realtà, ma in essa trova lo spunto per configurare i suoi simboli. Le anonime donne della società che trovava diletto in questa lettura non potevano certo venire proiettate in tali strabilianti avventure, né ci si poteva attendere che sapessero farvi fronte con tanta fermezza d'animo. Ma ai destinatari del romanzo era pur sempre concesso di identificare, nell' atteggiamento di Anzia e delle altre di fronte ai casi dell' immaginario, il grado compiuto e perfetto di qualcosa che, a un livello meno eroico, forse non era impossibile constatare nella realtà."

social prestige, and, at the same time, from wealth, 3.2.10, to poverty, and again to opulence, 5.9.1). This mirrors a social situation marked by individual mobility, even within the boundaries of the Hellenized world, and by economic instability.

The ruling class enjoys a considerable degree of prosperity. The young couple take on their honeymoon (1.10.4) plenty of gold, silver, victuals, and valuable slaves (1.13.1). All this wealth falls to the pirates (1.14.1). Violence is the quickest and most widespread way to promote the circulation of wealth: aside from the romantic τόπος, this is in all likelihood a real circumstance. The quality of Perilaus' estate is stated (2.13.6 περιβολὴ χρημάτων οὐκ ὀλίγη); fields are mentioned (3.3.7), a hoard of cash (3.5.9), from which Anthia secretly draws as many as 20 silver minas (we do not see by what right). All this wealth receives further attestation through a lavish banquet (3.5.1) and the imposing grave prepared for Anthia (3.7.3f.). In this episode the three fundamental moments of human life are effectively blended: food, love, and death (though the latter is only assumed). The consistency of Hippothous' old wife's estate at Tauromenium is known (5.9.1 crowds of slaves, fine clothes and furniture; no mention of cash is made). And when the enterprising and lucky youth (having happily become a widower) moves to Ephesus, he is forced to rent a big ship to load all his luggage (5.11.1; 5.15.1). The Indian maharajah is wealthy (4.3.1f.), and duly so, as in popular imagination the Far East was inseparable from the idea of luxury and lavishness. Leucon and Rhode receive a considerable legacy from their old and benevolent master, Xanthus (5.6.3): therefore they are able to erect at Rhodes a stele inscribed with letters of gold (5.10.6). Anthia's prospective buyers must command a great amount of money, given the girl's high price (5.7.3). The governor of Egypt also has money (4.4.1). The wealth of Aristomachus, a Byzantian, is mentioned in passing (3.2.5 πλούτῳ καὶ περιουσίᾳ). Hippothous' economic and patrimonial situation varies, as already mentioned. At Perinthus he is a wealthy free citizen; after his rival's murder, he cashes in all his belongings and emigrates (3.2.10). In the sea voyage he loses everything, including his ἐρώμενος, owing to a storm (3.2.12). He then wanders through Phrygia and Pamphylia and joins a gang of bandits, in which he is only a subordinate (3.2.14 ὑπηρέτης λῃστηρίου). After becoming leader, he has his men slaughtered or enslaved first by Perilaus (2.13.4), then by Polyidos, in Egypt, and his belongings plundered. Having become poor again, he flees to Sicily (5.3.3), where a welcome marriage and widowhood raise him to ease and respectability again (5.9.1). Hippothous' vicissitudes record the making of a well-disposed but rash individual;[35] he finally recovers his standing, but his estate is precarious at a time when multiple hostile forces could shove individuals from one end to the other of the social and economical scale— which is to say at the time of the Roman Empire. Actually, the same is also recorded in the case of Habrocomes, with the very same words (5.10.5 ἀπορίᾳ ... τῶν ἐπιτηδείων ~ 5.9.1 ἀπορίᾳ τῶν ἐπιτηδείων). The cycle or alternation of wealth and poverty must have not appeared incredible to the novelist's readers; it was probably considered possible, and was therefore a credible reason for unhappiness and despair.

Activities typical of a middle class are briefly mentioned. There are soothsayers and priests (1.5.6). Sailors are common in a novel where people often flee from shore to shore (1.10.8; 1.11.6; 1.12.1; 1.12.3; etc.) on freight ships that also take on passengers (3.2.11; 5.6.4; 5.9.3; 5.10.1; 5.11.2; etc.) The occupation of the wealthy (2.10.4 ἐν ἀφθόνοις ... πᾶσιν) and kindly old man of Xanthus is unknown. Honest but unlucky merchants from Cilicia are at the port of Antioch (2.11.9). Aristomachus of Byzantium, a fake rhetorician, is wealthy (3.2.5), whereas Eudoxus of Ephesus, a capable physician, is poor (3.4.1ff.): in order to go back home he first asks for the most prominent Tyrian citizens' help (3.4.2 which means that human solidarity is not unheard of), then accepts valuable necklaces and money from Anthia (3.5.5ff.). Habrocomes, while a slave, lives in Nuceria[36] working as a stone carver (5.8.2). At Syracuse there lives unpretentiously, presumably by his trade's revenues, a citizen of Sparta, once preeminent in his city (5.1.4 τῶν τὰ πρῶτα ἐκεῖ δυναμένων). We may glean a few indications of agricultural activities: there is a goat farm (2.9.4) and horses and donkeys are in circulation (2.14.5); no mention of work in the fields is found. Commercial trading is carried out mainly by sea (at 4.3.1f. a land convoy is short-lived); but navigation is still very dangerous. A free middle-class certainly exists, but its size, occupations and economic consistence are not explained. Xenophon's society is clearly polarized:[37] the wealthy aristocrats (who are some-

---

[35] Schmeling (1980) 66: "Hippothous is the best delineated character in the novel."
[36] On the probable geographical location of this city, see Scarcella (1993).
[37] Billault (1991a) 129ff.: "Le monde romanesque est décidément rude et périlleux, à l'image du monde réel. Les Grands y détiennent la puissance et la richesse. Le reste de l'humanité cherche, avec des fortunes diverses, à s'accomoder de cet ordre ...

times political officials) on the one side, the miserable outcasts (sometimes originally from the wealthy classes) on the other.

There are popular, often nondescript masses, which are generally called πλῆθος (1.2.3) or δῆμος (1.10.5; 5.13.3), with a clear terminological inaccuracy. Their most conspicuous mark is a certain docility and also naivety and impulsiveness. Their normal occupations are religious practices (1.2.3 for Artemis; 5.11.2 for Helios; etc.) or the expression of lively feelings of admiration, joy, and awe for the protagonists (1.12.1; 5.13.2), and also of solidarity for their suffering (1.11.1). If a murderess denounces a crime to the people (3.12.6), this is just a trick to escape a well-deserved punishment (4.4.2). These crowds are masses rather than people: they have no relevance in the narrative, since they have no social status. Their only object is to enliven romantic invention, so that this may become more captivating.

Slaves are certainly present. As usual, the slave market is replenished by pirates (1.13.2; 1.14.3; 4.9.4; etc.). Slaves have different assignments: they take care of the education of well-to-do youngsters (1.14.4 τροφεύς), the care of prisoners (2.2.5), the delivery of a letter (2.5.3f.). Occasionally, they are also executioners (2.6.2 the οἰκέται of Apsyrtus; 2.11.3 Manto's goatherd; etc.). So their occupations vary. Unfortunately there is little terminological consistency: οἰκέτης (25 occurrences) and δοῦλος (3 occurrences) are sometimes used in reference to the same person. Atrocities against these forsaken people are anything but wanting; they even seem to be customary. They certainly have an historical foundation: Habrocomes is tortured, bound (3.5.3) and thrown into a dungeon (2.7.1 ἐδέδετο ... ἐν εἰρκτῇ); he is sentenced to crucifixion or, alternatively, to be burned at the stake (4.2.8), not in connection with his being a slave, though, but because he is believed to be a criminal; Anthia is tied to a tree (2.13.2) to be pierced with arrows; she also risks having her throat cut, being buried with a corpse, or being crucified (4.6.2). Finally she is thrown into a ditch with vicious dogs; she is tortured by Polyidus' wife (5.5.4), and—most intolerable of all—exhibited in a brothel (5.7.1). Incredibly, the girl is considered by Habrocomes (2.8.1) and considers herself a

---

Ce décor humain que les romanciers offrent souvent aux aventures de leurs héros correspond à une réalité. Sans doute l'époque impériale connaît-elle, dès le second siècle, un déclin du nombre des esclaves, mais il ne s'agit pas d'un effondrement. Une domesticité nombreuse peuple encore les demeures des riches et des puissants ... Ils (i.e. the novelists) mettent en scène un monde à la hiérarchie sociale rigoureuse et qui est loin d'être sans rapport avec le monde réel."

prisoner of war (2.9.4 τὴν αἰχμαλωσίαν). Habrocomes is about to be branded and scourged (2.6.2 πῦρ καὶ μάστιγας); he calls himself δοῦλος (2.4.4), but claims his freedom of mind. The situation of Aegialeus and Thelxinoe of Sparta is peculiar. They have eloped and are sentenced to death in their own city (5.1.8). The sentence is inflicted by a legally appointed court assembly, which has been given authority on the matter. Kyno dies by crucifixion (4.4.2). At other times threats or punishments against slaves remain vague (2.3.5 Manto against Rhode; 2.9.3 the same woman is sent to forced labor with Leukon). The most dreaded and commonest fate that can befall slaves, as well as free men fallen into slavery, is being sold: the young protagonists and other slaves are sold and resold everywhere to anybody who can buy them (1.13.2; 2.2.1; 2.2.5; 2.11.7; etc.). The longing for their lost freedom (and nobility) is then the most excruciating pain. In the actual tale, however, the most atrocious punishments are inflicted not so much upon slaves as upon the two anguished protagonists. There are also some freedmen (2.10.2). It must be said that slaves are not overworked, nor are they despised because of their nature or behavior. Next to the fictional need to emphasize the two protagonists' pitiful fate we may assume some tolerance and understanding towards slaves.

Pirates and bandits are separated from society. They may be physically good-looking (1.13.3 Corymbus, ἔξαρχος of the pirates), courageous (1.13.1 the Phoenician pirates), gentle and humane (2.10.2 οὐ γὰρ ἑκών σε ἠδίκησα Apsyrtus; at 4.6.3ff. Amphinomus protects Anthia from the ferocious Egyptian dogs). The pirates command copious and splendid riches: so Corymbus (1.16.4), his companion Euxinus (1.16.7), and Apsyrtus, their leader (2.2.1 πολλά... θαυμάσια... χρήματα). The profits of the slave trade (or other trades) are indeed considerable (1.13.2; 2.2.1 μέγα κέρδος; 2.2.5 ὡς μεγάλα κερδανῶν; 2.11.7; 3.9.1; 3.11.1 πολύ... ἀργύριον; Psammis too pays ἀργύριον... πολύ for Anthia: 3.11.3; 5.5.8; etc.). It is probably a matter of precious metal, perhaps minted (1.13.1 χρυσὸς καὶ ἄργυρος; 2.7.3; 3.8.3; 4.3.2). The merchandise sold consists precisely of male and female slaves—with the protagonists among them (1.13.2; even the most precious part of the load is looted). Quick circulation of money is therefore induced by pirates and bandits; the former rob sea voyagers, the latter land travellers or even whole villages and cities (5.2.1f.). Strangely enough, the pirates also possess land property (1.14.7 πλησίον... χωρίον; 2.9.4 ἐν τῷ χωρίῳ), which is run by a bailiff (2.10.3): as the location is near Tyre and the pirate lives unharmed on his estate, we must think of some kind of extra-territoriality, which ensures immunity. Hippothous is an unusual bandit: he also knows the language of Cappadocia (3.1.1.ff.) and his purchases befit a refined person: "attractive young servants, and maidservants, and all the other extravagances of a man of means" (5.9.2ff.). This impression is strengthened by the fact that he and his gang normally take refuge in caves[38] (2.14.1; 2.14.5 ἄντρον; 3.3.4; 4.1.5 they lie there in ambush to rob travellers; 4.3.6; 4.4.1; 4.5.1; 4.5.3; 4.5.6 twice; 5.2.3.) The use of caves as refuge in an often deserted territory is likely enough but it can also contain a symbolic meaning. Hippothous seems to hide in these caves, in the earth's entrails, as though he were descending into the realm of the most dreadful abjection and death (which, as a matter of fact, he inflicts upon his guiltless victims, 4.3.5). Finally, Hippothous emerges from this moral and social degradation to reenter society and legality and to take up a new living standard, being surrounded by comfort and respect (5.9.1ff.). He is a completely original character, for whom the happy ending dovetails with recovery of legality, dignity, and wealth. If a murder takes place in those caves (4.5.5), it is precisely from one of those caves that mercy takes a start (5.2.3 Amphinomus temporarily hides in a cave, waiting for Anthia's arrival, whom he later will save): and Hippothous becomes a supporter of such mercy (5.9.13). On the other hand, Hippothous and Anthia had met in a cave without recognizing each other (4.3.6) and the reformation of this youthful epitome of bandit also starts from a cave.

Xenophon Ephesius' novel exhibits original behaviors and convictions. Anthia's suitors hail from the remotest corners of the Mediterranean: they are foreigners, no matter how prominent and wealthy,

---

[38] This is another widespread τόπος of Greek novels. Létoublon (1993) 74f.: "Un des lieux préférés des romanciers grecs semble être le tombeau, avec comme variante la grotte et la caverne... l'héroine est enterrée vivante à plusieurs reprises, ou à defaut vit dans une caverne souterraine... Xenophon d'Ephèse montre le thème à l'état 'brut': la recherche par les brigands du supplice le plus douloureux pour Anthia les conduit à l'enterrer vivante avec deux molosses sauvages. C'est donc une variante aggravée du thème topique de la prison et du supplice... Heureusement pour Anthia, le brigand préposé à sa surveillance est amoureux d'elle, et lui donne de la nourriture pour sa survie et pour que dans son tombeau elle puisse apprivoisier les chiens féroces (*Ephésiaques* VI,6—actually IV,6,4ff.). Dans l'épisode précedent Anthia était prisonnière dans une grotte, gardée par l'un des brigands, nommé Anchialos, lui aussi amoureux d'elle. Il avait tenté de la violer, et elle l'avait tué en se défendant." But, if we are not mistaken, in Xenophon Ephesius the τόπος takes on a symbolic meaning. See also Scarcella (1995b).

and therefore, the girl has one more reason (besides faithfulness to her young husband: 2.1.5f.; 2.7.5; etc.) to despise them. These characters' legal position, though well enough defined (the είρηνάρχης of Cilicia, the maharaja of India, the governor of Egypt: the είρηνάρχης is elected, the Egyptian governor's assistant is a relative of his and is freely chosen by him), leaves their prerogatives unclear. Upper class members have credible, rather than romantic, estates; but pirates and bandits too, with their illegal trades and robberies, boast considerable properties, and strangely enough, even real estate. And Apsyrtus' immunity at Tyre, as though crimes could only be prosecuted in the countries where they have been committed, cannot but surprise. Hippothous himself returns safely to Ephesus, though he has committed a murder at Byzantium. He is therefore a symbol, which is confirmed by the use of caves we have just emphasized. The use of slaves is obvious but scanty; they are sometimes freed (2.10.2), sometimes benefited (5.6.3), and, except for verbal threats, are generally immune from the atrocities so common in ancient society (2.6.3 βασάνων... οίκετικών).

Longus'[39] society is confined to a small geographical area and has well-defined features and a closely-knit structure. Social differences are limited, though diversities in relation to legal status are quite evident. The island of Lesbos, free from outside influences, is divided into two πόλεις and enjoys self-rule, though no mention is made of public offices. Military commands are entrusted by election to στρατηγοί. The well-to-do are well represented: they own real estate as well as movable property, but are exposed to sudden economic disaster. They are mindful if not solicitously so, of their own business, and pay no heed to city government, which is run by the people's assembly. Labor is amply available: besides slaves, free workers (and farmers) are hired, no doubt owing to a shortage of slave labor. Comfort and culture are widespread, but so is a sense of precariousness, as shown by a recurrent fear of poverty. It is an industrious and yet violent world, where social differences tend to fade and disappear.

The island of Lesbos[40] is thought of as independent and divided into two communities of equal wealth and prestige. These freely decide their policy concerning relations with each other. There is no mention

---

[39] Guiding text: Vieillefond (1987).
[40] Scarcella (1968a). The description of Lesbos is considered realistic by Kloft (1988).

of any ἀρχή (at 1.8.3 the ἀρχή is wielded by the two youths only over their herds). There is no ἄρχων. There is, on the contrary, an assembly of the Methymneans (2.19.1 ἐκκλησίαν ... τῶν πολιτῶν), which has the power to decide the immediate waging of war against the πόλις of Mytilene. An old man[41] acts as δικαστής: he is a sort of justice of the peace (2.15.1; 2.17.1 Philetas). Chloe's judgment on two suitors of hers is totally personal and private (1.15.4). At a different time a full-fledged trial appears desirable (2.14.4 δικαιολογήσασθαι). Στρατηγοί appear on several occasions: Bryaxis (2.19.3) is the admiral of Methymna's fleet, comprising ten ships, which is sent to plunder the twin city's coasts (though there is no sense of an enmity between the two communities). He has both civil (2.26.5; 2.28.2) and military powers (2.25.1 he lets the crew rest; 2.28.1 he summons the ships' commanders; 2.28.2 he personally escorts a woman prisoner back with his own ship). At Mytilene the στρατηγός Hippasus commands 3,000 infantrymen and 500 cavalry (3.1.2): but there is no mention of the city magistracy that orders him to march against Methymna. It is his personal decision to approach the city without resorting to pillaging and plundering, which he deems robber-like acts (though they are regrettably frequent in the feuds between neighboring cities). Though he has been elected a commander with full power, when a messenger with the enemy's peace proposal arrives (3.2.2), he sends to his city for instructions (3.2.4). So the war ends as suddenly as it had begun without causing any casualty on either side.

In both cities there are well-to-do families[42] (if not belonging to the aristocracy in the full sense of the word): this is made plain by the γνωρίσματα of the two exposed infants (1.2.3; 1.5.3), among which are many precious objects. The assumption is then confirmed by reality (4.19.5; 4.21.1). The exposed boy is the son of Dionysophanes, a middle-aged man, who is tall, handsome, and strong (4.13.2), and also richer than most, and generous. His wealth is certainly newly-acquired, as in the past, when he already was the father of three, he has judged his fourth child (Daphnis) to be in excess, and has therefore exposed him (4.24.1). He comes to the country with his one

---

[41] Liviabella Furiani (1992) 90: "Il vecchio ... nel romanzo d'amore, non è percepito nè rappresentato come 'l'altro', nè come 'l'altro' si percepisce; egli, felicemente inserito nella società, non sembra appartenere ad una categoria sociale separata o ostile ... Generalmente tra le varie classi d'età si instaura una collaborazione amichevole, largamente positiva, mediante la quale gli individui giovani e maturi, anzichè considerare la vecchiaia un antivalore, ne utilizzano ogni potenzialità".

[42] Scarcella (1970).

surviving son, Astylus: the two brothers will have to share the estate (4.24.3), for which the father apologizes to the son who thought he would be the only heir. But even so, they will vie with kings in wealth (4.24.3 χρημάτων ἕνεκα βασιλεῦσιν ἐρίζετε). Dionysophanes will bequeath land, many skilled servants, gold, silver, and whatever riches are owned by wealthy families, to Astylus; Daphnis will receive the farm on which he has grown up, the two servants that act as his parents, and his own flock (4.24.3f.). Dionysophanes' property also includes an unusual number of slaves, both male and female (4.23.1), who live in his city palace, and also enough means to prepare lavish banquets (4.26.1; 4.34.2), organize a hunting party (4.11.1), and, finally, present Dryas, Chloe's foster father, with 3,000 drachmas. Chloe comes from an equally distinguished family, which was equally hit by economic straits at the time the girl was exposed (4.35.4). As there is a two-year difference in the youths' age (1.4.1), we gather that in that period of time the island (or at least the city of Mytilene) was facing serious economic problems. When the girl is found again, her family is enjoying an ever increasing prosperity (4.35.4). This is proved not only by the words of Megacles, the head of the family, but also by his 4,000 drachma present to Dryas (4.37.2). The rich banquets that are offered to all the preeminent citizens of Mytilene (4.34.2 πάντας τοὺς ἀρίστους), as well as a lavish wedding celebration (4.38.1), strengthen the impression of a current solid and ample wealth. Besides the two families so intimately involved in the story, at Mytilene there are other very wealthy women (4.33.4 πολλαὶ τῶν μέγα πλουσίων). There are prominent families at Methymna (2.19.3; 3.27.1 Chloe's suitors are very rich). Dionysophanes' extended property, about 200 stadia from the city, is extremely fruitful (1.1.1 ἀγρός ... κτῆμα κάλλιστον), affords a magnificent garden (4.2.1 ὁ παράδεισος), just like the royal ones, and buildings appropriate to the good running of the farm (1.6.2 τὴν ἔπαυλιν; 1.22.3; 2.8.1; 2.24.3; 4.15.4 the owners dine there, which means the place must be comfortable enough; 4.23.2). Other country dwellers also have their own ἔπαυλις (2.33.2 Philetas; 4.29.2 Lampis). There are rivers and springs (1.23.2; 1.30.4; 2.7.3; 4.26.4; etc.). Dionysophanes runs his land property himself, but with a detachment suggesting a man-of-leisure's indifference (4.1.1 his inspections must be many years apart if the existence of the foundling is news to him). The women[43] of the several families, both wealthy

---

[43] Scarcella (1972a).

and humble, appear mostly as wives; generally speaking when unnamed women are mentioned, they are mostly mothers. Lycaenion is an exception: she lives with the old Chromis, being perhaps his παλλακή (3.15.1); her pregnant neighbor (3.16.1) is a free woman. In Mytilene's well-to-do families Cleariste is Daphnis' mother (4.13.1), and Rhode Chloe's (4.36.3). They always behave with the utmost chastity and modesty; families are monogamous, and weddings take place among fellow-citizens (there are young maidservants, however, who might be kept for pleasure, 4.27.2). Lycaenion is the exception; her urgings may be understood if not approved of (she is unhappily matched). Wives are respected. Cleariste travels with her husband (4.13.1), debates with him (4.20.2), and decides with him to expose the infant (4.21.3; the horrible deed does not apparently cause any suffering to her, though she rejoices when the boy is found again: 4.23.1). Rhode is perhaps kept a little aside (at 4.36.3, though, her husband looks for her). These prominent women's only task seems to be procreation (not the education of their children), and later, caring for their offsprings' weddings (4.31.3). As for the offspring itself, Cleariste has had four children (though two died at a tender age: 4.24.2), Rhode only one (4.35.3ff.): it is probably owing to fictional daintiness that the former has only surviving boys, the latter only a girl. Chloe herself will bear two children of different sexes (conforming to the balanced structure of the whole: 4.39.2): but the first-born will be a boy, owing to persistent male-oriented prejudice. Amaryllis is more prolific; but only one of her and Philetas' children, Tityrus, is involved in the tale (2.32.1).

The economic features of Lesbos' society bear the marks of prosperity. In the cities, in the palaces of well-to-do families, banquets are prepared, but rustic meals are to be had in the country too (4.38.1f.). Some of the farmers live in an αὐλή, which allows a yard (3.5.1; 3.6.1; 3.6.2; 3.10.2 of Dryas; 4.18.2 of Lamon). Activities are pastoral rather than agricultural (2.1.1ff.). Anyway, they leave time for refined diversions (2.36.1; 2.37.1 a mime dance; 2.37.3; 4.38.3 harvesting songs, σύριγξ and αὐλός playing). Other occupations are hunting and fishing (2.12.3; 3.10.2). The presence of craftsmen is to be inferred from the numerous objects and working tools, but is not expressly mentioned. On the other hand, there are merchants (2.12.4; 2.12.5; 3.21.1; etc.). However, these farmers consider themselves poor (3.26.2 Lamon is οὐκ... πλούσιος; 3.27.5; 3.30.3 the barley harvest is less than the seeds sown; 1.16.2 Daphnis, in Dorcon's words, "is so poor he cannot keep a dog"; 3.26.4 Myrtale states πένητές έσμεν, ὦ παῖ). As a solace, it can be said (3.31.1) that honest poverty is preferable to wealth. In spite of this, there is a constant desire and effort to get rich. Money circulates in considerable amounts: Dryas receives a 10,000 drachma reward (3.29.4; 4.33.2; 4.37.2). Lesbos is no happy island, however: it is familiar with wars, pirates' incursions, accidental or untimely deaths (1.30.3ff.), killings at the hands of pirates (a current τόπος), rapes (though only expected: 3.25.2), and hard and unremitting toil (3.15.2 ἕωθεν εἰς νομήν, νύκτωρ ἐκ νομῆς). The shepherds have only small things at their disposal (at 4.10.3, though, they offer the delicious Lesbian wine), which they laboriously saved by depriving themselves of their daily necessities, as one might think (1.19.2 a wedding dowry; 4.7.1 cheeses, a kid, hides; etc.).

A limited middle class includes people who live in the country working for a salary: vintagers, both male (2.1.3) and female (2.2.1); there are numerous cow and goat herders and general farmers (2.5.3 Philetas' children; 2.12.4; 2.17.3 they live in villages; etc.). They are all free, though there exists a naive hierarchical difference between respected cow herders and despised goat herders (1.16.1 but this is a love rival's contention). The lands are either (2.1.1ff.) low-lying vines or meadows and woods (1.9.1 τὰ ἐν δρυμοῖς, τὰ ἐν λειμῶσι καὶ ὅσα ὄρεια); no plowed fields are mentioned, though there is ample consumption of bread[44] (1.16.4 ἄρτος ὀβελίας; 2.12.5; 3.6.3; 3.7.1; 3.9.1; 3.11.2.; 3.20.3), which is baked in individual homes (3.10.2 τῆς ... Νάπης ἀρτοποιούσης), in different types. The countryside is densely populated and settlements are very close to one another (2.12.4; 3.1.1; 3.2.3; 3.3.1; etc.). We receive detailed information about the old Chromis, a free man and an independent farmer (3.15.1 γείτων, γεωργὸς γῆς ἰδίας); he lives with a woman who came from the city, and is undoubtedly experienced and refined: Lycaenion (3.15.1 γύναιον ... ἐπακτὸν ἐξ ἄστεος, νέον καὶ ὡραῖον καὶ ἀγροικίας ἁβρότερον). Also free, wealthy and respected is Dorcon (1.15.1). In spite of the countryside being densely settled, farmers live in separate family units. There is no communal vision, in as much as they do not feel themselves part of a community (the word δῆμος is missing, and πλῆθος is either a flock of birds: 3.5.2; 3.10.2, or is used in reference to Chloe's suitors: 3.25.1, or to servants: 4.23.1; ὄχλος refers to servants of the retinue: 4.14.1, or to the crowd collecting at the palace: 4.33.3).

---

[44] Scarcella (1993).

None of these terms, therefore, has a political relevance. The island, however, is not conceived of as a primitive or wild land; on the contrary it distinguishes itself by a varied and refined culture, which is spread everywhere in the form of music,[45] song, dance, ability and zest for telling stories (2.33.3ff. the story of Syrinx told by Lamon). Such cultural learnings are not recorded for the city, though slaves too are credited with them.

Slaves appear in great numbers (2.12.1; 4.13.1; 4.15.4; 4.24.4 οἰκέτης; 3.31.3; 4.17.1; 4.17.4; 4.28.3; 4.29.4 δοῦλος; at 4.19.5 the two words are used to indicate the same person, Daphnis). Lamon and Myrtale are certainly slaves (at 4.1.1 the slave messenger[46] is called ὁμόδουλος of Lamon); later they are freed (4.13.4; 4.33.2). For reasons of balance one would expect Dryas and Rhode to be slaves too, but the fact that the request for Chloe's hand in marriage is addressed to Dryas (at 4.30.1ff. we see his intermediation with the boy's parents) and his receiving great sums of money, speak against this. Being delivered of the burden of procreation, women slaves take on the education of foster children (1.6.3 Nape). Another difference, as compared to city ladies, is the harsh treatment they occasionally receive (3.26.2f. Myrtale). The main difference lies in their functions within the family: baking bread, leading the herds to pasture (2.22.1 it is a toilsome task indeed, especially when the animals disband), curdling milk (1.23.3), making cheese (3.33.1), preparing meals and pouring wine for the vintagers (2.1.3). In town, instead, girl slaves may be expected to provide pleasure for their masters (4.27.2). The same would be expected of Daphnis, had he been given to Gnathon (4.11.2f. the danger is very real, given the affection Astylus shows to Gnathon, whom he call Γναθωνάριον: 4.16.4). In general, in town

---

[45] Maritz (1991) 65: "Music in *Daphnis and Chloe* fulfills various functions. Firstly it sets the scene... Specific music can be used, as highlights in painting, to focus attention on 'foreground' characters or events. Often, it is symbolic of order and control... Music symbolizes the erotic, in its joyous as well as its aggressive aspects... In each case the unchanging element is music."

[46] Liviabella Furiani (1990) 218ff.: "La rete informativa si dispiega in Longo più con i ritmi della favola che con quelli della realtà; anche l'innegabile base di realismo che sostiene il romanzo è soggetta all' intonazione e all' intenzione favolistica, come confermano l'assenza di ogni comunicazione scritta e la marcata presenza della comunicazione divina... Tuttavia la comunicazione orale riveste in Longo una fisionomia e un rilievo ben definiti... La preminenza dell' elemento favolistico su quello realistico è testimoniata anche dalla condanna della manipolazione delle informazioni... L'ambientazione favolistica comporta un' espansione dei metodi di comunicazione non verbali, ma musicali, con gli animali."

men and women slaves accompany their masters (4.23.1), whom they look up to with awe and respect (4.8.2 ὑπ' ἐκπλήξεως; 4.8.4 fear of being hanged at the master's command; 4.10.1 his wrath; etc.). None of the masters, however, is ever cruel to his slaves in the course of the tale; quite the contrary, they are kindly and generous to them (4.25.2; 4.33.1 a meal together). We witness even drawing-room manners with a series of introductions (4.37.2). On the other hand, the two foundlings' stories prove the (social and cultural, if not economical) affinity of the two groups: the free aristocrats on the one side, the slaves on the other. Life is certainly not free of worries, owing to unremitting toil and human wickedness (at 1.28.2 Daphnis is kidnapped; at 2.20.3; 4.28.1 it is Chloe's turn), but nothing makes it sorrowful or degraded. And, in fact, the two young protagonists, once married, decide to settle down in the country (4.39.1).

In Longus also pirates are outcasts: they are the object of general reprobation. They come from Tyre, but sail on a Carian schooner for camouflage (at 1.28.1 the difference is not clear); they are rather theatrically equipped with armor and scimitars; they steal wine, a great amount of wheat and honey, some cows, and, most importantly, they kidnap the young herder (1.28.2) and inflict deadly wounds on Dorcon (1.29.1). Other pirates are mentioned elsewhere (2.32.2 remembering is actually gratifying; 4.7.5 an enemy's, rather than a bandit's, ravages). They are not downright cruel and their actions cannot be called ferocious; and, if they commit a crime, they are immediately punished for it.

Longus' society is therefore homogeneous. Nobility does not boast an ancient lineage and a famous name; we often meet unnamed wealthy people, and the two protagonists' families have gone through economic straits, even though they soon recovered their wealth. Farmers and herders consider and call themselves poor (thus justifying their greed), but they enjoy free use of their humble properties (1.15.2; 3.11.2: etc.). City dwellers draw their precarious well-being from their land property income. They take care of it themselves, but from afar (at 4.1.1 it appears as though Dionysophanes visits his land for the first time—witness the fact that Daphnis does not know him). As compared to the city's luxury and waste, in the country a healthy variety of experiences is offered: if one cannot be happy in the country, then again, one can be happy in no other place but the country. Slaves are well represented, and their situation is certainly not abject or degrading; on the contrary, their unaffected behavior makes them resemble liberally educated city dwellers. Political institutions are ossified; if a war breaks out on frivolous pretexts, it is immediately over and causes no victims or hatred. Appreciation of culture is implied: music has something magical about it (2.28.3; 4.15.2ff. goats perform their usual acts to the syrinx' strains). In spite of the intrinsic hardships of the life of these shepherds, so many naively languorous scenes cause us to imagine a world of tender and unblemished gentleness.

Heliodorus'[47] society is very complex. As the tale takes place in politically and socially different countries, Heliodorus depicts strongly divergent social and economic structures. There are similar elements, however, based on common ethical principles. Athens appears as a democratic but frivolous city, where the people have a part in community rule (at least in the judiciary). Delphi is seen in a folkloristic religious atmosphere. Egypt is a peripheral province of the Persian empire with a largely oriental legislation. Ethiopia is a kingdom strongly influenced by the priestly class. The ratio of each of society's components varies from region to region: economic activities are well represented in Egypt, but neglected in Ethiopia; in the latter country human sacrifices are practiced, which are unheard of elsewhere; in other countries, however, a stern legislation is in force (1.13.4ff. the sentencing of the guiltless Cnemon at Athens; 8.3.2; 8.6.2; etc., torture and threats of torture and death, in Egypt). Even the nature of available information varies: it is extremely matter-of-fact in Egypt, but has a strong ideological slant in Ethiopia.

The cities of Delphi[48] and Athens[49] have likely, if highly manneristic, societies. Aristippus, the hero of a sorrowful story at Athens, is

---

[47] Guiding text: Rattenbury-Lumb (1960).
[48] Rougemont (1992) 94ff.: "il y a... à la fois discordance avec la topographie delphique et concordance avec le cérémonial habituel des grandes processions... Chaque fois que le lecteur moderne relève chez Héliodore une concordance précise avec les faits delphiques, aussitôt sa mémoire lui fournit un grand texte littéraire classique où figure justement le détail en question... Je ne prétends pas qu'il (i.e. Heliodorus) n'ait jamais visité Delphes; simplement son roman ne permet pas de l'affirmer."
[49] Oudot (1992) 105f.: "Athènes se réduit... à un décor savamment construit à partir de références culturelles et légendaires... Delphes, en effet, est le lieu de la rencontre romanesque (loin de simuler la passion, loin de ruser pour séduire, les deux héros 'se reconnaissent'); Delphes est à la fois le lieu de l'éclat religieux et celui de l'explication rationelle du monde; Delphes, enfin, qui s'offre au monde grecque, est le lieu où le spectacle fait sens, et Athènes, scène de comédie, devient son double négatif."

an elderly man (1.9.2; at 1.12.3 he has gray hair) and a member of the Areopagus; he shows a rather detached interest and participation in political activities (2.26.3 ἱερομνήμονα, the Amphictyonic assembly), and is of middle economic standing (1.9.1 τὴν περιουσίαν τῶν μέσων). Demaenete, his wife and a mother leaning to incest,[50] comes from a good family (1.11.4 εὐγενής ... φάσκουσα), enjoying solid kinship ties (2.9.2) and widespread social relations (1.14.6); her family is economically powerful (2.9.2 ἐπὶ πολλοῖς χρήμασιν). Cnemon, their son, who is subjected, nay accused of incest, has had a free man's education (1.13.1), but leads a dissolute and wanton life (1.10.4), as it was easy at Athens for free and wealthy youths. Moments of daily life are mentioned; so are details referring to the city (1.10.1 the Panathenaea; 1.10.2 the night banquet in the Prytaneum; 1.16.5 the gardens of Epicurus; etc.). Great relevance is given to the court,[51] whose procedure is portrayed (1.13.4 the questioning by the γραμματεύς; 1.14.1 the 2,700 judges casting their ballots—of whom 1,000 decree the defendant's exiling; 1.13.4 the people's noisy assent: ἀνεβόησαν ἅπαντες; 1.13.5 ἀκαταπαύστῳ θορύβῳ). So the political weight of the δῆμος is considerable (1.13.1 it can inflict the penalty; 1.17.6 it listens to and approves Aristippus' report on his wife's story; 2.9.3; 6.2.3 it takes part in the new trial of appeal, which ends with the confiscation of Aristippus' property and his exile). The picture of Athens is captivating, not owing to some theatrical details (e.g. Demaenete's suicide in the ditch of the Academy). There are slaves in the houses of these obscure people of Athens. They are often mentioned by name and possess a personality of their own. Thisbe is a young girl slave (1.11.3 παιδισκάριον; 1.15.2 θεραπαινίδα; 2.10.3) who is not devoid of some culture: she plays the lyre (2.8.2) very well (2.26.8) and writes effective and elegant letters (2.10.1ff.). From Aristippus' house she goes to live

---

[50] Scarcella (1985a).
[51] Both the court's composition and the procedure show this must be the ἐκκλησία, the meeting of all male citizens who were of age. This was Athens' most democratic institution (and yet the behavior of some of the present raises some doubts as to their actual open-mindedness). The number of yearly meetings—at least in the 5th century B.C.—had already risen to forty: nothing prevents us from thinking that a special meeting may have been called to discuss a case of attempted parricide. However, judicial power was normally the prerogative of citizens sitting in the various sections of the Heliaea. Sometimes, though [Biscardi (1982) 64]: "era l'Ecclesia stessa ad emanare il proprio giudizio, come quando l'accusa fosse stata presentata direttamente ad essa, mediante εἰσαγγελία, per reato flagrante contro la sicurezza dello Stato, e più tardi anche per delitti contro la morale pubblica, quali l'adulterio: ed in questa ipotesi, con riferimento alla pena, l'assemblea aveva poteri illimitati." The writer's effort to conform to historical reality must be appreciated.

with the merchant Nausicles, and dies tragically at the hands of Thyamis (2.14.4). Next to her is Arsinoe, a flute player (1.15.6; 2.8.5): she too rents out her art and her body (2.8.4f.). It is perhaps her mistress' confidence that drives Thisbe to her downfall (1.15.3 φιλτάτη; 1.15.6 ὦ γλυκεῖα Θίσβη). No fewer than two deaths and two exiles mark the short Athenian episode, in accordance with the city's frivolous and reckless atmosphere.

For Delphi we have the description of some of the city's most famous places and features (2.26.2): the cult of Artemis practiced by Charikleia (2.33.4) is emphasized, though the city is of course consecrated to Apollo (2.26.1) and houses his venerable oracle (2.26.5). Ample space is dedicated to the ceremonies honoring Neoptolemus (2.34.3; 2.34.7; 2.35.3; 3.2.4 twice; 3.5.3; 3.10.1). There are no public officials, just priests. Kalasiris stands out among them; he has been singled out to be a priest since childhood (2.25.3), is a priest of Isis (2.25.2; 3.11.2f.) and a widower with two sons, who keeps chaste (2.25.4). He has a venerable appearance (2.21.2). The city hosts a holy embassy of the Enians (2.34.1), a Thessalian people of great nobility (2.34.2), causing awe and admiration (3.3.8) in men and women witnessing their progress. These crowds eagerly hurry to the procession (2.36.2) and annoy Charikleia with their noisy frivolity. Charikles, a Gymnosophist (2.31.1f.) and a follower of Apollo (2.35.1), is the most authoritative among the citizens of Delphi (4.6.6 Δελφῶν ἐστι τὰ πρῶτα). He is appointed ambassador to the satrap of Egypt (2.31.3), thus uniting priestly status and lay function. In the city a sacred atmosphere can be felt everywhere (4.16.3 the banquet in honor of Heracles; 4.1.2 Charikleia's attendance at the Phythian games, with the torch and the palm; 4.2.2 her arbitration, in spite of the presidency being conferred on the Amphictyons; 4.3.3 the girl's passionate participation; 4.3.4; the rejoicing of all present, perhaps of all Greece, 4.3.2 πᾶσα . . . ἡ Ἑλλάς). Charikles' behavior merges priestly and democratic attitudes: he summons the people's assembly (4.19.4 εἰς βουλὴν καλεῖ τὸν δῆμον) to an evocative night session (4.19.5). The στρατηγός Hegesias suggests immediately pursuing the kidnappers, capturing and impaling them (4.20.2 ἀνασκολοπίσαι)—a punishment perhaps exorbitant, certainly gruesome and foreign to Greek custom (though mentioned also by Chariton 3.4.18; 8.7.8). He also proposes to deprive their descendants of all their rights[52] (4.20.2 ἀτιμῶσαι).

---

[52] The penalty meant for the kidnappers, after their capture, suggests total ἀτιμία,

The decision is taken by popular decree (4.21.1 δόγματι τοῦ δήμου) by hand-raising (4.21.1 ἐπικεχειροτονήσθω) and unanimously (4.21.2 μιᾷ ψήφῳ καὶ χειρὶ τῇ πάντων; also 4.21.3; 5.1.1 ἡ... πόλις ἡ Δελφῶν). Servants are only fleetingly mentioned (4.19.1 οἰκετῶν... ἀφιγμένων: messengers; 4.19.8 people in charge of a ceremony, but they are not really servants). The organizing of the celebration entails the performing of dances (4.17.1 Assyrian) and music (4.16.3 σὺν αὐλήμασιν at the banquet; 4.17.1 ὑπὸ πηκτίδων). Within the sacred atmosphere that seems to envelop everything (even love is part of the religious event), mention of working activities is rather scanty (4.16.6 merchants from Phoenicia,[53] and therefore foreign, with a shipload of Indian, Ethiopian and, of course, Phoenician goods).

Egypt[54] is a satrapy of the Persian empire, and therefore subject to the Persian king (5.9.2 τῷ κοινῷ δεσπότῃ, common to all his subjects and officials). Egypt is ruled by the satrap Oroondates, by the king's appointment (2.24.2; 5.9.1; 6.13.1 μεγάλου βασιλέως ὕπαρχον; 6.13.4; 7.3.3; etc.); he is the first among all Persian satraps (7.12.5 μεγίστῳ σατραπῶν), though we do not know the reasons for this hierarchical primacy. His prerogatives are listed in detail: he organizes and leads a military expedition from Thebes against Ethiopia (7.29.2), which ends in disaster (9.5.1ff. Syene is besieged by the Ethiopian and surrenders; 9.19.1 the satrap flees; 9.20.5 he is captured; 9.27.1 he receives and accepts the satrapy from the hands of the enemy Hydaspes). He lives in Oriental luxury; he has a harem (8.2.2. his women are strangely enough called παλλακίδας), uses precious weapons (9.23.4 his sword is worth many talents), and lives in a palace (8.12.2). In this Egypt, where war (of peoples against peoples and individuals against individuals) prevails and violence and deception (Arsake's; Achaemenes') are rampant, the satrap can ostensibly be both proud (8.2.1; 8.3.1) and humble (9.27.2), and inwardly evil (9.10.2). In spite of his ample power and the ruthlessness he shows to his subjects

---

to be extended to their offspring—except this, at least at Athens, was only applicable in the case of insolvency to the state or legally equivalent debts. Capital punishment was applied to those who, after being declared ἄτιμοι and expelled from the city, would again settle there [Biscardi (1982) 85f.].

[53] Briquel-Chatonnet (1992).

[54] Cauderlier (1992) 225: "Nous pouvons voir dans le romancier un esprit curieux de tout, bien informé, sans doute par des traités spécialisés, mais sachant admirablement retenir le détail essentiel, éviter l'érudition sèche, et faire vivre ses personnages."

(8.3.2) and his wife (7.2.5; 7.3.5), he is basically only a servant of the despotic central power.

Arsake is a young and pretty woman (7.17.3) of imposing height (7.2.1) and lively intelligence. Her noble birth and high social rank make her haughty (7.25.2). She is the Persian king's sister (7.3.3; 7.11.7; 7.12.5; etc.). During her husband's absence from his post, she takes his place. She is capable of taking wise military decisions (7.3.1ff.; 7.4.3; etc.). She is surrounded by Persian officials (7.19.1 τῶν ἐπὶ δόξης ... προέδρων), who are of course foreigners in Egypt. She performs the administration of justice and gives audiences sitting on the throne (7.24.3). She is fully conscious of the extent of power (8.5.3: "you can make all the fine speeches you like, with your meaningless definitions of equity, propriety, and expediency. He who holds absolute power needs none of these things: his will serves for them all"). And she takes the utmost and haughtiest advantage of it, not refraining from torture (8.8.3) and death (8.9.1) sentences. She is entitled to order arrest and imprisonment (8.9.5), but cannot inflict the death penalty without a trial (8.7.1; 8.9.9): this power is reserved for the Persian dignitaries (8.9.1 ὑπὸ κρίσει τῶν ἐν τέλει Περσῶν). Aside from this limitation, Arsake is the epitome of a new kind of feminine power which was intolerable to the Greeks. Her haughtiness receives a confirmation by the luxuriousness of her life (7.3.2; 7.8.6; etc.)—which is of course frequent enough in Oriental ruling classes. On the contrary, the inclination to wantonness is just her own (7.26.10 τὰ πάντων αἴσχιστα καὶ παρανομώτατα; 8.5.4: "the only holy order that love knows is its consummation"). She entertains friendly relations with her female slave (7.12.6 Kybele is a Greek woman from Lesbos, who was captured in an unspecified war, ὑπ' αἰχμαλωσίας). The woman is self-presuming enough to consider herself extremely important for her mistress (7.12.6 νοῦς ἐκείνῃ καὶ ὦτα καὶ πάντα τυγχάνω); she calls her "my darling", or "child" (7.9.5), and is herself called by Arsake "mother" (7.10.1), "mommie" (7.10.3 μητέριον; 7.10.5 μαμμίδιον), and "my dear Kybele" (7.10.6 Κυβέλιον φίλτατον). This kindness echoes perhaps a certain familiarity between masters and slaves, which was typical of Oriental courts; but it may also mirror a new sensibility. Theagenes too, in Arsake's palace, calls Kybele "mother" (7.13.1), while on her part the slave calls the two youths "my children" (7.12.4) and "my darling children" (7.17.2 γλυκύτατα τέκνα, and the like). In Arsake we witness the merging of traditional assumptions and new humanity. The deceptions and atrocities perpetrated in the palace and in the country are an effective backdrop to her figure.

Next to the satrap and his court, but in a subordinate position, is Mitranes, who commands the garrisons at Chemmis (2.24.2) and other villages (5.9.1). He has the title of φρούραρχος (5.9.2; 7.16.2) and πολέμαρχος (5.8.2); the difference between the two titles is unclear. He directs an operation against the Βουκόλοι (6.3.4): this seems to be a police assignment, though prompted by personal reasons (6.13.2 ἀγανακτήσας). The limits of morality (and allowability) are wide and unsettled (2.24.2 ἐπὶ χρήμασι μεγάλοις ~ 5.8.2 ἐπὶ χρήμασι πολλοῖς). He does not show great competence (8.1.6 his opponents not only take away Theagenes from him, they also kill him). Oroondates' revenge, which is announced by Arsake (8.5.2), and the details of the deadly clash, are left vague (6.3.4; 6.13.1ff.; 7.16.2; 7.24.2; etc.) in spite of some moving moments. Finally Mitranes' decision to send Theagenes to the Great King has the appearance of flattery, coming from a man who, aside from his functions, is spiritless and conceited (5.8.5 χαυνωθεὶς τοῖς ἐπαίνοις). Achaemenes' legal situation is clearer, but his political position is ambiguous. He is the son of the Greek woman slave Kybele (7.14.3) and must therefore be a slave too. His name, however, is illustrious, being the same as that of the Persian dynasty's founder—we may wonder whether he was so named because he was born in the palace, after his mother's capture. He is first cup-bearer at court (7.23.4; 7.27.7): and cup-bearers could form a rank of their own. A prominent prisoner, with whom he had been entrusted, is taken away from him (7.24.2), and he barely escapes himself. He is privy to Arsake's lapses, perhaps through her mother, who had been a party to those intrigues. He denounces her to Oroondates (8.1.6ff.; 8.5.6). He treacherously tries to kill the satrap on the battlefield but is himself hit by an Ethiopian (9.20.5f.). He may be a minor court official who has become close to the satrap. Heliodorus, however, despises him: he is envious (7.19.4), insolent (7.25.1), violent (7.26.8), vindictive (7.26.10), hypocritical (7.27.5); even his own mother considers him a chatterbox (7.22.4 ἀδολεσχεῖς). His spiritual meanness is still enhanced by an eye disease (7.14.3) and his habit to spy through keyholes[55] (7.15.2ff.). Aside from his moral peculiarities, he typifies low standing people cheating their way up toward

---

[55] Heliodorus' novel has a wealth of such swift, evocative touches: gestures, poses, winkings, changes of color, etc.; all lend the characters autonomous life and psycho-

the powerful. Another official is the satrap Bagoas, a eunuch (8.17.2 his mutilation affects even his looks). He is one of Oroondates' most trusted men (8.2.3; 8.17.3; 9.25.5 τῶν Ὀροονδάτου κτῆμα τὸ τιμιώτατον). He is therefore entrusted with a very delicate assignment (8.12.2ff.), which he fulfills, giving proof of understanding and solidarity (8.13.3; 8.14.4; 8.15.2). His military capabilities do not seem high: though he has fifty cavalrymen at his command (8.2.3), he is caught in an ambush by the Ethiopians (8.16.1) and is wounded (8.16.6 the detail adds a dramatic touch). The head-eunuch, Euphrates, lives at court, in Memphis (8.3.2; 8.6.1) and has a hand in palace intrigues (8.3.2 he receives a confidential letter from Oroondates). Other eunuchs have less dignified functions (7.18.1f. they serve food; 7.11.1 they escort Kybele; they do the same with Theagenes, 7.19.3, and two young prisoners, whose fate they bemoan, 8.13.5). They are not devoid of sympathy. The description of a provincial court interior is extremely colorful, but the unhappy eunuchs' plea triggers the author's pity. Political structures are vague and sink to folklore and theatricality, though mirroring reality to a certain extent. The eunuchs' importance for the sovereign is expressly stated (8.17.4: "eunuchs act as eyes and ears to the courts of Persian royalty, since they have no children or family, love for whom might divide their loyalties, but are entirely dependent on him who places his trust in them"). So we understand why the head-eunuch is entrusted with assignments of special disagreeableness (8.5.12; 8.6.5 torturing guiltless prisoners), importance (8.9.1; 8.9.20; 8.12.3ff. guarding high-ranking prisoners), or responsibility (8.15.2 confidential communications). Obviously, eunuchs, like any subject, are subordinates of the king and may incur his wrath (8.3.2). However, in spite of such limitations and their submission to the holders of power, eunuchs have their functions and importance in the running of the state. The dignitaries of the Persian empire in Egypt, being free citizens, are much above them, but their tasks are greatly reduced (even too much so): "the Persian lords in whom power was vested to discuss matters of state, to pronounce judgments and decide sentences, summoning them to hear the case the following day. The judges arrived at daybreak and took their seats on the bench" (8.9.5; see also 8.9.16 τοῖς δυναστεύουσι Περσῶν). They have a consultative function for Arsake, with whom

---

logical depth [Liviabella Furiani (1995), the article offers an in-depth inquiry and clever conclusions].

they have some familiarity (7.19.5 they take part in a banquet with her). Their opinion (or sentence) is compulsorily asked for (8.9.1) in the case of capital trials (8.9.9). They do not appear to fulfil the same task with Oroondates. The framework of government in Egypt appears to be well contrived, surely because it is based on Persian experience. Popular masses are the other social component in Egypt.[56] People in power owe their position to the King's unappealable authority or to dynastic or legal reasons (Arsake is the king's sister and the satrap's wife); lower-ranking officials are chosen for their social standing (Persian dignitaries belong to aristocratic families), and the crowds of humbler agents are appointed at the leaders' whim. The lowest class, though free, is devoid of any share in government and administration. These masses sometimes produce a single authoritative citizen (7.1.4 a respectable old man, τῶν ἐπὶ δόξης, suggests informing Arsake; 9.5.9 another old man exhorts to make peace with the enemy). More often these masses identify with a whole city (7.1.3; 7.2.2 πανδημεί; 7.8.3; 9.22.2) or a village (1.33.1 τὰς πέριξ ... κώμας; 1.33.2; 2.18.4; Chemmis 2.19.6; 2.20.1; etc.). They fulfil the fictional needs for choreography. At times the masses of civilians are not separated from police or military forces, as occasionally a meeting is immediately followed by a battle (4.21.2) and the whole city population, hastily armed, turns into a military corps (7.1.3 τὸν ἀστικὸν δῆμον) at a time when only a few cavalrymen and archers are the military professionals. And, if a city is besieged, everyone takes part in the defence (9.2.3; 9.3.8; 9.6.1 at Syene and elsewhere; 9.8.3). The reasons for war between Persian Egypt and Ethiopia are explained in detail (8.1.1ff.): they are credible enough as they touch on economy (the fixing of the boundaries and possession of emerald mines). Even so the Egyptians, who are led by foreigners, seem at times reluctant (9.5.10 the people of Syene insist on peace), generally indifferent, and even ill-informed. The population is also weighed down by frequent and violent police operations (1.30.1: "war in all its forms was loudly raging: the inhabitants of the lake put up a stout and spirited resistance, but their opponents had the immense advantages of strength of numbers and suddenness of attack; some they slew on land; others they sent to the bottom of the lake with their very boats and homes"); it is quite understandable that Egyptians take part in these operations with anger and frustration. The Βουκόλοι make war their normal life

---

[56] Futre Pinheiro (1989).

condition (1.29.5): but to them fighting means trying to survive in a country constantly upset and ransacked by foreign military forces.

A conspicuous, if anomalous, component of Egyptian society is the priestly ranks. A lively witness to his is the fight between two brothers (7.6.1ff.) for a hereditary priesthood (7.8.7 the winner is proclaimed by their father, formerly a priest). Priests and soothsayers possess true wisdom (3.16.4), which comes from Ethiopian sources (9.22.7), Ethiopia being the mother of all wisdom. As these people, especially the priests, also act as counselors to the rulers, their influence, though indirect, is extremely real. They know and read holy books (2.28.2; 3.8.1). There are sacred instruments (7.8.5), laws (7.11.9), letters (8.11.8), and even poses (7.7.2). The sacred salt of hospitality is also mentioned (4.16.5). In the novel priests are wandering, highly evocative figures, though we cannot ascertain how well they mirror reality.

The middle class is poorly recorded, perhaps because of its smallness and irrelevance. As it is, the story unfolds among foreigners—Greeks, Persians, Ethiopians—who are not part of the Egyptian environment. Kalasiris of Memphis (2.24.5) and his two sons, however, are Egyptian. They are priests leading a roving life (2.24.5 βίος ... νῦν ... ἀλήτης) and preach cosmic-oriented doctrines (2.24.6 their conception of fate seems Stoic). Aside from priests, few people belong to the middle class: the merchant Nausicles is of intermediate social standing; he is a Greek and extremely wealthy (2.8.5 ἔμπορος ὑπόχρυσος). There are Tyrian merchants, travelling with their foreign goods (4.16.6); unfortunately merchants are currently considered as greedy as the Persians (5.12.2 φιλοπλούσιον: 5.22.6; 6.6.3; etc.). Trade seems to be an activity reserved for foreigners, that is for outcasts, who are also made such by this very activity. Humble ferrymen ferry people across rivers for money (2.22.1 ἐπὶ μισθῷ); herders pasture oxen (2.19.4 ποίμναις); the offer of a thousand rams and one hundred oxen to the Bessan community suggests there will be more herders in the future (7.8.4 each of them also receives ten drachmas, surely a very small sum to start a new activity after the waste and the exhaustion caused by the fight); the shipwrecked people at the Heracleian mouth of the Nile are able to buy animals, as they have a considerable amount of money (5.27.9). Precious metals are in circulation, both in coins (1.3.2 χρυσοῦ ... καὶ ἀργύρου; 1.22.3; 2.17.2) and in the form of jewels (4.8.7 a ring, though made in Ethiopia; 5.11.5 a necklace, also from Ethiopia; 5.13.3; 7.8.6 Arsake's jewels;[57] 7.27.1 the jewels worn by the reluctant Theagenes: ἑκών τε τὸ μέρος καὶ ἄκων; 9.14.1 the Persian soldiers' precious armor; etc.). Most of these, however, seem to come from abroad. Wealth in the form of movable property does not seem to be widespread among the Egyptians: it is a privilege of the powerful (and the occupying foreigners). Beggars are not missing among the people of Egypt. Kalasiris and Charikleia disguise themselves as beggars (6.11.3)—surely a likely disguise. Poverty prompts compassion, is the author's noble and original statement (6.10.2).

Beyond the protection of the law in Egypt too there are slaves (though themselves not completely deprived of some legal protection). First of all, Theagenes and Charikleia themselves are slaves: they are called δοῦλοι (7.24.1; 7.24.4; 7.26.2; etc.), and also δούλους τοὺς αἰχμαλώτους (8.3.8): rightly so, as they have been captured in a police, if not a military, operation. As a matter of fact, it is commonly accepted (8.4.1) that "while it is in the nature of war to make slaves, it is in the nature of peace to set them free; the former act is a tyrant's whim; the latter shows the judgment of a true king". Some perhaps are born in slavery (7.26.10 Achaemenes). Free people, the masters, pass merciless judgments on slaves (7.26.10: "A man subject to master tends to hate the master to whom he is subject"). On the contrary, slaves consider themselves to be loyal cooperators (7.27.8). Actually, in spite of the threats of atrocious punishments, the slaves' condition appears tolerable in Egypt (8.7.2ff.; but 9.20.5ff., Kybele and Achaemenes succumb to a cruel death, victims to their own wickedness).

In Heliodorus' novel Ethiopia[58] conveys the picture of a society

---

[57] Conde Guerri (1988): a valuable attempt to date the *Aethiopica* on the basis of the jewels mentioned in the work (176: "pués, por el material ofrecido en las escavaciones, la tipologìa del ceñidor de la heroìna se ajusta en sus elementos sustanciales a *modelos reales* que, con clara herencia artistica oriental y helenìstica, se difunden en la joyeria romana de época imperial y estàn patentes a lo largo del siglo III... y en las primeras decadas del IV."

[58] Lonis (1992) 233: "Si les Ethiopiens que met en scène Héliodore et l'Éthiopie qu'il nous décrit relèvent incontestablement de la fiction, c'est une fiction largement sous-tendue par une réalité historique qui lui sert de toile de fond"; p. 234: "le regard qu' Héliodore pose sur les Éthiopiens est un regard attentif, chaleureux, admiratif, et, pour tout dire, complice"; p. 238: "Ni utopiste, ni sophiste, mais peut-être bien visionnaire, l'Emésien semble vouloir montrer à ses contemporaines la seule ambition qui pouvait être à la mesure de leur époque, celle d'un rapprochement entre d'une part, les diverses cultures qui s'épanouissaient dans l'Empire et, d'autre part, les cultures des mondes que l'on disait encore barbares."

founded upon lofty values with a monarchical form of government. The reign of Meroebus is a lesser actualization of this; the young man, a black (10.24.2 ἐν μελαίνῃ τῇ χροιᾷ), is physically handsome (he is taller than most of those present); he has risen to the throne thanks to the help of his uncle Hydaspes, king of Ethiopia. Escorted by a colorful train, he is cordially received by the king. Hydaspes treats him with a father's affection and makes him sit next to him. Meroebus (and his reign) almost epitomize Ethiopian ideology, which is supported by the other peoples who come to pay homage to the sovereign: the Seres (10.25.2), the people of Arabia Felix (10.26.1), the Troglodytae (10.26.2), the Blemmyes (10.26.2), the Auxomitae (10.27.1). All bring presents, such as rare animals (10.27.1 the giraffe, which surprises and excites the assembled crowds), unusual weapons (10.26.2), precious materials (10.25.2). No less surprising are the presents Meroebus receives in exchange (10.25.2 an elephant matched with the gigantic athlete offered by him). On this occasion Hydaspes shows a sense of humor and a politically well-balanced mind (10.26.3 a ten-year total exemption from taxes). Most significant of all presents are Arabia's perfumes[59] (10.26.1): they typify, as if a premonition, what offers become the powerful and the gods. Hydaspes is king of both the Eastern and the Western Ethiopian (9.6.2). The kingdom's inheritance seems to be transmitted through the feminine line too, which explains the queen's behavior, as she fears possible suspicions concerning her honesty: in fact she has borne a strange looking girl, who still might be the heiress to the throne. Here moral and dynastical reasons merge. The king of Ethiopia holds several powers at the same time: he is the head of the armed forces (of immense numbers: 9.1.2 μυριάσιν ἀπείροις), directs the operations by ordering the continuance of exceptionally imposing military works (9.2.3 πολιορκίᾳ μεγαλουργῷ καὶ ἀφύκτῳ), and makes wise tactical decisions (10.1.1). He is lenient towards the vanquished (9.5.4; 9.20.1ff.; this is the same noble attitude, becoming a priest better than a king, that has been taken by Thyamis: 7.5.4; 9.13.1); as a matter of fact, he reinstates the vanquished Oroondates in his office (9.26.3). He holds sway over the prisoners, gives slaves and releases free men (9.26.1 at least on

---

[59] Lallemand (1992) 81f.: "nous avons constaté le manque d'intérêt des romanciers grecs pour l'aptitude des parfums à exprimer les sentiments de leurs héros... Ils ont privilégié la vue, et se sont méfiés des parfums chargés d'érotisme qui auraient rabaissé l'amour au niveau du simple désir charnel."

this point his morals are not above traditional ethics). Politically, the king can decide to give up a part of the national territory (9.26.2 Philae and the emerald mines) and is entitled to fix the country's boundaries to his liking (9.26.2 the Cataracts, judged to be natural boundary between Egypt and Ethiopia). In the notification to the Persian king he treats him as an equal. He gives the people of Syene a ten-year tax exemption, as an effort towards general pacification (9.26.3). He is surrounded by a council of Ethiopian dignitaries (9.25.1), but his decisions are autonomous. Even so, he grants other people's requests, even though he may judge them inappropriate (10.16.7; 10.17.3; etc.).

The king, though a layman, is also the most prominent personality among cult ministers: Ethiopia is therefore a theocratic monarchy. It is he who orders the search for a new victim to sacrifice, when Charikleia turns out to be ineligible (10.12.3; 10.22.5). He is in charge of carrying out the human sacrifice,[60] if under pressure of popular will (10.7.1; 10.16.7ff.) and the law's provisions (10.16.5). The masses can and do directly influence the rule of Ethiopia as far as religious affairs are concerned. As the people change their mind so does the king: he saves the girl by resorting to a legal ploy, whereby he can sacrifice foreigners, but not his own children (10.12.3 τεκνοκτονεῖν: the suggestion comes from the victim herself, who is in fact his daughter).[61] On the other hand, the law, in its frigid mercy, allows the sacrifice of prisoners of war (10.7.2). The final push is given by Sisimithres, the president of the Gymnosophists' college (10.9.6ff.), who refuses to attend the sacrifice. The order to arrest the reluctant victim must be issued by the judges (10.12.4 the double

---

[60] Liviabella Furiani (1985b) 38: "Il sacrificio umano di ringraziamento agli dèi, diventato una rappresentazione ambiguamente teatrale, ha perso le caratteristiche del sacro, approdando nel profano. Che Eliodoro nutra insistenti dubbi su un tal genere di credenze e culti religiosi, è palese, ma... egli non si arresta al momento negativo, distruttivo e, oltre ad ipotizzare, per bocca dei Gimnosofisti, la mancata accettazione da parte degli dèi di simili sacrifici (X 9,6; 39,2 sg.), auspica una più elevata forma di religione, in cui non sia ammessa neanche la θυσία, il sacrificio cruento animale, e sia praticata invece la sola offerta di preghiere e aromi (X 9,6)."

[61] Pernot (1992) 47: "L'habilité sophistique de Chariclée appelle une double explication. Si l'on se place à l'intérieur du roman, il suffit d'observer que la jeune fille a bénéficié d'une éducation particulière, qu'elle est poussée par la nécessité et mue par la passion. Mais si l'on tente de cerner le projet du romancier, on aperçoit la volonté de présenter une figure hors du commun placée dans une situation exceptionnelle, une héroïne au sens plein du terme."

testimony, both written and oral). The sovereign appears ready to accept the objections raised from several sides, and in general declares himself ready to talk things out (9.12.3; 10.6.4). His doubts are caused by the conflict between law and custom and between the latter and his own private humanity. This places the figure of an Oriental king in a new and captivating light, crediting him with an even finer sensibility than the Greeks. Greek ideas, on the contrary, are not exceeded by the recognition of the right to approach the king to men only; women are excluded, surely because they are considered impure (10.4.4ff.). We have reasons to believe that this matter was regulated by a written code (2.28.2), as in Heliodorus' society laws are written. With blatant inconsistency, to be attributed either to the presumed code of law or to the author's carelessness, a council sits by the king, but the latter can ignore it by appealing to the people's will. The reason for this questionable behavior is once more to be sought in the common opinion that the king is his people's father (10.17.2) and in the fact that the violation of the law in refusing to perform the sacrifice is just apparent not real (10.17.2). This is followed by a reversal of the decision just taken and by the granting of pardon to the two youths, with an appeal to the gods' inscrutable will (10.40.1 θεῶν νεύματι τούτων οὕτω διαπεπραγμένων). Further prerogatives of the king are his personal management of the sacrifice (10.41.1), the conferring of the priestly mitre (10.41.2), and the consecrating of Charikleia to Selene and of Theagenes to Helios: with which the king expressly sanctions the religious syncretism—thus far only implied—by which Helios and Apollo are one and the same god (10.36.3). The *proskynēsis* (kowtow) in front of the king is absolutely normal (10.25.1); so is the kissing of his foot (10.34.6); but he expressly refuses excessive praises, which might displease the gods (9.23.1). It is somewhat surprising, instead, that his actions receive express assent and acclaim on the part of the army (10.41.1). So, the Ethiopian king's basically theocratic power is tempered (and completed) by popular reactions and even by the armed forces' approval. Next to the king and in comparison with him, the queen's functions are greatly reduced: she organizes the procession and invites the kingdom's wise men (10.2.2) by personally going to the temple of Pan, where they reside (10.4.1); she waits for her husband, the king, in the temple's porch, as an act of homage (10.6.1); she takes part in the wedding train moving towards the city, Meroe (10.41.3). The queen's main, perhaps essential, function is providing offspring to the king[62] (10.13.4ff. Charikleia is her only child; 10.7.4; 10.18.2).

The Gymnosophists' authority is unobtrusive and yet conspicuous. They have no well-defined institutional position. Their credentials are of a spiritual nature: they profess an extremely noble doctrine, which does not allow them to relinquish a soul enclosed in a human form (2.31.1 ψυχὴν ἅπαξ ἐνανθρωπήσασαν: the formulation of the idea is extremely bold); they speak Greek,[63] a mark of cultural distinction (9.25.3) but also of elitist conceit (10.9.6): they are counselors to the king (10.2.1 σύνεδροί τε καὶ σύμβουλοι) and receive him with unaffected familiarity (10.6.1 hand shaking and embraces); they are the object of awe (10.4.1 their presence gives prestige to a ceremony); they kowtow only to the god (10.6.2); only the god's platform is higher than the one where they sit (10.6.3); they are given an escort to keep the crowd away (10.6.4); finally, they are the only ones entitled to pass judgment on kings (10.10.2), though they declare themselves unprivileged in regard to justice (10.10.3). Their dignity, which equals and in some ways exceeds the king's, stems from moral convictions (10.10.4). They live up to their doctrine by external behavior too (10.9.6 they refuse human sacrifices to the god and only approve of the offering of prayers and perfumes). Their diet is moderate and simple (2.22.1ff.; 2.23.4ff.; 3.11.2); they have the gift of prophecy (10.2.1) and sit in a venerable council (10.2.1 τῷ θειοτάτῳ συνεδρίῳ). Their numbers and nationality are unknown (though they enjoy universal prestige); they rise to the highest dignity through an apprenticeship (10.11.1). The legal position, however, is not clear; they seem to be the equivalent of Egypt's priestly ranks. They shun contact with the people but have an indirect part in political decisions, as they influence and condition the king's acts.

Ethiopia's free citizens appear as a crowd rather than as individuals.

---

[62] Scarcella (1976).
[63] Saïd (1992) 178: "Avec Héliodore la différence des langues et l'incompréhension qui en découle deviennent un moyen de nourrir un intérêt proprement romanesque... Il est clair que de Chariton à Héliodore, les romanciers grecs ont prêté une attention beaucoup plus grandes aux autres et à leur langue et qu'ils ont peu à peu renoncé à la convention littéraire commode de l'incompréhension des personnages. Il est tout aussi clair que Philostrate et Héliodore, qui se rejoignent par l'intérêt qu'ils portent aux problèmes de la communication, incarnent deux attitudes totalement différentes qui sont peut-être le reflet de deux siècles. L'Atticiste Philostrate s'inscrit en effet dans un milieu profondément persuadé de la supériorité du grec, qui est la langue naturelle de la culture et de la philosophie. Le Syrien Héliodore vit dans un monde où cette supériorité ne va peu-être plus autant de soi."

They easily give themselves up to rejoicing (both in public and private), and excitement (10.4.6), both in Ethiopia and elsewhere; they receive the king, whom they honor like a god (10.6.1). They are opposed to departing from traditional cult practices (10.7.6 they are a πλῆθος), but their religious scruples do not rule out mercy (10.9.5); their feelings are strong but unsteady (10.16.3; 10.27.4; 10.28.5; 10.30.5; 10.37.3; etc.). Aside from such repeated shows of passion, the people of Ethiopia do not seem occupied with, or even interested in, any socially lucrative activity. They often provide men for the army, to the extent that civilian masses and armed forces seem sometimes to identify (but at 10.6.4 soldiers keep the crowd away). In a country at war, troops have demanding duties and are constantly present. The army comprises special detachments: hoplites (9.5.4; 9.13.1; 9.14.2), heavy-armed soldiers (9.16.2), scythed chariots (9.14.3; 9.20.4), elephants fitted with turrets (9.16.3 the king himself is mounted on one), the Blemmyans' light infantry (9.18.1). So the Ethiopian army is made up of troops of different nationalities with an incredible variety of armament and tactics. Single individuals have specific functions: there are mounted messengers (10.3.2; 10.4.4), and heralds (10.16.3); it cannot be determined whether these are civil officials or, more plausibly, military personnel from a communications corps, and also whether they are free citizens or slaves. Their dedication to the king is unfaltering: they have no nationalistic motivation nor any notion of the economic and territorial reasons that have caused the war between Ethiopia and Egypt (in the 5th and 4th centuries B.C. during which the story supposedly takes place).

Mention and presence of slaves are extremely rare. If they are already slaves when captured in war, they remain so (9.24.1), but free men captured on the battlefield are released. The men who look for victims to sacrifice in the crowd are perhaps slaves (10.8.1 οἱ ὑπηρέται); so those who publicly carry the picture that startles the pregnant Persinna[64] (10.15.1); or those who detain Charikleia (10.10.1). So, there are few of them, they are scarcely and seldom employed, and—most of all—completely exempt from the threats and sufferings

---

[64] The biological and genetic details accompanying Charikleia's conception and birth are totally incredible. Kudlien (1989) 37: "bleibt nur der Schluß, daß hier ganz ungehemmt ein 'Thaumaston/Mirabile', ein 'Apiston' oder 'Paradoxon', etwas durchaus unwahrscheinliches eben ohne jede weitere Hinterabsicht, präsentiert wird." There are also useful notations on the two infants' exposure in Longus and the practice of exposure in antiquity.

which slaves are exposed to in other countries. At least in the upper classes, Ethiopian society seems not to approve of slavery, though it cannot be said that the latter is unheard of or unpracticed.

The complexity and wealth of the societies in the various countries described by Heliodorus' novel is certain and conspicuous. Athens is the somewhat frivolous and inconsiderate community it has become, if not in reality, certainly in popular imagination; the glimpses with which the novelist presents us take us inside an ordinary family's house. Their resources are limited. Their democratic beliefs are strong and earnest—which doesn't spare their dismay and suffering (Demaenete commits suicide, Thisbe has her throat cut, Aristippus and Charikles are sent into exile in a context of theatrical suspicions and violence). Political regimes appear to be irrelevant as far as people's conscience—and happiness—are concerned. Delphi is steeped in a religious atmosphere; but in the small social universe of this little town a few personalities stand out, including some lay people; in the first place, of course, this applies to the protagonists: they meet in this crucible, where they display the mark of cult and religion (Theagenes is a member of a mission, Charikleia is attached to the cult of a goddess); at the end of the story they receive not just permission to marry (10.21.3; 10.40.2), but rather a personal sanction to priesthood. Criminal actions are not missing (a kidnapping and the hunt for the culprits). The mass of citizens takes part in its city's life as a whole: but the presence of groups of foreigners is a fostering factor for conflicts that not even the holiness of the temples or the solemnity of the Panhellenic games are able to appease. Egypt is a peripheral province of the Persian empire and itself a melting pot of races:[65] there Greek exiles, Persian officials, Egyptian people (enrolled in the army or lurking in threatening concealment), Ethiopian kings and troops meet, sometimes by mutual consent, sometimes against their will: it is an extensive and colorful universe in which the story unfolds with a wealth of great acts, that are at the same time the

---

[65] The terms βάρβαρος and βαρβαρικός appear rather frequently in Heliodorus; they refer to the rashness of non-Greeks (1.30.6), their violent acts (5.7.3) and psychological rudeness (8.9.4), however not impervious to compassion (1.4.3; 1.19.2). Some disdain towards these populations is shown (1.25.5; 5.8.5; 7.29.1). Some philters (2.10.4), as well as some cruelties (7.25.4) or inclinations to wrath (2.12.5), are considered worthy of a barbarian; so is whatever does not exceed irrationality of behavior. And yet Heliodorus' characters, or at least some characters, are less given to hostility and spiteful intolerance than other writers and novels. In general, see on this Scarcella (1986), Kuch (1989d).

acts of the great. The social ranks, involved in the story are the higher ones, which compete for and handle power, for which they are ready, or are condemned, to die. In the midst of all this there are the priests, the bearers of a universal message of their own. Everywhere a tense, exasperated and even despairing atmosphere prevails (witness the two brothers' fight watched by their father): fear (and death) grips or threatens even those who might be protected by legal status or family power (the satrap, his wife, the young lovers, and also lesser or minimal characters). In Egypt slaves move and act at court too, being protected by their masters' condescension or foolishness, or stimulated by their confidence in an open, emotional, and sometimes delirious personal relationship (Arsake and her slave accomplice, the good and not-so-good eunuchs). War overwhelms and destroys unnamed and guiltless crowds; pride and fury, and other people's blindness, sunder others from society, turning them into bandits. At the other end (or rather at the summit) we find a priestly class, juridically self-contained, but ideologically open to outside suggestions, actually itself advocating a lofty creed of its own. Some of its members (such as Kalasiris and his sons, who bear the conspicuously Egyptian names of Thyamis and Petosiris) are of native stock. They testify to a very complex social situation in which the religious area is what has retained authenticity: under Persian occupation and in the general indifference towards economic activities, which are left to foreigners, Egypt protects its cultural identity by producing a priestly class endowed with universal views. Ethiopia is the goal of the young protagonists' travel (and spiritual formation). Its monarchical government is enlivened by the sovereign's absolute personal humanity. By their presence and influence the religiously and philosophically oriented group of the Gymnosophists contributes to the ennobling of the ruling class (though it is not sure that after the death of the auspiciously reigning king it will be the young protagonists' turn to be the embodiment of that class). Economic activities and slave labor are excluded from this picture. Outcasts, so tenaciously present in other societies, have no place here. A policy of fusion in a multi-racial society is pursued thanks to the king's enlightened generosity (in return for the picturesque presents he has received from the neighboring populations, Hydaspes gives them tax exemptions). The embarrassing action of a council and a priestly guild does not relieve him from the obligation to consult the people's will, though this, in turn, is often influenced by irrational impulses and is therefore blind and contradictory. In spite of the king's readiness to grant his subjects' requests, Ethiopia remains a monarchical and centralized state. And yet the masses' intervention prevents it from becoming a crudely theocratic country. The suspicion cannot be eliminated that, in this vision, or rather invention, of an ennobled state and society, ideology may have prevailed over the needs of the narrative. To what extent an historical reality in which absolute, imperialistic, and violent monarchies were paramount, may have contributed, by contrast, to the portrayal of an ideal state, is not possible to ascertain.

11. MODERN CRITICAL THEORIES AND THE ANCIENT NOVEL

Massimo Fusillo

I. *The Novel: An Open Genre*

In the history of Western literature the polarity between tragedy and novel seems to be a basic one: as much as the first is a closed form, old, noble, sublime and rigidly coded, so the second is an open one, (relatively) new and low, without strong rules. Maybe it is not by chance that the novel flourishes especially in the ages when tragedy is declining or has already declined. These statements should not be interpreted as an abstract truth, transcending the infinite variations of historical contexts; it is just a way to introduce an important datum for our perspective: that the novel became a very late object of theory just because of its fluidity. The ancient works of aesthetics do not even mention the novel, although there is a strong relationship between this genre and rhetoric (its "inventor" must have read Aristotle's *Poetics*).[1] Even in modern times a true theory of the novel began very late, not before the baroque period (the Renaissance treatises only discussed where they should put the romances of chivalry in their Aristotelian system):[2] the *Traité sur l'origine des romans* (1670) by Daniel Huet was a first interesting experiment, but a century later the Gothic novelist Clara Reeve with her *The Progress of Romance* (1785) is still in search of legitimacy. In both cases—ancient rhetoric and modern theory before the Romantic Revival—the ground for such an evaluation seems to be the same: the novel is considered pure entertainment, low literature.

At the end of the eighteenth century this situation changes completely: the novel acquires slowly the hegemonic position it still holds today, becoming the genre par excellence of the middle class society that grew up with the Industrial Revolution. Consequently the aesthetic of the nineteenth century gave to it a new universal role: we can

---

[1] Cf. in general Barwick (1928); on Aristotle Cicu (1982).
[2] See the material quoted and discussed by Biagini (1983), and by Meneghetti (1988) 6–10.

mention only Hegel's great work, with his famous definition of the novel as a bourgeois epic.[3] It is a historicist theory, limited therefore to the modern "realistic" novel, and does not extend to the romance or to ancient fiction; nevertheless it could be illustrative to put in parallel this vision of the genre with the late birth of the Greek novel in the Hellenistic period, in a historical context with some features of a middle-class society.

Among Hegel's followers the young Lukács turns out to be particularly stimulating: his *Theory of the Novel* sketches the successful idea of this genre as an "open form".[4] Open from the stylistic point of view, because the absence of rigid norms allows the oscillation among the most various expressive levels; and open from the thematic one, because the novel tends to express the totality of the world, while tragedy tends to an essential selection.

This idea of "open form" can be related to a more recent critical perspective, very widespread now, intertextuality, that is, the dialogue between texts and cultures. It is a perspective involving of course every kind of literature, and the openness of the novel strengthens the attitude to rewrite literary patterns. This general statement is particularly true for ancient fiction: the Greek novel looks like an encyclopaedia of all literary genres, relived at a more private and sentimental level. Actually the five erotic novelists have a very ambivalent attitude towards literary tradition: they use it to ennoble a freshly born genre, and at the same time they lower it to their everyday-life and bourgeois level. That happens in particular for epics (especially the *Odyssey*), tragedy (especially Euripides), historiography, rhetoric, while more recent genres, like epistolography or paradoxography, and humbler genres, like the fable or novella, are reused just to enrich the spectrum of literary voices: to give the sense of totality.[5] The intertextuality of the Roman novel is more refined: the *Satyricon* plays with the very concept of genre, deluding every expectation of its reader and creating thus a unique work of art.[6] Among the multiple literary patterns distorted by Petronius' incredibly expressive

---

[3] Hegel (1836–1838) part III.
[4] Lukács (1920) 110–132; one can read similar definitions already in Reeve (1785); Wolff (1841) 8; and later in Koskimies (1935) 111–115; Kristeva (1970) 15–19; Robert (1972) part I.
[5] See Manso (1802) 202–206; Fusillo (1989) chap. 1; on the particular reutilization of historiographic patterns see Müller (1976); Scarcella (1981).
[6] Zeitlin (1971).

violence there is also the Greek novel in its more popular and sentimental phase (represented for us by Chariton and by papyrological fragments): it offers the narrative structure of a travelling couple. In its more literary phase, the Sophistic one, even the Greek novel reaches a complex internal intertextuality not too far from that of Petronius: Achilles Tatius' *Leucippe and Clitophon* is an ironical and metaliterary pastiche of the erotic novel, playing with its conventions in a quite ambivalent way;[7] a play which, however, does not have the disruptive character of the *Satyricon*: Achilles Tatius always remains within the schemes Petronius always breaks.

The term "intertextuality" was coined in 1970 by Julia Kristeva, and applied not by chance to a medieval romance.[8] But a very similar perspective had been articulated in 1929 by the most prominent theorist of the novel in this century, Michael Bakhtin, although his works did not circulate in Western countries before the late seventies. According to Bakhtin the novel is a unique genre: the only one in progress, relativistic, dialogical, polyphonic.[9] Actually these features cannot be reserved only for the novel; moreover it is more and more difficult to consider it a unitarian genre because of the large number of subtypes (the concept itself of genre is one of the most controversial).[10] On one hand Bakhtin includes in his model a lot of non-novelistic texts; on the other he defines "monological" many important novels, such as those by Tolstoy. To express better his nuanced position: the dialogical character of literature—the confrontation of different languages and voices without dominant perspective—can be realized at best by the open form of the novel.

Bakhtin's approach is mostly anthropological: from Aristophanes to Dostoevskij he seeks to find a culture of the low, of the grotesque, of hierarchic subversion: in a word, a carnevalesque culture. One can surely object that he privileges thematic constants and neglects historic variations; but one cannot deny the infinite suggestions this new vision gives to the understanding of Western literature. Among

---

[7] Cf. Durham (1938), although papyri undermined his theory of this novel as parody of Heliodorus; Calderini (1913) 85; Reardon (1971) 362; Heiserman (1977) 117–129; Anderson (1982) 27–28; Fusillo (1989) 98–109.

[8] Kristeva (1970) 139–146.

[9] Bakhtin (1975) (all the essays were written in the thirties and forties); see also the reading of his works in terms of intertextuality by Todorov (1981) 8–23 and 77–90.

[10] Cf. in general Scheffer (1986); Fowler (1982) on the subgenres of the novel; a large vision of the novelistic genre in antiquity is proposed by Kuch (1989b).

those suggestions we must include the ancient novel, to which Bakhtin gave special prominence. While his vision of the Greek novel is too schematic and static, according to popular opinion, his Menippean interpretation of Petronius and Apuleius is still very stimulating,[11] especially if we understand "Menippean" not as a definite genre (whose features would be very difficult to single out), but, more metaphorically, as a cultural constant, based on comic degradation, free structure, grotesque corporality.

II. *The Narratology of the Histoire*

The theory of literature as an autonomous field of research had an incredible development in the sixties, when structuralism and semiotics dominated human sciences. It is remarkable that at the beginning of this modern movement we find the same lack of interest for narrative we found in ancient rhetoric: neorhetoric was first and foremost a rhetoric of poetic figures, of single tropes; the study of the transphrastic level and narrative figures began later, mostly under the influence of Benveniste's linguistics.[12] More precisely the special number of the French review *Communications* in 1966 marks by convention the birth of a specific science of narration, so-called narratology.

Russian formalists were the first to distinguish between the *sjužet*, the narrated story, and the *fabula*, the narrative discourse, the plot, although a similar opposition can be traced already in Aristotle's *Poetics* and in Renaissance treatises.[13] This distinction was resumed in the semiotics of narration following the famous Saussarian dichotomy between signifier and signified, and can be used to recognize two essential branches of narratology: a first one describing narrative content and defining its functions; a second one analyzing narrative structure, its figures and its expressive technique. Although some authors made contributions in both branches, the difference between the branches is drastic.

The narratology of "histoire" is represented essentially by the works

---

[11] Cf. especially Bakhtin (1975) 3.1–2; on Menippean tradition see the collection by Kirk (1980); see also the Petronian readings by Courtney (1962) and Adamietz (1987).
[12] See the collection of his most important essays published in 1966.
[13] See Tomaševskij (1928); Todorov (1966); Genette (1972); a fourfold division is proposed by Segre (1974) 3–5; on Aristotle see Ricoeur (1983) 65–71, 101–109; Fusillo (1986).

of Greimas and by the *Logique du récit* of Bremond, who brought this method to its ultimate consequences; but it has a very influential precedent in the *Morphology of the Folktale* by Vladimir Propp (1928), a rigorous research on a definite corpus of Russian fables, which should not be extended, in the author's opinion, to every kind of literature. Actually this approach seems to be much more productive in the fields of mythology, folklore and anthropology, than for literary texts, because it reduces the narrative to abstract schemes; textual dynamics are in fact excluded: the basis of research is generally the summary of the narrative content, not the complex semantic strategy.

Applying this method to the erotic novel we might recognize some narrative constants, like, for example, the function of the opponent which is always performed by the rivals, who try to seduce a member of the leading couple; but we will not catch the various nuances differentiating single texts and single episodes: the uniformity of plots often criticized in the Greek novel is in fact less consistent than one might expect. A very organic study by Consuelo Ruiz-Montero (1982) tried this approach, which resulted in a valuable analysis of variations and in an equally valuable attention to semantic implications; but my impression of unproductivity here remains in the end unaltered. This kind of approach would be totally unproductive for Petronius' complex narrative strategy, which confuses every hermeneutic path, or for the rich ambiguity of Apuleius' novel.

III. *The Narratology of the Récit*

If Propp is the antecedent of the narratology of the "histoire", that of the second branch is the Anglosaxon theory of the novel: Henry James' *Prefaces* and E.M. Forster's *Aspects of the Novel*. The most representative work of this critical method is certainly Gérard Genette's *Figure III* (1972), which outlines a complete theory of narrative discourse following the path of grammarian categories: time, mode, voice. Time is the essential dimension of narrative, as space is that of drama: that is the reason why it can be divided into some subcategories (succession, duration, frequency) and studied from different perspectives.

Generally speaking the temporal structure of the Greek novel is rather linear: a progression starting with the main couple falling in love and ending with their reunification after a series of parallel adventures; they actually form the largest portion of narration, representing no development of idealized love at first sight.[14] This pattern, implying a linear narration of a circular story, is submitted to many interesting variations. The first "popular" phase of the genre—Chariton and Xenophon of Ephesus—follows it in a rather rigid way: the discrepancy between the time of the narrated story and the time of the narration is quite strong, while the parallel plots of the separated couple play the leading role. This is particularly true for the second novelist: the *Ephesiaca* shows an incredible alternation of simultaneous actions, narrated with a frantic rhythm,[15] like a silent movie (a feature which might, however, depend on the epitomization of the text, but this is a controversial matter).[16] Though the same basic structure, Chariton's narration is more wide-ranging, especially if we refer to the temporal level of duration and to the large use of scene and direct speech; Xenophon uses almost exclusively very synthetic summaries (a dialectic somehow similar to the Jamesian opposition "showing/telling").[17]

On the other hand the novels of the sophistic phase show more nuances; Achilles Tatius greatly reduces adventures and separation, and generally the extension of the story: a narrative choice in accordance with his thematic peculiarities, that is with his reduced exaltation of the leading couple and with his ironic pastiche of the erotic novel. In Longus' novel we find not a simple reduction, but a drastic elimination of adventures: they become just allusions in miniature to a literary convention. Thanks to the contamination between the erotic novel and pastoral poetry the spatial movement in *Daphnis and Chloe* is replaced by an inner evolution of the couple: by the discovery of sexuality.

These two variations to the temporal pattern of the erotic novel do not affect its basic linearity: we find no big deviations forwards (prolepsis) or backwards (analepsis) from the primary time of narration. Thanks to the innovative choice of a first person narrator, some

---

[14] Cf. Bakhtin (1975) 236–250 on "adventurous chronotope".

[15] See Hägg (1971a) 171–177: the most organic study on time in the Greek novel (excluding Longus and Heliodorus), inspired more by Anglosaxon methods.

[16] First proposed by Bürger (1892), this thesis was largely discussed and refuted by Hägg (1966).

[17] For Jamesian concepts see Lubbock (1935) 93–119 and 188–189; Wellek-Warren (1942) 301; Friedman (1955) 108–117; on scene/summary Genette (1972) chap. 2. A narratological reading of Xenophon's novel is offered by Scarcella (1979); see also Schmeling (1980) chap. 4.

parts of Achilles Tatius' plot (especially Leucippe's second apparent death in 5.7.4) are left indeed in mystery with a narrative ellipsis, and cleared up only at the end of the novel by an analepsis (8.16); but this is not yet a structural change. Heliodorus is the first and the only one to break completely with this convention, using a narrative device directly inspired by the *Odyssey*, the beginning *in medias res*. The *Aithiopika* does not begin with a clear presentation of the leading couple, their native city, their family, their age and physical aspect, as the other Greek novels do, but with a mysterious scene of abduction which will be completely clarified only at the middle of the novel (5.33), where a long analepsis tells all the first part of the story. Although the narrative time is no longer linear, the narrated story is no longer circular: the leading couple does not go back to the starting point at the end of the novel, but finds on the contrary a new fatherland: the utopian Aethiopia.[18] And this outcome is often foreshadowed by a series of vague prolepses which gives a strong closure to the novel: *Aethiopica* is in fact a dense and stratified architecture.

In presemiotic narratology mode and voice were often confused, mistaking for example first person narration for restricted point of view. On the contrary, as Genette points out, "Who sees?" and "Who tells?" must be always distinguished.[19] The first level concerns the point of view from which the reader perceives the action, or, in specular terms, which focalization the narrator uses towards its characters (to these problems Henry James devoted all his theoretical activity);[20] the second level regards only the figure of the narrator and its various forms. Nevertheless the two categories can be interrelated to sketch the "narrative situation" of the novel: a very productive critical concept.[21]

The novels by Chariton and Xenophon of Ephesus belong to the same narrative situation: an external narrator, basically using a zero focalization, that is superior to its characters, without subjective identifications. Even in this case there are interesting variations: Xeno-

---

[18] See Szepessy (1957).
[19] Genette (1972) 203-206.
[20] In general on the kinds of focalization see Pouillon (1946); Todorov (1966) 254-256; Uspensky (1970); Genette (1972) 205-211; Lanser (1981); Danon-Boileau (1982) chap. 1; Segre (1984) chap. 6; Pugliatti (1985) chaps. 2-3.
[21] The concept goes back to Stanzel (1955 and 1979), who confuses however mode and voice to build a Hegelian triad; see Genette (1972) 251-259 and (1983) 77-89, where he adds the focalization axis; and the book by Lintvelt (1981). An application to the Greek novel in Fusillo (1988b).

phon's narrator is absolutely impersonal and objective, while that of Chariton intervenes often with ideological or metaliterary commentaries (an "intrusive" narrator),[22] and adopts sometimes (even if just for short-cuts) the point of view of its characters, especially that of the heroine.[23] One technical difference which has, however, semantic consequences: the model of the world expressed by Xenophon is quite pragmatic, totally oppressed by Fortune, while that laid out by Chariton gives more space to psychological dynamics.

This is also the narrative situation on which Longus' novel is based; its innovations are in fact not technical, but expressive: the narrator makes few explicit comments, but in all its narration we perceive a subtle kind of irony towards the two young herders; the bucolic novel discloses thus a voyeuristic and urban nature.[24]

Achilles Tatius' narrative situation is completely different from those above: an internal narrator ("homodiegetic"), using basically a zero focalization—that is the I-author superimposing on the I-actor its a posteriori information[25]—but with long and consistent exceptions: passages where the reader perceives events with the same limited knowledge that the narrator-character, Clitophon, had at the moment of the experience. The immediate function of these exceptions is obviously to create suspense: for example the narration of Leucippe's first apparent death, a long grandguignolesque human sacrifice which later turns out to be a theatrical fiction (3.15).[26] At a deeper level the choice of such a new narrative structure has multiple meanings: it gives to the work a more everyday-life character; it breaks the parallelism between the leading couple, and consequently lowers their idealization, giving to the heroine an elusive nature; it eliminates the Olympian character of the narration especially typical of Xenophon's

---

[22] On the various kinds of omniscient narrator see Delasanta (1967) 23–26; Sternberg (1978) 256–260; on authorial interventions by Chariton see Hägg (1971a) 95–96.

[23] See Segre (1984) 100 and Pugliatti (1985) 11–12 in general on the impossibility of a pure zero focalization; on Chariton's exceptions see Hägg (1971a) 114–119; Reardon (1982) 16–19; Auger (1983); Stark (1984) 260.

[24] See the reading by Effe (1982); see also Rohde (1937); Scarcella (1968b); Mittelstadt (1970); Longo (1978); and especially Saïd (1987).

[25] See Genette (1972) 251–261; Stanzel (1979) 109–148, on the dialectic between the two I; in general on first person novel (a feature whose importance was too stressed by presemiotic narratology) see Booth (1961) 150–151; Romberg (1962); Rousset (1973).

[26] Cf. Hägg (1971a) 133; Effe (1975) 150–151.

novel in favour of a relativistic one.[27] All these operations make *Leucippe and Clitophon* closer to the comic tradition, and cooperate in its ironical pastiche.

Heliodorus' novel is the most complex in the ancient Greek corpus: it has an external narrator, like the other erotic novels except that of Achilles Tatius, but with a variable focalization and with large sections delegated to I-narrators like Clitophon. Here the semantic function is even clearer: as John Winkler pointed out, the *Aithiopika* is dominated by the idea of progressive decipherment of the divine in an enigmatic world; a Neoplatonic idea imbuing forms, themes, and reader's responses.[28] That is the reason why we find chiefly in the first half of the novel the internal focalization creating a sense of mystery: characters and readers must gradually interpret a series of clues.

In ancient narrative Heliodorus is the author who best exploits this technique of internal focalization with a pregnant semantic function: a technique systematically used and theorized first at the end of last century, notably by Henry James. To show this peculiarity we can quote the *Aethiopika*'s fascinating and cinematographic incipit, which became very famous and canonical in the baroque period (Philip Sydney exalted it in his *Defense of Poetry*, and imitated it in the *Arcadia*):[29]

> The smile of daybreak was just beginning to brighten the sky, the sunlight to catch the hilltops, when a group of men in brigand gear peered over the mountain that overlooks the place where the Nile flows into the sea at the mouth that men call the Heracleotic. They stood there for a moment, scanning the expanse of sea beneath them: first they gazed out over the ocean, but as there was nothing sailing there that held out hope of spoil and plunder, their eyes were drawn to the beach nearby. This is what they saw: a merchant ship was riding there, moored by her stern, empty of crew but laden with freight. This much could be surmised even from a distance, for the weight of her cargo forced the water up to the third line of boards on the ship's side. But the beach!—a mass of new slain bodies, some of them quite dead, others half-alive and still twitching, testimony that the fighting had only just

---

[27] See Fusillo (1989) 158–170; Maeder (1991); see also Schmeling (1981).

[28] Winkler (1982); on Heliodorus' Neoplatonism see Szepessy (1976), defending so the date to the third century.

[29] See Bühler (1976) on its visual qualities; on suspense and focalization Keyes (1922) 50; Helm (1956) 40; Hefti (1950) 7–9; Winkler (1982) 95–101; on its Byzantine and modern reception see Delasanta (1967) 62; Gärtner (1969); Molinié (1982) 57–65.

ended. To judge by the signs this had been no proper battle. Amongst the carnage were the miserable remnants of festivities that had to come to this unhappy end. There were tables still set of food, and others upset on the ground, held in dead men's hands; in the fray they had served some as weapons, for this had been an impromptu conflict; beneath other tables men had crawled in the vain hope of hiding there. There were wine bowls upturned, and some slipping from the hands that held them; some had been drinking from them, other using them like stones, for the suddenness of the catastrophe had caused objects to be put to strange, new uses and taught men to use drinking vessels as missiles. There they lay, here a man felled by an axe, there another struck down by a stone picked up then and there from the shingly beach; here a man battered to death with a club, there another burned to death with a brand from the fire. Various were the forms of their deaths, but most were the victims of arrows and archery. In that small space the deity had contrived an infinitely varied spectacle, defiling wine with blood and unleashing war at the party, combining winning and dying, pouring of drink and spilling of blood, and staging this show for the Egyptian bandits.

They stood on the mountainside like the audience in a theater, unable to comprehend the scene: the vanquished were there, but the victors were nowhere to be seen; the victory was unequivocal, but the spoils had not been taken, and the ship lay there by herself, crewless but otherwise intact, riding peacefully at anchor as if protected by a great force of men. But although they were at a loss to know what it all meant, they still had an eye for plunder and a quick profit. So they cast themselves in the role of victors and set off down the hillside (trans. Morgan).

The Roman novel falls within the same typology we saw in Achilles Tatius, but with a stronger presence of internal focalization—actually it becomes the dominant level—and with more refined semantic games. Though its condition is fragmentary, Petronius' *Satyricon* shows a very complex dialectic among author, I-narrator and I-character: in every part of the work we perceive the destructive irony of the first and the constant tension between the second and the third, that is the various attempts of Encolpius to interpret his experience as the main actor of adventures.[30] A very recent interpretation by

---

[30] See Veyne (1964); Beck (1973) and (1982a); Jones (1987); however the irony of the I-narrator against the I-character is very difficult to recognize; some quite clear examples are: 41.5; 49.7; 65.4–5; 69.9; 72.7; 83.7; 100.2; 127.5; 128.5; 133.1; 135.1; 136.12.

Gian Biagio Conte tries to fix this dialectic in a systematic way: Encolpius reads every event in terms of sublime literature (especially the epic and tragedy), while the author always puts him in melodramatic situations inspired by the Greek novel and by popular literature; a contrast having a very original effect.[31]

The relationship between I-narrator and I-character distinguishes the *Golden Ass* by Apuleius: *Auctor and Actor* is not by chance the title of Winkler's narratological reading of this novel (1985). Until the last book of the novel the reader lives a series of grotesque adventures without any kind of proleptic hint of the final mystical initiation to Isis: they are in fact all narrated with a strict internal focalization on the I-actor. The ending (notably added to the Greek *Ass* novel) would give a retroactive pattern to the previous narration,[32] imposing an allegorical reading: from the condition of the lowest beast to the highest role of an Isiac priest. Nevertheless a strong and fascinating ambiguity remains unsolved: an ambiguity between mystical closure and picaresque plot, *docere* and *delectare*, edifying moral and polyphonic dialogue.[33]

Among the problems of narrative voice a central role was recently played by the tale-within-the-tale technique, and by the consequent representation of the narratee.[34] Both in the Roman and Greek novels we read a lot of lateral stories, narrated by various characters; we find also a characterization of the internal audience, usually stressing its curiosity, its emotionalism, its sentimental involvement: all reactions the authors wanted to produce in their external audience, in their public. Even in this case Heliodorus is the only one to use this mechanism in a structural way: the relationship between the narrator Calasiris and the narratee Cnemon, involving the basic plot of the novel, is a complex semantic performance, where Cnemon represents the ingenuous sentimental reader (a partial, not false reading),

---

[31] Conte (1996).
[32] On this closural device in fiction see Smith (1968) 117–121.
[33] See Heine (1978): the allegorical ending might have been conceived during the composition of picaresque chaos; on *delectare/docere* and on sociological implications of the ass condition see Gianotti (1986) chap. 1 and 4.
[34] The concept was first introduced by Genette (1972) 265–267; see also Prince (1973) and (1982) 1.2, with a wider meaning, distinguishing between external narratee and virtual reader; against this distinction see Genette (1983) 90–93.

while Calasiris tries to raise his aesthetic response to a deeper philosophical interpretation.[35]

IV. *The Reader-Response Criticism*

Aesthetic response and implied readership became the leading themes of criticism twenty years ago, often in polemic opposition to the immanent approach of semiotic theories and American New Critics. The literary text is no longer a closed unity to describe and to decipher, but a dynamic horizon to be viewed by every public in accordance with its cultural codes. This approach has a rich linguistic background (especially the speech-act theory and pragmatics) and no unitarian physiognomy; as Susan Suleiman synthesizes: "Audience-oriented criticism is not one field but many, not a single widely trodden path but a multiplicity of crisscrossing, often divergent tracks that cover a vast area of the critical landscape in a pattern whose complexity dismays the brave and confounds the faint of heart".[36] After this discouraging statement she recognizes, however, a series of basic trends: semiotic-structuralist, phenomenological, sociological, hermeneutical; they often intersect, sometimes are incompatible, but certainly have changed completely our way of understanding literature and fiction.

For every audience-oriented perspective applied to the Greek novel it is important to stress the distinction between the first "popular" phase and the more refined sophistic second phase. From a few external traces (rather a large amount of papyri, judgements of other writers)[37] and from the internal evidence, we can infer that Chariton's and Xenophon's novels would represent for us something similar to so-called *Trivialliteratur*: the entertaining literature that is now a preferential object of criticism.[38] The repetition of topoi and conventions,

---

[35] See Winkler (1982) 139–147, stressing too much Cnemon's negativity; Fusillo (1989) 174–177; a different interpretation of Cnemon incarnating the aesthetic response Heliodorus aims at is held by Morgan (1991); see also Futre Pinheiro (1991a); and in general on the theoretical implication of Heliodorean metadiegetic narrations Molinié (1992).

[36] Suleiman (1980) 6; the entire book edited by her and I. Crosman is a very valuable view of the various trends in this field.

[37] The three most important passages are a short letter by Philostratus (66), a verse by Persius (1.134), both about Chariton but not quite certain; and a letter by the Emperor Julian (89b, 301b); see Reardon (1991) chap. 1.

[38] A recent theoretical reflexion in Couégnas (1992).

the schematic psychological characterization, the snobbish setting in the high society, the preponderance of sentimental themes, the use of recapitulations to help the reader, the consolatory happy end, are all typical features of nineteenth century *feuilletons* and current TV serials we already find in this ancient fiction, although we cannot forget the different cultural systems.[39]

This (para) literature has usually a kind of reception which tends to cancel every boundary between art and life: referential illusion and identification with heroes are indeed quite emphasized. Karlheinz Stierle defined it "quasi pragmatic reception", because the illocutionary character is almost the same as in everyday life communication.[40] In Heliodorus' novel we find a clear representation of this reader-response in the narratee Cnemon: especially when he really believes he sees Theagenes and Chariclea thanks to the vivid and effective description made by Calasiris.

At the beginning of the last book of *Chaireas and Callirhoe* we read an incredibly valuable passage for this perspective: the only passage of a Greek novel directly addressed to the reader:

> And I think that this last chapter will prove very agreeable to its readers: it cleanses away the grim events of the earlier ones. There will be no more pirates or slavery or lawsuits or fighting or suicide or wars or conquests; now there will be lawful love and sanctioned marriage. So I shall tell you how the goddess brought the truth to light and revealed the unrecognized pair to each other (trans. Reardon) (8.1.4).

With sharp metaliterary conscience and explicit Aristotelian terminology (καθάρσιον)[41] this passage evokes a strong solidarity between the author and its implied readership, which expects a long series of melodramatic events, grouped in fixed topoi, and a final triumph of love and marriage. The same solidarity is represented at the end of the novel, when the protagonist Chaireas tells the entire plot in front of the Syracusan assembly (exceptionally it also includes women) that listens with incredible passion and asks for linearity and totality: a narratee probably reflecting, with the effect of "mise en abyme",[42] the external audience and its collective aural fruition.

The novels of the Sophistic phase have a quite different character,

---

[39] See Scobie (1969); Reardon (1971); García Gual (1972); Heiserman (1977); Anderson (1982); Holzberg (1986) 7-8; Fusillo (1994) §1.
[40] Stierle (1980); see also Mendel (1970).
[41] See Cicu (1982); Rijksbaron (1984).
[42] On this concept due to André Gide see the book by Dällenbach (1978).

more complex and literary: therefore their relationship with the audience seems to be no longer one of solidarity, but on the contrary of dialectic conflict. In fact they play with conventions, delude expectations, establish a confrontational relationship with their reader, called to construct its interpretation. This is certainly true for Longus' *Daphnis and Chloe*, where the contamination between pastoral poetry and the erotic novel needs a sophisticated reading in order to catch the deep dialectic between nature and culture and the ironic ambivalence towards the ingenuity of the characters. Achilles Tatius' attitude towards generic norms and the reader's horizon is really contradictory, oscillating between participation and irony: his reader should have the kind of "ironical identification" defined by Jauss.[43] Heliodorus' implied reader must really be an ideal reader, who has to cooperate at every moment to build a Neoplatonic architecture, making continuously "inferential walks" (Eco)[44] without clear paths, even for the happy end.[45]

According to Hans Robert Jauss the shorter the distance is from the horizon of expectations, the closer the literature comes to "culinary" reading;[46] with this evaluative point of view we can distinguish between the pure entertainment of the first Greek novelists (Xenophon more than Chariton), and the different complexity of the last three, not by chance much admired and imitated especially in the baroque age.

Choosing ekphrasis as a very important issue in imperial culture, Shadi Bartsch (1989)—in a very good application of reader-response criticism (especially Jauss and Iser) to the ancient novel—showed how much Achilles Tatius' and Heliodorus' novels are imbued with the theme of reading and interpreting: descriptions of paintings, dreams, oracles, oracular dreams, ethnographic digressions, spectacles give to the reader false clues, ambiguous signs, hermeneutic puzzles; the result is very far from the "unconscious reception" presupposed by Chariton and Xenophon: it is rather a semantic game that rewrites and ennobles a popular genre.

---

[43] See Jauss (1982) II 10.5.
[44] Eco (1979), chap. 7.
[45] See Morgan (1989b), especially the "conclusions and closures" (318–320) about the "scrupulous unpredictability" of this novel, with a method inspired by Barthes' notion of "proairetic code": (1970), chap. XI.
[46] Jauss (1970) 15.

This kind of complex response is required even more by Petronius and Apuleius; as we have already hinted, the *Golden Ass*' most striking peculiarity is the contrast between the picaresque level, which is dominant in the first reading, and the mystical level, which applies in the last book and would inform every later reading, nevertheless leaving a great deal of ambiguity. Generally speaking, a first and second reading must be always considered, in my opinion, as two different approaches simultaneously present in each interpretative act: an ingenuous one, following the cognitive paths of the text even if the outcome is already well-known; and a conscious one, a kind of "metareading" analyzing the construction of meaning. In the prologue Apuleius makes a clear pact with his reader: he declares his choice of obscene Milesian novellas, of Ovidian baroque surprise, of stylistic freedom, promising a pure entertainment: *lector, laetaberis*! The two other addresses to the reader imply a different response: in 9.30 he prevents the objection of a *lector scrupulosus* about the narrative information of the ass, pointing to a public aware of focalization problems. At the beginning of the rewriting of the Phaedra story, he warns the *lector optime* (10.2) that he is going to read a tragedy, not a comedy, showing the wide range of his intertextuality (a tragedy however comically rewritten with a happy ending).[47] And in fact the implied reader of Apuleius' novel must always catch the oscillation of expressive registers: a voyage from low and grotesque novella to Psyche's symbolic fable up to the Isiac mystery.

The delusion of generic expectations seems to be the essential peculiarity of Petronius' *Satyricon*, escaping in fact every classification into fixed patterns. As Froma Zeitlin affirms, its audience was "accustomed, far more than we, to an organizing literary form": its "incongruous, unexpected juxtaposition or fusion of genres" must have therefore been really shocking.[48] Of course this impression might derive also from the fragmentary condition of the text we read, which inhibits a structural inquiry. But we have enough to judge how baffling this reading was and still is. Incongruity is indeed a Petronian basic device: the reader receives multiple textual signs, always transferred in a different context, parodically distorted, contaminated with dissonant material. The confusion is at the same time related to emotive identification: if the Greek novel has a clear distinction between "bad"

---

[47] See Scarcella (1985a).
[48] Zeitlin (1971) 635.

and "good" characters—although not that rigid, as we shall see soon—Petronius' world does not have any clear axiology. There is certainly a sharp criticism of Encolpius' scholastic culture, of Eumolpus' false poetry, of Giton's fatuity, but their ductility and their ability to face the polyphony of the real awakens a kind of contradictory empathy. A very good example could be Lichas' death (115): he is certainly a negative figure, a classical opponent of the main characters, but when he dies, the Petronian text assumes unexpected tragic tones, and makes even his enemy Encolpius pronounce a pastiche of rhetorical declamations and consolations, completely incongruous with the narrative context, and therefore absolutely paradoxical and comical.[49]

A more extreme part of audience-oriented criticism denies any common textual basis of the reading process: every public would retransform literary texts according to its culture and its tradition; or, coming down to a singular reception, every reader would recreate the text according to her/his primary fantasies and private stories. The consequence of this theoretical view is to forsake any form of literary analysis, choosing instead a sociology of collective kinds of public or a psychology of individual readings. The latter is the position held by Norman Holland, who investigated first the interaction between textual processes and the reader's subjectivities, and came later to the negative conclusions that this interaction does not exist, and that only the reader's responses do.[50]

Apart from theoretical discussions, the basic problem for the ancient novel is our poor information about authors, the public and book circulation, i.e. about the first presupposition of any sociological research. If we think of the rather large amount of papyri,[51] and of the fluid textual transmission of some novels (especially the *Historia Apollonii Regis Tyrii*, or, among the non-erotic novels, the *Romance of Alexander*, the *Aesop Romance*), we can deduce a free circulation of narrative motifs, which had to correspond to a large demand of an increasing reading public—maybe, for the erotic novel, mostly feminine. A public which could even influence the reworking of narrative material, or for which one could make epitomes of more complex

---

[49] See Labate (1988).
[50] Holland (1968) and (1975); very close to the second book is the position held by David Bleich (1975).
[51] On papyrological evidence as support for research about different kinds of public cf. Cavallo (1986); on some important papyri a very important recent contribution is Kussl (1991).

novels, like that of Achilles Tatius, as a famous papyrus proves.[52]

Creative rewriting is a special kind of reception showing in a pregnant way the transformation of a text in the course of time. In such an intertextual perspective one can recover the classical comparative method, getting over the restriction of source problems and coming to a dialogue of cultures. The reception of the Greek novel has a striking complexity, with various shifts in evaluation, classification of genre, activation of meaning: from the allegorical reading of the Byzantines, who interpreted adventures like religious proofs and exalted the chastity ideal, to the epic interpretation of the baroque age, when Heliodorus was juxtaposed to Homer and Virgil, and when ancient fiction was a model of scenographic descriptions, theatrical emotions and erotic passions; from the depreciation of last century, when these novels were considered typical products of a decadent age, to the actual new interest in terms of *Trivialliteratur*.[53]

V. *The Thematic Structure: A Psychoanalytical Approach*

Psychoanalytic criticism has almost always neglected the textual dimension of literature, focusing either on the author's psychic story, or on fictive characters taken as living subjects, or finally on the reader's unconscious mechanisms. The first two approaches dominated for a very long time and fall within so-called wild psychoanalysis, while the third is a part of the reader-response criticism, although the book by Simon Lesser *Fiction and the Unconscious* (1957) was already oriented in this direction (and even some of Freud's literary analyses, for example that of *Oedipus Rex*). This lack of interest in literary forms and dynamics is one of the reasons why psychoanalysis and literature is still a very thorny relationship. "One resists labelling as a 'psychoanalytic critic' because the kind of criticism evoked by the term mostly deserves the bad name it has largely made by itself": so writes one of the best critics in this field, Peter Brooks.[54] Nevertheless, especially if psychoanalysis ceases to be imperialistic towards literature, and to use it as a confirmation of its theories, it

---

[52] See Russo (1955).
[53] On the baroque age see Oeftering (1901); Wolff (1912); Gesner (1970); Molinié (1982); in general see Loicq-Berger (1980); Hägg (1983) 193–213; and the contribution by Sandy in this volume.
[54] Brooks (1986) 1; recently a Lacanian theory of fiction is held by Gunn (1988).

can be a very fruitful perspective not only because of the simple statement that literature has much to do with unconscious logic, but also because it offers the right way to see the interaction between thematic structure and form of expression: to go "beyond formalism", as the famous title by Geoffrey Hartman (1970) puts it. A way suggested for example by Francesco Orlando in a series of theoretical and critical essays, which sees literature as "return of the repressed" and sketches consequently a "Freudian rhetoric".[55]

Love and adventure are the two basic themes of the Greek novel, narrated with rigorous parallelism: the two young people are both extraordinarily beautiful (beauty is the only real divine trace in a secular world),[56] of the highest social rank,[57] of the same age (the mythicized adolescence), and both live the same peripetiai in the phase of separation till the final triumph. To understand this view of eros we can refer to a Chilian psychoanalyst, Ignacio Matte Blanco;[58] according to his mathematical rewriting of Freud, the so-called unconscious follows in fact a specific logic, a non-Aristotelian one, which does not know the non-contradiction principle and the separation between individuum and class. This symmetric logic tends to see the world in terms of an indistinct and homogeneous totality (corresponding to the original symbiosis with maternal body); it can be read only by conscious asymmetrical logic, and looms out especially in emotive experience, in its purest form in the strongest emotion, obviously love. These concepts can explain some universal constants of the erotic (and mystical) language we find also in the Greek novel, like desire of fusion, indifference to space and time (for example the sensation of a previous acquaintance), idealization of the love object, monomaniac concentration. Perhaps the best exemplification of this unconscious dynamic is the myth told by Aristophanes in Plato's *Symposium*: human beings were previously androgynous, female or male spheres; after the traumatic cut decided by Zeus each of them tries to regain the other half: a myth that so justifies every kind of eros and sexuality as longing for a lost unity.

The obsessive parallelism giving shape to the Greek novel[59] can be

---

[55] Orlando (1973) (1979) (1982).
[56] See Miralles (1968); Diaz (1984).
[57] See Baslez (1990).
[58] Matte Blanco (1975).
[59] In general on parallelism as narrative figure see Todorov (1967) 70–73; on its use in the Greek erotic novel see Marcovaldi (1969) 57–58 and 69–74; Ruiz-Montero

read as a narrative concretization of this trend to symmetry peculiar to unconscious logic and particularly to erotic emotion. In fact each component of the main couples is absolutely specular to the other: a feature sounding like a typical wish-fulfillment of an entertaining literature and of its sentimental reader; as Gérard Mendel states, paraliterature is a direct expression of desire.[60] Anyway this issue can be only a first step, that does not accomplish the interpretation of this genre.

To find a connexion between a psychic process and a literary text is a very common device in psychoanalytical criticism, especially regarding fictional texts because of their closeness to primary fantasies and daydreams; we can remember the Freudian concept of "family romance", developed by Marthe Robert in *Roman des origine et origines du roman* (1972), or the previously quoted book by Simon Lesser. But if we carefully choose a perspective of textual dynamics and literary formalization this can be just a starting point to sound out the various expressive solutions. These variations in the thematic structure are usually parallel to the different narrative techniques we have already seen in the narratology chapter, showing how the Greek novel cannot be considered a monolithic corpus.

The representation of a triangle acts often as a disturbing element of reciprocal eros and therefore of parallelism. According to René Girard, this is the essential theme of the modern novel, disclosing the deep structure of desire opposed to the "romantic falsehood" of dual love.[61] The Greek novel does not generally reach this psychological depth, but it cannot be confined, however, to a simplistic sentimentalism. A rival trying to seduce one of the two young protagonists is one of the most widespread topoi in this genre; usually these actors receive a very bad characterization, in order to stress the heroic resistance of the chaste and faithful couple: they are violent, sensual, barbarian, often of low social rank (pirates, slaves). But sometimes a new ambiguity replaces this Manicheism: the text activates then a latent empathy towards the figure of the third. Making reference to Orlando's Freudian rhetoric, we can describe this dialectic as a compromise formation between a repressive instance—the exaltation of the couple—and a repressed one—the unconscious

---

(1982) 230–231; Molinié (1982) part 1; Fusillo (1989) 186–196; Létoublon (1993) chaps. 4–6; Konstan (1994a).
[60] Mendel (1970) 441–466.
[61] Girard (1961).

identification with the rivals—and thus sketch a typology of various degrees of empathy.

Xenophon of Ephesus represents for us a kind of zero degree of the corpus, showing conventions in their purest form. His rivals are almost always completely negative, without any space left for identification. On the other hand his protagonists are absolutely specular, without any difference in characterization and in their parallel adventures. This rigid duality is shaken only by the unconscious empathy the text communicates towards the erotic suffering of two figures: Manto, the lady who owns Habrocomes as a slave, falls in love with him, and finally slanders him according to the Potiphar (or Phaedra) motive;[62] and Perilaos, the governor of Cilicia who saves the life of Anthia, falls in love with her, tries to marry her and finally mourns for a long time her (apparent) death. There is a third, more important exception: the brigand Hippothous, who oscillates between the classic role of opponent (one who rapes and condemns the heroine to death) and the positive role of Habrocomes' true friend; at the end of the adventures he loses his ambiguity and takes part in the happy triumph with his lover Cleisthenes.

Although *Chaireas and Callirhoe* is the first ancient novel completely preserved, it already shows interesting variations to the pattern of the erotic novel. These innovations are chiefly of a psychological nature (that is the reason why Chariton was preferred by Ben Edwin Perry even in his idealistic perspective),[63] and involve the representation of rivals. If the satrap Mithridates falls still within the category we called "unconscious empathy"—an empathy provoked especially by a Sapphic description of his erotic suffering and by his incredible rhetorical skill—with king Artaxerxes and noble Dionysius we switch to a different degree: to the situation of a "conscious but not accepted" repressed.[64] That is to say: a part of the text communicates in a clear and consistent way ("conscious") a content in contrast with its moral code and with that presupposed in its addressee ("but not accepted"). In both cases the main device of empathy is the inner conflict—a feature usually considered totally absent in the Greek novel: the king

---

[62] On this motive see in general Braun (1934); on the rewriting in the Greek novel see Scarcella (1985a).

[63] Perry (1930) 116–123, especially regarding minor characters; see also Packcinska (1968) 600–602; García Gual (1972) 201–203 and 218–220; Ruiz-Montero (1982) 325–326; Hägg (1972).

[64] Orlando (1973) 74–79, quoting as example Racine's *Phèdre*.

considers adultery absolutely inconsistent with his way of life and with the laws promulgated by himself, and fights for a long time against the attraction issuing from Callirhoe's divine beauty, trying many forms of sublimation; at the end eros and desire win the battle, but they never come to the extreme of rape and violence, as in other triangle situations. The empathy towards Dionysius is particularly strong and marked: he receives a quite positive characterization as a noble, well-educated and self-controlled man according to a Menandrean pattern;[65] he has to fight not only his moral code, but also the memory of his dead wife (2.4); his destructive passion finally finds the only canonical and acceptable expression for the ideology of the Greek novel, marriage. A marriage accepted by Callirhoe—after a long inner conflict lost by a dream of Chaireas—only to save Chaireas' son from slavery (she deceives Dionysius about his true paternity). The exaltation of the main couple's eros is apparently not compromised by this second marriage: Callirhoe solemnly affirms that it has been the worst proof sent by Fortune. But in the happy end, after the topos of reunification with her true husband, Chaireas, she secretly sends a letter to Dionysius, expressing her gratitude (8.4.4–6): it is a part of the text where the repressed empathy towards this unusual rival emerges in a pregnant way, even if it cannot change the strict narrative logic of the genre.[66]

Chariton's novel realizes the pattern of parallelism in the same structural way as in Xenophon: the two main characters live similar adventures (slavery, dangerous travels), experience for a long time the anxiety of separation (they both believe in the other's death even celebrating a funeral: 1.6, 4.1), reacting in the same self-destructive way; but thanks to certain ambiguities, to a better characterization of Callirhoe's emotivity (even from a narratological point of view) and to the topos of the triangle, the duality shows a latent inclination towards the heroine.

In the novels of the Sophistic phase parallelism has always a more problematic aspect. Because of his Neoplatonic ideology, Heliodorus did not pay such a strong tribute to the topos of the triangle as Chariton did; his main couple became a vehicle of mystical ideals, stressing virginity and fidelity as absolute values and giving an even

---

[65] See Borgogno (1971) 260.
[66] On this figure see Ruiz de Elvira (1953) 102; Marcovaldi (1969) 81–84; Fusillo (1989) 227–228.

clearer predominance to the heroine. Rivals are therefore represented in a Manichean way, as incarnations of the devil; there is a single exception, the noble brigand Thyamis, son of Calasiris—a figure similar to Xenophon's Hippothous.[67] But there is a much more fascinating case where the most perverse and negative characterization coincides with the strongest unconscious empathy of this genre: Arsake, the sister of the king of Persia, is a sadistic, luxurious, violent woman preserving nevertheless a kind of sublime tragedy, an object of passionate admiration by Jean Racine (who imitated this figure in the tragedy *Bajazet*).[68] Her erotic suffering is narrated at length in terms of eros-folly and eros-disease, a typical Greek idea that reduces individual responsibility and favours the reader's identification.

Parallelism undergoes the biggest alteration in Achilles Tatius' novel; here one can perceive best the cooperation between thematic structure and narrative discourse already found in the other novels. First and foremost the choice of an I-narrator inevitably breaks the rigid duality typical of this genre: the reader perceives events from Clitophon's male perspective, while Leucippe remains almost always an elusive being; his voice is really the orientation center for the reader: rarely a mouthpiece of the author, he restricts often the point of view to his experience as I-actor. Then the free and comprehensive structure, the ironical pastiche, the absence of historical ennoblement, the trend to comedy and everyday life, are all elements which lessen the idealization and heroicization of the couple. However, the parallel structure realizing unconscious symmetrical logic is still the dominant cipher of the work: Achilles Tatius plays with the conventions but does not break them; we read about love at first sight, pathetic monologues, passionate letters, attempted suicides, dreams and descriptions, battles and processes, erotic intrigues, until the inevitable reunification in the happy ending, although the latter is narrated in a very rapid way, without any strong closure, on the contrary with a kind of anticlosure.[69] The biggest infraction to the rules of reciprocal eros, chastity and fidelity is the sexual intercourse between Clitophon and Melite, although even this infraction is not destructive and recedes

---

[67] See Rohde (1876) 428–429 and 477; Marcovaldi (1969) 47–48 and 59.
[68] Tüchert (1889) 31–36 and 39–43; Oeftering (1901) 142.
[69] Cf. Hägg (1971a) 125; Plepelits (1980) 28; Hunter (1983) 38–40; and especially Bartsch (1989) 168–170: "an intentional omission . . . a deliberate artistic creation"; Fusillo (1996); on the contrary, a sharp criticism by Romberg (1962) 33–38.

in the convention with a dialectic movement. Clitophon marries Melite because he believes Leucippe dead: this is quite unusual for a Greek novel, where lovers cannot endure the other's death and regularly attempt suicide; but the anomaly is reabsorbed, since Clitophon does not consummate marriage out of respect for Leucippe's memory. Paradoxically, intercourse takes place when it is open adultery, because Leucippe and Melite's husband are both "resurrected"; Clitophon narrates the episode stressing that he did it just to regain Leucippe and to heal a sick soul, but he will cover it with total reticence. At the end Melite will be able to conceal the adultery even on sacred oath, a parodic transgression to the convention of the genre. Even more than Chariton's Dionysius, Melite is a quite anomalous and positive rival: she is represented as a cultivated, refined, humorous woman, incarnating the worldly and materialistic ideology typical of Achilles Tatius; towards this full sense of life, not very far from that expressed by the Ephesian widow in Petronius, the text activates a clear empathy of a stronger degree, the strongest we can find in the Greek novel: an "accepted but not supported" repressed.[70]

In Longus' novel we find the same kind of infraction, but with different function and tonality. The young and ingenuous herdsman Daphnis is taught to make love by Lykaenion, a woman from the city: he will remember this lesson about sex and violence in his first night with Chloe at the end of the novel. There is certainly an ironic attitude of the urban author towards the bucolic world, but the episode acts more as a culminating point of the dialectic nature-culture, and does not affect radically the parallelism: the point is not fidelity, but sexual dynamics.[71] On the other hand *Daphnis and Chloe* shows an incredible dual structure: every episode is narrated once for each protagonist, beginning from the antecedent (the two dreams of the parents);[72] a thematic and narrative feature which is reflected even on the expressive form, rich in balance and echoes: Longus seems really obsessed by symmetry.

The second prominent psychoanalytic movement, that inspired by Carl Gustav Jung, had an equally telling influence on literary criticism; here the distance from textual dynamics turns out to be even

---

[70] Orlando (1973) chap. 5; on Melite see Cresci (1978); Segal (1984); Fusillo (1989) 228.
[71] See Levin (1977); and later, §7.
[72] See Hunter (1983) 16–37.

stronger: the search for universal archetypes inhibits interpretation of texts, contexts and variations. Of course there are many valuable exceptions and many nuanced positions we cannot deal with here. Regarding the ancient novel one can ascribe to a not strictly Jungian method in the famous book by Kerényi (1927), with its depreciation of literary dimension and with its mystical clue-reading carried to extremes by Merkelbach (1962); or *The Secular Scripture* by Northrop Frye (1976), who sees in Greek fiction the archetype of a long lasting constant, romance; or finally Apuleius' symbolic interpretation by Marie Louis von Franz (1980), however with precise literary analysis.

VI. *Poststructuralist Trends: An Anthropology of Desire*

"Poststructuralism" is a very vague and ambiguous term, like every term with this prefix: it should designate all the critical production of the last decade, dominated by the crisis of French structuralism and semiotics, and by deconstructionism. Here we cannot discuss the philosophical implications of this movement (with many of them I would personally disagree, especially regarding its negative hermeneutic); we can state only what unifies the various critical trends: the refusal of the idea that texts must have an organic wholeness, an absolute truth to be discovered, deciphered and fixed. It was certainly an idea connected with the structuralist pretence to be an exact science (a concept denied even by theorist of science). Nevertheless I still think that many of those methods, their break-up, segmentations and articulations, can be recovered, if we do not give up the need of interpretation and if we intend for theory of literature a theory of the models of the world expressed by the constants and variants of different cultures. That is to say, if we link formalistic methods with reborn "thematic criticism".[73]

Anyway because of their ideological presuppositions poststructuralist trends usually do not focus on expressive strategies or on implied readerships, but make the text react to some important issues for contemporary readers: thematic issues of anthropological relevance, which can be significant for the marginal perspectives repressed for

---

[73] *The Return of Thematic Criticism* is the nice title of a recent interesting collection of essays edited by Werner Sollors (1993); see also the collection edited by Cohen (1989).

many centuries by the dominant culture and now finally exploited by gender studies, gay and lesbian studies, black studies and so on.

The ancient novel offers very stimulating material from this point of view: it gives rich information about social relationships, mentalities, sexual behaviour, much more than strictly coded genres like tragedy or epic. In his unfinished *History of Sexuality* (1984) the late Michel Foucault attached much importance to the role of the Greek novel in a long lasting process of mentality: the exhaustion of classical erotic, i.e. pederasty, and the formation of a new erotic based on marriage. In the classical age marriage was based in fact only on economic grounds, excluding any decisional role of the woman and any affective dynamic, reserved to love for young boys. Beginning with some texts of the fourth century (Isocrates and the *Laws* by Plato), and especially with late Stoicism we can recognize a progressive exploitation of marriage in terms of personal relationship, culminating in Plutarch's *Amatorius*: the exaltation of the heterosexual couple made by the Greek novel is the literary correspondent to this process. The parallelism between the two protagonists we analyzed from a narrative and psychoanalytic point of view is an important novelty even from a sociological one: the canonical relationships of classical Greece implied always a difference of age which was of course a difference of power; the man in marriage or in extraconjugal stories with concubines, or the lover in pederastic loves, was necessarily older and dominant. Here at the center of the narration we have instead a couple of early adolescents, aged between 13 and 15 years.[74] In the first two novels we read expressions of surprise towards this kind of relationship: in Chariton the deluded rivals lament the very young age of Chaireas, preferred, though he is a juvenile character (1.2); in Xenophon the pirate Euxinous says to Habrocomes that at his age he does not yet need a female lover, ignoring that the couple is just married (1.16). In this first phase marriage takes place indeed at the beginning of the plot: therefore it is reciprocal fidelity—a stoic principle—to be hyperbolically exalted by the longer series of adventures.

The novels of the second phase focus instead on chastity and virginity, but with very important differences: the moral elasticity of Achilles Tatius presents at the beginning of the novel a quite comical intrigue, with the slave helping the male protagonist to reach the bed of the assenting loved girl; preconjugal intercourse does not take

---

[74] See Fusillo (1989) 228–234.

place only for an external reason: a dream of Leucippe's mother which saves at the same time the heroine's virginity and the conventions of the genre. Later in the novel preconjugal virginity becomes an acquired ideal: during their peripetiai the protagonists avoid sexual intercourse again thanks to an oneiric intervention; two parallel dreams of Aphrodite and Artemis convince the two young people this time (4.1). Nevertheless a certain margin of ambiguity and inequality remains: Clitophon tells his friend Menelaos that he has previously had sexual experiences with prostitutes (2.37.5), and writes to Leucippe reassuring her he has preserved his virginity, "if there is a male virginity" (5.20.5: again in 8.5.7). After this letter he loses this supposed virtue with the Ephesian widow Melite, while Leucippe's virginity and fidelity undergo a heroic trial echoing Christian martyrdoms, told with an emphatic tone quite unusual for this ironic novelist. At the end of the novel the sacred test of Melite's fidelity and Leucippe's virginity gives an ironic touch to the conjugal ideology of the erotic novel: Melite wins with a trick, while Leucippe's virginity was preserved only because of her mother's dream.

On the contrary in the *Aethiopica* by Heliodorus virginity is quite a parallel ideal and has roots in worship: both Theagenes and Chariclea grow up with an anomalous refusal of any erotic involvement; after mutual falling in love, told by Chalasiris with Neoplatonic undertones (3.5.4–6),[75] they sublimate physical attraction waiting for their final goal (a sublimation however harder for Theagenes). At the end of the novel, the positive outcome of the sacred test (here narrated in a quite serious way) awakens the general astonishment of the large Aethiopian public: they cannot believe that such a beautiful girl could preserve her virginity having long travelled in pirate ships and that an equally beautiful boy had not yet tried sex. Such an idealization of preconjugal virginity, much more marked than in Achilles Tatius' novel, as opposed to the demonic characterization of sensual love incarnated by Arsake, would inevitably remind one of Christian culture, and it is easy to understand how Heliodorus was Christianized by ancient and Byzantine sources. Nevertheless there are some differences in general between this pagan exaltation of marriage and

---

[75] Feuillâtre (1966) 125–127; Kövendi (1966) 157–159; on the widespread motive of Western fiction see the book by Rousset (1989), especially chapter 5 about the Platonic theme of mutual recognizing, exploited, among others, by Novalis, Flaubert, Nodier, Proust, Wagner; see also Barthes (1977) 223–229.

the Christian moral: according to the latter, sexuality and marriage are subordinated to procreation; the erotic novel remains instead still in the frame of Greek ethics, which never considered pleasure a negative phenomenon: marriage and virginity are just a way to control the morbid destructivity of eros.[76]

Even from this point of view *Daphnis and Chloe* stands apart in its genre; the point here is neither fidelity nor chastity (there are no separations and travels), but the discovery of sexuality. An illuminating reading by the late John Winkler in terms of gender studies interpreted the pastoral novel by Longus as a problematic reflection on the impossibility of sexual development resulting only from nature: sexuality indeed needs culture, that is social constraints and codes.[77] This is the meaning of the "lesson" made by Lykaenion— the woman coming not by chance from the city—to Daphnis, a lesson implying another very important issue: violence; to the young boy eager to repeat with Chloe what he had learnt, Lykaenion adds an appendix on the loss of virginity as a traumatic experience for young girls, an appendix that actually terrifies Daphnis. The motifs of rape, male penetration and violation often recur in the novel, for example in the metadiegetic tales[78] or in the metaphor of the garden,[79] disclosing a disturbing message beneath the sweet and naive textual surface. It is a dialectic affecting also the closure of the text:[80] after a typical folk-tale prolexis (very similar to that of Xenophon) about the happy and bucolic future of the couple, Longus goes back to the primary time of narration, to the first night after the wedding:

Daphnis did some of the things Lycaenion taught him; and then for the first time, Chloe found out that what they have done in the woods had been nothing but shepherds' games (ποιμένων παίγνια) (transl. Gill) (4.40).

According to Winkler Longus does not limit himself to the statement of this "inevitable" element of violence in sexuality, but presents it as problematic; anyway he leaves open the question if this

---

[76] Foucault (1984a) II 233–237.
[77] Winkler (1990b); see also Zeitlin (1990).
[78] See Philippides (1980); Hunter (1983) 52–58; Pandiri (1985) 130–133; Vox (1986) 311–317.
[79] Forehand (1976), Zeitlin (1994).
[80] On the complex dialectic of this ending and of its vision of sexuality see Winkler (1990b) 124–126; Zeitlin (1990) 457–460; Fusillo (1996).

can be considered really an intentional message directed towards the implied audience or a modern superimposition making Longus a forerunner of polemics against phallocratic and patriarchal ideology; the most important issue for cultural studies should be to recover not the authorial meaning, but to make explicit the ambiguities, inconsistencies and contradictions in dominant sexual ideology.

This feminist reading of Longus can certainly sound as a "violence" to his text, but it has a consistent ground in the general attitude the Greek novel shows towards women; an attitude which justified the hypothesis of female authors, or, at least, of a mostly female audience.[81] The basic parallelism between the two main characters does not conceal a certain emphasis on the heroine, from the psychological depth of Callirhoe to the pragmatic initiative of Anthia up to the absolute centrality of Chariclea—the true protagonist—who refuses first any feminine activity in favour of an "intellectual" life as priestess, and plays then the leading role in the adventures, incarnating the Odyssean pattern of shrewdness. There are in all the novels still many traces of classical conceptions of femininity like passivity and subordination, but the incredible adventures the Greek heroines experience seem to correspond to the phantasy of omnipotence of a new different public.[82]

The fact that the Greek novel represents a new heterosexual erotic giving a special space to women does not imply that homosexuality is excluded or condemned; it is rather confined to lateral stories, like those of Hippothous in Xenophon of Ephesus, Cleinias and Menelaos in Achilles Tatius: tragic love stories which never come to a happy ending—the transience of adolescence sung by epigrammatists seems to find here a narrative realization in a wicked and paradoxical destiny. There is only one important exception in Xenophon's novel, where the homosexual couple takes part in a happy ending and in the prolexis about the pleasant future, while Achilles Tatius is the only one to give a theoretical space to this issue: at the end of the second

---

[81] Hägg (1983) 95–96; Holzberg (1986) 42.

[82] See the illuminating reading by Egger (1988), conjugating gender studies with *Rezeptionsaesthetik*; see also Liviabella Furiani (1989a); Johne (1989a), and her contribution in this volume; Del Corno (1989); Wiersma (1990); García Gual (1991). For a theoretical introduction see the contributions by Stimpson and by Gilbert and Gubar in the already quoted collection edited by Cohen (1989) (the literature is already quite large).

book we read a long debate about pederasty and heterosexual love, with an almost explicit preference for the former (Chariton and Heliodorus follow instead the epic norm imposing reticence or vague allusion to this theme).[83]

In Petronius' *Satyricon* the choice of a homosexual couple is not easy to interpret. Richard Heinze considered it a clear parody of the Greek sentimental novel;[84] if we remember the Stoic character of the exaltation of marriage expressed by that genre, and think of the Epicurean attitude usually ascribed to Petronius, this narrative choice can carry also a cultural value: a polemic against a fanatic emphasis on conjugal fidelity. Even in this case there is the danger of an excessive modernizing of ancient texts; moreover, for any gay criticism applied to ancient literature there is always a strong obstacle in the fact that homosexuality, as David Halperin stated, is a modern concept, only one century old: classical antiquity did not know such a scission of desire.[85] Nevertheless it is quite remarkable that Petronius recovered the classic pederastic erotic to express an ambiguous, polyphonic, dialogic model of reality, linked with a Menippean and "promiscuous" view of sexuality (not excluding anyway a strong sentimental involvement). His paradoxes strike every idealization of the couple, as the most comical reverse of dual love and of fidelity we find in ancient fiction (80): when the beloved Giton is forced to choose between the lover Encolpius and his rival Ascyltos, he candidly chooses the second.

---

[83] See Effe (1987).
[84] Heinze (1899).
[85] Halperin (1990); see also Devereux (1968); Dover (1978); Cantarella (1988).

12. MAJOR AUTHORS

GREEK (A–E) AND ROMAN (F–H)

A. CHARITON

B.P. Reardon

I

The divinely beautiful Callirhoe is the daughter of Hermocrates, the leader of Syracuse who was victorious against the Athenian expedition of 415 B.C. Eros makes her fall in love at first sight with the handsome Chaereas after a festival of Aphrodite; he returns her love. Despite the bitter rivalry of their families, and at the urgent instigation of the assembled people of Syracuse, the pair are married. Disappointed rival suitors for Callirhoe's hand mount a plot to make Chaereas think that his wife is unfaithful; he kicks her in the stomach, and she falls down apparently dead. Chaereas, suicidal with remorse, condemns himself, but is acquitted of guilt, and Callirhoe is entombed in a funeral vault. The wealth displayed at her sumptuous funeral attracts tomb-robbers; but on entering the vault they find Callirhoe alive after all and awaking from what was really a deep coma—lack of food, Chariton tells us, restored her suspended respiration. Their leader Theron decides to carry her off; their ship carries them to Miletus, and Callirhoe is sold as a slave to Leonas, the steward of a wealthy and recently widowed seigneur, Dionysius. Dionysius, who at first takes her for Aphrodite, immediately falls in love with her; but being an honourable and cultivated man he respects her person and treats her royally. At this point, Callirhoe discovers that she is two months pregnant—by Chaereas, of course, to whom, despite his treatment of her, she is still passionately devoted, but whom she thinks forever lost to her. She holds anguished debate with herself: should she kill her child or let it be born a slave? An adroit slave, Plangon, persuades her rather to marry Dionysius and pass the child off as his, in order to assure it of a decent life.

In the meantime, Syracuse has learned of her disappearance and organised a search for her; Chaereas sets out to sea, and his ship meets that of Theron, who reveals Callirhoe's whereabouts and is crucified. Sailing to Miletus, Chaereas and his faithful friend Polycharmus land on Dionysius' estate. Dionysius' bailiff Phocas learns of their arrival and incites Persian troops to attack the Syracusan ship as hostile to the king of Persia (Ionia being represented as part of the Persian empire at this time). Most of the crew are killed, but Chaereas and Polycharmus are taken prisoner and set to work in a chain gang on the estate of Mithridates, the Persian satrap of Caria. Callirhoe now gives birth to a son, whom Dionysius, although he has now learned of her earlier marriage, unsuspectingly accepts as his own. She is led to believe that Chaereas is dead. Dionysius, though not himself certain that Chaereas was killed, holds a funeral ceremony for him to console Callirhoe. To it he invites Mithridates, who instantly falls in love with Callirhoe; back on his estate Mithridates discovers Chaereas' identity just in time to save him from crucifixion, and in the hope of manipulating the situation to his own advantage persuades him to write a letter to Callirhoe to tell her he is alive. The letter is intercepted and given to Dionysius; wilfully blind, he decides it is a trick devised by Mithridates, and complains of Mithridates' behaviour to a neighbouring satrap, Pharnaces, an enemy of Mithridates (and yet another of Callirhoe's admirers). Pharnaces relays the charge to the King of Persia, Artaxerxes, who summons Mithridates and Dionysius to Babylon for a formal trial; Callirhoe, of whom the King has already heard, is also summoned; and Mithridates takes Chaereas with him as a surprise weapon.

The trial has all Babylon agog at Callirhoe's beauty, and taking sides. In a dramatic debate, conducted according to proper rhetorical procedure, Dionysius accuses Mithridates of forging the letter and attempting to seduce another man's wife. Mithridates retorts that Dionysius' marriage is not valid, and sensationally produces Chaereas in court to prove it. But the lovers are restrained from reuniting; Mithridates is acquitted and returns home, and the question at issue now becomes the rival claims to Callirhoe of Dionysius and Chaereas. The King adjourns the trial and, pending decision, gives Callirhoe into the neutral charge of his Queen, Statira, who receives her kindly, though she is suspicious of her husband's sudden interest in visiting the women's quarters. Babylon is in a ferment. By now, however, the King has himself fallen violently in love with Callirhoe, and postpones decision by proclaiming a month-long sacrifice. He too, like Dionysius, will not force himself on her, but Callirhoe rejects persistent overtures made on his behalf by his eunuch Artaxates, who as a barbarian cannot comprehend her attitude, and threatens her with torture for herself and Chaereas.

This desperate situation is resolved by the news that the Persian province of Egypt has rebelled. The King marches out against the rebels; Dionysius goes with him, as following Persian custom do Statira and his entourage; and the King contrives to take Callirhoe as well. Chaereas, learning of Callirhoe's departure, is in despair. Polycharmus, though he has already prevented his suicide several times, at this hopeless juncture of events encourages him in his plan of killing himself, but persuades him to do so by joining the rebels and fighting against the King. Chaereas wins the Egyptian king's confidence, and with a hand-picked force of Greeks serving as mercenaries successfully (though by deceit) storms Tyre. This success leads to his being appointed commander of the Egyptian navy. In that capacity he defeats the Persian fleet and captures the small island of Aradus, where the Persian King has left his possessions and non-military entourage. On land, however, the Egyptians are defeated, and the revolt is suppressed. Dionysius distinguishes himself in the fighting, and in return the King awards Callirhoe to him (though she is on Aradus with the Queen and other Persian women).

At this point, at the beginning of the last book, Chariton himself enters the story. After summarizing events so far, he tells us that Tyche—Fortune—had intended Chaereas not to learn that Callirhoe was herself among the women on Aradus, and in his ignorance to leave her there, an outcome "as cruel as it was paradoxical"; but Aphrodite, thinking that Chaereas has paid dearly enough for his original misplaced jealousy, overrules Tyche and decides to reunite the lovers. "I think that readers will find this last episode most enjoyable," we are told; "it will clear away the grim events of the early ones ... now there will be rightful love and lawful marriage" (8.1.4). So in the nick of time, and as it were by the skin of their teeth, Chaereas and Callirhoe do at last find each other again. Chariton wraps up the story conscientiously. Chaereas, himself undefeated, disengages himself from the fighting, and generously sends Statira back to Artaxerxes; Callirhoe—surreptitiously, because she knows Chaereas' jealous nature—gives her a letter for Dionysius in which, in saying goodbye, she entrusts her son to him, bidding him send the boy to Syracuse when he grows up. Dionysius, appointed by the King governor of Ionia, goes sadly back to Miletus. The lovers return in triumph to Syracuse, with all the Persian treasure; Chaereas settles his crews generously, and gives his own sister in marriage to Polycharmus. While Chaereas recounts his and Callirhoe's adventures to the assembled citizens, Callirhoe goes to the temple of Aphrodite to thank the goddess for restoring Chaereas to her and express the wish, no doubt prophetic, that they will live happily ever after. "That," says Chariton finally, "is my story about Callirhoe."[1]

II

Assessment of a literary work must take account of its cultural context, but the literary-historical problems raised by the story outlined here are not easy to resolve. This is because there is little evidence outside the work itself to guide us: at the same time, in examining the story we are conditioned by the assumptions we bring to it regarding its nature, and those assumptions may themselves be open to question. In particular, the date of the work cannot be established with confidence, within a period of some hundred years or more— plausible dates range from the late first century B.C. to the early second century A.D. In consequence we have only a rather loose idea of its position within the genre; we can be reasonably sure that it is the first fully extant specimen of its kind, but are on less sure ground in assessing its degree of sophistication, the extent of its author's ambitions, and the nature of the audience for which it was written. For a long time in the modern world, from the first publication of *Callirhoe* in 1750, the simplicity of its language, the exiguity of its textual tradition, and its reception in antiquity contributed to its neglect and unflattering reputation; indeed, from 1876, all of the novels long suffered from the contempt meted out to them in the massive and erudite standard work of Erwin Rohde, *Der griechische Roman*, although it was made out of date by subsequent papyrological discoveries that radically changed our knowledge of the history of the genre. For *Callirhoe*, the first modern study to treat it with sympathy as a literary-historical phenomenon and as a work of literature was that of Perry in 1930, but it remained relatively isolated for several decades. Even

---

[1] There is a much fuller account of the plot in Perry (1967) 124–37. On Chariton's novel see above all Ruiz-Montero (1994a) for comprehensive, systematic and thoroughly documented coverage of the topics here discussed. There is a general study in Schmeling (1974). Schmid (1899) is now out of date but gives much basic information. For editions see n. 5 below. Modern translations: English, Blake (1939), Reardon (1989b), Goold (1995); French, Grimal (1958a), Molinié (1989); German, Plepelits (1976), Wehrhahn (1983), Lucke-Schäfer (1985); Italian, Nuti (1958), Annibaldis (1987); Spanish, Mendoza (1979).

in 1976 Northrop Frye, in *The Secular Scripture*, a comprehensive analysis of romance as a genre, could disregard totally the first prose romance in European history, though he often refers to Longus and Heliodorus. With interest growing, however, in Greek pagan culture of the imperial period, it has risen markedly in academic esteem, and is now more generally thought to merit serious scholarly and critical attention.

All that is firmly known of Chariton himself is what he tells us in the opening sentence of his story:

Χαρίτων 'Αφροδισιεύς, 'Αθηναγόρου τοῦ ῥήτορος ὑπογραφεύς, πάθος ἐρωτικὸν ἐν Συρακούσαις γενόμενον διηγήσομαι

I, Chariton of Aphrodisias, secretary of the lawyer Athenagoras, shall tell you a love story that took place in Syracuse.

Even his name ("man of graces") was once thought to be a pseudonym, suitable for the author of a love-story; but inscriptions found at Aphrodisias in Asia Minor attest the existence in the area of both Chariton and Athenagoras as proper names.[2] Besides this, there is mention of a writer called Chariton in a "literary letter" appearing in a collection written by Philostratus, early in the third century A.D.:

Χαρίτωνι· Μεμνήσεσθαι τῶν σῶν λόγων οἴει τοὺς ῞Ελληνας, ἐπειδὰν τελευτήσῃς· οἱ δὲ μηδὲν ὄντες, ὅποτε εἰσίν, τίνες ἂν εἶεν, ὅποτε οὐκ εἰσίν;

To Chariton. You think Greece will remember your writings when you are dead. But if people are nothing when they are alive, what can they possibly be when they are not alive?[3]

The letter itself strongly suggests that "Chariton" is not alive at the time of writing, and certainly other letters in the collection are addressed to men already dead. While it cannot be shown that this Chariton is the novelist the identification is too good not to be true; we know of no other author of that name. On this highly likely assumption, we know at least that Chariton lived not later than the later second century, and that his novel earned the contempt of the

---

[2] Rohde (1914) 520 = (1876) 489. For Aphrodisias see Erim (1986).
[3] Letter 66. It is worth observing at this point that the word here translated as "writings" (λόγοι) may be a real plural (rather than designating only one book); it is quite possible that Chariton wrote other novels, of which we have fragments; see n. 19 below.

highly sophisticated author of a *Life of Apollonius of Tyana* and of *Lives of the Sophists* (an account of many of the "concert orators" of the period).

Both of these pieces of information are consistent with what we know of the textual tradition of *Callirhoe*, which is the only other concrete evidence we have for its author's date and place in the literary scene of the period. That evidence consists of the only extant complete manuscript, one of four novels in a late 13th century volume containing religious and historical texts as well, known as Conventi Soppressi 627, and now in the Laurentian Library in Florence (whence it is usually designated as F—the Budé edition calls it L); together with several brief papyrus fragments and a late parchment codex of a larger fragment, these fragments covering among them some 6% of the text.[4] The manuscript is unreliable; the fact that the tradition is so scanty suggests that the novel was not held in high esteem by the educated and was lucky to survive antiquity[5]— though, as will be seen, in all probability educated people did read it, much as educated people may read thrillers today without rating them highly. The papyrus fragments number four, two being from the same papyrus, and were found at remote country sites in Egypt; this suggests that the story was at least known to a fairly widely distributed readership.[6] They can be dated on palaeographical grounds to around A.D. 200, give or take perhaps a quarter of a century; this, given that it would no doubt take quite a long time for the novel to reach rural Egypt, suggests a date of composition certainly not later than the middle of the second century, probably earlier, and perhaps much earlier. The parchment codex acquired in Egyptian Thebes by U. Wilcken and known as Thebanus (Wilckenus in

---

[4] Conventi Soppressi 627 contains also texts of Xenophon Ephesius and the more sophisticated Achilles Tatius and Longus. Xenophon—commonly paired with Chariton as a "pre-sophistic" writer—shares with him the feature of having survived only in this manuscript. For the Budé edition see next note.

[5] It has not fared well in modern times either until recently. It did not surface until the 18th century, and until 1938 none of the scholars who edited it had themselves seen the only evidence for its text; see Blake (1931 and 1938, introduction). Modern editions are D'Orville (1750); Beck (1783); Hirschig (1856); Hercher (1859); Blake (1938) (indispensable); Molinié (1979) (Budé; cosmetic improvements in 2nd ed., 1989) see Reardon (1982a).

[6] See Grenfell (1900) (*P.Fay.*1); Grenfell (1910) (*P.Oxy.*1019); Crawford (1955) (*P.Mich.*1); Weinstein (1972) (*P.Oxy.*2948). For the superiority of the fragments to F see Lucke (1985a).

the Budé), was written in the 6th or 7th century.[7] It offers a "rogue" text, clearly less good than that of F and the papyri.[8] The scribe has clearly made alterations and additions of his own, which suggests that the story had passed into the public domain, like the Alexander Romance, and was considered fair game for rewriting in the process of transmission; it is interesting that at one point the scribe invents an obviously sentimental passage.[9] All of this suggests that *Callirhoe* was popular in antiquity as a tear-jerking story; and it all fits Philostratus' remark.

One further line of inquiry may confirm this. The novel has so far generally gone under the title *Chaereas and Callirhoe*, which is what it is called in F at the beginning of each book. This *Jack and Jill* kind of title is one of the standard forms for the genre *(Daphnis and Chloe, Leucippe and Clitophon)*. Chariton himself, however, says in his last sentence "this is my story about Callirhoe (τοσάδε περὶ Καλλιρόης ἔγραψα), not "about Chaereas and Callirhoe". It is certainly true that Callirhoe is more prominent in it than Chaereas, and other novels were sometimes known by the name of the heroine alone.[10] Further evidence turned up in a quite recently published second-century papyrus which contains the text of the end of Book 2, followed immediately by the colophon "The story of Chariton of Aphrodisias about Callirhoe, Book 2.[11] While neither of these items is necessarily decisive in itself, they do tend to support each other.

A final piece of information, furthermore, points in the same direction. The Roman satiric poet Persius refers to some form of literary production as *Callirhoe*:

---

[7] On acquiring the codex (a palimpsest) in 1898 Wilcken transcribed about half of it in Egypt, but did not have the facilities to examine the more difficult passages. On his return to Hamburg in 1899 the codex was destroyed in a fire. See Wilcken (1901).

[8] See Zimmermann (1922).

[9] At 8.5.15 Dionysius has learned that he has definitively lost Callirhoe, who has returned to Syracuse with Chaereas. The Thebanus represents "his" baby son (in reality Chaereas' son) as saying to him "Daddy, where's Mummy? Let's go to her." Blake (1938, apparatus *ad loc.*) observes that the scribe is developing, rather untelligently, a sentimental motif sketched at 5.10.4–5.

[10] It is not impossible, however, that the text of F is defective in Chariton's last sentence—it not infrequently omits words or groups of letters—and should read "This is my story about <Chaereas and> Callirhoe." For the shorter form of title cf. Achilles Tatius' *Leucippe (Leucippe and Clitophon)* and Heliodorus' *Charicleia (Theagenes and Charicleia)*. Yet another form of title is geographical: *Ethiopica, Ephesiaca*.

[11] *P.Mich.*1; see Crawford (1955) 1.

his mane edictum, post prandia Callirhoen do.

To these people I offer in the morning the programme of public entertainment, and in the afternoon Callirhoe.[12]

"These people" are the object of Persius' satire, contemptible people incapable of appreciating his own elegant verse; all *they* are fit for is, as it were, pop TV and Barbara Cartland. Persius lived from 34 to 62, so his poem was certainly published in Nero's reign (it has been dated in 59). If he is indeed referring to Chariton's novel, the reference seems to clinch a number of matters: the relatively early date, the reputation of the novels among highbrows, and the short form of the title. It seems hard to come to any other conclusion.

Some questions remain, however. First, we do not know for sure that Persius' *Callirhoe was* Chariton's novel; although it seems almost self-evident, and although we do not know of anything else it could have been, it may have been some kind of literary work by someone else. There may, for instance, have been a mime or other dramatic work called *Callirhoe*; there were versions in mime of other novels, *Ninus* and *Metiochus and Parthenope*.[13] If that is so, Persius is recommending to lowbrows that they read the entertainment guide in the morning and then in the afternoon go to see the show announced in it: "have a look at *TV Guide* and watch *Dallas*." In that case, of course, we cannot know whether Chariton's novel antedates or postdates the stage spectacle; but the analogy of *Ninus* would suggest that the novel came first, and was successful enough to inspire a staged version, which would no doubt have appeared soon afterwards (as happens nowadays when "the film of the book" is made). Second, although all educated Romans of the period knew Greek, it is not clear that "these people" would be of that kind (elsewhere in the poem Persius seems to suggest that they were). Thirdly, it has been held that a mid-1st century date for *Callirhoe* does not fit certain other

---

[12] Persius, *Satires* 1.134. The *edictum*, in this context, was the official public announcement of forthcoming games or other spectacles.

[13] See, most recently, the full discussion, with extensive bibliography, of Quet (1992). *Ninus* is certainly early (see n. 17 below); *Metiochus and Parthenope* is stylistically similar to *Callirhoe*, so probably of similar date (and conceivably by Chariton himself—see n. 19 below). It is of course possible that the mosaics discussed by Quet were inspired directly by the stories. Persius may be referring to a written work other than Chariton's novel, rather than to a staged entertainment. This speculation, however, seems to create more problems than it solves: what would be the relation between such a work and Chariton's novel?

kinds of evidence. Chariton's language has been thought to place him a generation later, or even two generations, while other linguistic researches have put him as much as a hundred years *earlier* than the reign of Nero; and the contemporary historical circumstances that appear to lie behind his story, which in general reflect the Roman Empire, have seemed to some scholars more suited to the early second century A.D. than the middle of the first. But such arguments are notoriously unreliable, relying as they do on evidence that is incomplete, susceptible of various interpretation, or simply too lacking in firm concrete detail to be convincing. They are discussed further below, in connection with other aspects of the novel; for immediate purposes we may say, summarily, that in the view of the present writer the balance of probability is that Chariton's story was called simply *Callirhoe*, was written in or before the earliest years of Nero's reign (54–68), and was thought of by the literary establishment as sentimental and cheap. That does not preclude literary ambition on the part of its author, nor does it preclude skill.

III

The question of literary ambition is in fact of much importance in the study of Chariton. In the early Roman Empire there occurred a cultural movement that goes by the name of "Atticism". Atticism is a fairly complex phenomenon. In its original manifestation it was in one aspect a reaction against "Asianism", which marked a florid style of oratory that developed in the Greek world in the period after Demosthenes, and inevitably affected Roman oratory as well, since its practitioners were trained in the Greek tradition. From the time of Cicero a return to sober Attic style and imitation of classical (that is, fourth-century) models were advocated by many teachers of rhetoric. Atticism and Asianism, however, were by no means simple opposites. In the Greek world, increasingly throughout the first and second centuries A.D., the Atticist movement took the form of the imitation not so much of Attic sobriety as of Attic vocabulary. With the spread of Greek civilization after Alexander, the Greek language had evolved in the direction of syntactical and morphological simplicity and of lexical change, as was inevitable with a language learned in non-Greek countries as a second language. This resulted in the development of a "common language", a κοινὴ διάλεκτος known as the Koine, the simplified international Greek notably of the New Testament.[14] For the nature of the differences, one could draw a partial analogy with those between English English (classical, Attic Greek) and American English (Koine). With the definitive establishment of the Roman Empire, and especially after the troubled Julio-Claudian period, there came to the Greek world a degree of prosperity that led to a period of renewed self-confidence and cultural self-consciousness—sometimes known as the Greek Renaissance—and in particular to an attempt on the part of many educated Greeks to reestablish the Greek of the classical period in place of "debased" Koine; this was in fact the origin of the distinction in modern Greek between formal *katharevousa* and informal *demotike*. The Atticizing movement in this form, beginning in the first century A.D. and at its height in the second, affected the language and particularly the vocabulary of writers who wished to be respected. Linguistic pundits, especially in the second century, drew up lists of words and usages to be replaced by their Attic counterparts.[15] One way of approaching the assessment of a writer's place in the literary scene is to chart his vocabulary in terms of his use of Atticizing language. Lucian, for instance, in the third quarter of the second century, who as a non-Greek (he was Syrian) had particular reason to be careful about his Greek, Atticized extensively; at the same time, he castigates those who carried the habit to extremes and resuscitated words that had always been exotic even in classical Greek ("eftsoons", "verily"). By this criterion Chariton appears less ambitious than many in that in the main his language is a form of fairly high-level Koine. Since, however, in other respects he clearly does have literary ambitions— as will be seen—one should probably draw one or both of two conclusions: (a) he was writing at a time when the Atticizing movement had not yet attained its peak, or (b) he did not feel any strong need

---

[14] Browning (1983) chs. 2, 19–52, "Greek in the Hellenistic World and the Roman Empire", gives a concise comprehensive treatment of the phenomenon. The principal features are: optative and dual largely disappear; verb voices (active and, middle) are confused, as are verb tenses (aorist and perfect); differences in case (dative replaced by accusative or genitive) and use of prepositions (e.g. εἰς + acc. instead of ἐν + dat.); periphrastic verbal expressions (εἰμί or ἔχω + active participle for indicative); changes in participial usage; syntactical change (δοκῶ ὅτι); morphological simplification (οἶδα οἶδας); and lexical change.

[15] As examples: Phrynichus (2nd century) recommends the use of ἔδομαι (Attic) instead of φάγομαι (Koine) (Luke 14.15) for "eat"; his contemporary Herodian observes that κελεύω should take the accusative (Attic), not the dative (Koine).

to write a work *of this kind* in fashionable literary language. Atticism of the kind here described is one of the marked features of the Second Sophistic, the renaissance of rhetoric as an art form which constitutes the context of Philostratus' *Lives of the Sophists*. Philostratus, who coined the term "Second Sophistic" to distinguish the phenomenon from the classical sophistic art of Gorgias and his contemporaries, although he maintains that the movement is fundamentally an extension of that first sophistic, in fact indicates a distinct renewal of it in the last two or three decades of the first century A.D.[16] From this point of view, therefore, it seems unlikely that Chariton wrote later than, say, the reign of Nero—which fits the other evidence. It is relevant to add here that Petronius' *Satyrica* (commonly known as the *Satyricon*, but the nominative plural form is more likely to be correct), a work certainly of the Neronian period and in all probability written about A.D. 65, clearly parodies the Greek sentimental novel of love and adventure. There is thus nothing intrinsically unlikely in a date in the mid-first century A.D. or earlier for Chariton's novel.[17]

IV

Whatever its precise date, *Callirhoe* is nothing less than the first fully extant European novel, or romance if the less realistic term is preferred.[18] Not only that, but it seems to have marked an important stage, possibly a crucial stage, in the early history of the genre, the stage at which prose fiction itself comes of age,[19] although still having a long way to go even in antiquity, where it is followed by more self-consciously sophisticated specimens. Its signal success is probably

---

[16] Philostratus, *Lives of the Sophists* 19; the main influence was Nicetes of Smyrna.

[17] The genre existed before Nero's time; the Ninus Romance, the surviving fragments of which are securely dated by documentary evidence to A.D. 100–101, was probably written in the 1st century B.C.; see Wilcken (1893).

[18] Early scholarship saw in *Callirhoe* the last of the line of novels, not the first. Rohde (1914) dated it in the 5th or 6th century precisely on account of the simplicity of its language, which he took to indicate decadence. It is now clear that it indicates, on the contrary, an early stage of the form.

[19] Chariton may well have written other novels, to judge by the style and manner of some extant fragments: see Dihle (1978), Gronewald (1979b), Lucke (1984); the *Chione* fragment was in the same codex as the Thebanus fragment of Chariton. He could thus be a key figure in the development of the genre; or he may have been the "leader" of a group of early novelists ("school of Chariton").

what is marked by the subsequent popularity of the story as witnessed by the dismissive remark of Philostratus in the third century—for evidently Chariton *was* a familiar name in the early third century!—the relatively numerous and scattered fragments, and the additional fact that at some point in the second century he is manifestly (and clumsily) imitated by Xenophon of Ephesus in his novel the *Ephesiaca*. This distinctive place in the early history of the genre holds good, to the best of our knowledge, even if we accept a later date for the composition of *Callirhoe*.

To return to the linguistic evidence mentioned above, the first point to make is that the Greek language of the early Empire has not been studied systematically enough for any reliable map or chart to be constructed on which a given author can be situated accurately with confidence. There is a very considerable body of Greek literature extant from the first two or three centuries, and although there exist indices and linguistic studies of a number of individual authors, there is not enough by way of modern comprehensive analytical study. The principal tool available is still the massive study by W. Schmid, *Der Atticismus*.[20] But it was never perfect. Such a project, to be carried out thoroughly, involves an amount of work perhaps beyond the powers of any single scholar, especially without complete indices and mechanical aids such as computers can now provide. Above all, a hundred years ago much less was known than is now known, thanks to the very extensive papyrological discoveries since Schmid's day, about the development of the Greek language in the Hellenistic and (especially) Roman periods, discoveries that have enabled us to set Koine, and hence other forms of language, in perspective. Furthermore, Schmid's study was based on some simplistic and untenable assumptions about the linguistic phenomena of the period: for him, Asianism and Atticism were opposed phenomena, and Atticism was fundamentally an unnatural attempt simply to turn back the clock. Finally, and this is extremely important, the texts he had to work with had themselves been established often on Atticizing assumptions; as an illustration of this attitude, directly pertinent to the present case, earlier in the century Cobet had gone through the text of *Callirhoe* not so much correcting the errors of the Byzantine manuscript as

---

[20] The full title, cumbrous as it is, is of relevance here: *Der Atticismus in seinen Hauptvertretern von Dionysius von Halikarnass bis auf den zweiten Philostratus*; that is, it is a study of major authors from the time of Augustus to the early third century.

"correcting" Chariton's Greek to make it conform to classical usage—about which, be it said, Cobet assuredly knew much more than Chariton—and on every page snorting with disgust at Chariton's "ignorance".[21]

This reservation is important. An imperfect knowledge of the total picture can crucially affect details of that picture. That said, however, Chariton's language has been studied, and recently; but there is no agreement on the matter. In 1973 Papanikolaou examined several aspects of Chariton's language in an attempt to situate it in relation to Koine and Atticizing usage.[22] The study is not a complete account of the matter, and is by no means free from errors, but does accumulate evidence that shows extensive Koine usage as opposed to Attic. Papanikolaou's conclusion is categorical: "Chariton's language shows no trace of Atticism, although he was a very well-read man";[23] on the strength of that, he not only declares *Callirhoe* the first of the extant novels but sets Chariton firmly in the pre-Atticizing period, "when Atticizing tendencies first began to have a gradual influence"; that period, he maintains, coincides with the beginning of the Atticizing reform, in the middle or second half of the first century B.C.[24] Papanikolaou establishes a *terminus ante quem* from a reference at 6.4.2 to a Chinese bow and arrows; China first became known to the Greco-Roman world in the early first century B.C., and is referred to several times by Augustan poets.

While the general thrust of Papanikolaou's argument is sound, some substantial reservations are necessary. First, of method: not enough attention is paid to the Atticisms that can be shown to exist and

---

[21] See especially Cobet (1859) (his review of Hercher's edition).

[22] For reviews of Papanikolaou (1973) see Giangrande (1974) and Reardon (1976c). There is a study of Chariton's language by Gasda (1860), but it is based on the view that Chariton is to be dated late—not before the later 4th century, and perhaps as late as the 6th century.

[23] Papanikolaou's first chapter is an examination of Chariton's quite numerous borrowings from classical literature, especially Homer and historical writers; see text and n. 29 below.

[24] For this dating see Papanikolaou (1973) 160–63, Zusammenhang. The other candidate in recent times for the distinction of being the earliest extant novel has been that of Xenophon Ephesius. There are some episodes and expressions in which one of the two has clearly imitated the other, notably at Char.3.5.4 and Xen.1.14.4, scenes of impassioned pleading on the part of distraught elders. Papanikolaou (ch. 10) argues convincingly for the priority of Chariton, in whom the impassioned pleading is clearly more in place than it is in Xenophon. At Char.6.6.4 and Xen.5.5.5, Callirhoe and Anthia respectively lament their treacherous beauty in similar language (κάλλος ἐπίβουλον).

have recently received more detailed study. Hernández Lara analyses some 500 words, from Chariton's vocabulary of 3000, that are listed as Atticist either in Atticist lexica or in *Der Atticismus*.[25] Many of these are excluded on the grounds that they also occur in the New Testament, Koine authors, or non-literary papyri; but nearly 300— 10% of Chariton's vocabulary—are apparently genuine Atticisms. In some 30 cases Chariton uses doublets of the Atticist term—that is, he uses both the Atticist and the Koine terms for the same thing in different places. To these researches it may be added that in some cases the way in which the term is used may be significant. Chariton normally uses the Koine term, but does know the Attic form and will use it, exceptionally, when he has specific reason to do so.[26] It may, however, be just as significant, for a different reason, that often he appears to use the two interchangeably; either way, he seems not to be particularly concerned to establish himself as an Atticist.

In a related study, Ruiz Montero analyses the degree of coincidence between Chariton and a number of possible contemporaries, mostly Atticizing writers (Diodorus Siculus, Philo, Josephus, Dio Chrysostom, Plutarch), as well as Koine texts (the New Testament, papyri), in the light of Atticist lexica and *Der Atticismus*.[27] It would be disproportionate here to go into the detail of this complex examina-

---

[25] Hernández Lara (1990, 1994).

[26] For example, for "to buy" Chariton normally (7 times) uses the standard Koine word ἀγοράζειν (which in Attic is intransitive—"to be in the market-place"). At 1.14.4 however, and only there, he uses the transitive Attic ὠνεῖσθαι—but at the end of a sentence, τοὺς ἐθέλοντας ὠνεῖσθαι, where it produces one of his favourite clausulae or rhythmical sentence endings (- ⏑ - - x) instead of the dribble of short syllables that ἀγοράσαι would give (- ⏑ ⏑ ⏑ ⏑ x) [see Heibges (1911) for Chariton's clausulae]. Similarly, Attic ἀποδίδομαι occurs only twice in place of Koine πωλέω, which appears 18 times for "sell" (in Attic πωλέω more properly means "offer for sale", but again the nuance disappears in Koine). The occurrences are 1.10.8 and 6.7.4. In the first, the sentence runs ἀποδώσομαι τὴν γυναῖκα μᾶλλον ἢ ἀπολέσω—"I shall sell the woman rather than kill her" (the pirate Theron is discussing what to do with his captive Callirhoe); Koine πωλήσω would produce a jingle with ἀπολέσω, and Chariton uses the Attic word. At 5.7.4 there is no similar circumstance; but it occurs in a speech of Mithridates which is deliberately written in a more flamboyant style than the corresponding speech of his opponent Dionysius. It seems likely that in both cases the use of the Attic term is fully conscious and deliberate. In some cases, however, the unreliability of F prompts a certain caution. At 2.1.5, and only there, the Attic term φιλογύνης appears, for no very apparent reason; at 12.2.7 and 8.6.7, and only there, the form is the late Greek φιλογύναιος, producing a favourite clausula in one case but not in the other. This may be an instance of simple whimsy on Chariton's part, or could be a case of error on a scribe's part, perhaps abetted by his pronunciation of -ης/-αιος.

[27] Ruiz-Montero (1991).

tion, but some significant figures may be given. First, of Chariton's total vocabulary of 3000 words, over two-thirds occur in the New Testament and papyri—although most of these also occur in the more literary texts. The study concentrates on some 200 less common terms, of which two-thirds are drawn from the Atticizing or otherwise literary stock (Attic prose, comedy, poetic terms, Ionisms). Ruiz-Montero's conclusions are markedly different from Papanikolaou's: she attributes to Chariton "a knowledge of Atticist precepts which the author follows when he wants... Atticisms are indeed present in Chariton, although in moderate quantity." Chariton, she maintains, employs "a mixed language in which various levels of language are combined" (p. 489), While this study is not exhaustive, and its method may need modification, it produces workable results, which are certainly much nearer the mark than Papanikolaou's exaggerated conclusions.

Ruiz-Montero's formulation corresponds well to the impression Chariton makes on the reader, of a writer of generally unpretentious but literate enough prose, by no means devoid on occasion of a degree of modest elevation. It fits also with the picture of a man distinctly living in his own times, rather than a bookworm, a pedant, or a scholar. Engaged as he was in the legal profession, he was necessarily involved in the society of his day—he shows his legal knowledge on a number of occasions, particularly in the episode of the "sale" of Callirhoe.[28] He was also well aware of the tradition of Greek *paideia* that was certainly a feature of the world he lived in, and that forms one of the most prominent motifs in his story. Chariton was fairly well-educated: he certainly had a decent secondary education, perhaps more. To call him "a very well-read man", however—"ein sehr belesener Mann"—is an overstatement. He quotes or alludes to the classics of Greek literature: Homer very often (he clearly knew him well), historical writers quite often (especially Xenophon of Athens), orators and drama occasionally.[29] He similarly has a general knowledge of some of the more familiar events in Greek history, notably

---

[28] Zimmermann (1957).
[29] Papanikolaou (1973) ch. 1 collects the following: Homer, over 30 quotations and allusions; historians (Hdt., Thuc., Xen.), especially similarities and reminiscences of expression and vocabulary (quite frequent); orators, a handful of passages, from Dem. in particular; Menander, a few cases; Sophocles, one reference. Some of Papanikolaou's instances are questionable. On the use Chariton makes of his principal borrowings see Bartsch (1934), Zimmermann (1961) (historiography), and Scarcella (1971) 54–59 (Homer).

the Athenian defeat in Sicily (which recurs with tedious frequency in the text) and some principal features of fourth-century history (to be discussed in another context below). But very little of this goes beyond standard texts, a "reading list" of predictable "prescribed books". Homer was the basis of all Greek education, as is demonstrated for the Hellenistic period and later by the considerable number of papyri of the *Iliad* and *Odyssey*, obviously school texts. Chariton's whole novel is set in the fourth century as a "historical novel", and both his opening and closing sentences recall formulations from the beginning and other parts of the histories of Herodotus and Thucydides—which again were familiar works in antiquity; while Xenophon was a favourite author of the early Empire.[30] Menander was another favourite—Plutarch preferred him to Aristophanes; the great speeches of Demosthenes (such as *De Corona*) and other orators were standard models for speakers. Chariton had in fact a standard "classical education", remarkably similar to that of today. But his quotations and literary references are not really more "well-read" than standard quotations from Shakespeare ("The quality of mercy is not strained"), or Winston Churchill ("Never in the field of human conflict . . ."), or Abraham Lincoln ("government of the people, for the people, and by the people"). This is by no means to denigrate him; he is culturally fairly well equipped. But he is not erudite; his knowledge of Greek literature and cultural tradition bears no comparison with that of Callimachus in the Hellenistic period, or nearer his own time Dionysius of Halicarnassus, Dio Chrysostom or Plutarch—or his successors as novelists, Longus, Achilles Tatius and Heliodorus.

Nor is his language notably that of an intellectual. Nowhere in the narrative passages does one find anything like the elaborate prose of Heliodorus, or the tortuous language of Achilles Tatius' ecphrases; throughout, he employs a straightforward, uncomplicated manner and simple Greek, although on a higher level than the New Testament, that can fairly be called literary Koine. He is rather given to clichés of vocabulary and stereotyped diction; his language often gives the impression of reflecting contemporary speech, the *Umgangssprache*, especially in the more rapid exchanges of dialogue; and he does not often employ metaphor, certainly not colourful metaphor.[31] It is in

---

[30] Several writers used his name as a nom de plume, notably Arrian (who calls himself a "second Xenophon") and the novelist Xenophon Ephesius. Others are mentioned in the Suda; see Perry (1967) 167.

[31] See Zanetto (1990) 236–37.

fact rather ordinary language. But this is not due to any lack of schooling; rhetorical schools flourished throughout the Hellenistic and imperial periods, and in the more emotional direct speech, such as Callirhoe's monologues, Chariton uses a whole battery of rhetorical figures—antithesis, anaphora, amplification, chiasmus, homoioteleuton, and many others.[32] He is careful about his prose rhythms, and he avoids hiatus;[33] and as we have seen, he does show signs, though they are not extensive, of being aware of the linguistic and stylistic currents of his time. Given this picture of careful and moderately ambitious writing, he should be dated a good deal later than Papanikolaou's date of the middle or end of the first century B.C. How much later it is hard to say; but it seems likely that if he had been writing at the end of the first century A.D., or *a fortiori* in the reign of Trajan or Hadrian, where he has been placed on a variety of criteria,[34] he would have Atticized more than he does. The reference in Persius—more concrete than a rather fluid linguistic or historically-based dating—would seem to place him a generation or two earlier; and his language fits there quite well.

V

To turn to the setting and atmosphere of *Callirhoe*: it purports, as has been seen, to be a historical novel, in the sense that some of its characters and its background are supposedly drawn from Greek

---

[32] Ruiz-Montero (1991a) shows that there is a marked correspondence between Chariton's practice and the precepts set out in Aelius Theon, *Progymnasmata* or "Preliminary Exercises", (2nd century A.D.), one of a number of manuals of rhetoric in common use in the imperial period. See also Hernández Lara (1990).

[33] Prose rhythms: Heibges (1911); hiatus: Reeve (1971b).

[34] Late 1st century/Trajan/Hadrian: Ruiz-Montero (1994a) 489; C.P. Jones (1992a) 165; Baslez (1992) 204. Other estimates are conveniently summarized in Plepelits (1976) 4–9, Ruiz-Montero (1980) 64–67, and Hernández Lara (1994) 7–10. Briefly: early or mid-1st century A.D. is favoured by Perry (1967) 108–109, García Gual (1972) 374, Plepelits (1976) 8, Reardon (1982) 1 and (1991) 17, Holzberg (1986) 52. The extreme date of late 2nd century A.D. (Petri 1963) is based on the thesis of Merkelbach (1962) that the novels are almost all mystery-texts, that is to say literary elaborations of the proceedings of the mysteries of various divinities. Chariton's story, in this theory, does not fit the mystery-pattern; this is taken to mean that his novel was written not according to any such programme, but in uncomprehending imitation of earlier (mystery-) novels such as the *Ephesiaca* of Xenophon Ephesius. This entails the assumption of a date later than the 2nd century models and near the date of the papyri (see n. 6 above). The theory has been universally rejected; see e.g. Reardon (1971) 394–98.

history. But this is superficial; not only are there anachronisms, but more importantly, the unconscious assumptions underlying the story are consistently those of the early Roman Empire. Some of the anachronisms are major and blatant. Hermocrates is represented as being alive and pre-eminent in Syracuse when Artaxerxes (Artaxerxes II Mnemon) is on the Persian throne; in fact Hermocrates died in exile in 407—the novel does not report his death—but Artaxerxes ruled from 404 to 358. Some of the "history", furthermore, appears to reflect the reign of Artaxerxes III; and Miletus did not come under Persian domination, in the fourth century, until 386. Other departures from historical accuracy are less flagrant, and are integrated into the story plausibly enough. Hermocrates did have a daughter, who was the first wife of Dionysius I, the first tyrant of Syracuse and originally a supporter of Hermocrates; we do not know her name, but we are told by Plutarch that she committed suicide after being brutally raped by rebels.[35] At the end of Chariton's story, Callirhoe leaves her baby (by Chaereas, but thought by Dionysius to be his own) with his putative father in Miletus, and it is predicted that he will one day come to Syracuse to come into Hermocrates' heritage. Now, Syracuse was in fact later ruled by the son of *a* Dionysius— Dionysius II, the son of Dionysius I. The name of Dionysius is admittedly common enough, but it is clear that this Syracusan background is the origin of Chariton's name for his character. Chariton's names for his actors are usually felicitous and generally authentic.[36] Besides Artaxerxes himself, Artaxerxes' wife Statira figures in the novel under her own name, though assuredly with no more verisimilitude than her husband or Hermocrates. The name Chaereas resembles Chabrias, the name of a celebrated historical Athenian general who fought as a mercenary for the Egyptian king Tachos during an Egyptian revolt against Persia. The revolt represented in the novel thus again reflects a historical event; and again it constitutes an anachronism, because it took place in 360, more than forty years after the

---

[35] So says Plutarch, *Dion* 3; the charge of rape is a fair inference from his phrase "grave and outrageous abuse of her person". Diodorus 13.112 reports that she died of blows inflicted by soldiers.

[36] "Callirhoe" means "lovely stream"; the name is not uncommon (and we do not know that it was *not* the name of Hermocrates' daughter). "Chaereas" suggests "rejoicing", although he does little enough of that until the end of the story; the name occurs in an inscription from Aphrodisias, as belonging to a lawyer (the profession of Chariton's employer Athenagoras); see C.P. Jones (1992a) 162.

opening events of the novel.[37] Other names in the story—Rhodogune, Mithridates, Pharnaces, Artaxates, Megabyzus—are equally suggestive and authentic, being actually borne by historical people at various times, although they do not fit Chariton's characters accurately. Finally, Chaereas' capture of Tyre strongly resembles the exploit of Alexander in 332 (except that Chaereas achieves it by deceit), and thus is yet another anachronism. In fact the episode resembles even more closely a later siege of Tyre, in 312;[38] but Chariton is less concerned with historical accuracy than with recalling a tradition about Alexander, in which procedure he is perfectly capable of conflating events. And there are anachronisms of another kind, in which the text makes reference to conditions that did not obtain until imperial times. Thus, we find civic assemblies held in a theatre (3.17.3); chain-gangs (4.2.5); women participating in the assembly (8.7.1) and present at banquets (4.6.2—so that the host can see Callirhoe!).[39]

In short, Chariton's so-called "historical" background amounts rather to a general evocation of fourth-century history than to accurate exploitation of a given historical situation. None of the anachronisms has any serious incidence on the credibility (or incredibility) of the story; it is doubtful, in fact, whether it is justifiable to call it a historical novel at all.[40] It is clear, however, that the author is referring, in these historical reminiscences, to Greek historical tradition, as did the Alexander Romance, and as, apparently, does the fragmentary and probably roughly contemporary, novel *Metiochus and Parthenope* (which could be by Chariton). Certainly, the sarcastic criticism once levelled at him for his "ignorance" of history is totally misplaced. He never aimed at historical accuracy, but only at a general colouring of Greek history, to titillate the interest of readers, who could be expected to recognize and respond to a familiar tradition, in history as in literature. The story itself is of course not in the slightest degree historical. Nor is Chariton concerned, as a modern historical novelist would be, to represent the society and mentality of his story's dramatic date. The geographical, social and moral setting is very largely conventional, but where it has some specific reference, that reference is to the conditions and mores of the early Roman Empire:

---

[37] Salmon (1961) examines in detail this situation and associated circumstances.
[38] See C.P. Jones (1992b).
[39] See Plepelits (1976) 14–17 and his notes, esp. 118, 127, 144, 182, 185.
[40] See especially the important articles of Hägg (1987a) and Hunter (1994).

broadly speaking, in the first century A.D., although some would say the early second.[41]

For the geographical setting, Chariton clearly knows Caria, and in particular Miletus and the region around it. The town did have several harbours, as Dionysius says at 4.1.5; Chariton actually names one of them, Dokimos (3.2.11), the name being possibly a reflection of an episode in Hellenistic history.[42] It is entirely possible that in the early Empire it would have had a Temple of Concord (Homonoia); although we have no knowledge of it, other such temples are known at this period, and the general theme of *homonoia*—civic harmony— is common in the period, particularly from the later first century (it is the theme of speeches by Dio Chrysostom and Aelius Aristides, for instance). There did exist, at the right distance from Miletus, an anchorage similar to the one used by the pirate Theron when he brings Callirhoe to Caria (he does not use the harbour, presumably in order not to be conspicuous—he himself tells Dionysius' steward it was in order to avoid the tax-collectors—1.11.8, 1.13.4). Likewise, there was a local cult of Aphrodite, with a temple similar to that in which Dionysius first sees Callirhoe. Aphrodisias was, as its name implies, a centre of Aphrodite-worship, and had close ties with Miletus; its *floruit* is precisely the early centuries of the Roman Empire, so that the prominence of Aphrodite in the plot is accurate for the period. At the same time, this is after all a love-story, and Aphrodite is very much in place in it. Chariton may simply be cashing in on his local deity, rather than expressing any profound religious enthusiasm. Aphrodite's intervention in the action, whether in her own person or through her son Eros, is something less than systematic, and the religious impulse in the story is active only at a few points, for instance when finally Aphrodite decides that the lovers have been tormented enough and countermands Tyche's plans for further tribulations (8.1.1–3; this is a convenient way for the author to bring his story to an end).[43] *Tyche*—Chance—is in fact represented as a deity of major importance in human affairs, although in practice Chariton usually (not always) manages to motivate the action naturally and to eliminate unlikely coincidence from it. This concept of *tyche*, Helle-

---

[41] Notably C.P. Jones (1992a), Baslez (1992), and Ruiz-Montero (1980, 1989, 1994a).

[42] See C.P. Jones (1992b); this article and Jones (1992a) should be consulted for Chariton's own context and knowledge.

[43] For a different view of the importance of Aphrodite in *Callirhoe*, see Edwards (1985) and Ruiz-Montero (1994a) 1032–35.

nistic in origin, was certainly still a feature of popular belief in the pre-Christian imperial Greek world.

The structure of the society represented in *Callirhoe* is realistic enough, for the early imperial period. This is notably the case of the figure of the prosperous land-owner and public benefactor Dionysius, whose activities and estate correspond to those known from other sources. Other figures and elements in the story also fit perfectly well in the period: freedmen and slaves running the great man's estate, other estates worked by slaves in chain-gangs, lawyers, bankers, tax-collectors, pirates—who continued to operate despite Pompey's campaign against them in the last century of the Republic, and the best efforts of the Roman navy in the Empire. One detail may be thought seriously out of keeping: the option price paid by Dionysius's steward Leonas for the "slave" Callirhoe (1.14.5). A talent of silver would be a quite inordinate price at the dramatic date, since such a sum would have bought twenty or thirty slaves in the fourth century; even in Chariton's own time it would still be far too much.[44] But like much else in the story, this price is intended above all to produce an effect. Leonas, having just seen the stunning beauty of Callirhoe, is willing to risk a great deal of his master's money so as to secure her for him against the competition he is sure she would inspire; and Dionysius can be represented as rich enough, and magnanimous enough, to accept the loss of such a sum with equanimity, even before he has seen Callirhoe.

To turn to less tangible aspects of *Callirhoe*'s world, the dominant moral values are especially conventional. Dionysius, in effect a second hero in the story, is shown as humane, civilized, cultured, idealist, in fact a model ruler; and for all that these are timeless virtues, they do find an echo in the Empire, as in Pliny's *Panegyric* in praise of Trajan and Dio Chrysostom's speeches *On Kingship*. Dionysius is also the embodiment of specifically Greek *paideia*; throughout the story stress is laid on the comprehensive superiority of Greeks to "barbarians", which here means Persians—the theme is traditional from classical times; along with an interest in, but only limited knowledge of, exotic Persian customs, Chariton expresses the standard Greek repugnance towards despotic rule.[45] The heroine Callirhoe herself is

---

[44] A talent was 6000 drachmas, and at the time Hermocrates was alive a drachma per day was what a skilled workman earned (Thuc.3.17).
[45] See Bowie (1991) for Greek attitudes towards "barbarians".

obviously an idealized portrait, but again this fits with contemporary official emphasis (as in Augustus' legislation) on chastity, fidelity, stable marriage and family values—which is not of course to say that Chariton is drawing a realistic picture of early imperial society. Callirhoe's apparently facile abandonment of her son, at the end of the story, does strike a discordant note. Readers have been worried by this apparent cold-heartedness on her part—and, it must be said, on the part of Chaereas too, since he seems singularly undisturbed at losing a son he has never seen; it is the more puzzling in that Chariton could easily have had Callirhoe bring the child back to Syracuse, and does not attribute to Callirhoe any reason for her action (he might, for instance, have adduced pangs of guilt on her part for the way she has treated Dionysius). But as we have seen, this is one element in the vaguely historical background; it also has the merit of leaving Dionysius, for whom Chariton clearly has much affection, with at least a consolation prize, to add to the honours piled on him by the King. One can only conclude that in this respect Chariton's sentiment, or rather sentimentality, did not coincide with ours. He was prepared to make the trade-off for the benefit of his plot.[46] As for Chaereas, for most of the story he is too tear-stricken and ineffectual to command our admiration—indeed, one wonders what Callirhoe saw in him—but does finally emerge as a natural leader of men, brave, successful, generous to friend and foe, and beloved by his men; these are traditional terms of Greek historiography, as found in Xenophon's *Cyropaedia*, and again they find contemporary echo in (notably) Plutarch's idealizing pictures of earlier Greek leaders. This is another structural trade-off: if one wants to have two heroes but only one heroine, something has to give. But whatever the needs of Chariton's plot, it remains true that the combined qualities of the trio of principals are a reflection of his own age as much as they are traditional.

VI

Some aspects of *Callirhoe* have been indicated in passing, in discussing its date and context; they may here be gathered up in an overall view.

---

[46] Perry (1930) 102n contends that Chariton "must have been following some

The story is clearly melodramatic and sentimental, with abundant scope for pathetic representation of the three principal characters: Callirhoe, Chaereas and Dionysius indulge at every opportunity in soliloquies lamenting their sad lot, as *tyche* lands each of them in one desperate situation after another. It is in short an early popular romance. Early, but not primitive; if popular, not therefore cheap; and if relatively unsophisticated, in comparison with its successors, certainly not naive and not clumsy. *Callirhoe* is consciously conceived to produce by sensational means a strong emotional effect, and within its conventions is carefully and skilfully executed. Those conventions comprehend several spheres: moral values, literary structure, and writing. In each of these Chariton operates by clearly visible formulae.

In respect of moral values, human behaviour and the assumptions underlying it, what matters above all is love. Love makes the world go round; beauty begets love, love leads to marriage, and marriage brings happiness. This life-process is traditionally symbolized and engineered by Eros, but Chariton gives the ultimate credit to Eros' mother Aphrodite, as is only proper for a writer from Aphrodite's city; it is Eros, however, who is the principal operator. Eros is notoriously capricious, and his interventions lead to unpredictable adventures and mortal perils. He is abetted by *tyche*, *Fortuna*, herself virtually a deity in Hellenistic times, and the embodiment of another cliché: life is uncertain. But virtue will ultimately triumph; keep faith, and the gods will bring you through to happiness. In literary structure, this world-view takes the shape of other clichés. A handsome couple meet by chance and at once fall in love; they are separated and wander all over the world, meeting mounting dangers at every turn, but remaining true to each other until the gods bring them to final reunion. The mise-en-scène is just as formulaic. Characters are recognizable New Comedy types: hapless heroine, vapid hero, villain (Theron), resourceful slave (Plangon), rival (here a series of rivals, culminating in the King of Persia himself), noble seigneur (who is himself the principal rival and alternative hero, which causes problems for Chariton).[47] In the actual writing it is paradox and antithesis, apostrophe and monologue, hyperbole and rhetorical question;

---

tradition that obliged him to make this concession"—a singularly weak explanation given the liberties that Chariton takes with the genuinely existent tradition about Callirhoe herself when he actually resuscitates her from the dead!

[47] On Chariton's character portrayal see Helms (1966).

and linguistic figures, homoioteleuton, isoteleuton, hyperbaton; that is to say, rhetorical formulae.

Conventions and rhetorical figures are workman's tools. Like tools, they can be used well or badly. Chariton has certainly learned his lessons, and is clearly familiar with the whole range of literary equipment and devices by now accumulated in the Greek tradition. The conventions themselves, however, even if used well, can become tedious to modern readers, generally no longer used to so formal a vocabulary, such codes and devices, in literature (although often they will be perfectly happy to accept similar forms of stylized expression in opera). Chariton shares with contemporary Latin writers (notably Lucan) an appetite for whipping up the emotions, for increasing the tension at moments of crisis—they are numerous—that can be tiring; in Callirhoe's arias, paradox and antithesis can pile up to a point where the reader finds them so strident, so artificial, that they miss their effect. This of course is a matter of taste, and in the matter of rhetoric modern taste is not always the taste of Chariton's age. But beyond convention there is the author's personal contribution. Chariton, we have seen, does have literary ambitions, and they are visible in the way he approaches his story and the way he handles it. He clearly wants to fit it into the Greek literary and cultural tradition, and he handles the narrative, confidently, in such a way as to fit his specific purposes.

The historical setting of *Callirhoe*, it was suggested earlier, is meant to titillate the reader, who will feel pleasure at recognizing it. He can bring something to the story himself, and thus enter into complicity with the author. That is true, but there is more to it than that: there is the question of just what it is that the reader himself contributes. The setting is a classical Greek setting, so that author and reader are tacitly embracing Greek tradition; Chariton is to that extent already putting himself alongside earlier Greek writers, laying claim to *paideia*. That is reinforced by overt reference in his opening and closing sentences to his predecessors, the historians Thucydides and Herodotus, and further reinforced by quite frequent echoes of the historian Xenophon of Athens. The whole story is, after all, a history, or a biography, albeit of non-existent people, written for emotional effect as was some Hellenistic historiography. Polybius (2.56) describes how Phylarchus "in his eagerness to arouse the pity of his readers and enlist their sympathy through his story ... introduces graphic scenes of women clinging to one another"—compare the description of the

Persian queen, captive on Aradus, in *Callirhoe* 7.6.5, where "Statira laid her head in Callirhoe's lap and wept"; such parallels could easily be multiplied. Going beyond the historiographical parallel, the most frequent of all Chariton's literary references are to Homer. He is always ready with a familiar and apposite quotation, and is obviously conscious of the parallel between the warrior Chaereas and the warriors of the *Iliad*, as well as that between the wanderer Chaereas and the wandering hero of the *Odyssey*.[48] Chariton, in setting out his terms of reference, is staking his claim to participation in the cultural tradition; no doubt Philostratus found that especially pretentious.

So much, briefly, for Chariton's explicit ambition. The way he conducts his narrative displays another side, a somewhat more covert side, of that ambition: his self-conscious skill marks the craftsman. The principal feature of *Callirhoe*'s structure is the way in which, by the actual manner of his narrative, Chaereas plays the events in his story against the emotion they generate. This is achieved by the interplay between narrated action and dramatic presentation of selected episodes: between "summary" and "scene", to use the critical technical terminology employed by Hägg in his fundamental study of Chariton's narrative technique.[49] Thus, to take a particularly vivid example, the episode of the tomb-robbery is treated in this way. Chariton brings Theron into the action; his status as a pirate is established in a few lines, then we have a close-up of his thoughts as he soliloquizes about his criminal project. This is followed by the rapid description of the assembling of his gang, and then once more by dramatic representation, in direct speech, of their deliberations; all of which serves both to put us in the picture and to generate excitement as we are invited, by the mimetic presentation, to put ourselves in the gang's place. The scene switches to Callirhoe, entombed alive. The sensational revelation is made quickly: "she came back to life!" Follows a detailed account, *rallentando*, of Callirhoe's gradual return to consciousness and realisation that she has been buried alive. As the awful truth dawns on Callirhoe, we have no

---

[48] At 8.1.3, recounting Aphrodite's reconciliation with Chaereas, Chariton explicitly refers to the very language of the *Odyssey*'s exordium: διὰ μυρίων παθῶν πλανηθείς... γυμνάσασα διὰ γῆς καὶ θαλάσσης. For Chariton's references to the world of legend see especially Hunter (1994); for his use of Homer, Müller (1976) (exaggerated).

[49] Hägg (1971a) discusses the topic in great detail, in a comparative study of Chariton, Xenophon Ephesius and Achilles Tatius. See also Gerschmann (1975) for a study of the unfolding plot; and Reardon (1982) for Chariton's handling of his story.

more narrative but once more a direct representation of her terror, in her actual words: "Oh, what a terrible fate! Buried alive!"; and the tension mounts with Callirhoe's emotions. As Theron's men enter the vault the process is repeated: rapid narrative passing ("gliding" is Hägg's apt term) to dramatic presentation, in the characters' very words, of the girl's excited emotions, the pirates' panic, and their leader's scornful resolution of the situation: "a fine brigand you are—scared of a mere woman!" Throughout, the reader is first put rapidly, by authorial narration, in possession of the situation, then his emotions are whipped up in sympathy with those of the characters. Hägg literally measures the proportions of these passages, and they are striking: in round figures, nine-tenths of the story is presented in emotive "scene", and half of that dramatically, in direct speech.

Thus, it is not—or not only—the story itself, the plot, that is at the centre of Chariton's mind; it is the reactions it generates in the reader. This is particularly noticeable in the trial scene, in Babylon. Chariton, drawing on his legal experience, pulls out all the stops in the episode: the build-up to it, the impassioned and carefully written debate between Dionysius and Mithridates, and above all the startling climax as the "dead" Chaereas steps forward in court, to see Callirhoe for the first time since her "funeral" (the theme of *Scheintod* is standard in such novels). "Who could fitly describe that scene in court?" asks Chariton, who then proceeds to do so himself; "what dramatist ever staged such an astonishing story?" And there is proof, were proof needed, that Chariton, who explicitly acknowledges his debt to historiography and epic, is just as fully conscious how much he has borrowed from his third major model, drama. What is equally striking, however, is that although this is perhaps the most exciting moment, the emotional climax, of the whole story, it is not structurally of great importance, since for all its glamour it does not advance the plot at all; Callirhoe remains where she was before the trial, in the hands of Dionysius—or more accurately, of the King of Persia, and that is worse. The central issue—possession of Callirhoe—is resolved not by a passionate scene in court, but by a war related in the medium of narrative.

For all his drama, however—his melodrama, in fact, with its coloratura arias from Callirhoe, its blood-and-thunder Verdi-esque passions—Chariton does pay as much attention to his plot, his *mythos* in Aristotelian terms, as to his emotional effects. One of the marked features of his storytelling is the number of recapitulations he distributes throughout his narrative. Some of these are major. At two points he recalls to us in detail "the story so far", before inviting us to read on, and they are significant points: the middle of his tale, just before the sensational trial in Babylon (which might well throw a reader off track), and the beginning of his last book, a point at which he takes care to inform a reader now perhaps nearing emotional exhaustion that he is nearly home and everything is now going to be good news and plain sailing—quite literally, as Chaereas' ship, with Callirhoe now on board, heads for Syracuse. Other summaries are brief, but still carefully put together. There are some twenty of these recapitulations, as well as numerous brief phrases to keep the reader aligned as the narrative proceeds. This is the demonstration that Chariton is conscious of the need to keep his story straight, through all the emotion. He is willing, and eager, to play story and emotion off against each other; but he has a craftman's conscience. Conscience shows also in the care he takes to motivate action credibly as far as possible. He will go to a good deal of trouble in the matter, as in the episode wherein Mithridates learns the identity of his slaves Chaereas and Polycharmus; this could have been achieved quite summarily, but Chariton mounts a slave revolt purely to cover it plausibly. Likewise, the interception by Dionysius of Chaereas' letter to Callirhoe is justified by the rowdy behaviour of slaves left without supervision, which results in intervention by the forces of authority. *Tyche* is frequently represented by Chariton as being an ever-present driving force in human affairs, but in fact pure chance and coincidence do not figure excessively in the unfolding of the story. They are invoked sometimes, as when rebellion breaks out in Egypt just in time to solve Artaxerxes' (and Chariton's) insoluble problem of what to do with Callirhoe; but in general, here also Chariton's *trompe l'oeil* tends to hide a writer's conscience that is commensurate with his ambition.

Add, to all of this, the care for language and style already noted, and there emerges a picture of an early writer, working in clearly marked romantic conventions, who is by no means the poor thing he was once thought, by critics and scholars of more austere taste. Chariton, as a writer of love stories, is no Stendhal; no-one in antiquity was. One can reasonably reject the conventions of Greek romances. But they tell us something about their age, and at their best can be relished. Chariton is worth serious attention.

B. XENOPHON OF EPHESUS

Bernhard Kytzler

The narrative prose texts from classical antiquity, which we have come to call—somewhat anachronistically—the ancient "novels", comprise about one and a half thousand pages in modern editions or translations. Within this quite impressive corpus, the tale of a young couple and their adventures, that has survived under the name of Xenophon of Ephesus, is a mere sixty pages, thereby qualifying for the distinction of being the shortest of all ancient Greek novels.

I. *The Text*

Two codices conserve the text in question. Whereas the London cod. Musei Brit. Add. 10378 is a product of the eighteenth century and therefore of no use for the *recensio*, the cod. Laurentianus conv. soppr. 627 in Florence has been produced in the thirteenth century. It thus serves as *codex unicus*. Its spelling and its syntax are far from being standardised;[1] yet all the sentences are essentially clear from beginning to end, and our understanding of the tale is generally not impaired by the shortcomings of the transmitted text. Certainly, emendations are necessary in many places,[2] but looking at the whole, the only details not fully comprehensible are minor ones. The progression of the narration is surely questionable, though never on textual grounds. It is rather the context which occasionally baffles the modern reader.

II. *The Story*

There are five books of varying lengths which narrate the story. The work provides a rich texture woven of threads which originate from a common point (one is tempted to add, from a common place),

---

[1] Dalmeyda (1926) XXXVI–XXXVIII; Papanikolaou (1978) XI–XII.
[2] See Appendix.

which then diverge over most of the Mediterranean world and eventually are brought together at the end in a happy finale: the closing scene shows a group of virtuous people enjoying their life and one another's company whereas the evil-doers are eliminated one by one during the course of the story.

It all begins with love. There is a young man of exceptional beauty in Ephesus who spurns the god of love. Since he himself is the only one whose looks are capable of enchanting everyone, he feels himself superior to any divine power. And there is also a lovely virgin in the city, the fairest of them all, the same age as Juliet and Lolita. Predictably, the two meet during a religious celebration, and when they see each other, immediately fall in love: this is the classical *coup de foudre*, and both victims, inexperienced in love but sufficiently well versed in rhetoric by the author, utter long monologues about the unhappiness produced by their new feelings and their intolerable separation. These declamations are accompanied by ominous physical phenomena such as pale complexions, weary eyes and a slow physical wasting away of the whole physique. Diviners try their arts on the couple in vain; the distressed parents feel the need to consult Apollo himself in his temple in nearby Kolophon. The nine oracle verses—the text of which is not fully clear at some points—indicate that their lives are endangered by endless toils and hardships, but promise a *lieta fine*. Like the modern reader, the parents of the two unhappy lovers are not sure what the oracle really means. They decide to unite their children in marriage and "to send them on a trip abroad for the time after their marriage".[3]

The narration indulges in descriptions of the wedding and its joy as well as of the departure and its sadness. The journey takes the newly-wed couple via Kos and Knidos to Rhodos, where they disembark, admired by all Rhodians for their radiating beauty. "They toured the whole city and gave as an offering to the Temple of Helios a gold panoply and inscribed on a votive tablet an epigram with the donors' names." After this they go to sea, sailing towards Egypt. And it is from this point onwards that the ill fate predicted by Apollo's oracle, begin to manifest themselves.

A certain pattern becomes dominant: the exceptional beauty of the two young people arouses the desire of pirates, robbers, maharajahs, commanders and other strange people. The aforementioned

---

[3] Translation here and in the following by Anderson (1989a).

oracle of Apollo is also relevant here: the same source of danger is also the source of salvation. Wherever one of the evil-doers threatens the chastity or lives of the victims, another one, beguiled by their so extraordinarily attractive appearances, sets out to help them. They both find few true friends but numerous unexpected helpers willing to save them for egotistic reasons, until the next encounter repeats the pattern in a slightly altered way. The weaving of this texture of plot may be termed "Theme and Variations".

First, pirates seize their ship and burn it, taking along with them Anthia and Habrokomes, a few of the servants and most of the cargo. Immediately the pattern begins to manifest itself: pirate A, named Korymbos, falls in love with Habrokomes, pirate B, named Euxeinos, with Anthia. However, pirate C, Apsyrtos, the chief of the robbers, takes both for himself "since he hoped to make a large profit if he could sell them at their market value." But this soon leads to the next turn of the pattern: in Tyre, Apsyrtos' daughter Manto falls in love with Habrokomes. He proudly spurns her insinuations and replies to her letters with stern contempt. What comes next is not unexpected: Manto, feeling offended and degraded, complains to her father that Habrokomes has tried to rape her. Why should the father distrust his daughter? He puts Habrokomes into jail to be tortured, while at the same time sending Anthia away to Syria with their two servants, Leukon and Rhode. There, our heroine is given to a goat-herd named Lampon. However, she tells him her story in such heart-moving tones that he "took pity on her and swore that indeed he would not molest her, and tried to reassure her."

From this point on, there are two disparate threads of the story to follow: hero and heroine are separated, and each has to resist many different trials. While Anthia is unhappy but at least safe with Lampon, Habrokomes is still in jail. His master Apsyrtos discovers his innocence in a rather predictable way: by chance, he finds the correspondence between his daughter and the handsome young man, understands Manto's calumny, and becomes aware of the injustice of his punishment. As a consequence, he not only frees his slave but puts him in charge of his entire household. The parallel to the Old Testament story of Joseph, Potiphar and his wife is evident. In a short aside we learn that Leukon and Rhode, the two servants, are taken to Xanthos in Lykia, where they are bought by a friendly old man so that they are enabled to lead a comfortable life, "but sorely missed the sight of Anthia and Habrokomes."

And this brings us back to Anthia. This time it is Moeris, the husband of her arch-enemy Manto, who falls in love with her. When Manto becomes aware of this turn of events, her fury leads her to order Lampon to kill Anthia; Anthia laments her situation thus: "Ah, this beauty conspires against both of us at every turn! Because of his all too attractive appearance Habrokomes has perished in Tyre, and I here." Again, Lampon takes pity on her and instead of killing the girl, he sells her in the harbour to some merchants who sail with her to Kilikia. However, as is typical of an ancient Greek novel, they never arrive there: a storm wrecks their ship, and only a few people survive, Anthia among them. But she is not destined to enjoy her freedom for long: a robber called Hippothoos, who will become an important figure in the tale, appears with his band out of the darkness and takes her prisoner.

Meanwhile, Habrokomes discovers from a letter written by Manto to Apsyrtos that Anthia has been sold. Manto unwittingly reveals the truth when she tries to deceive her father about her plans to murder Anthia. The husband seeking his wife does not hesitate for a moment: he leaves Apsyrtos's household, travels to the estate where his wife has been living, and since this is a Greek novel, he immediately encounters Lampon, whom he questions about "a girl from Tyre". Lampon shares his knowledge with the unknown stranger, and thereupon Habrokomes sets out for Kilikia to find Anthia.

She is, as we know, in the hands of the robbers. They hold a celebration in honour of Ares, the god of war, with Anthia chosen to be the victim. However, the danger to the heroine is averted: at the very moment of the sacrifice, Perilaos the Eirenarch, "Peace Officer" of Kilikia, appears, and his soldiers capture or kill all the robbers. Only one escapes—Hippothoos. And Anthia? It is easy to predict her fate: Perilaos takes her into his care, brings her to Tarsos and all too soon falls deeply in love with her. So insistent is he about wedding her that she cannot refuse to comply: she promises to consent to their marriage after a delay of thirty days—a clever tactic that she will again employ later in the tale.

Re-enacting the pattern of his fortuitous encounter with Lampon, Habrokomes now meets the sole survivor, Hippothoos, who persuades the young man to join him, leaving Kilikia to journey to Kappadokia and Pontos, where there are many wealthy people to rob. Although Habrokomes has set out to find Anthia in Kilikia, he now agrees to his new friend's suggestions; we are told that he "also hoped in the course of their long travels to find Anthia."

And so Book III proceeds with the two new friends on their way to the town of Mazakos. There, Hippothoos briefly recounts his own story: he had been the lover of a fine young boy in Perinthos until a rich man seized the object of his desire and took him to Byzantium. Since Hippothoos saw no other alternative, he stabbed the rich man one night and escaped with his beloved boy. However, when a shipwreck took the life of his friend, he decided to become a robber. When Habrokomes in turn recounts the events of his life, Hippothoos remembers that a beautiful young girl had been taken prisoner by his men; they realize that she must have been Anthia, and set out to find her in Kilikia.

Meanwhile, the thirty days having come to an end, Anthia must keep her promise to marry Perilaos. In order to avert this fate, she obtains from a doctor a poison which will kill her on the night of her wedding. When Perilaos enters the bridal chamber, she appears to be dead. Anthia is much bewailed and laid to rest in her grave. But, like her counterpart, Juliet, the potion, that she has taken, proves to be a harmless sleeping drink, so that she awakens in horror in her tomb.

Instead of Romeo, robbers come to her rescue. Recognizing her value on the slave market, they ship her to Alexandreia, where no less a personage than a real Maharajah from India buys her for his pleasure. But Anthia employs her delaying tactic again: she tells him that he must wait a full year because she is under the protection of Isis until then. Psammis, her owner, is superstitious enough to believe this and reluctantly agrees not to touch her.

Habrokomes learns news of his wife in Tarsos—her sudden death, the disappearance of her corpse. Spontaneously he runs to the harbour and boards a ship which by mere chance is sailing to no other place than Alexandreia where, as we know and he does not, Anthia is waiting. But there are many more detours. The ship goes off course, and in the Nile delta all aboard are captured by a band of vicious knaves and sold in Pelusion. Habrokomes, again a slave, is sold to old Araxos, whose lascivious wife, aptly called Kyno (bitch), murders her husband in order to live with Habrokomes. He detests her, deplores her deed and flees. In obvious congruity with the Manto story, the tale proceeds: Habrokomes ends up in jail again, falsely accused by Kyno of having murdered his master and of attempting to rape his mistress.

At the beginning of Book IV, the shortest one, there are now three simultaneous plots to follow. Hippothoos, attempting to find his runaway friend Habrokomes, eventually arrives in Egypt with more than five hundred robbers and practices his profession there. While Anthia waits there for the end of her year's delay, Habrokomes is sentenced to death. Tied to his cross, he addresses a prayer to the sun and the god of the Nile, and behold, a storm pushes his cross into the waves, so that he reaches the sea unharmed. But this cannot suffice, as Tamino and Pamina tell us. He is recaptured and this time sentenced to be burnt. Again he prays, and again the mighty river's waves extinguish the fire and save his life for the second time. Thereupon he is returned to jail "till they could find out who he was and why the gods were looking after him like this."

The unfortunate Psammis falls into the hands of Hippothoos on his return to India and is killed. Anthia and the precious goods carried by the caravan fall prey to the robbers, but strangely enough, neither Hippothoos nor Anthia recognize each other. By contrast, Habrokomes is released and, quite unexpectedly, decides to travel to Italy but instead is driven by adverse winds to Syracuse in Sicily. During this period one of the robbers tries to rape Anthia; she resists and succeeds in stabbing him. On his return, Hippothoos, enraged by the loss of his man, orders Anthia to be placed into a deep trench together with two wild dogs. But how can the rancour of a robber prevail against the power of Eros? Predictably, the guard falls in love with Anthia, feeds the dogs so that they do not harm her, and brings her some food and water to survive.

Book V, the final one, shows Habrokomes in the hut of a Sicilian fisherman, to whom he tells all his troubles and who responds with his own quite extraordinary story. As enigmatically as Habrokomes had decided to journey to Italy, so too Hippothoos mysteriously decides to go there. He has lost his men in a battle with Polyidos, a kinsman of the prefect of Egypt, while Anthia has been persuaded by the strong oaths of her guard to trust him and to accompany him to Koptos. Here, Polyidos seizes the robber and also finds Anthia. The continuation of the story is no surprise: Polyidos falls in love with her on the spot, but once again she contrives to make him promise not to take her by force. His wife Rhenaia is none too pleased about her new rival, and while her husband is away on duty, she arranges for Anthia to be sold to a brothel and puts her aboard a ship bound for a far away place:—Italy, of course. In Tarent Anthia finds herself in the hands of a greedy brothel keeper. At the same time Hippothoos comes to Taormina, whereas Habrokomes leaves Syracuse and sets out to sail home via Italy.

This is the moment when the author returns to two almost forgotten places. One is Ephesus: here the parents of the hero and the heroine end their life subdued by grief at not knowing the whereabouts of their children. And the other one is Xanthos in Lycia. Only very attentive readers will recall that it is here that the former servants of our couple, Leukon and Rhode, live a comfortable life. They now also decide to go back to Ephesus, and proceed on their journey via Rhodos. There they learn that their young master and mistress have still not returned home, and make up their mind to remain in Rhodos until they hear news of them. Here then is the widest divergence of the plot with no fewer than five different places and situations to remember: Ephesus, where the parents die and which all the other characters in the tale make their destination; Xanthos, from where the servants make their journey to Rhodos; Taormina, where Hippothoos has landed against his will; Italy, to where Habrokomes is travelling; and finally Tarentum, where Anthia is incarcerated in the brothel.

Anthia's story proceeds in the usual way: the brothel keeper wants to sell her, but she is able to deceive him: "She fell to the ground, let herself go, and pretended to be afflicted with the divine disease," i.e. epilepsy. To fully convince him, she tells him a gruesome story about a revenant who had infected her one night, in her early youth, with that disease.

Habrokomes and Hippothoos experience quite different fates in Italy: whereas the robber succeeds in Taormina, finding an old, rich widow who marries him quickly and then dies even more quickly, Habrokomes has a very difficult time at Nuceria, where he labours in a quarry.

As a man of means, Hippothoos now lives in luxury, but "always kept Habrokomes in his mind and prayed that he would find him; he was determined to share with him his whole way of life and his wealth." In the meantime, he shares his possessions with a good-looking young Sicilian aristocrat. By chance Hippothoos is present when Anthia is exhibited for sale in the market place of Tarentum. He remembers having seen her in Egypt and buys her; and falls in love with her; and is repudiated by her; and insists all the more. And so finally she tells him her life story, with the result that he now realizes that he has found his friend Habrokomes's wife, Anthia. From now on she is safe—except that Habrokomes is absent.

Habrokomes now sets his course back to Ephesus. During his stopover in Rhodos, he finds not only the golden panoply dedicated by him and Anthia such a long time ago, but also sees next to it a pillar, erected in honour of Habrokomes and Anthia by Leukon and Rhode. They come along by chance while he is bemoaning his fate; after the recognition scene they care for him, while he continues to mourn for Anthia.

She is, as we know, with Hippothoos in Italy, and fortunately he now sets sail to bring her back home; of course his journey leads him to Rhodos too. And so the way is paved for a long drawn out anagnorisis, for a second wedding night with tales recounted of all these hardships suffered and so bravely overcome. Soon the three couples enter Ephesus and dwell there happily for the rest of their lives—Hippothoos and his boyfriend, Leukon and Rhode, and Habrokomes and Anthia.

III. *Characterization*

The tale's torrential account of journeys, encounters, complications, torments, rescues and many other opposing elements depicted in the course of the narrative is certainly entertaining. Yet it is also confusing. In fact Xenophon's is a kafkaesque world: characters set out for a certain place but never arrive there. They suddenly leave places without convincing reasons for doing so. Friendships suddenly develop, one wonders why. Goals are set but soon abandoned without sufficient explanation. People are buffeted in a world, beset by obstacles which they are unable to overcome. It is only by mere chance that they survive their torments unharmed or at least not too seriously damaged. Whenever one of the characters decides to adopt a certain plan of action, the reader may be sure in advance that he will not succeed. The host of Anthia's suitors never really possess her, outwitted as they are by the clever girl or restrained by some unexpected fate. Habrokomes never finds Anthia even though he constantly travels in search of her. Hippothoos never manages to keep his gang of robbers together, since the forces of the law repeatedly destroy his bands. However, neither are the regular troops ever capable of taking him prisoner; he always is the single solitary survivor of the military disaster inflicted on his men.

This summary is all correct and yet, at the same time, much too simplistic to be entirely correct. For as much as details contradict each other, as much as goals are unfulfilled and plans and schemes mysteriously abandoned, it is none the less evident that the central motif, Eros, is triumphantly dominant, not only at the end in the reunion of the loving couple, but also throughout the story; Habrokomes and Anthia both succeed in remaining faithful to each other even under the most incredible circumstances and the most cruel hardships. Although they never actually accomplish what they undertake they are rewarded finally for their endurance and faithfulness. Fate has been cruel to them without reason or justice; but the granting of pardon and their ultimate reunion are equally inexplicable. The figures in the narrative find themselves in a world that cannot be rationally explained; however, the irrational aspect of human existence is operative, even dominant during the entire tale.

By contrast, whereas all the endeavours of Xenophon's characters are to no avail, their prayers and vows and donations bring about marvelous changes. Virtually every time they address a god or goddess they are rewarded with some consolation or even salvation. In fact the story commences, in accordance with the great models provided by the *Odyssey* and the *Aeneid*, with the revenge of an offended deity. And the story ends with a joyful reunion under the protection of another mighty god. In between there is a series of divine interventions on a higher or lower scale. Even if reason fails, piety rewards.

The two main characters complement each other very well. While the girl waits to be found by her lost husband, not taking any steps to find him on her own, he wanders through almost the whole of the then known world to discover her whereabouts. And only while he takes action by moving around, resisting all temptations, he proves himself as an active "male" hero. Anthia, on the other hand, uses many different means to preserve her life and her virtue: she not only resists all suitors, when necessary with force (even by killing one of them), but she also is quite clever in devising ruses and tactics of evasion, making up stories about herself, about religious vows that must be obeyed and even by performing a spectacle of the "divine illness"—epilepsy—performing so well and lying so convincingly that she achieves complete success. Comparing both characters, she is the shrewd, inventive, resourceful partner, much more colourful than Habrokomes, who is portrayed as a figure of endurance and resistance but not so much as a deviser of clever schemes or a performer of heroic deeds.

Interestingly enough, Hippothoos is portrayed as a "noble" robber, a man who has been brought down to this corrupt and degrading way of life through the experience of a lost love, and one who returns to an honest way of life as soon as fate has bestowed on him a fortune adequate for a comfortable existence. As long as he leads his band of robbers, he is characterized as a savage, even vicious person; but his origin is noble, and his later life proves him to be a good friend to Habrokomes, unselfish and congenial.

The threads interwoven in the fabric of the text are manifold, the changes of place and mood are numerous and rapid. This "cinematic" technique is a prominent feature of Xenophon's narration. Yet who was Xenophon? What do we know about him?

IV. *The Author*

In contrast to the much more famous Xenophon of Athens, author, disciple of Sokrates and cavalry officer, whose life is well known and amply documented, the personality of Xenophon of Ephesus is hardly known at all. Even the attribute "of Ephesus" may be no more than a result of his narrative which begins and ends in Ephesus; it may indicate not so much "the man from Ephesus" as rather something like "the author of the Ephesian tale". There is only one single testimony to his existence, to be found in the Suda.[4]

TESTIMONIVM
DE XENOPHONTE EPHESIO

Suda s. v. Ξενοφῶν (ed. A. Adler, pars III, 495)· Ξενοφῶν, Ἐφέσιος, ἱστορικός. Ἐφεσιακά· ἔστι δὲ ἐρωτικὰ βιβλία ί περὶ Ἀβροκόμον καὶ Ἀνθίας· καὶ Περὶ τῆς πόλεως Ἐφεσίων· καὶ ἄλλα.

"Xenophon from Ephesus, historiographer, (author of) The Ephesiaka, an erotic narration in ten books concerning (the fates of) Habrokomes and Anthia; (further) of 'About the City of the Ephesians' and other topics."

Even this short testimony is problematic. The most obvious inconsistency is that if mentions ten books, whereas only five have been transmitted.[5] We have already speculated about the meaning of the

---

[4] F Gr H 419 T1.
[5] On this see below pp. 348–350.

place of origin attached to the name. The definition *historikos* is equally enigmatic: certainly it could indicate to what modern scholars would term a historiographer, as exemplified by writers such as Herodotos, Thukydides, or Xenophon of Athens; but since one of the synonyms which were used in antiquity for the then not yet existent "novel" was *historie* (or "story"), Xenophon could also be described here as a "story-teller", or in modern terminology, an author of a novel.

Equally dubious is the title cited at the end, referring to a work "About the City of the Ephesians": is it a text that provides evidence about Xenophon's birth or life? What is written about Ephesus itself in the novel, is actually very little and at that, not particularly informative. On the basis of the evidence, the writer may have been (a) a born Ephesian citizen; (b) a visitor to Ephesus; (c) a stranger who had never seen the place with his own eyes and was not so much a keen observer of reality as an attentive reader of books. So the reference to the work "About the City of the Ephesians" may be no more than a lengthy circumlocution about our Ephesian-based novel. Or it may refer to a description of the city, lost to us but still available in the Suda's time. *Adhuc sub iudice lis est*... At least the information provided by the Suda about the novel makes sense: it appears in the same format in which Heliodoros speaks of his own work;[6] and could therefore indeed be Xenophon's own words for his title. Again, this is a hypothesis, as such quite probable, but not a cogent proof.

Although the Suda calls Xenophon an Ephesian, the manuscript does not mention his origin at all. It is, in fact, difficult to proceed further. The evidence provided is too slight to enable us to draw a more detailed picture of the author. And unfortunately there is very little further light shed when we investigate the date of his life and work.

V. *The Date*

The data-base to establish the date of Xenophon's lifetime and his work's composition is very limited. There are no direct documents, only doubtful conclusions drawn from details of the text itself. The

---

[6] Gärtner (1967) 2080/81 discusses the parallel material common to both Xenophon and Heliodoros; see also Ruiz-Montero (1994b) 1089.

learned *communis opinio* places him in the second century A.D. Two prior sources of evidence for fixing the date are available: the first is a number of expressions and other information provided in the text, the other the relation of Xenophon's novel to the work of Heliodoros and other novel authors such as Chariton *et al.* Unfortunately, here we encounter the same kind of dilemma with regard to the priority problem as that arising between Horace *Epode* XVI and Vergil *Eclogue* IV or between Tertullian's *Apologeticus* and the *Octavius* of Minucius Felix. As Adolf von Harnack wisely remarked long ago, the value of all the arguments is like the sand in an hour-glass; one turn of the instrument, and everything points to the opposite direction. Suffice it here to say that Heliodoros seems to belong to the third century A.D.; but some scholars see him, while others see Xenophon as the imitator of the other author's text. It should he noted, that this method of argumentation—i.e. the use of common patterns of narration or scenarios or personal profiles—is thus of minimal value. After the loss of so many more similar texts, any affiliation between two of the surviving ones is hazardous to establish, unless we have a verbatim quotation or the name of the author cited or the title of his work quoted. None of this is the case in Xenophon's text, so that although many close parallels might be drawn between parts of his novel and others, there is no certainty at all as to whether they establish a real link or a clear chronology. In fact both writers might have followed a source now lost to us. They might also have read many related texts and thus followed common patterns instead of a single example.[7]

If intertextuality is of no assistance in establishing precise data for the *Ephesiaka*, perhaps historical evidence could clarify the matter further? Unfortunately, however, there is little to be achieved by employing this method. If the ruler of Egypt is referred to repeatedly as ἄρχων τῆς Αἰγύπτου[8] we really learn no more than that this terminology points to a period in the time after Augustus. When the "Peace Officer of Kilikia" is mentioned[9], historians refer to an inscription of 116/7 A.D. which is a firm *terminus post quem*; but this could also be terminology already in use for some time earlier.[10] There also seems

---

[7] For the material of parallels between Xenophon and other authors see note 31; the consequences drawn from this material are subject to different evaluations of the sources and cannot provide more than vague hypotheses.

[8] 3.12.6.; 4.2.1.9.; 5.5.2.

[9] 2.13.3.; 3.9.5.

[10] See Ruiz-Montero (1994b) 1092, ann.18.

to exist a *terminus ante*: when Xenophon talks about the Temple of Artemis at Ephesus he mentions it as if it were fully functioning. This would place his writing before the destruction of the temple by the Goths in 263 A.D.; however, he might also have written later (although this is improbable) and decided to set his narrative some time in the past. Finally there is mention[11] of "herdsmen" in the Nile Delta, who act as robbers and thus might be identified with the revolt of 171 A.D.[12] Certainly, such lawless people might well have been found for some time prior to 171; the connection between the revolt and the novel texts seems obvious, but even this provides no more than an approximation of the date.

To conclude, it is impossible to refute the assumption that Xenophon lived in the second century; however, it is equally impossible to prove this assumption beyond doubt or to give it a more precise profile.

VI. *The Epitome Theory*

As mentioned previously, the Suda informs us that the *Ephesiaka* comprise i = ten books; the extant manuscript, however, contains only five. There are three possible ways to resolve this dilemma: to explain the incorrect figure in the Suda, or to provide evidence to show traces of an epitomator's work in the text, or finally to reconcile all the contradictions in one way or other. The story is well rounded at the end and has a proper beginning, thus mechanical damage is certainly excluded. Has a scribe misread e = five as i = ten? Or was it possibly a lapse of memory on the author's part when he construed confusing contradictions? It is easier to try to explain away the figure ten than to make any sense of it. In fact there seems to be only one other possible solution: to recognize the extant text as an epitome which has survived whereas the original full text of ten books has perished in the course of time. This is certainly a highly probable explanation, but can it be proven?

Many philologists have tried to discern traces of the process of abbreviation or condensation. In fact one is tempted to regard some

---

[11] 3.12.2.
[12] Schwartz (1985) 197–204, includes Ach. Tatios 3.13 and 5.18.1.1; Shaw (1984) 3–52.

of the contradictions which exist in the text as defects resulting from the clumsy work of an epitomator. On the other hand, they are details which might also have other causes, be it the carelessness of Xenophon himself or the lack of attention by an editor in his own time. Here again the evaluation process operates; what for one scholar is irrefutable proof of the epitome theory, is for another an enigmatic detail that might have various other explanations. And while scholars normally think of only one epitome, Kerényi[13] postulates no fewer than three: one dating from the first century A.D., the next one, under the influence of Chariton, in the second, and the final one, which is the extant text, in the third. It serves no real purpose to consider all the other possible theories, for example that the author himself might either have shortened his own book for selling purposes, which would make him his own epitomator,[14] or that once it had proved to be popular, he expanded his successful small novel of five books to ten books which still existed in the Suda's time but are now lost.[15] Suffice it to say that more than a century ago, K. Bürger's study, backed by the authority of Erwin Rohde,[16] usurped the *communis opinio* within the learned world: according to him, only Book I, half of Book II and also Book V—with the exception of chapter 2–10—are original, whereas the reworking by the epitomator accounts for the lack of logical progress in the plot as well as the variations in the lengths of the individual books.[17]

However, the issue is further complicated by the fact that T. Hägg's study of 1966 marked a turning point. He was able to refute most of the arguments in favour of the epitome theory. Although it has not been entirely abandoned, it is understood at least that once again there is no definite proof of the theory, nor any unequivocal refutation of it either.[18]

This leads, in some way, to a disappointing conclusion: the person of the author is unseizable, the text itself presents contradictions as

---

[13] 1973², 232 sqq. See also Merkelbach (1962) 337.
[14] Cf. Weinreich (1962) 14.
[15] Cf. Miralles (1967) 76f.
[16] Rohde (1914) 429.
[17] For a discussion of difficulties supposedly caused by the epitomator see Gärtner (1967) 2072–2080. O'Sullivan (1995) argues that the extant text of Xenophon is not an epitome, that it reflects a background of oral story-telling, and that Xenophon's novel pre-dates Chariton's.
[18] For linguistic and metrical points related to this question see Ruiz-Montero (1994b) 1096 and 1112–1119.

350 BERNHARD KYTZLER

does its description by the Suda; the date cannot be determined precisely, and the epitome question offers disheartening evidence as to how deeply these discussions are based on biases. There is more light shed, however, when we consider the little book's literary value.

VII. *Style and Language*

It is obvious to any reader of Xenophon's work, be it in the original Greek or in any of its numerous translations into various languages,[19] that he is using an unrefined, rather simple language. It is not accidental that J.B. Bauer was able to point to certain parallels between Xenophon's text and the New Testament in its *koine*.[20] Without getting lost in statistics it might be helpful to survey the figures of similes used by the authors of Greek novels:[21] Heliodoros 120, Achilles Tatios 110, Longus 107, Chariton 49, Xenophon no more than 4. Although some of the other texts are considerably longer, the enormous disparity of the figures is highly significant. Xenophon's style is to abandon virtually all the rhetorical ornamentation which abounds in other novels. It is only in his numerous lamentations and his few descriptions that some elements of rhetorical commonplaces are used ostentatiously. This author is not unable but apparently unwilling to disguise his tale in flowery language.

This is in fact a wise decision: the vigorous, even rapid pace of his narration, the repeated sudden changes of place, the many schemes which are carried out by different actors in locations far away from each other, could all easily convey too intense a conflict. The tension of the tale itself should not be intensified further by the language in which it is presented to the reader, or the reader would react negatively to an excess of literary means coming from devices duplicated by both plot and phrasing. We may assume that it is Xenophon's awareness of this that prevents him from using too many rhetorical devices. Moreover within the kaleidoscope of different environments and contrasting actions and counteractions, the style em-

---

[19] Schmeling (1980) provides a survey over fourteen translations into seven languages, to be supplemented by further items recorded by Ruiz-Montero (1994b) 1133. See also above no. 3.
[20] See Schmeling (1980) 78/79.
[21] See Schmeling (1980) 77.

ployed minimizes confusion and helps provide clarity and coherence. In the same way that the story repeats certain thematic patterns, the language reiterates certain set expressions which might be termed formulae.[22] The phrase "the most important people of the area" appears in our short text no less than six times, "(s)he was distressed" seven times and "was no longer able to endure" five times. A voyage frequently ends with the remark "having finished a voyage of many days they arrived..."; and a bridging of two episodes is habitually phrased as "on the one hand (s)he..., on the other hand (s)he..." This technique helps the reader to reorientate himself within the cataract of events; he recognizes a specific situation within the rapid flow of scenes as he recognizes a familiar description of a situation within the narrative. What the modern scholar sometimes is inclined to call monotonous,[23] the ancient reader (and especially listener) has accepted thankfully as a signpost on his way through an action-filled story.

All in all, Xenophon does not blind his readers with verbal pyrotechnics of word play and ornamentation; his diction is far removed from that of Apuleius. Again and again he uses the simple "and" to begin a new section or to combine two phrases which other writers might have worked out more elaborately as a well rounded sentence with numerous clauses. His is not the sophisticated style adopted by schools of rhetoric but the simpler way of addressing an audience used by (oral) narrators—that is, the language of life, not of school. His readers certainly derived their entertainment from his text; they were not in need of stylistic bravura but enjoyed a story which, packed with action, did not require—actually precluded—artistic verbal virtuosity.

VIII. *Religion*

More than anything else in Xenophon's *Ephesiaka*, the religious allusions throughout the work indicate the probability of a second century A.D. composition date. It is a deity, after all, who sets the entire plot in motion. In this respect, Xenophon seems to model his

---

[22] For the following see Schmeling (1980) 78.
[23] Schmeling (1980) 75 and 77, aptly quotes Turner (1968b) who felt that Xenophon "gives the impression of being almost illiterate... the style is "referential... to the point of being slipshod".

work on those of Homer, Vergil and Petronius, in which the wrath of Poseidon, Juno and Priapos control the destinies of the heroes, Odysseus, Aeneas and Encolpius. In a similar manner, it is Habrokomes's offence against Eros which precipitates the god's taking vengeful action against Xenophon's hero. However, as the story proceeds, other deities are introduced. In Ephesus it is Artemis, during whose celebration the protagonists meet for the first time. In Rhodos it is Helios, in whose temple they make an offering, one which ultimately brings about their reunion. Further on, it is Isis who, in the Egyptian sections of the story, aids Anthia. Above all, it is Fate, the Greek goddess Τύχη in control of all aspects of human destiny, who plays such a dominant role in the story. Most of the events in the plot occur "by chance": Fortuna reigns unpredictably, and there is no way of influencing her inexplicable and inexorable decisions.

This array of deities is typical of the second century A.D., during which a number of oriental and traditional cults competed for popular attention. Indeed, there are many others such as Mithras, Asklepios, Kybele—not to mention Jesus Christ—who do not even appear in Xenophon's text. The fact that there is no reference to Christ or to the Church could conceivably point to an earlier date of composition but the absence of other major gods and goddesses vitiates this argument considerably.

Scholars such as Kerenyi and Merkelbach have used the religious discrepancies in the text as evidence that the original novel was modified for other purposes into something else. In their view, the primary text, dedicated to celebrating Isis, was revised into a new text in honour of Helios. Such views are a strange combination of acute subtlety and modern narrow-mindedness. In a pantheistic society, one god may be perceived to be more powerful than another, but there is never any need to reconcile opposing religious beliefs or to eradicate contradictions. One belief is no worse than another; a believer may worship one divinity here, another there, just as a Christian pilgrim may pray to St. James in Santiago de Compostela, to the Holy Virgin in Lourdes, to St. Anthony in Padova and to the Black Madonna in Czestochowa. This is precisely what happens in Xenophon's romance. When our protagonists are in Ephesus, they worship Artemis; in fact the novel both begins and ends in the temple of Artemis in Ephesus, a cyclical composition pattern that is typically classical. When in Rhodos, they worship Helios, when in Egypt, Habrokomes prays to the sun and the god of the River Nile for his salvation, whereas Anthia visits the Temple of Isis and Apis. It is quite natural for them to honour the local deities, and the divine presence so honoured is in no way shown to be offended when somewhere else another deity is revered. An analysis of religious allusions is useless as a means of determining chronology, since the only thing revealed is geography, and this revelation serves no useful purpose.

Habrokomes and Anthia are not Christian missionaries, nor Artemisian ones, for that matter. They have no intention of acquiring followers of their local goddess in other places. They are merely pious enough to pay homage to foreign deities when they enter realms protected by such deities. Had they been transported by the author to Athens, they would have paid homage to Pallas Athene; had they gone to Cyprus, they would have worshipped Aphrodite. When they travel to places where other divine powers reign, they join the local populace and share the prevalent beliefs. Having left one place, they must reorientate themselves and ascertain in this new locale, who represents the divine heavenly forces there. Given the colourful variety of local cults, reflecting the fact that diverse regions are subject to the power of different deities, it is to be expected that only some of the gods and goddesses of the time are portrayed in Xenophon's novel. This should not mislead anyone into seeing these deities as providing a clue to the chronological genesis of the text.

IX. *Structure*

If any ancient novel offers a well-rounded structure, it is the tale of Habrokomes and Anthia.[24] The story both begins and concludes in Ephesus; it is based on the cult of the Ephesian Artemis. When the young couple commence their voyage, they are soon separated, and the rapid shift of focus back and forth from Habrokomes to Anthia gives the narrative not only a lively pace but also a balanced structure. However, in the course of the narrative the perspective diverges: it shifts from one local point at the beginning to a dual vista, and then, after the separation, it spreads out further, weaving in a third

---

[24] Some structural points are made in the report of the telling of the story by Gärtner (1967) 2060–2070; Schmeling (1980) 21–74; Ruiz-Montero (1994b) 1096–1105.

thread—the figure of Hippothoos who meets here Habrokomes and there Anthia, sometimes deliberately and sometimes by chance, sometimes recognizing each other, sometimes not. Before the final spectacle no fewer than five scenarios are displayed before the reader: even peripheral figures are reactivated, such as the parents of the couple in Ephesus and their servants in Xanthos. And with authorial dexterity, the whole company is suddenly regrouped and reorganized: the parents die; the servants come to Rhodos; and Hippothoos finds Anthia in Italy, from where they have both taken their way to Ephesus via Rhodos. There in the temple of the sun god, the lovers, so long separated, finally are reunited. In the *lieta finale*, three couples journey home to Ephesus where they will spend the rest of their lives together in joy. It is evident that this is not a simple way of telling a tale but a sophisticated method of structuring a narrative. None the less, misled by Xenophon's simple language, philologists have insisted on seeing the text as an unsophisticated piece of prose. Yet, even though it utilizes linguistic patterns (as noted earlier), it slowly, steadily, increasingly widens its horizon, not only geographically, moving from the eastern Mediterranean Sea via Rhodos, Egypt and Anatolia on to Sicily and Italy, but scenically. Moreover the plot is orchestrated to retain the reader's attention by shifting the focus of attention to several figures and diverse places. This narrative method renders the ending, when all are reunited, even more effective.

It is both astonishing and confusing how little the units of the single books are used for structure. Not only are the books of strikingly different lengths (I and V are equal, as are II and III, whereas IV is paradoxically short, no more than a third of the enclosing books): so far, no principle has been discovered to explain the reason for the books ending where they do. Nor is there any evidence to point to the inner unity of any single book or to parallels and correlations between the books with regard to their content. It seems that we must be content with a survey of the work's overall structure (as outlined above) and leave aside all questions related to the internal structure of the various books.

X. *Names, Dreams, Lies*

Three prominent features of the novel should be discussed briefly, since they add colour to the narrative combining traditional *topoi* with the personal style of the prose. T. Hägg[25] has drawn scholars' attention to the distinctive way in which names are used in Xenophon's composition. Given the short length of the volume, the mention of no fewer than forty-four characters is an astonishingly high number. Three quarters of them, mostly marginal figures, are given names by the author, the rest remain nameless. Many of these names carry a message, like Kyno = bitch, Habrokomes = soft-haired, Anthia = fresh bud, Hippothoos = swift horse. Ruiz-Montero has grouped these names into three separate categories:[26]

1. names which reflect the function of the characters,
2. names which reflect their professions,
3. names which reflect physical or moral qualities (the largest distribution of the three categories)

It should be noted that six of these names are found for the first time in Homer's epic, six others in Herodotos's historiography. Eighteen names, more than half, are found in the mythographical works of Apollodoros and Hyginos.[27] Even more significant than such links to literature is the fact that almost all the names in the novel are also mentioned in contemporary inscriptions: that is, Xenophon utilizes the real world much more than scholarship has generally acknowledged.

* * *

Dreams frequently recur in ancient literature, and Xenophon's work is no exception. However there are only three which are integrated into the text. Are they really "integrated"? The first (1.12) serves as a means of heightening the tension: it occurs immediately before the ill-fated separation of the star-crossed lovers commences, when Habrokomes dreams "that a woman stood over him, fearful in appearance and superhuman in size, and dressed in a blood-red robe; and the vision seemed to set the ship alight; the rest perished, but he swam to safety with Anthia". On this occasion, the author successfully places the dream into its proper context; he continues: "As soon

---

[25] T. Hägg (1971b) 25–59.
[26] Ruiz-Montero (1994b) 1107–1109.
[27] To assume that this is proof of Xenophon's using these handbooks (Ruiz-Montero (1994b) 1107 is going much too far.

as he dreamt this, he was in panic and expected his dream to portend some dreadful outcome, as indeed it did." In fact in the very next line, the pirates appear.

Quite different is the second dream (2.8): immediately before their separation, when Anthia has told him the calamitous news and said farewell, Habrokomes, imprisoned, dreams that his father comes and frees him from his jail cell. The second part of his dream depicts Habrokomes as a horse pursuing a mare through many lands, before finally finding her and being transformed back into human shape. As a consequence of his dream, he "was a little more hopeful".

The only dream that Anthia has (5.8) is an expression of her suppressed fears and jealousy: she envisions Habrokomes approached by a beautiful woman who is determined to take him away from her. Even though this is only a dream, Anthia begins to lament her plight. It is easy to see how different these three dreams and their functions are.

Such dreams are linked to the numerous forebodings of disaster interwoven in the romance and used "in most cases somewhat ambiguously".[28] The clues which are offered to the reader "are not always reliable, a situation which aggravates the already capricious appearance of the plot: Anthia is given up to pirates who do not ravage her (1.14), to a goat-herd husband who does not violate her chastity (2.9), to a kind of priest who does not sacrifice her (2.13), to a physician who promises but then does not poison her (3.5), to killers who do not kill her (4.6), and finally to a pimp who does not use her (5.7)".[29] What is revealed here is an author writing for an audience that does not mind being confronted with fearful threats which are never carried out; such an author is not addressing himself to scholars who compare and criticize but to simpler folk, who read and enjoy the story more naively.

* * *

Lies are one of the ploys which Anthia uses to fight off her suitors, and she masters this technique with ever increasing skill. At first, she achieves, on the grounds of fictitious divine protection, a thirty day

---

[28] Schmeling (1980) 90.
[29] Schmeling, *ibid.*

delay of her enforced marriage which she asks—and receives—from Perilaos (2.13.8); next, she insists on a full year in a similar situation with Psammis (3.11.5). Her final triumph is an artfully contrived performance (5.7): forced by her owner, the brothel keeper, to sell herself on the street, she pretends to suffer an epileptic seizure and subsequently relates a horror story of how this illness had been transmitted to her in her youth by a phantom. From a month to a year, from a story to a spectacle—it is easy to see how Xenophon intensifies his heroine's mastery of the lie, in terms of both quantity and quality. Surely the street scene marks the climax not only of Anthia's self defence but of the whole romance. And it is markedly superior to similar scenes depicting other heroines' escapes from degradation in brothels, as found in the *Acta Apocrypha* and in the *Historia Apollonii*.

XI. *Nachleben*

The terminus *Nachleben* is a coin with two sides. In one way it designates the physical survival of the ancient text, its transmission via scrolls and codices, papyri and inscriptions, quotations and allusions, later on editions of the original and translations into modern languages. On the other hand it means the influence that the work exerted on later writings, be it in the realm of the style, the story or the composition; be it the same genre or in other ones, on traditional forms or on modern inventions such as opera and film. There is not very much to say about both sides of this coin with relation to Xenophon's romance. There are no papyri, no direct quotations nor inscriptions, and before looking at some probable parallel texts, we have to keep a golden rule in mind,[30] namely "that much of the later influence realized by ancient prose fiction was exerted by the total corpus of ancient novels and not so very much by individual works." Now there are indeed some phrases in the letters of Aristainetos which might in fact be formed after the model of Xenophon.[31] Remarkably enough, Photios in the tenth century gives no summary of the *Ephesiaka*, whereas Hesychios around 500 takes notice of them.

---

[30] Schmeling (1980) 139.
[31] Xen.1.2.6 = A. 1.10; Xen.1.3.2 = A. 1.27; Xen.1.9.1 = A. 1.5; Xen.1.9.4 = A. 2.7; Xen.1.9.9 = A. 1.16; Xen.2.11.2 = A. 1.25; Xen.5.5.3 = A. 1.5; see Gärtner (1967) 2087.

The only transmitter of the text, the codex in Florence, is written in the thirteenth century. Xenophon's novel here is copied alongside the romances of Longos, Achilleus Tatios and Chariton, all of them embedded amidst a host of theological writings. Angelo Poliziano has seen it, a fact proven by his Latin translation of the description of the procession in honour of Artemis in Book I, included in his *Liber Miscellaneorum* (LI). Astonishingly late came the *editio princeps* in 1726, arranged by A. Cocchi, accompanied by his Latin translation and preceded by an Italian translation of A.M. Salvini in 1723.

If we turn now to the other side of the coin, we come across an obvious connection of our text with *Historia Apollonii Regis Tyri*, where—in a Latin translation of a Greek novel—a number of traces of Xenophon's work may be found. Since this text found its way into the medieval *Gesta Romanorum* (153) it was later read by Shakespeare and used as the basis for his *Pericles*. Also Heliodoros's romance seems to be influenced by Xenophon. There are numerous parallels in the *Acta Apocrypha*, but before jumping to any conclusion we should remember the golden rule quoted above. However, there should be added a general observation which supports the view of genre influence over individual influence:[32] "The fact that the ancient novels cease to be written about the time that saints' lives and hagiographic romances begin, supports the notion that the latter grew out of the former." The so called *Recognitiones* must be mentioned in this connection, a work which, in a Christian context, uses many of the motifs that are part of the pagan stories: travel, defence of chastity, miraculous salvations, dreams and even the *Scheintod* motif.

Still following the first golden rule, we assume that the parallels from Shakespeare's *Romeo and Juliet* and *Cymbeline* with similar scenes in Xenophon's text are most probably genre-based. English romances in the nineteenth century by Henry Fielding and Charlotte Brontë may also be seen more as followers of tradition than of one single text.[33]

In conclusion, it is difficult to distinguish between Xenophon the author and Xenophon the object of research. In the latter part he falls in with the other Greek novelists as a member of a renowned group, not as a leader. In the former, he has not yet found the

---

[32] Schmeling (1980) 142. Cp. also B. Kytzler (1996) "Spätantike narrative Prosa," in *Neues Handbuch der Literaturwissenschaft*, ed. H. Hofmann.

[33] For a detailed discussion see Schmeling (1980) 148–153.

scriptwriter for the opera libretto or the film scenario which his colourful story deserves. Despite the numerous translations into modern languages, his text has remained widely unrecognized and probably will remain so in the future. It is strange enough that someone who apparently wrote for the entertainment of the masses in his time has been neglected so far by the entertainment industry of modern times.

APPENDIX

TEXTS

Dalmeyda, G., ed. (1926) *Xenophon d'Ephèse: Les Ephésiaques*. Budé. Paris.
Papanikolaou, A., ed. (1973a) *Xenophon Ephesius: Ephesiacorum Libri V.* Teubner. Leipzig.

TRANSLATION

English: Anderson, G., trans. (1989a) *Xenophon of Ephesus: An Ephesian Tale*, in Reardon, B.P., ed., *Collected Ancient Greek Novels*, 128–169. Berkeley.
French: Dalmeyda, G. (see above).
German: Kytzler, B. trans. (1968) *Xenophon von Ephesus: Die Waffen des Eros*. Berlin.
Kytzler, B. trans. (1986) *Xenophon von Ephesus: Abrokomes und Anthia*. Leipzig.
Italian: Cataudella, Q., trans. (1958) *Il romanzo di Sinofonte Ephesio*, in Cataudella, Q., ed., *Il romanzo classico*. Rome.
Spanish (= Catalan): Miralles, C., trans. (1967) *Xenophont d'Efes*. Barcelona.

GENERAL

Gärtner, H. (1967) "Xenophon von Ephesus," in *Realencyclopädie der classischen Altertumswissenschaft* 9A.2, 2055–2089. Stuttgart.
Schmeling, G. (1980) *Xenophon of Ephesus*. Boston.
Ruiz-Montero, C. (1994b) "Xenophon von Ephesus: ein Überblick," in *Aufstieg und Niedergang der römischen Welt* II 34.2, 1087–1138. Berlin. (Ample bibliography)
O'Sullivan, J.N. (1995) *Xenophon of Ephesus: his Compositional Technique and the Birth of the Novel*. Berlin.

C. LONGUS, *DAPHNIS AND CHLOE*

Richard Hunter

I. *A Summary*

Proem

A nameless narrator declares that while hunting on Lesbos he saw, in a grove sacred to the Nymphs, a series of painted scenes depicting "women giving birth, others dressing the babies, babies exposed, animals suckling them, shepherds adopting them, young people pledging love, a pirates' raid, an enemy attack—and more, much more, all of it romantic (ἐρωτικά)".[1] This painting inspired a wish "to depict the picture in words" (ἀντιγράψαι τῆι γραφῆι), and so the narrator sought out an "expounder" (ἐξηγητής) of the painting and then wrote an account of it in four books as a dedication to "Eros and the Nymphs and Pan".

Book 1

On a large estate not far from Mytilene a goatherd named Lamon finds a baby boy being suckled by a she-goat; with the boy are expensive recognition-tokens. He and his wife, Myrtale, adopt the child, call him Daphnis, and allow the goat to continue feeding him. Two years later the pattern is repeated when a shepherd on the estate, Dryas, finds a sheep suckling a female child in a cave sacred to the Nymphs; this child too has expensive recognition-tokens with her. Dryas and his wife, Nape, adopt the child and call her Chloe.

When the children are, respectively, fifteen and thirteen, they are put out in the springtime to look after the goats and the sheep in response to a dream which Lamon and Dryas have on the same night; in this dream the Nymphs hand over Daphnis and Chloe "to a very pretty boy, with a very arrogant manner, who had wings growing from his shoulders and carried little arrows and a miniature bow".

---

[1] Translations from *D & C* are either my own or those of Christopher Gill in Reardon (1989), sometimes amended.

As they begin their life together with their animals, Eros introduced a note of seriousness (σπουδή) into their play. As Daphnis is chasing two he-goats which have been fighting, both he and one of the goats fall into a pit which had been constructed in an attempt to catch a wolf which had been ravaging the flocks. Chloe hauls him out of the pit by taking off her "breast-band"[2] and lowering it down to him; they then go to the Nymphs' shrine where Daphnis washes himself in a spring while Chloe watches and helps. When they go home in the evening, "Chloe felt nothing unusual except the desire to see Daphnis washing again". This she persuades him to do the following day, and having touched his skin again "she went away praising him, and that praise was the beginning of love", though Chloe has no idea why she feels so strange. Chloe is now the object of the attentions of a cowherd called Dorkon who knows "the name and the deeds of love", but Daphnis defeats him in a "beauty contest" in which the two young men compete in self-praise. The prize is a kiss from the judge, Chloe, and it is that kiss which is the start of Daphnis' love: "I have often kissed kids; I've often kissed new-born puppies and the calf that Dorkon gave her—but this is a new kind of kiss". Dorkon now resorts to force, wraps himself in a wolfskin and lies in wait for Chloe. Before he can grab her, however, he is attacked by the dogs who think he is a real wolf; he is rescued by Daphnis and Chloe who just assume it was a game "because they lacked experience of the daring strategies of lovers".

Their first summer together is full of opportunities for nakedness and kissing and what we, but not they, recognise as lovers' games. In the following autumn Daphnis is seized and carried off, together with some of Dorkon's cattle, by pirates who are ravaging the coast. Dorkon has been beaten up by the pirates, and as he dies he gives Chloe his pipe and is rewarded with a kiss. Chloe plays on the pipe, and Dorkon's cattle, recognising the sound, leap overboard thus causing the pirate-ship to capsize; the pirates drown, but Daphnis is carried on the backs of the cattle safely to shore. There is a joyous reunion—though Chloe conceals the kiss she had bestowed upon Dorkon—and they bury their benefactor with proper rustic honours. Chloe then washes Daphnis and herself bathes for the first time under his gaze, a sight which merely increases his suffering: "The bath seemed more terrible than the sea. He thought he must have left his

---

[2] ταινία, a band of material which functioned as a bra.

life (ψυχή) behind with the pirates—for he was young and a country boy and still ignorant of the piracy of love".

Book 2

After helping with the vintage, Daphnis and Chloe return to their usual pursuits and meet an old countryman called Philetas[3] who tells them about an encounter he had in his garden with a little boy whose "skin was white like milk, and his hair was reddish-gold like fire, and his body glistened as though he had just bathed". This little boy who, despite his appearance, claimed to be "older than Kronos and of all time (χρόνος) itself" told Philetas that he was "shepherding" Daphnis and Chloe, and at the end of his speech Philetas identifies the little boy as Love (Eros). In response to their questions, Philetas explains the great power of Eros and also gives them some advice: "There is no medicine (φάρμακον) for Love, no potion, no drug, no spell to mutter, except a kiss and an embrace and lying down together with naked bodies". Daphnis and Chloe recognise that their condition corresponds to Philetas' description and resolve to try his remedies (despite the cold weather). When it comes to it, however, they cannot bring themselves to lie together naked—except in the erotic dreams which haunt them—although their kissing becomes ever fiercer.

Some young men from the city of Methymna come into their territory to hunt, having secured their boat by a willow-shoot, because they had lost the rope. When the Methymnaeans' dogs scare Daphnis' goats, the goats run down to the shore and one of them eats the willow-shoot, thus freeing the ship to be carried out to sea. A violent dispute follows which leads to a trial presided over by Philetas. The Methymnaeans' prosecution of Daphnis fails, and when they try to carry him off by force a battle ensues in which the locals drive off the rich intruders. Back in Methymna, however, they deceive the citizens into declaring war with Mytilene, and coastal raids are launched; Chloe is carried off in an attack, while Daphnis hides in a tree. In a dream, however, the Nymphs tell him that they have asked Pan to look after Chloe, and they promise him that he will

---

[3] On the spelling of his name cf. Bowie (1985b) 72 n. 27; Müller (1990). The Hellenistic poet after whom this character is probably named was very likely "Philitas" of Cos, a well attested Coan name from the third century B.C.E., cf. Fraser (1987) s.v.

resume his life with her because the two of them are being cared for by Eros. Sure enough, out at sea the Methymnaean ship suffers from the weird manifestations of an attack of "Panic"[4] and the god himself appears to the captain in a dream, rebuking him "because you have dragged from the altars a young girl (παρθένος) from whom Eros wishes to create a story (μῦθον ποιῆσαι)" and warning him to restore Chloe and the animals at once. The ship is now borne supernaturally to the shore where there is another joyous reunion, with much kissing, and then a rustic party during which Lamon tells the myth of Pan and Syrinx (the goat-herding maiden who became the original "pan-pipes") and Philetas presents Daphnis with his own set of pipes. Finally, Daphnis and Chloe exchange oaths of eternal fidelity, Daphnis by Pan and Chloe by the Nymphs.

Book 3

The Methymnaeans sue for peace with Mytilene, and a bitter winter descends upon the land which keeps everyone at home, and so Daphnis and Chloe apart. To overcome this, Daphnis decides to trap the birds which nest outside Chloe' house, because "love can fight its way through anything—fire, water, or Scythian snow". He is in luck, because not only is the trapping successful, but he is discovered by Dryas who invites him in to share their celebration of the winter festival of Dionysus. There is a joyous reunion, and Daphnis stays the night, sharing Dryas' bed: "he embraced him and kissed him often and dreamed he was doing all this to Chloe". In the morning the young people have a chance for hurried conversation and kissing, the first of many such visits that winter.

When spring comes, the sight of the rutting sheep and goats encourages Daphnis to ask Chloe to lie down naked with him, as Philetas had advised, so that they could imitate the animals. Chloe, however, points out that not only do the animals do it standing up, they also do it "with their clothes on". Daphnis and Chloe therefore do not take their clothes off, but first try lying down together; when nothing happens, they stand up and Daphnis embraces Chloe from behind "imitating the he-goats", but again to no effect. Daphnis' "salvation" comes in the shape of Lykainion ("little wolf"), a lady who was "young, pretty, and rather sophisticated for the countryside" and who was

---

[4] Cf. Meillier (1975); Bourgeaud (1988).

married to a neighbour who was past his prime. She wanted to seduce the good-looking young goatherd, but realised that he loved Chloe and had also observed their unsuccessful attempts to discover how to make love. She therefore tricks him into coming into the forest with her, sits him down and tells him that the Nymphs have instructed her in a dream to teach him "the deeds of love". This she proceeds to do: "When he had sat down, kissed, and lain down, and she discovered that he was capable of action and was swollen with desire, she lifted him up from where he was lying on his side, slipped her body underneath, and guided him skilfully on the road he had been searching for until now. After that, she did nothing exotic (ξένον); from then on, nature herself taught him what had to be done". After the lesson Daphnis wants to rush off to practise his new found skill upon Chloe, but Lykainion warns him that Chloe "will groan and weep and bleed profusely", which rather puts Daphnis off. He does not tell her what happened in the wood, and indeed becomes less keen than before to allow Chloe to undress in front of him.

As summer comes around again, suitors are asking Dryas for Chloe's hand, and so Daphnis is forced to speak to Myrtale about his love for Chloe. Lamon reacts badly to the news, because Daphnis' recognition-tokens have always suggested that one day he and they might become rich. Again, however, the Nymphs intervene in a dream to Daphnis, telling him where he can find a great sum of money, washed up on the coast from a wrecked ship. Armed with this money, he approaches Dryas and Myrtale who immediately promise Chloe to him. Dryas then, with some difficulty, persuades Lamon of the desirability of the match, which is however postponed until after the visit of "the master" in the following autumn. Daphnis can now kiss Chloe openly "as his future wife", and he climbs a tree to pluck one lovely apple which was too high for the pickers, presenting it to her with the analogy of Aphrodite who received an apple as a prize for beauty. In return he received "a kiss that was better than an apple—even a golden one".

Book 4

As autumn approaches, the master's visit is announced, and so everything is done to prepare the estate. In particular, a very lovely formal garden, whose centrepiece is a shrine of Dionysus, is meticulously groomed by Lamon and Daphnis. One night, however, this garden is vandalised by a cowherd called Lampis who has his eye on Chloe and who hopes in this way to turn the master against Lamon. After bewailing their fate, they decide to reveal all to the master's son, Astylos, who is to arrive ahead of his father. This they do, and Astylos promises to make up a story to pacify his father, and so this danger passes.

Astylos had brought with him a parasite named Gnathon ("Jaws") who knew only how to "eat and to drink till he was drunk and to have sex when he was drunk. He was nothing but jaws and a stomach and what lies underneath the stomach". Being "by nature fond of boys (φύσει παιδεραστής)", he is attracted by the sight of Daphnis, and at night asks him to "let himself be used as he-goats use the she-goats". When it slowly dawns on Daphnis what is being requested, he observes that he has never seen one male animal mount another male; Gnathon must then resort to rape, but Daphnis is far too strong and quick for the drunken sot. The arrival of the master, Dionysophanes, and his wife, Kleariste, is now described; Daphnis wins much praise for his splendid goats which put on a performance for the visitors from the city. Gnathon, however, pleads with Astylos to give him Daphnis to take back to the city, arguing with elegant sophistry for the wondrous charm of goatherds. The possibility that Daphnis will become "a plaything for Gnathon's drunken lust" is too much for Lamon who now reveals the full story, together with the recognition tokens, to Dionysophanes. The master knows them at once, and Daphnis is recognised as the son of Dionysophanes and Kleariste, exposed at birth because Dionysophanes thought then that Daphnis was one child too many. A great celebration is held, and under cover of these amazing events Lampis seizes Chloe and carries her off. She is, however, rescued by Gnathon, who sees here a chance to recover his position which was obviously precarious now that Daphnis' real identity had been discovered. When she is returned, Dryas decides to tell her story also, and he allows Dionysophanes to understand that Daphnis and Chloe wish to marry. Further rustic parties are held.

They all then proceed to Mytilene to search for Chloe's parents. In a dream Dionysophanes sees Eros, at the request of the Nymphs, "undo his bow, put off his quiver, and tell him to invite all the best of the Mytileneans to a party, and when he had filled the last mixing bowl, to show each person the tokens of Chloe's identity—and then sing the wedding song". Dionysophanes does this, and the tokens are recognised by Megakles ("Big Man"), who explains that he had exposed his baby daughter because he had been impoverished by public demands on his money. After Chloe is reunited with her parents, they all decide to return to the estate to celebrate the marriage in the grand, rustic manner. The narrator tells us that after their marriage Daphnis and Chloe continued to live the pastoral life, and

> When they had a baby boy, they put him under a she-goat for nursing, and when their second child was born to them, a little girl, they had her suck the teat of an ewe. They called the boy Philopoimen ("Lover of Flocks"), and the girl Agele ("Herd"). They also decorated the cave and set up images in it and established an altar to Love the Shepherd, and gave Pan a temple to live in instead of the pine, calling him Pan the Soldier.

This anticipation is, however, not the end of the novel, as the wedding night is still to be described. Daphnis and Chloe are escorted to their bed-chamber to the harsh sounds of peasants singing the wedding-song.[5] In the chamber "Daphnis and Chloe lay down naked together, embraced and kissed, and had even less sleep that night than owls. Daphnis did some of the things Lykainion had taught him, and then Chloe discovered for the first time that what they had done in the woods had been nothing but shepherds' games (ποιμένων παίγνια)".

II. *Author and Transmission*[6]

Nothing is known about Λόγγος, the name which the manuscripts give to the author of *Daphnis and Chloe*.[7] The name is, of course, a very common Roman one—it is even attested on Lesbos where the

---

[5] Winkler (1990b) 124–5 sees here a disturbing element in the sexuality of the novel; at the very least we should connect this with the claim in the scholia to Theocritus 18 that epithalamia were sung to drown out the cries of the bride as she was deflowered, cf. Montague (1992) 242–3.

[6] For fuller accounts of these matters, and the evidence upon which my statements are based, cf. Hunter (1983) 1–15; Reeve (1986) v–xv; Vieillefond (1987) *Introduction*.

[7] We do not know what the original title of the novel was, and it is not unlikely that, if it was at all widely read (which cannot be shown, cf. below p. 369), it was known by more than one title; analogy from the other novels, and the evidence of the MSS, suggest that ποιμενικά ("Stories of Shepherds") or τὰ περὶ Δάφνιν καὶ Χλόην ("The Story of Daphnis and Chloe"), or some combination of these, will not be far from the mark.

novel is set—but many Greeks of the imperial period had Roman names, and no strong argument about the author's race can be based upon it. It has been argued that the novel contains allusions to some classical Latin poetry (notably Vergil); we can hardly rule out the possibility that an educated Greek of the later second century C.E. (cf. below p. 369) was familiar with major Latin verse, though I do not in fact believe that the case has been proved.[8] The case of a poet such as Vergil also makes it unreasonable to deny outright that a native Latin-speaker could have produced a Greek text of such allusiveness as *Daphnis and Chloe*, though it may be thought inherently unlikely. Whether or not the author reveals detailed knowledge of Lesbian topography has been much disputed,[9] but the stylised and rhetorical way in which Longus writes suggests that it would be fundamentally mistaken to seek topographical or climatic particularity. The opening of the proem, "When I was hunting in Lesbos, I saw in a grove of the nymphs...,"[10] suggests the *persona* of someone from outside Lesbos, who must be instructed by a local expert in the details of a famous local *muthos*. A similar conclusion may be drawn from a much discussed passage which describes how Chloe helps at grape-picking time: "... she picked the grapes off the vines that were nearer the ground. In Lesbos all the vines are low; they do not grow up high and are not trained on trees, but they let their shoots hang down and are spread out like ivy. In fact, a baby who had only just got his hands out of his shawl could reach a bunch" (2.1.4). The passage has been criticised, somewhat pedantically, for internal inconsistency, but it clearly assumes a non-Lesbian audience, and it perhaps also carries the flavour of a narrator relating the ethnographic information he has collected on his travels, rather than an inhabitant of the island telling of its traditions. The choice of Lesbos, an island famous for wine and love-poetry (Sappho), as the setting of the novel need not have a very complex explanation,[11] but there is no reason to deny that the author may well have had a personal connection

---

[8] Cf. Hunter (1983) 76–83.

[9] For recent surveys and bibliography cf. Bowie (1985b) 86–90; Vieillefond (1987) c–cv; Bowie (1994b) 451–2. For related considerations concerning the presentation of the natural world cf. Arnott (1994).

[10] The rhythmical structuring, ἐν Λέσβωι θηρῶν ἐν ἄλσει Νυμφῶν, seems to point to this translation, rather than (e.g., Dalmeyda and Vieillefond) "On Lesbos, while I was hunting in a grove of the Nymphs...." This, of course, does not mean that it was not the hunting which brought the narrator into the grove.

[11] For further speculations cf. Bowie (1985b).

with the island. It may indeed be that there is much in the novel which speaks to those with a privileged knowledge of the island and some, at least, of its people; unfortunately, we cannot identify any such material.

We are equally badly provided with information to assist in dating the novel. There does not seem to be a clear allusion to it until a poem of Constantine of Sicily in the (?) late ninth century C.E.[12] and then imitations in the twelfth century; no papyri have been identified. Nevertheless, there is a broad consensus among scholars that the linguistic style and "atmosphere" of the novel point to that marvellous period for Greek culture which falls roughly between the middle of the second and the middle of the third century C.E.; it is, at any rate, unlikely to be later than this. Greater specification within that period has been sought through hazardous arguments based upon Longus' literary affiliations and borrowings,[13] the cultural, economic and political conditions assumed by the narrative,[14] and the similarities between Longus' narrative technique and particular styles of ancient painting;[15] none of these methods inspires confidence.

There are two reasonably complete and independent witnesses to the text of *Daphnis and Chloe*: (i) Florentinus Laur.Conv.Sopp.627, written in the thirteenth century, and rediscovered in 1809. This is normally called A, though Reeve designates it F (for Florence). (ii) Vaticanus Gr.1348 of the early sixteenth century, usually cited as V or B. The other extant MSS are descendants of V,[16] and the *editio princeps* was published by Raphael Colombani at Florence in 1598.[17] F and V diverge very greatly, and F in particular presents a large number of very strange readings, perhaps the work of a careless scribe. The largest lacuna in V runs from 1.12.5 to 1.17.4 (five folios), and

---

[12] Cf. R.C. McCail, "Did Constantine of Sicily read *Daphnis and Chloe*?," *Byzantion* 58 (1988) 112–22.

[13] To the discussion in Hunter (1983) add H. Bernsdorff, "Longos und Lukian (Zu *Verae Historiae* 2, 5)," *Wiener Studien* 106 (1993) 35–44, who argues for a borrowing from Longus by Lucian.

[14] The description of Dionysophanes' estate is highly stylised, but there is nothing which defies belief for Lesbos of, say, the late second century C.E., cf. Bowie (1977) 94; Alcock (1989); Kloft (1989).

[15] For visual attitudes in *D & C* cf. below pp. 376–7.

[16] Cf. van Thiel (1961); Reeve (1986) *Praefatio*; id., *Journal of Hellenic Studies* 99 (1979) 165–7.

[17] Reeve (1986) xvi lists twenty-six editions of the Greek text up to 1960; since then there have been two more (Reeve and Vieillefond), and more are currently in preparation.

when Paul-Louis Courier discovered F in 1809 he transcribed the missing pages, with the assistance of the two librarians Del Furia and Bencini, only to obliterate them again by inserting a piece of paper covered in ink at the crucial point of the manuscript. Whether or not this was a deliberate act has been the subject of heated scholarly wrangling,[18] but whatever the truth, the text of that section of the novel is particularly uncertain.

III. *Reading for Pleasure*

The summary given above will have shown just how different *Daphnis and Chloe* is from the other Greek novels which survive. Instead of "love at first sight" we have an account of how love grows and how lovers come to recognise their condition, which is no longer a "given" of the narrative, but rather its very substance. As a consequence, the narrative does not unfold across the wide sweep of the Mediterranean in a maelstrom of adventures which carry the protagonists ever forward toward the inevitable conclusion, a maelstrom in which the main driving force of the narrative is the separation of the central pair. Rather, the "action" takes place, but for one brief scene in Mytilene, on the one estate, with a small cast of characters, and the two protagonists spend much more time together than apart; moreover, although the climax of the narrative is indeed, as in the other novels, the sealing of a permanent union between the happy pair, the central narrative interest, at least until the fourth book,[19] is "psychological" and emotional. The forward movement of the "plot" takes place in the minds and attitudes of the characters. There are, of course, motifs and scenes which we recognise from the other novels, but here played out in microcosm:[20] both lovers are threatened by admirers prepared to resort to rape if necessary; there are separations followed by joyous reunions; there are pirate attacks, shipwreck, a small-scale war between Mytilene and Methymna, and frequent dream interventions by helpful deities. The listing of these similarities, however, merely emphasises the differences.

The static quality of this novel by comparison with the others is

---

[18] See the helpful survey in Vieillefond (1987) xli–xlviii.
[19] On the special status of Book 4 cf. below p. 375.
[20] Cf. in general Anderson (1982) 41–2; Hunter (1983) 64–5.

part of its debt to the bucolic and pastoral tradition, represented for us largely by the poems of Theocritus and the *Eclogues* of Vergil. These poems are played out within a circumscribed world in which the dramatic and often erotic suffering of "little people" is contextualized by the limited horizons of the setting. In the principal "bucolic" poems of Theocritus,[21] as opposed to some at least of Vergil's poems, it is broadly true that nothing "happens": the situation at the end of the poems, or of the bucolic songs included within them, is unchanged. The bucolic world is a series of scenes which are always there, into which we can enter whenever we open a book. So it is that the relationship of Daphnis and Chloe is structured in a loose series of independent panels or episodes which allow us to view Daphnis and Chloe separately, then together.[22] These panels not only recall the painted scenes of the proem, but also emphasise the essentially static nature of the narrative at the level of the "action"; in one sense, nothing "happens". At another level, however, the narrative moves forward with the pattern of the seasons which both shape and (in a version of the pathetic fallacy) respond to the developing sensibilities of the young people.[23] This structuring by the seasons is not in fact a direct inheritance from the bucolic tradition, though it obviously draws upon imagery which is very familiar in all ancient erotic literature (the fire of summer corresponds to the fire of love etc.). Nevertheless, in joining his protagonists to the onward, but ever repeating,[24] cycle of the seasons, Longus makes them "a part of nature (φύσις)", just like the characters of Theocritus. That this also means that we must ask the same questions of their relationship as we ask of nature as it is constructed in the novel is a matter to which I shall return.[25]

The poetry of Theocritus advertises itself as ἡδύ, "sweet",[26] and *Daphnis and Chloe* is likewise τερπνόν, "pleasing", "delightful" (*Proem* 1,

---

[21] *Idylls* 1, 3, 4, 5, 6, 7, 8, 9, 10, 11, 14, 21. I make no distinction between genuine and spurious poems. *Idyll* 27 really belongs in this list, particularly in the context of *Daphnis and Chloe*, but something does "happen" in the narrative of that poem.

[22] Cf. Schissel (1913b) proposing twelve such panels; for some reservations cf. Hunter (1983) 65-6 (with notes). For rather different, "specular", structures in the novel cf. MacQueen (1990).

[23] Cf. especially Chalk (1960).

[24] The repetitiveness is stressed by the stylised and "ideal" form in which all the seasons are described: thus winter (3.3) is as we "imagine" winter, and so forth.

[25] Cf. below pp. 382-3.

[26] Cf. *Idyll* 1.1-2. It cannot, of course, be demonstrated that *Idyll* 1 was intended by Theocritus to head a collection of his poems, but *Eclogue* 1.1 picks up these

3). In part this acknowledges the bucolic tradition; in part too it marks the style of the novel as γλυκύ, a kind of style fully described in the surviving rhetorical treatise of Hermogenes of Tarsus (second century C.E.).[27] This is a style characteristic of "mythic" narrative—Hermogenes cites, *inter alia*, the story of the cicadas from Plato's *Phaedrus*—or of ecphrastic descriptions of scenes which appeal to the senses (Sappho is a standard example), and indeed of bucolic simplicity in general. "Sweet" too are texts in which quotations from and allusions to poetic texts are interwoven in the prose narrative, exactly as happens in *D & C*. Finally, "all thoughts of *eros* are sweet", and in this we see how closely subject and style are bound together in the novel; here again, *D & C* is truly the heir of Plato's *Phaedrus*[28] in which the link between a style which appeals to the emotions and senses and a similar content is firmly established. "Sweet" style is rhythmical, and characterised by short, matching cola in which "the arrangement of words produces pleasure for the senses". Closely similar, in another ancient classification, is the "middle style", called ἀνθηρόν, *floridum*, ("flowery") by Quintilian (12.10.59), a style whose primary function is *delectare* or *conciliare*. Thus, the narrator's entry into a "lovely grove, full of trees and flowers, well-watered" (*Proem* 1) marks entry into a particular literary style designed to appeal to our senses, to offer us heightened impressions.

Longus' vocabulary[29] is for the most part that of late *koine* Greek; there are few obvious poeticisms, despite the extremely rich literary texture of the whole. The more straightforwardly narrative sections of the work are characterised by a simplicity and a syntactical lucidity which is obviously appropriate to the "naive" subject matter of the work. There are, however, also more elaborate set pieces—the proem, the descriptions of the seasons, Philetas' *ekphrasis* of *eros* and of his garden—marked by a highly mannered symmetry and patterning which draws attention to the artifice of the composition.[30] The most typical form for this patterning is the arrangement of words in groups of two ("dicola") or three ("tricola"), in which the groups

---

verses, and Longus may well have seen this poem as programmatic. Cf. in general Cairns (1984).

[27] Cf. Hunter (1983) 92–8. "Style" is perhaps a misleading translation of what Hermogenes called ἰδέαι, "stylistic types or qualities found in all authors" [D.A. Russell and M. Winterbottom, *Ancient Literary Criticism* (Oxford 1972) 561].

[28] Cf. in general Danek and Wallisch (1993); Hunter (1996).

[29] See especially Valley (1926).

[30] Cf. Castiglioni (1928); Hunter (1983) 85–91; Teske (1991) 77–85.

are often linked by assonance, rhyme, chiasmus or matching synonyms. Such mannerism is not merely the display of the brilliant sophist, but is intimately bound to the work's central concern with "art" and "nature".[31] It also shows us how "the appeal to the senses" can never, in such a rhetorical culture as that of Greek élite literature of the second century C.E., be divorced from an intellectual appeal. The "Gorgianic" style of Longus has the incantatory effect of Gorgias' own prose, but our "pleasure" derives—as indeed it does in bucolic poetry—because we are challenged to see how this textual effect operates.

A closely related phenomenon is the dense texture of allusion to archaic, classical and Hellenistic Greek literature;[32] the phenomenal virtuosity displayed here turns the novel into what has been well described as "a hallucinating echo text that is constituted as a secondary or even tertiary signifying system".[33] Particularly important are Homer, Sappho—as we would expect in an erotic work set on Lesbos—and, of course, Theocritus. Thus, for example, Philetas' advice to the children on how to cure their condition (quoted above p. 363), which becomes a major motive force for much of the action of Books 2 and 3, is a rewriting—with significant changes—of the famous opening of Theocritus' eleventh *Idyll* (the love-song of the Cyclops). The closing scene of Book 3 in which Daphnis climbs an apple-tree to secure a symbolic gift for his bride-to-be is a prose expansion of a famous fragment of Sappho's wedding poetry (fr. 105a). Even the "war" between Mytilene and Methymna is given a marked "Thucydidean" colouring. In this feature also *D & C* stands with the bucolic tradition which "had always been highly literary-allusive as part of its insistence that it is not an unmediated representation of reality".[34] I shall consider the relationship of art and nature in the following section, but here we may note how this allusiveness, this constant challenge to our reading skills, is an integral part of the pleasure, the τερπνόν, offered by this text.

This aesthetic dimension of the text, in which the very patterning of the words appeals visually to the reader as well as aurally to the listener, is clearly connected to the presentation of the whole work as

---

[31] Cf. below p. 382.
[32] Cf. Valley (1926) 79–104; Hunter (1983) Chapter 3, with further bibliography; Vieillefond (1987) cxiv–cxl.
[33] Zeitlin (1990) 438.
[34] Zeitlin (1990) 438.

a written elaboration of a "sweet" series of painted scenes. It is not uncommon indeed to associate the narrative technique and structuring of *D & C* with known techniques of "narrative" wall-painting of the first two centuries C.E., in which scenes from different stages of a single story were depicted within one space.[35] It is also clear that the modern theoretical interest in the different possibilities and imperatives of literary and visual narratives[36] was anticipated at least in the second century C.E., as is most obvious in the *Imagines* literature evidenced for us by Philostratus and Callistratus. It is at best doubtful whether specific links can be drawn, with consequences for dating, between the novel and any particular "style" of painting, but the importance of the general concept is clear. A pictorial style of representation is perhaps most obvious in those scenes in which the countryside is "on display" for the delectation, not just of sophisticated readers, but of characters from the city.[37] When Dionysophanes and his wife visit their estate, Daphnis and his goats perform for them:

> Daphnis stood there, with a shaggy goatskin wrapped around him, a newly sewn bag hanging from his shoulders, holding in one hand some freshly made cheeses, and with the other some unweaned kids. If Apollo ever did work as cowherd for Laomedon, he must have looked just as Daphnis looked then.... Daphnis made them all sit down like the audience in a theatre, while he took his stand under the oak tree. Producing his pipes from his bag, he first of all gave a gentle blow on them: the goats stood still and raised their heads. Then he blew the grazing tune: the goats lowered their heads and started to graze. Then he struck up another tune, clear and sweet: they all lay down together. He piped a high-pitched tune: they ran away into the wood as if a wolf was coming. A little later, he sounded a rallying cry: they came out of the wood and ran together near his feet. You wouldn't see human slaves so obedient as this to the orders of their master. (4.14.1–2, 15.2–3)

Daphnis' performance is focalised by the master and his wife; as city-dwellers they assimilate what they "see" to the familiar pictures of the countryside with which house-walls were decorated; this is, in fact, what they do "see", in part because the countryside is specially prepared for their visit to accord with their expectations (4.1.2–3). Part of the grape-pressing is delayed "so that those who came from

---

[35] For bibliography cf. Hunter (1983) 4–5, adding Brilliant (1984) 18, 76, 86.
[36] For a summary cf. Brilliant (1984) 15–19.
[37] On the presentation of the countryside in the novel cf. Effe (1982), with a helpful summary of earlier views, and Saïd (1987).

the city should enjoy the image (εἰκών) and pleasure of the harvest" (4.5.2); this image was one shaped by painted representations, and this is one important reason why the whole work is presented as a series of painted scenes. In this respect at least, Longus has written his readers into the text in the shape of the new characters who invade the pastoral space in Book 4.

In literary terms, the change which comes over the novel in Book 4 may be represented as a shift from the bucolic-pastoral mode to a comic mode, which is made most manifest in the characters of Dionysophanes' son, Astylos, and his parasite, Gnathon. Just as Theocritus is the classical validating model for the presentation of the countryside, so New Comedy fulfils the same role for urban life. The stories of unwanted children, exposure and recognition, which Dionysophanes and Megakles tell, follow a pattern familiar from New Comedy, just as comedy and the novel share a narrative movement towards marriage as resolution and closure. We are also invited to view the characters with the mixed response demanded by the characters of comedy: we are pleased and amused at their success and their likeness to us, but also disturbed and unsure what this likeness means. If these characters are so easily ironised, where does that leave us?

The complex irony which is essential to bucolic literature from its very inception does not require lengthy demonstration. In *D & C* this pervasive irony is merely strengthened by the naivete about sex which the two protagonists reveal.[38] Our knowing "superiority" is inscribed into the text at every turn; given that this "superiority" is about how to make love, the pleasures of this text are distinctly erotic. The complaints of critics of earlier ages that *D & C* is a salacious or even pornographic text may seem old-fashioned today, but this is perhaps rather because those critics were aiming at the wrong target, than because there is nothing of this kind in the work which needs description.[39] The scene in which Lykainion instructs Daphnis in how to make love (3.18) is teasingly decorous,[40] but elsewhere Longus exploits our knowledge of the veiled and coded vocabulary of sex to make otherwise "innocent" scenes rather more complex;

---

[38] For a further aspect of this naivete cf. below p. 385.
[39] Good remarks in Effe (1982) 79–81, and for more general considerations cf. Elsom (1992); Montague (1992); B. Egger, *Petronian Society Newsletter* 24 (1994) 14–16.
[40] Cf. Goldhill (1995) 23–30.

this strategy is made explicit when Philetas' advice that they should "lie down together" (συγκατακλιθῆναι) produces no good result, as "euphemism" is meaningless for those who are entirely ignorant (2.7.7).[41] A very simple case is the episode of the cicada which takes refuge from a pursuing swallow in the sleeping Chloe's lap (κόλπος):[42] "Taking this opportunity, Daphnis put his hands between her breasts and took out that obliging cicada, which did not go quiet even when it was in his hand. Chloe enjoyed seeing this; she took hold of the cicada, kissed it, and put it back, chirping, inside her clothes (ἐνέβαλε τῶι κόλπωι)" (1.26.3).[43] A rather more complex example is the episode which first leads to the stirring of *eros* in Chloe (1.12). It is spring and two he-goats are fighting; Longus has no need to tell us what it is that he-goats fight about. The loser breaks a horn (κέρας) and dashes off in pain (ἀλγήσας), with the victor in hot pursuit. Daphnis "was grieved at the horn" (ἀλγεῖ περὶ τῶι κέρατι) and himself takes off after the victor (ἐδίωκε τὸν διώκοντα), with the result that both Daphnis and the goat fall in a heap at the bottom of the wolf-pit; from there he is hauled out as he clutches hold of Chloe's breast-band. The situation and language obviously create an analogy between Daphnis and a he-goat in springtime, and the fact that "horn", κέρας, is a common euphemism for "penis" invites a "knowing" reading of the scene.[44] Opinions will differ about precisely when and where Longus invites such readings, but that he does do so can hardly be doubted; moreover, as the text itself makes clear, this is a matter in which different readers will inevitably read in different ways.

An appeal to the reader as voyeur is clearest in those scenes which foreground the rôle of vision, such as the bathing scenes. After the incident of the he-goat referred to above, Chloe washes the dirt off Daphnis' body: "She washed his back, and as she did so, his flesh yielded so gently to her touch that she surreptitiously felt her own several times to see if his was more delicate than hers" (1.13.2). The appeal to vision and touch is sharpened by our familiarity with an

---

[41] Cf. Bretzigheimer (1988).

[42] For the anatomical sense of κόλπος "vagina", which surely hovers over this scene, cf. *LSJ* s.v. I 2.

[43] For a rather similar scene cf. 3.34.3 in which Daphnis places an apple in Chloe's lap.

[44] For κέρας cf. (apart from the standard lexica) R. Pretagostini, "ΚΕΡΑΣ. Nascita e Storia di una Metafora: da Archiloco (fr. 217 T. = 247 W.) a Meleagro (*AP* 12,95,5–6)," in *Lirica Greca da Archiloco a Elitis. Studi in Onore di Filippo Maria Pontani* (Padua 1984) 51–60.

art "criticism" which stresses the lifelike realism of painted or carved figures.[45] The best known literary representations of such an attitude are Hellenistic poetic texts such as Theocritus 15.78–86 (women admiring Adonis-tapestries) and Herodas 4.59–62: "If I scratch this naked boy, won't he bleed, Kynno? For the flesh pulses warmly on him on the painted panel". Daphnis and Chloe too are, as the proem has made clear, painted figures, and Chloe's "naive" reaction to Daphnis' nakedness both suggests and ironises our inclination to vivify and "believe in" the creations of art.[46] When in a parallel scene Daphnis bathes in the middle of summer—the traditional time for women's sexual desires to be fiercest—[47] "Chloe, seeing Daphnis naked, was lost in gazing at his beauty and felt weak (ἐτήκετο), unable to find fault with any part (μέρος) of him" (1.24.1).[48] Here clearly we are invited not only to wonder *which* part of Daphnis Chloe is likely to find unsatisfactory, but again ourselves to imagine and contemplate Daphnis' naked form.

These aspects of *D & C* are to varying degrees shared with the other novels. What sets *D & C* apart is not only the bucolic setting of the whole, but the explicit statements in the proem and elsewhere which suggest that these pleasures are not idle, but that they serve a specific paideutic purpose. It is to this aspect of Longus' novel which I now turn.

IV. *Reading for Profit*

I searched out an interpreter of the picture and with great effort created (ἐξεπονησάμην) four books, as an offering to Eros and the Nymphs and Pan, and a sweet possession for all men. It will heal the sick and console the pained, stir the memory of he who has loved, and educate (προπαιδεύσει) he who has not loved. For certainly no one has escaped Eros, nor will escape, while beauty exists and there are eyes to see; for myself, may the god grant that I may describe the experiences of others and retain my self-control (ἡμῖν δὲ ὁ θεὸς παράσχοι σωφρονοῦσι τὰ τῶν ἄλλων γράφειν).

(*Proem* 3–4)

---

[45] For further use of this idea in ancient novels cf. Hunter (1994).
[46] For another aspect of this passage cf. below pp. 382–3.
[47] Cf. Hesiod, *WD* 586 etc.
[48] For the motif cf. Ovid, *Amores* 1.5.18,23.

With these words the narrator both universalises the relevance of his story and, partly by an allusion to Thucydides' famous assertion (1.22) that he has written a "possession for all time" because the clarity of his account will render it useful (ὠφέλιμον), lays claim to the usefulness of his work. These two claims—universal relevance and educational benefit—are closely connected, because what this book will remind us of or teach us is precisely the universal experience of Eros. The *muthos* of Chloe (2.27.2) is to have "the sense of a founding paradigm which underwrites the coherence of the larger erotic experience that takes place in the more expanded settings of romance. The air of a sacred tale enhances (and protects) this authority...".[49] From this perspective, the complete sexual "naivete" of the children takes on a new importance. They do not merely discover love and sex in the way that all adolescents do, but in some sense they actually "invent" it, as though it did not exist before.[50] In seeking to imitate the animals as they learn to enjoy the pleasures of the countryside, Daphnis and Chloe conform to a standard ancient conception of how "civilisation" developed; Longus freely exploits the obvious similarities between the traditional bucolic *locus amoenus* and the natural plenty which was associated with ideas of a "Golden Age".[51] Thus their story has something of the doubleness of, say, Hesiod's Pandora: both an *aition* for our present condition and a representation on the "mythical" level of what happens every day.

The "mythical" quality of the events of the novel is reinforced by three short included narratives, which tell of loss and metamorphosis.[52] In 1.27 Daphnis tells Chloe the story of how a beautiful young girl who looked after cows was metamorphosed into the wood-pigeon (φάττα) after she lost some of her cows who were lured away by the strong male voice of a boy (παῖς) who looked after a nearby herd. In 2.34 Lamon tells Daphnis and Chloe the tale of Syrinx, a nymph who hid from Pan's advances in the reeds, and was killed when the god cut the reeds down; when he realised what he had done, Pan invented the pan-pipes from the cut reeds, "fastening together reeds of unequal length because their love had been unequal". Finally, in 3.23 Daphnis tells Chloe the story of Echo, a nymph whom Pan

---

[49] Zeitlin (1990) 422.
[50] Cf. A. Carson, *Eros the Bittersweet* (Princeton 1986) 87.
[51] Cf. Hunter (1983) 20-1.
[52] On these stories cf. Hunter (1983) 52-7 (with bibliography).

caused "the shepherds and the goatherds" to tear apart, because he was jealous of her musical skill and she scorned his sexual advances; the earth, however, preserved her songs as a favour to the Nymphs. Like the novel which frames them, these stories both tell a "once upon a time" story which explains something in our world (wood-pigeons, pan-pipes, echoes), and also present a mythical paradigm for crucial features of the relations between the sexes, as Daphnis and Chloe come to know them: the strength of the male, the loss of the female, and the inevitable violence of male desire.[53] These included stories follow the development of the narrative in as much as the absence of an *explicit* relationship of *eros* between the two cowherds in the *phatta* story reflects the fact that in Book 1 Daphnis and Chloe do not know what *eros* is, and the word and its cognates are used only by the narrator. The cowgirl's sense of loss and helplessness after the musical victory of the young man suggests Chloe's despair that she is not as beautiful and musical as Daphnis (1.13–14) and also, we might suspect, a male author's representation of the perceived female desire to share the privileged status of the male. The increasing violence through the three stories must, at some level, reflect the approaching consummation of the young people's love, and the fact that it is again Daphnis who tells the echo story suggests his new status as possessor of special knowledge after his lesson from Lykainion. He can now take over the rôle of *praeceptor* which, until that time, had been held successively by Philetas and Lykainion. His knowledge of echo (εἰδὼς τὸ πραττόμενον) in fact points to a wider knowledge, recently acquired.

Through these stories it is also possible to see how Longus constructs his picture of *eros* at two complementary levels, that of *muthos* and that of *logos*,[54] a dichotomy which may be glossed in several ways—"imagination/science", "description/metaphor", "fiction/truth". Thus, for example, one of the "lessons" of the included narratives is much the same as the lesson about what happens when a girl loses her virginity which Lykainion teaches Daphnis (3.19). Lykainion is very much a creature of *logos*, but she must first approach Daphnis through the realm of "myth" (3.16–17) before the serious business begins.[55]

---

[53] On these features of the novel cf. especially Winkler (1990b).
[54] For a more detailed discussion cf. Hunter (1996).
[55] Cf. Bretzigheimer (1988) 539–41. For a differently nuanced appreciation of Lykainion cf. Stanzel (1991).

The two levels are indeed juxtaposed in the echo episode, when the narrator's "scientific" account of the production of echo is followed by the *muthos* which Daphnis relates to Chloe; though now possessed of "scientific" knowledge about love-making, Daphnis must still use the mythic level when talking about these things to Chloe. Her lesson must wait until the very end of the novel when, after a textual reprise of Philetas' instructions to them ("they lay down together naked, embraced each other, and kissed", cf. 2.7.7),[56] Daphnis is able to pass on what he has learned. Moreover, in the third book Daphnis' knowledge is still incomplete, he is ἀρτιμαθής (3.20.2), and he can only engage in reasoning (λογισμός, 3.20.1) within his own limited horizons: "he shrank from pestering (διοχλεῖν)[57] Chloe for more than kisses and embraces. He did not want her to cry out at him as though he was an enemy or weep as if she was hurt or bleed as though she had been killed.[58] For being newly instructed, he was frightened of the blood and thought it was only from a wound that blood came". The transition to *logos* through *logismos* is a gradual one. A similar pattern is played out in Book 2 after Philetas' speech:

> When they were left on their own, now that they had heard for the first time the word "love" (τὸ Ἔρωτος ὄνομα), they felt a spasm of pain in their souls; and when they went home to their farms at night, they compared their own experiences with what they had heard.
> "Lovers feel pain—and so do we. They neglect their food—and we have neglected ours in the same way. They cannot sleep—and that is happening to us at this moment. They seem to burn—and there is a fire inside us. They long to see each other—and that is why we pray for the day to come more quickly. Surely this is "love", and we are "in love" with each other without realising it. Or is it that this is love and

---

[56] It is not, I think, merely stylistic considerations which dictate that the three elements are repeated in chiastic order at the end of the book. Philetas' order—kissing, embracing, lying down together—is indeed followed by Daphnis and Chloe, but to no satisfactory outcome (2.9–11); the reversal of the order at the end of the work not only leads to success, but also (I suggest) evokes the "sanctioned" and regular love-making of a married couple, rather than intercourse which results from kissing which "gets out of hand". Relevant here is Konstan's discussion [(1994a) 86–90] of the clear distinction in the novel between erotic play and genital sex.

[57] This and related expressions are regularly used to mean "to importune, pester for sexual favours" (cf., e.g., Plato, *Alc*.I 104d; Xen. *Symp*.8.4), and so the use here—with Daphnis as "embedded focaliser"—reveals the quantum leap in his knowledge since his lesson with Lykainion. For his "shrinking", ὄκνος, cf. Alcibiades' mistaken view of Socrates at Pl. *Symp*.218c.

[58] Castiglioni's deletion of καθάπερ πεφονευμένη from Lykainion's speech at 3.19.2 is surely correct (though it is retained by Schönberger and Vieillefond).

that I alone am in love?[59] But why then do we feel the same pain? Why do we seek each other? Everything that Philetas said is true."
(2.8.1–4)

Like Lykainion, Philetas is a *praeceptor* from the world of *logos*, but has approached the children through the realm of *muthos* (a dichotomy made explicit at 2.7.1). Sexual "progress" will require that they come to see what the connection between the two worlds is.

If the process of reasoning through which Daphnis and Chloe pass in their ascent towards "knowledge" sounds rather like a version of the philosophical acquisition of wisdom, particularly in its Socratic and Platonic instantiations, then this is no accident.[60] The obvious debt of the novel to Plato's *Phaedrus* and *Symposium*, works which had a privileged status for the erotic prose of the second century C.E., and the repeated stress on ignorance and knowledge of the "name" or "definition" of *eros* suggest an analogy between the "getting of (sexual) wisdom" and the philosophical pursuit of truth. The Platonic works in which sexual arousal and the contemplation of physical beauty were represented as a stimulus to this pursuit were clearly suited to Longus' project. The analogy is, of course, an ironical and humorous one, suggesting as it does that Platonic *eros* is nothing more than a nice-sounding excuse for hanging around with pretty boys. The character of the paederastic parasite Gnathon may also be seen as a satirical exposure of Platonic (and neo-Platonic) pretentiousness. Certainly, his plea to Astylos that beauty is a universal which may be as manifest in a goatherd as in a plant or a river (4.17.4) can be read as a debased reflection of Platonic "form" theory, which is particularly amusing in the mouth of a character who would appear to lack any higher, Platonic aim. Similarly, the "shame", αἰδώς, which prevents Chloe from asking Daphnis why he is no longer so keen for her to take her clothes off (3.24.3) may be seen not only as an inversion of the "shame" about things sexual which would be proper for a young girl, but also of the αἰδώς which should govern the relations of *erastes* and *eromenos* in Plato. Nevertheless, the philosophical structuring of the pursuit of *eros* is not merely comic, for this novel is not simply about two people who do not know how to have sex; it is also about how we construct the world in which we live.

---

[59] The text at this point is uncertain.
[60] For what follows cf. especially Bretzigheimer (1988) and Hunter (1996).

It is obvious that the contrast and interplay between art and nature, and between nature and culture, lies at the heart of much of *D & C*, as of bucolic and pastoral literature in general.[61] Just as the description of the "natural" world is a highly stylised one, partly indeed created from reworkings of earlier poetry, so the behaviour of Daphnis and Chloe itself problematises any easy assumptions about what is natural. When Daphnis' feelings have been stirred by a kiss from Chloe, his soliloquy employs bucolic versions of some of the most hackneyed of amatory *topoi*:

> Whatever is Chloe's kiss doing to me? Her lips are softer than rose petals, and her mouth is sweeter than honeycombs, but her kiss is sharper than the bee's sting. I've often kissed kids; I've often kissed new-born puppies and the calf that Dorkon gave her—but this is a new kind of kiss. My breath comes in gasps; my heart leaps out of my breast; my spirit dissolves—and yet I want to kiss her again. Oh, what a terrible victory! Oh, what a strange disease! I don't even know what to call it (τὸ ὄνομα)! Did Chloe take poison before she kissed me? But then why didn't she die? . . .
>
> (1.18.1–2)

Here we see Daphnis acting like a "lover" before he knows what "love" is; this may seem to us the most "natural" thing in the world, but the familiarity and literary texture of what he says raises the question of whether or not this is actually the case.[62] Does our behaviour in fact become less "natural", once our condition has been identified as "love"? Do we have to "understand" love in order to feel embarrassed about taking our clothes off? We may contrast the nameless goatherd who serenades the cave-dwelling Amaryllis in Theocritus, *Idyll* 3: he too "bucolicises" familiar amatory *topoi*, but the difference is that he "knows" what he is doing, as the opening word of the poem, κωμάσδω, "I go on a *komos*", makes clear. Daphnis suffers in ignorance as he "tastes for the first time the deeds and words of love", and Chloe's naive awakening to the pleasures of the flesh (1.13.2, quoted above p. 376) carries with it a first lesson in sexual difference between the genders which also poses the question of the origin of our category of "the beautiful" (τὸ καλόν): "because that was the first time she had thought him beautiful, she reckoned

---

[61] All modern work on *D & C* touches on this subject, but see especially Hunter (1983) 45–6; Pandiri (1985); Zeitlin (1990); Winkler (1990b); Teske (1991).

[62] A very similar argument could, of course, be put for Chloe's matching soliloquy in 1.14. On this whole subject cf. Zeitlin (1990); Kennedy (1993), Chapter 4.

that the bath was responsible for the beauty". Moreover, it finally requires an intrusion by people from the very "unnatural" world of the city to effect the proper socialisation (in marriage) of the relationship between Daphnis and Chloe. When they subsequently seek to allow their own children to repeat, as nearly as possible, what they themselves had experienced—being suckled by animals, "pastoral" names (4.39.2)—we are strongly aware that this is no less of a pretence than was the vintage enjoyed by Dionysophanes and his family. "Nature", like "love", is something created by culture.

In this context the figure of the paederastic parasite Gnathon occupies a special place, for it is through him that the standard argument that homosexuality is "contrary to nature" is subverted.[63] Daphnis' appeal to the animal world (4.12.2) in refusing Gnathon's request, which itself is couched as an analogy from animal behaviour, is a familiar *topos* of prose literature, and as such paradoxically and ironically "unnatural". "Nature" both shows Daphnis how to satisfy Lykainion (3.18.4) and is responsible for Gnathon's sexual orientation.

These themes are presented at the very opening of the work in the presentation of the novel as the story behind a painting, i.e. as the result of two separate acts of *mimesis*; the barriers which any single act of *mimesis* puts between us and "reality" are analogous to the "artificial" construction of nature. The paintings themselves display τέχνη περιττή, "outstanding art", and are thus not presented as any simple, unmediated means of access to "what actually happened". All the extant novels, to greater or less degree, are programmatically concerned with their own truth status and with the idea of fiction,[64] and Longus' ecphrastic device obviously fits centrally into this concern. "Fiction" itself is an idea bound up with "art" and "nature", for in fiction art claims to create (or imitate) nature. From this perspective it is perhaps surprising that the ancient world took so long to get around to "bucolic" fiction, as bucolic poetry, on one hand, and fiction, on the other, seem to have much in common.

---

[63] For this argument cf. Dover (1978) 175–80; Goldhill (1995) 48–66.
[64] Cf. Reardon (1991), together with my remarks at *Classical Journal* 87 (1992) 180–1, and Hunter (1994).

V. The Mysteries of Love

In universalising the experience of Daphnis and Chloe and making them paradigms for ourselves, Longus exploits the pre-existence of the myth of Daphnis, the legendary cowherd whose "suffering for love" formed the originary and validating subject of bucolic song.[65] Moreover the children's mysterious origin and fortuitous salvation suggest divine origins, which though not in fact the case are reinforced by the assimilation of them to Pan and his beloved Pitys. These and other aspects of the novel have given rise to a major school of interpretation,[66] the weaker version of which sees the young people's initiation into love and sex following the patterns of initiation into "mystery cults" such as those of Dionysus and Orpheus, both gods with prominent associations with Lesbos; the stronger version of the theory sees one level of the novel, at least, addressed to initiates into one of these mystery cults, so that full understanding of what is going on requires access to the details of those cults. We are in fact reasonably well informed, from both inscriptional and iconographic evidence, about the structure and activities of Dionysiac associations of the second century C.E.[67] Such associations—if one can generalise across what were presumably wide local differences—stressed the rural aspects of Dionysus, used titles such as βουκόλος within a rigid scheme of hierarchical stratification, and "dressed the part" for their bucolic meetings; many will have promised their members a blessed afterlife.

There is much in the various versions of the theory which can be accepted with few qualms. It is obvious that the pattern of *eros* as it develops through the work follows the pattern of the seasons, and this latter pattern had always been associated with Dionysus as a primal force of vegetation. In the centre of the splendid garden which Lamon tends is a temple and altar of Dionysus (4.3), and in as much as the garden may be seen, by the familiar technique of *mise-en-abyme*,

---

[65] For allusions in *D & C* to this "Daphnis" cf. Hunter (1983) 22–31.

[66] The crucial discussions are Chalk (1960); Merkelbach (1962), with the remarks of R. Turcan, *Revue de l'Histoire des Religions* 163 (1963) 186–93; Geyer (1977); and Merkelbach (1988). I have considered many of the primary arguments in Hunter (1983) 31–8.

[67] To Merkelbach (1988) add M.P. Nilsson, *The Dionysiac Mysteries of the Hellenistic and Roman Age* (Lund 1957); E. Simon, "Dionysischer Sarkophag in Princeton," *Mitteilungen des deutschen archaeologischen Instituts (Röm.Abt.)* 69 (1962) 136–58; A. Henrichs, "Greek Maenadism from Olympias to Messalina," *Harvard Studies in Classical Philology* 82 (1978) 121–60.

as descriptive of the work as a whole, it is not difficult to see the god at the centre of the meaning of the work.[68] Moreover, the parallelism between this garden and that of Philetas in Book 2 confirms an analogy or complicity between Dionysus and *eros*, something which is only too comprehensible in the light of contemporary iconography. The resolving appearance in Book 4 of Daphnis' father, Dionysophanes, "appearance of Dionysus", is not unnaturally a focal point for those who would see in the work a coded description of the progress of an entirely innocent child towards knowledge of a revealed mystery. That this name is of a common type attested in the Aegean is not a conclusive counter-argument,[69] for even the most ardent searchers after allegory would have the novel operating on at least two levels, not all of which are accessible to all readers. Seen in this light, the otherwise absurd naivete of Daphnis and Chloe, which I have already associated with the novel's dialectic between the realms of *muthos* and *logos* (above p. 378), may be seen as a function of their status as initiates, and the characters of Philetas and Lykainion function as helpers or "expounders", ἐξηγηταί, like the priest of Isis in the eleventh book of Apuleius' *Metamorphoses*.

The "universal" experience of the young people is also that of the narrator, who also requires an ἐξηγητής to expound the painting to him; immediately before we learn this, the description of his experience of sight, wonder, desire, and longing for rivalry (*Proem* 3) is clearly parallel to that of Daphnis and Chloe themselves as they fall in love with each other, and the narrator's "dedication" (ἀνάθημα) to "Eros and the Nymphs and Pan" is also parallel to the images which Daphnis and Chloe set up after their marriage (εἰκόνας ἀνέθεσαν, 4.39.2).[70] These similarities, however, point away from the "strong" version of the "mystery" theory towards a more purely literary interpretation. The undeniable "religious" elements and motifs of the novel, and the religious language of many scenes, do indeed suggest an analogy between the experience of the protagonists and "initiation" into deeper mysteries; the "religious" element is thus rather like the

---

[68] For the garden and its importance cf. especially Zeitlin (1990). I am reminded of Caesar at the centre of the poetic temple which Vergil promises at the opening of *Georgic* 3, and which many interpret as a foreshadowing of the *Aeneid*.
[69] Cf. Fraser (1987) s.v.; Διονύσιος, Διονυσιφάνης, Διονυσιφάης, and Διονυσόδωρος are all common names, and are all attested on Lesbos, cf. Fraser (1987) s.vv.
[70] That Longus wants us to understand that the narrator actually sees the images set up by his protagonists is an easy and common assumption, cf. Wouters (1990).

"philosophical" structuring of the narrative (above p. 381), and an educated reader of the second century C.E. would, of course, not understand the distinction between "religious" and "philosophical" in the way we might wish to draw it. Framing the efforts of Daphnis and Chloe to lose their virginity is thus a heavy intellectual superstructure, both philosophical and religious, but one built with incredible lightness of touch, and as we prod the structure, we are offered glimpses of hidden knowledge and of *eudaimonia*; to "get the message", however, to be "in the know", is a matter of intellectual and cultural privilege, not of religious initiation.

D. ACHILLES TATIUS

Karl Plepelits

Biography of the Author

We have hardly any certain or undisputed information about the author of *Leucippe and Clitophon*. He himself, unlike other Greek novelists, avoids giving biographical data in his work. As he is not mentioned by other ancient writers, we are thrown back upon the scanty information given by Byzantine sources, first and foremost the *Suda* (10th century), whose relevant article reads:[1]

> Achilles Statius (Achilleus Statios) of Alexandria, the author of the stories of Leucippe and Clitophon and of other love stories in eight books. Finally became a Christian and a bishop. Wrote besides on the celestial sphere and on etymology as well as a miscellaneous history making mention of many great and admirable men. His style in all these works is similar to that in the love stories (*or, with less probability*: his style is in all his works similar to that of other authors of love stories).

This shows that not even the form of his name is beyond possibility of doubt, for even several manuscripts of the novel give in the title the form *Achilleus Statios* as the author's name. The vast majority of the manuscripts, however, present the form *Achilleus Tatios*, and so do the rest of the Byzantine testimonia.

The only biographical item unanimously transmitted by the manuscripts of the novel as well as the Byzantine testimonia is the fact that Achilles Tatius was a native of Alexandria. The text of his work bears out this assertion; for he quite obviously knows Egypt and Phoenicia well: his descriptions of these two countries are vivid and colourful. On the other hand there can be no doubt that he has no first-hand knowledge of Ephesus, the last of the three geographical areas in which the action is set: there is hardly any local colour in the relevant passages, not even an attempt at describing the temple of Artemis, which is of decisive importance to the action and was after all one of the seven wonders of the world (whereas at 5.6.3 another one of the seven wonders of the world, the lighthouse on

---

[1] Ed. A. Adler, vol. I, p. 439.

Pharus, is described briefly, but most vividly, although it is of no importance whatsoever to the action), and the few facts mentioned are either of general validity or downright unhistorical.[2]

As regards the dating of Achilles Tatius, until the beginning of the 20th century no clue whatsoever was to be found. He was usually dated to the 4th, the 5th, or even the 6th century. It was however always agreed that the was an imitator of Heliodorus and therefore to be dated later than he. The same opinion was already held by the Byzantine critics.[3] The only exception was F. Ast, who in the epilogue to his German translation of *Leucippe and Clitophon*[4] designated Achilles Tatius as the older, Heliodorus as the younger.

He was to prove to have been in the right. The change was brought about, in two stages, by the papyri. The first papyrus fragment from *Leucippe and Clitophon* was published in 1914;[5] it dates, as the forms of the letters indicate, from the end of the 3rd or the beginning of the 4th century. This instantly made the hitherto universally accepted dating to the latest antiquity untenable. Nevertheless, Achilles Tatius was still unanimously considered to be an imitator of Heliodorus; as the latter is dated to the second quarter of the 3rd century by most scholars, Achilles Tatius was now dated to the second half of the 3rd century. But how big was the surprise when in 1938 a second papyrus was published,[6] which the papyrologists unanimously attribute to the 2nd century! This was tantamount to a downright revolution, because it not only made the dating to the late 3rd century untenable, but in particular suddenly reversed the temporal succession Heliodorus—Achilles Tatius and brilliantly rehabilitated the latter from the accusation of slavish imitation so often brought against him. In the meantime more papyrus fragments from *Leucippe and Clitophon* have been discovered or attributed to it. Most of them date from the 3rd century and are therefore no longer relevant to its dating; one, however, published only in 1989, dates equally from the 2nd century, thus corroborating the new findings.[7]

Thus a *terminus ante quem* was gained. As regards a *terminus post*

---

[2] For details see Plepelits (1980) 3–6.
[3] Dyck (1986) 94 1.66 (English translation on p. 95): "In my opinion Leucippe's book was crafted in imitation of Chariclea."
[4] Leipzig 1802, p. 72.
[5] B.P. Grenfell and A.S. Hunt, *The Oxyrhynchus Papyri* 10 (London 1914) 135–142, no. 1250.
[6] Vogliano (1938) 121–130.
[7] See the section on the history of the text below.

quem, the text itself provides two clues. One of them is the passage at 2.18.3, where eight men disguised as women are referred to: they are wearing women's clothes and have shaved off their beards. The latter remark, however, is meaningful only if men normally grow beards. Now, we know that both in Greek lands and in Italy from about 300 B.C., apart from short exceptions, beardlessness was the general custom. It ended with emperor Hadrian (A.D. 117-138), who grew a beard, allegedly for the purpose of covering natural scars that disfigured his face—thus his biographer.[8] From that time the emperors and after their example the mass of the adult male population with the only exceptions of Caracalla (212-217) and Elagabalus (218-222) were bearded for almost two centuries, until in the early 4th century Constantine introduced beardlessness again. The change of fashion under Hadrian was so thorough that Cassius Dio, who wrote his Roman History at the turn from the 2nd to the 3rd century, felt obliged to explain the statement that emperor Trajan (A.D. 98-117) was having his beard shaved by the words: "For this was from of old the custom of all other men and also the emperors themselves; for it was only Hadrian who introduced the beard."[9] Since Hadrian, according to pictorial representations from the time before his accession to the throne, seems to have grown a beard even then, it is surely legitimate to suppose that the change of fashion took place immediately with his accession. However, the naturalness with which it is taken for granted that men normally grow beards admits of the conclusion that since the introduction of the new fashion quite a long time must have elapsed.

The other clue was already recognized by Ch. Picard;[10] unfortunately it is not absolutely certain. It is furnished by the description of Alexandria at 5.1: Clitophon is narrating how he entered the city by the "so-called Sun-Gate" and was immediately dazzled by the beauty of the perfectly straight colonnaded street reaching from the Sun-Gate to the Moon-Gate. This is the earliest reference to these particular gates; the one next in time belongs to the 4th century.[11] John Malalas (6th century)[12] reports about them as follows:

---

[8] 26.1.
[9] 68.15.5 in Xiphilinus' epitome.
[10] *Ephèse et Claros. Recherches sur les Sanctuaires et les Cultes de l' Ionie du Nord* (Paris 1922) 52 n. 4.
[11] In a papyrus from A.D. 335 (?) in *Jews and Christians in Egypt*, ed. H.I. Bell (London 1924) 1914 no. 35.
[12] *Chronographia* 11.280 Migne gr. 97, p. 424B.

Antoninus Pius (138–161) made war upon the Egyptians, who had committed violence and murdered the governor Dinarchus, and after the punishment and the victory he built in Alexandria, the big city, having come there, the Sun-Gate and the Moon-Gate and the colonnaded street.

Obviously the building activities referred to by Malalas can at best have been a restoration of structures that had already existed before but had perhaps suffered in the course of the riots or hostilities.[13] The salient point here is the question whether the two city gates had already been called Sun-Gate and Moon-Gate before or were renamed so on the occasion of their restoration. The question cannot be decided with absolute certainty, but it seems as if the wording of Malalas' report spoke rather in favour of the latter possibility. Add to this the fact observed by J. Vogt[14] that emperor Antoninus Pius and his consort Faustina are frequently conceived as sun god and moon goddess, particularly in pictorial representations, but also in written sources. Moreover, by naming the governor murdered by the Egyptians, Malalas enables us to determine a little more precisely the date of the events in question. Unfortunately, this particular Dinarchus is not known to us by any other source. For his term of office, therefore, we have to take into consideration all those periods for which as yet no other governors are testified. These are the intervals between 26 August 142 and 12 May 144, between 11 November 148 and 17 April 150, and the year 153 until 28 August 154 at the latest. Vogt himself[15] dates the disturbances Dinarchus fell a victim to "with great probability" to the years 153 and 154. But whatever the exact historical details, the reference to the Sun-Gate and Moon-Gate seems to provide a *terminus post quem* about the middle of the 2nd century.

As a consequence, it seems appropriate to date Achilles Tatius and his novel roughly to the second half of the 2nd century or, in view of the papyri written in the same century, somewhat more precisely to the third quarter of the 2nd century.

Of the other works attributed to Achilles Tatius by the *Suda* the one on etymology and the miscellaneous history are not preserved. However, of the work on the celestial sphere we possess considerable

---

[13] See Hunger (1978) I, 321.
[14] *Die alexandrinischen Münzen. Grundlegung einer alexandrinischen Kaisergeschichte* (Stuttgart 1924) I 114ff.
[15] (See n. 14) p. 128f.

fragments transmitted in the manuscripts under the title *Introduction into Aratus' Phaenomena* (an Hellenistic didactic poem on the celestial "phenomena") and the author's name *Achilleus*; it was one of the numerous commentaries to Aratus.[16] Formerly, when *Leucippe and Clitophon* was dated to the latest periods of antiquity, it was regarded as certain that the author of the novel and the author of the astronomical work were not identical, because the latter is likely to be the very *prudentissimus Achilles* quoted by Firmicus Maternus in his astrological treatise *Mathesis*[17] written about A.D. 335–337 (a *terminus post quem* is provided by the fact that he himself quotes authors of as late as the middle of the 2nd century). Since we learned that the novel belongs to the 2nd century, those declaring in favour of the identity of the novelist with the astronomical writer have been in the majority.

History of the Text

Achilles Tatius must have been a much-read author in the late 2nd, 3rd and early 4th centuries, even if he is never mentioned in contemporary literature, for no fewer than seven papyri, i.e. fragments of ancient text editions, from that period have been discovered and published. They are usually indicated by the logogram Π or P and an exponent denoting the chronological order of their respective discovery or publication. They are:

1. Π[1] and P[1] = Pap.Oxyrhynch.1250 (= no. 2 Pack[2]), published in 1914, from the end of the 3rd or the beginning of the 4th century, containing 2.2.1–2.3.2 and 2.7.7–2.9.3 in an order, however, different from that of the medieval manuscripts: chapters 2 and 3 (§§1–2) of book 2 have been placed between chapters 8 and 9; at the junction of the first two passages the papyrus inserts this transitional phrase: "When evening came, we drank together again as before." This divergence helped to nourish for some time the theory enunciated by Salmasius, the second editor of the text (1640), of the double redaction of the novel.[18] M. Laplace[19] stands for

---

[16] Ed. E. Maass, *Commentariorum in Aratum Reliquiae* (Berlin 1898) 25–86.
[17] 4.17.2.
[18] Cf. Cataudella (1940) (1954); Grimal (1958) 872 (cf. the criticism of his reviewer R. Flacelière in *Revue des Études Grecques* 72 (1959) 447.
[19] Laplace (1983c) 53, 59.

conserving the disposition of the text presented by Π^1. E. Vilborg[20] considers the order of Π^1 to be superior from the point of view of continuity, but in editing the text shrinks from changing the order of the manuscripts, arguing as follows: "We should in fact change a text which is possibly in disorder, into one which is completely arbitrary and uncertain." Other scholars[21] hold that the text of Π^1 came from an abridged edition or an anthology of selected passages of the novel, in which motifs used twice (such as the dinner in 2.2 and 2.9) had been merged (Π^1 knows only one dinner).

2. Π^2 Vilborg = P^3 Conca = Pap. Schubart 30 (= no. 1 Pack²), published by W. Schubart (1950), p. 59f., from the 3rd century "at the latest" (thus Schubart), containing 2.2.4–2.2.5 and 2.14.5–2.14.7. This papyrus now seems to be lost. Not even the editor had it at hand when he published it; he possessed only an incomplete copy.
3. Π^3 Vilborg = P^2 Conca = Pap. Mediolanensis = Pap.Mil.Vogl. no. 124 (= no. 3 Pack²), published by A. Vogliano (1938), pp. 121–130, from the end of the 2nd century, containing 6.14.1–6.15.3 and 6.16.6–6.17.3.
4. $\Pi^4 = P^4$ = Pap.Colon. inv. 901, published by A. Henrichs (1968), pp. 211–226, from the end of the 3rd century, containing 3.17.5–3.18.1, 3.18.3–3.20.1, 3.21.2–3.21.6, and 3.23.1–3.24.1.
5. Π^5 = Pap.Oxyrhynch.3836, published in 1989, from the 2nd century, containing 3.21.4–3.23.3.
6. Π^6 = Pap.Oxyrhynch.3837, published in 1989, from the 3rd century, containing 8.6.14–8.7.6.
7. Π^7 = Pap.Oxyrhynch.1014 (= no. 2258 Pack²), published by M. Gronewald (1976), pp. 14–17, from the 3rd century, containing 4.14.2–4.14.5.

The earliest extant manuscripts date from the 12th and 13th centuries: W = Vaticanus Graecus 1349 (12th century; contains the complete text), M = Marcianus Graecus 409 (beginning of the 13th century?; leaves off at 8.16.3; also contains Heliodorus' novel, whose editor, A. Colonna[22] dates M to the 11th century), F = Laurentianus conv. soppr. 627 (13th century; leaves off at 4.4.4; this is the famous manuscript that alone has preserved to us the novels of Chariton and Xenophon Ephesius and gives us Longus' text in full) and V =

---

[20] Vilborg (1955) XLIf.
[21] Russo (1955); Rattenbury (1956); Dörrie (1959); Conca (1969).
[22] Rome 1938, p. XIII; cf. Colonna (1956) 184.

Vaticanus Graecus 114 (end of the 13th century; contains the complete text). There are only a few more medieval manuscripts: D = Vaticanus Graecus 914 (excerpts) from the 14th century, G = Marcianus Graecus 607 and some excerpts not yet known to E. Vilborg (1955), published by A. Guida (1981), contained in the MS Olomouc, municipal library I.VI.9, both from the 15th century, and finally probably E = Ambrosianus Graecus 394, which is one of the best single authorities for the text, from the 15th or 16th century. In the 16th century no fewer than 16 manuscripts[23] appeared, almost all of which were based on the work of the two humanists Fulvio Orsini and Henricus Stephanus. The youngest manuscript was copied from the editio princeps and consequently, as will soon be seen, written after 1601.

According to E. Vilborg there is no doubt that all manuscripts originate from one archetype, which, if written in uncials, as there is reason to assume, was written in the 9th century at the latest. Its descendants are divided into three lines: firstly α, represented by W, M and D and their descendants, and secondly β, represented (among others) by V, G and E; the third line is represented by F alone.

There is also a certain amount of indirect tradition: some anthologies and collections of sentences from the 7th to the 15th and beginning 16th centuries have excerpted several passages. E. Vilborg lists them all precisely and has included their variants in his apparatus criticus.

The editio princeps of Achilles Tatius appeared in 1601, long after Latin, Italian, French and English translations had been published (see below under *Nachleben*). It was prepared by the Heidelberg printer H. Commelinus and finished by his nephews I. and N. Bonnvitius. It was simply a publication of the text of a manuscript in the Palatine Library, which was then still at Heidelberg, no doubt C = Palat.Gr.52, now in the Vatican. The first edition based on a comparison between the readings of different manuscripts (viz. Θ, A and a copy of the editio princeps) was the one made by the French humanist C. Salmasius (Saumaise) and published at Leyden in 1640. B.G.L. Boden's edition (Leipzig 1776) did not essentially improve upon that of Salmasius, nor did C.G. Mitscherlich's (Zweibrücken 1792). Much progress was, however, made by the edition of F. Jacobs

---

[23] Including cod. Sinaiticus gr. 1197 unknown to Vilborg (1955); see Hagedorn and Koenen (1970).

(Leipzig 1821), who gave the text a much surer basis than the earlier editors. The two other editions published in the 19th century, viz. by G.A. Hirschig (Paris 1856) and R. Hercher (Leipzig 1858), added nothing to the work of Jacobs, nor did the one published in 1917 in the Loeb Classical Library by S. Gaselee, except that he was the first to be able to exploit Π^1 for his text.

The first and hitherto only edition that meets all scholarly requirements is the one published by Vilborg, who in his elaborate introduction gives a full description and evaluation of the three papyri and the 23 manuscripts known to him.

In 1980 a Lexicon to Achilles Tatius by J.N. O'Sullivan appeared in Berlin and New York. It constitutes a complete philological dissection of the text, concerned extensively with textual *examinatio* and taking into account anything that has come to light since E. Vilborg's edition appeared, even two papyri that were still unpublished when the Lexicon was being prepared, viz. Π^5 and Π^6, thus creating a textual basis that has considerably improved even upon E. Vilborg's edition.

Achilles Tatius' Relationship to Heliodorus

It has already been mentioned that Achilles Tatius and Heliodorus have a great number of motifs in common and that until quite recently it was universally agreed that Achilles Tatius was an "almost slavish imitator" of Heliodorus.[24] Meanwhile Achilles Tatius has proved to be the earlier and therefore the one giving, Heliodorus the one taking. Now, a comparison shows that Heliodorus consistently changed the motifs he borrowed from Achilles Tatius in the sense of greater idealization, or, in other words, that parallel motifs in Achilles Tatius are always more realistic, more profane, more human.

Thus, whereas in Heliodorus (and in most other novels) the lovers' love at first sight is mutual, in Achilles Tatius it is not: Clitophon indeed falls in love with Leucippe at first sight (1.4.4f.), but not vice versa, and this gives occasion for an elaborate description of his wooing. At last he wins her over, and she is prepared to let herself

---

[24] So J. Maillon in the introduction (vol. I, p. XCIII) to his French translation of Heliodorus published together with an edition of the text attended to by R.M. Rattenbury and T.W. Lumb (1935). Even later an attempt was made to interpret Achilles Tatius as a parodist of Heliodorus: Durham (1938).

be seduced—inconceivable in Heliodorus and a breach of the ideal of virginity, though probably not of the realities in actual life. It is by pure chance that she preserves her virginity after all. Later, however, Artemis appearing to her in a dream (4.1) causes her to comply with the ideal until legal marriage, although she finds the delay hard enough (cf. 4.1.5).

At 2.37.5 Clitophon casually remarks that as yet he has "only had intercourse" with prostitutes—thus being characterized quite realistically, whereas Heliodorus idealizes his hero, Theagenes, by describing him as perfectly virginal, pointing out himself that this does not correspond to actual life at a passage where the virginity of ten young men and ten young girls is being tested by means of an ordeal and among the girls the heroine and two or three others prove to be virginal, among the young men, however, only Theagenes; and "everybody", he adds, "was surprised... that such a blooming man was inexperienced in the works of Aphrodite" (10.9.1).

Attempts at seducing the hero or the heroine are common to all Greek novels. However, the Clitophon-Melite episode in Achilles Tatius has a clear parallel in the Theagenes-Arsace episode in Heliodorus. Melite, as it seems, has hitherto been leading a stainless life (cf. 6.10.2). Now, her husband having been reported dead, there is no legal or social obstacle whatsoever for Melite to marry again.[25] In Alexandria she meets Clitophon and passionately falls in love with him. For months she keeps imploring him to become her husband or at least lover. Finally, at his friends' insistence, he agrees on condition of postponing the consummation of the marriage out of piety towards Leucippe, whom he thinks to be dead, until their arrival at Melite's home town Ephesus. In Ephesus we witness the pity she has for a maltreated female slave, who proves to be none other than Leucippe. As a consequence Clitophon still refuses to consummate his marriage with Melite. Shortly afterwards Melite's allegedly dead husband turns up, falls on Clitophon and locks him up. Melite, visiting him in his prison, at first gives vent to her grief and fury, then, changing her mind, beseeches him amid tears to heal the pain of her desire by one single embrace. And now at last, after he has found Leucippe

---

[25] Since classical times in Greece it had been the rule for a widow to remarry, and remarriage immediately after the husband's death was by no means unusual; we do not even learn of an obligatory mourning-time such as in Rome. See W. Erdmann, *Die Ehe im alten Griechenland* (Munich 1934) 408.

again and Melite can no longer be called a widow, he surrenders to her wooing. After he has "healed" her (6.1.1), she movingly takes care for his and Leucippe's safety, pays him compliments, gives him a large amount of money and, since for reasons of safety they change clothes, asks him to keep her dress as a souvenir, promising for her part to keep his. Thus, as E. Vilborg has put it, Melite appears as an almost pathetic personage who remains for a long time in the reader's memory. Clitophon, for his part, has naturally been harshly criticized for his "lapse". E. Rohde[26] reproaches him for a "particular lack of dignity". Perhaps rightly so; and yet with all his "lack of dignity" Clitophon appears thoroughly human.

In Heliodorus Theagenes is desired by Arsace, the sister of the Persian king and wife of the satrap of Egypt and accordingly a person of the greatest importance and power. To heighten the idealization of the hero even more, she is delineated in the blackest colours. She has always been leading a dissolute life; now fascinated by Theagenes' beauty, she desperately wants him as her lover despite the fact that she very well knows him to have a fiancée, Chariclea, and she has herself a husband who is alive and well, although absent for the time being. Having brought Theagenes and Chariclea under her power by a trick, she at first showers him with her attentions and then, failing to make him waver in his fidelity to Chariclea, has him thrown into prison and cruelly tortured. Finally she even tries to do away with Chariclea by poison, failing in this attempt only because the poisoned cup is mistaken for another one and a servant dies in Chariclea's stead (8.8.2).

This particular incident has led us to a set of parallel motifs where in Heliodorus supernatural events, indeed downright miracles, happen, whereas in Achilles Tatius everything can be explained by perfectly natural causes. For Chariclea accuses herself of poisoning Arsace's servant in order not to have to die by her own hand. Therefore she is condemned to burn at the stake, but its flames do her no harm thanks to a certain gem she is wearing (8.9.13ff.; cf. 8.11.8f.). It is for the same reason of not having to die by his own hand that Clitophon accuses himself of having murdered Leucippe in complicity with Melite, however with the better motivation of thus being able to cause Melite, the supposed murderess, to get her deserts. He, too, is condemned to death—*nota bene*, to the more humane death

---

[26] (1876[1]) 480 = (1900[2]) 511.

by the cup of hemlock customary in Greece (cf. 8.8.5)—and is saved from this fate in a perfectly natural way.

How do gods make their will known to the humans? In Achilles Tatius (4.1), it is in dreams that Artemis appears to Leucippe, Aphrodite to Clitophon, to give them intimations about the future and to guide their behaviour in the present. In Heliodorus (3.11.5–3.12.1) Apollo and Artemis appear to the priest Calasiris at midnight to consign Theagenes and Chariclea to his care. At first he is uncertain as to whether it was a dream or reality, but then he cannot help realizing that he experienced a genuine appearance of deities.

Both novels are characterized by ordeals towards the end of the narrative. In Achilles Tatius the two ordeals testing Leucippe's virginity and Melite's chastity (8.12–8.14; cf. 8.6) aim at a decision in a lawsuit and are recounted, as it were, with a mischievous smile. For Leucippe is indeed still a virgin, but hardly by her own merit (cf. 2.23.3ff.), and Melite's oath not to have had sexual intercourse with a man during her husband's absence is indeed technically correct, though not in the least by her own merit, and her intercourse with Clitophon took place only after her husband's return (5.27). The test examining her chastity is therefore a mere farce and, as D.B. Durham[27] has put it, "is an insult to the god who holds jurisdiction".

In Heliodorus (10.7–10.9), on the other hand, the ordeal serves purely religious purposes: a human sacrifice of either sex is to be offered to the Sun and the Moon, and only virginal persons are worthy of such an honour. Therefore the candidates for this honour must undergo an examination which consists in mounting a golden sacrificial hearth barefooted; whoever is no longer virginal burns the soles of his feet on it, but whoever is free from guilt, suffers no harm. How the examination ends has already been described: several girls and among the young men only Theagenes pass it; all others burn their soles. This is obviously a miracle, and Heliodorus recounts it with holy earnestness and solemnity.

No miracle, on the other hand, takes place in Achilles Tatius. Indeed during Leucippe's examination "sweet music" is heard from inside the cave of Pan in which she has been locked, and subsequently the door of the cave opens "of its own accord". But the priest, who describes the process of the ordeal, besides the supernatural explanation, which he qualifies as the less likely one, viz. that Pan blows his

---

[27] Durham (1938) 12.

syrinx, hints at a natural one himself—"because there is some musical breeze"—, and this latter explanation is almost certainly the accurate one; there is sufficient evidence that the priests' achievement of effects which were to simulate supernatural events was quite common. And during Melite's examination nothing in reality happens at all.

Moreover, whereas for understandable reasons no parallels from real life can be found for the ordeal in Heliodorus, rituals such as those described by Achilles Tatius have actually been performed, if, at least in historical times, extremely rarely and never as a part of legal proceedings.[28]

Finally, in both novels a priest plays an important part. In Achilles Tatius it is the (unnamed) priest of Artemis at Ephesus, in Heliodorus the Egyptian priest Calasiris. They have quite comparable function, giving the respective hero and heroine their protection and support. And yet it would be unimaginable for Calasiris to be criticized and suspected of moral misdemeanour, indeed obscenely reviled as his counterpart in Achilles Tatius is, no less than to use "Aristophanic" language as he does (8.9.1) in order to accuse an adversary of immoral conduct. Calasiris, every inch a member of the Egyptian sacerdotal caste, is far above such profanity.

Style

Every modern reader who, without being especially prepared, opens Achilles Tatius' novel at its first page and begins to read, is in for a surprise at the unfamiliar, quasi-poetical diction. Now, Achilles Tatius, being a child of his time, could not help complying with its fashions and obeying its laws, and the 2nd century A.D. happened to be the center of that literary-rhetorical movement which has usually been called "Second Sophistic" since Philostratus (ca. A.D. 200).

Greek artistic prose as a whole has been superbly characterized in these terms:[29] viewed as a whole, the history of Greek artistic prose presents the spectacle of a continued struggle between two principles of style. The one, which might be called the principle of baroque style, claims for artistic prose, for the "beautiful speech", as the Greeks have it, the resources of poetry. It excludes only the verse proper;

---

[28] For details see Plepelits (1980) 38–40.
[29] Cf. E. Schwartz (1896) 147ff.

everything else is virtually admissible. In addition, it feels justified to employ the entire stock of artifices of rhetoric. The other principle, the one of classicism, strictly separates poetry and prose and confines prose to those resources that are adequate to it, developing them with diligent consideration and respect of moderation and lucidity.

Now, in the epoch of the Second Sophistic that struggle had intensified to a vehemence unheard of before. Naturally, a sophisticated and ambitious writer could not escape its influence. Achilles Tatius is open to it as is no other Greek novelist. He gives both principles of style their due: in the purely narrative passages he usually writes quite plainly and unpretentiously, often refreshingly vividly, indeed even casually; in purple patches, on the other hand, he takes advantage of all artifices of contemporary rhetoric and writes, to use an ancient judgement on such a style, "poetry in prose".[30] One of his most conspicuous peculiarities is the affected naiveté of stringing together extremely short sentences of similar structure without a verb; the ancient critics called it ἀφέλεια ("simplicity").[31] This "baroque style" is to be met not only in the various declamations of high pathos and sometimes perfect bombast and the fairly adroitly structured forensic speeches, but especially in the frequent descriptions and digressions, essayistic studies, in which erudition of the most diverse kinds in the mode of the Second Sophistic is displayed and which used to be called ἐκφράσεις ("descriptions").[32] These *ekphraseis* are not always, but very often inserted at structurally important places of the narrative, such as the beginning and the end of a book, and their subject is not always, but very often connected with the narrative proper, either directly or in symbolic refraction. For example, the description of a painting representing the abduction of Europa by the amorous Zeus as a prelude to the narrative proper is doubtless meant to be a symbol of its two main subjects, love and abduction. A park-like garden as described in 1.15 is held to be a symbol of love; indeed the gardens of love, in which Eros brings the lovers together, are an important feature in literature. In two instances (3.6.2 and 5.3.3f.) the narrator explicitly points out the immanent symbolism of descriptions of paintings by conferring upon them the value of portents.

---

[30] Athenaeus 14 p. 639A.
[31] A really long sentence is to be found only once in the whole novel: 7.4.4f.; it contains an elaborate comparison.
[32] An exhaustive treatise has been devoted to them by Rommel (1923).

It cannot be denied that the modern reader, largely unaccustomed to rhetorical or poetical diction, is occasionally required to summon up a little patience. However, it hardly does the author's art justice to speak in a sweeping manner of bad taste, as has been done. It is well known that taste is a very changeable quantity. To the age of baroque Achilles Tatius' diction appealed far more than to ours; P.D. Huet in his famous *Essai sur l'origine des romans* (Paris 1670) actually voiced the opinion that in his style he surpassed Heliodorus and all other Greek novelists.

Description of the Novel

Book 1

The story opens with the author ("I"), having landed in Sidon, "presenting an offering of thanks to the Phoenicians' Aphrodite[33]—Astarte the Sidonians call her" (1.1.2). Walking around the town, he is then fascinated by the implied eroticism of a painting representing Europa and the bull together with Eros, which he describes in great detail. Finally, he becomes aware of the presence of a young man who cannot help sighing at Eros' power and mentions the large number of trials inflicted upon him by Eros. Made curious by these words, the author leads him to a lovely spot depicted after the famous model set by Plato in the introduction to his dialogue *Phaedrus* (228E–230E) and causes him to tell him his story; and this young man's tale is the novel proper.

He introduces himself as Clitophon of Tyre. It was when he was in the 19th year of his life that "Tyche initiated the drama" (1.3.3). He was by then betrothed to his paternal half sister Calligone. Now, his father's brother, who lived in Byzantium, sent his wife Panthea and daughter Leucippe to Tyre to stay with them for a while. As soon as Clitophon caught sight of Leucippe, who was extremely beautiful, he fell in love with her. Being rather inexperienced, he turned to a cousin of his by the name of Clinias, who was two years his senior and in love with a boy. Clinias gave Clitophon useful advice about the art of seduction. In the meantime, however, his boy-friend

---

[33] The word "Aphrodite" is not transmitted, but goes back to a convincing conjecture by Diggle (1972); cf. Plepelits (1980) 65.

met his death by the shying of the horse Clinias had given to him as a love present. The book finishes with the exquisite description of the wonderful garden of Clitophon's family and the talks he had in it with his servant Satyrus about Eros' power over the animate and inanimate nature in order to impress Leucippe, who, in company with her maid Clio, seemed to be listening "not without pleasure" (1.19.1).

Book 2

For ten days Clitophon risked no more than fiery looks, but then he asked Satyrus for help, who, of course, had already noticed everything and now supplied him with encouragement, good advice and the promise to help. Now several delightful wooing scenes follow showing Clitophon getting nearer and nearer to Leucippe's heart, interrupted by pangs of conscience because of Calligone. Meanwhile, Clitophon's and Calligone's wedding was delayed by a bad omen, and a certain Callisthenes from Byzantium, who had passionately fallen in love with Leucippe without ever having seen her, abducted Calligone, mistaking her for Leucippe. Several days later Clitophon at last succeeded in persuading Leucippe to receive him into her bedroom at night. However he had hardly lain down in bed with her when her mother, deeply alarmed by a disquieting dream, dashed in and harshly disrupted their tête-à-tête. Clitophon managed only a narrow escape. Panthea, beside herself with rage and disappointment, did not believe her daughter's protestations that she had no idea who the visitor had been and that her virginity had not been dishonored. Furious at her mother, Leucippe expressly begged Clitophon to elope with her. A couple of nights later, therefore, at night, as soon as everybody else in the house was asleep, Clitophon, Leucippe and Satyrus sneaked out into the street; at the town-gate, they met Clinias, who had been waiting for them with a carriage, and by it they, together with Clinias, went hurriedly as far as Berytus, where they boarded a ship just about to set sail for Alexandria. On board the ship they made friends with a young Egyptian by the name of Menelaus. The book finishes with a lengthy discussion on sensual pleasure with Clitophon advocating heterosexual love, and Clinias and Menelaus homosexual.

Book 3

On the third day of the voyage, a heavy storm caused the ship to be wrecked. Clitophon and Leucippe managed to sit on a plank, and were thus driven to the Egyptian shore at Pelusium, thinking all the others to have perished in the waters. After staying there for two days and recovering from the shipwreck, they rented rooms on a boat sailing to Alexandria using the delta of the Nile. At a narrow spot, however, the boat was attacked by the so-called herdsmen, brigands, who at that time held sway over the whole delta, and all passengers were captured. Leucippe was wrenched out of Clitophon's arms and taken away to be sacrificed for the sake of the herdsmen's band, the others however were soon rescued by a regiment of regular soldiers. Its commander, after listening to Clitophon's story, was deeply moved by it and made him his companion at table, even giving him an Egyptian servant. Yet they could not do anything about the robbers as long as they had Leucippe as a hostage. The next day, they discovered a huge robbers' army on the other side of a canal; in front of them there was a makeshift altar, and beside it a coffin. And suddenly Leucippe was led to the altar and ritually sacrificed; her entrails were roasted on the altar, cut in small pieces and eaten by all of them; the corpse was then laid into the coffin, and finally the robbers ran away. Meanwhile, Clitophon and all the soldiers had been watching the gruesome spectacle, but it was not until evening that they managed to fill up the canal and cross over. Although the commander did his best to console Clitophon in his despair, the latter, under cover of night, taking his sword, went to the coffin with the intention of killing himself. He was, however, prevented by two men shouting and running toward him; they turned out to be Menelaus and Satyrus! They opened the coffin and out came Leucippe, alive and perfectly well, and she clasped Clitophon in her arms. They then told the marvelling Clitophon how after the shipwreck the two of them had been thrown on to the Egyptian coast, had been captured by the "herdsmen" and had manipulated the sacrifice of Leucippe by means of a stage sword and a sham belly filled with animal entrails and animal blood. The book finishes with the commander telling Clitophon and Menelaus the story of the bird phoenix.

Book 4

It was because of the appearance of the phoenix that the expected reinforcements were delayed. Therefore, the troops returned to the village where they had camped earlier, and Clitophon and Leucippe were assigned a house of their own. And as soon as they had moved in, he wanted to sleep with her, but she refused, justifying her refusal with a dream in which Artemis had appeared to her. So he no longer tried to pester her. Meanwhile, Charmides, the commander, had set an eye on Leucippe and put pressure on Menelaus to persuade her to take him as a lover. While Menelaus was deliberating with Clitophon on this problem, it was reported to them that Leucippe had obviously gone crazy; and the report was true. She had to be bound with cords and treated by the surgeon, for the time being, however, without any success. In the meantime, an envoy from the governor of Egypt arrived with a letter for the commander, and the result of it was an immediate attack upon the "herdsmen's" capital village, which, like all villages in the Nile delta, lay on an island, or rather peninsula, because a narrow access connected it with the mainland. By means of a succession of most interesting stratagems, however, the brigands managed to annihilate almost the entire regiment, including the commander. On the tenth day of Leucippe's mental illness, Clitophon learned about its cause from a certain Chaereas: Gorgias, an Egyptian soldier, who had become a victim of the "herdsmen", desiring her, had brewed an aphrodisiac and prevailed on Clitophon's Egyptian servant to mix it into her drink; the latter, however, had served it to her undiluted, and that had caused her illness. Now Gorgias' servant, who was still alive, knew how to prepare an antidote. Thus, Leucippe was healed. Meanwhile, the "herdsmen" were utterly conquered by a greater army. Now that the region was freed from terror, Clitophon and Leucippe continued their journey to Alexandria in the company of Chaereas, who had become their friend; he lived on the island of Pharus. The book finishes with the praise of the water of the Nile and the description of the crocodile.

Book 5

The book begins with an enthusiastic description of Alexandria. Menelaus rented an apartment for Clitophon and Leucippe. Chaereas, who had for quite a long time been in love with her, invited them to his house on Pharus near the famous lighthouse. There he had a band of pirates abduct her. Clitophon, although wounded in the scuffle, begged the mayor to pursue them on a ship, but when it came near to theirs, they cut off Leucippe's head and pushed the rest of her body into the sea. Thus, they escaped pursuit, for Clitophon besaught the others to retrieve the corpse in order to have it buried. Back in Alexandria, his wound was treated, and as Menelaus never tired of comforting him, he finally forced himself to live on.

Six months had already passed when he happened to run into Clinias, whom he had thought to be dead. He had been saved by a ship bound for Sidon and had learned there that one day after their departure from Tyre a letter from Leucippe's father had been delivered in which he betrothed her to Clitophon, whereupon the latter's father had inquired where they had gone and had actually already found out about his whereabouts. So he, Clinias, had immediately come to Alexandria to search for Clitophon and tell him. When Clitophon concluded that he had no choice but to flee from Alexandria before his father arrived, Satyrus suggested that his master accept the good luck Aphrodite had offered him; for a beautiful and wealthy young widow from Ephesus named Melite had become infatuated with him and desired to marry him, or at least to be his mistress, but he refused obstinately. Clinias, however, earnestly advised him to listen to Satyrus and to comply with Eros, and so he surrendered on the condition that no intimacies should take place before they arrived at Ephesus. The next day, the wedding was performed in the temple of Isis, and one more day later, they departed for Ephesus, taking leave from Menelaus, but accompanied by Clinias. During the entire five-day-journey, Melite constantly tried to talk Clitophon into sleeping with her, but he remained firm. Having arrived at her home, Melite was showing Clitophon her nearby country-estate, when a female slave threw herself at Melite's feet and begged for mercy. She had been badly mistreated by Sosthenes, the steward, who had bought her from pirates; her name was Lacaena, and she came from Thessaly. Melite suspended Sosthenes on the spot and had Lacaena bathed, dressed in clean clothes and taken to town. That evening, Clitophon was thunder-struck when Satyrus handed him a letter in Leucippe's hand-writing, in which she asked him to see to it that she was freed and wished him all the best in his new marriage. "Lacaena" proved to be none other but Leucippe! That night, Clitophon felt it to be impossible to consummate his marriage with Melite, and so he feigned some illness to prevent it, a fact to which she resigned herself only with extreme reluctance. The next morning, she called for "Lacaena", told her everything about her supposed husband, and asked her to prepare an aphrodisiac for her; for she understood that Thessalian women knew the art of charming a man by magic. Not knowing how to refuse, Leucippe answered that if Melite permitted it, she would go to the country-estate to search for herbs, and set off immediately. Later that day, during a banquet Melite's husband, Thersander, who had been thought dead, suddenly stormed into the house, fell on Clitophon, beat him, tied him up and locked him up in a room. While that was happening, Leucippe's letter dropped to the ground, and Melite picked it up and, reading it, learned the whole truth. After Thersander had rushed out to one of his friends' house, she, having talked to the man who was entrusted with Clitophon's custody, entered the room where he was lying on the floor, and at first she heaped reproaches on him, but then, changing her tone, she begged and entreated him to heal her love-sickness and eventually undid his ties. And Clitophon, finally persuaded by her "wise lecture", actually "healed" Melite.

Book 6

This being done, Melite saw to it that Clitophon should escape safely: she made him change clothes with her so that the guard would think him to be her, and she gave him a large amount of money; besides, a young freedman of hers was to lead him to where he would find Clinias and Satyrus and where Leucippe would come. At the same time, however, Thersander was returning home in the company of Sosthenes, who had meanwhile talked him into desiring Leucippe as a mistress and had, at Thersander's request, seized hold of her and locked her up in some remote shack on the country-estate. And all of a sudden Clitophon was face to face with them, and they caught hold of him and took him to prison, and Thersander instituted legal proceedings for adultery against him. As for Leucippe, they pestered her several times, indeed Thersander tried to force her, but they met with complete failure, so that he finally reviled her and even hit her in the face. He learned, however, that Clitophon was her husband.

Book 7

Infuriated, he rushed out without saying one more word to Leucippe and turned to the prison-governor, asking him to do away with Clitophon by poison; as he could not talk him into that, he came up with a second request, viz. to lock up a spy together with Clitophon, as if he were a prisoner as well. This ostensible spy's task was in truth to mention that Melite had caused Leucippe to be murdered. And Clitophon believed every word of it and decided to die and told Clinias, who had come to see him, how: in court he would confess that he and Melite had had an affair and had therefore jointly done away with Leucippe; in this way Melite would get her just deserts as well. And Clinias and Satyrus consoled him indefatigably and went out of their way to dissuade him from his intention. This was, however, all to no avail; for when the trial opened, he made exactly that declaration to everybody's surprise. Although Clinias delivered a brilliant speech, setting matters straight, Thersander's lawyers shouted that the murderer who accused himself should be executed. But then Melite challenged Thersander to hand over Sosthenes for questioning; for perhaps he was the one who had killed Leucippe. Thereupon Thersander secretly sent one of his friends to Sosthenes, telling him to disappear as quickly as possible. And Sosthenes, who at that time was in Leucippe's shack, on hearing that news became greatly alarmed and, mounting a horse, hurriedly galloped away towards Smyrna, even forgetting to close the door of the shack. Meanwhile, Thersander had addressed himself to the judges, declaring that Sosthenes was missing for the third day and suspecting Clitophon and Melite to have murdered him as well. After he had sworn to not knowing what had happened to Sosthenes, Clitophon was sentenced to death; besides, being condemned, he was to be put to the torture so as to find out about Melite's participation in the murder. Preparations for the torture were already being made, when the priest of Artemis, adorned with a laurel wreath, was seen to approach. This is always a sign of an embassy having arrived in the honour of the goddess; in this case every punishment must be suspended until the envoys have performed the sacrifice. Therefore, Clitophon was untied. The embassy had come from Byzantium, and its head was Sostratus, Leucippe's father. At the same time, Leucippe fled from the shack and sought refuge in the nearby temple of Artemis. While in the law-court, after Sostratus had recognized Clitophon, a dramatic scene was taking place, one of the temple-attendants came running towards the priest and reported that Leucippe had taken refuge with Artemis. Thereupon everybody rushed towards the temple. Clitophon, however, was stopped by the guards and would have been dragged back to the prison, had the priest not engaged to keep him in his personal custody. Thus they continued their race to the temple, where, at last, they found and greeted Leucippe.

Book 8

They were just about to sit down and talk when Thersander arrived with several witnesses and made a huge row, even using violence against Clitophon; finally, those present in the temple dragged him out, but in leaving, Thersander threatened Clitophon with capital punishment and Leucippe with the syrinx. As it was time for dinner, the priest invited them very kindly and asked them to tell him their story. Naturally, it was Clitophon who did most of the talking; in doing so, he laid particular stress upon the fact that Leucippe was still a virgin. Asked to explain Thersander's final remark about the syrinx, the priest told the myth of Syrinx and Pan and how Pan's own syrinx in a grotto nearby was used as a test of virginity, whereupon Leucippe declared herself to be perfectly prepared to undergo that ordeal.

The next day was devoted to the matters of the embassy, and the day after that was appointed for the court trial. This time the priest proved to be the main target for Thersander's and his lawyers' invectives; the priest, for his part, retorted (ostensibly) in the manner of Aristophanes. Finally, Thersander put forward two challenges, one for Melite and one for Leucippe: he challenged Melite to undergo the ordeal of the holy Styx and Leucippe to undergo the ordeal of the syrinx. His challenges were promptly accepted. The water of the Styx was a fountain, which had originally been a virgin who had thrown away her virginity, and was occasionally used as an ordeal of chastity.

The following day both Leucippe and Melite victoriously passed their respective ordeals. Thersander, therefore, seeing himself utterly defeated, stole away and fled into his house; besides, just then, Sosthenes happened to be dragged along. For this reason Thersander secretly left Ephesus on the following night. When Sosthenes reported everything plainly, Thersander was, in absence, sentenced to exile.

At dinner that evening Leucippe told the story of the pirates of Pharus, thus clearing the mystery of the cut-off head. The woman whose head had been cut off had been a courtesan, whose clothes they had exchanged with hers. After that, it was Sostratus' turn to tell the others about Calligone, who had been abducted by Callisthenes, because he had thought her to be Leucippe. Having realized his mistake, he nevertheless ardently fell in love with her, in fact so much so that he completely changed his character and became a model youth. He spared her virginity and even made up his mind to ask her father for her hand in marriage.

After that night, they stayed at Ephesus for three more days in order to wait out maturity. Then they sailed to Byzantium, and, having celebrated their much-desired marriage there, they sailed to Tyre. They arrived two days later than Callisthenes and Calligone, who were about to get married the following day. So they took part in those celebrations and decided to spend the winter in Tyre and then to go to Byzantium.

The Time of the Action

What is the setting of Achilles Tatius' novel? Very often the opinion has been held that like Heliodorus' novel it is set in the epoch of the Persian empire, because at 4.11.1 the "satrap" of Egypt (τοῦ τῆς Αἰγύπτου σατράπου) and at 4.13.4 the residence of the "satrap" (τὰ σατραπεῖα) are referred to and, besides, at 7.12.1 it is mentioned that the chairman of the body of judges at Ephesus was a member of the "royal" family (τοῦ βασιλικοῦ γένους). This opinion is, however, inconsistent with the entire remaining historical background, which consistently reflects the conditions of Hellenistic and Roman times. This is by no means limited to the fact that Alexandria (founded 332/331 B.C.) and the lighthouse on the island of Pharos (built in the first half of the 3rd century B.C.) are described as existing. An essential part of the action is set in areas that were not yet Greek in Persian times, but—with one significant exception—appear completely Hellenized, a situation which evolved in the Hellenistic era and intensified under Roman rule. This applies first and foremost to Sidon and Tyre, two ancient Phoenician cities that since Hellenistic times, at least as far as the culturally and politically leading class of their populations is concerned, were purely Greek. In the same way all characters in Achilles Tatius' novel—apart from the exception just hinted at—are Greek in language and civilization, no matter if they are natives of Byzantium and Ephesus or of Phoenicia and Egypt, have Greek names and Greek-Hellenistic customs. The one significant exception concerns the brigands-herdsmen of the Nile delta. These barbarians unfamiliar with Hellenistic civilization "babble in a strange tongue" (3.9.2), viz., as the reader learns later (3.10.2; 3.15.3), in Egyptian, and at 3.10.2f. Clitophon, a native of Tyre, bewails the double misfortune of having fallen into the hands of Egyptian robbers: "A Greek robber might be moved by speaking . . . But, as things are, with what kind of words are we to make our prayers (*considering that we cannot make ourselves understood*)?"

In all this there is a substantial difference to Heliodorus' novel, whose action is indeed set in the epoch of the Persian empire and consequently in pre-Hellenistic times. In Heliodorus all Egyptians, not only the brigands-herdsmen, speak Egyptian and have Egyptian names.

The indications of Persian rule referred to at the outset, on the other hand, prove invalid if one considers the fact that the term "satrap" in a writer of the era of the Roman Empire need not mean a Persian governor, but may denote the governor of a Roman province. The reason for this was a stylistic fashion which made writers who wanted to be respected use, as far as possible, only words that were (so to speak) legitimated by the Attic classics of the 5th and 4th centuries B.C. This is how it happened that the realities of the contemporary Roman state could be indicated with terms of the late Persian empire, the governor of a province as "satrap", the emperor as "king".[34] Consequently, since the Hellenistic background excludes the time of Persian rule, it is precisely the reference to a "satrap" that helps us to determine the time of the action as intended by the author more accurately. For during the epoch of Hellenism (in the narrower sense) a "satrap" of Egypt did not exist, because Egypt was a sovereign kingdom. It was only since it had become a Roman province in 30 B.C., in other words since the beginning of the Roman Empire, that Egypt was again ruled by a "satrap". As to the member of the "royal" family, it was never more likely or at least credible for him to live at Ephesus and to be the chairman of a

---

[34] See H.J. Mason "The Roman Government in Greek Sources. The Effect of Literary Theory on the Translation of Official Titles," *Phoenix* 24 (1970) 150ff.; *Id.*, *Greek Terms for Roman Institutions: A Lexicon and Analysis* (Toronto 1974).

body of judges into the bargain than after Ephesus had become the capital of the province of Asia in 29 B.C., succeeding Pergamum in this rank.

Having thus ascertained the Roman Empire as general setting of Achilles Tatius' novel, we have to ask further whether he means his own contemporary world or some particular time in the recent past during the period between emperor Augustus' accession and his own age. Unfortunately, the question cannot be answered with certainty. An argument for the former alternative seems to be the initial situation, where he ("I", i.e. seemingly the author) recounts how he met the hero of his novel, who was then a young man, in Sidon and was told the story by him. On the other hand, an earlier date seems to be pointed at by two details. One of them is the war that Byzantium is forced to wage with the Thracians and which is the reason for Leucippe's coming to Tyre with her mother. Now, the raids and attacks of the restless and warlike Thracians had been a constant problem for Byzantium and even for the Romans, after the North coast of the Aegean had become their possession as part of the province Macedonia in 148 B.C., so that in about 15 B.C. the whole country was made a tributary state under a native prince dependent on Rome. Subsequently Thrace seems at first to have been quiet in the main, but in A.D. 21 and 26 there were rebellions against Roman hegemony, and finally in about A.D. 45 heavy fighting broke out, which, the account in Tacitus' *Annals* being lost, is scarcely attested in literature and about whose cause, development and duration we consequently know nothing; yet this much is certain that in A.D. 46 Thrace was transformed into a Roman province. From now on peace and quiet prevailed in and around Thrace; it was only during the pretenders' fights consequent on emperor Commodus' death (A.D. 193–196) that it again became a theatre of war without being actively involved in them. A passage in Tacitus' *Annals* (12.63.3) belonging to A.D. 53 refers to the hostilities previous to the final pacification of the country: "(*The Byzantines*) begged for exemption (*from*) or alleviation (*of their financial burdens*). The emperor supported them, arguing that their exhaustion from recent wars in Thrace and the Crimean Bosphorus entitled them to relief. A remission of tribute was granted for five years."[35] This passage proves that Byzantium was involved in the last Thracian war as well. Byzantium was at that

---

[35] Translation by M. Grant.

time tributary indeed, but still sovereign, and it was therefore free to wage war and conclude peace at will. As a consequence, Achilles Tatius seems most likely to mean this last historical war of about A.D. 45 by his Thracian war.

At 3.24.3 it is reported that at Heliopolis in Egypt the Phoenix appeared, delaying the departure of armed forces against the brigands-herdsmen. Now, the ancient tradition knows several appearances of the Phoenix occurring at vast intervals in earlier times and of three occurring during the Roman Empire, viz. in A.D. 34, 36 and 47; at a later date no such occurrence is attested. Provided that Achilles Tatius really refers to an historical appearance of the Phoenix, one of the three appearances recorded in the 1st century A.D., most of all the one in A.D. 47, would go excellently with the temporal frame of the last Thracian war.[36]

Compared to that, the author's assertion to have met the hero of his novel and have been told his story by him seems to weigh less and is most probably a mere fiction. As a result, it can be conjectured with a certain probability that Achilles Tatius means the year A.D. 47 to be the setting of his novel.

Nachleben

Apart from Achilles Tatius' influence upon Heliodorus mentioned above,[37] he never enjoyed any recognizable *Nachleben* in pagan antiquity. Strangely enough, however, some traces of acquaintance with him can be found in the Christian literature of late antiquity. E. Vilborg lists five paraphrases of certain passages of Achilles Tatius' novel from the commentary to *Hexaëmeron* wrongly attributed to Eustathius of Antiochia (died A.D. 337), which is to be dated to the 4th or 5th century.[38] Another trace is a martyr story transmitted in two versions in the *Acta Sanctorum* of November 5th.[39] In it the parents of a saint are named Clitophon and Leucippe. This being not an historical report, but a legend,[40] there can be no doubt that these

---

[36] For details see Plepelits (1980) 24–27.
[37] See the section on Achilles Tatius' relationship to Heliodorus.
[38] According to M. Geerard, *Clavis patrum Graecorum* II (Turnhout 1974) no. 3393.
[39] November, vol. 3 (Brussels 1910) 33ff.; the second version also in Migne gr. 116, p. 93ff.
[40] Thus the editor of the text in the *Acta Sanctorum*, H. Delahaye, p. 33f.

names have been taken over from Achilles Tatius, all the more so since there is in addition distinct evidence of Heliodorus' influence in the legend in question.

The article of the *Suda* on Achilles Tatius quoted above in the section on the biography of the author affirms that he "finally became a Christian and a bishop", an account that was formerly believed by many and passionately discussed for centuries, but is universally dismissed nowadays, particularly since the same is reported about Heliodorus. Today it is the *communis opinio* that these parallel reports were invented in order to protect the two novels from annihilation, for it is supposed that the vast majority of the doubtless considerable novelistic production was purposely destroyed by the Christians.

Achilles Tatius' influence upon Byzantine literature was most important after the 9th century. Whereas a man of the church such as Photius, patriarch of Constantinople in the 9th century, condemns his "obscenity and shamelessness", a secular scholar of the same century, Leo surnamed "the Philosopher" wrote a poetical homage to him,[42] praising the virtuousness of the two lovers and of the entire narrative. In the 11th century the polyhistorian, Psellus[43] testifies that both Achilles Tatius and Heliodorus were popular reading matter, "even among highly educated people", and reports about a vivid and learned debate as to which of the two novels should rank higher. In a critical essay he compares them in great detail, coming to the conclusion that Achilles Tatius proves inferior on most counts. Later in the 11th century, possibly in the 1080s, the first Byzantine novel was published, *Hysmine and Hysminias*, by a man whose name is given in the codices with apparently deliberate variation as Eustathios Makrembolites or Eumathios Makrembolites or Eustathios Parembolites (almost certainly pseudonyms, probably for the Caesar John Ducas, a close friend of Psellus').[44] It constitutes a close imitation of *Leucippe and Clitophon*, avoiding, however, its alleged faults, as listed by Psellus:

---

[41] *Bibliotheca*, cod. 87, latest edition in Vilborg (1955) 163.; cod. 94, latest editions *ibid.* p. 164 and in Habrich (1960) 2, 4.

[42] *Anthologia Graeca* 9.203; the manuscript attributes the authorship to "Photius, patriarch of Constantinople, according to others: Leo the Philosopher". What has just been reported about Photius should, however, exclude his authorship.

[43] *Essay on Heliodorus and Achilles Tatius*, ed. Vilborg (1955) 165–167 = Dyck (1986) 75–118 (with English translation). *Id.: About the Style of Some Literary Works* in J.F. Boissonade: Psellos, *De Operatione Daemonum* (Nürnberg 1838) 48ff.

[44] For details see Eustathios Makrembolites, *Hysmine and Hysminias*. Eingeleitet, übersetzt und erläutert von K. Plepelits (Stuttgart 1989), Introduction.

the everyday language, the sensational motifs and the obscenity, so that its author's intention seems to have been to "correct" Achilles Tatius. Its language, therefore, is throughout like the one Achilles Tatius uses in his "purple passages", in other words, "poetry in prose".[45] Consequently, its successors, the novels in the literary language as well as those in the vernacular, all use the verse form. In them Achilles Tatius (together with Heliodorus) continued to serve as a pattern; imitations of his description of a garden at 1.15 are particularly popular.[46]

In the West the natal hour of Achilles Tatius' *Nachleben* struck in 1544. It was in that year that a Latin translation by Annibal Cruceius (Annibale della Croce) appeared in Lyon. It was, however, as was expressed in the title of the translation (*Narrationis amatoriae fragmentum e graeco in latinum conversum*), only a fragment, viz. books 5 to 8, and besides the author was still unknown. This fragmentary translation for its part was translated into Italian in 1546 by the Venetian poet Lodovico Dolce. It was in 1551 that the first complete translation (into Italian) after a complete manuscript appeared in Venice and the author's name became known. In 1554 Cruceius completed his Latin translation. In 1556 the first French translation was published, in 1597 the first English one, in 1617 the hitherto only Spanish one, 1644 the first German one and in 1652 the hitherto only Dutch one.[47]

These and subsequent translations were frequently reprinted and were permanently available; they were read by a large audience and, which was of even greater importance, by the writers of every nation taking part in the civilization of the Renaissance. For, together with Heliodorus and Eustathius Makrembolites, Achilles Tatius embodied the classic model of epic prose narrative and was placed on a level with Homer and Virgil. As a consequence their translations, which were usually rather "free", in particular expurgating Achilles Tatius' obscenities, led to imitations, sometimes so close ones that they have been regarded as translations, and thus to the rise of the Spanish

---

[45] See the section on style above.
[46] See O. Schissel von Fleschenberg, *Der byzantinische Garten, Seine Darstellung im gleichzeitigen Romane* (Vienna 1942) *passim*. The same author points out that the famous epic or rather romance of *Digenis Akritas* is partly no more than a versification of Achilles Tatius' novel: "Digenis Akritis und Achilleus Tatios," *Neophilologus* 27 (1942) 143f.
[47] For later translations see Appendix.

and French novel of ideal tendency, whose offspring was to be the modern novel. As far as Achilles Tatius is concerned, the first work written under his influence appeared as early as 1552 in Spain: the *Historia de los amores de Clareo y Florisea y de los trabajos de Ysea* by Alonso Núñez de Reinoso; Lodovico Dolce's Italian translation of 1546 having served as a model, it corresponds to *Leucippe and Clitophon*, Books 5 to 8. A similar case, but already corresponding to the complete Achilles Tatius, is, in England, *Arbasto* by Robert Greene (appeared 1584). Incidentally, Sir Philip Sidney's influential main work *Arcadia* (written 1577–1585, published posthumously 1590) combines influences from Longus, Heliodorus and Achilles Tatius.[48] Finally, it should be mentioned that Achilles Tatius' novel was even dramatized in the French tragicomedy *Clitophon et Leucippe* by Pierre Du Ryer (1622).[49]

---

[48] For further details see Wolff (1912).
[49] See K. Philipp, *Pierre Du Ryers Leben und dramatische Werke*, Diss. Leipzig (Zwickau 1905) 19ff.; cf. Plepelits (1980) 56–58.

APPENDIX

I. *Editions*

Bonnvitius, I. and N. (Heidelberg: ex officina Commeliana, 1601; reprinted 1606).
Salmasius (Saumaise), C. (Leiden 1640).
Boden, B.G.L. (Leipzig 1776).
Mitscherlich, C.G. (Zweibrücken 1792).
Jacobs, F. (Leipzig 1821).
Hirschig, G.A. (Paris 1856) 27–127.
Hercher, R. (Leipzig 1858) 37–213.
Gaselee, S. [London and Cambridge (Mass.) 1917, reprinted 1947; with an English translation].
Vilborg, E. (Stockholm-Gothenburg 1955).

II. *Translations*

Latin

Cruceius, Annibal (Annibale della Croce) (Lyon 1544). Only books 5–8.
Id. (Bâle 1554).

English

Burton, W. (London 1597; reprinted Oxford 1923).
Hodges, A. (Oxford 1638).
[Anonymous] (London 1720).
Smith, R. (London 1889).
[Anonymous] (Athens 1897).
[Anonymous] (Philadelphia 1902).
Gaselee, S. In the same volume as his edition (section I above).

French

Rochemaure, Jacques de (Lyon 1556, reprinted 1572 and 1573).
Comingeois, B. (Paris 1568, reprinted 1575).
Annibal, L. (Lyon 1586).
Baudouin, J. (Paris 1635).
Perron de Castera, L.A. du (Amsterdam 1733; reprinted Paris 1785, 1796 and 1930).
Monthenault d'Egly, C.P. de (Paris 1734; reprinted The Hague 1735).
Clément, J.M.B. (Paris 1800).
Zevort, M.C. (Paris 1856).
Pons, A. (Paris 1880).
Grimal, P. (Paris 1958).

German

[Anonymous] (Frankfurt am Main 1644).
[Anonymous] (Frankfurt am Main 1670).
Seybold, D.C. (Lemgo 1772).
Ast, F. (Leipzig 1802).
Plepelits, K. (Stuttgart 1980).

Italian

Dolce, Lodovico (Venice 1546): Only books 5–8.
Coccio, F.A. (Venice 1551; frequently reprinted until 1833).
Cataudella, Q. (Rome 1958) 353–523 and 1382–1388.
Monteleone, C., and Annibaldis, G. (Bari 1987).

Spanish

Agreda y Vargas, D. de (Madrid 1617).

Dutch

Nispen, A. van (Dordrecht 1652).

III. *Commentaries*

Jacobs, F. In the same volume as his edition (section I above).
Vilborg, E. (Gothenburg 1962).

E. HELIODOROS

J.R. Morgan

I

Author and Date

Heliodoros concludes his novel with a *sphragis*, in which he identifies himself as ἀνὴρ Φοῖνιξ Ἐμισηνός, τῶν ἀφ' Ἡλίου γένος, Θεοδοσίου παῖς Ἡλιόδωρος "a Phoenician from the city of Emesa, one of the clan of Descendants of the Sun, Theodosios' son, Heliodoros", 10.41.4.[1] There is no reason to doubt the authenticity of this final sentence.[2]

Emesa (modern Homs), a Syrian city in the hinterland of the Phoenician coastal area, became the capital of the newly formed Roman province of Phoinike Libanesia in 194, from which time its inhabitants, though not racially Phoenician, could be referred to as "Phoenicians".[3] The town was the centre of a major solar religion, imported to Rome by the emperor Elagabalus, himself a native of Emesa, in 218. Clearly the novelist, whose very name (presumably a Greek version of a Syrian theophoric name) enshrines his solar connections, and who describes himself as a "descendant of the Sun", was connected in some way with the Emesan cult.

Here certainty ends. Estimates of the date of composition of the novel range from the reign of Hadrian (117–38)[4] to the fourth century. On the strength of the Emesan connection, E. Rohde[5] influentially assigned the novel to the reign of Aurelian (270–75), who adopted the cult of the Sun as the official religion of the empire. Rattenbury

---

[1] The text is quoted from Rattenbury and Lumb (1935–1943); the translation from Morgan (1989a).
[2] As Hefti (1950) 131, who drew attention to the third-person form, suggesting addition by a later copyist. However, the careful style and pose of objectivity are characteristic of Heliodoros.
[3] For example, Herodian refers to Julia Maesa as "a Phoenician woman by race from a city named Emesa in Phoinike", and thinks that the name of the local god, Elaiogabalos, is a Phoenician word (5.3.2ff.).
[4] Feuillâtre (1966) 147–8, arguing from the prominence of Delphi in the novel. This suggestion has found few followers.
[5] Rohde (1914) 496–7.

and Lumb opted for a date earlier in the third century, but after the reign of Elagabalus; this was also the view of Altheim, who revived the identification, first advanced in the *editio princeps* of 1534, of the novelist with the sophist Heliodoros the Arab mentioned by Philostratos (*Vit.Soph*.2.32), who died in Rome around 240.[6]

The argument for the fourth century is based on striking similarities[7] between the fictitious siege of Syene in Bk. 9 and the third siege of Nisibis by the Parthians under Shapur II in 350 as described in two panegyrics of Constantius by the future emperor Julian (*Orations* 1 and 3). In both cases a river is diverted to form a lake around the walls of a city, ships sail on the lake, a section of the city wall is undermined by the water and collapses, but the attackers are unable to press home their advantage because of mud left by the waters, and because of continued resistance by the defenders who make good the breach in their walls. There can be no doubt that the two narratives are somehow related. The problem is to decide which is prior.

Clearly the central issue is the accuracy of Julian: if his account of the siege is historically correct, Heliodoros must be the borrower and so must be dated *after* the siege; on the other hand, if there are reasons to doubt Julian's accuracy, the similarities can be taken as allusion, conscious or unconscious, to the *Aithiopika*, which can thus be dated at any period *before* Julian's speeches.

There appear to be two versions of the siege of Nisibis: Julian's and an alternative tradition, represented in Greek primarily by Theodoretos, and in Syriac by the *Historia S. Ephraemi* and Michael the Syrian. In this Shapur dams the river that flows through the town,[8] and then releases its waters like a battering-ram, flattening a stretch of the walls. Colonna (1950) found corroboration of Julian's version in the Syriac hymns of Saint Ephraim, who was inside the city during the siege, but his interpretation of the relevant details has been questioned.[9]

Thus far scholars have approached the discrepancies between the

---

[6] Rattenbury and Lumb (1935–1943), vol. 1, xiv–xv; Altheim (1948) 113. The identification is also accepted by, among others, Merkelbach (1962) 234 and Bowie (1994b) 443.

[7] First noted by van der Valk (1941); the argument is refined by Colonna (1950) and Keydell (1966); see also Chuvin (1990) 321–5.

[8] This is the river Mygdonios. In fact it flowed past, not through, the city. In this detail at least, Julian is correct.

[9] By Szepessy (1975 and 1976); Maróth (1979); and Lightfoot (1988), who finds Julian's version simply incredible.

versions in terms of irreconcilable traditions about the same event, one of which must in the end be preferred to the other. However, it makes better sense to sort the evidence on the basis of two quite separate, though mechanically similar, sieges.[10] Theodoretos and the Syriac sources agree in assigning an important role to Jacob, the bishop of Nisibis, whose death occurred between 337 and 339: if they were describing the siege of 350 his presence could only be explained as contamination from the events of an earlier siege. It is much more straightforward to accept them as describing the otherwise elusive first siege of Nisibis, dated by Jerome to 338. That would be the occasion when the river was used as a battering ram,[11] leaving Julian's orations as an essentially accurate account of the third siege in 350, when the river was diverted to form an artificial lake. Ephraim's hymns appear to corroborate him at least in assuming a situation where the town was surrounded by water for some length of time.[12] The siege was clearly an impressive feat of engineering, but when allowance is made for rhetorical embellishment it is not incredible.[13]

With Julian thus salvaged, the conclusion is inescapable that Heliodoros wrote *after* 350. This does not necessarily mean that Julian was Heliodoros' source. It is arguable that the resemblances between the authors, which are confined to the accounts of the siege, are better explained as independent use of a common source, perhaps a history of Constantius' campaigns. In either case, Heliodoros' motive can only have been to exploit public awareness and interest, and he cannot, therefore, have been writing very long after the event: the novel was probably completed in the years between 350 and 375.[14]

Our earliest biographical testimonium of Heliodoros occurs in the church historian Sokrates. In a passage discussing variations between

---

[10] Lamy (1886) 22; Dodgeon and Lieu (1991) 164–171, 193–207, a useful compendium of all the source material.

[11] These sources also agree that the duration of the siege was two months or 70 days, and that the Parthians were forced to withdraw by a plague of gnats.

[12] Other sources which can be definitely assigned to 350 do not contradict Julian in any material particular. They agree in fixing the length of this siege at four months or 100 days.

[13] We can, for instance, read Julian's description of ships sailing an inland sea as rafts on a marsh whose water-level had risen an inch or two. See Peeters (1920) 285ff., for discussion of Parthian tactics.

[14] Support for a fourth-century dating on linguistic and religious grounds comes, respectively, from Wifstrand (1944–5) 36–41 and Nilsson (1961) 545ff.

the practices of local churches,[15] he notes that in Thessaly a married man who is ordained must cease to sleep with his wife, on pain of excommunication.

ἀλλὰ τοῦ μὲν ἐν Θεσσαλίᾳ ἔθους ἀρχηγὸς Ἡλιόδωρος Τρίκκης τῆς ἐκεῖ γενόμενος, οὗ λέγεται πονήματα ἐρωτικὰ βιβλία, ἃ νέος ὢν ἔταξε καὶ Αἰθιοπικὰ προσηγόρευσε

The originator of the practice in Thessaly was Heliodoros, on becoming <bishop?>[16] of Trikka there, who was the author, it is said, of an erotic book, which he wrote in his youth and entitled *Aithiopika*.

We know nothing else of this Thessalian bishop. Sokrates' reference to him occurs formally under the year 384, but the chapter is organised associatively rather than chronologically and provides no evidence for dating. All we can say for certain is that he must have lived before Sokrates compiled his history in the second quarter of the fifth century. Sokrates qualifies his identification of bishop with novelist; but he grounds his knowledge of Thessalian practice in personal knowledge of the area, and the word λέγεται probably denotes uncorroborated oral information acquired during his visit. That suggests that the bishopric of Heliodoros fell within living memory, reducing the likelihood of confusion between two homonymous individuals. We can thus reconstruct a speculative biography: Heliodoros wrote the *Aithiopika* around 360, and was holding high office in the Thessalian church around 400.[17] The evidence does not say that he was a Christian when he wrote the novel, and it is not unusual at this period to find former pagans, even priests, in the Christian hierarchy. It is striking that Heliodoros' hero is a Thessalian and that the novelist seems well informed about the Thessalian sport of bull-tossing (10.30). The novel's strict sexual ethic and emphasis on chas-

---

[15] *Hist.Eccl.*5.22 = Colonna (1938) Test.I.

[16] There is no word for 'bishop' in the Greek, contrary to Sokrates' normal usage; but it is difficult to see how else the sentence can be understood.

[17] There is no further reference to Trikka as the seat of a bishop before Hierokles' *Synekdemos* early in the sixth century. The city was not of great importance during the early empire, but its walls were rebuilt by Justinian (Procop. *de aed.*4.3.5), which suggests some prior expansion. The point is that a bishop at Trikka becomes more credible as the date gets later. Despite the coincidence of period, I can see no reason to connect either novelist or bishop with the Heliodoros who succeeded Eusebonas and Abibion as head of the monastery at Teleda in Syria; according to Theodoretos (*Hist.Relig.*26.4) he entered the monastery aged three, and knew so little of the world that he did not know what pigs and chickens looked like.

tity might also be felt to suggest a personality not too far removed from that of the bishop.[18]

In the ninth century, Photios too knew Heliodoros as a bishop, as did the eleventh-century chronicler Theodosios Melitenos, who dates his office to the reign of Theodosios (379–95).[19] This coheres with the biography suggested here, but may be just a lucky chance arising from a confusion between the emperor and Heliodoros' father. Sokrates' information is further expanded by the fourteenth-century writer Nikephoros Kallistos Xanthopoulos, according to whom the local synod at Trikka, concerned at the effect of the *Aithiopika* on the morals of youth, gave Heliodoros the choice of renouncing and burning the novel of his youth or resigning his see; he chose the latter. The source of this additional information at so late a date is unclear; the story is probably too good to be true.

II

The Title

The author's own subscript describes the novel as τὰ περὶ Θεαγένην καὶ Χαρίκλειαν Αἰθιοπικά, ("Ethiopian Story concerning Theagenes and Charikleia") combining a reference to the heroes' names with the geographical form of title characteristic of works of history and attested for some other novels. The earliest external evidence, a reference in the church historian Sokrates, gives τὰ Αἰθιοπικά alone as the author's own title. This form is found at the head of some manuscripts (CVM), and, as some of the impact of the early scenes of the novel derives from the reader's uncertainty as to who are the main characters, it is unlikely that the author intended to give the game away by identifying them before the novel begins. Elias of Crete in the eighth and Photios in the ninth century also knew the novel simply as τὰ Αἰθιοπικά.[20] As early as the seventh century, however, it was circulating under the title of Χαρίκλεια, this being the rubric under which quotations are given in the collection of Maximus

---

[18] The identification of bishop and novelist is disputed by Rohde (1914), but accepted by Rattenbury (1927), though for an earlier date, and by Lacombrade (1970).

[19] Colonna (1938) Test.III and XIV. For the authorship of the second item cf. Colonna (1950) 86–7.

[20] Colonna (1938) Test.IV, IX.

Confessor, and most references to the work by Byzantine writers are in this form.[21]

III

Testimonia

About 400 the medical writer Theodorus Priscianus recommended the reading of erotic novels as a cure for male impotence: among the writers he mentions is an otherwise unknown Herodianos, and it has recently been suggested[22] that this is a corruption of Heliodoros' name. Apart from the passage of Sokrates already discussed, the next trace we have of the *Aithiopika* is a scrap of parchment from a codex written in the middle of the sixth century and discovered in Egypt.[23] In the seventh century Maximus Confessor included seven sententiae from the *Aithiopika* in his *Florilegium*.[24]

There is extensive evidence for knowledge of the *Aithiopika* at Byzantium, where its reputation was no doubt enhanced by the belief that its author was a Christian.[25] Photios summarised it in the ninth century, though the principles on which the *Bibliotheke* was compiled imply that it was not a widely read text at that period. He finds the *Aithiopika* morally superior to other novels, such as those of Iamblichos and Achilleus Tatius.

In the eleventh century Michael Psellos composed a comparison of Heliodoros and Achilleus Tatius,[26] which he presents as a contribution to a learned debate about the merits of the two novels. His own preferences lie with Heliodoros, but his apologetic tone suggests that the novel was coming under criticism on grounds of morality and characterisation. Unlike Photios, Psellos appreciates the sophistication of the construction of the novel, which he compares graphically to a coiled snake.

---

[21] Cf. Colonna (1938) Test.II (Maximus Confessor), X (the Souda), XI, XII (Michael Psellos), XIII, XVI, XVII, XIX, XX.

[22] Bowie (1994b) 447.

[23] Gronewald (1979).

[24] Contained in Migne *PG*.91. The sententiae in question are 1.15.3, 1.26.6, 2.6.4, 2.29.5, 4.4.4, 4.5.7, 6.10.2.

[25] See Gärtner (1969). Most of the testimonia are conveniently gathered in Colonna (1938) 361–72.

[26] Full text edited with commentary in Dyck (1986). The section on Heliodoros = Colonna (1938) Test.XII. See too Wilson (1983) 172ff.

In the twelfth century, Heliodoros (along with Achilleus and, to a lesser extent, Longus) was extensively imitated by the learned novelists of the Byzantine renaissance, especially Theodoros Prodromos, who took over the temporal dislocation of Heliodoros' narrative, as well as details of theme and incident.[27]

More extensive critical treatments of the *Aithiopika* survive from Philippos Philagathos[28] in the twelfth and John Eugenikos in the fifteenth centuries.[29] Both defend the novel against accusations of frivolous immorality by interpreting it allegorically. The former is offered ostensibly in response to a public debate by scholars in Rhegion, and begins by interpreting the novel as παιδαγωγική ... καὶ ἠθικῆς φιλοσοφίας διδάσκαλος, "educational, and a teacher of moral philosophy", with its main characters as archetypes of the four cardinal virtues. The author then proceeds to an ingenious neoplatonic allegory, supported by Pythagorean number symbolism,[30] whereby the heroine symbolises soul and mind, her sojourn at Delphi the acquisition of philosophical wisdom, her love for Theagenes the desire of the initiate for union with god, and her adventures the tribulations and temptations of the earthly life which threaten to block the return of the soul to its true home. Eugenikos praises the novel as a source of encyclopedic information and improving dicta, before he too expounds it as an allegory of the virtues, comparing its use of an outwardly erotic form to the biblical Song of Songs.

In addition there is a sprinkling of citations throughout the Byzantine period. Five sententiae are included in the *Gnomologion* of Ioannes Georgides Monazon,[31] and four in the *Melissa* of Antonius (10th century);[32] from such collections they passed into the paroemiographies of Apostolios and Arsenios. Elias of Crete quotes the opening of the novel in his commentary on Gregory of Nazianzos' 19th oration. The novel is cited once by title in the *Souda*. An anonymous 12th century

---

[27] See Rohde (1914) 563-5.
[28] Colonna (1938) Test.XIII. For the author of this piece see Lavagnini (1974); Wilson (1983) 216-7 gives a partial translation. Mosino (1979-80) raises the possibility that the manuscript from which X and Z were copied was the very one (or at least closely related to the one) from which the learned men of Rhegion were reading.
[29] For text Gärtner (1971).
[30] The Greek characters of the heroine's name when read as numerals total 777, a perfect Pythagorean number. Is this a coincidence?
[31] Text in Boissonade's *Anecdota Graeca*, vol. 1, and *PG* 117. The sententiae are from 2.6.4, 5.7.3, 5.29.4, 7.12.4, 10.16.1.
[32] 1.26.6, 2.6.4, 4.5.7, 5.29.4.

rhetorician recommends the *Aithiopika* as a model of χαρίτων μετὰ σωφροσύνης "charm with chastity".[33] Eustathios of Thessaloniki seems to be using the accumulation of material on the Nile in Hld.9.22 in his note on Dionysios Periegetes 222, and the twelfth-century natural scientist Michael Glykas twice quotes Heliodoros without acknowledgement.[34] Incongruously in Nikolas Kataskepenos' *Life of Cyril Phileotes* (early 12th century), the saint quotes Heliodoros in a discussion with his wife about love.[35] In the 14th century Thomas Magister cites Hld.2.10.1 on a grammatical point and Rhakendytes uses the novel as an example of narrative and of the middle style for orators.[36] A poem attributed to Theodoros Prodromos expresses the reader's love for the heroine, while another anonymous and undatable epigram on the novel has been discovered in a manuscript in the British Library.[37]

IV

Manuscripts and Editions

Twenty four manuscripts of the *Aithiopika* are known. Of these, six are of primary importance for the constitution of the text:[38]

i. Vaticanus gr.157, late 11th century (V)
ii. Venetus Marcianus gr. 838 (formerly 409), 11–12th century (Z)[39]
iii. Vaticanus gr.1390, 13–14th century (C)
iv. Monacensis gr.157, early 15th century (M)
v. Vindobonensis 130, late 15th century (B)
vi. Parisinus gr.Bibl.Nat.2905, 15–16th century (Q1)[40]

---

[33] Colonna (1938) Test.IX, X, XV.
[34] On the reasons why cocks crow (1.18.3 = *PG*.158.109), and on the causes of the Nile flood (2.28 = *PG*.158.56).
[35] 3.7, p. 51 (Sargologos), quoting Hld.4.4.4, without acknowledgement of course. Possibly the quotation reached Kataskepenos through the collection of Maximus.
[36] Colonna (1938) Test.XV, XIX, XX.
[37] Colonna (1938) Test.XVIII; Browning (1955).
[38] On the manuscript tradition I follow primarily Rattenbury and Lumb (1935–43) vol. 1, xxiv–xlvii. Dörrie (1935) reaches broadly similar conclusions, with a few differences of detail. For criticism see Colonna (1940), particularly on the question of the presence of the end of the novel in the β group.
[39] The first twenty pages of the novel are in a later hand (13th century). Readings of Z should be compared with those of Marcianus 410, 13th century (X), which appears to be an independent copy of the same original.
[40] This manuscript was written by Andreas Eparchos. Rattenbury and Lumb (1935–

C terminates at 7.7.1, in the middle of a sentence at the foot of a page, indicating the loss of some leaves. B stops at 9.13.3, in the middle of a page, in such a way as to suggest that its exemplar contained no further text; it also has lacunae at 3.15.3–19.4, 4.19.9–21.3.

There is a high level of agreement among these witnesses, and the text they present is generally of a good quality. There seem to be two main families, with BCQ1Z frequently in agreement against MV, suggesting descent from two distinct subarchetypes (respectively β and γ). Within the β group, however, Z sometimes has readings in common with VM against BCQ1, demonstrating that it was collated against a γ manuscript. BQ1 are closely related, presumably deriving from a common ancestor, possibly at one remove: both show signs of influence from γ, but Q1 appears to have undergone further contamination from a representative of the γ group which had already begun to develop the minor deviations found in M when compared to V. C is of somewhat problematic status: although it thus seems to be left as the purest exemplar of β, its palpable errors are numerous. At 1.15.3, it agrees, against all other significant manuscripts, with a manifestly inferior reading contained in Maximus' collection of sententiae, suggesting that there were already two branches of the tradition by the seventh century. Rattenbury and Lumb tend to overvalue it, but at the same time Colonna can hardly be correct in assigning it to a separate third family. It is not possible to give consistent preference to either branch of the tradition, and editors must still use their judgement as to what constitutes acceptable Heliodoran Greek.

After 9.13.3 the relationship between those manuscripts containing the final section of the novel appears to be altered; there are fewer significant divergences, with VZ generally agreeing against MQ1, and generally presenting preferable readings. This state of affairs is best explained by Rattenbury's hypothesis that β had lost the last book and a half of the novel before any of the surviving copies were taken from it. This implies that C was never complete, and the final section found in Z is a result of the knowledge of γ evident elsewhere.

In a handful of places Q1 and its relatives contain words not found

---

43) generally cite, however, the readings of Palatinus 125, 15–16th century (P), which they take to be an apograph of Q1.

in other manuscripts, which certainly have the true Heliodoran flavour (most strikingly at 10.9.3 and 10.13.5). However, to accept them is to posit access to true readings through a third branch of the tradition independent of all extant manuscripts. These insertions are more likely concoctions by a clever scribe.

Some later manuscripts (such as Vindobonensis 116, 16th century; Taurinensis B.III.29, 16th century; and Laurentianus LXXX.36) contain interesting, and possibly correct, readings against the consensus of earlier manuscripts, but these are best considered the work of intelligent emendators. They do not afford adequate reasons for positing additional lines of transmission.

Of the few witnesses to the text antedating the earliest surviving manuscript, I have already mentioned Maximus Confessor's citation of sententiae. The single papyrus of the *Aithiopika* (P.Amh.160 = Pack²2797) contains barely legible fragments from 8.16.6–7 and 8.17.3–4, including one attractive reading not found in any manuscript. Fragments of the *Aithiopika* in an 11th century hand survive in a largely illegible palimpsest in Jerusalem (Hierosolymitanus 57 gr. S. Crucis): they show a sound text firmly in the β tradition, but do not add anything of importance.

The *editio princeps* of Heliodoros was published in Basle in February 1534.[41] The editor, Vincentius Obsopoeus, simply transcribed M, with a fair sprinkling of misreadings and misprints. The next complete text to be printed was that of Commelinus (Heidelberg 1596, reprinted Lyon 1611), a major advance in that the editor collated four sources: the *editio princeps* (i.e.M), P (which he inspected himself), and variant readings from V and Z (or a lost manuscript closely related to it), reported to him by Andreas Schottus and Xylander respectively. The editions of I. Bourdelotius (Paris 1619), D. Pareus (Frankfurt 1631) and I.P. Schmid (Leipzig 1772) simply reprint Commelinus' text with minor editorial alterations, but that of C.G. Mitscherlich (Strasbourg 1798) was a more scholarly reworking of Commelinus, making full use of his critical notes. The famous edition by A. Korais (Paris 1804) added some new readings which came to him from manuscript notes by Amyot,[42] but the text is still fundamentally Commelinus, in places brilliantly emended. The accompa-

---

[41] On editions see Mazal (1966).
[42] On the source of these, see Rattenbury and Lumb (1935–43) vol. 1, lxv–lxx. They seem to be mainly from Z.

nying commentary, however, guarantees this edition a permanent place in Heliodoran studies. Two editions appeared in consecutive years in the middle of the nineteenth century. The Teubner of I. Bekker (Leipzig 1855) is straight from Korais, while the Didot of C.W. Hirschig (Paris 1856) goes back to Mitscherlich, with a few good readings derived from B, and rather more bad ones from later and insignificant manuscripts.

Again in the middle of the twentieth century, two editions appeared almost simultaneously. The Budé of R.M. Rattenbury and T.W. Lumb (Paris 1935–43) was the first scientific edition, and remains the standard text. A. Colonna's edition (Rome 1938, reprinted with a few alterations Turin 1987) is sometimes eccentric in its choice of reading. Rattenbury and Lumb's *apparatus criticus* is fuller and more accurate.[43]

V

The Story

Book 1: The novel opens with some Egyptian bandits looking at a scene of carnage near the mouth of the Nile. Among the wreckage of a feast by a richly loaded merchant ship, they find an amazingly beautiful young woman tending a wounded young man: who they are is unclear, but they speak Greek. The bandits are driven off by a larger gang, who take the young couple captive and convey them back to their hideout in the swamps,[44] where they are entrusted to the care of another Greek captive, Knemon. Their own words reveal their names: Theagenes and Charikleia. During the night Knemon tells them his story:

> he is an Athenian, whose stepmother Demainete developed an infatuation with him. When her advances were refused, she used her sexually skilled slave-girl Thisbe to carry through an intrigue against Knemon, culminating in his arraignment before the Areiopagos for attempted parricide. Escaping the death penalty on a technicality, Knemon fled Athens. Later he learned that Demainete had killed herself after being lured to a false assignation by Thisbe, who then informed his father.

---

[43] At the time of writing, a new Loeb edition by G.P. Goold is in preparation.
[44] These bandits are Boukoloi, or Herdsmen, an historically attested group, who also figure in the novels of Achilleus and (perhaps) Lollianus.

That same night, the robber-captain, Thyamis, has a dream which he interprets as a divine instruction to make Charikleia his wife. Next day he proposes marriage, revealing that he is the rightful high-priest at Memphis, driven from office by his younger brother. Charikleia procrastinates, claiming that she and Theagenes are brother and sister, a priest and priestess from Ephesos; she must be allowed to lay down her priesthood in a temple before the marriage is celebrated. Thyamis consents, and prepares to march on Memphis. When Theagenes and Charikleia are alone again, their conversation makes it clear that they are in fact chaste lovers. Now the bandit stronghold is under attack. Thyamis commands Knemon to conceal Charikleia in a secret cave, but as the fighting goes against him he reinterprets his dream, and runs to the cave where, in the darkness, he kills a woman who speaks Greek to him. Theagenes and Knemon stay out of the fighting, but Thyamis is taken alive. The attackers are in fact the first gang of bandits from the beach, in the pay of his treacherous brother Petosiris.

Book 2: Next day Knemon takes Theagenes to the cave, only to stumble over a corpse. As Theagenes laments and prepares to kill himself, Knemon, to his horror, discovers that the dead woman is in fact Thisbe: Charikleia is safe, deeper in the cave. Knemon explains that

> after Demainete's death, to escape punishment by her relatives, Thisbe had eloped with Nausikles, a merchant from Naukratis; Knemon had pursued her.

A message on the body explains that she was being held in erotic captivity by one of the bandits, who (the author explains) had hijacked her a few days previously. Thisbe's lover, Thermouthis, who had secreted her in the cave during the fighting, returns to reclaim her—only to find her dead. Next day Knemon reluctantly sets off with Thermouthis in search of Thyamis: the plan is to give him the slip and rejoin his friends at a nearby village, Chemmis. By pretending to have diarrhoea, Knemon loses Thermouthis, who is conveniently disposed of by a poisonous snake. On the outskirts of Chemmis Knemon encounters a mysterious old man, who intriguingly bewails his plight in Greek. He declares that he has lost his children, whom he names, to Knemon's amazement, as Theagenes and Charikleia; he also lets drop that his host is Nausikles, who is at present trying to recover Thisbe with the help of a Persian officer, Mitranes. The old man now proceeds to tell his story.

He is Kalasiris, a high-priest who had fled Memphis to escape sexual temptation and to avert a prophecy that he would see his sons take up arms against each other; he incidentally reveals that his elder son is Thyamis. In the course of his self-imposed exile Kalasiris found his way to Delphi, where he was welcomed by the oracle. Here he made the acquaintance of Charikles, priest of Apollo, who had a story to tell:

> After tragically losing his wife and child he had travelled the world, ending up by the Nile cataracts. Here an Ethiopian, on an embassy to the satrap of Egypt about disputed emerald mines, had offered him fabulous wealth to take care of a beautiful child, explaining that:
>> he had saved her life after her mother had exposed her along with an embroidered account of her circumstances. For seven years he had kept the girl a secret, but now feared that her exceptional beauty would draw attention to her.
>
> The Ethiopian was forced to leave before he could tell Charikles the whole story. Charikles took the child back to Delphi, where she grew up as his daughter: Charikleia, devoted to the service of Artemis.

Charikles wanted Kalasiris' help, to break down her resistance to marriage to her cousin. The two priests attended a ritual performed by a sacred mission from Thessaly, led by a young man who claimed descent from Achilleus. As the ceremony was about to begin, the Delphic priestess produced an enigmatic oracle (the reader can recognise allusions to the names of Theagenes and Charikleia), prophesying a journey to the "black land of the sun".

Book 3: (Kalasiris' story continues)

At the ceremony, Charikleia and the leader of the mission, Theagenes, fell in love at first sight, though no one but Kalasiris realised. After the ceremony Charikleia and Theagenes were both ill, but only Kalasiris realised the cause, duping Charikles with pseudo-scientific lore about the Evil Eye.[45] That night a vision of Apollo and Artemis told him to take the lovers back to Egypt. At dawn he was visited by Theagenes, who in great embarrassment confessed his love for Charikleia. Acting up to Theagenes' perception of him as an Egyptian magician, Kalasiris promised his assistance, and put his powers at Charikles' disposal to cure Charikleia of the Evil Eye.

Book 4: (Kalasiris' story continues)

Next day in the Pythian games Theagenes won the race in armour, inspired by the thought of receiving the prize from Charikleia. Perplexed

---

[45] On this, cf. Capelle (1953) 175–80, Yatromanolakis (1988), Dickie (1991).

as to how to carry out the gods' instructions, Kalasiris decided he must see the embroidered message from Charikleia's mother. Her condition continued to worsen, but, despite Kalasiris' play-acting, modesty kept her from revealing the cause. On Kalasiris' advice, Charikles consulted a doctor, who diagnosed her condition as love, but the sight of her cousin produced a violent response. Claiming that his spells were being blocked by a counter-power contained in the embroidery, Kalasiris persuaded Charikles to let him read it. It was embroidered in the Ethiopian royal script, and contained the following narrative:

Persinna, queen of Ethiopia, long childless, eventually conceived. But when the child was born, she had a white skin because at the moment of conception Persinna had seen a painting of white-skinned Andromeda.[46] Fearing that the king, Hydaspes, would accuse her of adultery, she exposed the baby with recognition tokens, including a magic ring.

Kalasiris now understood the gods' will. He informed Charikleia that he knew she was in love, and reassured her it was reciprocated. Then he told her who she was, and revealed that he had been commissioned by Persinna to seek out her lost daughter at Delphi. Charikleia placed herself in his hands, and he started to make arrangements for their departure. Providentially he encountered some Phoenicians who were due to sail next day. That night, Theagenes' Thessalians staged an abduction, but in fact the lovers had taken refuge with Kalasiris. On Charikleia's insistence, Theagenes swore to respect her chastity, as the Delphians set off in pursuit of the supposed kidnappers.

Book 5:

Meanwhile Kalasiris and the young lovers set sail.

At this point Nausikles returns, claiming to have a "better Thisbe". In terrified insomnia, Knemon wanders the house, and overhears a woman lamenting and referring to herself as Thisbe. The author intervenes to explain that it is Charikleia: she and Theagenes were captured by Mitranes, and Nausikles quick-wittedly identified her as the woman he was looking for; Theagenes has been sent off to the satrap, as a gift to the Persian king. Next day Kalasiris and Charikleia are reunited, and at a sacrificial feast Kalasiris continues his story:

they rested up on Zakynthos, where they took lodgings with a deaf fisherman, Tyrrhenos. One of the Phoenicians was in love with Charikleia, but Kalasiris, posing as the pair's father, kept him at bay with promises. However, Tyrrhenos learned that some local pirates, led by Trachinos who was also madly in love with Charikleia, were planning

---

[46] This phenomenon was widely accepted as scientific fact; see Reeve (1989).

to ambush the ship. Kalasiris persuaded the Phoenicians to put to sea at once, but just before leaving he was visited by a vision of Odysseus, foretelling suffering for him but giving Penelope's blessing to Charikleia. Off Crete Trachinos and the pirates boarded the Phoenician ship, casting everyone adrift, except Charikleia and her "father" and "brother". A fearful storm wrecked them on the coast of Egypt, where Trachinos proposed to marry Charikleia there and then. Kalasiris induced his lieutenant, Peloros, to claim her for himself, and in the ensuing fracas, all the pirates were killed and Theagenes wounded.

Nausikles promises his help in securing Theagenes' release.

Book 6: Next day Kalasiris, Knemon and Nausikles set off to see Mitranes, but on their way they meet a man who tells them that he has gone to fight the bandits of Bessa, who under the leadership of Thyamis have snatched the young Greek. A banquet is held, at which Nausikles offers his daughter in marriage to Knemon, who accepts, despite his remorse at abandoning Charikleia. Kalasiris comforts her and they decide to continue their search for Theagenes alone, disguised as beggars. Outside Bessa they stumble across a battlefield where an old woman is lamenting her dead son. The Bessaians have defeated Mitranes, and are now marching on Memphis to forestall reprisals and reinstate Thyamis. As they wait for daybreak, they accidentally witness a scene of necromancy: the old woman revives her dead son to learn the fate of her surviving child, but instead the corpse predicts a happy ending for Charikleia at the end of the earth. As the witch runs to attack the eavesdroppers, she impales herself on a spear.

Book 7: At Memphis the gates have been closed against the Bessaians just in time. The satrap, Oroondates, is fighting the Ethiopians over the mines, but his wife, Arsake, is in residence. She is sister of the Great King, and has a voracious sexual appetite. Once she had a passion for Thyamis, which his brother Petosiris exploited to oust him from the priesthood. She now proposes a single combat between the two brothers, but her interest is kindled by the sight of Theagenes. Petosiris runs from Thyamis, but just as he is on the point of being caught Kalasiris and Charikleia arrive. A theatrical recognition takes place and hostilities are abandoned. Thyamis is installed as high-priest, but meanwhile Arsake is in a frenzy of desire, which she confides to her intimate servant Kybele, who undertakes to procure Theagenes for her. Kalasiris dies in the night, and Kybele seizes the opportunity to bring Theagenes and Charikleia into the palace, assuring them of Arsake's friendship. Theagenes suspects a hidden agenda, and they keep up the pretence of being brother and sister. Kybele's son, Achaimenes, spies on them through a keyhole: he falls in love with Charikleia, but recognises Theagenes as the young man he had been escorting to the satrap. He guesses Arsake's intentions. Kybele does everything she can to dispose Theagenes towards her mistress but he is obdurate, forcing her to become more and more explicit and threatening. She is at crisis point, when Achaimenes offers to secure Theagenes for Arsake if he can have his "sister" for himself. Theagenes' position as Persian property is thus revealed and he enters service in the royal household, but saves Charikleia from Achaimenes by disclosing that she is not his sister but his bride, hoping thus to induce Achaimenes to betray his mistress to her husband. Further humiliated by Theagenes' virtuoso performance as wine-waiter, Achaimenes steals away to inform Oroondates, who is mustering his army at Thebes.

Book 8: By this time the Ethiopians have taken Philai. Achaimenes arrives and tells Oroondates everything, firing him with desire for Charikleia. Oroondates sends the eunuch Bagoas to fetch Theagenes and Charikleia from Memphis. Meanwhile Thyamis comes to the palace in search of his friends, but is rebuffed by Arsake, whose situation is desperate: she is getting nowhere with Theagenes and foresees trouble from Achaimenes. On Kybele's advice she has Theagenes thrown in a cell and tortured, but still the name of Charikleia is ever on his lips. She decides to get rid of Charikleia, but the plan goes wrong and Kybele drinks the poison herself, with her last breath accusing Charikleia of murder. She is arraigned before a Persian court, but makes no defence, having agreed in the cells with Theagenes to accept death as release from continued suffering. She is condemned to be burned at the stake, but to universal astonishment the flames do not harm her. Despite public outcry, she is thrown back into the cell, where, recalling a dream of Kalasiris, she realises that her salvation was due to the magic powers of her mother's ring. Theagenes has also dreamed of their mentor, who prophesied that they would reach Ethiopia, which he takes to mean death. As the lovers ponder their future, Bagoas arrives. On their way to Thebes news reaches them that Arsake has hanged herself, but before they reach Oroondates they are ambushed by an advance party of Ethiopians. The lovers allow themselves to be captured, recognising the fulfilment of Theagenes' dream.

Book 9: Oroondates is besieged in Syene. Theagenes and Charikleia are brought to Hydaspes. Despite his instinctive response to his daughter, he commands that, as the first captives of the war, they are to be kept as sacrificial victims for the Ethiopian gods. By diverting the Nile, the Ethiopians succeed in breaching the walls of Syene, but treacherously Oroondates gets away and reappears at the head of his army from Elephantine. In the ensuing battle the Ethiopians are victorious; Achaimenes is killed in the act of settling his score with the satrap, and Oroondates himself is captured alive. Nevertheless, the wise and merciful Hydaspes spares him. Charikleia and Theagenes are again brought before the king, who again fails to understand his own response, but Charikleia still does not reveal her identity, arguing that she must wait for her mother's presence. Peace and friendship are concluded between Hydaspes and Oroondates.

Book 10: Hydaspes returns to Meroe, where he is greeted by Persinna and the Gymnosophists, naked wise men who are his advisers. The populace demands the traditional human sacrifice, but Persinna is moved with compassion when she sees Charikleia. In a ritual test on a magic gridiron, both the lovers are shown to be virgins. Charikleia realises that the leader of the Gymnosophists, Sisimithres, is the very man who saved her as a baby and throws herself at his feet, claiming she cannot be sacrificed as she is the king's own daughter. Hydaspes is only fully convinced when the painting of Andromeda is produced and shown to be an exact likeness. All the same, he offers to go through with the sacrifice, until the people demand that Charikleia be spared. Theagenes, however, is still condemned. Charikleia is too modest to do more than hint at their relationship, but cannot make her parents understand. Hydaspes even betroths his daughter to his nephew. Theagenes performs two heroic exploits, recapturing a runaway bull and defeating a colossal Ethiopian wrestler by intelligence. Charikleia is on the point of confessing all when an embassy arrives from Oroondates, with an old man who has lost his daughter. This happens to be Charikles and he dramatically accuses Theagenes of kidnapping. At last the truth is revealed by Sisimithres and Persinna, and in recognition of the gods' will human sacrifice is abolished forever. Theagenes and Charikleia are formally betrothed and inaugurated as priest and priestess of the Sun and the Moon. As the novel ends Charikles recalls the enigmatic Delphic oracle and finds it fulfilled in every detail.

VI

Setting and Dramatic Date

The story is set in the real world. All 79 place names which occur in the novel are authentic; the names of Chemmis and Bessa are attested, although apparently misapplied by Heliodoros. The emerald mines were real enough. The story is further anchored in perceived reality by the use of local colour familiar to most readers. The picture given of Meroitic Ethiopia for instance relies on literary traditions of its exotic flora and fauna, wealth and piety which can be traced back through historians to a world view already present in the Homeric poems. Ethiopia is, almost by definition, the land of the sun. Even details which have no absolute historical validity are authorised by their presence in the literary tradition which governed perceptions of reality. The Gymnosophists, who are usually located in India, are in Ethiopia on the precedent of Philostratos' *Life of Apollonios*, and their importance in Hydaspes' administration reflects Greek beliefs on the power of the Meroitic priesthood. The geography and ethnography are equally grounded in ancient belief.[47]

Similarly, the realia of the Delphic portion of the story also support an impression of reality, although some aspects required by the story, such as the role of Charikleia as acolyte of Artemis, seem to be an invention.[48] Many of the details of Egypt too are conventional and can be paralleled from other ancient writers.[49] The different races in the story also conform to widely perceived stereotypes. The Persians are cruel, corrupt and sensual. The Egyptians combine arcane wisdom with cunning and barbarity. The Ethiopians are just and pious subjects of a theocracy. Knemon's Athens is very much the world of New Comedy: Heliodoros plays with the names of places and institutions, but details of the legal system, for instance, bear little relation to the realities of the fifth century B.C.[50]

---

[47] See Morgan (1982) for a general treatment of Heliodoros' realism. The realia of the novel are fully treated by Kowarna (1959). On its picture of Ethiopia specifically see Vycichl (1977), Lonis (1992). The world-view which it echoes is expounded by Lesky (1959). Glava (1937) is too ready to accept Heliodoros' representation of Ethiopia as of independent historical value.

[48] On Delphi see Feuillâtre (1966) 45–67; Pouilloux (1983 and 1984); Rougemont (1992).

[49] Cf. Capelle (1953); Brioso Sánchez (1992); Cauderlier (1992).

[50] For example the technicality on which Knemon evades execution never existed; cf. Russell (1983) 25.

None of this implies any first-hand knowledge. The learning is derived from literature and deployed for literary purposes, to encourage an imaginative belief in the reality of the fiction. Most of it is accurate but Heliodoros is quite happy to include items such as gold-digging ants and gold-guarding griffins, which were part of the accepted decor of Ethiopia and India. The veneer of realism can easily be pierced: the Delphic ceremonies he describes could never have taken place in the confined spaces of the real sanctuary, and there are things that he gets wrong, even within the limits of ancient knowledge. For instance, he seems not to realise that Philai and Elephantine were built on islands in the Nile, and believes there was an important administrative centre at Katadoupoi. There is little awareness of contemporary events, although the special position granted to the city of Axum in the Ethiopian alliance may reflect its emergence as a major power in the fourth century. The Egyptian bandits, or Boukoloi, reflect events of the second century.

The novel is set in the period of the Persian occupation of Egypt. The very opening is located near the site of Alexandreia but before the foundation of the city. Kalasiris' self-imposed flight from Memphis is motivated by his encounter with the Greek courtesan Rhodopis famous from Herodotos (2.134f.), which suggests a setting in the sixth century B.C. There are some minor anachronisms, such as the existence of an historically inappropriate but ethically apt Epicurean monument in Knemon's Athens, or the presence of cataphract cavalry in the Persian army, but generally the setting is well enough sustained for Heliodoros' purposes.

The impression of reality is abetted by the device of feigning uncertainty concerning the material Heliodoros has himself invented, expressed directly, or through deliberately obtrusive approximations, or through the multiplication of explanations for fictional events (the extreme example being the suggestion of four possible reasons for the collapse of the Ethiopian earthworks at Syene). This pretends to imitate the limitations of knowledge inherent in any factual writing. It is also possible to point to some mannerisms which Heliodoros has borrowed from classical historiography as a literary genre, such as the insertion of encyclopedic digressions, transitions modelled on those of Herodotos, and ironic use of pious reticence in matters of religious practice.[51]

---

[51] On the "historiographical pose" see Morgan (1982) 227-34.

VII

Models and Sources

Heliodoros' greatest debt is to Homer. The whole structure of the novel, beginning in the middle of the story and filling in the earlier portions by means of a retrospective narration, which concludes about halfway through the whole work, is modelled on that of the *Odyssey*.[52] Further, the *Aithiopika*, alone of the extant novels, is cast as a *nostos* ending in marriage and recognition of the protagonist by a father. The episode of necromancy in 6.14ff. corresponds to the Odyssean *Nekyia* with fairly precise reminiscences in the description of the magic rites. The narrative structure puts Kalasiris into Odysseus' role as secondary narrator, and apart from the ambiguous duplicity of character the connection is made explicit by a series of specific allusions. Kalasiris begins his lengthy narrative by alluding to the opening of Odysseus' (2.21.5), and later expounds to Knemon the doctrine that Homer was Egyptian, in fact the son of Hermes, exiled from his native land because of an accident of birth, a growth of hair on his thigh (ὁ μηρός) which would have given rise to suspicions of illegitimacy (3.14). Although the notion that Homer was Egyptian is attested elsewhere, Heliodoros has invented new details of his biography to accommodate it to the figures of Kalasiris (Egyptian, wise and exiled in Greece) and Charikleia (accident of birth leading to suspicions of illegitimacy avoided by exile). Odysseus himself makes an emblematic appearance in a vision to Kalasiris (5.22.1ff.), in which he suggests a comparison between Charikleia and Penelope, though, of course, she also plays some aspects of the role of Odysseus. When Charikleia and Theagenes disguise themselves as beggars Knemon even (mis)quotes the *Odyssey* to make sure no one misses the parallel (2.19.1). Theagenes claims descent from Achilleus, and is specifically compared to him at the beginning of the Delphic foot-race (4.3.1), which he wins, evoking his formulaically "swift-footed" ancestor. Charikleia, on her bed of love-sickness, can only repeat a line from the *Iliad* naming Achilleus (4.7.4). He is linked to Odysseus too, through a scar which he got hunting boar, which like the famous scar of Odysseus is the surest sign of his identity (5.5.2). The scene

---

[52] On the Odyssean structure, cf. Keyes (1922), but with impossible views on layers of composition of the novel.

at Memphis when Thyamis chases his brother Petosiris three times around the city walls (7.6.) clearly evokes Achilleus' pursuit of Hektor around Troy.

The effect of all this is to locate the protagonists in a literary world which ranks with that of epic. But there are also some more decorative allusions to Homer in matters of motif and diction. For example when Thermouthis dies, he sleeps the brazen sleep of death (2.20.2), like a victim of Agamemnon in *Iliad* 11, and Knemon sleeping beneath a blanket of leaves ironically recalls Odysseus (2.20.3f.). As an element of his characterisation, Kalasiris expounds Homer in a deliberately implausible way to prove that Apollo and Artemis manifested themselves to him in physical form rather than as a dream (3.12ff.).[53]

Heliodoros' novel is also permeated by references to the theatre, often exploiting quite abstruse technical theatrical vocabulary.[54] This serves a complex of several functions. Firstly it helps to redefine the relationship between reader and text as one between spectator and spectacle, which is central to the author's narrative technique, and guides the reader's response. Secondly, it underlines the emotional force and tragic status of the narrative, as for example when lamentations are introduced with a verb such as ἐπιτραγῳδεῖν (as at 1.3.2, 7.14.7). Finally it self-referentially comments on (but also mitigates) the theatrical and artificial nature of the novel's plotting. Thus surprising and unexpected events (such as the appearance of Thisbe in the Egyptian cave, or the sudden arrival of Charikles at Meroe) are regularly compared to the μηχανή, a crane-like device in the Attic theatre which was used to stage the epiphany of a god to resolve the action (*deus ex machina*).

These functions can all be illustrated in a striking episode from the seventh book (7.6.4ff.) when Kalasiris supervenes to stop the duel between his sons. The population of Memphis, who provide the reader's lens on the action, are described as the presiding judges in a theatre, not only watching the action but (like the reader) enjoying and evaluating it. Their responses of surprise, puzzlement and joy provide cues for the reader's own reactions. The sudden arrival of

---

[53] For lists of Homeric allusions cf. Feuillâtre (1966) 105–14. The fullest treatment is Gabert (1974). See also Garson (1975).

[54] Walden (1894) is still fundamental. For recent discussions see Marino (1990); Montes Cala (1992). Paulsen (1992) uses the theatrical metaphor as the basis of a fine reading of the novel as a whole.

Kalasiris is ascribed to some divine power which καινὸν ἐπεισόδιον ἐπετραγῴδει τοῖς δρωμένοις ("made the drama take a new and tragic twist") by bringing Kalasiris on to the scene ὥσπερ ἐκ μηχανῆς. Then as Kalasiris is recognised, Charikleia arrives as another "unexpected entry" (παρεγκύκλημα τοῦ δράματος) and as she is eventually recognised and falls into Theagenes' arms the watching crowd is "enraptured by this miracle of theatrical art" (σκηνογραφικῆς ... θαυματουργίας). This "happy ending" is then described as a modulation from tragedy to comedy, but the aspect of the drama which everyone appreciates the most is its love-interest (τὸ ἐρωτικὸν μέρος τοῦ δράματος).

Besides the use of theatrical metaphor to control response and provide metaliterary commentary, some specific dramatic works are used as intertexts. In outline the story of Knemon resembles that of Hippolytos: it may even be that Heliodoros was using the first version of the Euripidean play.[55] The role of Phaidra is shared between Demainete and Arsake: Demainete calls Knemon a new Hippolytos (1.10.2), and Arsake's death is marked by a close allusion to Euripides' play (8.15.2, echoing Eur. *Hipp*.802). But the tragic implications of the story, which are seen by Knemon himself, are undercut by the decidedly New Comedy ambience (including Knemon's own name) and the nature of Thisbe's intrigue. He gradually moves away from a tragic towards a comic model. In this sense the dramatic subtext is used to differentiate him morally from the tragic protagonists. His conduct with Demainete and Thisbe is implicitly compared with that of Theagenes with Arsake and Kybele, and he is disqualified from reaching Ethiopia and what it represents.[56]

The action of the novel evokes other tragic archetypes. The confrontation of Kalasiris' two sons over the priesthood recalls the quarrel between the sons of Oidipous over the throne of Thebes, while Kalasiris himself acts out an Oidipodean story of a man's inability to avoid or change the destiny written for him. The final book plays on the two Iphigeneia plays of Euripides, with the threat of human sacrifice in a barbarian land, and a father confronting the possibility of slaying his own daughter for the sake of the community he leads.

Again there are numerous verbal allusions, quotations and references to tragedy, particularly Euripides.[57]

---

[55] Cf. Rocca (1976); Donnini (1981); Scarcella (1985a).
[56] Cf. Paulsen (1992) 82–101.
[57] Assembled by Neimke (1889); cf. also Feuillâtre (1966) 115–21.

The other literary form against which the *Aithiopika* is written (apart from a few passing allusions to lyric poets and orators) is historiography. Heliodoros' use of history takes two main forms. Firstly, he exploits historical texts for narrative situations in much the same way as he does epic and tragedy. This is particularly marked in the military narrative of book nine, whose subject matter of course approximates much more closely than any other part of the novel to that of canonical historiography. For instance the flight of the Persian satrap from the battlefield (9.19.1) recalls the behaviour of the Persian king Dareios at the battle of Gaugamela, and the scene between Hydaspes and Oroondates after the battle (9.21) resembles the famous interview between Agesilaos and Pharnabazos found in both Xenophon (*Hell*.4.1.32ff.) and Plutarch (*Ages*.12). Elements of the characterisation of Hydaspes as ideal monarch are taken from Xenophon's Kyros and from general traditions about Alexander, as well as Hellenistic treatises on ideal kingship. Secondly, Heliodoros will use historiographical mannerisms to reinforce the impression that he stands in the relation of investigator and recorder rather than inventor of his material: we have already mentioned his pose of uncertainty, but his digressions on geography and other subjects, some of his transitions, and his pose of religious silence all mimic historians.[58]

Finally, we must note the place of the novel in the romantic tradition itself. The consensus is that this is the latest of the extant novels, by a large margin if the dating proposed above is accepted. The late date as such need not be a difficulty, as papyrus fragments show that novels were still being copied and read as late as the seventh century: the market still existed, even if it was shrinking. In much of its substance, however, the *Aithiopika* is something of a throwback, disregarding the new moral and psychological possibilities opened up by Achilleus Tatius and Longus, and reverting to the historical setting of the earliest novels. Its ambition seems to be to stay in the mainstream but excel. It is easily the longest and most sophisticated of the novels; its heroes are of even nobler extraction,[59] emphasised by the epic ambience, and their beauty and moral worth exceeds that of their predecessors. While it retains the conventional furniture

---

[58] See Morgan (1982) 227–234.
[59] The only other princess heroines seem to be Semiramis in the *Ninos Romance*, who is reduced to a bourgeois debutante; and Chione in the fragmentary *Chione Romance*.

of the genre, love at first sight, bandits, pirates, shipwreck, apparent deaths, and unwanted rivals, it presents the old story in a brilliantly innovative way. Precisely because his material is deliberately conventional, it is difficult to be sure whether Heliodoros knew any of the extant novels, though his exploitation of the Boukoloi may suggest an affinity to Achilleus.[60]

VIII

Structure and Narrative Technique

Although the basic story of the *Aithiopika* is very much in the mould of the standard romance plot, Heliodoros' presentation is highly innovative. Firstly, the story itself is not the familiar circular one. Its protagonists do not simply end up where they started and resume their lives as if the intervening adventures had occurred outside time and place. Heliodoros has replaced the romantic pattern of separation and reunion with one of return and recognition. It is notable that the protagonists are physically separated only for a short period in the novel.

Secondly, the story is both more complex and more economical.[61] Instead of a series of episodes which could stand alone, the action is very much more unified. Material is presented through a series of secondary narrators, and at one point (2.31) we are reading Kalasiris' relation to Knemon of Charikles' account of what had been told to him by the Ethiopian ambassador, presented in a triple chinese-box of direct speech. Characters like Thisbe, Nausikles and Thyamis act as bridges from one section of the novel to another and their causative importance is often not obvious at first sight. There is a new sense of intricate parts of the narrative mechanism functioning just out of sight. While the focus remains constantly on the protagonists, other stories are going on, which emerge only as they impinge on the main plot: Nausikles' liaison with and loss of Thisbe; the conflict of Thyamis and Petosiris over the priesthood of Memphis; the international facedown over the emerald mines. There is, by comparison

---

[60] Cf. Szepessy (1978) linking Thyamis' attempt to kill Charikleia with episodes of human sacrifice by the Boukoloi in Achilleus and Lollianus.
[61] See Sandy (1982a) 21–74 for analysis of the complexity of the intrigue. For less positive opinion cf. Wolff (1912).

with some other novels, a marked absence of non-functional digressions.[62] Most encyclopedic material is allocated to Kalasiris as part of his characterisation as an Egyptian wise man.

Thirdly, and most importantly, the narrative does not follow a linear chronological sequence. The novel opens with a scene from the middle of the story, and it is not until the end of the fifth book that the reader is fully informed of the events leading up to that striking opening tableau. By this single stratagem Heliodoros has redefined the impulse of reading. Normally we read on to be told what happens in the end; in the *Aithiopika* that motive is not lost, especially in the second half of the novel, but it is supplemented by a desire to discover what has gone before in order to understand fully what is already known. The reader must not only follow the story as it develops, but reassemble and interpret it. The opening scene is a riddle which it takes five books to disambiguate. On a smaller scale, the same textual strategy pervades the whole work. Thisbe's presence in Egypt is known before its reasons. The reasons for Charikleia's miraculous escape from the stake are only revealed *post eventum* when she recalls a dream of Kalasiris alluding to the magic powers of her mother's ring. In the ninth book, Oroondates' duplicitous intentions are revealed only as they attain fruition, and the apparently crazy stratagem of contingents in the Ethiopian army is explicated only at the moment of its vindication.[63]

The effects of this new hermeneutic demand on the reader translate down to the details of Heliodoros' narrative technique.[64] In general terms, there is a movement away from telling to showing, from diegesis to mimesis; this is one aspect of the work's explicit theatricality. The omniscient author subtracts himself from most of the text, and the reader is often presented with a visual description of what an observer of the imaginary scene might have seen. Sometimes the narrative is focalised and presented from the point of view of a character or group inside the fiction who act as an imaginative point of identification for the reader, but sometimes the narrator represents himself as simply a more articulate version of the reader, recording sense data with no surplus of information. This narrative mode is

---

[62] Cf. Rommel (1923) 59–64.
[63] On narrative as riddle cf. Morgan (1994a).
[64] Hefti (1950) is still basic here. For a full-scale Genettian analysis cf. Futre Pinheiro (1987); good concise treatment in Fusillo (1989).

familiar to us from modern novels, but unique in the ancient genre.

Thus, on the first page of the novel, the tableau of the ship and the bodies on the beach is seen through the eyes of Egyptian bandits, who are ignorant of what it signifies.[65] The reader is only told what they can see, and what they can deduce. The author does not explain what has caused the carnage, or who the beautiful young pair are. As the text proceeds, information is released to the reader only as it is released to the characters in the novel, and even this channel is teasingly obstructed. Charikleia's first speech, in which she might have revealed something about herself, is cut short by the inability of her fictional audience, the bandits, to understand Greek, and when at last the protagonists are given a Greek speaker, Knemon, to whom they could confide, they insist on hearing his story instead of telling him (and thus the reader) theirs. Even then, the first communication that Charikleia is able to make about herself turns out to be a false one, when she tells Thyamis that she and Theagenes are brother and sister from Ephesos. This causes the reader to question even whether the assumption, based on acquaintance with the genre, that Theagenes and Charikleia are the romantic hero and heroine is correct. Only afterwards do we learn, from Charikleia's words to Theagenes, that she was lying to Thyamis. Nearly a whole book passes before the reader knows for certain who are the protagonists of the story, and even then he knows nothing about them. So the reader, instead of being a passive consumer of an unambiguous story, is recast as an active participant in the actuation of the text, constructing the parts of the story not directly communicated to him by the narrator.

Audiences and spectators do not act only as channels through which visual information about the action can be conveyed to the reader. They function also as cues to emotional response. So, for instance, the Ethiopian populace in the last book, from whose point of view much of the action is described, is constantly reacting, with amazement, joy and excitement, in ways that reflect and provoke the reader's responses: the reader is projected almost as a member of the crowd. We have already seen how the metaphor of theatricality is important in this respect.[66]

The narrative of Kalasiris and Knemon's response to it thus ac-

---

[65] For analysis of this scene see Hefti (1950); Bühler (1976); Morgan (1991).
[66] Cf. Bartsch (1989); Morgan (1991).

quire an emblematic significance.[67] This is the only audience in the fiction which is responding to a verbal text, and the situation closely corresponds to that of Heliodoros and his reader. Heliodoros uses the figure of Kalasiris self-referentially to make clear what sort of work he himself is writing. He is, as his structural role implies, a quintessentially Odyssean character. Even before his narrative proper begins Knemon comments on his Protean elusiveness, and Kalasiris apologises for the apparently sophistic arrangement of his story (2.24.4–5). Within the plot he acts with an element of duplicity, or at least ambiguity. Although he sometimes speaks with serious learning, for instance on the sources of the Nile (2.28), he manipulates the whole of the intrigue at Delphi through false appearances and half-truths, concealing the truth of Charikleia's condition from her adoptive father with pseudo-science (3.8), tricking him into parting with the embroidered message and recognition tokens but never revealing Charikleia's true identity, and deliberately leading him to misunderstand a dream (4.14); he even stages a blatantly charlatan charade of Egyptian magic to impose on each of the protagonists (3.17, 4.5).

His guile as a narrator is similarly ambivalent. It is most clearly seen in what has become a celebrated crux.[68] Kalasiris seems to have two contradictory reasons for being at Delphi. Initially, he presents his narrative as if Delphi were just one port of call in his exile, where he chanced upon Charikleia, came gradually to understand who she was, and undertook a god-given role in her restitution. He later divulges, however, that he has visited Ethiopia, where Persinna consulted him about her daughter, and commissioned him to seek her out, after he learned "from the gods" that she was living in Delphi.[69] Earlier scholars interpreted this as a simple lapse by the author, resulting either from defective memory or failure to handle his own intricate structure, but more recent work suggests that it is better seen as the product of Kalasiris' narrative technique. Like Heliodoros as narrator, he does not immediately put his audience in full possession of all the relevant facts, but withholds material to make the presentation more effective. What is stressed in the presentation is

---

[67] Winkler (1982), centred on the narrative of Kalasiris, is indispensable for the hermeneutic strategy of the whole novel.
[68] First analysed by Hefti (1950); Winkler (1982) offers the reinterpretation followed here; see also Futre Pinheiro (1991a), Fuchs (1993) 174–88.
[69] Although he (or Heliodoros) equivocates slightly by suggesting that this was not the primary reason for his being in Delphi (4.13.1).

the way in which Kalasiris gradually attained full comprehension of what already existed by reassembling the story from a number of different sources (Charikles, Persinna's embroidery, the gods' instructions). The narrative does not inform its audience so much as re-enact Kalasiris' own discovery.

Throughout Heliodoros is interested in situations where characters are engaged in some interpretive activity, directed at a dream or oracle for example.[70] The reader too is obliged to speculate on the real meaning. Structurally most important is the oracle delivered just before Theagenes and Charikleia meet for the first time, which is not completely disambiguated until the last page of the novel, when Charikles compares it to the final outcome. Heliodoros exploits the reader's attempts to understand it to generate a series of expectations which can be reversed or questioned so as to prevent the novel tailing off into generic predictability, as the plot throws up incidents which seem to fulfil the oracle in unexpected ways. For example, its reference to ἀριστοβίων μέγ'ἀέθλιον ("the reward of those whose lives are passed in virtue") can be presumed at first to predict the happy ending required by the conventions of romantic fiction, but in the last book seems for a moment to refer instead to death by human sacrifice for which virginity is a required qualification.[71] A similar device operates with the dream of Kalasiris which Theagenes sees in Arsake's dungeon (8.11.3–5): the different interpretations of the two heroes point to two different endings, both of which are lent credence by signs that apparently point to now one, now the other.

An interesting example is Thyamis' dream of Isis, which tells him

τήνδε σοι τὴν παρθένον παραδίδωμι· σὺ δὲ ἔχων οὐχ ἕξεις, ἀλλ' ἄδικος ἔσῃ καὶ φονεύσεις τὴν ξένην· ἡ δὲ οὐ φονευθήσεται

This maiden I deliver to you; you shall have her and not have her; you shall do wrong and slay her but she shall not be slain. (1.18)

At first he wishfully understands this as a reference to marriage and defloration; but later reinterprets it as an injunction to kill her. Actually neither of his interpretations is correct, but the act of interpreting is foregrounded, and it is only by acting on his misinterpretations

---

[70] On the pressure placed on the reader to take "inferential walks", see Bartsch (1989) 80–108; on dreams cf. MacAlister (1987) 153–90 and (forthcoming); on the effects generated by the principal oracle see Morgan (1989b).

[71] Theagenes himself draws out the irony to make the point at 10.9.

that Thyamis brings about the dream's true fulfilment, just as the reader must make wrong speculations about the plot to enjoy it to the full.

Some critics read this hermeneutic hothouse of a novel in a self-referential and narratological way, seeing its characters as surrogate readers, and the novel as a sort of parable of what it means to read a novel, focusing attention on the genre's conventions for producing meaning.[72] It is beyond doubt that Heliodoros was the most self-aware of the Greek novelists, and that he was deeply interested in what we might call the theory of the novel. Apart from the metaliterary theatrical metaphors, and the role of Kalasiris, we can point to the scene in 9.24, when Charikleia's reasons for not revealing her identity to her father read like an aesthetic justification of Heliodoros' own strategies:

ὧν γὰρ πολυπλόκους τὰς ἀρχὰς ὁ δαίμων καταβέβληται, τούτων ἀνάγκη καὶ τὰ τέλη διὰ μακροτέρων συμπεραίνεσθαι

a story whose beginnings heaven has made convoluted cannot be quickly resolved.

The entire divine plan which supports the plot is, in one sense, a cypher for the author's own control of a properly formed story.

Nevertheless, we should avoid attributing to the author articulate theories which anticipate our own too closely. The alternative is to read Heliodoros' narrative technique as a primarily a means for affording the reader a new immediacy and intensity of experience. (S)he is encouraged to stand inside the fiction and watch it as a spectator. The removal of the omniscient narrator fosters the illusion that it is not a mediated fiction at all. The fondness for aporetic situations demanding interpretation can also be read as an approximation to reality, where sense-making is partial, provisional and retrospective.[73]

---

[72] Most influentially Winkler (1982); cf. also Bartsch (1989). For a different kind of self-referential reading, see Laplace (1992).
[73] Fuller discussion in Morgan (1991 and 1994a).

IX

Religion and Morality

Heliodoros, as a real life individual, had a connection of some sort with the cult of the Sun of his native Emesa. The question naturally arises of whether and to what extent this religious affiliation is present in his novel. Scholarly opinion falls into four broad categories:[74] i) the position originated by Kerényi (1927) and developed by Merkelbach (1962) that the novels are cult texts of mystery religions; ii) the view of scholars like Altheim (1948) and Weinreich (1950) that the Emesan cult pervades the novel, but in some less precise form; iii) that the *Aithiopika* is a religious novel in a much more general sense, whose concern to demonstrate the working of divine providence (however that divinity might be individuated) dictates the very structure of the work;[75] iv) that the divine apparatus of the novel is no more than a resource of narrative technique with no reference beyond the boundaries of its own fiction.

Merkelbach's argument is that the *Aithiopika* was written for initiates of the solar cult, as a coded allegory of its myths and initiation rituals. Ethiopia, land of the Sun, represents a state of union with god which a human soul leaves on entering the earthly life, and to which it is enabled to return through religious observance. Charikleia embodies the experience of the devotee, enduring ordeals at various stages of initiation on a journey back to his or her heavenly home. This myth of the fall of the soul is characteristic of neoplatonist thought of the period, which supplied a philosophical framework for religious practice, and there is nothing inherently implausible in the idea of a novel being written to allegorize it. But the *Aithiopika* is not that novel. The strict allegorical interpretation denies importance or interest to the very literary innovations which distinguish Heliodoros from the other novelists. The theme of return applies only to one of the protagonists, leaving Theagenes as a non-meaning appendage, and the cause of the fall of the soul (Charikleia's infant exposure) seems to reside in the very entity (her mother) to which she must return. A

---

[74] I leave aside the attempt of Korais (1804) to trace Christian ideas in the novel. The almost direct quotation from Philon's *Life of Moses* 2.195 at 9.9.3 does not necessarily indicate membership of Judaeo-Christian circles as this is one of Philon's exoteric works.

[75] As, for example, Reardon (1969) 302–3; Heiserman (1977) 186–202.

more fundamental problem is that not enough is known of the actual practices of the cult to control this reading: ritual practice is deduced from details in the novel which are given a mystic sense because the argument demands that they must have one. To interpret the entry of Charikleia and Theagenes into Arsake's palace as a voluntarily undergone ordeal in mystic initiation, for instance, is to ignore the episode's function in a self-sufficient literary and moral structure.[76]

The wider case for seeing the novel as promoting the Emesan cult rests on the postscript as a keystone from which meaning flows back into the rest of the work. The argument demands that the Sun be seen, if only retrospectively, as the controlling power of the novel. Admittedly Apollo dominates Delphi, but he is the god of Delphi, and it is realistic for him to take centre stage in his own city. Apollo is left behind in Delphi, and the Sun only becomes important again in the last book, again as the local god of Ethiopia. Charikles does, it is true, identify Delphic Apollo with Ethiopian Helios: τὸν πάτριον ὑμῶν θεὸν Ἀπόλλωνα, τὸν αὐτὸν ὄντα καὶ Ἥλιον ("Apollo, who is one and the same as the Sun, the god of your fathers") 10.36.3; but this is a rhetorical point to assert some sort of claim over the Ethiopians. The motive for the identification is directly contrary to the outcome desired by reader and god, and Charikles is hardly a satisfactory mouthpiece for a vital piece of authorial theology. Nor is the Ethiopian Sun-cult, whose human sacrifices present the last and greatest danger to the happy ending, presented as a religion to attract converts. It is best taken as an element of ethnographic realism.[77]

Although its orgiastic excesses were sanitised after Elagabalus, there is no evidence that the real solar cult ever demanded sexual purity of the type positively valorised through the whole novel. The readiness of the *Aithiopika* to accommodate a wide range of gods and divine powers on more or less equal terms, sometimes operating against the "right" direction of the plot, sits uneasily with the profound monotheism of the religion of Helios. Heliodoros was, when he wrote the novel, an adherent of his local religion, but that item of biography is not a key to unlock the meaning of his novel.

The two final approaches are different ways of interpreting the

---

[76] For more detailed criticism of Merkelbach (1962) see Turcan (1963), and Kövendi (1966).

[77] It is widely attested in the historiographical tradition: cf. Morgan (1982).

same corpus of evidence. The divine is tightly written into the *Aithiopika*. The love of the protagonists originates at a religious ceremony at Delphi (whose classical deities contribute to the idealised characterisation of the protagonists),[78] and reaches its fulfilment at another at Meroe. The action is distributed around the three sacred sites of Delphi, Memphis and Meroe, each of which contributes a priest who acts as father to Charikleia: Charikles, Kalasiris, and (at beginning and end) Sisimithres. These priests even seem to be arranged in their own hierarchy, so that the heroine's progress back to Ethiopia is articulated by an ascent towards wisdom and spirituality.[79]

The forward movement of the plot itself is provided by a system of divine intervention.[80] Apart from the oracle, Kalasiris experiences a theophany of Apollo and Artemis which motivates his plan for the lovers' elopement (3.11), and the encounter with the Phoenicians which provides the means of escape is ascribed to divine forethought (4.16.3ff.). The gods also exercise control through dreams, which often have the effect of moving the action on to a new stage, sometimes in direct contradiction of the characters' intentions. A dream of Hydaspes, prompting him to make love to his wife, sets the whole story going (4.8.4). Thyamis' two interpretations of his dream combine to have Charikleia hidden in the cave and Thisbe killed in her stead, with all the consequent complications of the intrigue. Charikles' misunderstanding of his dream (4.14.2), encouraged by Kalasiris, motivates him to present Charikleia with her recognition-tokens, which are destined to play a role in her ultimate salvation and restoration.

On a few occasions the omniscient narrator attributes an event to divine agency. The striking tableau with which the novel opens is said to be the work of ὁ δαίμων (1.1.6). When Knemon is perplexed by the apparent resurrection of Thisbe he is at first described as the victim of τι ... δαιμόνιον ("a supernatural power"), which is then glossed as ὃ καὶ τὰ ἄλλα χλεύην ὡς ἐπίπαν τὰ ἀνθρώπεια καὶ παιδιὰν πεποίηται ("whose habit it is in general to make mock of all human life and use it as its plaything", 5.4.1). Kalasiris' intervention at his sons' duel is attributed within the space of a few sentences to τι δαιμόνιον ("some divine power"), τύχη τις τὰ ἀνθρώπεια βραβεύουσα ("some fortune that

---

[78] At her very first appearance Charikleia is represented as an icon of Artemis; her Delphic robes are a crucial element of the emblematic scenes at Arsake's stake and on the Ethiopian griddle.
[79] Cf. Szepessy (1957).
[80] The material is usefully collected by Futre Pinheiro (1991b).

arbitrates over human destiny"), ἡ εἱμαρμένη ("fate"), οἱ θεοί ("the gods"), and τὸ προωρισμένον ἐκ μοιρῶν ("what the fates had foreseen"). At the end of the novel Charikleia's recognition is described as ἡ σκηνοποιία τῆς τύχης ("destiny's stage-management", 10.16.3). On several occasions divine agency is mentioned as one of several possible explanations for an event (e.g. 8.9.2, 9.8.2, 10.28.2, 10.38.3).

There are numerous passages where a character senses the hand of god. Often, of course, these perceptions arise from error or limitation of viewpoint, but some authority must be allowed to Sisimithres' climactic explanation that the process of Charikleia's recognition and reprieve, and beyond it the whole of her life, are the expression of the gods' will (10.39.2ff.).[81] Two of the novel's profoundest moments occur when characters attain an epiphany of comprehension as they glimpse the fullness of the divine economy: Kalasiris on reading Charikleia's embroidered message (4.9.1), and Charikles who on the very last page finally sees that the oracle has been fulfilled exact in every particular. Elsewhere characters speak of οἱ θεοί, ἡ τύχη, τὰ πεπρωμένα, αἱ μοῖραι, ἡ εἱμαρμένη, τὸ θεῖον, τὸ δαιμόνιον and οἱ κρείττονες, and characteristically see themselves as the charge of a personal δαίμων who oversees their lives, for good or ill, ὁ εἰληχὼς δαίμων (as at 2.25.3, 6.12.1).[82]

The characters' sense is almost invariably of malign powers, expressing a profound metaphysical pessimism, deeply at variance with the novel's structural progression towards a preordained happy ending. But even authorially, Heliodoros can attribute events to divine malevolence: the divine dispensation is not unitary. Nor, it must be said, is Heliodoros' multiplication of agencies intellectually coherent. The important word δαίμων for instance is loosely used: sometimes it denotes a malign or vengeful power operating at a level between gods and men, at other times it seems interchangeable with other words for divine entities for no reason more profound than stylistic variation.[83] Nor is any attempt made to distinguish between gods and concepts like destiny or chance.[84]

---

[81] This speech serves precisely the same structural function as that of the priest of Isis in Apuleius. It is striking that Sisimithres' name combines those of Isis (reversed) and Mithras.
[82] Cf. 2.25.3, 5.2.7, 6.8.3, 6.12.1, 7.25.7. The phrase is a cliché of popular thinking.
[83] For an attempt to classify Heliodoros' usages cf. Puiggali (1981).
[84] Chance (*Tyche*) plays a relatively small role in Heliodoros, but perhaps one better defined than in the other novels; cf. Robiano (1984).

The problem of course is how far the fictional representation of the divine is intended to have any referential truth-value, either as a description of the way the world works, or as a polemical, didactic tool to alter the reader's perception of and response to reality. Clearly the divine system presented in the novel made sense to its intended readers, but its intelligibility derives as much from conformity to the received rules of literature as from similarity to religious belief in the real world.[85] The action of the gods is just as fictitious as the action of the human characters, and the overarching divine purpose in the *Aithiopika* coincides with the novel's literary structure: at the deepest level god and author are indistinguishable, both as guarantor of ultimate moral sense and as site for the fully reconstituted version of the story, which in this, alone of the Greek novels, exists outside and before the text.[86] The *Aithiopika* is a religious novel, but the religious experience it offers is that of artistic completion, without necessary reference to the real world.

At the centre of the novel's moral universe stands love, elevated almost to the status of a sacrament.[87] The love of the protagonists is ideal: mutual, permanent and exclusive. Their ultimate union is what gives a sense of purpose and meaning to their sufferings. Here we may contrast the novels of Chariton and Xenophon of Ephesos, in which marriage and the consummation of love form a prelude to the adventures of separation, rather than a goal of moral and structural direction. Heliodoros is markedly more rigorous than the other novelists in identifying emotional devotion with physical purity. In Chariton's novel, for instance, Kallirhoe's emotional and spiritual fidelity to Chaireas is apparently not compromised by her inability to sustain strict physical monogamy. But for Heliodoros love is of such moral and structural importance that it is a matter of overriding concern to Charikleia that it should not reach its fulfilment in the wrong circumstances and without the proper formalities. Chastity is thus afforded a very high value. It is enjoined on Charikleia

---

[85] A parallel is provided by the Byzantine romances, whose Christian readers were quite happy to accept a fictional world governed by the same pagan gods who had always governed fiction.

[86] Perhaps the point emerges most clearly in the idea of the divine as playwright (e.g. at 1.1.6, 7.6.4, 10.16.3, 10.38.2): the gods' activity is closely assimilated to that of the author himself, as expressed through the pervasive theatrical metaphor; cf. Bartsch (1989) 135–43.

[87] For fuller discussion see Morgan (1989c), Fusillo (1989).

by her mother as befitting her royal station (4.8.7), and dominates her thoughts throughout the novel. It generates one of the novel's iconic scenes when Charikleia's virginity is proven by the magical ordeal of the Ethiopian gridiron and she stands in the radiant splendour of her purity, protected by her virtue (10.9.3ff.).[88] Theagenes subscribes to the same sexual ethic and, when forced to take an oath to respect Charikleia's virginity, is resentful that his restraint should be made to appear the result of coercion rather than volition (4.18.5f.). He refuses even to pretend to compromise with Arsake, even at Charikleia's suggestion (7.21.5). But, despite the prominence of piety and purity as elements in the characterisation of an ideal heroine, the *Aithiopika* is not an anti-sexual work: its climax is the long-postponed betrothal of the lovers θεσμῷ παιδογονίας ("in accordance with god's ordinance for the bearing of children" 10.40.2), simultaneous with their induction into the solar and lunar priesthood; its structure and its moral economy do not condemn the sexual act as something to be avoided, but, by reserving it so long and so strictly, valorise it as a matter of supreme and symbolic importance in human life.

The sexual code of the protagonists is illuminated by the story of Knemon, which presents its exact converse. The world of Demainete, Thisbe and Knemon revolves around an eroticism which is unreciprocated, selfish, ephemeral and promiscuous. It deals in disparities of social status, age and authority, in coercion, seduction and deception. Love is degraded into a meaningless physical act, which can be exploited and subordinated as a means to other ends, of power and wealth for example. The stories of Demainete and Thisbe both end in underground darkness and death, and that of Knemon in exile, in counterpoint to Charikleia's which culminates in return, light and a reunion which is portrayed as a rebirth. Thisbe in particular is presented as an anti-Charikleia, a *Doppelgänger* whose identity criss-crosses with the heroine's: she is mistaken for Charikleia by Thyamis who kills her, by Theagenes who grieves over her body; Charikleia in her turn is constrained to pass herself off as Thisbe by Nausikles, and is then taken for her by the terrified Knemon who hears her lamenting.

The figure of Charikleia has impressed readers from the Byzantine period onwards. Her beauty arouses the love of all who see her, but for the reader it is the token of other, inner, qualities. In her

---

[88] The obvious irony of the scene, that the proof of her virtue qualifies her for death, does not negate the powerfully positive image.

piety and purity she certainly embodies the ideals of her period,[89] and there are occasions when she seems to possess more initiative and composure than her partner. Structurally she is the dominant character, both as object of Kalasiris' investigations and as centre of the themes of return and recognition. However, part of the impression of dominance which she gives is due to the author's wish to stress the characteristically romantic equality of the central relationship: conventional gender roles are not reversed but combined.[90] Theagenes must not make all the running, and conversely must be shown to be subject to the same doubts and vulnerabilities as the heroine. At the last he is allowed his due moment of heroic glory, in his two wrestling exploits at Meroe. Though strictly redundant, they are necessary preparation for the emotional climax of the novel.

The figure of Kalasiris is morally much more complex and ambiguous. We have already examined the Odyssean duplicity of his narrative technique. But his whole character seems split between the personae of holy man and charlatan swindler, in a way that is perhaps an authentic depiction of a certain type of late antique figure.[91] He distinguishes two sorts of wisdom, a lower kind of magic χαμαὶ ἐρχομένη . . . καὶ περὶ σώματα νεκρῶν εἰλουμένη ("that crawls upon the earth . . . and skulks around dead bodies") which is delusive and perverted (3.16),[92] and a higher variety practised by priests like himself, directed towards the gods and the good; but he is quite prepared to represent himself as employing the lower sort of spell-magic in order to achieve his ends. Although he has the sympathy of the reader because his intrigues are directed at bringing about the right end to the story (as well as being conducive to narrative pleasure in the interim), he himself is problematically aware of the effect of his actions on the unfortunate Charikles (3.15.3).[93] The novel never actually makes clear why Kalasiris chooses not to be completely open with Charikles: apart from the generic presumption that fathers obstruct love-matches, there is no reason supplied in the text for think-

---

[89] Cf. Hani 1978.
[90] On the equality of the genders, characteristic of romance, see Konstan (1994a).
[91] For these aspects of Kalasiris see Sandy (1982b).
[92] This lower magic and its effects are illustrated explicitly, with verbal repetitions, in the episode of the necromancy at Bessa, leading to the death of the practitioner.
[93] There is an isolated hint that Charikles "deserved" what happens to him at 4.19, when he speaks of the loss of his daughter as a god-sent punishment for his having seen some forbidden sight in a shrine. But though this makes sense of the gods' dispensation from Charikles' point of view, it does not exculpate Kalasiris.

ing that he would have opposed Charikleia's love for Theagenes, had he known about it, or that he would have stood in the way of her return to Ethiopia, had he ever been informed of her true identity. Ultimately Kalasiris' ambivalent and devious procedures have to be read as indices of his ambivalent and devious personality.

As to the philosophical orientation of the novel, there is a strong current of Platonism, particularly in the scene where the two protagonists meet and fall in love at first sight ὥσπερ εἴ που γνωρίζοντες ἢ ἰδόντες πρότερον, ταῖς μνήμαις ἀναπεμπάζοντες ("as if calling to mind a previous acquaintance or meeting").[94] Here the *Phaidros* is very much in the air, but this was a text widely read and exploited in the period of the Second Sophistic and it would be unwise to read Heliodoros' use of it as anything much more profound than literary colouring. However, some scholars have seen more pervasive influence from the neoplatonic or neopythagorean schools of the empire.[95]

In part this involves the specific relationship between the *Aithiopika* and another "Emesan" text, Philostratos' romantic biography of the neopythagorean guru Apollonios of Tyana, commissioned by the Emesan empress Julia Domna. We have seen, however, that the role of the Sun (which would form the main ideological linkage between the two works) is easily exaggerated in the *Aithiopika*. Heliodoros clearly knew Philostratos' biography, but the connections are mostly fairly superficial.[96]

Other elements in the *Aithiopika* appear at least to originate in the intellectual climate of neoplatonism. The discussion of Egyptian mysteries in Bk. 9 for example presupposes a hermeneutic hierarchy, with a literal meaning for the majority and allegorical subtexts accessible only to the initiated. Kalasiris combines aspects of asceticism (including vegetarianism) and theurgy which are found in neoplatonist thinkers, many of whom looked to Egypt as a source of revealed

---

[94] See especially Kövendi (1966) 153–9.
[95] Neopythagoreanism is traced by Rohde (1914) and J. Maillon in Rattenbury and Lumb (1935–43) vol. 1, lxxxiiiff. Cf. Geffcken (1929) 88: "eine neuplatonische Tendenzdichtung", and Nilsson (1961) vol. 2, 565–6.
[96] Philostratos provides Heliodoros' precedent for locating Gymnosophists in Ethiopia, but is explicit about their inferiority to their Indian forebears in a way that would be highly inconvenient for the novelist. The scene in the last book where the Gymnosophists retire from a blood sacrifice recalls Apollonios' refusal to participate in a sacrifice (1.31), and their foreknowledge of Hydaspes' letter (10.4.3) is similar to the prescience of the Indian Iarchas (*Vit.Apoll.*3.16). Both texts also exploit the paradox of a black man blushing (10.24.2/*Vit.Apoll.*6.12).

wisdom. He is able to extract hidden meanings from Homer with a tortured ingenuity typical of an authentic neoplatonist.[97] The difference of course is that his exposition is distanced by its context within an ironic characterisation of an ambivalent individual. Likewise aspects of his apparently neoplatonist demonology, such as the ἀντίθεος which allegedly blocks his efforts to make Charikleia fall in love, belong to the playacting aspect of his double persona.[98]

It is in the theology and demonology of the novel if anywhere that traces of neoplatonism and neopythagoreanism are to be found. As we have seen Heliodoros' world is thickly populated by δαίμονες, some of which are conceived, by the characters at least, as being personal spirits. Neoplatonism also postulated a mechanism of powers or δαίμονες as intermediaries between the worlds of gods and men. However, Heliodoros' demonology is not systematic when pressed: the supposed levels of supernatural power often seem interchangeable in his vocabulary. The difference is one of perceived intention rather than power, the gods being benevolent and the δαίμονες generally malign or retributive. One is left with the impression that these things are in the novel because they were part of the general mental furniture of the period rather than because the author was propagandising a particular intellectual system with any precision.

X

Language and Style

The Byzantine critics were much interested in Heliodoros' style. Photios is the most conventional and least perceptive, singling out its appropriateness to the subject matter, its simplicity and sweetness (καὶ γὰρ ἀφελείᾳ καὶ γλυκύτητι πλεονάζει), its purity and clarity of diction and metaphors: oddly he sees the sentence structure as well-proportioned (σύμμετροι) and compressed (πρὸς τὸ βραχύτερον οἷα δὴ συστελλόμεναι). Psellos on the other hand notes its grandeur (τῷ μεγαλοπρεπεῖ διαπρέπον) but also its charm and pleasure, its graceful and beautiful vocabulary, and the lofty effect achieved by the nov-

---

[97] Cf. Lamberton (1986) 149–61.
[98] Fullest treatment in Sandy (1982b); for the *antitheos* see Puiggali (1984).

elty of its style (τῇ καινοτομίᾳ τῆς φράσεως πρὸς τὸ ὑψηλότερον συγκεκρότηται). Eugenikos comments on Heliodoros' rhythm and his ἠκριβωμένη λέξις and perceptively notes the poetic qualities of the style with rhymes and balanced clauses. His judgment is that there is a perfect balance of clarity, charm and elevation.

Heliodoros is a highly literary writer. Even in the relatively straightforward narrative sections of the novel, he uses a wide range of unusual but evocative vocabulary and his sentences, while made up of elements that are simple enough in themselves, tend to be long and complex. A favourite pattern is to allow participles to carry much of the meaning and to accumulate in co-ordinate strings. Word order is artificial, with mannered hyperbaton. Simple narrative is interspersed, however, by passages where he has allowed his undoubted gifts for rhetorical embellishment to have their head.

Perhaps the most striking feature of these is their use of expressive symmetry.[99] Pairs or larger groups of syntactically parallel clauses and especially participial cola are arranged to produce exact or nearly exact balance, or in patterns of ascending length, and the grammatical parallelisms are often underlined with heavy homoeoteleuton, usually produced through end-placement of participles. The formal patterns within sentences can often become quite complex, with multiple participial cola framing and articulating a series of main verbs. Antithesis is constantly deployed, most often underlined by the use of μέν and δέ: sometimes these particles are used to create an antithesis that is more formal than organic.

Within these structures Heliodoros is fond of word-play of a number of types. Near homophones are juxtaposed, verbs with the same prepositional prefix are allowed to saturate a context, words are repeated (either by anaphora or in different forms in the same sentence; sometimes different senses of the same word, or literal and transferred usages will be brought into proximity), there is plentiful alliteration and assonance.

He exploits a wide range of metaphors from many areas of experience.[100] For the most part these, and the relatively small number of explicit similes, are fairly straightforward. The vocabulary is extremely wide, often poetic in flavour, and Heliodoros often has the knack of

---

[99] See especially Mazal (1955 and 1958).
[100] Cf. Feuillâtre (1966) 74–93.

hitting upon the *mot juste*.[101] Although broadly Atticist, he is tolerant of neologisms,[102] and allows a number of words to extend their usage in ways not attested in earlier extant authors: verbs in particular are allowed to govern infinitives or direct objects in ways that would have been impermissible in classical Greek, but which can sometimes be paralleled from other writers of the empire.[103] He is fond of expressing abstracts through the use of the infinitive or neuter participle as a noun, the latter often governing a partitive genitive. Like many writers of post-classical prose he is drawn to the middle voice, even of verbs employed exclusively in the active by strict Atticists, largely for the possibilities of assonance. His use of tenses is also fluid: he slips in and out of the historic present, usually for a discernible dramatic effect; and uses the imperfect and perfect as narrative tenses, in a way which can nearly always be justified but not always predicted. Like the other novelists he rigorously avoids hiatus.[104] Preferred clausulae are combinations of trochaic and cretic.[105]

In general critics have been harsh on Heliodoros' style, finding fault with its artificiality and excesses, as well as with its departures from a strictly conceived correctness.[106] It certainly is not the sort of language which would ever have been spoken, but taken at its own terms it is a richly nuanced prose of great exuberance and emotional effect, whose devices combine with the author's characteristic narrative technique to produce an experience of immediacy and involvement with the action. One cannot expect Richard Strauss to sound like Haydn.

---

[101] On vocabulary see Rohde (1914) 489–93.

[102] Full lists in Colonna (1938) 378 and Colonna (1987).

[103] For Heliodoros' Atticism, cf. Fritsch (1901–2) and Zanetto (1990); for all aspects of usage of verbs see Barber (1962). For a small number of solecisms see Cobet (1857) and Naber (1873).

[104] Perhaps the major fault of Rattenbury and Lumb's edition is their tolerance of hiatus, sometimes introduced through needless conjecture. See Reeve (1971b) 518–21.

[105] Statistics in Mazal (1955).

[106] Cf. Rohde (1914) 489–90: "Leider entspricht dem Willen die Kraft nur wenig: die Feierlichkeit artet vielfach in eine schwülstig großsprecherische Redeweise aus; ein leeres und hohles Pathos, immer festgehalten, verdriesst uns, weil die Gedanken einer so umständlichen weitgebauschten Einkleidung allzuwenig würdig erscheinen... Sein sprachlicher Ausdruck ist ein echtes Sophistenwerk."

F. THE *SATYRICA* OF PETRONIUS

Gareth Schmeling

Petronius the Historical Figure

Though a few sceptics and unbelievers from time to time arise and haunt scholarly halls, most critics hold that the Petronius of Tacitus (*Annales* 16.17–20) is also the author of the *Satyrica*.[1] Much of the romance, however, and some of the appeal clinging to the *Satyrica* originate from uncertainties surrounding its author and his fragmentary text and the portrait of its author recorded by Tacitus. Even if the Petronius of Tacitus is the author of the *Satyrica*, we cannot be certain that we know his full name; it seems, however, that Titus Petronius Niger, consul A.D. 62, is our best bet.[2] According to Tacitus Petronius died in a palace intrigue because he got himself on the wrong side of Tigellinus, notorious Prefect of the Praetorian Guard, and Nero ordered Petronius to kill himself. The story has many elements of a Hollywood extravaganza: Nero, orgies, marble halls of power on the Palatine and in the Forum, riotous banquets, nude dancing girls, sexual excesses, in short everything hinted at in the mysteries of the *Revelation of John* and referred to as the root of all evil by American televangelists. As a classical wag has recently noted, Petronius would lose much glamour and appeal had he written under Vespasian.[3]

As portrayed by Tacitus, Petronius is an exceedingly complex person:

> nam illi dies per somnum, nox officiis et oblectamentis vitae transigebatur; utque alios industria, ita hunc ignavia ad famam protulerat,

---

[1] The most serious recent challenge to the orthodox dating of Petronius to the reign of Nero was mounted by Marmorale (1948), who, if nothing else, encouraged scholars to use historical information very carefully. Rowell (1958) is typical of the scholarly world's reaction to Marmorale dating of Petronius to the late second century. In his text and commentary Smith (1975) doubts the connection between the Tacitean Petronius and the author of the *Satyrica* and dates the novel to the reign of Tiberius-Caligula. Rose (1971) seems to me to settle the question once and for all in favor of a Neronian date for the novelist. For Petronian questions cf. Bowie (1993).
[2] K. Rose (1971).
[3] Vessey (1991–1993) 149.

> habebaturque non ganeo et profligator, ut plerique sua haurientium, sed erudito luxu. (*Ann*.16.18)

> He spent his days sleeping and his nights working and enjoying himself. Industry is the usual foundation of success, but with him it was idleness. Unlike most people who throw away their money in dissipation, he was not regarded as an extravagant sensualist, but as one who made luxury a fine art.

And then in an antithetical style so beloved of our historian he adds:

> ac dicta factaque eius quanto solutiora et quandam sui neglegentiam praeferentia, tanto gratius in speciem simplicitatis accipiebantur.

> His conversation and his way of life were unconventional with a certain air of nonchalance, and they charmed people all the more by seeming so unstudied.

Petronius serves as proconsul in Bithynia where he proves himself an able administrator, and then returns to Rome where he enters Nero's inner (but not innermost) circle and holds the (unofficial) post of *arbiter elegantiae*. The title *arbiter* sticks to Petronius in succeeding generations until finally he is referred to simply as Petronius Arbiter—as though it were his name or official title.[4] When the twenty-nine year old emperor orders the death of Petronius, the novelist responds in an original way:

> flagitia principis sub nominibus exoletorum feminarumque et novitatem cuiusque stupri perscripsit atque obsignata misit Neroni. (*Ann*.16.19).

And so Petronius kills himself—but even here he is original—compared with Seneca, e.g.:[5]

> neque tamen praeceps vitam expulit, sed incisas venas, ut libitum, obligatas aperire rursum et adloqui amicos, non per seria aut quibus gloriam constantiae peteret.... iniit epulas, somno indulsit, ut quamquam coacta mors fortuitae similis esset. (*Ann*.16.19)

> Not that he was hasty in taking leave of his life. On the contrary, he opened his veins and then as the fancy took him, he bound them up again. Meanwhile he talked to his friends, but not on serious topics or anything calculated to win admiration for his courage.... He began a

---

[4] Fantasy and scholarship are combined in Bagnani (1954). For a balanced view cf. Corbett (1970). For Petronius as an Epicurean cf. Raith (1963).
[5] van Hooff (1990) 52.

lavish dinner and took a nap, so that death, although forced on him, should appear natural.

The description of the life of Petronius and in particular his almost-attractive manner of dying could be the by-product of Tacitus' love for rhetorical antithesis, an example of coercive rhetoric influencing its own creator. Tacitus' focus is on the contradictions in Petronius' life, certain episodes are exaggerated or highly colored, while the ordinary acts in his life are passed over. Some support, however, of Tacitus' portrayal of Petronius' life as unusual is offered in references made in passing by Pliny the Elder and Plutarch. Pliny (*NH* 37.20) records that when Petronius was ordered to commit suicide, he went out of his way to break a wine-dipper valued at 300,000 sesterces so that the emperor could not inherit it, and Plutarch (*Mor.*60 d–e) tells us that Petronius chided Nero, who was extravagant with money, for being frugal: Nero has enough faults, says Plutarch, but Petronius chooses to criticize a virtue he does not have. And in so doing Plutarch may support Tacitus' description of him as an eccentric. In any attempt we make to re-construct a biographical sketch of Petronius, we must always be alert not to transfer descriptions of the narrator of the *Satyrica* to the author of the novel.[6] The narrator and narrative are fiction.

And so the myth of Petronius begins. His death is translated into the archetypal death of noble Romans popular in literature and becomes an important part in such works as Jeremy Taylor's *The Rule and Exercise of Holy Dying* (1678), Henryk Sienkiewicz' *Quo Vadis* (1896), Nicholas Blake's mystery *The Worm of Death* (1961), and Federico Fellini's movie *Fellini-Satyricon* (1969).

Though the author is enshrined in myth, his claim to lasting fame rests on his novel, which is not, however, alluded to until late (A.D. 400)[7] by Macrobius, and no title is offered until much later. The spelling of the title of the novel is now generally accepted as *Satyrica*. For many years we had seen *Satyricon* for Σατυρικῶν *libri*, *Saturae*, *Satirae*, but to align the title of this novel with those of other ancient

---

[6] Sullivan (1968) 98, reads the eight lines of verse at 132.15 (*quid me constricta...*) as an "aside of the author to his audience."

[7] In Frag. 19 of the *Satyrica* we see that the late second century grammarian Terentianus Maurus mentions the "Arbiter" as having written a certain type of verse, which is not found in the extant text. Maurus may not have been alluding to the *Satyrica*.

works (*Aethiopica*, *Ephesiaca*, etc.), *Satyrica* is now used regularly.[8] Petronius perhaps is punning on Σάτυροι (sexual subjects) and *lanx satura* (subjects in traditional Roman satire) and creates a hybrid term.

Satyrica *the Novel*

The *Satyrica* is a long narrative work in prose with sections of verse, of varying lengths, set in here and there. What is extant today of the *Satyrica* comes from a part of Book 14, all of Book 15 (*Cena Trimalchionis*), and Book 16—assuming an original of 24 books. It is not certain that the *Satyrica* is the only work written by Petronius. The standard editions of the *Satyrica* list numerous fragments attributed to Petronius for which no home can be found in the novel itself; perhaps these fragments belong to lost sections of the *Satyrica*.

Our extant Latin text is fragmentary, some fragments are very short and their order in dispute; the *Cena Trimalchionis* is a complete episode, but in the context of the whole it too is a fragment. In addition to, and because of, the work's fragmentary state, many controversies and doubts surround the *Satyrica*. We have just seen the controversy surrounding the identity of the author and his date and are about to consider problems of the novel's length, arrangement of the surviving fragments, genre, literary intent (if any; is it a parody?).

The *Satyrica* is a first-person narrative, but our narrator Encolpius is so unreliable that he adds to our problems instead of helping to solve them by filtering all elements of the story through a common point of view.

Possible Systematic Reconstruction of the Plot of the Satyrica

The notion that the completed *Satyrica* consists of 24 books is highly speculative.[9] We do not know if Petronius had completed the *Satyrica* at the time of his death in A.D. 66, or if he had even an idea of a systematic *Satyrica*. From the evidence we can speculate that the *Satyrica* in the original might have looked something like this:[10]

---

[8] K. Müller (1983) 491–492.
[9] Sullivan (1968).
[10] For a reconstruction of the *Satyrica*, cf. Sullivan (1968) 34–80, Walsh (1970) 73–109, van Thiel (1971a) 25–65, 76–78.

THE *SATYRICA* OF PETRONIUS

Books 1–10 (In the North)	– Beginnings at Massilia (Frags. 1, 4) – Introduction of Encolpius as narrator – Sacrilege against Priapus – Encolpius as scapegoat – Interlude with Doris (126.18) – Introduction of Giton
Books 11–12 (Moving South-Baiae)	– Introduction/Episodes with Tryphaena – Affair with Lichas and his wife (?) Hedyle – Insult to Lichas and escape
Book 13 (Baiae-Puteoli)	– Introduction of Ascyltus – Introduction of Lycurgus – Robbery of Lycurgus' villa
Book 14 (Puteoli)	– Introduction of Quartilla – Diverse episodes with Quartilla – Theft of gold coins – Loss of gold coins – Theft of cloak – Second loss of gold coins
Book 15 (Puteoli)	– (Opening is missing) – Introduction of Agamemnon via Menelaus – Episode with Menelaus – *Cena Trimalchionis* – Departure of Ascyltus, arrival of Eumolpus
Book 16 (Moving South)	– Begins with ch. 100, departure from Puteoli – Meeting with Lichas and Tryphaena – *Matrona Ephesi, Bellum Civile* – Toward Croton
Book 17 (Croton)	– Legacy-hunters defrauded – Introduction of Circe – Episodes of Proselenus, Circe, Oenothea – Final scheme of Eumolpus
Book 18 (Moving further South)	– Eumolpus leaves story – Departure of Encolpius and Giton from Croton.
Book 19 (Moving South)	– Eumolpus replaced by someone – Movement toward the East
Books 20–24	– Arrival in Lampsacus – Encolpius expiates offenses against Priapus – Encolpius initiated into cult of Priapus – Encolpius finds new troubles

Summary of the Novel

The Opening Scenes

The *Satyrica* is a fragmentary work, and the order and arrangements of the pieces, as they have come down to us, are almost certainly not correct in detail. The summary which follows, however, offers the traditional arrangement of fragments made in the Middle Ages and Renaissance.

As our *Satyrica* opens [in Book 15, after a lacuna],[11] the reader finds himself in the middle of a speech by Encolpius (who turns out to be the novel's narrator), berating the wretched state of modern education. [The *Satyrica* in its original state may have begun in Massilia; cf. Frags. 1 and 4.] He calls for a "back to basics" movement; the subject is hackneyed and discussed by many others including Tacitus and Quintilian. The vehemence with which Encolpius attacks current educational practices is out-of-proportion to his own beliefs, but he is an actor and performs for even small audiences, in this case for Agamemnon, who owns a nearby school of rhetoric. The setting could be the seaside resort of Puteoli near Naples. Encolpius may have been introduced to Agamemnon by his assistant Menelaus (27.4; 81.1) whose interest in finding students may have been more erotic than educational. For his part Encolpius is probably more interested in obtaining free meals and other handouts through his association with Agamemnon than in gaining educational insights. These discussions about education and literature have been taken seriously by some. (1–5).[12]

Even as he listens to Agamemnon, Encolpius notices that Ascyltus (a friend of Encolpius and unknown up to this point to the reader) is leaving and tries to follow him. An old woman leads him straight into a brothel, where (fictional coincidence) he discovers Ascyltus. The text is very fragmentary, but an escape is effected. (6–8).

Encolpius catches sight of Giton (a boy-love of Encolpius and unknown up to this point to the reader) who blurts out that Ascyltus tried to force him to have sex. A fight ensues, but the tempers and fists turn out to be play-acting and stage-management.[13] [Lacuna]. After some reflection the two youths agree that their current *modus vivendi* is not working, and Ascyltus agrees that he will move out

---

[11] Square brackets indicate lacunae.
[12] Nelson (1956); for a balanced view cf. Kennedy (1978).
[13] Schmeling (1994b).

tomorrow after the dinner tonight to which they have been invited. [Lacuna] While Encolpius and Giton are making love in bed in their locked apartment, Ascyltus knocks the doorbolts loose, catches the pair, and playfully sets about Encolpius with a strap. (9–11)

[Lacuna, but this episode (12–15) probably belongs to Book 14]. Our threesome joins together in an evening trip to the forum to flog a valuable cloak stolen earlier. It appears that they live from hand-to-mouth through petty theft, begging, selling sex, and cadging meals by pretending to be teachers (with a pretty attendant in tow). As fictional fortune would have it, Ascyltus spies their lost old tunic draped over the shoulder of a farmer and upon closer examination discovers that the gold coins hidden in the stitching are still there [refers to earlier—but recent—lost episode]. In a scene out of New Comedy, the farmer who owned the cloak which the boys had stolen grabs the valuable cloak even as our heroes grab for the old tunic. It is clear from the tone of the closing lines that the coins are soon to be lost again. (12–15)

[The next episode, that of Quartilla (16–26), is generally believed to be out of place and to precede the opening scene with Agamemnon; it might belong to Book 14.]

[Lacuna]. Our three heroes are together in their room, when a blow to the door knocks the bolt loose and a woman with a covered head enters and accuses the three of having disrupted the religious services of her mistress, Quartilla. Priestesses and religious scenes are comic in the *Satyrica*. In a rambling speech Quartilla never actually names the unforgivable sins the youths are supposed to have committed at the shrine of Priapus: the affair is somehow a mime. [The section is full of lacunae.] She announces that the sacrilege of the youths has caused her to be stricken by a fever and that she and her two maids will seek a remedy from the three youths. (16–19). Ch. 20 is very fragmentary, but the contents describe various sexual actions of the inhabitants of the room. Quartilla and her maid Psyche then hatch the brilliant scheme to have their seven-year old attendant Pannychis deflowered by the young Giton. At 21.7 we learn that this celebration by Quartilla and friends is a *Priapi genio pervigilium*, and now she will conclude it with a sacrifice of a girl named Pannychis. Was this whole episode arranged to be a wordplay on *pervigilium— pannychis*?[14] When Encolpius questions Quartilla about the physical

---

[14] Schmeling (1971b) (1991).

capabilities of Pannychis to undergo the ritual, she replies: *minor est ista quam ego fui, cum primum virum passa sum? . . . hinc etiam puto proverbium natum illud, posse taurum tollere, qui vitulum sustulerit.* To add insult to injury Quartilla drills a little hole in the door to observe the cult ritual of Priapus. (20–26.6)

The Banquet of Trimalchio

Our youths have been invited to dine at Trimalchio's, a man with a large but regional reputation. [There is a lacuna between the Quartilla story and the Banquet.] At ch. 27 the unholy trinity enters the baths attached to Trimalchio's house and at that point runs into the great man himself: *senem calvum, tunica vestitum russea . . . ad . . . signum matellam spado ludenti subiecit. exonerata ille vesica aquam poposcit ad manus.* One of the most memorable introductions in classical literature. After the *frigidarium* the assembled group begins to make its way into the house proper, but a dog painted on the wall almost scares Encolpius into a faint. This is the first of many extant examples of scenes misinterpreted by Encolpius. After reviewing murals near the entrance of the house depicting the rise of Trimalchio from slave to master, Encolpius' attempt to enter the house is delayed by a slave who informs him that he must enter "right foot first". Finally the three youths are seated in the *triclinium.* (26.7–31)

Probable Table Arrangement

MEDIUS

	Habinnas	Ascyltus or Agamemnon	Encolpius (summus in medio)	
I M U S	Fortunata and Scintilla			Hermeros
	Proculus			Ascyltus or Agamemnon
	Diogenes (imus in imo)			Trimalchio (summus in summo)

SUMMUS (right side) / IMUS (left side)

To the sound of music the host is carried into the dining room, and his outlandish costume elicits snickers from the guests. Eggs are passed around to the guests and the host announces that he hopes that they are still fresh. Encolpius, again misunderstanding the ritual of the meal, almost throws away a rich pastry egg. Trimalchio is a man of dramatic action—each carefully orchestrated: he has slaves beaten, dropped silver thrown out with the trash, wine (instead of water) poured over guests' hands to clean them, and a silver skeleton brought out to remind all guests of their mortality:[15] Trimalchio is superstitious and seems to be fascinated with death. (32–36)

Trimalchio has no children, but at ch. 37 we meet his wife, Fortunata, who is in attendance at, and to some degree managing, the feast: she controls the purse strings. Hermeros, one of the guests, gossips about Trimalchio and then points out Diogenes, one of the freedmen in the *triclinium* who like Trimalchio began from nothing and acquired great wealth. Hermeros tells a fascinating history of Proculus another freedman at table, when Trimalchio interrupts to give his *learned* version of the zodiac and astrological signs. Trimalchio leaves the festivities for the toilet and gives his guests a chance to talk among themselves. (37–41)

Seleucus, another freedman at the table, takes up the conversation. Like the other freedmen he has a predictable point of view but relates an interesting story. The reader discovers here a principle behind Petronius' method of narrative-construction: Trimalchio monopolizes the table conversation for a time with pre-arranged set-pieces designed to show off his learning (usually the opposite is achieved); just as his speech begins to bore the guests (or the reader), one of the freedmen launches into an engaging story of some kind. The conversation of Seleucus is too much concerned with the dead, and Phileros breaks in to note that Chrysanthus (the dead man under consideration) lived and died well and that is the best anyone can expect. In his turn Ganymedes brings the conversation down to the price of bread and the lack of rain: he is a lower class *laudator temporis acti*, bemoaning the sad state of ancient religious practices. At ch. 45 Echion the ragmerchant interrupts to argue that life is really pretty good—and there is a three-day gladiatorial show coming. The speech of Echion is a veritable goldmine of material for the linguistic capabilities of freedmen in the first century A.D. (42–46).

---

[15] Dunbabin (1986).

Trimalchio returns at ch. 47 and becomes a wet blanket on the free conversation: he complains that he is constipated. At a cue a huge pig is carried in, and we are witnesses to a scene from New Comedy. Without missing a beat Trimalchio explains (without explaining) why he is the only person to have real Corinthian bronze. All those at the table who know how to get regular invitations to keep their snouts in Trimalchio's trough, applaud his every effort—even if they must hide their smiles in their hands. The wine is beginning to have an effect on Trimalchio who encourages someone/anyone to dance with his wife. While the reader cannot decipher the plan behind the actions of the cast assembled by Trimalchio, he is witness to a kind of surrealistic choreography. Using as an excuse a slave's accidental (on purpose) clumsiness, Trimalchio composes a short poem for the occasion, adds a 16-line effort purportedly by Publilius, and then addresses *philosophical* issues. (47–56)

Beneath the jovial surface of the banquet's events it seems that there has been running a subtext of conflicts between classes. We see a bit of that at ch. 46 where Echion feels compelled to defend himself against the contempt he imagines Agamemnon harbors against people in the lower classes. Ascyltus' repeated laughter at the freedmen finally arouses Hermeros to strike out. His speech is another linguistic jewel, but is interrupted by the delivery of novel foods through openings made in the roof by the removal of ceiling panels. After this excitement Trimalchio gives a cue to a silent freedman, Niceros, to entertain the guests with a story, the first extant interpolated narrative (61.3–63) in the *Satyrica*,[16] the well-known "Werewolf Tale". Not only are the freedmen at Trimalchio's table able to relate interesting events about their past and current lives, they are marvellous raconteurs. Not to be outdone by Niceros, Trimalchio regales the guests with a scary story about witches—similar to stories in Apuleius—and proves he is a better story-teller than poet. (57–64)

The focus of attention at the banquet shifts to the entrance of what appears to be some kind of magistrate with a large retinue. In fact it is only Habinnas, a wealthy mason and minor priest and his wife, Scintilla—friends of the family. The wine has made Trimalchio maudlin and he invites his slaves (*et servi homines sunt* 71.1) to join the feast and take a place at the table (even before this invitation to the

---

[16] Sandy (1970).

slaves there were more guests at the table than there was space for them—assuming three tables and nine places). By ch. 71 Trimalchio is weepy and drunk and reads out his will to all assembled so that all those mentioned will love him now while he is living. Another bath and new dining-room do not sober up the host or guests, and Trimalchio begins to tell his life's history (a nightly monologue?) beginning with his days as a slave in Asia (75.10–77). In order to make his friends love him even more Trimalchio pretends that he is dead and orders that he be covered with a shroud and that the funeral trumpets be blown. The trumpets are so loud that the fire brigade believes them to be signals of a fire, rushes to Trimalchio's house, and breaks down the door. Encolpius, Ascyltus and Giton use it as an opportunity to escape the banquet. (65–78)

Eumolpus Arrives and Stays

As soon as the *Cena* concludes, the old jealousies among Encolpius, Ascyltus and Giton re-emerge, and when Giton chooses Ascyltus for a lover, Encolpius is crushed. [Lacuna] Left to himself Encolpius visits an art gallery and there encounters a white-haired old man named Eumolpus, whose entry into the gallery might profitably be compared with that of Trimalchio into the bath and triclinium. Eumolpus confesses to being a poet, but we will remember him as a great raconteur (79–84). "The Story of the Pergamene Youth" (ch. 85–87) is one of the jewels of Latin literature, an interpolated tale by Eumolpus about 1) how he found a youthful lover, 2) how he won him, 3) how he kept him, 4) how he rid himself of a lover (cf. Ovid). It is a verbally brilliant, magnificently crafted short story. Eumolpus acts as Encolpius' guide through the art gallery and, a propos of nothing, delivers a 65-line poem, *Troiae Halosis* (a topic of interest to Nero), whereupon the patrons of the gallery pelt him with stones. [Lacuna] Encolpius happens to find Giton, whom Ascyltus is treating more like a slave than a lover, and Giton consents to go home with Encolpius. At home Eumolpus is so pleased with the pretty Giton that Encolpius attempts to throw Eumolpus out of the apartment. [Lacuna] Accompanied by a policeman, Ascyltus is making a house by house search for Giton and finally lands in Encolpius' apartment. [Lacuna] Encolpius, Giton, Eumolpus and one slave (at least) board a ship. (85–99)

Travel by Shipwreck

As fate would have it, Eumolpus has booked passage on a ship owned by a man named Lichas who is escorting Tryphaena to Tarentum into exile. Both are enemies of Encolpius and Giton for offenses committed in (lost) Books 11–12. Eumolpus, ignorant of the past, puts all the enemies into one boat: this is a time-tested narratological device. Lichas and Tryphaena both have dreams (topos) that Encolpius and Giton are on board ship. [Lacuna] At ch. 107 the reader becomes witness to a kind of trial in which Eumolpus, the word-merchant, defends the youths (trial scenes are a favorite topos in the ancient novel). A peace treaty with terms laid down for all belligerent parties is drawn up by Eumolpus who goes on to tell the story of the "Widow of Ephesus" in order to divert the crowd. Eumolpus the mediocre poet is the master of short story narrative, and the Widow of Ephesus is a masterpiece: a widow is determined to die in her husband's tomb but is persuaded to live by her love for a good man. The story appears in many forms in Western and Eastern literature and may not be original with Petronius.[17] The crew and passengers are captivated by Eumolpus' story and fail to see the approaching storm in which Lichas is drowned, the ship is wrecked, and our triad is abandoned on the shore. (100–115). [Lacuna]

On the Road to Croton

It seems that our heroes had not necessarily intended to head for Croton, but it is nearby. Learning that the town is full of legacy-hunters, the mediocre poet but marvellous story-teller Eumolpus creates a legend for himself, Encolpius and Giton: Eumolpus will spread the story that he is a childless but wealthy man from Africa who was shipwrecked nearby and is daily awaiting the arrival of bags of money—and his cough indicates poor health (116–118). To make the journey into Croton more enjoyable Eumolpus unleashes a 295-line poem (chs. 119–124.1) entitled the *Bellum Civile*. The poem proves that he is a better prose raconteur than poet; however, the poem may be intended as a parody of Lucan's *Pharsalia*.

Encolpius, operating under the assumed name of Polyaenus (one of many references to the *Odyssey*), is approached by Chrysis, a maid of Circe who claims that Circe is in love with him. Encolpius notes

---

[17] Huber (1990).

that Circe is beauty itself, but their physical union is spoiled by Encolpius' continued impotence. (Perhaps he has been impotent from time to time since early in the *Satyrica*.) Circe is deeply offended and after an exchange of letters in which Encolpius pledges his love, she arranges for a witch named Proselenus to work some charms on him. In the clinch, however, he fails again. [Lacuna] Several rather good poems by Encolpius are interspersed here with his complaints about his offending member. [Lacuna] Proselenus finds Encolpius in her temple and escorts him to the priestess' quarters where she introduces Encolpius to Oenothea, priestess of Priapus. The mood is gloomy because of his impotence but also because he "murders" one of the geese sacred to Priapus who had attacked him. Encolpius finally flees his treatment in the temple, as Oenothea inserts a leather dildo up his rectum. [Lacuna] Chrysis seems to have fallen in love with Encolpius. (124.2–139) [Lacuna]

A legacy-hunter named Philomela arranges to leave her young daughter and son in the charge of Eumolpus, on the pretext that he can teach them things; in reality she prostitutes them for a legacy. The episode has many narrative possibilities but is fragmentary and never rises anywhere near the level of the "Widow of Ephesus". The legacy-hunters of Croton are very unhappy that no ship laden with money has arrived for Eumolpus from Africa. Eumolpus announces that he has made a will, and all those with legacies in it will get their money only if they agree to eat his body after he dies. A man named Gorgias agrees to the terms, and the extant *Satyrica* comes to an end. (140–141)

Manuscripts, Editions and Scholarship on the Satyrica

Like many other ancient works the *Satyrica* has a very messy history which connects the original to the manuscripts extant today. Except for the *Cena*, the *Satyrica* consists of a more or less connected series of short fragments which for the most part probably represents the arrangement prepared by Petronius.[18] The basis for the current sequence of events is Scaliger's manuscript of 1571 (1). The stemma below illustrates just how difficult is the reconstruction of the text.[19]

---

[18] Cf. van Thiel (1971a) 76–78.
[19] This stemma and list of manuscripts are not comprehensive. For more detailed information the reader should consult K. Müller (1961) (1983), Reeve (1983), and Richardson (1993).

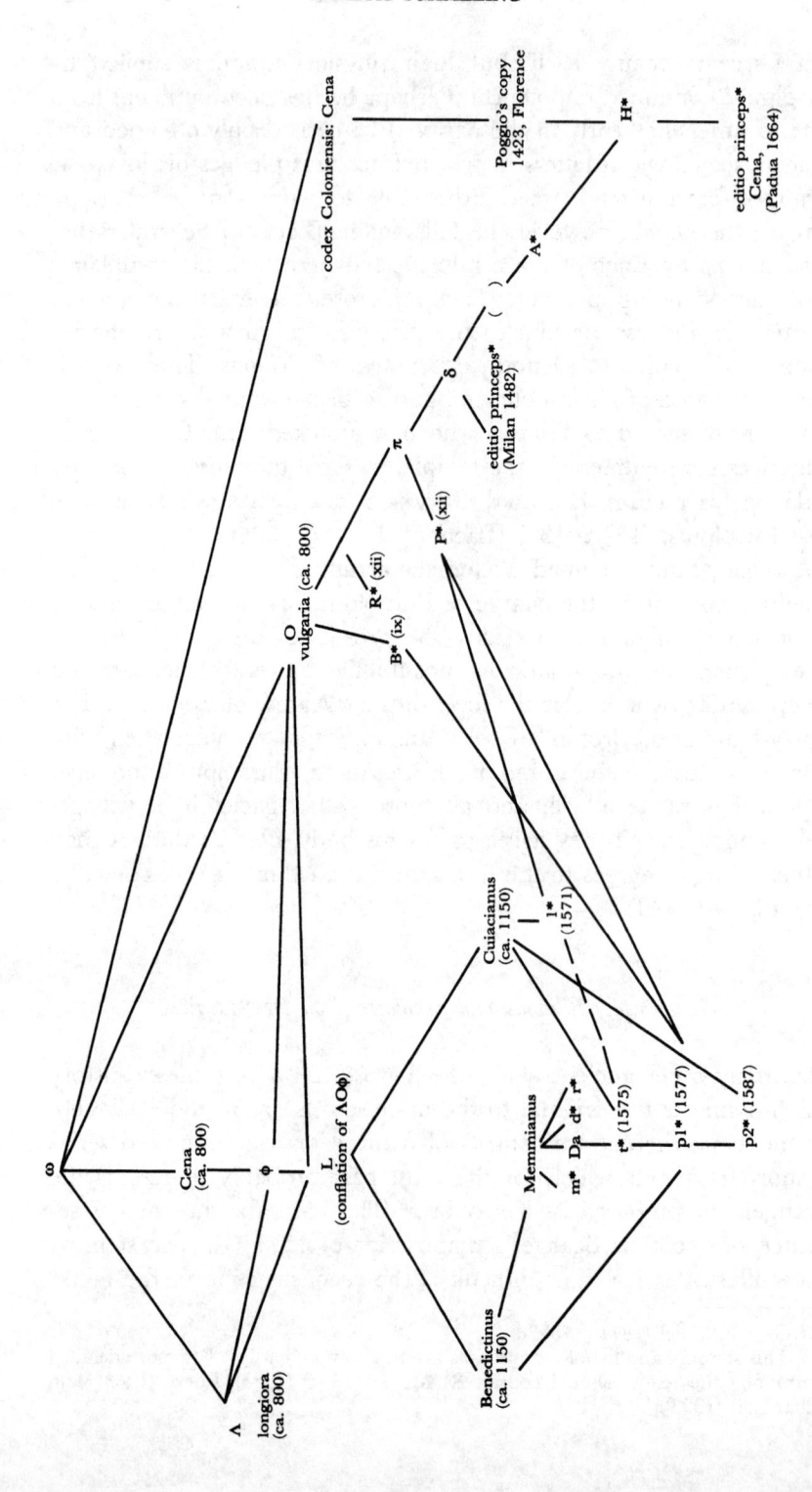

THE *SATYRICA* OF PETRONIUS

Key to the stemma (all items in the stemma marked with asterisks are still extant):

B	Bern, Bernensis 357 together with Leiden, Vossianus lat.Q.30, ninth century.
R	Paris, Parisinus lat.6842D, twelfth century.
P	Paris, Parisinus lat.8049, twelfth century.
π	lost manuscript of twelfth century.
δ	lost manuscript of Bucolica Calpurnii et particula Petronii found in England by Poggio in 1420.
A	Paris, Parisinus lat.7989 (Traguriensis), part containing vulgaria of O.
codex Coloniensis	manuscript from Köln, seen by Poggio, containing XV liber Petronii.
Poggio's copy	copy of codex Coloniensis sent to Poggio in 1423.
H	Paris, Parisinus lat.7989 (Traguriensis), part containing the *Cena*, dated 1423, discovered in Trogir in 1650 by Statileo.
ω	archetype of the *Satyrica*, consensus of Λ, O, *Cena*.
Λ	hypothesized manuscript, excerpted from ω ca. 800, of the so-called longer sections; source with O of φ and L.
O	hypothesized manuscript, excerpted from ω ca. 800, of the so-called shorter sections; source with Λ of φ and L, and consensus of BRP.
φ	archetype of the florilegia, extracted from Λ, O, *Cena*, dated to ca. 1100.
L	hypothesized manuscript representing conflation of Λ, O, φ; parent of lost manuscripts Benedictinus and Cuiacianus.
Benedictinus	lost manuscript from ca. 1150, descendant of L, ancestor of Memmianus, employed by Pithou.
Cuiacianus	lost manuscript from ca. 1150, descendant of L, employed by de Tournes and Pithou.
Memmianus	lost manuscript, copied from Benedictinus, antecedent of d, m, r, Da.
m	Vat.Lat.11428, ca. 1565.
d	Bern, Bong.IV.665, ca. 1564.
r	London, Lambethanus 693, 1570.
Da	Dalecampianus, lost manuscript of sixteenth century, copied from Memmianus, used by de Tournes.
l	Leiden, Scaligeranus 61, ca. 1571.
t	printed edition of de Tournes, Lyon 1575.
p[1]	first printed edition of Pithou, Paris 1577.
p[2]	second printed edition of Pithou, Paris 1587.

In this stemma I have done some violence to the manuscript history of the *Cena*: the *Cena* is entered twice in the scheme only so that I could illustrate the stemma in one drawing. How the *Cena* could come between ω and φ, and thus be excerpted, and still remain intact in another tradition, would make an interesting story to report, if we knew it.

It appears that the ancient world did not bequeath much of the *Satyrica* to the Middle Ages, and what it did pass on seems to be from the later parts of the novel. It is conjectured that by ca. 800, the archetype (ω) of the *Satyrica* had been excerpted in various ways and survived in only four forms. Why each of the four forms was copied so selectively is unknown: the form of Λ is in the most part narrative and contains the racy bits of the novel; at times Λ seems to be little more than a collection of unrelated fragments. O presents shorter pieces of the *Satyrica* but these are better connected and contain materials in dialogue and poetry; the *Cena Trimalchionis* (26.1–78), MS H, representing about a third of the extant *Satyrica*, survives in its entirety; florilegia.

ΛOHφ were conflated into an hypothesized MS known as L, which can be proved from its two lost descendants Cuiacianus and Benedictinus. When the editio princeps was published about 1482 in Milan, however, its editor seems to have known only the shorter excerpts of O, and the resultant first edition represented less than one-third of our extant text. Within 100 years the editors, Scaliger, de Tournes and Pithou, using now lost MSS of L together with MSS of O had doubled the size of the *Satyrica*. Because these editors made use of a printed text which they then enlarged and corrected from MSS lost and/or unnamed, they produced, as it were, a new conflation which remains an enigma to modern scholars.

The last third of the text appeared in print in 1664 in Padua. The story behind this edition reads like a mystery novel. It begins in 1423 with a letter of Poggio in Rome to Niccoli: *allatus est mihi ex Colonia XV liber Petronii Arbitri, quem curavi transcribendum modo, cum illac iter feci.* Poggio's copy of the codex Coloniensis has been lost and is without descendants except for the Traguriensis, now Parisinus lat.7989 (H), which apparently was made in Florence and transported to Trogir in Dalmatia. The date of H seems to be late 1423, and the date of Poggio's letter, 28 May 1423, connects Poggio's lost copy to H. For some years the *Cena* (H) was held to be a forgery; in 1669 was printed the first edition to contain everything we have in our extant text.

The oldest MS of the *Satyrica* is B, written at Auxerre in the ninth century. It is interesting to speculate with Reeve that the post-ancient history of the *Satyrica* might have begun at Auxerre or at Fleury, because a reference to the *Satyrica* in one of its MSS might indicate that it possessed a much larger *Satyrica* than the one we have. It would add to the romance of the novel if John of Salisbury (twelfth century) made a copy (excerpted or not) of one of the MSS of the *Satyrica* at Fleury and took it with him to England, where use is later made of it in the *Canterbury Tales*.

Though many editions of the *Satyrica* are important for various reasons, I would like to mention just a few. The variorum edition of P. Burmann (1709)[20] is a treasure of comparative learning, but the first consistently scientific approach to the *Satyrica* is found in F. Bücheler's 1862 editio maior.[21] The pride of place, however, among Petronius editors must go to K. Müller, whose four editions (1961, 1964, 1973, 1983) have set a very high standard.[22] These magisterial studies have produced both a text and an analysis of the manuscript tradition which are accepted by scholars of all countries. If I have any objections to Müller's editions, one is that his later apparatuses are too brief (I trust his judgment to identify those MSS which are copies of MSS which are still extant) and another is that many items he had bracketed as interpolations in 1961 have been restored to the text: the resultant text, it seems to me, is more uneven than necessary. Whether there was one Carolingian interpolator, as Fraenkel suggested and Müller believed at first,[23] Sullivan's systematic exposition of interpolations in the *Satyrica* has not been seriously shaken.[24]

For one reason or another Petronian studies have attracted more than their share of eccentrics. In 1693, shortly after the discovery and publication of the *Cena* MS, a Frenchman named Nodot published what he said was a more complete MS of the *Satyrica*; this was followed in 1800 by the publication of a hitherto unknown small piece of the *Satyrica* found by the Spaniard Marchena and which filled in a lacuna in ch. 26. Both Nodot and Marchena were forgers.[25] The fragmentary nature of the *Satyrica* seems to attract special notice.

---

[20] Burmann (1709).
[21] Bücheler (1862).
[22] K. Müller (1961) (1983).
[23] K. Müller (1961) XXXVIIff.
[24] Sullivan (1976).
[25] Stolz (1987).

Though there is no commentary on the whole *Satyrica*, commentaries do exist for the *Cena* and I cite the research efforts of Friedländer, Maiuri, and Smith.[26] Our computer age has, however, produced a most useful concordance in which the Latin context is given for each word cited.[27] The ever increasing number of published materials on the *Satyrica* is reported annually in the *Petronian Society Newsletter*,[28] and there exists a bibliography covering the years through 1975.[29] There are translations of the *Satyrica* into most modern languages, from Bulgarian to Welsh, but I cite only those of Sullivan (English), Heinse (German), Marzullo/Bonaria (Italian), Grimal (French).[30]

The Language of the Satyrica

Not only does Petronius tell an engaging story, he is a master of the Latin prose in which it is told. Even those who object to the infrequently obscene content of *Satyrica* admit that the Latin style of Petronius ranks him high on the list of ancient authors.[31] A great virtue of Petronius, it seems to me, is his ability to say everything simply, which makes his language appear healthy and in touch with the living, spoken language. The *Satyrica* is marked by casual simplicity or off-hand stylishness which we envy because it appears to cost nothing to achieve. Though this simplicity is, I believe, the end product both of *labor limae* and *ingenium*, it is imbued with such confidence and maturity that it embraces the reader as naturally and perfectly as erotic rapture or coming to terms with mortality. Whatever Petronius *intends* for the *Satyricon* (if anything) or *means* for his reader to see (if anything), he is in complete control of its language: the coercive strength of his rhetoric encourages the adventurous reader to carry through to the end, even if some of the subject material might be disturbing.

As the *Satyrica* violates most rules of the doctrine of ancient literary decorum ("... it exhibits no rigid unity to tone, no stylistic pu-

---

[26] Friedländer (1906), Maiuri (1945), Smith (1975).
[27] Korn (1986).
[28] Schmeling (1970-present).
[29] Schmeling (1977).
[30] Sullivan (1986), Heinse (1773), Marzullo (1962), Grimal (1958).
[31] Council of Trent 1545-1563; cf. J. Mansi, ed. (1902) *Sacrorum Conciliorum Nova et Amplissima Collectio* 33.230. Paris.

rity and simplicity, no concentration on a single emotion, and probably not on a single plot or theme . . .),[32] we are not surprised that it breaks the rule of the decorum of language and presents freedmen sounding like real freedmen. The freedmen's speeches in the *Cena* offer us a rare glimpse of the vulgar Latin excluded from the classical canon: freedmen in the *Cena* can utter (46.1) *qui potes loquere, non loquis*, (42.5) *malus fatus*, and construe (45.7) *delecto* as a deponent verb (example of hyperurbanism), but the uneducated slave in Apuleius' *Metamorphoses* (3.27) plays *by* the rules of decorum and *on* the famous opening line in Cicero's *Catiline* 1, *quo usque tandem*. We could call the level of speech of the freedmen *sermo plebeius* to differentiate it from the lofty style of the speech of rhetoricians *sermo grandis* (*Sat*.2.6, 4.3), and the "careful and rhythmical style which is the chief narrative medium, a kind of artistic *sermo urbanus*"[33] (111–112). To illustrate Petronius' *sermo urbanus* I have chosen a passage (116.4–9) from late in the story which shows the power of language to manipulate the narrative.[34] The numbers in parentheses are used merely to divide the seven sentences in the paragraph.

> (1) "o mi" inquit "hospites, si negotiatores estis, mutate propositum aliudque vitae praesidium quaerite. (2) sin autem urbanioris notae homines sustinetis semper mentiri, recta ad lucrum curritis. (3) in hac enim urbe non litterarum studia celebrantur, non eloquentia locum habet, non frugalitas sanctique mores laudibus ad fructum perveniunt, sed quoscumque homines in hac urbe videritis, scitote in duas partes esse divisos. (4) nam aut captantur aut captant. (5) in hac urbe nemo liberos tollit, quia quisquis suos heredes habet, non ad cenas, non ad spectacula admittitur, sed omnibus prohibetur commodis, inter ignominiosos latitat. (6) qui vero nec uxorem umquam duxerunt nec proximas neccesitudines habent, ad summos honores perveniunt, id est soli militares, soli fortissimi atque etiam innocentes habentur. (7) adibitis" inquit "oppidum tamquam in pestilentia campos, in quibus nihil aliud est nisi cadavera, quae lacerantur aut corvi qui lacerant.

The above speech of the *vilicus* is not intended to provide accurate information about Croton or about the level of Latin spoken by overseers in Bruttium. Rather Petronius is setting the stage with the speech for the comedy to follow (117.2 *utinam quidem sufficeret largior scaena*). We should probably read 116.4–7 as the dramatist's prologue to his

---

[32] Zeitlin (1971) 635.
[33] Sullivan (1968) 164. Cf. also Horsfall (1989).
[34] Petersmann (1977), Sullivan (1968), George (1966).

work: the speech conforms to the setting in which it appears. The *vilicus* has become either the announcer of the play or the orator laying down the outline for a *controversia*,

> a pestilence has fallen on Croton, and there are dead bodies everywhere because many people indulge in the evil practice of *captatio*. In order to survive, however, newcomers to Croton with no money must become *captatores*. Is it a serious sin then to pretend to be rich and to let greedy *captatores* give you gifts?

which the performers will then act out. Whatever Encolpius' part is in the hoax perpetrated at Croton, when he comes to record the events from memory, he surely reshapes his deeds as one of the actors and reframes reality to make it appear more impressive and to metamorphose it into the literary genre of comedy. Legacy-hunters turn out to be no match for Eumolpus who confuses them and disguises reality in the best tradition of artists, poets and storytellers.

"*o mi hospites*," the first words out of the mouth of the *vilicus*, whom our triad of heroes has just met on the road to Croton, ring false: the implied relationship of whatever kind does not exist. At best the *vilicus* and Encolpius should be wary of each other's presence and actions on the country road. Petronius, however, has no desire here to describe for his reader what really happens when three recently shipwrecked males meet a *vilicus* on the road to Croton—any more than Apuleius in *The Golden Ass* 1 wishes to describe how travellers greet each other on Greek roads: both wish to entertain through story-telling. As Beck points out, however, it is not only the content of the account of the story of the *vilicus* which strikes the reader as implausible but the language and literary style in which it is delivered.[35] As we can see from the *Cena* (e.g., the speech of Echion at 45ff.), Petronius is a master of capturing the vulgar level of Latin spoken by slaves, freedmen *vilici*, and those with little formal education. The language of this *vilicus*, however, rivals in quality the best Latin prose: Eumolpus in telling the Widow of Ephesus story does not rise above the *vilicus* who comments on Croton. But in all of this we must remember the sage advice of von Albrecht that even the conversations of freedmen in vulgar Latin are shaped by a skillful author: the wheat for the *Satyrica* has been carefully winnowed so that the results which we read are in fact the product of a careful,

---

[35] Beck (1973) 46.

artistic arrangement of form imposed on a content of grain and varying amounts of chaff.[36] For a linguistic analysis of first century A.D. vulgar Latin we are on much safer ground with *Wandinschriften* from Pompeii. The charm of this passage (116.4–9) lies in its swift and nimble language and in its apparent simplicity: the reader grasps it at first reading; the narrative is lucid and flowing—even if the argumentation is at times ambiguous. Encolpius, our narrator, assumes so completely the role of the *vilicus* who tells our heroic triad about Croton that the reader might forget that the passage is a re-telling of an earlier narrative: the nature of the re-told narrative is captured very simply by opening the first and last sentences (1 and 7) with *inquit* and framing the speech. One reason for the freshness of style is that Petronius is a master at varying the particles (and means) with which he begins sentences: (2) *sin autem*, (3) *enim*, (4) *nam*, (5) preposition, (6) *vero*. Comments about the people of Croton in third person verbs are mixed with imperative forms addressed to the listeners, and the combination gives the narrative a kind of intimacy. The middle sentence (4) of the speech contains only five words and is the core of the presentation: *nam aut captantur aut captant*. Sentences 3 and 5 surround 4 with an interestingly arranged example of anaphora: (3) *in hac enim urbe*... *in hac urbe*... (5) *in hac urbe*. With some regularity the actors in the *Satyrica* meet individuals who act as interpreters and explain the current situation: the *vilicus* functions here as such an *interpres* and just like all the others is unreliable.[37] The people of Croton are not *in duas partes divisos* but *in tres* at least: people rich enough to leave legacies, legacy-hunters, and Eumolpus who as actor/director of this unfolding mime hoodwinks all parties and preys upon both the good and the bad.

The prose rhythms of Petronius are never chance affairs, as Müller has shown:[38] sentences 1 and 2 show ⏑‐ ⏑⏑ and ‐‐ ⏑⏑, in which the last word is a mirror image of the preceding one, while sentences 3 and 5 show a reduplicated clausula, ⏑‐‐ ⏑‐‐, ⏑‐ ⏑⏑; sentences 4, 6, and 7 are favorites: ⏑‐‐, ⏑‐ ⏑ ⏑, ‐‐⏑⏑. Not only is there a rhythm or pace to the narrative, there is the rhythm of Petronius' favorite cretics and trochaics. Each of the seven sentences of the speech ends with a verb; sentence 1 ends in chiasmus and 4

---

[36] von Albrecht (1989) 125–135.
[37] Schmeling (1994c).
[38] K. Müller (1983) 449–470.

in a play on voices active and passive, *captantur... captant*, which play is repeated in the last (7) sentence, *quae lacerantur... qui lacerant*. Because of its somewhat asyndetic character the narrative gains vigor;[39] *et* does not make an appearance, and *-que* occurs only twice.[40] Negatives (*non* [5 times], *nemo* [once], *nec* [twice] *nihil* [once], *nisi* [once]) imbue the text with an almost legalistic flavor, while at the same time plays on words and sounds disconfirm this with a ludic atmosphere (sentences 2–3): *ad lucrum... non... locum... non... ad fructum*; negatives used in anaphora (5) *non ad... non ad*; or negatives in play (6) *nec... necessitudines*. One of the most subtle negative sentences in the *Satyrica* contains no negative word and at first reading may appear positive: the *vilicus* offers one ray of hope to those travelling to Croton (sentence 2), *sin autem urbanioris notae homines sustinetis semper mentiri, recta ad lucrum curritis*. Only men with a clear stamp of breeding (cf. 132.12) have the necessary fortitude to lie at all times. The humor rests on *semper*,[41] which turns a positive quality negative, and on *sustinetis* which even in a positive context usually connotes an unfavorable sense.[42]

The speech of the *vilicus* concludes (fragmentary) with the note that Croton is full of *cadavera*, a word which will assume importance later: the theme in the prologue is developed afterwards in the comedy. At 134.1 Proselenos who is attempting to cure Encolpius of impotence asks him if he happened to step on a *cadaver* at the crossroad. The reader's mind immediately retreats to the speech by the *vilicus* who describes Croton as a place *in quibus nihil aliud est nisi cadavera*. How can Encolpius *not* step on a *cadaver*? And in the final chapter (141.2) of the extant *Satyrica* Eumolpus announces that those cited for receiving legacies in his *testamentum* must eat his dead body (*corpus* = *cadaver*) in order to get their hands on the cash. The speech of the *vilicus* is thus woven tightly into the fabric of the plot.

As Encolpius comments about the sad state of education, rhetoric, and literature in the opening chapters of the *Satyrica*, and Eumolpus at 83.8ff. on the accumulation of money as the chief virtue in life

---

[39] Beck (1973) 45–46; Baldwin (1992) 6–7.

[40] In the freedmen's speeches in the *Cena* it seems that *-que* is used only once, at 64.7 by Trimalchio to describe his dog as *praesidium domus familiaeque*. This, however, may not be a direct quotation but Trimalchio's expression redone into Encolpius' *sermo urbanus*; or it may be some kind of proverb picked up by Trimalchio and not part of his speech pattern.

[41] Stöcker (1969) 100.

[42] *OLD ad loc.*, 6.

(*amor ingenii neminem umquam divitem fecit*), so the *vilicus* runs through the litany of evils besetting Croton, all of which had been for some years, and continued to be, subjects of discussion among writers: (sentence 3) literature is ignored, decay of rhetoric is complete, *frugalitas sanctique mores* win no plaudits; (4) city is full of *captatores*; (5) *nemo liberos tollit*;[43] (6) *nec uxorem umquam duxerunt*. This litany adds a rich literary texture to the *Satyrica* by connecting it firmly to motifs employed by Greek and Roman satirists and historians. (The shipwreck which precedes ch. 116 and the entry of our triad into Croton are a re-created mosaic from the *tesserae* of Virgil's *Aeneid* 1, in which Aeneas suffers from the winds and waves and then enters Carthage.)[44] The evil in which Croton excels and about which the *vilicus* waxes eloquent is *captatio* (with its attendant malignancies of *nemo liberos tollit . . . nec uxorem umquam duxerunt*), a vice central to the outcries of many ancients: Horace, *Serm*.2.5, *Ep*.1.1.77–79; Martial 6.63; Juvenal 12.93–130; Pliny, *Ep*.2.20; 4.2; 9.30; Seneca, *Ep*.95.43; *de Ben*.1.14.3,4.20.3;[45] Tacitus, *Ann*.3.25; Lucian, *Dial.Mort*. (Macleod) 15–19.

Relation of the Satyrica to Other Ancient Novels

It is of course an anachronism to refer to the *Satyrica* and the other ancient works of extended narrative prose fiction as novels. The label, however, has been used for some years by classicists, now even by scholars in modern languages, and seems to have stuck to its object.[46] The *Satyrica* of Petronius is certainly the best known in our day of the novels from antiquity: it probably appeared as vibrant, entertaining, and responsive to the interests of the ancients even as it does to us. Though the *Satyrica* is in some ways radically different from the other Greek and Latin novels, it retains enough similarities to be subsumed with them under the generic title of novel.[47] Macrobius (*Comm. in Somnium Scipionis* 1.2.8) links Petronius to Apuleius and calls

---

[43] The *vilicus* again proves to be an unreliable *interpres*. Philomela in ch. 140 has two children and uses them as bisexual tools of *captatio*. She takes *captatio* to extremes.

[44] Walsh (1970) 37–38.

[45] The language of Petronius is very close to Seneca's here (a parody?): *ut aves, quae laceratione corporum aluntur . . . circa cadavera volat*. I owe this reference to John Bodel.

[46] Frye (1976), followed by Reardon (1991), makes a strong case for reading ancient Greek novels as "romances". Heiserman (1977) cleverly blurs distinctions by calling ancient fiction novels before there were novels.

[47] Schmeling (1971a) 49–53; Konstan (1994) 113–125; Reardon (1991) 42ff.

their work *argumenta*[48]—I assume that he is referring to the *Satyrica* and the *Metamorphoses*. In the opening chapter of the first book of his novel Apuleius in his address to the reader twice refers to his creation as a *fabula: at ego tibi sermone isto Milesio varias fabulas conseram . . . fabulam Graecanicam incipimus. lector intende: laetaberis*. Apuleius' use of the adjective Milesian and his close ties to the *Satyrica* have encouraged scholars to find in Petronius examples of Milesian Tales (e.g., Widow of Ephesus tale, chs. 111-112). And from Milesian Tales these two novels are then connected with the Greek novellae of much earlier literature.[49] Classical scholars seem unwilling even to entertain the theory that it is Petronius who helped to give birth to a new genre, since the natural classical prejudice supports the idea that the Greeks created everything. Parsons states it succinctly: "Natural reason long ago revealed that Petronius had a Greek model."[50] While Petronius surely borrows ingredients for his new work from earlier Greek writers, it is probably more valid to suggest that Petronius creates the ancient novel and that the earliest classical vehicle is Latin, than to suggest *aut ex nihilo aut e comparatione iniqua* that natural reason tells us it is a Greek invention. In any case Macrobius' linking of Petronius and Apuleius has proved most elucidative, and the two novelists are regularly lumped together and studied as a duo.

Even in its fragmentary state we recognize that the *Satyrica* is episodic, and it seems possible that Petronius delivered it orally in a serial fashion to Nero's literary coterie,[51] all of which could account for the great length of the original novel which Sullivan feels it had.[52] The *Satyrica*, however, is not merely a collection of episodes or tales, whether Milesian or of some other kind, sewn together without motivations, causes, effects or unifying characters. Nor do the *Cena*, episodes at rhetorical schools, adventures at Croton belong to the subgenre of Milesian tales.[53] If the *Satyrica* must have an ancestor, Sullivan suggests that we look to the *Odyssey*, the ancestor of all *Reiseromanen*.[54]

---

[48] There is no technical term in antiquity for the novel. On the apparent lack of interest in defining the novel, cf. Reardon (1991) 3-14.
[49] Trenkner (1958); Müller (1980).
[50] Parsons (1971) 66; Schmeling (1996a).
[51] If the first audience of the *Satyrica* was in fact spectators at a presentation, we might wish to reconsider our generic terminology for the work; cf. Schmeling (1994c).
[52] Sullivan (1968) 36.
[53] On Milesian tales cf. Trenkner (1958) 168ff., Perry (1967) 92ff., Walsh (1970) 10ff., Müller (1980).
[54] Sullivan (1968) 96; theory first put forward by Klebs (1889).

Is there a relationship between the *Satyrica* and the other ancient novels? Each is a work of extended narrative prose fiction, but do they depend on each other (as Xenophon of Ephesus depends on Chariton, e.g.)? or do most of them borrow from a common source? or in the case of Petronius, does he feed off the so-called ideal Greek novel, making of the *Satyrica* a long parody?[55] Whether the *Satyrica* is a novel or not or related to the Greek novel, is it a parody of the Greek novel—or perhaps a prose parody of the *Odyssey*? If the whole is not a parody, then perhaps at least parts parody earlier or contemporary writers like Plato, Virgil, Seneca and Lucan.[56] The advantage for the critic in labeling the *Satyrica* a parody is that he is spared the shame of improperly identifying what it really is. A review of some of the constituent parts, or ingredients, or influences (or parodies), which scholars have found in (or read into) the *Satyrica*, shows something like the following: the *Odyssey* (Priapus hounds Encolpius as Poseidon dogged Odysseus); Milesian Tales and *Sybaritici libelli*; novellae e.g. a *Priapea*; a burlesque periplous or *Reiseroman* tempered by the literature surrounding utopias or sentimental epics like the *Argonautica*; symposium literature; mimes and theatrical productions; earlier examples of the novel; Menippean satire; earlier Roman satire; works like Seneca's *Apocolocyntosis*. Once the ingredients have been identified, then the critic needs to discover only the correct recipe, or in literary terms, the correct synthesis. For Rohde the magic synthesis of the *Satyrica* is one of erotic poetry and travel stories, which, though it results in a kind of novel, is unrelated to the Greek novel; for Walsh the *Satyrica* is a "synthesis of Greek fiction with Roman satire and mimic motifs."[57]

The rich literary texture of the *Satyrica* ensures that it shares numerous elements with many other ancient works including novels: a wandering hero, an angry deity, sea-storms and shipwrecks, threats of suicide, motifs like *Scheintod* and love-at-first-sight, legal/court proceedings, rhetorical outbursts, pathetic monologues, interpolated tales.

---

[55] Heinze (1899).
[56] Sullivan (1968) 186–213; 67; 168–169. On the literary feud between Petronius and Seneca and Lucan cf. Sullivan (1968a). Cameron (1969) notes Petronian borrowings from Plato. Bodel (1994) gathers together many kinds of parodies or travesties in the *Satyrica*, as he demonstrates how Petronius fashioned Trimalchio's *Cena* as a funeral and his house as the underworld. It is a proper antidote to Arrowsmith's view of the *Satyrica* as a moral work; Arrowsmith (1966). Panayotakis (1995) makes a strong case that Petronius is influenced by the theater.
[57] Rohde (1914) 248; Walsh (1970) 7.

With Apuleius' *Metamorphoses* only, the *Satyrica* shares two important features: no (apparent) attempt at unity or desire to present his work as a "coherent whole",[58] and a cynical, often unedifying, tone which undercuts the ideal. Though the *Satyrica* shares many characteristics with the other ancient novels, I would apply Sandy's observation about the *Metamorphoses*' relationship with the other novels to the *Satyrica's*: "more often than not the supposed parallels turn out to be part of the common stock of classical Greek and Latin literature rather than *distinctive* features of the prose fiction of classical antiquity."[59] Sandy likens the *Metamorphoses* to the Greek novels in at least seven areas and concludes that they run parallel courses rather than that they are influenced by each other. The *Satyrica* and the *Metamorphoses* are related to each other and to the Greek novel by virtue of their umbrella genre, not their influence on each other or any kind of *contaminatio*. Just as the modern novel occupies a wide literary spectrum, so the ancient novel.[60] By genre Petronius, Apuleius and Chariton are related. But when Petronius borrows and adopts scenes and language, or parodies, mocks, or misapplies for humorous (?) effect, he looks to the major writers inside the traditional canon: lines borrowed from a touching scene in *Aeneid* 6 are used to describe Encolpius' limp member, to amuse the reader, and to give a new twist to intertextuality. There could be no parody of "popular" literature by Petronius:[61] "It is Petronius' practice to incorporate into the texture of his work the 'standard' authors and the conspicuous men of letters belonging to Nero's court: Homer, Virgil, Ovid, Seneca, Lucan. A Chariton or Xenophon would be out of place in this illustrious company."[62]

---

[58] Sandy (1994a) 1529.
[59] Sandy (1994a) 1517.
[60] Schmeling (1996b).
[61] Winkler (1980a) 155: "The great silence of the ancient world which hampers research into mystery cults is also a barrier in the area of popular entertainment. For contrary reasons, both mysteries and popular literature are not well known to us in anything like the extent of their actual existence. The silence of serious reverence enshrined the one, the silence of critical disdain dismissed the other."
[62] Sandy (1994a) 1544; cf. also Mayer (1982) 316: "If we are correct in identifying Neronian literature as a new and self-conscious imitation of the forms and standards of Augustan literature, then it is appropriate to read Neronian texts generally in this light.... Eumolpus quotes Horace (*odi profanum vulgus et arceo*), and requires a knowledge of his poetry ... By praising Horace, Eumolpus shows himself to be in the vanguard of current taste." For an intelligent approach to placing Petronius and the Roman novel into the larger mosaic of Latin literature, cf. von Albrecht (1992) 955–981.

Forms in Search of a Genre

There is more than a little disagreement about the genre designation of the *Satyrica*.[63] Often critics claim that it is unique in classical literature and thus, I assume, that for them it has its own genre and that they are spared the need to find a home for it. The *Satyrica* is a work of extended narrative prose fiction, which in today's tolerant classification system we would simply call a "novel", but then quibble for hours about how we define "fiction".[64] Petronius employs a first-person narrator in an episodic structure often obscured by the fragmentary state of the extant work. E.M. Forster offers a definition of the novel better than most—and it seems to fit the *Satyrica*.

> [T]he novel is a formidable mass, and it is so amorphous—no mountain to climb.... It is most distinctly one of the moister areas of literature— irrigated by a hundred rills and occasionally degenerating into a swamp. I do not wonder that the poets despise it, though they sometimes find themselves in it by accident.[65] And I am not surprised at the annoyance of the historians when by accident it finds itself among them.[66] Perhaps we ought to define what a novel is.... This will not take a second... [it is] a fiction in prose of a certain extent.[67]

The "outer form" of the *Satyrica* is usually described as (choose one) a Menippean satire, an epic in prose, theater in prose, a novel (including an extended prose parody of the Greek novel, or a pornographic novel, or a kind of picaresque novel), prose satire; the "inner form"[68] is (choose one) a satire of some kind, a sympathetic portrayal of reality, parody, entertainment, all of which strike a respondent chord in the modern reader who feels some affinity to the concerns of the actors in the work. Since the term novel is so elastic, there should be little disagreement in applying it to the outer form of the *Satyrica*. About the inner form there is almost no agreement. My own

---

[63] Schmeling (1971a) 49–53, (1996a).

[64] M. Abrams, *A Glossary of Literary Terms* (New York 1971³) 110: "The term novel is now applied to a great variety of writings that have in common only the attribute of being extended works of prose *fiction*."

[65] Modern critics often comment that the *Satyrica* is a prosimetric work, prose with verse, as if the addition of verses rendered the prose some other genre.

[66] Forster would be amused to observe the self-doubt of modern historians who now realize that their "scientific" histories are a kind of literary work with much in common with fiction; cf. H. White, *Metahistory* (Baltimore 1973) and *The Content of the Form* (Baltimore 1987); cf. Gill (1993).

[67] E.M. Forster, *Aspects of the Novel* (London 1974 [1927]) 2.

[68] The terms come from Wellek (1956).

preference is to respect the old link between the *Satyrica* and the *Metamorphoses*, to focus also on the fact that both have first-person narrators, and then to read the inner form of the *Satyrica* as a confession which has the effect of entertaining the reader.[69] Like Sandy and Beck I would remove the traditional label of classical satire from the *Satyrica*; like Zeitlin[70] I would read the work as a clash in understanding/misunderstanding reality. One approach I have in common with these three scholars plus Sullivan[71] is that I doubt Encolpius knows at all times what is real, that his imagination frequently runs wild and that he has only a superficial appreciation of the situation around him.[72] I stress this point because one of the most common appreciative adjectives bestowed on the *Satyrica* is that it is "realistic", in fact, one of the most realistic works of ancient literature, and that it can be used as a primary historical source to provide us with a picture of life in the first century A.D.[73] Any *Realien*, however, coming to us from the ancient world in this novel must arrive via Encolpius, who arranges facts the same way a plastic surgeon arranges silicon.

The most common classification of the outer form of the *Satyrica* is Menippean satire: Frye, Sullivan, Walsh, Courtney, and many others have so termed it. They all, however, do not mean the same thing by Menippean satire and do not see the same inner form in the *Satyrica*. Frye, for example, sees Petronius as a disciple of Varro as a disciple of Menippus, and reads the *Satyrica* as satirical: "[it] deals less with people as such than with mental attitudes ... and differs from the novel in its characterization, which is stylized rather than naturalistic."[74] Sullivan and Walsh are not dogmatic about the term Menippean satire, and feel comfortable also classifying the *Satyrica* as a novel—with some satire, parody and heavy doses of mime: Petronius writes *in the form of* Menippean satire (he does not write Menippean satire) which indicates literary conservatism exploiting the prosimetric

---

[69] Schmeling (1994b) and (1994c).

[70] Sandy (1969) 295, offers the best definition of satire in the *Satyrica*: "... a principal object of Petronius' satire is artificiality and self-delusion which intervene between individuals and reality." Beck (1973) and (1975), questions the narrator's unwillingness to report what really happened, and Zeitlin (1971), carefully chronicles the narrative of Encolpius as the expression of one youth's (in)ability to make sense of the real world.

[71] Sullivan (1968) 119.

[72] Schmeling (1994b).

[73] D'Arms (1981) 97–120.

[74] Frye (1957) 309. On the genre of the ancient novel see Müller (1981), Holzberg (1986), Kuch (1989a).

(mixture of prose and poetry) sub-genre.[75] Courtney reads the inner form as a parody of the novel.[76] But the most recent Teubner editor of Varro's *Saturae Menippeae*[77] finds no connection between Menippean satire and the *Satyrica* save "the use of prosimetrum".[78] The moralizing of Menippean satire, once found in so many places in the *Satyrica*, seems on closer examination not to be there.

It is difficult to find another classical work with a richer or more widely diversified literary texture. Even in the small portion of the *Satyrica* extant today, the number and variety of intertextual usages boggle the mind.[79] Do all of these intertextual references signal parody? We are admonished to remember that "to parody everything is to parody nothing". Perhaps Petronius is assembling the ultimate mosaic—*tesserae* borrowed from every kind of literary work, the composite equaling the sum of all forces attacking the reader's senses. Dear to the heart of most classicists is the search for allusions. Perhaps for the *Satyrica* this inquiry ought to be turned on its head, and a search conducted to ascertain if there is any kind of literary work from which Petronius does not borrow, to which he does not allude, or which he does not treat in some fashion. A review of the list of works/genres avoided by Petronius might be most elucidative.

Is the *Satyrica* to any great extent a satire? Occasional satire is hard not to write. A satire must, it seems to me, have at least two attributes: a position (moral, ethical, philosophical) from which it speaks in a relatively consistent manner; an object (person, belief, etc.) which the satire can attack. On both counts the *Satyrica* is found wanting. As I said many years ago, "If the *Satyricon* is to be called . . . satire, it must be a satire of such loose definition as to be almost meaningless. If Petronius must have a *Weltanschauung*, it might be the negative approach *nil* admirari."[80]

While the *Satyrica is* generally subsumed under the generic listing "satire" and grouped with the satirists, it is the modern poet and critic T.S. Eliot who seems to me to be responsible for the most recent attempt to make Petronius a card-carrying satirist. As the epigraph to *The Waste Land* (1922) Eliot uses a quotation from *Satyrica*

---

[75] Sullivan (1968) 90–91, 100; Walsh (1970) 19ff.
[76] Courtney (1962) 86, followed by Heiserman (1977) 58.
[77] Astbury, R., ed. (1985) *Saturae Menippeae*. Leipzig.
[78] Astbury (1977) 30.
[79] Collignon (1892).
[80] Schmeling (1971a) 50.

48 (*nam Sibyllam . . .*), and Eliot's image of the modern world is transferred back in time to Petronius and transformed into his view of Nero's waste land.[81] Bacon and Arrowsmith[82] were convinced by Eliot and along with Gilbert Highet[83] convinced a generation of scholars to believe "that the *Satyricon* is a fundamentally serious and even moral work."[84] Sullivan was able to stomp out this heresy by the application of common sense: "Of course the chief objection to the theories that Petronius is . . . a . . . moral satirist is the sheer difficulty of reading the work in that way."[85]

My own reading of the inner form of the *Satyrica* convinces me that it is a confession. By understanding the *Satyrica* as a confession, the reader will, I believe, get a relatively unbiased view of the novel. The narrator of the *Satyrica* is the only element of the *Satyrica* which remains unchanging from first to last, and around which we can wrap our genre theory.

The voice of the *Satyrica* is always that of Encolpius, but it is so unreliable, his perception so conditioned by his fantasy world, his statements of facts so regularly contradicted, his contexts so steeped in literature, that we are forced to treat all words out of the mouth of this narrator with caution. At the same time we function at the mercy of Encolpius to obtain all information. From time to time Encolpius relates events in which he states that he did something inappropriate: he accuses, as it were, himself. Then again he reports the speeches of other persons (e.g., 9.8), in which they state what improper deeds he has committed. Because Encolpius is the narrator, it makes no real difference whether he admits something about himself or reports what others say about him: both types of statements rest on the same authority and can be read as confessions of the narrator or as autobiography. In addition to confessing that he has made mistakes, he seems, like the follower of the Syrian goddess in Apuleius' *Metamorphoses* (8.28, see below), to confess to crimes he has not committed.

Each offence to which Encolpius confesses seems to have only a small basis in reality and takes place, as described, only in his imagination. Events in his life have a way of being blown into larger than

---

[81] Schmeling (1975).
[82] Bacon (1958), Arrowsmith (1966).
[83] Highet (1941).
[84] Arrowsmith (1966) 305.
[85] Sullivan (1968) 110.

life scenes and of being interpreted and repackaged into well known literary forms.

At 80.3 Encolpius reports that he is engaged in a heated argument and draws his sword. Of course no one is harmed or even scratched, but in his narrative he describes the quarrel as if it were the epic struggle of brothers at Thebes.

Encolpius' confession at 81.3 (*effugi iudicum, harenae imposui, hospitem occidi*) swells at 130.2 to *proditionem feci, hominem occidi, templum violavi*. He confesses (130.1) *fateor me ... saepe peccasse*. There is apparently no limit to his crimes. More likely, however, Encolpius has a confession-compulsion. With his active imagination which sees all events in his life as episodes from literature worthy of inclusion in literary trappings, Encolpius cannot portray himself as ordinary. If we are to take seriously his confession (130.2), *hominem occidi*, we must also take seriously his offer a few words later to provide a sword to Circe so that she can vent further her anger on him for sexually frustrating her. An examination of the whole confession reveals its theatrical nature.

A few chapters after Encolpius confesses to Circe (130.2), we find him confessing to Priapus (133.2ff.): *positoque in limine genu... non sanguine tristi/perfusus venio, non templis impius hostis/admovi dextram....* According to his confession/prayer to Priapus not only had he not desecrated a temple, he had not killed anyone. There is some similarity here with what Winkler called a "hypocritical confession" of a follower of the Syrian goddess in Apuleius' *Metamorphoses*.[86] Encolpius is the *confessor gloriosus*,[87] and if I ask serious questions about the internal consistency, nature, and frequency of detailed confessions, I wish to cast no aspersions on him as narrator. Like Eumolpus, Encolpius is a first-rate story-teller. By making his confessions conform to literary genres, however, Encolpius encourages his reader to see the artifice in which his narrative is couched.

Nachleben of the Satyrica

Until the number of manuscripts of the *Satyrica* became substantial in the fifteenth century, the survival of Petronius was precarious. From

---

[86] Winkler (1985) 109; Apuleius, *Met*.8.28: *infit vaticinatione clamosa conficto mendacio semet ipsum incessere atque criminari... exposcere*.
[87] Schmeling (1994b).

antiquity to the Renaissance the *Satyrica* seems always to have been known—even if only to a few scholars.[88] For example, John of Salisbury in the twelfth century knew the *Satyrica* well and may have had more of it than we do today.[89] Most readers, however, knew the *Satyrica* in the same way that they knew other classical writers—from *florilegia*.[90]

We might say that in modern times the first real influence of the *Satyrica* on secular literature appeared in the Spanish picaresque novel.[91] This early beginning of influence in Spain, however, does not continue. For a Nachleben of the *Satyrica* which has been potent for many centuries we must look first to writers in Italy and France: Rini and Collignon have provided us with splendid (though now outdated) studies of the influence of the *Satyrica* in Italy and France.[92]

A brief review of the Nachleben of the *Satyrica* in England shows that from early on Petronius, his biography in Tacitus, and the style of his death were often divorced from the influence of the *Satyrica* itself. For instance, the prelate Jeremy Taylor in his influential *The Rule and Exercise of Holy Dying* (1678) comments favorably on the suicide of Petronius and the elegance of the story of the Widow of Ephesus but ignores the *Satyrica* as a work of art.[93] The vibrant force called Nachleben can be found in Tobias Smollett's novel *Adventures of Roderick Random* (1748). Lord Strutwell is speaking and trying to seduce Roderick: "'Here's a book,' said he, taking one from his bosom, 'written with great elegance and spirit, and though the subject may give offense to some narrow-minded people, the author will always be held in esteem by every person of wit and learning.' So saying, he put into my hand Petronius Arbiter..."

The Nachleben of the *Satyrica* in nineteenth-twentieth century Britain and in twentieth century America is truly impressive: everyone, it seems, knows the *Satyrica*. Even a partial list of writers reads like "Who's Who of English Literature". I mention the poets Lord Byron, Coleridge, Rossetti, and Yeats; the novelists Peacock, Stevenson, Wilde,

---

[88] Cf. M. Manitius (1911–31) *Geschichte der lateinischen Literatur im Mittelalter*, 3 vols. Munich.

[89] Cf. J. Martin (1968) *John of Salisbury and the Classics*. Dissertation, Cambridge, MA.

[90] Cf. L. Reynolds (1974²) *Scribes and Scholars*, Oxford, who makes the telling remark (p. 100): "... second-hand learning had come to stay."

[91] Walker (1971).

[92] Rini (1937), Collignon (1905).

[93] Stuckey (1966).

Joyce, D.H. Lawrence, several in the "Bloomsbury Group", Aldous Huxley, Lawrence Durrell—and popular, English translations of Sienkiewicz' *Quo Vadis* and Huysman's *A Rebours*; and the playwrights John Synge and Christopher Fry. Among American writers I cite F. Scott Fitzgerald who modeled his *The Great Gatsby* on the *Satyrica*, Ezra Pound who quotes from it, and Henry Miller who notes that it was one of the most influential books on his career. Pride of place among writers in the English language who admired the *Satyrica* probably belongs to the Anglo-American T.S. Eliot. This may surprise some because we do not usually associate Eliot with "underground" literature. The solemn black-suited warden of St. Stephen's in Kensington, self-professed classicist in letters, royalist in politics and Anglo-Catholic in religion was nevertheless under the spell of the *Satyrica*. He quotes from the *Satyrica* no fewer than ten times, the most famous quotation being the one used as the epigraph for *The Waste Land* (*Sat.*48.8 *nam Sibyllam* . . .).[94]

In 1969 the *Satyrica* achieved a level of fame/notoriety rarely bestowed in modern times on any ancient work. The Italian moviedirector Federico Fellini brought out a full-length cinema "adaptation" entitled *Fellini-Satyricon*. Classicists are still divided about the quality of the film. Like the novel, the film has become a classic.[95] The year 1969 also saw a musical version of the *Satyrica* at the Stratford (Ontario) Summer Festival, and in 1979 the German artist Manfred Henninger continued the pictorial interpretation of the *Satyrica* with a show in Stuttgart of fifty-five illustrations.[96]

Petronius the man and advisor of Nero has for many years been separated in the minds of many from the novel. There is a Petronius reeling through history, who seems to have been Nero's confidant in orgies. He is a name only and is used by those who have no time to check sources or skill to read any language. Hence we get *New York Unexpurgated: an Amoral Guide for the Jaded, Tired, Evil, Non-conforming, Corrupt, Condemned and the Curious—Humans and Otherwise—to the Underground Manhattan*, and the author listed is Petronius.[97] The Western business community which prides itself on historical research and

---

[94] For references to all items cited here, cf. Schmeling (1975).
[95] For a classicist's view, see Highet (1970); for a film critic's view, see P. Bondanella (1992) *The Cinema of Federico Fellini*, 239–261. Princeton.
[96] A book is available: M. Henninger (1979) *Zeichnungen und Pastelle zum Satyricon von Petronius*. Galerie der Stadt Stuttgart.
[97] New York: Grove Press, 1966.

computer-driven accuracy continues to reprint in their professional journals a short piece attributed to Petronius called *Reorganizing:* "I was to learn later in life that we tend to meet any new situation by reorganizing; and a wonderful method it can be for creating the illusion of progress while producing confusion, inefficiency, and demoralization."[98] Of course, this quotation which appears often each year does not come from Petronius, but the business community is not overly concerned with such obligations as checking sources.

1994 saw the *Satyrica* again return to the stage in *Satiricon* 94, this time in Geneva at the summer Théâtre Poétique de l'Orangerie.[99] The *Satyrica* continues to enjoy a vibrant Nachleben, even if the visual expression in Geneva was "interdit au moins de 14 ans". But then the *Satyrica* has been recommended to mature audiences while being forbidden to the young since the Council of Trent (1545–1563):

> Regula VII. Libri, qui res lascivas seu obscaenas ex professo tractant, narrant, aut docent, cum non solum fidei, set et morum, qui huiusmodi librorum lectione facile corrumpi solent, ratio habenda sit, omnino prohibentur; et qui eos habuerint, severe ab episcopis puniantur. Antiqui vero ab Ethnicis conscriptis, propter sermonis elegantiam et proprietatem permittuntur: nulla tamen ratione pueris praelegendi erunt.[100]

Among the writers and works of elegance and purity of language exempt from the Council's ban, we find listed in the Council's index "Petronius Arbiter in Satyra".

---

[98] Cf. R. Townsend (1984) *Further Up the Organization,* 192. New York.
[99] Book by P. Lüscher (1994) *Satiricon* 94. L'Age d'Homme: Lausanne.
[100] J. Mansi, ed. (1902) *Sacrorum Conciliorum Nova et Amplissima Collectio,* 33.230. Paris.

G. APULEIUS' *METAMORPHOSES*

S.J. Harrison

I. *Apuleius—Life and Works*

Information concerning Apuleius' life comes largely from his extant works, with some information from his fellow-African St. Augustine, who was educated in Apuleius' birthplace and knew his works well.[1] He was born in the middle 120's A.D.[2] at Madauros in Africa Proconsularis (Augustine *Ep*.102.32, *Civ*.8.14.2), now Mdaurouch in Algeria, a Roman *colonia* founded in the Flavian period some 150 miles S.W. of Carthage. His family was prosperous (cf. Augustine *Ep*.146.19); his father had risen to the duumvirate, the chief magistracy of Madauros, and had left Apuleius and his brother the substantial sum of 2,000,000 sesterces on his death, some time before 158/9 (*Apol*.23.1). As a citizen of an inland *colonia* in Africa Proconsularis, far from the cosmopolitan sea-coast, he is likely to have spoken Latin before Greek,[3] and probably Punic as the local vernacular, though he never reveals knowledge of the last and despises it in public (*Apol*.98.8). He received a high-grade literary education in Latin and Greek, first at Carthage, the proconsular seat and provincial capital (*Flor*.18.15,20.3), then at Athens (*Flor*.20.4), where he learned enough Platonic philosophy to be called a *philosophus Platonicus* by himself and others (*Apol*.10.6, Augustine *Civ*.8.19), though he never claims to have studied at the Platonic Academy itself;[4] he tells us of further "distant travels and long studies" which reduced his patrimony (*Apol*.23.2)—these included a stay in Rome (*Flor*.16.36–7) and perhaps visits to a number of sophistic centres in Greece and Asia Minor (cf. e.g. *Flor*.15, suggesting a possible visit to Samos).

During his time in Athens, probably in the early 150's, Apuleius met and became mentor to a young fellow-student from Roman Africa named Pontianus; a few years later, probably in the winter of 156,

---

[1] For Augustine's knowledge of Apuleius cf. Hagendahl (1967) 1.17–28 and 2.680–89.
[2] For the date cf. Walsh (1970) 248.
[3] For the evidence cf. Harrison (1990a) 508 n. 4.
[4] Cf. Glucker (1978) 139–41.

he rested at Pontianus' home town of Oea, the modern Tripoli in Libya, on the way to the great cultural and sophistic centre of Alexandria (*Apol.*72.1), and was prevailed upon by Pontianus to stay there for a year and eventually to marry his mother Pudentilla, a wealthy widow. The consequences of the marriage are set out in Apuleius' *Apologia*, his speech in his own defence in his trial for magic (see below) which naturally gives the story from Apuleius' point of view. Apuleius was accused by certain relatives of Pudentilla, who hoped to gain control of her and her fortune, of inducing her to marry him through the use of magic. The case against Apuleius was heard in the proconsular year 158/9 at Sabathra, modern Sabratah in Libya, the assize seat closest to Oea;[5] the publication of the *Apologia* is good evidence that he was acquitted. The speech itself is an impressive advertisement for Apuleius' rhetorical talents, combining Ciceronian forensic force and fireworks with a wide range of learned allusions to literature and philosophy.[6]

Apuleius' career as a speaker and lecturer, a Latin-speaking African version of the great Greek sophists of his day such as Lucian and Aelius Aristides, seems to have been established by the time of his trial (*Apol.*55.10,73.2). The chief evidence for his subsequent activities comes from the *Florida*, an extant collection of extracts from his speeches and declamations, some of which may be dated to the 160's, a decade in which Apuleius clearly operated as a public speaker in Carthage (*Flor.*18.16). *Flor.*9 and 17 are delivered in the presence of the proconsuls of 162–3 and 163–4, while *Flor.*16 gives thanks for the honour of a statue voted to Apuleius by the senate and people of Carthage and notes his election to the chief priesthood of the province, a major honour (cf. Augustine *Ep.*138.9, a somewhat jaundiced view). Also likely to belong to this period, though it gives no indication of date or place of delivery,[7] is the brilliant lecture *De Deo Socratis*, on the guardian spirit claimed by Socrates as his guide, a topic also discussed by Plutarch in his *De Genio Socratis*.

Nothing is known of Apuleius' activities or life after the 160's. That he retained some connection with his home town of Madauros is likely from a famous inscription found there to *a philosophus Platonicus*, which has been plausibly assumed to be Apuleius (*ILA* 2115—cf.

---

[5] For the date cf. Syme (1959).
[6] Cf. Helm (1955).
[7] Cf. Beaujeu (1973) xxxv.

Flor.16.37),[8] but there is no evidence that he returned to live there. One much-debated question is when he wrote the *Metamorphoses*, his greatest work. Some have followed Rohde in regarding it as a product of Apuleius' earlier years,[9] but apart from the novel's sophistication of style and technique which suggests some maturity, there are two main arguments for dating it after the *Apologia*. First, the fact that the *Metamorphoses*, a work which openly recounts magical and obscene stories, was not raised against Apuleius at his trial for magic, a safe deduction from the *Apologia*. Second, the fact that the novel seems obliquely to allude to some events in Apuleius' own life, including his marriage and trial.[10] Considerations of *Realien* in the text, such as details of Roman law, do not help to give an accurate date;[11] a further possibility for dating through literary parody is raised in 8 below.

The other extant works commonly ascribed to Apuleius are the *De Mundo*, a version of the Aristotelian work περὶ κόσμου, the *De Platone*, a treatise on Platonic philosophy in two books, the περὶ ἑρμηνείας, a work on Aristotelian logic, and the *Asclepius*, a translation of a Greek Hermetic treatise. The last two are unlikely to be genuine Apuleian works;[12] the authenticity of the *De Platone* and the *De Mundo* has also been powerfully impugned, though both are still defended as Apuleian by some.[13] Medieval copiers add three spurious works from late antiquity, the *De Herbarum Medicaminibus*, the *De Remediis Salutaribus*, and the *Physiognomonia*.[14] There was also a wide range of works ascribed to Apuleius but now lost, many of which were undoubtedly genuine; the remaining testimonia and fragments show that they included poetry, speeches, another novel (*Hermagoras*), a translation of Plato's *Phaedo*, works on proverbs, history, medical botany, agriculture, astronomy, zoology, music and arithmetic.[15] This list justifies Apuleius' own boasts of wide versatility in his writings (*Flor*.9.27–8,20–5–6), and provides with the extant works an overall picture of a sophistic intellectual of remarkable range, talent and energy.

---

[8] Cf. Tatum (1979) 106–8.
[9] Rohde (1885).
[10] Cf. Kenney (1990a) 203, Walsh (1970) 250, van der Paardt (1971) 91.
[11] Cf. Summers (1973).
[12] On the spuriousness of the περὶ ἑρμηνείας cf. Beaujeu (1973) vii–viii, on that of the *Asclepius* Nock (1945) 277–84.
[13] On the issue see Beaujeu (1973) ix–xxix, Hijmans (1987) 408–12.
[14] For these works see the bibliography gathered by Schlam (1971).
[15] Best collected and discussed in Beaujeu (1973).

II. The Metamorphoses: *Manuscripts and Editions*

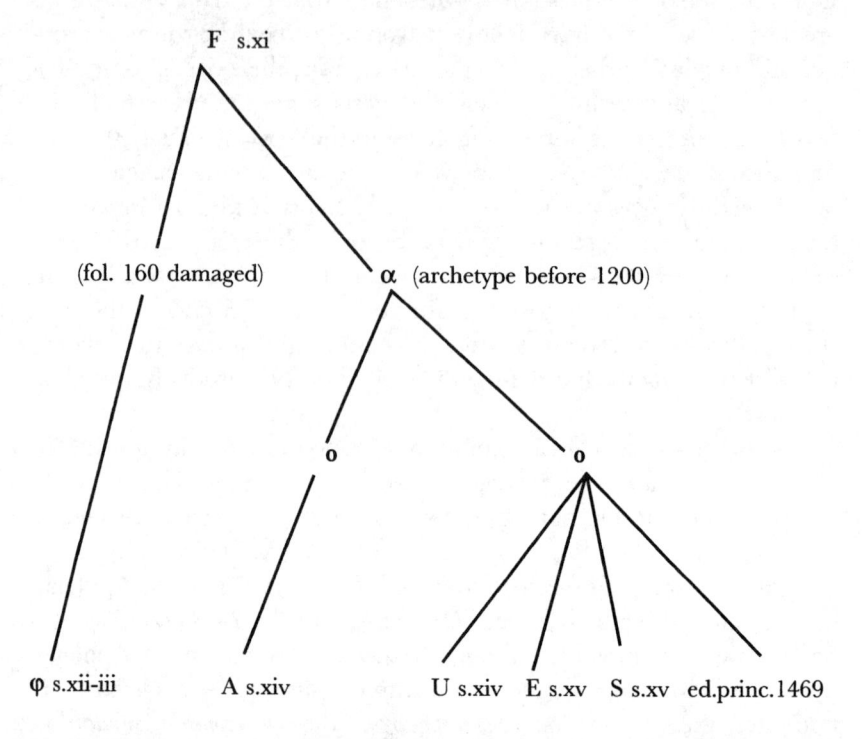

```
                    F s.xi
                   /    \
                  /      \
   (fol. 160 damaged)    α  (archetype before 1200)
         /   \            /    \
        /     \          /      \
       /       \        o        o
      /         \                /|\
     /           \              / | \
    /             \            /  |  \
   φ s.xii-iii   A s.xiv    U s.xiv  E s.xv  S s.xv  ed.princ.1469
```

As indicated in the above stemma, all known manuscripts of the *Metamorphoses*, usually preserved in a group with the *Apologia* and *Florida* in the order *Apol.Met.Flor.*, are generally agreed to be descended from F, a Florentine MS. (Laur.68.2), written at Montecassino in the second half of the eleventh century and the earliest extant manuscript of the work.[16] The text in F goes back ultimately to a double revision made in A.D. 395 and 397, as the subscription to *Met.*9 usefully records. F is the most valuable witness for any constitution of the text, but is in parts illegible and can be usefully supplemented from two further sources. The first is φ (Florence, Laur.29.2), copied from F in s.xii/xiii after damage to f. 160 of F; this contains the famous *spurcum additamentum* at *Met.*10.21, an obscene passage written in the margin, probably in the hand of the 14C scholar Zanobi di Strada.[17]

---

[16] For a brief survey of the tradition cf. Marshall (1983), for detailed analysis Robertson (1924) and Robertson and Vallette (1940–5) l.xxxviii–lv.

[17] Cf. Billanovich (1953) 1–3.

The second is a group of four MSS. of s.xiv/xv, descended from another copy of F made before the damage (A, U, E and S). The discovery in 1942 of C, another Beneventan MS perhaps contemporary with F and containing only ten leaves of the *Apologia* (Assisi 706) led briefly to hopes that another tradition of *Apol., Met.* and *Flor.* might have been preserved, but it seems probable that C too is derived from the tradition of F.[18]

Popularised in the Italian Renaissance, notably by Boccaccio, a copy in whose hand is preserved (Florence, Laur.54.32),[19] Apuleius was early into print (*editio princeps* Rome, 1469), and had a number of significant editions in the sixteenth and seventeenth centuries.[20] The two older editions of the complete works of Apuleius which are still most useful are products of the eighteenth and nineteenth centuries: that of G.F. Oudendorp, published posthumously by D. Ruhnken (1786), and that of G.F. Hildebrand (1842), both of which give commentaries with good accounts and summaries of earlier work. The three most important modern editions of the *Metamorphoses* are those of R. Helm (1931), C. Giarratano (1929) and D.S. Robertson (1940–45); Robertson's is the best and the most reliable in the constitution of the text, though Helm and Giarratano must still be consulted for a full range of reported conjectures. These textual editions have been complemented by useful commentaries on the individual books of the *Metamorphoses*, many by Dutch scholars—Book 1 by M. Molt (1938) and A. Scobie (1975), Book 2 by B.J. de Jonge (1941), Book 3 by R.Th. van der Paardt (1971), Book 4.1–27, Book 6.25–32 and Book 7, and Book 8 all by the Groningen collective led by B.L. Hijmans Jr. (1977, 1981, 1985), Book 5 by J.M.H. Fernhout (1949). The episode of Cupid and Psyche (*Met.*4.28–6.24) has been particularly popular, edited by L.C. Purser (1910), P. Grimal (1963) and E.J. Kenney (1990) amongst others, as has Book 11, the Isis-book, edited by J.-C. Fredouille (1975) and J. Gwyn Griffiths (1975). Many individual points of textual criticism and interpretation are made in these commentaries, and it is hoped that the whole of the *Metamorphoses* will soon be covered.[21]

---

[18] Cf. Robertson (1956).
[19] Cf. Scobie (1978) 212–13 and Haight (1945) 122–41.
[20] For a list cf. Robertson and Vallette (1940–5) l.liii–lxii, and for discussion Purser (1910) ciii–cvii.
[21] At the time of writing commentaries are being prepared on *Met.*9 by the Groningen team [published 1995] and *Met.*10 by Maaike Zimmerman.

III. The Metamorphoses: Plot-Summary

Book 1 After the prologue which promises an entertaining series of tales from a Greek source, Lucius tells of his journey to Hypata in Thessaly, on which he encounters Aristomenes. Aristomenes tells him of his friend Socrates, who while in Aristomenes' company was murdered by magic after becoming sexually involved with a witch. The travellers arrive at Hypata, where Lucius is received by his miserly host Milo. Forced to find his own dinner, he goes to the market, where he encounters an old school-friend, Pythias, now a magistrate, who rejects as unfit the fish Lucius has bought and destroys it. Lucius goes back to Milo's house still unfed, and, after a conversation with him but still no dinner, goes to sleep.

Book 2 The next day, Lucius meets Byrrhaena, an old family friend, and visits her house, where a statue of Diana and Actaeon clearly prefigures his metamorphosis. Byrrhaena warns him of the magic arts of Pamphile, Milo's wife; far from heeding this, Lucius rushes back to Milo's house to investigate. There he makes an assignation with Pamphile's slave, Photis. Meanwhile, he dines with Milo, and they talk of the prophet Diophanes, believed in by Lucius but discredited by a story of Milo's. After dinner, he retires to bed with Photis, and they become sexually involved. A few days later, Byrrhaena invites him to dinner, where he hears the story of Thelyphron, who tells how he was humiliated and physically maimed through incautious contact with witches at Larissa. On his way back to Milo's, late and drunk, Lucius is set upon by three robbers at Milo's door; he kills them all with his sword.

Book 3 The next day, Lucius is arrested and tried for murder. Surprisingly, the people laugh at him. Despite an elaborate and exaggerated plea of self-defence, he is convicted and forced to uncover the bodies of the three victims, which turn out to have been wine-skins. All laugh uproariously, and the chief magistrate explains that the trial is a practical joke to celebrate the Festival of Laughter in the city. Lucius is angry and offended, but pacified by civic honours. Back at Milo's house, Photis confesses that she is to blame: the animated wine-skins resulted from her own errors in aiding her mistress' magic activities. Lucius begs to be initiated into the mysteries of magic; Photis reluctantly agrees, and a few nights later allows Lucius to see Pamphile turning herself into a bird. Photis tries to provide the same metamorphosis for Lucius, but uses the wrong ointment and turns him into an ass. She promises to provide him with the antidote, roses, at dawn the next day and puts him in the stable for the night. That same night, robbers break into Milo's house, and steal Lucius with the other animals to carry away their booty.

Book 4 Lucius suffers as the robbers travel on, but decides against collapsing when another ass who does so is killed. They arrive at the robbers' cave, where their companions tell over dinner of their three expeditions which ended in comic failure and the loss of the great robbers Lamachus, Alcimus and Thrasyleon. The same night, the robbers go out and return with a prisoner, a beautiful young girl of high birth, kidnapped on the very point of marriage. She is distraught, and the aged housekeeper of the robbers tells her a tale to soothe her, that of Cupid and Psyche.

"There was once a princess so beautiful that she was worshipped as Venus. Venus, outraged, asked Cupid to ensure that the princess made the most degrading of marriages. But none dared to marry her (her name was Psyche) because of her extreme beauty; the Delphic oracle, consulted, said she should be placed on a cliff and would marry a terrifying winged monster. Her parents sadly complied with the oracle; no monster appeared to Psyche, but a gentle breeze carried her down and set her in a grassy valley."

Book 5 "When she woke up, she saw a beautiful palace, equipped with disembodied voices, which answered her bidding and provided for all her comforts. When she went to bed, she was visited by an unknown male who slept with her, and who returned each night. Eventually, Psyche asked her unknown partner for contact with her family; he objected but eventually allowed her to summon her sisters to the palace, on condition that she resist any pressure on their part to discover his identity. The sisters visited and were jealous of Psyche's luxurious lifestyle, especially when they heard that she was pregnant. They tricked her into fatal curiosity and finding out her husband's identity—he was Cupid, who had taken her for himself; on the discovery he left her. Psyche, realising her loss and her sisters' trick, took deadly revenge on them. Venus, informed of Cupid's activities with Psyche, was enraged with both the lovers."

Book 6 "Psyche began her search for her lost Cupid. Ceres and Juno were sympathetic, but could not help for fear of Venus' wrath.

Venus asked Mercury to advertise for Psyche's return to her as a runaway slave, but Psyche gave herself up of her own accord. To punish and humiliate Psyche, Venus set her a number of almost impossible tasks to do, which friendly animals under Cupid's influence helped her to complete. The final task was to descend to the Underworld to get a little of Proserpina's beauty for Venus in a box. Psyche managed to fill the box and bring it back, but at the last moment her curiosity again got the better of her; she opened the box and a deadly sleep flew out, making her unconscious. Cupid rescued her, and persuaded Jupiter to allow him to marry Psyche; even Venus agreed, and Psyche was made an immortal and Cupid's wife, giving birth to a daughter, Pleasure."

Shortly afterwards, Lucius takes the opportunity of the robbers' absence to try to escape; the girl jumps on his back, but they are recaptured. The robbers plan a dire fate for Lucius and the girl.

Book 7 The next day, these plans are intercepted by the arrival of a stranger, who claims to be the famous bandit Haemus. Telling the robbers tales of bravado, which include a story of a resolute wife who takes male disguise and saves her husband, he offers himself as leader to them. They accept; he advises them not to kill the girl as planned, but sell her instead. Lucius the ass is indignant at Haemus' overtures to the girl and her warm response, but soon realises that Haemus is her fiancé Tlepolemus in disguise. Tlepolemus/Haemus drugs the robbers' wine and then, with the help of his fellow-citizens, rescues the girl, now named as Charite; he and the girl are married. Lucius is rewarded by being sent to their country estate. Remaining there for some weeks, he is mistreated by a herdsman's wife and a cruel boy. Eventually, the boy is eaten by a bear; Lucius is blamed and attacked by the boy's mother, but repels her.

Book 8 A slave arrives at the estate from the town, bringing the dreadful news that both Tlepolemus and Charite are dead; Tlepolemus has been treacherously murdered by Thrasyllus, in love with Charite, who, after discovering the murder and blinding Thrasyllus by a trick, has killed herself. All the slaves panic at a change of ownership, and run away, taking Lucius with them. On their perilous journey they risk attack by wolves, have dogs set on them, and encounter an old man who turns out to be a devouring serpent in disguise. Eventually, they reach the safety of a town, where Lucius is sold to a group of travelling priests of the Syrian Goddess. They are charlatans, dedicated to making money and homosexual gratification, and visit various places, exploiting the superstition of the locals. In the course of their travels, Lucius is faced with the possibility of being butchered to replace a stolen joint of venison.

Book 9 He escapes this fate by pretending to be rabid. Travelling on with the priests, Lucius hears the tale of a deceived husband. The priests are arrested for stealing from a shrine; Lucius is sold again, this time to a miller, who puts him to arduous work in a mill. There he is mistreated by the miller's adulterous wife and overhears her conversation, which includes a tale about the exploits of her potential new lover; her new lover visits, but the pair are surprised by the miller's return. The wife hides the lover; he remains hidden while the miller narrates yet another tale of adultery, but is discovered by Lucius' help, and punished appropriately by the miller. The miller's wife, expelled from her home, takes dreadful revenge, killing the miller by witchcraft. Lucius is sold to a gardener and endures more hardship; the pair encounter a rich man whose family is tragically destroyed. Finally, a soldier attempts to commandeer Lucius; the gardener resists, escapes and hides with the ass, but Lucius' appearance at the window betrays them, and the gardener is arrested.

Book 10 The soldier takes Lucius for himself, and leaves him temporarily at a house where he learns the story of a wicked poisoning stepmother whose crimes were discovered by the good sense of a doctor. The soldier sells Lucius; he is bought by a pair of cooks, and enjoys their food secretly; they discover him and turn his apparently strange eating into a spectacle for public entertainment. Their master buys Lucius for himself, and has him taught more tricks and taken to Corinth. There a noble matron enjoys sex with Lucius as the ass; this leads Lucius' master to plan to display him in sexual congress in the arena with a condemned woman, another vicious poisoner, whose story is then narrated. Lucius dreads this as the ultimate degradation. The show in the arena begins with an elaborately-staged pantomime; Lucius escapes just before his own ordeal is due, runs to Cenchreae, the port of Corinth, and falls asleep.

Book 11 He wakes, and seeing the moon, prays to the universal mother-goddess for help. She appears to him in the form of Isis, and gives him instructions for his re-transformation through participation in her festival, about to occur in that very location, and for future happiness as her initiate. The festival is described; Lucius follows Isis' instructions and is changed back to human form. A priest of Isis explains that Lucius' ass-form and sufferings were just punishment for his former curiosity and slavish pleasures. Lucius becomes a devotee of the goddess, and receives initiation, with some payments needed; he then travels at her suggestion to Rome. There he undergoes two further initiations into the mysteries of Osiris, a surprise to him, each requiring more payments and accompanied by dream-instructions from the god; money is provided through Lucius' work as an advocate, and he ends the novel as a minor priest of the cult in Rome, joyfully performing his duties.

IV. *The* Metamorphoses *and Other Ancient Novels*

(a) *The* Metamorphoses, *the* Ὄνος, *and the Greek* Metamorphoses

Preserved amongst the works ascribed to Lucian, though probably by a contemporary rather than Lucian himself,[22] is a short work Λούκιος ἢ Ὄνος, of second-century date. This gives in outline the same ass-tale as that told in Apuleius' *Metamorphoses*, told in the same first person of the hero Lucius, but minus all the inserted tales, the prologue and the Isiac ending, and with a number of the details modified; a number of illogicalities and unexplained references indicate that it is a shortened version of a longer work. Given that the Ὄνος shows many close verbal similarities with Apuleius' Latin version, and that its approximate second-century date allows it to have been written either before or after Apuleius' *Metamorphoses*, it would seem at first glance to be its source, an original short version of the ass-tale which Apuleius dramatically expanded. The prologue to the *Met.* freely admits that the story of the novel is a Greek one (1.1.6 *fabulam Graecanicam incipimus*). However, this simple picture is overturned by the existence of a passage in the ninth-century *Bibliotheca* of Photius (cod. 129). Photius, who had access to many lost texts of Greek literature, claims to have read the *Metamorphoses* of Lucius of Patras, a work containing astonishing stories, and states that the first two books of that work are "practically copied out" in the Ὄνος of Lucian (clearly the extant Ὄνος) which, he says, uses the same words and phrases in shortening its original.

---

[22] Cf. Macleod (1967) 49–50.

Few have doubted that the Ὄνος is a shortened version of the Greek *Metamorphoses* recorded by Photius, but his other assertions have been highly controversial.[23] If what he says is reliable, then the more likely source for Apuleius is the longer Greek *Metamorphoses*, rather than the Ὄνος. The former provides Apuleius with a title (the title *Golden Ass*, also commonly used, is first attested in St. Augustine, and if it goes back to Apuleius may have been a second or alternative title),[24] and the verbal parallels between Apuleius' *Metamorphoses* and the Ὄνος are easily explained as coincidental, with the Ὄνος merely repeating the wording of the Greek *Metamorphoses* it summarises, as Photius explicitly states and as was normal in ancient epitomising. If the section of the original Greek *Metamorphoses* shortened (perhaps not by much) in the Ὄνος was only two books long, as Photius states, this would leave plenty of room for Apuleian innovations in his eleven books (such as the tale of Cupid and Psyche). The notion that the Ὄνος and Apuleius are independently derived from the Greek *Metamorphoses* seems more economical than postulating both the Ὄνος and Greek *Metamorphoses* as Apuleius' sources (why should he use both?), and more plausible than postulating the Ὄνος alone as source, given the apparent use by Apuleius of features of the Greek *Metamorphoses* not found in the Ὄνος.[25]

The fundamental differences between the Ὄνος and Apuleius are the narrative complications of the inserted tales, the difficulties about the identity of the speaker of the narrative at both beginning and end, and the Isiac material. These are the elements also fundamental to the character of Apuleius' novel (see below), and must largely be his insertions (no doubt from other sources) into the original ass-tale, with the proviso that some at least of the inserted tales might well have been in the original Greek *Metamorphoses* (e.g. that of Aristomenes in Book 1).[26] As it stands, the Ὄνος is a relatively unsophisticated

---

[23] For the problems of the Photius passage cf. Kussl (1990); for the issue of Apuleius' relation to the Ὄνος and the Greek *Metamorphoses* cf. van Thiel (1971), Bianco (1971), Walsh (1974), Mason (1978), Holzberg (1984).

[24] Augustine (*Civ*.18.18) insists that *Golden Ass* (*Asinus Aureus*) was Apuleius' own title, but *Metamorphoses* alone appears in the manuscripts; perhaps we should suppose a double title generated through circulation such as those known for some Greek novels (e.g. those of Xenophon, *Ephesiaka* or *Anthia and Habrocomes*, and Heliodorus, *Aethiopika* or *Theagenes and Charikleia*). For a recent argument for *Golden Ass* cf. Winkler (1985) 292–320.

[25] Cf. conveniently Macleod (1967) 48; Apuleius' prologue may echo that of the Greek *Metamorphoses*—cf. Scobie (1975) 65.

[26] Cf. Effe (1976).

narrative in Lucianic Attic with a satirical slant, its major interest being its relation to more complex works.[27]

(b) *Apuleius'* Metamorphoses *and Other Ancient Novels*

It might naturally be expected that Apuleius' novel should show some links with its only surviving Latin predecessor, the *Satyrica* of Petronius. The general resemblances of satirical tone and erotic/low-life interests, especially sex and magic, a narrator who is at least partly himself satirised, and the general structure of a long narrative interspersed with tales are evident, but the prosimetric form of Petronius is an evident difference, and individual imitations are not perhaps as numerous as we would expect, though it must always be remembered how little we possess of Petronius' novel. Some linguistic imitation seems clear,[28] and several parallel motifs stand out, for example the melodramatic attempted suicide in the inn, in both cases using a bed (*Sat.*94.8 and *Met.*1.16), the humble hospitality of Milo at *Met.*1.23.4 and that of Oenothea at *Sat.*135.15, both explicitly compared to that of Callimachus' *Hecale*, or the two ghost-stories at the feast told at the host's insistence by Niceros and Thelyphron (*Sat.*61.1–62.5 and *Met.*2.20.5–30.9).

The *Metamorphoses* also shares with the *Satyrica* something of an inversion of the traditional motifs of boy-girl romance central to the Greek ideal novel. The *Satyrica* parodies the traditional *Liebespaar* by presenting a homosexual *ménage à trois*, while in Apuleius' novel Lucius, both in human form and when metamorphosed into a macrophallic ass, experiences sex but no romance, an inversion of the usual chastity of the hero and heroine of the Greek novel, and ends up not by marrying a heroine but in chaste service to the gods. Lucius' vague wanderings in the byways of central Greece and narrow escapes from undignified fates as an ass also reflect and parody the more dramatic and glamorous element of travel and perilous adventure crucial to the Greek novel tradition. But in other ways the *Met.* conforms to the Greek model; it reflects its element of *Bildungsroman* in the depiction of Lucius' growing experience of the world, however naive he remains, and many parts of the novel, especially the Charite-episode and the tale of Cupid and Psyche, include romantic colouring trace-

---

[27] Cf. Anderson (1976b) 34–49.
[28] Cf. Walsh (1978).

able to Greek novels. It also, of course, shows connections with the low-life Greek novels which have come to light in recent papyrus discoveries, especially the *Phoinikika* of Lollianus.[29]

But there are also two general features shared with the tradition of the Greek novels, though Apuleius develops them well beyond their original use. First, the complication and problematising of the narrative and narrator, achieved by Apuleius through uncertainty in his prologue about the narrator's identity and through the final switch which seems to introduce Apuleius himself as narrator rather than Lucius (see 7(b) below). This complication is reflected in Longus, who makes his work the summary of an account given by an exegete of a picture, in Achilles Tatius, who presents his novel as the words of Clitophon spoken to the author without returning at the end to this original frame, and by Heliodorus through his enigmatic opening *in medias res* and the long tale of Calasiris, which appears to give the reader necessary information but may also mislead.[30] Second, Lucius' tribulations at the hands of fortune and his rescue by Isis: though these elements are extensively developed in Apuleius and there is much disagreement about how profound and sincere the Isiac religious content is in his novel (see 7(c) below), there is no doubt that the caprice of Fortune and the ultimate guiding hand of a particular divinity are an important feature in most of the Greek novels,[31] and that in Xenophon's *Ephesiaka*, probably written before Apuleius, the directing goddess is again Isis.[32] In conclusion, Apuleius' *Metamorphoses* shows some generic resemblance both to Petronius and to the Greek ideal novels, but (as in its relation to the Ὄνος) is original and creative in its treatment of inherited material.

V. *The* Metamorphoses *and Apuleius' Other Writings*

As argued in 1 above, Apuleius was in effect a professional sophist, and the *Metamorphoses* has been aptly described as "a sophist's novel";[33] like the more sophisticated amongst the Greek novels, it reflects very

---

[29] For romantic colouring cf. e.g. Kenney (1990a) 117 and 135 and Mason (1978) 8–9; for links with Lollianus cf. Jones (1980) and Winkler (1980a).
[30] Cf. Winkler (1982).
[31] Cf. Walsh (1970) 174–5 and Reardon (1991) 25.
[32] Cf. Xenophon *Eph*.1.6,5.13 and Witt (1971) 243–54.
[33] Tatum (1979) 135.

much the concerns of its author and its age. Its interest in rhetoric, clearly something central for the author of the *Apologia* and *Florida*, is beyond dispute, especially in passages such as the formal praise of Photis' hair (*Met*.2.8.2ff.) or the splendid set speeches of the mock-trial scene at the Festival of Laughter (*Met*.3.3.1ff.); we can also detect from time to time the flavour and themes of traditional Roman declamation, which Apuleius had no doubt been trained in and practised.[34] The novel's interest in ἔκφρασις and formal description is also clear,[35] matching several instances in the *Florida* and the currency of the technique in sophistic literature in general,[36] and the general level of literary learning and allusion is very considerable, just as in the literary pyrotechnics of the *Apologia*; all the works of Apuleius are clearly the writings of a man of high education determined to demonstrate what he knows. Occasional allusions to the dialogues of Plato,[37] and indeed other Platonising elements in the novel (see 8 below) fit well with one who was by his own account a *philosophus Platonicus*, probable translator of the *Phaedo* and possible author of two books *De Platone* (see 1 above). The novel also shows some miscellaneous scientific learning on matters as diverse as medicine, elephant pregnancy or the workings of a water-clock,[38] appropriate for a writer who can discourse in the *Apologia* on the anatomy of fish (*Apol*.36) and who is credited with works on medical botany, agriculture, astronomy and zoology (see 1 above). We find too a plausible smattering of legal knowledge, perhaps not entirely accurate,[39] appropriate enough for Apuleius, who had appeared as advocate in cases other than that of the *Apologia*.[40] But the element which links the *Metamorphoses* most closely to the other extant works of Apuleius is that of a common style of writing, to which we now proceed.

---

[34] E.g. the rich oppressive neighbour at *Met*.9.35.3ff.—cf. Seneca *Contr*.5.5.
[35] Cf. e.g. *Met*.2.4.1–10,4.6.1–6,5.1.2–7,6.14.2–3,10.30.1–32.4,11.3.4–4.3, 11.8.1–11.4.
[36] Cf. *Flor*.6, 12 and 15. For the prominence of ἔκφρασις in the literature of the Greek Second Sophistic cf. Bartsch (1989) 3–39.
[37] Most notably to the *Phaedrus*, at *Met*.1.18.8 [cf. Tatum (1979) 27–8] and at *Met*.5.24.1 [cf. Walsh (1970) 206–7]. For further Platonic imitation cf. n. 68 (below).
[38] Medicine: *Met*.1.18.4. Elephant pregnancy: *Met*.1.9.6. Water-clock: *Met*.3.3.1.
[39] Cf. Summers (1970) (1972) and (1973).
[40] *Apol*.1.5. For Apuleius' self-proclaimed legal learning cf. *Apol*.88.3.

VI. *Style, Expression and Literary Colour in the* Metamorphoses

The notion that Apuleius and some other second-century writers also born in Africa, such as Fronto, wrote "African Latin" has largely been discredited.[41] As Norden stressed in his classic treatment, the exuberant, archaizing and alliterative style which characterises Apuleius' genuine works should be viewed not as deriving from colonial vernacular origins, but as continuing and bringing to its culmination the Latin version of the Asianic style known at Rome well before the age of Cicero.[42] Apuleius' style is supremely euphonious, colourful and above all rhythmical, an effect achieved not only by the regular use of standard Ciceronian clausulae but by syntactical balance of clauses, homoeoteleuton, and rhyming effects of every kind. His syntax is markedly expansive and pleonastic, very often providing three or more parallel clauses in theme and variation, especially in elaborate passages; its structure is rarely complex or difficult, differing much in this respect from e.g. Tacitus earlier in the century, and generally prefers paratactic clauses to subordinate ones.

In vocabulary, Apuleius follows the choice selection from archaic and poetic sources practised by Fronto and other advocates of the *elocutio novella*, and seems to coin words with some freedom, resembling in this and other respects a poet rather than a prose-writer; he is relatively restrained in the use of Graecisms. In more colloquial passages, his frequent use of the diction of archaic Roman comedy produces a tone which is both familiar and distant. The level of style and expression can vary considerably, from basic narrative and Plautine dialogue to epic imitation, high rhetoric and lofty description; it is the flexible tool of a rhetorical virtuoso, which may be turned to suit the context and occasion, but which nevertheless retains its individual mark in every situation. In sum, the style of Apuleius is unique in Latin; its qualities are difficult to capture in mere description, but the reading of a few pages in the original will give a stronger and more immediate impression.[43]

Another aspect of the *Metamorphoses*' use of language is that of wordplay. This comes partly from the alliterative tendencies noted above,

---

[41] But cf. Kenney (1990a) 29–30, who, following Lancel (1987), suggests that Apuleius' language reflects "the experimental exploitation of an adopted tongue".
[42] Norden (1915) 588–605.
[43] The standard treatments of Apuleian style are Bernhard (1927) and Callebat (1968); for a recent stimulating introduction cf. Kenney (1990a) 28–38.

where similar-sounding words are placed together both for euphony and for quasi-etymological play (e.g. 9.14.4 *saeva scaeva*). The fact that the novel is plainly written for a readership which has at least some Greek also means that translingual puns are possible; this comes out above all in the use of significant names, most of which may be Apuleius' own inventions in the manner of Plautus rather than inherited from sources. Thus for example Lucius' hostess who is unfaithful to her husband is called Pamphile, "lover of all" (πᾶς, φιλεῖν), two of the robbers whose deaths are narrated in Book 4 are called Alcimus, "mighty" (ἄλκιμος), and Thrasyleon, "bold as a lion" (θρασύς, λέων), and a woman-chasing youth is called Philesitherus, "lover of the chase" (φιλεῖν, θήρα).[44]

Finally, literary imitation and allusion also form a strong strand in the reader's experience of the novel's language and expression. The *Metamorphoses* is written for an educated reader of the second century A.D. and is full of references to and clever adaptations of Greek and Latin classics. The extent of these allusions to other texts is still being investigated, but many imitations of well-known literary episodes and vocabulary are evident, and this patchwork technique is clearly fundamental to Apuleius' mode of composition in the *Metamorphoses* (see further 8 below).

VII. *The* Metamorphoses: *Issues and Controversies*

The main controversies in the interpretation of the *Metamorphoses*, apart from that of its relation to the Greek ass-narratives, already dealt with in 3(a) above, may be grouped under three headings: unity, narrative complexity and religious sincerity. As will become clear, these areas are necessarily closely related, and answers to one problem will often depend on those to another.

(a) *Unity*

B.E. Perry famously viewed the *Metamorphoses* as lacking essential unity, and saw the last book as added to give the work an intellectual and moral weight lacking in the first ten books of scandalous and entertaining stories.[45] This implies a serious and literal interpretation of

---

[44] For this type of name in Apuleius cf. Hijmans (1978b).
[45] Perry (1967) 244–5.

the Isiac material in the last book (see (c) below), but more significant for the moment is Perry's explicit denial that the novel had any coherent structure or meaning as a whole. This view, previously widespread but not universal, has generated much persuasive work in opposition, seeking to prove the unity of the novel and the coherence of the main narrative with the inserted tales and the Isis-book, and it is now difficult to maintain Perry's position.[46] For example, it is now generally agreed that the appearance of the Egyptian goddess Isis in Book 11 is prepared for in foreshadowing allusions which begin as early as the novel's prologue, that Lucius' relations with and erotic slavery to the slave-girl Photis, ironically named for the illumination she fails to give (φῶς), are in some sense an inferior version of his ultimate joyous "union" with and service of the all-illuminating female Isis, and that the theme of *curiositas* unites Lucius' adventures in human form with the tale of Cupid and Psyche and with his experiences in Book 11, where his *curiositas* is sated by initiation and reversed into keeping due silence. In particular, it is now generally agreed that the tale of Cupid and Psyche provides a parallel to the plot of the whole novel (see 8 below), though not all would agree with the strong thesis of Merkelbach that almost every detail in the story of Cupid and Psyche indicates that it is an allegory of Isiac initiation.[47] Most also agree that many of the other tales in the novel, particularly those told to Lucius before his transformation, contain prefigurations and warnings of his future fate (see 8 below).[48] More recently, too, Winkler has stressed that hermeneutic playfulness and the setting of puzzles is a constant feature of the novel which draws it together, and which applies to Book 11 just as much as to the first ten books (see (b) and (c) below).[49]

(b) *Narrative Complexity*

The *Metamorphoses* begins with a prologue in which the speaker is not named or closely identified, and which indeed raises explicitly the question of the speaker's identity (1.1.3 *quis ille?*), a question which

---
[46] For a statement of unity and coherence before Perry cf. Riefstahl (1938); for subsequent treatments cf. (e.g.) Wlosok (1969), Walsh (1970), Tatum (1979), Winkler (1985), Schlam (1992), Alpers (1980) and several of the pieces in Hijmans and van der Paardt (1978a).
[47] Merkelbach (1962).
[48] Cf. esp. Tatum (1969) and Walsh (1970) 177–82.
[49] Winkler (1985).

cannot easily be answered; the story opens at 1.2.1 in the voice of Lucius, but it is not clear that Lucius speaks the prologue (cf. 8 below). Such deliberate problematising of narrator and narrative at such an early stage clearly sets an agenda for the novel as a whole; the problems of the prologue are famously redoubled at the novel's end, where the hero/narrator, up to now clearly Lucius of Corinth, is apparently named by the god Osiris appearing to the priest Asinius Marcellus as *Madaurensem, sed admodum pauperem* (11.27.9), apparently identifying him with Apuleius himself, born at Madauros. Some have tried to emend *Madaurensem*, but most regard it simply as a signal that the initiation-narrative in Book 11 is in some sense autobiographical.[50] Though there are clear similarities between Apuleius himself and the Lucius of his novel, for example their common profession of public speaker (cf. *Met.*11.28.6) and shared experience of religious initation (cf. *Apol.*55.8), this notion that they are effectively identical at its end and that fiction becomes personal witness is a sudden and unprepared metamorphosis, even in a text where the identity of the narrator was prominently marked out as a problem in the prologue. It has been relevantly pointed out that Apuleius the author clearly intervenes in his narrative *in propria persona* at another point,[51] but this is not a full explanation or parallel for the dramatic shift of identity. Winkler's sophisticated interpretation of it as a deliberate puzzle for the reader which admits of no authoritative solution seems too indeterminate; more attractive are interpretations which stress that Asinius Marcellus misinterprets the true words of the god, and that *mitti sibi Madaurensem* truly predicts that Apuleius (not Lucius) will be "sent" to Asinius in the sense of including him in his novel.[52]

(c) *Religious Sincerity*

Until recently, most interpreters of the *Metamorphoses* were agreed that the narrative of Lucius' initiations into the mysteries of Isis and Osiris in Book 11 represented a sincere personal testament of religious experience; this judgement was in most cases linked with an interpretation of 11.27.9 *Madaurensem* as a signal of autobiographical data

---

[50] For good discussions of the problem cf. W.S. Smith (1972) 530–4, van der Paardt (1981) and Penwill (1990) 224–6. Typical of the autobiographical approach is Walsh (1970) 184.
[51] Cf. van der Paardt (1981) 105–6.
[52] Winkler (1985) 218–9; Smith (1972) 530–2, Penwill (1990) 224–6.

and therefore of authorial sincerity (see (b) above). This has been used not only to reconstruct the details of the cult of Isis, of which Apuleius clearly had considerable knowledge,[53] but also to describe the mentality of conversion and personal religion in the second century A.D.[54] This last step demands that the account given in Book 11 is either significantly autobiographical for Apuleius (see above), or represents his sincere and even evangelistic attempt to portray participation in a particular mystery-religion.

Recently, but not without precedent,[55] Winkler has pointed out in his crucial interpretation of the novel that this view of Book 11 as wholly serious and sincere need not be accepted. He stressed that the character Lucius, whether or not he intersects with the author Apuleius, retained his *naïveté* and gullibility throughout the last book, especially in terms of being financially exploited by the officials of the cults, and that therefore the reader is not sure whether his account is that of genuine religious experience or foolish self-deception; the bald-headed Lucius at the end may be either a venerable priest or a ridiculous clown.[56] While not all may accept the open-ended indeterminacy of Winkler's own account, his subversion of the "sincere" view of the Isiac material in Book 11 is very powerful. The personal encounter with Isis and her cult which has struck so many as the statement of a believer is after all the narrated experience of the youthful and gullible Lucius, who as a naive character who has endured much suffering is perhaps likely to have such an experience at this point in the novel. Lucius' moving rhetoric in his prayer to Isis, and the grand epiphany of Isis herself are meant to convince in context but need not retail the author's own views. Furthermore, the satirical edge to the almost interminable stages of initiation, each time involving expenditure by the impoverished Lucius and strongly marked in the text by pointed remarks and false endings, argues that this is not the heart-felt narrative of a convert's own experience.[57] I shall suggest in 8 below further reasons for pursuing this view.

---

[53] Clear from the work of Gwyn Griffiths (1975).
[54] Cf. Nock (1933) 138–55, Festugière (1954) 68–84, Dodds (1965) 3.
[55] For a reading of *Met.*11 which is at least partly satirical cf. Anderson (1982) 83–5.
[56] Winkler (1985) 223–7.
[57] Winkler (1985) 219–23.

VIII. *The* Metamorphoses: *An Interpretative Essay*

The prologue to the *Metamorphoses* (*Met*.1.1.1–6) points to many of its central themes and problems. As mentioned in 7(b) above, this self-conscious opening of the novel gives no clear indication of the identity of its speaker, and the autobiographical details it supplies apply strictly neither to the author Apuleius nor the novel's main narrator Lucius, who clearly picks up the story at 1.2, the following section. Whether one solves this difficulty by postulating a separate Plautine-type prologue-speaker or by presenting the book itself as the speaker of its own prologue,[58] such an initial enigma marks out what kind of work the *Metamorphoses* is—one involved with questioning the status and authority of its own narrator and narrative, an "interrogative" text, to use a convenient critical term.[59] The prologue also makes clear the different levels on which the work can be read. The initial reference to Milesian tales (*sermone isto Milesio*) and the final promise of pleasure (*laetaberis*) suggests a series of racy stories for the purposes of entertainment in the Milesian mode,[60] but the allusion to Egypt (*papyrum Aegyptiam argutia Nilotici calami inscriptam*) also anticipates the unity provided by the Isiac closure, though it significantly makes no serious religious claims for it; the Egyptian reed provides cleverness (*argutia*), not revelation or illumination.[61]

These elements of foreshadowing and anticipation in the prologue are followed by many others, and self-conscious reference to the events of its own narrative is a chief feature of the work. One of the chief agents of this reflexivity is the technique of the inserted tale.[62] The earlier tales told to Lucius before his metamorphosis can be seen as specific warnings to him by narrators who cannot know his future against the course of action which leads to that disastrous climax; that of Aristomenes in Book 1 states the dangers of becoming tied up with witches and magic through sexual liaisons with women when

---

[58] For the first cf. W.S. Smith (1972), for the second Harrison (1990a).

[59] Cf. Belsey (1980) 90–102, esp. 91: "[in the interrogative text] the position of the author inscribed in the text, if it can be located at all, is seen as questioning or as literally contradictory ... the interrogative text ... does literally invite the reader to produce answers to the questions it implicitly or explicitly raises."

[60] For brief accounts of the Milesian tales cf. Trenkner (1958) 172–7, Mason (1978) 7–8.

[61] For a more "serious" interpretation of this passage cf. Grimal (1971). For *argutia* as "cleverness" cf. *Met*.10.17.2, *TLL* 2.555.76ff.

[62] Cf. the references in n. 48 and van der Paardt (1978) 80–84.

one is away from home, while that of Thelyphron in Book 2, where an Egyptian priest finally reveals the humiliation of another man incautiously involved with magic and witches, adds to this same warning against magic a suggestion of the means by which Lucius will be able to escape his enchanted asinine shape—the ministrations of an Egyptian priest. Again, the description of the statue of Diana and Actaeon in the atrium of Byrrhaena's house provides a different means of anticipating the narrative: *tua sunt . . . cuncta quae vides* says Byrrhaena as Lucius surveys the statue, meaning to offer the facilities of the house as the polite hostess,[63] but in fact unwittingly pointing to the impending metamorphosis of Lucius, inflicted like that of Actaeon as deserved punishment by a goddess following sexual transgression; this point is finely underlined through the links of iconography between Isis and this statue of Diana.[64] Once more Lucius, presented with a foreshadowing of his own fate, fails to take the hint. Similarly, after Lucius' metamorphosis, the great tale of Cupid and Psyche clearly contains hints at his future, though once again he fails to perceive them, saying only that the tale is a *bella fabella* (6.25.1). The Psyche who falls from grace through *curiositas*, endures many sufferings through divinely-inflicted punishment and is finally raised to godhead in a divine union seems an obvious analogue for Lucius, whose experience of *curiositas* and suffering is similar, and whose chaste "union" with Isis parallels the marriage of Cupid and Psyche; the issue of that marriage is Voluptas, "pleasure", just as the issue of Lucius' divine service is religious joy, another kind of pleasure.[65]

The notion that the narrative of the *Metamorphoses* works simultaneously on different levels, like the notion that it is fundamentally unified (cf. 7(a) above), is common ground to most modern interpretations. It is, for example, shared by the very different views of Merkelbach, who sees Books 1–10 and particularly the tale of Cupid and Psyche as an allegory of Isiac initiation preparing for the literal Isiac initiation of Book 11,[66] and Winkler, who sees the novel's multiple levels of interpretation as indicative of its ultimate indeterminate "message" as conveyed in Book 11: "[the novel] is a philosophical

---

[63] Cf. *Met.*5.2.1 *tua sunt haec omnia*, the polite words of the disembodied voice to Psyche, newly-arrived in Cupid's palace.
[64] For the element of anticipation cf. (e.g.) Merkelbach (1962) 339 n. 3; for the iconographical resemblance cf. Peden (1985).
[65] Cf. Gwyn Griffiths (1978a) 155–8.
[66] Merkelbach (1962).

comedy about religious knowledge. The effect of its hermeneutic playfulness, including the final book, is to raise the question whether there is a higher order that can integrate conflicting individual judgements."[67] The philosophical element in the *Metamorphoses* is also significant here in explaining why the novel works on more than one level, why it is more than a simple set of entertaining stories. Its use of Platonic ideas is natural for a writer who called himself *philosophus Platonicus*; though Apuleius may well have used the syncretistic and Platonising account of the myth of Isis and Osiris given by Plutarch, his chief philosophical debt is owed directly to Plato himself,[68] and extends beyond a few allusions to prominent passages of the *Phaedrus* and the Platonic links of the term *curiositas*.[69]

In its own terms as a narrative, which must be distinguished from any personal view or ideology of the author, the *Metamorphoses* presents us with a series of events which are shown in the final book to have a coherence and meaning not fully apparent before. The priest's words at *Met.*11.15 make it clear that Lucius' experiences in the first ten books have been controlled by a divine force, which has, through punishing him by metamorphosis and suffering, shown him the inappropriateness of the sensual existence which he previously sought, and which now offers him the "true" existence of divine service. His previous ideas and view of the world were wrong, and he is now being given a chance to correct it with the benefit of "true" perception. Photis' initiation of Lucius into the false and enslaving mysteries of sex and magic can now be identified as an inferior and negative version of the true and final initiation into the chaste cult of Isis, where the service of the god is not shameful but true pleasure; the resemblances between Photis and Isis are not coincidental, but reflect the fact that the first is a negative foreshadowing of the second.[70] This distinction between the partial and false knowledge of the non-initiate and the true knowledge of the initiate clearly recalls Platonic epistemology and the theory of Forms, with which Apuleius as translator of the *Phaedo* had some acquaintance. There only the

---

[67] Winkler (1985) 124.
[68] For Apuleius and Plutarch's *De Iside et Osiride* cf. Walsh (1981); for his direct debt to Platonic texts cf. (e.g.) Thibau (1965), Gianotti (1986), Kenney (1990b), Fick-Michel (1991).
[69] For the *Phaedrus* cf. n. 37 (above); for the Platonic aspect of *curiositas* cf. De Filippo (1990).
[70] Cf. e.g. Wlosok (1969) 78–9, Alpers (1980).

trained and "initiated" philosopher can perceive the true version of the world in the dimension of the Forms, while most mortals move in the shadowy world of sense-perception.[71] In terms of the famous analogy of the Cave in the *Republic*,[72] those elements of Lucius' unenlightened experience prefiguring his future as an initiate are mere dark shadows on the wall of the Cave, whereas the real knowledge of Isis achieved by Lucius in the last book corresponds to the sun-lit knowledge of the Good, which Plato describes, as Apuleius describes Isis, as the source of light and illumination.[73]

This use of Platonic epistemology does not necessitate that the story of Lucius is a moral fable presented for a didactic purpose, though this has been strongly argued;[74] like other elements in the novel, it is part of the intellectual apparatus of its writer, deployed for clever literary effect and as a mode of structuring the narrative, and need have no particular "message" to the reader—this is not a work written to promote Platonic epistemology, but a work which uses Platonic epistemology as one of its structuring principles. This lack of ideological thrust can also extend to the account of the Isiac cult itself; it has already been stressed, following Winkler, that it is presented in something of a satirical mode (cf. 7(c) above), and that it is unlikely to be a straightforward narrative of religious experience, as it has so often been taken to be. One important purpose of the narrative of Book 11 is to stress that Lucius is no less naive or incautious in his dealings with the Isis-cult than he had been in his dealings with magic, but that narrative of Book 11 also seems to have a specific relation to the religious literature of its period. The traces of Isis-aretalogies in the initial prayer of Lucius and Isis' reply are plain and well-known (and themselves say nothing about the "seriousness" of the Isiac material),[75] but there is a further significant connection with another religious text.

In A.D. 170-1 the famous rhetorical performer Aelius Aristides

---

[71] For a recent exposition of Plato's Theory of Forms as argued in the *Republic* cf. Fine (1990).

[72] *Republic* 7,514a ff.

[73] For the illumination shed by the Good, by analogy with the Sun, on every aspect of the world of Forms cf. *Republic* 6,507b ff.; for the comparable function of Isis cf. *Met*.11.2.3 *ista luce feminea conlustrans cuncta moenia*, 11.15.3 *quae suae lucis splendore ceteros etiam deos illuminat*. Compare also the generative functions of Isis (*Met*.11.25.4) with those of the Good (*Republic* 6,509b).

[74] Cf. Gianotti (1986), Fick-Michel (1991).

[75] For the details see Gwyn Griffiths (1975), esp. 137.

wrote down the visions of the god Asclepius and other deities by which his life and particularly his health had been directed over nearly thirty years.[76] This text, extant as the Sacred Tales ('Ιεροὶ Λόγοι), has a number of interesting parallels with the narrative of Lucius' experiences of the Isis-cult in *Metamorphoses* Book 11. In both texts the narrator is presented as an initiate and priest of a particular deity (though it is not clear how strictly true this is for Aristides),[77] receives and obeys divine instructions in repeated visions, including detailed predictions which come true and orders to go to a different place,[78] expresses his inability adequately to describe the ineffable deity,[79] and acquires or improves his powers of public speaking through the god's agency.[80] We even find Isis as one of the several deities appearing to Aristides, and an explicit refusal to tell of the unspeakable mysteries of Isis which offer salvation to the initiate, a point prominently made by Apuleius.[81]

It seems difficult to believe that these parallels are coincidental. If they are not, parody in Apuleius' playful novel of the work of Aristides, evidently sincerely intended as an account of the writer's experiences, seems the most likely relation; there is no problem about chronology, since Apuleius could easily have written the *Metamorphoses* some time after A.D. 170–1 (see 1 above). Apuleius, then, would be sending up his age's taste for writing about religious cults and personal religious experience, a satirical attitude found elsewhere in the *Metamorphoses* (e.g. the wicked but monotheistic baker's wife and the quack priests of the Syrian Goddess).[82] This satirical outlook is shared with a famous contemporary, Lucian, who showed in general a humorously sceptical attitude to religion and who in his *Alexander* devastatingly exposed after his death a well-known religious charlatan and those who were credulous enough to be deceived by him.[83] Thus the *Metamorphoses* would have something of the same parodic relation to

---

[76] For the date cf. Behr (1968) 108–10. The six *Sacred Tales* are *Orations* 47–52 in Keil's standard numeration of the works of Aristides.
[77] For Aristides as initiate and priest of Asclepius cf. *Or*.47.41,48.28,50.102.
[78] *Or*.49.21–22,52.1—cf. *Met*.11.26.2.
[79] *Or*.47.1,48.8,48.49—cf. *Met*.11.3.3.
[80] *Or*.47.31,50.8—cf. *Met*.11.28.6,11.30.2.
[81] *Or*.49.6,49.48—cf. *Met*.11.23.7,11.27.4.
[82] On these two episodes (*Met*.8.24ff. and *Met*.9.14) cf. Gwyn Griffiths (1978a) 152–3.
[83] For Lucian's attitude to religion cf. Jones (1986) 33–45, 133–48; his view of the Syrian Goddess in *De Dea Syria* may have been similar to that of Apuleius—cf. Anderson (1976b) 68–82.

the contemporary literature of religious experience as it does to the Greek ideal novel (see 3(b) above), and its initial promise to provide entertainment is fulfilled right through to the end, rather than stopping at the beginning of Book 11.

Having considered issues of meaning, overall interpretation and ideology, I now turn (finally) to questions of literary form. What kind of text is the *Metamorphoses*? It seems right to classify it with the *Satyrica* of Petronius and the Greek romances as a novel,[84] though the term is not beyond question in ancient literature,[85] given both the considerable variety of the few texts which represent ancient prose fiction and attractive ideas such as Bakhtin's that the novel necessarily falls outside generic categories.[86] As already stressed, the *Metamorphoses* is full of literary allusions to many kinds of writing, but it seems to be particularly concerned with highlighting its similarities with and differences from the epic in particular; as has been pointed out, the ancient novel is essentially the successor of the epic as the vehicle of lengthy fictional narrative.[87] The epic affinities of the *Metamorphoses* are evident from its structure. It has eleven books, almost but not quite an epic number; the two-book inserted tale of Cupid and Psyche, taking up approximately one-sixth of the work, clearly recalls inserted tales of similar size in epic, such as that of Aeneas in Books 2 and 3 of the twelve-book *Aeneid* and that of Odysseus in Books 9–12 of the twenty-four-book *Odyssey*. Even the way in which the tale of Cupid and Psyche begins before the end of Book 4 and ends before the end of Book 6, evidently not matching the Homeric or Vergilian model where the tales of Odysseus and Aeneas begin and end with books, clearly derives from the tension between episode and book in the structure of Ovid's *Metamorphoses*.[88]

Epic imitations are also found in significant number in specific episodes of the *Metamorphoses*, as well as in its overall structure. Best-known are the echoes of the *katabasis* of *Aeneid* 6 in the descent of Psyche to the Underworld,[89] but epic imitation in the *Metamorphoses* is not confined to the loftier style of Cupid and Psyche; for example,

---

[84] So rightly Barchiesi (1991).
[85] Cf. Callebat (1992).
[86] Bakhtin (1975).
[87] Perry (1967) 45–55.
[88] Cf. e.g. Ovid *Met.*1–2, where the story of Phaethon is carried over, or *Met.*8–9, where that of Hercules and Achelous likewise bridges the two books.
[89] Cf. Walsh (1970) 56–7, Finkelpearl (1990).

the journey of Lucius to Hypata and his dealings with strangers in the opening books recall those of Telemachus in the opening books of the *Odyssey*,[90] the Haemus/Tlepolemus episode echoes the cunning of Odysseus,[91] the story of Charite echoes that of Dido,[92] and Lucius' time as an ass is specifically compared with the adventures of Odysseus as a formative learning process.[93] Of course, Apuleius is conscious of the tradition of the Greek ideal novel, which owes more than a little to the *Odyssey*,[94] but Apuleius' detailed reworkings of both Greek and Roman epic in particular episodes are meant to be noticed as such, and are of a different order of imitation from the use of epic in the Greek novel, which usually provides only themes and a general narrative framework. As already stressed, epic provides the only long fictional narrative genre before the novel, and is therefore a natural quarry, but the epic episodes mentioned above are almost all transformed in their new novelistic context; reworked with the comic or sensational tone of Milesian stories, their metamorphosis stresses the difference of literary kind between a low-life novel and the lofty epic level.

This generic transformation of epic material, though designed to show literary learning, is interestingly analogous with the use of Isiac religion and Platonic philosophy already discussed above. In each case, material from more "serious" contexts is absorbed into, and made to serve the purposes of, a lighter and amusing literary form, with an overarching unity and coherence. Overall, Apuleius' novel should be viewed as a confident written performance by a consummate stylist, who orchestrates his disparate matter into an artistic and carefully-constructed whole; despite its deployment of both religion and philosophy, its main purpose is not to improve the reader's morals or convey philosophical truth, but to provide entertainment of a subtle and challenging kind, and above all to demonstrate the talents and knowledge of its author.

---

[90] Cf. Harrison (1990b).
[91] Cf. Harrison (1990b), Frangoulidis (1992).
[92] Cf. Forbes (1943), Walsh (1970) 54.
[93] *Met.*9.13.4: cf. Winkler (1985) 165-8.
[94] Cf. Perry (1967) 50-53, Reardon (1991) 15-17.

H. *HISTORIA APOLLONII REGIS TYRI*

Gareth Schmeling

The *Historia Apollonii* not only contains riddles, it is a riddle, a problem-piece to be solved: the name of the author is unknown, the language of the original is in dispute, the place of composition can only be guessed at, the date of composition is placed anywhere over a four century period (A.D. 200–600), and the extant Latin text itself is considered (1) a translation from Greek, (2) epitome(s) of a Greek original, (3) altered over time by re-writers so severely that little if anything of the original survives, (4) a collection of corrupt texts but worth the effort to speculate about and to try to improve.

Summary of the Story

The plot of the *Historia* like that of many ancient novels is deceptively simple: the devil, however, hides in the details.

Overview

The narrative of the *Historia* seems to fall into three uneven sections, while the disposition of the chief protagonist's life follows the formula laid down in Campbell's *Hero with a Thousand Faces*,[1] and the structure of the plot follows Propp's *Morphology*.[2] In section one Apollonius leaves home and becomes a suitor of a king's only child (motherless) whom he deserves to have won by his learning and riddle-solving ability (storm at sea). In section two Apollonius is again made a suitor by solving a riddle set by another king's only child (motherless), when she rejects all others, having fallen in love (she says) with his great learning; birth of their daughter and apparent death of his wife (storm at sea). In section three Apollonius sets out to fetch his daughter (storm at sea) but lands instead in Mytilene, where he solves riddles

---

[1] Campbell (1949). See also Frye (1976) 50ff.
[2] Propp (1928). See also Chiarini (1983) and Ruiz-Montero (1983).

set by his daughter and delivers her to an acceptable suitor. The symmetry is readily apparent and the (roughly) same pattern is followed in each section.[3] Progress in the story is made by shipwreck, and communication is conducted by riddle.

Prelude (chs. 1–3)

Unlike in introductions to most other ancient novels we do not meet the chief protagonists of the story in the opening chapters. In a twist of structure we come first upon a villain, king Antiochus, who has no role to play after ch. 8 (his death in ch. 24 causes more problems than did his living), and his unnamed daughter. Chapters 1–3 form a kind of prelude to the plot and establish the novel's dominant leitmotiv (without revealing any specific background for the plot; information revealed in the prelude is not vital): there exists a special relationship of trust between daughter and father, and Antiochus incestuously violates all acceptable norms. Though the *Historia* is notorious for the paucity of physical and psychological details, the prelude (plus the ballgame scene in ch. 13 and the auction of Tarsia in ch. 33) contains graphic scenes, which heighten the horror and set in our minds the monstrosity of the actions of the villainous Antiochus (ch. 1): *puella vero stans dum miratur scelestis patris impietatem, fluentem sanguinem coepit celare: sed guttae sanguinis in pavimento ceciderunt.* At this point the reader has no idea where the story is going; while the father is clearly evil, the plot seems to have come to an abrupt end with incest completed.[4] Rohde[5] and Perry[6] hold that the episode involving Antiochus is a later addition to the Apollonius story. Behind the fictional account of the incest of Antiochus probably lies a garbled version of the historical incident in which Antiochus I (324–262 B.C.) fell in love with his stepmother Stratonice, and his father Seleucus I scandalously handed over his own wife to his son (Plutarch, *Demetrius* 38). Archibald proposes that the fictional Antiochus can reasonably be viewed as a composite of the Antiochuses I–IV, seeing in Antiochus IV Epiphanes, as described in the Books of Maccabees, the embodiment of many evils including incest.[7] Then returning to an old ob-

---

[3] Fusillo (1989) 186–196.
[4] See Chiarini (1983).
[5] Rohde (1914) 445ff.
[6] Perry (1967) 297ff.
[7] Archibald (1991) 38ff.

servation of Perry,[8] that non-historical stories often grow up around or are attached to significant historical names, Archibald adopts a productive approach to names in the *Historia*.[9]

The princess' nurse encourages her to comply with her father's sexual desires and so sets herself off as the bad nurse in the pattern bad nurse-good nurse with Tarsia's good nurse in chs. 29–30.

Riddles, Rogues and Wrecks: the Appearance of Apollonius (chs. 4–12)

Life at court in Antioch has settled down to a ritual: Antiochus shows himself to his citizens as a proper father, inside the palace commits incest on a regular basis, and just as regularly murders every suitor of his daughter. A young, rich man from Tyre named Apollonius comes to Antioch as a suitor, acknowledges the penalty for failure to solve the riddle and then is asked to solve it: "I am carried by crime; I eat my mother's flesh; I seek my brother, my mother's husband, my wife's son. I do not find him." Pausing briefly Apollonius replies that the "I" of the riddle is Antiochus himself. The riddle set by Antiochus seems to be faulty, unless we understand the family relationships to include in-laws (e.g., mother-in-law); Apollonius' solution does not explain how Antiochus can represent all parts of the puzzle.[10] Why the king would pose a riddle whose correct answer would expose him is one of those questions whose answer the author does not care to offer us. In any case the king tells Apollonius that his solution is wrong but then inexplicably grants him thirty days to reconsider his answer. Apollonius retreats (in fact, he escapes) to his library, which is a kind of sanctuary for him, reconfirms his correct solution and, realizing now that the king intends to kill him, loads his ship and heads to Tarsus. Dispatched by Antiochus to murder Apollonius, Thaliarchus cannot find him in Tyre and reports this to the king who offers a bigger reward for Apollonius dead than alive—which attracts even Apollonius' supposed friends to betrayal (ch. 7). In Tarsus a man named Hellenicus informs Apollonius of the king's actions but refuses a cash reward (he accepts it in ch. 51). From Stranguillio, a friend in Tarsus, Apollonius obtains help in hiding himself from Antiochus and then offers the citizens of Tarsus, suffering from a

---

[8] Perry (1967) 151ff.
[9] Archibald (1991) 37.
[10] See Goolden (1955) and Taylor (1938); Ohlert (1912).

famine, wheat at a low price. The good citizens erect a statue to Apollonius with his name on it—a strange tribute to a man trying to hide. Like Antiochus' riddle about himself and his thirty day reprieve of Apollonius, the erection of the statue of Apollonius is inexplicable. After a brief period in which gratitude wears thin Stranguillio and his wife in a move which anticipates their treachery (chs. 31–32) encourage Apollonius to leave Tarsus and (I suspect) avert any problems with Antiochus. In a storm scene told in dactylic hexameters (garbled and fragmentary) reminiscent of Virgil's *Aeneid* 1, the rich Apollonius is shipwrecked near Cyrene in North Africa (Aeneas suffers the same fate in North Africa), loses all his possessions, but is rescued by a fisherman, who like St. Martin gives him one half of his cloak (he is rewarded in ch. 51).

Perry[11] questions the structure of the incest episode and asks why the unwilling party to incest did not go into exile like Mattidia in the Pseudo-Clementine *Recognitiones* (and many others) and thus conform to the pattern for the motif. It is, however, Apollonius, an external suitor, who is driven into exile, a condition which provides the motivation for his travels and adventures. Had the original story of Apollonius made him a son of Antiochus, exposed or driven from home by some pronouncement, then his return as suitor would have made him susceptible to incest and his exile made the episode conform to the motif.[12] The reader does want to know, however, why Apollonius, who recognizes that Antiochus' daughter has been in a long-term incestuous relationship, continues to act the role of suitor and seek the princess in marriage.

From Storms to Marriage to Storms (chs. 13–25)

Dressed in one-half of the fisherman's old cloak Apollonius makes his way into Cyrene and hearing that the baths are open enters and is soon engaged in something like pat-ball or medicine-ball with Archistrates, king of Cyrene.[13] As in all games, musical events and

---

[11] Perry (1967) 300ff.
[12] Müller (1991).
[13] Gillmeister (1981) speculates that the ballgame in the *Historia* may be the *pila trigonalis* and in Note 9 provides an interesting glimpse of Roman ballgames. Some of his conclusions, however, cannot be taken seriously. Unfortunately he follows those scholars who have postulated a fifth century origin for the Latin *Historia* and bases conclusions on that as though it were proven. He compounds the error in this

literary contests, Apollonius is an expert and quickly attracts the attention of the king, who orders a slave to invite him to dinner: both soon learn (and the king soon forgets) that Apollonius has been shipwrecked and has no clothes for dining. At the rich feast Apollonius looks around and, remembering what it was like to be rich, begins to weep. The king's beautiful daughter enters at this point (ch. 15) and father and daughter agree that she should cheer up Apollonius with her singing and lyre playing. Amused by her amateur performance, Apollonius demonstrates how the lyre is to be played and how actors should perform,[14] and in reply she wheedles two hundred talents of gold, forty pounds of silver, twenty slaves, a king's wardrobe, and a royal apartment in the palace out of her father, and gives them to Apollonius. Like Antiochus' daughter she seems to be motherless, but unlike her she is indulged without limit by her father. Early the next morning she rushes into her father's room and easily convinces him to make Apollonius her tutor.

At this point our author explicitly compares the love-struck princess with Dido, after she had met Aeneas, by borrowing lines from Virgil's *Aeneid* (4.2) *vulneris saevo carpitur igne* at 12.27[15] and (4.4) *regina gravi iamdudum saucia cura* at 13.19. Both Aeneas and Apollonius had been cast upon the North African shore by a storm and both were rescued by royal personages. It is possible that our author had also intended a comparison between Archistrates' daughter and Nausikaa in *Odyssey* 6.[16]

It seems (ch. 19) that Archistrates' daughter like Antiochus' is beset by suitors—she is not only his only heir but is also exceedingly beautiful. In a quasi-comic episode (Perry sees it as a scene from New Comedy)[17] three suitors corner Archistrates and request that he stop avoiding them and that he name one of them his son-in-law. The king replies that his daughter is ill but that if each suitor would write

---

way: in the second century Greek version he is confidant that the contest between Archistrates and Apollonius was a wrestling match, "which had fallen into disrepute; it also shows how a Roman ball game . . . was substituted in its place by the fifth century reviser of the work." For a pictorial illustration of a ballgame there is a fresco from a tomb in Rome; cf. Eugenia Salza Prina Ricotti (1983) *L'Arte del Convito nella Roma Antica*, p. 124, fig. 67. Rome.

[14] Archibald (1988) shows how important learning is to Apollonius, his wife, and daughter. The value placed on learning is one of the "patterns" in the novel.

[15] All page and line references in the *Historia* refer to my Teubner edition, Schmeling (1988).

[16] See Holzberg (1990) on borrowings from the *Odyssey*.

[17] Perry (1967) 306–307.

down the amount he is willing to pay as a dowry,[18] he would pass on the notes to his daughter. In fact Apollonius delivers the sealed bids for her hand to her (see ch. 33 and the bids for Tarsia), and after she asks him if he is not a little sad that she is about to marry, she writes back to her father (only a few feet away) that she desires to marry the shipwrecked (this is set as a riddle) man. At the end of a comedy of errors Apollonius identifies himself as the answer to her riddle. He is a polite young man who seemingly without passion agrees to marry the king's daughter, who has enough passion for two. No sooner are they married (ch. 23) than Apollonius learns that Antiochus and his daughter have been killed *in flagrante* by lightning and that (for reasons left unexpressed) the kingdom of Antiochus is being kept for him. With his bride some months pregnant he sets sail for Antioch (ch. 25), but the ship is hit by a storm, and in childbirth his wife dies. She is buried at sea with great riches (like Callirhoe), and her water-tight coffin floats off leaving Apollonius with his infant daughter as his only consolation.

Tarsia: The Heart and Heroine of the Novel (chs. 26–36)

The coffin enclosing Apollonius' wife is washed ashore near Ephesus, and owing to the perceptiveness (praise of learning—a pattern) of a physician's assistant (cf. Ephesian physician in Xenophon of Ephesus 3.4) she is revived, adopted by the physician and placed in the care of Diana, protectress of virgins (ch. 27). After ch. 27 the story shifts from Apollonius to his daughter Tarsia, whom he takes to Tarsus and entrusts to Stranguillio and Dionysias for upbringing, while he himself goes off to Egypt as a merchant, leaving Tarsia in the care of the nurse Lycoris. It is at this nurse's deathbed (ch. 29) that Tarsia aged fourteen learns that Stranguillio and wife are not her parents, and we get our first glimpse of the sterling character of Tarsia as she cares for her nurse. While sterling character has often led to a person's downfall, Tarsia finds herself in trouble for a much more mundane reason, her beauty, and especially her beauty compared with the plain features of Dionysias' own daughter: it is clear to the mother that Tarsia will attract all the suitors. Attracting suitors is a powerful motif in the *Historia*, and perhaps for this reason Dionysias' defense of her own daughter should be treated more kindly. As Dionysias

---

[18] See Schmeling (1988) XXI.

(and her husband) had not long protected Apollonius in the face of Antiochus' threats, so she does not watch over his daughter: she calls her overseer Theophilus and orders him to kill Tarsia, but he acts so slowly that pirates are able to snatch her. Like Thaliarchus, Theophilus is promised his freedom from slavery, if he commits murder. While we are led to believe that Thaliarchus was freed by Antiochus, Dionysias goes back on her promise and by comparison appears worse than Antiochus. To explain the disappearance of Tarsia, Dionysias confesses to her husband, blaming the whole affair on strangers' insults of their daughter and praise of Tarsia. In a speech slightly reminiscent of Adam's remarks to God about Eve, Stranguillio claims total innocence for himself. As the citizens of Tarsus had raised a monument in praise of Apollonius (ch. 10), so they now build another in memory of Tarsia (ch. 32).

The pirates take Tarsia to Mytilene where she is paraded at a slave auction, and in one of the most memorable sequences of scenes in the *Historia* the plucky Tarsia is seen fighting for her honor. During a spirited auction a greedy pimp who recognizes the profit potential in a noble virgin is pitted against Athenagoras, a local prince, who dreams of the pleasures in deflowering (cf. ch. 1) the same noble virgin: this confrontation is worth revisiting when Athenagoras later marries Tarsia. Greed, as usual, wins out over lust, and the pimp advertizes Tarsia at a half pound of gold for her first customer, after which the price falls to one *aureus* (ch. 33). Though Athenagoras loses the bidding, he stands first in line at Tarsia's crib. Like Sheherazade who puts off death by telling a good story, Tarsia with her own sad tales regales Athenagoras, who pays the price but spares the virgin; each succeeding (but unsuccessful) patron treats her in the same way. Athenagoras approaches the affair in a light hearted way and tricks his friends standing in line into thinking that they are soon to have a great experience. The pimp is amazed that Tarsia is able to bring in so much money and yet remain a virgin; she adds even more money and fame by performing musical numbers, and Athenagoras begins to watch over her, as a good father would. In Tarsia's performances of music the reader can recall to Tarsia's advantage the musical performances of her mother: Tarsia is an educated young woman, whereas her mother had simply displayed natural abilities; education is equated with royalty.[19] Chapters 29-36 seem to be rich

---

[19] Archibald (1988).

in a profusion and confusion of literary motifs, from that of the beautiful girl who becomes a threat and is sold into slavery from the lost *Alcmaeon* of Euripides,[20] to those of pimps and brothels in the comedies of Plautus,[21] to that of Seneca (*Controversiae* 1.2) where a girl preserves her virginity in a brothel by the power of her rhetoric.[22] While it is difficult to know how much clear light such inquiries into the history of motifs throw on our understanding of the story, the results (however indeterminate) do point to an author of wide interests and reading.

The Return of Apollonius and the Return of Tarsia (chs. 36–47)

The first part of the *Historia* is devoted to Apollonius, the second to Tarsia, and now the third to both of them as the unit father-daughter. After a fourteen year absence Apollonius returns to Tarsus and is informed by Dionysias that Tarsia is dead. Confining himself to the bilge level of his ship he is for a third time caught up in a storm at sea but this time deposited in the harbor at Mytilene during the Neptunalia—a subtle indication, perhaps, that the gloom is passing and merriment entering the plot. As it happens, Athenagoras is walking along the harbor and noticing the fine quality of Apollonius' ship asks whose it is. Learning that it belongs to an Apollonius and remembering that Tarsia's father is so named, Athenagoras descends into the hold, asks Apollonius to leave the filth, but is rebuked. Athenagoras, who for some reason still allows Tarsia to live in the brothel, demands that she be sent to him and then challenges her to entice Apollonius to the Neptunalia: if she can convince Apollonius to leave the hold, he will purchase her from the pimp. By her learning she can save herself. At first she is rejected by Apollonius who then agrees to answer a series of riddles, most of which seem to have a thematic connection with his life (chs. 42–43). Though he is clearly entertained by Tarsia, he refuses to give up the ship, and she resorts to grabbing his clothes and dragging him out. In a passage (ch. 44) of which I have tried to make much, Apollonius pushes Tarsia away, causes her to fall, and *de naribus eius sanguis coepit egredi*. The last time there was a mention of blood in a violent setting was ch. 1 and

---

[20] Krappe (1924).
[21] Klebs (1899) 305–306.
[22] Perry (1967) 314.

the rape of the princess: *fluentem sanguinem coepit celare*. The incest of Antiochus leading to the flowing of blood stands in marked contrast to the blood here: where Antiochus' daughter thought of suicide, Tarsia resorts to tears and an account of her life story, which causes a chain reaction and leads to her recognition by Apollonius as his daughter. Tarsia's ability to tell stories had saved her in the brothel and now restores her to her father (ch. 45). Ever the opportunist, Athenagoras steps forward, claims that he helped to preserve Tarsia's chastity, and then asks for her hand in marriage.[23] While the pimp is burned alive, Apollonius is given a bath, new clothes and a new life (ch. 46).

Finale: Rewards for the Virtuous, Punishment for the Guilty (chs. 47–51)

Apollonius thanks the people of Mytilene, and a grateful people erect a statue to both Apollonius and Tarsia—a sign of the denouement. Almost as an afterthought our author notes that Athenagoras and Tarsia are married; the important part of the story is that the father recovers his daughter. On board ship again Apollonius is not buffeted by another storm but by a dream in which he is advised to sail to Ephesus, visit the temple of Diana, and sail then to Tarsus. A second recognition scene occurs in the temple of Diana at Ephesus, and the immediate family of Apollonius is reunited (ch. 49). In Tyre Apollonius appoints Athenagoras king, according to the RB redaction, and the entourage goes off to Tarsus, where Stranguillio and Dionysias are first arrested and, then on the testimony of Theophilus (who plea-bargains to save his own skin), are stoned to death by the people (ch. 50). Finally the group sails for Cyrene and is welcomed by Archistrates who after all these years sees his granddaughter. The fisherman from ch. 12 is rewarded as is Hellenicus from ch. 8, in reverse order of their appearance but in keeping with the precepts of ring-composition. Apollonius names his new son from Archistrates' daughter as king of Cyrene to replace the deceased Archistrates; as ruler of Antioch he himself lives with his wife until ripe old age, when both die peacefully (ch. 51). RB does not record the death of Apollonius and his wife, but it does note that he wrote down an account of everything that happened to him and deposited one copy of it in the temple of Diana at Ephesus and another in his own library.

---

[23] Schmeling (1989) and (1994a).

Manuscripts and Texts

The known manuscripts of the anonymous *Historia* number some 114, and, since the pioneering work of Klebs,[24] have been divided into nine or so redactions or groups, which are often termed recensions when employed for other ancient works but which here defy the usual meaning of that word. The nine groups are R(ecension)A (3 MSS), Rα (16), RB (8), RC (22), RT (12), RSt (20), RE (8), Rber (5), Rß (9), and eleven MSS await assignment of a home in a group. There is a rational approach behind these designations: it is believed that RA represents the earliest and best tradition of the MSS of the *Historia* and that Rα, while grounded to a great extent on RA, shows some little influence of RB. Klebs[25] was almost surely mistaken to postulate a stemma for the *Historia* which showed that RA and RB were separate and independent witnesses of the original; it is much more probable that RB derives mainly from the tradition of RA, perhaps influenced by early but no longer extant manuscripts of that group. To the fulsomeness and even wordiness of the vulgar RA, RB seems to offer remedial doses of classical restraint, to include additional information which helps to clarify situations, and even on occasion (a little in RB MS b, more in ß) to set forward revisions in content and Latinity. RB, however, appears from time to time not to have as direct a line to the original *Historia* as does RA: even with its striving for classical form, RB fails to recognize or to preserve intact at ch. 11 the verses written in imitation of Virgil's storm scene from *Aeneid* 1.81–141. From such we can speculate that RB derives from manuscripts in the RA tradition but does not have its origin in the group of MSS (A, P, Va^c) we know as RA.

RA is comprised of A (the best if fragmentary MS of the *Historia*, written in Monte Cassino in the ninth century and now in Florence), P (fourteenth century Italian MS, excellent, now in Paris), and Va^c (the corrected portion represents RA, in a twelfth century Italian MS of the RC group, now in the Vatican); RB is made up of b (a fragmentary ninth century MS from Tours, excellent, now in Leiden), ß (twelfth century MS from England, now in Oxford), and two lesser thirteenth MSS, M (now in Madrid) and π (now in Paris).

The RC group, while borrowing in almost identical proportions

---

[24] Klebs (1899).
[25] Klebs (1899) 32.

from RA and RB, regularly displays a penchant to rewrite its sources. Although it is true that RC contributes little to our ability to improve RA or RB, our primary and secondary redactions, MSS in RC often share readings and mistakes with the best MSS of RA and RB, and in addition RC is exceedingly influential in the later development of the novel in modern languages. A MS in the RC group was used in the earliest vernacular translation (eleventh century) of the *Historia*, a translation into Old English: "The Old English version preserved in Cambridge... is remarkable as the first vernacular translation, an early witness to the long-standing popularity of the story in England, and... the first English romance."[26] In a curious way RC became allied to RA through the actions of a scribe who took MS Va from RC and, in comparing it with a MS from RA, corrected Va (Va^c) and made it read in part like a MS from RA: is it just a coincidence that the scribe chose a MS from RC to compare with RA?

The groups RT (Tegernsee Redaction), RSt (Stuttgart Redaction), RE (Erfurt Redaction), Rber (Bern Redaction), all named for the location of the most important MS in their group, can all be traced back for the most part to RB. Though these four groups together with Rα, derived from RA, have only limited importance, an edition making them readily available to scholars is a clear desideratum.

A special curiosity among the MSS of the *Historia* is φ, a fragmentary tenth-eleventh century work written in Werden an der Ruhr, containing about one-third of the novel, and now housed in Budapest. This MS is illustrated by a series of thirty-five drawings which Hägg refers to as "comic strips" and which Weitzmann estimates numbered about two hundred in the original, complete MS.[27] Our artistic scribe follows an old custom of illustrating MSS with drawings: "There is hardly another illustrated text known to us in which the scenes follow each other in such a close approximation of a cinematic narration, and it does not seem to be accidental that this should occur in an ancient romance for which the quick change of action and locality is most typical."[28]

From the report above the reader already realizes that the numerous groupings, which are not at all the usual recensions we see in

---

[26] Archibald (1991) 184.
[27] Hägg (1983) 150; Weitzmann (1959) 103.
[28] Weitzmann (1959) 104. The MS that lies behind Welser's 1595 edition was also illuminated.

most ancient texts, defy reconciliation and result in a different text for each grouping. These problems were not fully appreciated by the editor of the editio princeps in Utrecht in 1474, or by Welser in his 1595 Augsburg edition, or by Riese in his first Teubner edition (1871). In his second Teubner edition (1893) Riese corrected his attempt to offer one text for all MSS (after Ring uncovered MS P and published his own edition in 1888) and divided RA and RB into discrete redactions—RA occupying the top half of the page, RB the bottom.[29] Tsitsikli in 1981 corrected many of Riese's most glaring mistakes and again printed both RA and RB; the 1978 edition of Waiblinger contains only RA, but it is intelligently done; in 1985 Konstan and Roberts produced a most useful text of RA together with a set of helpful notes; in her 1991 study of the *Historia* in the medieval world Archibald included a very conservative version of the text of RA.[30] In 1988 [1989] I brought out an edition in which RA, RB, and RC were printed consecutively, which attempts to break away from the conservative mold in which recent editors had placed the text and which tries to shift the focus from problems in MSS to those in the text.[31] The works of J.M. Hunt on the text were influential in my approach to the text and are listed in my edition. For English readers the *Historia* is available in good translations by Pavlovskis and Sandy;[32] translations into modern languages are cited in my edition.

Issues and Controversies: Latin-Greek-Christian Original, Epitome, Date

One reason why the text of the *Historia* could seem to present few problems is that it is deceptively simple. The straight-forward, often paratactical Latin, the use of high-frequency vocabulary, the often inartistic arrangement of words, and the lack of subtle philosophical explanations or psychological motivations all seem to conspire to encourage editors not to question the usual human failings of scribes. The conservative editor then prints that which scribes dictate, and the result is a needlessly inelegant text.

---

[29] Riese (1871); Ring (1888); Riese (1893).
[30] Archibald (1991).
[31] Schmeling (1988). Cf. Hunt (1994).
[32] Pavlovskis (1978); Sandy (1989).

A way to explain away problems is to posit that the anonymous *Historia* is a translation from Greek into Latin. Under the influence of the powerful intellect of Rohde who held that the *Historia* was a re-working, if not exactly a translation in the sixth century of a Greek original, many scholars were persuaded to agree.[33] If all the ideal and sentimental ancient novels are Greek and the Latin ones are realistic, there is a kind of logic in assuming that the *Historia* was originally Greek. Among some classical scholars there appears to be a natural bias that, for example, behind every pedestrian Roman marble sculpture there is a better Greek bronze. H.J. Rose after all has taught us that Greeks had an "active imagination" but that Roman creative thought by comparison was "narrow and sluggish".[34] This bias extends even to the study of the ancient novel where Parsons has pronounced: "Natural reason long ago revealed that Petronius had a Greek model."[35]

An examination of the text does reveal a number of Greek words, phrases and grammatical constructions. These, however, do not make it any more a Greek work than do all the things Greek in the *Satyrica* render it any less a monument of Latin literature.[36] Scholars who believe in a Greek original for the *Historia* cite inter alia *nodus virginitatis* (1.14),[37] an un-Latin combination of words, which they contend was translated directly from Greek to Latin with little understanding of the Latin idiom: *nodus virginitatis* is unique to the *Historia*, reflects a literal translation of ἄμμα παρθενίας and in the hands of a Latin author (as opposed to a Latin translator) would most likely have been rendered as *zonam solvere* (Catullus 67.28) or something similar.[38] The expression *nodum virginitatis eripuit*, the argument goes, is not Latin. I would like to suggest a different explanation: the expression, though unique in Latin is easily understandable; perhaps it was chosen to jolt the reader with an "estranging and defamiliarizing effect",[39] because the author had great plans for the word *nodus* later in the

---

[33] Rohde (1914) 435–453. Unpersuaded by Rohde is Perry (1967) 294–324; see bibliography in Archibald (1991). Comments by Ziegler (1984) are cogent. Cf. also Schmeling (1995a).
[34] Rose (1959) 1.
[35] Parson (1971) 66.
[36] Salonius (1927).
[37] Weyman (1909).
[38] MS A reads *nodum*; MS P was apparently confused by *nodum* and changed it to *florem* (cf. Catullus 62.46).
[39] Eagleton (1983) 3–4.

novel.[40] The expression is used at 1.14 in a scene of father-daughter incest (*prima luce vigilans irrumpit cubiculum filiae suae . . . nodum virginitatis eripuit*), and then re-employed as a point of contrast for the proper father-daughter relationship of Apollonius-Tarsia at ch. 41 (33.24): Tarsia asks her father, who is at the time still unknown to her, to *absolvere nodos parabolarum mearum*. This is a striking work-play because *solvere* is the recognized verb in the sexual euphemism with *zonam*, for which our author has substituted *nodum*. The reader's mind goes back to 1.14 where wicked Antiochus deflowered his daughter and then hid his crime by setting a riddle whose *nodus* Apollonius solved to open the novel as he solved Tarsia's *nodos* to end it.

RA, the oldest redaction of the text, contains (ch. 11) seventeen lines of dactylic hexameter about a storm at sea, which is a clear borrowing from Virgil's *Aeneid* 1.81–141. In ch. 23 (17.18–22) there are strong echoes of Ovid, and in ch. 48 (40.18–19) Apollonius' wife is described as a new Dido in words from *Aeneid* 1.496–497, 4.136. If this were originally a Greek text, we could expect some borrowings from classical Greek authors. Since all the imitations arise from Latin authors, we can be forgiven for assuming that the work was from its origin Latin. Klebs has produced a substantial list of the borrowings in the *Historia* from Latin authors (pp. 280–293) and also shown that the inscriptions recorded in the novel are set up in the style of Latin inscriptions (pp. 196–205) and that all references to metals, coins, monetary values and measures are Latin (pp. 191–196).[41] I would add that all terms of endearment and little words of politeness are Latin. While attempts have been made to connect the *Historia* to several Greek papyrus fragments[42] and through these back to the influence of the *Odyssey*, little enthusiasm has been generated for them: the name Apollonius appearing in a narrative setting written on papyrus does not constitute a prior occurrence or textual connection. The riddle about incest which Antiochus poses to Apollonius at ch. 4, however, does have a Greek parallel. In a bathhouse in Pergamum Hepding[43] reports that there is a Greek inscription which reads like our riddle; the date of the inscription, however, is termed "Byzantine" by the epigraphers and may, in fact, be quite late.[44]

---

[40] Schmeling (1994a).
[41] Klebs (1899).
[42] Mazza (1985); Holzberg (1990).
[43] Hepding (1913) 180–181.
[44] Hexter (1988) 189; Archibald (1991) 24.

Hexter sums up the arguments against a Greek original very nicely: "... Grecisms do not necessarily allow us to posit a Greek original; rather they bespeak the degree to which Greek, and the extensive literature of translation from Greek, had become part of the language;"[45] the strongest statement that the *Historia* is a Latin novel in origin and not a translation from the Greek is made by Perry.[46] In his literary analysis of the *Historia* Konstan comes to the conclusion that it should not be grouped with the Greek novels but with the Latin: "... the *History of Apollonius*.... is in its essential theme and structure entirely different from the pattern that informs all the surviving Greek novels.... It is possible, of course, to posit a comparable tradition in Greek, but in the absence of firm evidence for such a type, it seems economical to treat *Apollonius* as distinctly Latin in structure and theme as well as in language."[47]

The text is held by some to be not only a translation into Latin from Greek but also of Christian origin, whose translation was subjected to Late Latin influences from the Itala and Vulgate. An example of this influence is cited in ch. 37 (29.7), *ut quid* for the classical *quid* (= why). The explanation goes something like this: the Greek original read ἵνα τί which was translated not by the Classical *quid* but by the Late Latin *ut quid*, because the translator was a Christian who knew that the expression ἵνα τί in the Greek New Testament was regularly put into Latin as *ut quid*; an alternative explanation is that the pagan author wrote *quid* but a late scribe changed *quid* to *ut quid* under the influence of the Itala and Vulgate. Since the evidence for a Greek original of the *Historia* is weak at best, the first explanation ought to be rejected. If the second explanation for *ut quid* is valid, then the *ut quid* can easily be changed to its original form. If *ut quid* is the regular way for the *Historia* to express the classical *quid* (= why), then we can expect *ut quid* to appear regularly, as it does in the Itala, Vulgate, writings of St. Augustine, etc. Upon investigation, however, we discover that *ut quid* for *quid* appears only once in all RA (and not at all in RB).[48] It thus seems logical to conclude that a late scribe under the influence of Late Latin usage of *ut quid* erroneously at this one point added *ut* to *quid*, and that the editor should thus delete it.

---

[45] Hexter (1988) 189.
[46] Perry (1967) 294–324.
[47] Konstan (1994a) 113; cf. Schmeling (1996a).
[48] The *ut* of *ut quid* at 29.7 in MSS AP could easily have entered the tradition

Other linguistic evidence to support the thesis that the *Historia* is a religious text rests on such expressions *deo volente* at ch. 20 (14.31).[49] The use of the singular *deus* instead of the plural is thought to indicate the Christian *deus*. It is more likely, however, that such expressions lie within the range of standard pagan literature; Virgil for example uses it at *Aeneid* 1.303, Petronius at 38.9, and we find τοῦ θεοῦ βουλομένου in the non-Christian novel of Xenophon of Ephesus (1.7) and θεοῦ νεύοντος in Heliodorus 1.22 and 7.5. In ch. 50 (42.19–21) we read after the words *lapidibus eos occiderunt* the scribal insertion *et ad bestias terrae et volucres caeli . . . negarentur* which Klebs[50] deleted as a biblical addition from Vulgate *Ierem.*7.33, *Ezech.*29.5, 1 *Reg.*17.46 and an interpolation from ch. 44 (37.21). Some editors do not delete such interpolations because they hold that the text of the *Historia* has been contaminated so thoroughly that corrections are futile or because they believe that the earliest redaction dating to the sixth century is a Christian document, and that the best an editor can hope to do is to print an apographon of the best MS of each redaction. The text of the *Historia* is considered by some not to be fixed to a particular time, e.g., to the time of its composition in the early years of the third century but to be defined only by its earliest and best MSS of the ninth century.

If the *Historia* is a Christian work which can be recognized by the faithful, how can we explain the ordination of Apollonius' wife into the priesthood of Diana, or the comparison of Apollonius to the god Apollo, or the celebration of the festival of Neptune? The emphasis in the *Historia* on virginity can be seen as a Christian sentiment, along with the belief that slaves should be treated as equals of free people. In ch. 51 (43.31–32) the expression *in pace atque senectute bona defuncti sunt* could be a Christian sentiment. Sentiments, however, are unreliable gauges: protection of virginity at any cost is a sentiment which runs through most Greek novels, Seneca (*Ep.*47) expresses fine Christian sentiments about slaves and (*de Cons. ad Marc.*19.6) about dying in peace. All of this, however, has not kept Hexter from stating categorically that the anonymous author of the *Historia* was a Christian: "I feel . . . that the *H(istoria) A(pollonii)* is profoundly, albeit never

---

from *ut vidit* at 29.6. *quid* in RB ch. 44 (76.17) is supported by MS βMπ, *ut quid* by the MSS of RT and Riese (1893); MS V in RC at 126.8 offers *ut quid*.

[49] Merkelbach (1962).
[50] Klebs (1899) 41–42.

explicitly, Christian.... I can well imagine a Christian writer setting the romance in a pagan world for appropriate generic color."[51]

I can see the pagan references in the Latin but, except for the frequent uses of *deus* in the singular, I cannot find specifically Christian material in the *Historia*. What would make it and its author Christian? Thirty years ago Merkelbach[52] put forward the thesis "that all the surviving novels, except that of Chariton, are in fact Mysterientexte, a kind of ancient romans-à-clef meant to be fully intelligible only to the properly initiated into the mysteries."[53] Initiated Christians read Christian sentiments into the *Historia* (and Virgil's *Fourth Eclogue*), but that is far from meaning the same thing as a Christian novel. What Hexter is certain is a Christian novel, Merkelbach is sure is an "Isisroman".[54] In the same way that the ancient novels cannot be Mysterientexte, so the *Historia* cannot be Christian: there should be a sign. Winkler proposes for the sake of argument (a theory to resolve a mystery) that the *Asinus Aureus* is an Isisroman in the guise of a confession: "One of the most interesting and suggestive approaches to the *AA* is that which locates the implied occasion of its narration ... in a temple precinct. A visitor to any of the great public sanctuaries of the ancient world would have encountered among the crowds of ... devout worshippers two kinds of storytellers: exegetes and confessors."[55] But, continues Winkler, this "finally fails as an explanation on two counts: its proponents can explain neither why Isis is a secret for ten books nor why if the entire *AA* is a bearing-witness the narrator *never* says so to us."[56] For similar reasons the designation of the *Historia* as a Christian novel fails. What would be necessary for the *Historia* to be taken as a Christian document? The author could have stated it openly, but because he is creating a literary product he can be expected to be creative; the narrator could have told us in the closing words of the novel that Apollonius presented a copy of his adventures to his local Christian church. Instead we learn (in RB and RC) that Apollonius deposited "one copy of his adventures in the temple of Diana at Ephesus and a second copy in his

---

[51] Hexter (1988) 188.
[52] Merkelbach (1962).
[53] Hägg (1983) 101.
[54] Merkelbach (1962) 161–171.
[55] Winkler (1985) 233.
[56] Winkler (1985) 241.

own library" (ch. 51). The reader is led to believe that the work is entrusted to Diana.

In addition to its many other troubles the *Historia* is held by some to be an epitome. As early as 1876 Rohde had considered the *Historia* to be a crazy patchwork of different stories sewn together—not too artfully, and thus a kind of epitome.[57] Garin and Merkelbach see it as a much shortened work, basing their judgments for the most part on the skeleton-like narrative, summaries instead of scenes, and a sloppiness in handling details of fact, motivation, and story-line.[58] When emphasizing the joints in the chain, the critic can question whether or not the chain will hold; when all the joints are not well made, the critic may lose sight of the whole chain in his eager pursuit to point out problems in construction. The judgment of history, however, does not always follow the opinions of negative critics: "The *Historia Apollonii* is a unique example of 'a novel' from late antiquity which was known and enjoyed throughout the Middle Ages and into the Renaissance and maintained unbroken popularity... from the fifth century to the seventeenth."[59] It is interesting to note that among the ancient novels the *Ephesiaca* of Xenophon of Ephesus is often regarded as the one most similar to the *Historia* and also regarded as an epitome.[60] Observing the uneven rhythm, spasmodic time-line, faulty narrative composition and plot-structure, as many of the seams holding the novel together are exposed to view, some critics label the *Historia* and the *Ephesiaca* as epitomes.[61] Looking at the same shortcomings in these two novels, Hägg comes to a different conclusion:

> ... both the *Historia Apollonii* and the *Ephesiaca* have now and then been taken as unskillful abbreviations of originally homogeneous and well-written novels. To me, however, this seems about as well founded as it would be to maintain that modern detective stories or adventure films which are lacking in logic and characterization are really cut versions of more accomplished representatives of those genres.[62]

A practical problem for those who subscribe to the epitome theory is to explain how all redactions, which differ greatly in dates of origin, could be turned into almost identical epitomes.

---

[57] Rohde (1914) 435ff., especially 447ff.
[58] Garin (1914); Merkelbach (1962) 161ff.
[59] Archibald (1991) 3.
[60] Rohde (1914) 440ff.; Garin (1914); Riese (1893) XVI–XVII.
[61] Bürger (1892).
[62] Hägg (1983) 152–153.

The text of the Latin *Historia* appears to have been composed early in the third century. Evidence for such a date is provided by an examination of the relative values of coins cited in the text. The version of the text available to us today seems to go back to a redaction made in the fifth-sixth century by a Christian writer; our oldest MSS date from the ninth century. The comparative numismatic data, the only hard-evidence for dating the *Historia*, gathered by scholars such as Duncan-Jones, Callu, Lana, Nocera Lo Giudice, and Ziegler seem to point with some certainty to a date of composition in the early third century.[63] Attempts to see in several Greek papyri fragments, which mention a certain Apollonius and which are probably datable to the third century, a connection with the *Historia*, are not convincing.[64] Had the papyri in fact any connection with the *Historia*, the task of dating the novel would become simpler. Depending on which redaction the reader has before him, he will find ten or fewer riddles in chs. 42-43; these same riddles are found scattered in Symphosius, a shadowy figure usually dated to the fourth-fifth century. Did Symphosius compose the metrical riddles, did he collect them, or were they simply credited to him when someone mistook *symphosius* for *symposius*?[65] In any case no help with dating comes from this quarter. Hepding found an inscription in a bathhouse in Pergamum which offers us a Greek version of the incest riddle of Antiochus in ch. 4. Because the inscription is only generally datable to the Byzantine period, it is not helpful for our purposes.[66]

The earliest reference (of which we can be quite certain) to the *Historia* comes from Fortunatus (*Opera Poetica* 6.8.5-6) and dates to about 566—after he had suffered certain experiences in traveling:

> tristius erro nimis patriis vagus exul ab oris
> quam sit Apollonius naufragus hospes aquis.

A second sixth century reference is found in the anonymous work *de Dubiis Nominibus*, a manual on the correct use of genders of nouns:

> GYMNASIUM generis neutri—sicit "balneum"—: in Apollonio: gymnasium patet.

---

[63] Duncan-Jones (1982); Callu (1980); Lana (1975); Nocera Lo Giudice (1979); Ziegler (1977) and (1984).
[64] Mazza (1985); Holzberg (1990); Kussl (1991).
[65] Murru (1980).
[66] Hepding (1913); Hexter (1988) 189; Archibald (1991) 24.

The phrase *gymnasium patet* occurs at ch. 13 in RA, RB, RC. The next reference to the *Historia* dates from 747 when Abbot Wando of St. Wandrille donated a copy of the *Historia* to the library of the monastery.[67]

It is not a sterile academic pursuit to try to discover whether the *Historia* was composed in Latin or Greek, or at what date, or if it is a Christian novel: such attempts do not constitute a biographical fallacy. To begin at the beginning: our problem with the *Historia* is that what it was, when it was composed in the third century, became something else by the sixth century when we get our first look at it. If the *Historia* was written originally in Greek, then our version is a substantial re-working and not a translation. This would mean, for example, that where our Latin version borrows lines from Virgil and Ovid, the Greek original would have quoted Greek writers; the Latin translator would have been highly gifted in comparative literature. If the *Historia* is a Greek work, then it was meant for a Greek speaking audience, and, only after it was re-worked into Latin, would it have come under the influence of those familiar with the Latin bible. If it is a Greek work, then it is the only extant Greek novel in which the two main actors are not the Liebespaar, in which the driving force or efficient motif is not erotic love but paternal affection. While all extant Greek novels are concerned with erotic love between a young woman and man, it is the Latin novels which experiment with new subject matter.

Because of the corroboration offered by the numismatic evidence (see above) I feel some confidence in dating the *Historia* to the early third century. Once I have accepted this date, I am encouraged to correct expressions like *ut quid* added to the text (see above) and to delete phrases imported from the Vulgate like *ad bestias terrae* (see above), which if left as they stand represent anachronisms. To say that there are Grecisms in the language of the *Historia* and to conclude from this that the original language of the *Historia* is Greek is not really convincing. We are not at all surprised to find that Greek words, expressions, and grammatical constructions appear in a Latin work of the third century. References are made in the text to pagan deities, but there is not one specific mention of the Christian god. It is clear that by the fifth-sixth century several expressions from well

---

[67] A list of references can be found in Archibald (1991) 217ff.

known stories in the Vulgate had crept into the text, added to be sure by pious scribes who knew by heart many of the stories. If the *Historia* were, however, a Greek or Christian work we could expect it to look or to be presented as such. Since in the so-called Pseudo-Clementine *Homilies/Recognitiones* we possess a kind of early Christian novel in Greek together with a Latin version, we need not speculate about its nature: the Christian novel is clearly Christian.

Hägg points out for us that "*The Pseudo-Clementines* ... may rightly claim to be called the first genuine Christian novel, even though it is built on the remains of a pagan one."[68] Clement is the narrator and a protagonist, not the author, of the two extant works, the Greek *Homilies* and the Latin *Recognitiones*, both of the fourth century and both probably adaptations of a second-third century Greek work called something like *Periodoi Petrou*. These "Journeys of Peter" are a collection of debates and sermons ostensibly made by Peter to strengthen the faithful, convert the heathens, and refute the pagans. Though the bulk of the *Homilies* and *Recognitiones* is consigned to sermons of Peter, Clement embellishes the religious material by adding the novel-like story of his family's history. Clement leaves Rome and travels to Palestine where he accompanies the itinerant preacher and acts the part of Watson reporting the exploits of Holmes. It is not until *Recognitiones* 7.8 that Clement tells Peter (and the reader) the story of his life (= novel). He is the youngest son of Mattidia and Faustus and has older (twin) brothers Faustinus and Faustinianus. Saying that she was ordered to do so in a dream, Mattidia takes the twins and boards a ship for Athens—this is the last known about them. After sending messengers and waiting many years, Faustus leaves Clement in Rome and goes in search of his wife. That was twenty years ago, says Clement. Later on the island of Arados (where hero and heroine of Chariton's novel are reunited) Peter strikes up a conversation with an old beggar woman who says that she left home with her twins to escape the incestuous advances of her brother-in-law. As it turns out she is Mattidia, and Peter oversees her recognition with Clement. Then on their journey to Antioch Peter and Company first discover the twins, who had been captured by pirates, and soon thereafter Faustus. The plot of Clement's story of his family could easily be an adaptation of a pagan novel, to which the author grafted the larger sayings of Peter with the intention of leavening the flat

---

[68] Hägg (1983) 162-163.

dough of Peter's preaching and making the whole more palatable. Whatever the origin, the final product is clearly Christian.

Language and Style

The language of the *Historia* is straightforward, often paratactic rather than syntactic, and behind the unassuming vocabulary lie simple thoughts. Even if the reader should skip over the first eighteen chapters, he can make sense of the uncomplicated plot at ch. 19, to which I would like now to direct his attention:

> rex autem post paucos dies tenens Apollonium manu forum petit et cum eo deambulavit. iuvenes scholastici tres nobilissimi, qui per longum tempus filiam eius petebant in matrimonium, pariter omnes una voce salutaverunt eum. quos videns rex subridens ait illis: "quid est hoc quod una voce me pariter salutastis?" unus ex ipsis ait: "petentibus nobis filiam tuam in matrimonium tu saepius nos differendo fatigas...." rex ait... "sed ne videar vos diutius differre, scribite in codicillos nomina vestra...." illi tres itaque iuvenes scripserunt nomina sua.... rex accepit codicillos anuloque suo signavit datque Apollonio dicens.

From the first sentence the reader is exposed to the author's fondness for present participles: *tenens* stands in place of a third finite verb in a short sentence and allows the author to avoid a subordinate clause—also to miss an historical period. In the third sentence the reader comes upon a regular feature in the language of the *Historia*, two present participles modifying the same noun but remaining asyndetic = *videns rex subridens*. *rex* is both the connector by syntax of the participles and by its position in the line their divider; the internal rhyme is not particularly pleasing, and the hissing of the "s" sounds with which five of the six words in the phrase end (*quos videns rex subridens ait illis*) deceives the readers into thinking that the sweet nature of the speaker does not extend to those wooing his only daughter. The juxtaposition of *omnes una*, however, is a nice touch. In the long Latin quotation above the last word (*dicens*) illustrates the most common use of the participle in the *Historia*: a main verb plus participle just before a quotation (e.g., *respiciens... ait*, or *intrat... dicens*). In the final sentence the reader is brought up short by the sequence of tenses: *accepit... signavit... datque... dicens*. It is unlikely that *dat* is a late scribal error and unlikely to be an error e perseveratione (unless *signAvit → dAt*), and with *desiderat* eighteen words forward an error ex expectatione is also unlikely; nor is *dat* a "correction" for something like *dans Apollonio et dicens*. This is in fact only one example of many problems with the sequence of tenses.

Much repetitive language is found between the third person narrative and the dialogue—as if the actors in the scene could overhear the comments of the narrator, who states that the suitors *pariter omnes una voce salutaverunt eum*; the actor picks up the line as though it were an on-stage utterance and says: "*quid est hoc quod una voce me pariter salutastis?*" The reply to a statement is recast by the second party in the words of the first: "*saepius nos differendo fatigas*" becomes "*sed ne videar vos diutius differre*". On every page these re-phrasings are found and seem to be one way in which the author creates a tight weave in the fabric of his narrative.

Rhetoric and point for the most part seem not to have much influence on the language of the *Historia*, and the level flow of the narrative is rarely broken by witty or striking *sententiae*: sentences seldom rise to a climax or fall to a quiet paradox. Tricola when used do not really ascend or descend (1.9–10): *qui cum luctatur cum furore, pugnat cum dolore, vincitur amore*; we are aware only of *-ore, -ore, -ore*. The anonymous author of the *Historia* is not, however, without art. Apollonius' comment at ch. 16 to Archistrates about his daughter's musical talent is designed not to offend (12.13): *filia enim tua in artem musicam incidit, sed non didicit*. It is a diplomatic criticism of the young princess who likes music but does not care much for the work associated with acquiring the skill. Then after listening to Apollonius' musical offering, she surprises her father by saying that she is now willing to study and wants Apollonius for a teacher. The father is amused (ch. 18) by his youthful daughter who in her eagerness to learn has risen before midday (13.22): *filia dulcis, quid est quod tam mane praeter consuetudinem vigilasti?* The author plays with the two verbs *incidit ... didicit: -dicit* is an inverted form of *-cidit*. At times the language can be almost cantabile as at 27.16: *plus dabis plus plorabis*. The gentle humor of the father toward his daughter in *praeter consuetudinem*, is returned by the daughter in ch. 23 where she tries to persuade her father that, since she is pregnant, he should allow her to accompany her husband on a trip (17.27): *unam dimittis, en duas recipies*. Also the dark side of humor surfaces at ch. 39 as Athenagoras offers a sailor two gold coins to descend into the hold of a ship and question a man who has threatened to break the legs of anyone who disturbs him; the sailor replies (31.6–7): *si possum de duobus aureis quattuor habere crura*. We find that

Antiochus can produce a modest *sententia* in ch. 7, as he calculates the chances of a person escaping his clutches (5.6–7): *fugere quidem potest, sed effugere non potest.* Svoboda demonstrates that our author, while skillfully employing numerous literary tropes, conspicuously shuns the common metaphor.[69]

The author of the *Historia* is also able to orchestrate his language on a larger stage. A plaintive speech of Stranguillio in ch. 32 is neatly framed by parallel words (24.30–31) and constructions: *equidem da mihi vestes lugubres, ut lugeam me, qui talem sum sortitus sceleratam coniugem. heu mihi!*, and the concluding words (25.10–11): *heu mihi, caecatus sum! lugeam me et innocentem virginem, quia iunctus sum ad pessimam venenosamque serpentem et iniquam coniugem.* The beginning and ending are enhanced by a figura etymologica, *lugubres . . . lugeam* and *iunctus sum . . . coniugem*. Such framing is not an accident and occurs at other places, e.g., 14.14–15.23–24.

What arrests the reader's sympathy and saves the story from often artless narrative scenes is poignant direct speech. As soon as the nurse of Antiochus' daughter realizes that the young woman has been raped, she blurts outs (2.6): "*cur ergo non indicas patri?*" The desperate girl replies: "*et ubi est pater?*" Or there is the episode at 15.3–7 where Archistrates' daughter, though hopelessly in love with Apollonius, is so shy that she can discuss her loved one even with her father only in a letter and then only without mentioning his name: "*bone rex et pater optime . . . illum volo coniugem naufragio patrimonio deceptum. et si miraris . . . quod pudica virgo tam impudenter scripserim: per certam litteram mandavi, quae pudorem non habet.*" Clearly more at home with dialogue than with scenes, our author may have some experience writing for the theater, and Perry offers supporting evidence for this, when he states that several episodes in the *Historia* seem to have been prepared for the stage.[70]

Relationship of the Historia to Other Ancient Novels

The *Historia* is unlike the extant Greek novels, which are focused on the Liebespaar, a heterosexual relationship of two young people which blossoms into a love affair and marriage. As the young daughter of

---

[69] Svoboda (1962).
[70] Perry (1967) 306–307.

king Antiochus stands in her bedroom and watches as the (1.17) *guttae sanguinis in pavimento ceciderunt*, the *Historia* departs from the norm of the Greek novel and charts new waters.

Affinities between the *Historia* and the Greek novel exist in abundance in details and in incidents, but, as we go on to discover, the *Historia*, while clearly related to, is fundamentally different from, the Greek novel. As the *Satyrica* of Petronius and the *Metamorphoses* of Apuleius on the one hand stand within the magical generic circle of the ancient novel, but on the other are radically different in tone, attitude and structure from the Greek novels, so the *Historia* has positioned itself apart from the Greek novels—not, however, by moving more closely to the other two Latin novels. For many years scholars have compared the *Historia* with Xenophon of Ephesus' *Ephesiaca*, and this comparison is still useful: both novels are marked by skeleton-like narratives which encourage critics to brand them as epitomes. While the *Satyrica* and *Metamorphoses* are ego-narratives, the Greek novels (with a partial exception for Achilles Tatius' work) and the *Historia* utilize third-person narrators.

Pirates and brothelkeepers play similar and important roles in both the *Historia* and the *Ephesiaca*. Xenophon offers us an episode (perhaps borrowed from Chariton 1.9) in which Anthia, believed dead, is buried but rescued by pirates (3.8) and later sold to a brothelkeeper (5.5); Tarsia is thought to have died (similarly her mother) and been buried, but in reality was rescued by pirates and sold to a brothelkeeper (chs. 31–33). In Chariton (1.5), Xenophon (3.6–7), Achilles Tatius (3.15), Longus (4.35), Heliodorus (1.30), Petronius (111), and the *Historia* (ch. 25), a heroine is erroneously taken for dead (cf. Scheintod motif, Aarne Type 990).[71] Anthia appears to have died from a poison supplied by a physician from Ephesus who, however, was a kind man and had prepared only a sleeping draught; Tarsia's mother, assumed dead, was brought back to life by a young physician's assistant in Ephesus. Both the *Ephesiaca* and the *Historia* (ch. 38) have episodes about the construction of tombs and both record the epitaphs. As Habrocomes is befriended by a fisherman (5.1) after his shipwreck, so is Apollonius (ch. 12); as Perilaus delays his marriage to Anthia for thirty days (2.13), so Athenagoras agrees to buy Tarsia after a thirty-day interval. In the last chapter of both novels the narrators note that copies of the adventures of the heroes and heroines (sc. the

---

[71] Aarne (1964); cf. Schmeling (1980) 21ff. for analysis by motif.

novels themselves) have been deposited in the temple of Diana at Ephesus. The adventures become memoires.

From short incidents let us go on to compare an episode in the *Historia* with one in the *Ephesiaca*. I do not wish to imply that one novelist borrowed from the other; it is much more likely that, since they work in the same genre, they borrow from a common store. Variations on the motifs in this episode are found in other authors. At *Ephesiaca* 5.5 Rhenaea discovers that her husband Polyidus is in love with Anthia and so orders her servant Clytus to sell Anthia to a brothel: Anthia pleads for mercy, and Clytus at first relents but then sells her. As Rhenaea lies to Polyidus about Anthia's fate, Clytus reports that Anthia has been sold. Anthia's owner dresses her in fitting clothes and displays her before the brothel (5.7). Customers are eager to purchase her services, but the resourceful Anthia feigns epilepsy, and the customers take pity on her. Hippothous, a friend of Anthia's husband, purchases her (5.9) from the brothelkeeper, restrains himself when he learns her story, and eventually helps to restore her to her husband. In the *Historia* (ch. 31) Dionysias discovers that her daughter has no suitors because Tarsia (her ward) distracts them, and so she orders her servant Theophilus to kill her. As Tarsia pleads with him for her life, pirates appear, seize her and sell her to a brothelkeeper. After Theophilus reports that Tarsia has been killed, Dionysias lies to her husband that in a moment of insane rage she killed her young ward. Tarsia's crib at the brothel is beautifully adorned (ch. 34) and customers line up. With great verbal skill in pleading her case, Tarsia extracts fees from her would-be clients without delivering any services. Athenagoras, her first customer and future husband restrains himself after hearing her story, decides to become her guardian (ch. 36), and eventually helps to restore her to her father.

The opening paragraphs of the ancient novels are important and perhaps even signal the genre of the works. The formula for the opening would run something like: "In city X there lived a man and woman who had a daughter so beautiful that ... and also another husband and wife who had a son so handsome that...." We see this formula in Chariton, Xenophon and the *Historia* (and in the interpolated story of Cupid and Psyche in Apuleius' *Metamorphoses* 4.28–6.25), and a modified formula in Longus and Achilles Tatius. An ingredient of the opening formula is the early confirmation of the hero's and heroine's identity. Another ingredient which serves as a genre marker is, as Fowler[72] has noted about the early English novel, "... the pretense of factuality... Fictional narratives were presented as Memoires or Adventures or Histories. So we have *The History of Tom Jones*...." The title of our novel, *Historia Apollonii Regis Tyri*, seems to imply that same pretense of factuality. The introduction of an historical king named Antiochus, after whom the city is named, is further indication of a desire on the part of our novelist to allow the reader to connive at fiction as fact. Chariton opens his novel with at least one historical figure and then adds that he will narrate for us something that had already taken place, and Xenophon implies that his characters are real. The games of fact/fiction are rarely abandoned completely by the ancient novelists.

While from the evidence of the extant works it seems that most ancient novelists shun narratives about kings and queens and prefer to write about somewhat more lowly folk (albeit exceptionally beautiful ones), the anonymous author of the *Historia* puts royalty at the center of his story, and in this respect the *Historia* shares something with *Aethiopica*.

Now that we have stressed similarities between the *Historia* and other ancient novels with an eye toward proving that the *Historia* is one of the ancient novels, we must also point out how it stands apart from the Greek novels—while at the same time remaining within the genre. Because the author of the *Historia* on page one introduces to the reader a most beautiful young woman and provides her with a specific historical setting—novelistic procedures with which the reader would have some familiarity—the author can play with the initial expectations he has raised. Instead of a handsome suitor to match the beautiful maiden, the reader is introduced to her father who murders all suitors. Before the reader has the opportunity to miss the appearance of the handsome young man in love with the beautiful princess, we discover that the father has assumed the position and that instead of the expected heterosexual love story we have a story of incest: the princess, no matter how beautiful, cannot be the heroine of the story nor can she marry the man in love with her (marriage is de rigueur in the Greek novels); instead of a Liebespaar we have an incestuous father-daughter relationship. From the beginning the author is announcing to the reader, who cannot see it at this point, that his novel will concern itself primarily with love stories, not those

---

[72] Fowler (1982) 93.

of young men and women, but those of fathers and daughters. And in the opening chapters we meet the evil kind of father-daughter relationship against which all the later good ones will be judged.

Recently Szepessy has argued that a new class or sub-genre of ancient novel, which he terms the Family Novel, should be used when one speaks of the *Historia*, because it is so radically different from the other ancient novels.[73] Basing his study of the *Historia* on its themes and the structure of the male/female roles, Konstan would agree partially with Szepessy but sees the *Historia* as a Latin novel: "On the basis of the preceding description, it is easy to see that... *The History*..., which is frequently taken to be a close relative of the Greek novels, is in fact cut to an entirely different pattern."[74]

Interpretive Essay

> However beautiful the strategy, you should occasionally look at the results.
>
> Churchill

From time to time in the *Historia* the reader is allowed to see into the feelings of an actor (Antiochus' daughter after her rape, Dionysias in fear of Tarsia, Apollonius at the death of his daughter), and at those times the author seems to have chosen as the approach to the narrative what Kettle calls "life" (an interest in the feelings/joy/sadness of living); much more often, however, our author shows an interest in what Kettle calls "pattern" (the point or significance of living).[75] Novels usually embrace both "life" and "pattern" but with a preference of one over the other, and Archibald makes much of the *Historia* as a "pattern" narrative: "... it is a carefully patterned and symmetrical story which derives its unity from the recurrence of some important themes ... but motivation and characterization receive short shrift."[76] Our author emphasizes that the significant items in life follow a structure: good fathers prosper, honest slaves are rewarded, and irony does not often apply to the micromanagement of lives.

---

[73] Szepessy (1985–1988).
[74] Konstan (1994a) 100; cf. Schmeling (1996a).
[75] Kettle (1967) 20ff.
[76] Archibald (1991) 12–13.

We see a different emphasis or bias in the *Satyrica*, e.g., where Petronius develops Trimalchio into a particular individual who is unique in classical literature and who, it seems to us, conveys the feelings of life from A.D. 66. Though an individualized character, Trimalchio may nevertheless represent a particular kind of person (pattern), a type of successful entrepreneur in the early Empire who exhibits acquisitive skills (pattern) but at the same time such a "Lust am Leben" (life)[77] that we feel some connection to his world. In the *Historia*, then, we the readers seem to confront a narrative more of pattern than of life.

Of the three ancient novels in Latin (four if we include the Christian Pseudo-Clementine *Recognitiones*) only the *Historia* has an external (to the novel), third-person, omniscient, unpersonalized narrator, and so the reader of the *Historia* unlike that of Petronius and Apuleius feels no tension between the narrator of the story and the story itself. Lucius, the first-person narrator of Apuleius' *Metamorphoses* confronts his reader in the opening paragraph,[78] and Encolpius in the *Satyrica* clearly tries to manipulate his reader,[79] who become suspicious of both these narrators-in-the-story because from personal experience readers know that individuals who tell stories about themselves tend to exaggerate, to choose only interesting details, or to lack the proper perspective, i.e., narrators internal to the story can easily become unreliable. A narrator like the one for the *Historia* appears to be more reliable because he seems to defend no character, and, since he is perceived to be able to see all sides, he has a certain authority: our narrator hates incest, admires respectability and tradition, and praises all generally accepted societal values and hierarchies.[80] Thus the focus in the *Historia* is not on the narrator but on the narrative told, and the language of the third-person narrator, whether formal or informal, whether spoken by king or slave, used in thought or employed for description, is diaphanous and does not call attention to itself as something made strange, but encourages the reader to focus on the story. If the RB redaction of the *Historia* (ch. 51) can be trusted, the implied medium of the narrative is the record of events set down in writing by Apollonius himself (assumed source) and stored

---

[77] Müller (1980) 111.
[78] Harrison (1990).
[79] Schmeling (1991).
[80] Eagelton (1983) 194ff.

in the temple of Diana in Ephesus for visitors (implied audience) to read and in his own library for his descendants (implied audience) to find—and discovered and made into a story by our narrator. When reading this novel we realize that we are being told a story which took place earlier and which the narrator is re-counting from his perspective for us. Chariton (1.1) says that he will tell us something that γενόμενον. All the reader need do (it is implied) is to trust that the narrator has a good memory; though the reader of the *Historia* like that of the Pentateuch may be unfamiliar with the plot, his inferior position vis-à-vis the omniscient narrator does not really allow for tensions to develop between himself and the narrator. There is no remark, however offhand, to suggest that our narrator is male, female, young, old, Western or Eastern: he—or is it a she?—is simply omniscient. If the implied medium of the *Historia* is the record from the temple of Diana and the assumed source is Apollonius himself (RB. ch. 51), then the reader will have a different attitude toward the narrative than if he believes that an omniscient narrator invented it and that the authority of the author rests on invention only. In either case, however, the narrator is seen as reliable and not intimate; by comparison the personified narrators in the *Satyrica* and *Metamorphoses* are unreliable and intrusive. The implied reader or narratee of the *Historia* could be either (1) no one in particular or (2) someone in Apollonius' library or in the temple of Diana in Ephesus.[81] If the intrusive narrator like Encolpius or Lucius seems to bridge the gap between the fictional and real world (and thus to hint at its fictionality) and to speak almostly directly to the reader, i.e., builds a relationship with the reader, then it appears to follow that the narrator of the *Historia* is likely the creator of a world closed to reality. Where the narrators of the *Satyrica* and *Metamorphoses* hint that their creations, in which they play a major role, are, at least in part, fiction, the narrator of the *Historia* encourages the reader to see an existence so real in his novel that he can deposit a record of it in a temple, while he himself is so remote as narrator so as to be even less substantial than an extrafictional raconteur.

Looking at the *Historia* from the actors' points of view, we see (among other things) that (1) Apollonius believes (erroneously) that

---

[81] Winkler (1985) 240 speculates that the occasion for the original narration of the *Metamorphoses* might have been structured by Apuleius to imitate confessions declaimed in temple precincts.

his wife and daughter are dead; (2) Tarsia believes (erroneously) that Stranguillo and Dionysias are her parents; (3) Tarsia's mother knows (correctly) nothing. The narrator who knows all speaks to the reader who knows only what the narrator chooses to tell: the reader may want to know what happened to Antiochus' wife, Archistrates' wife, Athenagoras' wife (wives as an endangered species), Apollonius' parents and siblings. The voice of the *Historia*, i.e., the point of view (A), is always that of the narrator, who in turn allows certain actors to know parts of the action by compartmentalizing the plot, as it were, and inside each compartment allowing the reader to see what the actor in that compartment can see. The perspective, i.e., the point of view (B), of the actor in each compartment is limited (but clear to the reader) until the end of the story, when the voice of the narrator and the perspectives of all the actors are more or less made the same.

The voice of the narrator tells the reader a few facts about the actors and their actions, and these he often arranges into patterns. Our author might be viewed as a movie director interpreting (via patterns) the real items in life, the most important of which for this novel is the relationship of fathers and daughters. We can see just how good a director our author is at controlling information, if we would imagine, e.g., the staging or filming of the opening scene of the *Historia*.

The film version of the *Historia* might open with a king brooding in a dark room or on his throne in his palace, and then the scene might switch to another room where a beautiful young but sad girl stands looking at an unused wedding dress. The viewer can see that she is beautiful, but only a narrator can tell us exactly why she is sad and that she is as lovely as a goddess; she could, however, be dressed and made up in imitation of a statue of a goddess. The scene switches back to the king who is visibly agitated, as he contemplates the beauty of the young woman, who might be his wife, mistress, sister, daughter, or a visitor. The "pattern" of father-daughter relationships which the author wishes to explore will be less clear to the viewer than it is at this time even to the reader, who at least knows that the girl is the king's daughter. To the modern viewer the rape scene in ch. 1 will be all too familiar; the uselessness of the young girl's resistance adds pathos to the setting, while the blood dripping on the floor represents the graphic detail so dear to the hearts of many fans of the cinema. When the young woman's nurse enters the room, she does not immediately understand the situation, because the girl insists on replying to her questions in riddles only. Eventually the girl conveys the information that the rape was incest and the rapist her own father.

Even from such a small sample, which is probably in many ways representative of the whole, it seems fair to observe that our author presents a narrative which has a straight-forward time-line and graphic settings. There are no flights of fancy in the narrative which other (later) novels develop and which film directors find almost impossible to reproduce, because they cannot restrict and confine the views of their audiences as can writers. What the author of the *Historia* narrates is almost always so concrete and linear that it seems an enactment rather than a narrative of the kind which other authors might manipulate and which would be fraught with nuance. It is perhaps this dedication to the graphic in a precise linear approach (which looks so unadorned) that makes the *Historia* often seem such a simple work. Our author, however, mixes the ways in which the reader learns about king Anthiochus, e.g.: he *tells* us about Antiochus' lack of control of his emotions and then *shows* (how unlike ancient stage productions) us the rape of his daughter. Later he will *tell* us that king Archistrates loves his daughter and then *show* us in many ways how the king expresses his love. This mixture of telling and showing is quite refreshing.

The characterization of Tarsia is probably the best drawn in the novel because our author not only has others tell us about her (ch. 31), allows us to form opinions of her by her deeds (ch. 30) and by her erudite conversation (ch. 42),[82] but also provides the reader with a symbol for Tarsia (ch. 32), by which our appreciation of her is heightened. At ch. 32 Dionysias (a Svengali to her puppet husband) erects a tomb for Tarsia, which reads *Dii Manes... Tarsiae*, and to all the world Tarsia ceases to exist; she is a non-person. Dionysias knows that Tarsia is not buried in the tomb but believes that Theophilus has killed her; Theophilus is convinced that in the hands of pirates she is as good as dead; Apollonius thinks that she is in the tomb; Tarsia's mother and grandfather do not know that she even exists. Whatever attributes she had as a person she loses when she is forced to become a prostitute (ch. 33). The symbolic nature of her tomb and of her name written on the poster above her crib in the brothel convey more to the reader about her condition than do all

---

[82] Archibald (1988).

her tears. Apollonius, too, is given a striking symbol and that is the wrecked ship: his life is in ruins even as his wrecked ships are symbols which he shares among others with Odysseus and Aeneas.

The reader's attention, interest and curiosity are especially piqued in two places in the novel because the reader is not told (an unusual event) what is happening: at ch. 27 Apollonius' wife is placed among the priestesses of Diana in Ephesus, and in ch. 28 Apollonius goes off into *ignotas et longinquas Aegypti regiones*. They remain respectively in Ephesus and Egypt for fourteen or fifteen years, separated from the story. Does Apollonius' wife become a kind of Penelope and Apollonius a latter day Odysseus enduring one adventure after another? Though these are not stories our author wishes to tell us, the ellipsis could be important both for the structure and for the interest of the reader.

Many critics hold that one of the many marks of a sophisticated narrative style is the frequency of variation in telling and re-telling the same event. Each time the same incident in a well executed story is retold, the reader learns more about it or has greater insights into its complexity and ramifications of meaning. While the narrative of the *Historia* is not often so well crafted that we can experience a growing appreciation with each retelling of an incident, the recounting of Tarsia's life-story by various people for different reasons signals, however, some sophistication in narrative: it appears that the story of her betrayal by Dionysias, of her supposed death/capture by pirates and (added at times) of her trials in the *lupanar*, is told/retold no fewer than twelve times:

1. ch. 31 Dionysias plans aloud (for the reader's benefit) Tarsia's murder so that her own daughter can find suitors.
2. She explains the plan to Theophilus who will execute the order to gain his freedom.
3. Theophilus explains the plan to Tarsia in order to shift the guilt to Dionysias.
4. ch. 32 The enactment of the plan, which goes awry, and Tarsia is seized by pirates who now control the situation.
5. Theophilus lies to Dionysias that Tarsia has been murdered and asks for his freedom which, because of her niggardly character, she refuses. Theophilus remembers this betrayal and lives to indict Dionysias in ch. 51 and seal her fate.
6. Dionysias incorrectly assumes that because she had ordered it, she knows what happened to Tarsia, and in her attempt to justify her ways to Stranguillio she enriches a fiction with a lie.
7. Stranguillio laments his wife's deeds (which are a fiction)

		but is more concerned with the debt they owe Tarsia's father.
8.	ch. 34	Tarsia tells her story to each of her customers in the *lupanar* and thus preserves her virginity. Like Scheherazade she saves herself with a narrative which has assumed the power of a talisman.
9.	ch. 38	Tarsia tells her story in the forum to a fee-paying public.
10.	ch. 41	Tarsia recounts her history in verse.
11.	ch. 41	Tarsia tells her story to, and is thus recognized by, her father.
12.	ch. 48	Apollonius tells his wife Tarsia's story.

The permutations (truthful and otherwise) and uses to which Tarsia and others put the narrative of her life are quite amazing when isolated and viewed separately from the novel. Each user of her story manipulates the narrative to serve her or his own ends, and our author thereby enhances the economy of the narrative: while the "voice" element of the point of view remains always the third person narrator, the "perspective" element shifts rapidly even when dealing with the same story.

The Nachleben of the Historia

One hundred and fourteen Latin manuscripts attest to the popularity of the *Historia* among literate people in the Middle Ages and Renaissance, but Archibald (1991) is quite correct to halt her study of the influence of the *Historia* at Shakespeare's (and others') *Pericles*, published in quarto in 1609, because after that date the Nachleben of the *Historia* goes into a serious decline—even though the modern poet T.S. Eliot uses the *Historia* in his work *Marina* (1930).

The first translation of the *Historia* into the vernacular was the Old English version of the early eleventh century, and Godfrey of Viterbo in the twelfth century included the *Historia* in his *Pantheon*, a world history. The twelfth century also saw the first translation (adaptation) into Old French, while in the thirteenth century we find the *Historia* translated (adapted) into Danish, Old Norse and Spanish. By the fourteenth century Heinrich von Neustadt had translated (greatly modified) it into German, and in the same period there appear Italian translations, followed by Czech, Dutch, and Byzantine Greek versions in the fifteenth century, and then Hungarian and Polish in the sixteenth.

Not only are there numerous Latin manuscripts of the *Historia*, there are also a considerable number of early translations and larger or shorter allusions to it plus many instances of borrowings or suspected borrowings from it [see Archibald (1991), Appendix I, Latin and Vernacular Versions and Appendix II, Medieval and Renaissance Allusions to the Story of Apollonius]. In the popular and often irreverent *Carmina Burana*, a collection of German and Latin poems assembled in the 13th century, we find a Latin poem (97) of ten stanzas which briefly tells the story of Apollonius. It seems that the *Historia* was read not only by the pious. In another larger and more influential collection from the fourteenth century, the *Gesta Romanorum*, we find that chapter 153 is the story of Apollonius. The *Gesta* is a compilation of tales mostly Greek and Roman plus a few of medieval origin by which the reader was expected to be morally uplifted and spiritually rejuvenated. In a long poem *Confessio Amantis* written by Gower in the late fourteenth century the tale of Apollonius is used as an *exemplum* for the young lover Amans to warn him off mortal sins. No less a writer than Chaucer in *The Canterbury Tales* ("The Man of Law's Tale", lines 77–90, the Introduction) was familiar with the story of Apollonius and commented on the incest motif from the *Historia*. In a lyric of three stanzas Hans Sachs, the Meistersinger von Nürnberg, tells about Apollonius' shipwreck near Cyrene and then rescue and marriage to the king's daughter. Perhaps the most interesting and important appearance of the *Historia* in later literature is in Shakespeare's *Pericles, Prince of Tyre*. How the tale came to the Bard is unknown; since he knew at least a little Latin, it is possible that he read it in one of the texts of the *Historia*, though he more likely got it from Gower or the *Gesta Romanorum*. Though not influential among the *litterati* of the last three hundred years, the *Historia* had been previously both influential and popular across the whole of Europe. Speculation that the *Historia* was also influential in twelfth century France on the *roman d'aventure et d'amour* has been rejected by Archibald.[83]

---

[83] Archibald (1991) 52ff.

13. NOVEL-LIKE WORKS OF EXTENDED PROSE FICTION I

A. LUCIAN'S *VERAE HISTORIAE*

Graham Anderson

I. *Genre*

In contrast to the writers of the five ideal romances, Lucian is well known outside his major excursion into fiction for his contribution to the world of sophistic belles-lettres and literary satire in the second century A.D. Indeed his temperament as a satirist may well account for the choice of parody as a medium for fiction in the first place. Hence too a reason why Lucian's *Verae Historiae*[1] is traditionally marginal in discussions of fiction as such: Perry classified it with comic romances written for a specific purpose,[2] and Lucian's own preface already offers as good a guide as any, mentioning the *Odyssey*, Ctesias and Iambulus as sources while inviting the reader to guess the rest.[3] The resulting parody and pastiche offers a corresponding variety of content,[4] a consideration which may have a bearing on the general layout of episodes.[5] "Lying geography", "bogus ethnography" or "travellers' tales" are at its centre,[6] and these can at least be approximated to "romance"; adventure is included automatically, but love-romance only incidentally and usually as "sexual misadventure".[7]

---

[1] Useful overview in Bompaire (1958) 658–673; *idem* (1988) 31–39. The change in the language of Lucianic criticism can be well measured by contrasting the latter with Fusillo (1988a) 109–135, who brings to bear the angles of vision of Genette and Bakhtin among others. But the basic problems are little changed, and Fusillo is able to present them sympathetically and succinctly.

[2] (1967) 88, cf. 234f.

[3] *VH* 1.2f.

[4] But not so large as to allow the suggestion that it should be allowed as Menippean Satire, or "Menippean Romance", as cautiously suggested by Relihan (1993) 202. Fusillo (1988a) usefully summarizes the secondary features: "dans les interstices de ce discours polémique s'insinue un autre sens, latent celui-ci: une ludicité libre, carnavalesque; un plaisir du paradoxe; un jeu de langage, une tension vers le récit fantastique" (129).

[5] See Anderson (1976b) 7–11.

[6] For the relationship of *VH* to Lucian's to Lucian's own treatise on historiography (*Quomodo historia conscribenda sit*), see Georgiadou and Larmour (1993) 1478–1487. I am not sure that Swain (1994) is fair to the tradition of Quellenforschung on *VH*: no-one who investigates the sources is likely to fail to accept that Lucian treats them as targets.

[7] E.g. *VH* 1.21; 2.25f.

The past decades have also seen serious consideration of *Verae Historiae* as Science Fiction. Reardon firmly rejected the notion, but it is argued at some length by Fredericks and Swanson.[8] The key criterion is really whether ancient concepts of scientific activity are upheld, and in this sense the label does indeed seem admissible. The emphasis on correct observation and inference and the insistence on precise measurements readily point to the literature of the *Periplus*, the genre which includes systematic accounts of voyages of exploration;[9] while the mirror effect of the moon is rationalised as that of a reflecting telescope.[10] Even the monster-fights so obligatory in the early B-science fiction film are already in place.

II. *The Problem of Antonius Diogenes*

One source-puzzle has tended to eclipse the rest: why it should be that Photius came to describe Antonius Diogenes' τὰ ὑπὲρ Θούλην ἄπιστα (*The Wonders beyond Thule*) as the πηγὴ καὶ ῥίζα ('source and root') of Lucian's work; the major recent challenge to current orthodoxy has come from J.R. Morgan.[11] The orthodox position is that Lucian imitates and parodies Antonius Diogenes' use of the (men in the) moon: Morgan argues that Lucian does not use Antonius; that Antonius does not himself put his characters on the moon; and that further he is wrongly thought by Photius to be the root of a number of romances on the basis of false chronological inference.[12]

The parameters of the problem are however such as to make it virtually impossible for Morgan to prove his case without the rest of Antonius Diogenes. In the first place it is not possible to disqualify such an author on the grounds that he is not eligible to be one of Lucian's declared targets anyway. Lucian's notorious "proofs" of

---

[8] Reardon (1965) xxiv, n. 19 ("*not* science fiction..., there is no 'science' in it"). Fredericks (1976) 49–60; Swanson (1979) 228–239.

[9] Inference: e.g. *VH* 1.7 (distinction between footprints of Heracles and Dionysus; river of wine as confirmation of visit of the latter); 1.10 (inference that the world below is the earth). Measurement: e.g. 9ff., cf. Scarcella (1985b) 249–257. The ethnographic sections such as 1.22–25 and 2.11–16 also have a "scientific" flavour over and above parody of specific sources.

[10] *VH* 1.26.

[11] (1985) 475–490.

[12] *Cod.*166.111b.

authenticity are enough to qualify Antonius as a lying historiographer—if any such criterion is really needed to ensure inclusion.[13] Morgan argues that a covering letter claiming the material as fiction disqualifies the work as one of Lucian's targets, which ought strictly speaking to be works where fiction masquerades as truth. This ingenious but in any case hypercritical argument can be neatly offset: Lucian could easily have used the disclaimer of fiction in Antonius' covering letter as the basis for his own preface disclaiming the truth of his following narrative.

Nor does it matter whether Antonius actually does put his characters on the moon: it is clear enough from Photius' summary that the moon figured prominently in Diogenes' ensemble, and that would have been enough for Lucian.[14] By far the weakest of Morgan's arguments is the implication that in order to produce effective parody by exaggeration, Lucian could not be using a writer who already had his characters visit so exotic a quarter already. As usual such an argument can be reversed. Antonius could have made his characters approach and study the moon, but without an actual visit; Lucian could easily have then supplied a long and detailed one, still effectively supplementing the absurdities of his target. But in any case such an argument is wrong in principle. By Morgan's notion of parody it would be inadmissible for example for Lucian to include a reference to Calypso's cave as being exactly as Homer described, precisely because Homer had already done so. It would have been within the bounds of Lucian's very resourceful and unpredictable parody to leave Antonius' moon much as Antonius had described it: there can be no consistent rules in these sorts of games with the erudite reader.

Moreover it seems impossible without Antonius' text to say whether it could not have been the root of the lost *Metamorphoses of Lucius of Patras* as well as *VH*. The fact that Antonius admitted substantial digression, including one on Pythagorean teachings, would leave room for continued uncertainty.[15] Swain entertains the interesting notion that Antonius was himself a parodist, and that accordingly "his relationship to Lucian is most likely one of being a fellow-parodist rather

---

[13] Morgan (1985) 481ff.

[14] Morgan (1985) 490: "What I am proposing to reject is not the testimony of someone better placed to the truth than we are". But how is Morgan entitled to make such a claim, unaware of the total contents of Antonius Diogenes and the Metamorphoses of Lucius of Patras alike?

[15] E.g. *Cod*.166.109b (Pythagoras); 110b/111a (wonders of the north).

than a 'source'".[16] But the two categories are obviously not exclusive. Rabelais had to imitate Lucian's treatment of the inside of the whale in his own treatment of "the world in Pantagruel's mouth" in order to parody it. It is still not established that Lucian ignored Antonius Diogenes in his palette of victims.

III. *Some Illustrative Passages*

Much of the interest in *Verae Historiae* should be concentrated in Lucian's handling of particular details: even the detail of why Helen escapes punishment for elopement has not escaped investigation.[17] I note several cases *en passant* to illustrate the breadth of materials which require to be considered. (A commentary is in preparation by Georgiadou and Larmour).

(a) *The Footprint of Heracles at VH 1.7*

Morgan[18] has advice for those who seek parallels to individual parodic details in Lucian:

> Obviously the one thing that we should *not* look for amongst Lucian's sources is a writer who recorded a footprint an acre large. To do so would spoil the fun. This is obvious and uncontested, but commentators have been curiously literal and straight-faced in the way in which they have approached some of Lucian's larger-scale jokes.

This is an ominous procedure: when dealing with a parodist one has to start with an open mind, rather than a preconceived idea of what *not* to look for. In this case it seems particularly worthwhile to note the first item in Aulus Gellius' contemporary *Noctes Atticae*: a note on how Plutarch said Pythagoras measured the footprint of Heracles (by comparing the length of a Heraclean racecourse with a normal-sized one, and computing the size of Heracles' footprint in proportion).

---

[16] Swain (1994) 178. Cf. the same author's discussion (1992) on the status of Antonius' claim to be "a poet of Old Comedy". Swain takes the claim figuratively, but that is not to take account of the versatility of later antique belles-lettres. A writer who writes a fantasy-novel might either describe such a work in just those terms, or also have tried his hand at dramatic imitations of Aristophanes.

[17] And not just once: Devereux (1979/80) 63–68; Levine (1991) 31–33. Helen retains her Homeric exemption.

[18] (1985) 147.

Such an enigma might have occurred in some well-known *Pythagorica*, or even in a some writer coloured by Pythagorean material, such as Diogenes himself; or might have simply been a current sophistic *quaestio sympotica*. None of these rules out parody of Herodotus as well; but this case warns us to be open to less literal and straight-faced approaches to parody.

(b) *The Vinewomen at 1.8*

I have made some attempt to account for these intriguing specimens solely from literary sources;[19] but it is worth noting a parallel from (ultimately oriental) folklore. A modern Yiddish source offers the charming fairy-tale of a shipwrecked sailor attracted not to a tree-woman identical with the tree, but to a young girl actually living inside one, and visible through a hole in it; he stays with her, and they marry and live inside the tree.[20] Lucian's version offers a crudely cynical version of the same motif.

(c) *The Sea-monsters at 1.30*

S. West[21] notes the parallel between Nearchus' account of an encounter with a school of whales at dawn, and Lucian's with the same creatures at the same hour. We should note that the parody might in this case not be of Nearchus direct, but of Lucian's contemporary and possible acquaintance Arrian, from whose *Indica* West quotes the fragment (30.1ff.). It should however be noticed that dawn is the naturally most vulnerable time at which mariners ancient and modern can expect to run into their enemies: one thinks of the naval engagement off the River Plate in 1939. And Ps.-Callisthenes should also be invoked here: Alexander's men mistake the outside of a whale for an island,[22] while in *VH* they find men and animals using the inside of the whale as one; such a parody would be supported by the obvious and frequent allusion to Ps.-Callisthenes or the tradition he represents elsewhere in *VH*.

---

[19] Anderson (1976a) 27f.
[20] Translated by H. Schwartz (1988) 49–55 from a 19th century East European version in Olsvanger (1931).
[21] (1991) 275.
[22] A III.17.5f. (Feldbusch 1976).

(d) *The Tritonomendetes at 1.35*

The late Jack Winkler[23] had noted that these creatures are to be seen not as weasels in the lower half but as swordfish, but he seems to misinterpret the sexual implications of this oddity. If creatures are thus compounded the sword part of the swordfish will be so positioned as to serve as the erect phallus of the new creature. This gives us a means of inferring why they should have been less unjust than their fellows: they were making love not war.

IV. *Some General Considerations*

The preoccupation of Lucian for corroborative detail based on large numbers has been studied by Scarcella,[24] who sees the enormous dimensions as paradoxically serving both to establish authenticity[25] and destroy it in turn by their Munchausenesque exaggeration.[26] It is worthwhile to note in this connexion the fun which Lucian has with figures in general in his tall stories: as when Menippus reckons the stages of his journey to heaven in the opening speech of *Icaromenippus*, or in the discussion at some length on corroborative detail in imaginative falsehoods in *Hermotimus*.

Two new frameworks emerge for *VH*: "Ends of the Earth" and "Truth in Fiction". On the former W. Fauth[27] usefully extends the study and bibliography of the Utopian islands describes by Lucian, an interest long ago annotated by Rohde; while B. Kytzler has discussed the genre of Utopian romance, both descriptive and prescriptive.[28] But it is two recent works not directly connected with Lucian which may nonetheless help most towards new thinking on the work as a whole. James Romm's *The Edges of the Earth in Ancient Thought*[29]

---

[23] (1980b), 304f.

[24] Scarcella (1985b) 249–257.

[25] Against the approach to authenticity in Robert (1980) 428f. and C.P. Jones (1986) 52–55, see Anderson (1993a) 1427. The use of recent or contemporary names for this or that individual figure does little to produce any sense of "contemporary relevance" for this piece; nor on the other hand are Lucian's literary preoccupations here any indication of his being somehow trapped in the past.

[26] For similar resourcefulness and inventiveness in the use of proper and generic names, Matteuzi (1975) 225–229.

[27] (1979) 39–58.

[28] (1988) 7–16.

[29] (1992) (on Lucian, 211–214).

collects together many hitherto scattered details on ancient ethnography and the ways it was used. Though Romm has relatively little to say on Lucian himself, and accepts Morgan's view of Antonius Diogenes, it is now possible to form a general overview of the formation of the Greek repertoire of 'exotic geography', and hence of the core of material which Lucian set out to parody.

In a completely different way C. Gill and T.P. Wiseman[30] stimulate study of *Verae Historiae* by omitting from a series of discussions on lies and fiction the very work that is perhaps the most consummate work of self-confessed lying to survive Antiquity. We have to ask ourselves how far Lucian's *jeu d'esprit* belongs with a thought-world where the theoretical basis for the separation of truth and fiction was not always available.

V. *Future Prospects*

The decades since Bompaire have seen little activity on this engaging work: Lucian's own clarity of intention has pointed to an absence of "problems": yet those illustrated above are only a minute sample; and this author at any rate remains suspicious that some kind of *Urwahrengeschichte* probably did exist, whether or not in Antonius Diogenes. There are considerable remains of "Journey to the other World" texts ranging from *Gilgamesh* and the *Odyssey* through the *Alexander Romance* to the *Seven Voyages of Sindbad* and the Rabbah bar bar Hannah Tales in the Babylonian Talmud.[31] It is not a case of throwing a net so wide as to include all known fantasy texts: underworld visits may be standard in much of this material, and easily reproduced; the motif of arriving at a foreign king and refusing his offspring's hand in marriage is a more specific motif, and the number of variations on it may have to be explained. There may be further variants on this and on the curious text quoted by Aelian (*VH* 3.18) from Theopompus; if placed together such materials might suggest a standard scheme for a Utopia which Lucian himself might in turn have known. The oriental epicentre of many of these texts has still to be taken into account; so has Lucian's own formative background in the Aramaic-speaking world.

---

[30] (1993).
[31] The core is in Tractate *Baba Bathra* 73a–74a; *exempli gratia* reconstruction by H. Schwartz (1988).

B. THE TRUTH AND NOTHING BUT THE TRUTH: DICTYS AND DARES

Stefan Merkle

"Dictys Cretensis" and "Dares Phrygius" are the pseudonyms of the authors of two fictitious eye-witness accounts of the Trojan War who wrote in imperial times; Dictys claims to have taken part in the War on the Greek side, Dares on the Trojan. Both works have survived in sober Latin prose versions, each one prefaced with a dedicatory letter informing the reader that the respective text was discovered under lucky circumstances and translated from Greek into Latin. In each case the traditional course of events in the War is changed decisively. The authors present "plausible", rationalistic accounts; the gods do not appear personally, and the archaic heroism of the protagonists is reduced to human scale.

Laying claim to αὐτοψία, Dictys and Dares—according to ancient standards—pretend to exceptional reliability. Both authors underline that pretension by putting their works into a formal historiographical context: Dictys' *Ephemeris belli Troiani* (hereafter *Eph.*) as well as Dares' *Acta diurna belli Troiani* (hereafter *Acta*) pick up the literary tradition of unpretentious records of individual combatants, or war diaries similar to the Latin genre of the *commentarius*. This choice of the fictitious genre had various consequences: For one, it meant for the authors that in order to stay within the tradition they had to forego rhetorical embroidery. Both kept strictly to these self-imposed limitations, and this, in its turn, influenced the "Nachleben" of their texts decisively. In the Byzantine period and in the Middle Ages the works were in fact regarded as authentic, and they were highly esteemed as historical sources. The Greek *Eph.* was taken by several Byzantine chronographers as a basis for the respective passages of their works, and its Latin version, and even more the Latin *Acta*, had a formative influence on the medieval adaptations of the Trojan material.[1] In modern times, on the other hand, it was exactly the authors' consistent

---

[1] The "Nachleben" of both texts still awaits thorough study. For a short sketch and further literature see Merkle (1989) 21–24.

avoidance of stylistic ornamentation that caused the eclipse of both works. As happened with other fictitious prose texts of antiquity, the *Eph.* and the *Acta* were exposed as "forgeries" in the Enlightenment, and thus interested scholars mainly as subjects of "Quellenforschung" and textual criticism. A thorough analysis of the works as literary texts was for a long time considered simply not worthwhile, since in the eyes of scholars they were "Machwerke", "artless and abrupt, barren of literary power".[2] The fact that the unpretentious style of the works is an essential part of their literary conception, was not taken into consideration.

It comes as no surprise, then, that a sensational discovery virtually silenced for more than half a century the philological discussion about the two texts. A papyrus fragment of the Greek *Eph.*, published in 1907, not only solved what was called the "Diktys-Frage"— the question of whether a Greek *Eph.* had ever really existed—, it also destroyed the philologists' dreams that this Greek original was of considerably higher literary quality than the preserved Latin version. On the contrary, it turned out that the Latin translator had even improved the text stylistically.[3] Thus the main conclusion drawn from the find was essentially negative. On analogy with Dictys, for Dares also the existence of a Greek original was assumed, and thereby the most interesting problem about the texts could be dropped. Apart from articles on questions of textual criticism and a new edition of the *Eph.* in 1958,[4] only a few papers on the works were published during the next 60 years.

Not even the fact that both texts were labeled quite early as "Troja-Romane" turned out to be advantageous. This fact did help them find their place in handbooks and monographs on the ancient novel, but given the lack of adequate special surveys of these works, scholars could hardly give more than short paraphrases of their contents. In retrospect it even seems that the label "Troja-Romane" rather stood in the way of a proper appreciation of the texts. Scholars working on the ancient novel of course concentrated on those texts which

---

[2] Helm (1956) 21; Marblestone (1970) 216.

[3] He, for instance, often borrows phrases from Sallust.—The papyrus fragment together with a second one, published in 1966, is added to the second edition of Eisenhut's text (1973) 134–140.

[4] Eisenhut (1958), replacing Meister's edition from 1872.—A new edition of Dares still is a desideratum; instead Meister's Teubner text from 1873 has been reprinted in 1991. For the manuscript tradition see most recently Pavano (1993) (1993a).

came closest to the modern picture of "novel", i.e., the "ideal" novels and their "comic realistic" counterparts. Therefore Dictys and Dares, together with many other fictitious prose texts of imperial times, were grouped under the somewhat inadequately defined category of "fringe novels", and thus they remained at the fringe of philological interest, too.

Since the late 1960s, this situation has gradually changed. R.M. Luminansky's committed plea for a discussion of the literary characteristics of the texts, published in 1969—typically enough in a book on medieval literature—did not meet an immediate response. Nor did H.J. Marblestone's dissertation on Dictys from 1970, but within the last 25 years several articles and even two books have appeared which step by step prepared the field for a more thorough and proper estimation of the two works.[5]

In His Majesty's Service: Dictys of Crete

In order to explain why his work had remained unknown for such a long time, the author of the *Eph.* created an anonymous editor who in a prologue provides the reader with the following information: Dictys of Crete, a participant in the Trojan War, was the official war correspondent of the Cretan King Idomeneus. Dictys ordered his *Ephemeris* buried beside himself in his grave, where it lay hidden until in the 13th year of the Roman Emperor's Nero reign an earthquake opened the grave. The find was taken to Nero himself who had the books translated from Phoenician into Greek and lodged them in his Greek library.[6]

Even though this prologue is preserved in one of the two major

---

[5] *Eph.*: Edition: Eisenhut (1973²). Translation and commentary: Marblestone (1970); cf. the translation of Frazer (1966). Comprehensive bibliography: Merkle (1989) 310–316. On Dictys and Homer: Gianotti (1979), and Venini (1981–82). On aspects of narrative technique: Milazzo (1984), and Timpanaro (1987). On various aspects: Eisenhut (1983), and Merkle (1989)—*Acta*: Edition: Meister (1873), cf. n. 4 above. (German) Translation, commentary and comprehensive bibliography: Beschorner (1992a); English translation: Frazer (1966). On various aspects: Schetter (1987), *idem* (1988); Eisenhut (1983), Merkle (1990), Beschorner (1992a).

[6] We find such stories several times in historical and in fictitious texts of antiquity, cf. Merkle (1989) 73–80. See, e.g., the story of the discovery of Pythagorean texts in the grave of King Numa in Pliny, *NH* 13.84–87, Livy 40.29.3–14, and Plutarch, *Numa* 22, the highly complicated construction of Antonius Diogenes, or Damis' role in Philostratus' *Apollonius of Tyana* [cf. Bowie's remarks (1994a) 188, 195f.].

groups of manuscripts of the Latin text, it originally was most certainly not part of the Latin version of the *Eph*. In the other manuscripts the text is prefaced with a dedicatory letter of the translator Septimius to a certain Q. Aradius Rufinus, in which Sepitmius tells roughly the same story and adds some information on his translation of the work. He explains that he maintained the number of the first five books which contained events of the war proper, but reduced into one the remaining books, which were about the Greek *Nostoi*.[7] Since Septimius changed some details of the text's discovery, we may assume that his letter was supposed to replace the prologue; the Latin prologue obviously is a translation of the Greek πρόλογος, added later to the text by a different author who had both the Greek and the Latin texts before him.

Prologue and dedicatory letter respectively form the first part of the carefully conceived "Beglaubigungsapparat" of the text, an elaborate "authentication strategy" designed to produce in the reader a belief in the text's reliability and genuineness. On the one hand this ploy answers why no one had ever heard of the text before, and on the other hand Dictys is introduced not only as an eyewitness, but even as a professional historian; moreover the title *Ephemeris* ensures the reader that he may expect sober, reliable information. This expectation is fulfilled in what follows not only through the simple style of the text and through devices like the offering of alternative explanations for certain events, but also by two passages in which Dictys introduces himself. In a delayed prologue (1.13) Dictys briefly expounds his historiographical method which consists in referring first to his αὐτοψία and second to information gained from other eyewitnesses; later, this scheme is underlined in a kind of *sphragis* at the transition from the war's events to the *Nostoi* (5.17).

Moreover, prologue and letter show that Septimius' method of transferring the Greek text into Latin—he himself calls it *ea, uti erant, Latine disserere*—obviously consisted in maintaining structure and contents, but also included the license to change some details and a stylistic improvement of the original; this corresponds to the evidence provided by the two Greek papyri of the *Eph*. (cf. p. 564 with n. 3). As for structural devices and for the contents of the work, then, we may be confident that any observation in books 1–5 of the Latin version had close equivalents in the Greek original.

---

[7] The Greek *Eph*. consisted of nine or ten books; cf. Timpanaro (1987) 205f.

This observation is of great importance for a proper appreciation of the text's literary conception, since a careful use of structural techniques was clearly the way the author tried to compensate for the narrow stylistic limits he had imposed on himself by adopting the genre *ephemeris*. His text shows the following quasi-dramatic macrostructure: Book 1 has an expository function. It contains the background of the War; the conflict is developed, the enemy groups are established, and the account is dominated by negotiations. In book 2 there is the first set of battles and of severe personal conflicts in the Greek camp. The central book 3, with Achilles as the protagonist, brings about the military decision of the War with Hector's death. At the beginning of book 4 the arrival of strong Trojan allies (Penthesilea and Memnon) constitutes a delaying factor, but after their defeat the last Trojan hopes collapse. Like the first, book 5 is dominated by negotiations until the catastrophe, the sack of Troy, is described. In similar fashion the inner structure of the books is the result of careful planning. The account is divided into single blocks of action which alternately either contain enumerations of different events in sober annalistic manner, or present single episodes in self-contained dramatic scenes.[8]

Dictys draws a multilayered and complex picture of the Trojan War. On the surface we find a clear anti-Trojan tendency. Dictys reports violent clashes in Troy after Helen's reception (1.7–10), and in the War itself the Trojans are hopelessly inferior to the Greeks in open fights, gaining military advantages mostly by making assaults during truces and funerals. The Greeks, on the other hand, are introduced as peaceful people, living together in harmony (1.1–4). It takes an assault on their legates at Troy (1.11) to make them decide to prepare for the campaign (1.12), and for a long stretch of the account they fight their enemies bravely and honorably.

But this black and white drawing is only one aspect of Dictys' account. In the course of the story the author does not refrain from giving unflattering descriptions of events on the Greek side, which he partly found in the extant tradition and partly invented himself. Regarding the dishonorable conduct of Greeks, we can distinguish three phases in the *Eph*. In phase 1, which reaches to the end of book 2, such events happen almost exclusively within the Greek camp;

---

[8] See, e.g., the Aulis-episode (1.19–23), the *Presbeia* (2.47–52) or the *Lytra* (3.20–27).

with only one exception,[9] here the Greeks behave blamelessly towards the Trojans. Dictys uses his very own versions of the Iphigenia-episode (1.19–23), of the assassination of Palamedes (2.16) and of the quarrel between Agamemnon and Achilles (2.28–34; 48–52) to create a three-way split among the Greeks, with Agamemnon, Menelaos, Odysseus and Diomedes on the one side, the Greek soldiers on the other, and Achilles, who is isolated from both groups.

In the second phase (book 3) dubious actions on the Greek side are aimed at the Trojans. But it is not the Greek army as a whole who act reprehensibly. It is Achilles who increasingly cedes the moral superiority to the Trojans which the Greeks had shown up to this point. He kills Hector not in an open fight, but in a deceitful ambush (3.15), he has some captured sons of Priam strangled at Patroclus' grave (3.14), mutilates another dreadfully before sending him back to Troy (3.15), and treats Priam contemptuously when he comes to ask for the return of Hector's body (3.20–27).

Finally, in the third phase (books 4 and 5), the moral quality of Greek warfare in general decreases dramatically, the events including the slaughter of the already defeated Penthesilea by the Greek soldiers (4.3), Achilles' cruel execution of captured sons of Priam (4.9), a deceitful peace treaty with the Trojans (5.10), and finally the sack of Troy itself with all the awful details tradition had to offer (5.12–13).

Achilles' role in this process is most carefully conceived by the author. The son of Peleus is doubtless the most emotional and passionate character of the account, and this trait has two sides. On the one hand Achilles is established in books 1 and 2 as a fierce and self-sacrificing fighter who is closely joined together with his fellow soldiers in mutual love and admiration, but on the other hand his deep disappointment about the lack of solidarity from the Greeks during his quarrel with Agamemnon even drives him to an attempted assault on his own comrades (2.37). With Achilles' isolation from the Greeks at the end of book 2 Dictys prepares his role in book 3, where his conduct towards the Trojans foreshadows the Greeks' behavior in the final phase of the Trojan War.

---

[9] In 2.16 the Greeks kill the captured young Polydorus in full view of the Trojans. Atrocious as this deed is, Dictys does not let it happen before the Greeks had tried to exchange Polydorus for Helen and had been harshly rejected and derided by the Trojans. Here, then, the Greeks have "good reason" for their conduct. In later parts of the work this is not the case.

In book 3, which in a large measure seems to be Dictys' very own creation, the anti-heroic tendencies of the work are focused on Achilles. Not only does Dictys turn famous Homeric passages—the duel between Hector and Achilles and the *Lytra*—upside down. He also changes the chief motive for Achilles' hatred towards Hector. It is not his grief about Patroclus' death which makes him vow horrible vengeance on Hector, but an unheroic love story which Dictys inserts into his account. At the beginning of book 3, Achilles sees Hector's beautiful sister Polyxena and is immediately smitten with love for her (3.2). From then on he is beside himself with desire, but when asking for her hand, he is brusquely rejected by Hector; therefore he swears to kill him as soon as possible (3.3).

The extant parallel versions[10] of the Achilles-Polyxena story indicate that Dictys has made decisive changes in order to adapt the material to his account: It is only in the *Eph.* that Hector is involved into the plot, and it is only here that the story is arranged in three parts: only Dictys reports a second encounter between Achilles and Polyxena which takes place at the end of book 3, at the *Lytra* (3.20–27). Here we see Achilles burst into tears at the sight of Polyxena (3.24), but nevertheless he rejects Priam's offer to marry her. Remembering his duty as a Greek leader, he hands over Hector's corpse, and sends Polyxena back to Troy, providing her generously with precious gifts; negotiations about the marriage are arranged at another place and time (3.27). The final part of this story is located in the middle of book 4, where Achilles' love for Polyxena causes his death. Alexander (Paris) and Deiphobus are able to kill him because he carelessly meets his enemies unarmed in order to negotiate for Polyxena (4.11). Thus the Achilles-Polyxena story is located at the beginning, in the center and at the end of the crucial phase of the War: The death of Hector (3.16) and of Penthesilea and Memnon (4.3; 4.6) bring about the military decision.[11]

---

[10] See Hyginus, *Fabulae* 110; Philostratus, *Heroicus* 51.1–6; Servius ad Vergil, *Aeneid* 6.57 and 2.321; Scholia ad Lycophron, *Cassandra* 269; Dares 27 and 34. For the question of the origin of the story see King (1987) 184–195.

[11] Loving a woman in the *Eph.* always has disastrous effects, and the respective passages appear in prominent places in the account: at the beginning, as established by tradition, with the story of Paris and Helen; in the center, where Dictys locates the Achilles-Polyxena-story; and at the end, again due to Dictys' arrangement, when Menelaus' love for Helen causes the death of Ajax (5.14): Meeting the approval of *multi boni*, Ajax plans to kill Helen after the Sack of Troy, but with the help of Odysseus, Menelaus, *amorem coniugii etiam tum retinens*, manages to save her life (5.14).

The presentation of Achilles' unpredictable behavior, his fluctuation between singular *virtus* and particular emotionality, is obviously the result of careful planning. Achilles is the only figure in the work who is set apart twice through a specific characterization. When he first appears in the text (1.14) and later, when Ajax finds him mortally wounded (4.15), the extreme polarity of his nature is explicitly stressed. With this mental disposition Achilles is in a way representative of almost every character in the work. As S. Timpanaro has observed, the figures in the *Eph.* generally show a marked "instabilità psicologica". To say it in his words: Dictys presents to his readers "lo spettaculo di un'umanità nel cui comportamento l'incoerenza è la regola e non l'eccezione".[12]

This characteristic of the Dictaean protagonists corresponds to another frequently employed device in the account: Dictys obviously loves to surprise his reader, to confront him with *aprosdoketa*. After Achilles' quarrel with Agamemnon and his retreat, for instance, we read that—as in the *Iliad*—the Trojans prepare an attack on the Greeks. Dictys even presents an exhaustive catalogue of their leaders, and the Greeks also draw up for battle. But surprisingly both sides withdraw without any fight, and instead Achilles tries to attack the Greek army (3.35–37).[13]

This aspect of the work is clearly aimed at readers who know the Trojan tradition well, and such readers find the author using two different methods in order to create his *aprosdoketa*. Sometimes Dictys simply turns famous scenes upside down, as in the *Lytra*; in other instances he combines different traditions or adds inventions of his own to the inherited course of events. For example, with Achilles' motive for killing Hector he does insert the Achilles-Polyxena story, but he nevertheless has Patroclus killed by Hector, and has Achilles react extremely violently (3.10–14). Sometimes such combinations cause logical problems: it is, for instance, hard to see why Iphigenia in the *Eph.* is sent to the King of the Scythians by the Greeks without

---

As a reward, the Atrides decide in the famous quarrel between Ajax and Odysseus in favor of Odysseus; Ajax vows vengeance, but the day after he is found killed.

[12] Timpanaro (1987) esp. 180–182, 185–191, 196–201 (citations from pp. 199 and 201). Besides some secondary figures like Nestor or Idomeneus, there is only one single character within the whole text whose performance is absolutely free of negative features: Ajax.

[13] Cf. the above mentioned replacement of the famous duel between Achilles and Hector with an ambush, or the course of the *Lytra*. For further examples see Timpanaro (1987) 176–184.

anybody telling Agamemnon (1.22). Or, at the end of the War, where the Greeks first deceitfully conclude a formal peace treaty with the Trojans and pretend to sail away, but nevertheless return and attack their drunken and sleeping enemies, one wonders how the Trojans could believe the Greeks, since they sailed away without Helen (5.10–12). Sometimes apparently even Dictys nodded.

But "mistakes" like these occur rarely in the *Eph*. Dictys' version of the destruction of Troy is the carefully prepared climax of the Greeks' increasingly immoral conduct towards their enemies, an unheroic combination of deceit and extreme cruelty. Nevertheless this behavior is not yet the nadir of the moral decline of the Greeks. Dictys ends his account with a final big surprise for his reader. Only here does the author place the famous quarrel between Odysseus and Ajax which results in Ajax' death (5.14), and thereby he can allow the tensions to erupt which had arisen within the Greek army in the course of the story, and construct an impressive finale. To this end Dictys not only changes the traditional position of the episode, he also significantly alters the traditional course of events (cf. n. 11). The Atrides and Odysseus are held to be guilty of Ajax' assassination and have to leave the camp disgraced and dishonored; murder and strife now prevail among the Greeks. Transported to the end of the story, the episode is a kind of "epilogue" to the Trojan War, and thus forms a marked contrast to the beginning of the account, the "prologue", where the Greeks are introduced as peaceful people reacting in complete solidarity to the rape of Helen (1.1–4).

Despite the harsh criticism of scholars, then, the *Eph*. upon closer examination appears as a quite carefully conceived text whose author handled his material within the self-imposed limits of an *ephemeris* with considerable skill. He tells, so to speak, two stories of the Trojan War: the story of a highly cultivated and peaceful nation which is dragged to a war by completely unscrupulous barbarians,[14] and the story of the gradual ethical decline of the victors in the course of the war. He does so by combining traditional material, later versions and inventions of his own into a unique and self-contained new story which is full of surprising twists and constellations.

---

[14] The strong anti-Trojan tendency of the *Eph*. is possibly an expression of the author's dislike of the heirs of the Trojans, the Romans. Their ancestor, Aeneas, does not cut a very good figure in the text (see esp. 5.17).

A View from the Trojan Side: Dares Phrygius

It is much harder to say anything certain about the *Acta diurna belli Troiani*[15] of Dares Phrygius than about the *Eph*. First we do not have any clear evidence for the existence of a Greek original despite the translator's claim in the dedicatory letter. Second we cannot even be sure if the preserved Latin version represents the complete text or an *epitome*. These two problems have dominated the philological discussion of the work up to the present. Moreover, scholars were even less inclined to work on the *Acta* than on the *Eph*.; Dares' text is much less sophisticated than Dictys', its style is even less ambitious, the narration is more compressed, the characters appear more schematic. This negative approach towards the text on the side of scholars has caused a third great difficulty: we do not have an even remotely satisfying critical edition of the *Acta* (cf. n. 4).

Nevertheless there is a broad consensus among scholars at least on the first point. It is commonly assumed that a Greek Dares did exist.[16] The second problem still remains unsolved, and this situation is unlikely ever to change unless a papyrus should provide us with new evidence. On the one hand we have scholars who either call the text wholesale "ein ganz dürftiges und unreines Exzerpt", or comb it meticulously for passages, which in their view must have been more detailed or better integrated into the original version,[17] on the other hand there are scholars who regard the preserved version as complete.[18]

Such discussions have their methodological problems. On the one hand the question of what we consider as "not acceptable" in a text depends to a high degree on very subjective criteria.[19] On the other

---

[15] As for the title of the work see Schetter (1988) 107–109.

[16] Only Eisenhut (1983) 18, firmly denies the existence of a Greek Dares; he is convincingly rejected by Schetter (1987) 213 n. 4. For a detailed discussion of the problem see Beschorner (1992a) 231–243; cf. n. 33 below.

[17] See above all Körting (1874) and Schetter (1988). The quotation is from Schmid (1906) 560, cf. 565; Schetter (1988) 104 agrees explicitly.

[18] Schissel von Fleschenberg (1907) and most recently Beschorner (1992a).

[19] Thus, the two most exhaustive surveys of scholars who regard the text as incomplete (see n. 17) find no fewer than 32 dubious passages, but only four times do their authors refer to the same section of the work. Not surprisingly, then, a large number of these objections have been rejected; see Beschorner (1992a) 204–230; cf. Merkle (1990) 509 n. 45, 517f. with n. 65.—Generally, the observations made in connection with the Dictys papyri (cf. p. 564) should warn us not to expect too much of Greek originals of such texts; Schetter (1988) 104 assumes, "daß das originale

hand it is not possible to prove definitely that the text is complete. Even though we can see clear structural principles in the *Acta*, this system could as well be the remains of a more complex original construction. Nevertheless, it seems more useful to analyze the text as we have it, than to conjecture as to the form of an ideal Dares; it is at least possible, that—as in the *Eph.*—the work's lack of literary shaping is a consequence of the authors conception which aims at producing in the reader a belief in the text's reliability and genuineness.

If so, Dares styled his work much more rigorously as a *commentarius* than Dictys.[20] In general, we can say that Dares tends more to the extreme than Dictys; it has long been observed that the *Acta* deviate much further from the traditional versions of the events than the *Eph*. This is already indicated in the dedicatory letter of the translator.[21] As in the *Eph.*, the author, when maintaining that his text finally tells the truth about the Trojan War, refers to Homer, but while in the *Eph.* this is only a subtle side-swipe, it forms half of the letter in the *Acta*.[22] This is the more noteworthy since the letter as a whole in the *Acta* is shorter than its counterpart in the *Eph.*; it starts right with the information that the translator had found the text accidentally in Athens, thus leaving out what is so elaborated in the *Eph.*: the answer to where the text had remained for so many centuries.[23] The author of the *Acta* obviously does not bother to tell the reader about that; he mainly concentrates on attacking Homer, and he continues in the course of his account by disproving the tradition

---

Daresbuch ein bedeutsames Werk war"; with such a premise we can enlarge the text however we like.

[20] This goes also for the representation of the supernatural element. Although the gods do not appear personally in the *Eph.*, there are passages where the author makes it possible for the reader to conclude that divine wrath overcomes Greeks or Trojans; see, e.g., the Aulis- and the Chryses-episode (1.19–23; 2.28–34), and, above all, the accumulation of ominous events and the relevant comments in speeches after the assassination of Achilles in a temple of Apollo (e.g., 4.18; 5.5); cf. Timpanaro (1987) 174 and Merkle (1989) 223–237. Dares has eliminated this factor more consistently.

[21] As in the *Eph.*, this letter forms the first part of the text's "Beglaubigungsapparat" which is strikingly similar to Dictys': As in the *Eph.*, we find a delayed prologue (ch. 12) and a *sphragis* (ch. 44) in the *Acta* in which the author, like Dictys, refers to his αὐτοψία and to his questioning of eyewitnesses.

[22] *Eph.*, p. 1, line 15 (*vera historia*), cf. the prologue, p. 3, line 9f. (*Troiani belli verior textus*)—*Acta*, p. 1, line 9–16. While in the *Eph.* Homer is not mentioned explicitly, in the *Acta* we even hear of legal proceedings against the poet because of assumed insanity.

[23] The translator compensated for this with another invention: His letter claims to be written by Cornelius Nepos and the addressee is the historian Sallust.

extensively. Hector, for instance, is killed quite early (ch. 24), and Dares presents Troilus as a second Hector (chs. 29–33) by depicting in detailed parallel their military achievements (chs. 19–24; 29–33), behavior in the Trojan Council (ch. 22; 31) and death scenes (ch. 24; 33). Achilles kills Hector, but he leaves his corpse on the battlefield (ch. 24), and so there are no *Lytra*. There is no quarrel between Agamemnon and Achilles, and, instead, the latter's wrath is motivated by his love for Polyxena (ch. 27f.). As in the *Eph.*, this love-story causes Achilles' death (ch. 34), and at the end of his account Dares even transforms the Trojan horse to a sculpture of a horse's head at the Scaean gate of Troy (ch. 40).

Dares' love of changing the traditional versions of the War of course also influences his presentation of individual characters. Besides the lovesick Achilles and the superheroic Troilus, we find, for instance, a completely irreproachable Agamemnon and a power-hungry Palamedes on the Greek side. On the Trojan side Antenor is a war-monger at the beginning (ch. 8), but at the end he, together with Aeneas, is a committed supporter of surrender, meeting a Priam who prefers death to capitulation; Priam even attempts to assassinate Antenor and Aeneas which they prevent only by betraying the city to the Greeks (chs. 37–41).

Dares' account, then, for a reader who is well acquainted with the Trojan tradition, offers a lot of surprises, and many of these surprises concern the presentation of the Greeks. Unlike Dictys, Dares does not disparage the "enemies"; in his version Greeks and Trojans are basically equal in every respect. At the beginning of his account he is at pains to make the Rape of Helen appear as the result of an exchange of blows between Greeks and Trojans (chs. 1–8), and during the War both sides fight bravely and honorably. But surprisingly Dares does even more to depict the Greeks positively. He consistently abstains from the problematic episodes on the Greek side which tradition provided and which Dictys does not hesitate to report. Iphigenia does not come to Aulis, Philoctetes is not abandoned, Palamedes is not murdered, Dolon does not die, there is no quarrel about Chryseis and none about Achilles' armor, and the Greeks treat the defeated Trojans honorably. But Dares does not just leave these episodes out; he uses them to create striking *aprosdoketa* proceeding in a way that surpasses Dictys' (cf. p. 570). Often he prepares the traditional situation, but shortly before the catastrophe occurs, he abruptly finishes the episode in an unexpected way. Thus, for instance, in ch. 22 Odysseus and Diomedes are sent to Troy, and on their way they meet Dolon. When Dolon asks them why they come to the city by night and in such heavy armor, the reader must expect him to be killed as in the *Iliad*. But surprisingly they identify themselves as legates, and Priam convenes an assembly.[24]

With this approach Dares not only is far away from the Trojan tradition, but also from the *Eph*. As for their contents, the *Acta* and the *Eph*. are not like mirror images, as the fictitious identities of the authors might suggest; Dares' story differs from Dictys' as much as from any other description of the War. The same goes for the structure of the *Acta*.

In the *Acta* there are two different structural principles overlapping each other. In the arrangement of material we find the following: chs. 1-11 give the background, and in chs. 12-13 there is the delayed prologue and the portraits of Greeks and Trojans.[25] Chs. 14-41 contain the campaign of the Greeks, which is introduced by a description of the crossing of the Greeks and troop catalogues in chs. 14-18, continued by the clashes between the Greeks and the Trojans in chs. 19-36, and finished by quarrels within Troy and the sack of the city in chs. 37-41. Chs. 42-43 show Greeks and Trojans after the War, and in ch. 44 there follows the *sphragis* (cf. n. 21). In the battles the Trojans are increasingly superior to the Greeks in chs. 19-33; then Achilles' victory over Troilus and Memnon at the end of ch. 33 marks the *peripeteia*, and in chs. 35-36 the Trojan resistance is broken despite the death of Achilles (ch. 34) and Ajax (ch. 35) and the arrival of a strong Trojan ally, Penthesilea (ch. 36).

The single phases of the military confrontation between Trojans and Greeks are marked by a change of the dominant characters. According to this principle we may subdivide chapters 19-36 into five parts. 1. ch. 19, where after the Greeks' landing we read the first *aristeiai* of several heroes on both sides; 2. chs. 20-24, with Achilles and Hector in the center; 3. chs. 25-28, with Palamedes as the leader of the Greeks; 4. chs. 29-33, dominated by Achilles and Troilus, 5. chs. 34-36, with the deaths of Achilles, Ajax and Penthesilea.

This model seems to be contradicted by the chronological structure of the work. Dares reports a number of armistices which endure up to three years, and while some of them do support the described

---

[24] For further examples of this technique see Beschorner (1992a) 206-215.
[25] On this problematic section see Beschorner (1992a) 106-127.

distribution of the events,[26] the majority does not, but rather takes place within the sections outlined above.[27] The main function of these armistices certainly is to make the 10-year campaign describable in such small space,[28] and the meticulous notices about time is of course part of the concept of an authentic and reliable *commentarius*, but their distribution at first sight seems quite arbitrary. On closer examination, however, it turns out that many of them do have a further function. It is within truces that Dares informs his reader either about the momentary situation or about important developments within the camps, as, for instance, Palamedes' attempts to gain the leading position in the Greek army (ch. 20; 25), Achilles' encounter with Polyxena (ch. 27), or his assassination (ch. 34); with the armistices the author, so to speak, gives his protagonists time to carry out their respective actions.

Moreover the differing length of the armistices seems just as little arbitrary as their position in the text. After the first battles following the arrival of the Greeks in ch. 19, the period of time which is bridged by the single sections decreases continuously: The second phase of the war (chs. 20–24) covers more than five years, the third (chs. 26–28) a bit more than one year, the fourth (chs. 29–33) about eight months, the fifth (chs. 34–36) does not endure longer than one or two weeks. In the following passage (chs. 37–41) the events of only two days are told in five chapters. This means that the elapsed time of the events narrated decreases rapidly in the course of the account, the narration intensifies up to the last two days of Troy, where the above mentioned conflict between Priam and Aeneas and Antenor is reported. And indeed here the account reaches its most dramatic tension.

Dares' account, then, differs remarkably from Dictys' both in its structure and contents. While the *Eph.* presents a pessimistic picture of the Trojan War with the completely reprehensible behavior of the Trojans and the ethically deteriorating Greeks, the *Acta* quite neutrally report a military conflict between basically equal contestants. Dares' main concern apparently was to change the tradition as far

---

[26] Ch. 20: 2 years; ch. 25: 2 months; ch. 29: 2 months; ch. 33: 20 days.

[27] Ch. 22: 3 years; ch. 23: a) 6 months, b) 30 days; ch. 26/27: 1 year; ch. 31: 6 months; ch. 32: 30 days; ch. 34; without precise information about time.

[28] Dictys solves this problem differently: he reduces the presence of the Greeks at Troy to one and a half year through arms production and an erroneous landing of the Greeks in Mysia (1.16–2.9).

as possible and to create a most surprising and unique "true story" of the Trojan War. Nevertheless the close parallels between the two texts with regard to their "Beglaubigungsapparat" (see n. 21), and moreover the authors' choice of the same fictitious genre, indicate that one author knew the other's text; as Beschorner has shown, it seems quite probable that Dictys' work is prior to Dares'.[29]

Time of Composition and Literary Context

As for the questions of the time of composition and the literary context of the works we paradoxically can say more about the Greek *Eph.*, which is lost for the most part, and even about the Greek *Acta*, which are lost completely, than about the preserved Latin versions. The Latin *Eph.* most probably is to be dated to the fourth century A.D. In this period we come across a great number of Latin works and translations from Greek into Latin that seem to respond to an intense and widespread interest in historical topics, as for instance the rather novelistic adaptations of the Alexander material, the *Breviaria* of Festus and Eutropius, or the *Corpus Aurelianum*. As a narrative in the form of a historical source, the *Eph.* seems to fit well in this context. The Latin *Acta* are most likely to be dated to the fifth century A.D.[30]

Although we cannot be absolutely sure whether the translators could see through the imaginary nature of the eyewitness construction, the recognizable alterations which Septimius made to the original, and above all the usurpation of the names of Cornelius Nepos and Sallust by the translator of the *Acta* (cf. n. 23) let us assume a certain mental familiarity of authors and translators. If this is true, both translations were probably aimed primarily at educated Romans who could appreciate the texts' manipulation of the tradition. Nevertheless the lack of closely related texts in Latin literature of the 4th and 5th centuries does not allow definite statements; it cannot be excluded that Septimius or "Cornelius Nepos" wanted his construction to be believed by his readers.[31]

---

[29] Beschorner (1992a) 250f.

[30] An earlier dating of the *Eph.* (3rd century) is suggested by Cameron (1980) 172–75, and Champlin (1981). For a detailed discussion of the problem see Merkle (1989) 263–283.—For the dating of the *Acta* see Beschorner (1992a) 254–263.

[31] Gianotti (1979) suggests that both texts were written primarily for readers of

The Greek original of the *Eph.* can be dated quite exactly: Its time of origin lies between A.D. 66 and A.D. 200, since the year 66 is mentioned in the prologue, and the older papyrus is dated to about 200. It is related to the Greek prose fiction of this period in various ways. To begin with, we do have three other works which contain pseudoeyewitness records of the Trojan War: The Τρωικὸς Λόγος (*Or.* 11) of Dio Chrysostom, a passage in Lucian's *Cock*, and Philostratus' dialogue *Heroicus*.[32] Correcting Homer and the canonical tradition in such way, then, obviously was a game that Greek *literati* of that time loved to play, and this indicates that there were readers who appreciated this sort of text.[33]

These three texts show a remarkably broad spectrum with regards to form, contents and intention. Dio offers a spirited epideictic speech, claiming that the Greeks had lost the War after they had attacked Troy arbitrarily and without cause.[34] Lucian, in his short passage (*Cock* 17), only playfully corrects some Homeric details; his text looks like a compressed parody on works like the *Eph.* Philostratus, adopting the tradition of the Platonic dialogue, wrote his *Heroicus* apparently not least to justify the Emperor Caracalla's extravagant worship of the heroes.

In this realm the Greek *Eph.* and probably the Greek *Acta* were placed by their authors, enlarging the spectrum with texts that are elaborately conceived as authentic historical sources, and therefore—unlike the others—lack rhetorical embroidery. With their marked anti-heroic and rationalistic tendencies, both works are diametrically

---

mediocre education who were not familiar with the Homeric texts. His arguments, however, are hardly convincing; cf. Timpanaro (1987) n. 11 and n. 27, and Merkle (1989) 286 n. 119.

[32] Dio names the chronicles of Egyptian priests that were based on a report of Menelaus himself as his source. Lucian's cock claims that in a former life he had taken part in the Trojan War as the Trojan Euphorbus, and Philostratus has his version of the events reported through a Thracian vintner who is in contact with the ghost of the hero Protesilaus.

[33] In my view this is a strong argument for the assumption of a Greek Dares. The marked hostility against Homer which forms the second half of the dedicatory letter of the *Acta* (cf. p. 10) fits perfectly with this tendency; in Latin literature of the fifth century we do not have any traces of a similar "fashion".—It seems that in general readers in this period of Greek literature were well acquainted with the Homeric works; the authors of Greek novels, too, are known to refer often to Homer in various ways.

[34] Dio, then, goes even further than Dares in constructing a pro-Trojan version of the events. This conception may be an expression of his sympathy for the heirs of the Trojans, the Romans.

opposed to Philostratus' dialogue, and the severely anti-Trojan and pessimistic picture Dictys draws is unique in this context. It even seems that Philostratus knew the *Eph.* and assumed that some of his readers did so, too, since he apparently bothered to undermine Dictys' claim to authority. While Dictys maintains that he wrote his work in Phoenician letters and as Idomeneus' official chronicler, we read in ch. 26 of the *Heroicus* that the use of writing was unknown at that time, and in ch. 30 that Idomeneus did not take part in the War.

But what about Dictys' and Dares' relation to the novels and to "fringe novels" like the *Alexander-Romance* or the *Vita Aesopi*? Despite basic differences between these texts with regards to plot, they all have one fundamental thing in common: they present "fiction in the form of history". This apparently was what their readers expected. But while in the "canonical" novels the respective historical features are hardly more than a framework for the main plot, and the readers were well aware that the protagonists and their adventures are fictitious,[35] things are fundamentally different in texts like the *Alexander Romance* and the *Vita Aesopi* and in Dictys and Dares: these texts are built around characters and events which antiquity regarded as historical.

Nevertheless Dictys and Dares do differ decisively from these "fringe novels". While the *Alexander-Romance* and the *Vita Aesopi* have one single protagonist, Dictys' and Dares' works have an event—the Trojan War—at their center, and while the authors of the *Alexander-Romance* and the *Vita Aesopi* take the opportunity to enrich their account with fantastic episodes and a series of *mirabilia* (*Alexander-Romance*) or even to construct a whole narrative consisting of comic anecdotes and fables (*Vita Aesopi*), thus verging on the limits of "historical plausibility", Dictys and Dares are at pains to reduce the "historically implausible" in their accounts to a minimum and to shape their works as authentic historical sources.

In this last respect they are closely related to another branch of ancient prose fiction which only recently has been established in classical scholarship as a veritable literary genre: the novels in letters.[36] Here, too, the authors pretend to present hitherto unknown authentic material about well-known historical figures and events, and they,

---

[35] On the various implications of "realism" in the novels see Morgan (1993) 197–215.
[36] See Holzberg (1994a).

too, stick to the rationally plausible. But differently front Dictys and Dares and from the authors of the fictitious biographies, they do not tell the respective story completely; they are mainly interested in the perspectives and feelings of the protagonist, and only single stages of the development of events are reflected in the letters.[37]

Fictitious biographies and novels in letters, then, make up another feature of the literary context of the *Eph.* and the *Acta*. Dealing with well-known events and figures of Greek history, being styled as authentic and reliable historical sources, and presenting their material in the form of a continuous, coherent narrative, the works are in a way somewhere in between these sorts of texts.

All these texts most probably had readers who believed their historiographical ruse. Others certainly saw through this construction, and for them the works provided what E.L. Bowie in connection with Philostratus' *Heroicus* calls "a self-indulgent *frisson* of satisfaction": On the one hand they were well aware of the fictional nature of the texts, but on the other hand they were allowed "to toy with the notion that this source might really provide extra information that only the privileged readers of this work can share."[38]

---

[37] This genre, too, could be used to "correct" canonical tradition. As Merkle/Beschorner (1994b) have shown, a considerable part of the *Letters of Phalaris* apparently represents the remains of a novel in letters which—according to a common tendency in Greek literature of imperial times [cf. Merkle/Beschorner (1994b) 116f. with n. 6]—drew a decidedly positive picture of the tyrant.

[38] Bowie (1994b) 185.

C. XENOPHON OF ATHENS: THE *CYROPAEDIA*

Bodil Due

Xenophon of Athens

I. *Biography*

Xenophon was born in Athens during the Peloponnesian War ca. 425 B.C. and died ca. 354.[1] He thus witnessed in his youth the two oligarchic revolutions in 411 and 404, the civil war, the return of democracy and Athens' total surrender in the Peloponnesian War. His family was well-to-do, and, in view of his lifelong interest in agriculture, horses and hunting, presumably landowners. He probably served in the cavalry as later did his sons. It is possible that he or his family had some, perhaps not quite voluntary involvement with the Thirty Tyrants, although he later in his Greek history criticized them severely, especially the radical wing under Critias.[2]

Xenophon was well educated and demonstrates in his works a thorough knowledge of literature, especially Homer, Herodotus and Thucydides. As a young man he had met Socrates, and although, according to most modern scholars, he did not understand him very well—at least not as well as Plato—he was deeply influenced by Socrates' ethical and pedagogical approach.[3]

In search of adventure or frustrated in his expectations in the afterwar climate, he left Athens in 401, in spite of Socrates' warnings,[4] to join the Persian prince Cyrus in what turned out to be a mutiny against his brother, the Great King, Artaxerxes II. After Cyrus' death Xenophon was one of the leaders in the retreat of the Greeks to the Black Sea. In 399 he handed the rest of the 10,000 Greek mercenaries over to the Spartan commander Thibron, but stayed on in Asia in Spartan service, from 396 under king Agesilaus whom he followed back to Greece in 394. So he was on the wrong side, i.e. against

---

[1] Apart from Xenophon's own works, especially the *Anabasis*, our best source is Diogenes Laertius 2.48–59.
[2] *HG* 2.3,11ff.
[3] D.L. 2.48.
[4] *An*.3.1,4ff.

Athens, in the battle of Coronea. Because of this, or because of his participation in the Persian mutiny, he was banished from Athens.[5] The Spartans rewarded him with an estate in Skillous near Olympia where he lived for some 20 years until he was expelled after the Spartan defeat at Leuctra in 371.[6] When Athens and Sparta were reconciled and joined in an alliance to fight Thebes, and a general amnesty was proclaimed, he probably returned to Athens; his last work deals with the Athenian economy.[7] One of his sons died for Athens in the battle of Mantinea in 362.[8]

II. *Literary Works*

Xenophon is often seen as a forerunner of Hellenistic literature, and he is so in many respects, e.g. in his many-sidedness as a writer. Most Greek authors in classical literature kept to one genre. But Xenophon did not, like Herodotus or Thucydides, content himself by writing history alone; he also composed technical treatises, philosophical or political essays, memoirs and pseudo-historical works or fiction. This versatility has not won him any credit with scholars in recent times, but created a certain suspicion. As a historian he has been compared to Thucydides and as a philosopher to Plato, and in both cases found wanting.[9]

Yet, however denigrated in these fields, Xenophon surely deserves some credit, in the eyes of posterity, for having been, in effect, the progenitor of what were to become two of the most popular literary genres of all time, biography and fiction: the first through his *Memoirs of Socrates*, *Anabasis* and *Agesilaus*, the second through his *Cyropaedia*. To explain these seminal innovations by an author otherwise considered dull and not very intelligent, it has recently been argued that they are but the accidental consequences of his failure to write Thucydidean, i.e. contemporary politico-military history:[10] the material

---

[5] The question has been and is still disputed: Breitenbach (1967) supports the first, Erbse (1966) the second view.

[6] Paus.5.6,5. Xenophon himself paints an idyllic picture of life at his country estate in *An.*5.3,7ff.

[7] Πόροι, *Revenues*.

[8] See D.L.2.54f. for a description of Xenophon's stoic reaction when receiving the message.

[9] To quote Strauss (1948) 5. A positive view is expressed by Zimmermann (1989) 97 and Hirsch (1985a) 66.

[10] Connor (1985) I.3.48.

which, according to the criteria for this kind of history, had to be excluded from his *Hellenica* was—it is argued—relegated to other genres. But apart from problems in dating, this is not the way authors work, using scissors and paste to stick pieces and scraps together. In any case, even if we were to admit the truth of these arguments, we would still have to speak of innovations. Another more fruitful way of explaining them is to try, as Perry has done,[11] to identify the author's intention with each work, and the audience he intended it for. Some of Xenophon's works are obviously didactic, and must have had a rather narrow and well-defined audience. Others, notably the *Cyropaedia*, seem to be directed at a wider, less specific audience and to have a large-scale pedagogical aim,[12] not to mention considerable entertainment value.

The Cyropaedia

I. *Description and Synopsis of the Action*

The title of the *Cyropaedia* Κύρου παιδεία means the upbringing and education of Cyrus; its subject is the life from cradle to grave, so to speak, of Cyrus the Great, the founder of the Achaemenid dynasty. Thus the setting is Asia in the 6th century.

It has been argued that only the first book answers to the title;[13] the description, however, of the Persian educational system makes it clear that education is to be taken in a wider sense, meaning education for life.[14]

The division into 8 books is not Xenophon's and cuts across the natural structure of contents, which is the following: a formal introduction where Xenophon speaks directly in the first person as the author to his reader (1.1) and as a complement to this an epilogue, again in the first person (8.8). These two chapters form a frame around the main story, which falls into three parts of very uneven length. The first part (1.2–1.6,46) deals with Cyrus' birth, his upbringing and education until his first military command. The second and by

---

[11] Perry (1967) 82.
[12] Gabba (1983) 11f. uses the expression "an audience of educated general readers" about the audience of Ephorus and Theopompus.
[13] Breitenbach (1967) 1707a.
[14] Higgins (1977) 54; Nickel (1979) 57; Tatum (1989) 90f. Due (1989a) 15.

far the longest (2.1–7.5,36) describes his adventures and conquests, among which Sardis and Babylon are the most important. And the third (7.5,37–8.7) gives an account of Cyrus' ideology and administration of his empire, ending with his death.

In the first part Xenophon combines the specific description of Cyrus' education with a general description of the Persian educational system. But the geographical scene is mainly set in Media where he visits his grandfather who is king of the Medes. Here Cyrus acquires some of his best friends, destined to play an important part later (Artabazus and Araspas). He is represented as member of a nuclear family consisting of his mother, father, grandfather and uncle. His father is king of Persia, his mother the daughter of the Median King. When the Assyrian king and his allies threaten the Median realm, his uncle, Cyaxares, who has succeeded to the throne, asks the Persians for help. They appoint Cyrus as leader. The last chapter is a short military manual cast in the form of a dialogue between father and son.

In the second part Xenophon extends both the range of protagonists and the geographical circuit of his work. Together with Cyaxares, Cyrus marches against the Assyrian king and his allies, regains a defected ally, the Armenian king, wins the first battle, acquires the Hyrcanians and later some of the former allies of the Assyrians, Gobryas and Gadatas as his allies, creates a Persian cavalry, conquers Chaldaea, Caria, Phrygia, Cappadocia and Arabia, wins the beautiful Pantheia as part of his booty and, through his chivalrous conduct, her husband Abradatas as a powerful ally. After the second and greatest battle, Cyrus alone conquers Sardis, meets Croesus, marches on to Babylon where Gobryas and Gadatas kill the Assyrian king. The Egyptian mercenaries are persuaded to join him. Cilicia and Cyprus, too, associate themselves with him. In between he has quarelled and made peace with Cyaxares, whom he completely surpasses in all areas, in strategy and tactics, in courage and morals. He further trains the army, entertains his soldiers on several occasions, and installs a meritocratic system of rewards, helped by some of his Persian friends, Chrysanthas, Hydaspas and Pheraulas.

In the third part he settles down in Babylon, creates a court with a life-guard of eunuchs, establishes a system of government and of satrapies, creates a postal system, a public health-care system, returns to Cyaxares in Media and to his parents in Persia, marries Cyaxares' daughter receiving half the kingdom of Media as dowry and the other half after Cyaxares' death. Finally, he dies, surrounded by his sons and peers, to whom he conveys his last will and advice.

This summary outline shows the dominance of the main character in the story. But it also illustrates how Xenophon has created around him a group of minor figures, relatives, friends, allies and foes who serve not only as a foil to Cyrus, but also as a source of entertainment and excitement. They are used to introduce some of the best "stories" of the work, arousing feelings of sympathy, pity, admiration or horror in the mind of the reader, and adding liveliness, romance and suspense to the main action. The most famous among these subsidiary characters are Pantheia and Abradatas; others are Pheraulas, Gadatas and Gombryas. The love story of Pantheia and Abradatas, in particular, not only points the way towards, but actually seems to have inspired, later romances. It thus deserves a detailed summary.[15]

II. *Pantheia and Abradatas*

The episode is actually in itself a novella or mini-romance, skillfully adapted to the context. Xenophon does not tell the whole story in a narrative continuum, but breaks it up into several scenes following the chronology of the main events.[16] It begins in book 4 where Pantheia is selected for Cyrus by the Medes as his part of the spoils. She is not mentioned by name, but identified by her nationality and her renowned beauty.[17]

At the beginning of book 5[18] she still has no proper name, but her husband Abradatas is mentioned. Cyrus orders his old friend from book 1, Araspas, to be her guardian. In a dialogue between Cyrus and Araspas we have a detailed description of her at the moment of her capture. Her nobleness and beauty make a strong impression upon all those present, especially upon Araspas who describes her face, neck and hands, so that the reader feels his attraction towards

---

[15] According to Philostratus *V.S.*I 22.524, Celer wrote a novel about Araspas and Pantheia under Hadrian, and according to Suidas, Pantheia was the heroine in an Epyllion by Soterichus under Diocletian. Schmeling (1980) 40f. takes the story of Pantheia and Abradatas to have been the model for Anthia and Habrocomes in Xenophon of Ephesus.

[16] 4.6,11–12; 5.1,2–18; 6.1,31–51; 6.3,35–6.4,11; 7.1,15; 7.1,24–32; 7.1,46–49; 7.3,2–16.

[17] 4.6,11. Ph.A. Stadter (1991) 481ff. analyses it as a story in four acts, making the passage in book 4 a prologue.

[18] 5.1,2ff.

her.[19] Cyrus' reaction is to avoid seeing her for fear he might be tempted to neglect his duties as commander. This refusal is the starting point for a discussion about love and free will. Araspas claims with great naïveté that love is subject to the power of will, whereas Cyrus in a humorous way tries to warn him against the fallacies beauty may involve. He ends the passage with a remark which prepares the way for Abradatas to appear on the scene as a powerful ally: φύλαττε τοίνυν, ἔφη (sc. ὁ Κῦρος), ὥσπερ σε κελεύω καὶ ἐπιμελοῦ αὐτῆς· ἴσως γὰρ ἂν πάνυ ἡμῖν ἐν καιρῷ γένοιτο αὕτη ἡ γυνή. (Keep her then, as I bid you, and take good care of her, for this lady may perhaps be of very great service to us in due time.) At this point Xenophon leaves the story by telling how Araspas—as might be expected—falls in love, contrary to all his promises and intentions.

The next instalment comes in 6.1,31. The beautiful lady is still anonymous, but we are told of her deep love and affection for her husband which makes her reject Araspas' proposals. At first she declines to reveal Araspas' attempts to seduce her. But threatened by violence she eventually sends one of her eunuchs to tell Cyrus. After Cyrus' intervention she proposes to atone for the loss of Araspas by sending for her husband who can then become a powerful ally in his stead. He will be motivated by his hatred for the young Assyrian king who, in contrast to Cyrus, has tried to "separate" her from her husband as she very delicately says. In this passage she is finally referred to by name. Cyrus is the first to use it when, after trusting Araspas with a mission as a spy, he asks him if he will be able to give up the beautiful Pantheia. From then on she is always called by that name. Shortly afterwards Abradatas, her husband, presents himself to Cyrus who courteously allows him to see his wife before anything else. This display of tact, and Pantheia's subsequent laudations of him, secure for Cyrus Abradatas' friendship and unswerving loyalty.

Afterwards Abradatas watches Cyrus develop his new tactical weapon, viz. τὰ δρεπανηφόρα ἅρματα (the scythe-bearing chariots). He has more of them built on his own account and prepares himself to become commander of this weapon.

This leads in book 7.1,15ff. and 29ff. to a description of Abradatas in the great battle, where he fights very bravely, but finally falls from his chariot and is killed. The description of the effect of the δρέπανα points forward to the final scene of the story in 7.3,2ff. However,

---

[19] Perry (1967) 169 takes this scene to be the model imitated in Chariton 7.6,7ff.

before the battle, in 6.4,2ff. there is a moving farewell scene with reminiscences of the parting of Hector and Andromache.[20] The Homeric model prepares the reader for a tragic end to the story. Pantheia gives her husband a suit of golden armour made from her jewels. In passionate words she swears by their mutual love that she would rather follow him into death, if he proves himself a brave warrior, than live in shame if he does not. She reminds him of the gratitude they owe to Cyrus, and of her promise that he would prove a better and more loyal ally than Araspas. Abradatas, in his turn, prays to Zeus that he may be worthy of Pantheia and Cyrus. There is a very moving description of Pantheia kissing the chariot and following her husband, unseen by him until he becomes aware of her and bids a final goodbye. She is then taken to her tent by her servants and Xenophon ends the scene with a refined reference to her beauty: οἱ δὲ ἄνθρωποι, καλοῦ ὄντος τοῦ θεάματος τοῦ τε Ἀβραδάτου καὶ τοῦ ἅρματος, οὐ πρόσθεν ἐδύναντο θεάσασθαι αὐτὸν πρὶν ἡ Πάνθεια ἀπῆλθεν. (And the people, beautiful as was the sight of Abradatas and his chariot, had no eyes for him, until Pantheia was gone.)

After the battle in 7.3,2 Cyrus enquires about Abradatas and is told of his death. He is also informed that Pantheia is mourning his dead body. The meeting between Cyrus and Pantheia is told in gruesome detail. When Cyrus clasps the dead Abradatas' hand, it comes off. It had been severed by the Egyptians with a saber, as Xenophon explains. Pantheia rearranges the corpse, indicating that all the limbs are in the same mutilated condition. To a certain extent she blames herself for pressing him to his death. Cyrus expresses his sorrow and admiration, and promises to send her to whomever she may wish under escort. Pantheia answers ambiguously and Cyrus, for once, misunderstands and leaves.

The sequel shows her real intention. She makes her eunuchs retreat a little and orders her old nurse to cover herself and Abradatas under the same blanket after her death. In spite of the nurse's protests, she commits suicide. She had, Xenophon adds, long ago secured herself a dagger. Her example is followed by the eunuchs. Hearing the tragic happening Cyrus rushes back, but too late. He can only mourn them and take care that they receive all due honours. A great monument is built over their tomb.

---

[20] *Iliad* 6.390–493. For an analysis see Rinner (1981) 151ff.

III. Date and Definition

The *Cyropaedia* was probably composed in the last part of Xenophon's life. If the last chapter is genuine, we have a terminus post quem of 362/1 B.C. with mention of the satrap revolt.[21] Because it long precedes the other Greek novels in date and because its author was also an historian, there has been much discussion about what to call it. It has been severally described as an historical novel, the description of an exotic milieu, a political utopia, a handbook for soldiers, a work of Panhellenic propaganda for the conquest of Asia, and a pedagogical treatise.[22] Or a biography.[23] But fundamentally, as already recognised by Cicero,[24] the *Cyropaedia* is not history or biography, but fiction in prose.[25] Thus, according to modern terminology, it is, in view of its considerable length, a novel, the very first in European history. According to its subject and setting, it can further be defined as an historical novel, and according to its aim as a pedagogical or educational novel. Among the ancient novels it is therefore more in line with the Ninus-novel, which Henri Weil actually called a Ninopedia,[26] and the Alexander-romance than with Chariton, Achilles Tatius, Longus and Heliodorus. Its main theme is ruling, not love, but it does contain an affecting story about two lovers separated by war and reunited again. And religion, morality, suspense, violence, sex, sentimentality, heroes and villains, in short all the usual ingredients in later novels, are given a place in it. The main story ends with the peaceful death of its hero, and Xenophon probably would have said that it has a happy ending. The love story however, ends with violent death and suicide.

Xenophon's Aims and Intention

But around the main story there is, as mentioned above, a kind of narrative frame consisting of an introduction and an epilogue: two chapters in which Xenophon talks directly to his audience. In the first he explicitly informs his reader of his subject, which is the art of

---

[21] 8.8,4.
[22] Tigerstedt (1965) I.177 and Tatum (1989) XV.
[23] Momigliano (1971) 46ff. Reardon (1991) 5, 61 uses the term "romantic biography".
[24] Cic. Q. fr. I.1,23. See Schmeling (1974) 29.
[25] Ph.A. Stadter (1991) 461ff. uses the term "fictional narrative".
[26] Weil (1902) 90ff., especially 105f.

ruling, and his aim in writing the work, *viz.* through Cyrus' example to understand what it takes to become an ideal leader. In the last chapter he returns from Cyrus' time to his own times and contrasts the degenerate Persia of now with the ideal Persia of then. Especially the last chapter has given rise to heated discussions. The general opinion today[27] is that the chapter was written by Xenophon, but earlier it was often assumed to be spurious;[28] this theory still finds support.[29] In the first chapter Xenophon describes the difficulties in ruling human beings in general through all ages and in all kinds of regimes, and then procedes from the general to the particular, i.e. to Cyrus. In the last chapter he stays within the Persian empire; he returns from the past to the present and from the ideal to the real state of affairs, but not from the particular to the general. The purpose of the last chapter has been seen as an effort to stress for the last time the greatness and exceptional nature of the hero and the absolute necessity of moral superiority and integrity; once that personal trait had gone, by inner logic the process of deterioration and degeneration started and has been going on ever since.[30] Another explanation maintains that reality imposed itself too forcefully upon the author after the death of Cyrus. The gap between the perfections of Cyrus and the imperfections of present-day Persia was too great for fantasy to continue.[31] Whatever the reason, it must be admitted that the last chapter has a strong, an almost shocking, effect upon the reader. And that of course may also have been the intention; Xenophon is always fond of working with contrasts.[32] He may also have been trying to avert too many protests from a Greek audience,[33] though not with the aim of urging a Greek invasion of Asia.[34]

In this context, however, the most important part of the narrative frame is the first chapter, which contains the raison d'être of the

---

[27] Tatum (1989) 218ff. in accordance with Eichler (1880), Due (1989a) 16ff. Delebecque (1946–7) 101f., (1957) 405ff. and (1978) 172 note claims that the chapter was written by Xenophon, but as a later addition.

[28] See Breitenbach (1967) 1741 with references and discussion. Bizos who edited the first volume of the Budé edition regards the chapter as an interpolation contrary to Delebecque, who edited the second volume.

[29] Hirsch (1985a) 91ff.; see also Sancisi-Weerdenburg (1987b) 119ff.

[30] Due (1989a) 19; Stadter (1991) 471ff.

[31] Tatum (1989) 237ff.

[32] He uses the same structure in Ἡ πολιτεία τῶν Λακεδαιμονίων, *The constitution of the Lacedaemonians*.

[33] Due (1989a) 20; Tatum (1989) 225.

[34] As suggested by Prinz (1911) and Luccioni (1947) 203.

composition.[35] Xenophon intended it to be his contribution to the discussion about leadership or the best possible way of governing. He wanted to learn for himself and to teach his reader something about the art of ruling, a subject of central importance in the debate of the 4th century, discussed also by Plato, Isocrates and Aristotle. Such an intention constitutes a marked difference from the later novels and might seem to place the *Cyropaedia* within the so-called politeia literature. Yet, Xenophon chose not to give an abstract discussion, but turned to fiction instead and wrote a dramatized paradigmatic account of the life of an idealized individual who, although belonging to the past, is meant to be an inspiration for Xenophon's contemporaries. His starting point is the sad reality of political instability and his aim is to show a way of improvement. Thus he intends to impart a moral lesson, but preferred to do so indirectly and allegorically through a historical παράδειγμα. The historical setting, the exotic surroundings and the dramatic action add a strong element of entertainment to the moral lesson. Xenophon wanted his reader to become wiser by reading, but also to be entertained.

Relation to Other Ancient Novels

I. *Intertextuality*

Chariton, too, used an historical setting and historical figures, but on a lesser scale.[36] Hermocrates in Chariton's novel is not a leading figure and was not as well-known. In Xenophon the main character is an historical figure, well known from literature and especially from Herodotus. Xenophon obviously knew Herodotus' first book very well and exploits it dexterously. Apparently he also supposed that at least some of his readers would have been familiar with it and able to relish the omissions, changes and differences his version represents. For the modern reader the intertextuality between the *Cyropaedia* and Herodotus provides an opportunity to acknowledge where Xenophon is most inventive, and to evaluate the result in order to understand the intention behind it.[37]

---

[35] Tatum (1989) 37ff.
[36] See Schmeling (1974) 76ff.
[37] Keller (1910) 252ff.; Höstad (1948) 77ff.; Riemann (1967) 20ff.; Cizek (1975) 531ff.; Hirsch (1985a) 68ff.; Tatum (1989) 147ff.; Due (1989a) 117ff.

In the context of the ancient novel, it is of special interest to note that many of the most purely entertaining scenes or dramatic anecdotes in the *Cyropaedia* lack a counterpart in Herodotus. This is the case of the meeting between Cyrus and his grandfather in Media, their conversation at dinner, Cyrus' first hunting experience and his return to Persia in the first part. This private side of Cyrus is later continued in the description of his relationship with his soldiers and friends at ease during meals or training. Likewise, figures unattested in Herodotus, but of great importance to the unity and structure of the composition, appear in the *Cyropaedia*. Most prominent is Cyrus' uncle, Cyaxares, who in the first and second part acts as a negative counterpart to Cyrus, but later, in part three, as his father-in-law bestows Media upon him.[38]

Conversely there are figures and dramatic episodes in Herodotus which are left out in Xenophon. These appear to be those which were irreconcilable with the moral message and educational intention of the *Cyropaedia*, such as the mésalliance between the princess of Media and a poor Persian, the cruel grandfather who tries to kill his daughter's child, the Harpagus story, Cyrus' war against his grandfather and subsequent conquest of Media, and his ignoble death. In Xenophon we find a picture of a peaceful and harmonious family without conflicts, where Persia and Media become united through marriage, and Cyrus dies a peaceful death surrounded by his nearest and dearest. In Xenophon Cyrus is flawless and perfect, a true hero.

Herodotus is not the only example of intertextuality. As in the later romances, there are many other more or less hidden quotations from other literary works, as well as allusions to historical figures or events. The well-read and painstaking reader is referred to Homer, to Plato, perhaps to Antisthenes and Ctesias, and certainly to Xenophon's own works. The farewell scene between Pantheia and Abradatas in 6.4,2–11 is reminiscent of the parting of Hector and Andromache in the *Iliad* 6,390ff. The death of Cyrus in 8.7 points to Socrates' death as described in Plato's *Phaedo* 118eff., and is reminiscent of *Apology* 40cff. and *Crito* 44a–b, even if it probably also owes something to Persian sources.[39] And Socrates likewise imposes himself in the delicate story in 3.1,38ff. about Tigranes' teacher, a sophist whom

---

[38] Riemann (1967) 39ff.; Tatum (1989) 115ff.; Due (1989a) 55ff.
[39] Sancisi-Werdenburg (1985) 459ff. and Knauth (1975) 53ff.

his father, the Armenian king, executes.[40] The battle of Leuctra in *Hellenica* 6.4,4ff. lies behind the battle in book 7.1,29ff.[41] Behind Cyrus the Great there lies much of Cyrus the Younger,[42] and so on.

II. *The World and Milieu of the* Cyropaedia

The world of Cyrus in geographical terms is to a very high degree the world of the ancient novels. Xenophon draws its contours in the introduction in 1.1,4 and repeats them in a shorter version in 8.6,21 and in the formal ending 8.8,1. The short version has a hint of folk tale: Καὶ ἐκ τούτου τὴν ἀρχὴν ὡρίζεν αὐτῷ πρὸς ἕω μὲν ἡ Ἐρυθρὰ θάλαττα, πρὸς ἄρκτον δὲ ὁ Εὔξεινος πόντος, πρὸς ἑσπέραν δὲ Κύπρος καὶ Αἴγυπτος, πρός μεσημβρίαν δὲ Αἰθιοπία. Τούτων δὲ τὰ πέρατα τὰ μὲν διὰ θάλπος, τὰ δὲ διὰ ψῦχος, τὰ δὲ διὰ ὕδωρ, τὰ δὲ δι' ἀνυδρίαν δυσοίκητα. (From that time on his empire was bounded on the east by the Indian Ocean, on the north by the Black Sea, on the west by Cyprus and Egypt, and on the south by Ethiopia. The extremes of his empire are uninhabitable, on one side because of the heat, on another because of the cold, on another because of too much water, on the fourth because of too little.) The long version, a litany of conquest and annexation, tickles the imagination: Κῦρος δὲ παραλαβὼν ὡσαύτως οὕτω καὶ τὰ ἐν τῇ Ἀσίᾳ ἔθνη αὐτόνομα ὄντα ὁρμηθεὶς σὺν ὀλίγῃ Περσῶν στρατιᾷ ἑκόντων μὲν ἡγήσατο Μήδων, ἑκόντων δὲ Ὑρκανίων, κατεστρέψατο δέ Σύρους, Ἀσσυρίους, Ἀραβίους, Καππαδόκας, Φρύγας ἀμφοτέρους, Λυδούς, Κᾶρας, Φοίνικας, Βαβυλωνίους, ἦρξε δὲ Βακτρίων καὶ Ἰνδῶν καὶ Κιλίκων, ὡσαύτως δὲ Σακῶν καὶ Παφλαγόνων καὶ Μαγαδιδῶν, καὶ ἄλλων δὲ παμπόλλων ἐθνῶν, ὧν οὐδ' ἂν τὰ ὀνόματα ἔχοι τις εἰπεῖν, ἐπῆρξε δὲ καὶ Ἑλλήνων τῶν ἐν τῇ Ἀσίᾳ, καταβὰς δ' ἐπὶ θάλατταν καὶ Κυπρίων καὶ Αἰγυπτίων. (But Cyrus, finding the nations in Asia also independent in exactly the same way, started out with a little band of Persians and became leader of the Medes by their full consent and of the Hyrcanians by theirs; he then conquered Syria, Assyria, Arabia, Cappadocia, both Phrygias, Lydia, Caria, Phoenicia, and Babylonia; he ruled also over Bactria, India, and Cilicia; and he was likewise king of the Sacians, Paphlagonians, Magadidae, and very many other nations, of which one could not even tell the names; he brought

---

[40] 3.1,38ff., *Mem*.1.2,49ff.; *Ap*.20f.; Münschner (1920) 118.
[41] J. Anderson (1970) 165ff.; Holden (1870) vol. I LIIf., vol. 3 196f.
[42] Tatum (1989) 179ff.; Due (1989a) 187ff.

under his sway the Asiatic Greeks also; and descending to the sea, he added both Cyprus and Egypt to his empire.)

The reader's curiosity and taste for the exotic is further whetted by picturesque descriptions of Cyrus' grandfather in his high-heeled shoes, make-up, and splendid dress,[43] the oriental court with its eunuchs,[44] the construction of the scythe-bearing chariots,[45] the king's table[46] and banquet, or the ecphrasis describing the first ceremonial procession from Babylon.[47]

Emotions of pity, fear and sorrow, are especially raised by the sad and sentimental story about Pantheia and Abradatas, but also by the vivid descriptions of the battles and their effects on women and children, as well as by the story of Gobryas and Gadatas. The former lost a son,[48] the latter his virility through the jealousy of the cruel Assyrian.[49]

Other features which link the *Cyropaedia* to later novels are the absolute morality and piety of its hero and his friends. The ideal characters of, e.g., Pantheia and Abradatas and their endeavours to be worthy of Cyrus make him appear even more admirable because they are such paragons of virtue themselves. He is shown to be the exact opposite of the oriental tyrant exemplified by the Assyrian.

His adversaries and enemies are by contrast materialistic (Cyaxares), cowardly (Croesus), and cruel (the Assyrian). Given the context, an antithesis between Greeks and Barbarians was out of the question and probably against Xenophon's feelings; instead he contrasted the Persians with the Medes and the Assyrians.

Style and Narrative Technique

Xenophon's style is lucid, graceful and apparently unpretentious. His wording is precise and his syntax simple. He mixes narrative, speeches and dialogues to form a varied texture. He is remarkable for his ability to make a scene or a situation come to life and unfold itself

---

[43] 1.3,2.
[44] 7.5,58ff.
[45] 6.1,27ff. 6.1,50ff.
[46] 8.2,4ff.
[47] 7.3,1ff.
[48] 4.6,2ff.
[49] 5.2,23ff.

before his reader's eyes. He has a reporter's sense for precise and revealing detail, and his descriptions are imaginative and visual. He is at once realistic and emotional. As an author he is omniscient and knows everything that goes on in the minds of his characters as well as what is happening around them. He has a tendency to establish parallels and to play on echoes and contrasts within the text, and is fond of describing persons antithetically as either heroes or villains. The summary of the Pantheia story exemplifies all these qualities.

In the *Cyropaedia* as a whole the narrative in general appears very straight-forward. Owing to the total dominance of the main character, Xenophon mostly operates on one level in linear simplicity. An exception is book 4 where Cyrus and Cyaxares are separated, the former pursuing his enemies, the second staying behind.[50] Proper flashbacks are rare too, the most obvious occurs in the Pantheia story where Xenophon in 6.1,31 in retrospect tells what had happened to Araspas. To this corresponds a prolepsis in 5.1,18 where he concludes the first act of the story by giving a glimpse of future events. On the other hand he makes frequent use of cross-references and short repetitions in describing the minor figures around Cyrus such as Artabazus, Hydaspas, Chrysanthas and others. This technique keeps the story and its different episodes together, and is a help for the reader as well as an economizing factor for the author. Very often Xenophon creates a sort of suspense or stimulus for further reading by letting a character appear without a proper name in one episode and then re-introducing him with name in another. Apart from the Pantheia story, this technique is used in the case of Artabazus, Araspas and Gadatas.[51]

Another interesting feature of the narrative technique is the handling of time. The *Cyropaedia* is supposedly the first comprehensive description of one particular individual from birth to death, thus covering in fictional time a rather long period.[52] But two rather sudden leaps forward in time show that these years are distributed very unevenly in narrative time, so that what we actually have is a description of its hero's childhood and youth, a narrative account of his actions within a very limited period, and a description of his

---

[50] 4.2,9ff.; 4.5,8ff.
[51] For Artabazus see 1.4,27; 4.1,22; 5.1,24 and 6.1,7; for Araspas 1.4,26 and 5.1,2 and for Gadatas 5.2,23ff.; 5.3,8; 5.3,10 and 5.3,15.
[52] For the terminology see Hägg (1971a) 23ff.

death. The first leap occurs in the first book where Xenophon 1.5,4f. compresses ten years of Cyrus' youth in three lines. The second and even more dramatic leap forward occurs in 8,7,1 where after a short enumeration of Cyrus' conquests and way of life after the first year in Babylon he suddenly interrupts his narrative and somewhat vaguely states: Οὕτω δὲ τοῦ αἰῶνος προκεχωρηκότος, μάλα δὴ πρεσβύτης ὢν ὁ Κῦρος ἀφικνεῖται εἰς Πέρσας τὸ ἕβδομον ἐπὶ τῆς αὑτοῦ ἀρχῆς. καὶ ὁ μὲν πατὴρ καὶ ἡ μήτηρ πάλαι δὴ ὥσπερ εἰκὸς ἐτετελευτήκεσαν αὐτῷ· (When his life was far spent amid such achievements and Cyrus was now a very old man, he came back for the seventh time in his reign to Persia. His father and his mother were in the course of nature long since dead.) Having disposed of Cyrus' later life in this way, Xenophon without further ado launches into a description of his death. It appears from the following that Cyrus has two grown-up sons so that about 20 years are left almost unaccounted for.

The illusion of comprehensiveness is created by three features 1) a tendency in general to give very vague chronological indications; 2) precise dating of particular episodes in relation to others (the predominant phrase being τῇ ὑστεραίᾳ), sometimes with exact information of the time of day; and 3) compression of several events into one particular scene which stands for the general pattern.

The first part of the story gives the best opportunity to estimate the passage of time.[53] Combining the few precise data about Cyrus' age with the general description of the Persian education it can be established that book 1 in fictional time covers ca. 25 years. But from book 2 until 8.6 19 there is only relative dating, and it is possible that the narrative covers only one year in fictional time.[54] After 8,6,19 Xenophon then covers the rest of Cyrus' life until his last three days in 5 paragraphs or one page in the Oxford edition, whereas the account of his last actions and death during those final three days takes up 7 pages. The shift in tempo or the ability to expand or compress episodes in narrative time is impressive and creates in the mind of the reader a feeling of extensiveness.

But the most interesting feature and greatest innovation is the third one, Xenophon's technique of transforming one episode from a specific incident into a general description of a pattern. The description in

---

[53] According to Ph.A. Stadter (1991) 474f. time in book 1 is developmental, in books 2–8 static.

[54] Due (1989a) 49f. As pointed out by Nylander (1995) Xenophon may in this be influenced by Persian sources.

book 1 of Cyrus' stay in Media may serve as an illustration. The narrative consists of a number of different scenes, one of welcome, one describing a dinner, one of hunting, one of war, and a final one of leave-taking. The scenes are interspersed with descriptive passages or dialogues to conclude the subject or introduce a new one.

The welcome scene[55] shows the immediate impact made on the young Cyrus by the impressive appearance of the Median king. Astyages promptly returns the boy's affection by presenting him with a very beautiful dress, στολὴν καλὴν ἐνέδυσε as Xenophon says, using the aorist tense for describing a single completed action. But he proceeds in imperfects and oblique optatives, suggesting repeated actions, thus giving the reader information not about a specific occasion but about a general pattern: καὶ στρεπτοῖς καὶ ψελίοις ἐτίμα καὶ ἐκόσμει, καί εἴ ποι ἐξελαύνοι, ἐφ' ἵππου χρυσοχαλίνου περιῆγεν, ὥσπερ καὶ αὐτὸς εἰώθει πορεύεσθαι (and he used to adorn him with necklaces and bracelets; and if he went for a ride he took the boy along upon a horse with a gold-studded bridle, just as he himself was accustomed to go). Obviously the function of this sentence is to broaden the picture given in the welcome scene and lead over to the next: the dinner.[56]

This scene opens with the words: δειπνῶν δὲ δὴ ὁ Ἀστυάγης σὺν τῇ θυγατρὶ καὶ τῷ Κύρῳ, βουλόμενος τὸν παῖδα ὡς ἥδιστα δειπνεῖν ἵνα ἧττον τὰ οἴκαδε ποθοίη, προσῆγαγεν αὐτῷ καὶ παροψίδας καὶ παντοδαπὰ ἐμβάμματα καὶ βρώματα (When Astyages dined with his daughter and Cyrus, he set before him dainty sidedishes and all sorts of sauces and meats, for he wished the boy to enjoy his dinner as much as possible, in order that he might be less likely to miss things at home.) The description then changes to indirect discourse depending on φασί (they say). So the reader is made to understand that the scene depicts the very first dinner during the visit. The charming naïveté, lack of sophistication and ignorance of etiquette, which Cyrus displays, point in the same direction. But gradually it dawns upon the reader that Cyrus has already been in Media for some time. He is familiar with many of the servants and has taken a strong dislike to Sakas, the royal cup-bearer. He has also witnessed his grandfather's birthday-party. However, the impression is still that the scene depicts one specific dinner rather early in the visit. But this impression, or

---

[55] 1.3,2ff.
[56] 1.3,4ff.

illusion, is suddenly broken when Xenophon ends the scene with the following comment: Τοσαύτας μέν αὐτοῖς εὐθυμίας παρεῖχεν ἐπὶ τῷ δείπνῳ· τὰς δὲ ἡμέρας, εἴ τινος αἴσθοιτο δεόμενον ἢ τὸν πάππον ἢ τὸν τῆς μητρός ἀδελφόν, χαλεπὸν ἦν ἄλλον φθάσαι τοῦτο ποιήσαντα· ὅ τι γὰρ δύναιτο ὁ Κῦρος ὑπερέχαιρεν αὐτοῖς χαριζόμενος (Such amusements he furnished them with at dinner; and during the days, whenever he saw his grandfather or his uncle in need of anything, it was difficult for anyone else to get ahead of him in supplying the need; for Cyrus was most happy to do them any service that he could). Again Xenophon passes from the specific to the general, as the imperfects and the oblique optatives show. And the plural τὰς ἡμέρας (the days) reveals that the singular number in ἐπὶ τῷ δείπνῳ (at dinner) is to be understood as a generic singular. Thus the specific dinner may be interpreted as a conglomerate of many dinners compressed for the sake of dramatic unity and vividness.

In book 2 Xenophon describes Cyrus' social life in the camp by the same technique, but there he starts with the general and then illustrates it through a series of particular events.[57] Both variations occur frequently in the third part in the description of Cyrus' government and administration.[58]

Another dominant feature in the narrative is the frequent parallels between Cyrus' time and the author's time, between then and now. Together with proper authorial comments they establish a dialogue between author and reader. They break the illusion of history and fiction by recalling the reader to reality and the present, and thus serve to stress the paradigmatic importance of the story. They enable Xenophon to repeat the message from the introduction and epilogue reminding the reader of the purpose of it all.

Xenophon's ability to make rather abstract ideas intelligible to all works in the same direction: the reader is invited to connect the exploits and abilities of Cyrus with his own problems and surroundings. Thus, he illustrates the somewhat abstract idea of the perfect ruler by stressing among the many different duties and qualities of Cyrus his ability to remember the names of his officers and soldiers.[59] Further, he uses analogies to the world of artisans, physicians and family-fathers to explain Cyrus' motives and reasons. The reader thus

---
[57] 2.1,30 and 2.3,17–24.
[58] 7.5,37ff.; 8.1,16ff. and 8.2,1ff.
[59] 5.3,46ff.

readily identifies them as valid for his own situation, too. Similarly, Xenophon compares military life in the camp to life in a household on several occasions, making it easy for the reader to find the work useful or exemplary for his own daily life.[60]

The Audience of the Cyropaedia

This tendency points towards an audience of general readers or ordinary citizens. There are parts of the work which would appeal strongly to experts in strategy or to leaders of different categories, but also parts which would appeal to pedagogues, slaveowners or hunters. Nobody has dared to claim that the Cyropaedia was written for the poor in spirit[61] or for the young as has been done in the case of the ancient novels.[62] Yet, it would be just as wrong to restrict its audience to a narrow circle of experts. Its literary allusions may only have been grasped and appreciated by an élite; however, even without this dimension, the story e.g. of Pantheia and Abradatas would have had a more universal appeal and retain its attraction to this day. The Cyropaedia can thus be claimed as a popular work in the best sense of the word.

The Message of the Cyropaedia

Ostensibly the Cyropaedia is a book about a king and about the ideal ruler. However, already the introduction with its parallels to householding and slaves shows that Xenophon is not just advocating monarchy as the ideal government. His message is much more general and universal; it enunciates the need for moral strength and integrity in leaders at all levels of life, whether in a state, an army or a family. Thus the work was instructive for everybody who had to make decisions of social importance.[63] Through Cyrus' actions and behaviour in different situations and towards different characters it describes the qualities which, according to Xenophon, were necessary

---

[60] 8,56ff.
[61] Perry (1967) 5, 98.
[62] Perry (1967) 98, 164; Hignett (1949) 165; criticized by Hägg (1983) 96ff. and Bowie (1992) 55f.
[63] Todd (1968).

to improve, or to redeem, the sad and confusing conditions of human life, qualities as kindness, clemency and concern for other people, combined with strength, discipline, especially self-discipline, and capacity for moral, as well as physical, endurance. And besides being instructive and educational, it contains much purely entertaining material.

If an author's success can be measured by his number of readers, Xenophon was fairly successful. The *Cyropaedia* was very popular with a differentiated audience from the Roman period through the Middle Ages and the Renaissance down to modern times.[64] It was read for all its aspects, for its moral instruction as "Fürstenspiegel" as well as for its charm as entertainment. In the present century, however, its popularity has diminished for many different reasons. Its author fell out of favour, its moralising seemed tedious,[65] its praise of a hierarchic system instead of a democratic one met with disapproval, other and newer works were available; in short it had become a classic read only, if at all, by specialists in philology and history. Recently however, a growing interest can be detected among scholars. The work is read for its importance for literary history and studied as a source for mentality, values and attitudes in the 4th century, as well as for Hellenistic ruler ideology and Iranian history.[66] New translations, though, are needed in order to reach a wider audience.

The standard editions of the Greek text of the *Cyropaedia* are by Marchant (OCT, 1910) and Peters (Bibliotheca Teubneriana, 1968); editions which include notes and translations are by Bizos, Delebecque (Budé, 1971–78, French), Miller (Loeb, 1914, English), and De Vegas Sansalvador (Bibl. des Gredos 108, 1987, Spanish). These translations are the best available ones. The few full commentaries, all from the 19th century, are by Hertlein (Berlin 1859–60), Breitenbach (Leipzig 1878) and Holden (Cambridge 1870).

---

[64] Münschner (1920) and the brilliant chapter: "The Classic as a Footnote" in Tatum (1989) 3ff.

[65] H. Sancisi–Weerdenburg (1985) 459: "In short, the *Cyropaedia* contains too much virtue for our age".

[66] Xenophon knew more about Persia than most of his contemporaries, and there can be no doubt that he used his personal knowledge and experiences to introduce many items from Persia in his own times into the world of Cyrus. He may also have had some knowledge of oral Persian tradition, but the nature of the *Cyropaedia* and Xenophon's intention with his work calls for much caution when we try to use it as a source for Iranian History. See, e.g., Briant (1987) 1–10; Sancisi-Weerdenburg (1987a) 35, (1987b) 117ff. and (1985) 459ff.

D. THE METAMORPHOSES OF THE *ALEXANDER ROMANCE*

Richard Stoneman

There is not one Alexander Romance but many. In the Middle Ages, as has been often remarked, the work was translated more often than any book except for the Gospels, and the study of its ramifications can be on a small scale a veritable cultural history as well as an object lesson in iconographic traditions. But even before the Alexander Romance arrived in the vernacular languages of medieval Europe and Asia it had undergone considerable changes in its Greek and Latin forms. It is the object of this paper to trace these developments and to outline the inter-relation of the several classical and early medieval texts both with each other and with related parahistorical texts about Alexander. (No systematic treatment of the historical writers is attempted).

The Alexander Romance survives in three Greek recensions: A (a single MS), β, which has a number of derivatives with additional material, notably λ and L, and γ, a complex of MSS which represent variant forms of a single version with strong Jewish-Christian elements.[1] In addition there is an abbreviated version, ε, based on α with some material from β.

Some of the later MSS of the β-recension attribute the work to Callisthenes, one of the historians who accompanied Alexander; this attribution is followed by the twelfth century Byzantine scholar Johannes Tzetzes. It is impossible because Callisthenes died before the conclusion of the expedition.

A in its present form dates from the third or very early fourth century A.D. A terminus ante quem is provided by the translation into Latin made, with little alteration, by Julius Valerius, consul in A.D. 338. At I.7 this translation refers to the philosophical author Favorinus (fl. A.D. 130); this reference was also in the Greek text followed by the Armenian translation (where the name appears as Paphovranos); a terminus post quem for A is therefore about A.D.

---

[1] Cf. Stoneman (1991) 28–32.

200. (Favorinus is not mentioned in any of the Greek recensions we have). A is our only witness to a hypothetical original known as α.[2] The date of composition of α is disputed: many scholars, including Reinhold Merkelbach,[3] hold that the date of composition of A is not only the earliest evidence for this recension but also the likely date at which it was composed. Merkelbach has analysed the form of the Alexander Romance, surely correctly, as an amalgam of several different kinds of text—Hellenistic history, the letters of Alexander and Darius (a form of which was circulating soon after Alexander's death),[4] the wonder-letters, and the account of Alexander's last days— put together on the model of the composition of the Greek novels of the Second Sophistic. However, new discoveries have pushed back the origin of the novel earlier and earlier than the third century A.D. period originally posited by Rohde.[5] Furthermore, numerous pieces of evidence suggest that the Alexander Romance in something like its present form was known to Philostratus, for example;[6] it is the opinion of the present writer that the work was already compiled in something like the form of A in Ptolemaic Alexandria, as early as the second or perhaps even third century B.C.[7]

Our manuscript of A has already suffered interpolation, as is shown by comparison with the Latin translation of Julius Valerius. The most notable addition to the hypothetical α is the inclusion after 3.6 of most of the monograph attributed to the fifth century bishop Palladius, *On the Life of the Brahmans*,[8] which expands Alexander's encounter with the Brahmans to much greater length. This interpolation is not found in any of the other Greek recensions. In addition, we have a witness to a purer form of α in the Armenian translation made in the sixth century A.D.—without reference to Julius Valerius—and wrongly attributed to the fifth century historian Moses of Choren.[9]

At this point it may be helpful to summarise the narrative of A,

---

[2] A hypothetical reconstruction of α is made by Ausfeld (1907), and translated by Haight (1955).
[3] Merkelbach (1977).
[4] Pieraccioni (1947); re-edited Norsa and Bartoletti (1951).
[5] Rohde (1914). On earlier novels: Rattenbury (1933), Sandy (1994b).
[6] Evidence that the Romance was known to Philostratus includes the latter's dispute with the Romance version over the location of the Brahmans (Stoneman (1995) and the reference to the Alexander-plaques at Taxila (Stoneman, 1994b).
[7] Stoneman (1991) 8–17; Gunderson (1980).
[8] Editions by Derrett (1960) and Berghoff (1967); translation in Stoneman (1994c).
[9] Wolohojian (1969).

and thus presumably of α, as an armature on which to attach the accretions of the later recensions.[10] (The chapter numbers were established by Müller in his edition of Pseudo-Callisthenes, and subsequent editors have used the same chapter numbers even where this entails some numbers being missing in any given recension.)

Alexander is represented as the son of Nectanebo, the last Pharaoh of Egypt, who has fled to Macedonia to escape the Persian conquest of Egypt. Nectanebo contrives to make love to Queen Olympias by disguising himself as the god Ammon, and explains her pregnancy to a suspicious Philip by sending an oracular dream to Philip to explain that his wife is pregnant by a god. When Alexander grows up, he murders Nectanebo who explains as he dies the truth about Alexander's paternity.

Alexander is educated by Aristotle and competes at the Olympic Games. On Philip's death Alexander begins a series of campaigns in Greece and then goes to Egypt where the oracle of Ammon instructs him where to found the city of Alexandria. The foundation is described in great detail. Alexander is then hailed in Memphis as the reincarnation of Nectanebo. These episodes, along with the prominence given to Nectanebo make it virtually certain that these elements of the story were composed in Ptolemaic Alexandria.

The next chapter finds Alexander beginning his march into Asia and leads to the campaign against Darius which is interspersed with a number of letters between Alexander and Darius. This narrative is interrupted by a return to the campaigns in Greece (the author being quite unaware of the geographical muddle) and the long debate in Athens about how the Athenians should react to Alexander, which has the marks of being derived from a Hellenistic rhetorical history, though its author cannot be conjectured.

Alexander uses the campaign against Darius to indulge his penchant for disguises, and on Darius' defeat burns the palace at Persepolis (unnamed). As he prepares to marry Darius' daughter Roxane he writes a letter to his mother describing strange adventures in India and Central Asia. This is the section which is expanded further and further in each succeeding recension, acquiring new adventures all the time. A contains only a limited number of these adventures, mainly concerning fabulous beasts and races of men, many details of which

---

[10] Cf. the fuller summary in Stoneman (1991) 5–7.

originate with the fifth century writer Ctesias.[11] Alexander meets two talking birds which admonish him not to seek heaven but to return and conquer India.

Alexander turns back, marches into India, conquering its king Porus, and goes on to visit the Brahmans and to interrogate them about their way of life. This episode was very popular and a version of it appears not only in Plutarch's *Life* of Alexander but on a papyrus of about 100 B.C.[12] There follows a letter of Alexander to Aristotle about India. This letter is very corrupt and lacunose in A and the text has to be substantially supplemented from the Armenian version. This letter took on an independent life in antiquity as the Latin *Letter to Aristotle about India* (see below).

Alexander visits Candace the Queen of Meroe (again in disguise). He subdues the Amazons by exchanging letters with them, not even meeting them face to face (whereas the vulgate historians, such as Quintus Curtius and Plutarch, allowed him to indulge in a long sexual dalliance with their queen Thalestris). He and his army visit the City of the Sun (the description of which contains elements both of Nysa, the shrine of Dionysus, and of the standard topoi used to describe the palace of the Persian kings.)

Alexander then reaches Babylon where he is poisoned by his cupbearer Iolaus (or Iollas). He makes his will, which is given in detail and dies. This episode is in effect a separate text interpolated here into the MS of A. It is given much more briefly in β and γ. It achieved independent life as a Latin text, *The Death and Testament of Alexander the Great*, substantially the same in content as the Greek.[13]

The succeeding recensions of the Alexander Romance belong either to the Greek or the Latin traditions. The first oriental version to derive from the Greek tradition is the Syriac Romance, which is based on A but also has a significant admixture of elements from the λ versions; this led Ausfeld[14] to postulate a lost source-recension, known as δ*. The Syriac version was translated into Arabic and Ethiopic, and into Pahlavi, whence its tales were absorbed into Persian legend. The translation of Julius Valerius had no further influence, but in the tenth century a second Latin translation was made by Leo the

---

[11] For detailed discussion see Stoneman (1994a).
[12] Berlin papyrus 13044; Wilcken (1923). There is another variant in Boissonade *Anecdota Graeca* I. 145.
[13] Thomas (1960); Heckel (1988).
[14] Ausfeld (1907).

Archpriest, which in turn gave rise to three variously interpolated versions known as the *Historia de Proeliis* (see further below). The texts of this work show a similar combination of topics to the Syriac, so that it appears that the lost δ* also influenced the western tradition. The earliest recension of the *Historia de Proeliis* dates from the eleventh century; it is therefore logical to treat the Greek versions before the Latin ones. There is little interplay between the two traditions until the Middle Ages, when Arabic versions began to exercise an influence on both Latin and vernacular medieval writers about Alexander: but this influence was confined to miscellaneous lore and did not influence the form of the various European versions of the Alexander Romance as such.[15]

The second recension, β,[16] is characterised by its considerable additions to the wonder tales of Book 2.23ff. (the Letter to Olympias). These focus on Alexander's expedition to the north, including encounters with strange beasts and a river with black stones which cause any who touch them to turn black. His army travels through a land of darkness, and his cook chances to discover the Water of Life when he sets out to cook a dried fish in water from a spring: the fish immediately comes to life again. Two birds appear and tell Alexander to turn back: "The East is calling you, and the kingdom of Porus will be subjected to your rule." Now, when it is too late, Alexander's cook tells him the story of the fish, and Alexander punishes him. The narrative then continues with the expedition to India and the visit to the Brahmans. However, β does not include the Letter to Aristotle about India (3.7–16 in A).

Other changes in this recension are as follows: the verse passages in Book 1.33 (the oracle of Sarapis) and 2.20 (the lament for Darius) are recast as prose, and the story of the foundation of Alexandria is curtailed. The long verse effusion of Ismenias about the destruction of Thebes (1.46) is omitted, as is the debate in Athens (2.1–5). These changes suggest an audience in some ways less literate, and certainly less interested in the specifics of fourth century B.C. Greek history. However, the author of β also makes some attempt to repair the chronology of Alexander's career by interpolating a brief account of Alexander's campaigns against Greece immediately after his accession

---

[15] See e.g. Hertz (1905); Düring (1957).
[16] Bergson (1965).

(1.26-29; these chapter numbers are omitted from the text of A). This includes not only the campaigns against the northern tribes and against Thebes, but also (next following) the Battle of the Granicus and then a visit to Sicily where Alexander receives envoys from the Romans. Then (30) he sails to Africa as in A. The result of this addition is that the Greek and Theban campaigns appear again, at much greater length, in the same place as in A (1.43ff.).

All these alterations and omissions are carried over from β to the remainder of the Greek recensions. Stylistically the text remains in a *koine* similar to that of A.

The date of β is fixed by its derivation from A, ca. A.D. 300 on the one hand, and the fact that it was used by the author of the Armenian translation, ca. A.D. 550, on the other hand. From β derives the MS L (fifteenth century) which contains substantial additions to the wonder tales of Book 2 and a smaller addition in 3. Most of these additions appear also in the sub-recension λ (five MSS of the fourteenth century), so that the version of L must be dated before 1400.

The additional material in L is as follows: 2.32-33: minor additions. 2.38-39: mysterious voices order Alexander to turn back from the island and utter an oracle about his destiny. After the appearance of the giant crabs (briefly in β), Alexander constructs a diving bell to explore the sea. The diving bell is seized by a fish and dragged away. Alexander emerges half dead from fright. The journey into the land of darkness is told at much greater length, adding the episode of the old man who advises leaving foals behind to guide the mares on the return journey. The story of the water of life is told more fully, including the name of the cook Andreas. 2.41: the rest of the story of the cook. Here Alexander's daughter Kale is also named. Alexander erects a signpost to the Land of the Blessed. (The medieval name of the cook, and the name of the daughter, recalling the folkloric Καλὴ τῶν ὀρέων, situate this version firmly in the Middle Ages.) Alexander then constructs a flying machine by attaching large birds to a receptacle of wood and leather, in which he ascends; in due course he encounters a flying creature which orders him to return to earth; he decides to make no more attempts on the impossible. 3.33: Alexander's letter to Olympias, dictated on his deathbed, includes the admonition to invite to a banquet all those who have known no sorrow: Olympias finds no one answering to this description, and takes the instruction as a consolation.

Independent of β is a much shorter version known as ε, represented by seven MSS.[17] This is a free re-telling of the same story, probably to be dated in the eighth century. Because of its distance from the other versions (though verbally it is often close), it cannot be edited according to the same chapter numbers which are to followed by editors of the other recensions. The language shows many elements of Byzantine vocabulary, syntax and spelling. The main differences from the preceding versions are the following. 1. Alexander's visit to Jerusalem (ch. 20). This apocryphal legend is certainly much earlier since it is already mentioned by Josephus (*AJ* 11.317-345). 2. The Land of the Blessed is now an island (ch. 31).[18] 3. The visit to the Gymnosophists or Brahmans is barely mentioned and none of the interview or the question-and-answer session is included. Some of the topoi of this meeting are however included in the speech of Euanthes (a character unique to this recension) whom Alexander encounters en route to the Land of the Blessed (ch. 31). 4. Alexander erects an arch to bridge a chasm (ch. 32). 5. The adventures in the diving bell and the flying machine are not included, but in their place is a visit to a lake from which the men catch a fish in whose belly is a gleaming stone. Alexander uses it as a lamp. In the night women emerge from the lake and sing around the camp (ch. 33). 6. The Letter to Aristotle about India is included (ch. 34). 7. The enclosure of the Unclean Nations Gog and Magog (or Goth and Magoth) behind the Caspian Gates is described (ch. 39). This episode is derived from the Apocalypse of Pseudo-Methodius, which dates from the sixth or seventh century (though the real Methodius died in 311). 8. As Alexander is dying, Bucephalus enters the room and tears apart his murderer (ch. 46).

In general the affinities of this text seem to be closer to the contemporary genre of Saints' Lives than to the history-plus-wonder-tale character of the earlier recensions.

Both β and ε were utilised as a source by the composer of the last and most complex of the Greek recensions, γ, represented by three MSS with often substantial differences between them. γ contains everything that is in β and L, and also the bulk of Palladius *On the Brahmans*, which otherwise occurs only in A. In addition, it contains

---

[17] Trumpf (1974).
[18] For the date of this change see Stoneman (1994a).

several new episodes.[19] These include: Alexander's visit to Rome (1.27); an extended version of Porus' response to Darius' letter (2.12); a different ending to the battle with Porus (3.3); and "obituary" (3.35). Several episodes also clearly originate in Jewish or Christian circles. These are: the visit to Judaea (from ε: 2.22); the proclamation of the One God in Alexandria (2.28);[20] the lake with the fish with a luminous stone in its belly (from ε), a battle with centaurs and a comic encounter with pigmies (2.28); the visits of Charmides and Bucephalus to Alexander on his death bed (from ε; 3.33). In several of these cases the narrative has been so altered or changed in order that the events of γ cannot be slotted into place in one of the earlier versions, but represent incompatible alternatives. In addition, the letter form of Alexander's letters is lost and the episodes in these become third person narratives, with the result that events now actually occur in the narrative at points where previously they were simply narrated, as having occurred earlier. The most important of these dislocations is that the Letter to Aristotle about India is moved to a position after the conquest of Porus instead of before, so that its events now follow the Indian sojourn. This dislocation is important because in later tellings of the Alexander story the Brahmans (already further east, on the Ganges, in Palladius), become a stage on the route to the Land of the Blessed or Paradise (as the Brahman-like character, Euanthes, already is in ε).

γ probably belongs to the ninth century, and with it ends the continuous reworking of the Greek Alexander Romance. The tale was retold in several medieval Greek versions including the "Byzantine Alexander Poem" (ca. 1388),[21] the so-called "Rimada" (published Venice 1529),[22] and a Byzantine prose re-telling which became the basis of the sixteenth century φυλλάδα τοῦ Μεγαλεξάντρου.[23] The *Rimada* at least shows cross-influence from the west, from the Italian *Alexandreida in Rima* (1512). It should be mentioned that these medieval Greek versions also make use of the abbreviated account of Alexander's career in the sixth century *Chronicle* of George the Monk

---

[19] See the appendices in my translation, Stoneman (1991); a list is given in Trumpf (1974) vii.
[20] Another Jewish story, preserved in Pseudo-Epiphanius, is that of Alexander's transportation of the bones of Jeremiah to Alexandria.
[21] Wagner (1881).
[22] Holton (1974).
[23] Pallis (1990/1); Veloudis (1977).

(or George the Sinner), which includes the story of Alexander's visit to Jerusalem.

The Latin versions of the Romance can be somewhat more briefly dealt with, though all of them are important for our reconstruction of the Greek original texts. As we have seen, the translation by Julius Valerius is a fairly close translation of α, without the addition of Palladius in Book 3 and with a very truncated version of the Letter to Aristotle. (The book numbers of Julius Valerius correspond to those of Pseudo-Callisthenes, but the chapter numbers do not). This work may have been known to the author of the *Itinerarium Alexandri Magni*, composed between 340 and 350,[24] which refers (ch. 53), to Alexander's expedition to the Pillars of Hercules in the Far East (not otherwise referred to in the vulgate historians).[25]

In the ninth century an epitome was made of Julius Valerius which was preserved in Metz Codex 500 (destroyed in 1944), from which it has the name of the Metz Epitome. The Metz Codex also included another Alexander text, namely the *Death and Testament of Alexander* (*Liber de Morte Testamentumque Alexandri Magni*), which is a Latin version of the concluding episode of the Greek Romance as given in A.[26] It is given in less complete form in Julius Valerius.[27]

Of more lasting influence is the second Latin translation of the Romance, made by Leo the Archpriest between 951 and 968/9.[28] This, which was entitled *Nativitas et Victoria Alexandri Magni*, is again a translation of an α- version. Leo's original is not extant, but a close approximation to it is MS E.III.14 (Ba) in the Bamberg Staatsbibliothek, which was written in South Italy about 1000 and contains also some other Alexander treatises, namely the *Commonitorium Palladii* (a Latin version of the introductory section of Palladius *On the Brahmans*,[29] the *Collatio Alexandri cum Dindimo* or Correspondence of Alexander and Dindimus, and a version of the Latin Letter of Alexander

---

[24] Mai (1835).
[25] Quintus Curtius 10.1.17 refers to the (western) Pillars of Hercules, introducing the reference while Alexander is in India; this may be the source of the displacement of these pillars to the far east.
[26] Both edited by Thomas (1960).
[27] See Heckel (1988) for full details.
[28] Leo the Archpriest ed. F. Pfister (1913).
[29] There are two other variants of the Latin Palladius, one a Vatican MS (of which Bamberg is an abridgement) and one heavily revised one falsely attributed to St. Ambrose: Wilmart (1933). Cf. Derrett (1960).

to Aristotle.[30] An independent partial copy of Leo's text is Lambeth Palace MS 342 (L). But the fullest tradition is that of the three recensions of the interpolated version of Leo which has become known as the *Historia de Proeliis*, after the title of MS Bodl. Rawlinson B.149, *Liber Alexandri Philippi Macedonum qui primus regnavit in Grecia et de preliis ejusdem*.[31]

The earliest of these, J^1, interpolates many episodes from λ, and also corresponds in many places to a version close to the Syriac translation of the Greek, so that it is presumed that both versions derive from a lost Greek recension, δ*, which has elements of both α and β.[32] The original of J^1 must date from the eleventh century, as it was used as a source for the first vernacular Alexander Romance, by Alberic of Besançon (ca. 1100). The episodes of this version additional to Leo's text include Alexander's visit to Jerusalem; the correspondence with Dindimus; Alexander's ascent in the basket borne by eagles and his descent in the diving bell; and the episode with the prophetic trees. The correspondence with Dindimus is drawn from one of the works included in the Bamberg MS which contains the text of Leo, the *Commonitorium Palladii*. The events of the Letter to Aristotle about India are incorporated in this recension, but are told in the third person (as in γ). The letters to Porus and the visit to the Amazons occur before the Indian section instead of after it.

J^2 was composed in the twelfth century. It is sometimes known as the Orosius-recension because it incorporates a number of episodes drawn from the *Historiae adversum Paganos* of Orosius. Verbally it remains close to J^1. In addition it has the episode of the enclosure of Gog and Magog (as in γ), and material drawn from Pseudo-Epiphanius concerning the removal of the bones of Jeremiah to Alexandria, as well as material from Josephus relating to the visit to Jerusalem.[33] Neither this recension nor J^3 contains the ascent in the basket or the descent in the diving bell.

J^3 belongs to the late twelfth or early thirteenth century, and is at any rate before 1326 when it was utilised by Quilichinus of Spoleto for his *Alexandreis* in Latin distichs. Additions in this text include a still longer account of the visit to Jerusalem, considerable details about

---

[30] Edited by Pfister (1910). For the letter: Boer (1953), Feldbusch (1976), Gunderson (1980).

[31] A good recent brief account of these three recensions is Pritchard (1992).

[32] See above; also Gunderson (1980) 41.

[33] Bergmeister (1975) ix.

the throne of Cyrus, and other minor additions. Verbal variations from J¹ and J² are significant.[34]

Other Latin versions were also composed, notably the *Liber Alexandri Magni* (Paris MS B.N., n.a.l.310), which is contaminated from all three recensions as well as other Alexander texts.[35] The first printed edition of the *Historia de Proeliis* was made in 1471. The printed editions likewise reflect different recensions, and all the recensions had their influence on the vernacular versions of the Alexander Romance.

Before concluding this survey of the Latin recensions we should mention the Latin *Letter of Alexander to Aristotle about India*,[36] which represents a version of this letter independent of, and longer than, the Greek version. It presumably represents a longer Greek letter which was epitomised in the Greek Romance, and is therefore important for the understanding of the development of the Greek version. The Latin translation was made certainly by the seventh century and may be earlier than the reign of Constantine.[37] A second version was made in the tenth century, in a modernised Italian-Latin, which shows only minor deviations in content from the first.[38] It is based not on the Greek original but on the earlier Latin text as is made clear by its occasional misunderstandings of the Latin original.

This concludes the survey of texts related to or deriving from the Greek Alexander Romance. However, one other text should be mentioned, namely the *Iter Alexandri ad Paradisum*,[39] a medieval Latin work recounting Alexander's journey up the Ganges to Paradise and the parable about the stone which resembles an Eye. Though the Latin text of this story belongs to the Middle Ages, we know from the appearance of the parable in the Babylonian Talmud, before A.D. 500, that the tale was circulating much earlier. It is just one indication that throughout antiquity there was a considerable fund of stories relating to Alexander which were drawn on for one or other legendary account. It shows also that the date at which stories first appear in our texts is of little value as evidence for their antiquity.

Alexander, very soon after his death, became an important "bearer

---

[34] Bergmeister (1975) viia, citing W. Kirsch's edition of Quilichinus of Spoleto (Skopje 1977).
[35] Schnell (1989).
[36] Feldbusch (1976); Gunderson (1980).
[37] Gunderson (1980) 35.
[38] Pfister (1910); Stoneman (1994c).
[39] Hilka (1935); Stoneman (1994c).

of meaning" for the preoccupations of the cultures in which the legends originated. If, as I believe, the Alexander Romance is in its origins a Hellenistic work, it encapsulates first of all the concerns (Egyptian history; the problems of world empire) of that era. As antiquity advances, it becomes able to support reflections in the medium of fiction on such topics as ambition and mortality (the Brahmans, the ascent in the basket and the prophetic trees); Alexander becomes, instead of a troubled adventurer, a culture-hero (the enclosure of the Unclean Nations; the preaching of God in Alexandria); he takes on characteristics of the Christian saint (the journey to the Land of the Blessed becomes a journey to paradise); and (to go beyond the limits of our period) in Greek tradition he becomes a folk-hero and even encounters—apparently—a character of folklore of Ottoman times in Candace's son Karagoz, while in Latin tradition he becomes a chivalric hero (the stone in the Parable of the Eye is a model for the Grail in *Parzival*).[40]

It is hard perhaps to identify the appeal and the reasons for the endurance of the artless farrago that is the Alexander Romance. In part it lies in the resonance of the great conqueror, in part in the variety and imaginative excellence of the tales incorporated in it. It is without doubt one of the most enduring legacies of Greek antiquity to the medieval world. With the invention of the printed book, it disappears from view almost instantly.

---

[40] Kratz (1973) 590–3.

E. PHILOSTRATUS ON APOLLONIUS OF TYANA: THE UNPREDICTABLE ON THE UNFATHOMABLE

Graham Anderson

The massive third-century confection by the Athenian Philostratus entitled τὰ ἐς τὸν Τυανέα Ἀπολλώνιον ("In honour of Apollonius of Tyana", henceforth *V[ita] A[pollonii]*) is difficult to classify under any label, and is often classified as fiction almost as a matter of default. Critical opinions have tended to bifurcate, and the equivocal nature of the author himself and his attitude towards his task have contributed to a certain sense of impasse. Philostratus' other major work, the βίοι σοφιστῶν (*Lives of the Sophists*) helps to define and illustrate the activities of a species of writer better equipped to produce flamboyant fiction than accurate reporting; while his two major *opuscula* embodied in the Ἡρωικός (*Heroic Tale*) and Εἰκόνες (*Pictures*) are largely concerned with mythological themes. We are rather predisposed to expect something less than a fully factual working of any of such an author's materials. But the *VA* is nonetheless valuable and illuminating, not least for its unique blend of the problems that characterise sophisticated fiction and popular devotional subliterature alike.

I. *Genre*

Relatively little work has been attempted on the question of genre, and perhaps rightly, since the general scale, disparate materials and author's expressed explanation would mark this massive ensemble as outside normal generic expectation. It purports to be biography of a first-century Pythagorean sage; its subject-matter belongs in large measure to hagiography, aretalogy or similarly pious material; while its difficulties with political truth in particular have traditionally pushed it into the realm of romantic fiction. The views of individual scholars on genre are often inseparable from their views on the author's veracity itself. What follows is intended to concentrate on those aspects of the *VA* most directly related to its contribution to fiction, rather than to examine the problems of the work as a whole.[1]

That some stratum of fiction accompanies Philostratus' treatment of Apollonius seems scarcely in doubt. Bowie in particular has stressed features which he regards as signals to the reader that this is how *VA* is to be read: these include the very claim that Philostratus obtained memoirs of Apollonios' alleged disciple Damis from his patroness Julia Domna and used them as his principal source.[2] Bowie's arguments have won a good deal of acceptance, but are open to challenge. In the first place comparison is adduced, converging with that offered by W. Speyer, with Dictys' purported reporting of the Trojan War, as well as with Antonius Diogenes' device of the "discovery" of cypress-wood tablets as the basis for his narrative.[3] But neither analogy obliges us to believe that "Philostratus ... could himself be responsible for the invention of Damis *in conscious evocation of a novelistic tone and setting*".[4] Such authenticating devices could just as easily perform their function because they imitate real life: people *do* accompany great men, and *do* find written memoirs. To suggest that such claims are probably false on the strength of their mere mention seems to prejudge the issue. Moreover Bowie's comparisons of *VA* with Iamblichus' *Babyloniaca* seem of unequal value. The "Babylonian" milieu seems a natural sphere of activity for a Cappadocian sage, as readily as it might for a Manichaean missionary. The eunuch in love seems a valid link, but primarily as a rhetorical rather than novelistic topos; the form of the *Scheintod* at *VA* 4.45 is in context and function far closer to hagiographical parallels than to its admittedly characteristic appearances in the novel. Any holy man can have his "Jairus' daughter" episode; but without a *Liebespaar* the theme of falsely presumed death does not suggest a novel. Nor does persecution by authorities, as Bowie himself as good as admits. Prophecies of kingship are similarly far more characteristic of holy men than of the heroes of novels.[5] Moreover title and structure take us little further:

---

[1] The following works are referred to by author's surname throughout: Bowie (1978); Anderson (1986) (on Apollonius, 121–239); Dielska (1986); Flintermann (1993) with the fullest biography to date; Anderson (1994).

[2] Bowie (1978) 1653–1670, refuting the excesses of Grosso (1954), 331–532; *VA* 1.3, cf. 1.19. The positions taken in Bowie (1994a) are considerably more circumspect, though the emphasis on fiction is retained in title and arguments alike. I was able to see this treatment only after completing the present survey.

[3] Bowie (1978) 1663, cf. Speyer (1974) 51; Antonius Diogenes in Photius cod. 166. 111a.

[4] Bowie (1978).

[5] Cf. Bowie (1978) 1664f.

the phrase τὰ ἐς 'Απολλώνιον does not really point to any connotations more specific than the subject Apollonius himself; eight-book division may well look back to the Xenophon's *Cyropaedia*—but perceived as biography or novel, or as a monumental literary model regardless of genre?[6]

It is perhaps more helpful to ask why it is so natural for the topoi of hagiographical works and love-romances to coincide. One factor is that holy men existed in real life, and were natural enablers (and preventers) in fiction;[7] a second, that the novel and hagiography alike move in a world of converging cultural tastes and relative imprecision of rhetorical expression. That does not oblige us to reject Bowie's position out of hand; but it might serve as a warning against the approach that anything with an air of *ben trovato* about it *must* be fiction; all that it ever seems safe to say about the *VA* is that much of it must remain suspect, a very different matter.

If we return to the problem of Damis' memoirs, there are four possible positions: (a) that Philostratus received genuine memoirs; (b) that he only mistakenly supposed that that was what they were; (c) that he invented them himself in order to deceive, or (d) that he invented them merely to entertain or amuse. Of these (a) is only really possible if the disciple wrote in a fanciful hagiographic manner not unlike that of portions of Apocryphal Gospels or Acts; while (d) requires a substantial *cui bono?*: why invent the memoirs for recognition as fiction, when one is already claiming licence to depart from them anyway? But it may be less a matter of Philostratus' wishing his work to be recognised as a sophistic novel than of making the most of the information available and patching it up into a rather ramshackle composition, protecting the sage's reputation from unsavoury accusation as the author does so. It ought perhaps to be insisted more strongly that this particular work is not really a very likely task for this particular sophist to have taken on, had it not accorded specially with the tastes of his philosophically inclined patroness Julia Domna. Had he taken his own path and written a work of fiction *ab initio*, we should have felt entitled to expect something with at least the fluency of the Philostratean *Heroicus*, if not of Heliodorus' *Aethiopica*:[8] instead

---

[6] Cf. Bowie (1978) 1665. On its aspect as fiction, cf. Tatum (1989), index s.v. fiction.
[7] Anderson (1994) 178–187.
[8] Cf. Anderson (1986) 230f.

we are looking at a very shakily constructed composition whose inequalities seem to proclaim a sophist fumbling with unreliable and characteristically incompatible materials,[9] and no less characteristically brazening out his task with a brave face.[10]

VA remains the classic example where popular and sophisticated jostle one another side by side without the author's seeming clearly aware of the fact. One senses that local and oral traditions on Apollonius are not always accorded a great deal of elaboration.[11] Perhaps this is due to the fact that some of them at any rate did not contain enough, or enough of the right sort of material, for Philostratus to feel that elaboration was justified or indeed possible; or perhaps true to his commission he set himself to elaborate only the "Damis archive" (of whatever sort it might have been).

II. *The Romanticising of the* Θεῖος Ἀνήρ

What seems clearly at the centre of the problem is the nature of Apollonius of Tyana himself. We should at least agree on why this is so difficult to judge. I have tried to argue elsewhere that the early Imperial holy man, Jewish, Christian or Pagan, is by nature a figure who remains effectively all things to all men, sometimes by speaking in laconic and enigmatic terms, and dashing in from the outer fringe of civilisation to the centre and out again. He is not the sort of man to commit himself if he can help it, and someone who purports to be a master of equivocatory epigram will be able to keep everyone guessing. The result is that such a figure is likely to run the risk of being the projection of other men's hopes and expectations, and one

---

[9] *Ibid.*, 236.
[10] Morgan (1988) 236, and Flintermann (1993) 312 question my suggestion of a "φασιν"-*Quelle* to account for Philostratus' less reliable information. In attempting to argue for a source signalled by φασιν or some evident variation I had not intended to include passages where Damis quite clearly forms part of an antecedent subject (e.g. in passages indicating an authorial Damis who includes himself together with Apollonius). I had taken it as self-evident that any passages of this kind had to be taken as part of any hypothetical Damis-Quelle. But the problem of difficult joins between sources, or of formulae fudged or obfuscated by Philostratus, is never far away, and both authors are right to raise it; a specific study of the language of Philostratus' editorial formulae is called for. For the difficulties of "Damis the Epicurean" see M. Edwards (1991) 563–566, a useful illustration of many of the impasses that confront the scholar in search of consistency in such a work.
[11] E.g. *VA* 4.6; 4.29; 7.5ff.

is never likely to be near enough the reality to check.[12] Two strands seem particularly consistent throughout the string of *apomnemoneumata* around Apollonius: his insistence on the proper worship of the gods, on which he appears to have a great deal of antiquarian information at his fingertips; and his general oneupmanship vis-à-vis his fellow men.[13] Both contribute to an aura or charisma surrounding the person of Apollonius that makes fictitious elaboration or secondary accretion of hagiographic cliché highly likely.

There is a constant credibility gap between those who see the normal forces of hagiography at work, and those who see Philostratus as always the inventor, making implausible connexions between Apollonius and such eminently attested cultural leaders as Dio of Prusa and Scopelian,[14] or as twisting the tried and tested chronology sanctioned by Roman Historians.[15] But it should be stressed that this view tends not take into account either the varied and versatile lifestyles of holy men in general, or the treachery of the popular traditions through which they are so often mediated.[16]

Two recent works have tried to place Philostratus' construction of Apollonius in a larger perspective. Dielska's main concern is the growth of the Apollonius-legend rather than the shape of Philostratus' work. She has much of interest to say in particular on the subject of Apollonius' magic; but it is perhaps worth pointing out the parallelism between charges of magic against Apollonius and against Jesus Christ, and the inevitable circularities of method which tend to result from pursuing them.[17] Much of Dielska's account seems to me to be based on little more than assertion. How is one to prove that the episodes of the incarnation of Amasis, the three-headed baby, or the accounts of the Lamia, Empousa, or satyr-like creatures are distorted by Philostratus "from the world of myths and folk imagination"? To all appearances Apollonius was not interested in the world of

---

[12] Anderson (1994) 16–33 (on perceptions of the holy man); *ibid.*, 73–85 (on their often evasive rhetoric).

[13] Of course this must apply to his superlative rhetoric as well: see now Billault (1993) 227–235. Philostratus however never seems quite fully aware of the ironies of a sophist discharging his professional duty in honour of the philosopher who must outdo rhetoricians in their own profession.

[14] Anderson (1986) 183.

[15] *Ibid.*, 176–182.

[16] Anderson (1994) 34–112 *passim*; 16–33.

[17] For the problems of Jesus Christ's magic, cf. among much the still controversial M. Smith (1978).

folk mythology".[18] Nor need he have been, perhaps: but that world was interested in him, and it is the world of popular tradition and its reflection of the sage that is here in question. Nor can it be assumed that Philostratus did not know of Apollonius as a creator of *telesmata*: only that the biographer did not use the material, for the obvious reason that it did not suit his anti-magical stance.[19]

The most compendious treatment of *VA* known to me hitherto, that of Flintermann, treads a much less credulous path than Grosso and a less sceptical one than Bowie: he concerns himself not with the defence of every historical detail, but rather with setting the political materials in particular within the framework of Philostratus' broad cultural assumptions, and showing sensitivity to the emergence of differing viewpoints between passages in the *VA* and the epistolary tradition where comparison is possible.[20] But the considerable scale of such a study of a relatively restricted aspect of the *VA* serves to emphasise the by no means decreasing difficulties of seeing it as a whole.

III. *Present and Future Prospects*

It is difficult to arrive at facile pronouncements on *VA* as an ensemble when so many other questions surrounding the work are themselves unsolved or have interdependent solutions. There seems little doubt that Philostratus is not always as scrupulous as he might be, and allows the licences of panegyric in biography, before any question of fiction is raised at all. Before arriving at any judgement in the future we should be aware of the strong degree of cultural convergence that has contributed to the production of such an ensemble. There is room for demonstrable resemblance to almost all known branches of Graeco-Roman fictional activity at some point or other; but then we have to bear in mind the exceptional length of the work, nearly twice as long as Achilles Tatius, himself no short novelist, for a start; while the sophistic pretensions and flourishes of Philostratus carry an air of obfuscation which superimpose on the professional obfuscations of the subject himself, let alone of any intermediate witnesses.

---

[18] Dielska (1986) 93f.
[19] Pace Dielska (1986) 100.
[20] Flintermann (1993) 311f.; 313f.

14. NOVEL-LIKE WORKS OF EXTENDED PROSE FICTION II

Niklas Holzberg

A. UTOPIAS AND FANTASTIC TRAVEL: EUHEMERUS, IAMBULUS

It was Erwin Rohde who first entertained the notion that the corpus of narrative prose fiction written in antiquity originally included at least two utopian novels, and the authors of all subsequent monographs on the ancient novel have subscribed to this idea.[1] Rohde's suggestion is based on two passages from Diodorus Siculus' world history (*Bibliotheca historica*) which describe the fabulous conditions on some islands in the southern Ocean (2.55–60 and 5.41–46) and which in each case represent Diodorus' summary of the contents of an older prose narrative or, as Rohde implies, of a novel which told the story of a fantastic journey.[2]

The text derived from the earlier of these two narratives, namely from the *Sacred Inscription* ('Ιερὰ Ἀναγραφή) of Euhemerus of Messene,[3] is in book 5 of the *Bibliotheca*, where Diodorus deals in the main with the islands in the Mediterranean and in the Ocean (5.41–46); in book 6, which has survived in fragments only, the foregoing account of Euhemerus' narrative is supplemented with further details of the contents of the lost work (6.1). We are told that Euhemerus, who claims to have made several journeys abroad in the service of King Cassander of Macedon (305–297 B.C.), talks of sailing on one of his trips to a group of islands opposite the farthest Ocean shores of *Arabia Felix*.

---

[1] Rohde (1914) 220–60; Helm (1956) 25–8; Hägg (1983) 117–8; Holzberg (1986) 20–1, (1995) 12–13.

[2] The lost text by Hecataeus of Abdera (ca. 350–290 B.C.) describing a utopian island to the north, *On the Hyperboreans*, is not defined as a "travel novel" by Rohde (1914) 226–30, but Jacoby (1912) 2755–8 classified it as such and several scholars later followed suit. However, Jacoby's suggestion that the description of the island was bedded in a narrative framework is pure speculation, resting as it does merely on F 10 and F 11. Equally unfounded is Rohde's designation of the report of one Amometus on the "Attacori" and the report of one Timocles on the "Snake-killers" as "phantastisch erbauliche Romane" [(1914) 233–4].

[3] On the question of date most recently and at length Winiarczyk (1991) 1–4, who cites older literature. Discussions of this problem have hitherto failed to take into consideration that "Euhemerus" could be a fictitious name for the person of the narrator and is not necessarily the author's real name. The premise for our discussion of the text being that it is quite definitely a work of fiction, we have chosen to leave aside problems of geography and the attempts made by some scholars to localize the island [e.g. by Hüsing (1929)].

The largest of these islands, Panchaea, is singled out as highly remarkable in two respects. Firstly, it boasts a magnificent temple dedicated to Zeus, this being situated in idyllic surroundings on unusually fertile land, and containing within a column on which are inscribed the origins of the Greek gods and their cults. Zeus and the other Olympians were once, according to this, mere mortals, kings who had been deified on account of their great services to mankind and civilization. Secondly, the social structure of the island, the inhabitants of which are divided into three castes—priests (together with the artisans), farmers, and soldiers (who are grouped together with the herdsmen)—, displays primitive communistic features.

The passage drawn from the other lost description of an island, a text which probably dates from the 2nd or 1st century B.C.,[4] was incorporated by Diodorus into book 2 (55–60), where it follows accounts of the Assyrians, Medes, Indians, Scythians, Amazons and Hyperboreans, and forms the last section of the book. Diodorus cites as his source a merchant by the name of Iambulus,[5] who had visited the island and written about it. On a journey to Arabia, Iambulus had been captured first by brigands and then by Ethiopians, and the latter had cast out Iambulus and a companion in a small boat, sending them south towards a "blessed island" in the belief that the trip would effect the purification of their own land. The climate and fertile soil, writes Diodorus, make Iambulus' island too an earthly paradise, and the islanders' social structure is, like that of the Panchaeans, characterized by principles of primitive communism such as community of property and wives, and division of labour. Other peculiarities described by Iambulus have to do mainly with the physical attributes of men and animals; all islanders, for example, have a split in their tongue which enables them to carry on two different conversations at once, and the blood of a tortoise-like creature can be used to glue severed human limbs back on to the body.[6]

---

[4] On this dating see Winston (1956); Ehlers' arguments [(1985) 83–4] are by comparison a throwback to former theories.

[5] Winston (1956) 59–60 quite rightly considers it more probable that Iambulus is the name given to the narrator rather than the author's own name. The conclusions about the biography of the author "Iambulus" reached by Altheim (1964) 83ff. on the basis of the name's probable Semitic origin are therefore of limited value.

[6] This animal and many other of the *mirabilia* on Iambulus' island are definitely not drawn from the "Bodensatz an ἄπιστα, mit dem man in antiker Historiographie oder Ethnographie selbst bei bedeutendsten Autoren rechnen muß" [Ehlers (1985) 76]. It therefore seems appropriate here, as in the case of Euhemerus (see above

Now, if the lost narratives of Euhemerus and Iambulus really were "utopian novels", as has been the general and quite automatic assumption since the publication of Rohde's book, then they would have to be considered in the company of More's *Utopia* and Bellamy's *Looking Backwards*. Or were they merely forerunners of the utopian novel? There is at least one good reason for caution here. To date only two discussions concentrating specifically on the literary context of utopias within the genre "ancient novel" have been published— one article by B. Kytzler (1988) and one by H. Kuch (1989)—, and neither of these have applied the findings and methodology of modern literary criticism to reconsider the question and decide whether or not the standard designation of both narratives as "utopian novels" is absolutely correct. Examinations of the two accounts given by Diodorus have otherwise been penned almost exclusively by scholars from the field of ancient history. They too have—forgivably—tended to leave aside the question of literary form, concentrating instead on the political intentions of the two original authors.[7] On this point, the general conclusion was until recently almost unanimous—that the two narratives rendered by Diodorus could be compared to modern utopias. The structure of the societies described by Euhemerus and Iambulus had been based in each case on conceptions of an ideal political constitution which both authors had wished to be interpreted as a viable alternative to the monarchies of their own age[8] or—and this applies solely to Euhemerus—as ideological justification of such forms of government.[9]

More recently, however, the view has been expressed that the accounts given by Euhemerus and Iambulus of the social systems on

---

n. 3), not to enter into the discussion of the island's actual position on the map [for this see again Ehlers (1985), also in particular Schwarz (1982) and the summary in Winston (1956) 69–78].

[7] von Pöhlmann (1925) vol. ii, 293–324; Jacoby (1907); Bidez (1932); T.S. Brown (1946); Polet (1947); T.S. Brown (1949) 54–77; Visser (1948); van der Meer (1949); W.E. Brown (1955); Vallauri (1956); Braunert (1963); Simon (1963); Dörrie (1964); Braunert (1965); Finley (1967); Braunert (1968) (1969); Mossé (1969); Fraser (1972) vol. i, 289–301; vol. iia, 447–61; Baldassarri (1973); Kytzler (1973); Aalders (1975) 64–73; Ferguson (1975) 102–10, 122–9; R. Müller (1975); Bertelli (1976); L. Giangrande (1976) (1976/77); Zumschlinge (1976); R. Müller (1977); Koch (1979); Manuel (1980) 81–92; Bichler (1983) (1984); Günther (1988) 79–88; Di Capua (1989); R.J. Müller (1993).

[8] Cf. esp. Simon (1963); Finley (1967); Mossé (1969); Aalders (1975) 64–75; R. Müller (1975); Koch (1979).

[9] Cf. esp. Dörrie (1964); Braunert (1968).

their respective islands were by no means as carefully thought out and as firmly founded on a philosophical base as might be expected of a political programme.[10] They are, say these critics, far more reminiscent of the unfulfillable dreams of a better world as presented in ancient visions of a Golden Age and of barbarian societies untouched by civilization.[11] From this point of view—and these recent conclusions certainly have the better arguments—the narratives of Euhemerus and Iambulus would have to be assigned to the same type of escapist literature as the early Greek idealistic novels of love and adventure now mostly are.[12] It therefore seems advisable to use the term "utopia" only in a very broad sense when applying it to these island impressions.

Any attempt to analyse the narratives of Euhemerus and Iambulus is faced with another problem, one which arises out of the findings of the latest studies on Diodorus' *Bibliotheca*. Whilst this historian was formerly dismissed as an artless compiler with no original ideas of his own and his renderings of the two island accounts were without further ado declared to be fragments of the narratives,[13] today's assessments of his work have to be considerably more circumspect. Several modern analyses have shown that Diodorus was in fact trying to present a view of history pieced together from his own reflections on the facts.[14] And we must consequently assume that the material offered in Diodorus' sources had to be moulded in some way to fit in with his intentions. In the preface to his world history he clearly states his belief in Stoic universalism, this being an ideal vision of fellowship amongst men within the individual states and within the commonwealth of states; Diodorus stresses at the same time that it is the function of historiography to point to the best possible course of action by presenting exemplary deeds performed in the past. In the case of Euhemerus and Iambulus then, who both describe an ideal form of human coexistence, we must take it virtually for granted that Diodorus adapted the narratives to suit the ten-

---

[10] Cf. esp. Zumschlinge (1976) 178–9 and 222–3; Bichler (1983) (1984); Ehlers (1985); R.J. Müller (1993) 299–300. Doubts as to the presence of any political intentions in the work of "Iambulus" had already been voiced occasionally in earlier studies: cf. Visser (1948) and Winston (1956) 89.

[11] Manuel (1980) 88; Bichler (1983) (1984).

[12] Hägg (1994); Holzberg (1995) 29–32.

[13] Cf. esp. Jacoby's collection of "Fragmente" of Euhemerus (= FGrHist63). Winiarczyk (1991), on the other hand, calls his textual gleanings "Testimonia".

[14] Cf. esp. Burde (1974) 43–59; Sacks (1990) 55–82 and Wirth (1992) 1–23.

dency of his own work. The fact that his two renderings bear considerable thematic resemblance not only to each other, but also to other reports he gives of social systems described by different authors, serves to confirm this.[15]

However, as far as the earlier of the two lost narratives is concerned, Diodorus' *Bibliotheca* is not our only source of information. Quite a number of surviving Greek and Roman texts written by authors who knew Euhemerus' *Sacred Inscription* make mention of his work. They do prove that it was still read in late antiquity, but further evaluation of these "fragments" calls likewise for a certain wariness. The majority of the references, and the most extensive of them, were made by Lactantius (ca. 300 A.D.), and he probably read Euhemerus' narrative not in the original, but in the also now lost Latin adaptation written by Ennius (239–169 B.C.). The Church Father Lactantius would obviously be very interested in Euhemerus', or rather Ennius', theory about the origins of the Greek gods, but are his paraphrases of relevant passages reason enough to conclude that it was theological and philosophical convictions that motivated the author of the Greek original to rationalize religious myths? This seems doubtful when one reads, for example, in Athenaeus (early 3rd century A.D.) that Euhemerus had styled Cadmus, Dionysus' grandfather, a cook in a royal household, and his wife Harmonia a flute-girl.[16] Even if in later times the term "euhemerism"[17] was coined because the author of the *Sacred Inscription* was supposed to have been the first exponent of this type of religious criticism, one other possible interpretation of his work ought not to be completely dismissed: it may have been intended as more or less disguised satire on, for example, the deification and cult worship of contemporary rulers, a practice which had become widespread in Greece since Alexander the Great.[18]

Nevertheless, since the references to and quotations from the *Sacred Inscription* by authors other than Diodorus almost all have to do with Euhemerus' reinterpretation of mythology, we may at least safely assume that this was also the central theme of the lost work and that the description of Panchaea and the other islands simply provided the necessary framework.[19] Now, is it likely that this same framework

---

[15] Cf. Sartori (1984); R.J. Müller (1993) 282.
[16] Athen.Dipn.14.658e–f = Winiarczyk (1991) test.77.
[17] Cf. esp. Vallauri (1960) and Thraede (1966).
[18] Early suggestions of such an interpretation appear in Hirzel (1895) vol. i, 392–8 and Schwartz (1943) 102–7.
[19] Cf. esp. Zumschlinge (1976) 238–40; R.J. Müller (1993).

was itself set within the broader frame of a long narrative telling the story of Euhemerus' sea-journey to Panchaea and his return to Macedon? This seems to have been the general assumption since Rohde, as the *Sacred Inscription* has frequently been labelled "travel novel".[20] The classification rests on a single sentence in Diodorus, according to whom Euhemerus mentioned at some point that his journeys were undertaken at the behest of King Cassander (6.1.14), but is this really conclusive evidence? Is it not equally conceivable that the original text also contained little more than this one sentence? That words to this effect preceded the report about the southerly group of islands as a brief introduction with information about the reporter himself, and that they were simply meant to give the text some degree of authenticity—in a word, a *Beglaubigungsapparat*?[21] The *Sacred Inscription* may, as has been shown above, quite legitimately be seen as a forerunner of the utopian novel, but to link it in addition to the travel novel would be stretching the available facts.

Iambulus, on the other hand, is known to have written not only about his outward journey to the island, but also about his return to Greece, a trip which took him through India and Persia and during which he met with a number of adventures. For those who see Iambulus' depiction of the island as a political utopia, the account of his experiences before and after his long stay there can have been nothing more than a narrative framework fitted around a purely descriptive text.[22] Was this central part of the original work therefore merely a list of *mirabilia* observed by Iambulus on the island, like the corresponding list in Diodorus? Rohde did note that the text offered by Diodorus seems "oddly confused",[23] and indeed, it is not a systematic enumeration with headings such as "life style of the islanders", "social structure" and "flora and fauna", but seems to jump back

---

[20] Rohde (1914) 237; most recently Kuch (1989c) 54 again.

[21] If this is so, it would be another indication that Euhemerus modelled his narrative very closely on Plato's account of Atlantis, which also begins with a *Beglaubigungsapparat* (Critias 113a–b), but cannot be called a novel because of it. For further similarities between the *Sacred Inscription* and Plato's famous utopia cf. Bichler (1984) 191–5.

[22] Cf. Rohde (1914) 244 ("In der Schilderung der Zustände auf jener glückseligen Insel bestand nun der eigentliche Inhalt der Erzählung des Jambulus") and most recently Kytzler (1988) 12 ("In diesem Rahmen werden nun die Besonderheiten jener glücklichen Insel geschildert"—here we can see how lasting the influence of Rohde's words has been!).

[23] Rohde (1914) 243 n. 1; cf. Winston (1956) 30: "Diodorus' excerpt is obviously disordered".

and forward at random from one subject to another. The blame for this "disorder" was to be laid yet again at the door of the foolish compiler Diodorus, thus allowing Rohde to clear up the muddle by ordering his own description of the contents according to the system which Diodorus had regrettably neglected to use.[24]

Of course, one may well ask what reason Diodorus could possibly have had for altering the structure of Iambulus' text, if this too was just a plain description of the island and its inhabitants. One other theory does seem more plausible: the first-person narrator in the original described the island phenomena in the order in which he himself was, in different ways, confronted with them. If this is correct, then the "disorder" in Diodorus' version could have a simple explanation—the historian (systematically!) omitted all passages in which Iambulus explained how he came to observe what he then described.[25] This would have created gaps which can no longer be filled in now, although we do know what might have been said in one of them. Diodorus tells us that, seven years after their arrival on the island, Iambulus and his companion were forced against their will to leave it because they were "evil-doers, brought up to have base habits" (2.60.1). In the eyes of the islanders, then, the two must have been guilty of some crime, but of which? It is reasonable to assume that the original offered more details of their disgrace, and in this light the following suggestion, based on the account given by Diodorus, as to the narrative structure of the lost work, could be ventured: 1. Iambulus first meets the islanders and becomes acquainted with their customs (56.1–58.6),[26] 2. he visits the other islands, becomes more and more familiar with the native way of life and is finally initiated in their cult (58.8–59.9). And then, at one of the religious festivals mentioned by Diodorus (59.7), Iambulus and his companion perhaps perpetrated their evil deed, one which the islanders considered a sacrilege and for which the two men were banished from the island.[27]

---

[24] Rohde (1914) 243–9. Altheim (1964) 88–9 is able to detect a principle of order in Diodorus' account, but this train of thought is rather difficult to follow.

[25] Similarly Ehlers (1985) 75–6.

[26] In 58.7 an observation on the island's social structure is followed by an observation on the sea surrounding the island and the stars visible from it, this in turn being followed by the first reference to the other six islands; it is reasonable to assume that there was a change of scenery here in the original story.

[27] Weinreich (1962) 11 thinks it possible that Iambulus related an erotic adventure then omitted by Diodorus—also a quite plausible theory.

There is, therefore, every reason to believe that with the tale told by Iambulus we have lost not only a forerunner of the modern utopian novel, but also a travel novel bristling with adventure. And the remark made by Lucian in his *True Stories* to the effect that Iambulus' travel novel was "not without charm"[28] gives us some indication of the magnitude of this loss.

---

[28] Ver.Hist.1.3 (... οὐκ ἂν ἀτερπῆ δὲ ὅμως συνθεὶς τὴν ὑπόθεσιν).

B. HISTORY: CTESIAS

Ctesias of Cnidus, the author of a novel-like historical text which will be discussed briefly in the following, was born in the sixth decade of the 5th century B.C.[1] and served 404–398/7 as physician to Artaxerxes II, the Persians having captured him probably as early as 415/4; between 393/2 and 385, after his return to Greece, he wrote a history of Persia (*Persica*) in twenty-three books and an ethnographical work on India (*Indica*) in one book.[2] The contents of his *Persica*, the actual text of which is, like that of his *Indica*, now lost, are relatively well documented. For books 7–23 we have a summary by the Byzantine patriarch Photius (9th century),[3] and we can moreover safely assume that the Hellenistic historian Diodorus Siculus (1st century B.C.) used books 1–6 of the *Persica* as the main source for a section on the Assyrians and Medes in book 2 of his *Bibliotheca historica* (1.4–34.7).[4] Only a very few fragments of the original Greek of the *Persica* have survived,[5] but one of these, a papyrus fragment (P.Oxy.2330),[6] contains a passage from the account of a love affair, and in its motifs and style this sample of Ctesias' work bears a strong resemblance to the kind of writing found in the Greek idealistic novel.

What is perhaps most striking about books 7–23 of the *Persica* as reproduced by Photius is that Ctesias' account of those periods in Persian history which are also covered by Herodotus sometimes differs considerably from the version given by the earlier historian; the most notable example is Ctesias' dating of the battle of Plataea back to a time before the battle of Salamis, which is quite definitely incorrect. However, Ctesias is at pains to stress that not he himself, but Herodotus is the liar; he insists that he was able to draw from the best of sources, having been permitted to use the Persian court archives and having once even been given his information by a member of

---

[1] For his vita see esp. Jacoby (1922) 2032–6; T.S. Brown (1978); Eck (1990).
[2] Cf. most recently Bigwood (1989) (1993).
[3] Bibl.72 p. 35b35–45a19 = FGrHist688 F 9ff. On Photius' rendering of Ctesias see esp. Goossens (1950) and Bigwood (1976) 2–6.
[4] On Diodorus' rendering of Ctesias see esp. Bigwood (1980) and Boncquet (1987) 13–6.
[5] See list in Del Corno (1962) 131–2.
[6] FGrHist688 F 8b. Editio princeps: Lobel (1954) 81–4.

the royal family, Artaxerxes' mother Parysatis.[7] Those familiar with the ancient novel as a literary genre will automatically be reminded here of Dictys and Dares, the "eyewitnesses" to the Trojan War who invariably know better than Homer. In point of fact, ancient history scholars believed for a long time that countless events recorded only by Ctesias were simply invented by him and that he treated other, historical happenings with what F. Jacoby called "the sovereign license of a novelist".[8]

The view generally held today[9] is that Ctesias did actually use Persian sources, and one simple reason for this could be that his account of the events which took place during Greece's conflict with her great Eastern opponent was designed to confront the Greek version of the facts with the Persian standpoint. Nonetheless, even scholars who are particularly friendly in their judgement of Ctesias as a historian readily concede that his obvious predilection for the sensational, for love affairs, palace intrigues and acts of sheer despotism meant that he was always in danger of recording such incidents without having found reliable proof that they had ever really happened. Ctesias' search for precisely this kind of material in the *chronique scandaleuse* of the Persian court was bound to lead him to written and oral accounts which imagination had embellished to such an extent that the actual historical truth was entirely blurred by fiction. Moreover, we have unmistakable evidence that, during the composition of certain episodes in his *Persica*, Ctesias was all too willingly influenced by other works of literature in which he found stories bearing a thematic resemblance to the events he wished to portray. For example, in a passage from which we still have some of the original wording as quoted in Ps.-Demetrius, Ctesias describes how a messenger brings Queen Parysatis news of the outcome of the battle of Cunaxa, and he clearly leans heavily here on similar scenes in Greek tragedy.[10]

Another example is the episode which has partially survived in the

---

[7] Phot.Bibl.72 p. 35b41–3 = FGrHist688 T 8; Diod.2.32,4 = FGrHist688 F 5; Phot.Bibl.72 p. 42b11–13 = FGrHist688 F 15,51.

[8] Cf. esp. Jacoby (1922) 2046–64 (*loc. cit.* col. 2055).

[9] Cf. esp. Bigwood (1965) (1976) (1978) (1983) and T.S. Brown (1973) 77–86, esp. n. 63 on p. 103.

[10] [Demetr.] De eloc.216 = FGrHist688 F 24; cf. Bigwood (1983) 346 and on Ctesias' use of tragedy in general Marasco (1988). On his literary sources see also Sancisi-Weerdenburg (1987a).

papyrus fragment mentioned above.[11] Sources documenting the contents of the *Persica* and of an adaptation of the work[12] fortunately provide us with the narrative context of the fragment: Zarinaea, wife of the king of the Sacae, is knocked from her horse during battle by the Mede Stryangaeus; she begs for her life and he spares her. Later Stryangaeus is captured by the Sacae, but Zarinaea is unable to persuade her husband to pardon the Mede; she kills her husband and sets Stryangaeus free. He falls in love with her, is rejected and decides to kill himself. Before committing suicide, however, he writes a letter, and it is from the beginning of this that the papyrus fragment gives us a relatively lengthy passage. Stryangaeus says, amongst other things, that his predicament and his love were not of his own choosing, but brought about by "the god":

ὅτωι μὲν οὖν εἴλεως ἔλθηι, πλείστας γε ἡδονὰς δίδωσιν, καὶ ἄλλα πλεῖστα ἀγαθὰ ἐποίησεν αὐτόν, ὅτωι δὲ ὀργιζόμενος ἔλθηι οἱονπερ ἐμοὶ νῦν, πλεῖστα κακὰ ἐργασάμενος τὸ τελευταῖον πρόρριζον ἀπώλεσεν καὶ ἐξέτρεψεν.

Whom he approaches in friendliness, to this man he brings a great many pleasures and bestows on him many other favours, but whom he approaches in anger as he does me now, to this man he brings a great many ills and in the end ruins and destroys him.

Thus this episode combines no fewer than three familiar motifs most commonly used in Greek idealistic novels: "unrequited love and ensuing decision to commit suicide", "love letter", and "wrath of the god (of love)". However, it is not only such thematic similarities that form the close parallels between the papyrus text and many other parts of the *Persica* on the one hand, and Greek idealistic novels on the other; the borrowing of motifs would not alone constitute sufficient grounds for discussing this historical work in a handbook on the ancient novel, since motifs used in novels also appear in texts belonging to various other literary genres. The comparison does nonetheless seem justified in this case when one other significant feature is taken into consideration, a feature which is recognizable even

---

[11] Cf. Del Corno (1962); Gigante (1962); Biltcliffe (1969); G. Giangrande (1976), who rejects the attribution of the text fragment to Ctesias, his arguments not being very convincing; Bigwood (1986); Boncquet (1987) 209–11; Toher (1989).

[12] Cf. FGrHist688 F 7 (= Anonym.De mul.2) and 8a (= [Demetr.] De eloc.213) and FGrHist90 (Nicolaus of Damascus) F 5.

in the short quotation above and which, moreover, one of Ctesias' readers in antiquity remarked upon as being typical of the *Persica*:[13] it is the almost primitive simplicity and clarity of style, with short sentences for the most part totally lacking in rhetorical embellishment and strung together so as to give the reader a quick grasp of what is being said.

For scholars studying the history of the ancient novel, Ctesias' use of a less sophisticated style to write about love and adventure is interesting for the following reason. This is for once a historian who makes no attempt to emulate the high stylistic level reached by Greek prose writers—including historians—long before his time. An historian who dispenses with well-turned periods and rhetorical "sound-effects", who is not afraid of literal repetition and narrates exciting stories in much the same way as an oral story-teller perhaps would have done. For an author such as this there must have been an audience, readers who preferred his packaging and presenting of historical knowledge to the usual methods, because they were not as erudite as for example readers of Thucydides. And this less educated circle of readers probably corresponds almost exactly to the circle for which in Hellenistic times the first authors of Greek idealistic novels wrote their stories of love and adventure. Ctesias of Cnidus can be said to have "whetted the appetites" first of readers for simple narrative prose and then of those novelists who were later to write for these same readers. It is, therefore, scarcely a coincidence that the earliest Greek idealistic novel known to us tells the story of Ninus and Semiramis, this pair of lovers having made their first appearance in Greek literature in book 2 of Ctesias' *Persica*.[14]

---

[13] [Demetr.] De eloc.209ff. = FGrHist688 T 14. Cf. also Phot.Bibl.72 p. 45a5ff. = FGrHist688 T 13.

[14] On the influence of the *Persica* on the *Ninus Romance* cf. Kussl (1991) 84–95.

C. FABLE: AESOP. LIFE OF AESOP

In his exhaustive analysis of ancient fable collections M. Nøjgaard was able to show that even the shortest form of narrative fiction used by Greek and Roman authors was generally composed in accordance with quite specific, recurrent structural patterns.[1] The "Collectio Augustana", for example, a prose *Aesopus Graecus* dating from the 1st or 2nd century A.D.,[2] comprises for the most part fables which can each be divided into three parts of roughly equal length: an exposition is followed by the story proper, and at the end the protagonist, or one of the several characters involved, comments upon what has happened, thus spelling out the moral of the tale. In 19 of the 231 fables in the "Collectio Augustana" someone reflects at the end on his/her own misfortune;[3] in fable no. 116, for instance, the crab who had come out of the sea to live alone on the shore and is about to be devoured by the fox, says: "It really serves me right for wanting to live on the land although I am a sea-dweller." The following discussion of the *Life of Aesop*, a fictional biographical novel written in the 2nd/3rd century A.D. by an unknown author,[4] will show that the structure of the text is strikingly similar to that of the above-mentioned type of fable.

First, however, a brief glance at the somewhat tangled textual history of the *Life*.[5] Like the *Alexander Romance*, Aesop's fictional vita is one of the Greek narrative works written in the imperial age which were destined to be subjected to a series of changes starting not long after their first appearance. The language of the *Aesop Romance* was revised at various times by various hands, from recension to recension

---

[1] Nøjgaard (1964–1967), vol. i, 142ff.
[2] On the question of date see Holzberg (1993a) 83 (further literature cited p. 104f.). The fables in the "Collectio Augustana" correspond to fables 1–231 in Perry (1952).
[3] Nos. 25, 74, 75, 76, 77, 80, 86, 115, 116, 120, 128, 131, 147, 148, 176, 181, 187, 203, 209; cf. also 139 and 144.
[4] For comprehensive studies, these however in the main concentrating on the question of sources, see Zeitz (1936); Hausrath (1940) 114–40; La Penna (1962); Holbek (1977); Adrados (1979) (1979–1987) vol. i, 661–97; Winkler (1985) 276–91; Jedrkiewicz (1989) 39–215; Patterson (1991) 13–43; detailed bibliography by Beschorner (1992b).
[5] Cf. Marc (1910); Perry (1933) (1936) (1952) 1–32 (1966); Hower (1936).

new adventures were added or the existing ones were epitomized. When European scholars began to rediscover Greek literature in the 15th and 16th centuries, the first *Life of Aesop* they encountered was merely an epitome which was probably not written before the Byzantine era and which is now labelled "Vita Westermanniana" ("Vita W"), after its first modern editor.[6] A Latin version of this abridged text, translated by the Italian humanist Rinuccio da Castiglione, was published in 1476/7, together with a German translation of the Latin text, in Heinrich Steinhöwel's "Esopus", and this book became one of the great best-sellers of early printing history. Over the next 100 years it was reprinted more than 200 times, and the languages into which the Latin and German texts were translated in various of these later editions include French, English, Spanish, Dutch, Low German, Danish, Czech, and even Japanese.[7]

The original text of the *Vita Aesopi* is irretrievably lost and we cannot be absolutely sure what form it took. However, we do have several fragments in five different papyrus rolls dating from between the 2nd/3rd and 7th centuries,[8] as well as an almost complete version of the novel surviving in one manuscript from the 10th century, and it is quite plain that these are all very closely related to the original text. The manuscript version was a surprise find made in 1928 in New York's Pierpont Morgan Library; it is now known as "Vita G", having formerly been preserved in Grottaferrata, Italy, and it was first edited in 1952 by B.E. Perry.[9] In the light of these discoveries we can now not only safely assume that we have the entire contents of the original novel, but also form a fairly clear picture of its diction and style, the work having namely been written in unsophisticated narrative prose.[10]

A comparison of the *Life* with earlier sources for Aesop's biography[11] leads to an observation which is of significance for the analysis

---

[6] Westermann (1845), now also in Perry (1952) 79ff.
[7] On 15th- and 16th-century reading of the *Life* most recently Hilpert (1992); Holzberg (1993b); Smits (1993); Dicke (1994); further titles included in Beschorner (1992b) and van Dijk (1994) 388.
[8] Edited by Zeitz (1935); Perry (1936); Haslam (1980–1986).
[9] New edition by Papathomopoulos (1991).
[10] On the *Life*'s language in general see Tallmadge (1938); Birch (1955); Hostetter (1955); Papathomopoulos (1989), also index to Perry's (1952) Vita G in Dimitriadou-Toufexi (1981). On chapter 6 in particular see Mignogna (1992).
[11] Enumerated in Perry (1952) 209ff.

of the narrative structure of the novel.[12] From the large stock of anecdotes which had been in circulation in Greece since the 5th century B.C., the anonymous author of the fictional vita chose to use only those relating to the end of the fabulist's life. According to these, Aesop had insulted the inhabitants of Delphi by telling a particular fable and the priests of Apollo had then conspired to kill him. A golden bowl from the temple had been smuggled into his luggage, Aesop had been accused of sacrilege and sentenced to death; although he had tried to save his skin by telling the Delphians fables designed to make them fear divine punishment, they had forced him off a cliff.[13] Now, shortly before the execution the Aesop of the novel makes two remarks which are reminiscent of the last words of a doomed protagonist in the type of fable mentioned above. After his arrest Aesop cries out: "How shall I, being a mortal man, manage to escape what is about to befall me?" (ch. 128, 11). And to a friend, who appears for the first time at the end of the novel and is therefore comparable to a typical fable character—to use Nøjgaard's terminology, the "survenant"[14]—, Aesop says: "I had lost what was left of my senses when I came to Delphi" (ch. 131, 16f.); this self-reproach bears a close resemblance to the words of the crab in fable no. 116 of the "Collectio Augustana", who sees what a mistake it was for a creature of the sea to live on land.

The following consideration makes it seem probable that the anonymous author of the *Life* in fact designed the plot of his novel with the end as his starting point. At the beginning of the vita, the very man who was renowned in antiquity for his exceptional talent as a story-teller, is entirely bereft of the gift of speech. In spite of his handicap he is able to do something here which later in Delphi, where he appears as a seasoned narrator—the Muses having endowed him with the gift of eloquence (ch. 7)—, he is quite incapable of accomplishing: he foils a plot against himself, using silent actions to do so.[15] The contrast between this and the end of the novel, together with the earlier biographical tradition, is evident, since there Aesop is unable to extricate himself from the situation brought upon him

---

[12] In detail Holzberg (1992b).
[13] For the account of Aesop's death see Perry (1952) 220–3; Wiechers (1961); Luzzatto (1988); Schauer (1992); Brodersen (1992); Merkle (1992).
[14] Nøjgaard (1964–1967), vol. i, 159–60.
[15] Chapter 2–3, the fig episode.

by the Delphian priests' schemes, although in his attempts to save himself he makes repeated use of his narrative skills. It is clear that the first chapters of the novel and the last (1–19.124–142) together form a framework for the rest of the story; since the remaining middle chapters relate how the mute Aesop rises by virtue of his eloquence from mere slavery to the position of a highly successful adviser in the service of a powerful king, the novel as a whole can therefore be divided into the three main sections "prelude", "plot" and "conclusion".

The central plot offers at first sight what readers would expect to find in the biography of a λογοποιός: a series of episodes in which the protagonist tells his λόγοι (why we prefer to use this term rather than the word "fable" will be explained presently). Aesop's adventures begin on the island of Samos where he serves as slave to the philosopher Xanthus, playing a number of practical jokes on his master, and is later given his freedom as a reward for helping Xanthus out of three difficult situations and for giving the Samians the correct meaning of a bird sign (chs. 20–91). He then manages to prevent what is forewarned by the omen, namely the conquest of Samos by King Croesus of Lydia, by telling the king a λόγος and thus winning his favour (chs. 92–100). After this Aesop goes off to Babylon and, during a short stay in Egypt, helps the Babylonian king solve a brain-teasing riddle of the type which rulers in that part of the world are wont to pose one another, and thereby secures for him high tribute payments from the Egyptian king (chs. 101–123); this particular part of the story is an adaptation of the *Ahiqar Romance*, a Syrian narrative of which the earliest extant fragments are found in an Aramaic papyrus dating from the 5th century B.C. and which was later translated into several other languages.[16]

Apart from this series of adventures, however, the central section of the novel also confirms and offers the explanation for Aesop's last words, in which he acknowledges that it was foolish of him to come to Delphi and that he himself (like the crab in the fable) is to blame for his plight. Right after his first big success as a λογοποιός, namely in negotiating peace between Croesus and the Samians, Aesop makes

---

[16] On parallels between the *Life* and the *Ahiqar Romance* see esp. E. Meyer (1912); Coneybeare (1913); Hausrath (1918); Perry (1952) 5–10; Degen (1977); Haslam (1980–1986); Lindenberger (1985); Wilsdorf (1991); Oettinger (1992); Kussl (1992) who establishes the relationship between the *Ahiqar Romance* and the *Tinuphis Romance*.

a serious mistake. In the temple which he has built for the Muses as a token of his gratitude for their gift of eloquence, he raises in the midst of their statues not a likeness of Apollo Musagetes, but of himself.[17] This enrages the god of Delphi so greatly that he later supports his priests in their conspiracy against Aesop (ch. 127, 4–6), thus aiding and abetting them in the murder. The narrative structure of the *Life*, then, clearly combines components used in the simple Aesopic fable with elements generally found in epic and in the novel. On the one hand there is a distinct division into three parts, the last of which offers the moral of the story: a slave whom the gods endow with the art of λογοποιία and whom this new talent brings high honours, is seized with hubris and pays with his life; this is a tale which could also be told in the form of a short fable. On the other hand, however, the motif "wrath of a god", which figures prominently both in epic and in the novel,[18] and the frequent changing of scene within the Greek world and the ancient Orient extend and diversify the plots.

The story does consist of a string of events, but not in the sense that single episodes were simply assembled at random, as has often been maintained.[19] For the composition of his novel the anonymous author in fact had a carefully designed plan which was based on the two following structural principles: 1. varying deployment of the three types of Aesopic λόγοι used in the novel, 2. three-stage development of story lines. To consider the first of these, it must be noted that the author has Aesop use three different types of λόγοι, rather than putting only simple "fables" into his mouth:

A. direct instruction (monologue, dialogue);
B. solution of a problem (difficult task, question, riddle);
C. fable applicable to a particular situation.

These three variants are distributed over the central section and the conclusion in the following manner. In the episodes where Aesop is a slave in Xanthus' household (chs. 20–91) and in Babylon and Egypt (chs. 101–123), only type A (direct instruction) and type B (solution of a problem) are used, the type A λόγος appearing in the Xanthus

---

[17] Here we follow Papathomopoulos' (1991) conjecture for ch. 100, 12–14.
[18] Cf. Holzberg (1990) 99.
[19] See esp. Zeitz (1936) 225 and 256; Birch (1955) 86; La Penna (1962) 313; Holbek (1977) 886.

episodes alone in a modified form where Aesop, like the German scapegrace Till Eulenspiegel, takes an order given by his master too literally and thereby teaches him a lesson. In those chapters which relate how Aesop helps the Samians to keep Croesus at bay (chs. 92–100) and in the Delphian chapters (chs. 124–142), only fables applicable to a given situation are used, the effect in the Samian section being always positive, in the Delphian always negative. We therefore find the following system of variation: A/B – C(+) – A/B – C(–).

The second structural principle, in accordance with which story lines are developed in three stages, can best be illustrated here, for the sake of brevity,[20] with a simple example. In the second half of the Xanthus chapters Aesop thrice helps his master find the solution to a problem: in chapters 68–74 Xanthus is asked by a pupil whether a man could drink an ocean to the last drop, wagers that he, Xanthus, could, and wins the bet only after Aesop advises him to request that all river mouths be blocked before he starts drinking; in chapters 78–80 Xanthus is unable to decipher the inscription on a grave, but, once given the meaning of the letters by Aesop, finds a hidden treasure; in chapters 81–91 Xanthus is asked by the Samians to explain the ominous significance of an eagle's behaviour and decides to commit suicide because he is unable to do so, but Aesop comes to the rescue with the correct explanation. If we connect the respective ends of these episodes, they form the gradual approach to a climax: in chapter 74 Aesop asks to be set free as a reward for helping his master, but his request is turned down; in chapter 80 he is put in fetters although Xanthus had promised him his freedom this time; in chapter 90 he finally becomes a freedman.

The careful structuring of a series of episodes is a compositional feature which links the fictional *Life of Aesop* to picaresque novels, the earliest of which, the *Vida de Lazarillo de Tormes* (1554), was, like the *Life*, written by an anonymous author.[21] And just as in this description of his Spanish hero's adventures the author uses coarse humour as a vehicle to illustrate the discrepancies between appearances and reality, so too the anonymous Greek author: narrative motifs such as "mute exposes people who can talk" or "slave smarter than his

---

[20] In more detail Holzberg (1992b) 53ff.
[21] He quite possibly knew the *Life*; cf. Holzberg (1993b).

master" are used in the *Life* to create a topsy-turvy world which opens the eyes of readers ancient and modern to what goes on behind the scenes in the real world. Criticism of moral defects by means of satire was in fact most probably one of the primary objectives of the *Life*,[22] and this, again, is something it has in common not only with many ancient fables,[23] but also with two outstanding novels of classical antiquity, Petronius' *Satyrica* and Apuleius' *Metamorphoses*.

---

[22] One first attempt at a sociohistorical approach is made by Hopkins (1993).
[23] Cf. Holzberg (1993a) 13ff.

D. RHETORIC: DIO CHRYSOSTOM

The insertion of a fable which is specifically relevant to the given situation and from which can be drawn some kind of moral applicable to the hero's behaviour or that of his audience—like the fables told by Aesop at several points in the *Life*[1]—is a literary device employed in a similar fashion by numerous ancient authors from the earliest days of Greek literature to Greek and Roman writing of imperial times. Poets, philosophers, rhetoricians and historians exemplify all manner of observations by telling fables either directly themselves or through the voice of one of the characters featuring in their work.[2] One of the authors who had a particular preference for this literary device was the orator Dio, named "Chrysostom", from Prusa in Bithynia (AD 40–120). In his speeches—these being for the most part Stoic-Cynic "sermons", some of which were held during his period of exile after Domitian had banished him from Italy and Bithynia—Dio uses a number of *Aesopica* or refers to such.[3] In one case his narrative exemplification is even of sufficient length and substance to allow it to stand as a *novella* in its own right; the tale found in the 7th Oration (§§2–80),[4] is generally given the title "The Hunters of Euboea" and has been aptly characterized by B.E. Perry in the following words: It "reads so much like a high class modern novel, in respect to its dramatic manner of presentation, its attention to character, and the social and ethical implications of its incidents, that one might as easily suppose it to have been written in the twentieth century as in the first".[5]

As so frequently in Dio's writings, the lesson to be learnt from the narrative is one which stems from popular philosophy. The 7th Oration is devoted to the notion that the simple life of a poor man is in every respect preferable to the life of a rich man. The beginning of the orator's discussion of this theme is, together with the

---

[1] *Life of Aesop* chs. 94, 97, 99, 125, 129, 131, 133, 135–139, 140, 141.
[2] Cf. most recently Holzberg (1993a) 13ff.
[3] Cf. or.6,41; 8,36; 12,7f.; 32,66; 33,16; 34,5; 47,20; 72,14f.
[4] Cf. the commentaries of Wilamowitz (1966) 9–14; Avezzù (1985); Russell (1992). The whole oration is commonly known as *Euboicus*.
[5] Perry (1967) 70.

beginning of the speech, unfortunately no longer extant,[6] but the words which lead up to the narrative exemplification have survived (§1). What he is about to relate, writes Dio, is something which he himself had experienced "almost in the middle of Greece", and, apologizing for the length of the narrative to come, he remarks that it is perhaps the way of the elderly to be so loquacious, or of widely travelled men. Dio was possibly both of these,[7] but the obvious similarity between these lines and passages in ancient narrative prose where the "credentials" of the first-person narrator are presented in preliminaries designed to create a ring of authenticity,[8] indicates that Dio deliberately composed this particular narrative exemplification along the lines of such texts and therefore intended to present here something more sophisticated than a fable.[9] What then emerged was indeed a narrative *tour de force*, and "The Hunters of Euboea" can compare to the great Greek and Roman novels of the imperial age. However, it does still have two things in common with many *Aesopica*: in contrast to the rest of the oration in which it stands, the language of the narrative is relatively unsophisticated,[10] and in itself the text can be divided into three main sections (§§2–20.21–63.64–80), each of which, in turn, comprises several three-stage story lines.

At the beginning of the narrative three compositional stages are used to unfold a dramatic scene. The narrator, who, as he tells us briefly at the outset, had put to sea from Chios in a small boat together with some fishermen and whom a storm had cast ashore by the cliffs of Euboea, is wandering lost and alone along the coastline. Suddenly he catches sight of a stag which had plummeted down from a cliff-top and now lies with the incoming waves breaking against it; he then hears barking and finally sees some dogs with their master, a man whose outward appearance and clothing identify him as a hunter (§§2–4). This sequence of sensory responses, which the reader experiences together with the narrator and which at the same time creates a build-up of suspense for the audience, bears a clear resemblance to the sequence of single "shots" at the beginning

---

[6] As von Arnim (1891) 393–406 showed; cf. also Russell (1992) 9–10.
[7] See, however, Russell (1992) 109–10 *ad loc.*, who sees this simply as a play on the literary topos *forsan et haec olim meminisse iuvabit*.
[8] Cf. esp. Petron.110,8; Lucian.ver.hist.1,4; Ach.Tat.1.2,1f. and Maeder (1991).
[9] Cf. however, epist.Anachars.9, where the letter writer opens a fable with the words ἄκουσον δὲ ἐμῆς ὄψεως ἱστορίαν.
[10] On the style of the narrative see Reuter (1932) 61–3.

of Heliodorus' *Aethiopica*, where skilful narrative technique also has the reader gradually focus on a figure now to play a central role in the ensuing plot.[11]

The narrator takes three steps to reach the subject proper of the tale. The opening scene (§§2–4) is followed by a dialogue between the narrator and the hunter, in the course of which the former is invited to the latter's home (§§5–8), and while they are on their way there (§§8–10), Dio—at first still through the mouth of the hunter— begins to describe what he sees as a perfect example for his theory of the moral superiority of the simple life over an existence ruled by craving and indulgence. It is the life led by the hunter and his brother-in-law with their respective families. Both are the sons of cattle-herdsmen who had once worked for a wealthy landowner, but who had become hunters after the death of their employer and the confiscation of his estate by order of the emperor. The hunters' life is described again in three sections, each forming a narrative unit in itself. The first (§§10–20) contains the above-outlined family history (§§10–12), a description of their idyllic country home where they used to put the cattle out to pasture in the summer (§§12–16) and of their life as hunters (§§16–20); the second section (§§21–63) describes a visit made by the hunter to the city and serves as a contrast to highlight the foregoing character portrayal of a modest man untouched by urban culture; in the third section (§§64–80) we have genre painting, a domestic scene in which, during the course of a simple meal in the hunter's cottage, a lively comedy of revelations leads to the decision on the part of the hunter and his brother-in-law to wed the one's daughter to the other's son two days hence.

This three-part description of the hunter's life and character is structured in such a way that only the information in sections 1 and 2 is given to us in the words of the hunter himself, while the domestic idyll is presented through the eyes of the first-person narrator. With this skilful device Dio manages to link section 1 and 2 more closely, these forming the contrasting pair country *vs.* city life, while section 3 creates together with the triptych of scenes at the beginning of the story (§§2–10) a framework for the whole, these being accounts given by the first-person narrator of his conversations with the hunter alone and with all the family.

---

[11] Cf. Bühler (1976).

Seen within the context of the ancient novel, the report of the hunter's visit to the city and the domestic scene at the end of the story are of particular significance. The hunter's experiences in the city are illustrated for the most part in a long and animated scene which stands almost exactly in the middle of the entire narrative (§§24–63). The hunter is taken to the people's assembly in the city theatre, where he has to defend himself against the charge that he and his family are illegal squatters on land which belongs to the city, that they owe rent for their tenancy and that they are wreckers who set up beacons to make ships run aground on the rocky shores, and then plunder the wreckage (§§27–32).[12] In his reaction to these accusations (§§41–53) the hunter has a two-fold similarity to the protagonists of the three ancient picaresque novels known to us, namely to Encolpius in Petronius' *Satyrica*, to Lucius in Apuleius' *Golden Ass* and to Aesop in the anonymous *Life of Aesop*. The hunter too is able on the one hand to give witty answers to some of the questions put to him, even to make puns, and then has the laughs on his side.[13] On the other hand his rustic *simplicitas* makes him seem at times so slow-witted and blundering that, like Lucius at the Risus Festival (Apul. *Met*.3.1–12), he himself is laughed at several times and owes the final escape from his predicament merely to chance: one of those present at the assembly had—like the narrator—been shipwrecked and taken in by the hunter some time ago and now recognizes the accused as the man who had saved his life (§§53–61).[14]

Both this ἀναγνώρισις motif and the γάμος motif in the final domestic scene have long been established as links between the narrative and the extant Greek idealistic novels;[15] *Daphnis and Chloe* in particular comes to mind at every turn, as Dio, like Longus, combines

---

[12] The speech in which the charges are brought forward is divided into three parts, the first-person narrator inserting two remarks which record his own reactions at the beginning of §29 and §30. The assembly scene as a whole is also divided into three sections: 1 (§§27–41) prosecutor's speech and the second speaker's answer, 2 (§§41–53) the hunter's answers to questions and his speech, 3 (§§53–61) ἀναγνώρισις and reaction of second speaker to this.

[13] Cf. in Plato's *Apologia* the dialogue between Socrates and Meletus (24d–25c), although here it is the defendant who asks the questions. That the Cynic Dio intends his hunter figure in a certain sense as an allusion to Socrates may also be inferred from the proposal made by the second speaker to the effect that the hunter be given a dinner in the prytaneum (§60).

[14] §§62–3, which close the episode, underlining again the contrast hunter/city-dweller, and §§21–6, where the same motif dominates, together form a framework for the assembly scene.

[15] Cf. Reuter (1932) 13–21; Canevari (1962); Jouan (1977); Hunter (1983) 66–7;

elements of the novel with elements of the bucolic idyll. The orator does of course take greater pains than the novelist to present in his description of social conditions on Euboea parallels to the social realities of his own age. The reference to the landowner whose estate is confiscated by the emperor (§12) and some thoughts expressed by a speaker in the assembly (§§33–41) are quite probably intended for the ears of Roman magistrates in the Greek provinces, the speaker touching amongst other things on the problem of creating employment for the proletariat in country towns.[16]

In the main, however, the predominant note in Dio's portrayal of the hunters' life is an unrealistic, even almost fantastical one. It is significant that the setting for their idyllic existence is an island, that the first-person narrator arrives there—as does Odysseus on the idyllic island of the Phaeacians—after being shipwrecked, and that the description of the *locus amoenus* where the hunters formerly put the cattle out to graze (§§13–16) shows certain similarities to descriptions of nature in the Golden Age. Like the report about Iambulus' islanders as paraphrased by Diodorus, what Dio tells us about the hunters and their families corresponds for the most part to idealistic notions of the simple life found in the popular philosophy of Hellenistic and imperial times. R. Vischer, whose study on this same motif in literature includes an analysis of Dio's narrative, has been able to demonstrate that the simple life led by the Euboean hunters fulfils the most important requirement set in ancient ethical codes for such an existence. In the way of outward characteristics of the simple life we find here harmony with nature and provision for only the barest essentials, and the mental outlook of the people here displays φιλανθρωπία, veracity and godliness, all of which together means that they possess inner freedom.[17] This being a utopian notion, Dio's similarity to the authors of idealistic novels therefore lies not only in his skill as a narrator, but also in the fact that "The Hunters of Euboea" can likewise be classed as escapist literature.[18]

Russell (1992) 8–9; Swain (1994) 170. Highet (1973) quite rightly points to similar motifs in New Comedy, but his conclusion that Dio used a now lost Νέα seems unnecessary. Anderson (1976b) 94–8, on the other hand, hits the mark when he compares these motifs with themes from Lucian and calls the *Euboicus* "the bridge between Lucian's rhetorique appliquée and the 'Pastoral Novel'" (p. 98).

[16] On topical references in or.7 cf. Day (1951); Brunt (1973); Jones (1978) 56–61; Salmeri (1982) 82–86; Russell (1992) *passim*.

[17] Vischer (1965) 157–70; cf. also Reuter (1932) 23–60.

[18] See above p. 624 and n. 12.

E. LETTERS: CHION

Handbooks and histories of classical literature have been content to cite I. Düring, who maintained in 1951: "In epistolary literature the letters of Chion hold a unique position as the only extant example of a novel in letters".[1] However, whilst the study of Greek epistolography more or less grinded to a halt in 1697 when R. Bentley published his famous exposure of the *Letters of Phalaris* as a forgery,[2] recent years have at last seen a revival of interest and historicism has given way to literary criticism in approaches to the subject, with the result that Düring's assertion now clearly needs to be modified. It would still be correct to say that the *Letters of Chion*, which can quite certainly be classed as pseudepigraphic, come closest to modern conceptions of the epistolary novel, since the first-person letter writer and the flow of events reflected in his letters are integral parts of a particularly compact whole.[3] Nevertheless, there are in fact another eight collections of letters—seven fully extant and one surviving in fragments only—which can quite plainly be classed as forerunners of the modern epistolary novel. The following is a brief, general account of all nine collections, after which a closer look will be taken, by way of specific example, at the *Letters of Chion*.

1. *The Letters of Plato* (13):[4] In the chronologically ordered[5] letters 1–4 and 7–8 the philosopher uses a retrospective view of his stay at the court of Dionysius II, tyrant of Syracuse, to present his philosophy;

---

[1] Düring (1951) 7; and similarly Lesky (1971) 970–1; Hägg (1983) 126; Holzberg (1995) 19–21; Johne (1989) 230; Rosenmeyer (1994) 152, 163.

[2] Bentley (1874). Brief résumés of earlier research, which followed Bentley and concentrated likewise on the question of authenticity, are found in Christ (1920) 482–5; Sykutris (1931a) 210–4; Gößwein (1975) 3–4; Städele (1980) 27–8; Holzberg (1994a) ix–xiii; detailed bibliography by Beschorner (1994).

[3] The elaborate narrative structure and, in addition, diction and style [Düring (1951) 14–6 and 108–16] are the most important arguments against the theory that the letters are genuine [*sic* most recently Cataudella (1980) and (1981)].

[4] Edited most recently by Moore-Blunt (1985).

[5] This structural principle and, similarly, the compositional compactness of the collection as a whole have hitherto only been noted by Dornseiff (1934) (1939). All other studies before and after Dornseiff's have tended to overlook the structural unity of the corpus in their efforts to prove the authenticity of single letters, but see now Holzberg (1994b) 8–13.

the remaining letters (5–6 and 9–13) are closely related to the above in theme, their main subject being the advice Plato gives to various statesmen, and two of them (10 and 13) containing again references to Plato's Sicilian period. This collection is the only one of the nine which perhaps contains genuine letters; scholars of note have brought forward convincing arguments for the authenticity of letter 7 and have seriously considered the possibility that one or two others may be genuine too.[6] Seen as a whole, however, the collection shows in its composition and in its use of certain leitmotifs such a strong similarity to the collections listed below as nos. 2–6—the letters in which are quite definitely pseudepigraphic—that the corpus must at least be assigned to the same genre as these forerunners of the epistolary novel.

2. *The Letters of Euripides* (5):[7] Chronologically ordered and written directly before the tragedian moved to the court of Archelaus of Macedon (1–4) and then from Pella (5), the letters combine two themes: a sort of *Fürstenspiegel* and a defence of Euripides' decision to accept the king's invitation.

3. *The Letters of Aischines* (12):[8] In exile on the island of Rhodes, the orator writes to various friends and to the council and assembly of Athens. Alongside graphic descriptions of Aeschines' journey to Rhodes, of his first experiences in his place of exile, and a trip to Troy,[9] the chronologically ordered letters discuss the orator's politics, combining retrospective glances at his activities in Athens with advice for his native city and justification of his own actions.

4. *The Correspondence of Hippocrates* (24):[10] Instead of going to Persia at

---

[6] The mountain of literature on the problem "genuine or spurious" is listed by Neumann (1967) and in the surveys on Plato scholarship in *Lustrum*: 4,20,25 and 30.

[7] Text, German translation and in-depth study: Gößwein (1975); see also Jouan (1983) and Holzberg (1994b) 13–17.

[8] Text and French translation: Martin (1952). For the most recent study (with references to previous ones), see Salomone (1985); see also Holzberg (1994b) 17–22.

[9] In letter 10, which gives an account of the erotic adventure of one Cimon. In studies on Greek epistolography dominated by the question of authenticity, this letter was always quite naturally considered spurious and therefore did not belong to the collection [cf. esp. Stöcker (1980)]. From the point of view of modern literary criticism, it seems a somewhat questionable step when a letter is excluded from what is known to be a pseudepigraphic collection on the grounds that it is "more pseudepigraphic", and its established structural and thematic position in the story recorded in the remaining letters, is ignored; see now Holzberg (1994b) 19–21.

[10] Text with English translation, commentary and bibliography: W.D. Smith (1990);

the invitation of King Artaxerxes, the physician complies with the request of the Abderites that he come to their city to cure Democritus, whom they believe to be out of his mind because he laughs all the time. In the course of a long conversation with Democritus, who talks at length of the insanity of men's actions—madness being the subject of a book he is currently writing—, Hippocrates realizes that Democritus is in fact the greatest of sages.[11] One particularly novel-like feature of this likewise chronologically ordered corpus is the gradual approach to a climax, built up in seven letters (10–16) written before Hippocrates' arrival in Abdera; moreover, what Democritus says in letter 17, which records a conversation on the theme "world as madness", is very closely related to the view of the world found in surviving ancient novels of the comic-realistic type (Petronius, Apuleius, *Life of Aesop*).

5. *The Letters of Chion* (17):[12] The assassination of the Heraclean tyrant Clearchus by the hand of one Chion, recorded for the year 353/2 B.C., forms the historical basis of this chronologically ordered collection; the anonymous author presents, through the eyes of Chion, the gradual thought processes which lead him to tyrannicide and has him explain the killing as a practical application of the knowledge and insight gained from the philosophy of Plato.

6. *The Letters of Themistocles* (21):[13] In letters written after his banishment from Athens at various points on his wanderings as an exile from Argus to Susa, Themistocles reflects on his situation. The letters are not arranged throughout in chronological order, they nevertheless convey the impression that their contents are in fact a dramatic sequence of events, the author placing more emphasis on his presentation of what is going on in the mind of his letter-writing "I" than on an account of what is going on outside. He allows himself, for example, the following device: almost directly in the middle of the

---

cf. also Sakalis (1989). Most recent studies: Brodersen (1994); Holzberg (1994b) 22–28.

[11] Christoph Martin Wieland used the letters for his novel *Die Abderiten* (first published in 1774).

[12] Text, introduction, English translation and commentary: Düring (1951). For further literature see notes 111–115.

[13] Recommended edition: Cortassa (1990). Text, English translation, commentary and in-depth study: Doenges (1981); cf. also Penwill (1978). Doenges and Penwill both offer a structural analysis, that of Doenges being to my mind more convincing; see Holzberg (1994b) 33–38.

collection three pairs of corresponding letters (8-13) each contrast an earlier situation for the letter writer with a later one; the author is thus able to heighten the inner struggle.

7. *The Letters of Socrates and the Socratics* (35):[14] The collection presents the letters in chronological order and begins with seven letters of Socrates. In them the reader is introduced to those of the philosopher's teachings which the epistolographer considered most important. Letters 8-13 form a group which reveals that, in Socrates' lifetime, not all of his pupils truly imbibed his teachings: Aristippus argues here with other Socratics as to whether a philosopher may justifiably attend the court of a tyrant like Dionysius or not. Letter 14, which gives an account of the conviction and execution of Socrates, opens the second half of the collection. This records the developments which lead to the rise of the Socratic "school". Letters 14-27 describe how the first generation of Socratics compose the first Socratic writings and how they entrust Plato with the leadership of the Academy. In letters 28-34 Speusippus has taken over from Plato and corresponds with, amongst others, his successor Xenocrates.

8. *The Correspondence of the "Seven Wise Men"*: The existence of such a collection and also its probable similarity to the epistolary novel formed by the letters of Socrates and the Socratics, may be inferred from the following fact: the letters inserted by Diogenes Laertius into his history of philosophy and attributed to the "Seven Wise Men" or personages connected with them, are in formal respects and in their content closely related and in some cases even refer directly to one another.[15]

---

[14] Text and German translation: Köhler (1928); text, English translation and extensive bibliography [to which add Harward (1932)]: Malherbe (1977); cf. also Sykutris (1933).

[15] For an attempt to reconstruct the epistolary novel see Dührsen (1994). Two papyri containing letters from and to Alexander the Great seem to suggest that there was possibly another epistolary novel which now survives only in fragments. One of the two texts, Pap.Hamb.129 (1st century B.C.), is a fragment from an anthology of letters, these ordered without regard to chronology. The other text, PSI 1285 (2nd century A.D.), contains five chronologically arranged letters which reflect one particular period in the events that followed the Battle of Issus and the capture by Alexander of Darius' family. Four of the letters in the papyri are almost identical in their wording with letters inserted into the 3rd-century *Alexander Romance*, and this formed the basis for R. Merkelbach's (1977) now well-known theory that there was an epistolary *Alexander* novel in existence around 100 B.C., which was later used, together with a (lost) Hellenistic biography of Alexander, by the author of the *Alexander Romance*. However, a recently published fragment of a *Tabula Iliaca*

9. *The Letters of Phalaris* (147[16]):[17] The collection combines letters which cover themes from popular philosophy, some being intended as a defence for the tyrant's actions, with letters which, on the basis of thematical references, can be divided into various groups and which, when read in their particular context, prove to be the responses to individual phases in a sequence of events; for example, 22 letters which are scattered over the whole collection and which each of the various manuscript traditions also place at different points,[18] actually form, when put in the "correct" order, an epistolary novel on the course of relations between Phalaris and the poet Stesichorus.[19]

Attempts to date these epistolary novels can be based for the most part on nothing more than vague assumptions. In Plato's or rather Ps.-Plato's case alone the ground is less shaky, since this collection is recorded as being in existence in the 3rd century B.C.: Diogenes Laertius tells us that the Alexandrian scholar Aristophanes of Byzantium, who lived around 200 B.C., included "letters" in his edition of Plato's works (3.62).[20] The other collections, with the exception of the *Letters of Phalaris*, were written during the period in which Greek narrative prose came into full flower: the late Hellenistic and early imperial age. The general view today is that the diction and style of the Phalaris collection in its extant form place it in the 4th century A.D.,[21] but we may assume that there was an earlier version (1st/2nd century A.D.) in which the above-mentioned groups of letters,

---

from the early 1st century A.D. [cf. Burstein (1989) and Merkelbach (1989)] contains shreds of a letter found both in Pap.Hamb.129 and in the *Alexander Romance*, and further text remnants in this same fragment can be identified as the beginning of the narrative following the letter in the *Alexander Romance*. This find means that, as early as the 1st century A.D., there could have existed a novel-like biography of Alexander which was comparable to the *Alexander Romance* and which included fictitious letters. The letters in the two above-mentioned papyri could, then, represent extracts from this biography. The whole question of sources for the *Alexander Romance* must therefore now be given a thorough re-examination, and until such a time as this has been accomplished, the two papyri ought not to be numbered amongst the surviving texts from Greek epistolary novels. For the reconstruction of a late antique epistolary *Alexander* novel see Grignaschi (1967).

[16] One further letter [No. 57 in Hercher (1873)] is from Abaris to Phalaris.

[17] Text and Latin translation: Hercher (1873) 409–59; cf. also Bentley (1874); Bianchetti (1987); Russell (1988); Merkle (1994b).

[18] Cf. Tudeer (1931).

[19] On this see Bianchetti (1987) 200–3; Russell (1988) 97–9; Merkle (1994b) 134–165.

[20] The number 13 is, however, mentioned by Diogenes only in connection with an edition of the letters included in the Plato edition ascribed to Thrasyllus (3.61).

[21] Cf. most recently Russell (1988) 96–7.

each re-tracing a brief course of events, formed the skeleton for an epistolary novel composed according to the chronological principle.²²

While eight of the nine collections of letters are associated with famous names, the anonymous author of the *Letters of Chion* chose as his letter writer a man who even in antiquity was probably not very well known. Nevertheless, a central motif of the collection—"tyrannicide"—links the *Letters of Chion* not only with the epistolary novels named above, but also with the other Greek epistolary texts. The motif "thoughts of letter writer on a ruler", especially when the latter is a tyrant, appears again and again in Greek letters; it is sometimes—although less frequently—accompanied by another, closely connected motif, that of the "letter writer's thoughts on exile".²³ In the various collections we very often find letters from a sage to a ruler, in which a previous request that the sage come to the ruler's court is refused.²⁴ There is every indication that the letters of Plato, which—whether genuine or spurious—can perhaps be regarded as the first "epistolary novel" and which focus repeatedly on Plato's difficulties with Dionysius II of Syracuse, established a thematic tradition for the whole genre.

In the Chion novel there are in fact several direct references to the letters of Plato,²⁵ and this seems in any case inevitable when one considers the plot. The pseudepigraphic letters—17 in all—give an account of how Chion, immediately before and during his studies under Plato, gradually becomes firmly convinced that he must murder Heraclea's tyrant Clearchus. Since very little was known about the historical Chion, the author of the epistolary novel could portray the character of his protagonist and the events in which he was involved with a greater degree of poetic licence than other authors of pseudepigraphic letters, and indeed he made ample use of this freedom. For instance, the Chion of the *Letters* writes that while on his

---

²² Merkle (1994b) 167–8.

²³ Used in Aeschines, Demosthenes, Euripides, Heraclitus, Phalaris (ep. 4, 18, 19, 49, 51, 95, 119), the "Seven Wise Men" and Themistocles collections.

²⁴ In the letters of Diogenes (4), Heraclitus (1 and 2), Hippocrates (1–9), Isocrates (6), Phalaris (23,56,57,74), Pythagoras (1), Socrates (1), Xenophon (7) and Zenon (= Diog.Laert.7.8). Sometimes the invitation is accepted: Anacharsis (10), Euripides, Pittacus (Diog.Laert.1.81), Plato and Aristippus in the letters of the Socratics (8–13). The motif also plays an important role in the complementary letters "Menander to Glycera/Glycera to Menander", Alciphro 4.18 and 19 [cf. Bungarten (1967) and the *Life of Aesop* (chs. 96–100)].

²⁵ Cf. ep. 4, 6 and 16, also Düring (1951) *ad loc.*

way to Athens he had met Xenophon in Byzantium, Socrates' pupil being on the homeward march after the expedition against Artaxerxes II (ep. 3). If we try to verify this, calculations show that it is an anachronism, since the "anabasis" of the Greek mercenaries fell in the year 400 B.C. and the assassination of Clearchus, which according to the Chion of the *Letters* took place five years after this meeting with Xenophon, is documented for the year 353/2 B.C. It is precisely such liberal handling of the given narrative material that links this anonymous epistolographer with authors of modern epistolary novels.[26]

Chion's meeting with Xenophon prompts him to expand on a thought which had previously been briefly referred to (ep. 1 and 2) and which now becomes a dominant theme in the remaining letters. Until now, he explains to his father Matris in an account of his experiences with Xenophon,[27] he had been afraid that the study of philosophy would steer him towards a quietistic life far removed from politics. Now, however, the example set in Byzantium by Xenophon, who in a bold speech had managed to persuade the Greek mercenaries not to plunder the city, had taught him that those who have applied themselves to philosophy are superior to others in terms of manliness (ἀνδρεία) too (ep. 3, 6). It therefore suits Chion well that Plato's philosophy is, as the student very soon sees in Athens, oriented towards both the practical side of life and leisurely contemplation far away from business and politics (ep. 5). Under Plato's guidance Chion thus gradually matures into a "good man" in the ethical sense and at the same time into a prudent citizen.

The letters in the novel can be divided into three groups,[28] the end of each group being marked by a display of Chion's ἀνδρεία. Letters 1–4 describe Chion's journey to Athens and the last major event recorded in ep. 4 is Chion's brave stand in Perinthus: the city is currently at war with the Thracians and Chion, armed with a spear, confronts three Thracian horsemen, forcing them to retreat. In the last of the letters which form the second group (5–13) there is a corresponding scene in which one of Clearchus' bodyguards

---

[26] For a comparison between ancient and modern epistolary novels see Arndt (1994) and Rosenmeyer (1994).

[27] Matris is the addressee of all the letters except 9,16 and 17, and this also contributes greatly to the compactness of the epistolary novel.

[28] This symmetry was first observed by Lana (1974) 266 and Konstan (1990) 264–5.

makes an attempt on Chion's life in Athens: the hero is able to foil the assailant in a clear improvement on his already impressive performance in Perinthus. And in the final letter of the last group, which, like the first, comprises four epistles (14–17) and deals with events taking place not in Athens but elsewhere, Chion tells his teacher Plato that he is going to murder the tyrant in two days' time. He describes here a dream in which a woman of divine beauty and stature crowns him with a wreath of wild olive and ribbons (ep. 17, 2). Chion thus achieves at the end of the novel precisely what he had hoped for at the beginning of his studies in philosophy when, in ep. 1, he had asked his parents, who had been worrying about him since his departure, instead to promise a trophy as a reward for the virtue (ἀρετή) he hoped to attain; this honour will be his, according to the dream, when he has passed the highest test of ἀρετή by assassinating the tyrant.

It would be impossible to unravel all the strands of the Chion novel here and demonstrate how skilfully the author weaves the 17 letters into an organic whole by linking together in the manner of leitmotifs certain ideas dominant in the philosophy espoused by his Chion; as those familiar with the technique will know, one of its typical devices is to delay the revelation of the full significance of a given theme, rather than let its first appearance say all. The following example must suffice:[29] In ep. 2 Chion commends to his father a certain merchant who, when Chion had wanted to see (θεάσασθαι) Byzantium, had shown him what is worth seeing (ἄξια θέας), who will himself, however, probably not wish to be given a sight-seeing tour (θέα) of Heraclea, having once taken part in a military expedition to the Pontus. In ep. 3 Chion again sees something at Byzantium (§2: ἐθεασάμην), this time Xenophon's inspiring performance. A comparison of the two passages where Chion's θεᾶσθαι occurs shows that the future philosopher's eye is gradually learning to focus on the essential. And if we now also keep in view the merchant, to whom in ep. 2 no great significance appears to be attached, we find a hint in ep. 3 and a clear indication in the complementary letters 7 and 8 that his two activities, "trading" (ἐμπορεύεσθαι) and "taking the field" (καταστρατεύεσθαι)—the latter being the only one he shares with Xenophon—, stand in Chion's thought for two diametrically opposed spheres. The said letters 7 and 8 talk of one Archepolis

---

[29] For further examples see Konstan (1990) *passim*.

whom Chion commends to his father, but with certain reservations. The man, writes Chion, had been of the opinion that Plato's pupils were a useless lot because they only talked about ἀρετή and not about money, and, in a later passage obviously intended ironically, Chion says: "I am sure that he is also a good merchant, since he studied philosophy before becoming a merchant".

The philosophical content of the *Letters of Chion* is, as has long been established, based essentially on those of Plato's writings with which the author was familiar, but is also interlarded with Stoic ideas.[30] The language of the letters points to the late 1st century A.D. as the date of composition,[31] and it must therefore at least be considered possible that the anonymous epistolographer was in some way associated with the numerous Stoic opponents of the Roman emperors;[32] the motif "tyrannicide" is widely used in various works of Greek and Latin prose and poetry written during the period when the *principatus* began to give way to *dominatio*,[33] and the reason for this was certainly not simply that it was a stock theme in rhetorical declamations. However, tyrannical forms of government being, as we have seen, a popular subject amongst Greek epistolographers, the specific political intentions expressed by the author of the *Letters of Chion* through his treatment of this motif can only be more narrowly defined when all letter collections have finally been carefully analysed.

---

[30] Cf. esp. Düring (1951) 20–2 and Lana (1974).
[31] Düring (1951) 14–6 and 108–16; Zucchelli (1986).
[32] Cf. Düring (1951) 16–7,21,24–5; Ballanti (1954) 84–91; Lana (1974); Billault (1977) 36; Zucchelli (1986) 24; Konstan (1990); Robiano (1991).
[33] Cf. esp. Fleskes (1914).

15. FRAGMENTS OF LOST NOVELS[1]

Susan Stephens

No survey of ancient fiction can be complete without some consideration of the body of material that has been lost to us, fragments of which increase at least threefold our inventory of Greek novels. Knowledge about these lost texts has been transmitted in several ways. An invaluable source of information has been the 9th century patriarch of Constantinople, Photius, who, in addition to summarizing the extant novels of Achilles Tatius and Heliodorus, left us epitomes of two others: a text that Photius, at least, considered to be the *fons et origo* of the novel-writing enterprise, Antonius Diogenes' *Incredible Things Beyond Thule*, and Iamblichus's *Babyloniaca*. A variety of other ancient sources provides testimony about the existence of ancient fictional works and even supplies us with quotations: John Lydus's *On Months* and Porphyry's *Life of Pythagoras* have given us several pages from Antonius Diogenes; the *Souda* Lexicon has provided a series of short fragments attributed to Iamblichus's *Babyloniaca* and Persian lexica an epitome as well as fragments from a Persian version of *Metiochus and Parthenope*, which now help to reconstruct the Greek original. Additionally we may learn something from incidental remarks in Lucian or from the existence of pavement mosaics whose subject matter was inspired by novels.[2] But by far, the largest and most varied supply of new material has been papyri from the sands of Egypt, recovery of which began in the 19th century. First to appear at the end of the century were eight columns from a romantic narrative about the young king of Nineveh, the legendary Ninus. This was followed in rapid fashion by the publication of other fragments, named by their editors for their main characters—*Calligone*, a tale set in the region of the Black Sea, *Chione* ("Snow White"), a princess plotting to escape a forced marital alliance, *Metiochus and Parthenope*, and *Herpyllis*. Finds in this century have yielded the sensational events of Lollianus's

---

[1] The views presented here are based on the analyses of novel fragments to be found in Stephens-Winkler (1995). Greek texts and translations of the fragments are also taken from that work. Line numbers for Greek texts are the same for all editions.

[2] For the most recent discussion of these mosaics, see Quet (1992).

Phoenicica, the Iolaus fragment, further fragments of *Metiochus and Parthenope*, *Sesonchosis*, a Hellenized romantic adventure about the legendary king of Egypt, as well as a handful of lesser pieces. Papyrus fragments of novels range in date from the first century A.D. (*Ninus*) to the fourth century A.D. (*Sesonchosis*), with the majority concentrated in the second century. Novel fragments come primarily from two sites, Oxyrhynchus and the villages surrounding the area of the Fayumic depression. This clustering in time and locality results from the vagaries of preservation at various ancient sites—the same phenomenon is apparent in other papyrus finds of Greek literature—and is not necessarily correlated to an increase or decline in novel writing as a cultural phenomenon.

Working with fragments of any genre presents limitations, but for novels, where even a relatively large fragment of several columns can represent only a tiny fraction of the whole text, reconstruction is not only difficult, but frequently idiosyncratic. The limited glimpse of characters and plot often encourage an editor to make a judgment or even indulge in an occasional flight of fancy that subsequent editors may regard, or new finds prove, misguided. The earliest published fragment of *Sesonchosis*, for example, was identified as Egyptian history,[3] and it was only recognized as belonging to a novel when another portion of the same papyrus came to light. F. Zimmermann identified *P.Oxy*.416 as belonging to Arrian's *Life of Tillorobus*[4] and it is so-listed in the standard handbook, Pack's *Greek and Latin Literary Texts from Greco-Roman Egypt*, although there is nothing about the papyrus, apart from the rather dubious reading of τι[, to permit such an identification. In the ensuing assessment of the range and significance of papyrus contributions to our understanding of the ancient novel as a whole, I have attempted to err on the conservative side, outlining positions in the main for which there is considerable consensus. On issues where there is genuine disagreement, I have tried to present each side of the argument. The following discussion is focused on broadly interpretative issues rather than grammatical particularities of the text or the reconstruction of scenes, although occasionally the two areas intersect.

Fragmentary novels seem to fall into four fairly distinct, but occa-

---

[3] See Rea (1962) 134–136.

[4] Zimmermann (1935). Our only information about this supposedly lost work comes from a comment in Lucian's *Alexander* §2: "He [sc. Arrian] thought it appropriate to record the life of Tillorobus the bandit."

sionally overlapping groups: (1) the so-called ideal-romantic is the best known, because it is the category into which the extant five Greek novels fall. The action of the ideal-romantic type is located in the heyday of Greek culture—the sixth or the fifth century B.C.— and centers on an adolescent couple of high station, who fall in love at first sight but undergo a series of harrowing adventures—kidnapping, shipwreck, slavery, even marriage to another party—before being reunited. (2) Next are novels that focus on the life of a non-Greek hero, like Ninus or Sesonchosis. These novels may be located in an even more remote past—Ninus was the legendary founder of Nineveh, Sesonchosis, a pharaoh of Egypt's Twelfth dynasty—though they share a number of features with the ideal-romantic novel, and may in fact be a subset of it. (3) The novels that concern themselves with criminals and the otherwise socially marginal are well represented in fragments, although only Petronius's *Satyricon* and Apuleius's *Golden Ass* provide examples of this type among the extant novels. (4) Finally, Antonius Diogenes' *Incredible Things Beyond Thule* is a novel that, we might say, fits the default category—none of the above. It seems better defined in terms of what it is not than what it is—it is not a love story, though it has several pairs of lovers; it is not a parody or satire, though it has elements of both; it is not a travelogue or a geography or an history, though it freely appropriates material from all of these ancient literary categories.

In order to see more easily the ways in which individual fragmentary novels adhere to or diverge from expectations based on extant Latin and Greek novels and how the fragments may relate to each other, the discussion of individual fragments below has been divided into these four groups.

Ideal-Romantic Novels

Metiochus and Parthenope is the best known fragment that belongs to this type. While its papyrus fragments date from the second or third century of the common era, *Metiochus and Parthenope* must have been one of the earliest Greek novels. On the basis of its language, A. Dihle placed it before the flowering of Atticism, even as early as the first century B.C.[5] Certainly it had been written no later than the first

---

[5] (1978) 54–55.

century A.D., because Lucian mentions its main characters Parthenope and Metiochus in his dialogues.[6] It was sufficiently popular that, like the Ninus novel, it served as the inspiration for pavement mosaics found in Antioch-on-the-Orontes.[7] There are two unique features of this novel: it was translated into Persian at a later date by Unsuri[8] and it came also to serve as the basis for a Coptic martyr tale.[9]

Metiochus and Parthenope is based on the historical events found in Herodotus (3.124–151, 6.39–41). Characters include Polycrates, the tyrant of Samos, his daughter, Parthenope, and Metiochus, the son of Miltiades. The Persian story opens with a marriage on the island of Samos between Polycrates (= Folikrat) and a woman named Yani. This is followed by the birth of their daughter Parthenope (= 'Adhra'). She is raised as a son, receiving the standard education of princes, training in the martial arts and in rhetoric. The Greek fragments begin with a romantic encounter. Metiochus,[10] having fallen victim to the machinations of a wicked step-mother, Hegesipyle, has fled his homeland. Arriving in Samos he meets Parthenope, accompanied by her mother, at a temple of Hera, and the two fall in love at first sight. Subsequent events include a banquet at which the poet Ibycus and the philosopher Anaximenes are present and where the young lovers are induced to discuss the nature of eros. Metiochus proposes the philosophically correct view of eros as a "stirring of the mind aroused by beauty and increasing with familiarity,"[11] while Parthenope defends the traditional image of love found in the poets, namely, that Eros is a winged boy. At this stage, the Greek fragment breaks off.

We learn more about the story from a Persian epitome published

---

[6] *De saltatione* §2: θηλυδρίαν ἄνθρωπον ὁρῶν ἐσθῆσι μαλακαῖς... μιμούμενον ἐρωτικὰ γύναια... Φαίδρας καὶ Παρθενόπας καὶ Ῥοδόπας... *Pseudologistes* §25: τὰ μὲν πρῶτα ἐν τοῖς θεάτροις εὐδοκιμεῖν ἐποίησα, νῦν μὲν Νίνον, νῦν δὲ Μητίοχον....

[7] Quet (1992) 129–34.

[8] Hägg (1985). The title in Persian was "Wamiq and '*Adhra*'" = "The lover and the virgin." According to M. Shafi (1967) 7–8, in Persian literature "Wamiq and '*Adhra*'" came to be used as a generic title for romantic tales. About 300 lines from the beginning of this poem have been published. Since it overlaps in detail with the Greek fragment it is most helpful in reconstructing the original story.

[9] Hägg (1984) convincingly links the Greek tale with the Coptic martyrology of St. Bartanuba.

[10] He is accompanied by a companion named Tufan (= Theophanes?) in the Persian text, though no trace of this character remains in the Greek. See Ritter (1948) 139.

[11] Col. II 60–62: ἔρως [δ' ἔστιν] κίνημα διανοίας ὑπὸ [κ]άλλους γινόμε[νον] καὶ ὑπὸ συνηθείας αὐξόμενον, Stephens-Winkler (1995) 86–87.

by Mohammed Shafi in the introduction to *Wamiq and 'Adhra'*.[12] The girl continues to attend dinner parties at which Metiochus (= Wamiq) is present. But when her conduct is reported to her mother, the girl confesses her love for Metiochus (= Wamiq) and threatens to kill herself if not allowed to marry him. Her father, Polycrates, apparently consents, but changes his mind when her mother dies. When her father is killed in battle, his secretary, Maiandrios ascended the throne and cast the lovers into prison. When Parthenope rejects the new tyrant's advances, she is sold into slavery. After four years of servitude she tells her story to her master, probably Anaxilaus of Rhegium, who recognizes her and sets her free.

Parthenope's wanderings must have taken her both east and west, because Lucian mentions that Parthenope wanders as far as Persia.[13] Also, events in the martyr tale of St. Bartanuba, which seems to have been based on this novel, may help to shed light on Parthenope's Persian adventure. The young saint is importuned first by the emperor Constantine, who respects her religious devotion, then by the king of Persia, who does not. In order to escape the latter's attentions she becomes a martyr by throwing herself into a fire. This self-immolation looks remarkably like a feigned suicide, a ruse employed by heroines in other novels to avoid unwelcome advances. It is easy to conclude that Bartanuba's martyrdom reflects Parthenope's pretended suicide in order to escape the attentions of a suitor, who is perhaps the king of Persia. We may infer, from the Persian poem, that after her adventures Parthenope finally returns to Samos, for at her birth, her father dreams that an olive tree grew up, was subsequently uprooted, and wandered through many lands before returning to spread its shade over his throne.[14] About the subsequent adventures of Metiochus, however, we know nothing. Given the very high incidence of happy endings in these novels, we may infer that the lovers were reunited, but it is also possible that this early novel was atypical and Parthenope's name proved to be prophetic—she may have remained a virgin throughout her life.[15]

P.Oxy.435 is a very small scrap, mentioning a character named

---

[12] Shafi (1967) 3. It was connected to the Greek story by Bo Utas (1984–86) and Tomas Hägg in Hägg (1985).

[13] *De saltatione* §54: . . .τὸ Πολυκράτους πάθος καὶ τῆς θυγατρὸς αὐτοῦ μέχρι Περσῶν πλάνη.

[14] Verses 16–22.

[15] See Utas (1984–86).

Δημο[. . . .], the Corcyreans, and παρθεν[. . .]. Zimmermann originally identified the piece as belonging to *Metiochus and Parthenope*,[16] though few have taken his conjecture seriously. A Persian fragment from this novel, however, includes a character named Damchasinos (= Demoxenus), who appears to have control of Parthenope.[17] If correctly assigned, *P.Oxy*.435 indicates that Parthenope traveled as a slave or captive to Corcyra, probably en route to Rhegium.

Chione was discovered by Wilcken[18] in an eighth century palimpsest papyrus codex that also contained Chariton's *Chaereas and Callirhoe*. The whole manuscript was lost when the ship's cargo caught fire in the harbor at Hamburg, hence its current name of *codex Thebanus deperditus*. Although Wilcken's transcription has survived, he was uncertain about the order of the three columns that he had succeeded in copying. As a result, much scholarly discussion has been devoted to the proper ordering of his text. Salient features include the heroine, Chione, her parents, the king and queen, and Megamedes, an outsider who has some claim to her hand. The characters have been given a period of thirty days to deliberate, after which either Megamedes arrives or Chione's marriage must take place, or both. The column Wilcken regarded as final breaks off with Chione's speech to a man generally assumed to be her lover: "I have not discovered any way to save us. But this one thing I declare to you, that if we are not able to live with each other, commanding him [Megamedes] . . . painful . . . ultimately is left to us. We must . . . nothing and consider how it may be done with due propriety. For if we secretly . . ."[19]

In 1979 M. Gronewald published another scrap from the same papyrus roll as P.Berol.10535,[20] suggesting that the two pieces belonged to the *Chione* novel.[21] Together they contain what appears to have been a marriage scene. The language of these scraps is remarkably close to Chariton, and since *Chione* was bound together

---

[16] Zimmermann (1935) 194–205.
[17] Ritter (1948) 138, Kussl (1991) 167 n. 7, Stephens-Winkler (1995) 95.
[18] See Wilcken (1901).
[19] Col. III 13–27: ἡ δὲ Χιόνη, "οὐιδ' ἐγὼ μέν, "φησιν, "εἰς | σωτηρίαν τι εὑρίσκω. | ἓν δὲ τοῦτό σοι λέγω, | εἰ μὴ δυνάμεθα ζῆν μετ' ἀλλήλων, προστά|ξαντες . . . τελευταῖον ἡμῖν | ἀπολείπεται. χρὴ δὲ | οὐδὲν . . . καὶ ὅ|πως εὐσχημόνως | γενηθῇ σκοπεῖν· λειληθότας γὰρ ἡμῖν . . ., Stephens-Winkler 296–7.
[20] P.Berol.10535 had been previously identified as "romance" and published by Zimmermann (1936) in his edition of the novel fragments.
[21] P.Berol.10535 and P.Berol.21234. See Gronewald (1979b) 15–20 and Lucke (1984).

with *Chaereas and Callirhoe* it is possible that both novels were written by the same author.

The fragment known as *Antheia*, although quite small, presents what appears to be a tale within a tale. The second, and most complete column, contains an embedded narrative between two men, one of whom addresses the other as "φίλτατε," and relates the following events:

> Speaker A: "Lysippos, having come to the sea with Euxeinos, asks the people he knows about the whole situation.... Thraseas is ruling... Thalassia, having commandeered Kleandros' boat is aiding Thraseas... when she sailed out having escaped notice of those in her care—for it is safe to give out... Thalassia's devisings—having taken Antheia's affairs in hand, she... Antheia, after she saw the poison and concealed it certainly....
> B: "About Antheia's affairs, is it not possible to speak, friend?"
> A: "I'm not sure," he said. "Lysander betrayed her... and Thraseas has been removed because of her (?). These things are clear to everyone. The rest is conjecture and talk, mingled with... holding the unbelievable and astonishing."[22]

The fragment shares several features in common with Xenophon's *Ephesiaka*: (1) the names of a main character, Antheia, and one minor character, Euxeinos; (2) the relative prominence (so far as the fragment allows us to tell) of Artemis; and (3) the fact that both Antheias have acquired poison. Unfortunately, the fragment is far too small to judge whether one novel is deliberately imitating or alluding to the other, whether borrowings are merely accidental, or indeed, whether they bear some relation to a third text (besides, of course, Xenophon's *Cyropaedia*).

Apollonius consists of two very small and disconnected fragments. One contains a banquet scene at the Persian court where the queen is described as possessing a beauty suitable to the gods and where the king toasts first a character named Dionysius, then another named Apollonius. In the smaller fragment, marked as column 14, there is a scene between Apollonius and a woman who appears desirous of

---

[22] Ll. 1–20: Λύσιππος δ' ἐ[λ]θὼν ἐπὶ θάλατ|ταν σὺν Εὐξείνῳ πυνθάνεται τῶν γνωl[ρί]μων τὴν κατάστασιν [π]ᾶσαν, ... Θρασέας μὲν ἄρχει.. Θαλασσία δὲ ἀναρπάσασα τὸ πλοῖ I[ο]ν Κλεάνδρου Θρασέαν περιέπει καὶ ... ὅτε ἐξέί[π]λευσεν λαθοῦσα αὐτὰ[ς ὢ]ν αὐτῆι μεἰλ[εῖ.]— ἀσφαλὲς γὰρ δοῦναι ... τὰς Θαλασlσίας βουλάς—τὰ δὲ Ἀvθ[εί]ας ἑλομένη ... Ἀνθείαν ἰδοῦσα τὸ φάρl[μ]ακον καὶ κατακρύψασα ὡς μάλιcτα...." "τὰ δὲ Ἀνθείας, I [ο]ὐδ' ἔχ[ει] λέγειν, φίλτατε;" "οὐκ οἶδα," ἔφη, I "σαφῶ[ς. ὁ] μὲν γὰρ Λύσανδρος αὐτὴν ὑπ[ὸ ἁ]ρlπαγῆς παρέδωκεν δ [..]..καὶ Θρασέα[ς] I ἐξήρητο ἐπ' αὐτῆι. δ[ῆλ]α ταῦτα ἅπασιν· I [τὰ δὲ] ἄλλα εἰκασία καὶ λόγος μεμιγμένος I [......]ατι ἔχοντι τὸ ἄπιστον καὶ παράδοl[ξον."], Stephens-Winkler (1995) 282–83.

an assignation later that evening. At this point the fragment breaks off. Some, though by no means all, editors have attempted to connect these scraps to the Greek version of the *History of Apollonius, King of Tyre*, a late Latin romantic tale for which a Greek original has long been posited. Although in their present form these fragments look quite unlike the extant Latin text, in his 1984 edition of the *HA*, Kortekaas observed that the "original Greek version would have undergone substantial Christianizing revisions in the process of its translation and transmission. So the original may look quite unlike its offspring."[23]

Nationalistic Novels

The category of the nationalistic novel is well-represented among the novel fragments, though no one of this type has survived intact. In general, these stories center on the youthful adventures of non-Greek historical or legendary characters, like Ninus, the founder of Nineveh or Sesonchosis, the Egyptian conqueror of Europe and Asia. The *Babyloniaca*, whose hero, Rhodanes, becomes the king of Babylon, belongs in this group as does *Calligone*, a story that takes place among the native peoples of South Russia and includes Amazons. While the characters of these nationalistic dramas may be known from non-Greek traditions, in these novels they appear to be reduced to a cultural homogeneity and their behavior assimilated to the social norms of the Greek-speaking educated classes within the Roman Empire. Thus, Semiramis, who is a fierce and independent queen in Diodorus's account of Babylonian history, becomes in the Ninus novel shy and tongue-tied, too embarrassed to tell her aunt that she loves her cousin. Further, explicitly foreign elements in the novels tend to be explained in Greek terms. In general, these novels support the thesis first put forward by Martin Braun, who observed that non-Greek figures like Ninus, Nektanebus, and Moses, along with obscure local legends, grew into subjects for Greek history as well as popular fiction in the Hellenistic period. Braun believed such characters and legends served as foci for native resistance to Greek rule;[24] though equally one might

---

[23] Kortekaas (1984) 130. For the most recent and complete presentation of the argument for assigning this papyrus to the *HA*, see R. Kussl (1991) 143–159.
[24] (1938) 1–31.

view such stories as attempts by non-Greeks to demonstrate the significance of their own cultural achievements, not by resistance, but by recasting their own local heroes in Greek garb *for* Greeks.

Ninus was the first of the fragmentary novels to come to light and is still among the most attractive. The drama centers on the tension between Ninus as warrior and Ninus as lover of his shy young cousin, between manly daring (θάρσος) and female modesty (αἰδώς). The central problem confronting editors has been the order of the two large fragments (A and B) published by Wilcken. Written on a papyrus that was later reused for a document dated in the time of Trajan, Wilcken assumed the roll was intact at the time of reuse and assembled *Ninus* accordingly.[25] The A fragment begins with a scene between Ninus and his cousin, manifestly in love and discussing the possibility of an immediate marriage. Both agree to approach their respective aunts, who are sisters, to plead their case. It is clear from Ninus's speech to his aunt that he has already returned from at least one military expedition. His argument employs the niceties of rhetorical style that have come to be expected in these novels:

> I am subject not only to the common calamities—I mean diseases and Chance which often strikes even those sitting quietly by their own hearth—but sea journeys too await me, and wars upon wars; and I am certainly no coward nor as an assistant to my safety will I hide behind a veil of cravenness. I am the man you know me to be, so I need not tiresomely proclaim it. Let royalty urge some haste, let strong desire urge some haste, let the uncertainty and incalculability of the times that lie ahead of me urge haste. Let the fact that each of us is an only child count somewhat in favor of our haste, so that even if Chance contrive some disaster for us, we may leave you a token of our union. You may call me shameless for speaking of these matters, but I truly would have been shameless if I had tried her virtue in secret.... I am not shameless in discussing a daughter's longed-for marriage with her mother, nor in asking you for what you have already offered, nor in begging that the common hopes of our house and for the entire kingdom be not postponed....[26]

---

[25] Wilcken (1893) 165. If the papyrus roll was not intact at the time of reuse, there is no reason to prefer the AB to the BA order. Sections might have been cut off of the original Ninus manuscript as needed and pasted on to the roll that formed the daily account book.

[26] A III 16–IV 11: καὶ οὐδὲ ǀ τοῖc κοινοῖc τούτοις ὑπευǀ[θυ]νός εἰμι μόνον, νόσοις λέǀ[γω] καὶ Τύχηι πολλάκις καὶ τοὺς ǀ [ἐπ]ὶ τῆς οἰκείας ἑστίας ἠρεμοῦνǀτας ἀν[α]ιρούσηι· ἀλλὰ ναυτιλίǀαι μ' ἐκδέχονται καὶ ἐκ πολέǀμων πόλεμοι καὶ οὐδὲ ἄτολǀμος ἐγὼ καὶ βοηθὸν ἀσφαλείας δειλίαν προκαλυπτόμενος, ǀ ἀλλ' οἷον [ο]ἶcθας, ἵνα μὴ φορτιǀκὸc ὦι λ[έ]γων· σπευσάτω δή ǀ τι βασιλεία, σπευσάτω τι ἐπιǀθυμία, cπευσάτω τὸ ἀστάθμηǀτον καὶ ἀτέκμαρτον

The girl, in contrast, finds herself speechless and can only weep on her aunt's bosom, a sign that her aunt nevertheless shrewdly interprets as modesty rather than reluctance. The aunts agree to the nuptials as the fragment breaks off.

Fragment B opens with a scene in which either Ninus or the girl are in a state of considerable distress with rending of garments and the traditional signs of emotional turmoil. Unfortunately, this scene is broken in such a way that either masculine or feminine forms can be restored throughout. Wilcken and Kussl, following him, have taken Ninus as the distraught subject and restored masculine forms; virtually all other editors have preferred feminine forms and understood the scene as Ninus interrupting his overwrought cousin and calming her with pledges of undying devotion. This is followed or interrupted by preparations for the military expedition against the Armenians that appears to have been Ninus's first command. The scene includes details of troop deployment[27] and the army's unexpectedly easy passage through the mountain passes. In fact, the ease which Ninus prepares for his first battle is in marked contrast to the difficulties in love he experiences with his young cousin and the delays in the marriage, occasioned by their youth.

Subsequent editors and commentators have pointed out that the fragments would be more coherent if assembled B A; then the Armenian expedition of B would be the command from which Ninus has returned in A—now a seasoned warrior; the impending expedition in B would serve as the rationale for the girl's distress as well as the pledges of affection; this would predate the lovers' conversation in A and make explicable the marriage that Ninus confidently mentions to his aunt as already promised.

Fragment C, from a different but nearly contemporary papyrus roll, is a scene from a shipwreck, resulting from natural causes. Since the Armenian expedition appears to have been entirely land-based, fragment C must belong to a later expedition, possibly the "sea journey," mentioned in A. The most curious feature of this fragment is

---

τῶν | ἐκδεχομένων με χρόνων | προλαβέτω τι καὶ φθήτω καὶ | τὸ μονογενὲς ἡμῶν ἀμφοῖτέρων, ἄνα κἄν ἄλλως ἡ Τύχη | κακ[όν] τι βουλεύηται περὶ ἡ|μῶν, καταλείπωμεν ὑμῖν ἐνέχυρα. ἀναιδῆ τάχα με ἐρεῖς περὶ τούτων διαλεγόμενον· ἐγὼ δὲ ἀναιδὴς ἂν ἤμην λάθραι | πειρῶν ... οὐκ ἀναιδὴς δὲ | μητρὶ περὶ γάμων θυγατρὸς | εὐκταίων διαλεγόμενος | καὶ ἀπαιτῶν ἃ ἔδωκας καὶ | δεόμενος τὰς κοινὰς τῆς | [ο]ἰκίας καὶ τῆς βασιλείας ἁπάσης εὐχὰς μὴ εἰς τοῦτον ἀ|ναβάλλεσθαι τὸν καιρόν, Stephens-Winkler (1995) 39–41.

[27] See Jenistova (1953) 216. These are remarkably accurate in comparison with other Hellenistic armies for which we have information.

the presence of a woman at its beginning, before the shipwreck. She is addressed as "γύναι," which would indicate a married woman, though not necessarily one's own wife.[28] If the woman is Ninus's wife, they must become separated shortly before the time of the shipwreck.

Other evidence for the plot comes from two pavement mosaics on which Ninus gazes longingly at the portrait of a woman. The mosaics were surely inspired directly or indirectly by the events of the novel. They suggest that an important or memorable feature of the story was the separation of Ninus from his beloved.

Sesonchosis consists also of two papyrus fragments, one from a fourth century codex, containing a scene between Sesonchosis and his father, in which the son is given his first military venture. The second papyrus, a third-century roll, contains details of a battle between Egyptians and Arabians, and also a scene in which Sesonchosis, apparently incognito, accompanied by a friend named Pamounis, encounters the young woman named Meameris, to whom he has been betrothed. She does not recognize him as her fiancé, which suggests that they had never met and must have been betrothed over a long-distance. As is the way in these stories she has fallen in love with him at first sight.[29]

Sesonchosis resembles *Ninus* in several particulars: both novels focus on the moment of coming of age of young men who subsequently become great kings or foundational heroes for their people. The first military expeditions of each are detailed; both include large components of the erotic—betrothal and passionate love—that do not appear in any historical tradition. Both seem to include separation from the beloved and perhaps disguise or temporary loss of status. This raises a question about the relationship between the two novels: does one imitate the other or do both partake of stock story motifs about the education of princes? The material out of which the *Sesonchosis* novel was fashioned probably belongs to the time of the Achaemonid conquest of Egypt and the subsequent Hellenistic period, during which native priesthoods promoted stories about several historical kingships in order to create native rivals to Darius and Alexander. Therefore, *Sesonchosis* could be very early, contemporary with, or even predating *Ninus*. In which case its existence would support the direction for the origin of the novel suggested by J.W.B. Barns, namely from Egypt

---

[28] In fact, in the extant novels γύναι is almost never used to address one's own wife.
[29] Quet (1992) 129–34.

into the Greek world.[30] Or it might be no earlier than its papyrus copies—produced in the third and fourth centuries of this era. In which case we probably have the already developed earlier Greek novel (*Ninus*) producing a later Greco-Egyptian imitation.

Two fragments of *Calligone* are currently known. The published fragment contains one column with a very powerful scene that takes place within a tent in an army camp somewhere in the vicinity of the Bosporus. Calligone, a Greek woman who is wearing military dress or is decked out as an Amazon, proclaims her great distress over the news about one Erasinus whom she first laid eyes on at the hunt. We must infer from her distress that she is in love and has learned either that Erasinus is dead or he has found another woman. She apparently intends to kill herself, but Eubiotus—the other participant in the scene—has hidden away her dagger or short sword. When she discovers the theft she turns her rage against him and threatens to kill him with her bare hands. From an unpublished Oxyrhynchus fragment,[31] we learn that Calligone's ship had run aground and both she and her crew were captured and taken before the Amazon queen, who is named Themisto.[32] Calligone identifies herself to the queen, mentioning the Milesian settlement of Borysthenes, that is, the Greek Olbia. Which of the two fragments comes earlier in the narrative is unclear. What is clear is that the characters—Greeks, Sauromatians, and Scythians in the area of the sea of Azov as well as the character Eubiotus—also figure in Lucian's *Toxaris*. This latter is a tale about friendship in which Eubiotus, the half-brother of the king of the Bosporans, assumes the kingship on his brother's death. Meanwhile he lived among the Sauromatians, the very people mentioned in the published papyrus fragment. Lucian's tale and the novel are not very similar, but the fact of their location in the same area and the inclusion of at least one historical character, lends credence to Rostovtseff's belief[33] in the existence of a cycle of stories featuring peoples of the Scythian Bosporus, which formed the basis for the *Toxaris* and also *Calligone*. Further there are two possible narrative connections between the *Toxaris* and *Calligone*:

---

[30] (1956) 29–34.

[31] The existence of the fragment was generously called to our attention by Peter Parsons.

[32] Körte (1927) 271 was the first to suggest that Themisto was an actual character in the novel.

[33] (1931) 98–99.

(1) events in the tent—dismissal of attendants, removal of weapon, circulation of a false report—are closely paralleled by events in the Ares temple in *Toxaris* §50. (2) Themisto's reaction to her first view of Calligone in the unpublished fragment is verbally similar to *Toxaris* §44, where Arsakomas first sees Mazaia. Obviously not enough remains even to conjecture about the relationship of these two texts, but, as was the case with the *Antheia* fragment above and Xenophon of Ephesus, these texts obviously exist in a narrative field that is both broader and more interrelated than has been hitherto imagined.

The *Babyloniaca* is known to us now from Photius's summary, from a series of quotations in the *Souda* lexicon, selected primarily for their exotic vocabulary, and three long fragments preserved in the manuscript tradition. C. Habricht's Teubner edition conveniently prints Photius's epitome to the left with the fragments on the right opposite the section in the epitome in which they may reasonably have been presumed to occur. The bulk of scholarship on Iamblichus has been devoted to identifying fragments of the *Babyloniaca* in other sources and fixing their probable location in the epitome.

The novel originally consisted of 16 books and was written in the time of the Second Sophistic. Internal references to Verus's campaign against the Parthian king Vologaeses III suggest a terminus post quem of 164–166. According to the scholium on Photius, Iamblichus was

> a Syrian by birth, both on his father's and his mother's side, not a Syrian in the sense of a Greek living in Syria but a native. He spoke Syrian and lived in that culture until a tutor, as he tells us, who was Babylonian, took charge of him and taught him the language and culture of Babylon, and their stories, of which the one he is writing is an example. The Babylonian was taken prisoner in the time when Trajan entered Babylonia and the booty merchants sold him to a Syrian. He was learned in the wisdom of the barbarians, enough to have been one of the king's scribes when he was living in his fatherland. So this Iamblichus, speaking his native Syrian, learned Babylonian as well, and after that he says that he worked hard practicing Greek too, so as to be an accomplished rhetor.[34]

With its raw emotional power and improbable events, the *Babyloniaca* would strain the credulity of modern soap opera watchers. Not merely located in the environs of ancient Babylon, it boasts characters named

---

[34] If the statement is true and not simply what had become a plausible pedigree for novel writers (cf. Chariton of Aphrodisias and Heliodorus).

Mesopotamia and her twin brothers Tigris and Euphrates. At both the beginning and near the end of Photius's plot summary one of the two main characters, Rhodanes, finds himself tied to a cross (the same cross as it happens), a tangible correlative to his position in the novel, pulled between the generous and noble friendship of the farmer's daughter and the suicidal jealousy of his beloved Sinonis, between the old king of Babylon, who covets Sinonis, and the young king of Syria, who succeeds in marrying her. Sinonis's jealous violence reaches such a pitch that she attempts to kill a farmer's daughter when she finds her alone with Rhodanes, and she is so relentless in her desire to punish the girl for fancied wrongs that she has her condemned to sleep with the public executioner. No shy miss who feigns suicide to avoid unwelcome advances, Sinonis stabs to death a dissolute rich man who is smitten with her charms, and in a vengeful moment abandons Rhodanes to marry the young king of the Syrians.

The plot turns on extraordinarily contrived incidents of mistaken identity combined with narrative doublets, like the crucifixion scenes at the beginning and end of the novel. Tigris and Euphrates, who are sons of a priestess of Aphrodite, are frequently mistaken for Rhodanes, even by their own parents. The farmer's daughter is mistaken for Sinonis as well as is a young woman whose corpse is partly consumed by Rhodanes's dog. When Sinonis' father sees the corpse, he judges it to be Sinonis and kills himself in grief. When Rhodanes and an older companion, Soraichos, arrive, they make a similar error in judgment and prepare, the one by the sword, the other by hanging, to duplicate the preceding scene and to follow Sinonis' father to the grave. When Sinonis herself arrives it is only with difficulty that she convinces them of their error.

Risky as it is to venture a critical judgment about this novel on the basis of Photius's epitome, it does look as if the very structure of the *Babyloniaca* is deliberately designed to undermine the reader's preconceptions of appearance and reality. The events of the narrative constantly violate normative expectations: too many characters look physically like one another; there are recurring incidents of parents who cannot identify their own children; we meet social inversions like a just tax collector, or a priest condemned to be an executioner, or a woman who kills a man with a sword. Our novel heroine chooses to marry someone other than the hero. The behavior of the farmer's daughter in her modesty, cleverness, and genuine good nature meets our expectations for the novel's heroine far better than the actual behavior of Sinonis. Consider for example, the various levels of illusion and deception implicit in the following events: when the farmer's daughter (who looks like Sinonis) is condemned to sleep with an executioner, the executioner in question turns out to be Euphrates (who looks like Rhodanes). He has taken on the job to save his father, who is a priest and has been falsely condemned to the task, from incurring blood pollution, and she helps Euphrates to escape from this fate by disguising him in her clothing. Euphrates and the farmer's daughter frequently act out selfless behavior, and by doing so call into question the conduct of their doubles—the alleged hero and heroine of the story, Rhodanes and Sinonis—who in contrast often behave irrationally or ignobly. This violation of normal expectations can, of course, be a source of pleasure, particularly for the sophisticated reader. But such inversions may also be intended to query the very nature of the social fabric as a whole.

Criminal-Satiric Novels

Novels that focus on the seedier side of ancient Mediterranean life are represented in Greek by Lollianus's *Phoenicica* and Iolaus, possibly the fragments of Daulis and Tinouphis, as well as a number of smaller pieces. Until they came to light, of the extant material, only the two Roman novels, Petronius's *Satyricon* and Apuleius's *Golden Ass*, fell into this category. The fragmentary evidence suggests, however, that the type might have been fairly widespread in Greek fiction also, and that such novels may have evolved in closer relationship to each other than to ideal-romantic types against which they could only be parodies or inversions.[35] The low survival rate of these novels in later Greek culture may have been determined by the taste of subsequent readers or by censorship.[36]

Pride of place for the sensational must be given to the fragments of Lollianus's *Phoenicica*, the title of which has come down to us on the codex itself. There are two published fragments from this novel, one from an Oxyrhynchus roll, the other the Cologne codex first published by A. Henrichs in 1972. Replete with apparitions of the

---

[35] Walsh (1970) 7–9.

[36] For example, Julian's interdiction (*Ep*.89b) against "erotic stories" gives us some indication that censorship might have been at work.

dead, defloration, ritual murder and cannibalism, and bandits dressing up like ghosts, the *Phoenicica* gains in significance for literary historians because of its clear connection to Apuleius' *Golden Ass*. Currently we have five scenes from the two papyri linked together only by the presence of an enigmatic character named Glaucetes. (1) In the Oxyrhynchus fragment (*P.Oxy.*1368), we find Glaucetes riding along when a ghost of a young man appears to him claiming: "there I lie beneath that plane-tree and with me a beautiful maiden, both of us slain."[37] Glaucetes, nods, then rides on until at dusk he finds a stable in which to spend the night. As he settles in we learn that "meanwhile a woman came down by a ladder which led down from the upper storey into the stable."[38] At this point the fragment breaks off. From the Cologne codex we have four more scenes: (2) a night party or festival celebrated on the rooftops; (3) a young man being initiated into the mysteries of Aphrodite by Persis, a lady who seems to have an inner or secret chamber in her house. The scene breaks off when her mother arrives. The relationship of these three scenes to each other and to the story as a whole is not certain, but these final two scenes (4 and 5) must follow each other: (4) a man dressed in a red sash or loin cloth appears to sacrifice a child or a servant (παῖς), then cut out the heart, slice it up, and feed it to his companions, who then swear an oath of fealty; and (5) a hideout in which a party seems to be taking place. A character named Androtimus complains about belching and flatulence induced by the food, which may or may not have included portions of the victim's heart, while wine is served to the company in a vessel bordered with a frieze depicting the battle of Lapiths and Centaurs. After drinking, the eleven guards, who have been left standing watch over some corpses, strip the bodies of the dead, hoist them out of the windows, and drop them over the side of a cliff.[39] The group then dresses up, some in black face, some painted white, and exits in the pre-dawn hours for further skulldug-

---

[37] Ll. 3–6: κεῖμαι δὴ ὑπὸ τῇ π[λα]ιτανίστῳ ἐκείνῃ καὶ μετ' ἐ|μοῦ κόρη καλή, ἄμφω ἀνῃρη|μένοι, Stephens-Winkler (1995) 326–27.

[38] Ll. 26–29: κἀν τούτῳ κάτεισι γυνὴ διὰ κλίμακος ἣ ἦν ἐξ ὑπερῴ[ου ἄ]γουσα κάτω εἰς τὴν ἐπί[πόστασιν]..., Stephens-Winkler (1995) 326–27.

[39] Accepting Stramaglia's restoration of B 1 verso 26: ἀφῆκαν κάτω εἰς τοὺ[ς κρημνού]ς, citing as a parallel Lucian's *Ass Tale* §24, where the robbers throw the body of the old crone who has hanged herself down over a cliff (ἐς τὸν κρημνὸν κάτω ἀφῆκαν). If correct, the supplement makes it even less likely that the location of the action could be Egypt, and it adds to the series of parallels between Lollianus and Apuleius outlined below.

gery. Androtimus is left with the guards. An escape may be in progress when the fragment breaks off.

Glaucetes is identified by name in scenes (1), (3) and (4); in none of these scenes is he an ego-narrator. Only in scene (5) can we be certain of Androtimus's presence, where he is speaking, though he is not the ego-narrator. Scene (3), however, is recounted in the first person,[40] though the name of the speaker is not known, and scene (5) shows some evidence of an ego-narrator.[41] Previous commentators have assumed that Androtimus was the central character, linked romantically with Persis as the *Liebespaar*. This has its attractions, especially given that Persis and Androtimus hint at a play on the names of Perseus and Andromeda, with roles reversed, as would have been the case if Persis took the lead in Androtimus' sexual initiation. But if scene (3) is narrated in Androtimus's voice, scene (5) is not.

The original editor identified the bandits as Egyptian boukoloi because of the clear parallels between the *Scheintod* in Achilles Tatius where, to the onlookers, Leucippe appears to have been eviscerated and her entrails consumed by a band of boukoloi and another incident of cannibalism of boukoloi recorded in Cassius Dio.[42] In point of fact, however, the criminal band in the Cologne codex are never called boukoloi and there are no indications that the action must be located in Egypt. Jones and Winkler have independently demonstrated that the sequence of events in scene (5) above is very close in detail to the incident of the robber cave in Apuleius.[43] Therefore, it is reasonable to consider the possibility that Lollianus's criminals are bandits similar to those in *The Golden Ass*, and that the action is taking place in a similar locale, not necessarily in Egypt. An inventory of coincidences between *Phoenicica* and *The Golden Ass* continue to mount: (1) we have a dead man lying under a plane tree in the Oxyrhynchus fragment, reminiscent of the location of the death of Socrates in Apuleius 1.18.8. (2) The scene of defloration is not unlike Lucius's encounter with Fotis.[44] (3) The belching and flatulence with which

---

[40] A 2 recto 8–9: καὶ τότε πρῶτον ἐπειρά[θ]ην συνου[σίας]. "And then I had my first experience of sexual intercourse."
[41] B 1 Verso 14 appears to contain the words ὡ]ς ἐμο[ὶ δ]οκεῖ, which suggests the presence of an ego narrator.
[42] See Achilles Tatius 3.15.4–6 and Cassius Dio 72.4.
[43] Jones (1980) 251–53, Winkler (1980a) 158–59.
[44] A. Henrichs (1972) 111 even conjectured that there is a female character named Notis in this scene.

scene (5) above opens is verbally reminiscent of Apuleius 4.3.10 where the ass spatters his attackers with a discharge of watery feces that serves as a distraction. The belching and flatulence in Lollianus, particularly if the sacrifice is a *Scheintod*, may also serve to deflect the group's attention. (4) Events take place in a similar order in the party scenes in both texts: the bandits enter, there is feasting, mention of Lapiths and Centaurs, drinking, singing songs, dressing up in white and black costume and exiting into night for criminal purposes, followed by an attempted escape in Apuleius and possibility of escape in Lollianus.[45] (5) A. Stramaglia[46] suggests that when the guards lift the corpses out of the windows they throw them down over a cliff, just as the bandits dispose of the body of the old crone who has hanged herself in the pseudo-Lucianic *Ass Tale* §24. If correct, it adds to our series of parallels. (6) The guards remove a breast band from an apparently dead girl in Lollianus;[47] this is described in very similar language to Apuleius 10.21.1: *taenia quoque qua decoras devinxerat papillas . . .*

What does this add up to? There are too many convergences in these two novels in too small a space for the pattern be accidental, but what relationship they bear to each other or to a common ancestor is difficult to assess. Given the fact that (at least as far as we can presently determine) the *Phoenicica* does not include a character who is transformed into an ass—a circumstance that seems to have been the central feature both of Apuleius and of his Greek predecessor—it is unlikely that Lollianus is the immediate predecessor to Apuleius. Lollianus could have borrowed from Apuleius directly, or from the original Greek ass tale, which Photius knew and compared— favorably—with the version attributed to Lucian,[48] but in doing so he omitted the metamorphosis. Why he might have done so, is of course impossible to judge, but it is fair to say that very many of the incidents in Apuleius as well as in the extant *Ass Tale* make exciting reading on their own terms, independent of the metamorphosis. One can easily imagine a novel constructed to tantalize the reader with expectations of a metamorphosis that was systematically denied.

---

[45] The parallels are even more striking when we consider that Apuleius 4.9–21 consists of three robber's tales inserted into the main narrative and 4.28–6.24 is another, much longer insert, the tale of Cupid and Psyche.
[46] See above, note 39.
[47] B 1 verso 24–25: τὴν ταινίαν Ι ἐν ἧι ἡ κόρη τοὺς μαστοὺς ἐδέδετ[ο.
[48] Photius cod. 129.

Iolaus was originally published as "A Greek Satyricon?"[49] less for any similarity in plot than for its combination of sacred and profane, if not downright vulgar, packaged in a combination of prose and verse. The fragmentary column contains a salacious account of one character "initiating" another into the rites of the galli—the castrated priests of Cybele—so that the initiate can effect a liaison with a young woman who has captured his fancy.[50] The text consists of a prose sequence followed by 20 lines of Sotadeans—a meter that had come in both Greek and Latin forms to be associated with the priesthood of the galli.

Tinouphis is another text in prosimetrum, this time featuring catalectic iambic tetrameters,[51] and set in an Egypto-Persian milieu. The cast includes a public executioner, who apparently saves the prophet Tinouphis with a trick involving a brick. Parallels that suggest themselves are the story of Rhampsinitus and the thief in Herodotus (2.121) and the various clever strategies of the executioners who populate Iamblichus—the priest turned executioner, the son who takes his place, and the farmer's daughter who takes the son's place. The fragment also contains a number of word games—the prophet is said to be the "king's savior," a play on the cult title of the Ptolemies, "king savior;" Magoas is reminiscent of the Persian eunuch Bagoas; Sosias[52] with his trick of the brick is the "savior" of the prophet, who in turn is the "savior" of the king.

Iolaus and *Tinouphis* raise the question of the relationship of Latin novels to Greek and the frequency with which novels may have employed prosimetry. Latin models for prosimetrum are well known. Petronius's *Satyricon* is the locus classicus. And within Latin literature the form of Menippean satire[53] popularized by Varro may be said to have taken firm root. On the Greek side, however, apart from the lost Menippus himself, we have only the Menippean satires of Lucian, which vary considerably in style from the Latin texts. *Iolaus* and *Tinouphis* are closer in style and subject matter to the extant Latin material than to Lucian, but does this mean that they are descendants of Latin prototypes (surely, a possibility by the second century)

---

[49] Parsons (1971).
[50] L. 30: ὅτι δόλῳ σὺ βινεῖν μέλλεις.
[51] M. West (1982) 15 believes this metric form may well be Latin in origin and "typically post-Hadrianic." For the opposite opinion, see Haslam (1981).
[52] Sosias's name is from the same root as σωτήρ = savior.
[53] Relihan (1993).

or were they part of a flourishing though now lost Greek prosimetric tradition? Again, no definitive answer presents itself, but it does suggest that it is wise to keep an open mind about the directions that literary influence might take. Though convention, aided and abetted by the Roman writers themselves, has dictated that Greek material must somehow precede Latin, among an international literary elite conversant in both languages, there is no reason why the reverse might not be true and a stunning tale like Petronius's *Satyricon* might lend itself to imitation by subsequent Greek writers.

The possibility that the fragment known as *Daulis* belonged to a novel narrative was first suggested by Stephanie West, who claimed that it was an "ugly duckling, an unobjectionable romance fragment which has been generally neglected on the assumption that it is a rather freakish specimen of some other genre."[54] Indeed, the three remaining columns of the papyrus roll contain an exchange that is both blood-curdling and rhetorically ornate. Daulis, the head of a band of men who intend to sack the shrine at Delphi and purge it of the false and thieving prophets who infest the place, begins with this imprecation: "He (sc. Ares) rejoices in slaughters of men, and I too take pleasure in them... Now as a worthy offering for him I shall pour out a libation of your blood."[55] As a devotee of Ares, Daulis provides himself with a fine literary pedigree: the host of criminals who populate the novels—the band in Lollianus, Hippothous in Xenophon of Ephesus, the leaders of boukoloi in Achilles Tatius, and Thyamis in Heliodorus. The prophet who is Daulis's potential victim in his turn asks "seer Apollo" and the Furies to accept Daulis as a sacrificial victim and immolate him upon those very altars.

Antonius Diogenes

Travel and adventure occur in all of the examples we have of ancient fiction, but Antonius Diogenes' *Unbelievable Things Beyond Thule* appears to have been unique. The *Liebespaar*—if that is what we should call them—of Antonius Diogenes' novel are well past their teen years and spend their time engaging in narrative flashbacks littered with

---

[54] (1971) 96. It was originally published as an aretology of Apollo.
[55] Ll. 1–2: χαίρει δὲ σφαγαῖς ἀνθρ[ώ]πων, αἷς καὶ ἐγὼ τέρπομαι τῶν ἐκείνωι καθοσιω[μέ]νων σπονδῶν καταρ|χόμενος, Stephens-Winkler (1995) 380–81.

geographical and philosophical lore, like the waxing and waning of Astraius's eyes. Further its narrative agenda appears to be too complex for it to be understood simply as a type of ideal-romantic fiction, or even a parody of that type. Photius believed it was the earliest example of novel writing, and whether or not we choose to accept his assessment, it must be acknowledged that Diogenes' sophisticated and intricate style puts him on a par with Heliodorus and Iamblichus for self-conscious manipulation of the narrative material. Apart from Photius's summary, there are two, three, or four papyrus fragments of Antonius Diogenes (see below), and several quotations from his Pythagorean books to be found in John Lydus's *On Months* and in Porphyry's *Life of Pythagoras*. Further, Diogenes is cited by ancient sources more than any other ancient novelist. This comparative wealth of secondary tradition no doubt results from several unusual features of his text: its fictionalization of geographical facts (or what could pass for such); what appears to have been a relative marginalization of the erotic elements in the story; and the inclusion of uplifting Pythagorean wisdom. The loss of this novel is perhaps the most seriously felt, because what we do know of it suggests that if we could read it whole, it might well require us to reevaluate the trajectory as well as the boundaries of Greek narrative fiction.

One of the most striking features of *The Unbelievable Things Beyond Thule* is the fact that there are so many narrators re-telling each others' stories. Diogenes sets in motion his Chinese box arrangement of receding narratives by prefacing the whole tale with a letter to Faustinus, in turn either incorporating or further prefacing another letter to a lady named Isidora.[56] In the letter to her, Diogenes quotes a letter of Balagrus, a soldier of Alexander, who discovered cypress wood tablets in a sepulcher outside of the city of Tyre and transcribed them for his wife, Phila. This letter includes a transcript of a text prepared by one Erasinides at the suggestion of Cymbas, who has visited Tyre and conversed with Deinias. It is only at this point that we encounter the central figure, Deinias, who recounts his journey from Arcadia around the world and then to Tyre. His travels take him in a north-easterly direction until he reaches Thule, the northernmost point on the ancient geographical landscape, and in his travels encounters a wide variety of characters who tell him of

---

[56] Isidora is generally taken to be Diogenes' sister, though Schissel von Fleschenberg (1912) 101 assumes she is Faustinus' sister.

their own adventures or of adventures that have been told to them. He meets, for example, Derkyllis and Mantineas, a brother and sister originally from Tyre, who have fled the evil attentions of the Egyptian sorcerer, Paapis, through whose designs their parents were cast into a deathlike trance. And they themselves were condemned to live by night and sleep by day. Derkyllis, with whom Deinias falls in love, in turn relates to him her experiences, including her visit to the underworld, her encounter with Astraius, and, in turn, what she learned from Astraius about Pythagoras and Mnesarchus. It is only at the point when he returns from Thule that Deinias relates his travels along with the tales he has heard to a friend (Cymbas) whom he instructs to have the material written on cypress wood tablets, thus setting off the narrative chain of events. The complexity of this interlocking structure will have forced the reader continuously to be aware of the presence of a narrator. Indeed this feature of the novel seems to require that the only present-time events are acts of narrating and listening. In contrast to the ideal-romantic type, the lovers Deinias and Derkyllis do not have adventures together, they tell tales.

Moreover, no other ancient novel for which we have evidence so deliberately constructs a self-presentation which is both serious and undercutting of its own seriousness. The letter addressed to Faustinus describes a work that has been laboriously assembled from a wealth of historical, geographical, and other material, and to which a list of the sources consulted is apparently appended. By this device, Diogenes would appear to be establishing the "truth" of his account by locating himself within a "serious" scholarly tradition. But the letter to Isidora confirms the "truth" of the tale, not by citing sources, but by meticulously accounting for the production and survival of the manuscript. Thus the letters offer mutually exclusive accounts of the production of the text and hence set up competing frames of reference for its truthfulness. By organizing the whole around two such contradictory letters Diogenes touts his seriousness in claiming to Faustinus that he has organized the scattered traditions of paradoxography into a single encyclopedia, citations and all; but by providing us with two letters and two verification procedures which contradict each other he forces us to question the veracity of his claims, and indeed seriousness of his narrative intentions in general.

It is well to focus on this characteristic of Diogenes' fiction when evaluating many of the statements made about his text. Photius, for example, specifically linked Antonius with Antiphanes of Berge, a writer of improbable tales if not downright falsehoods. So synonymous with mendacity was Antiphanes that the Greeks even coined the verb "to bergaize" (βεργαΐζειν),[57] which meant to tell outrageous lies. Further, Photius tells us that in his letter to Faustinus that Diogenes styled himself "a poet of Old Comedy."[58] Thus Diogenes deliberately links himself with notorious writers of fantasy like Aristophanes, whose heroes migrate to far-off lands such as Cloudcookooland. It is unwise to reject the literal sense of this,[59] considering that Lucian in his *True Histories* also links his fantastic adventure with Aristophanes: "I called to mind Aristophanes the poet, a wise and truthful man, whose writings were wrongly disbelieved" (1.29). The premises of the joke can hardly be missed.[60]

Which leads us to a consideration of the Pythagorean elements of this novel. Undoubtedly the fact that Diogenes included material from Pythagoras's life contributed to his relatively higher esteem in antiquity than other novels seem to have enjoyed. But is this a novel devoted to serious philosophical exposition adhering to doctrinal purity or is the Pythagorean lore, like the double credentials, pointing in two directions? Modern scholars have sometimes suggested that Diogenes was a committed Pythagorean and that his book promoted the truth of that philosophy.[61] Certainly the Pythagorean material was sufficiently convincing that it found its way into subsequent and seriously intended discussions like Porphyry's *Life of Pythagoras*. Reyhl is doubtless correct about the central position that Pythagorean material occupies in the novel (books 12–14).[62] But while it may be central, it is difficult to reconcile Pythagoras's injunction to truth-telling with Diogenes' rather more casual if not downright arbitrary attitude about fact and fiction. Note that the Pythagorean material is the most deeply embedded of the interlocked narratives. According to Photius, it is Derkyllis who recounts to Deinias the Pythagorean lore she had learned from Astraius just after her account of the underworld. Perhaps the Pythagorean material was placed at the core of the novel as a hard-won kernel of truth for the serious reader

---

[57] Steph.Byz. s.v. Βέργη.
[58] 111a34–5: λέγει δὲ ἑαυτὸν ὅτι ποιητής ἐστι κωμῳδίας παλαιᾶς. See Swain (1992).
[59] Rohde (1914³) 251/270 n. 2. Note that Di Gregorio (1968) 200 n. 1 also suspects a satiric or parodic element in Diogenes missed by Photius.
[60] For the relationship of Lucian and Antonius Diogenes, see Morgan (1985).
[61] Bürger (1903) 13, Merkelbach (1962) 225–33; Di Gregorio (1968) 211.
[62] See Reyhl (1969) 121.

who has finally succeeded in peeling off so many layers of narration. But there is another possibility. Pythagoras was praised for his stability: "... his bodily condition was invariant: it was not at one time healthy, at another time sick, not sometimes waxing fat, other times waning thin, and his soul too always displayed the same disposition through his face, not sometimes relaxed in pleasure, other times tense with pain. In fact, no one ever saw him laughing or crying."[63] This unvarying habit does not sit easily with Diogenes' stories of lunar-influenced waxing and waning, or indeed of characters like Derkyllis and Mantineas who systematically live by night and sleep by day. A cynic might even suspect that Diogenes chose to write about Pythagoras precisely because his philosophical position perceptibly gravitates to the furthest extreme from that of Diogenes, and because Pythagoras and his disciples in the details of their lives—at least the details that Diogenes chooses to tell us—constitute fair examples of unbelievable things.

Two papyrus fragments from this novel have been certainly identified: one contains an encounter between Derkyllis and her nurse Myrto, quite possibly as part of Derkyllis's trip to Hades. Her nurse, who cannot speak, nevertheless writes on school tablets a warning to her mistress about the Egyptian Paapis. A second papyrus, which comes from the beginning of a book roll (either Book 4, 14, or 24), is a scene between Derkyllis and Deinias in which she appears to be relating her travails to him.

Additionally, P.Mich.5 has been plausibly connected to this novel. In this fragment a father relates to someone who seems to be a magician that his daughter has fallen in love with a phantom or an apparition. The magician's speech should make us suspicious because, contrary to standard operating procedure for magicians, this one denies, in the most rhetorically elegant Greek, his ability to control love:

> if I order the moon, it will descend; if I wish to prevent the day, night will linger on for me; and again, if we demand the day, light will not depart; if I wish to sail the sea, I have no need of a ship; if I wish to

---

[63] Porphyry *Life of Pythagoras* §35: τὸ σῶμα... τὴν αὐτὴν ἕξιν διεφύλαττεν, οὐ ποτὲ μὲν ὑγιαῖνον ποτὲ δὲ νοσοῦν, οὐδ' αὖ ποτὲ μὲν πιαινόμενον καὶ αὐξανόμενον ποτὲ δὲ λεπτυνόμενον καὶ ἰσχναινόμενον, ἥ τε ψυχὴ τὸ ὅμοιον ἦθος ἀεὶ διὰ τῆς ὄψεως παρεδήλου. οὔτε γὰρ ὑφ' ἡδονῆς διεχεῖτο πλέον οὔθ' ὑπ' ἀνίας συνεστέλλετο, οὐδ' ἐπίδηλος ἦν χαρὰ ἢ λύπη κάτοχος, ἀλλ' οὐδὲ γελάσαντα ἢ κλαύσαντά τίς ποτ' ἐκεῖνον ἐθεάσατο, Stephens-Winkler (1995) 138–41.

move through the air, I shall become weightless. For love alone I find no drug, none with power to create it, none with power to abate it. For the earth in fear of that god bears no such plant. But if anyone has it to give, I beseech, I implore, "Give it to me—I wish to drink it down, I wish to rub it on."[64]

Reyhl has persuasively conjectured that the father is Mnason, the daughter, Derkyllis, and the magician, Paapis, and that, in fact, Paapis is engineering events by causing the girl to fall in love with an apparition.

A fourth papyrus (previously published as *Herpyllis*) also bears scrutiny in connection with *Unbelievable Things*. It consists of two characters—a man and a woman—who take leave of one another and disembark on separate ships just at the point when a storm comes up. Of course, the ships are separated. The bulk of the text is given over to a highly elaborated description of the storm, ending with the sailors sighting St. Elmo's fire, an omen of propitious outcome. The ships lose sight of each other near Lakter, a southern promontory on the island of Cos. Identification of the piece depends on a woman's name.[65] Although the original editors read the name as Ἑρπυλλίς,[66] Gallavotti suggested that the name might be Δερκυλλίς. The letters are both cursive and too broken to claim either reading with certitude. But the similarity of the two names, very like each other without much resemblance to the names of other female characters who inhabit the novels, should give us pause. Bury,[67] reading Ἑρπυλλίς believed that the fragment was an earlier predecessor of Antonius Diogenes. Equally it might be a later imitator. Apart from the matter of the name, there are other reasons to suspect that this text bears some relationship to Diogenes' novel. The narrator and the woman, whatever her name, have been generally taken as the *Liebespaar*, though there have always been doubters.[68] The language of departure—

---

[64] Ll. 2–20: κἂν σελήνῃ κελεύσω, καταβήσεται· κἂν | κωλῦσαι θελ[ή]σω τὴν ἡμέ|ραν, ἡ νύξ μοι μενεῖ· κἂν | δεήθωμεν πάλιν ἡμέρας, τὸ φῶς οὐκ ἀπελεύσεται· κἂν πλεῦσαι θελήσω | τὴν θάλατταν, οὐ δέομαι | νεώς· κἂν δι' ἀέρος ἐλθεῖν, | κουφισθήσομαι. ἐρωτικὸν | μόνον οὐχ εὑρίσκω φάρ|μακον—οὐ ποιῆσαι δυνάμε|νον, οὐ παῦσαι δυνάμενον. | ἡ γῆ γὰρ φοβουμένη τὸν | θεὸν οὐ φέρει. εἰ δέ τις ἔχει | καὶ δίδωσιν, αἰτῶ, δέομαι, | "δότε· πιεῖν θέλω, χρίσασθαι | θέλω," Stephens-Winkler (1995) 176–77.

[65] It occurs twice in the fragment, once missing all but -υλλις and again where the initial wedge-shaped letter might be a δε- ligature rather than ε- alone, followed by a clear ρ and the feet of a letter (either κ- or π- would fit).

[66] Most recently Kussl (1991) 129 n. 99 asserts the correctness of their reading.

[67] In Smyly (1909).

[68] See, e.g., O. Crusius (1897) 1–2.

lamentation, throwing kisses, halcyon wails of grief—are in fact not characteristic of erotic partings, but of mourning,[69] and it is worth considering that the pair are not lovers at all but, for example, a brother and sister who are grieving over a common misfortune, not necessarily their separation from each other, about which nothing is said.[70] The location may also be significant: it is in that general vicinity of Cos that Photius tells us that Diogenes' brother-sister were separated up after leaving Tyre.

Conclusions

Drawing conclusions from the growing number of fragments of Greek novels is, like reconstructing the texts themselves, a delicate and occasionally treacherous enterprise. Nonetheless, some conclusions about the identity of fragments, their style, their interdependence, and the boundaries of the field we call the "novel" will already have suggested themselves.

Daulis is typical of a number of smaller papyrus fragments that have come to light. They often contain a brief moment of exciting narrative such as a man and woman escaping from a palace at nightfall,[71] a man recognizing the person who induced him to commit suicide at the very moment he has completed the act,[72] a woman who abandons her infant son in a vineyard,[73] and a sudden appearance of a god before a group of fearful onlookers.[74] The elements in them are reminiscent of events that take place in larger texts, so it is easy to imagine that they belong in the growing corpus of narrative fiction, but they are so small that it is impossible to conjecture very much about their plots or their characters. Daulis, for example, might play a central role in a thrilling story of a counter-cultural hero or be no more than a vivid minor character in an otherwise typical ideal-romantic novel. It is always necessary to keep in mind

---

[69] Kussl (1991) 138–40, following Wilcken (1901) 269 n. 1, has argued that this scene is closely parallel to the Ceyx-Alcyone passage in Ovid's *Metamorphosis*.

[70] In this regard it should be noted that Diogenes' brother-sister pair are fleeing from Tyre after they have accidently caused their parents to enter a deathlike sleep. Surely cause for lamentation.

[71] "Goatherd and the Palace Guards," Stephens-Winkler (1995) 416–421.

[72] "Nightmare or Necromancy?," Stephens-Winkler (1995) 422–428.

[73] "Staphulos," Stephens-Winkler (1995) 429–437.

[74] "Apparition," Stephens-Winkler (1995) 409–415.

the possibility that these scenes belong to some other ancient genre like rhetorical exercise, and not to a novel at all.

Over the last century many fragments have come to be identified as "romance" when in fact they have turned out to belong in other literary categories. The most interesting (and consequential) examples of mistaken identity have been *The Dream of Nectanebo* and *The Story of Tefnut*. Both of these texts are translations from Egyptian into Greek, and they serve as the linchpin in J.W.B. Barns's influential argument that the translation of Egyptian narratives could have provided the stimulus for novel-writing in Greek. Undoubtedly both belong to the general field of narrative, but their fictionality is hardly of the same order as the material included in the discussion above as falling within the confines of "novel." *The Story of Tefnut*, is of course an animal fable, a fictional category for which there are many examples both within and without Greek literature. But no such fables are currently counted as "novels," even when the boundaries are expanded to include narratives beyond the canonical seven. Human-centered activity seems, at least for Greco-Roman sensibilities (in contrast to Egyptian), to have been a sine qua non for novel writing. Moreover, it is difficult to imagine that the translation of a work like *Tefnut* could have stimulated the writing of extended narrative fiction of such a different sort in Greek. Although the extant portion of *The Dream of Nectanebo* has the look of a picaresque adventure, in reality it belongs to a category of Egyptian writing known as *Königsnovelle*,[75] a subset of admonition literature, addressed to a king or new ruler, informing him of potential disasters within the land unless he takes corrective measures. Sometimes he does, more often he does not and the text presages social upheaval. As such, it is unlikely to have served as the basis for a nationalistic novel featuring Nectanebo, the last native king of Egypt. In fact a comparison between *Nectanebo* and *Sesonchosis* reveals interesting differences: the narrative of *The Dream of Nectanebo* is identifiably Egyptian even without the names, but without the names, we could have no reason to suspect that *Sesonchosis* was set in Egypt. This is not to deny categorically that the translation of either or both of these texts could have stimulated the writing of long fictional narratives in Greek prose, but it requires more than the mere fact of their existence to demonstrate that they did.

The style even of very small fragments, like the majority of the

---

[75] See Herrmann (1938); Koenen (1985).

larger ones, adheres for the most part to rules of ancient rhetoric, employing the series of highly artificial conventions that were taught and assiduously practiced in the schools. Connectives between sentences and clauses are meticulously employed, the vocabulary is usually restricted to Attic words, and clauses end in a small number of favored rhythmic patterns. Although two fragments, *Sesonchosis* and *Lollianus*, regularly admit hiatus, for the most part, hiatus tends to be avoided.[76] Many pieces boast an ornate syntax and full panoply of tropes. Narratives are complex, often employing framing devices, ecphrases, and literary allusions. The range in sophistication found in the fragments is considerable—the storm scene in *Herpyllis* is a narrative tour-de-force that would grace the oeuvre of any ancient rhetorician or novelist, while *Sesonchosis* distinctly lacks compositional finesse, evoking comparison with such stylistically unpretentious productions as the *Alexander Romance* or Christian martyr acts. *Sesonchosis* is markedly less sophisticated in its style than *Ninus*, although its fragments are to be dated much later, in the late third or early fourth century A.D. This raises a question: should we consider lack of stylistic sophistication as a mark of an early date of composition, and, as a consequence, should we suppose the *Sesonchosis* fragments to be later copies of a very early novel pre-dating *Ninus*, or do we suppose it merely to be late and not particularly stylish production within an already very sophisticated field? The question is not as naive as it might seem; in fact, style has often been used as a criterion for dating the novels and novel fragments, on the assumption that texts written during the Second Sophistic and in the heyday of Atticism must reflect those trends.

The relatively wider variety of type found among the fragments calls into question the apparent dominance of the ideal-romantic as the generic norm for Greek novels. There is a number of historical fictions centered on non-Greek characters, at least one of which (*Ninus*) is of a very early date and another of which (Iamblichus) holds its own with any of the extant novels. These, along with the greater abundance of criminal satiric material, suggest that the type that Chariton's novel came to represent may have been only one of a variety of narrative options for ancient fiction writers and the survival of this type to the exclusion of the others may have reflected

---

[76] See Reeve (1971b) for an analysis of incidence of hiatus in the novels and novel fragments.

the tastes of subsequent copyists and readers rather than those of the writers themselves and their contemporary audiences.

Perhaps the most unexpected picture that the fragments present is a much higher degree of fictional interactivity than the extant seven now allow us to infer. As the arguments above will have made clear, Lollianus' *Phoenicica* is much closer to Apuleius and to the *Ass Tale* attributed to Lucian than the original editor believed. The story now known as *Calligone* overlaps with Lucian's *Toxaris* not only in details of plot, character, and location, but even in narrative echoes. The *Antheia* fragment shares names and narrative elements with the plot of Xenophon's *Ephesiaca*. The fragment known as *Herpyllis*, if it is not actually by Antonius Diogenes, must exist in some close relationship to that work. In sum, consideration of fragments must bring us to a realization that ancient novels were at once more numerous, more complex in their stylistic and narrative range, and more heavily interdependent, not only upon other novels but upon the broader categories of narrative fiction, than was once thought to be the case. Further study of the fragments and further fragmentary finds will undoubtedly increase our appreciation for the variety and artistry of the novel writing enterprise in antiquity.

16. THE ANCIENT NOVEL BECOMES CHRISTIAN

Richard Pervo

Introduction

Among the problems confronting those who would sketch a profile of the ancient Christian novel are the definition of "ancient novel" and the properties that might make it "Christian." Must an ancient novel perforce focus upon the struggles of a heterosexual couple to achieve domestic tranquillity? Will these struggles necessarily include travel about the Mediterranean world? These questions reflect the influence of the most comprehensive study of the subject ever issued, Erwin Rohde's classic *Der griechische Roman und seine Vorläufer*.[1] This monograph exudes three major nineteenth century contributions and concerns: a genetic focus upon sources and origins, an emphasis upon original creativity, and an intellectual disdain for light fiction. The first of these items continues to intrigue (or plague) scholars,[2] while the last has lost its luster, but preference for "an entirely fictitious story narrated in prose and ruled in its course by erotic motifs and a series of adventures which mostly take place during a journey ... in a realistically portrayed world which, even when set by the author in an age long since past, essentially reflects everyday life ... [in the Graeco-Roman world]"[3] retains a strong and restraining grip upon critical study.

One reason for this orientation is the recognition that, although ancients had various terms for, and understandings of, "fiction," they had no designation for the genre now called "the novel."[4] Since this is a modern label employed for the purpose of contemporary analysis, it is best restricted to the prevailing modern use.[5] The novel is,

---

[1] First published in 1876, Rohde's monograph appeared with a valuable preface by W. Schmid in 1914 and has often been reprinted (Hildesheim: Georg Ohlms, 1974), with an additional essay by K. Kerényi in the more recent editions.

[2] Anderson (1984) is a recent example of the quest for origins.

[3] Holzberg (1995) 26–27.

[4] Bowersock (1994) 1–14 offers a recent discussion of fiction in antiquity. The question of ancient terminology for novels has often been discussed. A current example is Holzberg (1995a) 93–96.

[5] Selden, in an interesting essay (1994) esp. p. 43, stresses that the "ancient novel"

however, a genre of nearly matchless elasticity and includes many sub-types and variations. More importantly, behind the assignment of privilege to the "entirely fictitious" (if this actually exists)[6] stands the Romantic demand for unique and original creativity in literature and the arts, a value not shared by prior eras.[7] There is no question that even the romantic Greek novel first appeared in "historical" dress.[8] If any type should be given a privileged status, it is the "historical romance." Finally, the comparative study of literature and its forms requires that relatively "pure" types and representatives be studied in conjunction with "proximate genres." Kindred forms help delimit the options available and indicate both literary antecedents and the evolution/reception of particular genres and sub-genres. Therefore in this essay "novel" will be used in an inclusive sense, embracing a variety of prose fictions, in particular, historical novels.

The prefatory adjective "Christian" is less perplexing but requires brief attention, for it bears upon the reception and survival of ancient novels in general. In the first place, religious flavor or orientation, which might yield "Isiac," "Aphrodisian," and Jewish types of novels, for example,[9] is not the best criterion for the classification of this literature. It may mean no more than the adjectives "Greek" or "Latin" as used to qualify novels. Other possibilities include novels written by Christians, a difficult category to define,[10] novels that convey a form of Christian message, or novels used by Christians to edify and/or instruct the faithful and possibly to attract adherents. I shall employ the third of these options and thus include—without imperialistic intent—Jewish novels and novellas. Advantages of this approach

---

is a relatively modern invention. His observations are important, but he must also admit that Photius already perceived formal similarities. Many of Photius's literary values were shaped by antiquity. He is the only author known to have both read and commented upon both ancient novels and ApocActs.

[6] Even modern fiction often has bases in actual experiences, sometimes requiring warnings that any relation to actual persons or events is entirely coincidental. Ancient writers normally based their fictions upon sources.

[7] Romanticism permeates the famous claim of Perry (1967) 175 that the first novel was the creation of an individual who invented it on "a Tuesday afternoon in July."

[8] *Ninus, Parthenope,* and *Callirhoe* are obvious examples.

[9] Apuleius's *Metamorphoses* (and possibly *An Ephesian Tale*) might be called "Isiac," *Callirhoe* "Aphrodisian," and *Daphnis and Chloe,* "Dionysian," with considerable scholarly support. "Jewish" might be an ethnic or national category, as at least superficially in the (original?) Hebrew Esther.

[10] Byzantines were pleased to report that both Achilles Tatius and Heliodorus became Christians.

relate not only to antecedents, that is the degree to which Jewish fiction was source, model, and stimulus to Christian literary activity, but also to a kindred result: much ancient Jewish fiction has endured only because of Christian use.[11]

Jewish Fiction

The remains of this material have much to offer students of Greek fiction, expanding the contents of a rather slender corpus, showing a nexus between "Greek" and "Oriental" traditions, and illustrating the literary process of hellenization. In style and content they are, by and large, "popular." Jewish fiction thus helps to illuminate two of the classic issues surrounding ancient novels: where did they come from, and who read them? Since they can be placed within a chronological frame, these works also permit observations about literary development within an identifiable history and tradition.

Lawrence M. Wills offers a typology of ancient Jewish fiction.[12] One deals with "national heroes," such as Moses or Joseph. A second type includes novellas or short novels centered about figures who do not figure prominently in the traditional Israelite history, including Esther and Daniel. Although replete with historical errors, these works have a patina of historical color. Thirdly are more historical works, centered upon individuals of the relatively recent past. The items in this last category lie on the tenuous boundary between "bad" or novelistic history and historical fiction and will not be discussed here.[13]

A prime example of the "National Hero" type is the work of Artapanus, who wrote in Egypt, probably ca. 200 B.C.E. Only fragments of this work survive, excerpts culled by the Christian historian Eusebius (IV C.E.) from the work of an earlier universal historian,

---

[11] Examples include parts of Daniel (Susanna, Bel and the Snake), Judith, Tobit, and *Aseneth*. All save the last are in the Christian Bible but not the Hebrew Scriptures, indicating not only preservation but also official use. Modern discoveries (such as the Dead Sea Scrolls, unpublished elements of which include fragments of Hebrew narrative reminiscent of both Esther and Susanna) reveal that Jews once possessed these or kindred texts, but largely abandoned them or incorporated elements of them into a large corpus of haggadic (legendary) material.

[12] Wills (1994) and (1995).

[13] This hypothetical type appears to underlie some of the sources used by Josephus in his *Jewish Antiquities*. Examples are romantic accounts of the the powerful Tobiad clan (*Ant.*12.154–236) and the royal family of Adiabene (*Ant.*20.17–96).

Alexander Polyhistor. The extant fragments dealing with Abraham, Joseph, and Moses reveal a biographical focus with apologetic interests and admiration of the wondrous. Moses, for example, served the Egyptians both as a military leader and religious innovator. When not confounding enemies and founding animal cults, he engaged in the instruction of Orpheus. This portrait of an international *euergetes* in the context of ethnic and national rivalries has much in common with at least one important component of the traditions behind the *Alexander-Romance*. Such works may, of course, be read as "true" history, although we should classify them as biographical novels. Occupying an intermediate position are stories about the various patriarchs now found within a collection called the *Testaments of the Twelve Patriarchs*, some of which show Greek influence in their narrative sections,[14] which may be followed by visions, a structure reminiscent of the book of Daniel.

The first half of Daniel (chapters 1-6) features legends centered about Jews in the court of a foreign king.[15] Together with Judith and Esther these short stories and brief novels, which were probably intended to be read as fictions, illustrate the political background and literary popularity of a court theme, known also in romantic novels. Examination of these works shows a growing appropriation of Hellenism. Tobit is essentially "oriental," but the significance attached to proper burial of the dead reflects Greek influence (cf. *Antigone*), and motifs like threatened suicide appeal to Hellenistic taste. The Greek version of Esther sentimentalizes her encounter with the Persian king in a manner reminiscent of *Callirhoe*. Finally there is *Aseneth*, where influence from Greek novels is apparent enough to have attracted attention from classical philologists.

In sum, the history of Jewish fiction from ca. 200 B.C.E. to ca. 200 C.E. reveals, *inter alia*, the impact of Greek fiction, with which it seeks, so to speak, to keep up to date. Similar competitive or reciprocal elements may be noted in the development of early Christian narrative fiction. Researchers on the Greek novel will take note of the prominence of women in this material,[16] as well as the increasing

---

[14] Greek influence is most notable in the *Testament of Joseph*. See Pervo (1975).

[15] These are expanded in the Greek text, which begins with the tale of Susanna and closes with the account of Bel and the Snake, thus bracketing the book with novellas.

[16] Note the common use of a heroine's name alone as title.

use of erotic themes, baroque plots, and exotic settings. For students of early Christian literature this and kindred[17] literature established the literary pattern of the vindication of the suffering righteous person used to shape the Passion narrative of the canonical Gospels.

Christian Narrative Fiction

Gospels

Were space and tradition to permit, this chapter should include Matthew, Mark, Luke, and John, which can be understood as fictional biographies roughly analogous to the *Alexander-Romance*, the *Life of Aesop*, or Philostratus's novel about Apollonius of Tyana. The activity of shaping various independent stories about Jesus into a coherent narrative plot required compositional strategies very much like those of fiction.

The anonymous author of the work called The Gospel of Mark apparently initiated a process that long continued. Mark begins with Jesus's baptism and ends with the discovery of the empty tomb. Luke and Matthew expanded this work in both directions, as well as in the middle, adding more teachings and including birth and resurrection stories. Later gnostics fastened upon the last, producing "gospels" that have little narrative material and much celestial vision, often presented in the framework of a dialogue with the disciples. Infancy gospels continued to be written, as well as accounts attributed to figures of the Passion story, such as Pilate and Nicodemus.[18] Without the former both Western art and the paraphernalia of Christmas decoration would suffer major lacks; the latter are little more than shadows in the sad story of an apologetic enterprise that issued in Christian anti-Semitism. There is relatively little in this material that evokes comparison with romantic novels. In the case of the various Acts the situation is different.

---

[17] Of particular importance among works not discussed here are the books entitled "Maccabees" (II–IV Macc. in the biblical tradition), of varied genre.

[18] Discussions and translations of representatives of various gospel types may be found in the collections edited by Schneemelcher, Elliott, and Layton listed in the addendum to this article.

Acts

When the third of the canonical evangelists, traditionally called "Luke," prepared a sequel, known as "Acts,"[19] he set in motion a vital and enduring tradition. In contrast with the Gospel of Luke, Acts devotes more space to adventure than to instruction in recounting the work of early leaders, especially Paul, whose missionary career spans much of the territory over which the heroes of the romantic novels wander, and whose life is replete with intrigue, captivity, and a number of close brushes with death, including his famous escape from a wrecked ship. Affinities with ancient adventure-fiction are numerous and often noted.[20] Behind this endeavor stand narrative accounts of the suffering righteous, given Christian form in the Gospel of Mark. Literary investigation of the various gospels and acts reveals increasing facility in the composition of extended narrative and the creation of formal orations. The work of Luke displays both of these tendencies. While the Gospel is an advance over Mark in literary quality and contains a number of addresses, Acts replaces aphorism, anecdote, and concise miracle report with showpiece speeches that display some attention to rhetorical expectations and a rich mix of narrative episodes. The sincerest form of flattery soon began to manifest itself. Subsequent centuries saw a host of imitators, whose work flourished in conjunction with the production of hagiography. A primary focus of this essay is the major Apocryphal Acts of the Apostles (ApocActs).

Categorical Issues and General Observations

"Apocryphal" means "hidden," but in common use it denotes the fraudulent and fictitious. "Canonical," on the other hand, bears the cachet of the select and the official. One general understanding of the Christian Apocrypha is that they are pale imitators of their canonical models, wisely excluded by prudent churchmen. If some apocrypha utilize the same genres as canonical texts, they are not all

---

[19] The ascription of the third Gospel to Luke is traditional; the work itself is anonymous. The second volume was already called "Acts" in the second century; its original title (if any) is unknown. This title does indicate how early readers understood the work: historical narrative centered upon the deeds of extraordinary persons.

[20] The most thorough, but not the only, study of the affinities between Acts and ancient novels is Pervo (1987).

etiolated epigonids. Most of them ignore those texts later declared canonical.[21] Many of the Christian apocrypha long endured as spiritual resources. If the plastic arts were to serve as a criterion, they might appear to have exercised an influence at least as great as the canonical texts. The concluding sections of the various ApocActs found a permanent liturgical home in the readings for various saints days. Editors who were either unable or unwilling to seek their suppression revised them to conform to evolving theological taste. For centuries these books were translated into the new languages of the expanding Christian religion. For comparison one may again invoke the example of the *Alexander-Romance*.

The Major Apocryphal Acts

In the period from Antoninus Pius through Trajan Decius (ca. 150–250) there appeared five major ApocActs, relating the ministries of Andrew (*AA*), John (*AJn*), Paul (*APl*), Peter (*APtr*), and Thomas (*AThom*). Only the last of these is complete; none survives in its original condition. The *AThom* is also unique in that it was probably composed in Syriac. It is erroneous to view these works as a planned corpus; they became so under Manichean auspices in the fourth century. In fact, they utilized and, to a degree, competed with one another and other texts. Determination of intertextual relationships—who used whom—is an exasperating task, not least because of the difficulty in producing manageable critical editions from lacunose texts displaying numerous later adaptations. Most researchers would place *APl* at the beginning of the sequence and *AThom* at its end. *APtr*, *AJn*, and *AA* fall in between, possibly in that order.

Those who peruse this collection are likely to come away with impressions reminiscent of casual reports about romantic novels. A traditional stereotype is that the ApocActs are monotonously similar: wrecked temples, ruined marriages, routed demons, raised corpses, incredible wonders, intelligent animals, and insipid sermons, not to mention social deviance and a rather simple theology that is no less heretical for all that. In fact, the ApocActs display substantial differences in ideology, style, and structure. The range of difference is not

---

[21] One cannot use the term "canon" without anachronism until the fourth century, although the questions were not firmly settled then (or later).

unlike the gulf that distinguishes Xenophon of Ephesus from Achilles Tatius.

In a scholarly shift quite similar to that which has impacted the study of the romantic novel, ApocActs have become increasingly vogue in recent years, as sources for the exposure of other voices and as attractive targets for the application of new methods. ApocActs considerably expand the repertory of narrative fiction that can be called "popular"—in several senses of that word—and with much better external data, including both learned discussion and textual attestation, than applies in the case of *Callirhoe* and *An Ephesian Tale*.

If one were to use these works to create a broad index of the desires and values of those social groups standing at some distance below the elite aristocracy, they suggest that a leading concern is power to combat misfortune, whether in the form of illness, domestic oppression or official abuse. Longing for identity within a cohesive community is another factor, and it would be erroneous to overlook the palpable wish for experience that extends the drab horizons of daily existence. Similar concerns explain at least part of the appeal of romantic fiction. Many of the areas in which power is sought are those also addressed in the magical papyri, which illuminate this world from a more individualistic perspective. Not without reason are apostles called "sorcerers."[22] Just as love occurs at first sight and romantic heroes radiate a divine beauty of considerable potency,[23] so do the charismatic endowments of apostles and their followers work to their frequent apparent disadvantage while their exorcisms and cures operate instantly. In this regard the works manifest a popular fantasy still visible in commercial advertisements. Since it is almost unquestionably true that readers of romantic novels were well aware that "life isn't like that," it is likely that the readers and hearers of ApocActs were equally well informed. The critically sophisticated have long bewailed the credulity of the masses. This perspective may be unfair. In the case of the ApocActs there is ample room to suspect that readers were capable of grasping the symbolic character of the narratives before them. "Fundamentalism" is not restricted to those

---

[22] See Poupon (1981).

[23] Analogous to the beauty of Anthia and Callirhoe are the garments of Jesus and Paul (Mark 5:21–24; Acts 19:12). In most cases, however, Jesus and the apostles can manage the power they possess. "Erotic omnipotence" requires that there be no on/off switch.

of limited education; not all of the less educated are bound to literal understandings. By often assuming that these texts were to be taken quite concretely, critics of recent times have done both texts and audiences a disservice.

Having rejected stereotypes about the plots of ApocActs, I shall now proceed to set forth a typical plot. The apostle for whom the work is named tends to remain in the center of the narrator's eye. In novels and Acts divination is one means of launching plots. Like senior Roman senators determining who shall receive which province, the apostles cast lots for the twelve zones of the earth. By one means or another each proceeds to his missionary area. As they move about the world the apostles found and strengthen various communities, usually based upon households, do many great deeds, and suffer for them.

One, if not *the*, missionary position is an abhorrence of sexual intercourse, even within lawful marriage. Not all of their converts are charcoal burners and laundresses. Many are women of high standing within the community. Neither their withdrawal from the conjugal bed nor its motive escapes the attentions of their husbands, who, being civic leaders, are well positioned to do something about circumstances they find personally distressing and socially threatening. Persecution of both wife and apostle serve only to speed the latter on to new fields and more converts, until the last episode, when the crown of martyrdom is finally bestowed. The happily ever after of the ApocActs is in the hereafter, but it is none the less happy for that. Within this typical outline, employed not because authors lacked imagination but because audiences found it repeatedly satisfying, there is room for a great deal of variation.

The assertion that martyrdoms constitute happy endings anticipates one objection to labeling the ApocActs as novels. No one need waste words to prove that they are not romantic novels like *Callirhoe*. Both groups share themes and motifs, miraculous deliverances, for example, which might seem properly at home in ApocActs, and erotic scenes, in particular threatened rape, which might appear to belong to the realm of the romantic novel. (There is an apparent irony here: Jewish and Christian works tend to be much less delicate in sexual matters than are the standard *Scriptores Erotici*.)[24] These oft-discussed

---

[24] The bath provides an apt comparison. Callirhoe, in a rather atypical episode, is admired by her maids while bathing (2.2), in a passage that may have suffered

parallels indicate the popular appeal of both types. For the ApocActs romantic novels were, in some degree, competitors worthy of emulation. To this extent they are an important element in the history of the reception of the romantic novels. That matter is distinct from the question of whether they should be characterized as novels, a question long overshadowed by definitions based upon the presence or absence of certain motifs. The ApocActs are extended prose narratives crafted by authors who have fashioned from varied sources and forms an integral whole. They are fictions about famous figures of the past, historical novels in short.

In addition to objections based upon themes and motifs, the ApocActs (and some Jewish fiction) strike some[25] as distinct because they are ideological works, oriented to a particular group or cult. The danger of anachronism arises here, for Christian influence has fixed upon the western scholarly mind an understanding of mission as the acquisition of individual converts. *Callirhoe* leaves the reader in no doubt about the power of Aphrodite, just as the *APtr* leaves no doubt about the power of Jesus. Given the history of religion, it requires much less effort to imagine the impact of the *APtr* upon a body of Christian hearers assembled for devotion in second-century Rome than the effect of *Callirhoe* upon a group of women engaged in domestic industry in first-century Aphrodisias. The similarities may be greater than expected, although it appears more likely that one could read *Callirhoe* as "mere entertainment" than the *APtr*—at least until one reflects upon the Jewish and Christian names that permeate the Greek Magical Papyri. In its most concrete sense classification is a means for shelving books. It is doubtful that a librarian, ca. 175, faced with the Greek *Metamorphoses* attributed to Lucius of Patrae, *Leucippe*, *An Ephesian Tale*, and the *Acts of Paul* would unhesitatingly place the first three on one shelf, so to speak, and the last elsewhere. The two last items have much in common. Both are folkloristic, simple in style, and somewhat naive. *Leucippe*, too, is part of the reception of romantic novels like that of Chariton in so far as it displays a critical

---

from censorship. Susanna, on the other hand, is observed by male elders, who, in the more famous edition of the tale (Theodotion 15–27), gaze with lust in their hearts, followed by attempted blackmail. The apostle Peter's daughter attracted the interest of a man who saw her in the baths at age ten, while the *AA* described the death of a (presumably misbehaving) couple in the baths (see below).

[25] This blow struck B.E. Perry with considerable force. He regarded the ApocActs as "propaganda for a fanatical, antihumanistic creed," (1967) 85.

distance and a level of sophisticated humor. Reflections upon ancient prose fiction will do well to recognize both the differences among representatives of such groups as ApocActs and romantic novels as well as the affinities between the two groups and/or individual representatives thereof. To those representatives I now turn.

The Acts of Andrew
Alphabetical order, which avoids prejudice about date and dependence, assigns the first place to one of the less typical and by far the worst-preserved specimen of the group. The *AA* may be of Alexandrian origin and probably dates from the last quarter of the second century. Alexandrian Christianity then (and later) ran the gamut from "vulgar superstition" to the Christian philosophy of Clement, with a distinctly gnosticizing tinge, only gradually eradicated by leaders of a more orthodox orientation. Had one of Clement's more radical students decided to produce a sensational popular novel, the *AA* could have been his work.

In general, the final section of the various acts is the most complete and widely attested part of the work, although not the least edited, because these were excerpted and preserved for reading on feast days. This is also true of the *AA*. There are, in addition, a number of fragments and later versions as well as a Latin epitome. The last is due to the kind auspices of Gregory, late sixth century bishop of Tours, who found the work verbose and, at times, inappropriate, but worthy of use. Gregory gives us "the good stuff" in concise form. His catholic edition, clearly prepared in the face of the work's popularity, eliminated most of the long addresses, simplified the structure, and abbreviated many episodes. Some may appreciate a bishop who can find sermons dull, but scholars wish that a more intact edition survived. Out of these disparate pieces it is possible to grasp a glimpse of the original shape of these Acts. A vexing problem is the relation of the *Acts of Andrew and Matthias among the Cannibals* to the original *AA*. This may descend from the original text or represent a separate work.

The cannibal adventure has affinities with the roughly contemporary novel of Antonius Diogenes. The story begins with Matthias, chosen to fill the place of Judas. Matthias was not the last late-comer to get a less desirable assignment, for his territory included Myrmidonia, where cannibalism was all the rage. Matthias suffers the fate of other visitors: blinding and fattening up for the table. As the clock of doom ticks on, Andrew, on his mission to Greece, is alerted by a vision and dashes to the rescue, which includes a flood of (quite properly) biblical proportions and purpose, the deliverance of Matthias, and the division of the inhabitants into sheep, who repent and are saved, and goats, who perish. This story could have served Lucian as a source for his *True History*. To Christian readers it was an allegorical narrative. If this stood at the beginning of the original *AA*, it would have served as a kind of hermeneutical key urging readers to look beneath the surface flood of healings, exorcisms, and wrestlings with the flesh.

After scouring this sewer, the two make their way toward Greece. Patras served Andrew as missionary center and place of martyrdom. If the subsequent adventures are somewhat typical and occasionally coarse, the embedded sermons of Andrew lead discerning readers toward that symbolic perspective mentioned above. The *AA* offers no naive or unreflective theology, for there are indubitable allusions to Middle Platonism and contemporary Gnosis, with some borrowings from the ethics of the Stoa. Salvation comes through discovery, "birth," of the true self. With this realization believers can liberate themselves from all passions and happily elect an ascetic life that rejects the pursuits of both honor and pleasure. Andrew's final sermon on this subject has a most impressive setting: the cross upon which he hangs for days. There is but one God, hailed as either "Father" or "Son." This theology was less aberrant for its time than it would later become.

There is more than theological address and dialogue of a platonic sort. Novel approaches to the contrast between illusion and reality include the deceit of a husband by sending a lady's maid to his bed in her place and angels who can mimic female voices to protect women who are not in their proper place—at home rather than at prayers. Another woman is condemned to a brothel, not a rare fate in hagiography and fiction. Cleanliness is not adjacent to godliness; to prove the point a couple perish in the baths. Nor is every delivery overtly supernatural, witness the timely withdrawal of a proconsul to answer the summons of nature. The last incident would not be out of place in the *Life of Aesop* (or Aristophanes). This is a rather earthy condemnation of the earthly. Delicate readers might well take offense. To modern ears this presentation of an ascetic message in rowdy form may raise suspicions, but these result from the imposition of other value-systems.

Another roughly contemporary novel also relates an often bawdy and frequently boisterous picaresque tale with the apparent object of giving a platonic spin to an "oriental cult." The *AA* is a piece of narrative fiction rarely adduced in the quest for parallels to the *Metamorphoses* of Apuleius. Comparison of the two would be quite rewarding.

Dennis R. MacDonald has proposed that the *AA* is a Christian parodic re-casting of the *Odyssey*.[26] Given the fragmentary nature of the material and the consequent need to reconstruct rather than analyze the work's plan, his hypothesis is of necessity speculative, but he works from some strong clues in a worthy effort to break down the barriers that traditionally segregate "Christian" and "pagan" texts. The first of the ApocActs to be considered thus confirms none of the stereotypes about these works.

The Acts of John
Emerging orthodoxy identified the apostle John as the "Beloved Disciple" and the author of the Fourth Gospel, then found for him a resting place in Ephesus, a choice locale for the confusion of heretics. The *AJn* appears to exploit these associations from a rival theological perspective.

Like other ApocActs, this work has run afoul of theological controversy and survives only in part, although a much later and quite orthodox successor, the *Acts of John* by Prochorus, which contains some of the early *AJn*, exists in many manuscripts. *AJn* apparently appeared in Asia Minor or possibly in Alexandria ca. 190–220.

As is more or less *de rigeur* for ApocActs, the opening portion has not been recovered. The story evidently began in Palestine, probably at the Sea of Galilee, where the glorified Savior appeared to John and deterred him from committing matrimony. After adventures and experiences unknown this apostle found his way to Ephesus, where he is when the extant text opens. The object of his ministry is a wealthy couple, Cleopatra and Lycomedes. The former died from illness, the latter of grief. John raised her and led her to revive Lycomedes. Out of gratitude and admiration this good man commissioned a portrait of John, which he employed as an aid to his devotion. When the apostle came to learn of this, he used the occasion to contrast inner with outer appearance.[27]

---

[26] MacDonald (1994).
[27] The example may have been apt, but it did not enhance the text in the eyes

There follows a dramatic public healing of all the sick and elderly women of Ephesus, assembled for that purpose in the theater. The end of this episode is lost, although we need not doubt a satisfactory resolution.

From later references (with some support from artistic representations and a Manichean hymn) it appears that the conversion of one Drusiana brought John into conflict with her husband Andronicus. Both apostle and convert were jailed under threat of the most dire punishment should they not recant. In the end Andronicus repented and became a believer, saving not only himself but the others.

While she was in prison, Drusiana experienced a comforting epiphany of Christ. In fact, his manifold appearances confused her. The apostle's pastoral response took the shape of a lengthy speech that is nothing other than an embedded "gospel" presenting a unique perspective on the events from the Last Supper through the crucifixion. The former, it transpires, was a dinner dance, with an accompanying "Hymn of Christ."[28] During the latter the true Christ appeared to John in a cave while the earthly Jesus suffered apparent torment. Within this section are both theological developments rooted in the johannine tradition and apparently later additions designed to give it the character of a Valentinian Gnostic text. The many forms of both earthly Jesus and heavenly Christ illustrate the problem of the one and the many. Polymorphy thereby serves theology.

When the text resumes, following another lacuna, the apostle brings down the great temple of Artemis in Ephesus, surpassing even Paul, who could do no more than injure the tourist trade connected with this shrine (Acts 19:23–40). One of the casualties of this collapse was a priest of the goddess. He is returned to life to join a brother who had already converted.

The next episode is quite a moral tale about a young man caught up in an adulterous affair. Chastised by his father, he lost his temper and killed him. When this wretched youth came to terms with the effects of his libido, he determined to kill his inamorata, her husband, and, last of all, himself. Dissuaded by John, he witnesses the resurrection of his father. In a surprising and indicative switch, the

---

of iconodules, against whom it had been invoked. The Second Council of Nicea, which rejected Iconoclasm in 787, also condemned the *AJn*.

[28] The spirituality expressed in this hymn has fascinated many in the twentieth century, including Gustav Holst, who set to music his own translation of the text.

latter questions the utility of returning to a life of misery. John shows him the possibility of a better life. In response to all of this the youth once more takes up his blade and excises his genitals. The apostle did not approve.

At this point the wider field beckons. While John is absent on travels about Asia Minor, misfortune befell Drusiana, whose beauty, like that of any romance heroine—or B-movie actress—had not been in the least diminished by her severe regimen. The very sight of her had so aroused the lust of a leading man of Ephesus that she died of despair. Even death did not deter this Callimachus, who conspired to enter her tomb and have his way. Divine intervention thwarted these bestial ambitions. The foregoing transpires in a flashback narrated by Callimachus, raised for that very purpose. His conversion arguably removed all obstacles to the resuscitation of Drusiana. The argument convinced John, who restored her to the community. Not long thereafter these incidents, which, with miracles transformed into subterfuges, would not be out of place in *Leucippe*, John has the unique privilege of being the only apostle to die of natural causes.

The narrative and message of the *AJn* fit together hand in glove. The surviving episodes are vivid and varied; they also expound the work's theology. Physical resurrection, the dominant form of "healing," is useful only as a symbol of the ascent to genuine existence. Failing the latter, resuscitation is but a return to toil and trouble. The text employs a bewildering repertory of religious symbols, none of which is adequate to convey its message. Far from being a naive and credulous literalist, the author of *AJn* understood and propounded the limits of human language as a medium for the presentation of transcendent truth. Nascent orthodoxy tended to prefer unambiguous answers to the questions of the faithful. Against such compromise and presumed distortion the Acts delivers a staunch riposte. Once more an ApocActs displays considerable sophistication. In this instance Greek philosophy provided no immediate stimulus. There appears instead a distillate of the "heretical" elements within the "johannine" strand of early Christianity. Patristic authorities may have sensed this. In any case, the *AJn* lead the pack in the quantity and quality of ecclesiastical disapproval.

The Acts of Paul
The *APl* is probably the earliest of the ApocActs; in content and form it is closest to the canonical book (the major character in which

is Paul), and must be either a sequel or, more probably, a rival to it. During the last half of the second century *APl* was more popular among Christian readers than the Acts that eventually entered the Christian canon.[29] The *APl* appears in some lists of biblical texts and served church historians and panegyrists as a valuable source into the Middle Ages. That the *APl* long enjoyed a better fate than other ApocActs is due both to its stimulating content and its relatively innocent theology. The work was probably composed in Asia Minor in the third quarter of the second century.

Liturgical usage led to the separate preservation of two sections of the text: the martyrdom, as usual, and the "Acts of Paul and Thecla," probably the best known episodes of all the ApocActs, which were preserved and re-edited for use in the cult of Thecla. Almost nothing else of the work was known until the twentieth century. Papyrus recoveries of one large section in Coptic translation, another in Greek, and several smaller papyri in either Greek or Coptic have restored about two-thirds of the text, although not all of the portions come from a similar edition.

The opening is largely lost, as usual. From fragments and a later flashback it appears that the story began with Paul's conversion at Damascus. In due course the apostle arrived at Iconium, where Titus has prepared the way. His message quite captivated a wealthy young woman, Thecla, who subsequently rejects both family and fiancé. The latter joins her mother in a plot to have Paul expelled and the maiden burned. Readers of ancient novels will not be surprised to learn that an inspired shower aborted the execution.

Thecla pursues Paul, en route to Antioch.[30] In that city she had a run-in with a certain Alexander, evidently a priest of the imperial cult, who was overcome by her beauty. Firm rejection of his advances led to *damnatio ad bestias*. This condemnation generated the formation of a claque of female supporters and patronage from the wealthy Tryphaena, a queen. When the day of judgment came, the lions got first innings, but politely refused the opportunity. One of these (a lioness, of course) even devoured a bear sent in to save

---

[29] The Third Gospel (Luke) and Acts were written by the same author and linked through prefaces. In early Christian lists and collections, however, Luke was placed among the four gospels while Acts was most often associated with a group of epistles. The two books experienced different fates.

[30] This is evidently Pisidian Antioch, confused with the larger Syrian city. Similarly, Sidon may once have been Side.

the day. (When all is said and done, the king of beasts is no servant of the king of Rome in the *APl.*) Perhaps the third time would be the charm and place upon Thecla the seal of judgment. The seals selected for this task demurred, although their artificial aquatic habitat provided convenient water for a self-administered baptism.

Paul found these vindications convincing and commissioned Thecla to become a missionary. Modern research has taken note that, in these chapters, Thecla is really the leading character and Paul either a kind of absent lord (like Jesus) or an insensitive and negligent male authority figure. Thecla's support comes from other women rather than from the apostle or an adopted church family.[31]

The mission of Paul advances. One of his converts at Ephesus was the spouse of a high official. In a nice piece of symmetry this action led to his own condemnation to the beasts, lions as luck would have it. Providence, rather than fortune, took a hand here, for the very beast selected for this role had earlier benefited from Paul's ministrations and taken up a celibate life. The tale of Androcles has returned to the stage in new garb. Meanwhile, the show must go on, to Philippi and Corinth, with prison in the first and false teachers in the second. Paul, however, is destined for Rome.

One of the puzzles of the *APl* is that, contrary to the canonical Acts, Paul travels to Rome as a free agent. At the end of the canonical account Paul remains at Rome, practically a free person. In the *APl*, however, his revival and conversion of Patroclus, a cup-bearer (and Ganymede?) to that estimable Achilles, the Emperor Nero, set in motion a plot that will not end until Paul has been executed, with attendant miracles, conversions, and post-mortem experiences at his tomb, as well as an appearance to his repentant persecutor. This apostle has taken on a number of the qualities of his Lord.

As in other ApocActs, a message of radical renunciation, with particular attention to the ever-fascinating subject of sex, leads to constant opposition. In the surviving text there is a tendency to avoid accounts describing the disruption of extant marriages. This is probably the result of later revision to conform with the view that voluntary celibacy is a capital idea, and that some couples may live in mutual continence, but that lawful wives have no right to refuse their lords and masters.

---

[31] The independent account of Thecla's life rounds off the story by summarizing her subsequent ministry and ultimate vindication.

The original *APl* represent one pole in controversies about the life and teaching of Paul, with the canonical Acts somewhat right of center, and the Pastoral Epistles (1–2 Timothy, Titus) at the far right. Points of contact and opposition between 1 Timothy and the *APl*, especially the Thecla-material, are notable.[32] The spiritual milieu of *APl* seems to be an early phase of the intensely apocalyptic and charismatic movement that would explode in rural Asia Minor and be known as Montanism. The uncompromising moral rigor of this movement attracted the North African lay theologian Tertullian, who, ironically, strongly objected to the use made of stories about Thecla.

The Acts of Peter

If the *APl* reflects theological controversies about the apostle to the gentiles, the fate of the *APtr* has also been shaped by church history, most notably the prominence of the Bishop of Rome and the power associated with his presumed predecessor, Peter, leader of the disciples of Jesus. Perhaps two-thirds of the work is available, in different editions. Rome is prominent in the largest surviving portion, a Latin translation not earlier than the fourth century.

By this point it should not be necessary to mention that the beginning is lost and that its outline will be conjectured. Jerusalem appears to have been the setting of the first part, which included cooperation between Peter and Paul and an encounter between Peter and another Simon,[33] who is stigmatized as "wizard" and comes down in history as if Magus were his last name. Bested by Peter, Simon set out for the greener missionary pastures of Rome.

Two extracts, one Coptic, the other Latin, preserve edifying stories that apparently derive from an earlier section of the original *APtr*. Both prefer female virginity to life and health. In the Coptic text Peter is challenged in the midst of a Sunday healing service as to why he does not heal his own crippled daughter, a beautiful virgin. The beautiful virgin is healed, then immediately restored to her pathetic condition. The reason for this is that she had already become an occasion of temptation by the age of ten. One of those tempted was the wealthy Ptolemy, who saw her bathing with her mother. When Ptolemy's honorable proposals of marriage were

---

[32] See D.R. MacDonald (1983).

[33] Simon, a Greek name quite similar to one of the most common Hebrew proper names ("Simeon" in English), was Peter's original name.

spurned, he had the girl kidnapped. Shortly thereafter she reappeared on the parental door-step, crippled. Ptolemy repented and left his property to the church. The moral is clear (and, to most, abominable). A Latin text relates the fate of a gardener and his virgin daughter. In response to Peter's prayer that she receive what was best for her, she dropped dead. Her father did not appreciate this benefaction and demanded that she be raised. This Peter did. Within a few days she was seduced by a visitor with whom she eloped.

For better or worse, the largest extant section of the *APtr* lacks improving tales of the previous sort. The story as it now stands, with interpolations designed to display the harmony between Peter and Paul, opens in Rome, where Paul is minding the store. He departs for Spain, granting Simon a window of opportunity he does not neglect. Within a brief time he seduces nearly the entire community, including, most lamentably, Marcellus, a member of the Roman Senate and noteworthy benefactor. When all seems lost, Christ intervenes with a heavenly vision dispatching Peter to the rescue. The voyage includes a brief pause to baptize the vessel's captain, who will be of later service.[34]

Having arrived in Rome, Peter sets out to rebuild the shattered foundation of the church. At the center of this is a lengthy contest with Simon designed to demonstrate which has the most authentic power. Bible readers will recall the show-down between Moses and the wizards of Pharaoh; for readers of epic the competitions of heroes comes to mind. This is all quite entertaining and often droll, two factors that have earned it undying *odium theologicum*. Had Simon been a cheap magician, the battle would have had little interest. In fact he is quite skilled, but the apostle can both reduce Simon's accomplishments to nothing and improve upon them. An infant will give voice, as will a dog, and a dried fish comes to life, not to mention corpses revived in a public exhibition. When an expelled demon blasphemously shatters an imperial statue, Peter restores it.[35] The climax arrives when Simon proclaims that he will take flight.[36] Peter invents the science of anti-aircraft with a potent prayer that brings

---

[34] This baptism at (literally in the) sea is one incident shared by the *APl* and the *APtr*. Mutual contamination has rendered the decision about originality most difficult.
[35] Apollonius of Tyana (4.20) did much the same.
[36] Cf. Apuleius, *Met.*3.21.

Simon crashing to earth. Utterly vanquished, he withdrew from the city and soon perished from his wounds.

Sex then emerged as a more formidable enemy than magic. The chastity of converted wives and mistresses fired the wrath of their high-placed lords, with predictable results: persecution. At this juncture Peter imitated Simon Magus and took flight.

Once again Christ intervenes, with a famous shaming vision.[37] Denying Peter will repent and follow the path of his savior, suffering crucifixion upside down and offering (like Andrew) a stirring sermon on the cross. As in the *APl*, a revelation to Nero brings abatement of the persecution.[38]

The practice of managing theological dissension through displays of superior power rather than by intellectual refutation has, as noted, disappointed scholars. Little could be more "popular." Truth was useful, but for most people power was what counted. The *APtr* as it now exists promotes an ecclesiology with "catholic" features. Most of the ApocActs exhibit rather loosely organized bands of believers. In the *APtr* converts from the aristocracy serve not only to generate necessary persecution but also as sources of charitable contributions and buttresses to a solid organization that will serve the suppression of heresy. The *APtr* in present form is the least "novel-like" of the ApocActs. As a source for novels it has served long and well.[39] Many know the stirring "*Quo Vadis*" episode; few could identify its source.

Rome has been the terminus of the last two ApocActs surveyed. It is doubtless time for a visit to the exotic orient.

The Acts of Thomas

AThom is outstanding in several ways. Evidently composed in Syriac rather than Greek, it also survives in a complete (if edited) form. The *AThom* is not only the fullest but also the most theologically and literarily sophisticated of the ApocActs. This work probably came to light in the early third century in the bi-lingual, multi-cultural

---

[37] The *Quo Vadis* passage presents another instance of overlap between the *APtr* and the *APl*.

[38] The martyrdom section of *APtr* exists in Greek, as well as in a number of Latin editions.

[39] Henry Sienkiewcz's *Quo Vadis* appeared in a new English translation as recently as 1989 and has enjoyed repeated cinematic success. The once popular Thomas B. Costain delved deeply into the *APtr* for his 1952 best-seller *The Silver Chalice*, which presently became a major film.

environment of Edessa, a true crossroads of east and west. Given the number of Greek-speakers in the region, an edition in that tongue may have been nearly simultaneous.[40]

Christianity in eastern Syria during the early third century had distinctive features, including a general requirement for celibacy after baptism. By western standards *AThom* is heretical and aberrant. In its native environment it sets forth a Christianity that, if not "normative," was normal.

The structure of *AThom* has been a fruitful object of recent study. The work actually begins at the beginning, with a division of the world among the apostles. The lot of Thomas[41] falls to India. Unwilling to go there freely, he arrives as a slave. The first six of the thirteen chapters (called "acts") seem to lack organization and narrative development; acts 7–13 take place in and around the court of King Misdai (Misdaeus) and have literary unity. A quick reading suggests a string of episodes, all involving conflict, frequently over celibacy, with many last-minute rescues until, in the final scene, the apostle somehow achieves martyrdom. This is superficial.

The structure of acts 1–6 derives not from its surface but from an intertextual base of biblical narratives and themes. Not content with mere "parallels" or imitations, although these play a role, the author works with a system of symbols and typologies developed in scriptural exegesis. This is the *Pilgrim's Progress* of early Christian literature. When Judas Thomas is sold as a carpenter slave to serve a king and feeds the hungry, one thinks not only of Jesus the carpenter but also of the Judas who sold out Jesus, then of Joseph, father of Jesus and carpenter, and then of the Patriarch, who was sold as a slave but rose high in a foreign court and fed the hungry. Reading the *AThom* in quest of such associations is a rewarding experience to the biblically learned.

Within the *AThom* are two long poems, excellent representatives of Syriac prosody. The better-known of these is "The Hymn of the Pearl." On the surface this is a pleasant fairy-tale. When read in

---

[40] Although it is possible to argue for a Greek original, in this instance the advantage seems to lie with the Syriac. Continued use by Syriac-speaking Christians led to more revisions; in general the Greek edition reflects an earlier form of the text.

[41] Thomas is a Syriac nickname, "twin." In the Syrian tradition his proper name was Judas, i.e., Jude the brother of Jesus, happily exploited in the *AThom* through the theme of heavenly selves, "twins."

terms of its symbols, the hymn presents in poetic form the theology of the book. A very apt analogy in several ways is the embedded tale of Cupid and Psyche in the *Metamorphoses* of Apuleius, with its fairy-tale charm and symbolic meaning. In both cases the harmless story, told to prisoners in *AThom* and to a captive young woman in Apuleius, is a hermeneutical key to the text.

The theology of this work is quite dualistic, a kind of Gnosis not dependent upon any developed Gnostic system, and thus alien to most western readers. All can come to appreciate, however, the craft that has wrought from narrative episodes and poetic interludes a coherent religious novel of considerable depth. In its own cultural milieu, the *AThom* represents an achievement comparable to that of Longus or Apuleius.

The composition of new acts, centered upon both apostles and lesser figures, went on for centuries,[42] while the acts discussed above continued to be abridged, expanded, revised, and copied. Hagiography became the dominant genre, greatly influenced by these acts and influencing in turn their shape and preservation. In addition there were other types of Christian fiction, the most famous of which bears the ponderous name of the "Pseudo-Clementine Literature."

The Pseudo-Clementines and Other Texts

Homilies and Recognitions

There are a number of writings purporting to derive from St. Clement of Rome, by tradition a leader of that community in the late first century. The novel in question probably appeared in west Syria ca. 250. From extensive revisions there remain the *Homilies*, which betray the hand of an editor with Arian sympathies, and the *Recognitions*. The latter exist in Latin and Syriac translations. Ideologically, the *Ps-Clems* defy modern models, as they are rather rationalistic, yet tinged with something like Gnosis, but display a "Judeo-Christian" orientation, stridently anti-pauline.

Those who favor densely packed romances permeated with sex and violence should search elsewhere, for these works contain more than a sample of the teaching of Peter. (Perhaps the title of one edition is an adequate consumer warning label. How many will read a novel that rejoices in the name *Homilies?*)

---

[42] See the survey of A. de Santos Otero in Schneemelcher-Wilson 2:426–483.

The work does have a narrative line of considerable complexity.[43] The *Ps-Clems* are a Christian novel with a plot that resembles New Comedy. The center of action is neither couple nor individual but an aristocratic Roman family. Frightened by a dream, Clement's mother takes his older twin brothers and leaves the city. All disappear, as does their father, who had gone in search of them. For his part Clement enters into a quest for truth. None of the philosophical sects convince him. Learning that the son of God has appeared in Judea, he repairs to that place, meets Peter, who resolves his dilemmas, and becomes the apostle's companion on his travels, a major feature of which is the refutation of Simon Magus. Scorners of the *APtr* may now enjoy their reward. In fact, Simon's teachings are those of Paul. This is a smear-piece no less dreadful than it is tedious.

As the plot lumbers toward its conclusion, the various members of the family are happily recognized, rehabilitated when necessary from the degraded circumstances into which they have fallen, joyfully reunited, converted, and baptized.

The Christian novel behind the surviving editions exhibits a plot reminiscent of *Apollonius, Prince of Tyre*. The author may have plundered just such a text.[44] There is a coherence between the themes of recognition and quest pursued by Clement and the narrative plot, but it is difficult to see from the surviving texts that the narrator exploited this symmetry.

Xanthippe and Polyxena

This survey concludes with a brief examination of two other texts that will serve to illustrate the range and fate of ancient Christian fiction. The *Acts of Xanthippe and Polyxena*[45] is a third or fourth century work that makes rich use of various ApocActs in the construction of a short Christian novel. If one desires an example of a text that a bishop or matron might offer as a substitute for *An Ephesian Story*, this is it. The work falls into two parts, rather like *Aseneth*, with a conversion story in the first part and adventures in the second. Chapters 1–21 relate the conversion of Xanthippe by Paul during

---

[43] There is a delightful resumé of the plot by the late Bishop of Durham, Lightfoot (1890) 14–16.

[44] For discussion of these matters see Perry (1967) 285–293.

[45] The ms. title is "The Life and Conduct of the Holy Women Xanthippe, Polyxena, and Rebecca." *Bios kai politeia* is a conventional title for saints' lives.

his mission to Spain, with the normal marital difficulties, all resolved by the eventual baptism of her husband.

Now Xanthippe has a beautiful younger sister, Polyxena. The action accelerates in chapters 22–42, when a powerful rival of her suitor kidnaps Polyxena with the aid of bandits, who sail for Babylonia. A storm casts them upon the shore of Greece. Philip, warned by a vision, rescues her. When the bandits prepare to attack, Polyxena runs away. With the aid of a lioness and the apostle Andrew, Polyxena and a Jewish slave named Rebecca are baptized. Andrew left them to their own wiles. Soon a prefect kidnaps Polyxena, while a soldier seizes Rebecca. Polyxena is condemned but, like Thecla, finds a friendly lion. Eventually she returns to Spain in a voyage enlivened by another barbarian assault and an attempted suicide. Readers familiar with scripture, various Acts, and romantic novels would have found much to enjoy in this work, simple in style, often brief beyond belief (it reads like an outline for a narrator), and happy in its ultimate issue. This work, centered in Spain, conforms to the convention of "there and back." It is notable that, although Paul is a central authority, all of the tribulations and adventures are experienced by women. One can be a Thecla, get married, and live happily ever after. The readers of this low-calorie novel can have their cake and eat it too.

Baarlam and Ioasaph

This immensely popular work, a literary sensation in eleventh century Constantinople and beyond, once attributed to the eighth century Greek theologian John of Damascus, is now viewed as an originally Manichean text from central Asia, eventually transformed into Persian and Arabic Islamic dress, christianized in Georgia, and translated into Greek. Manicheans, whose admiration and adaptation of the ApocActs did much to ensure their decline, experienced the contrary fate. Christian fiction had come a full circle, from Jewish adaptations of tales of the Persian court to a medieval adaptation of a non-Christian tale mediated through Muslim Persia.[46]

---

[46] For a summary of the genesis and history of *Barlaam and Ioasaph* see D.M. Lang's introduction in Woodward and Mattingly (1967) ix–xxxv.

Conclusion

The various Jewish and Christian texts considerably enlarge the horizons and boundaries of the ancient novel, helping to bridge gaps across cultures and substantially illuminating what was actually "popular." Chronologically, they provide marks for the evolution of Greek fiction, since Jewish and Christian novels appear to keep pace with changing trends and demands. This is most apparent in the ApocActs, which flourished during the heyday of the romantic novel.

Those seeking to locate social and cultural bases for the less learned "pre-Sophistic" novels may learn something by comparison with Christian texts, which derive from groups with relatively well-known ideologies and social organizations.

Surveys always mislead in so far as they emphasize continuity and similarity. It is my hope that this survey has identified some generalities without neglect of diversity. There is a great deal of variation in form, style, object, and viewpoint within early Christian fiction. This essay invites investigators of romantic novels to be more comprehensive. At the same time it is clear that the primary task in the study of ancient fiction at the present time is the careful examination of individual works in all of their particularity and uniqueness.

ADDENDUM

I. Abbreviations used in Text and Notes

ABD. *The Anchor Bible Dictionary.* Chief Ed. D.N. Freedman, New York: Doubleday, 1992.
ANRW. *Aufstieg und Niedergang der Antiken Welt.* Eds. W. Haase and H. Temporini. Berlin: Walter De Gruyter.
Schneemelcher-Wilson. W. Schneemelcher, Ed., *New Testament Apocrypa*, Rev. ed., Trans. ed. R. McL. Wilson, Cambridge: James Clarke & Co., Ltd., 1992.
ApocActs. The Apocryphal Acts of Apostles.
AA. The Acts of Andrew.
AJn. The Acts of John.
APtr. The Acts of Peter.
APl. The Acts of Paul.
AThom. The Acts of Thomas.

II. Editions and Translations of Ancient Jewish and Christian Fiction

The standard edition of the ApocActs is
R.A. Lipsius and M. Bonnet, eds., *Acta Apostolorum Apocrypha*, two volumes in three parts, 1891–1898, reprinted Darmstadt: Georg Ohlms, 1959.

New editions are emerging under the auspices of the *Association pour l'Étude de la Littérature Apocryphe Chrétienne*, in the *Corpus Christianorum Series Apocryphorum*. These include introduction, commentary and French translation as well as the texts. Now available are:
E. Junod and J.-D. Kaestli. *Acta Johannis.* Two volumes. Turnhout: Brepols, 1983.
M. Prieur. *Acta Andreae.* Two volumes. Turnhout: Brepols, 1989.

Note also:
D.R. MacDonald. *The Acts of Andrew and The Acts of Andrew and Matthias in the City of the Cannibals. Society of Biblical Literature Texts and Translations. Christian Apocrypha Series.* Atlanta: Scholars Press, 1990.

English translations of the ApocActs are available in Schneemelcher-Wilson and
J.K. Elliott, ed. *The Apocryphal New Testament: A Collection of Apocryphal Christian Literature in an English Translation based on M.R. James.* Oxford: The Clarendon Press, 1993.

For Gnostic "gospels" see also
B. Layton, *The Gnostic Scriptures.* Garden City, New York: Doubleday & Company, 1987.

The current edition of the Greek and Latin texts of the *Pseudo-Clementines* is
B. Rehm. *Die Pseudoklementinen I.II. Griechische Christlichen Schrifsteller*, Berlin: Akadamie Verlag, 1965–1969. A new edition is appearing under the editorship of G. Strecker.

There is no recent edition of the Syriac text and no full English translation. Schneemelcher includes a partial translation. A fuller English version is to be found in the *Ante-Nicene Fathers*, vol. 8, ed. A. Roberts et al., Buffalo: The Christian Literature Company, 1886 (reprinted often), *Recognitions*, pp. 77–211 and *Homilies* 223–346.

There is an edition of *Xanthippe and Polyxena* in M.R. James, *Apocrypha Anecdota* 2. Texts and Studies 2. Cambridge: The University Press, 1893, 59–85, with an introduction on pp. 43–57. His text is translated in *Ante-Nicene Fathers*, vol. 9, ed. A. Menzies. New York: The Christian Literature Company, 1896 (reprinted often), 205–217.

Barlaam and Ioasaph is conveniently found in the Loeb series, with an edition of the Greek text and a translation by G.R. Woodward and H. Mattingly. In 1967 the work was issued with a new introduction by D.M. Lang: *Barlaam and Ioasaph*, Cambridge: Harvard University Press, 1967.

Daniel, Judith, Tobit, 2–4 Maccabees, and Esther may be found in editions of the Septuagint. There are a number of translations, including English versions of the Bible that include the "Deutero-Canonical" books.

A recent edition of Artapanus, with text, translation, and extensive notes may be found in Carl R. Holladay, *Fragments from Hellenistic Jewish Authors*, Vol. 1: Historians, SBL Texts and Translations 20 (Chico, California: Scholars Press, 1983), 189–243.

Aseneth exists in two editions and a number of versions. An edition of the shorter Greek text is M. Philonenko, *Joseph et Asenéth: Introduction, texte critique, traduction et Notes*. Leiden: E.J. Brill, 1968. Ch. Burchard is developing an edition of the longer text, given in preliminary form in "Ein Vorläufiger griechischer Text von Joseph und Aseneth," *Dielheimer Blätter zum Alten Testament* 14 (1979) 2–53. This is the basis for his English translation in "Joseph and Aseneth," *The Old Testament Pseudepigrapha*, ed. J.H. Charlesworth. Garden City, New York: Doubleday & Company, 1985, vol. 2:202–247, with an introduction 177–201, and many useful notes.

17. THE BYZANTINE REVIVAL OF THE ANCIENT NOVEL

Roderick Beaton

The ancient novels continued to be read and copied throughout the thousand years of the Byzantine empire—indeed a readership for the original texts among educated speakers of Modern Greek seems to have continued up till at least the early 19th century. It should never be forgotten that is very largely to Byzantine copyists that we owe our knowledge of Ancient Greek literature, and this is as true for the Hellenistic novels as for any other sphere. In the case of the novels, it also seems very probable that it was Byzantine taste that determined which of the novels were to be the ones to survive, and which condemned many of the more shocking examples of the genre to be recovered only in fragmentary form from the papyri dug up in more recent times.

Evidence for a Byzantine readership for the novels is scattered fairly widely: in the ninth-century *Bibliotheca* of the Patriarch Photios and the tenth-century compilation the *Suda*, in references to, in particular, *An Ethiopian Story* and *Leucippe and Clitophon* by Byzantine men of letters in the eleventh and twelfth centuries, and among the contents of private libraries at about the same period.[1] There is even the intriguing testimony of miniscule copies of, for example, *Daphnis and Chloe*, which may have been intended for surreptitious reading.[2] But the Byzantines did more than read and copy the novels of antiquity: they also, in the twelfth century and again two centuries later, wrote their own, and added significant innovations to the genre which perform an important bridging function between the earliest literary fiction and the apogee of the genre in more modern times. It is on this Byzantine, or as I have elsewhere termed it, medieval Greek contribution to fiction that the present chapter will concentrate.[3] And

---

[1] Documented in studies of the ancient novel. See for example Hägg (1983) 32–3. See also Gärtner (1969), Beck (1984) 87–96. On the evidence for library holdings in the eleventh century see Vryonis (1957) and Lemerle (1977) 15–63.
[2] See Beck (1984) 133.
[3] For a fuller treatment of the subject see Beaton (1989a), now in an expanded and updated edition (London 1996).

since all but one of these fictions are written in verse, not prose, I shall for the remainder of the chapter prefer the term commonly used to describe their contemporaries in the West, namely "romance".

The Twelfth Century

It is in the century of the *chanson de geste* and the earliest Arthurian romances in the West that we first find men of letters in the capital of the eastern empire, Constantinople, trying their hand at literary fiction on the model of the Hellenistic novels. Three of their romances have come down to us complete, and a fourth in the form of fragmentary excerpts. By contrast with the later period of the Greek verse romance, in the fourteenth and fifteenth centuries, there is no reason to believe that any more than these four romances were written at this time. All four appear to have been written within a few years of each other, by a coterie of writers some of whom certainly, and all of whom probably, were personally acquainted with one another, and more or less professionally employed by members of the imperial aristocracy. Large quantities of rhetorical literature were produced to order at this period in Constantinople, to be read or performed aloud either in public or before the more exclusive audience of a *theatron*—a precursor, perhaps, of the learned academies of the Renaissance. Writers seem to have vied with one another in winning the respect of their peers and the more substantial rewards implied by a commission from a highly placed personage. There is no surviving evidence, however, to tell us whether the romances were so commissioned, or were conceived solely by their authors; nor do we know anything of the audience or readership for which they were intended.[4]

We do at least know the names of the four authors of romances in the twelfth century, which, as we shall see, marks another contrast with their successors two centuries later. Theodore Prodromos was probably born around the year 1100 and lived until at least the mid 1150s. He was a prolific writer in the service of the imperial court at Constantinople, on both secular and religious themes, and may also have been the first man of letters to commit a form of the Modern

---

[4] The fullest study yet of the literary context of the Byzantine twelfth century is to be found in Magdalino (1993). On the *theatra*, see pp. 336–56.

Greek language to writing, in the four comic-satirical "begging poems" attributed to him by a (later) manuscript tradition and by some modern scholars.[5] Of Niketas Eugenianos, author of *Drosilla and Charicles*, we know only that he was a younger contemporary and quite possibly a pupil of Prodromos. The author of the remaining romance that has come down to us entire is harder to place: Eustathios or Eumathios Makrembolites, whose romance *Hysmine and Hysminias* is the only medieval Greek romance to be written in prose, is otherwise known so far only as the author of a book of riddles. Attempts to identify him more closely (for instance with the recipient of a letter addressed to someone of that name in the 1180s) or to pinpoint the composition of his romance more precisely in time have so far proved inconclusive.[6] Finally, the author of *Aristandros and Kallithea*, Konstantinos Manasses which survives only in the form of mostly moralizing extracts in later manuscripts, belonged to the same literary circles of the Byzantine court as Prodromos and Eugenianos. His best-known work was a chronicle of world history in verse which can be dated between 1143 and 1152. It is usually supposed that his romance was written after this work.

In the state of the evidence it seems most probable therefore that all four romances belong to the first half of the reign of Manuel I Comnenos (1143–1180).

The broad dependence of the three complete romances (and probably Manasses' fragmentary one as well) on Achilles Tatius and Heliodorus has been taken for granted at least since the time of Erwin Rohde, whose influential study of the ancient novel, originally published in 1876, extends to a brief survey of its Byzantine successors.[7] There are certainly copious allusions to *Leucippe and Clitophon* and the

---

[5] For Prodromos' dates and known career see Hörandner (1974), which includes an authoritative bibliography of his works and, more speculatively, Kazhdan and Franklin (1984) 92–100. The issue of Prodromos' authorship of the *Poems of Poor Prodromos* (*Ptochoprodromika*) has been debated inconclusively for almost a century. There is a good modern edition of these vernacular poems (with German translation and introduction) by Hans Eideneier (1991). On the poems and their literary and historical context see M. Alexiou (1986) and Beaton (1987).

[6] For discussion of the evidence and relevant bibliography see Beaton (1989a) 77–9; Magdalino (1992). Since then the case for Makrembolites' romance preceding the other two has been restated by Suzanne MacAlister (1991). I now accept, with Magdalino (1992; cf. 1993: 396–7), that all four should be dated close together in the middle part of the twelfth century, though I continue to believe that Prodromos' and Eugenianos' romances predate that of Makrembolites.

[7] Reprinted as Rohde (1914). There is no English translation of this book.

An Ethiopian Story in these romances, both in overall plot design and in many points of detail, but the reader who approaches them armed only with the damning words of Rohde and the drily judicious summaries provided by Herbert Hunger in the authoritative *Byzantinische Handbuch* volume devoted to secular literature,[8] is in for a surprise. Although at a very broad level of generality Prodromos and Eugenianos may be said to have followed the plot structure of Heliodorus, while Makrembolites has preferred Achilles Tatius, none of the three is the least like either of these ancient novels. In particular, it is precisely those features of Achilles' and Heliodorus' novels that most strikingly characterise them for modern readers, which their Byzantine successors have chosen to strip away: the vaudeville melodrama, the shock tactics and sadism of Achilles, the mysticism of Heliodorus.

The Byzantine romances of the twelfth century are works of remarkable, and surely deliberate, refinement. The rhetorical art which in the twelfth century had been given a new rein under the Comnenian dynasty at Constantinople is here shown off in abundance. Rhetoric and the power of artifice (whether verbal or visual) become the central props of the stories. And the quest for salvation that many have identified as an underlying theme in the ancient novels, reappears in a new guise, in the painstaking recreation of an imaginary pagan past by a group of writers who owed their allegiance to the most powerful Christian ruler in the world of their time.

Prodromos' romance, *Rhodanthe and Dosikles*, begins, like that of Heliodorus, *in medias res*. The hero and heroine are captured by pirates in a surprise attack on the town of Rhodes. In captivity, Dosikles compares life stories with a fellow-prisoner, Kratandros, whose ideal love has recently ended in tragedy. Dosikles and Rhodanthe, we learn, have eloped from their home in Abydos. A large part of the story is then taken up with the fortunes of their pirate captors, who are engaged first in diplomatic and then in armed conflict with the king of a fictitious state. As the battle goes against the pirates, Rhodanthe and Dosikles are separated, only to be reunited through the agency of Kratandros, whose parents, with Rhodanthe, arrive just in time to forestall the human sacrifice of the two men on a pyre. All their pleas are in vain, however, until a shower of rain, borrowed from Xenophon's *Ephesian Tale*, intervenes to save Dosikles and Kratandros. After a final test of their constancy, in the form of a hysterical pas-

---

[8] Hunger (1978) ii. 119–42.

sion for Dosikles conceived by Kratandros' mother, the lovers are finally reconciled to their home and their parents.[9]

Drosilla and Charikles by Niketas Eugenianos in many respects follows the plot-outline of Prodromos' romance quite closely. This romance too begins with a sudden attack, this time by Parthian raiders. And here too the tale of the lovers' meeting and elopement is told in retrospect to a fellow-captive, this time Kleandros, whose own tragic love-story, unusually in the genre, will continue in parallel to the main action almost to the end. Various assaults are made on the chastity of both hero and heroine but without success, and a war is again the cause of their separation (although Eugenianos, unlike Prodromos, leaves out the details). A comical-pastoral interlude follows, at the village where Drosilla and Charikles will be reunited, in which a bumptious yokel with a prodigious knowledge of classical literature presses his suit to the heroine, and the old woman who has given shelter to the lovers gets drunk and dances on the table to celebrate their reunion. Finally, news comes to Kleandros that his betrothed has died and he at once dies of grief, while a helpful merchant provides safe homeward passage to the more fortunate pair of the title. A notable feature of this romance is the inclusion in Book III of a number of love songs and letters, which represent the sum total of Byzantine lyrical love poetry up to this date.[10]

Makrembolites' *Hysmine and Hysminias* is narrated entirely through the persona of the hero, in this respect following a precedent set by Achilles Tatius but with much greater consistency, and without the device of the opening frame. The world of the previous two romances had been a mixture of the real geography of the eastern Mediterranean in Hellenistic or Roman times (Eugenianos extends the time-frame to include Arabs, but their enemies are the Parthians of an earlier period) with fictional placenames and peoples. Now, in Makrembolites' romance, the geography is pure fiction, as characters move around a world of invented Greek cities and specially devised pagan festivals.

Hysminias is sent from his city to another as herald in honour of Zeus. There, his attention is attracted by a series of allegorical paintings, and by Hysmine, the daughter of the house, who makes

---

[9] The text has been recently edited by M. Marcovich (1992) in the Teubner series. For discussion and further bibliography see Beaton (1989a) 67–73.

[10] For the text see Conca (1990), with editorial material in Latin. On this romance see Conca (1986); Beaton (1989a) 73–5; Jouanno (1989; 1992).

advances to him. In a dream Hysminias is arraigned before the throne of Eros, here not so much a god as an emperor with the full trappings of the Byzantine court, and swears terrified allegiance. In subsequent dreams (which include some of the most overtly erotic writing in Greek fiction to date) the way is prepared for Hysminias to fall irremediably in love with Hysmine. They then elope, but are separated when their ship runs into a storm and Hysmine (in a reminiscence of one of the fates meted out to Achilles Tatius' Leucippe) has to be thrown overboard to placate an angry god. Saved by a dolphin Hysmine is then sold as a slave, and in due course Hysminias too, who has been captured by the obligatory pirates, will find himself a slave in the same household. Only after the equally obligatory trials of their constancy will the pair be recognised as the free citizens they are and returned to Hysminias' home city to be married. Here the narrative ends, with the hero, still waiting for nightfall on his wedding day, promising to immortalize the love and adventures of the pair "in unfading timbers and in adamantine precious stones, with Hermes' pen and ink and in language breathing the fire of rhetoric" as an "imperishable monument".[11]

Finally, given the state in which it has come down to us, there is not much that can be said of the plot of Manasses' fragmentary *Aristandros and Kallithea*. It seems to have followed a similar pattern to the other three, with the hero and heroine passing through the hands of three sets of tyrannical masters and encountering a range of wild and exotic beasts, an innovation in the genre at this time.[12]

There are, then, common threads running through the Greek romances of the twelfth century, and these are actually a good deal stronger than their evident and undisguised links back to the novels of antiquity. What the Byzantine revivers of the genre have done is to adapt the skeletal structure of the ancient novels as a vehicle to pursue preoccupations of their own. And it is entirely characteristic of Byzantine conceptions of imitation, and of the authority of prece-

---

[11] There is no modern edition of this romance, which was edited twice in the last century: Hercher (1859) 159–286; Hilberg (1876). It has, however, been more extensively discussed than the previous two: see, in particular, Gigante (1960); M. Alexiou (1977); Beaton (1989a) 77–84.

[12] Two rather different attempts have been made to present the surviving fragments and reconstruct something of the plot: Tsolakis (1967) in Greek; and Mazal (1967) in German.

dent, that they should have chosen to adorn their work with many detailed, and sometimes playful allusions, to these and other ancient texts which their readers would no doubt have recognised and appreciated. One sometimes suspects that the pleasures of reading (or hearing a text spoken) for the Byzantines must have combined something of our own aesthetic interests in literature with the challenge of the crossword puzzle. But before we hasten to dismiss the authors of these romances as frivolous intellectuals, we might remind ourselves that there are both ancient and modern parallels for such recondite literary pastimes. The ancient novel itself affords a precedent, and the new currency given to such terms as "game" and "play" in contemporary discussions of the "postmodern" invites a comparison with today.

Between Epic and Romance

A discussion of the twelfth-century Greek revival of the ancient novel would not be complete without some mention of another text which is much better known, even in English, than the ones discussed in the previous section, but whose connection with the novel or romance as a genre is more problematic. This is *Digenes Akrites*, dubbed variously "the national epic of the Modern Greeks", a romance, a "proto-romance", or a compilation of heroic lays.[13] In many respects *Digenes* has more in common with the western, and contemporary, *chanson de geste* than with the romance: it is a tale, in verse, of daring deeds in the turbulent badlands that divide Byzantium ("Romania" in the text) from the Muslim Saracens to the south and east. But the most frequently recurring feat of daring in the story is the abduction, whether actual or attempted, of women; and in both halves of the story (the one dealing with the abduction and marriage of the hero's parents, the other with his own elopement with a bride whom he has then to defend against all comers) it is love rather than any more strategic or military objective that is won and held by feats of arms.

Digenes Akrites in its earliest form may then have represented a staging-post towards the fully fledged revival of the romance. In its

---

[13] Respectively by (among others) N.G. Polites (1906); Mavrogordato (1956); Beaton (1989a) 29–48; Ricks (1990). See most recently the essays on this work edited by Beaton and Ricks (1993).

subsequent elaborations, one probably dated to the mid-twelfth century, the very time of the revival of the romance, and the other no earlier than the fifteenth century, it certainly acquired many of the outward trappings of the romances that were current at each of these periods.[14]

Though the extent to which *Digenes Akrites* may have influenced the revival of the romance in the twelfth century remains uncertain, there is little doubt that it helped to pave the way for the second Byzantine revival of the genre in the fourteenth and fifteenth centuries. This is most evident in its language and its metre, which were to become standard for the Greek romance after the twelfth century. Although it is not known for certain what sort of Greek was used for the earliest written version of *Digenes Akrites*, its story fairly clearly derives from popular, local tales which must have been recited in the vernacular, and there is good evidence that a vernacular poem on the subject was known in Constantinople by about 1140. Although we can be fairly sure that this was not identical to the vernacular version of the poem we now possess, preserved in a manuscript of the fifteenth century,[15] it does seem certain that *Digenes Akrites* was the first fictional narrative of any length to circulate in written form in the vernacular (essentially, an early form of Modern Greek). In this it contrasts noticeably with the four romances of the same century, all of them written in a form of ancient Greek, which was the formal and official language of the Byzantine middle ages; and in this it would be followed by all subsequent attempts at literary fiction in Greek down to the seventeenth century.

The metre of *Digenes Akrites*, which among the twelfth-century romances it shares only with Manasses' *Aristandros and Kallithea*, is the fifteen-syllable accentual metre known to the Byzantines from this time on as "political" verse, a term whose precise significance is still

---

[14] The three oldest attested versions are: E (from a fifteenth-century manuscript in the Escorial, Madrid), in vernacular language and preserving material going back to the early twelfth century [edited by S. Alexiou (1985, 1990); translation with facing Greek text by Ricks (1990)]; G (from a thirteenth-century manuscript in the Grottaferrata monastery near Rome), in a mixed language, preserving an elaboration of the story from the mid-twelfth century [bilingual edition by Mavrogordato (1956), translation by Hull (1990)]; and "Z", the archetype of four later manuscripts which can be traced back to a deliberate compilation of the other two versions in the fifteenth century [reconstructed, in parallel with the E and G versions, by Trapp (1971)].

[15] This is the E(scorial) version of the poem. See note 14.

disputed, but probably meant something like "humdrum", "everyday".[16] "Political" verse had been in use for some two centuries before this in learned literature, and also, at some period unknown, became the dominant verseform for Modern Greek oral poetry. Though used by Manasses, both for his romance and for his chronicle of world history, it was not the choice of Prodromos (who did use it for other compositions in verse) or Eugenianos, both of whom preferred the Byzantine adaptation of the classical iambic trimeter for their romances. From the fourteenth century onwards, however—and indeed into the twentieth—the "political" verseform went on to establish itself as in effect the "national" Modern Greek metre, and is used without exception in the later vernacular romances.

The Later Vernacular Romances

By the time of the reappearance of the romance genre in Greek in (probably) the early fourteenth century, the Byzantine empire had shrunk considerably from its twelfth-century borders, and as it continued to dwindle before the combined pressures of western expansion into Greece and the Aegean, and the growing power of the Turks in Anatolia, more and more Greek-speakers found themselves living outside its borders. This is one reason why it is preferable at this period to speak of the "medieval Greek" rather than the "Byzantine" romance.

Another is that at this period the history of Greek fiction moves more closely into step with the history of fiction in western Europe. Several of the romances which appeared in Greek at this time are translations from Italian or French, and represent quite late adaptations of fictional stories widely disseminated in the west. It is possible that the western tales chosen to be translated into Greek at this time were picked for their distant thematic resemblance to the ancient novel.[17] The well-known tales of *Fleur et Blanchefleur* and *Pierre de Provence et la Belle Maguelonne*, which become respectively *Florios and Platzia-Flora* and *Imberios and Margarona* in Greek, involve (exceptionally in the western medieval genre) far-flung travels around the eastern Mediterranean.[18]

---

[16] See in particular M. Jeffreys (1974); Alexiou and Holton (1976) and Beaton (1989a) 94–7.
[17] The case for this is argued in Beaton (1989a) 132–42.
[18] Both are included in Kriaras (1955): *Florios* pp. 131–96; *Imberios* pp. 197–249.

The *War of Troy* tells a story whose tradition has never died out in Greek, although its direct source is French and its ultimate source is Latin.[19] Boccaccio's *Theseid* is set at an Athenian court seen through the filter of the early Italian Renaissance,[20] while *Apollonius of Tyre* is of course directly an ancient novel, although the two fifteenth-century Greek versions were translated from Italian.[21]

If these translated romances can be said to continue the tradition of the ancient novel at all, they do so in terms which had already by this time been fully laid down in the vernacular literatures of western Europe. On the other hand, from the same period (roughly the fourteenth and fifteenth centuries) we also have five original romances in verse. Most of these also show an awareness of western developments; but in three of them the tradition of the ancient novel, and particularly of its twelfth-century revival, can be more clearly discerned. It tends to be assumed that those romances which are translated from western languages took shape in the territories of Greece and the Aegean which were under western rule for all or part of this period.[22] Conversely, the original romances of the period, and especially the three which show the greatest familiarity with the ancient novel and with the Byzantine romances of the twelfth century, are more likely to have been produced in Constantinople. In what follows I shall concentrate on the three romances which may well, as we shall see, have been produced at the Byzantine court during the fourteenth century, and which undoubtedly represent the most developed contribution to literary fiction in Greek before the sixteenth century.

The Original "Constantinopolitan" Romances of the Fourteenth Century

All the Greek romances of this period have been transmitted anonymously (and are preserved in manuscripts copied in the late fifteenth

---

[19] The *editio princeps* of this 17,000-line poem, by Elizabeth Jeffreys and Manolis Papathomopoulos was announced in 1971. Although collation of the seven manuscripts and editorial work is reported to be complete, it is not yet certain when it will appear (Jeffreys and Papathomopoulos *forthcoming*).

[20] Printed in Venice in 1529. Only the first book has so far been published in a modern edition (Follieri 1959). For recent work see Olsen (1990) (1993).

[21] The older, unrhymed, version has not yet appeared in a modern edition [see Wagner (1870) 63–90]. A facsimile of the rhymed version, printed in Venice in 1553, has been published by Kechagioglou (1982b); cf. Kechagioglou (1986).

[22] See most recently on this E. Jeffreys (1993).

and sixteenth centuries, between one and two hundred years after the likely period of their composition). We have even fewer grounds than we did in the case of their twelfth-century counterparts for dating them more precisely, or for determining the sequence in which they were composed. Like the twelfth-century romances, they have many shared elements of plot and structure, although, no less than their counterparts of two centuries previously, they also show marked individual variations and each has a distinctive character of its own.[23] I begin with *Kallimachos and Chrysorrhoe* simply because, uniquely, we do have some circumstantial evidence to identify the author and thus to locate the composition of the romance in place and time.

The story told in this romance, in 2,407 lines of "political" verse, seems in its outer structure to be derived from fairytale, but in the detail of its unfolding reveals a literary sophistication comparable to that displayed by the Hellenistic and twelfth-century authors in the genre. The hero is the youngest of three brothers sent out on a quest. Venturing further than his elders, he braves the guardians of a magic castle to find inside a beautiful maiden, quite naked and suspended by her hair from a sumptuously painted ceiling. The girl is the prisoner of a cruel ogre (*drakon*), whom the hero kills; the pair then violate the strict Byzantine taboos on mixed bathing and go on to consummate their love by the poolside. So ends the first half of this bipartite tale. In the second, a new and powerful rival to Kallimachos appears, in the form of a foreign king who abducts Chrysorrhoe. Only after a long journey, and a complicated subterfuge including disguise as a gardener, is the hero able to be re-united with his love. Before he can rescue her, however, Chrysorrhoe has to plead the justice of their case before the king and court. Then, the original quest of the three brothers forgotten, the happy pair return to the ogre's castle to live happily ever after.[24]

The evidence we have about the authorship and context of this

---

[23] See Agapitos (1991) 64; 199; 319–20 and *passim*.
[24] The best available edition is by Pichard (1956), which includes (in French) introduction, commentary and parallel prose translation. For discussion of textual problems and useful emendations see Chatzigiakoumes (1977) 169–210 and (with caution) Agapitos (1990a) (1991). For discussions see Beaton (1989a) 101–2, 107–9, 115–7; Agapitos (1991). On the new sexual explicitness of this romance see Agapitos (1990b) and Garland (1990), a useful contrastive survey of the theme of sexuality in all the medieval romances. The first ever English version of this romance, together with *Belthandros* and *Libistros*, in a translation by Gavin Betts, appeared in the *Garland Medieval Library* series in 1994.

romance comes from an epigram by the court poet, Manuel Philes, which ascribes its composition to a cousin of the reigning emperor (who can be identified as Andronikos II Palaeologos), also called Andronikos Palaeologos. Philes gives a resumé of a tale written by Andronikos which in most respects quite closely resembles the romance as it has been preserved. The discrepancies (of which there are a number) can be attributed to two causes: Philes' unconcealed determination to extract a Christian allegory from the poem he is summarizing, and the distance of almost two centuries that separates the composition from the sole surviving manuscript. (It is a notorious fact, in Greek as in other medieval vernaculars, that texts of this sort undergo much greater alteration in the course of manuscript tradition than do those in the officially sanctioned "high" language.) The information provided by Manuel Philes enables us to date the romance between 1310 and 1340, and to place its composition in all probability in or close to the seat of the Byzantine court at Constantinople.[25]

Of this group of three romances, *Kallimachos* is the closest in language to its predecessors. (Although in most respects essentially Modern Greek, the language of this romance retains the largest number of features from the ancient language, such as the infinitive and the formation of the future tense.)[26] It includes long and elaborate *ekphraseis*—set-piece descriptions of the ogre's castle, of the richly painted rooms it contains, of the heroine, of the bathhouse, and so on—and the names of the principal characters allude to both the ancient novel and the 12th-century romance. (The name of the heroine in Chariton's novel, *Chaireas and Callirrhoe* has been split in two to give *Kalli*machos and Chrys*orrhoe*; and the heroine in Palaeologos' romance also has a name very similar to the heroine of the subplot in Prodromos' 12th-century romance, Chrysochroe.)

More fundamentally, this romance diverges from what had for long become the norm in both the ancient and the Byzantine genre in two respects: the two main characters are no longer the playthings of chance, tyrannized by (in the twelfth-century romances) a god of love who wields the absolute power of the Byzantine monarch; and

---

[25] The text of the epigram is most accessible in Knös (1962) 280–4, where the attribution of the romance is fully, but inconclusively, discussed. The attribution has been accepted by Pichard (1956) xxiii, and others, e.g. Beck (1971) 8, 124–5; Beaton (1989a) 101. For a contrary view see Agapitos (1993).

[26] See Apostolopoulos (1984).

the love-making of the hero and heroine, taboo in all previous examples of the genre, is narrated with both tenderness and gusto. (Other elements, such as the sadism of the scene in which the heroine is first introduced, and the spirited defence by the heroine of her rightful mate in a trial which takes place before the king who is his rival, can respectively be traced back to *Leucippe and Clitophon* and *Chaireas and Callirrhoe*). It is noticeable that the hero of this romance, in particular, is far more man of action than any Greek romance hero since Chaireas (who distinguishes himself in war before he can be reunited with his wife Callirrhoe). Kallimachos is never enslaved by Eros—he sets out at the beginning of the story to prove himself by his adventures, fearlessly pole-vaults into the magic castle, ambushes and kills the ogre who keeps the heroine prisoner there, and resourcefully traces the route taken by the abducted Chrysorrhoe and plans and executes an inventive strategy in order to gain access to her. This is a story of love in which the two principal characters have taken their destiny into their own hands.

Considerably shorter than *Kallimachos and Chrysorrhoe* at 1,348 lines, and possibly abridged in the single surviving manuscript, *Belthandros and Chrysantza* also sets its royal hero out in search of adventure, on a pretext which has nothing to do with the main story. A prince of the Romans (by which is meant the Byzantines), Belthandros leaves home to wander through Anatolia (the geography of this romance, unlike that of *Kallimachos*, is mostly real). Attracted by a river which contains a fiery star in its depths (an oxymoron which enacts in a novel way a conventional metaphor for love), the hero finds himself in an enchanted castle, which turns out to be the Castle of Eros. Here, in a mock-feudal ceremony, he is made to swear allegiance to the king of love, and chooses out of a fantasy beauty contest Chrysantza, daughter of the king of Antioch, to be his bride. Back in the real world, Belthandros travels on to Antioch, where he is recognised and loved at once by Chrysantza, who has never in reality set eyes on him before.

From here on the tale develops with a realism uncharacteristic of the genre. Belthandros and Chrysantza have become secret lovers in her father's palace. When an envious courtier spies on them and reveals their secret to the king, Chrysantza's lady-in-waiting, Phaidrokaza, is co-opted. Supposedly it is she, not the princess, that Belthandros has been visiting secretly at night, and Belthandros and

Phaidrokaza even go through a form of marriage. Eventually, however, the strain of this *ménage-à-trois* becomes too much for the real lovers, and all three flee the court of Antioch. On the way Phaidrokaza and their retainers are drowned in a river in spate, and the hero and heroine make a sorry sight when they are washed up on the riverbank, naked and destitute, each believing the other dead. Rescue comes in the form of a ship from Constantinople, where Belthandros is welcomed home with open arms. There he marries Chrysantza and is proclaimed heir to his father's kingdom.[27]

Apart from the striking realism of some scenes, and the highly allegorical, imaginative lyricism of others, this romance is notable for its almost perfectly symmetrical construction (if it has indeed been abridged, the job has been carefully done).[28] There is symmetry between the hero's alienation and departure from home and his welcome return with which the romance respectively begins and ends, between the river that leads to the Castle of Love near the beginning and the river that all but destroys the lovers near the end, between the phantasmagoric Castle of Love and the real court of Antioch, ruled by Chrysantza's father. In this romance, as in *Kallimachos*, the hero is capable of decisive action and the heroine is an active, at times resourceful accomplice. Western customs are more in evidence in this romance, particularly in the feudal relationship of king and vassal and the terminology which describes it. On the other hand, the spectacular iconography of Eros as king owes an evident debt to Makrembolites' romance of the twelfth-century,[29] and the anonymous author of this romance seems to have known the work of Prodromos and Eugenianos as well. There is little to connect this romance directly with any of the ancient novels, however. Of the three romances in this group, *Belthandros and Chrysantza* would seem to have travelled the most distance from the novel of antiquity.

The longest, and also the most complex, of the group is *Libistros and Rhodamne*. This romance has been preserved in five manuscripts, with sufficient textual divergences among them as to render impossible

---

[27] For the text see Kriaras (1955) 85–130, with emendations by Chatzegiakoumes (1977) 213–46 and Agapitos (1991). On literary aspects and narrative structure see Beaton (1989a) 102, 109–10, 118–22; Nørgaard (1989); Agapitos (1991).

[28] See Agapitos (1991) e.g. 69–70, 158.

[29] On the iconography of Eros as king in these and the twelfth-century romances see Cupane (1974); Beaton (1989a) 152–5; Garland (1990); Magdalino (1992).

the conventional task of an editor, of reconstructing a plausible approximation to the original text from which they derive. The full text must in its original form have been a little over 4,000 lines in length. The reason for this greater length does not lie in a greater density of narrative incident, but rather in two characteristics of this romance which make it unique among its contemporaries. First of all, like several of its predecessors in the genre, *Libistros* has a subplot in which the adventures of a second pair of lovers act as a foil to the main action; and like Eugenianos in *Drosilla and Charikles*, in particular, the author of *Libistros* has extended this subplot throughout the duration of the main action. Secondly (and this is the principal reason for the greater length), again following the example of Eugenianos which in this respect is otherwise unique in the tradition, *Libistros* has been hugely amplified by the verbatim inclusion of a large number of love letters and songs. These, taken together with the comparable, although many fewer, letters and songs in Eugenianos' romance, make up the sum total of the Byzantine love lyric.

The main story of the romance is that of Libistros, a prince of a fictional kingdom which may tenuously be linked to crusader Lebanon.[30] Like Belthandros, Libistros finds himself arraigned before Eros the King and promises himself his vassal. Faithful to his promise, he then sets out to find Rhodamne, who lives in a castle which is described in allegorical terms. Libistros, who temperamentally has more in common with his ancient and twelfth-century counterparts than with Kallimachos or Belthandros, pitches camp outside and is content, for the space of more than a thousand lines of the romance, to send love letters to the object of his affection, first of all by means of a carefully aimed arrow, latterly through helpful intermediaries. Finally his patience and persistence are rewarded, Rhodamne leaves the castle to go out hunting, and the love of the pair is consummated. But, as in the other two romances of this group, a snag now presents itself. Rhodamne had already been betrothed to the King of Egypt, who shortly afterwards abducts her. Libistros, not knowing where she has been taken, sets out to find her. In the course of his wanderings he falls in with another wanderer, also lovelorn (this is the point at which the romance begins), to whom he tells his story so far. The other wanderer is Klitovos, the hero of the subplot, who

---

[30] On the possible significance of the names of this romance (and also in *Belthandros*) see Beaton (1989b).

now becomes Libistros' helper. Using magical means, Klitovos first finds his way to Rhodamne, where she is living disguised as an inn-keeper, so far refusing the favours of her abductor, and paves the way for the reunion of the pair. Libistros and Rhodamne return home triumphantly to be married, along with Klitovos, who as a consolation is married off to Rhodamne's sister, although not before a lengthy exchange of lovesongs on the way. Libistros and Rhodamne live happily ever after. Klitovos' wife, however, dies, at which point he returns to his native Armenia to tell the whole story—Libistros' and his own—to his own first love who had been the cause of all his adventures.[31]

The most remarkable feature of this romance is its use of a first-person narrative, and the enormous complexity of the narrative structure that interweaves the stories told by Libistros to Klitovos, by Klitovos to his beloved Myrtane, and often further embedded stories within each of those. The use of first-person narrative places this romance in the tradition of *Leucippe and Clitophon* (from which the name Klitovos clearly derives) and of Makrembolites' twelfth-century romance in prose, *Hysmine and Hysminias*. Achilles Tatius had introduced his first-person narrative by a frame-story (the narrator meets a disconsolate young man in Sidon, admiring a painting of the abduction of Europa by the bull, and the young man turns out to be Clitophon, who then tells his story). By contrast Makrembolites, probably drawing on the Byzantine rhetorical exercise of *ethopoeia* or character study, a kind of precursor of the dramatic monologue,[32] couches the whole of his narrative within the point of view and the speech of the fictional Hysminias. The anonymous author of *Libistros* could be said to combine these two precedents, and has almost certainly also drawn on the elaborations of the frame-story in medieval Arabic and

---

[31] This romance is best approached through the edition of J. Lambert (1935), which prints the contents of the Escorial manuscript facing the first 979 lines of the Naples manuscript, and thereafter facing the Scaligeranus manuscript, whose first quarter is missing. The five manuscripts have been re-edited on computer file by Tina Lendari, who has also provided the *editio princeps* of the somewhat divergent Vatican MS [Lendari (1994), cf. (1993)]. A "synoptic" edition of the three versions which may be closest to the archetype has been announced by Agapitos (1992).

[32] See Beaton (1989a) 20–25, 85. The links between this romance and the highly sophisticated character studies of Nikephoros Basilakes, of the mid-twelfth century, are noted by Pignani (1983) 41–2 and documented in the footnotes to her edition of the *Progymnasmata* (Rhetorical Exercises) of this writer (1983). More recently Magdalino (1992) 203 has persuasively proposed that Makrembolites may have been Basilakes' pupil, and this suggestion, if accepted, would help to confirm the date of the romance.

Persian narratives, which had been available in Greek translation since the eleventh century.[33] *Libistros* retains the opening frame from Achilles Tatius, but unlike him develops it to become an organizing principle of the whole romance. Like Makrembolites, he puts into the mouth of his character only things which Libistros himself could have known and experienced, but unlike Makrembolites he introduces Klitovos as both the recipient of Libistros' narrative and as a narrator in his own right. Within the story, Klitovos and Libistros narrate their own stories to each other. But at the very beginning of the romance, and again in its final lines, it is indicated that everything is in fact being narrated by Klitovos, after the end of the whole story, to his former mistress Myrtane. The romance is thus teasingly open-ended, since Klitovos evidently hopes to regain the favours of the girl he had earlier loved and lost—precisely by recounting to her and her court the sum of his and Libistros' adventures!

In many respects, *Libistros* is the closest of this group of romances to its predecessors in the genre: hero and heroine are relatively passive victims first of Eros, later of a powerful rival; the allegorical use of *ekphrasis* extends the same device in the twelfth-century romances, particularly *Hysmine and Hysminias* with which *Libistros* has a marked affinity; the amplification of love letters and songs extends to an unprecedented degree the role of lyrical love poetry, otherwise unknown in Byzantium, that had first been exploited by Eugenianos in *Drosilla and Charikles*. It has been suggested that on these grounds *Libistros* should be dated the earliest of the fourteenth-century romances.[34] However, although *Libistros* reveals perhaps the closest knowledge of some, at least, of the earlier texts in the genre, *Kallimachos* is not far behind in its use of *Chaireas and Callirrhoe*, and indeed is much more conservative than *Libistros* in its language. On the other hand, as we have seen, *Libistros* is as innovative as any of the others in this group in extending the potential of the earlier genre in directions of its own, in this case towards lyrical amplification and narrative complexity. In the present state of our knowledge, we can conclude no more than that each of the three represents a significant and original contribution to the romance genre at this period, drawing on the past to break new ground in language, in subject matter, in the introduction of lyrical elements, and in narrative structure.

---

[33] See Kechagioglou (1982a) (1988).
[34] See Agapitos (1993).

Other Original Romances

Mention should more briefly be made of two romance-like tales of this period, also written in the vernacular using the fifteen-syllable "political" verseform. These are the *Tale of Achilles* (also known as *The Achilleid*) and the *Tale of Troy* (also known as *A Byzantine Iliad* and *Troas*). Both of these are reworkings of stories inherited from the classical tradition, possibly in the same spirit that some of the earliest ancient novels are thought to represent "romanticized" history.

The *Tale of Achilles* is linked to the Achilles of mythology only by its hero's name, by the fact that he is prince of the Myrmidons, and that he has a bosom-friend called Pandrouklos (Patroclus). In most other respects this work is a romance, in which the hero first distinguishes himself in war, is then visited by Eros and declares his love for the (unnamed) daughter of a defeated opponent, and fights another series of battles in order to abduct her. The wedding is celebrated with a tournament, which may imply a connexion with the West, but such things were also known in Byzantium in the twelfth century. And then the story parts company with the genre of romance. Achilles' wife falls ill and the last part of the story is taken up with their extended speeches of leavetaking as she dies. An epilogue which transports the inconsolable hero to the Trojan War, to be tricked and killed by Paris (the hero of the *Tale of Troy*) is almost certainly a later interpolation.[35]

Generically this seems to be a hybrid text. It displays no specific knowledge of the ancient novels, though its author certainly seems to know Makrembolites' twelfth-century romance and—the work with which the *Tale* has most in common—the equally hybrid *Digenes Akrites*. In date it could be placed anywhere between the thirteenth and the fifteenth centuries.

The *Tale of Troy* seems to be a late work, dating around the time of the fall of Constantinople in 1453. It contains a mishmash of elements deriving ultimately from Homer with much more that can be traced to the twelfth-century world chronicle in verse by Konstantinos Manasses and to the romances of the fourteenth century. If

---

[35] The fullest of the three surviving versions is published by Hesseling (1919); for a new edition, without introduction or commentary, of the abbreviated Oxford version see O. Smith (1990), forthcoming edition of all three announced in 1987, has been frustrated by that scholar's untimely death in 1994. For discussions and older bibliography see Beaton (1989a) 99–101, 196–7, 114–5; more recently see Smith (1988) (1993).

this curious text is to be regarded as a romance at all, it is a romance of Paris. The young hero is put out to sea in a basket, like Moses, to forestall the consequences of his birth prophesied to his mother in a dream. Later he sets out on his travels, and arrives at Helen's castle just as she is won by Menelaus in a tournament. Menelaus has then to depart on business, the hero and heroine fall in love and elope to Troy. The consequence is the Trojan War, and an episodic second half of the romance sees Paris eclipsed by Achilles, whom he treacherously kills (as in the interpolated epilogue to the *Tale of Achilles*) only to lose his own life as the Greeks avenge their fallen hero. Helen, by this time, has been completely forgotten.[36]

The *Tale of Troy* is not an impressive piece of literature. But it probably testifies to a trend in the fifteenth century, which seems to be characteristic of the final years of Byzantium and the aftermath of its fall, to put together new stories and to copy and adapt older ones for a more popular audience, perhaps in the spirit of preserving something of the legacy of the lost capital city. Certainly the *Tale of Troy* is the first Greek romance to indicate explicitly that it is addressed to a popular, rather than an educated, audience.[37] And there is evidence from the manuscript transmission of many other vernacular texts at this time, that older works not originally written for such an audience were copied and/or adapted for this purpose.

Finally, given the precarious manuscript transmission of those romances from this period that we do possess, it seems probable that many more romances or romance-like narratives were produced during the final years of the Byzantine empire than have come down to us. The chances of any of these coming to light now must be considered slim indeed. But we do have bibliographical evidence for two other tales which sound somewhat similar in genre and scope to the *Tale of Achilles* and *Tale of Troy*,[38] and this confirms that the romance and its offshoots were cultivated more widely in Greek at the end of the middle ages.

---

[36] The text has been edited by Nørgaard and Smith (1975); the fullest discussion and commentary is to be found in the Italian translation by Lavagnini (1988). See also Beaton (1989a) 104–5, 112–3, 130–1.

[37] "We have books of wise men and rhetors | but still I am 'writing down' to some of the young, | in hopes they will hear a little of the story of Troy..." (lines 886–8). Similar sentiments are found in other vernacular texts going back to the mid-fourteenth century, but not elsewhere in the romances [see also Beaton (1989a) 185–6, 233].

[38] *Story of Francesco and Bella* and *Story of Theseus, King of Athens*, reported among the

Afterlife of the Ancient Novel in Greek

The tradition of the ancient novel does not simply peter out with the fall of Constantinople, however. Around the turn of the seventeenth century, in Venetian-ruled Crete, the phoenix rose from the ashes in one of the most brilliant achievements of all Modern Greek literature, the 10,000-line verse romance *Erotokritos* by Vitsentzos Kornaros. This is loosely based on *Paris et Vienne*, one of the western romances of the late Middle Ages whose story of love and wanderings around the eastern Mediterranean can be placed, alongside *Fleur et Blanchefleur* and *Pierre de Provence* (which as we saw had also been translated into Greek), in the tradition of the ancient novel. With considerable success, Kornaros has excised from the story all those elements of far-flung adventure which may possibly have attracted him to *Paris et Vienne* in the first place, in order to create a finely balanced tale of love and war, refined to a new plane by the rhetoric and the human psychology of the Renaissance.[39]

Somewhat later, on the eve of Greek national independence in 1821, we find a spate of printed editions (not translations) of the ancient novels and some of their Byzantine successors, and the adventures of the ancient novel in Greek can be said to come full circle at the point where Adamantios Koraes, writing in 1804 in a preface to Heliodorus' *An Ethiopian Story*, can claim the *modern* European novel as an originally Greek invention. It was Koraes in the same preface who first coined a generic term in Greek to describe the novel or romance: *mythistoria*, and defined it by a slight modification of the definition proposed by Pierre Daniel Huet, whose *Traité de l'origine des romans* of 1670 had been one of the first European attempts to explore the origin of modern fiction in the ancient Greek world. Noting that many of the medieval Greek examples of this genre were not in prose but in verse, Koraes proposed to his Greek readers the definition of *mythistoria*: "a fictional, but plausible story of sufferings in love, written with artistry and dramatically, for the most part in prose".[40]

---

contents of a sixteenth-century library in Constantinople. See also Beaton (1989a) 104–5.

[39] The standard edition is by S. Alexiou (1980). For discussions see Holton (1991a) (1991b).

[40] For a fuller statement of this argument and relevant bibliography see Beaton (1994) 49–53.

In this way the modern Greek novel, as it has taken shape since the early nineteenth century, can be seen as the successor of Heliodorus' *An Ethiopian Story* and the other Greek novels of antiquity, and of the tradition of literary fiction in Greek as it has developed since the twelfth century.

18. THE HERITAGE OF THE ANCIENT GREEK NOVEL IN FRANCE AND BRITAIN

Gerald Sandy

Introduction

To make a long, complex story short and simple, the literary form now known variously as novel, romance or prose fiction evolved in the way it has because an unnamed, low-ranking German mercenary soldier completely ignorant of both Greek and Latin snatched the manuscript containing Heliodorus' *Ethiopian History* from the smouldering ruins of the Bibliotheca Corviniana of King Matthias of Hungary at the time of Sultan Suleiman's capture of Buda and destruction of the Royal Palace in 1526.[1] This manuscript served as the sole basis of the *editio princeps* of 1534. Its editor, Vincentius Obsopoeus, who purchased the manuscript from the soldier, while recognizing that good fortune had played a role in its preservation ("forte fortuna"), could not have foreseen that the serendipity of these events would be fabricated countless times by later imitators of Heliodorus and other ancient Greek novelists.[2] Obsopoeus' carelessly edited edition served in turn as the sole basis of the first translation of the *Ethiopian Story*, that of Jacques Amyot in 1547.[3] A direct line leads from these few events to Joseph Hall's declaration in the early part of the seventeenth century, "What Schole-boy, what apprentice knows not Heliodorus?"[4]

Most of this chapter will deal with late sixteenth- to early seventeenth-century French and English novels modelled directly or indirectly on ancient Greek prose fiction. Before serving as models, however, ancient Greek novels passed through a kind of homogenizing process that appears to have transmitted to post-mediaeval Western Europe a misleadingly saccharine product devoid of sensuality, vitality and variety. This process is more properly the business of other

---

[1] Dörrie (1935) 18, Csapodi (1973) 329–30.
[2] E.g. Fumée, Baudoin and Gerzan, who are discussed below.
[3] Sandy (1984–85).
[4] Sandy (1979) 41.

contributions to this volume that provide detailed accounts of the papyrus record, the ancient readership and, finally, the reception of the ancient Greek novel during the Byzantine period. However, because the process bears directly on the form of the ancient Greek novel that reached and, equally importantly, did *not* reach postmediaeval Western Europe, the next few pages will sketch some details of the mediation that prevented the full spectrum of ancient Greek prose fiction from having the impact on the development of the Western European novel that it otherwise would have had.

In my discussion of English and French imitations, I have restricted myself to the use made of the ancient Greek novel by postmediaeval novelists, omitting, for instance, Shakespeare's borrowings.[5] I have restricted the scope of this chapter even more by focussing principally on ancient Greek novels as models for the manipulation of complex narrative. Finally, I have not attempted to be exhaustive. Instead, I have selected English and French adaptations and imitations that highlight the attempts of their authors to master the medium of complex extended prose narrative. The bibliography will guide those who are interested to additional sources of information.

Transmission of the Ancient Greek Novel

The mediation, if not outright censorship, is in evidence as early as the time of the latest and most influential of the ancient Greek novels, Heliodorus' *Ethiopian Story*. Whereas this novel found favour with the ninth-century Byzantine patriarch Photius, who repeatedly cites it as the standard of moral propriety, the apostate emperor Julian at, apparently, approximately the time of its composition warns pagan priests against the titillating effects of reading *pathemata erotica*.[6] It is most unlikely that Julian would have voiced concern about any overtly pagan novel as patently devoid of lewd sensuality as the *Ethiopian Story*. Slightly more than a generation after Julian, however, the physician Theodorus Priscianus was recommending perusal of

---

[5] Sandy (1979) 55 for a critique of C. Gesner, *Shakespeare and the Greek Romance* (Lexington, Kentucky: 1970).

[6] Ancient readership: Macrobius, *Commentary on Cicero's Dream of Scipio* 1.2.7–8 (on Petronius and Apuleius); Julius Capitolinus, "Life of Clodius Albinus," 12 in *Scriptores Historiae Augustae* (on Apuleius); Julian, vol. 2, p. 326, of the Loeb edition of Julian, ed. W.C. Wright; Philostratus, *Letters* 66 (on Chariton).

Iamblichus' *Babylonian Story* and other novels to his patients who suffered from sexual impotence.[7]

Whether or not some ancient Greek novels were met with outraged hostility in late antiquity because of their lewdness, the papyrological record of Roman Egypt appears to reveal that the Greek novel reached a limited readership. Of the novels now extant, a total of eight papyrus fragments, four for each of two Greek novels, has surfaced; ancient Greek novels known only from summaries or in fragmentary form are represented by an additional twenty-six papyrus scraps. This total of thirty-four documented instances of the availability of Greek novels in Roman Egypt pales in comparison with the availability there of other kinds of Greek literature. To give only one example, the orator Demosthenes is represented by ninety-four fragments that have emerged from the sands of Roman Egypt.[8]

The unique combination of favourable climate and cultural heritage that has preserved for posterity fragments of novels that would otherwise have been lost for all time limits the value of the evidence, for in effect we have only a frayed and faded snapshot of a particular place at a particular time (principally, the second century). What this snapshot lacks in comprehensiveness is compensated for in the tantalizing glimpse that it provides of a literary tradition far more varied and vigorous than one would suppose on the basis of the extant Greek novels. Historical romance, murder and mayhem, cannibalism, fantasy, viragos, philosophical procurers and picaresque adventures—these are only some of the elements available to readers in Roman Egypt substantially absent from the models of prose fiction that reached post-mediaeval Western Europe.

We can only guess at the reasons for this distorted transmission. What affords little doubt is that the Byzantine patriarch Photius is at least partly responsible for the myopic view of ancient Greek prose fiction that helped to shape the tone and content of the earliest imitations and adaptations. At the end of his synopsis of the otherwise lost novel the *Wonders beyond Thule* by Antonius Diogenes, elsewhere labelled by Photius as "the father of fictional stories," he states:

> It seems that he is earlier than those who have made it their business to write this kind of fiction, such as... Iamblichus, Achilles Tatius [and] Heliodorus.... Dercyllis, Ceryllus, Thruscanius, and Dinias seem

---

[7] *Euporista* 2.33. See also Bowie (1994b) 435–59.
[8] Sandy (1994b) 135.

to have been the models for the romances about Sinonis and Rhodanes, Leucippe and Clitophon, Chariclea and Theagenes, and for their wanderings, love affairs, capture, and dangers.[9]

This putative norm—"wanderings, love affairs, capture, and dangers"—and Photius' predilection for what he calls a variety of occurring, hoped-for and unhoped-for incidents and last-second escapes from incredible dangers, we now know, falls far short of the thematic range of ancient Greek prose fiction. This, however, is the norm that prevails in the earliest post-mediaeval English and French imitations and adaptations.

Similarly, Photius' moral code seems to have precluded or reduced his summaries of some ancient Greek novels that would otherwise have been available to serve as models for Renaissance novelists. It is striking that his notice of Achilles Tatius' novel is much shorter (only fifteen lines in Henry's edition) than his summaries of the novels of Heliodorus (155 lines)—whose propriety he repeatedly praises—, Antonius Diogenes (259 lines) and Iamblichus (394 lines). The brevity of the notice of Achilles Tatius is even more striking because Photius emphasizes that all the writers cited above and some others named by him wrote works of the same genre. The explanation may be that he found Achilles Tatius' novel morally repellent:

> The excessively disgusting and filthy sentiments detract above all from the writer's [viz. Achilles Tatius'] serious purpose and cause those who wish to read the work to flee from it in disgust. It bears much resemblance in structural and thematic intention to Heliodorus' story except for... the loathsome obscenity.[10]

Similarly, his short notice (twenty-three lines) of Lucius of Patrae's *Lucius or the Ass* and even shorter notice (sixteen lines) of the unnamed novel of Damascius, both of which are grouped with the novels compared near the end of his summary of Antonius Diogenes, stress the "obscene vice" in the former writer and "the impossible and stupid and badly conceived marvellous tales worthy of Damascius' godless impiety."[11]

The final point to be made about Photius as a decisive influence on the range of novels available to post-mediaeval Western Euro-

---

[9] Reardon (1989) 782; see also Sandy (1994b) 141–2.
[10] Photius (1959–91) codex 87, 65b.21–28.
[11] Photius (1959–91) codex 129, 96b.28 (Lucius of Patrae); codex 130, 96b.44–97a.3 (Damascius); the grouping of the writers: codex 166, 111b.32–42.

pean writers of prose fiction is that he summarizes for the benefit of his brother Tarasius only works that were not commonly read by the Byzantine intelligentsia of the mid-ninth century. More precisely, in both the preface and the postface of the *Bibliotheca*, Photius states that he has intentionally excluded from his digest books that Tarasius himself has read and books that are commonly included in the syllabus of courses in the liberal arts and sciences.

Thus we must be mindful that Photius' choice of the novels to be summarized and the character of his summaries depend on several factors that may give a distorted impression of the range and nature of the ancient Greek novels available in the ninth century.

Hellenism in France

The link between Hellenism and sixteenth-century France, where both the development and the theory of the post-mediaeval extended prose fiction of Western Europe begin, is no less fragile than the adventitious preservation and discovery of papyri and the influence of the idiosyncratic taste and moral sensibility of late antiquity and the Byzantine period. It is, of course, impossible to prove that ancient Greek would not have become a subject of study in Western Europe if Byzantine intellectuals had not fled to Italy ahead of the invading forces of Mahomet II near the middle of the fifteenth century. What can be stated with certainty is that these events were to result in France becoming the pre-eminent centre of Hellenic studies in Western Europe within a century of the Turkish capture of Byzantium in 1453 and that Jacques Amyot, one of the second-generation beneficiaries of this body of knowledge imported to France via Italy, is above all others responsible for the impact that the ancient Greek novel had on the development of its equivalent in sixteenth- and seventeenth-century Western Europe.[12] This bald claim requires a few words of justification.

The military campaigns in Italy of Charles VIII of France resulted in more than the introduction of the *morbus Gallicus* to France. The illustrious Byzantine Hellenist Janus Lascaris accompanied or followed him in 1495 from Naples to France, where he helped Budé make rapid progress in his study of Greek. Until that time the sporadic

---

[12] Sandy (1982c) 169; Sandy (1984–5) 1–13; Sandy (1992) 892–7.

teaching of Greek in France had been conducted by a series of incompetent Italians and equally incompetent Greek émigrés and refugees, the most notorious of whom was Georgius Hermonymus. Erasmus, Reuchlin and Budé all describe him as an ignorant, "hungry" (*esuriens*) Greek, who, in Erasmus' words, "could not have taught if he had wanted to and would not have wanted to if he had been able to teach." Budé wrote of being cheated by him and being pestered to buy the Greek manuscripts that he had copied.[13]

None of Janus Lascaris' frequent visits to France while employed by the French Crown lasted long enough to allow him to teach "publicly," that is, in the colleges of the University of Paris. Instead, his teaching was restricted to a few eminent French humanists such as Budé, Lefèvre d'Étaples, Germaine de Brie, the first two professors of Greek at the Collège royal founded by François I in 1530 and the French king's personal physician Guillaume Cop.[14] Among the many services performed by Lascaris for French kings from Charles VIII to François I was the management of Louis XII's library at Blois and later, along with Budé, that of François I when it was transferred in the 1520s to Fontainebleau. The Greek nucleus of the latter library comprised some forty manuscripts brought to France in 1508 by Lascaris.[15] The collection of the Fontainebleau library was soon to be augmented by the addition of some sixty Greek manuscripts that François I commissioned the Italian Girolamo Fondulo to purchase in Italy. By 1545 the number of Greek manuscripts and printed editions had grown to 190.[16] In Paris around 1524 Fondulo taught Greek to Germaine de Brie, who had begun his Greek studies some fifteen years earlier with Lascaris. It should be evident from this limited selection of Lascaris' services to the French Crown and French humanists as "un ambassadeur de l'hellénisme" that his teaching of Greek had an immediate and lasting influence on important individuals who were positioned to influence its future development and that he put in place the foundations of the study of ancient Greek in France.

These foundations were to be occupied within the first decade of the sixteenth century by a Frenchman and an Italian who would

---

[13] Jovy (1899–1913) 11–2; II, p. 362 in the 1557 Basel edition of Budé's *Opera Omnia* (reprinted Farnborough: 1966).
[14] Knös (1945) 84–5, 93.
[15] Jovy (1899–1913) 12.
[16] Omont (1889) VII.

become the effective founders of the institutionalized, "public" teaching of Greek in France. When he went to Italy with the intention of completing his studies of law, François Tissard fell under the spell of the humanists Beroaldo and Guarino and soon began to study Greek with Demetrius of Sparta. Upon his return to Paris in the summer of 1507 he started teaching Greek "publicly" at the Collège de Boncour. The excitement with which this event was greeted is evident in a letter written by Bruno Amerbach of the humanistic Basel publishing house:

> A few days ago someone [viz. François Tissard] came here from Italy to give Greek lessons in public. I have immersed myself deeply in this language, which I have long desired and finally found and which, if I am not mistaken, will fill the maw of my ravenous mind.... Therefore, Father, I ask you to send me a monthly installment of my allowance so that I can take some Greek learning home.[17]

Tissard's arrival in Paris was to be followed within a year by that of Girolamo Aleandro from Venice. Provided with letters of introduction by Erasmus and in Paris enjoying the support of Lefèvre d'Étaples and Budé, he initially gave private lessons in Greek to a few wealthy individuals. By 1509, however, he was teaching Greek "publicly" in various Parisian colleges and continued to do so until he went to Belgium in 1514.[18] Beatus Rhenanus eagerly anticipated his "public" lectures in Paris:

> The University of Paris is at last going to receive the light and emerge from the deep darkness in which it has been buried for centuries.[19]

Like Tissard, he presented a humanistic curriculum to an enthusiastic audience, as the following extract from a letter that he wrote in 1511 to Michael Hummelberger illustrates:

> On 30 July I began to read [the Latin poet] Ausonius in public. You know how eagerly those readings were awaited. The crowd was so large that neither the portico nor the two courtyards of the Collège de la Marche could contain all the auditors! All the people of the highest stations in life..., so many that the number is estimated to be 2000.... Although the reading lasted 2 1/2 hours, not one person, in spite of the suffocating heat, showed the smallest sign of inattentiveness.[20]

---

[17] Allen (1907) 742–4.
[18] Hoyoux (1969).
[19] Jovy (1899–1913) 12.
[20] Jovy (1899–1913) 15–6. In Florence in the previous century Francesco Filelfo

Besides being charismatic teachers, Tissard and Aleandro ensured that the infrastructure to support the teaching of Greek in France was firmly in place. Both men recognized that Greek textbooks were a priority for their pupils, and they took steps to have editions of Greek authors, Greek-Latin lexicons and Greek grammar books supplied from Italy. As well, they arranged for several Greek books to be published in Paris, including the first Greek book to be published in France, the *Liber Gnomagyricus* (1507), and Aleandro was responsible for a major improvement in the publisher de Gourmont's Greek type.[21]

These are only a few of the French humanistic achievements of the first third of the sixteenth century that prompted Rabelais in 1532 to represent Gargantua writing to his son Pantagruel thus:

> Maintenant, toutes disciplines sent restituées, les langues instaurées: qrecque, sans laquelle c'est honte que une personne se die sçavant.[22]

The culmination of all this activity was the appointment by François I in 1530 of the first two *lecteurs royaux* for Greek to the Collège royal (now the Collège de France) that he had founded in the same year. Lefranc in his *Histoire du Collège de France* imagines a particularly piquant scene:

> Was it not a unique moment in history when Calvin, Ignatius of Loyola and Rabelais ... could have crowded together at the foot of the same chair [occupied by Pierre Danès, one of the first two *lecteurs royaux* for Greek]?

The private individual who deserves most of the credit for the achievements that I have outlined is Guillaume Budé. In the preface of his *Comentarii Linguae Graecae* (1529) he reminds François I of his promise to found a royal college for the study of the ancient languages. As we have seen, François was to fulfil that promise in the following year. Besides the three famous men named above who might have been classmates, Danès' illustrious pupils included Jean Dorat, Ronsard, Henri Etienne (Henricus Stephanus) and Jacques Amyot, to the last of whom I shall soon turn.[23]

---

claimed to have audiences of some 400 for his "public" lectures on Greek: Wilson (1992) 49.
[21] Omont (1891).
[22] I have retained the original spelling and even the typographical errors, of which there are many, in all quotations of the sixteenth- to eighteenth-century writers discussed in this chapter.
[23] Reverdin (1984).

The Hellenism that had taken root in France by the end of the first third of the sixteenth century has more direct bearing on the discovery and reception of the ancient Greek novel in France than is immediately evident. A manuscript that contains part of Achilles Tatius' novel is one of the codices sent to France from Italy in 1530 by Girolamo Fondulo on the orders of François I. The same codex contains Longus' *Daphnis and Chloe* and is the manuscript used by Jacques Amyot for his vernacular translation of the work in 1559, almost forty years before the Greek text of Longus was to appear in print. Another manuscript of Achilles Tatius travelled in the opposite direction, taken from Paris and given to St. Mark's Library in Venice in 1468 by Cardinal Bessarion. Much of the sixteenth-century activity in discovering, collating and copying manuscripts of Achilles Tatius was undertaken by H. Étienne (Henricus Stephanus) along with Fulvio Orsini, with the latter of whom the French statesman de Thou was associated during his searches for manuscripts in Rome and who himself possessed a now lost manuscript of the Greek writer's novel.[24]

Jacques Amyot also actively searched for manuscripts of Greek novelists and other Greek writers in Italy. Born in 1513 to "parentibus honestis magis quam copiosis," he received his matre ès-arts in 1532 from the Collège du Cardinal Lemoine, through which Erasmus had passed earlier, and sometime before the autumn of 1533 completed his studies at the now two-year-old Collège Royal, where, as we have seen, Pierre Danès was his teacher of Greek. In the spring of 1548 Amyot accompanied the French ambassador to Venice. He continued to consult manuscripts here until September 1550, when he continued his scholarly investigations at the Vatican Library until June 1551 "grâce au crédit du cardinal de Tournon."[25] Unlike most of his contemporaries, whose notion of textual criticism consisted of plundering the most readily available manuscripts for variant readings that agreed with their editorial preferences, Amyot made a complete collation of a Greek manuscript that did not always serve the immediate needs of his translation.[26] Similarly, at a time when most of his contemporary translators of Greek works had at best only a rudimentary knowledge of ancient Greek and based their translations on

---

[24] Vilborg (1955) I, xxxi, lxxiv–v.
[25] Sandy (1984–5) 1–2.
[26] Sandy (1984–5) 21–2.

Latin or Italian versions, Amyot was searching the libraries of Venice and Rome and discovering there uncollated manuscripts of Diodorus, Longus and Heliodorus. In the case of the last two authors, there were no translations in any language to which he could turn for guidance; and in the case of Longus there was not even a printed Greek edition available at the time of his translation of *Daphnis and Chloe*. As for Diodorus, Amyot revealed two books of his *Bibliotheca* that had been previously unknown to the humanists of the time. What makes Amyot's accomplishments even more remarkable is that he belonged to only the second generation of French Hellenists.

Discovery and Theory of the Novel

Amyot's accomplishments as a pioneer in the formulation of the theory of the novel have a greater claim on our attention than his philological achievements.[27] He combines practices that he observed in Heliodorus with precepts found in Aristotle's *Poetics* and Horace's *Ars Poetica* and in such diverse writers as Strabo, Plutarch, Lucian, Julian the apostate and the Byzantine intellectual Michael Psellos to create an *ars poetica* derived substantially from the theoretical underpinnings of heroic epic and drama but applied successfully to prose fiction.[28] Its recommendations that were to exert considerable influence on the earliest writers of prose fiction include the requirements of verisimilitude, surprise and realistic novelty, the epic-style—"in-medias-res" disposition of events, the resulting "flashbacks" and delayed dénouement. Amyot's contemporaries Julius Caesar Scaliger and Tasso make use of some of the same classical authorities and also Heliodorus and Amyot to formulate rules of fictional narrative.[29]

It was not until some one-hundred years after Amyot's pioneering efforts that a literary critic of independent judgment appeared on the scene to give prose fiction its due—an *ars poetica* designed specifically for prose fiction that did not conceptualize the *Ethiopian Story* as an epic poem or apply to it Aristotle's and Horace's "rules" of dramatic composition. Before turning to the early novels that were the products of the sixteenth-century theorizing, I shall remark on a

---

[27] Sandy (1982c).
[28] Sandy (1982c) 169–74.
[29] Sandy (1982c) 173–4.

few of the salient features of Daniel Huet's *Lettre-traité sur l'origine des romans*.[30] Born in Caen in 1630, he had a good Jesuit education but under cover of darkness resorted to the Protestant Samuel Bochart for help in teaching himself Greek and Latin. At the age of eighteen he translated *Daphnis and Chloe* into Latin. A few years later when returning from the court of Queen Christina of Sweden, where he had gone in the company of Bochart and Descartes, he visited Heinsius in Leyden and Vossius in Amsterdam. Huet had clearly made a favourable impression on the intellectuals of north-western Europe and at the age of forty he became one of Louis XIV's tutors. In that capacity he became the chief editor of the sixty annotated Latin texts intended *in usum Delphini*. Huet's contribution to the series, a critical edition of Manilius, has considerable merit and earned accolades from that author's next editor, Richard Bentley, who ranked Huet's conjectural emendations with those of Scaliger. Late in life, at the age of forty-six, Huet became an ordained Roman Catholic priest and eventually bishop of Avranches in Normandy until his retirement in 1689. He then moved to a Jesuit community house in Paris where he continued to reside until his death at the age of ninety-one in 1721. In the interval he was elected to membership in the Académie française.

In his memoirs Huet records that he wrote his *Lettre-traité sur l'origine des romans* in 1666 while staying at the convent of Malnoue. It is not clear whether the *Lettre-traité* emerged from there as a published monograph; in the form in which it now exists it appeared as a letter prefixed to the first volume of Mme Lafayette's *Zade* three years after the time of its reported composition. Huet distances himself immediately from his predecessors' indiscriminate mingling of the "rules" of epic poetry and "heroic" fictional prose. He too knows Aristotle and Horace and their "maxime... que le Poëte est plus Poëte par les fictions qu'il invente, que par les vers qu'il compose" but confidently declares:

> Romans... sont des histoires feintes d'aventures amoureuses, ecrites en prose avec art, pour le plaisir & l'instruction des lecteurs.[31]

Huet's observations on the origins of ancient prose fiction on the south-eastern shores of the Mediterranean will stand comparison with

---

[30] Huet (1670); Selden (1994).
[31] Huet (1670) 114, 116. Kok includes marginalia written by Huet himself in the

the most authoritative modern scholarship on the subject.[32] I do not mean to suggest that modern scholars such as Anderson, who remarks that "the Orontes had been surreptitiously flowing into the Springs of Helicon long before it reached the Tiber," resort to Huet's kind of intuitive stereotyping, as when he characterizes Oriental peoples as more imaginative and eager to communicate what they have imaginatively created than their counterparts in Western Europe.[33] Rather, like Anderson and other modern scholars, Huet recognized that the authors of the extant and fragmentary Greek novels whose native countries are known were natives of south-eastern Mediterranean countries; as well, the papyrus fragments of Greek novels published after the time of Huet such as the Ninus-romance and the *Phoenician Story* are set in the Levant.[34]

Perry devoted most of the first chapter of his book to debunking the then prevailing view that ancient prose fiction, on the biological model, either developed or degenerated from previously established prose forms such as history and tales of travel.[35] He concluded that cultural values and human concerns supplied the impetus for the spontaneous development of the new literary form. This is not greatly different from the position reached 300 years earlier by Huet:

> Il faut chercher leur premiere origine dans la nature de l'esprit de l'homme, inventif, amateur des nouveautez & des fictions, désireux d'apprendre, & de communiquer ce qu'il a inventé, & ce qu'il a appris.[36]

Huet adds that oriental peoples express everything—their theology, their philosophy, their political and moral codes—in fables and parables.[37] He discusses these in detail and regularly cites Aesop and Scripture as parallel manifestations of allegory. Again, Huet's consideration of oriental patterns of story-telling is not far removed from that of modern scholars such as Anderson, who looks to the East for parallels, and Reardon, who sees the ancient Greek novels as the post-classical equivalent of myth, i.e., parable.[38]

---

books that he bequeathed to the nation and that are now housed in the Bibliothèque nationale. In the two instances just quoted Huet acknowledges his debt to his friend Vossius, e.g. "Vide in argumentum priora capita libri Vosii *De artis poëticae natura et constitutione.*"

[32] Huet (1670) 120–41.
[33] Anderson (1984) 217; Huet (1670) ed. Kok, 120.
[34] Sandy (1994b).
[35] Perry (1967) 3–148.
[36] Huet (1670) 120.
[37] Huet (1670) 142–51.
[38] Anderson (1984); Reardon (1969).

Huet's analysis of Martin Fumée's *Du Vray et Parfait Amour* (1599) is a good test of his learning and scholarship.[39] The problems that Huet faced begin on the title page: "Du Vray et Parfait Amour. Escrit en Grec, par Athenagoras Philosophe Athenien." This ruse fooled at least two early seventeenth-century French writers. Pierre de Caseneuve in his novel *Caritée* (1621) writes in the "Au Lecteur" of "le Philosophe Athenagoras" and his "Theogenes, et Charide sous le titre du vray et parfait Amour," as does Mlle de Gournay in her defence of the "roman discourant," *L'Ombre de la Damoiselle de Gournay* (1626), "Nous apprenons d'Athenagoras, en son Livre du Parfaict amour."[40] Fumée's smoke-screen of ancient authorship is thickened by the alleged circumstances of publication. (They bear an uncanny proleptic resemblance to the publication of Huet's only published novel, *Diane de Castro ou le faux Incas*, which was found in a drawer of his desk after his death and published some fifty years after the time of its composition.) The prefacing epistolary "Au Lecteur" of Bernard de Sanjorry represents the writer of the letter as an old man who has been putting his affairs into order and has discovered the work among his papers. It had been sent originally to Monsieur Lamané, the secretary of Cardinal d'Armagnac. Sanjorry then undertook to learn whether the novel had ever been published by initiating enquiries in Toulouse. Discovering that it had never appeared in print, he has decided to have it published because of the purity of the language of Fumée's translation.[41]

After Sanjorry's prefatory letter there appears one dated October 1569 purporting to be from Fumée to Lamané in which Fumée describes himself as the translator of the work by Athenagoras, of which he has seen only the Greek manuscript entrusted to him by Lamané. He adds, as proof of the authenticity of the Greek work, that Athenagoras has resurrected disused words in the manner of the

---

[39] Huet (1670) 162–74. I have consulted one of the editions of 1612 of Fumée's work at the Bibliothèque nationale (Rés. Y². 1224). The only extant copy of the edition of 1599 is in the British Library. Dr J. Morgan has kindly confirmed for me that this copy, printed in Paris chez Michel Sonnius, bears an *extrait du privilege* dated 14 August 1599 and the colophon "Achevé d'imprimer le 25 Aoust. 1599." Küchler (1911) provides detailed discussion of Fumée's sources such as Plutarch and Heliodorus, both in Amyot's translations, and, unlike me, consulted the edition of Fumée annotated by Huet himself.
[40] Küchler (1911) 139.
[41] French philologists may find that Sanjorry's claims would repay study. He maintains, for instance, that the verb "decevoir" is not pure French, that "à parler le vrai François" one should use the verb "tromper."

Greek sophists of the Roman Imperial period. In other words, like the Greek novelists Achilles Tatius, Heliodorus, Antonius Diogenes and Longus, Fumée is attempting to place the imprimatur of authenticity on a work of fiction by distancing it at least one remove from the writer. He adds that the practice of writing-love-stories continued into the Christian era, as is proved by the example of Heliodorus:

> lequel ayma mieux quitter la charge de son Evesché que de condemner le petit livre qu'il avait faict des Amours de Theagenes et Chariclea.... De ce rang estoit aussi celuy [viz. Achilles Tatius] qui nous a laissé les Amours de Leucippé et Clitophon.

Fumée here reveals his awareness of, and exploits, the tradition that both Heliodorus and Achilles Tatius became Christian bishops, the former being forced by his synod either to burn his romance, which was "kindling the flames of love" in the young, or to give up his office. The tradition concerning Heliodorus, which derives from a few Byzantine authorities, would have been readily available from "Le proesme du translateur" of Amyot's second edition (1559) of his translation of Heliodorus' novel. The Byzantine *Suda* was the only source for the tradition concerning Achilles Tatius, however. Although it was a reference book regularly consulted by humanists and therefore available in several printed editions, the *Suda* was not a standard work in the humanistic Greek curriculum and, as far as I know, has never been translated into Latin or a vernacular language. It looks, therefore, as though Huet was pitting his wits against an erudite impersonator.[42]

It is from this cleverly contrived labyrinth of false authenticity that Huet attempts to emerge with the answer to the question of ancient Greek authorship. He notes that no Greek manuscript of the work exists in any library. This is not necessarily an idle remark since Huet knew before the *editio princeps* of 1750 of the existence in the Vatican Library of the complete manuscript of Chariton's novel and appears to have made enquiries about now lost manuscripts of Antonius Diogenes' *Wonders beyond Thule*.[43] On the positive side, Huet reasons that the nature of divinity as described in the novel accords with the beliefs of a Christian and that this makes Athenagoras'

---

[42] Montreux, who will be discussed later in this chapter, also expressed in his novel of 1595 awareness of the tradition concerning Achilles Tatius.

[43] Huet (1670) 181 and 156.

authorship possible. On the other hand, the author mentions the destruction of Greece, which can refer only to the Gothic invasions long after the time of Athenagoras.[44] "Mais je m'amuse à chercher en quel temps a vescu le Romancier, sans être assuré s'il a vescu, & si cét ouvrage qui porte son nom n'est point supposé," he muses.[45] Huet continues to be in two minds as he balances the inconclusive evidence. Eventually, however, he tires of the game:

> Mais enfin il faut se rendre à la verité, & vous confesser de bonne foy, qu'après une seconde lecture que j'en ay faite avec beaucoup plus d'attention que la premiere, je suis demeuré entierement convaincu qu'il est faux & supposé.[46]

Huet then remarks that several episodes in the novel are based on ancient writers such as Herodotus, Plutarch and Heliodorus but that there are other statements that could not have been made by an ancient writer, for instance:

> Il fait faire au milieu de la Grece une procedure criminelle, en la mesme forme qu'elle se feroit au Chastelet de Paris.[47]

Huet's deductive powers and storehouse of information are best evidenced in has discussion of the Scythian slave Brigittaire in the French novel:

> Le nom de Brigittaire qu'il donne à cette enclave Scythe, a esté indubitablement formé sur celui de sainte Brigide, vierge d'Ecosse, qui vivoit environ cent ans aprés le siécle du prétendu Athenagoras; ou plustost sur celuy de sainte Brigitte, qui a vescue dans ces derniers siècles, & qui estoit native de Suede, région voisine de la Scythie. Cette remarque, à mon jugement, fait tomber le masque d'antiquité, dont l'Auteur de la supposition s'est couvert.[48]

After acknowledging the erudition of Fumée and praising the literary qualities of the French novel, Huet infers its authorship from the architectural knowledge evident in it. Since the cardinal of Armagnac was keenly interested in building design and had in his circle of

---

[44] Huet has missed a clue here. Fumée's authorship is all the more likely in view of the fact that he translated Procopius' *Histoire des guerres faictes par l'empereur Justinien contre les Vandales et les Goths* (1597); and, as Küchler (1911) 143 observes, Bernard Sanjorry translated Athenagoras (1577).
[45] Huet (1670) 164.
[46] Huet (1670) 165.
[47] Huet (1670) 167.
[48] Huet (1670) 167-8.

friends the former architect and man of letters Philander, Huet supposes that Philander tricked Fumée into translating his original Greek composition and Lamané into publishing it.[49]

Thus approximately a century before the date of 1740 given as the date of the birth of the novel by standard surveys of English literature, Huet was already writing of its origins in the East and of its Western progeny. As well, he was criticizing earlier histories of the novel, as in the following example, which illustrates what Selden (1994) aptly labels Huet's complementary synchronic and diachronic configurations:

> L'erreur de Girali n'est pas supportable, quand il dit que la multiplicité d'actions est de l'invention des Italiens. Les Grecs & nos vieux François les avoient multipliées aver dépendance & subordination à une action principale, suivant les regles du Poëme Héroque, comme l'a fort bien pratiqué nostre faux Athenagoras; surpassant en cela Héliodore & Achillés Tatius, qui n'ont pas assez débroüillée. Nos vieux François les avoient multipliées sans ordonnace, sans liaison, & sans art. Ce sont eux que les Italiens ont imitez. En prenant d'eux les Romans, ils en ont pris les défauts. Et c'est une autre erreur de Giraldi pire que la précedente, de loüer ce defaut, & d'en faire une vertu.[50]

To judge by Huet's memoirs, he spent all his time either in cultivating his studies or in cultivating the friendship of the most learned Europeans of his time. The fruits of this cultivation have been preserved but modern scholarship seems scarcely to have tasted of them with the notable exception of Selden (1994).

Practice of the Novel

France

Imitations and adaptations of Greek novels begin in Western Europe with Nicolas de Montreux's *Oeuvre de la chasteté*; or, to give it its full title and its author's acronym as they appear on the title page:

> Oeuvre de la chasteté, Qui se remarque par les diverses fortunes, adventures, & fidelles Amours de Criniton & Lydie ... le tout l'invention d'Ollenix du Mont-Sacré, Gentill-homme du Mayne.

---

[49] Huet (1670) 172. The cardinal of Armagnac was one of the people employed by François I to search for and purchase Greek manuscripts in Italy (Omont [1889] IV).

[50] Huet (1670) 168.

The three parts of this work were published at two-year intervals beginning in 1595. For several reasons it will pay dividends to devote considerably more attention to this work than its negligible literary qualities merit. In the first place it vividly documents the transition from mediaeval-rooted romances of chivalry such as *Amadis de Gaule* to seventeenth-century sentimental French love romances based on Greek models. Second, King François I played a prominent part in this transition, as he had in the foundation of French Hellenism. As well, Montreux's clumsy attempts to control the complex narrative form—termed *multiplicité d'actions* by Huet (see above p. 750) that he borrowed from Heliodorus graphically illustrate how much still had to be learned before technical mastery could be achieved. Finally, it is evident from the preface that Montreux has consulted at least one Byzantine reference book that was available only in Greek. He refers to "Achilles Statius [i.e., Tatius] tresrenommé Chresten... [et] le docte Prelat Heliodore." The probably spurious biographical tradition that Heliodorus became a Christian bishop in his mature years would have been readily available in the preface of the second edition (1559) of Amyot's translation of the *Ethiopian Story* (see above, p. 748); the probably equally spurious account of Achilles Tatius' Christian status, however, as noted above (p. 748), occurs only in the Byzantine reference book the *Suda*, which was available only in Greek.

While a prisoner in Spain, François I became fond of *Amadis de Gaule*. He subsequently promoted French translations and original French compositions of the saga until the French amalgam numbered twenty-one books, one of which was written by Montreux. As it happens, his contribution owes nothing to the ancient Greek novel, but the Italian work that became book twenty of the French series is based closely and extensively on the *Ethiopian Story*. Thus Montreux's involvement in the enterprise may have contributed to his decision to model the *Oeuvre de la chasteté* on Heliodorus' novel.

Of the three parts of Montreux's ensemble, it is part two, *Les amours de Criniton et Lydie* (1597), that derives most substantially and noticeably from ancient Greek novels, above all Heliodorus and to a lesser degree Achilles Tatius. I have already described this work and will provide only enough description of it here to give an impression of the work and to flesh out some of my skeletal introductory remarks.[51]

---

[51] Sandy (1982a) 111–13 and Sandy (1982c) 175–6. See also Daele (1946) and Stone (1973) 36–49.

The ensemble opens with Criniton, who must wait until part three to unburden himself of his troubles, wandering about in abject despair, the victim of unrequited love. He meets the hermit Cléandre, who has withdrawn from human involvement because of the baleful attractions of women. In this respect he vaguely recalls the priest Calasiris in the *Ethiopian Story*, who also fled into self-imposed exile to escape the seductive charms of Rhodope. Cléandre proceeds to recount his star-crossed past for the rest of part one and all of part two until he grows tired and gives to his remarkably patient listener the script of the play *Cleopatra* that he saw performed in one of his ports of call while in search of his reluctant beloved Domiphille. The reader is also obliged to read or (as I did) skim the 116 pages of this intrusive drama before resuming the story. Finally, in part three, Criniton gets the opportunity to tell of his disappointments in love.

A few examples will suffice to establish that Montreux has closely imitated Heliodorus. In the course of reading hundreds of sixteenth- and seventeenth-century French and English romances during the past two decades, I have come to the conclusion that the single episode in the ancient Greek novel most often imitated by later writers is the incident in the *Ethiopian Story* where the heroine Chariclea is hidden in a cave by her jealously passionate captor.[52] When he returns to it to recover her, a series of accidents, contrived by Heliodorus for maximum suspense, results in another woman being mistaken for Chariclea. Montreux's appropriation of this series of events is unmistakable. In the course of eloping Domiphille and Cléandre are captured by a brigand who immediately becomes infatuated with her. As in Heliodorus, rival contenders intervene; and when the infatuated brigand rushes to the cave where Domiphille has taken refuge, he is thwarted in his attempt to recover her, as is the brigand in the *Ethiopian Story*.

Considerably later in the narrative, Domiphille thwarts the passionate advances of the king of Epirus by claiming that she is offering sacrifices to the goddess Isis in preparation for her marriage to the king. In fact, however, like Chariclea in the *Ethiopian Story*, she resorts to this religious pretext in order to delay the marriage while she prepares for her escape. At another point in the narrative of part two of the ensemble Princess Léodice becomes enamoured of Cléandre. He represents his beloved Domiphille to her as his sister,

---

[52] Sandy (1982c) 187.

a precautionary measure employed repeatedly by Theagenes and Charicles in Heliodorus' novel. The princess is modelled on Heliodorus' Arsace, the wife of the Persian satrap Oroondates, who has become infatuated with Theagenes. Like the son of Arsace's maid in Heliodorus, a messenger falls in love with Domiphille and betrays the message-sender. The threat of war between states caused by erotic jealousies and breaches of faith is reduced in both novels to individual combat. In Montreux, the successful contender is to win the hand of Princess Léodice; in Heliodorus, the winner is to recover the chief priesthood of the goddess Isis.

In another instance of obvious imitation, Montreux contrives to have the Delphic oracle require that an unbetrothed maiden be sacrificed. Cléandre urges that a foreign woman be sacrificed and declares that in any case Domiphille is betrothed to him. This string of events is patently modelled on the threatened immolation of the virginal heroine Chariclea and the last-minute, life-saving declaration of her true status in Heliodorus' novel. Finally, in Montreux, the Lady of the Island, upon examining Domiphille's right arm, discovers "une petite marque, comme d'une chapelet naturellement nee avecques Domiphille." She thereby recognises her long-lost daughter, who had been kidnapped at the age of four. In the same way, in Heliodorus, the ring of black skin on the upper part of Chariclea's right arm is recognised as vestigial evidence of her birth to black parents, the king and queen of Ethiopia.

These few examples of imitation of Heliodorus' novel could easily be multiplied. As well, at a greatly reduced rate, there is imitation of Achilles Tatius' novel. For instance, Princess Léodice, led at this point to believe that Domiphille is Cléandre's sister, is persuaded by him to send the sick Domiphille away from the theatre of war to the safety of one of her chateaux, just as Leucippe in Achilles Tatius is sent by her parents away from threatening warfare at Byzantium to the safety of her father's step-brother's home in Tyre. On some occasions Montreux blends material from the two Greek writers. For instance, soon after the episode described above where Domiphille is discovered to be the long-lost daughter of the Lady of the Island and is consequently spared from becoming a human sacrificial victim, Criniton, the narrator of part three and the listener to Cléandre's framed narrative comprising most of part one and all of part two of Montreux's novel, inadvertently kills the brother of his beloved Lydie while the two men are boar hunting. This accidental death is unmistakably modelled on the accidental death of Clitophon's cousin Charicles in Achilles Tatius' novel.

At this stage it will be more useful to examine Montreux's faltering attempts to imitate the narrative art of his Greek models than to rehearse his thematic borrowings from them. In the course of the more than 1,000 pages of the three-part ensemble there is very little actual action, as the pairs of lovers indulge in static declarations of everlasting love. As Coulet has observed, "On peut lire cinquante pages... sans voir l'action avancer d'un pas ni même comprendre quelle est la situation."[53] Perhaps the most blatant example of narrative retardation occurs at the end of part one of the ensemble. At this point in Cléandre's first-person narration, he and Domiphille have at last been reunited after a long separation caused by kidnapping, shipwreck and the malevolent designs of a wizard. The dramatized narrator Cléandre, like the ego-narrator Calasiris in Heliodorus' novel, suddenly announces to his listener Criniton that he is too tired to continue with his story. This ploy, probably as old as story-telling itself and evidenced in Greek literature as early as Homer's *Odyssey*, is undoubtedly derived from Heliodorus. The Greek author repeatedly suspends the narrative with delaying tactics that give rise to seemingly irrelevant subsequent events that eventually prove to be integral to the main lines of the plot, the object being to generate suspense.[54] On this occasion, however, as on others, Montreux aims unsuccessfully for the same effect by having Cléandre, as noted above (p. 752), present Criniton with the 116-page script of a play that he and, of course, the reader of the novel are to read during the interlude. Thus approximately one third of part one of the ensemble is padded with reading matter completely extraneous to the plot of the story and the emotional lives of the characters. At the earliest stage in post-mediaeval Western European attempts to master the manipulation of complex narrative, the lessons provided by Heliodorus, whom Julius Caesar Scaliger had called the best of models, have not yet been learned.[55]

To gauge the rapid progress made in the art of narrative manipulation, there is no better example than the *Histoire Negre-Pontique, Contenant la vie, et les Amours d'Alexandre Castriot ... et d'Olimpe* (1631).[56]

---

[53] Coulet (1967–8) I, 142; Sandy (1982c) 175–6.
[54] Sandy (1982a) 21–32 and Sandy (1970) 463–76.
[55] Sandy (1982c) 173.
[56] Sandy (1982c) 179–84.

The authorship of this work is no less confusing than the (intentionally confusing) fabricated authorship:

> Tirée des Manuscrits d'Octavio Finelli, de la Duché de Spolette, et recueillie par luy-mesme des Memoires d'un Caloyer Grec, en la Coste d'Ephese.

If, as the title-page states and as I prefer, the author is J. Baudoin (rather than Pierre de Boissat [or Boissac], as Segrais, slightly less than 100 years after the publication of the *histoire* states), then there is a certain satisfying harmony in the activities of the actual *auctor* and the invented *actor*.[57] For Baudoin translated, among others, Achilles Tatius, Lucian and Tasso, thereby duplicating the invented author's role in the transmission of a story that passed through the hands of a Greek monk and the Italian Finelli.[58] As well, like the prefatory "lettre du Caloyer Anselm," which vouches for the veracity of the *histoire*, Baudoin provides a prefatory endorsement of Gerzan's *Histoire africaine* (1627–8) (see below p. 762).

> La nuict n'estoit pas encore bien fermée, & le Soleil sembloit avoir du regret de laisser les royalles pompes d'Alger..., quand trois ou quatre personnes....

Not only is the *in-medias-res* opening of the *Ethiopian Story* duplicated, but the very syntax of Heliodorus' first sentence has been retained.[59] These "three or four people": actually, there are four people, the fourth of whom, Alexandre, is believed to be dead and therefore is left behind as the others make their escape from brigands attracted by the prospect of spoils presented by shipwreck. The uncertainty as to the exact number of people involved imitates Heliodorus' practice of restricting the dramatized narrators', even at this point the "omniscient" narrator's, and thereby the readers' knowledge and understanding of events to immediate impressions without benefit of hindsight.[60] The intended result, of course, is that the reader will experience the same bewilderment as the characters.

---

[57] Sandy (1982c) 180.
[58] Pellisson (1729) I, 320–3. Baudoin's translation of Achilles Tatius is somewhat uncertain. The *Catalogue générale des livres imprimés de la Bibliothèque nationale* s.v. and Lever (1976) 441 assign the same editions of *Les Amours de Clytophon et de Leucippe* (1635) to Baudoin's authorship. Arbour (1977–85), III, 300, however, does not assign them or any other copies to any author.
[59] Molinié (1978) 120–1.
[60] Sandy (1982a) 21–32; Morgan (1982).

The three refugees, Olympio (actually, Olympe disguised as a man), Euryale and Palemon, are then rescued in the Canary Islands by the wise hermit Hierosme Paleologue of the Isle de Negre-pont, who unburdens himself to them of his *histoire*. This turn of events is obviously modelled on Heliodorus' Isiac priest and sage Calasiris' account to the escaped Greek captive Cnemon of his *histoire*, which also encompasses that of the hero and heroine, Theagenes and Chariclea. As Hierosme was lying asleep in his room, "un homme sans barbe, delié de corsage" appeared to him and addressed him thus:

> Voici Hierosme, un present inestimable que le t'apporte: les Cieux veullent que tu le recoyes à gré.... C'est une fille baptisée à la haste, & née de parens Chrestiens.

Hierosme named her Olympe before she was kidnapped by Turkish pirates. He went in search of her but in despair of ever finding her became a hermit in a place far removed from her.

One can already see the advance in narrative art in evidence here. Whereas Montreux's many characters remain static and unconnected, Baudoin presents interlocked characters and points of view that resonate with past events and give impetus and shape to future events. In place of Montreux's still life, as it were, Baudoin has crafted engaging tableaux vivants.

Not only does Olympe, alias Olympio, share a past with Hierosme; Polemon, it transpires, is his brother Baptiste, "reduit à la vie des Coursaires, essayant à l'aide d'un vasseau, de persecuter selon mon pouvoir, ce cruel ennemy du nom du Iesus Christ." This surprising combination of piracy and religious mission also has a Heliodorean precedent, being modelled on the quarrel of the priest Calasiris' two sons, the elder of whom turns to a life of crime as he awaits the opportunity to claim the priesthood that is rightfully his.

Palemon/Baptiste is then prevailed upon to recount his *histoire*. He took up arms against Mahomet II, the quarrel over sacerdotal succussion in Heliodorus thus becoming transformed into a Christian crusade against infidels; and "la belle Amazone" Marulle becomes his beloved partner in the holy war. When they are captured by the pirate Machmut, Palemon/Baptiste manages to escape, but Machmut sees through Marulle's disguise:

> Il la donna en garde à l'un des siens, avec ces parolles: tien, Ibraim, conserve moy cette exquise Creature:... ie n'ay desiré que ce en tout mon voyage.

Palemon/Baptiste has been searching for her for the past seventeen years, all the while operating as a pirate against the Saracens.

At this point in the narrative Palemon/Baptiste interrupts his *histoire*:

> Mais parce qu'il est heure de prendre repos, ... ie suis d'avis, ... de differer à une autrefois la narration de cette avanture.

As we have seen, Montreux also employs this device of suspending the narrative, derived ultimately from Homer's *Odyssey* but more immediately from Heliodorus, as when in the latter author Cnemon threatens on grounds of fatigue to interrupt his account of his life. Heliodorus and Baudoin use the threatened interruption at a critical point in narration to arouse the dramatised listeners'—and the readers'—desire, like Scherezade's husband's, to learn what happens next. Montreux, however, fails completely to exploit the opportunity, inserting, instead of human interaction, a static, *extra-paginam* script of a play (see above pp. 752, 754).

Baudoin has learned other lessons from Heliodorus, such as manipulated surprise, as when Olimpe, sailing in disguise and believing herself to be alone overhears two people talking about her death:

> Car de voir qu'il y eust ... deux personnes, qui prinssent tant de soin de ses fortunes, & qu'encore l'une d'elles asseurat ..., l'avoir veuë vivante & morte, cela luy sembloit une illusion magique.

The setting in Heliodorus is landlocked, but the dynamics of the narration are patently the source of Baudoin's manipulation of the narrative and, more importantly, of the dramatized listener's response to it.[61] The story told about her by Olimpe's two fellow-passengers goes back three years and serves the same narrative purpose as Calasiris' framed *histoire* in the *Ethiopian Story*: that of filling in the background of one of the principal characters whose appearance in the narrative up to this point is at a stage far advanced in the chronological progression of the plot. The person to whom the story is being told interrupts: since you have known her only since she was thirteen or fourteen, let me tell you of her early childhood, whereupon "ils se mirent tous deux en estat, l'un pour ouyr, & l'autre de parler long temps." Like Heliodorus, Baudoin signposts the desired reader-response: "ils se mirent."[62]

---

[61] Sandy (1982a) 14–5.
[62] Sandy (1982a) 24–8.

Olimpe's early childhood parallels that of Chariclea in Heliodorus' novel. She was sent as an infant by her mother to Negre-pont, entrusted "entre les mains d'un Caloyer, appellé Hierosme," just as Chariclea was entrusted by her mother to the Delphic priest Charicles. Olimpe, eavesdropping on her own *histoire*:

> fut resoulte d'une doubte où elle avoit toujours esté, sçavoir est comment elle fut portee en la cellule, & comprit que le bon Hierosme avoit attribué à vision celeste une chose purement humaine.

As I have noted elsewhere, Baudoin's astute scrutiny of the *Ethiopian Story* has enabled him in this short passage to correct a glaring inconsistency in the plot of his model that was to remain otherwise unnoticed until 1940.[63]

Only rarely, and especially towards the end of the novel, where he confesses that "ie suis pressé par la grosseur de ce volume, de venir bien-tost à sa conclusion," does Baudoin fail to maintain artistic control of the highest order over the complex narrative form that he has adopted from Heliodorus. For instance, in the face of "un nouveau sujet d'estonnement"—namely that her long-lost lover Alexandre and even longer-lost parents Palemon/Baptiste and Marulle (alias Euryale) are aboard the same ship as she is and that she is overhearing them, while they themselves fail to recognize one another, exchanging details of her life and "death"—Olimpe falls asleep. Undoubtedly, this is Baudoin's poorly contrived way to delay the dénouement of the story, much as Heliodorus introduces a number of gratuitous and implausible complications for the same tactical reason in Books 9 and 10 of the *Ethiopian Story*.

I shall report only enough details of Martin Fumée's *Du Vray et Parfoit Amour* (1599) to establish the essential qualities of its mannered derivation from the ancient Greek novel, especially Heliodorus and far less substantially Achilles Tatius. Its sources have already been fully discussed by Küchler (1911), who consulted Huet's annotated copy, and, as we have seen, by Huet (see above pp. 747–50).

Like Baudoin, Fumée has borrowed Heliodorus' opening sentence, "Des-ia la belle lueur du Soleil prest a se monstre sur la terre...." The opening action is of a Roman triumphal procession, with vanquished Persians being led through the streets of Rome, as the residents, among them a young Greek woman, gaze down from their

---

[63] Sandy (1982c) 183.

windows at them. Among the friends and domestic staff of Philippe, the son of the defeated Persian king, is "un jeune homme beau." The young Greek woman exclaims, "'O dieux qu'est ce que ie voy...? Est-ce là Theogene?'" She is Charide, who gives vent to her anxieties for some twenty pages. Charide urges her female servant Melangenie to reassure her on the nature of love:

> Ma Dame, dit Melangenie, ce seroit une longue Iliade que de vous faire le discours entier de ce que vous demandez. La longueur de la nuict s'y passeroit, tant s'en faut que ce soit y fust suffisant.

Needless to say, Melangenie does eventually relate her "Iliade" of star-crossed love:

> Pensant que mon mal pourra adoucir le vostre, ie vous en feray volontiers le recit. Il y a vingt neuf ans, ainsi que la calammité...,

and her tale continues for over fifty pages until she is interrupted. Charide then recounts to Melangenie what Baudoin would have called her "histoire." When she was thirteen and the ward of a relative, a young man named Theogene came to her city. At the festival of Minerva they saw each other and "'nos yeux furent les premiers messagers de nos amours.'"

The rest—such as separation, misadventure, pirates and quest—can easily be imagined. The contents are in general and in particulars, such as the mention of "Brachmanes & Gymnosophystes" in Ethiopia, derived from Heliodorus and to a lesser degree from Achilles Tatius, as in the cases of the test of chastity and the human sacrifice practised by nomadic Scythians.

As for the literary merits of the work, there is some disagreement, some critics regarding it as a forerunner of French imitations of Greek novels while others dismiss it as a mediocre pastiche.[64] I am inclined to agree with the latter group but believe that it has historical importance: it confirms the authority of the ancient Greek novel at the dawn of extended prose fiction in post-mediaeval Western Europe. It also, as we saw earlier, attracted the attention of Pierre-Daniel Huet in the first critical history of prose fiction.

The authority of the ancient Greek novel is also evident in J. Herembert's *Les aventureuses et fortunées amours de Pandion et d'Yonice. Tirées des anciens Autheurs Grecs* (1599).[65] In her otherwise useful book Daele

---

[64] Küchler (1911) 146.
[65] Sandy (1982c) 176–9.

([1946] 161) states that "as far as can be ascertained, for a literary period still largely unexplored, the following are the earliest French Greek romances showing influences of Heliodorus," and she proceeds to enumerate the works of Montreux and Fumée (q.v. *supra*), M. Roussel and J. Herembert. In the case of Herembert she is mistaken, misled perhaps by the erroneous statement written by an unknown person on the inside of the copy now housed in the Bibliothèque de l'Arsenal (8° B.L. 17468): "Il semble . . . que l'auteur ait entiérement copié . . . en quelques endroits l'histoire ethiopique d'heliodor." As for Roussel's *Histoire de Cleophas et Sephora* (1601), the only possible traces of Heliodorean influence that I have been able to find are in the intentionally labyrinthine events associated with the threatened placatory sacrifice of the hero and heroine and the subsequent passionate pursuit of Cleophas by Arsinoé, which bear a generic resemblance to the last few books of the *Ethiopian Story*. Otherwise, Roussel's borrowings are restricted to mythological paradigms in accordance with his prefatory "Aux Lecteurs":

> Aussi pour orner dignement les vertus du Prince que je vous promets, & ceste Histoire mesme, j'ay emprunté force beaux traicts des anciens autheurs plus fameux.

As noted previously, Daele is equally mistaken about Herembert, but the lineage of his novel is of considerable interest. He derived it very extensively from that of Achilles Tatius, whose morally outrageous novel provoked indignant censure from the time of Photius in the ninth century to that of Herembert's compatriot Huet some 150 years after the publication of the French novel.[66] Since the editio princeps of the Greek text of Achilles Tatius' novel did not appear until 1601, two years after the publication of Herembert's novel, he probably based his French adaptation on the Latin translation of della Croce (Cruceius).

Apodeme, by his first marriage, has a son named Pandion, whom he betroths to Pandale. The match seems assured until the brother of Apodeme's second wife, Cleanthe Rhodien, sends his wife Ludipe and his daughter Yonice to the safety of Pandion's house, which is far removed from the theatre of war between Demetrius and Ptolomée. Predictably, for anyone who has read Achilles Tatius' novel, as Herembert has, Yonice immediately replaces Pandale in Pandion's

---

[66] Sandy (1982c) 176.

affections, "Dés la premiere veuë ceste incroyable beauté s'imprima tellement en son ame."

Pandion then confesses his dilemma to his cousin Lydus and the two of them engage in a Plato-inspired discussion of the nature of love exactly as in the discourse of Clitophon and his cousin Clinias in Achilles Tatius (1.8–11):

> Les affections qui d'un premier coup d'œil s'engendrent sans avoir esté causees ... sont sans doute divines et emanees du jugement des dieux ...:
> ... la principale piece du marriage, c'est une volonté et non forcee.

Thus encouraged, Pandion goes in search of Yonice, "qui se promenoit au jardin à l'endroit d'un petit boscage touffu d'une infinité de plantes" that corresponds to Achilles Tatius' *dignus amore locus* (1.8–11) and where in both novels the heroes profess their passionate attachment to the objects of their love at first sight.

A short time later and, as in Achilles Tatius, abruptly, the scene shifts to Therphant of Rhodes, who, rejected previously by Yonice because of his disgraceful behaviour, has followed her to her place of refuge and waits offshore aboard his ship for the opportunity to seize her. When the opportunity presents itself, he seizes instead Pandion's originally intended bride Pandale by mistake. This bizarre sequence of events is modelled closely on its counterpart in Achilles Tatius (2.13–18). The same is true of the immediately following sequence of events where the servant Bussaquet is persuaded by Pandion to allow him to enter Yonice's bedroom at night. As he is doing so, her mother Ludipe dreams that a robber is in the process of ravishing Yonice and cutting open her stomach. Ludipe immediately rushes into her daughter's bedroom and Pandion "faisoit sa retraite plustost qu'il n'eust desiré." This grotesquely symbolic sequence has an exact parallel in Achilles Tatius (2.23–4).

I have described only enough of Herembert's work to confirm that not all early French attempts to reinvent the novel were cast in the Heliodorean mould that from the outset prevailed as the dominant pattern in post-mediaeval Western Europe. Another issue that I have been concerned to confront in the preceding pages is the struggle on the part of French apprentice writers of extended prose fiction to master the manipulation of a complex narrative form. Montreux, for instance, as we have seen, patently failed to do so. The Greek writer Achilles Tatius also failed in this respect. Unable, apparently, to maintain the *à-tiroirs* structure initiated at the outset, he eventually allows the narrative to lapse into the more easily manageable third-person, omniscient point of view.[67] One may question Herembert's judgment in choosing Achilles Tatius' novel as his exclusive model, but one must respect his astuteness and literary skill in detecting and correcting its technical deficiencies. Achilles Tatius launches the *à-tiroirs* structure with the familiar device of an erotic painting that bears directly on the emotional history of the viewers, one of whom recounts his similar amorous misfortunes. A framed painting thereby occasions the framed narrative that serves as a component of the frame. To be consistent, the author must eventually resume the role of framing agent. Herembert has circumvented this potential narrative pitfall; but so committed is he to the contents of his model that he has his lovers elope needlessly to Sidon, where in Achilles Tatius the *ekphrasis* occurs, whence they flee to Alexandria instead of going directly in the first place to the Egyptian city as in the Greek author.

The last of the French adaptations of the ancient Greek novel that I shall pass in review is Gerzan's *L'Histoire afriquaine de Cleomede et de Sophonisbe* (1627-8).[68] As I confessed more than a decade ago, I have not read all of this vast work of some 2,000 pages. I have, however, read enough of it to verify or correct observations that have been made about it in the past.

Most fundamentally, it is this work of Gerzan and not a putative *Sophonisbe* of the much more famous Madeleine de Scudéry that was translated in 1646 into German by P. von Zesen and helped to condition public demand in Germany for romance novels *à la grecque*. Also noteworthy is the fact that the dedicatory "Ode" by J. Baudoin forges a link of continuing enterprise to his *Histoire Negre-pontique* (1631), which was discussed earlier. As well, Gerzan and Baudoin seem to have been in agreement on the appropriateness of Heliodorus as a model; for the opening sentence of the former's novel is modelled as closely on the first sentence of the *Ethiopian Story* as is Baudoin's opening sentence (see above p. 755). As well, Gerzan's imitation of the thematic contents and complex narrative structure of Heliodorus continue apace.[69] Gerzan and Baudoin also saw eye-to-eye on the desirability of authenticating the alleged ancient Greek provenance of their stories. In his "Preface Au Lecteur" Gerzan assures the reader that

---

[67] Sandy (1982c) 178-9.
[68] Sandy (1982c) 185-9.
[69] Sandy (1982c) 185-7.

he will, in the interest of "l'exacte Geographie & ... la vraye Histoire," recount what "un vieux Grec," like Baudoin's "Caloyer Grec," "me ... a monstré ... en mes voyages."

Perhaps the most noteworthy feature of Gerzan's work is that it combines with imitation of Heliodorus episodes unmistakably borrowed from Apuleius' *Golden Ass*, Achilles Tatius and Iamblichus.[70] Inclusion of material from the last of these three writers is startling, for Photius' résumé of Iamblichus' otherwise lost *Babylonian Story* did not appear in print until the Greek edition of 1601, to be followed in five years by Andreas Schott's Latin translation of the *Bibliotheca*. The only other contemporary instance known to me of combining material from Apuleius and Iamblichus occurs in Canto XIV of the *Adone* (1623) of Marino, who was in Paris at the very time of Gerzan's literary activity.

Gerzan is a fitting conclusion to this survey of French imitations and adaptations of ancient Greek novels. His opportunism in exploiting Iamblichus' *Babylonian Story* within slightly more than two decades of its initial appearance in print underscores that in France the literary enterprise that I have been discussing was also a humanistic enterprise rooted deeply in the development of French Hellenism during the first third of the sixteenth century. The French undertaking is comparable to the recovery, study and production of Latin translation of Greek works by Italian humanists during the fifteenth century. Amyot defined the ideals of the French enterprise. A member of the second generation of French Hellenists, he scoured the major libraries of Italy for new and better Greek manuscripts, produced vernacular translations directly from the Greek instead of from the intermediary of Latin translations, in some cases discovered and translated Greek works or parts of Greek works previously unknown in Western Europe, collated Greek manuscripts in order to improve his translations and, finally, derived from the example of Heliodorus and from ancient theorists the "rules" of extended prose fiction. In this way he implicitly fostered a reverence for the preeminence of Greek authority in the composition of novels that can be seen in the elaborate schemes of Fumée ("... Escrit en Grec, par Athenagoras"), Baudoin ("... Memoires d'un Caloyer Grec") and Gerzan ("Un vieux Grec me ...") to authenticate their modern creations as recently discovered ancient Greek works. Amyot's tour of

---

[70] Sandy (1982c) 187–9.

Italian libraries enabled him in the second edition of his translation of the *Ethiopian Story* (1559) to transmit biographical details of Heliodorus previously unknown in Western Europe that he had found in "un fort vieil exemplaire . . ., escrit à la main, en parchmin" housed in the Vatican Library. Similarly, Montreux must have consulted the *Suda*, a Byzantine reference book valued by humanists but unavailable in translations, for the prefatory statement of "Achilles Statius [sic] tresrenommé Philosophe Chrestien."[71] Finally, both Fumée and Baudoin, the latter of whom wrote the "Ode" that prefaces Gerzan's novel, were active in the humanistic enterprise of translating Greek works. Fumée's efforts are represented by *Histoire des guerres faictes par l'empereur Iustinian contre les Vandales et les Goths. Escrite en Grec par Procope et Agathias et mise en François par Martin Fumée* (1587).[72] In addition to his many translations of English, Italian, Latin and Spanish works, Baudoin produced versions of Achilles Tatius and the complete works of Lucian.[73] To judge by the scathing remarks of one critic early in the seventeenth century, however, the translation of Lucian seems to have owed more to a slightly earlier French version than to the Greek text.[74] In any case his translation of Sidney's *Arcadia* now takes us to the western shore of the English Channel.

Great Britain

Ancient Greek novels, particularly that of Heliodorus, had already been discovered, studied, translated, plundered and adapted in France before extended prose fiction makes its appearance in Great Britain. Thus the earliest British novelists first experience the literary form through continental European intermediaries. More specifically, the surprising combination of Plutarch and Heliodorus in the earliest English exploitation of the *Ethiopian Story*, James Sandford's *The Amorous and Tragicall Tales of Plutarch. Whereonto is annexed the Hystorie of Chariclia and Theagenes* (1567), suggests that this enterprise was inspired directly by Amyot's celebrated translations of the two Greek authors.[75] Just as "North's Plutarch" is really Amyot's Plutarch translated into

---

[71] Dyck (1986) 81; Wilson (1992) 38.
[72] Küchler (1911) 144.
[73] Pellisson (1729) I, 320–3.
[74] Lauvergnat-Gagnière (1988) 129, n. 24.
[75] Sandy (1982a) 9; Oeftering (1901) 92–3.

English and even Adlington's famous translation of a Latin work, Apuleius' *Golden Ass*, is based substantially on earlier French translations and its preface is a paraphrase of the Italian humanist Beroaldus' commentary of 1500, just so are the earliest English versions of the two most influential Greek novels, the *Ethiopian Story* and *Daphnis and Chloe*, based on previous translations. Angel Day's English version of *Daphnis and Chloe* (1587) is in fact a paraphrase of Amyot's translation of 1559, and Underdowne has based his translation of the *Ethiopian Story* exclusively on the Latin translation of Heliodorus by the Pole Warschewiczki.[76] There is some uncertainty about the details of publication of Underdowne's version.[77] These details are marginal to our purposes except in so far as they provide a striking illustration of the zeal with which Elizabethan writers of narrative fiction seized the most immediate opportunity afforded by the appearance of translations of Greek novels. Wolff has vividly characterized this process of urgent ransacking:

> The later date (1577) [of an edition of Underdowne's translation] still brings the "Aethiopica" into Elizabethan hands in plenty of time. "Euphues" is not yet out; Greene's first piece of fiction will not be licensed till three years later; Lodge's will not be printed till seven; Sidney has perhaps begun the "Arcadia" in desultory fashion, but will not finish it for several years, and will afterward, before his death in 1586, recast rather more than the first half of it, with the "Aethiopica" full in his view.—As for the subsequent edition of Underdowne, in 1587, this, though it comes too late for Sidney, is ready to give Greene a new impulse toward the imitation of Greek romance.[78]

Of the five major writers of Elizabethan narrative fiction—Greene, Lodge, Lyly, Nash and Sidney—, three are represented in Wolff's catalogue of writers eagerly awaiting fresh narrative grist; of the other two, Lyly may have been exposed indirectly to the ancient Greek novels through the medium of Italian *novelle*, and Nash, in Wolff's words, "makes no use whatever of the Greek Romances."[79] Nonetheless, this is an impressive progeny.

Angel Day's paraphrase of Amyot's translation of *Daphnis and Chloe* and one of the editions of James Underdowne's English version of

---

[76] Sandy (1982a) 102–3.
[77] Wolff (1912) 238.
[78] Wolff (1912) 239.
[79] Wolff (1912) 459.

Heliodorus Latinus were both published in 1587. In the words of Wolff again:

> In 1588, Greene is on the spot with his best known story, "Pandosto"... which is full of matter from both of them [viz. *Ethiopian Story* and *Daphnis and Chloe*], and which draws somewhat upon Achilles Tatius as well. "Pandosto" thus possesses a two-fold interest—first, and chiefly, as the main source of [Shakespeare's] "The Winter's Tale"; secondly, as exhibiting with the greatest fullness the influence of the Greek Romances upon Greene.[80]

There are other indications of the speed with which translations of the ancient Greek novels were converted to other artistic purposes in Great Britain. A play based on the *Ethiopian Story* was performed at Court in the winter of 1572–3. This supports the possibility that an edition of Underdowne's version appeared in print as early as 1569.[81] Two decades after the production of "the play of Cariclia," for which "ij spears" and "an awlter for theagines" were required as props, Stephen Gosson wrote that "*the Aethiopian historie*" had "been throughly ransackt, to furnish the Playe houses in London."[82] Some thirteen or fourteen years still later Shakespeare alludes to the *Ethiopian Story* in *Twelfth Night* and by 1620 Joseph Hall exclaims, "What Schole-boy, what apprentice knows not Heliodorus?"[83] Thus within a period of only fifty-three years, starting with James Sandford's versified, thirty-eight page retelling of the *Ethiopian Story* in 1567, the ancient Greek novel has come to occupy a prominent place in the minds of British writers, readers and theatre-goers.

In the pages that follow I shall devote considerably less attention to English-language adaptations of the ancient Greek novel than I did to their French counterparts for two reasons. First, as I have already mentioned, the French, in initiating the enterprise, set the pattern for Western Europe. Second, it is often difficult, if not impossible, to distinguish between the direct influence of the ancient Greek novel and the blended combination of Greek novel and French adaptation that was available to British writers. This complex line of descent is evident, for instance, in the prefatory "An Apologie for **ROMANCES**" of Sir George Mackenzie's *Aretina; Or, the Serious Romance* (1660):

---

[80] Wolff (1912) 376.
[81] Wolff (1912) 238, n. 5.
[82] S. Gosson, *Plays Confuted in Five Actions* (1582). Sandy (1982a) 103.
[83] Sandy (1982c) 41.

> Who should blush to trace in these paths, which the famous Sidney, Scuderie, Barkely, and Braghill hath beaten for them, besides thousands of Ancients...? I shall speak nothing of that noble Romance written by a Bishop [i.e., Heliodorus], which the entreaty of all the Eastern Churches could never prevail with him to disown.[84]

Similarly, M. Dalzie, the editor of a modern reissue of Charlotte Lennox's *The Female Quixote* (1752), remarks that the Heliodorean character Oroondates was so widely known from La Calprenède's *Cassandra* (1642-5) that eighteenth-century British writers casually mention him "as if expecting their readers to know who he is."[85] Conversely, in *Evagoras, A Romance* (1677) by "L.L. Gent. [leman]," the outward signs point to derivation from French adaptations. N. Brady's versified tribute links the author's Maiden Muse" to "Dedalean Scudery," i.e., the immensely popular, multi-volume romances of Madeleine and her brother Georges de Scudéry. As I have explained elsewhere, however, the seamless blending of distantly placed but thematically linked episodes from Achilles Tatius' novel suggest that the author of *Evagoras* has been influenced by the Greek author.[86]

In the next century, only four years before the "first" English novel, Richardson's *Pamela* of 1740, *Celenia: Or, the History of Hyempsal*, by "Zelis," resonates with a mishmash of thematic echoes of ancient novels. The queen of Numidia entrusts her youngest son Hyempsal to the faithful Merobanes in order to protect him from dynastic treachery. The child is declared in a written declaration by his mother to be "the rightful heir... of the Crown of Numidia, whereof this Mark of a Cross upon his right Arm, shall hereafter be a sufficient Evidence." In the ultimate source, Heliodorus' *Ethiopian Story*, Chariclea, the white daughter of the black king and queen of Ethiopia, is exposed by her mother with a swathe on which in Ethiopian hieroglyphics are embroidered the explanation of the child's exposure and a declaration of her royal birth. The phrase "The Mark of a Cross upon his right Arm" in *Celenia* corresponds to the vestigial ring of black skin above the elbow of Chariclea's left arm in Heliodorus.

The abrupt, *in-medias-res* opening of *Celenia*, like its counterparts in early French novels, is also Heliodorean, "Scarce had Phoebus rais'd up his Eye-lids... when Calomander...," of whom the reader knows

---

[84] Sandy (1982c) 54.
[85] Sandy (1982c) 46, n. 16.
[86] Sandy (1982c) 47-50.

nothing. To Calomander are told all the events leading to Hyempsal's recovery of the crown of Numidia. This account is interrupted on a few occasions and there are, as in Heliodorus, changes in the point of view, as when Antemora tells of her misfortunes in her love-affair with Philarchus. It began when the parents of Antemora and her newly wed husband Busídes, both of whom are pre-pubescent, separate the youthful couple at the enigmatic urging of Providence. She and Philarchus later employ a physician to poison both her husband Busídes and a witness to their adultery.

The few episodes from the inset "The Story of Antemora and Philarchus" that I have recounted owe nothing to the otherwise dominant Heliodorean pattern of events. Instead, their antecedents exist in a variety of ancient novels and are to be found in other post-mediaeval narratives. The combination of misjudged parental interference and divinely ordained separation of Antemora and Busídes recalls the springboard for all the subsequent misfortunes and adventures in Xenophon of Ephesus' *Ephesian Story* (1.6–7). The *editio princeps* of this rudimentary ancient Greek novel appeared in 1727, that is, ten years before the publication of *Celenia*. In her *The Progress of Romance through Times, Countries, and Manners* (1785), Clara Reeve mentions it in the same breath as the ancient Greek novels of Antonius Diogenes and Achilles Tatius, to which her interlocutor responds, "From whence, and to what purpose have you conjured up such a list of uncouth names—to frighten us?" From this we may conclude that Xenophon of Ephesus' novel was at least known if not familiar in Great Britain some fifty years after the publication of *Celenia* and possibly at the time of its composition.

The role of the physician in *Celenia* adheres to the (by then) predictable pattern of his substituting for a variety of reasons a harmless soporific for the ordered poison. This pattern is found in Apuleius' *Golden Ass* (10.11 and 24–5), Xenophon of Ephesus (3.5.11), the fragmentary novel of Antonius Diogenes and the anonymous *The Most Pleasant History of Tom A Lincoln* (1655).[87]

A character named Theophilus in *Celenia* converts Hydaspes to Christianity. This is similar to the proselytizing efforts of the Isiac priest Calasiris in the *Ethiopian Story*. As well, as Hyempsal is about to issue a challenge to an opponent, Celinia reminds him, "'Remember, Sir, you are now a Christian, and the Christian Religion

---

[87] Sandy (1982c) 46.

forbids Murder.'" However, there are other possible sources that were part of the common stock of narrative themes available to English-language novelists of this time. They include the goddess Athena's restoration of harmony at the end of the *Odyssey*, which was Heliodorus' model, similar French transformations of pagan discord into religious conflict between Christians and infidels (see above p. 756) and Spenser's *Faerie Queene* and Sidney's *Arcadia* and *their* sources, Achilles Tatius and Heliodorus.[88]

I have enumerated a few of the many links to ancient prose fiction still in force in the eighteenth century in order to bring to the forefront a fundamental critical problem: how are we to distinguish between direct imitation of ancient Greek novels and the French and earlier English-language adaptations and use of them? I do not claim to have an answer to this question. However, the late date of *Celenia* and its wily-nily proliferation of novelistic themes predispose me to decide in favour of indirect imitation of ancient Greek novels. In any case, the potential sources of themes first developed in ancient Greek novels that are employed by English-language novelists after approximately the first half of the seventeenth century become too numerous and widespread to be traced with any degree of certainty directly back to their originators.

To appreciate fully the effect of the ancient Greek novels on the development of prose fiction in Great Britain we must go back to the embryonic stage of the literary form during the Elizabethan period. John Grange's *Golden Aphroditis* (1577) and John Lyly's *Euphues. The Anatomy of Wit* (1578) are usually cited in literary surveys of the period as the earliest examples of English prose fiction, and I know of nothing that contradicts that judgment. These two works and most of their immediate successors lack what is now usually considered to be an essential component of traditional novels: a sustained and coherently developed plot. Instead, they rely on static colloquies, soliloquies and epistolary exchanges; and in this respect they are reminiscent of Montreux's three-part ensemble of 1595-99, the earliest Western European example of sustained, methodical imitation of ancient Greek novels.

Brian Melbanke's *Philotimus. The Warre betwixt Nature and Fortune* (1583) is representative of the type. It consists principally of a series of *sententiae* and *exempla* culled from a variety of ancient authors in furtherance of

---

[88] Sandy (1982c) 49, n. 23.

romantic suit. Heliodorus figures among the ancient writers whom Melbanke quarries, often in words unmistakably borrowed from Underdowne's translation of *Heliodorus Latinus*, which was published at most fourteen years earlier.[89] It seems unlikely that the *Ethiopian Story* has in that short span of time become a household book among the reading public; yet Melbanke provides very few clues for his readers. I wonder what an Elizabethan reader would have made of this passage, for instance:

> There he [viz. Philotimus] gave her a ring. . . . She [viz. Aurelia] bestowed on him an Amatist, whose force was to drive away all evil thoughts, and sharpen his understanding at his booke: when he behelde the Amatist, I think, quoth he, the force of this Amatist hath kept you working all this night, for such operation also do Lapidaries ascribe to it.

A reader familiar with chapters 13–5 of Book 5 of the *Ethiopian Story* might have had an inkling of some of the implications of the exchange. On other occasions Melbanke associates by name actions in his novel with their agents in Heliodorus. The names at least provide clues, but this is still some sixty years before La Calprenède made them familiar to the reading public (see above p. 767). In the following example Castibula checks Telamon's aggressive ardour with these words:

> If thou canst bringe under thy gadding appetites, and submit them to the friendshippe thou owest my husband, Cariclia was not halfe so glad, that her Theagenes overcame Ormenes in the race at Pithiaeas games, as I will rejoyce that my husbands deserts, hathe daunted the force of thy illegitymate desyres, and as the same Cariclia, rather purposed to receive that which is destined to deathe, then by having Alcamenes deceive Theagenes, so shall these handes first pull out this tonge.

On still other occasions Melbanke provides enough context to make the meaning clear whether or not a reader is familiar with the Greek source, as in the following example, where Laida is speaking to Cornelius:

> Thou wilt be found as phantasticall as Nausicles a Merchant in Naucratia, which being in love with Arsinoe, and often gratulated with her companye, began in process to loath his Arsinoe, bycause, when she sunge at entreaty, her cheekes swelled, and her eyes stared.

---

[89] Rollins (1935) 177–98.

Finally, on one occasion, in a sentence modelled very closely on Underdowne's translation of the passage, Melbanke identifies his source, "As Heliodorus Aethiopicus reports...." Before leaving Melbanke I want to emphasize that in spite of his many references to the *Ethiopian Story* he has made no use whatsoever of the plot of the Greek novel for the simple reason that his work has no plot whatsoever.

Wolff (1912) has dealt fully and admirably with the influence of the ancient Greek novel on the five major Elizabethan writers of narrative fiction and I shall follow in his footsteps only far enough to give an impression of the progress that was made and the lessons still to be learned by them in the manipulation of complex narrative. Of Sidney's *Arcadia* I shall say very little because pastoral narrative romance falls outside of the range of this chapter. In so far as its *narrative* qualities are concerned, it is worth noting that the augmented versions of 1590 and 1593, the latter of which has come to be known as *The Countess of Pembrokes Arcadia*, are characterized by Sidney's increased use of distinctive Heliodorean narrative techniques such as dramatized narrators, suspension of ego-narratives, the plunge *in medias res*, flashbacks and complications of plot. As Wolff explains:

> The Old Arcadia consisted of material largely derived from Heliodorus and wholly kept within a Heliodorean frame; the New Arcadia retains this material and this frame, and deliberately recasts it in the Heliodorean mould of narrative structure. Sidney has learned to write Greek Romance in English.[90]

It is worth noting as well that Spenser's *Faerie Queene*, in spite of being infused with a large amount of allegory in the mediaeval fashion and owing much of its inspiration to Italian narrative poetry, also benefits from the lessons in narrative manipulation provided by Heliodorus. As Lewis observes:

> This method—the immediate presentation of a figure already in action ["A gentle knight was pricking on the playne"]—was not... the method of Spenser's predecessors and contemporaries. He had perhaps no perfect model of it except in Heliodorus.[91]

One of Sidney's contemporaries, the poet Gervase Markham, states in the "To the Reader" of his *The English Arcadia* (1607) that "the

---

[90] Wolff (1912) 353.
[91] Lewis (1954) 389.

onely to be admired Sir Philip Sidney [drew] ... both from *Heliodorus*, and [Montemayor's] *Diana*."[92]

We can dispense with Thomas Lodge quickly as well. His debt to ancient Greek novels is restricted to two references to the *Ethiopian Story*. The So(u)ldan of Babylon in *The History of Robert, Second Duke of Normandy* (1591) defends his love for the daughter of the Roman emperor in these words addressed to his compatriots, "'Princes woonder not, Theagines a Greeke, loved Cariclia a Moore, & your Souldan a Mahometist, his Ermine a Christian.'"[93] The other reference, at the beginning of *Forbonius and Prisceria* (1584), in spite of its equally limited application, has some significance; for as Wolff remarks, "Lodge would have had no motive for professing to continue a story [viz. the *Ethiopian Story*] that was not widely and favorably known."[94]

Robert Greene deserves more of our attention than the previous Elizabethan writers of narrative fiction. It is true that his many borrowings from Achilles Tatius, Heliodorus and Longus function principally as isolated, inorganic incidents and decor in novelle inspired by the type written by Boccaccio, Bandello, Fiorentino and the queen of Navarre in her *Heptameron* and previously exploited in English in such collections of tales as Painter's *The Palace of Pleasure* (1566) and Fenton's *Certain Tragical Discourses of Bandello* (1567). It is nevertheless possible to conclude that instances of his more sustained development of plot derive from his continued exposure to the ancient Greek novelists, as he progressed from pamphleteering to full-fledged narrative. In *Gwyndonius. The Carde of Fancie* (1584), for instance, there are borrowings from Heliodorus that shape the structure of the work rather than providing only superficial ornament.[95] His use of Achilles Tatius has similar results. The structure of *Arbasto*, published in the same year as *Carde of Fancie*, is so completely influenced by *Leucippe and Clitophon* that it retains the failed first-person, framed narrative structure of the Greek model (see above, p. 762).[96] Elsewhere in Greene's corpus, in Wolff's words:

---

[92] A. Hamilton, "Sidney's *Arcadia* as Prose Fiction ...," *English Literary Renaissance* 2 (1972) 30 (of 29–60).
[93] Wolff (1912) 459–60.
[94] Wolff (1912) 459.
[95] Wolff (1912) 417.
[96] Wolff (1912) 393–5 and 407.

> The influence of Achilles Tatius... gives either single scenes,..., or, still more superficially, ornament that is non-structural, [and] that is easily detachable.[97]

Greene's continuing exposure to Heliodorus goes beyond the principally superficial details that Achilles Tatius contributes to his novelle. Heliodorus provides the forward thrust of plot and the resonance of integrated characters. In works such as *Pandosto* (1588) and *Menaphon* (1589) the plots advance coherently and the various characters contribute to, and are integrated with, their progression. "Here at last the story is the thing," as Lewis states, instead of serving as a vehicle of static colloquies and soliloquies as in *Planetomachia* (1585).[98]

Like the English language itself, English-language narrative fiction of the late sixteenth and the seventeenth centuries that displays traces of the ancient Greek novels tends to be an amalgam of various components. The Elizabethan examples of the form are characterized by their indiscriminately rapacious plundering of whatever was to hand: Italianate novelle, Greek and Latin myth and legend and English translations of translations of Heliodorus, Longus and Achilles Tatius. Greene is as guilty of the indiscriminate rapine as his contemporaries whom he castigates for the practice in the prefatory "To the Gentlemen Students of both Universities" in his *Menaphon*:

> Let other men (as they please) praise... the Italionate pen, that of a packet of pilfries, affoordeth the presse a pamphlet or two in an age, and then in disguised arraie, vaunts **Ovids** and **Plutarchs** plumes as their owne.

Almost without exception the resultant patchworks of borrowed material function principally as static, inorganic displays of derivative discourse. In the next century and even as late as *Celenia* (1736), when "at last the story is the thing," the sources of the story appear to be derived indirectly from ancient Greek novels by way of French adaptations. At this point the subject ceases to be the heritage of the ancient Greek novel and becomes instead the influence throughout Western Europe of the French novelists like the Scudérys and La Calprenède, who mastered the lessons taught by "ces fameux Romans de l'Antiquité" and advanced to the level of *inventing* their own "heroic" fictional narratives.[99]

---

[97] Wolff (1912) 407.
[98] Lewis (1954) 422.
[99] The quoted phrase comes from M. Scudéry's *Ibrahim* (1641).

19. THE NACHLEBEN OF THE ANCIENT NOVEL IN IBERIAN LITERATURE IN THE SIXTEENTH CENTURY

M. Futre Pinheiro

Introduction

It has been amply stressed that the novel was, right from the beginning, a popular and secular form of literature, profoundly rooted in a popular substratum. And the traditional view of literature inherited from Plato, which Christianity maintained alive, systematically rejected the novel as a valid form of artistic expression, making it take the last place in the hierarchy of literary genres. This traditional framework has rarely been challenged throughout the history of Western culture, so much so that critical appreciation of the genre has not been on a par with the attention that the reading public has always given to the novel.[1]

Unlike other genres, however, like epic or drama, that carry the weight of social and religious functions which lends them social importance and even authority, the novel, right from its remotest origins, has led a sort of nomadic existence, foreign to national or historical commitments. "Romance is the epic of the creature, man's vision of his own life as a quest".[2] With the older literary genres the novel establishes a peculiar polyphonic dialectic, which seems to derive its relevance from the shared inheritance in that which concerns structures, cross-references and allusions. Scholars have used various terms for this intertwining of themes, languages and styles belonging to different periods, and the kind of approach to the texts themselves varies according to schools of thought and opinion. They are all unanimous, however, in recognizing in this melting-pot process a

---

[1] Frye (1976) 23 highlighted this contradiction as follows: "Popular literature has been the object of a constant bombardment of social anxieties for over two thousand years, and nearly the whole of the established critical tradition has stood out against it. The greater part of the reading and listening public has ignored the critics and censors for exactly the same length of time."
[2] *Ibid.*, p. 15.

mysterious power of cohesion, supporting the construction of a large interconnected body of stories and legends with the "outlines of an imaginative universe also in it",[3] as well as a particular *Weltanschauung*. But the inner force which the novel derives from this magnetic welding generates, on the other hand, a contrary motion of irradiation and *contaminatio* in later literatures.

We can say, in fact, without too great a margin for error, that the conventions, the uniform pattern which underlies the use of certain themes, the storyteller's tactics and the narrative technique as a whole reveal only very small changes throughout the centuries. This leads us to state that the novel has broken all records where longevity and versatility are concerned. There is a visible continuity in the history of the narrative genre: for that reason, the genre we call the novel remains the same,[4] if we consider its main structural patterns or, should we prefer a different term, its system of *invariables* which could be used to create a *grammar* of the genre, subject to the occasional influences of historical, social, political and cultural determinants, which do not, however, alter its essential structure. Such a conservative outlook is surely the mark of intrinsic stability rooted somewhere within the genre itself.

Concerning Portuguese literature and the way it was influenced by the ancient novel, we will focus on sixteenth-century narrative which, from a thematic point of view, is usually divided into three broad sections: the sentimental novel, the pastoral novel and the chivalric novel.

It seems possible to find parallels between the flowering of the Greek novel, which Hegel called the *bourgeois epic*, and the snuffing out of the epic flame that, with the French and Castillian *chansons de geste*, lent a voice to the spirit of chivalry during the historic period in which it flowered. Love, which was not relevant in the old epics, became the main motivation for the heroes' actions. And the feminine element became prevalent in this type of literature. Europe never tired of hearing, for three centuries, the sad love stories of Tristan and Isolda, Lancelot and Guinevere and all the others who challenged traditional morals.

---

[3] *Ibid.*, p. 15.
[4] Cizek (1974) 421.

I. The Chivalric Novel

The Amadis de Gaula, a spurious but fascinating offspring of the old epic material related to Brittany, considered by the eminent Spanish philologist Menéndez Pelayo one of the greatest novels of all times,[5] derives from the so-called "spirit of chivalry" that swept across feudal France in the twelfth century, lending form and expression to the courtly novel which flowered there at the same time. *Amadis* also reveals the influence of medieval Iberian narratives connected with Arthurian legends, particularly *A Demanda do Santa Graal* (*The Quest of the Holy Grail*), which is one of the oldest pieces of literary medieval prose in Portugal.[6]

Amadis became a sort of breviary that touched the heart of Europe; and much later, it would blossom once more in a context both within and outside the Iberian Peninsula and fire the imagination of the Romantic movement, which Sainte-Beuve called a powerful "feminine insurrection".

Frequently mentioned in fourteenth-century texts, the work was only published in Castillian in 1508. This version is not the original one, but an amply reworked copy by the hand of Garci Rodríguez de Montalvo, who calls himself its "author". We know, however, thanks to the recent discovery of a fifteenth-century fragment,[7] that Garci Rodríguez added to the original three books a fourth book he wrote himself. Although the origin of *Amadis* is shrouded in uncertainty (and the question of priority over Castillian or Portuguese authorship has sparked considerable debate between Portuguese and Castillian adepts),[8] the frequent overlapping of Castillian and Gallician-Portuguese cultures during the Middle Ages, together with the subsequent impossibility of autonomously establishing authorship in either of the two languages, contribute to our not making a clear distinction between the two literatures during that period of time. The Renaissance ideals and the political relations between Castillia and Portugal, supported by frequent marriages between their crowns, also

---

[5] Menéndez Pelayo (1962) 350.
[6] García Gual (1990) 227–266 and Futre Pinheiro (1993) 147–154.
[7] Rodríguez-Moñino, Milares Carlo, Lapesa (1957). A more recent attempt to reconstruct the original text by Avalle-Arce (1990). New edition of *Amadis* by Cacho Blecua (1991) with a long introductory study.
[8] This question is looked into by Rodrigues Lapa (1981) 276ff. and (1970) 28 as well as by Cacho Blecua (1991) 57–81.

fostered the existence of bilingual writers. Furthermore, *Amadis* is representative of the primitive chivalric novel genre and, therefore, it seems relevant to include in this study a work which reveals itself to be such a rich and unexpected hunting ground for those who wish to understand the continuity of classical culture by way of the by-paths and uncharted trails of the transmission. One should not also forget that until the end of the sixteenth century Portuguese and Castillian cultures complemented each other, at least as far as the chivalric novel was concerned.

It was from its sixteenth-century edition that *Amadis de Gaula* became the new and exclusive model of practically all later chivalric novels. Other than the extraordinary success the work achieved during the Humanist period,[9] its narrative structure, the appropriateness of its chivalrous ideal to the values that the Iberian nobility still considered distinctive of its social group (honour, courage, elevated feelings, and the "worship" of an idealized feminine image)[10] made a prolonged success possible. This did not only happen at a popular level: the influence of *Amadis* can be felt right at the dawn of modern times, even in the typical mechanisms of the nineteenth-century and modern adventure novel.

Like the Greek novels, *Amadis* is a purely imaginative work, without any firm national or historical connections, made up of aspirations and affections which merge with the stereotype of universal sentiments and ideals. Here is, perhaps, the secret of its popularity. It is a totally artificial creation, where we can sense all the poetry of the Celtic world, in a fantastic scenery of giants and dwarves, fairies and dragons, wizards and witches, fountains and forests, looming with mystery.

The gravitational centre of the novel is transferred from East to West. But the scene of Amadis' heroic acts does not limit itself to the British Isles: it extends itself through Germany and Bohemia, Greece and the Mediterranean islands, up to the triumphant entry of the hero in Constantinople, after his victory over the Emperor of Rome.

As in the Greek novels, and now I shall use the narratological terminology developed by the Russian formalists, we can say that the nucleus of the fable is a love and adventure story. The typical

---

[9] The *Nachleben* of *Amadis* is studied by Menéndez Pelayo (1962) 369ff.
[10] Finazzi-Agrò (1978) 23.

plot in the Greek novels concerns the misfortunes that torment a pair of young lovers (pirates, wars, shipwrecks, cruel adversaries) and postpone the happy ending as well as the consummation of their love. In *Amadis* these themes recur again and again with an almost obsessive regularity. The topic of the exposed newly born baby, for instance, determines the story of the birth of Amadis, son of Elisena, who was the daughter of the King of Smaller Brittany. The hero's mother throws him in the sea, locked in a well-sealed casket, to conceal the fruit of her love affair, later legitimized by marriage, with King Perion of Gaul.[11] The new-born baby is found by a Scottish knight, Gandales, who adopts Amadis and brings him up with his own son, Gandalim, calling him the "Donzel do Mar", which in English means something like "young man from the sea". A sword without a scabbard, a ring and a parchment with an inscription are the signs which will make the *anagnorisis* possible when the young man's real parents recognize him in the kingdom of Gaul. This happens when Amadis had gone to Gaul to help Perion in the war against the giant king of Ireland, whom Amadis fights and kills.

The disguise motif,[12] which reminds us of well-known classical situations,[13] occurs before the test with the sword and the marvellous garland which Amadis and Oriana (whose idyll had been outlined with extraordinary delicacy and sobriety in Book I) will pass with flying colours.[14] For only he who loved his beloved with perfect love and only she who returned this love could remove half of the sword that was hidden in the scabbard and make the faded flowers of the garland blossom once more. Before this Amadis had already shown that he was the most faithful and perfect lover, having subjected himself to a fantastic test on the Enchanted Island, the outcome of which was the breaking of the spells that enabled Amadis to become lord of the island.[15]

---

[11] I.1. The motif of abandonment, with rich antecedents within folklore, is analyzed by Cacho Blecua (1991) 136–140, based upon a selected bibliography.

[12] II.13.

[13] E.g., the scene of Charikleia and Kalasiris's disguise in Chemmis before they set out for Bessa in search of Theagenes (*Aethiopica* VI,11,3ff.), which is, in turn, clearly evocative of Homer (*Odyssey* XVII.221–222 and XIII.430–438).

[14] II.14.

[15] See the tests that Theagenes and Charicleia are subjected to in the *Aethiopica*, particularly the chastity test (X.7ff.). The victims were commanded to step onto a gridiron made from a lattice of gold bars. Only the pure in body and soul would be allowed to walk painlessly over it, so as to be later sacrificed to the gods of the

Another *topos* which is shared by all the Greek and chivalric novels is the extraordinary beauty of the protagonists. Oriana's beauty is such that it outshines that of any other woman; and Amadis' procession of triumph is formed by more than three hundred characters (friendly or inimical knights, ladies, giants and dwarves, monsters and wizards), all of them brought to their knees by the hero's unbelievable beauty and by his indomitable courage, which shows itself at every occasion. Amadis is the focal point of the whole plot, the centerpiece where the main outlines of the story converge (these had been revealed in the prophecy given to Gandales by Urganda the "Unknown".[16] It would be pointless to insist on the importance of this narrative process, since similar instances are to be found in some of the Greek novels (the *Aethiopica*, for example, or the *Ephesiaca* of Xenophon of Ephesus), where we notice that the effect of the prophecy is to reduce the narrative scope of the adventures to the working-out of a preestablished ending. It is within this framework, guaranteed, so to speak, by Urganda's prophecy, that Amadis' heroic acts take place. The hero's portrait is also reminiscent of the Greek novel: here, as there, it would be out of place to speak of psychological insight, as we are confronted with the monotony of characterization brought about by unalloyed goodness, which we all know from examples such as Tristan, Lancelot and Galahad.

Defender of the weak, the unprotected and damsels in distress, this tireless hero is the perfect gentle knight, the mirror of bravery and chivalry. The following anecdote might illustrate something of the impact that the character of Amadis had among readers of the time: someone comes home one day and finds the whole family in tears in front of an open book. One of the mourners turns to the person who had entered and says "Amadis has just died". The hero's presumed death at the hands of Arcalaus the Enchanter had caused that lachrymose scene. The "presumed death" motif is, incidentally, a common *topos* in the Greek novel, as well as the "false identity" theme, which also occurs.[17]

---

country. Similarly, in *Leucippe and Clitophon* (VIII.13ff.), Leucippe is submitted to the virginity test, which she successfully passes.

[16] I.2.

[17] See the "presumed death" of Callirhoe in Chariton's *Chaereas and Callirhoe* (I.5ff.) and in *Leucippe and Clitophon* Leucippe's fake sacrifice (III,15) and his apparent death (V.7). In Heliodorus' *Aethiopica* Theagenes and Knemon assume that Charikleia is dead, because they mistake Thisbe's dead body for hers (II.3ff.). Charikleia will be

There is a certain dualism in Amadis' character, which also reminds us of the Greek novel. The hero is capable, in war, of the greatest acts of courage and also of typically medieval savagery; on the other hand, he pledges to his damsel Oriana a love which is faithful and boundless. He obeys her in everything, so much that his life depends on her.[18] This love materializes itself in constant tears, in pangs and yearnings *in absentia*, in raptures and fainting spells brought on by the mere mention of the beloved's name.[19] This is an integral part of the Portuguese troubadour tradition adapted from Provence, where we find a complex code of behaviour that the perfect lover must obey. This sentimental idealism, which seems more typically Portuguese or Gallician than actually Castillian, might be an argument in favour of the novel's Portuguese origin. According to Menéndez Pelayo,[20] the work's soft and doleful tone contrasts sharply with the harsh austerity of the Castillian epics, where we sense above all a grave and heroic tone, an attempt at historical objectivity and a profoundly male-oriented outlook. This attitude leaves no room for any kind of gallantry, since the wife is entirely dominated by the husband, as we can see, for instance, in the Cid poem.

All this leads us to expect a form of love, in *Amadis de Gaula*, that ends up by burning itself out in sterile and self-motivated sentimentalism. This is the direction in which a number of ingredients had pointed, such as the hyperbolic descriptions of the hero's emotions, the glorification of the fatalistic aspects of being in love and the unrealistic, almost divine presentation of the female sex. But in fact this does not happen: in the end, we realize that we are not very far from the world of the Greek novel, for the love that unites Amadis and Oriana is more than sensual fantasy or senseless devotion. As in the Greek novels, it is the foundation and mainstay of the narration as such, it is a "great and mortal desire that can only find satisfaction in the possession of a woman".[21] Far from burning itself out with this possession, it grows and flares up even more "as happens only with hallowed and true love".[22] In the opinion of the Portuguese

---

taken for Thisbe when Cnemon comes to believe she is "Thisbe brought back to life" (V.2ff.).

[18] E.g., I.4; I.30; I.35; I.40; I.48; and *passim*.
[19] E.g., I.9; I.10 and *passim*.
[20] Menéndez Pelayo (1962) 346–347 and Rodrigues Lapa (1981) 287.
[21] IV.45.
[22] I.35 and IV.49.

philologist Rodrigues Lapa, "there is a certain something that is classical and robust in the novel, particularly in the pronounced cult of physical beauty and in the strong and hygienic sensuality that comes across in some of the episodes".[23]

The attitude to femininity as a whole in *Amadis de Gaula* reminds us of Goethe's famous concept of *das ewige Weibliche*. As with the heroines of the Greek novels, in whom some pre-feminist traits have been discovered (not to mention a certain taste for transgression,[24] it is Oriana who controls the complex game of love. Thus, while Amadis seems shy and hesitant, Oriana confesses that she feels for him a "disordered love". This boldness enables her to take the lead, particularly at the end of the XXXV chapter where she offers herself to Amadis. Her attitude fits in with the hero's ardent but timidly expressed desire. In a recent book, David Konstan showed that, in contrast to the classical polarization of sexual roles, love is expressed in the Greek novel through an image in which both hero and heroine reciprocate their mutual affections.[25]

Amadis de Gaula differs from the other Breton chivalry novels in its conception of love. In our novel passion is not seen as sinful and adulterous, and here the similarities with the Greek novel are evident. The "Infernal Couple", as the subtitle of a recent book on courtly love will have it,[26] gives way to a completely different pair of lovers, who enact a long and faithful relationship, made up of tenderness and instinct in equal parts. Because of this, the work acquired such an important social and didactic value.

Amadis introduces a new ideal of chivalry, in the centre of which the complex code of love seems to have something to say about ethics and behaviour. The ideal of the Round Table seems to have been refined, purified, ennobled. This ethical "cleansing" has much to do with Garci Rodríguez de Montalvo's moralizing intents. Thus they are more visible in the last (fourth) book which he himself wrote, where the sententious style and the long moralizing tirades mirror the zest with which he imitated the ancient historians and moralists.

As in the Greek novel, speeches are an indispensable part of any chivalric novel. In the harangue that Amadis addresses to his men,[27]

---

[23] Rodrigues Lapa (1981) 284.
[24] Liviabella Furiani (1989a) 45–106.
[25] Konstan (1994a).
[26] Markale (1987).
[27] III.18.

the example of the Greeks and Romans is also mentioned as an incentive to fight the enemy and defend his damsel, Oriana. *Mutatis mutandis*, we could use Saraiva and Lopes' words[28] to speak of the Greek novel: "The grandiloquent speeches of knights who, to defend the honour of their ladies, have to joust with their opponents in the forest, the lovers' sweet-sounding and witty dialogues . . ., the letters . . ., provide rhetorical role models of courtly life, amidst endless exciting adventures."

Stripped of the mystic and symbolic concepts of the chivalric novel,[29] *Amadis* ends up by transforming itself in what someone already called a *bric à brac* fable.[30] In fact the narrator seems to enjoy the liberty of introducing new characters and situations whenever he likes. Something similar to this happens in the *Aethiopica* by Heliodorus. A prolonged study of this Greek novel[31] suggested to me that the various mechanisms of the plot are controlled by an artist who manipulates the rules of fiction without ever losing himself in the process. We could say the same about *Amadis*. Although we may be tempted, now and again, to reduce all these novels to a single *cliché*, it remains obvious that the variety of the "subject" (in the sense V. Shklovsky and Tomashevsky use the term) avoids the risk of monotony. We find out, finally, that everything is actually structured with a view to making the ending itself more expressive. Thus, what seems confused and tangled is integrated in a deliberate and precise mechanism. The brilliant manipulation of the flashback, anticipations, recapitulations and the interaction of different narrative levels used by Heliodorus to such effect in the *Aethiopica*, was also used by the narrator of *Amadis*. With his extraordinary imagination and "Heliodorus-like" technique he maintains the reader's curiosity through the most hair-raising and unlikely *peripeteiai*.

In the sixteenth century this work will give rise to a whole cycle, made up of twelve chivalric novels (the Amadis cycle); simultaneously, a new chivalric cycle inspired by it will flower: the Palmeirins cycle.

---

[28] Saraiva and Lopes (1992) 99.

[29] In the courtly novel adventures acquire a wider symbolic meaning which is connected with the knight's inner route and his spiritual and moral development. For example, in *The Quest of the Holy Grail* this route is represented by the conquest of the Holy Grail, the chalice holding Christ's blood. See Futre Pinheiro (1993) 147–154.

[30] Finazzi-Agrò (1978) 24.

[31] Futre Pinheiro (1987).

"Due to these two cycles and to their translations and adaptations, the Iberian Peninsula will become the last inspiring source of chivalric imagination for the whole of Western Europe..."[32]

The Portuguese sixteenth-century interest in chivalric literature is amply documented in *Crónica do Imperador Clarimundo* (1522). The book was written in his early days by João de Barros, the renowned historian who would later become the Titus Livius of the Portuguese adventures in the East.[33]

From the original outstanding geographical, economical and historical encyclopedia of the Portuguese Expansion we are only left with some sections today: a few *Decades* (a set of ten books) from *Asia* which belonged to the first part of this work, "Milícia", which would give an account of the Portuguese conquests in four different parts of the world (Europe, Africa, Asia and Santa Cruz). It is believed that João de Barros is the author of, at least, a large section of *Geografia (Geography)*, written in Latin. The third part is said to have been called *Comércio (Trade)*.

This work, dedicated to King João III, an enthusiastic reader of chivalric novels, centres upon an imaginary genealogy of Count Henrique (the father of D. Afonso Henriques, Portugal's first king), who is presented to the reader as being Clarimundo's grandchild.[34] João de Barros' aim is clearly to exalt the glorious deeds of the Portuguese crown. To do as much, he makes use of the literary genre in fashion at the time, the chivalric novel, and draws on themes and motifs inherited from previous centuries, associating the tradition of a medieval atmosphere with a clearly epic-apologetic intention.

Clarimundo, the son of King Adriano of Hungary and of the daughter of the King of France, becomes estranged from his parents due to a scheming nanny and is abandoned near a fountain. Grionesa, a noble Italian widow, takes him home and brings him up as a son. Still very young, Clarimundo is made a knight by the King of France who ignores his true identity. After going through endless adventures, he is finally recognized by his mother, and later meets his beloved Clarinda, the daughter of the King of Constantinople, who will become his wife.

Around this nucleus centered upon the protagonist and his adven-

---

[32] Saraiva and Lopes (1992) 100.
[33] Edition used, Marques Braga (1953).
[34] I.10–12.

tures unfolds a series of stories and secondary characters that thicken the plot and postpone the denouement. There is a repetition of formal patterns, situations and character types formerly dealt with, specially in *Amadis*. In the same way, familiar motifs from well-known genres such as drama, new comedy and the novel are also to be found here.[35] The author faithfully follows medieval conventions, specially in the first two books that are inspired by the heroic-chivalric tradition. He praises the virtues of the valorous knights who overcome the forces of evil and face all kinds of danger not only in pursuit of glory and immortality but also to defend their ladies' honour, justice and the Christian faith.

However, the true meaning of Clarimundo's story goes beyond this first reading, calling for a particular interpretation that sets it apart from other chivalric novels. Similarly to Galahad in *The Quest of the Holy Grail*,[36] our hero also reveals himself as being exceptional and predestined. His birth is shrouded in mystery and associated with the elemental forces of Nature. On the eve of the hero's birth there is a violent thunderstorm, lightning flashing across the sky over the rough seas.[37] This clearly symbolic episode marks the transition to a new era, a New World in which Darkness will yield to Light.

The hero bears a sign, a red sore on the right side of his heart,[38] which reveals his exceptional nature. Like Galahad, the trials he faces and overcomes bear witness to his heroic stature.[39] He will go through the test of the "Wisdom ark", fighting against giant statues that try to prevent him from getting to the treasure where a gold head of the Emperor of Greece is to be found and which, to Clarimundo's amazement, acquires a life of its own and starts to talk. However, while in *The Quest of the Holy Grail*, Galahad appears to be invested with a sovereignty which is not temporal and which transforms him into a kind of reincarnated Christ, Clarimundo, a legendary ancestor of the

---

[35] E.g., abandoning and exposing children who are raised by adoptive parents and who later on are recognized by their real parents. Such themes contribute to the unfolding of the plot of Longus's *Daphnis and Chloe* and Heliodorus' *Aethiopica*.

[36] In King Arthur's court, during the Whit Sunday festivities, the knights of the Round Table are struck with wonder as they witness Galahad's feat, who manages to draw the sword from the marble stone, thus proving he is the greatest knight in the world. The prophesy is fulfilled: that very day he is marked out as the knight who will achieve the Quest of the Grail.

[37] I.68ff.

[38] *Ibid.*, 70.

[39] E.g., access to the "perfect house" (II.324) or, still, access to the "enchanted grave" in the valley of the "enchanted forest" (*ibid.*, 202ff.).

Kings of Portugal, is also involved in daring feats, fighting for justice and the Christian faith. Yet, he appears as the herald of a new era, the genesis of the soul of a nation particularly predisposed to expansionism and who fulfils the mission it was destined to: spread the Faith and expand the Empire. This ascending movement reaches its climax when the wizard, Fanimor, prophesizes from the top of Sintra tower the glorious deeds of Clarimundo's future descendants, the kings of Portugal, who will expand his domains from the most eastern part to the most western part of the world.[40] The fantastic dimension is, therefore, conditioned by well-established historical and political objectives.

At a time when the Portuguese court and, in a way, the whole country was imbued with a strong sense of nationalism, João de Barros takes upon himself the task of furthering that general feeling and, thus, paves the way to *Os Lusíadas*, Camões' heroic epic poem. This explains why *Crónica do Imperador Clarimundo* was such a success at the time,[41] becoming more famous than other more important works by João de Barros, such as *Décadas* or *Ropicapnefma*.

In Heliodorus' *Aethiopica*, Theagenes and Carikleia advance through a tortuous path till they reach perfection and attain the "state of grace" through a spiritual wedding, a symbolic ceremony which, at the end of the novel, is celebrated between the priestess devoted to Selene (Carikleia) and the Helios priest (Theagenes). In his turn, Galahad, in *The Quest of the Holy Grail*, will meet death in the mystical ecstasy brought about by the radiant brightness of the Holy Grail, in total communion with God.

In his search for perfection Clarimundo also advances gradually till a climax is reached at the end of the second book. He is, then, ready to receive the charisma and, consequently, he is able to accomplish the heroic task of defeating the Grand-Turk's army that laid siege to Constantinople. Constantinople's defence is an old literary topic that was and will go on being used not only by writers of chivalric novels but also by the anonymous author of the sentimental novel *Naceo e Amperidónia*, to which I will refer later on in this study.

In *Clarimundo* love relationships follow a traditional pattern: love is a noble and sublime feeling. As in the Greek novels, it will be rewarded with matrimony, after the protagonists have overcome all the difficulties

---

[40] III.90–112.
[41] *Crónica do Imperador Clarimundo* is reprinted in 1555, and later on in 1601, 1742, 1791 and 1843.

they encountered along their long and arduous journey, at the end of which they will finally experience complete happiness.

In 1567, the third edition of the novel *O Palmeirim de Inglaterra*, by Francisco de Morais, which is part of the Palmeirins Cycle previously referred to, is printed in Évora.[42] This novel enjoyed immediate and lasting success[43] and unlike *Crónica do Imperador Clarimundo*, it does not have any epic or apologetic intentions. Its fame comes from the fact that, together with *Amadis*, it was spared by D. Quixote's friends (the priest and the barber) who burned all chivalry novels but for those two aforementioned.

The hero, Palmeirim, and his twin brother Floreano are the sons of D. Duardos (who was the son of King Fradique of England) and of Flérida, the daughter of the first Palmeirim. As newborns, they are stolen from their mother and brought up by adoptive parents and are later made knights. Once their true identity is discovered, they embark upon their heroic and sentimental adventures and Palmeirim falls in love with Polinarda, the daughter of the Emperor of Constantinople, whom he later marries.

This narrative complies with the classical canons of the chivalric genre, which is undoubtedly rooted in its original source: the Greek novel. Thus, from amidst the intricate adventures one can unearth motifs that are common to all chivalric novels. However, the author managed to lend it a stamp of originality by combining fantastic and autobiographical elements, legend and history, reality and fiction.

As it is usual in this type of work, several episodes are inspired by the spirit of the holy war against the infidels, namely the final great battle, in which the hero defeats the Turks who lay siege to Constantinople.[44]

With *Memorial das Proezas da Segunda Távola Redonda* (1567) by Jorge

---

[42] The *Palmeirins* cycle started with *Palmerín de Oliva* (1511) written in Castillian, and was followed by *Primaléon de Grecia* (1512), then *Platir* (1533) and *Flortir*, all anonymous works written in Castillian. The exact date of the *editio princeps* of *Palmeirim de Inglaterra* remains a mystery and the fact that there was an 1547 Castillian edition led some scholars to believe that authorship of this novel should be assigned to the Castillians. However, nowadays both Portuguese and Spanish experts (*e.g.*, Asensio 1974) 445–453 recognize and confirm that Francisco de Morais was in fact the author of these novels. *Palmeirim de Inglaterra* was published for the last time in Lisbon in 1952 and in Brasil in 1946.

[43] *Palmeirim* was translated into French in 1552–1553 and into Italian in 1553–1554; between 1587 and 1807 there were around eight editions of this novel in England.

[44] Stegagno Picchio (1979) 169–206 has studied the theme of Constantinople and its anti-Muslim implications.

Ferreira de Vasconcelos, reality is once more brought into the realm of Portuguese chivalric fiction. Sharing with *Clarimundo* a nationalist tendency, *Memorial* is dedicated to "His Royal Highness and Mighty King Sebastião", D. João III's grandson, and is published a mere five years before *Os Lusíadas*. Jorge Ferreira de Vasconcelos imagines a second Round Table presided by King Sagramor, who supposedly succeeded King Arthur in the throne. *Memorial* narrates the adventures and glorious feats of Sagramor and his knights who, in their majority, are the sons of the heros of Chrétien de Troyes' novels.

In the prologue, the author states the objectives of his work, which are to exalt Prince João, D. Sebastião's father, and through him, the Portuguese monarchy and aristocracy. But, if on the one hand, the choice of Arthurian themes should be almost compulsory in a work which, as the title clearly shows, is impregnated with a medieval atmosphere and symbology, on the other hand, the author soon steers away from this mythical world essentially classical and medieval.[45] In fact, he only makes use of it to set the frame within which he will give a thorough account of the tournament of Xabregas, where Prince João was made a knight, though he had already died at the time. This tournament did really take place in those days and it enabled the author to describe some very interesting scenes based on the life at the time he lived in.

As in *Crónica do Imperador Clarimundo*, it is the magician Merlinda who, thanks to her supernatural powers, makes it possible for King Sagramor to attend the tournament. Nevertheless Jorge Ferreira de Vasconcelos' work aims higher. *Memorial* is imbued with a humanistic spirit, combining an historical-apologetic intention with a pedagogic and political one. In the manner of *The Prince* by Machiavelli, this work aspires to become a genuine treatise on political science. However, unlike Machiavelli, J. Vasconcelos did not know how or chose not to disentangle myth from reality, thus lending an ambiguous meaning to his work. Despite the pervasive chivalric spirit, the novel lacks cohesion and "myth and reality are arbitrarily amalgamated, the heroic deeds of imaginary knights being misinterpreted as historic events".[46]

---

[45] Medieval characters intertwine with mythological figures, such as Bacchus' friends in India, the twin brothers Castor and Pollux, and historical personalities of the Antiquity, such as Alexander, Caesar and Augustus.

[46] Finazzi-Agrò (1978) 52.

Indicative of the pervading Renaissance spirit in *Memorial* is the way in which the author depicts the Moors, that is, under a much more "ecumenical" light than they are usually portrayed in other chivalric novels. This humanistic approach to the question of religion reminds me of that maxim which, according to Moses Hadas, is perhaps the most representative of the Hellenistic age: all men are potentially equal.[47] Vasconcelos, however, could not help but recognize the superiority of the Christian faith, as he himself was influenced by the prevailing ideological and doctrinal views of a court longing to rule over northern African fortresses. Inspired by this crusade spirit, D. Sebastião will embark on a reckless expedition to Alcácer-Quibir. However the chivalric ideal will be discredited in the battlefield and Portugal will lack its sovereignty over the period of sixty years, losing its independence over to Spain.

Chivalric themes will remain popular till the beginning of the seventeenth century when more stress is laid on fantastic and phantasmagoric elements and one goes further into the realm of Utopia. Besides the two works that are said to be sequels to *Palmeirim*,[48] there are fragments of a few more chivalric novels, of an allegorical and doctrinal nature, to be found in Portuguese manuscripts that were never published, what seems to substantiate the disappearance of this genre.

Massaud Moisés carried out a survey, though not a very comprehensive one, of the existing manuscripts in several Portuguese libraries.[49] Amongst the most representative texts of the genre a group is to be found (commonly known as the D. Duardos trilogy) whose authorship is still under discussion.[50] This set of manuscripts is made up of the sequels to *Palmeirim de Inglaterra* and includes *Vida de Primaleão* (or *Cronica de D. Duardos*), *Segunda Parte da Cronica do Principe dom Duardos* and *Terceira Parte da Cronica do Principe dom Duardos*.

Adopting a well-known technique typical of chivalric novels, like *Amadis*, which was supposedly a translation from an ancient Hungarian manuscript found in a Constantinople tomb, as can be read in its prologue, these three books are falsely ascribed to an imaginary English chronicler. In the same way, their translation into Portuguese

---

[47] Hadas (1959) 11.
[48] *Terceira e Quarta Parte do Palmeirim de Inglaterra*, by Diogo Fernandes (1587) and *Quinta e Sexta Parte do Palmeirim de Inglaterra*, by Baltasar Goncalves Lobato (1602).
[49] Moisés (1957) 47–52.
[50] Finazzi-Agrò (1978) 66–68.

is said to have been done by the famous historian Gomes Eanes de Zurara, long dead before the first *Palmeirim* was published in 1511.[51]

This custom of using a false *auctoritas* so as to grant authority and lend objectivity to narrative writing can be said to be a conventional device of the chivalric novel. João de Barros himself claims to have translated his *Clarimundo* from an ancient Hungarian chronicle. The appeal to a pre-existent work is a distinguishing feature of numerous medieval texts, ranging from early instances of Arthurian literature to *The Quest of the Holy Grail*. The *topos* is even older as it appears in some accounts of the Trojan legend as, for instance, in the prologue of *Ephemeris bello Troiani*, by Dictys Cretensis (fourth century).[52]

Apart from this trilogy, a record is kept of another work in manuscript divided into four parts, titled, in an abridged way, *História Grega*.[53] Curiously, up to this day it is still debatable whether its author was a gentlewoman, D. Leonor Coutinho, who lived in-between the late sixteenth century and the first half of the seventeenth century.[54] The main characters are closely linked to the chivalric tradition of the *Palmeirins* cycle: D. Beliandro, emperor of Greece and D. Belindo, a legendary prince of Portugal, who eventually marries the emperor's daughter, thus ascending the Greek throne. The story unfolds in an altogether fantastic and unreal atmosphere that will characterize Portuguese chivalric narrative from the seventeenth century onwards.

Besides the seventeenth-century codex of the chivalric novel *Cronica do Principe Agesilau e da Rainha Sodônia*, we know the existence of other manuscripts through *Biblioteca Lusitana* by Barbosa Machado. Amongst these there is one that stands out due to the classical resonance evoked by its title: *Argonautica da Cavalleria na qual se tratão as façanhas e aventuras de Lesmundo de Grécia. Dedicado a D. Francisca de Aragão, Condessa de Villa-Nova de Ficalho*.[55]

---

[51] See note 41.

[52] The influence exerted by the accounts of the Trojan war over the artistic shaping of *Amadis* was stressed both by Garcia de la Riega (1909) 89 and 131ff. and Lida de Malkiel (1969) 149–156. More detailed information in Cacho Blecua (1991) 39ff.

[53] Other names for the same novel are *Cronica do Imperador Beliandro* or *Cronica de D. Belindo*.

[54] Finazzi-Agrò (1978) 69–70.

[55] Barbosa Machado (1741) I.114.

II. *The Pastoral Novel*

In addition to the chivalric novel, sixteenth-century Portuguese literature encompassed other relevant manifestations, which were as important owing to either the number of books they originated or the poetic quality of some of them and because they became famous all over Europe. While the chivalric novel ceased to have an ethical or apologetic value, the bucolic element grew in importance. The bucolic myth replaces the myth of the knight, each one as conventional as the other, with the difference that the former adapts itself better to the aesthetic of the period, owing to its doctrinal and conceptual aspects and its mannered allegories, which seem to announce the precious aesthetic of the Baroque.[56] Nevertheless, the sixteenth-century Portuguese taste for the bucolic is far from being rooted in an attitude of sheer aesthetic "dilettantism", no matter how evocative it is of classical literature. The anti-urban controversy underlying some of Gil Vicente's *autos* (plays) and used as a source of inspiration for some of Sá de Miranda and António Ferreira's poems, is explained by the historical, social and ideological context. In truth, the anti-courtly attitude was a way of expressing opposition to the expansionist policy and criticizing the moral and material damages caused by it. It was thus in the sixteenth century that the taste for pastoral, combined with poetic models derived from Italy, and/or from the Greek/Roman world, found a more precise aesthetic and ideology, as well as the appropriate context in which to manifest itself.

It is to Bernardim Ribeiro that we can ascribe the first non-versified example of the bucolic sensibility, once, for the first time in prose, a story connected with a pastoral setting expresses itself in an original way. Little is known about Bernardim Ribeiro's life other than that he collaborated in *Cancioneiro Geral* by Garcia de Resende and that he wrote *Éclogas*, the novel *Menina e Moça* or *Saudades*, amongst other works.

The world of knights and chivalry is also present in Bernardim Ribeiro's novel *Menina e Moça*.[57] However here we have a highly poetic intertwining of chivalric and bucolic motifs, so much so that it is

---

[56] This idea comes from Finazzi-Agrò (1978) 75.
[57] There are two different versions of *Saudades*, one from 1554, published by Abraão Usque in Ferrara, and another longer version of the first, written anew in 1557, from Évora, printed by André de Burgos. The most recent edition of *Menina e Moça* is by Macedo (1990).

difficult to decide whether the novel is a romance about knights or a gentle pastoral narrative in the manner of Longus. Intertwining the chivalric and pastoral ideals, *Menina e Moça* discloses the reveries and pangs of a feminine soul born to love and be loved.

Bernardim Ribeiro's novel starts with the monologue of a young lady (*Menina e Moça*), which hints at unhappy love and the suffering that comes from the absence of the loved one. These feelings are conveyed "through vague allusions along a long inquiry into the reasons for being sad—once mentioned, each cause for suffering is immediately set aside, being replaced with a stronger motive, in an unbroken sentimental dialectic conveyed through antithetic sentences, puns, asides round brackets".[58] A closer look at *Menina e Moça* reveals that Longus is not as important, in terms of influence, as the Italian *dolce stil nuovo* poets, whose poetic world of love-lorn shepherds Bernardim Ribeiro reproduces in prose. The narrative structure of *Menina e Moça* is notoriously complex: sometimes it drags, other times it seems to loose track of all the sub-plots, and once in a while the reader feels that here is a genuine masterpiece, a complete maverick or *hapax*, that in its best moments is totally unlike any other work in any other language. The neoplatonic concepts of love that were prevalent in Renaissance Italy (for which the troubadour love *ethos* seemed, unwittingly perhaps, to provide an authentically European paradigm) are also echoed by Bernardim Ribeiro, although once again, as with Longus, it is difficult to determine just how much the Greek original (in this case Plato) can have influenced the Portuguese writer.

Nevertheless, a careful, accurate and mature analysis of the feminine psychology and intimacy, done "according to a psychological strategy based upon intuition and experience",[59] would only be successfully accomplished in the modern psychological novel. This feature, together with a fatalistic vision of the world and a tragic notion of love, clearly establishes a distinction between love in *Menina e Moça* and the "ideal" love portrayed in most chivalric or pastoral novels.

We must necessarily mention, in this study, a famous Renaissance novel written in the Iberian Peninsula, *Diana*, by Jorge de Montemor, a Portuguese writer, born in Montemor-o-Velho, which is twelve miles away from Coimbra, on the banks of the river Mondego. Jorge de Montemor was a poet and a musician in the Portuguese and Castillian

---

[58] Saraiva and Lopes (1992) 234.
[59] *Ibid.*, 238.

courts. He became famous due to his pastoral novel *Los siete libros de la Diana*,[60] that was never finished because he died abruptly and mysteriously in 1561, when he was in his early fourties. He used a Castillian version of his name, George de Montemayor, to sign his work, written in Castillian but, by no means, foreign to Lusitanian sensibility and lyricism. The poet Afonso Lopes Vieira, who translated into Portuguese and adapted Montemor's book, says that "With *Diana*, our soul was heard underneath a foreign language".[61] This statement coincides with that of Menéndez Pelayo who claims that our bilingual writers may have opted out of their native language but they retained their national spirit.[62]

Even though the famous Castillian philologist, Menéndez Pelayo, said that this work lacks "the perfume of classical antiquity",[63] it is obvious that *Diana* really shows a direct Greek influence: it would be utterly unthinkable that this novel could have been written if the author had not known Longus and Heliodorus, presumably in Jacques Amyot's translations.[64]

The most extraordinary thing about *Diana*, which appears at the same time the *Aethiopica* becomes famous all over Europe, is that Montemor managed to reconcile Longus with Heliodorus. The subject matter is clearly derived from the pastoral and bucolic genre, but the narrative technique, full of highly mannered and artificial demonstrations of literary brilliance, stems from that masterpiece of prose architecture, namely Heliodorus' *Aethiopica*.

Saraiva and Lopes describe *Diana* as:

> the entangled string of an odyssey of a shepherd (or two) looking for his shepherdess, which, along the way, becomes more and more entangled upon itself, enmeshed in repeated similar subplots, in a theatrical game of *quid pro quo*, of travesties and sentimental blindman's

---

[60] The first edition of *Diana*, written between 1554 and 1559, was published without a date. The second edition dates from 1560 and the third from 1561. Modern edition by López Estrada (1954).
[61] Lopes Vieira (1974) XXIII.
[62] *Apud* Lopes Vieira (1974) XXXVI.
[63] Menéndez Pelayo (1943) 270.
[64] Longus' fame starts both in Italy with the translation of the humanist Annibal Caro (1507-1566), which never got to be published while its author's was alive, but only much later in 1784, and in France with J. Amyot's translation (1559). Amyot was also the author of the first French translation of Heliodorus' work (1547), which was followed by the Castillian translations (1554 and 1587), the latter published by López Estrada (1954).

bluffs, with tearful unburdenings of the heart ... in order to slacken the plot's pace, where *recognitions* and even, sometimes, classical comedy pirate kidnappings do not fail to put in an appearance. Numerous bucolic poems interspersed in this entangled string that makes up the central plot. One could say that this is an amplified and prolific eclogue, where prose and verse alternate.[65]

Diana intertwines, with underlying complicity, the languid tone, inherited from Bernardim's long monologues, a certain bourgeois or popular picturesque and the "sacred/pagan wood atmosphere",[66] inhabited by nymphs and goddesses, lewd wild satyrs, framed within mysterious temples which are described to us in long ἐκφράσεις, confirming the very obvious nature of Montemor's debt to the Greek novel.[67]

Equally relevant is the omnipresent role played by music and the importance given to such a charming art within the novel. The surprising musicality of Jorge de Montemor's five-or-seven-syllable-line poems (*redondilhas*), which contributed so much to the popularity of his work, reveals a special gift and a lot of hard work as he himself admits in a letter addressed to Sá de Miranda.

Other motifs also present in this narrative, such as the *topos* of apparent death, prophetic dreams, the role played by recognition in the economy of the plot, represent the core of an old romanesque tradition.

At the end of the sixteenth century, there were seventeen editions of *Diana*, which was enthusiastically acknowledged all over Europe and deeply influenced several national literatures. In Portugal, Spain, France, England and Germany, Montemor's book exerted an impressive and lasting influence on writers such as Francisco Rodrigues Lobo, Lope de Vega and Cervantes, Honoré d'Urfée, Philip Sidney and Spencer, Shakespeare.[68]

A jewel of courtly gallantry, in which scenes of bucolic life become patterns of artful living, *Diana*, a gallant and mannered novel, fits entirely in the spirit of the time, whose aesthetic and literary expression will enhance the baroque.

---

[65] Saraiva and Lopes (1922) 393–394.
[66] The term is from Saraiva and Lopes (1992) 394.
[67] *E.g.*, the nymphs' description in Diana book II resembles that of *Daphnis and Chloe* I.4.2. The role they play as the characters' confidantes and advisers is another common point in both novels: see *Diana* book II and *Daphnis and Chloe* II.23.
[68] The *nachleben* of *Diana* is analyzed by Menéndez Pelayo (1943) 278ff.

III. *The Sentimental Novel*

We have already mentioned that in *Menina e Moça*, by Bernardim Ribeiro, which has been somewhat hastily called a sentimental novel, there is an intertwining of the three narrative categories of the Portuguese cinquecento: sentimental, bucolic and chivalric. This fact made it possible to combine in a single account a "first-person" introspective narrative, interspersed with letters and lyrical compositions which lend an autobiographical and expressive character to this work, and the bucolic and chivalric ideal, which becomes apparent through the predominance of recitative and dialogue, as well as through appeal to an appropriate allegorical apparatus.

Therefore, it is only for the sake of taxonomy that we establish this distinction, at times loose and arbitrary, between related genres, in which definition of the boundaries of a particular genre is only achieved through predominance of certain features.

Naceo e Amperidónia,[69] an anonymous sentimental novel, recently published, comes from a miscellany written between 1543 and 1546. Prior to *Menina e Moça*, this work of historical, literary and documental interest "may be somehow representative of an eventual series of romanesque texts dating from the same period that are unknown or have gone missing".[70]

Making use of a device typical of this kind of book, the narrator claims to be merely the translator of a pre-existent work. According to him, the book was his share of the booty, after a town was invaded, when he served in the East under the orders of the Grand Turk.[71]

As in Greek novels, the narrator begins by stating his decision to provide a good beginning for the story, leaving its ending in the hands of Fortune. He says he is going to tell a Greek story which was written in Latin and which he translated into Portuguese, at a friend's request who did not know the language of Latium. The love story takes place in the town of Solbia, at the mouth of the

---

[69] The manuscript was discovered by E. Asensio and includes, besides this novel, copies of *Menina e Moça* and of the eclogue *Jano e Franco*, both by Bernardim Ribeiro. Forgotten for four centuries, *Naceo e Amperidónia* was recently published by Hook (1985) 11–46, who organized the paradiplomatic edition of the codex. The following year, Fagundes Duarte (1986), drawing information from Hook, presented a new edition of this novel. It was upon this latest edition that I based my work in order to make this comment.

[70] See Fagundes Duarte (1986) 11.

[71] This is, probably, an allusion to the taking of Baghdad by the Turks in 1534.

river Jeto, where it is said the Greeks took Achilles(?) when Troy was conquered.

Naceo, a man ill-favoured by Fortune, goes to the town of Solbia to serve under a prince. Once there, in a house which took in young noble women, he meets Amperidónia, a woman of unrivalled beauty, with whom he falls in love at first sight. Most of the novel is filled with the letters exchanged between the two lovers, which include love songs and pastoral poems.

As in other sentimental novels, this work's main themes are Love and Fortune. Following in the footsteps of Greek novels of a more elaborate plot, such as those by Achilles Tatius and Heliodorus, the complex game of love is made clear through a subtle dialectic that underlines the rhetoric of impossible love, which culminates in Amperidónia's marriage. However, and as it is suggested at the ending of the story, this outcome is not an impediment to an extra-marital affair, which unconsciously carries the reader into the world of Provençal lyric. Recurrent themes such as suffering, death and blind love, pessimism and the grief of parting, jealousy and full obedience to one's lady, lead me to say that the code of courtly love and its poetic expression were, in this novel, transferred into prose.

On the other hand, and complementary, the judicious tone, the formal and stylistic sophistication which permeates the whole work anticipate, as in *Menina e Moça*, the mannerist style of the baroque.

We include in this section another book, contemporary of *Diana* and *Menina e Moça*, by the Castillian poet and writer Alonso Núñez de Reinoso, who was brought up and lived in Coimbra and probably ended his days in Italy.[72] An enthusiastic fan of Bernardim Ribeiro,[73] Reinoso also proclaimed his admiration for Sá de Miranda, whose works were a model and source of inspiration for many of his poetical compositions.

This book is part of a volume containing his *opera omnia* that was published by Gabriel Giolito de Ferrari, in Venice, in 1552, under

---

[72] According to Asensio (1974) 123 there is an old soldier saying which can be used with reference to Reinoso: "España mi natura, Portugal mi ventura, Italia mi sepultura". I am grateful to my collegue Leonor Neves for having brought to my attention Reinoso's book. I am also grateful to Mr. Fernando F. Portugal for his remarks concerning Camões', Bernardim Ribeiro's and Jorge F. de Vasconcelos' influence over *Clareo y Florisea*.

[73] Michaëlis de Vasconcelos (1923) I.113 had already made it clear that the novel *Elareo y Florisea* by Núñez de Reinoso was reminiscent of *Menina e Moça*.

the title *La historia de los amores de Clareo y Florisea y de los trabajos de la sin ventura Isea.*

C.H. Rose[74] calls this work a "Byzantine-chivalric phantasia", written in the manner of *Leucippe and Clitophon* by Achilles Tatius, and of *Ragionamenti amorosi*, by Ludovico Dolce, published in 1546.[75]

Clareo and Florisea has thirty-two chapters, the first nineteen being a close imitation of *Leucippe and Clitophon.* As Reinoso did not know the first four books of the Greek novel, or the reasons behind the main characters' journey, he had to make up a situation which would account for the arrival of the young couple in Alexandria. Clareo and Florisea are promised to each other in marriage. However, Clareo promises to marry only after a year has gone by, deciding to behave like a brother to Florisea during that period of time.

After the young couple's arrival in Alexandria, the imitation of Achilles Tatius' work starts. Reducing the work to the fictional element, Reinoso narrates the kidnapping and apparent death of the young woman at the hands of a pirate; the false widow's (Isea's) passion for Clareo and his resistance to her advances; their marriage; Clareo's excuses to postpone the consummation of their marriage as he, in the meantime, had discovered his beloved amidst his new wife's slaves; Isea's first husband's return; Clareo's imprisonment and his sentence to death; Isea's first husband's passion for Florisea; the clearing up of the whole situation and, finally, the return of the two lovers to their hometown, Byzantium, where they get married.

The narration of events, which in the Greek novel is done by Clitophon, is here left in charge of the unlucky Isea who, after Clareo and Florisea's reunion, gives an account to the reader, as a mere bystander, of the adventures she witnesses throughout her perilous pilgrimage over land and sea. According to C.H. Rose,[76] the character of Isea enables Reinoso "to extend the theme of Fortune throughout

---

[74] Rose (1971) 11.

[75] Lodovico Dolce translated the Latin fragment of Achilles Tatius' work which was used by Reinoso in the first part of his novel. The Latin edition, published in 1544 in Milan, is by Annibale Cruceio, who based his work on an unfinished Greek manuscript from which the first four books and the author's name were missing. There is an anonymous Portuguese version, undated. This is a version abridged from the original manuscript that, according to Michaëlis de Vasconcelos, may well be either the source for or a first version of Reinoso's novel. *Contra*, Rose (1971) 99 n. 15. The novel was printed in Spain in the nineteenth century and was included in the third volume of the BAE series: *Novelistas anteriores a Cervantes.*

[76] Rose (1971) 103.

the novel". As in Greek novels, Fortune is here depicted as an abstract and hostile force, with full and unlimited power over the character, being the main element responsible for her suffering in this world.[77]

When, in the second part of the book dealing with the travails of Isea, Reinoso abandons Achilles Tatius' story, his work becomes a chivalric novel, as confounding and full of incidents as any other.

Menéndez Pelayo[78] stresses the moral and aesthetic depuration present in Reinoso's work compared with the Greek model, which is consonant with the author's declared principles and moralizing aim of this story. Thus, Pelayo opposes Clareo's noble character to that of Clitophon and confirms the absence of any suspicion of adultery on the part of Clareo and Isea (Clitophon and Melite in Achilles Tatius).

The pastoral element constitutes another thematic frame of *Clareo and Florisea*. At the end of the book, Isea retires to "Ínsua Pastoril" where she finds temporary refuge from her travails and that, according to López Estrada,[79] like Utopia in Thomas More, "is the most appropriate place to achieve the ultimate perfection of pastoral yearning".

According to C.H. Rose, the rediscovery and vogue for the Byzantine novel among intellectuals, will have given Reinoso the chance "to depict the agonies of exile" with the "concomitant of endless wandering and travail".[80] This scholar adds that Núñez de Reinoso "found himself cast in the role of the Wandering Jew".[81] On the other hand, his choice of the pastoral expresses "the desire to discover a tranquil land immune from the mutability of fortune and the slings and arrows of quotidian existence".[82]

IV. *Conclusion*

The novels I cite throughout this paper show that classical culture did have an important part to play in the development of the novel in the Iberian Peninsula in the 16th century. Structural patterns and characterization are areas where the Greek novel and the chivalric

---

[77] The theme of Fortune in *Clareo e Florisea* is analyzed by Rose (1971) 104ff.
[78] Menéndez Pelayo (1943) 78ff.
[79] López Estrada (1974) 360.
[80] Rose (1971) 10 and 103.
[81] Rose (1971) 84.
[82] Rose (1971) 10.

novel seem to converge. The bucolic *ethos* had something special to say to the individual sensibilities of two Portuguese writers, Bernardim Ribeiro and Jorge de Montemor. Some of the novels referred to are an evident offspring of the Greek novel. We can conclude that there is still much to unearth and to discover in the transmission of classical culture, and that new approaches often reveal a wealth of material where it might be least expected.

20. MAPS (A–L)

Jean Alvares

THE WORLD OF THE ANCIENT NOVELS

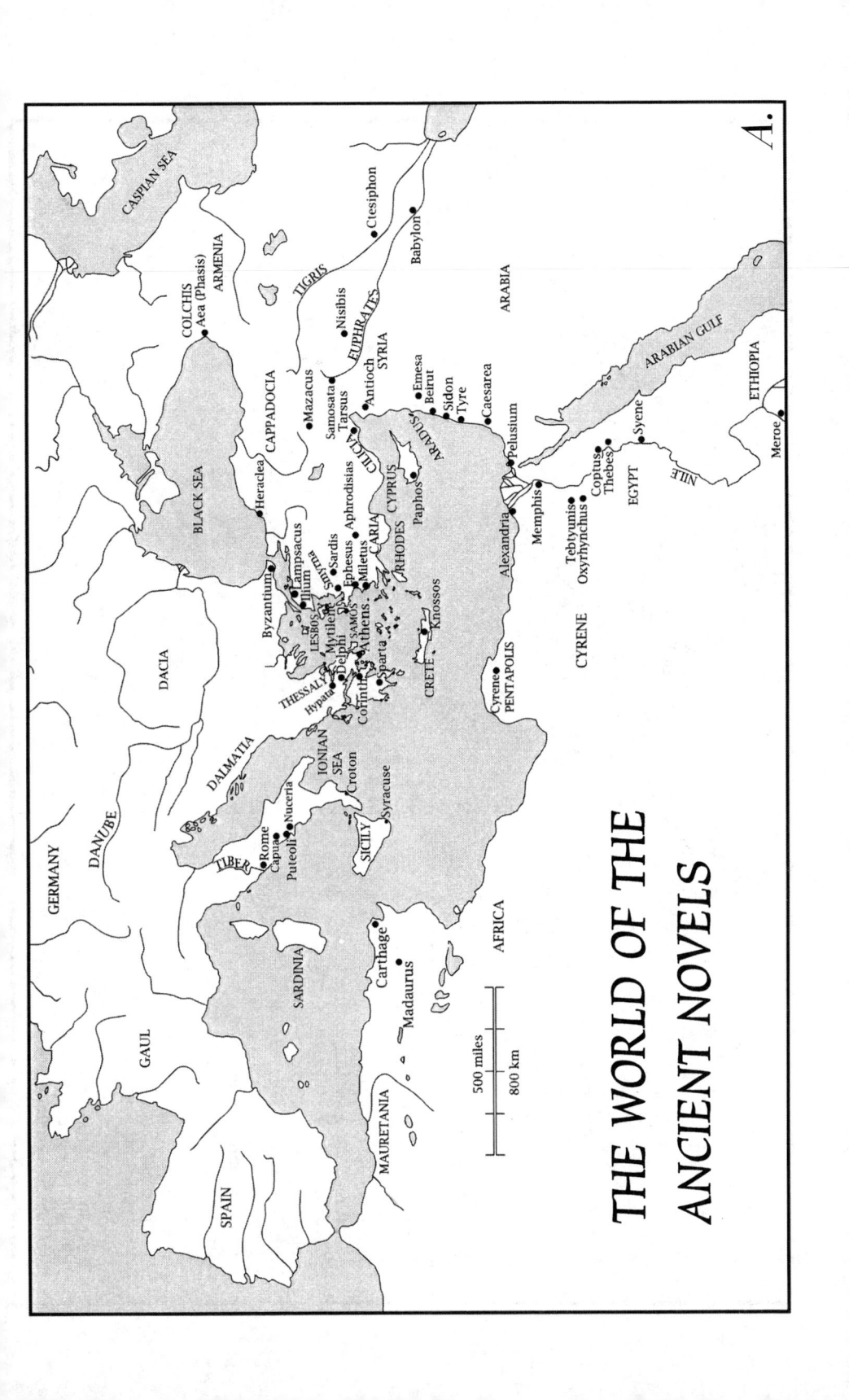

Chariton – Chaireas and Callirhoe

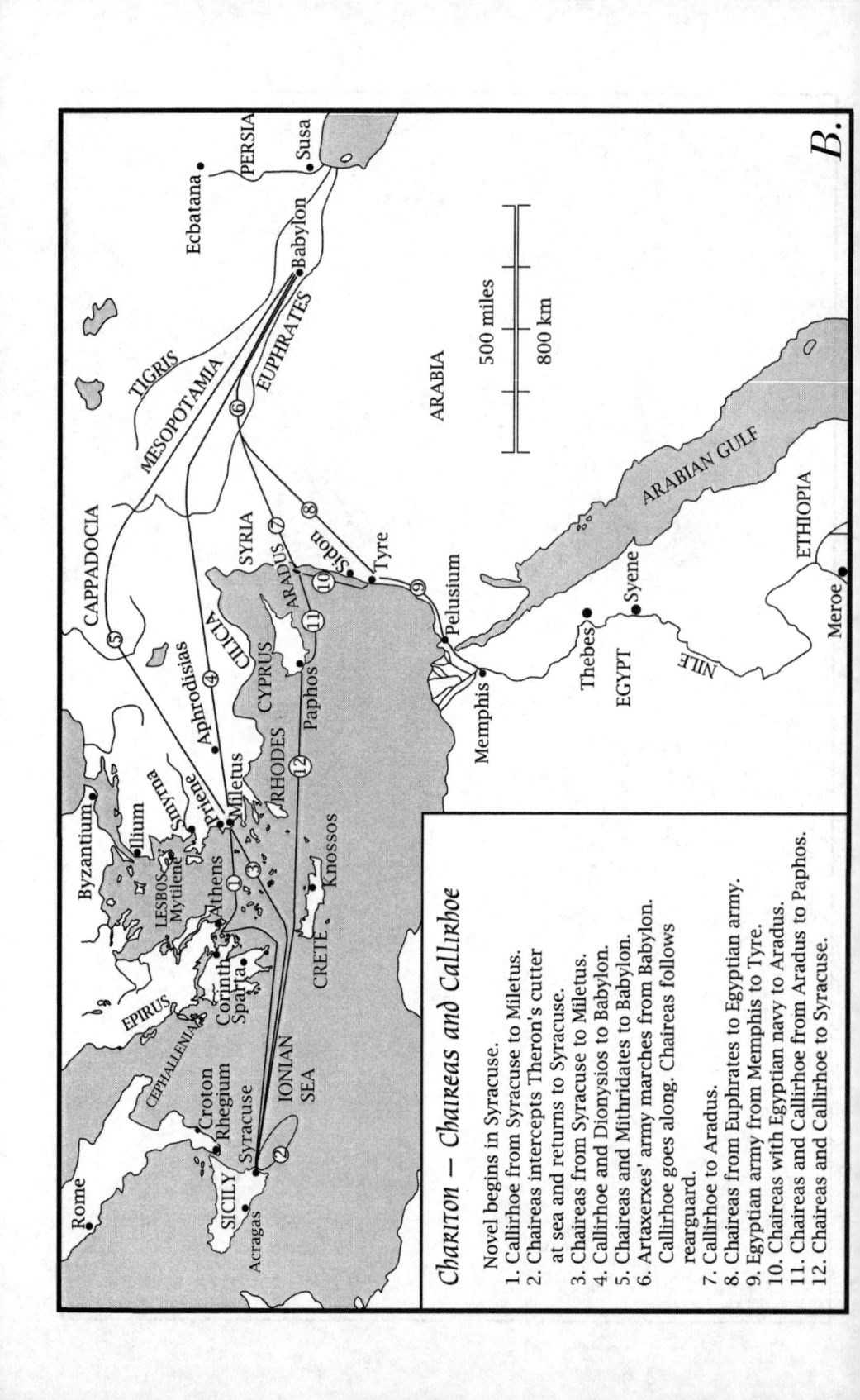

Novel begins in Syracuse.

1. Callirhoe from Syracuse to Miletus.
2. Chaireas intercepts Theron's cutter at sea and returns to Syracuse.
3. Chaireas from Syracuse to Miletus.
4. Callirhoe and Dionysios to Babylon.
5. Chaireas and Mithridates to Babylon.
6. Artaxerxes' army marches from Babylon. Callirhoe goes along. Chaireas follows rearguard.
7. Callirhoe to Aradus.
8. Chaireas from Euphrates to Egyptian army.
9. Egyptian army from Memphis to Tyre.
10. Chaireas with Egyptian navy to Aradus.
11. Chaireas and Callirhoe from Aradus to Paphos.
12. Chaireas and Callirhoe to Syracuse.

Xenophon of Ephesus – An Ephesian Tale

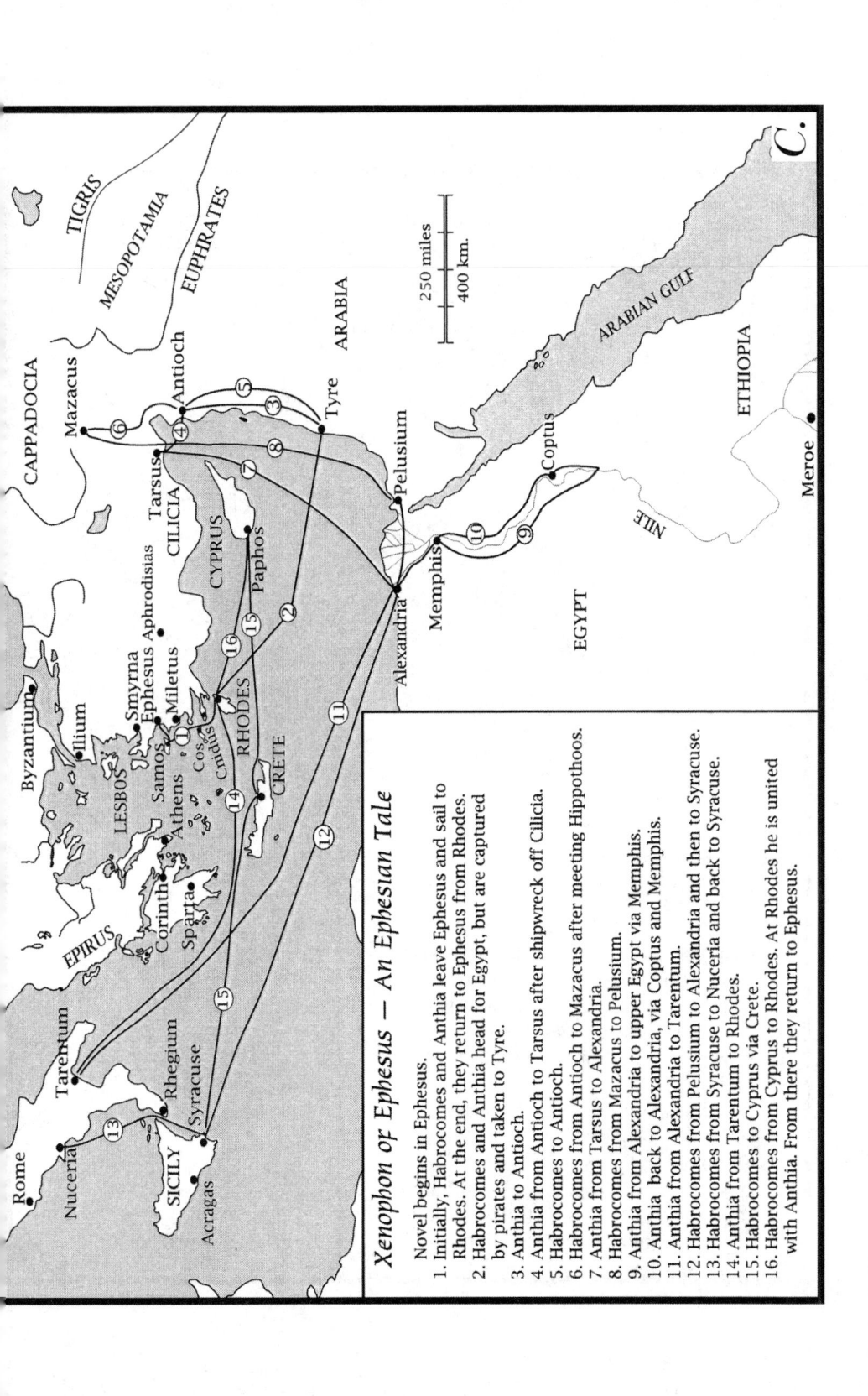

Novel begins in Ephesus.
1. Initially, Habrocomes and Anthia leave Ephesus and sail to Rhodes. At the end, they return to Ephesus from Rhodes.
2. Habrocomes and Anthia head for Egypt, but are captured by pirates and taken to Tyre.
3. Anthia to Antioch.
4. Anthia from Antioch to Tarsus after shipwreck off Cilicia.
5. Habrocomes to Antioch.
6. Habrocomes from Antioch to Mazacus after meeting Hippothoos.
7. Anthia from Tarsus to Alexandria.
8. Habrocomes from Mazacus to Pelusium.
9. Anthia from Alexandria to upper Egypt via Memphis.
10. Anthia back to Alexandria, via Coptus and Memphis.
11. Anthia from Alexandria to Tarentum.
12. Habrocomes from Pelusium to Alexandria and then to Syracuse.
13. Habrocomes from Syracuse to Nuceria and back to Syracuse.
14. Anthia from Tarentum to Rhodes.
15. Habrocomes to Cyprus via Crete.
16. Habrocomes from Cyprus to Rhodes. At Rhodes he is united with Anthia. From there they return to Ephesus.

ACHILLES TATIUS — LEUCIPPE AND CLITOPHON

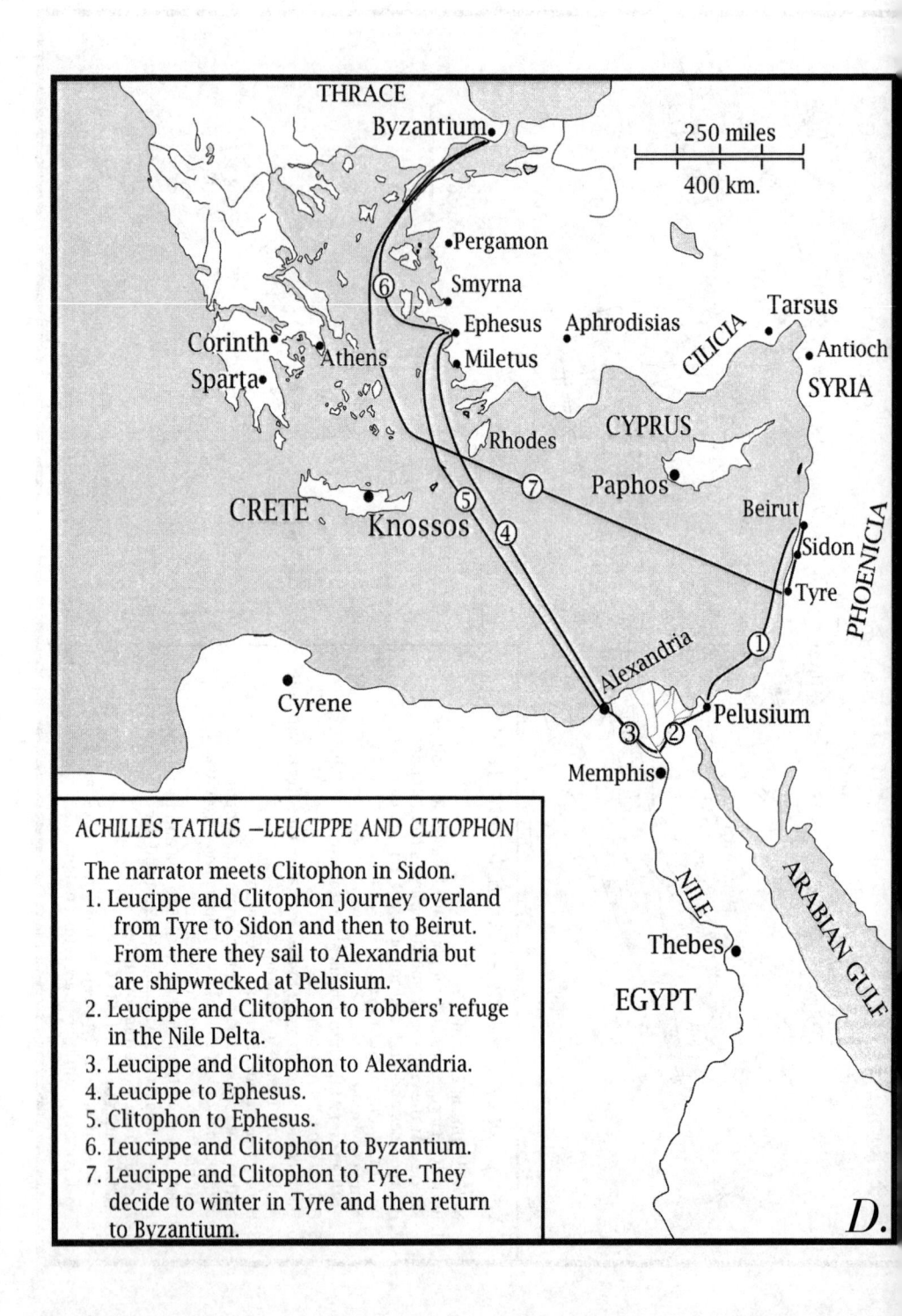

The narrator meets Clitophon in Sidon.
1. Leucippe and Clitophon journey overland from Tyre to Sidon and then to Beirut. From there they sail to Alexandria but are shipwrecked at Pelusium.
2. Leucippe and Clitophon to robbers' refuge in the Nile Delta.
3. Leucippe and Clitophon to Alexandria.
4. Leucippe to Ephesus.
5. Clitophon to Ephesus.
6. Leucippe and Clitophon to Byzantium.
7. Leucippe and Clitophon to Tyre. They decide to winter in Tyre and then return to Byzantium.

Heliodorus – An Ethiopian Tale

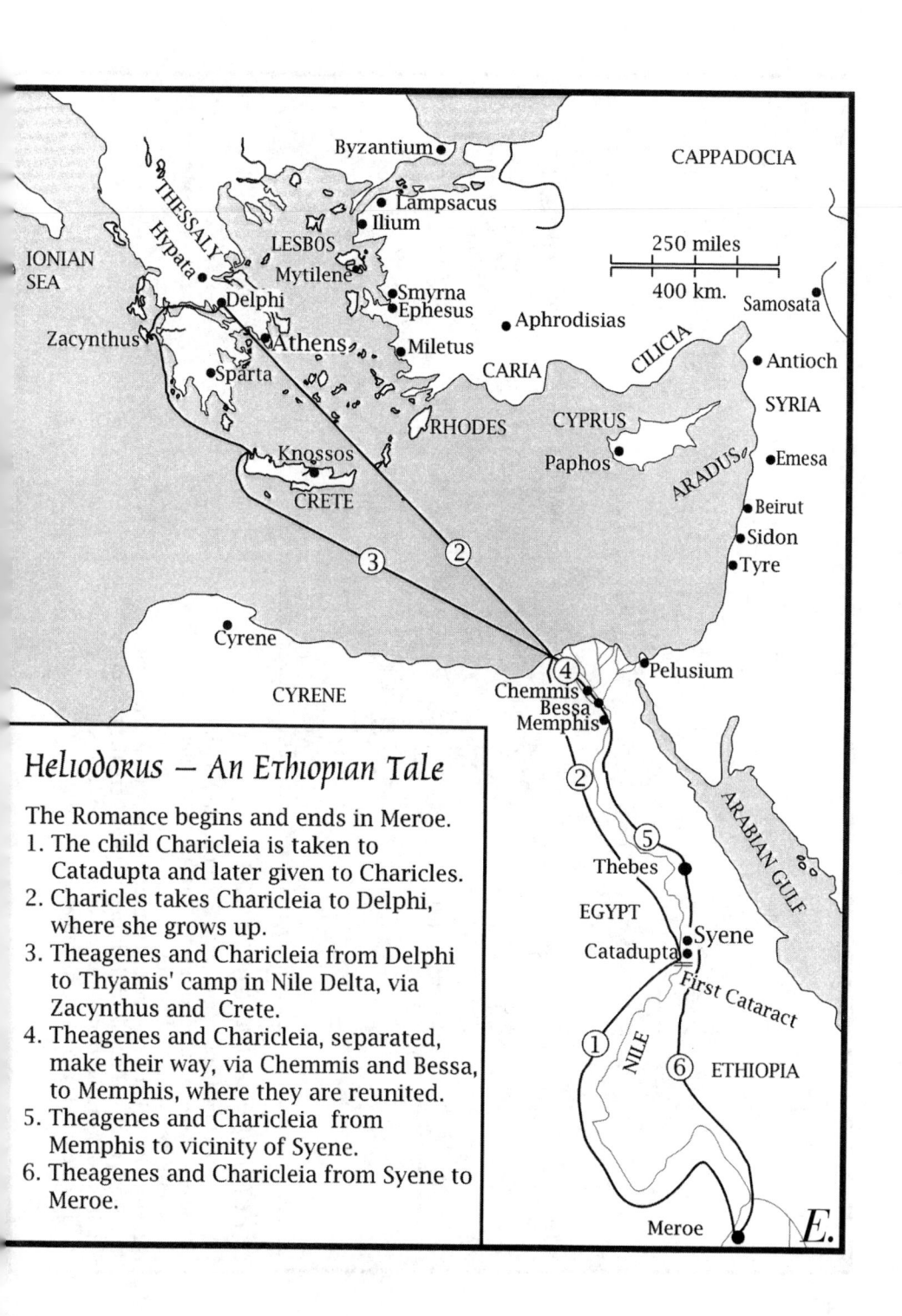

The Romance begins and ends in Meroe.
1. The child Charicleia is taken to Catadupta and later given to Charicles.
2. Charicles takes Charicleia to Delphi, where she grows up.
3. Theagenes and Charicleia from Delphi to Thyamis' camp in Nile Delta, via Zacynthus and Crete.
4. Theagenes and Charicleia, separated, make their way, via Chemmis and Bessa, to Memphis, where they are reunited.
5. Theagenes and Charicleia from Memphis to vicinity of Syene.
6. Theagenes and Charicleia from Syene to Meroe.

Petronius – The Satyricon

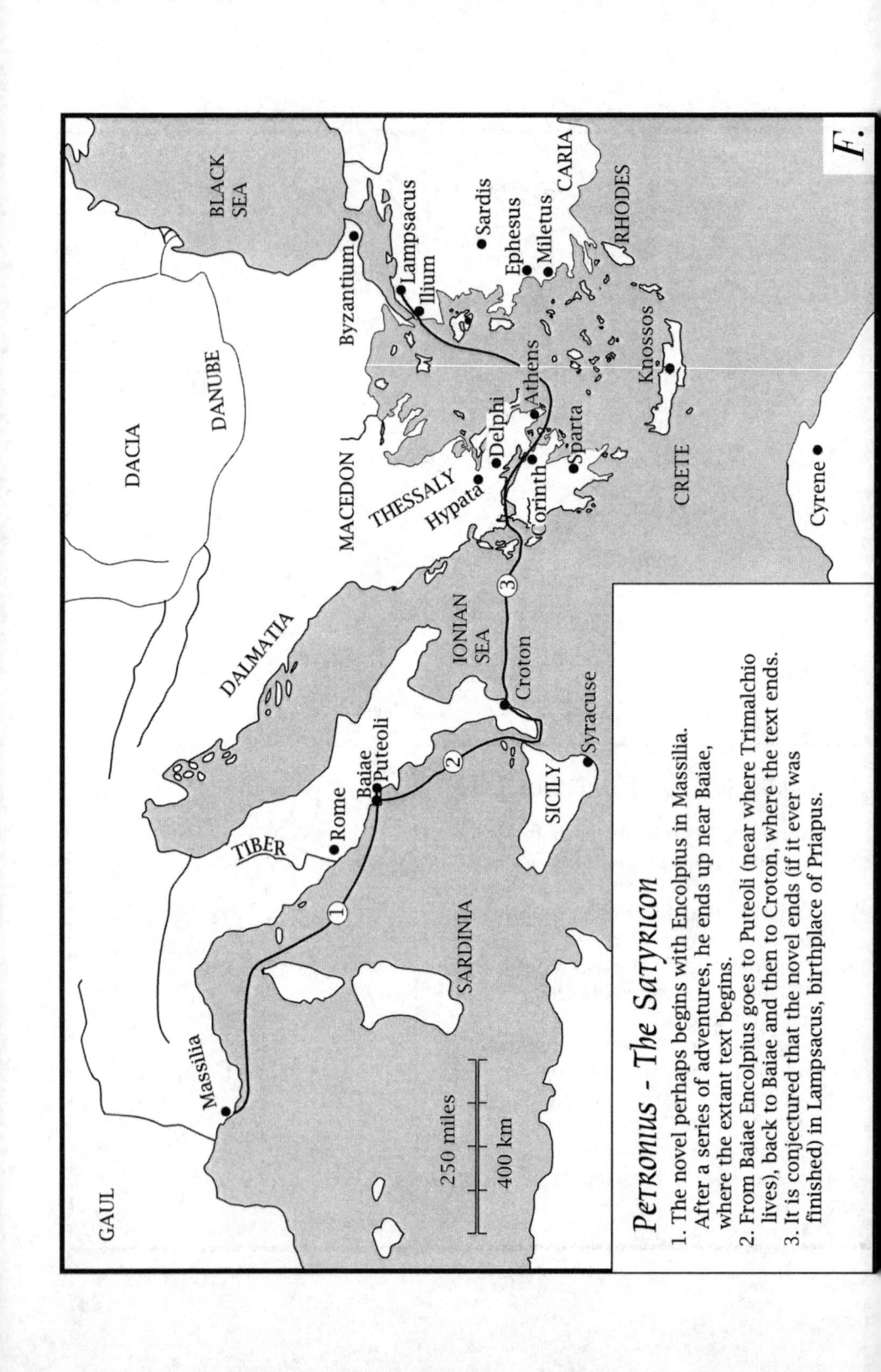

1. The novel perhaps begins with Encolpius in Massilia. After a series of adventures, he ends up near Baiae, where the extant text begins.
2. From Baiae Encolpius goes to Puteoli (near where Trimalchio lives), back to Baiae and then to Croton, where the text ends.
3. It is conjectured that the novel ends (if it ever was finished) in Lampsacus, birthplace of Priapus.

F.

Apollonius King of Tyre

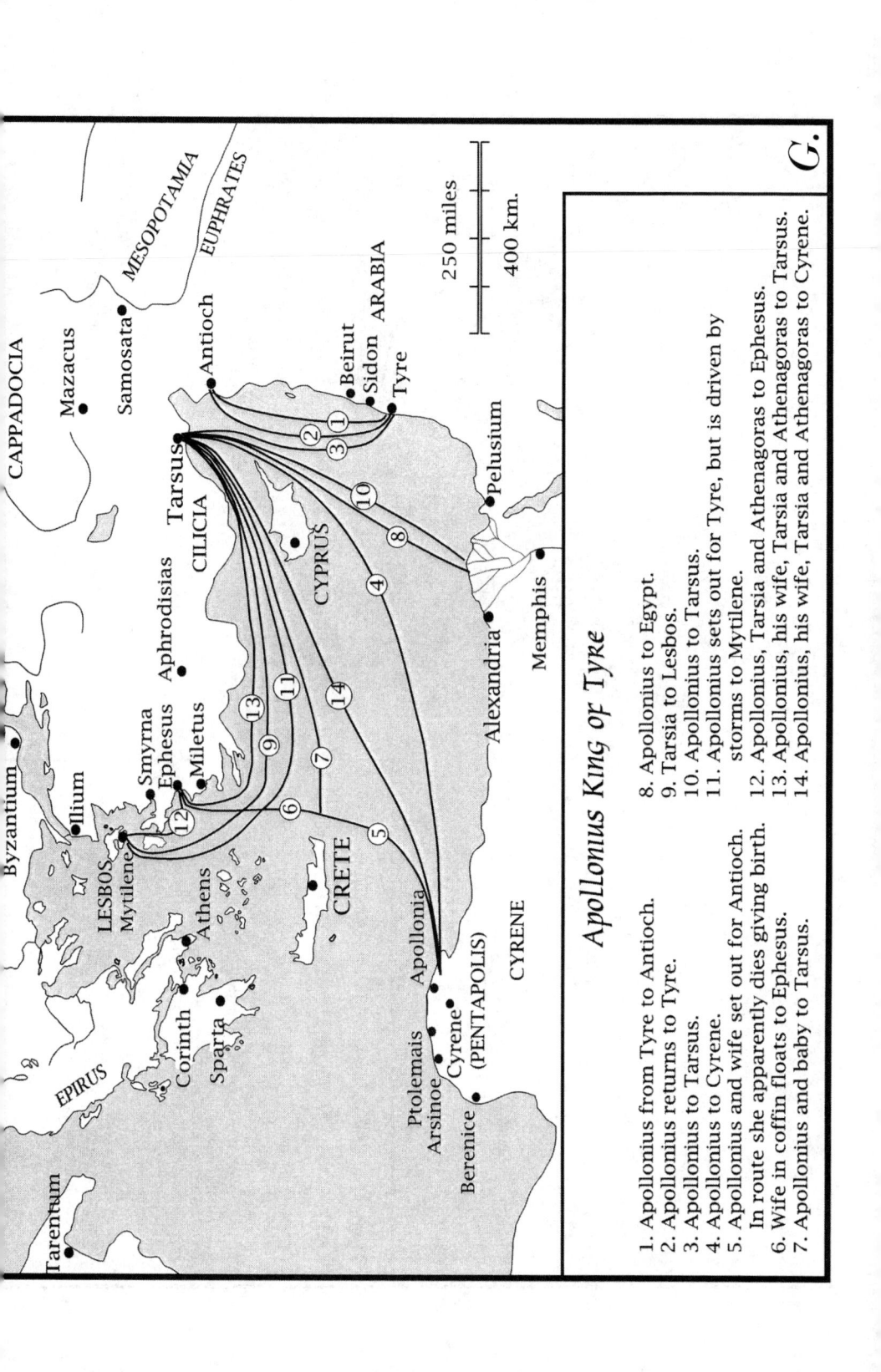

1. Apollonius from Tyre to Antioch.
2. Apollonius returns to Tyre.
3. Apollonius to Tarsus.
4. Apollonius to Cyrene.
5. Apollonius and wife set out for Antioch. In route she apparently dies giving birth.
6. Wife in coffin floats to Ephesus.
7. Apollonius and baby to Tarsus.
8. Apollonius to Egypt.
9. Tarsia to Lesbos.
10. Apollonius to Tarsus.
11. Apollonius sets out for Tyre, but is driven by storms to Mytilene.
12. Apollonius, Tarsia and Athenagoras to Ephesus.
13. Apollonius, his wife, Tarsia and Athenagoras to Tarsus.
14. Apollonius, his wife, Tarsia and Athenagoras to Cyrene.

G.

Homer – The Odyssey

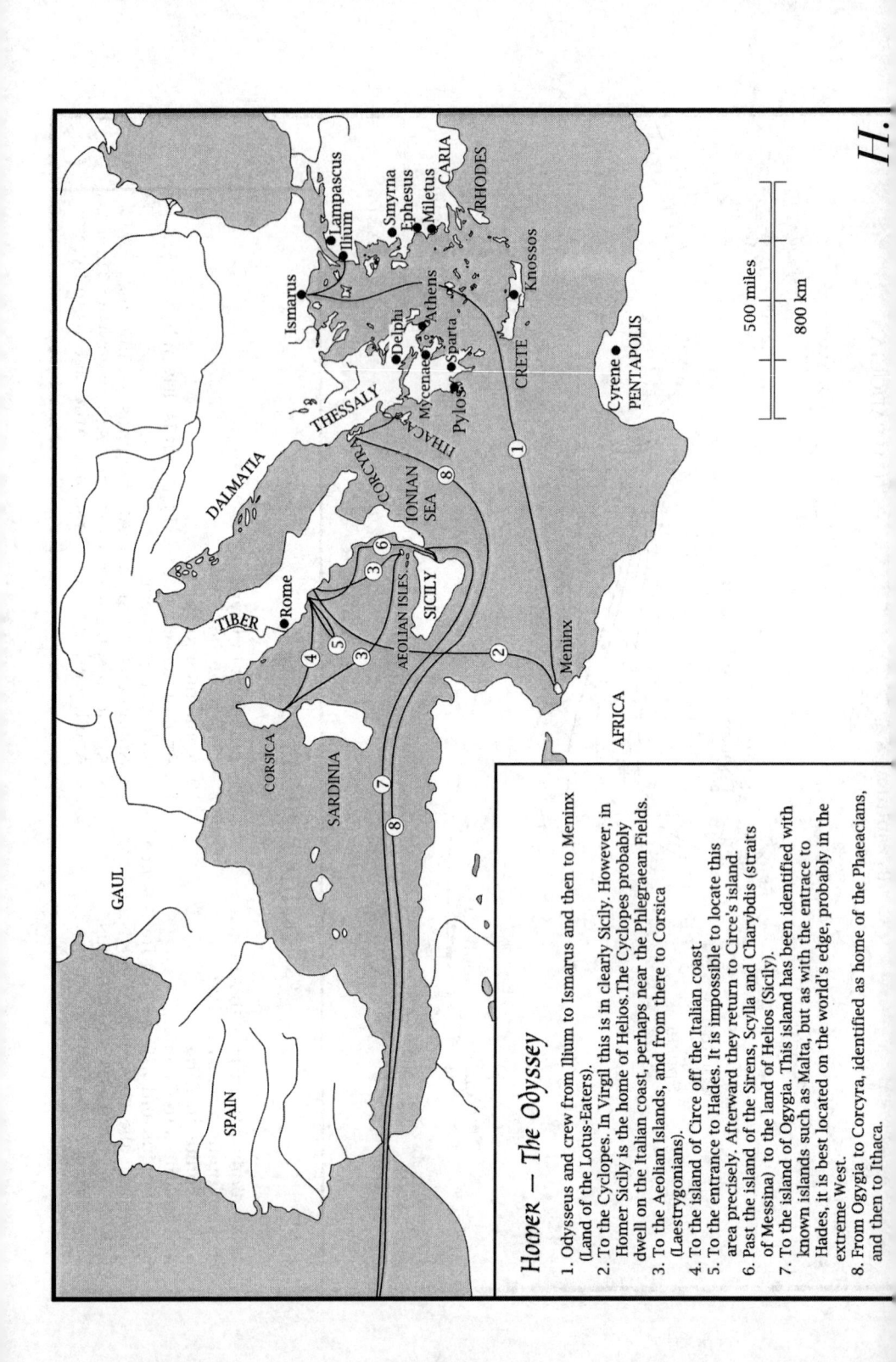

1. Odysseus and crew from Ilium to Ismarus and then to Meninx (Land of the Lotus-Eaters).
2. To the Cyclopes. In Virgil this is in clearly Sicily. However, in Homer Sicily is the home of Helios. The Cyclopes probably dwell on the Italian coast, perhaps near the Phlegraean Fields.
3. To the Aeolian Islands, and from there to Corsica (Laestrygonians).
4. To the island of Circe off the Italian coast.
5. To the entrance to Hades. It is impossible to locate this area precisely. Afterward they return to Circe's island.
6. Past the island of the Sirens, Scylla and Charybdis (straits of Messina) to the land of Helios (Sicily).
7. To the island of Ogygia. This island has been identified with known islands such as Malta, but as with the entrance to Hades, it is best located on the world's edge, probably in the extreme West.
8. From Ogygia to Corcyra, identified as home of the Phaeacians, and then to Ithaca.

Apollonius of Rhodes –
Voyage of the Argo

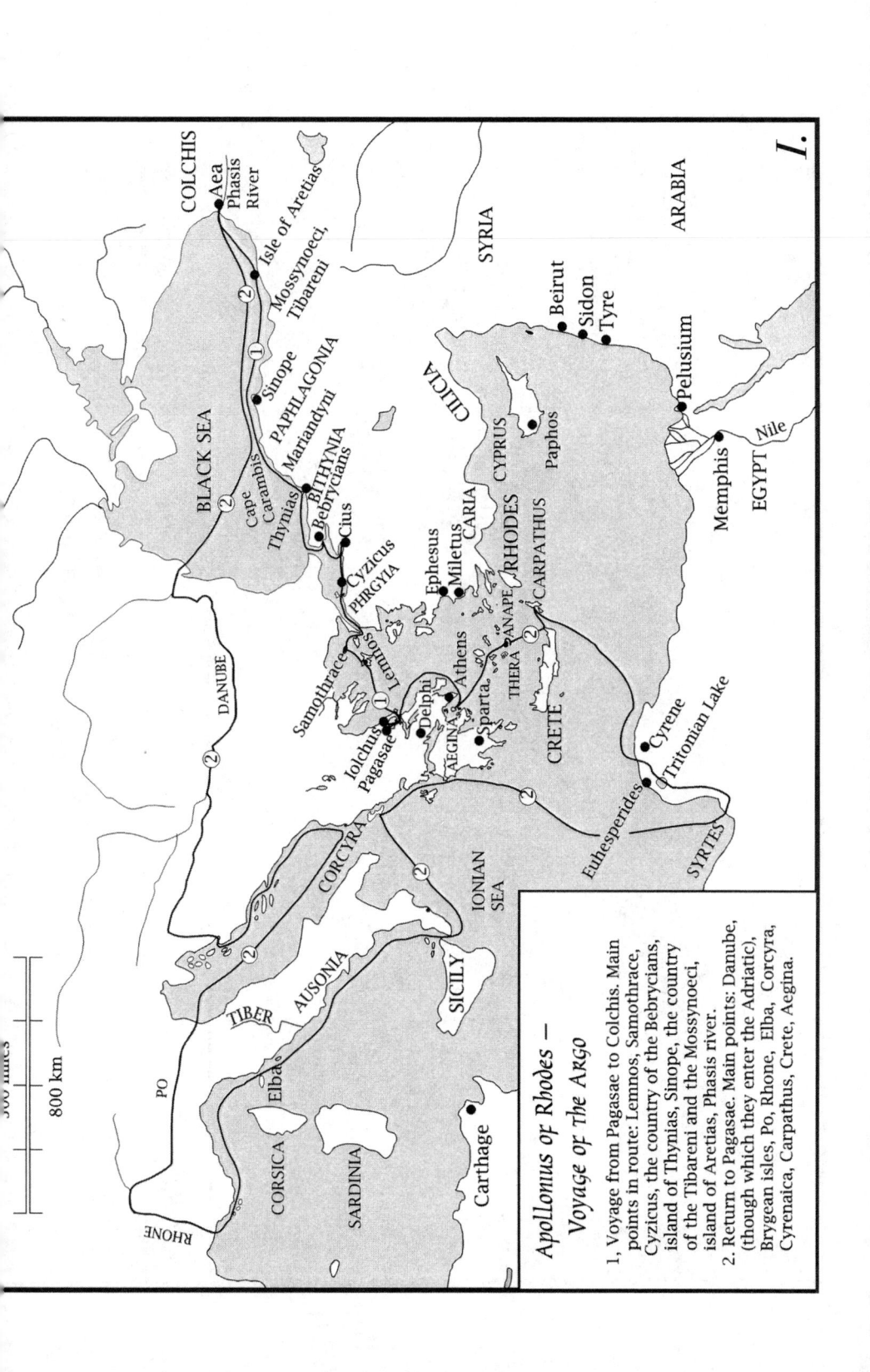

1. Voyage from Pagasae to Colchis. Main points in route: Lemnos, Samothrace, Cyzicus, the country of the Bebrycians, island of Thynias, Sinope, the country of the Tibareni and the Mossynoeci, island of Aretias, Phasis river.
2. Return to Pagasae. Main points: Danube, (though which they enter the Adriatic), Brygean isles, Po, Rhone, Elba, Corcyra, Cyrenaica, Carpathus, Crete, Aegina.

I.

Virgil – The Aeneid

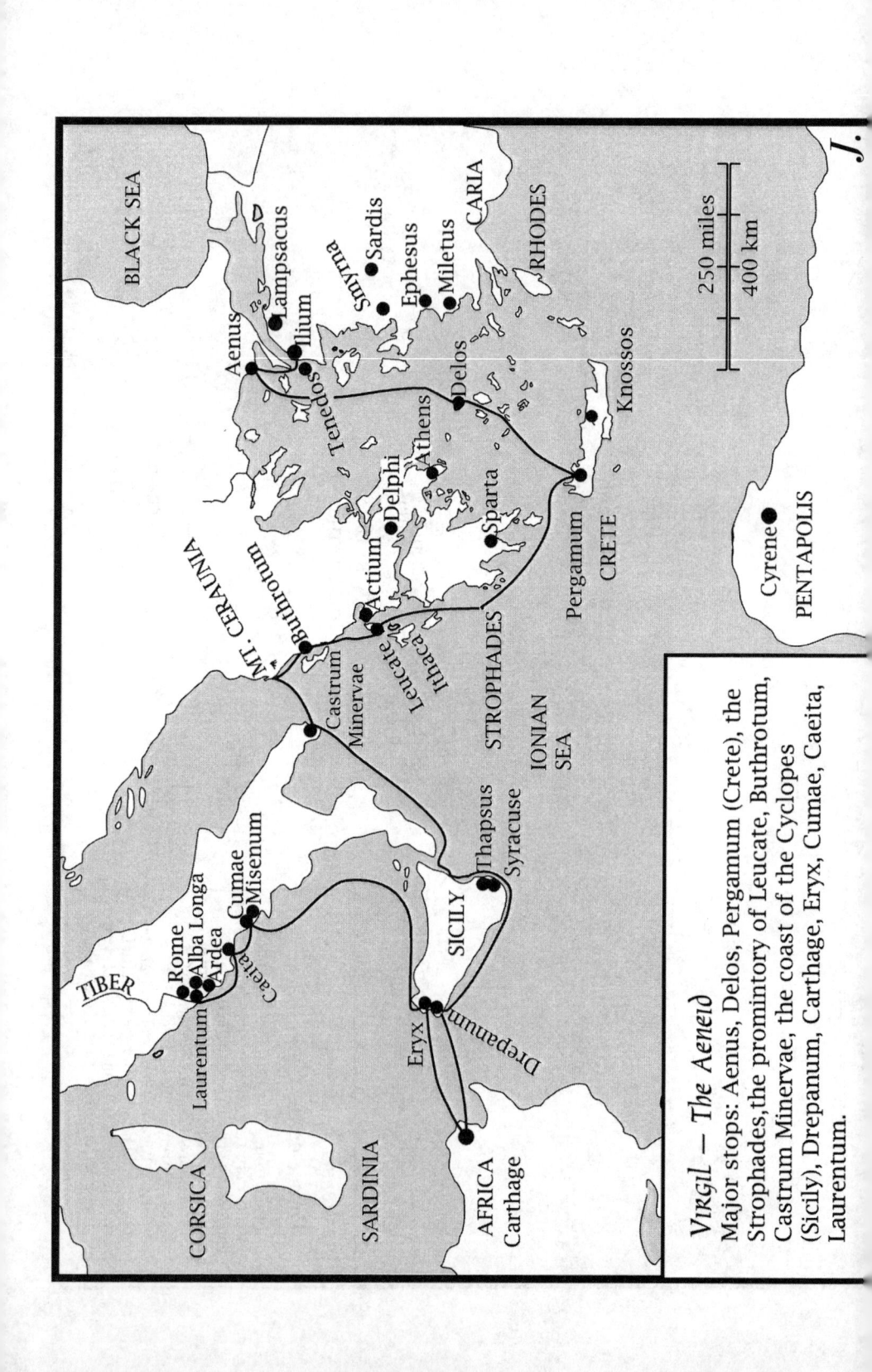

Major stops: Aenus, Delos, Pergamum (Crete), the Strophades, the promintory of Leucate, Buthrotum, Castrum Minervae, the coast of the Cyclopes (Sicily), Drepanum, Carthage, Eryx, Cumae, Caeita, Laurentum.

Paul's Journey to Rome

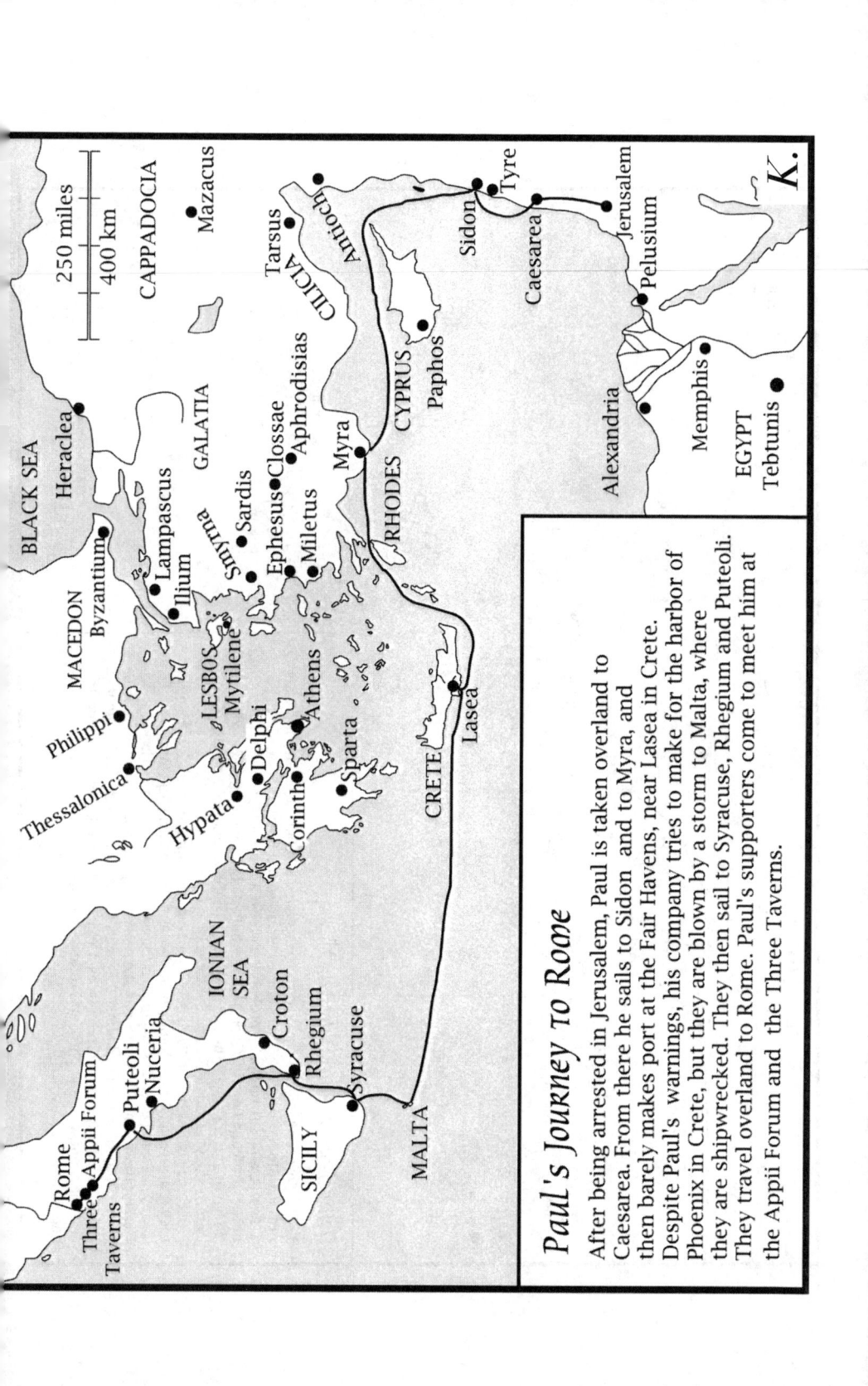

After being arrested in Jerusalem, Paul is taken overland to Caesarea. From there he sails to Sidon and to Myra, and then barely makes port at the Fair Havens, near Lasea in Crete. Despite Paul's warnings, his company tries to make for the harbor of Phoenix in Crete, but they are blown by a storm to Malta, where they are shipwrecked. They then sail to Syracuse, Rhegium and Puteoli. They travel overland to Rome. Paul's supporters come to meet him at the Appii Forum and the Three Taverns.

Travelers to the Holy Land

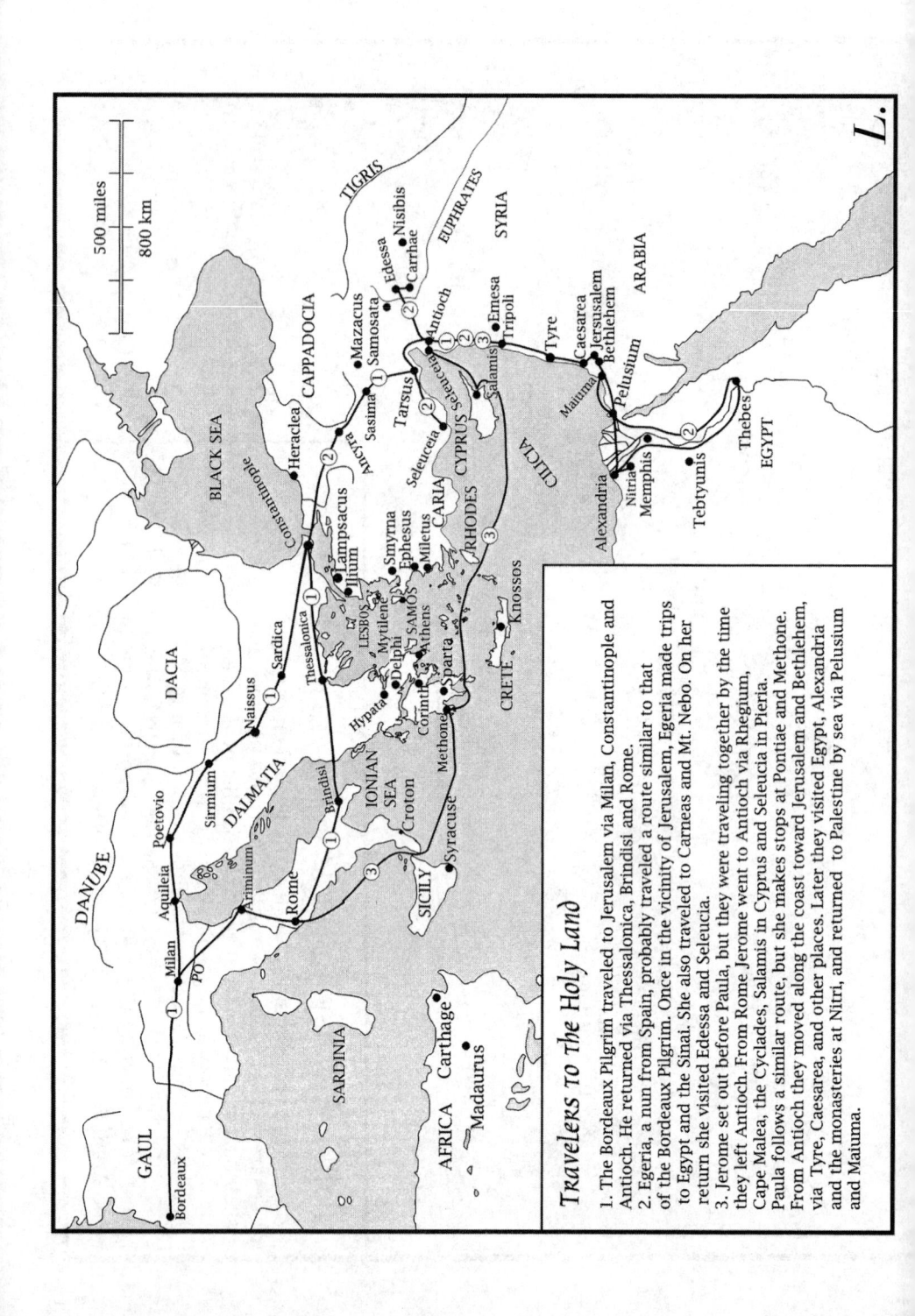

1. The Bordeaux Pilgrim traveled to Jerusalem via Milan, Constantinople and Antioch. He returned via Thessalonica, Brindisi and Rome.

2. Egeria, a nun from Spain, probably traveled a route similar to that of the Bordeaux Pilgrim. Once in the vicinity of Jerusalem, Egeria made trips to Egypt and the Sinai. She also traveled to Carneas and Mt. Nebo. On her return she visited Edessa and Seleucia.

3. Jerome set out before Paula, but they were traveling together by the time they left Antioch. From Rome Jerome went to Antioch via Rhegium, Cape Malea, the Cyclades, Salamis in Cyprus and Seleucia in Pieria. Paula follows a similar route, but she makes stops at Pontiae and Methone. From Antioch they moved along the coast toward Jerusalem and Bethlehem, via Tyre, Caesarea, and other places. Later they visited Egypt, Alexandria and the monasteries at Nitri, and returned to Palestine by sea via Pelusium and Maiuma.

BIBLIOGRAPHY

Aalders, G. (1975) *Political Thought in Hellenistic Times.* Amsterdam.
Aarne, A., Thompson, S. (1964) *The Types of the Folktale.* Helsinki.
Adamietz, J. (1987) "Zum literarischen Charakter von Petrons *Satyrica*," *Rheinisches Museum* 120: 329–346.
Adrados, F. (1979) "The *Life of Aesop* and the Origins of the Novel in Antiquity," *Quaderni Urbinati di Cultura Classica* n.s. 1: 93–112.
Adrados, F. (1979–1987) *Historia de la Fábula Greco-Latina.* 3 vols. Madrid.
Agapitos, P. (1990a) "Textkritisches zu *Kallimachos und Chrysorrhoe*," *Hellenika* 41: 33–41 = *Byzantion* 62 (1992) 34–44.
Agapitos, P. (1990b) "The Erotic Bath in the Byzantine Vernacular Romance *Kallimachos and Chrysorrhoe*," *Classica et Mediaevalia* 41: 257–273.
Agapitos, P. (1991) *Narrative Structure in the Byzantine Vernacular Romance. A Textual and Literary Study of Kallimachos, Belthandros and Libistros.* Miscellanea Byzantina Monacensia 34. Munich.
Agapitos, P. (1992) "Libistros und Rhodamne: Vorläufiges zu einer kritischen Ausgabe der Version a," *Jahrbuch der Österreichischen Byzantinistik* 42: 191–208.
Agapitos, P. (1993) "Ἡ χρονολογικὴ ἀκολουθία τῶς μυθιστορημάτων, Καλλίμαχος, Βέλθανδρος καὶ Λίβιστρος," in Panayotakis (1993) vol. 2, pp. 97–134.
Ahlers, H. (1911) *Die Vertrautenrolle in der griechischen Tragödie.* Diss., Gießen.
Albiani, M. (1989) "Ach.Tat.4.7.8 e Archil. frr.118–119W.," *Giornale Filologico Ferrarese* 12: 13–15.
Albrecht, M. von (1989) *Masters of Roman Prose.* Leeds.
Albrecht, M. von (1992) *Geschichte der römischen Literatur,* 2 vols. Munich.
Alcock, S. (1989) "Roman Imperialism in the Greek Landscape," *Journal of Roman Archeology* 2: 5–34.
Alexiou, M., Holton, D. (1976) "The Origins and Development of *politikos stichos*: a Select Critical Bibliography," *Mandatoforos* 9: 22–34.
Alexiou, M. (1977) "A Critical Reappraisal of Eustathios Makrembolites' *Hysmine and Hysminias*," *Byzantine and Modern Greek Studies* 3: 23–43.
Alexiou, M. (1986) "The Poverty of Écriture and the Craft of Writing: Towards a Reappraisal of the Prodromic Poems," *Byzantine and Modern Greek Studies* 10: 1–40.
Alexiou, S. (1980) Ερωτόκριτος: κριτικὴ ἔκδοση, εἰσαγωγή, σημειώσεις, γλωσσάριο. Athens. (Reprinted 1985 in small format with some editorial changes).
Alexiou, S. (1985) Βασίλειος Διγενὴς Ἀκρίτης (κατὰ τὸ χειρόγραφο τοῦ Ἐσκοριὰλ) καὶ τὸ Ἄσμα τοῦ Ἀρμούρη. Athens.
Alexiou, S. (1990) Βασίλειος Διγενὴς Ἀκρίτης καὶ τὰ ἄσματα τοῦ Ἀρμούρη καὶ τοῦ Υἱοῦ τοῦ Ἀνδρονίκου. Athens.
Alföldy, G. (1980) *Die Rolle des Einzelnen in der Gesellschaft des römischen Kaiserreiches, Erwartungen und Wertmaßstäbe.* Heidelberg.
Allen, P. (1907) "Some Letters of Masters and Scholars," *English Historical Review* 22: 740–754.
Alpers, K. (1980) "Innere Beziehungen und Kontraste als 'hermeneutische Zeichen' in den *Metamorphosen* des Apuleius," *Würzburger Jahrbücher für die Altertumswissenschaft* 6: 197–207.
Altheim, F. (1948) *Literatur und Gesellschaft im ausgehenden Altertum.* Halle. (In part a reprint of *Helios und Heliodoros von Emesa* [Albae Vigiles 12]. Amsterdam and Leipzig: 1942.)
Altheim, F. (1948a) *Roman und Dekadenz. Literatur und Gesellschaft im ausgehenden Altertum,* vol. 1., 13–47. Halle.

Altheim, F., Stiehl, R. (1964) *Die Araber in der alten Welt*, 1. Berlin.
Alvares, J. (1995) "The Drama of Hippothous in Xenophon of Ephesus' *Ephesiaca*," *Classical Journal* 90: 393–404.
Aly, W. (1936) "Novelle," *RE* XVII 1, 1171–9.
Anderson, G. (1976a) *Lucian: Theme and Variation in the Second Sophistic*. Leiden.
Anderson, G. (1976b) *Studies in Lucian's Comic Fiction*. Leiden.
Anderson, G. (1979) "The Mystic Pomegranate and the Vine of Sodom: Ach.Tat.3.6," *American Journal of Philology* 100: 516–518.
Anderson, G. (1982) *Eros Sophistes: Ancient Novelists at Play*. Chico, CA.
Anderson, G. (1984) *Ancient Fiction: the Novel in the Graeco-Roman World*. London.
Anderson, G. (1986) *Philostratus, Biography and Belles-Lettres in the Third Century A.D.* London.
Anderson. G., trans. (1989a) *Xenophon of Ephesus: an Ephesian Tale*, in Reardon (1989) 128–169.
Anderson, G. (1989b) "The Pepaideumenos in Action: Sophists and their Outlook in the Early Empire," *Aufstieg und Niedergang der römischen Welt* II 33.1, 79–108. Berlin.
Anderson, G. (1993a) "Lucian, Tradition versus Reality," *Aufstieg und Niedergang der römischen Welt* II 34.2, 1422–1447. Berlin.
Anderson, G. (1993b) "The Origins of Daphnis," *Proceedings of the Virgil Society* 21: 65–79.
Anderson, G. (1994) *Sage, Saint and Sophist: Holy Men and their Associates in the Early Roman Empire*. London.
Anderson, J. (1970) *Military Theory and Practice in the Age of Xenophon*. Berkeley.
Annibaldis, G., trans. (1987) *Chariton: Le Avventure di Cherea e Calliroe*, in Canfora (1987) 5–149.
Apostolopoulos, Ph. (1984) *La Langue du Roman Byzantin Callimaque et Chrysorrhoé*. Athens.
Arbour, R. (1977–85) *L'Ère Baroque en France: Répertoire Chronologique*... 4 volumes. Geneva.
Archibald, E. (1988) "'Deep clerks she dumbs': the Learned Heroine in *Apollonius of Tyre* and *Pericles*," *Comparative Drama* 22: 289–303.
Archibald, E. (1991) *Apollonius of Tyre: Medieval and Renaissance Themes and Variations*. Cambridge.
Arndt, C. (1994) "Antiker und neuzeitlicher Briefroman: ein gattungstypologischer Vergleich," in Holzberg (1994a) 53–83.
Arnim, H. v. (1891) "Entstehung und Anordnung der Schriftensammlung Dion von Prusa," *Hermes* 26: 366–407.
Arnott, G. (1994) "Longus, Natural History, and Realism," in Tatum (1994) 199–215.
Arrowsmith, W. (1966) "Luxury and Death in the *Satyricon*," *Arion* 5: 304–331.
Asensio, E. (1974) in *Estudios Portugueses*, 445–453. Paris.
Astbury, R. (1977) "Petronius, *P.Oxy.* 3010, and Menippean Satire," *Classical Philology* 72: 22–31.
Attridge, H. (1992) "Thomas, Acts of," in Freedman (1992) 531–534.
Auberger, J. (1991) *Ctésias. Histoires de l'Orient*. Paris.
Auger, D. (1983) "Rêve, Image et Récit dans le Roman de Chariton," *Ktema* 8: 39–52.
Ausfeld, A. (1907) *Der griechische Alexanderroman*. Leipzig.
Avalle-Arce, J. (1990²) *Amadís de Gaula: el Primitivo y el de Montalvo*. Mexico City.
Avezzù, E., Donadi, F. (1985) *Dione di Prusa. Il Cacciatore*. Venice.
Bacon, H. (1958) "The Sibyl in the Bottle," *Virginia Quarterly Review* 34: 262–276.
Bacon, H. (1961) *Barbarians in Greek Tragedy*. New Haven.
Bagnani, G. (1954) *Arbiter of Elegance*. Toronto.
Bakhtin, M. (1974) "Zeit und Raum im Roman," *Kunst und Literatur* 22.11: 1161–1191.

Bakhtin, M. (1975) *Voprosy Literatury i Estetiki*. Moscow. (English trans. *The Dialogic Imagination* 1981. Austin.)
Bakhtin, M. (1993) *Bakhtin and Ancient Studies: Dialogues and Dialogics*, ed. J. Peradotto, in *Arethusa* 26.2.
Baldassarri, M. (1973) "Intorno all'Utopia di Giambulo. I.II.," *Rivista di Filosofia Neo-Scolastica* 65: 303-333; 471-487.
Baldwin, B. (1992) "The Werewolf Story as Bulletinstil," *Petronian Society Newsletter* 22: 6-7.
Ballanti, A. (1954) "Documenti sull' Opposizione degli Intellettuali a Domiziano," *Annali della Facoltà di Lettere e Filosofia della Università di Napoli* 4: 75-95.
Barbosa Machado (1741) *Bibliotheca Lusitana*, vol. I. Lisbon.
Barchiesi, A. (1986) "Tracce di Narrativa Greca e Romanzo Latino: una Rassegna," *Semiotica della Novella Latina*, 219-236. Rome.
Barchiesi, A. (1988) "Il Romanzo," in Montanari (1988) 341-362.
Barchiesi, A. (1991) "Il Romanzo," in Montanari (1991) 229-248.
Barns, J.W.B. (1956) "Egypt and the Greek Romance," *Akten des VIII. Internationalen Kongresses für Papyrologie*, ed. H. Gerstinger, *Mitteilungen aus der Papyrussammlung der Nationalbibliothek in Wien*, new series 5: 29-36.
Barthes, R. (1970) *S/Z*. Paris. (Engl. trans. London 1975).
Barthes, R. (1977) *Fragments d'un Discours Amoureux*. Paris.
Bartsch, S. (1989) *Decoding the Ancient Novel: the Reader and the Role of Description in Heliodorus and Achilles Tatius*. Princeton.
Bartsch, W. (1934) *Der Charitonsroman und die Historiographie*. Diss., Leipzig.
Barwick, K. (1928) "Die Gliederung der *narratio* in der rhetorischen Theorie und ihre Bedeutung für die Geschichte des antiken Romans," *Hermes* 63: 261-287.
Baslez, M.F. (1984) *L'Étranger dans la Grèce Antique*. Paris
Baslez, M.F. (1990) "L'Idée de Noblesse dans les Romans Grecs," *Dialogues d'Histoire Ancienne* 16: 115-128.
Baslez, M.F., Hoffman, P., Trédé, M., eds. (1992) *Le Monde du Roman Grec*. Études de Littérature Ancienne 4. Paris.
Baslez, M.F. (1992a) "De l'Histoire au Roman: la Perse de Chariton," in Baslez (1992) 199-212.
Bauer, J. (1983) "Semitisches bei Petron," in *Festschrift für Robert Muths*, eds. P. Händel, W. Meid, 17-23. Innsbruck.
Bauer, J. (1987) "In Xenophontis Ephesii quem vocant fabellam commentariola," *Grazer Beiträge* 14: 229-238.
Beaton, R. (1987) "The Rhetoric of Poverty: the Lives and Opinions of Theodore Prodromos," *Byzantine and Modern Greek Studies* 11: 1-28.
Beaton, R., ed. (1988) *The Greek Novel, A.D. 1-1985*. London.
Beaton, R. (1989a) *The Medieval Greek Romance*. Cambridge.
Beaton, R. (1989b) "Courtly Romances in Byzantium: a Case Study in Reception," *Mediterranean Historical Review* 4: 345-355.
Beaton, R., Ricks, D. eds. (1993) *Digenes Akrites: New Approaches to Byzantine Heroic Poetry*. Aldershot, UK.
Beaton, R. (1994) *An Introduction to Modern Greek Literature*. Oxford.
Beaujeu, J. (1973) *Apulée: Opuscules Philosophiques et Fragments*. Paris.
Beck, C.D., ed., (1783) *Charitonis Aphrodisiensis de Chaerea et Callirrhoe Amatoriarum Narrationum Libri VIII*. Leipzig.
Beck, H.-G. (1971) *Geschichte der byzantinischen Volksliteratur*. Byzantinisches Handbuch. Munich.
Beck, H.-G. (1984) *Byzantinisches Erotikon: Orthodoxie – Literatur – Gesellschaft*. Bayrische Akademie der Wissenschaften, philosophische-historische Klasse, Sitzungsberichte: Jahrgang 1984, no. 5. Munich.
Beck, R. (1973) "Some Observations on the Narrative Technique of Petronius," *Phoenix* 27: 42-61.

Beck, R. (1975) "Encolpius at the *Cena*," *Phoenix* 29: 271-283.
Beck, R. (1982a) "*The Satyricon:* Satire, Narrator and Antecedents," *Museum Helveticum* 39: 206-214.
Beck, R. (1982b) "Soteriology, the Mysteries, and the Ancient Novel: Iamblichus *Babyloniaca* as a Test Case," in U. Bianchi, M.J. Vermaseren, eds., *La Soteriologia dei Culti Orientali nell' Impero Romano*. Études Préliminaires aux Religions Orientales dans l'Empire Romain 92, pp. 527-540. Leiden.
Beck, R. (1988) *Planetary Gods and Planetary Orders in the Mysteries of Mithras*. Études Préliminaires aux Religions Orientales dans l'Empire Romain 109. Leiden.
Behr, C. (1968) *Aelius Aristides and the Sacred Tales*. Amsterdam.
Belsey, C. (1980) *Critical Practice*. London.
Bentley, R. (1874) *Dissertations upon the Epistles of Phalaris, Themistocles, Socrates, Euripides, and upon the Fables of Aesop*. Edited, with an Introduction and Notes by W. Wagner. Berlin.
Benveniste, E. (1966) *Problèmes de Linguistique Générale*. Paris.
Berger, G. (1984) "Legitimation und Modell: dic *Aithiopika* als Prototyp des französischen heroisch-galanten Romans," *Antike und Abendland* 30: 177-189.
Berghoff, W. (1967) *Palladius de Gentibus Indiae et de Bragmanibus*. Meisenheim am Glan.
Bergmeister, H.-J. (1975) *Die Historia de Preliis Alexandri Magni: Synoptische Edition*. Meisenhem am Glan.
Bergson, L. (1965) *Der griechische Alexanderroman, Rezension β*. Uppsala.
Bernhard, M. (1927) *Der Stil des Apuleius von Madaura*. Stuttgart.
Bertelli, L. (1976) "Il Modello della Società Rurale nell' Utopia Greca," *Il Pensiero Politico* 9: 183-208.
Bertrand, J.-M. (1988) "Les Boucôloi ou le Monde à l'Envers," *Revue des Études Anciennes* 90: 139-149.
Beschorner, A. (1992a) *Untersuchungen zu Dares Phrygius*. Classica Monacensia 4. Tübingen.
Beschorner, A., Holzberg, N. (1992b) "A Bibliography of the Aesop Romance," in Holzberg (1992a) 165-187.
Beschorner, A. (1994) "Griechische Briefbücher berühmter Männer: eine Bibliographie," in Holzberg (1994a) 169-190.
Beta, S., De Carli, E., Zanetto, G. (1993) *Lessico dei Romanzieri Greci*, III (K-O). Hildesheim.
Beye, C. (1982) *Epic and Romance in the Argonautica of Apollonius*. Carbondale.
Beyer, F. (1991) *Die UFA-Stars im Dritten Reich. Frauen für Deutschland*. Munich.
Biagini, E. (1983) *Racconto e Teoria del Romanzo*. Turin.
Bianchetti, S. (1987) *Falaride e Pseudofalaride: Storia e Leggenda*. Rome.
Bianco, G. (1971) *La Fonte Greca delle Metamorfosi di Apuleio*. Brescia.
Bichler, R. (1983) "Utopie und gesellschaftlicher Wandel. Eine Studie am Beispiel der griechisch-hellenistischen Welt," in Acham, K., ed., *Gesellschaftliche Prozesse. Beiträge zur historischen Soziologie und Gesellschaftsanalyse*. Graz.
Bichler, R. (1984) "Zur historischen Beurteilung der griechischen Staatsutopie," *Grazer Beiträge* 11: 179-206.
Bidez, J. (1932) *La Cité du Monde et la Cité du Soleil chez les Stoïciens*. Bulletin de l'Académie royale de Belgique, Classe des lettres, 5e série, tome 18. Paris.
Bieler, L. (1967) Θεῖος 'Ανήρ. Reprint of 1935-36. Darmstadt.
Bigwood, J. (1965) *Ctesias of Cnidus*. Diss. Harvard [résumé in *Harvard Stadies in Classical Philology* 70: 263-265].
Bigwood, J. (1976) "Ctesias' Account of the Revolt of Inarus," *Phoenix* 30: 1-25.
Bigwood, J. (1978) "Ctesias as Historian of the Persian Wars," *Phoenix* 32: 19-41.
Bigwood, J. (1980) "Diodorus and Ctesias," *Phoenix* 34: 195-207.
Bigwood, J. (1983) "The Ancient Accounts of the Battle of Cunaxa," *American Journal of Philology* 104: 340-357.
Bigwood, J. (1986) "*P.Oxy.* 2330 and Ctesias," *Phoenix* 40: 393-406.

Bigwood, J. (1989) "Ctesias' *Indica* and Photius," *Phoenix* 43: 302-316.
Bigwood, J. (1993) "Ctesias' Parrot," *Classical Quarterly* 43: 321-327.
Billanovich, G. (1953) *I Primi Umanisti e la Tradizione dei Classici*. Fribourg.
Billault, A. (1977) "Les Lettres de Chion d'Héraclée," *Revue des Études Grecques* 90: 29-37.
Billault, A. (1986) "Hécate Romanesque: Mort et Fécondité dans les Mythologies," *Actes du Colloque de Poitiers, 13-14 mai 1983*, publiés par F. Jouan. Paris.
Billault, A. (1989) "De l'Histoire au Roman: Hermocrate de Syracuse," *Revue des Études Grecques* 102: 540-548.
Billault, A. (1991a) *La Création Romanesque dans la Littérature Grecque à l'Époque Impériale*. Paris.
Billault, A. (1991b) "Les Formes Romanesques de l'Héroïsation dans la *Vie d'Apollonios de Tyane* de Philostrate," *Bulletin de l'Association G. Budé*: 267-274.
Billault, A. (1993) "The Rhetoric of a 'Divine Man': Apollonius of Tyana as Critic of Oratory and as Orator according to Philostratus," *Philosophy and Rhetoric* 26: 227-235.
Biltcliffe, D. (1969) "*P.Oxy.* no. 2330 and its Importance for the Study of Nicolaus of Damascus," *Rheinisches Museum* 112: 85-93.
Biraud, M. (1985) "L'Hypotexte Homérique et le Rôle Amoureux de Callirhoé dans le Roman de Chariton," *Sémiologie de l'Amour dans les Civilisations Méditerranéennes*, 21-29. Paris.
Birch, C. (1955) *Traditions of the Life of Aesop*. Diss. Washington University, St. Louis.
Biscardi, A. (1982) *Diritto Greco Antico*. Milan.
Bizos, M., ed. (1971-1973) *Xénophon, Cyropédie I-V*. Budé. Paris.
Blake, W.E. (1931) "The Overtrustful Editors of Chariton," *Transactions of the American Philological Association* 62: 68-77.
Blake, W.E., ed. (1938) *Charitonis Aphrodisiensis de Chaerea et Callirhoe Libri Octo*. Oxford.
Blake, W.E., trans. (1939) *Chariton's Chaereas and Callirhoe*. Oxford.
Blanchard, A. (1983) *Essais sur la Compositon des Comédies de Ménandre*. Paris.
Blanchard, J. (1975) "Daphnis et Chloé: Histoire de la Mimesis," *Quaderni Urbinati di Cultura Classica* 20: 39-62.
Bleich, D. (1975) *Readings and Feelings: An Introduction to Subjective Criticism*. Baltimore.
Blümner, H. (1903) "Das Märchen von Amor und Psyche in der deutschen Dichtkunst," *Neue Jahrbücher für das klassische Altertum*. 11: 648-673.
Blumenthal, H.J., Markus, R.A., eds. (1981) *Neoplatonism and Early Christian Thought*. London.
Bobes, C. (1993) *La Novela*. Madrid.
Bock, G. (1983) "Historische Frauenforschung, Fragestellungen und Perspektiven," in K. Hausen, ed., *Frauen suchen ihre Geschichte*, 22-60. Munich.
Bodel, J. (1984) *Freedmen in the Satyricon of Petronius*. Dissertation, University of Michigan. Ann Arbor.
Bodel, J. (1994) "Trimalchio's Underworld," in Tatum (1994) 237-259.
Boer, W. (1953) *Epistola Alexandri ad Aristotelem ad Codicum Fidem Edita et Commentario Critico Instructa*. The Hague.
Boissonade, J.F. (1829-33) *Anecdota Graeca 1*, 145. Paris.
Bompaire, J. (1958) *Lucien Écrivain. Imitation et Création*. Paris.
Bompaire, J. (1988) "Comment Lire les *Histoires Vraies* de Lucien?," in Porte, D., Néraudau, J., eds. (1988) *Hommages à Henri le Bonniec*, 31-39. Brussels.
Boncquet, J. (1987) *Diodorus Siculus (II, 1-34) over Mesopotamie: een historische Kommentar*. Brussels.
Bonner, S. (1969) *Roman Declamation in the Late Republic and Early Empire*. Liverpool.
Booth, W. (1961) *The Rhetoric of Fiction*. Chicago.
Borgeaud, P. (1988) *The Cult of Pan in Ancient Greece*. Chicago.
Borgogno, A. (1971) "Menandro in Caritone," *Rivista di Filologia e di Istruzione Classica* 99: 257-263.

Bornecque H. (1967) *Les Déclamations et les Déclamateurs d'après Sénèque le Père*. Hildesheim.
Bovon, F., et al. (1981) *Les Actes Apocryphes des Apôtres*. Geneva.
Bovon, F. (1988) "Les Actes de Philippe," *Aufstieg und Niedergang der römischen Welt* II 25.6, 4431–4527.
Bovon, F. (1992) "Philip, Acts of," in Freedman (1992) 5: 312.
Bowersock, G. (1965) *Augustus and the Greek World*. Oxford.
Bowersock, G. (1969) *Greek Sophists in the Roman Empire*. Oxford.
Bowersock, G., ed. (1974) *Approaches to the Second Sophistic*. University Park, PA.
Bowersock, G. (1994) *Fiction as History: Nero to Julian*. Berkeley.
Bowie, E.L. (1977) "The Novels and the Real World," in Reardon (1977) 91–96.
Bowie, E.L. (1978) "Apollonius of Tyana: Tradition and Reality," *Aufstieg und Niedergang der römischen Welt* II 16.2, pp. 1652–1699. Berlin.
Bowie, E.L. (1982) "The Importance of Sophists," *Yale Classical Studies* 27: 29–59.
Bowie, E.L. (1985a) "The Greek Novel," in Easterling (1985) 683–699.
Bowie, E.L. (1985b) "Theocritus' Seventh *Idyll*, Philetas and Longus," *Classical Quarterly* 35: 67–91.
Bowie, E.L. (1991) "Hellenism in Writers of the Early Second Sophistic," in S. Saïd, ed. (1991) Ἑλληνισμός: *Quelques Jalons pour une Histoire de l'Identité Grecque*. Leiden.
Bowie, E.L. (1992) "Les Lecteurs du Roman Grec," in Baslez (1992) 55–61.
Bowie, E.L., Harrison, S.J. (1993) "The Romance of the Novel," *Journal of Roman Studies* 83: 159–178.
Bowie, E. L. (1994a) "Philostratus: Writer of Fiction," in Morgan (1994) 181–199.
Bowie, E.L. (1994b) "The Readership of Greek Novels in the Ancient World," in Tatum (1994) 435–459.
Bowman, A. (1986) *Egypt after the Pharaohs*. London.
Boyle, A., ed. (1990) *The Imperial Muse II: Flavian Epicist to Claudian*. Bendigo, Australia.
Boyle, A., ed. (1995) *Roman Literature and Ideology. Ramus Essays for J.P. Sullivan*. (A reprint in book form of *Ramus* 23.1-2 [1994]). Bendigo, Australia.
Braga, T. (1881) *Questões de Literatura Portugueza*. Lisbon.
Braun, M. (1934) *Griechischer Roman und hellenistische Geschichtsschreibung*. Frankfurt.
Braun, M. (1938) *History and Romance in Graeco-Oriental Literature*. Oxford.
Braunert, H. (1963) "Ideologie und Utopie im griechisch-hellenistischen Staatsdenken," *Geschichte in Wissenschaft und Unterricht* 14: 145–153, and in Braunert (1980) 49–65.
Braunert, H. (1965) "Die heilige Insel des Euhemeros in der Diodor-Überlieferung," *Rheinisches Museum* 108: 255–268, and in Braunert (1980) 153–164.
Braunert, H. (1968) "Staatstheorie und Staatsrecht im Hellenismus," *Saeculum* 19: 47–66, and in Braunert (1980) 165–190.
Braunert, H. (1969) *Utopia: Antworten griechischen Denkens auf die Herausforderung durch soziale Verhältnisse*. Veröffentlichungen der Schleswig-Holsteinischen Universitätsgesellschaft, N.F. 51. Kiel, and in Braunert (1980) 66–84.
Braunert, H. (1980) *Politik, Recht und Gesellschaft in der griechisch-römischen Antike: Gesammelte Aufsätze und Reden*. Kieler Historische Studien, 26. Stuttgart.
Breitenbach, H. (1967) *RE* vol. IX A2 cols. 1567ff., published as book *Xenophon von Athen*, 1966. Stuttgart.
Breitenbach, L., ed. (1878) *Xenophons Cyropaedie. Für den Schulgebrauch erklärt*. Leipzig.
Bremen, R. van (1983) "Women and Wealth," in Cameron (1983) 223–241.
Bretzigheimer, G. (1988) "Die Komik in Longos' Hirtenroman *Daphnis und Chloe*," *Gymnasium* 95: 515–555.
Briant, P. (1987) "Institutions Perses et Histoire Comparatiste dans l'Historiographie Grecque," in *Achaemenid History II. The Greek Sources* (1987). Proceedings of the Groningen 1984 Achaemenid Workshop, 1–10. Leiden.
Brilliant, R. (1984) *Visual Narratives. Storytelling in Etruscan and Roman Art*. Ithaca, N.Y.
Brioso Sánchez, M. (1981) "Notas sobre el Texto de Aquiles Tacio," *Habis* 12: 65–70.

Brioso Sánchez, M. (1989) "Caritón III 5 y sus Modelos," *Minerva* 3: 205-208.
Brioso Sánchez, M. (1992) "Egipto en la Novela Griega Antiqua," *Habis* 3: 197-215.
Briquel-Chatonnet, F. (1992) "L'Image des Phéniciens dans les Romans Grecs," in Baslez (1992) 189-197.
Brodersen, K. (1992) "Rache für Äsop. Zum Umgang mit Geschichte außerhalb der Historiographie," in Holzberg (1992a) 97-109.
Brodersen, K. (1994) "Hippokrates und Artaxerxes: Zu *P.Oxy.* 1184^v, P.Berol. inv. 7094^v und 21137^v + 6934^v," *Zeitschrift für Papyrologie und Epigraphik* 102: 100-110.
Brooks, P. (1986) "The Idea of a Psychoanalytic Literary Criticism," *Critical Inquiry* 13: 334-348 (then in *Discourse in Psychoanalysis and Literature*, ed. S. Rimmon-Kenan [1987] 1-18. London).
Brown, T. (1946) "Euhemerus and the Historians," *Harvard Theological Review* 39: 259-274.
Brown, T. (1949) *Onesicritus: a Study in Hellenistic Historiography* (repr. New York 1974). Berkeley.
Brown, T. (1973) *The Greek Historians.* Lexington, MA.
Brown, T. (1978) "Suggestions for a Vita of Ctesias of Cnidus," *Historia* 27: 1-19.
Brown, W. (1955) "Some Hellenistic Utopias," *Classical Weekly* 48: 57-62.
Browning, R. (1955) "An Unpublished Epigram on Heliodorus' *Aethiopica*," *Classical Review* 5: 141-143.
Browning, R. (1983) *Medieval and Modern Greek.* Cambridge.
Brunt, P. (1973) "Aspects of the Social Thought of Dio Chrysostom and of the Stoics," *Proceedings of the Cambridge Philological Society* 199: 9-34.
Bücheler, F., ed. (1862) *Petronii Arbitri Satirarum Reliquiae.* Berlin.
Bühler, W. (1976) "Das Element des Visuellen in der Eingangsszene von Heliodors *Aithiopika*," *Wiener Studien* 10: 177-185.
Bürger, K. (1892) "Zu Xenophon von Ephesus," *Hermes* 27: 36-67.
Bürger, K. (1903) *Studien zur Geschichte des griechischen Romans.* Vol. 2, *Die literaturgeschichtliche Stellung des Antonius Diogenes und der Historia Apollonii.* Wissenschaftliche Beilage zum Programm des Herzoglichen Gymnasiums. Blankenburg am Harz.
Bürger, P. (1948) *Eléments de Réalité chez Xénophon d'Ephèse.* Diss. Louvain.
Bungarten, J. (1967) *Menanders und Glykeras Brief bei Alkiphron.* Diss. Bonn.
Burchard, C. (1986) "Der jüdische Asenethroman und seine Nachwirkung: von Egeria zu Anna Katharina Emmerich oder von Moses aus Aggel zu Karl Kerenyi," *Aufstieg und Niedergang der römischen Welt* II 20.1, pp. 543-667. Berlin.
Burck, E. (1969) *Die Frau in der griechisch-römischen Antike.* Munich.
Burde, P. (1974) *Untersuchungen zur antiken Universalgeschichtsschreibung.* Diss. Erlangen-Nürnberg. Munich.
Burkert, W. (1987) *Ancient Mystery Cults.* Cambridge, MA.
Burkert, W., et al. (1990) *Hérodote et les Peuples non Grecs.* Entretiens sur l'Antiquité Classique 35. Vandoeuvres-Genève.
Burmann, P., ed. (1709) *Petronii Satyricon.* Utrecht.
Burstein, S. (1989) "SEG 33.802 and the Alexander Romance," *Zeitschrift für Papyrologie und Epigraphik* 77: 275-276.
Cacho Blecua, J., ed., (1991^2) *Amadís de Gaula.* 2 vols. Madrid.
Cairns, F. (1984) "Theocritus' *First Idyll:* the Literary Programme," *Wiener Studien* 18: 89-113.
Calderini, A. (1912) *Prolegomeni alle Avventure di Cherea e Calliroe.* Turin.
Calderini, A. (1913) *Caritone di Afrodisia, Le avventure di Cherea e Callirroe.* Turin.
Callebat, L. (1968) *Sermo Cotidianus dans les Métamorphoses d'Apulée.* Caen.
Callebat, L. (1992) "Le *Satyricon* de Pétrone et L'*Âne d'Or* d'Apulée sont-ils des Romans?," *Euphrosyne* 20: 149-164.
Callu, J.-P. (1980) "Les Prix dans deux Romans Mineurs d'Époque Impériale," *Les Devaluations à Rome: Époque Républicaine et Impériale* 2, pp. 187-212. Rome.

Cameron, Alan (1980) "Poetae Novelli," *Harvard Studies in Classical Philology* 84: 127-175.
Cameron, Averil (1969) "Petronius and Plato," *Classsical Quarterly* 63: 367-370.
Cameron, Averil, Kuhrt, A., eds. (1983) *Images of Women in Antiquity*. London.
Cameron, Averil (1989) "Women in Ancient Culture and Society," *Der altsprachliche Unterricht* 32: 6-17.
Cameron, Averil (1991) *Christianity and the Rhetoric of Empire*. Berkeley.
Campbell, J. (1949) *Hero with a Thousand Faces*. New York.
Canevari, A. (1962) "Aspetti dell' Euboico di Dione di Prusa," *Diadosis*, 16-18.
Canfora, L., ed. (1987) *Storie d'Avventure Antiche*. Italian trans. Bari.
Cantarella, E. (1988) *Secondo Natura. La Bisessualità nel Mondo Antico*. Rome.
Capelle, W. (1953) "Zwei Quellen des Heliodor," *Rheinisches Museum* 96: 166-180.
Carney, T. (1960a) *Leucippe and Clitophon, Book III*, ed. with Introd., Comm., Vocab., and Indices. Salisbury, Rhodesia.
Carney, T. (1960b) "Notes on the Text of Achilles Tatius, Book III," *Proceedings of the African Classical Association* 3: 10-14.
Castiglioni, L. (1928) "Stile e Testo del Romanzo Pastorale di Longo," *Rendiconti dell' Istituto Lombardo* 61: 203-223.
Cataudella, Q. (1927) "Riflessi Virgiliani nel Romanzo di Caritone," *Athenaeum* 5: 302-312.
Cataudella, Q. (1940) "Giovanni Crisostomo 'Imitatore' di Aristofane," *Athenaeum*, 18: 236-243.
Cataudella, Q. (1954) "Giovanni Crisostomo nel Romanzo di Achille Tazio," *La Parola del Passato* 9: 25-40.
Cataudella, Q. (1957) *La Novella Greca*. Naples.
Cataudella, Q., trans. (1958) *Il Romanzo di Senofonte Ephesio*, in Cataudella, Q., ed., *Il Romanzo Classico*. Rome.
Cataudella, Q. (1960) "Note Critiche al Testo di Achille Tazio," in *Studi in Onore di L. Castiglioni*, 171-177. Florence.
Cataudella, Q. (1980) "Sull' Autenticità delle Lettere di Chione di Eraclea," *Memorie della Classe di Scienze Morali e Storiche della Accademia Nazionale dei Lincei* 24: 649-751.
Cataudella, Q. (1981) "Revisioni e Scoperte. Chione di Eraclea," *Cultura e Scuola* 20: 78-84.
Cataudella, Q. (1990) *Luciano, Storia Vera*. I Classici della BUR 50. Milan.
Cauderlier, P. (1992) "Réalités Égyptiennes chez Héliodore," in Baslez (1992) 221-231.
Cavallo, G. (1986) "Conservazione e Perdita dei Testi Greci: Fattori Materiali, Sociali e Culturali," in *Società Romana e Impero Tardoantico IV. Tradizione dei Classici, Trasformazione della Cultura*, ed. A. Giardina, 146-150. Rome.
Centanni, M. (1988) *Il Romanzo di Alessandro*. Venice.
Cetta, G. (1967) "Il Romanzo Greco di Achille Tazio," in *Diadosis*, 39-43. Tortona.
Chalk, H.H.O. (1960) "Eros and the Lesbian Pastorals of Longus," *Journal of Hellenic Studies* 80: 32-51.
Champlin, E. (1981) "Serenus Sammonicus," *Harvard Studies in Classical Philology* 85: 189-212.
Chantraine, P. (1957) review of Vilborg (1955) in *Revue de Philologie* 31 (1957) 125f.
Chatzigiakoumes, M. (1977) Μεσαιωνικὰ ἑλληνικὰ κείμενα. Athens.
Chiarini, G. (1983) "Esogamia e Incesto nella *Historia Apollonii Regis Tyri*," *Materiali e Discussioni* 10-11: 267-292.
Christ, K. (1959) "Römer und Barbaren in der hohen Kaiserzeit," *Saeculum* 10: 273-288.
Christ, W., Schmid, W., Stählin, O. (1920^6) *Geschichte der griechischen Litteratur*. Vol. II, tom. 1. Handbuch der klassischen Altertumswissenschaft, VII, 1. Munich.
Chuvin, P. (1991) *Chronique des Derniers Païens*. Paris.

Cicu, L. (1982) "La *Poetica* di Aristotele e le Strutture dell'Antico Romanzo d'Amore e d'Avventure," *Sandalion* 5: 107-141.
Cizek, A. (1975) "From the Historical Truth to the Literary Convention. The Life of Cyrus the Great viewed by Herodotus, Ctesias and Xenophon," *L'Antiquité Classique* 44: 531-552.
Cizek, E. (1974) "Le Roman Moderne et les Structures du Roman Antique," *Bulletin de l'Association Guillaume Budé* 33: 421-444.
Clauss, M. (1992) *Cultores Mithrae*. Stuttgart.
Cobert, C.G. (1857) "Heliodori ἀκυρολογία," *Mnemosyne* 6: 454.
Cobert, C.G. (1859) "Annotationes Criticae ad Charitonem," *Mnemosyne* 8: 229-303.
Cohen, R., ed. (1989) *The Future of Literary Theory*. New York.
Cole, S. (1981) "Could Greek Women Read and Write?," in H. Foley, ed., *Reflections of Women in Antiquity*, 219-245. New York.
Collignon, A. (1892) *Étude sur Pétrone. La Critique Littéraire, l'Imitation et la Parodie dans le Satiricon*. Paris.
Collignon, A. (1905) *Pétrone en France*. Paris.
Colonna, A., ed. (1938) *Heliodori Aethiopica*. Rome.
Colonna, A. (1940) "Heliodorea," *Bolletino del Comitato per la Preparazione dell'Edizione Nazionale dei Classici Greci e Latini*. Supplemento a Rendiconti della Classe di Scienze Morali e Storiche della Accademia d'Italia 7.1: 41-60.
Colonna, A. (1950) "L'Assedio di Nisibis del 350 d.C. e la Cronologia di Eliodoro Emiseno," *Athenaeum* 18: 79-87.
Colonna, A. (1956) review of Vilborg (1955) in *Rivista di Filologia Classica* 34 (1956) 184.
Colonna, A. (1987) *Le Etiopiche di Eliodoro*. Turin.
Conacher, D. (1967) *Euripidean Drama. Myth, Drama and Structure*. Toronto.
Conca, F. (1969) "I Papiri di Achille Tazio," *Rendiconto dell'Istituto Lombardo, Classe di Lettere, Scienze Morali e Storiche* 103: 649-677.
Conca, F., De Carli, E., Zanetto, G. (1983) *Lessico dei Romanzieri Greci, I* (Α-Γ). Milan.
Conca, F., (1986) "Il Romanzo di Niceta Eugeniano: Modelli Narrativi e Stilistici," *Siculorum Gymnasium* 39: 115-126.
Conca, F., De Carli, E., Zanetto, G. (1989) *Lessico dei Romanzieri Greci* II (Δ-1). Hildesheim-Zürich-New York.
Conca, F., ed. (1990) *Nicetas Eugenianus, de Drosillae et Chariclis Amoribus*. London Studies in Classical Philology 24. Amsterdam.
Conde Guerri, E. (1988) "Joyas, Ajuar y Nuevas Reflexiones en las *Etiópicas* de Heliodoro como Indicios Cronológicos de la Historia Real," *Anales de Prehistoria y Arqueologia* 4: 169-181.
Connor, W.R. (1985) "Historical Writings in the Fourth Century B.C. and in the Hellenistic Period," in Easterling (1985) 458-471.
Conte, G.B. (1996) *The Hidden Author. An Interpretation of Petronius' Satyricon*. Berkeley.
Conybeare, F., Rendel Harris, J., Smith Lewis, A. (1913[2]) *The Story of Aḥikar: from the Aramaic, Syriac, Arabic, Armenian, Ethiopic, Old Turkish, Greek and Slavonic Versions*. London.
Corbato, C. (1968) "Da Menandro a Caritone. Studi sulla Genesi del Romanzo Greco e i suoi Rapporti con la Commedia Nuova. I," *Quaderni Triestini sul Teatro Antico* 1: 5-44.
Corbett, P. (1970) *Petronius*. New York.
Cortassa, G., Culasso Gastaldi, G. (1990) *Le Lettere di Temistocle*. 2 vols. Padua.
Couégnas, D. (1992) *Introduction à la Paralittérature*. Paris.
Coulet, H. (1967-8) *Le Roman jusqu' à la Révolution*. 2 vols. Paris.
Courtney, E. (1962) "Parody and Literary Allusion in Menippean Satire," *Philologus* 106: 86-100.
Crawford, D.S. (1955) *Papyri Michaelidae*. Aberdeen.
Cresci, L. (1976) "Citazioni Omeriche in Achille Tazio," *Sileno* 2: 121-126.
Cresci, L. (1978) "La Figura di Melite in Achille Tazio," *Atene e Roma* 23: 74-82.

Cresci, L. (1981) "Il Romanzo di Longo Sofista e la Tradizione Bucolica," *Atene e Roma* 26: 1–25.
Criscuolo, L., Geraci, G., eds. (1989) *Egitto e Storia Antica dall' Ellenismo all'Età Araba*. Bologna.
Crusius, O. (1897) "Die neuesten Papyrusfunde," *Beilage zur allgemeinen Zeitung* no. 145, July 3: 1–2.
Csapodi, C. (1973) *The Corvinian Library*. Studia Humanitatis, No. 1, trans. I. Gombos. Budapest.
Cunliffe, B. (1988) *Greeks, Romans and Barbarians. Spheres of Interaction*. London.
Cupane, C. (1974) "῎Ερως-Βασιλεύς: la Figura di Eros nel Romanzo Bizantino d'Amore," *Atti dell' Accademia di Arti di Palermo*, serie 4, 33/2: 243–297.
Daele, R.-M. (1946) *Nicolas de Montreulx: Arbiter of European Literary Vogues of the Late Renaissance*. New York.
Dällenbach, L. (1978) *Le Récit Speculaire. Contribution à l'Étude de la Mise en Abyme*. Paris.
Dalmeyda, G., ed. (1926) *Xénophon d'Ephèse: Les Ephésiaques*. Budé. Paris.
Dalmeyda, G., ed. (1934) *Longus, Pastorales (Daphnis et Chloé)*. Budé. Paris.
Danek, G., Wallisch, R. (1993) "Notizen zu Longos, Daphnis und Chloe," *Wiener Studien* 106: 45–60.
Danon-Boileau, L. (1982) *Produire le Fictif. Linguistique et Écriture Romanesque*. Paris.
D'Arms, J. (1981) "The 'Typicality' of Trimalchio," *Commerce and Social Standing in Ancient Rome*, 97–120. Cambridge, MA.
Davies, S. (1980) *The Revolt of the Widows*. Carbondale.
Day, J. (1951) "The Value of Dio Chrysostom's Euboean Discourse for the Economic Historian," in Coleman-Norton, P., Brown, F., Fine, J., eds., *Studies in Roman Economic and Social History in Honor of A.C. Johnston*, 209–235. Princeton.
De Figueiredo, F. (1946[3]) *História da Literatura Clássica* (2ª época, 1580–1756). São Paulo.
De Figueiredo, F. (1950[6]) *A Épica Portuguesa no Século XVI*. São Paulo.
De Filippo, J. (1990) "*Curiositas* and the Platonism of Apuleius' *Golden Ass*," *American Journal of Philology* 111: 471–492.
Degen, R. (1977) "Achikar," *Enzyklopädie des Märchens* 1: 53–59.
de Jonge, B.J. (1941) *Ad Apuleii Madaurensis Librum Secundum Commentarius Exegeticus*. Groningen.
Delahaye, H. (1921) *Les Passions des Martyrs et les Genres Littéraires*. Second edition 1966. Brussels.
Delasanta, R. (1967) *The Epic Voice*. The Hague.
Del Corno, D. (1962) "La Lingua di Ctesia (*P.Oxy*.2330)," *Athenaeum* n.s. 40: 126–141.
Del Corno, D. (1989) "Anzia e le Compagne, Ossia le Eroine del Romanzo Greco," in *Atti del II Convegno Internazionale. La donna nel mondo antico*, 73–84. Turin.
Delebecque, E. (1946–47) "Xénophon, Athènes et Lacédémone," *Revue des Études Grecques* 49–50: 101ff.
Delebecque, E. (1957) *Essai sur la Vie de Xénophon*. Paris.
Delebecque, E., ed. (1978) *Xénophon, Cyropédie VI–VIII*. Paris.
Delhay, C. (1990) "Achille Tatius Fabuliste?," *Pallas* 36: 117–131.
Derrett, J. (1960) "The History of *Palladius on the Races of India and the Brahmans*," *Classica et Medievalia* 21: 77–135.
De Vegas Sansalvador, Ana, ed. (1987) *Ciropedia. Intr. Trad. e Notos*. Bibl. dos Gredos 108. Madrid.
Devereux, G. (1968) "Greek Pseudo-Homosexuality and the 'Greek Miracle'," *Symbolae Osloenses* 42: 69–92.
Devereux, G. (1979/1980) "An Undetected Absurdity in Lucian's *True Story*," *Helios* 7: 63–68.

Diaz, J. (1984) "La Belleza en la Novela Griega," *Helmantica* 35: 243-266.
Di Capua, L. (1989) "L'Utopia di Giambulo tra Filosofia e Politica," *Atti della Accademia di Scienze morali e politiche della Società nazionale di Scienze, Lettere ed Arti di Napoli* 100: 223-240.
Dicke, G. (1994) *Heinrich Steinhöwels Esopus und seine Fortsetzer. Untersuchungen zu einem Bucherfolg der Frühdruckzeit.* Münchener Texte und Untersuchungen zur deutschen Literatur des Mittelalters, 103. Tübingen.
Dickie, M. (1991) "Heliodorus and Plutarch on the Evil Eye," *Classical Philology* 86: 17-29.
Dielska, M. (1986) *Apollonius of Tyana in Legend and History.* Rome.
Diepolder, H. (1931) *Die attischen Grabreliefs.* Berlin.
Diggle, J. (1972) "A Note on Achilles Tatius," *Classical Review* 22: 7.
Di Gregorio, L. (1968) "Sugli "Άπιστα ὑπὲρ Θούλην di Antonio Diogene," *Aevum* 42: 199-211.
Dihle, A. (1978) "Zur Datierung des Metiochos-Roman," *Würzburger Jahrbücher für die Altertumswissenschaft* n.f. 4: 47-55.
Dihle, A. (1987) *Die Entstehung der historischen Biographie.* Heidelberg.
Diller, H. (1962) "Die Hellenen-Barbaren-Antithese im Zeitalter der Perserkriege," in *Grecs et Barbares.* Entretiens sur l'Antiquité Classique 8, 37-82. Vandoeuvres-Genève.
Dimitriadou-Toufexi, E. (1981) "Index Verborum Vitae Aesopi Perrianae," Ἐπιστημονικὴ ἐπετηρίδα τῆς φιλοσοφικῆς σχολῆς τοῦ Ἀριστοτελείου πανεπιστημίου Θεσσαλονίκης 20: 69-153.
Dodds, E.R. (1965) *Pagan and Christian in an Age of Anxiety.* Cambridge.
Dodgeon, M., Lieu, S. (1991) *The Roman Eastern Frontier and the Persian Wars (A.D. 226-263).* London.
Doenges, N. (1981) *The Letters of Themistocles.* New York.
Dörrie, H. (1935) *De Longi Achillis Tatii Heliodori Memoria.* Diss. Göttingen.
Dörrie, H. (1959) review of Vilborg (1955) in *Gymnasium* 66 (1959) 428.
Dörrie, H. (1964) *Der Königskult des Antiochos von Kommagene im Lichte neuer Inschriften-Funde.* Abhandlungen der Göttinger Akademie der Wissenschaften, philosophisch-historische Klasse, 3, 60. Göttingen.
Dörrie, H. (1972) "Die Wertung der Barbaren im Urteil der Griechen. Knechtsnaturen? Oder Bewahrer und Künder heilbringender Weisheit?," in *Antike und Universalgeschichte. Festschrift Hans Erich Stier zum 70. Geburtstag am 25. Mai 1972,* pp. 146-175. Münster.
Donnini, M. (1981) "Apul. *Met.X*, 2-12: Analogie e Varianti di un Racconto," *Materiali e Contributi per la Storia della Narrativa Greco-Latina* 3: 145-160.
Dornseiff, F. (1934) "Platons Buch 'Briefe'," *Hermes* 69: 223-226.
Dornseiff, F. (1939) "Exkurs über die Platonbriefe," in Dornseiff, F., *Echtheitsfragen antik-griechischer Literatur: Rettungen des Theognis, Phokylides, Hekataios, Choirilos,* 31-36. Berlin.
D'Orville, J.P., ed. (1750) Χαρίτωνος Ἀφροδισέως τῶν περὶ Χαιρέαν καὶ Καλλιρρόην ἐρωτικῶν διηγημάτων λόγοι H. Amsterdam.
Dostálová, R. (1991) *Il Romanzo Greco e i Papiri.* Prague.
Dover, K.J. (1978) *Greek Homosexuality.* London.
Drijvers, H. (1992) "The Acts of Thomas," in Schneemelcher (1992) 2: 322-338.
Dubielzig, U. (1993) "Roman, Novelle und verwandte Gattungen," in *Kleines Lexikon des Hellenismus,* ed. H. Schmitt, E. Vogt, 688-707. Wiesbaden.
Duby, G., Perrot, M. (1993) *A History of Women in the West,* 5 vols.: Vol. 1, *Antike,* ed. P. Schmitt-Pantel; editor for the German edition B. Wagner-Hasel. Frankfurt.
Ducrot, O. and Todorov, T. (1972) *Dictionnaire Encyclopédique de Sciences du Langage.* Paris.
Due, B. (1989a) *The Cyropaedia: Xenophon's Aims and Methods.* Aarhus.

Due, B., ed. (1989b) *Pantheia og Abradatas, Text, Trad. and Commentary* (in Danish). Aarhus.
Dührsen, N. (1994) "Die Briefe der Sieben Weisen bei Diogenes Laertios: Möglichkeiten und Grenzen der Rekonstruktion eines verlorenen griechischen Briefromans," in Holzberg (1994a) 84–115.
Düring, I. (1951) *Chion of Heraclea: a Novel in Letters. Edited with Introduction and Commentary* (repr. New York 1979). Göteborg.
Düring, I. (1957) *Aristotle in the Ancient Biographical Tradition*. Göteborg.
Dunbabin, K. (1986) "*Sic erimus cuncti*... The Skeleton in Graeco-Roman Art," *Jahrbuch des deutschen archäologischen Instituts* 101: 185–255.
Duncan-Jones, R. (1982²) "The Use of Prices in the Latin Novel," *The Economy of the Roman Empire: Quantitative Studies*. Cambridge.
Durham, D.B. (1938) "Parody in Achilles Tatius," *Classical Philology* 33: 1–19.
Dyck, A.R. (1986) *Michael Psellus. The Essays on Euripides and George of Pisidia and on Heliodorus and Achilles Tatius*. Byzantina Vindobonensia 16. Vienna.
Eagleton, T. (1983) *Literary Theory*. Minneapolis.
Easterling, P., Knox, B., eds. (1985) *The Cambridge History of Classical Literature* I. Cambridge.
Eck, B. (1990) "Sur la Vie de Ctésias," *Revue des Études Grecques* 103: 409–434.
Eco, U. (1979) *Lector in Fabula. La Cooperazione Interpretativa nei Testi Narrativi*. Milan.
Edmonds, J., ed. (1916) *Daphnis & Chloe*. Loeb. Cambridge, MA.
Edwards, D. (1985) "Chariton's *Chaereas and Callirhoe*: Religion and Politics Do Mix," in K.H. Richards, ed. (1985) *Society of Biblical Literature 1985 Seminar Papers* 24: 175–181. Atlanta.
Edwards, D. (1987) "The New Testament and the Ancient Romance: A Survey of Recent Research," *Petronian Society Newsletter* 17: 9–14.
Edwards, M. (1991) "Damis the Epicurean," *Classical Quarterly* 41: 563–566.
Effe, B. (1975) "Entstehung und Funktion 'personaler' Erzählweisen in der Erzählliteratur der Antike," *Poetica* 7: 135–157.
Effe, B. (1976) "Der missglückte Selbstmord des Aristomenes (Apuleius *Met.*1.14–17). Zur Romanparodie im griechischen Eselsroman," *Hermes* 104: 362–375.
Effe, B. (1982) "Longos. Zur Funktionsgeschichte der Bukolik in der römischen Kaiserzeit," *Hermes* 110: 65–84.
Effe, B. (1987) "Der griechische Liebesroman und die Homoerotik. Ursprung und Entwicklung einer epischen Gattungskonvention," *Philologus* 131: 95–108.
Egger, B. (1988) "Zu den Frauenrollen im griechischen Roman: Die Frau als Heldin und Leserin," *Groningen Colloquia on the Novel* 1: 33–66.
Egger, B. (1990) *Women in the Greek Novel: Constructing the Feminine*. Diss., University of California-Irvine.
Egger, B. (1994) "Women and Marriage in the Greek Novel: The Boundaries of Romance," in Tatum (1994) 260–280.
Egger, B. (1994a) "Looking at Chariton's Callirhoe," in Morgan (1994) 31–48.
Ehlers, W.-W. (1985) "Mit dem Südwestmonsun nach Ceylon. Eine Interpretation der Iambul-Exzerpte Diodors," *Würzburger Jahrbücher für die Altertumswissenschaft* 11: 73–84.
Eichler, E. (1880) *De Cyrupaediae Capite Extremo*, Diss. Leipzig.
Eideneier, H. ed. (1991) *Ptochoprodromos*. Neograeca Medii Aevi, 5. Cologne.
Eisenhut, W., ed. (1973²) *Dictys Cretensis Ephemeridos Belli Troiani Libri a Lucio Septimio ex Graeco in Latinum Sermonem Translati, Accedunt Papyri Dictys Graeci in Aegypto Inventae*. (First edition 1958). Leipzig.
Eisenhut, W. (1983) "Spätantike Troja-Erzählungen—mit einem Ausblick auf die mittelalterliche Troja-Literatur," *Mittellateinisches Jahrbuch* 18: 1–28.
Elsom, H. (1992) "Callirhoe: Displaying the Phallic Woman," in Richlin (1992) 212–230.
Engelmann, H. (1963) *Der griechische Alexanderroman Rezension* γ. Vol. 2. Meisenheim am Glan.

Engelmann, H. (1975) *The Delian Aretalogy of Sarapis*. Études Préliminaires aux Religions Orientales 44. Leiden.
Erbse, H. (1966) "Xenophons Anabasis," *Gymnasium* 73: 485-505.
Erim, K. (1986) *Aphrodisias: City of Venus Aphrodite*. London.
Everson, S., ed. (1990) *Companions to Ancient Thought I: Epistemology*. Cambridge.
Eyben, E. (1980) "Family Planning in Graeco-Roman Antiquity," *Ancient Society* 11-12: 5-81.
Fagundes Duarte, L., ed. (1986) *Naceo e Amperidónia*. Lisbon.
Fauth, W. (1978) "Astraios und Zamolxis: Ueber Spuren pythagoreischer Aretalogie im Thuleroman des Antonius Diogenes," *Hermes* 106: 220-241.
Fauth, W. (1979) "Utopische Inseln in den *Wahren Geschichte* des Lukians," *Gymnasium* 86: 39-58.
Fehling, D. (1977) *Amor und Psyche: die Schöpfung des Apuleius und ihre Einwirkung auf das Märchen, eine Kritik der romantischen Märchentheorie*. Mainz.
Fehrle, E. (1910) *Die kultische Keuschheit im Altertum*. Gießen.
Feldbusch, M. (1976) *Der Brief Alexanders an Aristoteles über die Wunder Indiens. Synoptische Edition*. Meisenheim am Glan.
Ferguson, J. (1975) *Utopias of the Classical World*. London.
Fernhout, J. (1949) *Ad Apuleii Madaurensis Librum Quintum Commentarius Exegeticus*. Groningen.
Ferrini, M. (1990) "Le Parole e il Personaggio: Monologhi nel Romanzo Greco," *Giornale Italiano di Filologia* 42: 45-85.
Festugière, A.-J. (1954) *Personal Religion Among the Greeks*. Berkeley.
Fetzer, G. (1980) *Wertungsprobleme in der Trivialliteraturforschung*. Munich.
Feuillâtre, E. (1966) *Études sur les Éthiopiques d'Héliodore. Contribution à la Connaissance du Roman Grec*. Publications de la Faculté des Lettres et Sciences Humaines de Poitiers 2. Paris.
Fick-Michel, N. (1991) *Art et Mystique dans les Métamorphoses d'Apulée*. Paris.
Fine, G. (1990) "Knowledge and Belief in *Republic* V-VII," in Everson (1990) 85-115.
Finkelpearl, E. (1990) "Psyche, Aeneas and an Ass: Apuleius *Met*.6.10-6.21," *Transactions of the American Philological Association* 120: 333-348.
Finley, M.I. (1967) "Utopianism Ancient and Modern," in Wolff, K., More, B., eds. (1967) *The Critical Spirit: Essays in Honor of H. Marcuse*, 3-20, Boston, and in Finley, M.I. (1975) *The Use and Abuse of History*, 178-192. London.
Finazzi-Agrò, E. (1978) *A Novelística Portuguesa do Século XVI* (Port. transl.). Venda Nova-Amadora.
Flacelière, R., Chambry, E. (1976) *Plutarque. Vies, XI, Agis-Cléomène-Les Gracque*. Paris.
Fleskes, W. (1914) *Vermischte Beiträge zum litterarischen Porträt des Tyrannen im Anschluss an die Deklamationen*. Diss. Münster. Bonn.
Flintermann, J. (1993) *Politiek, Paideia & Pythagorisme: Griekse Identiteit, Voorstellingen Rond de Verhouding Tussen Filosofen en Alleenheersers en Politieke Ideeën in de Vita Apollonii van Philostratus*. Groningen.
Follieri, E. (1959) *Il Teseida Neogreco. Libro I. Saggio di Edizione*. Rome.
Forbes, C. (1943) "Charite and Dido," *Classical World* 37: 39-40.
Forehand, W. (1976) "Symbolic Gardens in Longus' *Daphnis and Chloe*," *Eranos* 74: 103-112.
Foucault, M. (1984a) *L'Usage de Plaisirs. Histoire de la Sexualité 2*. Paris.
Foucault, M. (1984b) *Le Souci de Soi. Histoire de la Sexualité 3*. Paris.
Fowler, A. (1982) *Kinds of Literature: An Introduction to the Theory of Genres and Modes*. Cambridge, MA.
Frangoulidis, S. (1992) "Epic Inversion in Apuleius' Tale of Tlepolemus/Haemus," *Mnemosyne* 45: 60-74.
Franklin, J. (1980) *Pompeii: the Electoral Programmata: Campaigns and Politics A.D. 71-79*. Rome.

Franz, M.L. von (1980) *Die Erlösung des Weiblichen im Manne. Der goldene Esel von Apuleius in tiefenpsychologischer Sicht.* Frankfurt.
Fraser, P. (1972) *Ptolemaic Alexandria.* 3 vols. Oxford.
Fraser, P., Matthews, E. (1987) *A Lexicon of Greek Personal Names* I. Oxford.
Fraustadt, G. (1909) *Encomiorum in Litteris Graecis usque ad Romanam Aetatem Historia.* Leipzig.
Frazer, R., trans. (1966) *The Trojan War: The Chronicles of Dictys of Crete and Dares the Phrygian.* Bloomington, IN.
Fredericks, S. (1976) "Lucian's *True History* as SF," *Science Fiction Studies* 3: 49–60.
Fredouille, J.-C. (1975) *Apulei Metamorphoseon Liber XI.* Paris.
Freedman, D., ed. (1992) *The Anchor Bible Dictionary.* New York.
Friedlander, L. (1906²) *Petronii Cena Trimalchionis.* Leipzig.
Friedman, N. (1955) "Point of View in Fiction: the Development of a Critical Concept," in *Theory of the Novel,* ed. P. Stevick, 108–137. New York.
Friedrich, H.-V., ed. (1968) *Thessalos von Tralles.* Beiträge zur klassischen Philologie 28. Meisenheim am Glan.
Frisk, H. (1960) *Griechisches etymologisches Wörterbuch,* Band 1. Heidelberg.
Fritsch, J. (1901–2) *Der Sprachgebrauch des griechischen Romanschriftstellers Heliodor und seine Verhältnis zum Atticismus.* Program des deutschen K.K. Staats-Obergymnasium in Kaaden. Kadaň.
Frye, N. (1957) *Anatomy of Criticism.* Princeton.
Frye, N. (1973) "Variedades de las Utopías Literarias," in *La Estructura Inflexible de la Obra Literaria, 151–182.* Madrid.
Frye, N. (1976) *The Secular Scripture: a Study of the Structure of Romance.* Cambridge, MA.
Fuchs, E. (1993) *Pseudologia.* Ψευδολογία: *Formen und Funktionen fiktionaler Trugrede in der griechischen Literatur der Antike.* Bibliothek der Klassischen Altertumswissenschaft, 2, 91. Heidelberg.
Fusillo, M. (1986) "'Mythos' Aristotelico e 'Récit' Narratologico," *Strumenti Critici* 1: 381–392.
Fusillo, M. (1988a) "Le Miroir de la Lune: L'*Histoire Vraie* de Lucien de la Satire à l'Utopie," *Poétique* 73: 109–135.
Fusillo, M. (1988b) "Textual Patterns and Narrative Situations in the Greek Novel," *Groningen Colloquia on the Novel* 1: 17–31.
Fusillo, M. (1989) *Il Romanzo Greco. Polifonia ed Eros.* Venice.
Fusillo, M. (1990a) "Le Conflit des Émotions: un Topos du Roman Grec Érotique," *Museum Helveticum* 47: 201–221.
Fusillo, M. (1990b) *Antonio Diogene. Le Incredibili Avventure al di là di Tule.* Palermo.
Fusillo, M. (1990c) "Il Testo nel Testo: la Citazione nel Romanzo Greco," *Materiali e Discussioni* 25: 27–48.
Fusillo, M. (1994) "Letteratura di Consumo e Romanzesca," in *Lo Spazio Letterario della Grecia Antica,* eds. G. Cambiano, L. Canfora, D. Lanza, vol. 1.3, pp. 233–273. Rome.
Fusillo, M. (1996) "How Novels End. Some Patterns of Closure in Hellenistic Narrative," in Roberts, D., Dunn, F., Fowler, D., eds. *Classical Closure: Reading the End in Greek and Latin Literature.* Princeton.
Futre Pinheiro, M. (1987) *Estruturas Técnico-Narrativas nas Etiópicas de Heliodoro.* Lisbon.
Futre Pinheiro, M. (1989) "Aspects de la Problématique Sociale et Économique dans le Roman d'Héliodore," in Liviabella Furiani (1989) 15–42.
Futre Pinheiro, M. (1991a) "Calasiris' Story and its Narrative Significance in Heliodorus' *Aethiopica,*" *Groningen Colloquia on the Novel* 4: 69–83.
Futre Pinheiro, M. (1991b) "Fonctions du Surnaturel dans les *Éthiopiques* d'Héliodore," *Bulletin de l'Association Guillaume Budé*: 359–381.
Futre Pinheiro, M. (1993) "Do Romance Grego ao Romance de Cavalaria: As *Etiópicas*

de Heliodoro e a Demanda do Santo Graal," in *Actas do IV Congresso da Associacão Hispânica de Literatura Medieval* 4, 147-154. Lisbon.
Gabba, E. (1983) "Literature," in *Sources for Ancient History*, ed. M. Crawford, 10-79. Cambridge.
Gabert, F. (1974) *Roman et Épopée dans les Éthiopiques d'Héliodore*. Paris-Sorbonne.
Gärtner, H. (1967) "Xenophon von Ephesos," in *Realencyclopädie der classischen Altertumswissenschaft* 2. Reihe, IX, 2055-2084. Stuttgart.
Gärtner, H. (1969) "Charikleia in Byzanz," *Antike und Abendland* 15: 47-69.
Gärtner, H. (1971) "Johannes Eugenikos Protheoria zu Heliodors *Aithiopika*," *Byzantinische Zeitschrift* 64: 322-325.
Gärtner, H., ed. (1984) *Beiträge zum griechischen Liebesroman*. Hildesheim.
Gaggero, G. (1989) "Testimonianze Tarde sul Faraone Sesostri," in Criscuolo (1989) 397-402.
Gallavotti, C. (1930) "Frammento di Antonio Diogene?," *Studi Italiani di Filologia Classica* n.s. 8: 247-257.
García de la Riega, C. (1909) *Literatura Galaica. El Amadís de Gaula*. Madrid.
García Gual, C. (1972) *Orígenes de la Novela*. Madrid.
García Gual, C. (1990) *Primeras Novelas Europeas*. Madrid.
García Gual, C. (1991) *Audacias Femeninas*. Madrid.
Garin, F. (1909) "Su i Romanzi Greci," *Studi Italiani di Filologia Classica* 17: 423-460.
Garin, F. (1914) "de *Historia Apollonii Tyrii*," *Mnemosyne* 42: 198-212.
Garland, L. (1990) "Sexual Morality in Byzantine Learned and Vernacular Romance," *Byzantine and Modern Greek Studies* 14: 62-120.
Garnaud, J.-P., ed. (1991) *Achille Tatius d'Alexandrie. Le Roman de Leucippé et Clitophon*. Budé. Paris.
Garson, R. (1975) "Notes on some Homeric Echoes in Heliodorus' *Aethiopica*," *Acta Classica* 18: 137-140.
Garson, R. (1978) "Works of Art in Achilles Tatius' *Leucippe and Clitophon*," *Acta Classica* 21: 83-86.
Garson, R. (1981) "The Faces of Love in the *Ephesiaka* of Anthia and Habrocomes by Xenophon of Ephesos," *Museum Africum* 7: 47-55.
Gasda, A. (1860) *Quaestiones Charitoneae*. Diss. Bratislava. Oels.
Gaspar Simões, J. (1967) *História do Romance Português*, Vol. I. Lisbon.
Geffcken, J. (1929) *Der Ausgang des griechisch-römischen Heidentums*. Heidelberg.
Genette, G. (1972) *Figures III. Discours du Récit*. Paris. (Trans. English 1980, Ithaca).
Genette, G. (1982) *Palimpsestes. La Littérature au Second Degré*. Paris.
Genette, G. (1983) *Nouveau Discours du Récit*. Paris.
Genette, G. (1986) "Introduction à l'Architexte," in *Théorie des Genres*, 88-159. Paris.
George, P. (1966) "Style and Character in the *Satyricon*," *Arion* 5: 336-358.
Georgiadou, A., Larmour, D. (1993) "Lucian and Historiography: *De Historia Conscribenda* and *Verae Historiae*," *Aufstieg und Niedergang der römischen Welt* II 34.2, 1448-1509. Berlin.
Gerschmann, K.H. (1975) *Chariton-Interpretationen*. Diss. Münster.
Gesner, C. (1970) *Shakespeare and the Greek Romance. A Study of Origins*. Lexington, KY.
Geyer, A. (1977) "Roman und Mysterienritual. Zum Problem eines Bezugs zum dionysischen Mysterienritual im Roman des Longus," *Würzburger Jahrbücher für die Altertumswissenschaft* 3: 179-196.
Giangrande, G. (1962) "On the Origins of the Greek Romance," *Eranos* 60: 132-159.
Giangrande, G. (1964) "Konjekturen zu Longos, Xenophon Ephesios und Achilleus Tatios," *Miscellanea Critica* I, 97-118. Leipzig.
Giangrande, G. (1974) review of Papanikolaou (1973), in *Journal of Hellenic Studies* 94: 197-198.
Giangrande, G. (1976) "On an Alleged Fragment of Ctesias," *Quaderni Urbinati di Cultura Classica* 23: 31-46.

Giangrande, G. (1984) "On the Origin of the Greek Novel," *Museum Philologum Londinense* 6: 41–44.
Giangrande, G. (1991) *Plutarco. Narrazioni d'Amore*. Naples.
Giangrande, L. (1976) "Les Utopies Hellénistiques," *Cahiers des Études Anciennes* 5: 17–33.
Giangrande, L. (1976/77) "Les Utopies Grecques," *Revue des Études Anciennes* 78/79: 120–128.
Gianotti, G. (1979) "Le Metamorfosi di Omero. Il Romanzo di Troia dalla Specializzazione delle Scholae ad un Pubblico di non Specialisti," *Sigma* 12: 15–32.
Gianotti, G. (1986) *Romanzo e Ideologia: Studi sulle Metamorfosi di Apuleio*. Naples.
Giarratano, C. (1929) *Apulei Metamorphoseon Libri XI*. Turin.
Gigante, M. (1960) "Il Romanzo di Eustathios Makrembolites," *Akten des XI. internationalen Byzantinistenkongresses (München 1958)*, pp. 168–81. Munich.
Gigante, M. (1962) "Lettera alla Regina o dello Stile di Ctesia," *Rivista di Filologia e Istruzione Classica* n.s. 40: 249–272.
Gigli, D. (1978) "Alcune Nuove Concordanze fra Nonno ed Achille Tazio," *Studi Ardizzoni*, eds. E. Livrea, G.A. Privitera, 433–446. Rome.
Gill, C., Wiseman, T.P., eds. (1993) *Lies and Fiction in the Ancient World*. Exeter.
Gill, C. (1993a) "Plato on Falsehood—not Fiction," in Gill (1993) 38–87.
Gillmeister, H. (1981) "The Origin of European Ball Games. A Re-evaluation and Linguistic Analysis," *Stadion* 7: 19–51.
Girard, R. (1961) *Mensonge Romantique et Vérité Romanesque*. Paris.
Glava, Z. (1937) *A Study of Heliodorus and his Romance the Aethiopica, with a Critical Evaluation of his Work as a Serious Source of Information on Ancient Aethiopia*. New York.
Gleason, C., ed. (1897) *Selections from Xenophon's Cyropaedia*. Boston.
Glucker, J. (1978) *Antiochus and the Late Academy*. Hypomnemata 56. Göttingen.
Gößwein, H.-U. (1975) *Die Briefe des Euripides*. Beiträge zur klassischen Philologie, 55. Meisenheim am Glan.
Goldhill, S. (1995) *Foucault's Virginity: Ancient Erotic Fiction and the History of Sexuality*. Cambridge.
Gomme, A. (1927) "The Athenian Hoplite Force in 431 B.C.," *Classical Quarterly* 21: 142–150.
Gomme, A. (1956) *A Historical Commentry on Thucydides*, vol. 2. Oxford.
Gomme, A. (1959) "The Population of Athens Again," *Journal of Hellenic Studies* 79: 61–68.
González García, J. (1986) *Estudios sobre el estilo de Jenofonte de Efeso*. Tesina inédita de Licenciatura. Murcia.
González García, J. (1989) "Los Conceptos Retíricos de ἀφέλεια y γλυκύτης en Jenofonte de Efeso," in *Actas del VII Congreso Español de Estudios Clásicos* II, 225–231. Madrid.
Goold, G.P., ed. (1995) *Chariton: Callirhoe*. Loeb. Cambridge.
Goolden, P. (1955) "Antiochus's Riddle in Gower and Shakespeare," *Review of English Studies* 6: 245–251.
Goossens, G. (1950) "Le Sommaire des *Persica* de Ctesias par Photius," *Revue Belge de Philologie et d'Histoire* 28: 513–521.
Grenfell, B.P., Hunt, A.S., Hogarth, D.G. (1900) *Fayûm Towns and their Papyri*. P. Fay. 1: 74–82. London.
Grenfell, B.P., Hunt, A.S. (1910) *The Oxyrhynchus Papyri* 7. P.Oxy. 1019: 143–146. London.
Griffiths, J. Gwyn (1970) *Plutarch's De Iside et Osiride*. Cardiff.
Griffiths, J. Gwyn (1975) *Apuleius of Madaura: the Isis-Book*. Études Préliminaires aux Religions Orientales 39. Leiden.
Griffiths, J. Gwyn (1978a) "Isis in the *Metamorphoses* of Apuleius," in Hijmans (1978a) 141–161.

Griffiths, J. Gwyn (1978b) "Xenophon of Ephesus on Isis and Alexandreia," in Boer, M. de, ed., *Hommages à Maarten J. Vermaseren* I, 409-437. Leiden.
Grignaschi, M. (1967) "Le Roman Épistolaire Classique Conservé dans la Version Arabe de Salim abu-l 'Ala'," *Le Museon* 80: 211-264.
Grimal, P., trans. (1958) *Pétrone, Le Satiricon*, in Grimal, P., trans., *Romans Grecs et Latins*. Tours.
Grimal, P., trans. (1958a) *Chariton d'Aphrodisias: les Aventures de Chéréas et de Callirhoé*, in Grimal (1958).
Grimal, P. (1963) *Apulei: Metamorphoseis (IV, 28-VI, 24)*. Paris.
Grimal, P. (1971) "Le Calame Égyptien d'Apulée," *Revue des Études Anciennes* 73: 343-355.
Grimal, P. (1992) "Essai sur la Formation du Genre Romanesque dans l'Antiquité," in Baslez (1992) 13-19.
Gronewald, M. (1976) "Ein verkannter Papyrus des Achilleus Tatios (P.Oxy.1014 = Achilleus Tatios 4.14.2-5)," *Zeitschrift für Papyrologie und Epigraphik* 22: 14-17.
Gronewald, M. (1979a) "Ein Fragment aus den *Aithiopica* des Heliodor," *Zeitschrift für Papyrologie und Epigraphik* 34: 19-21.
Gronewald, M. (1979b) "Ein neues Fragment zu einem Roman," *Zeitschrift für Papyrologie und Epigraphik* 35: 15-20.
Gronewald, M. (1993) "Zum Ninos-Roman," *Zeitschrift für Papyrologie und Epigraphik* 97: 1-6.
Grotanelli, C. (1987) "The Ancient Novel and Biblical Narrative," *Quaderni Urbinati di Cultura Classica* 27: 7-34
Gruen, E. (1993) "The Polis in the Hellenistic World," in Rosen, R., Farrell, J., eds., *Nomodeiktes. Greek Studies in Honor of Martin Ostwald*, 339-354. Ann Arbor.
Günther, R., Müller, R. (1988) *Das goldene Zeitalter: Utopien der hellenistisch-römischen Antike*. Stuttgart.
Guida, A. (1975) "Una nuova Collazione del Codice di Senofonte Efesio," *Prometheus* 1: 65-79, 279.
Guida, A. (1981) "Nuovi Testimoni di Longo e Achille Tazio," *Prometheus* 7: 1-10.
Gunderson, L. (1980) *Alexander's Letter to Aristotle about India*. Meisenheim am Glan.
Gunn, D. (1988) *Psychoanalysis and Fiction. An Exploration of Literary and Psychoanalytic Borders*. Cambridge.
Gutu, M. (1972) "Quelques Observations sur les Rapports entre le Roman Grec et la Rhétorique Antique," *Studii Clasice* 14: 129-140.
Habrich, E., ed. (1960) *Iamblichi Babyloniacorum Reliquiae*. Leipzig.
Hadas, M. (1959) *Hellenistic Culture. Fusion and Diffusion*. New York.
Hägg, T. (1966) "Die *Ephesiaka* des Xenophon Ephesios—Original oder Epitome?," *Classica et Mediaevalia* 27: 118-161.
Hägg, T. (1971a) *Narrative Technique in Ancient Greek Romances. Studies of Chariton, Xenophon Ephesius, and Achilles Tatius*. Stockholm.
Hägg, T. (1971b) "The Naming of the Characters in the Romance of Xenophon Ephesius," *Eranos* 69: 25-59.
Hägg, T. (1972) "Some Technical Aspects of the Characterization in Chariton's Romance," *Studi Classici in Onore di Quintino Cataudella*, vol. II, 545-556. Catania.
Hägg, T. (1983) *The Novel in Antiquity*. Oxford.
Hägg, T. (1984) "The Parthenope Romance Decapitated?," *Symbolae Osloenses* 59: 61-92.
Hägg, T. (1985) "Metiochus at Polycrates' Court," *Eranos* 83: 92-102.
Hägg, T. (1986) "The Oriental Reception of Greek Novels: A Survey with Some Preliminary Considerations," *Symbolae Osloenses* 61: 99-131.
Hägg, T. (1987a) "*Callirhoe* and *Parthenope*: the Beginnings of the Historical Novel," *Classical Antiquity* 6: 184-204.
Hägg, T. (1987b) *Eros und Tyche. Der Roman in der antiken Welt*, trans. K. Brodersen. Mainz.

Hägg, T. (1989) "Hermes and the Invention of the Lyre: An Unorthodox Version," *Symbolae Osloenses* 64: 36–73.
Hägg, T. (1994) "Orality, Literacy, and the 'Readership' of the Early Greek Novel," in Eriksen, R., ed., *Contexts of Pre-Novel Narrative: the European Tradition*, 47–81. Berlin.
Hagedorn, D., Koenen, L. (1970) "Eine Handschrift des Achilleus Tatios," *Museum Helveticum* 27: 49–57.
Hagendahl, H. (1967) *Augustine and the Latin Classics*. 2 vols. Gothenburg.
Haight, E. (1943) *Essays on the Greek Romance*. New York.
Haight, E. (1945) "Apuleius and Boccaccio," in ead., *More Essays on Greek Romances*. New York.
Haight, E. (1955) *The Life of Alexander of Macedon*. New York.
Hall, J. (1981) *Lucian's Satire*. New York.
Halperin, D. (1990) *One Hundred Years of Homosexuality and Other Essays on Greek Love*. New York.
Hani, J. (1978) "Le Personnage de Charicleia dans les *Éthiopiques*: Incarnation de l'Idéal Moral et Religieux d'une Époque," *Bulletin de l'Association Guillaume Budé*: 268–273.
Hansen, M. (1981) "The Number of Athenian Hoplites in 431 B.C.," *Symbolae Osloenses* 56: 19–32.
Harder, R. (1993) *Die Frauenrollen bei Euripides. Untersuchungen zu Alkestis, Medeia, Hekabe, Erechtheus, Elektra, Troades und Iphigeneia in Aulis*. Drama, Supplement 1. Stuttgart.
Harlan, E.C. (1965) *The Description of Paintings as a Literary Device and its Application in Achilles Tatius*. Diss. Columbia University, New York.
Harner, J. (1978–92) *English Renaissance Prose Fiction, 1500–1600: An Annotated Bibliography of Criticism*. 3 vols. Boston.
Harris, W. (1989) *Ancient Literacy*. Cambridge.
Harrison, S.J. (1989) "Two Notes on Achilles Tatius," *Philologus* 133: 153–154.
Harrison, S.J. (1990a) "The Speaking Book: the Prologue to Apuleius' *Metamorphoses*," *Classical Quarterly* n.s. 40: 507–513.
Harrison, S.J. (1990b) "Some Odyssean Scenes in Apuleius' *Metamorphoses*," *Materiali e Discussioni* 25: 193–201.
Hartman, G. (1970) *Beyond Formalism*. New Haven.
Harward, J. (1932) "On the Sokratic Epistles," in Harward, J. (1932) *The Platonic Epistles: Translated with Introduction and Notes*, 79–86. Cambridge.
Haslam, M. (1980–1986) "3331. Life of Aesop," *The Oxyrhynchus Papyri* 47: 53–56; "3720. Life of Aesop (Addendum to 3331)," *ibid.* 53: 149–172.
Haslam, M. (1981) *Papyri Greek & Egyptian: Edited by Various Hands in Honour of Eric Gardner Turner on the Occasion of his Seventieth Birthday* (= Graeco-Roman Memoirs 68) No. 8: 35–45. Oxford.
Hausrath, A. (1918) *Achiqar und Äsop: Das Verhältnis der orientalischen und griechischen Fabeldichtung*. Sitzungsberichte der Heidelberger Akademie der Wissenschaften, philosophisch-historische Klasse, 1918, 2. Heidelberg.
Hausrath, A. (1940) *Aesopische Fabeln: Zusammengestellt und ins Deutsche übertragen. Gefolgt von einer Abhandlung: Die Aesoplegende*. Munich.
Havelock, E. (1982) *The Literate Revolution in Greece and its Cultural Consequences*. Princeton.
Heckel, W. (1988) *The Last Days and Testament of Alexander the Great: a Prosopographic Study*. Stuttgart.
Hefti, V. (1950) *Zur Erzählungstechnik in Heliodors Aethiopica*. Vienna.
Hegel, G. (1836–1838) *Vorlesungen über die Aesthetik*. Berlin.
Heibges, S. (1911) *De Clausulis Charitoneis*. Diss. Münster. Halle.
Heine, R. (1978) "Picaresque Novel Versus Allegory," in Hijmans (1978a) 25–42.
Heine, S. (1986) *Frauen der frühen Christenheit. Zur historischen Kritik einer feministischen Theologie*. 3rd edition 1990. Göttingen.
Heinse, W., trans. (1773) *Begebenheiten des Enkolp*. (Often reprinted). Rome [Schwabach].

Heinze, R. (1899) "Petron und der griechische Roman," *Hermes* 34: 494–519.
Heiserman, A. (1977) *The Novel before the Novel. Essays and Discussions.* Chicago.
Helm, R., ed. (1931³) *Apuleius Metamorphoseon Libri XI.* Leipzig.
Helm, R. (1955) "Apuleius' *Apologie,* ein Meisterwerk des zweiten Sophistik," *Das Altertum* 1: 86–108.
Helm, R. (1956²) *Der antike Roman.* (First edition 1948). Göttingen.
Helms, J. (1966) *Character Portrayal in the Romance of Chariton.* The Hague.
Henne, H. (1936) "La Géographie de l'Egypte dans Xénophon d'Ephèse," *Revue d'Histoire de la Philosophie et d'Histoire Générale de la Civilisation* 4: 97–106.
Henrichs, A. (1968) "Achilleus Tatios, aus Buch III [17.5–24.1] (P.Colon.inv.901)," *Zeitschrift für Papyrologie und Epigraphik* 2: 211–226.
Henrichs, A. (1972) *Die Phoinikika des Lollianos.* Papyrologische Texte und Abhandlungen, No. 14. Bonn.
Henry, R., Schamps, J., eds. (1959–91) *Photius Bibliothèque.* 9 vols. Paris.
Hepding, H. (1913) "Hessische Hausinschriften und byzantinische Rätsel," *Hessische Blätter für Volkskunde* 12: 161–182.
Hercher, R. (1859) *Erotici Scriptores Graeci.* 2 vols. Leipzig.
Hercher, R. (1873) *Epistolographi Graeci.* (repr. Amsterdam 1965). Paris.
Hermann, A. (1938) *Die altägyptische Königsnovelle.* Hamburg.
Herrmann, L. (1956) review of Vilborg (1955) in *L'Antiquité Classique* 25 (1956) 181f.
Hernández Lara, C. (1990) "Rhetorical Aspects of Chariton of Aphrodisias," *Giornale Italiano di Filologia* 42: 267–274.
Hernández Lara, C. (1994) *Estudios sobre el Aticismo de Caritón de Afrodisias.* Amsterdam.
Hertlein, F., ed. (1859–60) *Xenophons Cyropaedie.* Berlin.
Hertz, W. (1905) *Gesammelte Abhandlungen.* Stuttgart/Berlin.
Hesberg-Tonn, B. von (1983) *Coniunx Carissima. Untersuchungen zum Normcharakter im Erscheinungsbild der römischen Frau.* Diss., Stuttgart.
Hesseling, D.C. (1919) *L'Achilléide Byzantine, avec une Introduction, des Observations et un Index.* Amsterdam.
Heubner, F. (1985) "Studien zum Barbarenbegriff bei Herodot," in *Kultur und Fortschritt in der Blütezeit der griechischen Polis,* ed. E. Kluwe, 91–108. Berlin.
Hexter, R. (1988) *Speculum* 63: 186–190.
Higgins, W. (1977) *Xenophon the Athenian.* Albany, N.Y.
Highet, G. (1941) "Petronius the Moralist," *Transactions of the American Philological Association* 72: 176–194.
Highet, G. (1949) *The Classical Tradition.* Oxford.
Highet, G. (1970) "Whose *Satyricon*—Petronius's or Fellini's?," *Horizon* 12: 42–47.
Highet, G. (1973) "The Huntsman and the Castaway," *Greek, Roman and Byzantine Studies* 14: 35–40, and in Highet, G. (1983) *The Classical Papers,* 58–62. New York.
Hijmans, B., Paardt, R. van der, Smits, E., Westendorp Boerma, R., Westerbrink, A. (1977) *Apuleius Madaurensis Metamorphoses Book IV.* 1–21. Groningen.
Hijmans, B., Paardt, R. van der, eds. (1978a) *Aspects of Apuleius' Golden Ass.* Groningen.
Hijmans, B. (1978b) "Significant Names and Their Function in Apuleius' *Metamorphoses,*" in Hijmans (1978a) 107–122.
Hijmans, B., Paardt, R. van der, Schmidt, V., Westendorp Boerma, R., Westerbrink, A. (1981) *Apuleius Madaurensis Metamorphoses Books VI. 25–32 and VII.* Groningen.
Hijmans, B., Settels, C., Wesseling, B., Paardt, R. van der, Schmidt, V., Westendorp Boerma, R. (1985) *Apuleius Madaurensis Metamorphoses Book VIII.* Groningen.
Hijmans, B. (1987) "Apuleius Philosophus Platonicus," *Aufstieg und Niedergang der römischen Welt* II 36.1: 395–475. Berlin.
Hikichi, M. (1965) "Eros and Tyche in Achilles Tatius," *Journal of Classical Studies* 13: 116–126. (In Japanese with summary in English.)
Hilberg, I. (1876) Εὐσταθίου Πρωτονωβελεσίμου τοῦ Μακρεμβολίτου τῶν καθ' Ὑσμίνην καὶ Ὑσμινίαν λόγοι ια'. Vienna.

Hildebrand, G., ed. (1842) *Apulei Opera Omnia*. 2 vols. Leipzig.
Hilka, A., ed. (1935) *Iter Alexandri ad Paradisum*, in L.P.G. Peckham and M.S. La Du, *La Prise de Defur and Le Voyage d'Alexandre au Paradis Terrestre*. Princeton.
Hilka, A., Steffens, K. (1979) *Historia Alexandri Magni: Rezension J¹*. Meisenheim am Glan.
Hilpert, R. (1992) "Bild und Text in Heinrich Steinhöwels 'leben des hochberümten fabeldichters Esopi'," in Holzberg (1992a) 131–154.
Hirsch, St. W. (1985a) *The Friendship of the Barbarians. Xenophon and the Persian Empire*. Hanover, NH.
Hirsch, St. W. (1985b) "1001 Iranian Nights. History and Fiction in Xenophon's *Cyropaedia*," in *The Greek Historians. Literature and History, Papers presented to A.E. Raubitschek*, ed. M. Jameson, 65–85. Saratoga.
Hirschig, W., ed. (1856) Χαρίτωνος Ἀφροδισέως τῶν περὶ Χαιρέαν καὶ Καλλιρρόην, in Hirschig, W., ed. (1856) *Erotici Scriptores*. Paris
Hirzel, R. (1895) *Der Dialog. Ein literarhistorischer Versuch*. 2 vols. Leipzig.
Höistad, R. (1948) *Cynic Hero and Cynic King*. Uppsala.
Hölscher, U. (1988) *Die Odyssee, Epos zwischen Märchen und Roman*. München.
Hörandner, W. (1974) *Theodoros Prodromos: Historische Gedichte*. Wiener Byzantinistische Studien, No. 11. Vienna.
Hofmann, H. (1993) "Die Flucht des Erzählers: Narrative Stategien in den Ehebruchsgeschichten in Apuleius' *Goldenem Esel*," *Groningen Colloquia on the Novel* 5: 111–141.
Holbek, B. (1977) "Äsop," *Enzyklopädie des Märchens* 1: 882–889.
Holden, H. (1870) *The Cyropaedia of Xenophon, Commentary in 4 volumes*. Cambridge.
Holland, N. (1968) *The Dynamics of Literary Response*. New York.
Holland, N. (1975) *5 Readers Reading*. New Haven.
Holton, D. (1974) *The Tale of Alexander: the Rhymed Version*. Thessaloniki.
Holton, D. (1991a) "Romance", in idem, ed., *Literature and Society and Renaissance Crete*, 205–237. Cambridge.
Holton, D. (1991b) *Erotokritos*. Studies in Modern Greek. Bristol Classical Press (UK); Caratzas: New York.
Holzberg, N. (1984) "Apuleius und der Verfasser des griechischen Eselromans," *Würzburger Jahrbücher für die Altertumswissenschaft* 10: 161–178.
Holzberg, N. (1986) *Der antike Roman: Eine Einführung*. Munich.
Holzberg, N. (1990) "The *Historia Apollonii Regis Tyri* and the *Odyssey*," *Groningen Colloquia on the Novel* 3: 91–101.
Holzberg, N. (1992a) *Der Äsop-Roman: Motivgeschichte und Erzählstruktur*. Classica Monacensia, 6. Tübingen.
Holzberg, N. (1992b) "Der Äsop-Roman: Eine strukturanalytische Interpretation," in Holzberg (1992a) 33–75.
Holzberg, N. (1993a) *Die antike Fabel: Eine Einführung*. Darmstadt.
Holzberg, N. (1993b) "A Lesser Known 'Picaresque' Novel of Greek Origin: the *Aesop Romance* and its Influence," *Groningen Colloquia on the Novel* 5: 1–16.
Holzberg, N., ed. (1994a) *Der griechische Briefroman. Gattungstypologie und Textanalyse*. Classica Monacensia, 8. Tübingen.
Holzberg, N. (1994b) "Der griechische Briefroman: Versuch einer Gattungstypologie," in Holzberg (1994a) 1–52.
Holzberg, N. (1995) *The Ancient Novel: an Introduction*. London.
Holzberg, N. (1995a) "Historie als Fiktion—Fiktion als Historie," in *Rom und der griechische Osten*, ed. Ch. Schubert, 93–101. Stuttgart.
Hooff, A. van (1990) *From Autothanasia to Suicide: Self-Killing in Classical Antiquity*. London.
Hook, D. (1985) "Naceo e Amperidónia: A Sixteenth-Century Portuguese Sentimental Romance," *Portuguese Studies* 1: 11–46.
Hopkins, K. (1993) "Novel Evidence for Roman Slavery," *Past and Present* 138: 3–27.

Horsfall, N. (1989) "The Uses of Literacy and the *Cena Trimalchionis*," *Greece and Rome* 36: 74–89, 194–209.
Hostetter, W. (1955) *A Linguistic Study of the Vulgar Greek Life of Aesop*. Diss. University of Illinois. Urbana.
Hower, C. (1936) *Studies on the So-Called Accursiana Recension of the Life and Fables of Aesop*. Diss. University of Illinois. Urbana.
Hoyoux, J. (1969) *Le Carnet de Voyage de Jérôme Aléandre en France et à Liège*. Bibliothèque de l'Institut Historique Belge de Rome, No. 18. Brussels.
Huber, G. (1990) *Das Motiv der Witwe von Ephesus in lateinischen Texten der Antike und des Mittelalters*. Tübingen.
Huchthausen, L. (1974) "Herkunft und ökonomische Stellung weiblicher Adressaten von Reskripten des Codex Iustinianus (2. und 3. Jh. u.Z.)," *Klio* 56: 199–228.
Hüsing, G. (1929) "Panchaia," in Mžik, H., ed. (1929) *Beiträge zur historischen Geographie, Kulturgeographie, Ethnographie und Kartographie, vornehmlich des Orients*, 99–111. Leipzig.
Huet, P.-D. (1670) *Traité de l'Origine des Romans*. Reprint 1942, ed. A. Kok. Amsterdam.
Hull, D.B. (1990) *Digenis Akritas: the Two-Blood Border Lord. The Grottaferrata Version Translated with an Introduction and Notes*. Athens, Ohio.
Hunger, H. (1978) *Die hochsprachliche profane Literatur der Byzantiner*. 2 vols. Byzantinische Handbuch. Munich.
Hunger, H. (1980) *Antiker und byzantinischer Roman*. Sitzungsberichte der Heidelberger Akademie der Wissenschaften, Phil.-hist.Kl.3. Heidelberg.
Hunt, J. (1994) review of Schmeling (1988) in *Gnomon* 66: 304–320.
Hunter, R. (1983) *A Study of Daphnis & Chloe*. Cambridge.
Hunter, R. (1993) *The Argonautica of Apollonius. Literary Studies*. Cambridge.
Hunter, R. (1994) "History and Historicity in the Romance of Chariton," in *Aufstieg und Niedergang der römischen Welt* II 34.2, 1055–1086. Berlin.
Hunter, R. (1996) "Longus and Plato," in *Der antike Roman und seine mittelalterliche Rezeption*. (Papers presented at a conference in Ascona, April 1995). Basel.
Irmscher, J., Strecker, G. (1992) "The Pseudo-Clementines," in Schneemelcher (1992) 2: 483–493.
Iser, W. (1978) *The Act of Reading: A Theory of Aesthetic Response*. Baltimore.
Jacoby, F. (1907) "Euemeros von Messene," *Pauly-Wissowa* 6, 1: 952–972, and in Jacoby (1956) 175–185.
Jacoby, F. (1912) "Hekataios von Abdera," *Pauly-Wissowa* 7, 2: 2750–2769, and in Jacoby (1956) 227–237.
Jacoby, F. (1922) "Ktesias," *Pauly-Wissowa* 11, 2: 2032–2073, and in Jacoby (1956) 311–332.
Jacoby, F. (1956) *Griechische Historiker*. Stuttgart.
Jauss, H. (1970) "Literaturgeschichte als Provokation der Literaturwissenschaft," *Jahrbuch für Internationale Germanistik* 2: 144–207.
Jauss, H. (1982) *Ästhetische Erfahrung und literarische Hermeneutik*. Frankfurt.
Jauss, H. (1986) "Littérature Médiévale et Théorie des Genres," *Théorie des Genres*, ed. G. Genette, T. Todorov, 37–76. Paris.
Jedrkiewicz, S. (1989) *Sapere e Paradosso nell'Antichità: Esopo e la Favola*. Rome.
Jeffreys, E. (1993) "Place as a Factor in the Editions of Early Demotic Texts," in Panayotakis (1993) vol. 1, pp. 310–324.
Jeffreys, E., Papathomopoulos, M. (forthcoming) Ὁ Πόλεμος τῆς Τρωάδος: *Critical Edition with Introduction, Notes and Glossary*. Thessaloniki.
Jeffreys, M. (1974) "The Nature and Origins of the Political Verse," *Dumbarton Oaks Papers* 28: 141–195.
Jeništová, V. (1953) "Nejstarší Román Světové Literatury (Zlomky reckého románu o Ninovi)," *Listy Filologické* n.s. 1: 30–54, pl. 4, 210–228., English summary 319.
Johne, R. (1985) "Dido und Charikleia," in *Die Frau in der Antike*. Kolloquium der Winckelmann-Gesellschaft, Beiträge 17: 75–82. Stendal.

Johne, R. (1987) "Dido und Charikleia. Zur Gestaltung der Frau bei Vergil und im griechischen Liebersroman," *Eirene* 24: 21–33.
Johne, R. (1988) "Vergleich und Analogie bei Frauengestalten in der Neuen Komödie und im antiken Roman," *Wissenschaftliche Zeitschrift der Universität Rostock* 37.2: 12–15.
Johne, R. (1989) "Übersicht über die antiken Romanautoren bzw. -werke mit Datierung und weiterführender Bibliographie," in Kuch (1989a) 198–230.
Johne, R. (1989a) "Zur Figurencharakteristik im antiken Roman," in Kuch (1989a) 150–177.
Johne, R. (1992) "Der 'Eccius Dedolatus' Willibald Pirckheimers als zeitgenössische Satire mit antiken Formelementen," *Renaissance-Hefte* 1.3: 48–59.
Jones, A.H.M. (1940) *The Greek City from Alexander to Justinian*. Oxford.
Jones, A.H.M. (1957) *Athenian Democracy*. Oxford.
Jones, C.P. (1978) *The Roman World of Dio Chrysostom*. Cambridge, MA.
Jones, C.P. (1980) "Apuleius' *Metamorphoses* and Lollianos' *Phoinikika*," *Phoenix* 34: 243–254.
Jones, C.P. (1986) *Culture and Society in Lucian*. Cambridge, MA.
Jones, C.P. (1992a) "La Personnalité de Chariton," in Baslez (1992) 161–167.
Jones, C.P. (1992b) "Hellenistic History in Chariton of Aphrodisias," *Chiron* 22: 91–102.
Jones, F. (1987) "The Narrator and the Narrative of the *Satyrica*," *Latomus* 46: 810–819.
Jones, F.S. (1992) "Clementines, Pseudo," in Freedman (1992) 1: 1061–1062.
Jouan, F. (1977) "Les Thèmes Romanesques dans l'*Euboicos* de Dion Chrysostome," *Revue des Études Grecques* 90: 38–46.
Jouan, F., Auger, D. (1983) "Sur le Corpus des *Lettres d'Euripide*," in *Mélanges Edouard Delebecque*, 183–198. Aix-en-Provence.
Jouanno, C. (1989) "Nicétas Eugénianos, un Héritier du Roman Grec," *Revue de Études Grecques* 102: 346–360.
Jouanno, C. (1992) "Les Barbares dans le Roman Byzantin du XIIe Siècle. Fonction d'un Topos," *Byzantion* 62: 264–300.
Jouve, V. (1992) *L'Effet Personnage dans le Roman*. Paris.
Jovy, E. (1899–1913) *François Tissard et Jérôme Aléandre*. Reprinted Geneva, 3 vols., 1971. Geneva.
Jüthner, J. (1923) *Hellenen und Barbaren. Aus der Geschichte des Nationalbewußtseins*. Leipzig.
Jüthner, J. (1950) "Barbar," in *Reallexikon für Antike und Christentum*, Band 1, 1173–1176. Stuttgart.
Junod, E. (1988) "Le Dossier des 'Actes de Jean': État de la Question et Perspectives Nouvelles," *Aufstieg und Niedergang der römischen Welt* II 25.6, 4293–4362.
Kasper, K., Wuckel, D. (1982) *Grundbegriffe der Literaturanalyse*. Leipzig.
Kazhdan, A. and Franklin, S. (1984) *Studies on Byzantine Literature of the Eleventh and Twelfth Centuries*. Cambridge.
Kechagioglou, G. (1982a) "'Ο βυζαντινὸς καὶ μεταβυζαντινὸς Συντίπας· γιὰ μιὰ ν°α ἔκδοση," *Graeco-Arabica* 1: 105–130.
Kechagioglou, G. (1982b) Ἀπόκοπος - Ἀπολώνιος - Ἱστορία τῆς Σωσάννης. Λαϊκὰ Λογοτεχνικὰ Ἔντυπα, vol. 1. Athens.
Kechagioglou, G. (1986) "Πρῶτες ἐκδόσεις τοῦ Ἀπολλωνίου: νέα στοιχεῖα," *Hellenika* 37: 145–159.
Kechagioglou, G. (1988) "Translation of Eastern 'Novels' and their Influence on Late Byzantine and Modern Greek Fiction (11th–18th centuries)?" in Beaton (1988) 156–166.
Keller, W. (1910) "Xenophon's Acquaintance with the History of Herodotus," *Classical Journal* 6: 252–259.
Kennedy, D. (1993) *The Arts of Love*. Cambridge.

Kennedy, G. (1978) "Encolpius and Agamemnon in Petronius," *American Journal of Philology* 99: 171–178.
Kenney, E.J., ed. (1990a) *Apuleius: Cupid and Psyche*. Cambridge.
Kenney, E.J. (1990b) "Psyche and her Mysterious Husband," in Russell (1990) 175–198.
Kenyon, F. (1951) *Books and Readers in Ancient Greece and Rome*. 2nd edition. Oxford.
Kerényi, K. (1927) *Die griechisch-orientalische Romanliteratur in religionsgeschichtlicher Beleuchtung*. (Reprint, Darmstadt 1964.) Tübingen.
Kerényi, K. (1971) *Der antike Roman: Einführung und Textauswahl*. Darmstadt.
Kestner, J. (1973) "Ekphrasis as Frame in Longus' Daphnis and Chloe," *Classical Weekly* 67: 166–171.
Kettle, A.,(1967²) *An Introduction to the English Novel*. Vol. 1. London.
Keydell, R. (1966) "Zur Datierung der Aithiopika Heliodors," in *Polychronion Festschrift für Franz Dölger zum 75. Geburtstag*, 345–350. Heidelberg. Reprinted in Gärtner (1984) 467–472.
Keyes, C. (1922) "The Structure of Heliodorus' Aethiopica," *Studies in Philology* 19: 42–51.
King, K. (1987) *Achilles. Paradigms of the War Hero from Homer to the Middle Ages*. Berkeley.
Kirk, E. (1980) *Menippean Satire. An Annotated Catalogue of Text and Criticism*. New York.
Kirsch, W. (1981) *Xenophon von Ephesos, Abrokomes und Anthia. Epilog*. Leipzig.
Kitto, H.D.F. (1939) *Greek Tragedy. A Literary Study*. London.
Klebs, E. (1889) "Zur Composition von Petronius Satirae," *Philologus* 47: 623–635.
Klebs, E. (1899) *Die Erzählung von Apollonius aus Tyrus. Eine geschichtliche Untersuchung über ihre lateinische Urform und ihre späteren Bearbeitungen*. Berlin.
Kloft, H. (1989) "Imagination und Realität. Überlegungen zur Wirtschaftsstruktur des Romans Daphnis und Chloe," *Groningen Colloquia on the Novel* 2: 54–61.
Knauth, W. (1975) *Das Altiranische Fürstenideal von Xenophon bis Ferdousi*. Wiesbaden.
Knös, B. (1945) *Un Ambassadeur de l'Hellénisme: Janus Lascaris*. Uppsala.
Knös, B. (1962) "Qui est l'Auteur de Callimaque et Chrysorrhoé?," *Hellenika* 17: 274–295.
Knox, B. (1985) "Books and Readers in the Greek World," in Easterling (1985) 1–41.
Koch, M. (1979) "Zur Utopie in der Alten Welt," in Sund, H., Zimmermann, M., eds. (1979) *Auf den Weg gebracht: Idee und Wirklichkeit der Universität Konstanz*, 399–417. Konstanz.
Köhler, E. (1974) *L'Aventure Chevaleresque*. Paris.
Köhler, L. (1928) *Die Briefe des Sokrates und der Sokratiker: Herausgegeben, Übersetzt und Kommentiert*. Philologus Suppl. 20, 2. Leipzig.
Koenen, L. (1985) "The Dream of Nektanebos," *Bulletin of the American Society of Papyrologists* 22: 171–194.
Körte, A. (1927) *Archiv für Papyrusforschung* 8: 271. Survey of Literary Papyri, no. 699.
Körte, A. (1937) *Die Menschen Menanders*. Berichte über die Verhandlungen der Sächsischen Akademie der Wissenschaften zu Leipzig, Phil.-hist.Kl.89.3. Leipzig
Körting, G. (1874) *Dictys und Dares. Ein Beitrag zur Geschichte der Troja-Sage in ihrem Uebergange aus der antiken in die romantische Form*. Halle/Saale.
Kövendi, D. (1966) "Heliodors Aithiopika. Eine literarische Würdigung," in *Die Araber in der alten Welt*, eds. F. Altheim, R. Stiehl, 3.136–197. Berlin.
Konstan, D., Roberts, M., eds. (1985) *Historia Apollonii Regis Tyri*. Bryn Mawr.
Konstan, D. (1987) "La Rappresentazione dei Rapporti Erotici nel Romanzo Greco," *Materiali e Discussioni* 19: 9–27.
Konstan, D., Mitsis, P. (1990) "Chion of Heraclea: a Philosophical Novel in Letters," *Apeiron* 23: 257–279.
Konstan, D. (1994a) *Sexual Symmetry: Love in the Ancient Novel and Related Genres*. Princeton.

Konstan, D. (1994b) "*Apollonius, King of Tyre* and the Greek Novel," in Tatum (1994) 173–182.
Korn, M., Reitzen, S. (1986) *Concordantia Petroniana. Computerkonkordanz zu den Satyrica des Petron*. Hildesheim.
Kortekaas, G., ed. (1984) *Historia Apollonii Regis Tyri*. Groningen.
Koskimies, R. (1935) *Theorie des Romans*. (Reprint 1966.) Darmstadt.
Kost, K. (1971) *Musaios, Hero und Leander*. Bonn.
Kowarna, R. (1959) *Das Weltbild Heliodors in den äthiopischen Geschichten*. Diss., Vienna.
Krappe, A. (1924) "Euripides' *Alcmaeon* and the *Apollonius Romance*," *Classical Quarterly* 18: 57–58.
Kratz, H. (1973) *Wolfram von Eschenbachs Parzival*. Bern.
Krenkel, W. (1971) "Erotica I: Der Abortus in der Antike," *Wissenschaftliche Zeitschrift der Universität Rostock, gesellschafts- und sprachwissenschaftliche Reihe* 6: 443–452.
Kriaras, E., ed. (1955) Βυζαντινὰ ἱπποτικὰ μυθιστορήματα. Athens.
Kristeva, J. (1970) *Le Texte du Roman. Approche Sémiologique d'une Structure Discursive Transformationelle*. The Hague.
Kroll, W. (1926) *Historia Alexandri Magni*. Recensio Vetusta. Berlin.
Krumeich, C. (1993) *Hieronymus und die christlichen Feminae Clarissimae*. Habelts Dissertationsdrucke. Edition Alte Geschichte 1, Heft 36. Bonn.
Kuch, H. (1976) "Nachwort" Zur Euripides-Übersetzung von D. Ebener, *Alkestis, Medeia, Hippolytos, Hekabe, Die Hilfeflehenden*. Reclams Universal-bibliothek 670, 237–260. Leipzig.
Kuch, H. (1985) "Gattungstheoretische Überlegungen zum antiken Roman," *Philologus* 129: 3–19.
Kuch, H., ed. (1989a) *Der antike Roman: Untersuchungen zur literarischen Kommunikation und Gattungsgeschichte*. Berlin.
Kuch, H. (1989b) "Die Herausbildung des antiken Romans als Literaturgattung: Theoretische Positionen, historische Voraussetzungen und literarische Prozesse," in Kuch (1989a) 11–51.
Kuch, H. (1989c) "Funktionswandlungen des antiken Romans," in Kuch (1989a) 52–81.
Kuch, H. (1989d) "Die 'Barbaren' und der antike Roman," *Das Altertum* 35: 80–86.
Kuch, H. (1992) "Zur Gattungsgeschichte und Gattungstheorie des antiken Romans," *Eikasmos* 3: 223–233.
Kudlien, F. (1989) "Kindesaussetzungen im antiken Roman: ein Thema zwischen Fiktionalität und Wirklichkeit," *Groningen Colloquia on the Novel* 2: 25–44.
Küchler, M. (1986) *Schweigen, Schmuck und Schleier. Drei neutestamentliche Vorschriften zur Verdrängung der Frauen auf dem Hintergrund einer frauenfeindlichen Exegese des Alten Testaments im antiken Judentum*. Göttingen.
Küchler, W. (1911) "Martin Fumée's Roman *Du Vray et Parfait Amour* (Ein Renaissanceroman)," *Zeitschrift für französische Sprache und Literatur* 37: 139–225.
Kussl, R. (1990) "Die *Metamorphosen* des 'Lucius von Patrai': Untersuchungen zu Photius, *Bibl.* 129," *Rheinisches Museum* 133: 379–388.
Kussl, R. (1991) *Papyrusfragmente griechischer Romane. Ausgewählte Untersuchungen*. Classica Monacensia, 2. Tübingen.
Kussl, R. (1992) "Achikar, Tinuphis und Äsop," in Holzberg (1992a) 23–30.
Kytzler, B., trans. (1968) *Xenophon von Ephesos: Die Waffen des Eros*. Berlin.
Kytzler, B. (1973) "Utopisches Denken und Handeln in der klassischen Antike," in Villgradter, R., Krey, F., eds., *Der utopische Roman*, 45–68. Darmstadt.
Kytzler, B. (1983) *Im Reiche des Eros: Sämtliche Liebes- und Abenteuerromane der Antike*, 2 vols. Munich.
Kytzler, B., trans. (1986) *Xenophon von Ephesos: Abrokomes und Anthia*. Leipzig.
Kytzler, B. (1988) "Zum utopischen Roman der klassischen Antike," *Groningen Colloquia on the Novel* 1: 7–16.

Labate, M. (1988) "Il Cadavere di Lica. Modelli Letterari e Istanza Narrativa nel *Satyricon* di Petronio," *Taccuini* 8: 83–89.
Lacombrade, C. (1970) "Sur l'Auteur et la Date des *Éthiopiques*," *Revue des Études Grecques* 83: 70–89.
Lafaye, G. (1904) *Les Métamorphoses d'Ovide et leurs Modèles Grecs*. Paris.
Lallemand, A. (1992) "Les Parfums dans le Roman Grec," in Baslez (1992) 75–83.
Lambert, J. (1935) *Le Roman de Libistros et Rhodamné*. Amsterdam.
Lamberton, R. (1986) *Homer the Theologian: Neoplatonist Allegorical Reading and the Growth of the Epic Tradition*. Berkeley.
Lamy, T. (1886) *Sancti Ephraem Syri Hymni et Sermones*. Antwerp.
Lana, I. (1974) "La Lotta al Tiranno nell' Epistolario Apocrifo di Chione di Eraclea," *Il Pensiero Politico* 7: 265–275.
Lana, I. (1975) *Studi su il Romanzo di Apollonio di Tiro*. Turin.
Lancel, S. (1987) "Y-a-t'il une *Africitas?*," *Revue des Études Latines* 63: 161–182.
Lane Fox, R. (1986) *Pagans and Christians*. Harmondsworth.
Lang, D.M. (1967) Introduction to Woodward (1914) ix–xxxv.
Lanser, S. (1981) *The Narrative Act. Point of View in Prose Fiction*. Princeton.
La Penna, A. (1962) "Il Romanzo di Esopo," *Athenaeum* n.s. 40: 264–314.
Laplace, M. (1980a) "Achille Tatius, *Leucippé et Clitophon* 4.19.6: un Locus Desperatus?," *Revue de Philologie* 54: 327–330.
Laplace, M. (1980b) "Sur un Lieu Commun d'Achille Tatius," *Revue des Études Grecques* 93: 516–519.
Laplace, M. (1980c) "Les Légendes Troyennes dans le 'Roman' de Chariton, Chairéas et Callirhoé," *Revue des Études Grecques* 93: 83–125.
Laplace, M. (1983a) "Achille Tatius, *Leucippé et Clitophon* 2.14.8: Sur un Fleuve Prétendument Ibérique," *L'Antiquité Classique* 52: 243–245.
Laplace, M. (1983b) "Légende et Fiction chez Achille Tatius. Les Personnages de Leucippé et de Iô," *Bulletin de l'Association G. Budé* 1983: 311–318.
Laplace, M. (1983c) "Achilleus Tatios, *Leucippé et Clitophon*: P.Oxyrhynchos 1250," *Zeitschrift für Papyrologie und Epigraphik* 53: 53–59.
Laplace, M. (1988) "Achilleus Tatios, *Leucippé et Clitophon* 3.21.3. L'Oracle des 'Bouviers' du Nil," *Zeitschrift für Papyrologie und Epigraphik* 74: 97–100.
Laplace, M. (1991) "Achille Tatius, *Leucippé et Clitophon*: des Fables au Roman de Formation," *Groningen Colloquia on the Novel* 4: 35–56.
Laplace, M. (1992) "Les *Éthiopiques* d'Héliodore, ou la Genèse d'un Panégyrique de l'Amour," *Revue des Études Anciennes* 94: 199–230.
Lasso de la Vega, J.S. (1957) review of Vilborg (1955) in *Emerita* 25 (1957) 265–269.
Lauenstein, U. (1962) *Der griechische Alexanderroman Rezension* γ. Vol. 1. Meisenheim am Glan.
Laurot, B. (1981) "Idéaux Grecs et Barbarie chez Hérodote," *Ktema* 6: 39–48.
Lauvergnat-Gagnière, C. (1988) *Lucien de Samosate et le Lucianisme en France au XVI*ème *Siècle*. Travaux d'Humanisme et Renaissance, No. 227. Geneva.
Lavagnini, B. (1922) *Eroticorum Graecorum Fragmenta Papyracea*. Leipzig.
Lavagnini, B. (1950) "Le Origine del Romanzo Greco," in *Studi sul Romanzo Greco*, 1–105. Messina-Florence.
Lavagnini, B. (1974) "Filippo Filagato Promotore degli Studi di Greco in Calabria," *Bolletino della Badia Greca di Grottaferrata* 28: 3–12.
Lavagnini, B. (1985) "Ancora sul Romanzo Greco," *Annali della Scuola Normale Superiore di Pisa* 15: 69–80.
Lavagnini, R. (1988) *I Fatti di Troia. L'Iliade Bizantina del cod. Paris Suppl. Gr. 926. Introduzione, Traduzione e Note*. Quaderni dell'Istituto di Filologia Greca della Università di Palermo, 20. Palermo.
Lefèvre, E. (1971) "Die Frage nach dem βίος εὐδαίμων. Die Begegnung zwischen Kyros und Kroisos bei Xenophon," *Hermes* 99: 283ff.

Lefkowitz, M. (1981) *Heroines and Hysterics* London.
Lefkowitz, M. (1986) *Women in Greek Myth.* London.
Lehmann-Haupt, C. (1929) "Der Sturz des Kroisos und das historische Element in Xenophons Kyropaedie," *Wiener Studien* 47: 123–127 and 50 (1932) 152–159.
Leipoldt, J. (1965) *Die Frau in der antiken Welt und im Urchristentum.* 3rd edition. Leipzig.
Lemerle, P. (1977) *Cinq Études sur le Xe Siècle Byzantin.* Paris.
Lendari, T. (1993) "*Livistros and Rhodamne*, Manuscript V," in Panayotakis (1993) vol. 2, pp. 135–147.
Lendari, T. (1994) *Livistros and Rodamne. A Critical Edition of Vat. gr. 2391.* Unpublished Ph.D., University of Cambridge.
Lesky, A. (1959) "*Aithiopika*," *Hermes* 87: 27–38.
Lesky, A. (1971³) *Geschichte der griechischen Literatur.* Bern.
Lesky, A. (1976) *Vom Eros der Hellenen.* Göttingen.
Lesser, S. (1957) *Fiction and the Unconscious.* With a preface by Ernest Jones. Boston.
Létoublon, F. (1993) *Les Lieux Communs du Roman. Stéréotypes Grecs d'Aventure et d'Amour.* Leiden.
Lever, M. (1976) *La Fiction Narrative en Prose au XVIème Siècle.* Paris.
Levi, D. (1944) "The Novel of Ninus and Semiramis," *Proceedings of the American Philosophical Society* 87: 420–428.
Levi, D. (1974) *Antioch Mosaic Pavements*, 2 vols. Princeton.
Levin, D. (1977) "The Pivotal Role of Lycaenion in Longus' Pastorals," *Rivista di Studi Classici* 25: 5–17.
Levine, D. (1991) "Lucian, *True History* 2.26 Reconsidered: Lust and Punishment," *Helios* 18: 31–33.
Lewis, C. (1954) *English Literature in the Sixteenth Century.* Oxford History of English Literature, No. 3. Oxford.
Lewis, N. (1983) *Life in Egypt under Roman Rule.* Oxford.
Lida de Malkiel, M. (1969) "El Desenlace del Amadís Primitivo," in *Estudios de Literatura Española y Comparada*, 149–156. Madrid.
Lightfoot, C. (1988) "Facts and Fiction: the Third Siege of Nisibis (A.D. 350)," *Historia* 37: 105–125.
Lightfoot, J. (1890) *The Apostolic Fathers.* Part One: *Clement*, vol. 1. Reprint 1981. Grand Rapids.
Lindenberger, J. (1985) "Ahiqar: a New Translation and Introduction," in Charlesworth, J., ed. (1985) *The Old Testament Pseudepigrapha*, vol. II, 479–507. London.
Lintvelt, J. (1981) *Essai de Typologie Narrative. Le Point de Vue, Théorie et Analyse.* Paris.
Liviabella Furiani, P. (1979) "L'Astrologia nelle *Etiopiche* di Eliodoro," *Giornale Italiano di Filologia* 31: 311–324.
Liviabella Furiani, P. (1984) "La Musica nel Romanzo 'Erotico' Greco, tra Natura e Cultura," *Quaderni Istituto di Filosofia, Università Perugia* 1: 27–43.
Liviabella Furiani, P. (1985a) "Achille Tazio 8.9.9 sgg. e Platone, *Leggi* 12.961A–B: Un Esempio di Imitazione e Deformazione," *Prometheus* 11: 179–182.
Liviabella Furiani, P. (1985b) "Religione e Letteratura nel 'Racconto' di Sacrifici Umani presso i Romanzieri Greci d'Amore," *Quaderni Istituto di Filosofia, Università Perugia* 3: 25–60.
Liviabella Furiani, P. (1988) "*Gamos e kenogamion* nel Romanzo di Achille Tazio," *Euphrosyne* 16: 271–280.
Liviabella Furiani, P., Scarcella, A., eds. (1989) *Piccolo Mondo Antico.* Perugia.
Liviabella Furiani, P., (1989a) "Di Donna in Donna. Elementi 'Femministi' nel Romanzo Greco d'Amore," in Liviabella Furiani (1989) 43–106.
Liviabella Furiani, P. (1990) "Metodi e Mezzi di Comunicazione Interpersonale nella Società dei Romanzi Greci d'Amore," *Giornale Italiano di Filologia* 42: 199–232.
Liviabella Furiani, P. (1991) "Il Tema del Sangue nei Romanzi Greci d'Amore," in *Atti della VII Settimana. Sangue e Antropologia nella Teologia Medioevale*, 519–560. Rome.

Liviabella Furiani, P. (1992) "I Vecchi e la Vecchiaia nei Romanzi Greci d'Amore," *Quaderni Istituto di Filosofia, Università Perugia* 11: 87-119.
Liviabella Furiani, P. (1995) "La Comunicazione non Verbale nelle *Etiopiche* di Eliodoro," in *Scritti in memoria di G. Forni*. Perugia. In press.
Lloyd, A. (1982) "Nationalist Propaganda in Ptolemaic Egypt," *Historia* 31: 33-55.
Lobel, E., Roberts, C. (1954) "2330. Ctesias, *Persica*," *The Oxyrhynchus Papyri* 22: 81-84.
Loicq-Berger, M. (1980) "Pour une Lecture des Romans Grecs," *Études Classiques* 48: 23-42.
Long, T. (1986) *Barbarians in Greek Comedy*. Carbondale.
Longo, O. (1978) "Paesaggio di Longo Sofista," *Quaderni di Storia* 4: 99-120.
Longo, V. (1969) *Aretalogie nel Mondo Greco. I. Epigraphi e Papiri*. Genoa.
Lonis, R. (1992) "Les Éthiopiens sous le regard d'Héliodore," in Baslez (1992) 232-241.
Lopes Vieira, A. (1974³) *A Diana de Jorge de Montemor*. Lisbon.
López Estrada, F., ed. (1970⁵) *Jorge de Montemayor, Los Siete Libros de la Diana*. Madrid.
Lubbock, P. (1935) *The Craft of Fiction*. London
Luccioni, J. (1947) *Les Idées Politiques et Sociales de Xénophon*. Paris.
Lucke, C. (1984) "Bemerkungen zu zwei Romanfragmenten," *Zeitschrift für Papyrologie und Epigraphik* 54: 41-47.
Lucke, C., Schäfer, K.-H., eds. (1985) *Chariton, Kallirhoe. Aus dem Griechischen. Übersetzung und Anmerkungen*. Leipzig.
Lucke, C. (1985a) "Zum Charitontext auf Papyrus," *Zeitschrift für Papyrologie und Epigraphik* 58: 21-33.
Ludvíkovský, J. (1925) *Recký Román Dobrodužný (Le Roman Grec d'Aventures: Étude sur sa Nature et son Origine)*. Prague.
Lukács, G. (1920) *Die Theorie des Romans*. Berlin.
Luminansky, R. (1969) "Dares' *Historia* and Dictys' *Ephemeris*: a Critical Comment," in *Studies in Language, Literature, and Culture of the Middle Ages and Later*, ed. E. Atwood, A. Hill, 200-209. Austin.
Luzzatto, M. (1988) "Plutarco, Socrate e l'Esopo di Delfi," *Illinois Classical Studies 13*: 427-445.
MacAlister, S. (1987) *The Dream in Greek Romance*. Ph.D. Diss., Sydney.
MacAlister, S. (1991) "Byzantine Twelfth-Century Romances: a Relative Chronology," *Byzantine and Modern Greek Studies* 15: 175-210.
MacAlister, S. (forthcoming) *Dreams and Suicides. The Greek Novel in Antiquity and the Byzantine Empire*. London.
MacDonald, D. (1983) *The Legend and the Apostle: the Battle for Paul in Story and Canon*. Philadelphia.
MacDonald, D. (1992) *"Acts of Andrew and Matthias,"* in Freedman (1992) 1: 244.
MacDonald, D. (1994) *Christianizing Homer: the Odyssey, Plato, and the Acts of Andrew*. New York.
Macedo, H. (1990) *Menina e Moça*. Lisbon.
Macleod, M., ed. (1967) *Lucian: VIII*. Loeb. Cambridge, MA.
Macleod, M., ed. (1972) *Luciani Opera. Vol. 1*. Oxford.
MacMullen, R. (1981) *Paganism in the Roman Empire*. New Haven.
MacMullen, R. (1984) *Christianizing the Roman Empire*. New Haven.
MacQueen, B. (1990) *Myth, Rhetoric, and Fiction. A Reading of Longus's Daphnis and Chloe*. Lincoln, NE.
Macuch, R. (1989) "Egyptian Sources and Versions of Pseudo-Callisthenes," in Criscuolo (1989) 503-511.
Maeder, D. (1991) "Au Seuil des Romans Grecs: Effets de Réel et Effets de Création," *Groningen Colloquia on the Novel* 4: 1-33.
Maehler, H. (1976) "Der Metiochos-Parthenope-Roman," *Zeitschrift für Papyrologie und Epigraphik* 23: 1-20.

Magdalino, P. (1992) "Eros the King and the King of *Amours*: Some Observations on *Hysmine and Hysminias*," in Cutler, A., Franklin, S., eds. (1992) *Homo Byzantinus: Papers in Honor of Alexander Kazhdan* (= *Dumbarton Oaks Papers* 46), pp. 197–204. Washington.
Magdalino, P. (1993) *The Empire of Manuel I Komnenos*, 1143–1180. Cambridge.
Magie, D. (1950) *Roman Rule in Asia Minor*. Princeton.
Mai, A. (1835) *Itinerarium Alexandri*, in *Classicorum Auctorum e Vaticanis codicibus editorum*, tom. VII. Rome.
Maiuri, A. (1945) *La Cena di Trimalchione di Petronio Arbitro*. Naples.
Malherbe, A. (1977) *The Cynic Epistles: a Study Edition*. Missoula, Mont.
Manganaro, G. (1958) "Novella e Romanzo," *Rivista di Filologia e di Istruzione Classica* 36: 376–392.
Mann, T. (1965) "Die Kunst des Romans," in *Gesammelte Werke*, Band 11: Altes und Neues. Kleine Prosa aus fünf Jahrzehnten, 457–471. Berlin.
Manni, E. (1991) "Bisanzio, l'Egitto e le Guerre Narrate da Achille Tazio," in *Studi di Filologia Classica in Onore di G. Monaco* I, 471–474. Palermo.
Manso, J. (1802) "Über den griechischen Roman," *Vermischte Schriften*, 2, 199–320. Leipzig.
Mantero, T. (1973) *Amore e Psiche. Struttura di una Fiaba di Magia*. Genova.
Manuel, F.E., Manuel, F.P. (1980) *Utopian Thought in the Western World*. Cambridge, MA.
Marasco, G. (1988) "Ctesia, Dinone, Eraclide di Cuma e le Origini della Storiografia 'Tragica'," *Studi Italiani di Filologia Classica* 6: 48–67.
Marblestone, H. (1970) *Dictys Cretensis: a Study of the Ephemeris Belli Troiani as a Cretan Pseudepigraphon*. Diss., Brandeis University, Waltham, MA.
Marc, P. (1910) "Die Überlieferung des Äsopromans," *Byzantinische Zeitschrift* 19: 383–421.
Marchant, E., ed. (1910) *Institutio Cyri*. Oxford.
Marcovaldi, G. (1969) *I Romanzi Greci*. Rome.
Marcovich, M. (1992) *Theodori Prodromi, de Rhodanthes et Dosiclis amoribus libri IX*. Stuttgart.
Marino, E. (1990) "Il Teatro nel Romanzo: Eliodoro e il Codice Spettacolare," *Materiali e Discussioni per l'Analisi dei Testi Classici* 25: 203–218.
Maritz, J. (1991) "The Role of Music in *Daphnis and Chloe*," *Groningen Colloquia on the Novel* 4: 56–67.
Markale, J. (1987) *L'Amour Courtois ou le Couple Infernal*. Paris.
Marmorale, E. (1948) *La Questione Petroniana*. Bari.
Maróth, M. (1979) "Le Siège de Nisibe en 350 ap. J.-Ch. d'après des Sources Syriennes," *Acta Antiqua Academiae Scientiarum Hungaricae* 27: 239–243.
Marques Braga, M., ed. (1953) *João de Barros, Crónica do Imperador Clarimundo*, 3 vols. Lisbon.
Marrou, H.-I. (1953) *L'Idéal de la Virginité et la Condition de la Femme dans le Civilisation Antique*. Paris.
Marrou, H.-I. (1957) *Geschichte der Erziehung im Klassischen Altertum*. Freiburg.
Marshall, P. (1983) "Apuleius," in Reynolds (1983) 15–16.
Martin, L.H. (1994) "The Anti-individualistic Ideology of Hellenistic Culture," *Numen* 41: 117–140.
Martin, V., Budé, G. de (1952) *Eschine: Discours Tome II: Contre Ctésiphon. Lettres: Texte Établi et Traduit*. Collection des Universités de France. Paris.
Marzullo, A., Bonaria, M., trans. (1962) *Il Satiricon*. Bologna.
Mason, H.J. (1978) "*Fabula Graecanica*: Apuleius and his Greek Sources," in Hijmans (1978a) 1–15.
Matte Blanco, I. (1975) *The Unconscious as Infinite Sets. An Essay in Bi-Logic*. London.
Matteuzi, M. (1975) "Sviluppi Narrativi di Giochi Linguistici nella *Storia Vera* di Luciano," *Maia* 27: 225–229.

Mavrogordato, J. (1956) *Digenes Akrites, Edited with an Introduction, Translation and Commentary.* Oxford.
Mayer, R. (1982) "Neronian Classicism," *American Journal of Philology* 103: 305–318.
Mazal, O. (1955) *Der Stil des Heliodorus von Emesa.* Diss., Vienna.
Mazal, O. (1958) "Die Satzstruktur in den *Aithiopika* des Heliodor von Emesa," *Wiener Studien* 71: 116–131. Reprinted in Gärtner (1984) 451–466.
Mazal, O. (1966) "Die Textausgaben der *Aithiopika* Heliodors von Emesa," *Gutenberg Jahrbuch*: 182–191.
Mazal, O. (1967) *Der Roman des Konstantinos Manasses.* Wiener Byzantinistische Studien, No. 4. Vienna.
Mazza, M. (1985) "Le Avventure del Romanzo nell' Occidente Latino: La *Historia Apollonii Regis Tyri*," *Le Trasformazioni della Cultura nella Tarda Antichità*, ed. C. Giuffrida, pp. 597–645. Rome.
McCulloh, W. (1970) *Longus.* New York.
McLeod, A.M.G. (1969) "Physiology and Medicine in a Greek Novel. Achilles Tatius' *Leucippe and Clitophon* (4.10.1–4)," *Journal of Hellenic Studies* 89: 97–105.
Meer, H. van der (1949) *Euhemerus van Messene.* Diss. Amsterdam.
Meillier, C. (1975) "L'Épiphanie du Dieu Pan au Livre II de *Daphnis et Chloé*," *Revue des Études Grecques* 88: 121–131.
Meister, F., ed. (1873) *Daretis Phrygii de Excidio Troiae Historia.* (Reprinted 1991). Leipzig.
Meletinsky, E. (1974) "Problem of the Historical Morphology of the Folktale," in *Soviet Structural Folkloristics*, ed. P. Maranda, 53–59. The Hague.
Meletinsky, E. (1993) *Introduzione alla Poetica Storica dell'Epos e del Romanzo.* Bologna.
Mendel, G. (1970) "Psychanalyse et Paralittérature," *Entretiens sur la Paralittérature*, eds. N. Arnaud, F. Lacassin, J. Tortel, 441–466. Paris.
Mendoza, J., trans. (1979) *Caritón de Afrodisias: Quéreas y Calírroe.* Madrid.
Meneghetti, M., ed. (1988) *Il Romanzo.* Bologna.
Menéndez Pelayo, M. (1962²) *Orígenes de la Novela*, Vol. I. Madrid.
Menéndez Pelayo, M. (1943) *Orígenes de la Novela*, Vol. II. Madrid.
Merkelbach, R. (1962) *Roman und Mysterium in der Antike.* Munich.
Merkelbach, R. (1967) "Achilleus Tatios 3.21.3," *Rheinisches Museum* 110: 287–288.
Merkelbach, R. (1973) "Fragmente eines satirischen Romans: Aufforderung zur Beichte," *Zeitschrift für Papyrologie und Epigraphik* 11: 81–100.
Merkelbach, R. (1977²) *Die Quellen des griechischen Alexanderromans.* Zetemata, 9. Munich.
Merkelbach, R. (1984) *Mithras.* Königstein/Ts.
Merkelbach, R. (1988) *Die Hirten des Dionysos: Die Dionysos-Mysterien der römischen Kaiserzeit und der bukolische Roman des Longus.* Stuttgart.
Merkelbach, R. (1989) "Der Brief des Dareios im Getty-Museum und Alexanders Wortwechsel mit Parmenion," *Zeitschrift für Papyrologie und Epigraphik* 77: 277–280.
Merkelbach, R. (1994) "Novel and Aretalogy," in Tatum (1994) 283–295.
Merkle, S. (1989) *Die Ephemeris belli Troiani des Diktys von Kreta.* Studien zur klassischen Philologie, 44. Frankfurt.
Merkle, S. (1990) "Troiani Belli Verior Textus: Die Trojaberichte des Dictys und Dares," in *Die deutsche Trojaliteratur des Mittelalters und der Frühen Neuzeit. Materialien und Untersuchungen*, ed. H. Brunner. Wiesbaden.
Merkle, S. (1992) "Die Fabel von Frosch und Maus: Zur Funktion der λόγοι im Delphi-Teil des Äsop-Romans," in Holzberg (1992a) 76–84.
Merkle, S. (1994a) "Telling the True Story of the Trojan War: the Eyewitness Account of Dictys of Crete," in Tatum (1994) 183–196.
Merkle, S., Beschorner, A. (1994b) "Der Tyrann und der Dichter: Handlungssequenzen in den Phalaris-Briefen," in Holzberg (1994a) 116–168.
Meyer, E. (1912) *Der Papyrusfund von Elephantine.* Leipzig.
Michaëlis de Vasconcelos, C. (1923), in Bramcamp Freire, ed., *Obras de Bernardim Ribeiro e Cristóvam Falcão*, 2 Vols. Coimbra.

Mignogna, E. (1992) "Aesopus Bucolicus: Come si 'Mette in Scena' un Miracolo (*Vita Aesopi* ch. 6)," in Holzberg (1992a) 76–84.
Milazzo, A. (1984) "Achille e Polissena in Ditti Cretese: un Romanzo nel Romanzo?," *Le Forme e la Storia* 5: 3–24.
Milbradt, J. (1974) "Der Charakter. Zu dem Menschenbild der Zeit der Poliskrise und seiner Aufnahme durch die römische Komödie," in *Hellenische Poleis*, ed. E. Welskopf, 1413–1449. Berlin.
Millar, F. (1981) "The World of the *Golden Ass*," *Journal of Roman Studies* 71: 63–75.
Miller, W., ed. (1914) *Xenophon Cyropaedia*. Loeb. Cambridge, MA.
Miralles, C., trans. (1967) *Xenofont d'Efes*. Barcelona.
Miralles, C. (1968) *La Novela en la Antigüedad Clasica*. Barcelona.
Mitchell, S. (1993) *Anatolia*. Oxford.
Mitteis, L. (1891) *Reichsrecht und Volksrecht in den östlichen Provinzen des römischen Kaiserreiches*. Leipzig.
Mittelstadt, M. (1970) "Bucolic-lyric Motifs and Dramatic Narrative in Longus' *Daphnis and Chloe*," *Rheinisches Museum* 113: 211–227.
Moisés, M. (1957) "A Novela de Cavalaria Portuguêsa (Achega Bibliográfica)," *Revista de História* VIII, 29 (S. Paulo) 47–52.
Molinié, G. (1978) *La Tradition Grecque dans le Roman Français (1600–1650): L'Art d'un Genre*. Thèse de Doctorat d'État, Université de Paris-Sorbonne, 2 vols. Paris.
Molinié, G. (1982) *Du Roman Grec au Roman Baroque*. Toulouse.
Molinié, G. ed. (1989²) *Chariton. Le Roman de Chairéas et Callirhoé*. Budé. First edition 1979. Paris.
Molinié, G. (1992) "Postérité du Roman Grec à l'Époque Moderne: pour une Sémiotique de Second Niveau," in Baslez (1992) 315–320.
Molt, M. (1938) *Ad Apuleii Madaurensis Librum Primum Commentarius Exegeticus*. Groningen.
Momigliano, A. (1971) *The Development of Greek Biography*. Cambridge, MA.
Montague, H. (1992) "Sweet and Pleasant Passion: Female and Male Fantasy in Ancient Romance Novels," in Richlin (1992) 231–249.
Montanari, F., ed. (1988) *Da Omero agli Alessandrini. Problemi e Figure della Lettertura Greca*. Rome.
Montanari, F., ed. (1991) *La Prosa Latina*. Rome.
Montes Cala, J.G. (1992) "En Torno a la 'Imposta Dramática' en la Novela Griega: Comentario a una Écfrasis de Espectáculo en Heliodoro," *Habis* 23: 217–235.
Montevecchi, O. (1973) *La Papirologia*. Turin.
Moore-Blunt, J. (1985) *Platonis Epistulae*. Leipzig.
Morel, W. (1964) review of Vilborg (1962) in *Gymnasium* 71 (1964) 545–547.
Moreschini, C. (1970–1971) "Un' Ipotesi per la Datazione del Romanzo di Senofonte Efesio," *Studi Classici e Orientali* 19–20: 73–75.
Moreschini, C. (1990) "Le Metamorfosi di Apuleio, la 'Fabula Milesia' e il Romanzo," *Materiali e Discussioni* 25: 115–127.
Morgan, J.R. (1982) "History, Romance, and Realism in the *Aithiopika* of Heliodoros," *Classical Antiquity* 1: 221–265.
Morgan, J.R. (1985) "Lucian's *True Histories* and the *Wonders Beyond Thule* of Antonios Diogenes," *Classical Quarterly* 35: 475–490.
Morgan, J.R. (1988) review of Anderson (1986), in *Classical Review* 38: 235f.
Morgan, J.R., trans. (1989a) *Heliodorus. An Ethiopian Story*, in Reardon (1989) 349–588.
Morgan, J.R. (1989b) "A Sense of the Ending: the Conclusion of Heliodoros' *Aithiopika*," *Transactions of the American Philological Association* 119: 299–320.
Morgan, J.R. (1989c) "The Story of Knemon in Heliodoros' *Aithiopika*," *Journal of Hellenic Studies* 109: 99–113.
Morgan, J.R. (1991) "Reader and Audiences in the *Aithiopika* of Heliodoros," *Groningen Colloquia on the Novel* 4: 85–103.

Morgan, J.R. (1993) "Make-believe and Make Believe: the Fictionality of the Greek Novels," in Gill (1993) 175-229.
Morgan, J.R., Stoneman, R., eds. (1994) *Greek Fiction: the Greek Novel in Context*. London.
Morgan, J.R. (1994a) "*The Aithiopika* of Heliodoros: Narrative as Riddle," in Morgan (1994) 97-113.
Morgan, J.R., ed. (forthcoming) *Daphnis and Chloe*.
Mosino, F. (1979-80) "Una Ipotesi sul Codice Marciano Greco 410," *Rivista di Cultura Classica e Medioevale* 21-22: 207-208.
Mossé, C. (1969) "Les Utopies Égalitaires à l'Époque Hellénistique," *Revue Historique* 241: 297-308.
Most, G. (1989) "The Stranger's Stratagem. Self-Disclosure and Self-Sufficiency in Greek Culture," *Journal of Hellenic Studies* 109: 114-133.
Müller, C. (1846) *Scriptores Rerum Alexandri Magni*. (Reprinted Chicago 1979.) Paris.
Müller, C.W. (1976) "Chariton von Aphrodisias und die Theorie des Romans in der Antike," *Antike & Abendland* 22: 115-136.
Müller, C.W. (1980) "Die Witwe von Ephesus—Petrons Novelle und die *Milesiaka* des Aristeides," *Antike und Abendland* 26: 103-121.
Müller, C.W. (1981) "Der griechische Roman," in *Neues Handbuch der Literaturwissenschaft*, Vol. 2, *Griechische Literatur*, ed. E. Vogt (1981) 377-412. Wiesbaden.
Müller, C.W. (1990) "Philetas oder Philitas?," in *Beiträge zur hellenistischen Literatur und ihrer Rezeption in Rom*, ed. P. Steinmetz (1990) 27-37. Stuttgart.
Müller, C.W. (1991) "Der Romanheld als Rätsellöser in der *Historia Apollonii Regis Tyri*," *Würzburger Jahrbücher für die Altertumswissenschaft* 17: 267-279.
Müller, K., ed. (1961) *Petronii Arbitri Satyricon*. Munich. (This edition is cited separately from those of 1965, 1978, 1983, because the 1961 edition is so radically different.)
Müller, K. (1983³) *Petronius: Satyrica*. Munich.
Müller, R. (1975) "Zur sozialen Utopie im Hellenismus," in Herrmann, J., Sellnow, I., eds. (1975) *Die Rolle der Volksmassen in der Geschichte der vorkapitalistischen Gesellschaftsformationen*. Berlin, and in Müller, R. (1981) *Menschenbild und Humanismus der Antike: Studien zur Geschichte der Literatur und Philosophie*, 189-201. Frankfurt.
Müller, R. (1977) "Sozialutopien der Antike," *Das Altertum* 23: 227-233.
Müller, R. (1983) *Sozialutopisches Denken in der griechischen Antike*. Berlin.
Müller, R. (1987) *Polis und Res Publica. Studien zum antiken Gesellschafts- und Geschichtsdenken*. Weimar.
Müller, R.J. (1993) "Überlegungen zur Ἱερὰ Ἀναγραφή des Euhemeros von Messene," *Hermes* 121: 276-300.
Münscher, K. (1920) *Xenophon in der griechisch-römischen Literatur*. Philologus Supplementband 13. Leipzig.
Murru, F. (1980) "Aenigmata Symphosii ou Aenigmata symposii," *Eos* 68: 155-158.
Naber, S. (1873) "Observationes Criticae in Heliodorum," *Mnemosyne* 1: 145-169, 313-353.
Napolitano, F. (1983-84) "Leucippe nel Romanzo di Achille Tazio," *Annali della Facoltà di Lettere e Filosofia della Università di Napoli* 26: 85-101.
Naumann, M. (1978) *Prosa in Frankreich. Studien zum Roman im 19. und 20. Jahrhundert*. Berlin.
Neimke, P. (1889) *Quaestiones Heliodoreae*. Halle.
Nelson, H. (1956) "Ein Unterrichtsprogramm aus neronischer Zeit, dargestellt auf Grund von Petrons *Satiricon* ch. 5," *Mededelingen der Koninklijke Nederlandse Akademie van Wetenschappen, Afdeling Letterkunde* 19.6: 201-228.
Neumann, W., Kerschensteiner, J. (1967) *Platon: Briefe. Griechisch-Deutsch*. Munich.
Nickel, R. (1979) *Xenophon*. Erträge der Forschung Bd.111. Darmstadt.
Nilsson, M.P. (1974³) *Geschichte der griechischen Religion*. Munich.
Nocera Lo Giudice, M. (1979) "Per la Datazione dell' *Historia Apollonii Regis Tyri*," *Atti della Accademia Peloritana dei Pericolanti, Classe di Lettere* 55: 273-284.

Nock, A.D. (1933) *Conversion*. Oxford.
Nock, A.D., ed. (1945) *Corpus Hermeticum* II. Paris
Nock, A.D. (1972) "Greek Novels and Egyptian Religion." Review of Kerényi (1927), reprinted in *Essays on Religion and the Ancient World*, ed. Z. Stewart (1972) 2 vols.: 1.169–175. Oxford.
Nøjgaard, M. (1964–1967) *La Fable Antique*. 2 vols. Copenhagen.
Nollé, J. (1994) "Frauen wie Omphale?," in *Reine Männersache?*, ed. M. Dettenhofer, 229–259. Köln.
Nolting-Hauff, I. (1974) "Märchen und Märchenroman," *Poetica* 6: 129–178.
Norden, E. (1915³) *Die Antike Kunstprosa*. 2 vols. Leipzig.
Nørgaard, L., Smith, O. (1975) *A Byzantine Iliad. The Text of Par. Suppl. Gr. 926.* Copenhagen.
Nørgaard, L. (1989) "Byzantine Romance—Some Remarks on the Coherence of Motives," *Classica et Mediaevalia* 40: 271–294.
Norsa, M., Bartoletti, V. (1951) *Papiri Greci e Latini*. Pubblicazioni della Società Italiana per la Ricerca dei Papiri Greci e Latini in Egitto XII. Florence.
Nuti, R., trans. (1958) *Caritone: le Avventure de Cherea e Calliroe*, in Cataudella (1958) 29–179.
Nylander, C. (1995) "Xenophon, Darius, Naram-Sin. A Note on the King's 'Year'," in *Festskrift till Gösta Säflunds 90-årsdag.*
Oeftering, M. (1901) *Heliodor und seine Bedeutung für die Litteratur*. Litterarhistorische Forschungen, No. 18. Berlin.
Oeri, H. (1948) *Der Typ der Komischen Alten in der griechischen Komödie, seine Nachwirkungen und seine Herkunft*. Basel.
Oettinger, N. (1992) "Achikars Weisheitssprüche im Licht älterer Fabeldichtung," in Holzberg (1992a) 3–22.
Ohlert, K. (1912²) *Rätsel und Rätselspiele der alten Griechen*. Berlin.
Oliver, S. (1979) "Xenophon of Ephesus and the Antithesis Historia-Philosophia," in Bowersock, G., ed., *Arktours. Hellenic Studies presented to B.M.W. Knox*, 401–406. Berlin.
Ollier, F. (1962) *Histoire Vraie*. Collection Érasme, Sér. Gr. 4. Paris.
Olsen, B. (1990) "The Greek Translation of Boccaccio's *Theseid* Book 6," *Classica et Mediaevalia* 41: 273–301.
Olsen, B. (1993) "The Model and Translation Method of the Greek *Theseid*," in Panayotakis (1993) vol. 2, pp. 313–318.
Olsvanger, I. (1931) *Rosinkess mit Mandlen: Aus der Volksliteratur der Ostjuden*. Basel.
Omont, H. (1889) *Catalogues des Manuscrits Grecs de Fontainebleau sous François Iᵉʳ et Henri II*. Paris.
Omont, H. (1891) "Essai sur les Débuts de la Typographie Grecque à Paris (1507–1516)," *Mémoires de la Société de l'Histoire de Paris*... 18: 1–72.
Orlando, F. (1973) *Per una Teoria Freudiana della Letteratura*. Turin. (Engl. transl. *Toward a Freudian Theory of Literature. With an Analysis of Racine's Phèdre*. Baltimore: 1976).
Orlando, F. (1979) *Lettura Freudiana del Misanthrope e Due Scritti Teorici*. Turin.
Orlando, F. (1982) *Illuminismo e Retorica Freudiana*. Turin.
Orsini, P. (1968) *Musée, Héro et Léandre*. Paris.
O'Sullivan, J.N. (1977) "On Achilles Tatius 6.6.3," *Classical Quarterly* 27: 238–239.
O'Sullivan, J.N. (1978) "Notes on the Text and Interpretation of Achilles Tatius 1," *Classical Quarterly* 28: 312–329.
O'Sullivan, J.N. (1980) *A Lexicon to Achilles Tatius*. Berlin.
O'Sullivan, J.N. (1995) *Xenophon of Ephesus: his Compositional Technique and the Birth of the Novel*. Berlin.
Oudendorp, F., ed. (1786) *Appulei Opera Omnia*. 3 vols. Leiden.
Oudot, E. (1992) "Images d'Athènes dans les Romans Grecs," in Baslez (1992) 101–111.

Paardt, R. van der (1971) *L. Apuleius Madaurensis: The Metamorphoses. A Commentary on Book III with Text and Introduction.* Amsterdam.
Paardt, R. van der (1978) "Aspects of Narrative Technique in Apuleius' *Metamorphoses*," in Hijmans (1978) 75–94.
Paardt, R. van der (1981) "The Unmasked 'I': Apuleius *Met.* XI. 27," *Mnemosyne* 34: 96–106.
Pack, R. (1965) *The Greek and Latin Literary Texts from Greco-Roman Egypt.* 2nd edition. Ann Arbor.
Pakcínska, M. (1968) "Chariton, Représentant le Plus Éminent de la Première Phase du Roman Grec," *Acta Conventus XI Eirene,* 597–603. Warsaw.
Pallis, A.A. (1990/1) Η Φυλλαδα του Μεγ 'Αλεξανδρου. Athens.
Panayotakis, C. (1995) *Theatrum Arbitri: Theatrical Elements in the Satyrica of Petronius.* Leiden.
Panayotakis, N., ed. (1993) *Origini della Letteratura Neogreca.* 2 vols. Venice.
Pandiri, T. (1985) "*Daphnis and Chloe:* the Art of Pastoral Play," *Ramus* 14: 116–141.
Papanikolaou, A. (1964) "Chariton und Xenophon von Ephesos. Zur Frage der Abhängigkeit," in *Festschrift K.I. Vourveris,* 305–320. Athens, and in Gärtner (1984) 279–294.
Papanikolaou, A. (1973) *Chariton-Studien.* Göttingen.
Papanikolaou, A., ed. (1973a) *Xenophon Ephesius. Ephesiacorum Libri V.* Leipzig.
Papanikolaou, A. (1983) *Index Xenophontis Ephesii.* Athens.
Papanikolaou, A. (1984) cf. Papanikolaou (1964).
Papathomopoulos, M. (1968) *Antoninus Liberalis. Les Métamorphoses.* Paris.
Papathomopoulos, M. (1989) *Aesopus Revisitatus: Recherches sur le Texte des Vies Esopiques,* vol. I: *La Critique Textuelle.* Ioannina.
Papathomopoulos, M. (1991²) Ὁ Βίος τοῦ Αἰσώπου. Ἡ Παραλλαγὴ G. Β΄ Ἔκδοση Διορθωμένη μὲ Εἰσαγωγὴ καὶ Μετάφραση. Ioannina.
Parsons, P. (1971) "A Greek *Satyricon*?," *Bulletin of the Institute of Classical Studies* 18: 53–68.
Parthe, F. (1969) *Der griechische Alexanderroman Rezension* γ. Vol. 3. Meisenheim am Glan.
Patterson, A. (1991) *Fables of Power: Aesopian Writing and Political History.* Durham.
Paulsen, T. (1992) *Inszenierung des Schicksals: Tragödie und Komödie im Roman des Heliodor.* Bochumer Altertumswissenschaftliches Colloquium 10. Trier.
Pavano, A. (1993) "A Proposito di una Presunta Seconda Redazione della *De Excidio Troiae Historia* di Darete Frigio," *Sileno* 19: 229–275.
Pavano, A. (1993a) "Contributo allo Studio della Tradizione Manoscritta della *De Excidio Troiae Historia,*" *Sileno* 19: 525–532.
Pavlovskis, Z., trans. (1978) *The Story of Apollonius, King of Tyre.* Lawrence.
Pearcy, L.T. (1978) "Achilles Tatius, *Leucippe and Clitophon* 1.14–15. An Unnoticed Lacuna?," *Classical Philology* 73: 233–235.
Pédech, P. (1963) review of Vilborg (1962) in *Erasmus* 15: 225–226.
Pédech, P. (1989) *Trois Historiens Méconnus, Théopompe-Duris-Phylarque.* Paris.
Peden, R.G. (1985) "The Statues in Apuleius *Metamorphoses* 2.4," *Phoenix* 39: 380–383.
Peeters, P. (1920) "La Légende de Saint Jacques de Nisibe," *Analecta Bollandiana* 38: 285–373.
Pellisson, (1729) *Histoire de l'Académie Françoise.* 2 vols. Paris.
Penella, R. (1979) *The Letters of Apollonius of Tyana.* Leiden.
Penwill, J. (1978) "The Letters of Themistocles: an Epistolary Novel?," *Antichthon* 12: 83–103.
Penwill, J. (1990) "*Ambages Reciprocae*: Reviewing Apuleius' *Metamorphoses,*" in Boyle (1990) 211–235.
Pepe, L. (1972) "La Narrativa," in *Introduzione allo Studio della Cultura Classica* I, 395–472. Milan.

Pernot, L. (1992) "Chariclée la Sirène," in Baslez (1992) 43–51.
Perry, B.E. (1930) "Chariton and his Romance from a Literary-Historical Point of View," *American Journal of Philology* 51: 93–134.
Perry, B.E. (1933) "The Text Tradition of the Greek *Life of Aesop*," *Transactions of the American Philological Association* 64: 198–244.
Perry, B.E. (1936) *Studies in the Text History of the Life and Fables of Aesop*. Haverford, PA.
Perry, B.E. (1952) *Aesopica: a Series of Texts Relating to Aesop or Ascribed to Him or Closely Connected with the Literary Tradition that Bears His Name. Collected and Critically Edited, in Part Translated from Oriental Languages, with a Commentary and Historical Essay*, vol. I: Greek and Latin Texts. (repr. New York 1980). Urbana, Ill.
Perry, B.E. (1966) "Some Addenda to the *Life of Aesop*," *Byzantinische Zeitschrift* 59: 285–304.
Perry, B.E. (1967) *The Ancient Romances: a Literary-Historical Account of their Origins*. Berkeley.
Pervo, R. (1975) "The Testament of Joseph and Greek Romance," in *Studies on the Testament of Joseph*, ed. G. Nickelburg, 15–28. Missoula, Montana.
Pervo, R. (1987) *Profit with Delight: The Literary Genre of the Acts of the Apostles*. Philadelphia.
Peters, J., ed. (1968) *Xenophontis Institutio Cyri*. Leipzig.
Petersmann, H. (1977) *Petrons Urbane Prosa. Untersuchungen zu Sprache und Text*. Vienna.
Petri, R. (1963) *Über den Roman des Chariton*. Meisenheim am Glan.
Pettinato, G. (1985) *Semiramide*. Milan.
Petzke, G. (1970) *Die Traditionen über Apollonius von Tyana und das Neue Testament*. Leiden.
Pfister, F. (1910) *Kleine Texte zum Alexanderroman*. Heidelberg.
Pfister, F. (1913) *Der Alexanderroman des Archipresbyters Leo*. Heidelberg.
Pfister, F. (1975) *Kleine Schriften zum Alexanderroman*. Meisenheim am Glan.
Philippides, M. (1980) "The Digressive *aitia* in Longus," *Classical Weekly* 74: 193–200.
Phillips, E. (1952) "A Hypochondriac and his God," *Greece & Rome* 21: 23–36.
Pichard, M. (1956) *Le Roman de Callimaque et de Chrysorrhoé. Texte Établi et Traduit*. Paris.
Pieraccioni, D. (1947) *Lettere del Ciclo di Alessandro in un Papiro Egiziano*. Florence.
Pieraccioni D. (1951) "1285. Lettere del Ciclo di Alessandro," in Norsa (1951) 166–190.
Pignani, A. (1983) *Niceforo Basilace, Progimnasi e Monodie*. Naples.
Pleket, H., ed. (1969) *Epigraphica II: Texts on the Social History of the Greek World*. Textus Minores 41. Leiden.
Plepelits, K. (1976) *Chariton von Aphrodisias: Kallirhoe. Eingeleitet, Übersetzt und Erläutert*. Stuttgart.
Plepelits, K. (1980) *Achilleus Tatios: Leukippe und Kleitophon. Eingeleitet, Übersetzt und Erläutert*. Stuttgart.
Plümacher, E (1978) "Apokryphe Apostelakten," *RE* Supp. 15: 11–70.
Plümacher, E. (1988) "Les Actes Apocryphes del l'Apôtre André: Présentation des Diverses Traditions Apocryphes et État de la Question," *Aufstieg und Niedergang der römischen Welt* II 25.6, 4384–4414. Berlin
Pöhlmann, E. (1988) "Mündlichkeit und Schriftlichkeit gestern und heute," *Würzburger Jahrbücher für die Altertumswissenschaft* 14: 7–20.
Pöhlmann, R. v. (1925³) *Geschichte der sozialen Frage und des Sozialismus in der antiken Welt*. 2 vols. Munich.
Polet, A. (1947) "La Panchaïe d'Evhémère et la Cité du Soleil de Jambule," *Fouad I University. Bulletin of the Faculty of Arts* 9: 47–62.
Polites, N. (1906) Περὶ τοῦ ἐθνικοῦ ἔπους τῶν νεωτέρων Ἑλλήνων. Athens.
Pollitt, J.J. (1986) *El Arte Helenístico*. Madrid.
Pomeroy, S. (1975) *Goddesses, Whores, Wives and Slaves. Women in Classical Antiquity*. New York.

Pomeroy, S. (1981) "Women in Roman Egypt. A Preliminary Study Based on Papyri," in H. Foley, ed., *Reflections of Women in Antiquity*, 303-322. New York.
Pomeroy, S. (1983) "Infanticide in Hellenistic Greece," in Cameron (1983) 207-222.
Pomeroy, S. (1985) *Frauenleben im klassischen Altertum*. Translated from English by N. Mattheis. Stuttgart.
Pouillon, J. (1946) *Temps et Roman*. Paris.
Pouilloux, J. (1983) "Delphes dans les *Éthiopiques* d'Héliodore: la Réalité dans la Fiction," *Journal des Savants*: 259-286.
Pouilloux, J. (1984) "Roman Grec et Réalité: un Episode Delphique des *Éthiopiques* d'Héliodore," in *Hommages à Lucien Lerat*, ed. Walter, H. (Publications du Centre de Recherches d'Histoire Ancienne 55 = Annales Littéraires de l'Université de Besançon 294), vol. 2, 691-703. Paris.
Poupon, G. (1981) "L'Accusation de Magie dans les Actes Apocryphes," in Bovon (1981) 71-94.
Poupon, G. (1988) "Les 'Actes de Pierre' et leur Remaniement," *Aufstieg und Niedergang der römischen Welt* II 25.6, 4363-4383. Berlin.
Prato, C. (1955) "Nota al Testo di Achille Tazio," *Annali della Facoltà di Lettere e Filosofia dell' Università di Bari* 2: 1.
Préaux, C. (1929) "Lettres Privées Grecques d' Egypte Relatives à l'Éducation," *Revue Belge de Philologie* 8: 757-800.
Préaux, C. (1959) "Le Statut de la Femme à l'Epoque Hellénistique, Principalement en Egypte," *La Femme. Recueils de la Société Jean Bodin* 11: 127-175.
Prieur, J.-M. (1992a) "Andrew, Acts of," in Freedman (1992) 1: 245-247.
Prieur, J.-M., Schneemelcher, W. (1992b) "The Acts of Andrew," in Schneemelcher (1992) 2: 101-118.
Prince, G. (1973) "Introduction à l'Étude du Narrataire," *Poétique* 14: 178-196.
Prince, G. (1982) *Narratology. The Form and Functioning of Narrative*. Berlin.
Prinz, W. (1911) *De Xenophontis Cyri Institutione*. Göttingen.
Pritchard, R. (1992) *The History of Alexander's Battles*. The J¹ version. Toronto.
Propp, V. (1928) *Morphology of the Folktale* (Engl. transl. Austin: 1968).
Prosch, C. (1956) *Heliodors Aithiophika als Quelle für das deutsche Drama des Barockzeitalters*. Diss. Vienna.
Pugliatti, P. (1985) *Lo Sguardo nel Racconto. Teoria e Prassi del Punto di Vista*. Bologna.
Puiggali, J. (1981) "Études de Démonologie I: la Démonologie dans les Romans Grecs ainsi que chez Certains Épistolographes," *Annales de la Faculté des Lettres et Sciences Humaines de l'Université de Dakar* 11: 57-69.
Puiggali, J. (1984) "Le Sens du Mot ἀντίθεος chez Héliodore, IV. 7.13," *Philologus* 128: 271-275.
Purser, L. (1910) *The Story of Cupid and Psyche*... London.
Quet, M.-H. (1992) "Romans Grecs, Mosaïques Romaines," in Baslez (1992) 125-160.
Radt, W. (1988) *Pergamon. Geschichte und Bauten, Funde und Erforschung einer antiken Metropole*. Berlin.
Raith, J., ed. (1956) *Historia Apollonii Regis Tyri, Text der englischchen Handschriftengruppe*. Munich.
Raith, O. (1963) *Petronius ein Epikureer*. Nürnberg.
Rattenbury, R.M. (1926) "Chastity and Chastity Ordeals in the Ancient Greek Romance," *Proceedings of the Leeds Philosophical and Literary Society. Literary and Historical Section* 1: 59-71.
Rattenbury, R.M. (1927) "Heliodorus, the Bishop of Tricca," *Proceedings of the Leeds Philosophical and Literary Society, Literary and Historical Section* 1: 168-180.
Rattenbury, R.M. (1933) "Romance: the Greek Novel" in Powell, J.U., ed. (1933) *New Chapters in the History of Greek Literature*. 3rd series, 211-257. Oxford.
Rattenbury, R.M. (1956) review of Vilborg (1955) in *Classical Review* n.s. 6 (1956) 229-233.

Rattenbury, R.M. (1959) "A Note on Achilles Tatius 3.21.3," *Revue des Études Grecques* 72: 116–118.
Rattenbury, R.M., Lumb, T.W., eds. (1960) *Héliodore. Les Éthiopiques (Théagène et Chariclée)*. Budé. First published 1935–1943. Paris.
Rea, J. (1962) *The Oxyrhynchus Papyri*, Vol. 27. 2466, 134–136. London
Reardon, B.P., trans. (1965) *Lucian: Selected Works*. New York.
Reardon, B.P. (1969) "The Greek Novel," *Phoenix* 23: 291–309, and in Gärtner (1984) 218–236.
Reardon, B.P. (1971) *Courants Littéraires Grecs des IIe et IIIe Siècles Après J.-C.* Paris.
Reardon, B.P. (1973) "The Anxious Pagan," *Classical News and Views* 17: 81–93.
Reardon, B.P. (1974) "Second Sophistic and the Novel," in Bowersock (1974) 23–29.
Reardon, B.P. (1976a) "Aspects of the Greek Novel," *Greece and Rome* 23: 118–131.
Reardon, B.P. (1976b) "Novels and Novelties, or Mysteriouser and Mysteriouser," in Williams, R.J., et al., eds., *The Mediterranean World: Papers Presented in Honor of Gilbert Bagnani*, 78–100. Peterborough, Ontario.
Reardon, B.P. (1976c) review of Papanikolaou (1973) in *Classical Review* 26: 21–23.
Reardon, B.P., ed. (1977) *Erotica Antiqua*. Acta of the International Conference on the Ancient Novel. Bangor, Wales.
Reardon, B.P. (1982) "Theme, Structure and Narrative in Chariton," *Yale Classical Studies* 27: 1–27.
Reardon, B.P. (1982a) review of Molinié (1979 = 1989^2) in *Revue des Études Grecques* 95: 157–173.
Reardon, B.P., ed. (1989) *Collected Ancient Greek Novels*. Berkeley.
Reardon, B.P., trans. (1989a) *Lucian: A True Story*, in Reardon (1989) 619–649.
Reardon, B.P., trans. (1989b) *Chariton: Chaereas and Callirhoe*, in Reardon (1989) 17–124.
Reardon, B.P. (1991) *The Form of Greek Romance*. Princeton.
Reeve, C. (1785) *The Progress of Romance Through Times, Countries and Manners, with Remarks on the Good and Bad Effects of it on Them Respectively*. Colchester.
Reeve, M.D. (1971a) "Eleven Notes," *Classical Review* 21: 324–329.
Reeve, M.D. (1971b) "Hiatus in the Greek Novelists," *Classical Quarterly*, n.s. 21: 514–539.
Reeve, M.D. (1981) "Five Dispensable Manuscripts of Achilles Tatius," *Journal of Hellenic Studies* 101: 144–145.
Reeve, M.D. (1983) "Petronius," in Reynolds (1983) 295–300.
Reeve, M.D., ed. (1986^2) *Longus, Daphnis et Chloe*. First edition 1982, third 1994. Leipzig.
Reeve, M.D. (1989) "Conceptions," *Proceedings of the Cambridge Philological Society* 215: 81–112.
Reichmann, S. (1963) *Das byzantinische Alexandergedicht*. Meisenheim am Glan.
Reinsberg, C. (1993) *Ehe, Hetärentum und Knabenliebe im antiken Griechenland*. Munich.
Reitzenstein, R. (1906) *Hellenistische Wundererzählungen*. (Reprint Darmstadt, 1974.) Leipzig.
Relihan, J. (1993) *Ancient Menippean Satire*. Baltimore.
Reuter, D. (1932) *Untersuchungen zum Euboikos des Dion von Prusa*. Diss. Leipzig. Weida in Thüringen.
Reverdin, O. (1962) "Crise Spirituelle et Évasion," in *Grecs et Barbares*. Entretiens sur l'Antiquité Classique 8, pp. 83–120. Vandoeuvres-Genève.
Reverdin, O. (1984) *Les Premiers Cours de Grec au Collège de France*. Paris.
Reyhl, K. (1969) *Antonios Diogenes: Untersuchungen zu den Romanfragmenten der Wunder jenseits von Thule und zu den Wahren Geschichten des Lukian*. Tübingen.
Reynolds, L.D., ed. (1983) *Texts and Transmission*. Oxford.
Richardson, W. (1993) *Reading and Variant in Petronius: Studies in the French Humanists and Their Manuscript Sources*. Toronto.

Richlin, A., ed. (1992) *Pornography and Representation in Greece & Rome.* New York.
Ricks, D. (1990) *Byzantine Heroic Poetry.* Bristol.
Ricoeur, P. (1983) *Temps et Récit I.* Paris..
Riefstahl, H. (1938) *Der Roman des Apuleius.* Frankfurt.
Riemann, K. (1967) *Das Herodoteische Geschichtswerk in der Antike.* Munich.
Riese, A., ed. (1893²) *Historia Apollonii Regis Tyri.* (First Edition 1871). Leipzig.
Rijksbaron, A. (1984) "Chariton 8, 1, 4 und Aristot. *Poet.* 1449b 28," *Philologus* 128: 306–307.
Ring, M., ed. (1888) *Historia Apollonii Regis Tyri.* Leipzig.
Rini, A. (1937) *Petronius in Italy from the Thirteenth Century to the Present Time.* New York.
Rinner, W. (1981) *Untersuchungen zur Erzählstruktur in Xenophons Kyrupaedie und Thukydides, Buch VI und VII.* Diss. Graz.
Ritter, H. (1948) review of Diwan-i Abu l-Qasim Hasan b. Ahmad 'Unsuri (Tahran 1323/1945), *Oriens* 1: 134–138.
Robert, L. (1980) *A Travers l'Asie Mineure: Poètes et Prosateurs, Monnaies Grecques, Voyageurs et Géographie.* Paris.
Robert, M. (1972) *Roman des Origines et Origines du Roman.* Paris.
Roberts, D. (1987) "Parting Words: Final Lines in Sophocles and Euripides," *Classical Quarterly* 37: 51–64.
Robertson, D.S. (1924) "The Manuscripts of the *Metamorphoses* of Apuleius," *Classical Quarterly* 18: 27–42; 85–99.
Robertson, D.S., Vallette, P., eds. (1940–45) *Apulée: les Métamorphoses.* 3 vols. Budé. Paris.
Robertson, D.S., (1956) "The Assisi Fragments of the *Apologia* of Apuleius," *Classical Quarterly* n.s. 6: 68–80.
Robiano, P. (1984) "La Notion de Tyché chez Chariton et chez Héliodore," *Revue des Études Grecques* 97: 543–549.
Robiano, P. (1991) "Cotys le Thrace: Anachronismes, Onomastique et Fiction dans les Lettres de Chion d'Héraclée," *Revue des Études Grecques* 104: 568–573.
Rocca, R. (1976) "Eliodoro e i Due Ippoliti Euripidei," *Materiali e Contributi per la Storia della Narrativa Greco-Latina* 1: 25–31.
Rodrigues Lapa, M. (1970) "A Questão do *Amadis de Gaula* no Contexto Peninsular," *Grial* 27: 14–28.
Rodrigues Lapa, M. (1981¹⁰) *Liçõeds de Literatura Portuguesa-Época Medieval.* Coimbra.
Rodríguez Monino, A., Milares Carlo, A., Lapesa, R. (1957) *El Primer Manuscrito del Amadis de Gaula.* Madrid.
Roeder, G. (1916) "Isis," in *RE* 9.2. 2084–2132.
Rogers, G. (1991) *The Sacred Identity of Ephesus.* London.
Rohde, E. (1885) "Zu Apuleius," *Rheinisches Museum* 40: 66–95.
Rohde, E. (1914³) *Der griechische Roman und seine Vorläufer,* ed. W. Schmid. (Reprinted Darmstadt 1974; originally published 1876). Leipzig.
Rohde, G. (1937) "Longus und die Bukolik," *Rheinisches Museum* 86: 23–49.
Rojas Alvarez, L. (1989) "Realismo Erótico en Aquiles Tacio," *Nova Tellus* 7: 81–90.
Rollins, H. (1935) "Notes on the Sources of Melbanke's Philotimus," *Harvard Studies in Philology and Literature* 18: 177–198.
Romberg, B. (1962) *Studies in the Narrative Technique of the First-Person Novel.* Lund.
de Romilly, J. (1993) "Les Barbares dans la Pensée de la Grèce Classique," *Phoenix* 47: 283–292.
Romm, J. (1992) *The Edges of the Earth in Ancient Thought.* Baltimore.
Rommel, H. (1923) *Die naturwissenschaftlich-paradoxographischen Exkurse bei Philostratos, Heliodoros und Achilleus Tatios.* Stuttgart.
Roscher, W.H. (1890–94) *Lexikon der griechischen und römischen Mythologie* II 1. Reprint 1965. Hildesheim.
Rose, C.H. (1971) *Alonso Núñez de Reinoso: The Lament of a Sixteenth-Century Exile.* Cranbury, NJ.

Rose, H.J. (1959) A *Handbook of Greek Mythology*. New York.
Rose, K. (1971) *Date and Author of the Satyricon*. Leiden.
Rosellini, M., ed. (1993) *Iulus Valerius: Res Gestae Alexandri Macedonis*. Stuttgart.
Rosenmeyer, P. (1994) "The Epistolary Novel," in Morgan (1994) 146–165.
Rossetti, L., Liviabella Furiani, P. (1993) "Rodi", in *Lo Spazio Litterario della Grecia Antica*, II, 657–715. Rome.
Rostovtzeff, M. (1931) *Skythien und der Bosporus I*. Berlin.
Rougemont, G. (1992) "Delphes chez Héliodore," in Baslez (1992) 93–99.
Rousset, J. (1973) *Narcisse Romancier. Essai sur la Première Personne dans le Roman*. Paris.
Rousset, J. (1981) *Leurs Yeux se Rencontrèrent. La Scène de Première Vue dans le Roman*. Paris.
Rowell, H. (1958) "The Gladiator Petraites and the Date of the *Satyricon*," *Transactions of the American Philological Association* 89: 14–24.
Rüdiger, H. (1963) *Curiositas und Magie. Apuleius und Lucius als Archetypen der Faustgestalt*. Frankfurt.
Ruffinato, A. (1981) "L'Analisi del Racconto dai Formalisti ad Oggi," in *Atti del Convegno Internazionale Letterature Classiche e Narratologia*, 67–101. Naples.
Ruiz de Elvira, A. (1953) "El Valor de la Novela Antigua a la Luz de la Ciencia de la Literatura," *Emerita* 21: 64–110.
Ruiz-Montero, C. (1980) "Una Observación para la Cronologia de Caritón de Afrodisias," *Estudios Clásicos* 24: 63–69.
Ruiz-Montero, C. (1981) "Los Orígenes de la Novela Griega: Revisión Critica y Nuevas Perspectivas," *Studia Philologica Salmanticensia* 5 (1981) 273–301.
Ruiz-Montero, C. (1982) *La Estructura de la Novela Griega*. Salamanca.
Ruiz-Montero, C. (1982a) "Una Interpretación del 'estilo KAI' de Jenofonte de Efeso," *Emerita* 50: 305–323.
Ruiz-Montero, C. (1983) "La Estructura de la *Historia Apollonii Regis Tyri*," *Cuadernos de Filología Clásica* 18: 291–334.
Ruiz-Montero, C. (1988) *La Estructura de la Novela Griega. Análisis Funcional*. Salamanca.
Ruiz-Montero, C. (1989) "Caritón de Afrodisias y el Mundo Real," in Liviabella Furiani (1989) 107–149.
Ruiz-Montero, C. (1989a) "*P.Oxy*.2466: the Sesonchosis Romance," *Zeitschrift für Papyrologie und Epigraphik* 79: 51–57.
Ruiz-Montero, C. (1991) "Aspects of the Vocabulary of Chariton of Aphrodisias," *Classical* Quarterly 41: 484–489.
Ruiz-Montero, C. (1991a) "Caritón de Afrodisias y los Ejercicios Preparatorios de Elio Teón," in L. Ferreres, ed. (1991) *Actes del IXe Simposi de la Secció Catalana de la SEEC*, Treballs en Honor de Virgilio Bejarano, vol. 2,709–713. Barcelona.
Ruiz-Montero, C. (1992) "Caritón de Afrodisias y Plutarco," in *Estudio sobre Plutarco: Paisaje y Naturaleza*, ed. J. García López, E. Calderón, 327–334. Murcia.
Ruiz-Montero, C. (1994a) "Chariton von Aphrodisias: ein Überblick," in *Aufstieg und Niedergang der römischen Welt* II 34.2, 1006–1054. Berlin.
Ruiz-Montero, C. (1994b) "Xenophon von Ephesos: ein Überblick," in *Aufstieg und Niedergang der römischen Welt* II 34.2, 1088–1138. Berlin.
Russell, D. (1983) *Greek Declamation*. Cambridge.
Russell, D. (1988) "The Ass in the Lion's Skin: Thoughts on the *Letters of Phalaris*," *Journal of Hellenic Studies* 108: 94–106.
Russell, D., ed. (1990) *Antonine Literature*. Oxford.
Russell, D. (1992) *Dio Chrysostom: Orations VII, XII and XXXVI*. Cambridge.
Russo, C.F. (1955) "Pap.Ox.1250 e il Romanzo di Achille Tazio," *Rendiconti della Classe di Scienze Morali, Storiche e Filologiche dell'Accademia dei Lincei*, Ser.8ª, 10: 379–403.
Russo, C.F. (1958) review of Vilborg (1955) in *Gnomon* 30 (1958) 585–590.
Sacks, K. (1981) *Polybius on the Writing of History*. Berkeley.
Sacks, K. (1990) *Diodorus Siculus and the First Century*. Princeton.

Saïd, S. (1987) "La Société Rurale dans le Roman Grec ou la Campagne Vue de la Ville," in *Sociétés Urbaines, Sociétés Rurales dans l'Asie Mineure et la Syrie Hellénistiques et Romaines*, ed. E. Frézouls, 149–171. Strasbourg.
Saïd, S. (1992) "Les Langues du Roman Grec," in Baslez (1992) 169–186.
Sakalis, D. (1989) Ἱπποκράτους. Ἐπιστολαί. Ἔκδοση κριτικὴ καὶ ἑρμηνευτική. Ioannina.
Salmeri, G. (1982) *La Politica e il Potere: Saggio su Dione di Prusa*. Quaderni del Siculorum Gymnasium, 9. Catania.
Salmon, P. (1991) "Chariton d'Aphrodisias et la Révolte Egyptienne de 360 B.C.," *Chronique d'Egypte* 36: 365–376.
Salomone, S. (1985) "Sull'Epistolario dello Ps. Eschine," *Maia* 37: 231–236.
Salonius, A., (1927) *Die Griechen und das Griechische in Petrons Cena Trimalchionis*. Helsinki and Leipzig.
Sancisi-Weerdenburg, H. (1985) "The Death of Cyrus: Xenophon's *Cyropaedia* as a Source for Iranian History," *Acta Iranica* 25, 2. ser. vol. 11, Papers in Honour of Professor Mary Boyce, Part 2, 459–471. Leiden.
Sancisi-Weerdenburg, H. (1987a) "Decadence in the Empire or Decadence in the Sources? From Source to Synthesis: Ctesias," in Sancisi-Weerdenburg, ed. (1987) *Achaemenid History I: Sources, Structures and Synthesis*. Proceedings of the 1983 Achaemenid History Workshop, 33–45. Leiden.
Sancisi-Weerdenburg, H. (1987b) "The Fifth Oriental Monarchy and Hellenocentrism," *Achaemenid History II. The Greek Sources*, Proceedings of the Groningen 1984 Achaemenid Workshop, 117–131. Leiden.
Sandy, G. (1969) "Satire in the *Satyricon*," *American Journal of Philology* 90: 293–303.
Sandy, G. (1970) "Petronius and the Tradition of the Interpolated Narrative," *Transactions of the American Philological Association* 101: 463–476.
Sandy, G. (1979) "Ancient Prose Fiction and Minor Early English Novels," *Antike und Abendland* 25: 41–55.
Sandy, G. (1982a) *Heliodorus*. Boston.
Sandy, G. (1982b) "Characterization and Philosophical Decor in Heliodorus' *Aethiopica*," *Transactions of the American Philological Association* 112: 141–167.
Sandy, G. (1982c) "Classical Forerunners of the Theory and Practice of Prose Romance in France...," *Antike und Abendland* 28: 169–191.
Sandy, G. (1984–85) "Jacques Amyot and the Manuscript Tradition of Heliodorus' *Aethiopica*," *Revue d'Histoire des Textes* 14–15: 1–22.
Sandy, G., trans. (1989) *The Story of Apollonius King of Tyre*, in Reardon (1989) 736–772.
Sandy, G. (1992) "Italy and the Development of Hellenism in France," *Studi Italiani di Filologia Classica* 10: 892–897.
Sandy, G. (1994a) "Apuleius' *Metamorphoses* and the Ancient Novel," in *Aufstieg und Niedergang der römischen Welt* II 34.2, 1511–1574. Berlin.
Sandy, G. (1994b) "New Pages of Greek Fiction," in Morgan (1994) 130–145.
Santos Otero, A. de (1992) "Later Acts of the Apostles," in Schneemelcher (1992) 2: 426–483.
Saraiva, A., Lopes, O. (1992[16]) *História da Literatura Portuguesa*. Oporto.
Sartori, F. (1985) "Italie et Sicile dans le Roman de Xénophon d'Éphèse," *Journal des Savants*, 161–186.
Sartori, M. (1984) "Storia, 'Utopia' e Mito nei Primi Libri della *Bibliotheca Historica* di Diodoro Siculo," *Athenaeum* n.s. 62: 492–536.
Scarcella, A.M. (1968a) *La Lesbo di Longo Sofista*. Roma = Scarcella (1993) 285–312.
Scarcella, A.M. (1968b) *Struttura e Tecnica Narrativa in Longo Sofista*. Palermo = Scarcella (1993) 221–240.
Scarcella, A.M. (1970) "Realtà e Letteratura nel Paesaggio Sociale ed Economico del Romanzo di Longo Sofista," *Maia* 22: 103–131 = Scarcella (1993) 241–257.

Scarcella, A.M. (1971) "La Tecnica dell' Imitazione in Longo Sofista," *Giornale Italiano di Filologia* 23: 34–59 = Scarcella (1993) 251–283.
Scarcella, A.M. (1972a), "La Donna nel Romanzo di Longo Sofista," *Giornale Italiano di Filologia* 24: 63–84 = Scarcella (1993) 313–328.
Scarcella, A.M. (1972b) "Testimonianze della Crisi di un' Età nel Romanzo di Eliodoro," *Maia* 34: 9–41 = Scarcella (1993) 329–356.
Scarcella, A.M. (1976) "Aspetti del Diritto e del Costume Matrimoniali nel Romanzo di Eliodoro," *Materiali e Contributi per la Storia della Narrativa Greco-Latina* 1: 57–96 = Scarcella (1993) 356–384.
Scarcella, A.M. (1977a) "Les Structures Socio-économiques du Roman de Xénophon d'Éphèse," *Revue des Études Greques* 90: 249–262 = Scarcella (1993) 185–197.
Scarcella, A.M. (1977b) "Noterelle al Romanzo di Senofonte Efesio," *Prometheus* 3: 79–86 = Scarcella (1993) 199–206.
Scarcella, A.M. (1979) "La Struttura del Romanzo di Senofonte Efesio," in *La Struttura della Fabulazione Antica*, 89–113. Genoa = Scarcella (1993) 165–184.
Scarcella, A.M. (1981) "Metastasi Narratologica del Dato Storico nel Romanzo Erotico Greco," *Materiali e Contribuii* 3: 341–367 = Scarcella (1993) 77–102.
Scarcella, A.M. (1985a) "Gli Amori di Fedra fra Tragedia e Romanzo," in Uglione, R., ed., *Atti delle Giornate di Studio su Fedra*, 213–239. Turin = Scarcella (1993) 385–408.
Scarcella, A.M. (1985b) "Luciano, le *Storie Vere* e il *furor mathematicus*," *Giornale Italiano di Filologia* 37: 249–257.
Scarcella, A.M. (1986) "Fremde und Barbaren im griechischen Liebesroman," = Scarcella (1993) 103–108.
Scarcella, A.M. (1987) "Caratteri e Funzione delle *gnōmai* in Achille Tazio," *Euphrosyne* 15: 269–280.
Scarcella, A.M. (1990) "Nomos nel Romanzo Greco d'Amore," *Giornale Italiano di Filologia* 42: 243–266.
Scarcella, A.M. (1992) "La Polémologie des Romans," in Baslez (1992) 63–74.
Scarcella, A.M. (1993) *Romanzo e Romanzieri. Note di Narratologia Greca*. Perugia.
Scarcella, A.M. (1995a) "Funzione Narratologica e Connotazione Ideologica del Cibo nei Romanzi Greci d'Amore," in *Scritti in Memoria di G. Forni*. In press.
Scarcella, A.M. (1995b) "Gli Emarginati Sociali e il Tema del 'Buon Cattivo' nei Romanzi Greci d'Amore," *Giornale Italiano di Filologia* 47: 3–25.
Schaeferdiek, K. (1992) "The Acts of John," in Schneemelcher (1992) 2: 152–171.
Schamberger, M. (1917) *De Declamationum Romanarum Argumentis Observationes Selectae*. Diss., Halle.
Schauer, M., Merkle, S. (1992) "Äsop und Sokrates," in Holzberg (1992a) 85–96.
Scheffer, J. (1986) *Qu'est-ce qu'un Genre Littéraire?* Paris.
Schetter, W. (1987) "Dares und Dracontius über die Vorgeschichte des Trojanischen Krieges," *Hermes* 115: 211–231.
Schetter, W. (1988) "Beobachtungen zum Dares Latinus," *Hermes* 116: 94–109.
Schissel von Fleschenberg, O. (1907) *Dares-Studien*. Halle/Saale.
Schissel von Fleschenberg, O. (1909) *Die Rahmenerzählung in den ephesischen Geschichten des Xenophon von Ephesus*. Innsbruck.
Schissel von Fleschenberg, O. (1912) "Die Komposition der *Apista* des Antonius Diogenes," *Novellenkränze Lukians*. Rhetorische Forschungen I, 101–108. Halle.
Schissel von Fleschenberg, O. (1913a) *Die griechische Novelle*. Halle.
Schissel von Fleschenberg, O. (1913b) "Die Technik des Bildeinsatzes," *Philologus* 72: 83–114.
Schlam, C. (1971) "The Scholarship on Apuleius since 1938," *Classical World* 64: 285–309.
Schlam, C. (1992) *The Metamorphoses of Apuleius: On Making an Ass of Oneself*. London.
Schmeling, G. (1969) "Petronius: Satirist, Moralist, Epicurean, Artist," *Classical Bulletin* 45 (1969) 49–50, 64.

Schmeling, G., ed. (1970-present) *Petronian Society Newsletter*. Gainesville, FL.
Schmeling, G. (1971a) "The *Satyricon*: Forms in Search of a Genre," *Classical Bulletin* 47: 49–53.
Schmeling, G. (1971b) "The *Exclusus Amator* Motif in Petronius," in *Fons Perennis. Saggi Critici di Filologia Classica Raccolti in Onore del Prof. Vittorio D'Agostino*, 333–357. Turin.
Schmeling, G. (1974) *Chariton*. New York.
Schmeling, G. (1975) "T.S. Eliot and Petronius," *Comparative Literature Studies* 12: 393–410.
Schmeling, G., Stuckey, J. (1977) *A Bibliography of Petronius*. Leiden.
Schmeling, G. (1980) *Xenophon of Ephesus*. Boston.
Schmeling, G. (1981) "The Authority of the Author: from Muse to Esthetics," in *Atti del Convegno Internazionale: Letterature Classiche e Narratologia*, 369–377. Perugia.
Schmeling, G., ed. (1988) [1989] *Historia Apollonii Regis Tyri*. Leipzig.
Schmeling, G. (1989) "Manners and Morality in *Apollonius of Tyre*," in Liviabella Furiani (1989) 197–215.
Schmeling, G. (1991) "*The Satyricon*: the Sense of an Ending," *Rheinisches Museum* 134: 352–377.
Schmeling, G. (1994a) "Notes to the Text of the *Historia Apollonii Regis Tyri*," Parts 1 and 2, *Latomus* 53: 132–154; 386–403.
Schmeling, G. (1994b) "Confessor Gloriosus: a Role of Encolpius in the *Satyrica*," *Würzburger Jahrbücher für die Altertumswissenschaft* 20: 207–224.
Schmeling, G. (1994c) "*Quid attinet veritatem per interpretem quaerere? Interpretes* and the *Satyricon* of Petronius," in Boyle, A.J., ed. (1995) *Roman Literature and Ideology: Ramus Essays for J.P. Sullivan*. Bendigo, Australia. A reprint in book form of *Ramus* 23.1–2 (1994): 144–168.
Schmeling, G. (1996a) "Apollonius of Tyre: Last of the Troublesome Latin Novels," in *Aufstieg und Niedergang der römischen Welt* II 34.4. Berlin.
Schmeling, G. (1996b) "Aspects of Genre, Narrative and History in the Ancient Novel," in *Aufstieg und Niedergang der römischen Welt* II 35.3. Berlin.
Schmid, W. (1887–1896) *Der Atticismus in seinen Hauptvertretern*, 4 vols. Reprinted Hildesheim 1964. Stuttgart.
Schmid, W. (1899) "Chariton," in Pauly-Wissowa, *Realencyclopädie der classischen Altertumswissenschaft* 3, 2168–2171. Stuttgart.
Schmid, W. (1906) "Ein übersehenes Citat aus einem griechischen Troiaroman," *Philologus* 65: 558–566.
Schmidt, S. (1989) "Verläuft die Entwicklung des Romans von Heliodor zu Goethe (und weiter)? Oder: Inkommensurabilität als literaturhistoriographische Kategorie," *Groningen Colloquia on the Novel* 2: 5–23.
Schmitt-Pantel, P. (1989) "Die Differenz der Geschlechter. Die Geschichtswissenschaft, Ethnologie und die griechische Stadt der Antike," in A. Corbin, ed., *Geschlecht und Geschichte. Ist eine weibliche Geschichtsschreibung möglich?*, 199–223. Frankfurt.
Schneemelcher, W., ed. (1992) *New Testament Apocrypha*, revised edition, translated and edited, R. McL. Wilson. Cambridge.
Schneemelcher, W. (1992a) "Act of Paul," in Schneemelcher (1992) 2: 213–237.
Schneemelcher, W. (1992b) "Acts of Peter," in Schneemelcher (1992) 2: 271–284.
Schneemelcher, W. (1992c) "Introduction to Second and Third Century Acts of Apostles," in Schneemelcher (1992) 75–100.
Schnell, R. (1989) *Liber Alexandri Magni. Die Alexandergeschichte der Handschrift Paris, B.N. n.a.l. 310. Untersuchungen und Textausgabe*. Munich.
Schneider-Menzel, U. (1948) "Jamblichos' Babylonische Geschichten," in F. Altheim, ed., *Literatur und Gesellschaft im ausgehenden Altertum*, Vol. 1, Part 1, "Der Roman," 48–92. Halle.
Schönberger, O. (1989[4]) *Longos, Hirtengeschichten von Daphnis und Chloe*. Griechisch und Deutsch. Berlin.

Schubart, W. (1920) "Aus einer Apollon-Aretalogie," *Hermes* 55: 188–195.
Schwartz, E. (1943²) *Fünf Vorträge über den griechischen Roman* (first edition 1896). Berlin.
Schwartz, H. (1988) *Miriam's Tambourine*. Oxford.
Schwartz, J. (1985) "Quelques Remarques sur les Éphésiaques," *L' Antiquité Classique* 54: 197–204.
Schwarz, F. (1982) "The Itinerary of Iambulus-Utopianism and History," in Sontheimer, G.-D., Aithal, P., eds. (1982) *Indology and Law: Studies in Honour of Professor J.D.M. Derrett*, 18–55. Wiesbaden.
Scobie, A. (1969) *Aspects of the Ancient Romance and its Heritage. Essays on Apuleius, Petronius and the Greek Romance.* Meisenheim.
Scobie, A. (1973) *More Essays on the Ancient Romance and its Heritage.* Meisenheim am Glan.
Scobie, A. (1975) *Apuleius Metamorphoses (Asinus Aureus) I.* Meisenheim.
Scobie, A. (1978) "The Influence of Apuleius' *Metamorphoses* in Renaissance Italy and Spain," in Hijmans (1978) 211–230.
Scobie, A. (1979) "Storytellers, Storytelling and the Novel in Graeco-Roman Antiquity," *Rheinisches Museum* 122: 229–259.
Scobie, A. (1983) *Apuleius and Folklore.* London
Sedelmeier-Stoeckl, D. (1958) *Studien zur Erzählungstechnik des Achilles Tatius.* Diss. Vienna.
Sedelmeier-Stoeckl, D. (1959) "Studien zu Achilleus Tatios," *Wiener Studien* 72: 113–143.
Segal, C. (1984) "The Trials at the End of Achilles Tatius' *Clitophon and Leucippe*. Doublets and Complementaries," *Studi Italiani di Filologia Classica* 77: 83–91.
Segre, C. (1974) *Le Strutture e il Tempo.* Turin.
Segre, C. (1984) *Teatro e Romanzo.* Turin.
Seidensticker, B. (1987) "Die Frau auf der attischen Bühne," in *Die Frau in der Gesellschaft. Vorträge und Beiträge zur Antike als Grundlage für Deutung und Bewältigung heutiger Probleme. Humanistische Bildung* 11: 7–42. Stuttgart.
Selden, D.L. (1994) "Genre of Genre," in Tatum (1994) 39–64.
Sellew, P. (1992) "Paul, Acts of," in Freedman (1992) 5: 201–202.
Shafi, M. (1967) *Wamiq-o-'Adhra' of 'Unṣuri*, 1–8. Lahore. (English preface).
Shaw, B. (1984) "Bandits in the Roman Empire," *Past and Present* 105: 3–52.
Siemens, K., ed. (1988) *Sexualität und Erotik in der Antike.* Darmstadt.
Simon, M. (1963) "Hellenistische Märchenutopien," *Wissenschaftliche Zeitschrift der Humboldt-Universität zu Berlin. Gesellschafts- und Sprachwissenschaftliche Reihe* 12: 237–243.
Smith, B.H. (1968) *Poetic Closure. A Study of How Poems End.* Chicago.
Smith, J.Z. (1978) "The Temple and the Magician," in *idem, Map is not Territory*, 172–189. Leiden.
Smith, M. (1971) "Prolegomena to a Discussion of Aretalogies, Divine Men, the Gospels and Jesus," *Journal of Biblical Literature* 90: 174–199.
Smith, M. (1978) *Jesus the Magician.* London.
Smith, M.S. (1975) *Petronii Arbitri Cena Trimalchionis.* Oxford.
Smith, O. (1987) "Versions and Manuscripts of the *Achilleid*," in H. Eideneier, ed., *Neograeca Medii Aevi*, pp. 315–325. Cologne.
Smith, O. (1988) "Notes on the Byzantine *Achilleid*: the Oxford Version," *Classica et Mediaevalia* 39: 259–272.
Smith, O. (1990) *The Oxford Version of the Achilleid.* Copenhagen.
Smith, O. (1993) "Literary and Ideological Observations to the *Achilleid*," in Panayotakis (1993) vol. 2, 182–187.
Smith, W.D. (1990) *Hippocrates: Pseudepigraphic Writings: Letters – Embassy – Speech from the Altar – Decree. Edited and Translated with an Introduction.* Leiden.
Smith, W.S. (1972) "The Narrative Voice in Apuleius' *Metamorphoses*," *Transactions of the American Philological Association* 103: 513–534.

Smits, I. (1993) "Aesopus in Japan; een zeventiende-eeuwse Best-Seller?," *Hermeneus* 65: 168–172.
Smyly, J. (1909) "Fragment of a Greek Romance," *Hermathena* 9: 322–330.
Snell, B. (1938) *Leben und Meinungen der Sieben Weisen: Griechische und lateinische Quellen aus 2000 Jahren. Mit der deutschen Übertragung.* Munich.
Söder, R. (1932) *Die apokryphen Apostelgeschichten und die romanhafte Literatur der Antike.* Stuttgart.
Sollors, W., ed. (1993) *The Return of Thematic Criticism.* Cambridge, MA.
Southwell, M. (1973) "Women under Christianity," *Arethusa* 6: 149–159.
Specht, E. (1989) *Schön zu sein und gut zu sein. Mädchenbildung und Frauensozialisation im antiken Griechenland.* Vienna.
Speyer, W. (1974) "Zum Bild des Apollonios von Tyana bei Heiden und Christen," *Jahrbuch für Antike und Christentum* 17: 47–63.
Speyer, W., Opelt, I. (1992) "Barbar I," in *Reallexikon für Antike und Christentum.* Supplement Band 1, Lieferung 5/6, pp. 813–895. Stuttgart.
Stadter, P. (1991) "Fictional Narrative in the *Cyropaedia*," *American Journal of Philology* 112: 461–491.
Städele, A. (1980) *Die Briefe des Pythagoras und der Pythagoreer.* Beiträge zur klassischen Philologie, 115. Meisenheim am Glan.
Stanzel, F. (1955) *Die typischen Erzählsituationen im Roman.* Tübingen.
Stanzel, F. (1979) *Theorie des Erzählens.* Göttingen.
Stanzel, K.-H. (1991) "Frühlingserwachen auf dem Lande. Zur erotischen Entwicklung im Hirtenroman des Longos," *Würzburger Jahrbücher für die Altertumswissenschaft* 17: 153–175.
Stark, I. (1984) "Zur Erzählperspektive im griechischen Liebesroman," *Philologus* 128: 256–270.
Stark, I. (1989) "Religiöse Elemente im antiken Roman," in Kuch (1989) 135–149.
Stechow, W. (1953) "Heliodorus' *Aethiopica* in Art," *Journal of the Warburg and Courtauld Institutes* 16: 144–152.
Steffens, K. (1975) *Die Historia de Preliis Alexandri Magni Rezension J*[3]. Meisenheim am Glan.
Stegagno Picchio, L. (1979) "Proto-história dos Palmeirins: A Corte de Constantinopla do *Cligès* ao *Palmerín de Olívia*," (Port. transl.), in *A Lição do Texto. Filologia e Literatura,* 169–206. Lisbon.
Steiner, G. (1969) "The Graphic Analogue from Myth in Greek Romance," in *Classical Studies Presented to B.E. Perry,* 123–137. Chicago.
Stephens, S. (1994) "Who Read Ancient Novels?," in Tatum (1994) 405–418.
Stephens, S., Winkler, J., eds. (1995) *Ancient Greek Novels: the Fragments. Introduction, Text, Translation and Commentary.* Princeton.
Sternberg, M. (1978) *Production de l'Intérêt Romanesque.* The Hague.
Stierle, K. (1980) "The Reading of Fictional Texts," in Suleiman (1980) 83–105.
Stimpson, C. (1989) "Woolf's Room, Our Project: The Building of Feminist Criticism," in Cohen (1989) 129–143.
Stöcker, C. (1969) *Humor bei Petron.* Dissertation, Erlangen.
Stöcker, C. (1980) "Der 10. Aischines-Brief: Eine Kimon-Novelle," *Mnemosyne* 33: 307–312.
Stolz, W. (1987) *Petrons Satyricon und Français Nodot: ein Beitrag zur Geschichte literarischer Fälschungen.* Stuttgart.
Stone, D. (1973) *From Tales to Truths.* Analecta Romanica, No. 34. Frankfurt am Main.
Stoneman, R. (1991) *The Greek Alexander Romance.* Harmondsworth.
Stoneman, R. (1992a) "Oriental Motifs in the *Alexander Romance*," *Antichthon* 26: 95–113.
Stoneman, R. (1992b) "Introduction" to Dakyns, H., trans., *The Education of Cyrus.* London.

Stoneman, R. (1992c) *Palmyra and its Empire. Zenobia's Revolt Against Rome.* Ann Arbor.
Stoneman, R. (1994a) "Romantic Ethnography: Central Asia and India in the *Alexander Romance*," *The Ancient World* 25: 93-107.
Stoneman, R. (1994b) "The *Alexander Romance:* from History to Fiction," in Morgan (1994) 117-129.
Stoneman, R. (1994c) *Legends of Alexander the Great.* London.
Stoneman, R. (1995) "Naked Philosophers: the Brahmans in the Alexander Romance and the Alexander Historians," *Journal of Hellenic Studies* 115: 99-114.
Stoops, R. (1992) "Peter, Acts of," in Freedman (1992) 5: 267-268.
Stramaglia, A. (1992) "Covi di Banditi e Cadaveri 'Scomodi' in Lolliano, Apuleio e [Luciano]," *Zeitschrift für Papyrologie und Epigraphik* 94: 59-63.
Strauss, L. (1948) *On Tyranny. An Interpretation of Xenophon's Hiero.* Ithaca, New York.
Strubbe, J. (1984-86) "Gründer kleinasiatischer Städte," *Ancient Society* 15-17: 253-304.
Stuckey, J. (1966) *The Reputation and Influence of C. Petronius Arbiter among English Men of Letters from 1660-1700.* Dissertation, New Haven.
Suleiman, S., Crosman I., ed. (1980) *The Reader in the Text. Essays on Audience and Interpretation.* Princeton.
Suleiman, S. (1980a) "Varieties of Audience-Oriented Criticism," Introduction to Suleiman (1980) 3-45.
Sullivan, J.P. (1968) *The Satyricon of Petronius: a Literary Study.* London.
Sullivan, J.P. (1968a) "Petronius, Seneca, and Lucan: a Neronian Literary Feud?," *Transactions of the American Philological Association* 99: 453-467.
Sullivan, J.P. (1976) "Interpolations in Petronius," *Proceedings of the Cambridge Philological Society* 22: 90-122.
Sullivan, J.P., trans. (1986) *Petronius the Satyricon.* (First Penguin translation 1965.) Harmondsworth.
Summers, R. (1970) "Roman Justice and Apuleius' *Metamorphoses*," *Transactions of the American Philological Association* 101: 511-531.
Summers, R. (1972) "Apuleius' *Juridicus*," *Historia* 21: 120-126.
Summers, R. (1973) "A Note on the Date of the *Golden Ass*," *American Journal of Philology* 94: 375-383.
Svoboda, K. (1962) "Über die Geschichte des Apollonius von Tyrus," in *Charisteria F. Novotný Octogenario Oblata*, ed. F. Stiebitz, 213-224. Prague.
Swain, S. (1992) "Antonius Diogenes and Lucian," *Liverpool Classical Monthly* 17.5: 74-76.
Swain, S. (1994) "Dio and Lucian," in Morgan (1994) 166-180.
Swanson, R. (1979) "The True, the False, and the Truly False: Lucian's Philosophical Science Fiction," *Science Fiction Studies* 6: 228-239.
Sykutris, J. (1931a) "Epistolographie," *Pauly-Wissowa*, Suppl. 5: 185-220.
Sykutris, J. (1931b) "Sokratikerbriefe," *Pauly-Wissowa*, Suppl. 5: 981-987.
Sykutris, J. (1933) *Die Briefe des Sokrates und der Sokratiker.* (repr. New York 1968). Paderborn.
Syme, R. (1959) "Proconsuls d'Afrique sous Antonin le Pieux," *Revue des Études Anciennes* 61: 310-319.
Szepessy, T. (1957) "Die Aithiopika des Heliodoros und der griechische sophistische Liebesroman," *Acta Antiqua Academiae Scientiarum Hungaricae* 5: 241-259. Reprinted Gärtner (1984) 432-450.
Szepessy, T. (1975) "Die Neudatierung des Heliodoros und die Belagerung von Nisibis," in *Actes de la XIIe Conférence Internationale d'Études Classiques "Eirene", Cluj-Napoca, 2-7 Octobre 1972*, pp. 279-287. Bucarest and Amsterdam.
Szepessy, T. (1976) "Le Siège de Nisibe et la Chronologie d'Héliodore," *Acta Antiqua Academiae Scientiarum Hungaricae* 24: 247-276.
Szepessy, T. (1978) "Zur Interpretation eines neu entdeckten griechischen Roman," *Acta Antiqua Academiae Scientiarum Hungaricae* 26: 29-36.

Szepessy, T. (1981) "Heliodoros und der griechische Liebesroman," *Homonoia* 3: 203–207.
Szepessy, T. (1982–84) "Rhodogune and Ninyas (Comments on Dio Chrysostomos' 21st Discourse)," *Acta Antiqua Academiae Scientiarum Hungaricae* 30: 355–362.
Szepessy, T. (1985–88) "The Ancient Family Novel (a Typological Approach)," *Acta Antiqua Academiae Scientiarum Hungaricae* 31: 357–365.
Tait, J. (1994) "Egyptian Fiction in Demotic and Greek," in Morgan (1994) 203–222.
Tallmadge, E. (1938) *A Grammatical Study of the Greek Life of Aesop.* Diss. University of Illinois. Urbana.
Tatum, J. (1969) "The Tales in Apuleius' *Metamorphoses*," *Transactions of the American Philological Association* 100: 487–527.
Tatum, J. (1979) *Apuleius and The Golden Ass.* Ithaca, N.Y.
Tatum, J., ed. (1988) *William Barker's Translation of Xenophon's Cyropedia (London 1567).* New York.
Tatum, J. (1989) *Xenophon's Imperial Fiction, On the Education of Cyrus.* Princeton.
Tatum, J., Vernazza, G., eds. (1990) *The Ancient Novel. Classical Paradigms and Modern Perspectives*, ICAN II, Proceedings of the International Conference, Dartmouth College 1989. Hanover, NH.
Tatum, J., ed. (1994) *The Search for the Ancient Novel.* Baltimore.
Taylor, A. (1938) "Riddles Dealing with Family Relationships," *Journal of American Folklore* 51: 25–37.
Teske, D. (1991) *Der Roman des Longos als Werk der Kunst.* Münster.
Thibau, R. (1965) "Les *Métamorphoses* d'Apulée et la Théorie Platonicienne de l'Eros," *Studia Philosophica Gandensia* 3: 89–144.
Thiel, H. van (1961) "Über die Textüberlieferung des Longus," *Rheinisches Museum* 104: 356–362.
Thiel, H. van (1971) *Das Eselsroman.* 2 vols. Munich.
Thiel, H. van (1971a) *Petron: Überlieferung und Rekonstruktion.* Leiden.
Thiel, H. van (1983) *Leben und Taten Alexanders von Makedonien.* Darmstadt.
Thomas, H. (1920) *Spanish and Portuguese Romances of Chivalry. The Revival of the Romance of Chivalry in the Spanish Peninsula and its Extention and Influence Abroad.* Cambridge.
Thomas, P. (1960) *Epitoma Rerum Gestarum Alexandri Magni.* Leipzig.
Thompson, S. (1966) *Motif-Index of Folk Literature,* 6 vols. London.
Thraede, K. (1966) "Euhemerismus," *Reallexikon für Antike und Christentum* 6: 877–890.
Thraede, K. (1972) "Frau," in *Reallexikon für Antike und Christentum* 8: 197–269.
Thraede, K. (1977) "Ärger mit der Freiheit. Die Bedeutung von Frauen in Theorie und Praxis der alten Kirche," in G. Scharffenorth, K. Thraede, eds., *Freunde in Christus werden...: Die Beziehung von Mann und Frau als Frage an Theologie und Kirche,* 31–182. Gelnhausen-Berlin.
Tigerstedt, E. (1965) *The Legend of Sparta in Classical Antiquity.* Lund.
Timpanaro, S. (1987) "Sulla Composizione e la Tecnica Narrativa dell' *Ephemeris* di Ditti-Settimio," in *Filologia e Forme Letterarie: Studi Offerti a F. Della Corte,* vol. 4, 169–215. Urbino.
Tissot, Y. (1988) "L'Encratisme des Actes de Thomas," *Aufstieg und Niedergang der römischen Welt* II 25.6, 4415–4430.
Todd, J. (1968) *Persian Paideia and Greek History. An Interpretation of the Cyropaedia of Xenophon. Book One.* Diss. Pittsburgh.
Todorov, T. (1966) "Les Catégories du Récit Litteraire," *Communications* 8: 125–151.
Todorov, T. (1967) *Littérature et Signification.* Paris.
Todorov, T. (1981) *Mikhail Bakhtine: le Principe Dialogique.* Paris.
Todorov, T. (1988) "El Origen de los Géneros," in *Teoría de los Géneros Literarios,* ed. M. Garrido, 31–48. Madrid.
Toher, M. (1989) "On the Use of Nicolaus' Historical Fragments," *Classical Antiquity* 8: 159–172.

Tomaševskij, B. (1928) "La Construction de l'Intrigue," *Théorie de la Littérature*, ed., T. Todorov. Paris.
Totti, M. (1985) *Ausgewählte Texte der Isis- und Sarapis-Religion*. Studia Epigraphica 12. Hildesheim.
Trapp, E. (1971) *Digenes Akrites—Synoptische Ausgabe der ältesten Versionen*. Wiener Byzantinistische Studien, No. 8. Vienna.
Trenkner, S. (1958) *The Greek Novella in the Classical Period*. Cambridge.
Treu, K. (1981) "Menanders Menschen als Polisbürger," *Philologus* 125: 211-214.
Treu, K. (1984) "Roman und Geschichtsschreibung," *Klio* 66: 456-459.
Treu, K. (1989) "Der antike Roman und sein Publikum," in Kuch (1989a) 178-197.
Trumpf, J. (1974) *Vita Alexandri Regis Macedonum*. Stuttgart.
Tsitsikli, D., ed. (1981) *Historia Apollonii Regis Tyri*. Königstein.
Tsolakis, E. (1967) Συμβολὴ στὴ μελέτη τοῦ ποιητικοῦ ἔργου τοῦ Κωνσταντίνου Μανασσῆ καὶ κριτικὴ ἔκδοση τοῦ μυθιστορήματός του "Τὰ κατ' 'Αρίστανδρον καὶ Καλλιθέαν". Epistemonike Epeteris Philosophikes Scholes, Panepistemiou Thessalonikes, No. 10. Thessalonike.
Tudeer, L. (1931) *The Epistles of Phalaris: Preliminary Investigations of the Manuscripts*. Helsinki.
Tüchert, A. (1889) *Racine und Heliodor*. Zweibrücken.
Turcan, R. (1963) "Le Roman Initiatique: à Propos d'un Livre Récent," *Revue de l'Histoire des Religions* 163: 149-199.
Turcan, R. (1989) "ΒΙΟΣ ΒΟΥΚΟΛΙΚΟΣ ou les Mystères de Lesbos," *Göttingische Gelehrte Anzeigen* 241: 169-192.
Turner, P. (1961) *Satirical Sketches*. Harmondsworth.
Turner, P. (1968a) "*Daphnis and Chloe*. An Interpretation," *Greece & Rome* 7: 117-123.
Turner, P. (1968b) "Novels, Ancient and Modern," *Novel* 2: 15-24.
Uspensky, B. (1970) *A Poetics of Composition. A Study of the Artistic Text and Typology of a Compositional Form*. Berkeley.
Utas, B. (1984-86) "Did 'Adhra' Remain a Virgin?," *Orientalia Suecana* 33-35: 429-441.
Vallauri, G. (1956) *Evemero di Messene: Testimonianze e Frammenti con Introduzione e Commento*. Università di Torino. Pubblicazioni della Facoltà di Lettere e Filosofia, 8, 3. Turin.
Vallauri, G. (1960) *Origine e Diffusione dell' Evemerismo nel Pensiero Classico*. Università di Torino. Pubblicazioni della Facoltà di Lettere e Filosofia, 12, 5. Turin.
Valley, G. (1926) *Über den Sprachgebrauch des Longus*. Uppsala.
Van der Valk, M.H.A.L.H. (1941) "Remarques sur la Date des *Éthiopiques* d'Héliodore," *Mnemosyne* 9: 97-100.
Vanhove, A. (1944) "De brieven in het eerste boek van Diogenes Laertios' compilatie," *Revue Belge de Philologie et d'Historie* 23: 5-23.
Vatin, C. (1970) *Recherches sur le Mariage et la Condition de la Femme Mariée à l'Époque Hellénistique*. Paris.
Venini, P. (1981-82) "Ditti Cretese e Omero," *Memorie dell'Istituto Lombardo* 37: 161-198.
Vessey, D. (1991-93) "Thoughts on 'the Ancient Novel' or What Ancients? What Novels?," *Bulletin of the Institute of Classical Studies*. 38: 144-161.
Veyne, P. (1964) "Le 'je' dans le *Satiricon*," *Revue des Études Latines* 42: 301-324.
Vidman, L. (1970) *Isis und Sarapis bei den Griechen und Römern. Epigraphische Studien zur Verbreitung und zu den Trägern dieses ägyptischen Kultes*. Berlin.
Vieillefond, J.-R., ed. (1987) *Longus. Pastorales (Daphnis et Chloé)*. French Translation and Notes. Paris.
Vilborg, E., ed. (1955) *Achilles Tatius: Leucippe and Clitophon*. Studia Graeca et Latina Gothoburgensia 1. Stockholm.

Vilborg, E. (1962) *Achilles Tatius: Leucippe and Clitophon. A Commentary*. Studia Graeca et Latina Gothoburgensia XV. Göteborg.
Vischer, R. (1965) *Das einfache Leben: Wort- und motivgeschichtliche Untersuchungen zu einem Wertbegriff der antiken Literatur*. Studienhefte zur Altertumswissenschaft, 11. Göttingen.
Visser, E. (1948) *Iamboulos en de Eilanden van de Zon*. Groningen.
Vogliano, A. (1938) "Un Papiro di Achille Tazio," *Studi Italiani di Filologia Classica* 15: 121–130.
Vogt-Spira, G. (1992) *Dramaturgie des Zufalls. Tyche und Handeln in der Komödie Menanders*. Munich.
Vox, O. (1986) "Dafni Lirico," *Belfagor* 41: 311–317.
Vryonis, S. (1957) "The Will of a Provincial Magnate: Eustathios Boilas (1059)," *Dumbarton Oaks Papers* 11: 263–277.
Vycichl, W. (1977) "Heliodors *Aithiopica* und die Volksstämme des Reiches Meroe," in *Ägypten und Kusch*, ed., Endesfelder, E., etc. *Schriften zur Geschichte und Kultur des alten Orients* 13, pp. 447–458. Berlin.
Wagner, W. (1870) *Carmina Graeca Medii Aevi*. Leipzig.
Wagner, W. (1881) *Trois Poèmes Grecs du Moyen Age*. Berlin. (βιος Αλεξανδρου, partial reprint 1990, Athens).
Wagner-Hasel, B. (1988a) "Das Private wird politisch. Die Perspektive 'Geschlecht' in der Altertumswissenschaft," in U. Becher, J. Rüsen, eds., *Weiblichkeit in geschichtlicher Perspektive*, 11–50. Frankfurt.
Wagner-Hasel, B. (1988b) "Frauenleben in orientalischer Abgeschiedenheit? Zur Geschichte und Nutzanwendung eines Topos," *Der altsprachliche Unterricht* 32: 18–29.
Wagner-Hasel, B. (1993) "Geschichte der Frauen. Epilog," in P. Schmitt-Pantel, ed., *Antike*, Vol. 1, 535–543. Frankfurt.
Waiblinger, F., ed. (1978) *Historia Apollonii Regis Tyri*. Munich.
Walbank, F.W. (1955) "Tragic History: a Reconsideration," *Bulletin of the Institut of Classical Studies* 2: 4–14.
Walbank, F.W. (1960) "History and Tragedy," *Historia* 9: 216–234.
Walden, J. (1894) "Stage-Terms in Heliodorus's *Aethiopica*," *Harvard Studies in Classical Philology* 5: 1–43.
Waldstein, W. (1983) "Zur Stellung der Frau im römischen Recht," in *Festschrift für Robert Muth zum 65. Geburtstag am 1. Jan. 1981*, 559–571. Innsbruck.
Walker, J. (1971) *The Satyricon, the Golden Ass and the Spanish Picaresque Novel*. Dissertation, Brigham Young University, Provo, Utah.
Wallace, P. (1968) "Μή with the Participle in Longus and Achilles Tatius," *American Journal of Philology* 89: 321–333.
Walsh, P. (1970) *The Roman Novel*. Cambridge.
Walsh, P. (1974) review of Bianco (1971) and van Thiel (1971), *Classical Review* 24: 215–218.
Walsh, P. (1978) "Petronius and Apuleius," in Hijmans (1978) 17–24.
Walsh, P. (1981) "Apuleius and Plutarch," in Blumenthal (1981) 20–32.
Warden, P., Bagnall, R. (1988) "The Forty Thousand Citizens of Ephesus," *Classical Philology* 83: 220–223.
Webster, T.B.L. (1974) *An Introduction to Menander*. Manchester.
Wehrhans, H., trans. (1983) *Chariton: Kallirhoë*, in Kytzler (1983) vol. 1, 513–672.
Wehrli, F. (1965) "Einheit und Vorgeschichte der griechisch–römischen Romanliteratur," *Museum Helveticum* 22: 133–154, and in Gärtner (1984) 161–182.
Weil, H. (1902) "La Ninopédie," in *Étude de Littérature et de Rhythmique Grecque*, 90–106. Paris.
Weinreich, O. (1909) *Antike Heilungswunder*. Giessen.
Weinreich, O. (1923) "Das Märchen von Amor und Psyche und andere Volksmärchen im Altertum," in L. Friedländer, *Darstellungen aus der Sittengeschichte Roms*, Bd. 4, 10th edition, 1923: 89–132.

Weinreich, O. (1950) "Nachwort," in Reymer, R., *Aithiopika*. Zurich. Reissued as *Der griechische Liebesroman*, Zurich 1962; partly reprinted in Gärtner (1984) 408–431.
Weinreich, O. (1962) *Der griechische Liebesroman*. Zürich.
Weinstein, M. (1972) *The Oxyrhyncus Papyri* 41. P.Oxy.2948, 12–14. London.
Weitzmann, K. (1959) *Ancient Book Illumination*. Harvard.
Wellek, R., Warren, A. (1956³) *Theory of Literature*. (Originally published 1942). New York. [Spanish trans. *Teoría Literaria* 1953. Madrid].
Wesseling, B. (1988) "The Audience of the Ancient Novels," *Groningen Colloquia on the Novel* 1: 67–79.
West, S. (1971) "Notes on Some Romance Papyri," *Zeitschrift für Papyrologie und Epigraphik* 7: 96.
West, S. (1991) "Sea-Monsters at Sunrise," *Classical Quarterly* 41: 275.
Westermann, A. (1845) *Vita Aesopi. Ex Vratislaviensi ac partim Monacensi et Vindobonensi codicibus*. Brunswick.
Weyman, C. (1909) "*Nodus virginitatis*," *Rheinisches Museum* 64: 156.
Wiechers, A. (1961) *Aesop in Delphi*. Beiträge zur klassischen Philologie, 2. Meisenheim am Glan.
Wiersma, S. (1990) "The Ancient Greek Novel and its Heroines: a Female Paradox," *Mnemosyne* 41: 109–123.
Wifstrand, A. (1944–5) "Εἰκότα. Emendationen und Interpretationen zu griechischen Prosaikern der Kaiserzeit. V: zu den Romanschriftstellern," *Kunglistiska Humanistiska Vetenskapssamfundet i Land -Årsberättelse*: 1–41 (69–109).
Wilamowitz-Moellendorff, U.v. (1966⁹) *Griechisches Lesebuch, II: Erläuterungen*. Dublin.
Wilcken, U. (1893) "Ein neuer griechischer Roman," *Hermes* 28: 161–193.
Wilcken, U. (1901) "Eine neue Roman-Handschrift," *Archiv für Papyrusforschung* 1: 227–264.
Wilcken, U. (1923) "Alexander der Grosse und die indischen Gymnosophisten," *Sitzungsber. Preuss. Akad. der Wissenschaften Berlin* (phil. hist. Klasse): 150–183.
Willis, W. (1984) "Identifying and Editing a Papyrus of Achilles Tatius by Computer," *Atti del XVII Congresso internazionale di Papirologia I*, pp. 163–166. Naples.
Wills, L. (1994) "The Jewish Novellas," in Morgan (1994) 223–238.
Wills, L. (1995) *The Jewish Novel in the Ancient World*. Ithaca.
Wilmart, A. (1933) "Les Textes Latins de la Lettre de Palladius sur les Moeurs des Brahmanes," *Revue Bénédictine* 45: 29–42.
Wilsdorf, H. (1991) "Der weise Achikaros bei Demokrit und Theophrast: Eine Kommunikationsfrage," *Philologus* 135: 191–206.
Wilson, N. (1983) *Scholars of Byzantium*. London.
Wilson, N. (1992) *From Byzantium to Italy*. London.
Winiarczyk, M. (1991) *Evhemerus Messenius: Reliquiae*. Leipzig.
Winkler, J. (1980a) "Lollianos and the Desperadoes," *Journal of Hellenic Studies* 100: 155–181.
Winkler, J. (1980b) "Lucian's *Tritonomendetes* (*True History* 1.35)," *Classical World* 73: 304f.
Winkler, J. (1982) "The Mendacity of Kalasiris and the Narrative Strategy of Heliodoros' *Aithiopika*," *Yale Classical Studies* 27: 93–158.
Winkler, J. (1985) *Auctor & Actor: a Narratological Reading of Apuleius's Golden Ass*. Berkeley.
Winkler, J. (1990a) *The Constraints of Desire. The Anthropology of Sex and Gender in Ancient Greece*. New York.
Winkler, J. (1990b) "The Education of Chloe: Hidden Injuries of Sex," in Winkler (1990a) 101–126.
Winkler, J. (1994) "The Invention of Romance," in Tatum (1994) 23–38.
Winston, D. (1956) *Iambulus: a Literary Study in Greek Utopianism*. Diss. Columbia University. New York.

Winston, D. (1976) "Iambulus's Island of the Sun and Hellenistic Literary Utopias," *Science Fiction Studies* 3: 219–227.
Wirth, G., Veh, O., Nothers, Th. (1992) *Diodoros: Griechische Weltgeschichte. Übersetzt, Eingeleitet und Kommentiert*. Vol. I (= Books 1–3). Stuttgart.
Witt, R.E. (1971) *Isis in the Graeco-Roman World*. London.
Wlosok, A. (1969) "Zur Einheit der *Metamorphosen* des Apuleius," *Philologus* 113: 68–84.
Woeller, W. (1963) "Der Märchentyp von Amor und Psyche und die Gestalt des Tierbräutigams," *Das Altertum* 9: 97–105.
Wolff, O.L.B. (1841) *Allgemeine Geschichte des Romans*. Jena.
Wolff, S. (1912) *Greek Romance in Elizabethan Prose Fiction*. Columbia University Studies in Comparative Literature 12. New York.
Wolohojian, A. (1969) *The Romance of Alexander the Great by Pseudo-Callisthenes*. New York.
Woodward, G., Mattingly, H., eds. (1914) *Barlaam and Ioasaph*. Greek Text with English Translation. London.
Wouters, A. (1989–90) "The ΕΙΚΟΝΕΣ in Longus' *Daphnis and Chloe* IV 39,2: 'Beglaubigungsapparat'?," *Sacris Erudiri. Jaarboek voor Godsdienstwetenschappen* 31: 465–479.
Wouters, A. (1994) "Longus, *Daphnis et Chloé*. Le *proemion* et les Histoires Enchâssées, à la Lumière de la Critique Récente," *Les Études Classiques* 62: 131–167.
Yatromanolakis, Y. (1988) "Baskanos Eros: Love and the Evil-Eye in Heliodorus' *Aethiopica*," in Beaton (1988) 194–204.
Youtie, H. (1975) "Hypographeus: the Social Impact of Illiteracy in Graeco-Roman Egypt," *Zeitschrift für Papyrologie und Epigraphik* 17: 201–221.
Zanetto, G. (1990) "La Lingua dei Romanzieri Greci," *Giornale Italiano di Filologia* 42: 233–242.
Zanker, P. (1979) "Zur Funktion und Bedeutung griechischer Skulptur in der Römerzeit," in *Le Classicisme à Rome*, ed. H. Flashar, 283–314. Vandoeuvres-Geneva.
Zegers, N. (1959) *Wesen und Ursprung der tragischen Geschichtsschreibung*. Köln.
Zeitlin, F. (1971) "Petronius as Paradox: Anarchy and Artistic Integrity," *Transactions of the American Philological Association* 102: 631–684.
Zeitlin, F. (1990) "The Poetics of *Eros*: Nature, Art, and Imitation in Longus' *Daphnis and Chloe*," in *Before Sexuality*, eds. D. Halperin, J. Winkler, F. Zeitlin, 417–464. Princeton.
Zeitlin, F. (1994) "Gardens of Desire in Longus's *Daphnis and Chloe*: Nature, Art, and Imitation," in Tatum (1994) 148–170.
Zeitz, H. (1935) *Die Fragmente des Äsopromans in Papyrushandschriften*. Diss. Gießen.
Zeitz, H. (1936) "Der Aesoproman und seine Geschichte: Eine Untersuchung im Anschluss an die neugefundenen Papyri," *Aegyptus* 16: 225–256.
Ziebarth, E. (1914) *Aus dem griechischen Schulwesen*. 2nd edition. Leipzig.
Ziegler, R. (1977) "Münzen Kilikiens als Zeugnis kaiserlicher Getreidespenden," *Jahrbuch für Numismatik und Geldgeschichte* 27: 29–67.
Ziegler, R. (1984) "Die *Historia Apollonii Regis Tyri* und der Kaiserkult in Tarsos," *Chiron* 14: 219–234.
Zimmermann, B. (1989) "Roman und Enkomium. Xenophons Erziehung des Kyros," *Würzburger Jahrbücher für die Altertumswissenschaft* 15: 97–105.
Zimmermann, B. (1994) "Liebe und poetische Reflexion. Der Hirtenroman des Longos," *Prometheus* 20: 193–210.
Zimmermann, F. (1922) *De Charitonis Codice Thebano*. Diss. Leipzig. Tübingen.
Zimmermann, F. (1935) "Verkannte Papyri," *Archiv für Papyrusforschung* 11: 165–175.
Zimmermann, F. (1936) *Griechische Roman-Papyri und verwandte Texte*. Heidelberg.
Zimmermann, F. (1949–50) "Die Ἐφεσιακά des sogenannten Xenophon von Ephesos: Untersuchungen zur Technik und Komposition," *Würzburger Jahrbücher für die Altertumswissenschaft* 4: 252–286.

Zimmermann, F. (1957) "Kallirhoes Verkauf durch Theron. Eine juristisch-philologische Betrachtung zu Chariton," in *Aus der byzantinischen Arbeit der Deutschen Demokratischen Republik*, vol. 1, 72–81. Berlin.

Zimmermann, F. (1961) "Chariton und die Geschichte," in *Sozialökonomische Verhältnisse in alten Orient und klassischen Altertum*, 329–345. Berlin.

Zucchelli, B. (1986) "A Proposito dell' Epistolario di Chione d'Eraclea," *Paideia* 41: 13–24.

Zumschlinge, M. (1976) *Euhemeros: Staatstheoretische und staatsutopische Motive*. Diss. Bonn.

INDEX

(numbers in bold type indicate a substantial discussion)

abbreviations *see* epitomes
abortion 180, 205
Achilleid, Tale of Achilles 730–731
Achilles 126, 198, 213, 436, 437, 567ff.
Achilles Tatius, *Leucippe and Clitophon* 13, 14, 15, 17, 29, 31, 34, 35, 36, 40, 50, 68, 85, 87, 88, 93, 95, 106, 108, 109, 111, 113, 116, 117, 118, 119, 120, 121, 122, 123, 126, 127, 128, 129, 131, 143, 158, 162, 163, 172, 174, **187–189**, 200, 201, 202, 203, 206, 210, 211, 213, 214, 215, 218, **235–244**, 279, 282, 283, 284, 285, 286, 290, 293, 298, 299, 301, 302, 304, 315, 324, 358, **387–416**, 422, 423, 439, 440, 503, 541, 618, 655, 671, 694, 699, 713, 715, 716, 725, 738, 743, 748, 751, 753, 754, 755, 758, 760, 761, 762, 763, 764, 767, 769, 772, 773, 797, 798
Acts of Andrew **695–697**
Acts of the Apostles (apocryphal) 19, 25, 358, 615, 690, 691, **691–706**
Acts of the Apostles (canonical) 143, 690
Acts of John **697–699**
Acts of Paul 26, **699–702**
Acts of Peter **702–704**
Acts of Thomas **704–706**
Acts of Xanthippe and Polyxena **707–708**
Aesop **633–639**
Aesop Romance see Life of Aesop
aesthetics 288
African Latin 505
Against Neaira 152
Ahikar Romance 75, 636
Aithiopika, Ethiopian Story see Heliodorus
Alcestis 168
Alcibiades 126
Alexander the Great *see Letters of Alexander the Great* and Pseudo-Callisthenes
Alexander Romance see Pseudo-Callisthenes
Alexandria 91, 92, 387, 389, 402, 408, 602, 603, 695, 697
allegory 446, 590
alliteration in Apuleius 505
allusions *see* intextuality 485
Amadis de Gaula, reworked by Garci Rodríguez de Montalvo 777, 778, 779, 780, 781, 782, 783, 785
Amazons 662, 666
Amor and Psyche *see* Apuleius
Amyot, Jacques 735, 739, 742, 743, 744, 751, 764, 765
anagnorisis 49, 440, 448, 449, 525, 643, 779
anaktoron 136
analepsis 283
Andromache 164, 587
Andromeda 127
Antheia fragment **661**, 667, 683
Anthia and Habrocomes see Xenophon of Ephesus
Antioch-on-the-Orontes 91, 92, 518, 519, 658, 726
Antiphon 65
Antisthenes 38
Antoninus Pius, emperor 390
Antonius Diogenes, *Wonders beyond Thule* 17, 29, 31, 34, 35, 40, 41, 84, 88, 90, 98, 103, 104, 105, 106, 161, 556, 559, 561, 655, 657, **674–680**, 683, 695, 737, 738, 748, 768
Antonius Liberalis 35
Aphrodisias 313, 315, 328
Aphrodite 77, 78, 116, 126, 152, 154, 155, 180, 195, 311, 312
Apollo 126, 337, 447
Apollonius fragments *see also Historia Apollonii* 661–662
Apollonius of Rhodes 55, 56, 57, 58
Apollonius of Tyana *see also* Philostratus 613–618
Apollonius of Tyre see Historia Apollonii Regis Tyri
apparent death *see* Scheintod
aprosdoketa 570, 574
Apuleius, *Metamorphoses* 13, 14, 15,

26, 29, 34, 62, 63, 64, 77, 103,
105, 111, 117, 118, 126, 128, 129,
131, 134, 139, 140, 144, 146, 147,
161, 162, 171, 175, 176, **181–184**,
205, 211, 219, 280, 281, 287, 291,
300, 385, 480, 482, 484, 487,
491–516, 533, 541, 545, 546, 639,
643, 647, 657, 669, 670, 671, 672,
683, 697, 706, 763, 768
Arabia 622
"architecture" 144
aretalogos 137, 140, 147
aretalogy and the novel 76, 78, 79,
131–150, 613
arete 652, 653
argumentum 15, 27, 28, 32
Ariadne 127
Aristandros and Kallithea see Manasses
Aristides, P. Aelius 68, 141, 492, 513, 514
Aristides of Miletus 62, 64
aristocrats 122
Aristophanes 38, 163, 169, 677
Aristotle 48, 49, 51, 53, 63, 99, 289, 590, 744
Arrian 103, 559, 656
art/nature 382, 383
Artapanus 687–688
Artaxerxes, King of Persia 310, 581
Artemis 13, 126, 159, 188, 195, 213, 348, 352
Asclepius 141
Asia Minor 122
Asianism 317, 505
Ass Romance, Lucius or the Ass see Pseudo-Lucian
assumed source 545–546
Athena 159
Athenaenus 625
Athenian Expedition 309
Athens 91, 154, 491
Atticism 68, 92, 94, 317, 318, 320, 321, 322, 323, 325, 456, 657
audience *see* reader
Augustine 491
authentication 566, 748, 790
author, female 164
autobiography 508, 509

Babylon 584, 593
Babyloniaca see Iamblichus
Bakhtin, M. 279, 280, 515
barbarians in the novel *see also* margin **209–220**, 593, 629

Barlaam and Ioasaph 708
de Barros, João, *Crónica do Imperador Clarimondo* 784–790
Bartanuba Romance 112, 659
Baudoin, J., *Histoire Negre-Pontique* 754, 755, 756, 757, 758, 762
Belthandros and Chrysantza **725–726**
Bildung 127–128, 191
Bildungsroman 502
biography 140, 143, 580, 588, 613, 617, 618
blood/symbol 365, 381, 518, 524, 525, 541, 547
Boccaccio 495, 722
boukoloi 214, 348, 384, 403, 409, 440, 671, 674
Brahmans 602ff.
brigands *see* pirates
Britain, Nachleben in **764–773**
Brontë, Charlotte 358
brothel 186, 249, 341, 523, 524, 541, 542, 548, 549
bucolic world 371
Byzantine novels **713–733**
Byzantine revival of ancient novel **713–733**
Byzantium 87, 161, 739

Calligone 655, 662, **666–667**, 683
Callimachus 59, 60, 158
Callirhoe, Callirhoe *see* Chariton
Callisthenes *see* Pseudo-Callisthenes
Callistratus 374
canon, literary 3–4
Caracalla, emperor 389, 578
Carmina Burana 551
Carthage 491, 492
Cassander of Macedon 621, 626
catharsis 99
Cena Trimalchionis see Petronius
Cervantes 40
Chaereas and Callirhoe see Chariton
characterization, character portrayal **115–129**
characters, compared with deities 126–127
characters, female: antagonist, intimate friend, mother 200–203
Chariton, *Chaereas and Callirhoe* 13, 14, 15, 17, 20, 21, 25, 26, 27, 28, 29, 30, 31, 33, 35, 36, 39, 40, 41, 42, 43, 44, 45, 46, 47, 48, 49, 50, 51, 52, 53, 54, 58, 59, 60, 64, 65, 67, 68, 70, 74, 75, 76, 77, 78, 81, 82,

83, 85, 88, 89, 90, 92, 95, 96, 97, 98, 100, 101, 102, 106, 111, 116, 118, 119, 120, 121, 122, 123, 125, 126, 127, 128, 129, 143, 159, 172, 178, 179–181, 185, 200, 201, 203, 205, 209, 210, 211, 213, 214, 217, 218, **222–235**, 279, 282, 283, 284, 288, 289, 290, 296, 297, 299, 301, 304, 305, **309–335**, 347, 349, 358, 392, 450, 481, 482, 590, 661, 682, 688, 692, 693, 694, 724, 725, 748
charisma 617, 692
chastity 115, 158, 197, 301, 450, 451, 525, 700–702, 704, 717
Chaucer, G. 551
children, exposure of 193, 203, 361, 367, 446, 778
Chion of Heraclea *see also Letters of Chion* 24, 28, 29, 69, 645, 647, **650–653**
Chion Novel *see* Chion of Heraclea
Chione, Chione 100, 113, 655, **660–661**
Choricius 66
Christian novel 12, 175, 176, 206, 531, 532, 533, 537, 538, **685–711**
Christianity 94, 133, 142, 412
chronique scandaleuse 630
Cicero 16, 32, 46
Cinderella story 113
cinema and the novel 345, 358, 359, 489
cities and readers 90
city/country 383
civilization 383
classification 613
clausulae 322, 324, 475–478
Clement *see* Pseudo-Clement
Cleopatra 153
Collectio Augustana 633
comic strips 527
commentarius 563, 576
concubines 230
condensed versions *see* epitomes
confession and the *Satyrica* 484–487
Constantine 659
Constantinople 714, 720, 726
contaminatio 776
controversia 65
conventions, literary 332
Correspondence of Hippocrates 19, 646–647
Correspondence of the Seven Wise Men 648
coterie, literary 714

Council of Trent 490
counter-culture 680
court proceedings 482
criminal-satiric novels **669–674**
critical theory and the novel **277–305**
  American New Critics 288
  Aristotle 277
  Bakhtin, M. 279, 280
  Beneviste, E. 280
  Bremond, C. 281
  Brooks, P. 293
  Forster, E.M. 281
  Foucault, M. 301
  Freud, S. 293, 294, 295
  Frye, N. 300
  Genette, G. 281, 282
  Girard, R. 295
  Greimas, A. 281
  Hartman, G. 294
  Hegel, G. 278
  Huet, D. 277
  Iser, W. 290
  James, H. 281, 282, 283, 285
  Jung, C. 299
  Kristeva, J. 279
  Lesser, S. 293
  Lukács, G. 278
  Matte Blaco, I. 294
  Mendel, G. 295
  Orlando, F. 294
  Plato 294
  Propp, V. 281
  Robert, M. 295
  Russian formalists 280
  Suleiman, S. 288
crowds 116
crucifixion 341, 668
Ctesias of Cnidus, *Persica, Indica* 18, 41, 42, 46, 48, 555, 591, 604, **629–632**
cultural hero 611, 612
"Cupid and Psyche" *see also* Apuleius 497, 498, 515
curiositas 507, 511, 512
Cyclops 127
Cyrene 520
Cyropaedia *see* Xenophon of Athens
Cyrus *see* Xenophon of Athens

Daphnis and Chloe *see* Longus
Dares Phrygius, *Acta diurna belli Troiani* 13, 16, 17, 19, 25, **563–580**, 630

Darius 602, 603
Daulis **674**, 680
deconstruction 300
deflowering 463, 464, 518, 523, 529
Defoe, Daniel 1
Deianeira 168
Delos 137, 138
Delphi 116, 443, 447, 448, 635, 636, 638
Demeter 150
democracy 223
Demosthenes 737
déracinement 87, 92
Derkyllis and Dinias see Antonius Diogenes
designer-text 90
dexiosis 169
dialectics 290
dialogics 279
Diana 532, 533
Dictys Cretensis, *Ephemeris belli Troiani* 16, 17, 19, 25, **563–580**, 614, 630, 790
Dido 170, 516
diegema mythikon/plasmatikon 16, 27, 28, 32, 64
Digenes Akrites **719–720**
digressions see interpolated stories
Dio Cassius 389, 671
Dio Chrysostom, Dio of Prusa, *The Hunters of Euboea* 41, 578, 617, **640–644**
Diodorus Siculus 39, 42, 78, 216, 217, 621, 622, 624, 625, 626, 627, 629
Diogenes, Cynic 38
Dionysus 76, 77, 126, 131, 132, 145, 146, 152, 384, 385
Diotima 168, 197
director 547
discourse 37
divine intervention 448
Domitian, emperor 23
drama and the novel **48–52**
Dream of Nectanebus see Nectanebus
dreams 138, 355, 356, 395, 444, 445, 448
dromena 134, 135
Drosilla and Charikles see Eugenianos
Dumuzi myths 113
Durrell, Lawrence 489
Du Ryer, Pierre 414

Eastern influences and the novel **70–80**, 205

economic structures see social and economic structures
ecphrasis 109, 290, 324, 361, 372, 383, 399, 400, 504, 724, 762, 794
Edessa 705
education/learning 204, 521, 523, 665, 693
ego-narrative see first-person narrative
Egyptian influences **71–76**, 111, 311, 337, 510, 522, 603, 681
Egyptian tales and the novel **71–76**
eirenarch 339, 347
Elagabalus, emperor 389, 417, 418, 447
elegy and the novel **59–65**
Eleusis 134
Elias of Crete 423
Eliot, T.S. 485, 489, 550
ellypsis 283, 549
Emesa 417
emotions, appeal to 331, 332–334, 593
enactment 548
entertainment 585, 590, 694
Ephesiaca see Xenophon of Ephesus
Ephesus 345, 346, 387, 395, 522, 697, 698, 701
epic and the novel **54–59**, 278, 516
Epictetus 103
Epiphanius 104
epistolary novel 23ff., 68–70, 162, 278, 580, **645–653**
epitomes 348–350, 517, 529, 534, 572, 655, 695
erastes/eromenos 381
Eros 78, 145, 146, 164, 166, 168, 171, 188, 195, 309, 331, 352, 363, 372, 376, 378, 379, 381, 400, 725, 726, 729
Erotica Pathemata see Parthenius
escapism 81
Ethiopia 417ff.
ethopoeia 728
Etruscans 155
eudaimonia 386
Eugenianos, Niketas, *Drosilla and Charikles* 715, **717**, 727, 729
Eugenikos, John 423, 454
Euhemerus 13, 38, 209, 210, 211, 216, **621–628**
Eumachia 155
eunuchs 233
Euripides 48, 49, 50, 51, 52, 59, 158, 168, 169, 438
Europa 399

INDEX

European novel 319
Eustathius of Antioch 411
exaggeration 560
execution of criminals 226
exegetes 140, 147
exotic 592, 593
exposure *see* children
extra characters 116–117
eye-witness (autopsy) 563, 566

fable 15, 32, 53, 55, 278, **633–639**
fabula 37, 280, 778
fairytale 184, 723
faithful friend 309
family novel 544
fantastic tales of travel 88, 555–561, **621–628**
fantasy texts 561
fate 170
father/daughter relationship 518, 521, 522, 523, 524, 525, 530, 544, 547
Faustinus *see* Isidora
Fellini, Federico 459, 489
female authorship 164
feminism 151
feminist readings 304
Ferreira de Vasconcelos, Jorge, *Memorial das Proezas da Segunda Távola Redonda* 787, 788
fiction 16, 32, 80–81, 555, 588, 685
fictionality 546
Fielding, H. 358
figura etymologica 540
first-person narrative 73, 286, 287, 410, 484, 715, 717, 718, 728, 795
Fitzgerald, F. Scott 489
flashback 594, 674, 675, 744
focalization 283, 284, 285, 286, 374
folktale 53, 113, 592
foreshadowing 97, 98, 99
Forster, E.M. 2, 483
Fortunatus 535
Fortune *see* Tyche
fragments of novels **655–683**
France, Nachleben in **750–764**
freedmen 475
fringe novels 14ff.
Fronto 505
Fry, Christopher 489
Frye, N. 313
Fumée, Martin 747–750, 758–759, 763

games 287, 291, 292, 502, 508, 514
Gellius, Aulus 558

gender studies 303
genre and the novel **11ff.**, **32–37**, 88, 107, 483–487, 567, 623, 775
genre for women, novel as 84
geography 561, 592, 593
Gerzan, François 762, 763
Gesta Romanorum 551
Gilgamesh 561
Gnostics 689, 695, 698, 706
god-ridden world 136
gods, portrayal of 128–129
Goethe, J.-W. von 191, 195, 206
Golden Age 378, 624
Golden Ass see Apuleius
Gorgias 65–66, 319, 373
Gospels (apocryphal) 615, 689
Gospels (canonical) 689–690
Gower, J. 551
Grange, John 769
Greene, Robert 765, 772, 773
Grimm Brothers 113
Groningen Colloquia on the Novel (GCN) 5
Gymnosophists 272, 434, 453, 607

Hadrian, emperor 389, 417
hagiography, hagiographic novels 613, 615, 616, 617
handbook 588
happy-ending 327, 354, 367, 444, 588, 693, 723
healing cults 173
Hecataeus 210, 211
Heliodorus, *Aethiopica, Ethiopica* 13, 14, 15, 31, 34, 35, 39, 40, 42, 55, 68, 85, 88, 93, 94, 95, 96, 113, 116, 117, 118, 119, 120, 123, 124, 125, 126, 127, 128, 129, 139, 143, 144, 145, 146, 158, 163, 170, 174, 176, 178, 192–199, 200, 202, 203, 206, 207, 211, 213, 214, 215, 218, 220, **259–276**, 283, 285, 287, 289, 290, 297, 298, 302, 304, 305, 324, 347, 388, 394–398, 408, 409, 411, 412, 413, **417–456**, 615, 642, 655, 674, 675, 713, 715, 716, 732, 733, 735, 736, 738, 744, 748, 749, 751, 753, 754, 755, 756, 757, 758, 762, 763, 765, 766, 767, 768, 769, 770, 771, 772, 773, 783, 786, 793
Helios 121, 131, 138, 139, 140, 214, 215, 337, 352, 417, 446, 447, 453, 604
Hellenism in France **739–744**
Hellenistic history 602
Hellenistic literature 582

870 INDEX

Heraclea 650, 651, 652
Heracles 127
Heraidous 153
Herembert, J. 759, 760, 761, 762
heritage of the ancient Greek novel in France, Britain **735–773**
hermeneutic playfulness 507, 512
Hermogenes 33, 34, 372
hero/heroines 31, 96, 101, 127, 128, 162, 178, 199, 589, 591, 593, 723
Herodas 377
Herodian 94
Herodotus 40, 45, 48, 65, 70, 324, 332, 346, 559, 581, 582, 590, 591, 629
Herpyllis 655, 682, 683
hetaira 152, 169
hiatus 325
hieros gamos 191
hieros logos 145, 147
high culture 107
Hippolytus 126, 438
histoire **280–281**
historia 15, 16, 32
Historia Apollonii Regis Tyri 16, 17, 27, 43, 76, 88, 109, 110, 111, 112, 113, 292, 358, **517–551**, 662, 707, 722
historiography and the novel **42–48**, 65, 278, 325–327, 439, 629, 686, 737
holyman 614, 615, 616, 617, 618
Homer, *Iliad, Odyssey* 54, 56, 58, 65, 80, 97, 101, 123, 157, 164, 175, 214, 324, 333, 344, 352, 373, 436, 437, 443, 452, 454, 481, 515, 516, 530, 567ff., 581, 586, 591, 697, 754, 757, 769
homonoia 328
homosexuality 338, 366, 383, 400, 401
Horace 744
Huet, P.-D. 745, 746, 747, 748, 749, 751, 760
human sacrifice 284, 444, 716
husband, first 203
"Hymn of the Pearl" 705
"Hymn to Isis" 135
Hypatia, Neo-Platonist 154
Hysmine and Hysminias see Makrembolites

Iamblichus, *Babyloniaca* 17, 29, 34, 35, 40, 41, 94, 95, 149, 172, **184–185**, 200, 210, 213, 214, 215, 220, 422, 614, 655, 662, 667, 668, 673, 675, 682, 738, 763
Iambulus 18, 39, 41, 210, 216, 220, 555, **621–628**
ideal novel 14, 88, 100
Iliad see Homer
illegitimate birth 193
illustrated text 527
implied audience 546
implied medium 545, 546
implied narrator 533
implied reader 288, 546
in medias res 283
incest 518, 519, 520, 530
initiation 133ff.
India 39, 604, 605, 608, 626, 705
inner form/outer form 483
intent 144
International Conference on the Ancient Novel (ICAN) 4
interpolated stories 73, 287, 483, 510, 511
interpreter/*exegetes* 377, 385
intertextuality 278, 279, 291, 485, 590–592
intrusive narrator 284, 311, 546
Iolaus 13, 29, 79, 88, 101, 104, 105, 106, 656, **673–674**
irony 279, 290, 375, 377, 451, 675, 677
Isidora, sister of Antonius Diogenes 84, 103, 161, 162, 163, 675, 676, 677
Isis, *Isisroman* 76, 77, 131, 135, 139, 145, 146, 147, 150, 154, 155, 291, 352, 353, 385, 507, 509, 511, 513, 514, 533
Isocrates 590

Jesus Christ 617
Jewish-Christian influence 601
Jewish novels 686, 687–689
John the Lydian 105, 655, 675
John of Salisbury 488
Joseph and Aseneth 113, 688, 707
judges, criminal 226
Julia: Domna, Maesa, Mammaea 153, 453, 614, 615
Julian, emperor 17, 18, 19, 25, 27, 34, 93, 148, 159, 418, 419, 736, 744

kalokagathia 175
katabasis 481, 515
kerygma 143

kidnapping 657, 708
king, by inheritance 223, 226
knowledge, hidden 386
Königsnovelle 681
koine 317, 318, 320, 321, 322, 323, 324, 350, 372
Kornaros, Vitsentzos, *Erotokritos* 732

Lactantius 625
Latin comedy 117
legacy hunters motif 468
legitimate union 169, 229, 364, 367
Leo the Archpriest 609, 610
Lesbos 361, 368
letters as novels *see* epistolary novel
Letters of Aeschines 19, 23, **646**
Letters of Alexander the Great see also Pseudo-Callisthenes 22, 69, 71, 602
Letters of Chion see also Chion of Heraclea 19, 647, **650–653**
Letters of Euripides 19, 24, **646**
Letters of Hippocrates see Correspondence of Hippocrates
Letters of Phalaris 649
Letters of Plato 19, 24, **645–646**
Letters of the Seven Wise Men see Correspondence of the Seven Wise Men 648
Letters of Socrates 19, 24, **648**
Letters of Themistocles 19, **647–648**
Leucippe and Cleitophon see Achilles Tatius
Libistros and Rhodamne 726, 727, 728, 729
libraries 519, 525, 533, 534, 546
Liebespaar 88, 108, 109, 112, 502, 536, 540, 543, 614, 671, 674, 679
lies 356, 357
life/pattern 544, 545, 547
Life of Aesop 18, 22, 28, 62, 75, 76, 110, 292, 579, **633–639**, 640, 643, 684, 696
Livia, wife of Augustus 153
locus amoenus 378, 644
Lodge, Thomas 765, 772
Lolita 337
Lollia Victorina 156
Lollianus, *Phoenicica* 17, 29, 88, 98, 104, 503, 655, 656, **669–672**, 674, 682, 683, 746
Longus, *Daphnis and Chloe* 13, 14, 15, 16, 17, 19, 29, 31, 35, 36, 41, 50, 68, 77, 85, 88, 93, 108, 109, 113, 116, 117, 118, 119, 120, 121, 122, 123, 124, 125, 128, 129, 132, 139, 140, 143, 144, 145, 146, 158, 162, 174, 187, **189–191**, 200, 201, 203, 206, 211, 213, **252–259**, 282, 284, 290, 299, 303, 304, 315, 324, 358, **361–386**, 423, 439, 503, 643, 644, 713, 743, 744, 745, 748, 765, 772, 773
lost novels **655–683**
love, love at first sight 52, 81, 116, 158, 164, 170, 190, 195, 204, 282, 309, 331, 337, 362, 370, 382, 451, 481, 586, 631, 692, 724, 725, 776, 779, 780, 781, 782, 786, 787, 792, 796
love letters 631, 727
love/mysteries 384–386
Lucan, *Pharsalia* 94, 332, 481
Lucian, *True History*, etc. 16, 18, 27, 41, 101, 103, 104, 105, 106, 141, 211, 318, 492, 514, **555–561**, 578, 628, 655, 658, 666, 667, 673, 696, 744, 755
Lucius of Patrae, supposed author of the lost *Metamorphoses* 103, 105, 111, 557, 694, 738
Lucius or the Ass see also Pseudo-Lucian 500–502
Lydus, John *see* John the Lydian
lying geography 555
Lyly, John 769

Macrobius 15, 26, 33, 459, 479, 480
Madaurus 150, 491
magic 511, 692, 694, 703
Makrembolites, Eustathius (Eumathios), *Hysmine and Hysminias* (prose) 412, 413, **717–718**, 728, 729
Malalas, John 389, 390
Manasses, Konstantinos, *Aristandros and Kallithea* 715, 718, 720, 721, 730
Mann, Thomas 211
Manuel I Comnenos 715
maps 7–8, **801–814**
margin, characters representing the: strangers, robbers, pirates, slaves **209–220**, 395, 523, 524, 636, 637, 657
marriage 151, 161
martyrs 112, 693
mass literature 84, 157
Maximus Confessor 422
Medea 168
medicine/love 363
medieval Greek contribution to fiction **713–733**

medieval Greek romance 721
Melbanke, B. 769, 770, 771
melodrama 109, 332–334
memoirs of Damis 614, 615
Menander 34, 53, 54, 59, 117, 169, 170, 297, 324
Menippean satire 280, 484, 485, 560, 673
Meroë 94, 116, 448, 604
mésalliance 338, 591
Mesomedes 135
message/intent 598
metaliterary 279, 289
Metamorphoses see Apuleius
Metiochus and Parthenope see Pathenope
Milesian Tales, Milesiaca see also Aristides 62, 63, 64, 76, 103, 291, 480, 510, 516
Miletus 309
mime 104
mirabilia 626
mise-en-abyme 384
de Montemor, Jorge, *Diana* 792, 793, 794, 798
de Montreaux, Nicolas 750, 751, 752, 753, 756, 757, 761, 764, 769
Mithras 76, 133, 145, 149
monogamy 450
Monazon, John Georgides 423
de Morais, Francisco, *O Palmeirim de Inglaterra* 787, 789
moral message 590, 591
morality 486
mosaics illustrating novels 101, 102, 159, 658, 665
motifs 106, 693, 694
Musaeus, Hero and Leander 95
mystagogos 145, 191, 405
mysteries/love 384–386
mystery religions, texts, and the novel **131–150**, 154, 352, 385, 386, 446, 447, 512, 533, 534
mythistoria 732
mythos/logos 15, 64, 127, 379, 380, 381, 385
Mytilene 363, 364, 366, 370, 373, 525

Naceo e Amperidónia 786, 795, 796
Nachleben 357–359, 411–414, 487–490, 550–551, 735–773, 775–799
names, naming 123–125, 345–346
narrative, narrative technique see also first-person narrative 107–113, 511, 507, 508, 510, 594:

Christian 112, **689–711**
high-brow 108
low-brow 107–109
middle-brow 111
popular 107–113, 598
romantic 113
sophisticated 107–113
narratives/wall paintings 374
narratology **280–288**, 445
narrator 539, 545–547, 755
narrator, unreliable 484, 545, 546
nationalism 72, 111, **662–669**, 786
naturalism 687
Nectanebus, *Dream of Nectanebus* 69–74, 603, 662, 681
Neoplatonists 446 see also Apuleius
Neopythagoreans 143, 453, 454
Nepos, Cornelius 577
Neptunalia 524
Nero, emperor 23, 457, 458, 459, 480, 486, 565
New Comedy and the novel 48, 50, **52–54**, 59, 100, 101, 110, 117, 169, 192, 199, 204, 205, 331, 375, 434, 438
New Testament 685ff.
Nile River 21, 341, 402, 403, 427ff.
Ninopedia 588
Ninus Romance (Ninus and Semiramis) 17, 30, 31 40, 42, 43, 44, 45, 46, 47, 48, 50, 52, 53, 54, 56, 57, 59, 61, 64, 67, 68, 70, 73, 74, 75, 76, 78, 79, 81, 88, 89, 90, 100, 101, 102, 178–179, 205, 207, 210, 316, 655, 656, 657, 662, **663–665**, 666, 682, 746
Nisibis 93, 418, 419
nostoi 566
novel 11–28:
 ancient labels 11–28
 and biography 18
 Christian **685–711**
 and comedy 14, 26 see also New Comedy
 criminal-satiric 669–674
 definition of **2–3, 11–28**
 digressions in see interpolated stories
 and epic see Homer, Virgil
 family 544
 and historiography see Herodotus, Thucydides
 origins of **29–85**
 as open genre (open form) 277–280

parody in   485, 502, 675
satire in   485
novella   61, 62, 63, 66, 74, 278, 585, 640
Núñez de Reinoso, Alonso *La Historia de los Amores de Clareo y Florisea*   414, 796, 797, 798
nymphs   126, 361, 378, 379

Odyssey   *see* Homer
oikos   202, 204
Olympias   603
oracles   39, 184, 337, 444, 449
orality   97, 99
ordeals   397, 407, 451
origins of the novel   **29–85**
Orpheus   384, 688
"others"   *see* margin
outcasts   233, 242, 249, 258
Ovid   59, 63, 100, 101

paideia   70, 74, 162, 323, 329, 332
paintings   361
Palaeologus, Andronikos, *Kallimachos and Chrysorrhe*   **723–725**, 726, 729
Palladius   602, 609
Pan   378
Pantheia and Abradatas   *see* also Xenophon of Athens   584, **585–588**, 593
papyri   93, 100, 104, 292, 293, 388, 391, 392, 530, 535, 564, 566, **655–683**, 700, 713, 736, 737, 739, 746
paradoxography   278
parallelism   294, 295, 297, 298, 302
Parthenius, *Erotica Pathemata*   35, 60, 61
Parthians   418
passivity   304
Parthenope, Metiochus and Parthenope   17, 30, 44, 45, 50, 63, 64, 70, 74, 78, 88, 89, 90, 92, 95, 96, 100, 101, 102, 106, 112, 316, 327, 655, 656, 657, **658–660**
Patroculus   126
pattern/life   544, 545, 547
"Paul and Thecla"   *see* "Thecla and Paul"
Peloponnesian War   581
Penthesileia   197
Pergamene Youth   467
Pergamum   91
Periodoi Petrou   537
peripeteia   575, 783

periplus   556
Perpetua   162
Persephone   150
Persia   39, 409, 584, 589, 626, 630
Persius   101, 159, 315, 316
personal features   123–126
Petronian Society Newsletter   3, 5
Petronius, *Satyrica*   13, 14, 15, 26, 29, 34, 64, 79, 101, 102, 109, 111, 117, 118, 123, 124, 126, 128, 171, 175, 219, 278, 279, 280, 286, 291, 292, 299, 305, 319, 352, **457–490**, 502, 503, 515, 529, 532, 541, 545, 546, 639, 643, 647, 657, 669, 673, 674
Phaedra   162, 168, 193, 291, 438
Philagathos, Philippos   423
Philes, Manuel   724
Philetas, Philitas of Cos   124, 363, 364, 376, 380, 385
Philip II   603
Philistion   104
Philodemus   79, 80
Philostratus, *Life of Apollonius of Tyana*, etc.   19, 24, 33, 34, 68, 102, 141, 143, 313, 314, 319, 320, 374, 398, 418, 434, 453, 578, 579, 580, 602, **613–618**, 689
Phoenicica (Phoinikika)   *see* Lollianus
Photius, *Bibliotheca*   34, 35, 40, 95, 103, 104, 357, 412, 421, 454, 556, 557, 629, 655, 668, 672, 676, 677, 680, 713, 736, 737, 738, 760
Phylarchus   46, 47
physical features   125–126
physicians   123, 174, 522
picaresque   681
pirates, brigands   *see* also margin   52, 233, 338, 362, 370, 523, 541, 549, 716
plasma   15, 17, 27, 32, 53, 159
Plato   32, 38, 66, 68, 153, 161, 166, 168, 372, 381, 453, 481, 491, 504, 512, 513, 581, 582, 590, 591, 651, 652, 653, 696, 775, 792
play   719
Pliny the Elder   459
Pliny the Younger   329
plot (mythos)   334, 693
Plutarch   35, 46, 47, 60, 63, 88, 95, 103, 134, 301, 459, 492, 604, 764
Poggio   472
point of view: voice/perspective   546–548
police   121, 237
politeia literature   590

Polybius 332
popular narrative 93, 282, 598, 692, 704, 709, 721, 775, 776
Porphyry 104, 655, 675, 677
Portugal, Nachleben in **775–799**
postmodern 719
poststructuralism and the novel **300–305**
Potiphar's wife motif 296, 338
prefect of Egypt 121
Priapus 463, 481, 487
priestesses 463
priests 398
Proclus 134
Prodromos, Theodoros, *Rhodanthe and Dosikles* 714, **716–717**, 721, 724, 725
prolepsis 594, 595
prose rhythm 322, 324, 455, 475–478, 682
prosimetrum 104, 485, 502, 673, 674
proskynesis 227
prostitutes 395
protagonists 116, 117
Proteus 127
Psellus 412, 422
Pseudo-Callisthenes, *Romance of Alexander* 18, 21, 22, 29, 45, 71, 73, 75, 76, 110, 210, 292, 315, 327, 559, 561, 579, 588, **601–612**, 682, 688, 689
Pseudo-Clement, *Homilies* and *Recognitiones (Clementines)* 19, 143, 358, 537, 545, **706–707**
pseudoeyewitness 578
Pseudo-Lucian, *Lucius or the Ass* 13, 14, 15, 29, 103, 105, 106, 111, 287, 672, 683, 738
pseudonyms 563
Psyche *see also* Apuleius 150
psychoanalytical approach to the novel **293–300**
pudicitia 81
Pythagoreanism 558, 559, 675, 676, 677, 678

Racine, Jean 298
readers, readership, audience, spectators **87–106**, 113, 115, 163, 288, 330, 373, 441, 442, 443, 451, 588, 597, 598, 713, 719, 737:
    actual 89, 93–95, 100–102, 104–105
    female 84, 95, 96, 97, 103, 159, 161–163, 199
    inexperienced 99
    intended 89, 92, 95–100, 103–104, 580
    as listeners 95–96
    as voyeur 376
reader-response criticism and the novel **288–293**
recapitulations 97, 98, 99, 334–335
recessed stories 675
récit **281–288**
recognition (anagnorisis) 49, 440, 448, 449, 525, 643, 779
Reeve, Clara 768
Reisefabulistik 41
Reiseroman 30, 481
religious models and the novel **76–80**, 351, 353, 508, 509
reporter 594, 626
representation 115, 450
resurrection 299
re-telling 549–550
rhetoric and the novel **65–70**, 278, 317, 373, 400, 539, **640–644**, 716
Rhodanthe and Dosikles see Prodromos
Ribeiro, Bernardin 791, 795, 796, 799
Richardson, Samuel 1, 767
riddles 110, 517, 519, 520, 522, 524, 530, 535, 548
rise of the novel **29–85**
Roman comedy 505
Roman Empire 410
romance *see* novel
Romance of Alexander see Pseudo-Callisthenes
Rome 155
Romeo and Juliet motif 337
Roxane 603
Rufinus, Q. Aradius 566
Rufus, C. Musonius 153

Sachs, Hans 551
sacred biography 144
sacred texts 132
St. Peter 537
Sallust 161, 577
salvation, individual 133ff.
Sandford, James 764, 766
Sappho 164, 166, 386, 373
Sarapis 137, 138
Satyrica (Satyricon, Satiricon) see Petronius
Scheintod 101, 147, 189, 296, 299, 309, 334, 337, 358, 408, 481, 517, 522, 524, 541, 547, 614, 671, 672, 780, 794

science fiction 556
season of the year/time structure 190, 362, 364, 365, 372, 384
Second Sophistic 30, 39, 41, 67, 70, 78, 399, 453, 602
seduction 364, 365
Segunda Parte da Cronica do Principe 789
Semiramis 179, 210, 662
Seneca 481
sententiae 539, 540
sentimentality 95
Seres 94
Servius 104
servus callidus 117, 309, 638, 639
Sesonchosis Romance 17, 43, 44, 45, 70, 72, 73, 75, 210, 656, 657, 662, **665–666**, 681, 682
Seven Wonders of the World 387
sexual abstinence 685–711 *passim*, 693
Shakespeare 337, 358, 550, 551, 736, 766
shipwreck 370, 468, 517, 520, 521, 522, 530, 551, 559, 643, 657, 708
showing/telling 282, 547, 548, 549
Sidney, Philip 414, 765, 771
Sienkiewicz, Henryk 459
similes/metapors 350
simplicitas 474, 643
Sinonis and Rhodanes *see* Iamblichus
Sisenna 103
sjužet 280, 783
slaves *see* margin, and social and economic structures
Smollett, Tobias 488
Snowwhite 113
social and economic structures **221–276**:
    crowds, popular masses 231, 235, 240, 249
    middle class portrayal 232, 240, 256, 267
    ruling classes 230, 236, 245, 253, 262
    slaves 233, 241, 257, 268, 273, 523, 524, 636, 637, 657
social contexts and the novel **80–85**
social position 122–123
society:
    portrayed in Chariton 222–235
    Achilles Tatius 235–244
    Xenophon of Ephesus 244–252
    Longus 252–259
    Heliodorus 259–276

Socrates, church historian 419, 420, 421
Socrates Scholasticus 94
sophists' novel 503
sophistic 30
sophistic novels 30, 39, 41, 105
Sophocles 51
Spain, Nachleben in **775–799**
sphragis 417, 508, 566, 575
spoils of war/beautiful woman as 585
Stesichorus 124, 649
Stoicism 624, 653
story within a story *see* interpolated stories
Suda, Souda, Suidas 43, 93, 345, 387, 390, 412, 423, 655, 667, 713, 748, 751
suicide 101, 587, 631
suitors 224, 309, 517, 519, 521
Sumer, origin of novels 75
summary *see* recapitulations
"superiority" 375
suspense 585, 594, 641
Syene 93
symbolism 548, 549
symmetry 299, 518
Symphosius 535
Synesius of Cyrene 104
Syracuse 91, 116, 309

table arrangement 464
Tacitus 410, 457, 458, 459
Tale of Troy, A Byzantine Iliad 730–731
Tarsus 519
Taylor, Jeremy 459
Tefnut, Tale of 73, 681
telesterion 136
Terceira Parte da Cronica do Principe 789
Terentia 155
Tertullian 702
theater and the novel 35, 437, 438, 449
theatron 714
"Thecla and Paul" 29, 143, **700–702**, 708
thematic criticism 300
Theocritus 124, 371, 373, 377
Theodorus Priscianus 94, 422, 423, 424
Theophrastus 53
Thessalus 141
Thucydides 35, 97, 151, 324, 332, 346, 378, 581, 582
Thule 104, 105 *see* also Antonius Diogenes

Tigellinus 457
time manipulation 594–596
time, temporal structure 281, 282, 283
Tinouphis, Narrative about **673**
topos 131, 382, 778ff.
tragedy 278, 630
tragic history 46
Trajan, emperor 384
travelers' tales *see* fantastic tales of travel
trial by ordeal 397, 407, 451
trial scenes 310
trivial literature 157, 288, 293
Trojan War *see* Dictys and Dares
Troja-Romance 564
truth 16, 560, 577, 676
Tyche 14, 54, 154, 161, 175, 188, 213, 284, 311, 328, 331, 335, 352, 449, 724
types of characters 331
Tyre 517, 518, 519, 525
tyrranicide 650, 652, 653

unity and the *Metamorphoses* 506–507
univira 156
utopian novels **38–42**, 176, 210, 212, 216, 283, 560, 588, **621–628**, 644, 789

Valerius, Julius 601, 602, 609, 615
Varro 673
verification 676
Vida de Primaleão 789
Virgil 110, 124, 170, 344, 352, 368, 371, 479, 481, 482, 515, 520, 521, 530, 532

virginity 158, 159, 189, 195, 197, 297, 301, 302, 407, 444, 451, 463, 523, 524, 532, 702
Volksbuch 110
Vulgar Latin 475, 476, 477

Wamiq and Adhra 657
war correspondent 565
werewolf tale 466
Widow of Ephesus 468
wife, role of 152
women in the ancient novel **151–207**, 304
women and the law 155
Wonders beyond Thule see Antonius Diogenes

Xanthus 636, 637
Xenophon of Athens, *Cyropaedia* 18, 20, 21, 33, 35, 38, 40, 45, 47, 66, 70, 88, 98, 323, 324, 330, 332, 345, 346, 439, **581–599**, 615, 651
Xenophon of Ephesus, *Ephesiaca* 13, 14, 15, 17, 29, 30, 31, 39, 48, 50, 62, 63, 64, 68, 77, 83, 89, 96, 97, 98, 99, 106, 109, 111, 112, 113, 116, 117, 119, 120, 121, 123, 125, 126, 128, 129, 131, 139, 140, 163, **185–187**, 201, 202, 205, 210, 211, 214, 217, 218, **244–252**, 282, 283, 284, 288, 290, 296, 298, 301, 304, 320, **336–360**, 392, 450, 481, 503, 534, 541, 542, 661, 674, 683, 692, 694, 707, 716, 768

Zenobia 154
Zola, E. 156